The Nonprofit Sector

THE NONPROFIT SECTOR

A Research Handbook

THIRD EDITION

Edited by Walter W. Powell and Patricia Bromley

STANFORD UNIVERSITY PRESS
Stanford, California

STANFORD UNIVERSITY PRESS

Stanford, California

©2020 by the Board of Trustees of the Leland Stanford Junior University. All rights reserved.

No part of this book may be reproduced or transmitted in any form or by any means, electronic or mechanical, including photocopying and recording, or in any information storage or retrieval system without the prior written permission of Stanford University Press.

Printed and bound by CPI Group (UK) Ltd, Croydon, CR0 4YY

Library of Congress Cataloging-in-Publication Data

Names: Powell, Walter W., editor. | Bromley, Patricia, editor.

Title: The nonprofit sector : a research handbook / edited by Walter W. Powell and Patricia Bromley.

Description: Third edition. | Stanford, California : Stanford University Press 2020. | Includes bibliographical references and index.

Identifiers: LCCN 2019021227 | ISBN 9781503608047 (paperback) | ISBN 9781503611085 (epub)

Subjects: LCSH: Nonprofit organizations—Management. | Nonprofit organizations. | Charitable uses, trusts, and foundations.

Classification: LCC HD62.6 .N67 2020 | DDC 338.7/4—dc23

LC record available at https://lccn.loc.gov/2019021227

Cover design: Rob Ehle

Text design: Kevin Barrett Kane

Typeset by Newgen in 10/13 Minion Pro

CONTENTS

PREFACE

The previous two editions of this handbook appeared at particular points in the history of nonprofit activity, and they reflect the scholarly attention of those specific periods. The first edition, published in 1987, brought together scholarship on a newly emerging space that was generally referred to as the independent sector. That effort was supported by Yale University's Program on Nonprofit Organizations (PONPO), led by the indomitable John G. Simon, Augustus Lines Professor at Yale Law School, who helped galvanize the first generation of scholarship on nonprofits. The first edition charted the terrain of the burgeoning domain of civic organizations. As this voluntary domain expanded, it evolved from informal activities of charitable citizens to highly formalized endeavors by enterprising individuals. Nonprofits became more professional.

I co-edited the second edition of the handbook, published in 2006, with economist Richard Steinberg. The task of surveying the research landscape was more than could be done alone. That edition focused on the ways in which nonprofit organizations attempted to influence society, interact with governments, influence public policy, and find new sources of revenue. One line of attention focused on why there was a particularly large nonprofit presence in certain sectors of society, such as health care, education, the arts, and social services. The second volume drew on work from scholars in the newly established Center on Philanthropy at Indiana University—Purdue University—Indianapolis (IUPUI) and Stanford University. James R. Wood, professor of sociology at Indiana University, and Robert L. Payton, founding director of the Center on Philanthropy, were both very supportive of the volume.

The current edition arrives at a time when scholars are arguing that civic action and social purpose can be found not only in nonprofit organizations but also in the public and business domains, and that nonprofits are increasingly intertwined with both. Many of the chapters in this edition reflect the age of fracture in which we live, grappling with questions of power, access, and inequality. The contributors also reflect on the changing expectations that social purpose organizations face. The Stanford University Center on Philanthropy and Civil Society, which supported this edition, has a mission to explore how and when civil society organizations contribute to or contravene the public good and to examine the role of philanthropy in enhancing, channeling, or diverting these efforts.

Woody Powell

ACKNOWLEDGMENTS

It takes commitment and care from an extended network of people to create a volume like this, and we are grateful to all those involved along the way. As a start, we are deeply appreciative of our forty-five authors for their hard work and bearing with us through multiple rounds of revisions and deadlines. We know it wasn't an easy task to produce chapters that are simultaneously forward-looking and convey the rich history of prior research, but they have done it and we are proud of the result. We are also indebted to the remarkable editors who read the chapters and commented on them—Elisabeth Andrews, Kelly Besecke, Adrienne Day, James Holt, Mike Levine, Kathleen Much, and Michael Slind. They provided excellent advice in helping shape the chapters in the volume. We have also had the great fortune of expertise from past and present editors at Stanford University Press, especially Margo Fleming and Kate Wahl, whose support and advice was instrumental in shaping the volume.

Organizationally, we have relied on the exceptional team at the Stanford Center on Philanthropy and Civil Society, and we particularly want to thank Valerie Dao, who helped organize the conference at which initial draft chapters were presented. Val has been involved in every stage of the book development process, continuously going above and beyond to ensure its success. Without her, this volume would not have come to fruition in a timely fashion. We are indebted to her for her steady hand. We also appreciate the encouragement from colleagues at the Center to move ahead with the volume, especially Faculty Co-Directors Paul Brest and Rob Reich and Executive Director Kim Meredith. Importantly, both the Center and the volume have benefited from generous support from the Rockefeller Foundation. The Foundation's work to promote high-quality academic research on the nonprofit sector will be seminal in shaping the future of the field.

Although the volume looks to the future, we build on the prior contributions of several decades of nonprofit scholarship. We owe intellectual debts to the authors and co-editor who contributed to previous editions of the Handbook, many of whom provided advice on presentations and drafts of the chapters here. We also relied on feedback from many nonprofit scholars beyond our past and present authors, as is evident in the acknowledgments in each chapter. The graduate students in the workshop on Philanthropy and Civil

Society also contributed by commenting on many of the chapters. We very much appreciate the wider interest and engagement with ideas in the chapters, and hope the work here contributes to stimulating and productive future research. These scholarly exchanges are what make taking on a large, collective, and collaborative project like this worthwhile. Relatedly, Tricia and Woody want to thank each other. This was a huge undertaking that could not have been done without a lot of faith and support by one another. Colleagueship does not get any better than this. Finally, we are thankful that our respective families have tolerated us over the past year as we mumbled that we have to work on the Handbook. Without their support, the work could not have happened.

Tricia Bromley and Woody Powell

INTRODUCTION

1 WHAT IS THE NONPROFIT SECTOR?

Walter W. Powell

SCHOLARS AND PRACTITIONERS ROUTINELY REFER to the wide array of activities pursued by voluntary and social purpose organizations in the United States as "the nonprofit sector." In different contexts and at different points in history, this domain has gone by a host of names: charitable organizations, civil society, the third sector, the independent sector, the social sector, and, more recently, social purpose organizations. My intention in this introductory chapter is to problematize the terms and concepts used to capture such activities and to preview how the chapters in this volume assess the current landscape and chart future directions. Each section of the book also contains an introduction presenting the unifying theme of those chapters and describing how the analyses within that section collectively elucidate current knowledge and research gaps within a specific area of nonprofit scholarship.

Our goal with this book is to advance research on a number of protean questions: What is a nonprofit organization? What is the relationship between formal nonprofit organizations and the wider sphere of civil society? Why do nonprofits exist in market economies? What roles do voluntary organizations play in democratic and autocratic societies? How do we explain variation in the contributions of nonprofits in fields such as health care, education, and the arts? When do voluntary organizations erode rather than encourage civic capacity? Why does the nonprofit realm have different social and economic footprints in different countries? The authors of this volume take up these and other important questions.

The first question concerns the conceptual framing of nonprofits. What does it mean to describe an entity in terms of the actions it *does not* take? Were we chemists, this would be a terrible way to go about research. In contrast, physicists often theorize about things with respect to the absence of particular features. The study of nonprofits has more in common with physics than chemistry in this regard, examining underlying principles and dynamics rather than discrete and predictable interactions. What are the common limiting elements associated with nonprofit organizations? Perhaps the most central idea is that of the nondistribution constraint (Hansmann 1987). Nonprofit organizations operate without distributing profits to their stakeholders. Simply put, if there are funds left over at the end of the year, nonprofit executives cannot pocket them. Nonprofit leaders do not focus their energy on enriching shareholders, as do managers of firms, nor do they feel the need to spend every penny of their budgets as if they were state agencies.[1] Accordingly, some scholars have argued that nonprofits are, in principle, more trustworthy than firms or government bureaus (Nelson and Krashinsky 1973; Hansmann 1987). The nondistribution constraint is centrally tied to the tax exemption given to nonprofits, which comes with an obligation to respond to society's needs at a particular time.[2] Of course, this temporal feature means that nonprofit organizations turn to the legal tools of organizing available resources in particular countries at specific moments in history. As several chapters of this volume discuss, this legal protection varies markedly across place and time.

What are other "negative" elements that characterize nonprofit organizations? Nonprofits are voluntary; that is, they do not coerce participation. In many countries, young people are required to perform either military or social service. Both are for public benefit, but they are demanded, and length of service is not negotiable. In contrast, people may move readily between nonprofits; participation is fluid and consensual. Nonprofits also exist without clear lines of ownership and accountability, precisely because they serve multiple masters (Frumkin 2002): nonprofits must be responsive not only to their constituents and clients but also to staff, members, volunteers, and donors.

Although these negative features describe what nonprofits lack or are not allowed to do, civil society organizations can also be framed through positive concepts. Whether referred to as civil society (Cohen and Arato 1992) or the public sphere (Habermas 1989), the space for voluntary activity is characterized by debate, contention, and engagement. These expressions reflect the interests of diverse members of society, whether a political regime is democratic or autocratic. In places where the tools of formal representation are available, nonprofits exist because ideas and resources are mobilized and formalized by activists, volunteers, donors, and social entrepreneurs. These diverse elements are the forces that supply energy and ideas. In this sense, nonprofits exist as the medium for the expression of values and commitment.[3] Put differently, nonprofits serve as "the organizational infrastructure for civil society" (Anheier 2014). They result from the legal incorporation of activities that represent the varied interests and identities that members of civil society hold. As Nancy Rosenblum and Robert Post (2002:4) nicely put it, "civil society affords individuals the experience of pluralism."

Political scientist Lester Salamon (2012:6–15) stresses this organizational nature. He emphasizes that nonprofits are formal entities distinct from their officers, capable of holding property, making contracts, and persisting over time. The right of people to come together to build community is distinct from the right of organizations to access the legal tools that enable them to grow larger and exist longer. Although this crucial distinction has become taken for granted in the United States, the ability to ensure organizational persistence is lacking in many countries.

Salamon also points out that nonprofits are self-governing and must provide a public benefit. This expressive view suggests that moral energy for a cause can exist independent of large-scale societal demand for its objectives. Civil society organizations can keep the home fires burning, so to speak, until the political winds blow in the right direction (Taylor 1989). Consider the abolitionist movement, the movement against child labor, advocacy for consumer safety, the fair trade movement, and, today, environmental conservation. Each of these activities was first championed and protected inside a small set of nonprofit organizations and social movements that worked to keep the issues alive until support came from a broad swath of society.

Such commitment or moral energy has enabled the nonprofit sector in the United States to garner political support from both conservatives and progressives. Both ends of the political spectrum use nonprofit organizations to achieve their aspirations and advance their divergent understandings of the public good, although their forms of organization can vary by political beliefs. Theda Skocpol (2011) argues that among contemporary U.S. civic organizations, those on the left create public interest groups that are staff-centered, whereas those on the right, such as the Tea Party and the National Rifle Association, create chapter-based membership federations. In some periods in U.S. history, nonprofits have acted as laboratories for experimentation, and successes were subsequently passed on to the government (Hall 1987). At other times, such as the era in which we now find ourselves, nonprofits may provide the space to raise opposition to the government. Civic engagement is also moving into more temporary and experimental vehicles that quickly spring up and disappear. Such minimalist organizations may have distinctly circumscribed goals; when these are met, the organization dissolves (Tufekci 2017; also see Walker and Oszkay, Chapter 21, "The Changing Face of Nonprofit Advocacy").

A sharp, clean image of a nonprofit *sector*, however, is problematic in several respects. First, the term has a geometric connotation that implies clear and firm boundaries. The sector imagery draws attention to formal entities rather than charitable activities or altruistic efforts. Acts of compassion and charity are as old as humankind, whereas the tax code is a modern legal entanglement. Although the U.S. tax code acts like a border patrol, policing which organizations qualify for tax exemption (Simon 1987; Barman 2013), basing the concept of a sector primarily on a single nation's tax code inhibits comparative analyses. In other countries, comparable organizations can be defined differently, as either nongovernmental organizations (NGOs), voluntary associations, a social economy, or part of a larger civil society. Recently, observers have noted that in North America, Europe, and the Asia Pacific region, nonprofit organizations have attained increasing importance as providers of health, social, educational, and cultural services (Anheier 2009). In Chapter 4, "The Organizational Transformation of Civil Society," Patricia Bromley chronicles the increasingly formal organization of associational life around the globe. Similarly, there has been international growth in the number of foundations and trusts, most notably in Asia but to a lesser extent in other regions as well (Johnson 2018).[4] Evan Schofer and Wesley Longhofer also explore the global growth of NGOs in Chapter 27, "The Global Rise of Nongovernmental Organizations."

Second, the concept of a sector leads scholars to try to classify and catalog types of organizations, often failing to capture what these entities actually do or promote. In the United States, nonprofit organizations are assigned subsector codes intended to categorize what they do, but such codes may mask an underlying commonality. For example, a variety of organizations in different subsectors, such as housing or the arts, may work with the elderly or children, but the codes assigned to these organizations do not reflect the recipients of their services. Beyond these internal classification challenges lies a bigger question: What purpose does an organization serve? The general public or constituents of different types of organizations are much more concerned with the quality and care of the service provided than with organizations' tax status. From this vantage point, depicting altruistic or charitable activity requires a broad canvas rather than a divided triptych of commercial, governmental, and nonprofit work.

How, then, did we come to think of the wide array of voluntary activities and donative organizations as belonging to a single common category? The boundaries between the market, the state, the family, and civil society are fluid and varied, depending on both the historical moment and the societal context. Consider, for example, health care in the United States. Jill R. Horwitz offers a fresh view in Chapter 17, "Charitable Nonprofits and the Business of Health Care." At the beginning of the nineteenth century, medical care in the United States was primarily private, delivered by solo practitioners, with some modest contribution from almshouses, where charitable care was given to the poor (Starr 1982). Over time, health care evolved to a much larger organizational scale and became primarily nonprofit and publicly provided. An unexpected consequence of the Medicare Act of 1964, which extended health care to many more citizens in the United States, was to turn health care into an activity that could be priced. This change drew new for-profit entrants into the field (Scott et al. 2000). Today, health care in the United States is a vast industry, populated by large chains that are primarily nonprofit and private. However, in other advanced industrial nations health care is provided to a greater extent by governments, with a small for-profit presence and a relatively limited nonprofit component.

Similarly, if we consider higher education, the current mix of public and private nonprofit universities in the United States (with a small for-profit component) looks very different from the arrangements in other nations, where higher education is largely public. Nevertheless, some of the most prestigious universities and research centers are nonprofits (e.g., McGill in Canada; Cambridge, Oxford, and the London School of Economics in Britain; Bocconi in Italy; Keio in Japan; and the Max Planck Institutes in Germany). In the United States, the costs of attending college are converging across private nonprofit and public state schools and becoming vastly more expensive. Chapter 18, "Education and the Nonprofit Sector," by Richard Arum and Jacob L. Kepins reviews the many factors that have reshaped the boundaries of educational institutions.

An Independent Sector?

To a certain extent, the porous boundaries in the United States between the market, the state, and nonprofits are policed by the tax code. However, the tax code is not an abstract entity that exists separately from the organizational realm, as Daniel J. Hemel emphasizes in Chapter 5, "Tangled Up in Tax." Tax policy is also deeply political, as Aaron Horvath and I detail in Chapter 3, "Seeing Like a Philanthropist," discussing the power struggles associated with various eras of elite philanthropy. The current IRS tax code that regulates 501(c)(3) organizations was the outcome of a two-decade political battle fought in the U.S. Congress. Indeed, the genesis of the concept of an "independent sector" was a response to contentious debates over the unchecked power of philanthropy. In May 1961, Texas congressman Wright Patman took to the floor of the House of Representatives to deliver a series of speeches inveighing against foundations and other tax-exempt organizations that had become "a vehicle for institutionalized, deliberate evasion of fiscal and moral responsibility" (Hall 1992:72). Distressed at the disproportionately rapid growth of foundations, Patman worried about the economic consequences of granting tax exemptions to these privately controlled entities. Over the next decade, through the efforts of the House Select Committee on Small Business, Patman focused on the favorable treatment that philanthropy gave to the very wealthy. Patman's efforts helped foster a growing belief that foundations were tax dodges and that those that existed in perpetuity were costs to the government (Brilliant 2000). Patman's eight-year campaign led to hearings by the House Ways and Means Committee in 1969, with the expectation that Congress would curb the activities of foundations (see detailed discussion of this debate in Hall 1992:66–80). The resulting 1969 Tax Reform Act, however, proved to be less stringent than the heated rhetoric might have suggested.

The foundation world and other tax-exempt entities did not sit idly by as these congressional debates ensued. John D. Rockefeller III and other elite foundation officials and academics sought to alter public opinion about the contributions of foundations to American life. Rockefeller understood that damping down further outbreaks of regulatory zeal would require foundations and tax-exempt entities to come up with a coherent and compelling rationale for the existence of nonprofits and the privileges they enjoyed. The Tax Reform Act set limits on charitable contributions to foundations and increased requirements of accountability and transparency. Penalties for violations were set on foundations, their managers, and their contributors. However, the proposed harsher limitation on the life of a foundation to just twenty-five to forty years was not passed.

In May 1973, John D. Rockefeller created a working group called the Advisory Group on Private Philanthropy. By the end of the summer, he had formed a prestigious and diverse commission, "exquisitely balanced by geography, party, gender, race, occupation, and religious denomination" (Hall 1992:77) and brought together under the leadership of John Filer, a corporate lawyer and the chief executive officer of Aetna Life & Casualty. The commission would come to be a joint effort of Congress, the Treasury Department, and the private sector, aided by a distinguished panel of experts. In 1977 the Department of the Treasury published the results of the Filer Commission's work in six large volumes as *The Report of the Commission on Private Philanthropy and Public Needs*. The work gave substance to a new idea: that charitable tax-exempt organizations composed a coherent sector of American political, economic, and social life.

This unified conception of nonprofits *and* foundations as together forming an independent sector laid the groundwork for establishing that these disparate organizations shared common interests. Before the work of the Filer Commission, there is little evidence in either tax records or scholarly research that the broad analytic category of "the nonprofit sector" existed at all (Hall 1987, 1992). The first two editions of this book had chapters that reflected herculean efforts to map the size and scope of the U.S. nonprofit sector (Rudney 1987; Boris and Steuerle 2006; also see Weisbrod and Long 1977). Today, however, this pioneering work has been supplanted by *The Nonprofit Almanac*, regularly compiled and published by the Urban Institute. Moreover, data on foundation giving is now available from Candid, the new entity formed through the merger of the Foundation Center and GuideStar, and various nonprofit rating services that assess nonprofits' efficacy.

The Filer Commission's vision of the sector brought donors and recipients together as actors with a common purpose. This unification of fund-raising bodies, foundations, and such diverse organizations as soup kitchens and symphony orchestras was a remarkable political and social achievement, cast in economic terms. Rather than seeing grant givers, advocacy organizations, and service providers as distinctive entities, this new view "carried an organizational conception modeled on business enterprise" (Karl 1987:985). The Filer Commission made the case that the independent sector should be viewed for its economic contributions rather than only its moral or social benefits.

But what does *independent* mean? Does it imply *free of government*? Surely not, as the effort to create this new sector was in direct response to the activities of Congress and the Treasury Department. Does it refer to independence from corporate influence? Again, the defense of the new sector was led by elite business and civic leaders who, although concerned with efforts to correct abuses by some foundations, nevertheless wanted to maintain a space for the power and influence of elite private philanthropy. Clearly, the claim of independence is misleading, politically constructed to suggest a separation from business and government interests that never existed in practice.

How Do the State and Civil Society Interact?

Perhaps a different way to think about independence is to consider open-access organizations (Lamoreaux and Wallis 2017). *Open access* implies that groups in society have the ability to associate with one another and create special-purpose organizations. The freedom to establish organizations that are designed to pursue purposes independent of government is relatively recent. Moreover, there is an important complementarity between government-granted freedoms allowing citizens to (1) assemble as a public right and (2) establish private organizations. The assumption that these two freedoms inherently arise together is, in many respects, naïve, both historically and in the contemporary global context. Two striking illustrations highlight this point. The French Revolution led to the influential Loi Le Chapelier (1791), which expressly stated that no intermediary associations were allowed to exist between the individual and the state as an expression of the public will (Anheier 2014:41). Citizens could assemble but not create associations. Prussians lacked the freedom to associate without government permission for most of the nineteenth century. Full freedom of association and the capacity to form organizations did not come about in either country until the twentieth century. In Germany, such freedom was not permitted until the Weimar Republic after World War I (Brooks and Guinnane 2017).

Britain and the United States were the first countries to undergo the dramatic transformation to open access, permitting citizens the power to form organizations without constraints or control by the government (see Lamoreaux and Wallis 2017). By the middle of the nineteenth century, both countries had shifted toward open access, although the process occurred very differently in the two settings. In Britain, a century and a half after the Glorious Revolution of 1688, the change occurred suddenly and with apparently little conflict. Joint stock companies were formed, and a shift toward greater tolerance for all kinds of organizations occurred. To be sure, both men and women had formed a growing number of clubs and voluntary associations since at least the mid-seventeenth century, but organizations that posed questions about the established political or religious order had led a shadowy existence on the margins, protecting themselves from repression by touting their charitable activities. Over the course of the nineteenth century, clubs and voluntary associations proliferated in Britain. These organizations served charitable, educational, recreational, political, and even whimsical goals.

By contrast, the transformation to open access in the United States was more halting, uneven, and organizationally and regionally variegated (Hilt 2017). Peter Hall (2006) has emphasized the profound ramifications of the religious differences between the New England, mid-Atlantic, and Southern states. The plantation South imposed the most restrictions on what types of organizations could be created and what kinds of people could participate. In the North, sharp differences between the states could be seen in rules of incorporation and charter as well as levels of political, religious, and ethnic tolerance. The Tocquevillian image of nineteenth-century America as a "nation of joiners" is far too rosy; Ruth Bloch and Naomi Lamoreaux (2017) convincingly argue that although white (male, and to a lesser extent female) U.S. citizens could form all manner of associations, they depended on state government approval for the tools to make their organizations long-lasting. Benjamin Soskis chronicles these developments in Chapter 2, "A History of Associational Life and the Nonprofit Sector in the United States."

More recently, scholars of American political development have argued that civic life in the United States has been reorganized from member-based associations to civic organizers and donors (Putnam 2000; Skocpol 2003, 2011). This transformation has two components. (1) It represents a movement from fellowship associations, with citizens joined in fraternal, religious, or veterans' groups, to more specialized organizations that advocate for causes on behalf of constituents. The staffs of these organizations do not directly interact with these constituents except when asking them for donations or specific actions such as signing petitions or contacting political representatives. (2) These new, professionally managed organizations operate as public-interest groups with considerable political clout (Berry 1999). Arguably, however, they do not create civic capacity, as they do not teach constituents the skills of interacting with one another to resolve differences and enhance sociability. Thus the paradox of contemporary civic life: more voices, but less participation; more causes, but less consensus. Additionally, in comparison to earlier eras, more time is now spent raising money, particularly chasing the wealthy for funds to support advocacy for less advantaged individuals (Skocpol 2011).

Another important question for contemporary scholars of nonprofits is how the private formation of organizations operates differently in legal settings that permit the creation of associations, in contrast to legal regimes that force associational activity outside the law and into the shadows. As we think about comparative differences in the shape and scale of the nonprofit sector across countries, it is critical to understand the ways in which some societies developed to achieve open access while others evolved in directions that keep such access restricted. This dynamic between societal development and associational freedoms is important because, as sociologist Arthur Stinchcombe (1965) argued many years ago, the spread of organizations becomes a self-reinforcing process, creating the groundwork for more organizations to be formed. Anheier and Salamon (2006) have made this argument most clearly, suggesting that the nonprofit sector has different historical "moorings" and reveals different social and economic "shapes" across countries. In a related vein, in Chapter 29, "Social Movements in a Global Context," sociologists Breno Bringel and Elizabeth McKenna argue that transnational activism takes on distinctly different shapes in specific historical eras.

Private organizations may rein in governments by providing focal points for resistance against abuses of power (Rosenblum and Post 2001: chap. 1). For much of the twentieth century, civil society was seen as a formidable force in sustaining democracy. In this view, private, nonprofit organizations serve as training wheels for democracy, teaching individuals how to function as citizens through both participation in organizations and commitment to associational life (Clemens 2006). As such organizations spread and become common, they enhance wider civic capacity. The organizations become separate from their founders; they can live on even as membership changes. This feature offers a different understanding of the "independence" of the sector. Civil society allows people to see themselves as agentic citizens, independent of their participation as employees, consumers, or voters at a ballot box. Furthermore, in our current illiberal era, with democracy challenged around the globe by elected autocrats in many countries, independence may take on a new meaning. Civil society may be "the last defense" against leaders who run roughshod over the rule of law and a free press (Acemoglu 2017).

Such tensions and counteracting dynamics have long characterized the historical relationship between civil society and the state. Indeed, many scholars consider the sequence and timing of associational and state development to be important in explaining the size and composition of the nonprofit sector (Esping-Anderson 1990). On the one hand, if a modern state developed before associational activity became widespread among its citizens, then the government is likely to carry out most social service activities. On the other hand, in nations where associational life either predated large-scale government or developed in tandem with it—such as the United States, Britain, Canada, and Australia—these same social service activities are conducted by voluntary organizations. Not surprisingly, in the latter circumstance the extent of associational life and nonprofit organization tends to be larger.

This developmental trajectory argument, or social origins theory, also helps us understand the differing composition of nonprofit sectors (Anheier and Salamon 2006). For example, social democratic countries such as Norway, Sweden, and Finland have a considerable array of nonprofit organizations, but they are concentrated among membership organizations, such as football and hockey clubs, rather than social service organizations. In contrast, many more social services are either performed directly by nonprofits or contracted to nonprofits by governments in the liberal market democracies of Anglo-American origin. The central argument in the social origins theory is that there is (1) an inverse relationship between the extent of government social welfare spending and the size of the nonprofit sector and (2) a difference across societies in the predominant types of nonprofits that is shaped by historical development and class relations. Helmut K. Anheier, Markus Lang, and Stefan Toepler revisit and amend this line of argument in Chapter 30, "Comparative Nonprofit Sector Research."

Despite this overarching framework, broad generalizations about international differences in civil society are nevertheless difficult to make. It is not only the size of the nonprofit arena across nations that is challenging to explain but also its composition.

The economist Burton Weisbrod (1975, 1988) attempted to develop such an argument, with important contributions added by the economist Estelle James (1987). Their general explanation of the presence of nonprofit organizations is based on two ideas: the heterogeneity of the population and the concept of a median voter. With heterogeneity, Weisbrod (1989) referred to the degree of consensus among citizens for collective services, such as medical services and famine relief, and trust services, such as day care and nursing homes. If members of a society have disparate interests, in, say, medical research or environmental conservation, governments will have difficulty catering to these diverse tastes. In a heterogeneous society, with differences also marked by religion, race, or ethnicity, one would expect to see more nonprofit organizations than in a homogeneous society. This argument rests on the belief that politicians cater to a "median voter" who represents the largest segment of the demand for public goods. Government spending is aimed at the median voter and leaves other members of society unsatisfied. Nonprofit organizations, in this view, step in to satisfy those who have an interest in public goods not provided by government.

Other factors may loom large alongside heterogeneous demands, however. By and large, more-developed countries have a larger nonprofit sector than less-developed countries. Some observers argue that democratic societies have larger nonprofit sectors than autocratic societies, but associational life in such settings can occur in the shadows and appear in unanticipated ways. Contemporary China, with its massive new middle class of more than 350 million people, has considerable (albeit not necessarily formalized) support for environmental goals and progress. Despite the extensive reach of a powerful state, there is an unruly, contentious online space where millions of Chinese citizens raise questions about their society (Lei 2018). Grassroots organizations spring up in the shadow of the state (Spires 2011). Furthermore, as more middle-class Chinese residents become homeowners, housing associations are becoming more active in expressing the views of neighbors and citizens (Lin 2020). Part of the challenge of studying civil society across nations is that organizing models are deeply conditioned by political struggles, media access, and legal tools.

Ideological movements also influence the contours of the nonprofit sector. In the 1990s, many advanced industrial nations saw a general move toward shrinking government (Hood 1995; Pollitt and Bouckaert 2011). This trend—whether referred to as retrenchment, decentralization, new public management, or neoliberalism—resulted in a sharp reorganization of the public sector. Much more emphasis was placed on accountability and contracting with both private for-profit organizations and private nonprofit entities. As the scale and activities of government shifted, an array of public–private partnerships appeared in many fields, as discussed in Chapter 9, "Toward a Governance Framework for Government–Nonprofit Relations," by Nicole P. Marwell and Maoz Brown.

General secular trends also shape the size of the nonprofit sector. As two-income families become more common, demand grows for professional child care. Increases in life expectancy raise the demand for elder care. Rising levels of educational attainment produce more heterogeneous tastes, creating a wider variety of artistic, athletic, and cultural interests. The kinds of associations created by the well-to-do are quite different, however, from mass participatory organizations; they are more likely to involve doing for others rather than with them (Skocpol 2003). Meanwhile, increased rates of immigration and forced migration put pressure on governments, and nonprofits have stepped in to provide relief in many countries, as described by Irene Bloemraad, Shannon Gleeson, and Els de Graauw in Chapter 12, "Immigrant Organizations." Greater awareness of the effects of climate change increases the role of environmental nonprofits (see Chapter 15, "Nonprofits and the Environment," by Magali Delmas, Thomas P. Lyon, and Sean Jackson), and when greater severity of events caused by climate change combines with increased frequency, pressures develop that governments cannot meet. These secular trends can to a large extent be understood as increasing the heterogeneity of demands discussed earlier, leading to greater nonprofit activity as predicted by Weisbrod (1988).

If explaining the size and scope of the nonprofit sector across countries is difficult, it is perhaps still harder to gain a purchase on how volunteering varies. There are competing definitions of what constitutes a volunteer in different nations, making it challenging to assess the amount of such activity. Even in the United States (as Nina Eliasoph shows in Chapter 25, "What Do Volunteers Do?"), volunteering carries a wide variety of meanings. Sorting out the relationship between formal employment and volunteering is not easy. Research by Salamon and his colleagues in the Johns Hopkins University comparative nonprofit sector project found a general trend: the larger the paid employment in the nonprofit field, the higher the volunteer workforce (Salamon et al. 2012). Paid work does not, therefore, displace volunteers. Countries with the largest nonprofit sectors, such as the United States, Australia, New Zealand, Belgium, and Israel, also have the highest rates of volunteering. Volunteering roles differ notably, however. In Europe, volunteers are often involved in sports activities, whereas in the United States religious congregations attract the most volunteers (see Brad Fulton's analysis in Chapter 26, "Religious Organizations").

Nonprofits and the Market

A complex relationship of interdependence has long existed between governments and nonprofits. Salamon (1987) was one of the first analysts to stress the idea of third-party government, in which governmental monies go to nonprofit organizations to deliver public services. This characterization raises the following question: Why don't governments contract with firms instead of nonprofits? And, relatedly, why don't we see more for-profit day care centers, art museums, or elder care facilities? To answer these questions, we need to examine the spaces nonprofits occupy in the market and how the value of these organizations is calculated, a topic Jennifer E. Mosley explores in Chapter 10, "Social Service Nonprofits."

Scholars have developed several arguments to account for which industries have the largest nonprofit presence and what kinds of evaluative criteria are typically used for nonprofit enterprises. Economist and legal scholar Henry Hansmann (1987) argued that nonprofits most commonly arise in situations where consumers feel unable to assess a good or service accurately. In this model, nonprofit organizations have less incentive to take advantage of consumers' informational disadvantages. Put differently, when it is difficult to monitor an activity or when the recipient of an activity is not the person paying for it (as in the case of professional child care), the informational asymmetry between the consumer and the provider could be exploited by commercial entities. The nondistribution constraint means that, as Weisbrod (1989:543) puts neatly, "the incentive to chisel is weak-ened." Consider, for example, the informational challenges faced in trying to find quality care for a developmentally disadvantaged family member or state-of-the-art medical interventions for older loved ones. These situations pose a moral hazard problem—that is, a circumstance in which someone other than the purchaser of the service bears the risk of misbehavior by the service provider.[5]

In a mixed economy, nonprofits should have some performance benefits over for-profits. And indeed they do. For example, nonprofit hospitals provide more uncompen-sated care to the indigent; nonprofit nursing homes and psychiatric care facilities are more likely to use waiting lists than raise prices; nonprofits provide higher-quality day care. In contrast, for-profits in these domains tend to pursue profitable niche markets (Krash-insky 1998; Mauer 1998; Schlesinger and Gray 2006; Horwitz, Chapter 17, "Charitable Nonprofits and the Business of Health Care"). Nobel laureate economist Oliver Hart and his colleagues take this incentive design argument further, demonstrating that in the case of prisons, for-profits are even more extreme in their revenue-oriented behaviors than chiseling on conditions or failing to focus on recidivism. They also use excessive force and have lower-quality personnel (Hart, Shleifer, and Vishny 1997).

The "stylized" theory assumes that nonprofits have less incentive to take advantage of people with fewer resources, but the companion implication is that they also have weaker motivations to be efficient or to innovate. Such trade-offs in incentives began to change in the 1990s. Despite the broad view that nonprofit organizations are more concerned with mission than maximizing output, a movement began at that time to promote the use of evaluative criteria to document nonprofits' impact. Paul Brest examines the motivations to measure outcomes and traces the emergence of such methods in Chapter 16, "The Outcomes Movement in Philanthropy and the Nonprofit Sector." This trend was driven by a host of factors. A turn toward more professional and professionalized employees, alongside demands for performance metrics by government funders, spurred efforts to develop new ways to measure nonprofit activity (Hwang and Powell 2009). A new gen-eration of philanthropists, flush with money made in tech sectors, drew on metrics from the for-profit sector to guide their donations. As Aaron Horvath and I discuss in Chapter 3, "Seeing Like a Philanthropist," the Bill & Melinda Gates Foundation was pivotal in this transformation; it launched initiatives in hopes that it would obtain measurable and verifiable results. Some funders extended this idea to conclude that if program results don't have a number attached to them, they are not valuable. The cultural climate in the United States thus shifted markedly in the 1990s and early 2000s, altering the criteria by which nonprofits are valued.

A change in the relations between nonprofits and the market has gone hand-in-hand with the shrinking of government. People with altruistic motives increasingly looked to work in civil society organizations rather than government service. As both evaluative criteria and public support shifted, there was widespread public enthusiasm for social enterprises of varied forms (see Chapter 14, "Social Entrepreneurship," by Johanna Mair). Many nonprofits have long relied on fees for their services and competed in a limited way with for-profit alternatives. The newer social enterprises reflect a stronger embrace of market forces, however, as Maitreesh Ghatak discusses in Chapter 13, "Economic Theories of the Social Sector." Whether in a nonprofit or hybrid form, these new models often share the view that social problems can be ameliorated with market-based, technical solutions. Examples abound, including digital platforms for informal labor markets and novel health care programs.

This entrepreneurial spirit has spread not only to nonprofits but also to philanthropy. As private giving for public purposes becomes more professional and businesslike, it changes from patronage to a more hands-on style (Skocpol 2016). This shift has many ramifications. Stephen Teles (2016) argues that foundations are turning to shorter-term projects that will show quick results, whereas Horvath and Powell (2016) suggest that patronage has moved away from projects that are contributions to the public sphere toward disruptive agendas that offer alternatives to existing governmental institutions. Other scholars speculate that philanthropy is highest when social inequality is greatest (Gilens 2012; Berry 2016; Levy 2016), leading us to ask why the superwealthy have the right to speak for others through philanthropic initiatives. This question of the imposition of tastes or values is taken up by Francie Ostrower in Chapter 19, "Nonprofit Arts Organizations," in her discussion of tensions between inclusion and exclusivity in the world of cultural organizations.

Philanthropic donations have also become a potent tool for policy advocacy, as Sarah Reckhow discusses in Chapter 8, "Politics, Philanthropy, and Inequality." One focus has been on "changing the conversation," that is, altering the policy formulation and implementation process. In the domain of political advocacy, we find a surprising twist. Progressive donors have tended to follow the entrepreneurial mind-set: project-based, incentive-laden, short-time-horizon donations. Many of the activities supported by these donations also entail some form of service provision. By contrast, conservative donors have played a long game (Hertel-Fernandez 2016; Hertel-Fernandez, Skocpol, and Sclar 2018). They have focused on building an institutional infrastructure, at the state level and in think tanks, with large gifts to a small number of entities. This contrasting focus raises questions about the meaning of voice in civil society.

Nonprofits and Voice

Despite wealthy donors' outsized influence on political affairs in relation to that of other citizens, the political activity of donors needs to be viewed in context to accurately gauge its impact. Funds from large donors, and philanthropic gifts in general, constitute but a small portion of the overall budget of most operating charities. In Chapter 23, "What Influences Charitable Giving?," Pamela Paxton surveys the scope of individual charitable giving in the United States, and Laura K. Gee and Jonathan Meer explore the motivations for giving in Chapter 24, "The Altruism Budget." Notwithstanding the media attention given to signers of the Giving Pledge,[6] the considerable philanthropic contributions of these donors make up only a small fraction of overall charitable gifts. Further, although the contemporary activities of the wealthy have garnered much public and scholarly attention, their current influence is not unrivaled. The more striking contrast is between the present celebration of philanthropists and the vilification of such individuals in the late nineteenth century (Horvath and Powell 2016; Levy 2016). Further, the remarkable political capacity-building of conservatively oriented philanthropists over the past thirty years was undertaken in response to the perception that large U.S. foundations had historically supported, in the main, liberal causes of integration and inclusion (Useem 1984:80–85; Teles 2008). Philanthropy has thus been altered both in reputation and orientation.

In addition to considering the role of donors and foundations in advocacy, the chapters in this volume analyze voice inside nonprofit and civil society organizations and discuss their external influence. Who speaks inside nonprofit organizations? Do nonprofits have a seat at the table when important decisions are made in their communities and cities? Chapter 6, "Political Theory and the Nonprofit Sector," by Ted Lechterman and Rob Reich, and Chapter 7, "Nonprofits as Boundary Markers," by Elisabeth S. Clemens, consider the effects of membership in nonprofit organizations on political socialization and attitudes. The classic writings of Alexis de Tocqueville spawned a line of work, perhaps most vividly expressed by Robert Putnam, Robert Leonardi, and Raffaella Nanetti (1993), that emphasized participation and associational life as means of fostering civic engagement. This "training ground" view has been buttressed by a good deal of empirical work. For example, Daniel McFarland and Reuben Thomas (2006) show that participation in student clubs and student government in high school leads to much stronger civic engagement in adulthood. Putnam and his colleagues (1993) argued that civic engagement is central to the subsequent success of political institutions because civic participation creates norms of trust and reciprocity that enable citizens from different backgrounds to work together.[7]

These arguments go right to the heart of what makes associational life distinctive. In Chapter 7, "Nonprofits as Boundary Markers," Elisabeth S. Clemens focuses on the processes that connect associational life and civic engagement. Does participation create a habit of involvement that is translated from nonprofits to the realm of the polity? Or do civic norms and practices depend on the character and functioning of specific organizations? Do nonprofit organizations provide a voice for their employees and volunteers through participation in strategic planning or other critical decisions? How much is the wider community drawn in, via meetings, focus groups, or social media? Powell, Horvath, and Brandtner (2016) have shown that nonprofits in the San Francisco Bay Area have become much more porous with regard to their external publics, inviting constituents in via their websites, blogs, chat rooms, and focus groups. Do internal and external participation go hand in hand, or are they subject to different influences?

Some participatory organizations, however, have values that are inconsistent with democracy (Fiorina 1999). The socialization role of such organizations can also work against democratic institutions. Sheri Berman's (1997) research on Weimar Germany is a vivid example, showing that associational life was rampant during this heady period. But absent a stable democratic government, many civil society groups worked to undermine democracy. In societies where cleavages among groups are significant, associational life may further aggravate tensions. Dylan Riley (2010), for example, argues that fascist regimes in Italy, Spain, and Romania arose, somewhat paradoxically, out of strong, prefascist civil societies. Some may ask whether we are at such a moment today in the United States—do nonprofits evince more bonding of like-minded people rather than bridging across different groups of people?

In the United States, members of churches, synagogues, and mosques are among the most generous citizens with regard to donations of both money and time (see Chapter 26, "Religious Organizations," by Brad Fulton). But do religious communities teach values of participation or toleration, especially toward others who are not members of their specific community? Recent research by Wesley Longhofer, Giacomo Negro, and Peter Roberts (2018) suggests that schools can unite diverse communities, whereas churches tend to divide them. In Chapter 11, "Nonprofits as Urban Infrastructure," Christof Brandtner and Claire Dunning explore how civic organizations function as either inclusive or exclusive communities. Their focus on the reciprocal relationships between civic associations and the wider society sheds light on the values of associational life for the vitality of cities.

Most research on civic participation has been carried out in countries that are broadly democratic. With democracy in retreat in many nations, it becomes imperative to study and theorize how associations operate under autocratic governments. In recent years, both autocratic and even ostensibly democratic regimes, such as Austria and Canada, have moved to limit the involvement of international NGOs in their local polities. These restrictions make it difficult or impossible for domestic NGOs to receive funding from international sources and restrict travel on both sides. Kendra Dupuy and Aseem Prakash argue in Chapter 28, "Global Backlash Against Foreign Funding to Domestic Nongovernmental Organizations," that such restrictions can be viewed as a form of border control, in which states seek to regulate foreign donors' influence on domestic politics.

Counterbalancing these limiting forces are a number of trends that expand civil society. As countries become more developed and larger middle classes arise, a number of features spark associational life. Environmental pollution prompts citizens to take action, independent of government, as discussed in Chapter 15, "Nonprofits and the Environment," by Magali Delmas, Thomas P. Lyon, and Sean Jackson. Homeownership fosters attachment to place and a sense of community. Addressing these local concerns requires some degree of organizational skill. Accordingly, the neo-Tocquevillian argument developed by Putnam and others may prove applicable in contemporary nondemocratic settings.

The internal organizational dynamics that develop in these new contexts will be as critical to determining outcomes as the external situations that nonprofits seek to rectify. The relationship between internal voice within organizations and external political advocacy is a central topic in this volume. Nonprofit organizations frequently advocate on behalf of their members, and the manner in which they do so both reflects and influences the way that citizens exercise their rights. As Ted Lechterman and Rob Reich discuss in Chapter 6, "Political Theory and the Nonprofit Sector," many of the most fundamental rights of liberty are expressed in the context of nonprofit organizations. It is to be expected, therefore, that voluntary associations function as sources of countervailing power challenging existing structures. How this countervailing force is exercised will be critical to its outcomes. Is voice exercised through influential mass membership associations, as was common at the end of the nineteenth century and the beginning of the twentieth century (Skocpol, Ganz, and Munson 2000), or is advocacy championed by organizations run by skilled managers with few members (Walker, McCarthy, and Baumgartner 2011)? If large national membership organizations have declined in size and influence, is civic voice reduced even as policy advocacy is more actively pursued by a growing number of special-interest nonprofits? The relationship between different types of nonprofits and their effects on public policy is a focus throughout Part VI of this volume.

Any argument that suggests strong swings of the pendulum from mass movements to special-purpose entities is, of course, subject to exceptions. It may well be that new forms of civic and social action are emerging that have largely escaped our view because of a scholarly focus on formal organizations. In a study of urban Chicago, Robert Sampson and his colleagues (2005) found a rich, blended associational life in which cookouts, bake sales, and barbecues, often sponsored by churches and neighborhood associations, were combined with efforts to influence local policy decisions. A picnic to save a local park and a cookout in support of a library are examples of community activism and policy advocacy going hand in hand (Han 2016). One question that remains to be answered is whether such activity channels advocacy and protest to the local level, away from large-scale social change, or is a wellspring for nationwide movements. The complex web of relationships among local, national, and international movements for political and human rights, and the attending backlash against these efforts, is explored in Chapter 28, "Global Backlash Against Foreign Funding to Domestic Nongovernmental Organizations," by Kendra Dupuy and Aseem Prakash.

Conclusion

In an earlier era, scholars sought to develop a body of theory to explain why and where nonprofit organizations existed (Hansmann 1987; Weisbrod 1988). Interestingly, this effort dovetailed with a period in American political development when nonprofits were perhaps most distinctive as an institutional form, separate from both government and business in their motivations. This tripartite scheme was an ingenious model; however, it proved challenging to apply to other nations with different political economies and at different stages of institutional development. Today, clear boundaries are harder to find even in the U.S. context. Social movements create markets, as discussed in Chapter 15, "Nonprofits and the Environment," by Magali Delmas, Thomas P. Lyon, and Sean Jackson, and markets create movements, too—consider, for example, the invention of the birth control pill (Eig 2016). Nonprofits rely on funding not only from earned income and individual donors but from governments, businesses, foundations and other nonprofits, tying all three sectors together.

In my own work on public and private science in the biomedical field, I have used the distinction between organizations that were "in science to do business" and "in business to do science." We found this contrast much more analytically crisp than a distinction based on legal form in explaining divergent behaviors (such as following norms of open as opposed to private science and developing new medicines rather than copycat drugs) (Powell and Sandholtz 2012). Nonetheless, some of the most pathbreaking work in biomedical research has come out of private nonprofit research centers such as the Salk Institute in La Jolla, California; the Gladstone Institutes in San Francisco; the Broad Institute in Cambridge, Massachusetts; the Genomics Institute of the Novartis Research Foundation, also in La Jolla; the Institute for Systems Biology in Seattle; and the Cleveland Clinic (Powell and Owen-Smith 2012). These entities combine the freedom of discovery associated with university science with the sense of urgency for tackling big questions associated with commercial firms. Yet not all nonprofit research centers have such sterling reputations; some fall victim to greed and malfeasance. In short, our analytical lens should be directed at behavior rather than legal form, and we cannot assume that behaviors and form march in lockstep.

There is little doubt that civil society is found in many places. The coffeehouses cele-brated by Jürgen Habermas (1989) have been joined by brewpubs, public and nonprofit parks, libraries, museums, incubators, and, for all their vitriol, online discussion platforms. Nonprofits now give microloans to small businesses, and limited liability corporations are gaining prominence as an alternative to foundations because they allow donors to fund businesses and engage in political advocacy (see Chapter 4, "The Organizational Trans-formation of Civil Society," by Patricia Bromley). More businesses have moved beyond viewing corporate social responsibility as a publicity matter and are thinking seriously about their social purpose. In the overall scheme of the economy, the number of such businesses is small, but it may be growing as some firms think about adding to the econ-omy rather than extracting from it. Furthermore, cities around the world have pursued challenges such as climate change by engaging with local civic actors and collaborating to develop bottom-up solutions rather than top-down imposed policies that seldom work (Brandtner 2019). Clearly, social purpose occurs across organizational forms rather than only in neatly segregated spaces.

Thus, our goal with this volume is to chart the current research terrain, identify gaps in our understanding of the shape and impact of associational life, and prioritize questions for future study. We have assembled an interdisciplinary cast of contributors, bringing economists, historians, philosophers, political scientists, and sociologists together with researchers from schools of communication, education, governance, law, management, and public policy. We aim to move beyond familiar tropes that nonprofit organizations are more trustworthy, that they are fountains of civic engagement, that the boundaries between sectors are blurring, or that the sector is expanding rapidly across the globe. The chapters in this book ask the hard questions: Under what conditions do we see such effects or changes, and in what domains? Do arguments made in the U.S. context apply across nations, or are they limited to specific political systems? How do we conceptualize the different meanings of participation, and in what kinds of organizations? What insights are gained from well-crafted comparative and historical perspectives? Perhaps most cru-cially, what role can nonprofits play in the future, particularly as democracy appears to be receding? In tackling these thorny questions, this volume aims to make fundamental contributions to the study of civil society in ways that can inform many fields throughout the social sciences.

PART I

EMERGENCE, TRANSFORMATION, AND REGULATION

THE CHAPTERS IN THIS OPENING PART PAINT the nonprofit world on a broad canvas, capturing its history, financing, global proliferation, and tax treatment. There is a deep and lasting influence of founding beliefs and models from Britain and the U.S. colonies on the field's development over the first century of the young republic and up to the present day. These liberal origins underpin the development of civil society into a more formally organized sector over time, certainly in the United States but also in countries around the world with the globalization of liberal and neoliberal models. The nonprofit sector's trajectory is linked not only to its cultural and political origins, but also to the growth of capitalism and economic imperatives. In the United States, elite philanthropists used the tools and models by which they made their fortunes and applied those to their charitable strategies and organizations. In so doing, they shaped the recipients of their patronage and influenced public debates in the process. Relatedly, the federal tax system is interwoven with the U.S. nonprofit sector. Tax policy intervenes in the functioning of nonprofits, conditions their involvement in the political arena, and shapes how nonprofits engage in income-generating activities. The accounts of emergence and development of the sector spelled out here bring us up to the present day, where historical legacies interact with contemporary pressures to change the sector in novel and unprecedented ways.

In Chapter 2, "A History of Associational Life and the Nonprofit Sector in the United States," Benjamin Soskis describes the development of associational life in the United States over the span of four centuries. Many have described the United States as a special case of "benevolent exceptionalism," but Soskis is skeptical of such a claim. He notes that in colonial times there was an active transatlantic network that connected Britain and the main port cities of the United States—Boston, New York, Philadelphia, and Charleston. As reform movements developed and matured in Britain, they crossed the Atlantic, spurred on by trade, print media, and the ties of church and family. The densest associational "ecology" was found in Philadelphia, with its charity schools, ethnic aid societies, and the first public hospital. The American Revolution changed associational life in the former colonies, in both the nature of voluntary activity and its governance. The connection of voluntary organizations with democratic practice meant that how associations were organized and who was allowed to participate in them became subjects of debate. Formal charitable organizations did not emerge in any great number until well into the nineteenth century, and their regional distribution was highly uneven.

Soskis charts numerous moments of crisis that have characterized the sector through its history; he argues that these crises mark changes in the relations of power in the larger society. The nonprofit sector has been a crucible for political contestation over most of the defining issues in US history, from slavery to immigration. But nonprofits are not just sites for deliberation and advocacy. Soskis shows how the activities of nonprofits have reflected the changing distribution of power and service in America, with voluntary action deeply implicated in the practice of democracy, for all its faults and strengths.

Philanthropy represents an attempt at transferring economic wealth into social influence. In Chapter 3 "Seeing Like a Philanthropist," Aaron Horvath and Walter W. Powell seek to understand how the influence of the wealthy has changed over time. The business successes of elite philanthropists become a kind of *idée fixe*—how you earn conditions how you give away, as does one's stage of life. They trace five different eras of philanthropy, distinguishing the visions of elite philanthropists, the organizations they built, and the controversies their attempts at intervening in American society provoked. The aim of their chapter is to both reveal how philanthropists "see" the world and show how the philanthropic field of vision has changed from the time of Andrew Carnegie and John D. Rockefeller to today's era of Bill Gates and Mark Zuckerberg. They view philanthropy not as "mere" acts of generosity but as reflective signposts that mark collective understandings of democracy, wealth, and the kind of society we have become.

Wealthy donors from the past are not the peers of those in the present, but the philanthropic practices they adopted leave their imprint on successive generations. Yet even as organizational models persist, new forms of wealth create new philanthropic endeavors alongside the old. The visions of new generations interweave with the organizational models of past generations. This braiding is reflected in the myriad ways that established foundations are influenced by new entrants, with their novel approaches. Charitable donations are more than a mere medium of exchange, however; they are imbued with different meanings. Alms, contributions, gifts, grants, and investments mark not only distinctive monetary forms, but also very different relations between benefactor and beneficiary. Different conceptions of recipients (such as the contrast between the donee and the grantee) imply divergent relationships and obligations. For example, twenty-first century, ultra-rich philanthropists impose on recipients a new set of requirements and routines; nonprofits today have to act like start-ups or incubators, produce metrics, and talk about scaling in order to attract attention.

Horvath and Powell begin their chapter by observing that during the first Gilded Age there was keen awareness of the contradiction between Andrew Carnegie's philanthropic vision of how to improve "the general condition of the people" and the ruthless manner in which he ran his railroads and steel mills. Both Carnegie and Rockefeller faced strong headwinds, as the marriage of monopoly corporate power and elite philanthropy did not sit well with a vision of democracy. Today in our new Gilded Age, powered by an interconnected global economy, the relationship between corporate wealth, elite philanthropy, and political legitimacy has changed. The new vision is to bring benevolence to business, in the hope that corporate enterprises may be less extractive and can be harnessed to solve public problems. Philanthropy has undergone a profound shift from something once contested to now venerated, carrying hopes that its legitimacy can rub off on the private sector.

In Chapter 4, "The Organizational Transformation of Civil Society," Patricia Bromley argues that the nonprofit form has expanded massively worldwide in countries that differ politically, economically, and institutionally. Moreover, she asserts, within countries large nonprofits are increasingly formal, complex organizations that can look like their counterparts in the business and government sectors. Consequently, she states, all types of organizations work to demonstrate their accountability and responsiveness to the members of a pluralist society.

Bromley develops a cultural argument for the rise of formal nonprofit organization that accounts for why this form has proliferated and expanded so markedly. Her argument has both historical and cultural components. Seen through the lens of long-term historical change, the growth of formal organization is tied to broad political changes related to the evolution of a feudal religious polity with medieval governance structures into the secular, administrative, and legal structures of most modern nation-states. In tandem, she chronicles a profound social transformation in which the individual has become the locus of both rights and action. The twentieth century witnessed an explosion of human rights treaties, organizations, and doctrines that spread liberal principles worldwide. More rights were constructed, and for more types of people, expanding agency to more members of the general population. In addition, diverse realms such as education, art, and music have become matters of interest to the general public, rather than restricted to an elite few.

Of course, there has been a backlash in many countries to the expansion of scientific principles, accompanied by a loss of respect for the rights of individuals. The core foundations of the liberal world order are under assault; hence we might expect a decline in the growth of formal nonprofit organizations, or a movement where they are more purveyors of special interests than the public good. Her chapter concludes with a rich discussion of possible research directions to explore these arguments.

Daniel J. Hemel argues in Chapter 5, "Tangled Up in Tax," that nonprofit organizations in the United States are caught in a complex web of nonprofit-specific tax provisions, and that even seemingly unrelated tax statutes often tie back to the sector in complicated ways. He distinguishes among three types of entanglements—administrative, political, and market—and explains how society's decisions to support the sector through tax exemptions and deductions both respond to and result in entanglements. The two main ways in which the federal tax system supports the nonprofit sector are exemption and deduction. Exemption allows nonprofit organizations to earn income without paying any entity-level tax; deduction allows donors to a subset of nonprofit organizations to reduce their taxable income by the amount of a gift. But such support comes with strings attached. He reminds us that the familiar term *tax exemption* is a misnomer of sorts, as exemption comes with a heavy load of compliance burdens, disclosure obligations, and other behavioral restrictions that dictate the day-to-day lives of nonprofits.

Administrative entanglement involves the tax authorities in the lives of nonprofit organizations, whereas political entanglement refers to the participation of nonprofit organizations in the political sphere. Administrative entanglement and political entanglement both involve the nonprofit sector with the organs of government; a different type occurs when nonprofit organizations engage with the market—for example, by operating profit-seeking enterprises. Such activities prompt worries over "unfair competition" between nonprofit organizations that enjoy the benefits of tax exemption and for-profit firms that pay full freight. A second fear is that excessive entanglement with the market will divert nonprofits from their core missions. A third is that nonprofit managers will prove ill-equipped to succeed in commercial ventures and that they will squander their organizations' resources when they try.

Hemel asks why the tax system should support nonprofit organizations in the first place. He notes that both public goods and redistribution arguments apply to a minority of the organizations in the sector. Moreover, if the goal is to redistribute wealth from rich to poor, then we might ask why policy makers have chosen to do so indirectly via tax-favored treatment for nonprofits rather than directly through cash assistance, food stamps, housing vouchers, and the like. Hemel suggests that three other rationales fare somewhat better in justifying the federal tax system's support for the nonprofit sector. One—the *Tocquevillian account*—emphasizes the importance of nonprofit organizations as checks on governmental power. A second—the *Hayekian account*—highlights the ability of the nonprofit sector to aggregate information and preferences without succumbing to the pathologies of the political process and central planning. A third—which he calls the *Pigouvian account*—posits that gifts to nonprofit organizations generate positive externalities (i.e., social benefits that the giver of the gift does not fully capture), and that government subsidies are necessary to ensure that a healthy amount of gift giving occurs.

Hemel further explores the key provisions of the US Internal Revenue Code affecting the nonprofit sector and explains how these provisions balance a set of seemingly irreconcilable policy objectives with varying degrees of success. He also surveys recent legislative changes that significantly reduce the tax system's support for the nonprofit sector, while also generating greater entanglement along several dimensions, raising the possibility that some nonprofit entities will opt out of tax-exempt status altogether.

The authors in the opening chapters attend to large-scale trends, both looking back into the past and questioning the future contours of voluntary activity. Whether the influences come from elite money, global political trends, or battles over US tax policy, it is clear that much change is afoot, and the nature and character of voluntary activities are becoming altered.

2   A HISTORY OF ASSOCIATIONAL LIFE AND THE NONPROFIT SECTOR IN THE UNITED STATES

Benjamin Soskis

WHETHER OR NOT JOHN WINTHROP ACTUALLY addressed his fellow Puritans sailing aboard the *Arbella* in 1630 on the subject of "A Modell of Christian Charity," that sermon represents one of the earliest intimations of a powerful discursive strain in American thought: benevolent exceptionalism (Curti 1961). This conviction holds that Americans, faced with extraordinary challenges and graced with exceptional resources, have long distinguished themselves through acts of personal generosity. Yet in the sermon, Winthrop did not call for the establishment of formal associations to practice good works. There was no need for them, for the entire covenanted body of those who "by mutual consent" had dedicated themselves to the Massachusetts commonwealth would be "knit" together by "the bond of love" (Hammack 1998:24, 25; Dawson 1998).

The relationship between voluntarist activity and the formal organizational structures and networks that harbor it would remain a powerful theme in the development of what we now call the *nonprofit sector*. In fact, outside the church, the first century of American settlement exhibited minimal *formal* nongovernmental associational activity. Well into the nineteenth century, most education and charitable care for the young, infirm, and elderly was provided informally in the home. There were, of course, some modest exceptions, such as the Societies to Suppress Disorders, modeled on English societies for the reformation of manners, that sprang up in a handful of New England towns in the early 1700s. The emergence of such societies reflected the dissolution of Winthrop's corporate commonwealth; they offered a space within the polity where the ecclesiastic elite, faced with declining political power, could continue to exert authority (Bernard 1998; Hammack 1998; Hall 1992). Such a calculation marks another prominent theme in the history of American voluntarism: the complex, and sometimes strained, relationship between voluntary action and democratic practice.

The Modest Colonial Roots of American Associational Activity

Throughout the colonial period, no clear line marked the boundaries between a public and a private realm. This lack of demarcation was especially notable in colonies with a strong religious establishment, where the tax-subsidized church (Anglican in Virginia,

Congregational in Massachusetts) was central to the apparatus of public governance and also the locus of charitable, religious, and educational service provision. In colonies marked by religious toleration, such as Pennsylvania, on the other hand, "self-supporting and self-governing congregations enjoyed an autonomy that anticipated the status of voluntary associations in the nineteenth century" (Hall 2006, 33).

Corporate charters, which allowed a charitable body to receive, alienate, and hold property beyond the lives of its members, were rarely granted by the British government, and only slightly more frequently by colonial proprietors, governors, and assemblies. When charters were issued, it was for some enumerated *public* purpose—constructing toll roads or managing schools, for instance. Not only did a considerable part of the funding of such corporations come from colonial legislatures, but public officials often sat on their boards (Hammack and Anheier, 2013; Levy 2017).

In the colonial period, few charitable institutions amassed significant endowments. Legislatures often refused to grant equity jurisdiction to courts, making charitable and testamentary trusts unenforceable and leading several early charitable trusts to fail (Hall 2006). Exceptions included the mission societies of Britain's established churches and a few denominational colleges, such as Harvard, the oldest eleemosynary corporation in the colonies, founded in 1636 and chartered in 1650 (Hall 1992; Thelin 2011). Only a few colonists had sufficient wealth to make large-scale donations to charitable corporations. Those who did, such as Puritan merchant Robert Keayne, who left more than a quarter of his considerable fortune to fund public works and the relief of the poor in Boston, helped secure a reconciliation between Winthrop's caritative ethics and the economic rationalism of an emerging mercantile elite (Dalzell 2013; Heyrman 1977).

By the middle decades of the eighteenth century, colonial cities—especially the port cities of Boston, New York, Philadelphia, and Charleston—were developing a richer associational ecology. The growth of such associations tracked the maturation of the formal and informal social groups, fraternities, and joint-stock companies that had sprung up in English cities at the end of the seventeenth century. In fact, major colonial port cities existed within a transatlantic network of reform. That network would be strained by the Revolutionary War but would survive it. Humanitarians were thus linked by trade, consumer and print culture, family and religious ties, and a shared concern for distant others (Moniz 2016).

The densest thicket of associational activity was in Philadelphia, at the time the colonies' largest city. Philadelphia boasted charity schools, a host of ethnic aid societies, and the nation's first public hospital. The hospital's funding was raised by Benjamin Franklin from a combination of private donations and what would now be called a challenge grant from the Pennsylvania Assembly. Reflecting Franklin's distinctive approach to voluntarism, the city hosted other institutions and organizations that melded self-help and civic betterment, including the Junto, a debating and moral improvement society founded by Franklin; the colonies' first volunteer fire company; and their first subscription library (Moniz 2016; Morgan 2002; McCarthy 2003).

The Revolutionary Surge in American Voluntarism:
Pluralism and the Private Sphere

A late-eighteenth-century surge in voluntary activity was spurred by the American Revolution. Associations like the Sons of Liberty and the Freemasons linked communities in common political purpose, and the Revolutionary rupture itself seeded further associational development. The break from Great Britain necessitated the formation of new associations to replace those whose support had come largely from the metropole (Wright 1992; Moniz 2016). The constitutional provisions guaranteeing freedom of speech, religion, and the press forged in the wake of the Revolution at the state and federal level nurtured associational activity; state and federal constitutions were models for many of the societies that formed in the early Federal period (Butterfield 2015). Independence itself fostered a sense of national identity and purpose, which found an outlet in expanding charitable enterprises. "Can there be a union of the people for political purposes, and not one for those of a moral and religious nature?" asked one clergyman advocating a national Bible society in 1816 (Fea 2016:15).

Yet the Revolution also reshaped America's legal and cultural landscape in ways not always favorable to formal associational life. Independence led several states to reject English law, thus untethering the regulation of charities from the 1601 Elizabethan Statute of Charitable Uses, whose enumerated categories of giving had provided the legal basis for donors to entrust property for eleemosynary purposes during the colonial period. More generally, the Revolutionary struggle and the republican principles that animated it forced Americans to grapple more directly with the relationship between voluntary organizations and the public systems of governance they were erecting. Republican thought provoked concerns that associational membership might undermine the individual autonomy essential for citizenship (Neem 2008; Butterfield 2015).

Thus if voluntary organizations would become increasingly prominent in the new nation's civic and social life, so too would suspicion of them as potential loci of concentrated power. A deep ambivalence regarding the compatibility between private organizations and democratic principles was built into American voluntarism. In the first half century of the new nation, this ambivalence was chiefly expressed in two areas of contestation: battles over the corporate privileges and legal rights that the state could grant to private organizations, and debates over the moral legitimacy and political consequences of private association, in relation to the public good.

The latter issue emerged as a commitment to pluralism reshaped the realms of religion and electoral politics, a consequence of legal disestablishment and the rise of electoral partisanship. The Federalists who stood at the helm of the new nation insisted on subordinating the right of association to the public good, which the government had been formed to promote, and which its elected leaders would define and superintend. For Federalists, behind the promise of association lurked the dangers of faction, which often served, as George Washington warned in his Farewell Address, "a small but artful and enterprising minority of the community" (Neem 2008:34). The Federalists' Republican challengers, on the other hand, insisted that extragovernmental associations could be a safeguard against public corruption and tyranny. This was the function they assigned to Democratic-Republican societies, more than fifty of which were formed during George

Washington's second term, in the cities of the Eastern Seaboard as well as in backcountry towns (Neem 2008; Butterfield 2015).

For Federalists, these extraconstitutional "self-created societies," as Washington termed them, represented the fracturing of an Edenic, unitary commonwealth (Neem 2008:46). Yet on the victory of Jeffersonian Democratic-Republicans, Federalists established their own Washington Benevolent Societies, signaling a general, if grudging, acceptance of the prismatic splintering of the public good into a contending array of associational forms.

Debates on the development of charitable institutions were subsumed by broader clashes over the place of private corporations in the new nation. In the post-Revolutionary decades, states in the Mid-Atlantic and the South tightened restrictions on corporate power, including on corporations formed for eleemosynary and religious purposes. These restrictions were especially pronounced in Virginia, which refused to incorporate many charities, limited the ability of those incorporated to accumulate property, and, in 1802, confiscated the endowments of the established Anglican church and turned the funds over to county control (Hall 1992; Wyllie 1959).

Other Southern states adopted elements of this restrictive "Virginia doctrine," which affirmed a preference for public institutions over private ones (as exhibited by the founding of the University of Virginia in 1819) (Hall 1992; McCarthy 2003; Neem 2008). Even some Northern states that later in the century would provide safe harbor for charitable corporations initially proved less hospitable, limiting the number of corporations (as in New York) or the amount of property they could hold (as in Connecticut).

In general, northeastern states were more solicitous of charitable corporations, in part because the political elite in those states tethered corporations closely to their governing authority (Hall 1992, 2006). In Massachusetts, which by the beginning of the nineteenth century led the nation in the number of corporations created, Federalists granted corporate privileges to institutions headed by their political allies, often installing ex officio representatives on their boards and insisting on their essentially public character. Democratic-Republicans, on the other hand, regarded exclusive grants of power as a threat to civic equality (Neem 2008). Yet Federalists began to reconsider their understanding of charitable corporations when their hold on political power began to slip. Instead, they grew attracted to an alternative vision in which voluntary corporate organizations belonged to a distinctively private sphere, insulated from political interference and the whims of electoral majorities (Hall 1992; Neem 2008).

The legitimacy of this private sphere for voluntarist activity was secured through a legal battle over control of Dartmouth College. The school was founded in 1769 under a royal charter, which named the major donors as trustees and gave them sole authority to name their successors. In the ensuing decades, Dartmouth received financial support from the New Hampshire legislature and was the site of clashes between orthodox and republican forces in the state, though it remained in Congregationalist hands even after a republican faction gained political power. In 1816, the Democratic-Republican governor of the state sought to reorganize the college as a fully public, secularized institution, appointing trustees to its governing board, establishing a body of overseers appointed by the state legislature, and expanding the institution's commitment to religious freedom. The old trustees challenged the governor's authority to alter the charter, and the case, *Dart-*

mouth College v. Woodward, arrived at the Supreme Court, where it was argued by notable Dartmouth alumnus Daniel Webster. Webster insisted that although the corporation was a creature of government, its identity was defined by the private relationship between donors and the college, not by its public purpose. This relationship was embodied in the charter, which represented a private contract between donors and trustees that the state was constitutionally bound to honor. In its 1819 decision, the Court sided with Webster. In the words of Justice John Marshall, the justices realized that one "great inducement to these gifts is the conviction felt by the giver that the disposition he makes of them is immutable" (Hammack 1998:135; Hall 2006; Wyllie 1959; McGarvie 2003).

Dartmouth College v. Woodward affirmed a sort of eleemosynary disestablishment, laying down rough lines of demarcation between public and private realms. It highlighted the dangers to states of delegating public purposes to private entities over which they could claim little control; henceforth, tasks that public authorities deemed vital would need to be met with governmental funds. Other objectives could be addressed by private voluntary associations, largely sustained through philanthropic contributions, whose rights to be free from government interference the Court grounded in their formal corporate status. As Justice Marshall wrote in his decision, "These eleemosynary institutions do not fill the place which would otherwise be occupied by government, but that which would otherwise remain vacant" (Neem 2008; McGarvie 2003:102).

Yet the boundaries remained indistinct. Elected officials sat on the governing boards of colleges like Harvard and Yale until the 1870s. And the *Dartmouth* decision did not mark the dissipation of the public's ambivalence toward charitable corporations. In fact, in another case from the same session, *Philadelphia Baptist Association v. Hart's Executors*, the Court ruled against a Virginia testator whose bequest to a Philadelphia Baptist association was challenged by his heirs, who pointed out that the association was unincorporated at the time of the gift. The Court argued that because Virginia had repealed the Statute of Charitable Uses, the state court lacked the equity power to enforce the trust (Wyllie 1959; Katz, Sullivan, and Beach 1985).

Following that decision, Virginia, Maryland, and Pennsylvania struck down other gifts and imposed additional limitations on charitable bequests (Neem 2008). The Court did not resolve the underlying legal issue until 1844, in *Vidal v. Girard's Executors*, issuing what one scholar called a "declaration of philanthropic independence, a plea for less reliance on English precedents and prohibitions" (Wyllie 1959:210). It affirmed that charitable trusts owed their legal standing to the common law and thus were not threatened by the repeal of the Elizabethan Statute of Charitable Uses.

Disestablishment and the Post-Revolutionary Frenzy of Association

In the nation's first half century, America's voluntary realm was marked by the somewhat paradoxical combination of the precariousness of its formal organizational terrain and the vitality of its associational activity. Alexis de Tocqueville famously celebrated this dynamism in his visit to the United States in the early 1830s. "Wherever at the head of some new undertaking you see the government in France, or a man of rank in England, in the United States you will be sure to find an association," he remarked. Americans united to form associations of a thousand other kinds, religious, moral, serious, futile, general or restricted, enormous or diminutive. The Americans make associations to give entertainments, to found seminaries, to build inns, to construct churches, to diffuse books, to send missionaries to the antipodes; in this manner, they found hospitals, prisons, and schools. (Hammack 1998:150)

But associational development was not uniformly distributed throughout the new nation. It was particularly pronounced in the Northeast (Tocqueville had depicted the New England town as a model voluntary association) and in certain parts of the Mid-Atlantic region. In New England, for instance, the number of charitable institutions grew from about fifty at the time of the Revolution to as many as two thousand by 1820 (Wright 1992). Between 1830 and 1850, voluntary associations spread to the upper South and the Midwest. In the lower South, their growth was checked by informal kinship networks. Nat Turner's 1831 slave rebellion also led Southern elites to clamp down on the formation of independent reform organizations (Gross 2003; McCarthy 2003; Green 2003).

The first wave of associations was often composed of mutual benefit and fraternal societies. They were followed by groups dedicated to humanitarianism and moral reform (Wright 1992). Before 1810, most were autonomous, stand-alone organizations. But by the 1820s, rich regional and even transnational networks had emerged, with a central headquarters and filigrees of local auxiliaries. Information—on local conditions, on fund-raising techniques, on organizational structure—flowed throughout these networks, feeding "a national culture of philanthropy" (McCarthy 2003:82). The adoption of the term *philanthropy* in the 1780s itself marked the expanded scope and ambitions of an organized approach to benevolence.

What caused this post-Revolutionary "frenzy of organization" (Wright 1992:5)? Historians have offered a host of explanations, none of which seems adequate singly. But in combination they suggest the maturation of a propulsive and increasingly self-conscious commitment to private association, closely aligned with the nascent culture of civic republicanism (Butterfield 2015). The factors historians most frequently cite include a transatlantic surge in humanitarian thought, driven by a belief in the innate human capacity for sympathy, the autonomous self, and natural rights that crested at the end of the eighteenth century, leaving fertile ground for organized efforts at social reform (Moniz 2016; Butterfield 2015). They also include expanding commercial markets and global industrial capitalism, which not only produced dislocations that humanitarianism could address but created a middle class with the disposable income to sustain humanitarian efforts and amplified individuals' sense of their agency and responsibility to shape distant lives (Haskell 1985).

Others have highlighted technological improvements in transportation and communication systems, which allowed for the more rapid dissemination of printed publications—annual reports, newspapers, constitutions—that familiarized Americans with voluntary associations (Neem 2008). The U.S. Postal Service—which after its establishment in 1775 quickly outpaced European systems in its sophistication and scope—allowed associational networks to extend from larger cities and towns into the hinterland. The blossoming of associational life that Tocqueville celebrated has often been attributed to the absence or weakness of early American government, but in this respect, it depended on a system of state support (Skocpol 1997).

Profound transformations in American religious belief, practice, and institutional development in the first half century after independence also reconfigured the associational landscape. The Second Great Awakening, which sparked evangelical revivals from Cane Ridge, Kentucky, to the coast of Maine, fired the converted with a sense of millennial possibility and a heightened sensitivity to the moral failings of society, fueling commitments to social reform. Evangelicalism itself, with its emphasis on personal conversion and spiritual agency, subtly nurtured voluntarism.

So too did religious disestablishment. "On the eve of the Revolution, nine of the thirteen colonies recognized established churches supported by public tax dollars" (McGarvie 2003:92); Massachusetts became the last of these to lose its established church in 1833. Voluntarism had occupied a place in American religious life before then—some states with an established church had allowed dissenters to opt out of supporting it, with their taxes directed to their preferred religious institutions. But disestablishment amplified voluntarism. It required denominations to compete for members and for funds, and the more fluid and volitional nature of religious identity that it encouraged boosted religious pluralism and provided a model for associational engagement more generally (Butterfield 2015; McCarthy 2003). In the early decades of the nineteenth century, states granted corporate status to dissenting Protestant and Catholic churches and to Jewish synagogues, many of which created affiliated charitable organizations or institutions; states also exempted these religious institutions from property taxes. Denominational organizations proliferated in the wake of disestablishment: denominations created their own seminaries, colleges, and reform and mission societies, to train ministers and promote their distinctive doctrines. Some of these institutions, as well as the denominations themselves, held significant funds and had a national scope and wide-ranging ambition that anticipated the general-purpose foundations of the Progressive era. Indeed, for the rest of the century, most "local schools, poverty-relief organizations, clinics and hospitals drew their support through religious networks" (Hammack 1999:53; Hammack and Anheier 2013; McGarvie 2003).

Both the orthodox religious establishment and its challengers could find some favorable elements in disestablishment. Jeffersonian Democratic-Republicans had pushed for disestablishment as a means of breaking up the concentrated power of the established churches. But leaders of the religious establishment, such as Connecticut Congregationalist minister Lyman Beecher, also came to embrace the development, worrying that state-funded churches could be controlled by an unpredictable democratically expanded electorate.

Beecher found value in voluntarism. When Connecticut eliminated state funding for Congregationalist churches in 1818, he declared it *the best thing that ever happened to the State of Connecticut* (italics in original) because it "threw [churches] wholly on their own resources and on God" (Hammack 1998:120). Moreover, the newly enlarged voluntarist realm created by disestablishment provided territory for the orthodox to set up fortified camp, where they could reconsolidate power through the establishment of reform societies after electoral defeats at the hands of the Jeffersonians. "Local voluntary associations of the wise and the good," Beecher explained, could serve as "a sort of disciplined moral militia," exerting a moral force "distinct from that of government" and helping the "Standing Order" to "retrieve what we have lost" (Boyer 1978:13). Voluntary associations, in Beecher's view, offered an antidote to democratic excesses and a means of checking the advance of secularism. Through them, he argued, the influence of orthodox ministers on the public actually increased after disestablishment (Hammack and Anheier 2013).

Reform associations like those championed by Beecher formed the backbone of what scholars have termed the Benevolent Empire, a loose network of organizations, often interdenominational, that developed by the third decade of the nineteenth century. They were dedicated to causes such as temperance, the establishment of Sunday schools and lyceums, the training of missionaries, and the distribution of Bibles and religious tracts. These associations were the first to harness the power of mass advocacy. Petition campaigns opposed President Andrew Jackson's Indian removal policy and pushed for the federal government to stop delivering mail on Sundays (John 1990). Women took an especially active role in the campaigns (Ginzberg 1990; Neem 2008; McCarthy 2003). The pressure that associations brought to bear on government policy compelled authorities to grapple with the legitimacy of private citizens lobbying to change the nation's laws (Zunz 2012).

The Benevolent Empire, with its particular moral vision of a redeemed Protestant nation, could not make exclusive claims to the field of reform. Its societies were part of a broader associational efflorescence that included groups with more radical ambitions, such as the handful of utopian communities that sprang up in the antebellum decades, and workers' associations and trade unions advocating for the rights of laborers (Laurie 1989). The Benevolent Empire also met with strong opposition from Democrats, immigrant groups, and others who resented its moralistic imperialism. Yet in response, Democrats did not seek to constrict the role of voluntary associations, but to expand access to them through general incorporation acts, many of which included property tax exemptions for "benevolent societies" or those devoted to "nonpecuniary" purposes. "No longer a discretionary grant of sovereignty, a corporate charter became a free entitlement of citizenship," writes historian Jonathan Levy (2016:22). In 1848, New York offered general incorporation to all "benevolent, charitable, scientific, and missionary societies." The act became a model for other legislatures; by 1860, twenty-four out of thirty-eight states offered some form of general incorporation (Levy 2016:30).

Nineteenth-Century Organized Benevolence, Urban Moral Reform, and Immigrants' Associational Vitality

The spread of voluntary associations over the first half of the nineteenth century was marked by the development of formalized organizational characteristics: elected officers and salaried employees, corporate charters, and written bylaws (Wright 1992; Hall 2006). In these decades, reform associations occupied the place that railways would at midcentury, as the most territorially expansive, bureaucratically complex, technologically advanced, and commercially sophisticated organizations of the period (Gross 2003). The American Bible Society, for instance, formed in 1816 through the merging of several state-based societies, had 1,200 auxiliaries by 1849; by the 1850s it had produced and distributed more than six million Bibles, pioneering the use of a steam-powered press as well as national marketing techniques (Fea 2016).

Fund-raising methods became more sophisticated, with coordinated annual collections, fund-raising auxiliaries (often headed by women), and invested endowments. In many communities, these endowments allowed for the accumulation of significant capital that could be reinvested, a development that did not merely reflect the growth of a market economy but spurred it on (McCarthy 2003). During these decades, small donors still provided most of the funds for voluntary associations, yet the accumulation of the first industrial fortunes initiated a slow shift toward reliance on the wealthy to sustain charitable institutions (McCarthy 2003; Dalzell 2013).

Although associations and charitable institutions sprang up in the hinterland, their growth was particularly pronounced in cities. In the three decades before the Civil War, the nation's urban population increased from 500,000 to 3.8 million, with new arrivals both domestic and foreign. For the middle class, the city surpassed the frontier as the primary arena for reformist zeal (with the threat of revolutionary violence hovering in the background). Urban public institutions—asylums and hospitals for those who could not care for themselves and workhouses for the able-bodied poor—had been an early response to such fears (Rothman 1971; Nash 2004). Private reform organizations, often led by prominent local merchants and bankers, sprang up from Pittsburgh to Louisville to combat what were considered distinctive urban vices: intemperance, gambling, sexual immorality. These associations represented attempts to re-create the moral order of village life amid the anonymity of the city and to counter the solicitations of urban political machines. In the decades before the Civil War, reformers made early efforts to systematize and rationalize city-based charitable work. A new corps of organizations, such as the Association for the Improvement of the Condition of the Poor (AICP), the Children's Aid Society, and the Young Men's Christian Association (YMCA), emerged, promoting increasingly moralistic approaches to poverty (Boyer 1978; McCarthy 2003).

If the voluntary realm expanded in response to the perceived threat of religious and ethnic diversity, it also came to reflect that diversity. Immigrants who arrived in the United States in the nineteenth century quickly established their own charitable networks, featuring mutual banks and credit unions, building associations and soup kitchens. Jews were particularly organizationally prolific. Jews in Charleston incorporated a Hebrew Orphans Society as early as 1802 (McCarthy 2003). As immigration increased from Germany and then from Eastern Europe, so too did association-forming. "Between 1848 and 1860, when Jews made up somewhere between two and five percent of [New York's] total population," writes Hasia Diner, "they supported more than ninety-three philanthropic associations. The rest of the city maintained only ninety-six similar institutions" (Diner 1992:102). Jewish institutions did not just address the needs of patrons and clients, but of staff as well. Barred from membership or professional advancement in Protestant-dominated social clubs and charitable institutions, Jewish immigrants founded their own. The Jews' Hospital, established in New York in 1851 (in 1866, it would change its name to Mount Sinai, to signify that it would care for non-Jewish patients as well), trained Jewish doctors who had difficulty securing positions at non-Jewish institutions (Hall 2006; Diner 1992).

Russian and Eastern European Jews who arrived at the century's end, like many other immigrants from those regions, formed thousands of *landsmanshaftn,* mutual aid societies for natives of the same hometown that offered unemployment, health, and burial benefits (Diner 1992). For Jewish Americans, as for Americans from a diverse range of religious and ethnic backgrounds, associational activity provided avenues for assimilation and acculturation, as well as opportunities to affirm and preserve religious and ethnic difference. The tension between these two imperatives has often been managed creatively. When Rebecca Gratz founded the first Jewish Sunday school in Philadelphia in 1838, she used books taken from the Protestant Sunday schools on which her own was modeled, but with slips of paper pasted over passages that posed especially stark challenges to Jewish religious teaching (McCarthy 2003).

For American Catholics, a consolidation of ecclesiastical authority channeled through the parish system both encouraged and constrained associational growth. In the early nineteenth century, lay trustees presided over the government of parish affairs, gaining vital experience in voluntary service; by the middle of the century, bishops asserted episcopal authority over the laity, presiding over a program of diocesan-based institution building. They also contended with the powerful impulse toward ethnic particularism that animated the voluntary efforts of Catholic immigrants. National parishes often started with the establishment of a mutual benefit society; regional or transnational ethnic-based secular voluntary associations, such as the Ancient Order of Hibernians (1836) and the German Central Verein (1855), followed, often championing broad programs of social insurance (Dolan 1985; Brown and McKeown 1997). As immigration, especially from Ireland, swelled in the 1840s, these voluntary associations came under strain, attracting the unwanted attentions of Protestant moral reformers. In response to these interventions and to the failure of public institutions to respect the religious needs of Catholics, a handful of leading bishops, led by New York's John Hughes, pushed for the establishment of an independent parochial school system ("build the school-house first, and the church afterwards," Hughes insisted). By 1865, such schools were instructing a third of the city's Catholics. Catholic bishops organized a broader campaign of institution building—orphanages, protectories, hospitals—that established a parallel voluntary realm, free from Protestant moralizing and proselytism. Although the construction of this private system of education and social service was in part precipitated by the perceived hostility of public officials to Catholic sectarian interests, Catholic institutions soon came to receive substantial public subsidies from state, county, and city coffers, as political machines became more sensitive to immigrants' electoral clout (Dolan 1985:263; Brown and McKeown 1997).

Similar patterns emerged on the West Coast as well. Immigrants turned toward voluntary associations and mutualism to negotiate the challenges of new and often hostile surroundings. In the Southwest, which did not experience the church-building surge of the East, Mexican Americans built their religious lives around the confraternity, the *confradia*, and formed *mutualistas*, self-help organizations. Chinese immigrants to California and the Pacific Northwest relied heavily on mutual aid organizations and credit societies, and early Japanese immigrants formed *kenjinkai*, voluntary associations to help newcomers find employment, food, and shelter; obtain legal residency; and arrange marriages and funerals (Dolan 1985; Carson 1999; Camarillo 1991).

Voluntary Associations as Spaces of Confinement and Liberation: African Americans', Women's, and Antislavery Activism

The American immigrant experience reflected a broader dynamic at play with respect to the associational life of marginalized or minority communities. The heavy investments they made in voluntary associations and private nonproprietary institutions often were

reactions to a degree of disempowerment, whether due to restricted access to certain political rights or to de facto forms of discrimination. But the voluntary realm also provided
opportunities for collective and individual advancement and *empowerment*. It provided a
beachhead allowing groups to assert those rights, lay claim to the privileges of citizenship,
and challenge the very structures of their discrimination. Voluntary associations could
function as spaces of both confinement and liberation.

This tension defined much of nineteenth-century women's voluntarism. The ideology
of Republican Motherhood that predominated during the Revolutionary era envisioned
women as uniquely equipped for charitable work through the exercise of their innate
maternal capacities, which were deemed too precious to be tainted by the vulgarities of
the political realm. Middle-class women, who made up the majority of church members
during the evangelical revivals of the early nineteenth century, swelled the ranks of the
benevolent associations that proliferated in the revivals' wake (women religious provided
much of the labor for Catholic charity institutions as well) (McCarthy 2003; Cott 1997;
Fitzgerald 2006). Women at first formed auxiliaries to male benevolence societies—by
1838, there were eighty-two female auxiliaries of the American Bible Society, for instance—
but by the early decades of the nineteenth century, they began to establish independent
organizations (Ginzberg 1990). Women's engagement with charitable corporations gave
them opportunities denied them in the domestic sphere. As historian Lori Ginzberg has
noted, through the control of charitable corporations, women, who if they were married
forfeited nearly all their property rights to their husbands, could acquire a measure of
independence. Women-led corporations could sue, make contracts, accept bequests in
their own name, and own, buy, and sell property (Ginzberg 1990:49). Through their voluntary labor organizing fairs, paying salaries of employers, investing revenues, conducting
petition campaigns, and even speaking before "promiscuous" (i.e., mixed-gender) audiences, women gained important training in entrepreneurial, commercial, and political
activity (McCarthy 2003).

Similarly, in the early Republic and antebellum decades, African Americans in northern cities threw themselves into the associational domain as a response to their restricted
access to the political one. Self-help organizations met the needs of communities neglected
by public and private social welfare organizations, and through their contributions to the
common good, they laid claim to African Americans' civic worth (Sinha 2016). Through
a network of churches, schools, and mutual aid societies, a black civil society flourished.
Philadelphia became the center of this "counter public" (Sinha 2016:130). It birthed, for
instance, the African Methodist Episcopal Church, the first national independent denomination under African American control. Under the leadership of Richard Allen, it was a
center of antislavery activism and reform. By 1835, Philadelphia could claim eighty black
mutual aid societies, and by 1848, nearly half of the adult African American population in
the city was affiliated with one. African Americans enjoyed considerably less associational
autonomy in Southern cities, because most states outlawed independent black fraternal
and mutual aid societies after Nat Turner's 1831 slave rebellion (Sinha 2016; Carson 1999;
McCarthy 2003).

Much African American associational activity channeled resistance toward Southern slavery and northern racial discrimination. In fact, the antislavery movement in the

United States exemplifies many of the characteristics of antebellum associational life more generally: in its transnational character, its intersection with evangelicalism, the heavy participation of women, and its assimilation of market culture and commercialism.

A group of Philadelphia Quaker artisans and shopkeepers formed the first organized American abolition society, the Society for the Relief of Free Negroes Unlawfully Held in Bondage, in April 1775. It represented the first wave of antislavery activism and formal associational activity, one nourished by republican and Enlightenment thought, which joined a rich transatlantic reformist network. The American Colonization Society (ACS), established in 1816, crested the second wave, directed by concessions to American racism toward the goal of settling free or manumitted blacks in Africa. The organization was led by some of the nation's preeminent citizens (James Madison served as its president), with particularly heavy representation from the South. In one of the nation's most striking early public–private ventures, the ACS received federal funding to purchase land in what is now Liberia to set up a colony (McCarthy 2003; Sinha 2016).

The first stirrings of the third wave were generated by the evangelical revivals of the Second Great Awakening, as well as by the opposition of African Americans to the colonization movement. It introduced a more militant, immediatist strain into antislavery activism. As early as 1787, free blacks in Philadelphia formally organized a society to protest slavery and protect community members from enslavement; counterparts that combined self-help, moral reform, and political advocacy were soon established in Boston, New York, and Newport. Black-led protection and vigilance societies established in the 1820s attacked not just slavery but racism in all its manifestations, in the North as well as in the South, taking aim at disenfranchisement and the segregation of public facilities like streetcars and schools (Sinha 2016).

The third wave of antislavery activism was marked by the publication of William Lloyd Garrison's journal *The Liberator* in 1831 and by the establishment of the American Anti-Slavery Society two years later. The AASS pursued immediate abolition through moral suasion and the mobilization of public opinion; it sponsored traveling speakers (including escaped slaves and, controversially, female orators), organized petitions to Congress, and supported abolition newspapers and journals. The AASS and other abolitionist associations harnessed consumer culture toward antislavery ends. They raised funds through fairs and instigated boycotts of slave-produced goods; some also developed a critique of capitalism that linked the emancipation of slavery to that of all laboring people. Antislavery was a mass movement, raising funds from a donor base of farmers, artisans, and workingmen. It was also a transatlantic one: Garrisonian abolitionists formed alliances with progressive antislavery forces in Britain and other European countries. By 1838, the AASS could claim more than a thousand auxiliaries throughout the North (Sinha 2016; Walters 1976).

Women served as the society's foot soldiers, raising much of its funds and making up as many as 70 percent of signatories on its petitions. Antislavery activism gave many women's rights activists their first education in networking, canvassing, and mobilizing (debates over the proper scope of women's activism produced organizational fissures within the antislavery movement) (Sinha 2016; McCarthy 2003). For some women, it also highlighted the limits of voluntary action itself and pushed toward a demand for suffrage.

The passage of the Fugitive Slave Act in 1850 and its enforcement throughout the North provoked an even more militant surge of antislavery activism. Vigilance committees fought off slave hunters through acts of civil disobedience. In both the North and the South, proslavery forces confronted antislavery activism with a countermobilization of repression and vigilante violence, responses that must be included within any honest reckoning of the history of American voluntarism. Mobs, often including some of the community's most distinguished citizens and enjoying the tacit support of local authorities, attacked abolitionist meetings. Garrison himself was nearly lynched. Southern states seized and destroyed abolitionist material dispatched from the North, with the backing of the U.S. Postmaster General (the dependence of associational activity on the mail system for its expansion proved a vulnerability). Anti-abolitionist violations of civil liberties galvanized bystanders into antislavery activism, until the struggle over slavery became intertwined with debates over the openness of American civil society. Threats to white citizens' freedom of expression in the North were as much at issue as the denial of freedom to African Americans in the South (Sinha 2016).

The Civil War and the Reconstruction of American Voluntarism

Battles over slavery fractured the nation's associational landscape. In the decades before the Civil War, the three major Protestant denominations—Presbyterians, Methodists, and Baptists—all split along sectional lines over a potent combination of theological disputation and the slavery question, "both portent and catalyst of the imminent national tragedy" (Goen 1985, 6). War itself would deepen this voluntarist sectional divide, as it fed on and boosted associational networks and capacity in the North to a greater extent than in the South (McCarthy 2003).

The initial mobilization in the North relied heavily on private voluntary action. According to the *New York Times*, individuals donated some $23 million in the first two weeks of the war, and most of the Union forces were volunteers. In fact, the war transformed the dominant modes of voluntarism, amplifying an emphasis on efficiency, bureaucratization, and professionalization that had been building over the preceding decades, and demoting in status a more traditional humanitarian culture closely associated with women's participation (Attie 1998; Ginzberg 1990; Skocpol 2003).

In the early months of the war, women took the lead in performing voluntary "war work," transforming an existing network of charitable associations into soldiers' aid societies. A band of elite women sought to coordinate and rationalize this wartime voluntarism; in October 1861, their efforts were incorporated into the Sanitary Commission, "a volunteer and unpaid bureau of the War Department," whose (male) leaders took responsibility for the public health of soldiers on the battlefield and in military encampments (Lawson 2002; Attie 1998:91). The Sanitary Commission championed an approach to humanitarianism that promoted scientific rationality harnessed in the service of efficiency, professional expertise, and bureaucratic rigor. It was sympathetic to the expanding national reach of the federal government, and it sought to quell "religious feeling, localism, and sentimentalism" in charitable work (Ginzberg 1990:159).

That commitment to scientific rationalism, bureaucratic organization, and a critique of traditional institutions and practices of benevolence would inform much of postbellum reform and would later achieve its apotheosis with the establishment of the private foundation. The approach was closely aligned with the managerial and industrial capitalism that provided the funds and the corporate model for those foundations (Hall 2006; McCarthy 2003).

During the war, the moral authority of the Sanitary Commission was challenged by the Christian Commission, which represented an older, evangelically oriented benevolent tradition. The Christian Commission relied largely on volunteers to minister to the physical and, especially, spiritual needs of soldiers. Unlike the Sanitary Commission, it encouraged provinciality in its donors, allowing them to target specific military units with their gifts. The contending approaches represented by the two commissions—a national, centralized, scientific system and a localized, religiously inspired one—would continue to clash in the decades to come, both in efforts to "reconstruct" the South and later in initiatives to relieve urban poverty (Ginzberg 1990; Attie 1998).

Indeed, in the years after the war, the South saw intensive associational activity, while undergoing a sort of voluntarist occupation that accompanied the brief military one. Scores of secular freedmen's aid societies formed throughout the North, joining denominational and interdenominational missionary agencies to send funds and volunteers to "uplift" the freed slaves. These societies worked closely with the Bureau of Refugees, Freedmen, and Abandoned Lands (the Freedmen's Bureau), established by Congress in March 1865. Bureau leaders actively courted the participation of voluntary societies. They initiated a division of labor in which the organization would fund the construction of hospitals and school buildings (more than 2,700 of them throughout the South), and the voluntary societies would fund upkeep and salaries (McCarthy 2003; Ginzberg 1990; Foner 1988). Former slaves carried an increasing share of the financial burden as donations began to dry up after the northern public came to assume that freed slaves' welfare was largely the government's responsibility. W.E.B. Du Bois estimated that freedmen donated $786,000 between 1866 and 1870 for the construction and upkeep of their own primary and secondary schools. In the decades after the war, African American Southern denominations established more than twenty colleges in the region (McCarthy 2003:198; Ginzberg 1990; Attie 1998; Foner 1988; Finkenbine 2003).

Divisions like those during the war emerged within northern voluntary interventions in the Reconstruction-era South, with evangelical groups focusing on proselytism and traditional charity and northern reformers seeking to transform the South along capitalist lines. This latter category included philanthropists who began to regard the South as their primary area of focus, a problem to be solved much as the city had been. To support Southern education, in 1867, for instance, financier George Peabody created what is often considered the first endowed grantmaking philanthropic foundation. Northern philanthropy flowed toward a network of black colleges and vocational schools that promoted a conservative gospel of black self-help, such as Alabama's Tuskegee Institute, founded by Booker T. Washington. By 1900, three fifths of Tuskegee's annual nontuition income came from a single foundation, the John F. Slater Fund, established in 1882 by a northern mill owner. Northern funders and their Southern agents largely accommodated Southern segregation in part to avoid provoking white hostility but also because they often held racist views regarding the capacities of freedmen and women (Harmon 2017; Anderson and Moss, 1999; Finkenbine 2003).

The failure of Reconstruction to fulfill its early radical visions of redistributive justice and racial egalitarianism is ultimately a political story. North and South sacrificed the rights of freedmen and freedwomen on the altar of sectional reconciliation. Yet that story must take its place within the history of American voluntarism as well. Not only did the ideals of free labor and racial uplift that animated much of the work of the Freedmen's Bureau's voluntarist partners offer little resistance to the entrenching of a system of racial oppression, but another, reactionary and indigenous wave of voluntary action helped secure that system. The Ku Klux Klan, begun as a social club in Pulaski, Tennessee, in 1866, soon spread throughout the South. It targeted African American and white leaders for assassination; it also conducted a campaign of terror to suppress Republican political activism; undermine institutions of black autonomy, such as schools and churches; and enforce labor discipline on white farms and plantations (Foner 1988).

Sectional reconciliation set the stage for a postbellum surge in the membership of voluntary associations and the creation of many that would develop national scope (although sectional divisions still persisted, because membership in these organizations was often less strong in the South) (Skocpol 2003). The half century after the Civil War marked a "golden age of fraternity" (Kaufman 2002). By one estimate, between 1870 and 1910, up to half of all adult Americans participated in fraternal societies, service clubs, or leisure organizations. This growth was not merely a product of urbanization, industrialization, and immigration. As Gerald Gamm and Robert Putnam have argued, "associational life was most vibrant . . . in the small cities and towns of the hinterland, rather than the great cities of the Northeast or Midwest" (Gamm and Putnam 1999:514). The associations provided vital training in civic engagement, linking Americans together in a shared associational culture.

Federations that bridged class and ethnic divides, such as the General Federation of Women's Clubs (1890) and the National Congress of Mothers (1897), which ultimately became the PTA, flourished (Skocpol 2003). Yet associational culture could fracture society as well. Many of the associations founded in these decades, such as the Knights of Columbus (1881) or, more parochially, the German Bakers' Singing Society of Paterson, New Jersey, allowed "individuals of different genders, races, ethnicities, and birthplaces to socialize in private, self-segregated groups" (Kaufman 2002:8, 21).

Some of the more prominent associations that formed in these decades channeled emerging social and political discontents and harnessed reformist energies. Farmers organized to demand the regulation of railroad freight rates and federal support for agricultural extension through the Patrons of Husbandry (the Grange) and the Farmers' Alliance; the Women's Christian Temperance Union, led by the indomitable Frances Willard, could claim more than a million members at the turn of the century and mobilized them in the push for Prohibition (Skocpol 2003). The first national labor federation, the National Labor Union, was founded in 1866; other labor associations, such as the Knights of Labor and the American Federation of Labor, soon followed (Laurie 1989). Groups emerged to promote reformist schemes of nearly every shape and hue: Greenbackers, single-tax supporters, Nationalist clubs championing the cooperative commonwealth ideas of reformer Edward Bellamy (Thomas 1983).

In the midst of this associational surge, the contours of an eleemosynary organizational realm, distinguishable from the domains of for-profit enterprise and public governance, became more distinct (though it could by no means yet be categorized as an intelligible "sector"). In 1874, after a speech before the Massachusetts General Court in which Harvard president Charles Eliot declared that the state owed its preeminence to "eight generations of people who have loved and cherished Church, School, and College," Massachusetts revised its charities statute, expanding the list of charitable purposes for which institutions and organizations might receive tax exemption (Hall 1992:43; Neem 2008). Over the next several decades, this "broad construction" of tax-exempt charitable activity was copied by a handful of other northern states, where private schools, colleges, and charitable organizations proliferated. States with a narrower construction of tax-exempt activity, in the South and West, experienced more modest growth, and public institutions often developed instead (Hall 2006).

In the same year as the Massachusetts revision, Pennsylvania passed a general incorporation law that determined corporate status with reference to three categories: religious corporations (exempted from property tax), taxable for-profit corporations, and not-for-profit corporations. This differentiation signaled the final dissolution of the commonwealth ideal, which had undergirded corporate status in the past, severing public and private purpose. For-profit corporations were thereby untethered from adherence to a public purpose enumerated in their charter; legally, they could be dedicated instead strictly to the pursuit of private profit. That focus hewed out a not-for-profit space for nonproprietary corporations animated by a different intent; indeed, at this time, rising real estate taxes led to the emergence of institutions organized along not-for-profit lines in fields such as arts, culture, education, and health care that previously had just as often been marked by commercial, for-profit enterprise. Many professional schools shifted from a proprietary model, in which the school was operated and owned independently by the faculty, to a salaried model, in which students paid tuition to the institution, which then paid a salary to instructors. Decoupling faculty income and academic policy allowed a greater institutional focus on academic rigor and achievement (Coquillette and Kimball 2015). Yet during the same period, many small private community hospitals developed into larger bureaucratic organizations, staffed by professionals and focused on providing medical treatment for paying customers, drawing closer in some respects to a for-profit corporate model (Rosner 1987).

Indeed, for-profit and not-for-profit corporate identity diverged only to be engaged in a complex pas de deux, each lending the other meaning and social significance. Indeed, the Pennsylvania law heralded the emergence of a social order tied to the ascension of industrial capitalism. Alongside mounting inequality, burgeoning private fortunes funded the private charitable institutions that would legitimize and rationalize the social and economic order and try to alleviate the ills that order perpetuated (Hall 1992, 2006:38; Levy 2016, 2017).

Immigration and the Rise of Scientific Charity

Successive late-nineteenth-century waves of immigration, originating beyond the traditional depots of western Europe, shaped the association building of the period. Between 1870 and 1890, for instance, more than forty-nine Czech mutual aid societies were formed in Chicago and more than thirty-five Italian mutual aid societies were established in Cleveland (Carson 1999). In the early decades of the twentieth century, *mutualistas* continued to sprout up in the West and Southwest, providing sickness and death benefits, loans, and legal aid for Mexican Americans and promoting festivities to mark Mexican national holidays; by the early twentieth century, Texas harbored an estimated one hundred of them. National organizations or convenings to promote the interests of immigrant populations and to defend against discrimination soon emerged, such as the Sons of Norway and the Alliance of Poles in America, both established in 1895, or El Primer Congreso Mexican-ista, held in Laredo in 1910 (Carson 1999; Camarillo 1991). Internal migration patterns also reconfigured the associational landscape. The failures of Reconstruction sparked a mass exodus of Southern African Americans to northern cities, where they joined rural workers and demobilized soldiers to rebuild black civil society. The black church, and the women's clubs and auxiliary societies that it sponsored, were at its center (Carson 1999; Hall 2006; Collier-Thomas 2010).

Steady immigration swelled the American Catholic Church and encouraged the creation of lay-led and parish-based societies to tend to the material and spiritual needs of the new arrivals. The ecclesiastical leadership also recommitted to the program of institution building that had begun earlier in the century. Public subsidies to Catholic charitable institutions continued to grow. In 1875, for instance, the New York Assembly agreed to fund Catholic institutions caring for poor children on a per capita basis and committed to move Catholic children housed in public institutions into Catholic ones. By 1880, 199 Catholic hospitals were in operation in the United States, as well as 267 orphan societies, staffed largely by women religious (comprising a labor force of some fifty thousand by the turn of the century) (Dolan 1985:324; Brown and McKeown 1997). More generally, public subsidies to private charitable institutions grew significantly during the close of the nineteenth century; in New York City, for instance, the city's payments to private charitable institutions for the care of prisoners and paupers grew from 2 percent of total city expenditures on the poor in 1850 to 57 percent in 1898 (Salamon 1987).

Immigration triggered an associational counterreaction as well. Over the last century and a half, nativist organizations have tended to peak in membership in tandem with the creation or expansion of ethnic associations (Skocpol 2003). The Ku Klux Klan experienced a resurgence in the 1920s after another burst of immigration, reaching membership in the millions. It spread throughout the nation, adapting its hate regionally. It focused on Latinos in the Southwest, Japanese in the Pacific Northwest, and blacks, Jews, and Catholics everywhere. The Klan managed to insinuate itself deeply into local politics in many communities throughout the nation (Gordon 2017).

The more visible nature of urban poverty in the closing decades of the nineteenth century stoked middle-class alarm over the potential spread of radicalism. Such concerns, coupled with more general fears about the working class abandoning the pews, drove many church leaders toward a "social Christianity." The adherents of its more progressive variant, such as Congregationalist minister Washington Gladden, preached a "social Gospel" in which the regeneration of the social order took precedence over individual salvation (May 1949). Other reform groups developed a more militant, moralistic approach to urban poverty, heralded by the arrival of the Salvation Army in the United States in 1880 (Winston 1999) and more aggressive policing of urban vice (Boyer 1978).

Reformers also sought to impose greater rationalization and coordination on private welfare provision, extending the work of antebellum organizations like the AICP and the Sanitary Commission. Charity organization societies (COSs), which originated in London in the late 1860s and first appeared in the United States in Buffalo in 1877, stood at the forefront of this movement. By the mid-1890s, more than a hundred COSs were clustered in the larger cities of the Eastern Seaboard and the Great Lakes region, as well as a number in the smaller towns of the Midwest, the West Coast, and the South. Charity organization leaders disdained the indiscriminate almsgiving that they claimed defined the benevolent approach of many traditional charitable agencies. They insisted on investigating charity applicants, registering those deemed deserving of help, and facilitating cooperation among charitable organizations. Like antebellum scientific charity societies, they also promoted "friendly visits" to the poor in their homes by volunteers, a practice that combined elite moral prescription and dispassionate social investigation (Soskis 2010:38; Ruswick 2013; Huyssen 2014).

The charity organization movement helped incubate the nascent social work profession; several of the earliest schools of social work emerged out of COS educational initiatives (Lubove 1965; Ruswick 2013). Over the next decades, paid professional social workers displaced volunteers within many charitable organizations. As a consequence, the public's charitable obligations came to center less on voluntary service than on monetary contributions necessary to sustain a professionalized workforce. Some regarded this development as a mark of progress, others as a sign of moral declension.

The economic depression that began in 1893, with unemployment rates that climbed by some estimates to as high as 15 percent, compelled many middle-class families to turn to private and public relief. Scientific charity leaders could not comfortably attribute this state of dependency to individualistic moral failings. The jarring sight of respectable citizens in bread lines pushed the movement to shift focus toward structural causes of poverty and to seek related legislative reforms. Progressive campaigns for increased governmental regulation and provision of social welfare sparked the establishment of a host of associations, the stirrings of an inchoate advocacy subsector. Much as at the turn of the previous century, a robust transatlantic network of reformers, who toured European and American cities, expanded the range of public policies and philanthropic initiatives under consideration (Rodgers 1998; Adam 2002).

The scientific charity drive toward centralization spread widely throughout the voluntary realm. Even the Catholic Church, which had been the charity organization movement's chief adversary, now assimilated its principles. It established centralized diocesan charity bureaus, overseen by the bishop and staffed by professional social workers. By World War II, all major urban dioceses had centralized their welfare services; these would ultimately be consolidated into Catholic Charities, the largest private system of social provision for the final half of the twentieth century (Oates 1995; Brown and McKeown 1997).

The Development of Modern American Philanthropy
and the Emergence of the Grantmaking Foundation

The massive personal fortunes accumulated by leading industrialists and financiers in the closing decades of the nineteenth century reshaped the realm of organized and institutional charitable activity. There were about a hundred American millionaires in the 1870s; by 1892 there were more than four thousand, and by 1916 more than forty thousand. At the start of the twentieth century, 8 percent of American families controlled more than three quarters of the nation's property (Zunz 2012:8; Sealander 1997:1). These fortunes—which were often the product of remorseless campaigns to drive down production costs (including labor) and anticompetitive tactics—provided the resources for an expanded philanthropic reservoir. The surge of large-scale giving raised questions about the relationship between ethically dubious means of accumulating wealth and the ways in which that wealth was redistributed. Critics worried about philanthropy's power to whitewash corporate depredation, and college presidents and charity officials grappled with the legitimacy of accepting "tainted money." The economic elite, meanwhile, sought to refashion traditional attitudes toward the responsibilities of wealth for an industrial age (Soskis 2010).

The Scottish émigré and steel magnate Andrew Carnegie, whose own fortune was premised upon the violent breaking of union power, which allowed him to slash wages and impose a twelve-hour workday at his steel works, offered what would become the best-known version of this refashioning in an 1889 essay titled "Wealth." (It gained its more famous title, "The Gospel of Wealth," in a subsequent British edition.) Carnegie's "Gospel" was notable in several respects. It secularized the traditional language of stewardship, embedding it within a social Darwinist framework, in which elite philanthropy was paired with inequality of resources. And it established philanthropy as an essentially public vocation, operating outside the realm of personal moral discretion and worthy of public scrutiny.

"The problem of our age is the proper administration of wealth," the essay opens, "so that the ties of brotherhood may still bind together the rich and poor in harmonious relationship." Carnegie's solution to the problem was philanthropy. It would not eliminate the gap between rich and poor, which Carnegie assumed to be a condition of progress. But philanthropy could provide "ladders upon which the aspiring can rise," and in doing so, it could legitimize concentrated wealth. The millionaire, using the skills and temperament that led to the accumulation of his fortune, would be called to serve as "a trustee for the poor, intrusted for a season with a great part of the increased wealth of the community, but administering it for the community far better than it could or would have done for itself" (Carnegie 2006:1, 12).

The more profit an entrepreneur could extract from the economy, the more he could return to the public as philanthropy. This powerful syllogism could work only if wealthy citizens abandoned two traditional means of disposing of personal fortunes: leaving them to their families or bequeathing them to some charitable cause at death. Entrepreneurs must take on an active engagement with their giving. In a subsequent essay, Carnegie listed a number of appropriate objects of philanthropic attention—parks, schools, public baths, music venues, and museums among them (Carnegie 2006:29).

In fact, all of the categories Carnegie invoked received large-scale infusions of philanthropic capital in the closing decades of the nineteenth century. The Gilded Age fortunes, which had been alchemized into spectacular private art collections, seeded some of the nation's most prominent art museums, such as New York's Metropolitan Museum of Art and the Art Institute of Chicago. Carnegie himself focused much of his giving on the establishment of a system of some 1,671 libraries in 1,412 communities throughout the nation (and hundreds more overseas) (Wall 1970; Nasaw 2006).

Gilded Age philanthropy also underwrote the rise of the research university in the United States, based on the German model. Whereas higher education in the United States had previously been dedicated largely to the training of clergy, with philanthropic prompting it would be directed to the production of a professionalized, technocratic elite, able to populate a swelling network of business corporations and government bureaucracies (Hall 2006; Hammack 1999). Philanthropy imposed academic standardization on unruly fields such as medical education and helped develop the modern university hospital. It also pushed institutions of higher education toward a more secular, nondenominational identity. In order to qualify for Carnegie Foundation faculty pensions, which were offered only to schools lacking denominational affiliations or tests for students, faculty, or trustees, a handful of colleges and universities loosened their church ties and excised their denominational affiliations from their charters (Thelin 2011; Marsden 1994; Lagemann 1983, 1989).

Indeed, whereas before the Civil War the largest single gift to an American college was Amos Lawrence's $50,000 contribution to Harvard, the postbellum decades brought forth a rush of million-dollar donations. Schools such as Johns Hopkins (funded with a $3.5 million gift in 1873), Stanford (funded with $20 million from Leland and Jane Stanford in 1885), and the University of Chicago (the beneficiary of $34.7 million from John D. Rockefeller over the course of several decades) sprouted (Hall 2006; Thelin and Trollinger 2014:20).

This new corps of philanthropists frequently intervened to shape educational policies and hiring decisions. At the same time, colleges and universities were developing social science departments in which scholars began to investigate sensitive issues in political economy and social policy, brushing awkwardly against the interests of their benefactors. At a handful of institutions of higher education across the nation, donors insisted on disciplining, and at times dismissing, professors who made public statements that they found politically, economically, or morally objectionable. The resistance of scholar-teachers to such intrusions produced a movement for academic freedom (Hofstadter and Metzger 1955). But as the most sophisticated critics of philanthropy appreciated, the pressures applied by benefactors were often subtler; the mere presence of a potential patron could warp academic practice and scholarly priorities. The turn of the century witnessed a pronounced shift among academics away from a commitment to advocacy and toward an ideal of "objectivity." Attaining that goal required avoiding certain inflammatory issues, which also happened to be those most likely to upset prospective donors (Furner 1975; Soskis 2010).

The themes that animated Carnegie's "Gospel" would become some of the most salient in the development of twentieth-century civil society, but the essay's immediate impact on elite giving practice is difficult to discern. More significant in that regard was the development of a legal landscape favorable toward philanthropy. This was especially the case in New York, where much of the new industrial wealth collected, and where restrictions on charitable and testamentary trusts buckled under the pressure of the promise of pooling philanthropic largesse. In the 1870s and 1880s, judges had invalidated several testamentary gifts to charitable trusts because of concerns about indefinite beneficiaries or violations of property limits established in corporate charters (Katz et al. 1985; Zunz 2012; Hall 1992). Public concerns about the squandering of these philanthropic resources mounted. A $5 million trust set up by former New York governor Samuel Tilden to establish a free library in the city failed after a legal challenge by Tilden's nephews; in response, the legislature passed an 1893 act allowing bequests to be made with indefinite beneficiaries, leaving the particular disposition of funds to the discretion of trustees (Zunz 2012; Wyllie 1959; Hall 1992).

The New York decision paved the way for the emergence of the general-purpose grant-making foundation, which became one of the most distinctive features of the twentieth-century nonprofit landscape. The modern philanthropic foundation expanded the orbit of the nineteenth-century charitable endowment. It adapted the bureaucratic structure of the business corporation, with a board of trustees and a staff of professional managers who oversaw an endowment whose invested returns were directed to charitable ends. Olivia Sage, the widow of the financier Russell Sage, established what is widely considered the first general-purpose grantmaking foundation in 1907. It focused on supporting policy and social research, including several pathbreaking surveys, and helped nurture the field of social work. By 1915, there were twenty-seven philanthropic foundations in the United States; by 1930, the number grew to three hundred (Zunz 2012; Crocker 2006; Sealander 1997). A handful of these were committed by charter to perpetual existence; others left institutional lifespan to the discretion of the trustees. Most still maintained circumscribed ambitions, supporting local social service providers. The few that claimed a broader, regional or national scope generated intense apprehension and scrutiny from the public. Foremost in this group was the Rockefeller Foundation (1913), which arrived at the end of a series of incorporated philanthropic institutions created by the Standard Oil founder, including the Rockefeller Institute for Medical Research (1901) and the General Education Board (1903).

Rockefeller's philanthropy would be animated by two principles, as defined by his philanthropic adviser, the former Baptist clergyman Frederick Gates. It would be scientific, meaning that it would address itself to root causes as opposed to palliatives, and it would be wholesale, meaning that when possible, it would be channeled through intermediary institutions and organizations that took up a position between benefactor and beneficiary. The Rockefeller Foundation's charter defined its aims as to "promote the well-being of mankind throughout the world," though Rockefeller's philanthropy largely came to focus on education, public health, and scientific and medical research (Fosdick 1952:20).

Like Andrew Carnegie and the longtime Sears, Roebuck head Julius Rosenwald, who founded schools for African Americans in the South, Rockefeller did not regard his philanthropy as rivaling the state. Instead, he often sought to boost state capacity, by paying salaries of public employees, for instance (Carnegie and Rosenwald conditioned their gifts on buy-in from local communities in the form of tax payments). But critics regarded the rise of the philanthropic foundation as a threat to democratic institutions and a direct challenge to federal authority. A cartoon in the *New York Press* expressed this apprehension by depicting the Rockefeller Foundation as a massive fortress with oilcan turrets, looming over Washington, D.C., and dwarfing the Capitol (Soskis 2010:255, 349). In part for these reasons, Congress rejected the Rockefeller Foundation's request for a congressional charter (though the foundation soon received one from New York State).

The leaders of the early major foundations were chastened by this opposition and subsequently largely avoided direct interventions in the policy arena. If it's true that the early philanthropic foundations were in the vanguard of efforts to promote a nationalized social policy before the New Deal, it was also the case that they bore that preeminence cautiously (Karl and Katz 1981). Most significantly, northern philanthropy directed to the support of Southern education worked within the confines of Jim Crow segregation (Nielsen 1972; Anderson and Moss, 1999). To the extent that foundations sought to shape public policy, they often did so indirectly, through the cultivation of private institutions and through the development and distribution of expert knowledge, which, as philanthropic leaders appreciated, provided an alternative means of governance (Lagemann 1989; O'Connor 1999).

The Growth of Mass Philanthropy and Voluntary Action in the Shadow of World War I

The ascendance of elite philanthropy in the first few decades of the new century coincided with, and in fact helped provoke, the growth of mass philanthropy. At times, the relationship between the two was complementary: wealthy citizens, who increasingly shouldered much of the burden of supporting the nation's expanding constellation of charitable institutions, sought to broaden the base of givers—though without necessarily yielding power to them. At times the relationship between the two was more adversarial: leaders of giving campaigns that targeted the lower and middle class framed their efforts as a necessary counterbalance to elite philanthropic power.

The dynamics between elite and mass giving were on particularly vivid display in Cleveland. In that city, powerful private business associations, led by the chamber of commerce, worked closely with local government, a collaborative relationship that was a hallmark of Midwestern communities more generally. Out of these public–private partnerships emerged several novel charitable institutions that soon spread throughout the United States: the charity federation and community chest, and the community foundation.

The seeds of the Cleveland Federation for Charity and Philanthropy were sown with a 1909 survey. It showed that the city's wealthiest 1 percent contributed more than 96 percent of funds collected for its social welfare agencies. In an effort to broaden the base of givers, the chamber of commerce joined forces with leaders of the city's chief social service agencies, including Catholic, Protestant, and Jewish charities. They adapted an innovation first developed by Jewish charities in Boston, in which various charity appeals were federated into a single, coordinated campaign. The Cleveland Federation allowed donors to designate their gifts to one of the participating agencies or place their funds' distribution at the discretion of the federation's board. Within a few years, half of all adults in the city were participating. The model soon spread to other cities in the form of community chests, which nurtured the ideal of nonsectarian social service provision (Hall 1992:64; Zunz 2012; Cutlip 1965; Hammack 1999).

Cleveland lawyer Frederick Goff, the head of the Cleveland Trust Company, devised the nation's first community foundation in 1914. Like the charity federation, the community foundation managed charitable trusts, whose funds could be directed to particular beneficiaries within the community or left to be distributed by a committee that included representatives selected by the Cleveland Trust Company, the city's mayor, and two of the region's senior judges. Not only would the community foundation extend giving op-portunities available to the city's financial elite to its middle-class and modestly wealthy residents, but also, through the active stewardship of community representatives, it un-dermined the power of the "dead hand" of the past to extend obsolete perpetual charitable gifts into the future. Goff evangelized throughout the country on behalf of the "Cleveland Plan." The model spread widely, first throughout the Midwest and then the Northeast (Hall 1992; Hammack 1998; Zunz 2012).

The community foundation, Goff declared, represented a way for "even greater foun-dations" than those that had been created by "men of great wealth" to be formed "out of the contributions of many citizens" (Hall 1992:165). Even more generally, the early twentieth century saw the growth and celebration of mass-based fund-raising campaigns that courted small-donor contributions, using sophisticated coordination, planning, and publicity techniques (while also tapping into earlier revivalist traditions of promotion). These campaigns often emphasized the collective power of ordinary Americans and pre-sented charitable giving as a democratic entitlement. Efforts that targeted disease proved some of the most successful, such as the American Red Cross–led charity seal campaign to fight tuberculosis, which brought in more than $1 million by 1916. Over the following decades, medical charities, such as the American Society for the Control of Cancer (which became the American Cancer Society in 1944) would become some of the nation's largest. They took the lead in pushing Congress to increase funding for medical research and, in the case of the March of Dimes and the polio vaccine, organized the medical trials themselves (Cutlip 1965; Zunz 2012). Mass philanthropy also swelled the endowments of the major universities. Harvard innovated with a campaign begun in 1912 that targeted alumni. Venturing beyond a traditional reliance on a few major donors, it brought in $12 million. Veterans of this campaign split off to form the first professional fund-raising firm, John Price Jones, Inc., which went on to lead hundreds of similar campaigns for colleges and universities across the nation over the next decades (Kimball 2014).

World War I intensified many of the trends toward institutionalization, coordination, and professionalization that had reshaped the voluntary realm in the United States over the preceding decades. It also deepened cooperation between the federal government and voluntary associations. The federal government quickly recognized that it could not achieve the massive mobilization of troops and resources necessary for the war effort with-out engaging in active partnership with the largest national membership federations, such as the Red Cross, the YMCA, and the Knights of Columbus. Yet it should be noted that, if war was the health of the state, as the radical Randolph Bourne famously argued, it was not *uniformly* the health of the voluntarist realm. Socialist and radical groups, as well as ethnic associations allied with the Central Powers, suffered disfavor and often persecution; after a congressional investigation into its alleged disloyalty, the German-American Alliance, for instance, disbanded and handed over its funds to the Red Cross (Barnett 2011; Skocpol 2003). Often voluntary organizations were themselves the agents of repression. The Justice Department turned to the American Protective League to investigate opponents of the war; state and local governments gave wide-ranging authority to volunteer-run councils of defense to track down draft dodgers and expose disloyal citizens (Schaffer 1991).

By the time the United States entered the war, thousands of relief organizations were contributing to the war effort, a superfluity that called out for coordination. Protestant, Catholic and Jewish leaders centralized their charitable efforts through organizations like the National Catholic War Council and the Jewish Welfare Board, and in turn partnered with each other and with the federal authorities (Skocpol 2003:53; Cutlip 1965:136; Zunz 2012).

The war gave an enormous boost to mass giving campaigns (Kimball 2015). When the United States entered the war in April 1917, the federal government threw its weight behind mass philanthropy by officially sponsoring appeals by the American Red Cross (ARC). The ARC received a congressional charter in 1900, which granted it "a unique and elevated status among American charitable organizations" as a "quasi-official, if still privately-funded, instrumentality of the U.S. government" (Jones 2013:94). Its first national fund-raising campaign raised more than $273 million in 1917 and 1918. The organization, which had been less than vital at the start of the new century, gained increased public confidence with its response to the 1906 San Francisco earthquake. By the war's end, it had become the nation's largest charity; its membership grew from 16,708 in 1914 to more than twenty million four years later (Zunz 2012). Wartime patriotic exhortations blurred the lines between compulsory and voluntary contributions and between private and public service, especially as governmental war bond campaigns, which engaged more than 66 million Americans as subscribers, adopted the techniques of mass philanthropy. Charitable giving became regarded as a mark of one's commitment to the American cause, and the failure to give generously, as a membership director of one association explained, could "cast a suspicion that one is not an American" (Cutlip 1965:121; Zunz 2012; Schaffer 1991).

The fund-raising demands led to the creation of community "war chests" to coordinate wartime solicitations. After the war, scores of these converted into community chests, which used surveys and statistical analysis to determine community needs. By 1920, in many cities, three quarters of families were listed as community chest contributors. Hospitals, colleges, and libraries also incorporated wartime fund-raising techniques in the decades after the war and employed the professionals who had honed them (Cutlip 1965; Zunz 2012). The patriotic fizz of war mobilization also boosted corporate giving. Donations continued to rise in the following decade, reaching significant levels even before Congress included a corporate charitable contribution deduction in the Revenue Act of 1935. Between 1920 and 1929, some thirty-five thousand corporations gave more than $300 million to community chests in 129 cities (Hall 1992:58; Cutlip 1965; Knauer 1994).

The need for wartime government revenue, which fueled skyrocketing taxation rates and sinking exemption levels, introduced a new fiscal order, which would soon engulf much charitable giving itself. No charitable deduction was included in the 1913 federal income tax, but one was added to the War Revenue Act of 1917. Exemptions from taxation for institutions organized for a charitable, education, or religious purpose had been included in the federal income tax enacted in 1894 and declared unconstitutional soon after; "subsequent enactments of the income tax code have all contained exemptions derived from this wording" (Fremont-Smith 2004:56). The charitable deduction was motivated by fears that war taxation would soak up the surplus wealth of wealthy citizens, depriving charities of needed resources. There was particular concern for the fate of higher education. A cartoon in the *New York Times* featured a top-hatted banker being held up at gunpoint by a robber labeled "Income Tax" and an impoverished figure in the background, with hands beseechingly outstretched, labeled "Charity."[1] Advocates made anti-statist arguments as well, warning that if wealthy citizens could no longer support charities for lack of private funds, the government would step in to provide those services. The fiscalization of charitable activity inaugurated by the 1917 act tied the voluntary realm even more closely to the state by instituting direct governmental subsidies for elite giving (Levy 2017).

The war bolstered the status of a few particular forms of nonprofit institutions. The pressures of mobilization and demobilization exposed the limited nature of the data available to government officials about the nature and workings of the economy. This realization led to the creation of a handful of influential new research institutions committed to collecting and analyzing data and, when appropriate, issuing guidelines to assist economic managers and policy makers. Institutions such as the National Bureau of Economic Research (NBER; founded in 1920) and the Brookings Institution (created in 1927) received significant funding from philanthropic foundations and formed the template for what would come to be known as the think tank (J. Smith 1991; Karl and Katz 1987). They sat within a web of privately governed institutions—alongside universities, foundations, and professional societies—that became vital instruments of public governance (Hall 1992).

The Associative State, the New Deal, and the Limits of Voluntarism

World War I was also a watershed moment for the development of mass humanitarianism and its relationship to state authority. The International Red Cross won the 1917 Nobel Peace Prize for its work monitoring prisoners of war, and the American Red Cross moved from its previous focus on domestic disaster relief into foreign aid. A number of other humanitarian organizations that would achieve high status in the following decades emerged out of the postwar period, including Save the Children, founded in 1919 (Barnett 2011; Irwin 2013).

One of the most ambitious humanitarian enterprises was conducted by the American Commission for Relief in Belgium, established in 1914 by Herbert Hoover to ship and distribute aid to Belgium, whose food supply had been decimated by German pillaging and by a British blockade. The commission's independence from any of the belligerent nations allowed it to distribute more than five million tons of food to Belgium during the war, yet in many respects it conducted operations on a scale and with the logistical sophistication associated with governmental authority. It was, as one British official quipped, "a piratical state organized for benevolence" (Nash 1988:94). It negotiated the purchase of food supplies, largely from offices in North and South America; arranged their transport across the Atlantic via convoys traveling under the commission's neutral flag; managed the unloading of the supplies at a port in Rotterdam and their stocking in French and Belgium warehouses, and then oversaw the distribution of the supplies to those in need. Flying under the flag of voluntarism, the commission, with its quasi-public status, presaged the emergence of international nongovernmental organizations in the final decades of the century (Cabanes 2014; Barnett 2011).

Hoover's work in Belgium made him the nation's most celebrated humanitarian. The future president's renown was amplified through his work heading the American Relief Administration, the government's postwar relief mission to Europe and Russia, whose establishment affirmed the government's continued commitment to harnessing humanitarian assistance to American foreign policy objectives. Appointed commerce secretary by President Warren Harding in 1920, Hoover pursued a program that built on the wartime voluntary collaboration between government, business, labor, and charitable organizations, one that he would also champion after he was elected president in 1928 (Hall 2006). He promoted a vision of what historians have termed the "associative state," a "nonstatist alternative" to both "welfare statism" and "atomic individualism," through the coordinated work of private organizations and cooperative institutions such as trade associations, professional societies, and agrarian and labor fraternities. These would work together to address national needs, acting as a "higher government" that would provide "permanent managerial mechanisms [of a] national system." The associative state would require only modest government direction and would preclude the erection of a significant governmental bureaucracy (Hawley 1974, 1998:162, 163, 167).

The agricultural and ecological devastation and economic depression of the early 1930s exposed the limits of Hoover's approach. As the demands on charitable agencies around the nation grew more intense, Hoover maintained his commitment to locally rooted voluntarism and resisted calls for the federal government to intervene in relief work. Congressional Democrats called for a $25 million federal appropriation for the Red Cross, but the organization refused the public funds, believing they would threaten its voluntarist essence. Hoover instead called for Americans to increase their donations to the agency, insisting this was the "the American way" of meeting a crisis (Cutlip 1965:300; Clemens 2010).

Yet as widespread unemployment strained the resources of nearly all private charities, the leaders of social welfare agencies became some of the first to draw attention to the "limits of voluntarism" (Morris 2009). Between 1929 and 1932, a third of all private charitable agencies closed their doors because of a lack of funds (Zunz 2012). In fact, leaders of those agencies, who had previously jealously guarded the preserves of voluntarism from the encroachment of public aid, were some of the most vocal in pushing for the first major federal relief effort in response to the Depression, the Reconstruction Finance Corporation in January 1932, which provided loans to states to fund welfare and public works (Morris 2009).

With the establishment of the Federal Emergency Relief Administration (FERA) in May 1933, President Franklin Roosevelt achieved a dramatic recalibration of the relationship between tax-supported government social welfare and private charity that had been at the root of Hoover's "associative state." Roosevelt placed at FERA's head Harry Hopkins, whose experience at charitable agencies such as the New York AICP had schooled him in the limits of voluntarism. Roosevelt and Hopkins determined that the federal relief that FERA oversaw would be administered only at the local level through public agencies; states would no longer be able to partner with private agencies to administer public funds (Morris 2009; Zunz 2012; Brown and McKeown 1997).

Compromises in the implementation of the policy softened the break with past practice that it initiated. In several cities, public agencies drafted the executives of private organizations into their service. The most prominent exception was made in Chicago, where, in a concession to Catholic electoral strength, Catholic Charities was allowed to register as a public agency, with its staff administering relief serving as public officials (Zunz 2012; Brown and McKeown 1997; Morris 2009).

Preferring that state and local government direct relief efforts and fearful of creating a permanent federal bureaucracy, in 1935 Roosevelt and Hopkins ended federal funding of direct relief. Yet even with funding pared back, the establishment of FERA initiated a "new alignment" between voluntary organizations and the burgeoning welfare state. A new division of responsibility emerged. With the New Deal's commitment to publicly provided social insurance—old-age pensions, unemployment compensation, and disability payments—the federal government assumed responsibilities that had previously been borne largely by fraternal and voluntary organizations (Hall 2006). Federal funding of social welfare was limited, and many Americans fell outside the public social safety net. These included domestic workers and agricultural laborers—categories that in the South included most of the region's African Americans—whom Southern congressmen successfully excluded from social security benefits. Many would still need to rely on private sources of aid. Yet broadly speaking, charity would assume a supplementary role in this regard. In many cases, voluntary organizations began to offer therapeutic and professional services such as family counseling, child care, vocational training, and mental health treatment that would appeal to both the poor and the middle class (Morris 2009). The expanded client base that would sustain these organizations in the decades to come points to the limits of spatial metaphors denoting the bounds of voluntary action. They suggest a finite landscape, hemmed in and compressed by the expansion of governmental welfare provision, as opposed to an elastic one capable of expansion with governmental subsidy and partnership.

Indeed, in other respects, the New Deal enlarged the voluntarist realm's scope. The Works Progress Administration (WPA) supported cultural institutions like Chicago's Art Institute and New York's Metropolitan Museum, helping them survive the Depression (Young and Casey 2017). The New Deal legislative barrage also created enormous demands for policy expertise, expanding the role of policy research institutions like the NBER and the Russell Sage Foundation (J. Smith 1991). The prospect of increased governmental activity and regulation also sparked the mobilization of private interest lobbies (including business groups like the National Association of Manufacturers, which opposed much of the New Deal), advocacy organizations, and "organized beneficiary groups" (Smith 1991; Hall 2006:51).

World War II, Voluntarism, and the State

World War II drew voluntary associations even closer into the arms of the state. As the federal government increasingly came to regard humanitarian intervention in strategic terms, it imposed greater oversight on voluntary associations working overseas. In 1941, the government required that all appeals for aid to foreign countries be registered with the State Department. The next year, President Roosevelt placed these associations under the regulatory authority of an independent agency, the War Relief Control Board (WRCB). All war relief societies were required to register with the board, which oversaw decisions regarding the organizations' fund-raising, publicity, and budgets. The WRCB drastically reduced the number of operating agencies, from several hundred in 1941 to just sixty-seven in 1943, with wartime strategic interests a central consideration determining institutional life or death (Barnett 2011; Zunz 2012).

The gravitational tug of the state led to the establishment of the American Council of Voluntary Agencies for Foreign Service, representing the leading voluntary organizations distributing relief in war zones. The council addressed twined imperatives: the state's demand for interagency cooperation and coordination and voluntary agencies' desire to defend their interests against governmental intrusion. On the home front, the pressure to federate multiplying wartime appeals into a national war fund was even more intense than during World War I. For the first time, labor leaders were willing to put aside suspicions of the community chest movement, traditionally dominated by business interests, and supported the federation, the National War Fund. It worked closely with the WRCB and raised, along with local war chests, nearly $750 million during the war (Zunz 2012; Cutlip 1965).

American giving to the war zone during combat and reconstruction was heavily shaped by ethnic and religious particularism. American Lutherans founded Lutheran World Relief in 1945 to focus on German and Austrian Lutherans; Catholic bishops, with the support of the federal government, established Catholic Relief Services in 1943. American Jews raised funds to help Jewish refugees in Europe and often to resettle them in Palestine. In 1948, the United Jewish Appeal, which managed much of this fund-raising, brought in nearly $100 million, much of it directed to the new state of Israel (Barnett 2011; Zunz 2012).

A host of new humanitarian agencies, such as Cooperative for American Remittances in Europe (better known as CARE), the Oxford Committee for Famine Relief (Oxfam), and World Vision International, emerged to address wartime humanitarian and postwar reconstruction and refugee crises. The religious ethos that had dominated humanitarian work in the previous century persisted in many organizations, but it was now dominated by a "secularized discourse of humanity" (Barnett 2011:119). After the war's conclusion, many of these organizations expanded their scope beyond European borders to the Global South, embracing not merely aid distribution but "development" more generally; in a reflection of this shift, in 1953 CARE adapted its acronym to stand for Cooperative for American Relief Everywhere. These organizations became vital institutions within a "global aid society" populated by what would be termed *nongovernmental organizations* (NGOs). They played key roles in the postwar decades in the fields of humanitarian relief, peace activism and arms control, environmentalism, education and cultural exchange, and human rights (Barnett 2011; Iriye 2009).

The NGOs were drawn into the orbit of the institutions of global governance developed to steward the postwar order, most under the aegis of the United Nations, established in 1945. In an American context, despite an avowed commitment to impartiality, independence, and neutrality, humanitarian groups often worked as implementing partners of government programs, which regarded humanitarian aid in the context of the Cold War, and were increasingly dependent on the state for funding. CARE and Catholic Relief Services, for instance, gave critical assistance in carrying out the federal government's postwar food aid program. Yet the identities, interests, and values of these NGOs were never entirely subsumed by the state, and they sometimes clashed with governmental agencies. The relationships between federal agencies and early NGOs anticipated the contracting-for-services dynamic that developed between the federal government and nonprofits to implement domestic programs in the 1960s (Barnett 2011; Iriye 2009).

The war also fostered new relationships between the federal government and private research institutions, which became important nodes within the modern military-industrial complex. The Department of Defense, as well as new federal agencies such as the Atomic Energy Commission, the Office of Naval Research, the National Institutes of Health (NIH), and the National Science Foundation (NSF), directed a torrent of research funding to outside agencies on a contract basis. These included universities as well as freestanding nonacademic institutions (J. Smith 1991; Geiger 1993:22). The prototype of the new think tanks was the RAND (for Research and Development) Corporation, which broke off from the Douglas Aircraft Company in Santa Monica, California, to form a separate nonprofit in 1948. The RAND model of the contract-based research institution proliferated in the 1960s, expanding beyond research in military and national security affairs to domestic policy (J. Smith 1991; Nielsen 1985; Hall 1992).

Federal support for nonprofit institutions grew across the board, until in the postwar decades it became the largest source of funding in many charitable domains, displacing private philanthropy for primacy. The transition was especially striking in higher education, though it could be detected in health care as well (after the passage of the 1946 Hill-Burton Act, which provided construction funds for public and nonprofit hospitals) (Hall 1992). In 1913, for instance, the Carnegie Corporation spent more on higher education than did the federal government (approximately $5 million, mostly for land grant colleges). Yet by 1964, the Carnegie Corporation spent a little more than $12 million on higher education, whereas federal expenditures reached $2 billion (Nielsen 1972). Basic and applied research's importance to the war effort led to increased government funding of private universities; such funding became their major source of income by the beginning of the 1940s (Hall 1992). By 1951, NIH was providing about half of all grants in support of medical research, whereas only a third came from private sources (Geiger 1993:27).

The other major trigger of the federal government's ascendance as the primary funder of higher education was the Servicemen's Readjustment Act of 1944, better known as the G.I. Bill, which provided tuition vouchers for veterans of World War II. With such a massive government subsidy, college enrollment doubled between 1938 and 1948, with veterans accounting for most of the increase (and with a rough parity between attendance of public and private universities). "By 1948 the Veteran's Administration was paying 56 percent of student fees in private universities" (Geiger 1993:41). The bill did not merely bolster a central institution of the voluntarist realm; it was also the product of voluntarist civic engagement. The G.I. Bill had been drafted and championed by the American Legion, and thousands of Legion posts around the country participated in a lobbying campaign to push Congress to support it (Skocpol 2003).

Postwar Philanthropy, Mass Giving, and the Regulation of Cold War Voluntarism

If an expanded federal bureaucracy demoted the status of private foundations within the polity, it also spurred a tremendous upsurge in their creation. A rise in business profits during the postwar boom, coupled with increased income, inheritance, and excess profit taxes to fund domestic programs and the Korean War, incentivized the creation of foundations as a means of tax avoidance (this had not been a significant motivation for the first generation of foundation founders, whose philanthropic vocations predated the advent of the federal income tax) (Nielsen 1972; Brilliant 2000). There were only 203 foundations with total assets over $1 million in 1929; by 1959, there were 2,058, and most had been created in the 1950s (Hall 1992).

Towering over all of them, and dominating the public's imagination, was the Ford Foundation. It was created by Henry Ford's son, Edsel, in 1936, not long after steep increases in the estate tax raised rates to as high as 70 percent for fortunes over $50 million. Establishing the foundation allowed the family to avoid the tax and to pass the Ford Motor Company to the next generation without ceding control. Edsel Ford died in 1943 and his father four years later. Henry Ford bequeathed the bulk of his Ford Company (nonvoting) stock to the foundation; it instantly became the largest in the world. Its assets were conservatively valued at $417 million in 1954, and by the late 1960s at $3.7 billion, a value equal to one third of the largest thirty-three foundations (Nielsen 1972:78). This top-heaviness, or what one philanthropy observer termed a "macro-cephalic" character—the dominance of a relatively small number of very large organizations (in relation to a very large number of smaller organizations)—has defined, and at times troubled, the foundation sector ever since (Soskis and Katz 2016).

The largest foundations—Ford, Carnegie, Rockefeller—sat at the center of a network of elite private institutions, which interlaced in informal yet powerful ways with governmental agencies. Philanthropic executives often passed back and forth between foundations and high-level government offices, and as they turned their focus overseas, they became critical agents within the liberal foreign policy establishment. In 1950, the Ford Foundation named as its head Paul Hoffman, who had administered the Marshall Plan. At Ford, Hoffman oversaw a sort of continuation of that plan, directed both domestically and globally, in which the foundation promoted economic development and democratic institutions as a means of thwarting communism. The foundation worked in close collaboration with the U.S. government, with Ford officials consulting frequently with State and Central Intelligence Agency (CIA) officials (though Hoffman did turn down a CIA request to use the foundation as a secret channel for agency funds) (Zunz 2012).[2]

The tangle of humanitarian and geopolitical considerations lay at the root of perhaps the most celebrated philanthropic initiative of the twentieth century, the Rockefeller Foundation's financial cultivation of a "Green Revolution." The program can be traced to Rockefeller's early-twentieth-century work to boost agricultural productivity through farm demonstration projects in the American South. By the early 1940s, Rockefeller Foundation officials had partnered with the Mexican government to implement a similar program focusing on increasing yields of corn, beans, and wheat. Prompted by Cold War fears that hunger would drive Asian farmers toward communism, Rockefeller staff next developed similar programs in India and Pakistan. The Ford Foundation joined the effort, funding an International Rice Research Institute in the Philippines. By some accounts, the high-yield agriculture generated through the Green Revolution has saved more than a billion lives, although scholars have also highlighted its dark side, in its promotion of monoculture at the expense of ecological diversity and its contribution to the dispossession of rural small farmers by commercial landowners (Zunz 2012).

Even as foundations grew in numbers and in total assets in the 1950s, so too did mass giving. The coincidence reflected a political economy that produced widely distributed income gains among the middle class, as well as the maturation of the fund-raising techniques that had been pioneered during the preceding two world wars. A 1950 analysis from the Russell Sage Foundation estimated that 80 percent of all charitable contributions came from those with incomes of $5,000 or less (Zunz 2012:176). "By 1950, 1,318 [community] chests . . . received contributions from 57 percent of the U.S. population" (Zunz 2012:177). In several cities, community chests, which in the past had focused largely on local causes, incorporated national charities; by the 1970s, the consolidated United Funds would join together under a national governing body known as the United Way. In factories and offices, the advent of charitable payroll deductions also boosted mass giving, though the practice would raise questions about the scope and diversity of participating organizations (Brilliant 1990; Barman 2006). Mass and elite giving flourished in tandem, but the former gained a privileged status relative to the latter within the tax code. A 1943 law made the first statutory distinction between charitable organizations supported by a broad range of donors, whose operation within a charitable marketplace imposed on them a degree of accountability, and tax-exempt organizations that relied on a small number of donors, which required additional scrutiny (in this case, filing annual information returns) (Brilliant 2000; Troyer 2000).

High levels of mass giving reflected broader voluntarist vigor. As in the early decades of the nineteenth century, when Benevolent Empire activism stoked notions of American millennial purpose, in the throes of midcentury Cold War liberalism, voluntarism again was coupled closely with American exceptionalism, though now its power was largely conservative. Tocqueville, whose *Democracy in America* had gone out of print at the turn of the century, was rediscovered; Eisenhower became the first president to quote him in public remarks. The French nobleman was embraced as a patron saint of American civil society, which was increasingly regarded as representing America's native immunity against the totalitarian threat tormenting Europe (Kloppenberg 1998; Skocpol 2003; Levy 2017; Neem 2008).

The Cold War also amplified voluntarism's status as a bulwark of capitalism. The 1953 New Jersey Supreme Court decision *AP Smith Manufacturing Co. v. Barlow* promulgated this view by authorizing corporate giving to private universities (and by extension, to the institutions of civil society more generally), on the grounds that such institutions were essential to maintaining the entire free enterprise system that sustained the corporate order (Knauer 1994). Yet the relationship between voluntarism and social order was always fraught. In 1956, Alabama sought the membership list of the National Association for the Advancement of Colored People (NAACP) after charging it with violating a state law as part of an effort to expel the civil rights group from the state. The NAACP refused, and the case made its way to the Supreme Court. In a 1958 decision, the Court sided with the NAACP, affirming that "the freedom to engage in association for the advancement of beliefs and ideas is an inseparable aspect of the 'liberty' assured by the Due Process Clause of the Fourteenth Amendment" (Levy 2017).

Voluntarism's potency as a Cold War and capitalist ideal allowed it to remain capacious and loosely defined, as long as it upheld the contrast to totalitarianism and communism. Yet the postwar years also witnessed efforts to impose regulatory demarcations between various tax-exempt organizations and to delimit what would become called the nonprofit sector from the realms of political activity and for-profit enterprise. One motivation was to check the abuse of "nominally charitable and educational organizations for the purpose of bestowing tax exemptions on private interests" and income-generating activities (Troyer 2000:53). (The most famous case involved a charity that operated the world's largest pasta factory and whose sole charitable activity was donating the income generated to NYU Law School, a "feeder corporation" in more than one respect.) The Revenue Act of 1950 limited charitable tax-exempt status to organizations that were organized and operated for an "exempt" purpose; it also mandated that any income derived from business activity unrelated to an exempt purpose would be taxed (Levy 2017; Hall 2003; Fremont-Smith 2004).

Regulations also deepened the long-standing divide between charitable organizations and political and partisan activity. With the adoption of a federal income tax, Treasury officials favored a narrow definition of authorized tax-exempt activity directed to the political realm, including within those bounds education, but restricting all partisan activity or promotion of "propaganda." In 1934, this distinction became law when Congress issued a vaguely worded prohibition on political lobbying done by charities. The revisions to the tax code were, somewhat paradoxically, themselves partially the result of a campaign by the American Legion, reacting to the lobbying efforts of a rival tax-exempt organization that had pushed for the restriction of veterans' benefits (Zunz 2012). The prohibition was extended two decades later when Senator Lyndon Johnson inserted an amendment into the Revenue Act of 1954 that prohibited tax-exempt charitable organizations from engaging in any electoral activity. Johnson, like the backers of the American Legion, was angered by the support a political opponent received from a rival charitable organization (Zunz 2012; Fremont-Smith 2004).

That same year, Treasury officials issued regulations requiring all organizations seeking exemption to file an application and to receive a determination of exempt status before operating. The revised classification system for tax-exempt entities, part of a broader rationalization of the Internal Revenue Code conducted in 1954, imposed greater differentiation on tax-exempt status. Previously, the sections of the code that dealt with charities, in the estimation of one scholar, were a "conglomeration of inconsistencies, inaccuracies, and omissions."[3] Indeed, before the late 1940s, the IRS had developed minimal oversight or enforcement mechanisms for charities. In the 1954 revised code, tax regulators herded together "the various types of nonproprietary entities—nonstock and mutual benefit corporations, charitable trusts, voluntary associations, cooperatives—and place[d] them in a common regulatory framework": a new section, 501(c), for tax-exempt organizations (Hall 2006:53). Unlike the previous undifferentiated categorization, section 501(c) had some two dozen subsections and assigned various tax privileges and degrees of regulatory oversight to each (Hall 2006, 2003). Tax-deductible public charities were covered in section 501(c)(3), though the Internal Revenue Service (IRS) did not impose tighter definitional clarity on the religious, charitable, scientific, literary, or educational nature of the work these organizations were meant to do. Through codifications over the next half decade, social welfare organizations were assigned to section 501(c)(4) and were authorized to conduct legislative advocacy and unlimited lobbying related to exempt purpose, though not to receive tax-deductible contributions.

Somewhat paradoxically, this taxonomic differentiation increased the coherence of what would soon be termed the nonprofit sector (the term came into use only in the 1960s). It represented a more deliberate surveying of boundaries, a registry of an organizational diversity that existed within a common regulatory framework. Indeed, it was only in 1967 that the IRS began to tally the total numbers of tax-exempt organizations in the United States (Hall 1992). Yet the soundness of this framework was precarious, since it was premised on an unruly heterogeneity. Exempt status was an unstable foundation to support a common, defining voluntarist identity.

The Nonprofit Boom and the Rise of Third-Party Government

The more rigorous, variegated classification system was initiated in time to absorb a massive expansion of nonprofit institutions (largely in the public charities category) and a dramatic transformation of the landscape of institutionalized voluntarism. The growth in the number of tax-exempt organizations began in the 1940s but accelerated in the following decades. Between 1950 and 1968, the number of charitable tax-exempt organizations increased by more than a factor of six to some 309,000 (and by a factor of nearly twenty by the late 1980s, to more than one million) (Hall 1992, 2006).

The explosion was the result of another major shift in the relationship between the federal government and nonprofit organizations: a reliance on NGOs to deliver publicly financed services and goods. Similar forms of what Lester Salamon has termed "third-party government" had grown at the state level for more than a century, but the federal government's vigorous embrace of the arrangement, with the vast resources at its disposal, was a novel development, and it became a central component of Great Society liberalism (Zunz 2012; Young and Casey 2017; Salamon 1987). Indeed, by the late 1960s, "federal government spending on social welfare and education surpassed state and local government spending for the first time" (Salamon 2012b:88). During the Kennedy and Johnson administrations, federal funding flowed to a wide range of voluntary agencies, and the availability of such funding called many new agencies into being. To take advantage of these funding streams, proprietary educational and health care institutions converted to nonprofit status (Hall 2006). By the early 1980s, the share of public benefit nonprofit revenue coming from the federal government was twice that coming from private charitable support (Hall 2006, 1992; Salamon 1987; O'Neill 1989). And whereas nonprofits had provided less than a quarter of state-funded welfare services in the 1950s, by the late 1970s they provided the majority (Levy 2017).

This burgeoning "mixed political economy of social services" advanced along a variety of fronts (Zunz 2012:214). Amendments to the Social Security Act in 1962 and 1967 overturned the New Deal prohibition against the federal government contracting with nonprofit organizations to provide social services. States were authorized to use nonprofit resources as seed money to attract federal matching funds, and, in what one consulting group termed in 1971 a "private sector conspiracy," these amplified funds were then often used to "purchase" the services of the contributing nonprofit agencies (Morris 2009:200). The Social Security Act Amendments of 1965, creating Medicare and Medicaid, explicitly sanctioned contracting with nonprofits and opened up new private markets for health care that nonprofits were statutorily authorized to meet (Levy 2017:232). Hundreds of new federal programs for housing, employment training, and poverty alleviation were developed and funded through competitive government grants open to nonprofit providers. Through these and other mechanisms, federal spending on social services, often provided by nonprofits, soared. By 1976, expenditures for "purchase-of-service" agreements accounted for nearly half of all federal social service spending (Young and Casey 2017; Salamon 2012a). Medicare, along with social security, accounted for 60 percent of the growth in total government social welfare spending between 1965 and 1980. These programs disproportionately flow to the middle class, and so much of the expanded welfare state spending channeled to nonprofits did not directly benefit the nation's poorest (Salamon 2012a).

The period also witnessed intense collaboration between leading foundations and the federal government in the realm of domestic policy, as officials transitioned back and forth between high-level positions within each sector. John Gardner, to cite one example, moved from the presidency of the Carnegie Corporation to serve as Lyndon Johnson's secretary of health, education, and welfare from 1965 to 1968 (Levy 2017; O'Connor 1999). If third-party government involved the privatization of policy implementation, private organizations also had a significant, if lesser, hand in public policy *formulation*. As the Rockefeller, the Carnegie, and especially the Ford Foundation increasingly focused on urban poverty as a prime field of interest, they worked closely with the Kennedy and Johnson administrations, as well as with cities around the nation, to fund policy experimentation in the inner cities that would form the basis for War on Poverty programs. The Ford Foundation, for instance, provided "seed grants, technical assistance, and intellectual brokering" for the community action programs created through the Economic Opportunity Act of 1964 (O'Connor 1996:588, 1999). The implementation of these policies often relied on novel nonprofit forms, such as community development corporations. These initiatives exhibited both the power of philanthropy and its self-imposed limits, as they tended to buttress individualistic behavioral interventions over deeper structural reform. They sought to remedy supposed cultural deficiencies of marginalized groups rather than overturn the political and economic systems that marginalized them. And they worked within the ideological boundaries erected by government policy rather than seeking to challenge these boundaries (O'Connor 1996, 1999; Kohl-Arenas 2016).

The Great Society's promotion of third-party government raised a host of questions regarding the nature of nonprofit–government relations. Social service agencies proliferated in subfields that offered the promise of increased dedicated federal funding, such as drug and alcohol counseling (Morris 2009). Did this tropism toward public funding represent a diminution of voluntarist independence? Would grantees' commitment to experimentation be dampened? In some cases, private charity officials who resisted accepting federal funds resigned and were quickly replaced by others more amenable to government patronage (Zunz 2012). Federal funding imposed greater reporting requirements and higher administrative costs more generally, introduced heightened volatility to budgeting, and encouraged the trends of professionalization and bureaucratization within the sector. How would these developments shape voluntary norms and practice (Morris 2009; Hall 2003; O'Connor 1996)?

Observers puzzled over the ideological valence of this mixed political economy. Third-party government reconciled two competing strains in American political discourse: "a desire for public services and hostility to the governmental apparatus that provides them" (Salamon 1987:37). Yet the balance between the two perspectives was always ambiguous. Did federal funding of nonprofits encourage privatization and a diminution of public authority, or was it a means of augmenting the federal government's reach? Did third-party government bolster the welfare state, or did it temper its power, as conservatives urged, through the support of "mediating institutions" (Salamon 1995)?

Voluntarism and the Rights Revolution

Alongside third-party government, the other powerful impetus in reshaping associational life and the nonprofit sector in the 1960s was the "rights revolution"—a new wave of legal and political activism, propelled by a surge of rights- and identity-based claims. Nearly every existing arena of organized social concern (and many new ones) were transformed by a movement-based mobilization of activists who promoted their causes through political agitation and litigation. The rights revolution ultimately led to important legislative advances for the rights of women, physically disabled people, racial and ethnic minorities, older people, gays and lesbians, consumers, and the environment. In nearly all these cases, protest precipitated a countermobilization of oppositional activists to check and roll back advances.

At times, rights claims were asserted through direct action. Disruptive protests sought to enact change outside traditional mechanisms of government lobbying. Some of them were informal and spontaneous; others benefited from formal organizational planning and coordination. The civil rights movement of the 1950s and 1960s provided many of the archetypal instances of direct action: the Montgomery Bus Boycott of 1956, the Greensboro lunch counter sit-ins of 1960, the march from Selma to Montgomery in 1965. The aim of nonviolent direct action, as Martin Luther King Jr. explained in his "Letter from Birmingham Jail," was "to create such a crisis and foster such a tension that a community which has constantly refused to negotiate is forced to confront the issue." The moral logic of this approach had tremendous influence on American activism in the half century since. As journalist and organizer L. A. Kauffman notes, "the civil rights movement's acts of resistance to racial segregation and white supremacy have become so emblematic of transformative collective action that every major movement since"—from AIDS Coalition to Unleash Power (ACT UP) in the 1980s to Occupy Wall Street in the 2000s—"has referenced them in some way" (Kauffman 2017:xi).

By the mid-1970s, however, protest had largely yielded to policy advocacy as the chief tactic of social change (Skocpol 2003). Professionally managed, centralized social change organizations, staffed by lobbyists and policy experts, clustered in the nation's capital and directed their attentions to the national government and media. These organizations in a sense deposed the more established volunteer federations, such as the General Federation of Women's Clubs or the American Legion, for whom membership was defined in participatory, cross-class, transnational, and fraternal/sororal terms. For the new advocacy groups, mass participation was realized largely through monetary contributions. Unlike the older federations, these organizations rarely allowed members to elect leaders or to participate in important strategic decisions (Skocpol 2003).

The first wave of what Jeffrey Berry has termed an "advocacy explosion" involved organizations pushing for the rights of marginalized communities. Groups acting on behalf of women, African Americans, Hispanics, and Asian Americans multiplied nearly sevenfold, from 98 groups in 1955 to 688 in 1985 (Berry 1997; Skocpol 2003). The next wave encompassed groups promoting various dimensions of a broadly conceived "public interest," defending, for instance, the environment, consumers, or children. In 1969 the environmental movement employed only two full-time lobbyists. By 1975, the largest twelve environmental organizations employed forty lobbyists, and a decade later, the number had grown to eighty-eight.[4] In what Berry has termed the "interest group spiral," the growth of these advocacy groups prompted a countermobilization of business and industry lobbying groups, which then in turn sparked the formation of additional public-interest advocacy organizations (Berry 1997; Skocpol 2003).

The black freedom movement and allied movement-based activism of the 1960s occupied a volatile interregnum between the ascendance of participatory federations in the first decades of the twentieth century and the reign of professionalized advocacy groups by the century's close. In the struggle for African American civil rights, an earlier generation of organizations, led by the NAACP (and the NAACP Legal Defense Fund) and the Urban League, achieved significant legal victories, most notably *Brown v. Board of Education* (1954), which ended legally mandated segregation in public schools. These groups collaborated and at times clashed with a host of newly established organizations focused largely on legislative politics (which also clashed among themselves). Their diversity reflected the broad range of approaches to social change across the spectrum of moderation and radicalism, integration and separatism. Several major organizations themselves journeyed across that ideological terrain. The Southern Christian Leadership Conference (SCLC), led by Martin Luther King Jr., marshaled the moral authority of the black church for the cause of nonviolent protest. The Student Nonviolent Coordinating Committee (SNCC) harnessed burgeoning student activism to the cause of black freedom, organizing sit-ins and voter registration drives (by the decade's end, it had dropped its commitment to nonviolence and changed its name). The Congress of Racial Equality (CORE), a nonviolent, interracial organization that by 1961 claimed more than fifty chapters across the country, helped organize the Freedom Rides, which sought to challenge segregation in interstate travel (and also moved toward militancy by the decade's end). The combined labors of these organizations, along with the efforts of black colleges and churches in the South and hundreds of grassroots, informal protest groups, fostered tensions that the nation's political leadership was forced to confront. The result was the landmark civil rights acts of 1964 and 1965.

The black freedom (and black power) movement inspired similar activism among other marginalized groups, helping to spark the American Indian, Chicano, and women's liberation movements, as well as the establishment of new civil rights organizations, such as the Native American Rights Fund, the Mexican American Legal Defense and Educational Fund, and the National Organization for Women, as well as hundreds of smaller grassroots organizations (Camarillo 1991; Carson 1999; Chafe 1991). Most of these movements mirrored the black freedom struggle in the divides they developed between organizations that followed moderate and integrationist approaches and those with more radical and separatist commitments.

These divides were often deepened by the pressures applied by philanthropic funders, or by their selective attentions. Most foundations, whose leaders were loath to court public controversy, kept a safe distance from contentious issues. One survey conducted in the late 1960s determined that only 1 percent of foundations reported making any "controversial" grants, and that those grants made up only 0.1 percent of total outlays. "The race problem" was deemed especially perilous (Nielsen 1972, 1985). Few foundations directed funding to African Americans. Even fewer targeted the issue of civil rights specifically. The Field Foundation's support for the NAACP Legal Defense Fund during the *Brown* litigation was a prominent exception. Most grassroots civil rights organizations received little funding from organized philanthropy. They were chronically short on cash, relying on small donations and volunteer labor from members (O'Connor 2010; Dobson 2014).

Of the large foundations, Ford took the most aggressive stand in support of civil rights, especially under the presidency of McGeorge Bundy, Kennedy's and Johnson's national security adviser who assumed the foundation's presidency in 1966. "Never in the history of American philanthropy had anything comparable in scale and aggressiveness to the Ford Foundation's assault on the problems of race and poverty been seen," noted Waldemar Nielsen, a philanthropy watcher who often upbraided foundations for their timidity (Nielsen 1985:64; O'Connor 1999). Ford's prominence helped spur the "emergence of a social change orientation in organized philanthropy" in the coming decades (O'Connor 2010:335).

Ford made significant contributions to the institutionalization of social movements in the final decades of the century (O'Connor 2010). The foundation provided essential funding to develop the infrastructure of public interest law, seeding organizations such as the Mexican American Legal Defense and Educational Fund, the Natural Resources Defense Council, the Native American Rights Fund, and the ACLU Women's Rights Project, among many others. These groups were at the forefront of the period's dominant liberal reformist paradigm, "in which the federal courts were seen as the key agents of social reform and professionally managed nonprofits as their partners in that effort."[5] Ford preferred to focus on "important but comparatively safe vehicles such as voter education, policy analysis and advocacy," professional development and leadership training (O'Connor 2010). But the foundation was also willing to support movement-based direct action organizations, such as CORE; the foundation funded voter registration campaigns, among them one in Cleveland, led by a local chapter of CORE, that helped elect the city's first African American mayor (Diaz 1999; Zunz 2012).

Ford used funding as ideological leverage. As one foundation official explained, offering financial support to groups like CORE helped to convince them "to operate within the system" (Zunz 2012:221). Such a strategy exemplified a principle governing philanthropic support of social activism more generally, in which funding has tended to temper radicalism and to "channel" social movements away from militancy and a commitment to structural reform and toward gradualism, moderation, and conciliation (Jenkins 1998; O'Connor 2010; Ferguson 2013). The pressures were sometimes subtle, and not always consciously applied, as donors' preferences for professionalized, Washington-based advocacy organizations steered resources away from more radical and disruptive forms of protest.

The Tax Reform Act of 1969 and Its Aftermath

Even if Ford's activism was firmly delimited by the consensus liberalism of the philanthropic establishment, many still perceived it as a threat to that establishment. In fact, it provoked a backlash to institutional philanthropy more generally. Traditional alarm over unaccountable, concentrated power merged with politicians' worries about foundations' potential to sway elections and Southern segregationists' fears about interference with the dominant racial hierarchy (Zunz 2012). In the late 1960s, the convergence of these concerns led to calls for further restrictions on foundations' political activity and a new congressional investigation of philanthropy.

In the 1950s, Congress had conducted two such investigations, the first initiated by Georgia Democratic congressman E. Eugene Cox and the second by Tennessee Republican congressman B. Carroll Reece. They were provoked by a host of apprehensions, high among them suspicions that many foundations were increasingly serving as little more than vehicles for tax avoidance. These attacks, which targeted the largest foundations, came from an opposite ideological position from those earlier in the century, and focused more on international affairs. As the lead counsel of the first investigation explained, if in the age of Rockefeller and Carnegie, congressional critics feared that foundations would become "the tool of reaction," by midcentury "the most articulately expressed fear has been that the foundations have swung from that position far to the left, and now they are endangering our existing capitalistic structure" (Lankford 1964:34; Brilliant 2000; Zunz 2012:193).

Neither congressional investigation managed to score any direct hits or lead to legislative reform. But alarm over the erosion of the tax base, the steady public exposure of various foundation abuses (largely implicating small, family foundations, which had grown exponentially over the previous decades), and concern with the increased social and political activism of the largest foundations laid the groundwork for a third, more consequential investigation led by the populist Texas congressman Wright Patman. This investigation sparked a separate study conducted by the Treasury Department, which acknowledged serious abuses within a minority of foundations, recommended regulations targeting "self-dealing, payout failure, and business holdings," and also insisted that foundations could serve as "powerful instrument[s] for evolution, growth, and improvement in the shape and direction of charity" (Troyer 2000;57–58). Patman saw few of these virtues. As chairman of the House Select Committee on Small Business, he placed particular emphasis on the ways that foundations used tax-exempt status to compete unfairly with private business. Patman called for a twenty-five-year time limit on foundations, a 20 percent tax on foundation income, and strict restrictions on their business activities (Hall 1992; Lankford 1964).

In February 1969, the House Ways and Means committee began hearings on foundations, with Patman as lead witness. The Senate Committee on Finance held hearings as well. Investigations focused with particular intensity on Ford, its political activism, and its support for civil rights (the Urban League regarded this attention as evidence that the investigation was motivated largely by racism). After considerable debate, in which critics highlighted foundations' undue political influence, hoarding of charitable resources, and lack of transparency, and in which defenders celebrated the vital support foundations gave to charities in communities across the nation, Congress passed the Tax Reform Act of 1969. It was the most significant piece of legislation aimed at the nonprofit sector in the last half century (Nielsen 1972; Brilliant 2000; Zunz 2012).

The act did not include the most draconian restrictions promoted by Patman, such as time limits for foundations. But it did tighten regulations on foundation lobbying and political activity; placed a 4 percent "audit fee" on foundation income to cover the costs of IRS regulation (later reduced to 2 percent); and imposed stricter public reporting requirements on foundations, prohibitions on self-dealing, and a mandated payout rate (initially set at 6 percent of foundation assets, later reduced to 5 percent). The act also deepened the distinction between private foundations, which rely on a single individual or family for funding, and community foundations and public charities, funded through contributions from multiple donors. The latter two were granted greater privileges (Brilliant 2000; Zunz 2012; Troyer 2000).

Congressional deliberations over the bill—and the ill will exposed among significant swaths of the political class—made clear to philanthropic leaders that they would need to demonstrate foundations' institutional legitimacy more actively. As Waldemar Nielsen remarked, they could no longer simply assume that invocations of Tocqueville and the glories of American civil society would ward off demands for increased regulation (Nielsen 1985). Yet there was little consensus about what sort of defensive position should be assumed, beyond the need for more and better communication to justify the privileges foundations and nonprofits enjoyed, and more and better research with which to support those claims.

During the run-up to the Tax Reform Act, John D. Rockefeller III (the Standard Oil founder's grandson) took the lead by pushing for the establishment of two private research commissions. The first was chaired by industrialist (and future secretary of commerce and financier) Peter Peterson; the second, more consequential of the two was headed by John Filer, CEO of Aetna, a large insurance company. The funding for the Commission on Private Philanthropy and Public Needs came from private sources, yet it received sponsorship from the Treasury Department, which lent staffers to direct research. The Filer Commission, as it became known, brought into its ambit the wide expanse of the 501(c)(3) tax-exempt charitable universe, "from giant grant makers through grassroots activist organizations" (Hall 1992:247). Notably, the commission incorporated feedback from a "donee group" representing grant-receiving public-interest organizations. It called for more diversity and greater grantee representation on foundation boards, and for more funding directed toward the most marginalized, disempowered Americans (Brilliant 2000).

Although the final shape of the Tax Reform Act was something of a relief to foundation leaders, its passage provoked a crisis of confidence within the philanthropic community. It led to a decrease in the number of new private foundations created and an increase in the number of community foundations established in the decade after the bill's passage (Nielsen 1985; Frumkin 1999). Anecdotal evidence emerged that foundations became more cautious, directing grants to well-established charities and steering clear of controversial causes (Brilliant 2000; Frumkin 1998). The increased regulatory scrutiny of foundations led to a more prominent role for legal and accounting expertise and to a professionalization of foundation staffs more generally. By one estimate, foundations' legal and accounting fees doubled between 1969 and 1970 (Brilliant 2000; Frumkin 1999). Total foundation administrative expenses increased from 6.4 percent of grant outlays in 1966 to nearly 15 percent in 1972, and at large foundations the jump was even more pronounced (Frumkin 1998).

These developments flowed throughout the entire voluntarist ecosystem. The increased devotion to evaluation that some foundation leaders embraced as a response to heightened public scrutiny placed greater reporting requirements on grantees, compounding the administrative burdens imposed by government funding (Hall 1992, 2004). Foundation professionalization encouraged program officers to shift from offering general-operating support to more project-based grants, thus further increasing reporting requirements for grantees. Philanthropic professionalization also laid the groundwork for sectorwide associations to represent common interests, such as regional associations of grantmakers, issue area affinity groups, and sectorwide infrastructure groups (Frumkin 1998, 1999; Nielsen 1985).

The Filer Commission had recommended the formation of a permanent advisory commission made up of private and public figures, potentially housed within the Treasury Department, to oversee nonprofit and philanthropic institutions (Brilliant 2000). This vision faded in the ensuing decade. The idea of an entirely private organization prevailed, and it was partially realized with the merger in 1980 of two previously created groups, the National Council on Philanthropy and the Coalition of National Voluntary Organizations, to form Independent Sector. The choice of the organization's name was as much aspirational as it was descriptive. Its leaders chose to promote the voluntary realm's "independence" at a moment when the government's entanglements with charitable tax -exempt organizations had become increasingly visible. In fact, Independent Sector's chair, the former Carnegie Corporation president and health, education, and welfare secretary John Gardner, hoped the new organization would protect the nonprofit sector from a "steadily increasing dependence on the federal government" (Zunz 2012:242). The term *independent sector* itself had been coined in a similar spirit of protest by the libertarian Richard Cornuelle, who in a 1965 book lamented the damage done to the voluntarist ideal by federal financing of private social service provision.[6]

Independent Sector brought together both public charities (including religious groups) and private foundations into one organization. It sought to make its multivalence a virtue, championing pluralism as a defining feature of civil society that required vigilant nurturing. The organization would not attempt "to bring order to a field whose tumultuous variety is its greatest source of creativity," John Gardner insisted (Zunz 2012:242). To the extent that it would take on a leading advocacy role for the nonprofit sector, it would promote voluntarism and the public good. It would resist, its organizers pledged, developing "a trade association reputation" that might be earned by focusing inordinately on "the financial and organization needs of the sector" (Hall 1992:79). Avoiding that focus would prove a challenge, given that the common identity of the organizations joined in Independent Sector was supplied by their organizational form and tax status. Yet in confronting this challenge, in seeking to meet the needs of both voluntarist spirit and its institutional embodiment, the organization grappled with a tension that has defined associational life in the United States since its earliest days.

Independent Sector would also come to provide important research and data collection functions for the nonprofit sector. The more rigorous research scrutiny applied to the sector was both cause and effect of the sector's increased formal coherence, as it focused scholarly and public attention on the sector's relationship to government and business (Hall 2006). The Filer Commission had produced what was at the time the most comprehensive research foray into the voluntary realm, publishing six volumes of research papers to accompany its final report, *Giving in America: Toward a Stronger Voluntary Sector*. John D. Rockefeller III along with a number of foundations provided funding for the first academic research center devoted to the study of nonprofits, Yale University's Program on Nonprofit Organizations (PONPO). The new multidisciplinary scholarly attention directed toward the nonprofit sector was reflected in the establishment in 1971 of the Association of Voluntary Action Scholars (AVAS), which in 1989 became the Association for Research on Nonprofit Organizations and Voluntary Action (ARNOVA) (D. Smith 1993). In 1983, Independent Sector convened a Research Committee, which over the next few years encouraged the establishment of twelve research centers on nonprofits in various universities around the nation. By 1993, there were thirty-five university-based academic centers focusing on the nonprofit sector (Hall 1992:251; Brilliant 2000). Academic institutions also met the growing demand for credentialed nonprofit professionals (even absent a consensus on whether, in the words of nonprofit scholar Peter Dobkin Hall, "there is such a thing as a nonprofit sector for which there is a generic core body of management skills and competencies").[7] In 1990, seventeen universities offered a graduate concentration on nonprofit management. By the new millennium, the number had increased to ninety-one (Mirabella and Wish 2001).

If professionalization contributed to centripetal forces within the sector, promoting standardized norms and practices, there were also centrifugal pressures, brought on by the growth of a new and diverse set of actors and organizations. The Immigration and Naturalization Act of 1965, which eliminated national immigration quotas from Africa, Asia, Latin America, Central America, and South America, had a profound effect on the nation's associational life. Whereas in the nineteenth and early twentieth centuries, most immigrants had come from Europe, in the decades after the act, 90 percent came from Latin America and Asia (O'Neill 1989). These immigrants developed a wide array of philanthropic, charitable, educational, and religious organizations that provided social services, political advocacy, and opportunities for social and religious activity. The number of mosques in the United States, for instance, jumped from 120 in 1960 to 290 in 1970.[8] The *mutualistas* that Mexican Americans had created at the turn of the century developed in the postwar years into more formal nonprofit organizations. In the 1960s, increased immigration, foundation support, funding from federal programs, and the model of the civil rights movement led to a significant increase in the number of voluntary organizations with a mission to serve Latinos. Whereas in the 1940s and 1950s, "the formation of new Latino nonprofits occurred at a rate ranging from 1 to 14 per year," in the 1960s, the rate of Latino nonprofits granted tax-exempt status by the IRS increased from 4 to 71 per year. That rate continued to climb in the 1970s and 1980s, with nearly half of the new organizations concentrated in the Southwest (Camarillo 1991; Cortés 1998:446).

This diversity strained the claims of the nation's dominant charitable institutions to represent the interests of the broader public. By the 1970s, challenges mounted, for instance, to the United Way's monopoly on soliciting workplace giving. "Alternative funds" were created that reflected a broader range of "communities of purpose," including those defined by ethnic and racial identity (Barman 2006). A particularly pronounced homogeneity presided over the philanthropic realm. When Waldemar Nielsen surveyed the donors behind the nation's thirty-three largest foundations in the early 1970s, he found that none was Catholic and only one was Jewish. Their board members were also almost exclusively white, Anglo-Saxon, and Protestant men. Some geographic diversity did develop, however, as concentrations of wealth spread beyond the East Coast and the Midwest, and major foundations emerged on the West Coast (Nielsen 1972; Soskis and Katz 2016). In the final decades of the century, women made steady gains in representation on foundation staff and at the leadership level: a 1990 survey of 723 foundations conducted by the Council on Foundations reported that women made up 43 percent of the chief executives of foundations for which information was available. Advances made toward ethnic and racial inclusion were considerably more modest. According to a 1991 study by Emmett Carson, for instance, 14 percent of foundation program staff were African American, and only 5 percent were Hispanic (Soskis and Katz 2016; Diaz 1999).

The Rise of the Conservative Counterestablishment
One form of diversity that did gain more recognition from philanthropists was ideological: the 1970s witnessed the development of a network of conservative nonprofit institutions devoted to promoting the principles of limited government, anti-communism, free enterprise, and "traditional" social values. Of course, voluntary organizations dedicated to these causes and fueled by a militant opposition to the perceived moral failings of the dominant institutions in public life were not new. They had proliferated in response to the New Deal and had been sustained through the support of a handful of conservative donors, such as members of the du Pont and Pew families. Yet these funders and organizations had previously exhibited little political sophistication or coordination (Nielsen 1985; O'Connor 2008; Zunz 2012).

By the 1970s, the sense of beleaguered crisis cultivated by leading conservatives had grown especially severe. They were galvanized by the fear that policy making in the Nixon administration had been captured by the network of progressively tilting private research institutions that had grown in the postwar years. There were also pressures applied from a rising tide of consumer, environmental, and workplace safety activism. In response, business interests, led by the U.S. Chamber of Commerce and the Business Roundtable (established in 1972), championed and funded an associational countermobilization, bankrolling a sharp increase in corporate lobbying and precipitating the move of corporate trade associations to headquarters in Washington (Berry 1997).

Conservative luminaries such as future Supreme Court justice Lewis Powell, neoconservative patriarch Irving Kristol, and former secretary of the Treasury William Simon elaborated a broader philanthropic strategy to overthrow progressive dominion. They insisted that the business community stop undermining corporate interests by providing financial support to the nonprofit establishment, which they claimed sat at the center of a broad-based attack on the capitalist system. Instead, they urged conservatives to construct a counterestablishment, an "alternative infrastructure of conservative thought, jurisprudence, 'private'-interest law, legal defense funds, policy advocacy, and public policy think tanks" (O'Connor 2010:342) to fight against what Simon called the "dominant socialist-statist-collectivist orthodoxy" (O'Connor 2008:158; Zunz 2012; J. Smith 1991).

A new crop of conservative funders proved receptive to this pitch. They actively sought to counter the influence of liberal foundations, self-consciously matching and extending the Ford Foundation's activism to adopt a countervailing philanthropic program to support conservative causes and reverse the ascendency of liberalism itself (Nielsen 1985; O'Connor 2010). By the mid-1970s, funders such as the Sarah Mellon Scaife, Smith Richardson, John M. Olin, and Lynde and Harry Bradley Foundations had engaged in a strategic campaign of institution building, often involving long-term and unrestricted general support to individuals and institutions. They directed funding across the entire line of policy production, funding student fellowships and campus publications, professional school organizations like the Federalist Society, think tanks and university-based research institutes, and advocacy organizations. To cite one example, the Olin Foundation helped develop the field of law and economics, funding efforts to establish beachhead programs at some of the nation's elite law schools (Covington 1997; Teles 2008).

Conservative philanthropy made a particularly robust investment in think tanks (Hammack and Anheier 2013). The older academic model of a nonpartisan research institution that focused on addressing technical policy questions, seemingly resistant to the pull of politics and insulated from the taint of ideology, had already been eroded by the rise of contract-based research institutions. But institutions like the American Enterprise Institute (AEI; founded in 1943 as the American Enterprise Association) and especially the Heritage Foundation (established in 1973 and funded in part by the beer magnate Joseph Coors) posed an even starker challenge to this model. These institutions developed explicitly conservative policies, crafted marketing and promotional strategies to promote them, and worked closely with advocacy groups to secure their enactment. The Heritage Foundation adopted these tactics most vigorously, skirting the boundary separating legally permissible research and education from the lobbying allowed only in limited amounts. Heritage's crowning moment arrived in the weeks after the election of Ronald Reagan, when the think tank's president delivered to the head of the White House transition team a thousand-page blueprint for the administration's first ninety days; Reagan asked that it be distributed at his first cabinet meeting, and Heritage's leaders later claimed that nearly 60 percent of its more than two thousand recommendations for appointments and policies were implemented by the end of Reagan's second term (J. Smith 1991). Although the report's influence has been exaggerated—many of those policies would have been implemented even without Heritage's intervention—its impact achieved mythic status within conservative circles and encouraged the establishment of additional research and advocacy institutes.[9]

The conservatives who led these institutions appreciated the novelty of their tactics while also insisting that they were not introducing ideology into an unspoiled realm of academic inquiry. Rejecting mainstream philanthropy's self-conceived identity as "politically and ideologically neutral protectors of the public interest" (O'Connor 2010:345), they claimed to be leveling a playing field that had so long been dominated by the ideology of the liberal establishment that its reign often advanced unregistered. Indeed, AEI's aim to challenge what it perceived as the liberal intellectual monopoly of research institutions fit into the valuation of pluralism so comfortably that even the Ford Foundation offered initial funding on those grounds (J. Smith 1991). Yet unrestrained by a public commitment to nonpartisanship, conservative institutions were able to engage in their ideological mission more deliberately and strategically and with less internal conflict than were liberal institutions.

By doing so, conservatives further weakened disinterestedness as an ideal in the realm of private research. It was overtaken by metaphors of the marketplace or the battlefield, with think tanks either peddling ideological wares or engaging in ideological combat (J. Smith 1991). This approach led to a sort of institutional arms race (to favor the military idiom), both within the conservative camp, as research institutions competed for contributions from conservative donors by staking out ideologically advanced and unclaimed territory, and between conservative and progressive think tanks. Progressives sought to emulate conservatives in establishing more explicitly ideologically directed research and advocacy-oriented institutions, with each side appropriating the organizational innovations of their ideological antagonists (J. Smith 1991; Soskis and Katz 2016).

Besides the funding it received from a small cohort of conservative philanthropists, the Heritage Foundation also received financial support from a larger contingent of small donors, engaged through an innovative computerized system of direct mail solicitations (up to 40 percent of the institution's budget in its early years was funded by small donations) (Zunz 2012; Nielsen 1985). More generally, the transformation of the top-down campaign to advance conservative social and economic policies into a social *movement* was accomplished by precisely such a convergence of elite and populist grievances and voluntarist enthusiasms. In Orange County, California, for instance, the combined grassroots forces of John Birch Society anti-communism, evangelical Christian political engagement, and the coffee klatch mobilization of suburban women, bolstered by donations from local conservative businessmen, helped push the Republican party firmly to the right (McGirr 2001).

In California as throughout the nation, the conservative movement was spurred by the growing politicization of evangelical Christians in the 1960s. Evangelicals channeled their activism through previously existing congregational networks and created new voluntary organizations, operating at the national, state, and local levels, to oppose the Equal Rights Amendment, gay rights, and abortion rights, among other issues (Martin 1996; Skocpol 2003). The Heritage Foundation provided key organizational assistance both to grassroots activists, such as fundamentalist Christians in Kanawha County, West Virginia, protesting sex education programs in public schools, and to evangelical leaders seeking to marshal Christians in organized political agitation. The key episode in galvanizing what became known as the Religious Right, formalizing a spirit of "co-belligerency" that brought together conservative evangelical Protestants and Catholics in a common political purpose, was the successful campaign in the 1970s to stop efforts by the IRS to strip segregated Christian schools of their tax-exempt status. This cause, more than opposition to abortion rights (which only came to define Christian Right political activism at the start of the following decade), strengthened the link between evangelical identity, hostility to government regulatory overreach, and a keen perception of the manifold threats posed by liberalism. It paved the way for the establishment in 1979 of the organizational embodiment of this coalition, the Moral Majority, which in the following decade formed chapters in states across the nation (Martin 1996).[10]

The Reagan Revolution, Fiscal Retrenchment, and Nonprofit Commercialization

The voluntarist campaigns of business, religious, and social conservatism, of both elite and grassroot varieties, scored their triumph with the election of Ronald Reagan in 1980. The president in fact styled himself an evangel of voluntarism, what he termed "the tradition of neighbor helping neighbor" (Bremner 1988). "The Reagan Administration came into office in 1981 with more awareness of, and more feelings and ideas about, the nonprofit sector . . . than any previous one," wrote Waldemar Nielsen in 1985 (Nielsen 1985:48). Yet the administration's promotion of voluntarism was marked by powerful contradictory forces that undermined that support (Lyman 1989).

Central to conservative attacks on liberalism was the repudiation of a "New Class" whose ranks included nonprofit professionals allied with government bureaucrats; conservatives instead held up visions of a neo-Tocquevillian idyll, populated by religiously committed volunteers. Yet in office, Reagan officials seemed to devote more energy to weakening the New Class, through efforts to defund the Left and to make it more difficult for nonprofits receiving federal funding to engage in political advocacy, than to boosting the tradition of neighbors helping neighbors (Salamon 1995). The 1981 Tax Act did include a time-limited experiment with the non-itemizer charitable deduction, which had been a policy recommendation of the Filer Commission (Brilliant 2000). Reagan also pushed deep spending and tax cuts, justified in part by the boost he assumed these would give to private initiatives. "We have let government take away too many of the things that were once ours to do voluntarily," he insisted in one of his early speeches, rekindling the Hooverian ideal (Salamon 2012b:22).

Yet the assumption animating these convictions, that there was a fundamental antagonism between state and voluntary action, overlooked the nonprofit sector's growing dependence on federal funding. In fact, the proposed cuts would have fallen hardest on those areas where federal support to nonprofits had been the most pronounced. According to estimates produced by nonprofit scholars Lester Salamon and Alan Abramson, by 1985, "after adjusting for inflation, the [Reagan] administration's proposed reductions in federal spending would have reduced the federal support to nonprofit social service organizations by 64 percent below" its levels in 1980 (Hall 2006; Salamon 1995:154, 2012b).

Ultimately, Congress resisted enacting the steepest proposed cuts, and, by 1984, total federal spending on "programs of relevance to nonprofit organizations" had dropped only 3 percent below 1980 levels (Salamon 1995). Another key factor that prevented nonprofit revenue from falling too precipitously were the indirect federal subsidies to nonprofit agencies through Medicare and Medicaid payments, which escaped the budgetary retrenchment and in fact continued to grow (Salamon 2012b).

Ultimately, the apocalyptic prognostications of nonprofit officials regarding the damage that would be done to the sector by the Reagan administration did not come to pass; in fact, the number of charitable tax-exempt entities actually increased by nearly a third over the course of Reagan's two terms (Hall 2006). This does not mean, however, that Reagan's budgetary policies did not have dire consequences for a significant number of nonprofit workers and clients, outcomes obscured by an understanding of the nonprofit sector as an undifferentiated whole. When payments to health services, boosted by Medicare and Medicaid subsidies, are excluded from the calculations, the value of federal support to nonprofits dropped by around a quarter in real dollar terms from 1980 to 1984 and did not return to 1980 levels until late in the following decade. Agencies that had relied heavily on federal funding in the past, that primarily served the poor, and that had only limited potential for raising additional funds from client fees, such as those within the fields of legal services, community development, employment and training, and social services, were hit particularly hard. Others, such as those devoted to arts and culture or mental health, experienced only modest reductions in federal funding (or had relied less heavily on federal funding in the past) and fared better. The disparate impact of Reagan's budget policies throughout the "independent sector" highlighted its variegated composition even as sector leaders sought to coalesce around a common voluntarist identity (Salamon 1995, 2012b).

Faced with declining federal support, many nonprofits increased their reliance on earned income to make up lost revenue. Salamon has estimated that 75 percent of the income that nonprofits generated to fill in the funding gap produced by budget cuts in the early years of the Reagan administration came from user fees and service charges (Salamon 1989). Of course, voluntarist organizations have long incorporated commercial activity into their practice, and this included, for many organizations, charging fees to those who made use of their services. The leading antebellum tract and Bible societies were major commercial enterprises, and nonproprietary primary schools, colleges, and hospitals have relied on client fees for centuries. In the early twentieth century, charity organization societies often featured wood yards where aid recipients performed work in return for assistance. More recently, in the 1940s and 1950s, many human service nonprofits increased their reliance on client fees as a means of differentiating their practice from charitable and welfare agencies, though the proportion of revenue such agencies derived from private contributions declined with the surge of federal funding in the 1960s (Brown 2018). Additionally, the inflation of the 1970s drove up administrative costs for many nonprofits at a time of declining charitable giving, requiring organizations to turn to alternative sources of revenue generation (Hall 1992).

Given this history, Maoz Brown suggests that the commercial ethos many human service nonprofits embraced in the 1980s should be regarded not as a break with past practice but as a resumption of trends interrupted by the War on Poverty (Brown 2018). Those trends, however, were not just recommenced but amplified during the 1980s. In the fields of social and legal services, the percentage of revenue that came from dues, fees, and charges for service nearly doubled between 1977 and 1987, to nearly 19 percent (Brown 2018). That increase did not merely compensate for declining governmental payments; it also ate into the proportion of revenue that nonprofits gained from charitable gifts. Indeed, overall, private giving as a share of total nonprofit income fell in the 1980s and 1990s, from 26 percent in 1977 to 17.5 percent in 1997 (Salamon 2012b).

These developments produced much consternation among some sectoral leaders about a deviation from an ideal donative model. They perceived the commercialization of the sector as a sign of a capitulation to alien market values and of a blurring of sectoral boundaries that threatened nonprofits' distinct identity. For instance, whereas earlier in the century, for-profit, public, and nonprofit hospitals relied on different sources of funding (patient fees, tax revenue, and charitable contributions, respectively) and diverged accordingly in the types of patients treated and in the types of care delivered, by the 1970s, they had begun to converge on these grounds, in part because of a common reliance on fees paid by insurance companies, Medicaid, or Medicare (Ferris and Graddy 1989).

Indeed, the growing commercialization of the nonprofit sector did not merely reflect a defensive accommodation to budgetary exigency. It registered the affirmative incorporation of market-oriented approaches and a consumer-oriented ethos into nonprofit practice (a facet of a broader political reorientation often identified with the ascent of neoliberalism and with the New Public Management approach to the delivery of public services adopted during this period by governments throughout the Western world). A number of factors encouraged this development. One was a feature of the growth of "third-party government": the shift in governmental support for social services from funding given directly to nonprofit service providers—producer subsidies—to aid channeled through the purchasers of those services—consumer subsidies. Between 1980 and 1986, the proportion of federal aid that reached nonprofit organizations via producer subsidies fell from 47 percent to 30 percent; this reduction in revenue was matched by an equal increase in the proportion of aid distributed in the form of consumer subsidies (which rose to 70 percent by 1986). The federal government also indirectly subsidized nonprofits through tax expenditures, as with the granting of tax exemptions for the purchase of services that nonprofits often provide. For instance, even as federal funding to day care providers through block grants fell during the 1980s, the federal tax credit for child care and dependent care expenses more than compensated for the decline (Salamon 1989; S. Smith 2017).

Conservatives championed the use of vouchers and tax expenditures as a means of empowering consumers (and of undermining the New Class alliance of government bureaucrats and nonprofit professionals). Doing so often entailed a channeling of government subsidy from the poor toward the middle class, whose appetite for nonprofit services was boosted by a number of demographic and socioeconomic developments; the "graying" of the population, for instance, led to increased demand for elder care services, while the continued entrance of women into the labor force increased demand for child care (Young, Salamon, and Grinsfelder 2012). Nonprofits were compelled to compete to attract these consumers, both with other nonprofit organizations and with for-profit firms that entered into fields previously dominated by nonprofits, such as nursing and child care, that were drawn in by the gravitational pull of federal subsidy (Salamon 2012b; Young et al. 2012).

Additionally, the increased demands imposed by revenue diversification and the need to incorporate and balance earned revenue, government grants, and charitable contributions encouraged many nonprofits to adopt more businesslike, entrepreneurial approaches to management and to court corporate leaders for executive positions and board service. These adaptations encouraged a more aggressive importation of the rhetoric and style of business culture into the nonprofit realm. As Salamon has written, nonprofits increasingly came to "market" their products and to seek out "market niches," to view their clients as "customers," and to formulate "business plans" (Salamon 2012b:54; Hall 1992).

Religious conservatives also came to endorse government-subsidized vouchers as a form of "charitable choice" that could direct public funds to faith-based charities, a move facilitated in the 1980s by a more permissive turn in Supreme Court jurisprudence toward governmental aid to religious institutions. Religious conservatives' embrace of "charitable choice" represented both an accommodation to and a critique of the development of "third-party" government. "After years of trying to limit federal funding to nonprofits, [religious] conservatives changed tactics and looked for ways to increase federal funding to" church-based and religiously-oriented social service providers (Zunz 2012:256). This effort was meant to address "the tragedy of American compassion"—to cite the title of an influential book by Marvin Olasky, a writer who served as adviser to Texas governor and president George W. Bush—brought on by the professionalization and bureaucratization of charity, which had been encouraged by government subsidy. Whereas secular charity focused only on clients' material needs, religious organizations could address their spiritual needs as well. Turn-of-the-century charity organization societies had made this claim as well, and in fact Olasky looked to them for inspiration. Religious conservatives often focused on a handful of cases in which government officials seemed to discriminate against religious organizations—insisting that Catholic hospitals remove crucifixes, for instance—and overlooked the long history of cooperation between government and religious organizations regarding social service provision. They also tended to assume that most religious congregations were intensely involved in social service activity, which was not the case (Chaves 2003).

The 1996 Welfare Reform Act contained a "charitable choice" provision, requiring states that contract with social service organizations to treat religious organizations as eligible contractees, though it prohibited faith-based organizations from proselytizing to clients. Both George W. Bush and Al Gore championed "charitable choice" during the 2000 presidential campaign. Once in the White House, Bush set up an Office of Faith-Based and Community Initiatives, as well as centers to promote faith-based initiatives in multiple federal departments. Many state and local governments followed suit, establishing similar offices and task forces that went beyond the statutory requirements of nondiscrimination with regard to faith-based charities to actively encourage and facilitate religious organizations taking on publicly funded social service provision (Chaves 2003). These developments generated enthusiasm among some evangelicals. They also produced considerable apprehension regarding the degree of government oversight that would follow federal subsidies, a concern summed up by the admonition that "with government shekels will come government shackles" (Zunz 2012; Hall 2006). Ultimately, the ambivalence of the evangelical community, compounded by a lack of funding and attention in the wake of the September 11 terrorist attacks, vitiated the impact of Bush's faith-based initiatives.[11]

Lastly, the permeation of a commercial ethos throughout the American nonprofit sector reflected broader geopolitical currents and geostrategic preoccupations. After the fall of communism, Western leaders held up a robust civil society as a defining feature of the "free world" that could be implanted within the former Soviet satellites to nurture the growth of democracy. Funders such as the financier George Soros and the Ford Foundation directed resources to nascent civil society organizations in Eastern Europe (Zunz 2012). The emergence of new nations, especially in Africa, following postwar decolonization also led to calls to support civil society institutions that built upon indigenous voluntarist traditions. This enthusiasm was part of a broader "global associational revolution" in the final decades of the century, an explosion of nonstate, nonproprietary organizations in nearly every region of the world, which marked the maturation of the "global community" that emerged in the aftermath of World War II. By the late 1990s, there were more than twenty thousand internationally oriented NGOs, often boasting cross-national agendas as well as local branches in multiple continents. The growth of such NGOs was particularly pronounced in the United States, rising from around six hundred in 1960 to over fifteen hundred by the mid-1980s (Salamon 1994; Iriye 1999).

The expansion of global civil society reflected the declining confidence in the welfare state that afflicted many developed nations in the final decades of the century. In the United States, private philanthropic and governmental funders distributing international aid grew increasingly suspicious of corrupt government bureaucracies in recipient nations and of the capabilities of states to perform effectively as agents of development. Fueling this suspicion was a countervailing belief in the flexibility, efficiency, responsiveness to community needs, and entrepreneurialism of NGOs, and a desire, among many donors, to support grassroots, indigenous organizations (Barnett 2011; Salamon 1994; Casey 2016).

Funders also developed a deepening enthusiasm for an emerging corps of "social entrepreneurs," a term popularized in the 1980s by the organization Ashoka, which formed to promote them. These were individuals with "breakthrough insights" who often tapped the power of market-based forces, and with leadership skills modeled on the corporate sector, whose activism and enthusiasm could bypass failed establishment institutions of governance (Bornstein and Davis 2010). Perhaps the most prominent social entrepreneur was Muhammad Yunus, the founder of Grameen Bank in Bangladesh, which gave out small loans to local women. In the 1980s and 1990s, the bank received hundreds of millions of dollars in financial support from governmental and multilateral aid agencies and foundations and inspired a host of microfinance enterprises worldwide (Zunz 2012; Bornstein and Davis 2010).

Associational Life, Voluntary Action, and the Nonprofit Sector in the Twenty-First Century

The last several decades have brought an amplification of many of the trends that reshaped the nonprofit sector in the second half of the twentieth century—the sector's expansion in size, its reflection of a changing demography, its absorption of commercial and market-based practices and values, the increased prevalence and prominence of public–private partnerships, and the transformative impact of technological advances that facilitate association. It has also been marked by a sense of crisis. "A struggle is under way . . . for the 'soul' of America's non-profit sector," one of its leading scholars has recently written (Salamon 2012b:3).

That experience of crisis is itself an enduring characteristic of American benevolent exceptionalism, one that has long provided landmarks linking key episodes in the history of American voluntarism. Indeed, surveying the past and present of American associational life and voluntary action produces an uneasy balance between an appreciation of historical continuities and contemporary impressions of discontinuity and novelty. Yet in the present moment, even developments for which historical lineages can be easily identified can seem exceptional because of their scale and intensity.

In many respects, the nonprofit sector's growth since the start of the new millennium has been remarkably consistent, given the upheavals that have defined the period. Public charities, for instance, managed to weather the recession of 2001 and the Great Recession without experiencing significant contractions in the aggregate number of organizations, total revenue, or assets (although charitable giving did drop by 7 percent in 2008 and another 6 percent in 2009, and revenue growth has not yet caught up to pre-recession rates).[12] Approximately 1.5 million nonprofits were registered with the IRS in 2015, representing an increase of 10.4 percent from a decade before. The growth of the sector has been particularly sharp in the realm of human services, where the number of nonprofits nearly doubled between 1995 and 2016 (S. Smith 2017).[13]

The growth in the sector reflects, albeit imperfectly, the major demographic shifts that will bring the nation to "majority–minority" status in a few decades. The surge in immigration over the last several decades increased and transformed demands for nonprofit services and changed the composition of the nonprofits offering them. Changing demographics have heightened calls for the introduction of greater diversity and equity into the sector, while also highlighting the gaps that remain between rhetoric and reality (Dighe 2012). Those changes are on vivid display in California, which achieved majority–minority status in 2000. According to a study by the Urban Institute, in 2009 people of color accounted for 57 percent of the state's population but held only a quarter of the executive director positions within the state's nonprofits (excluding hospitals and higher education), with Latinos accounting for less than 10 percent. People of color held 28 percent of nonprofit board positions in California. Though less than the actual proportion of people of color in the state, those totals are higher than national nonprofit figures. A recent survey from BoardSource, for instance, found that 90 percent of nonprofit CEOs and 84 percent of board members were white, numbers that have changed little since the organization first began conducting surveys on the issue in 1994.[14]

Commercialization, Marketization, and the Rise of Philanthrocapitalism

If demographic shifts help account for the nonprofit sector's growth over the last several decades, so too does the sector's increased commercialization. Nonprofit revenues have outpaced the growth of the economy as a whole during this time, and growth in commercial income accounted for nearly 60 percent of total nonprofit revenue growth from 1997 to 2007. In 2014, fees for services and goods made up 72 percent of the revenue for nonprofit institutions serving households, up from nearly 66 percent in 2004 (Salamon 2012b; McKeever, Dietz, and Fyffe 2016).

This growth represents an intensification of past trends yet also suggests some novel elements. The last decades have seen, for instance, a marked increase in "social enterprise," in which a nonprofit adopts a commercial venture not just as a means of generating income but as an intrinsic component of its charitable mission (Salamon 2012b). This approach has encouraged a further blurring of boundaries between for-profit and nonprofit enterprise. "Who cares about the tax status," the chief executive of a nonprofit that supports for-profit entrepreneurs told the *Chronicle of Philanthropy* in 2017. "The for-profit-nonprofit binary is officially over." This increasingly seems to be the case, discursively, at least, as market-based paradigms and financial metaphors of investment and capital have come to dominate discussions surrounding the definition of nonprofit aims and the assessment of nonprofit performance.[15]

In the philanthropic sector, the rise of impact investing has had a similar effect. The roots of the practice extend back at least to the turn of the last century, with the emergence of "philanthropy and 5 percent" below-market-rate housing loans. As early as the 1960s, the Ford Foundation experimented with "program-related investment" from its program budget (Adam 2002; Zunz 2012). Yet recently, a vanguard of individual philanthropists and foundations have placed even greater emphasis on the promotion of social good through for-profit investments. In 2017, Ford committed \$1 billion from its endowment to mission-related investments, the largest commitment by a private foundation to date. Several smaller foundations, such as the Heron Foundation, have committed to directing the entirety of their corpus to mission-related investments. Despite the hype surrounding these advances, however, the practice has not yet caught on among most large foundations, which still maintain firm boundaries between their investments and their program spending.[16]

These shifts are allied with the broader movement of *philanthrocapitalism*. It has two prongs: the idea that the market is the most powerful force for the promotion of social good and that the business leaders and entrepreneurs most adept at harnessing those forces must "save the world" (Bishop and Green, 2008). Neither of these is a novel conviction; they are both embedded, for instance, in Carnegie's "Gospel of Wealth." Yet their elaboration and permeation throughout the philanthropic sector, the variety of ways in which they have been implemented by funders, and the sophistication with which they have been adopted by the nonprofit grantees and social entrepreneurs those funders have favored is indeed exceptional.

The ascendance of philanthrocapitalism over the last decades reflects distributional trends in the American (and global) economy, increasingly characterized by income and wealth concentration (Soskis and Katz 2016). In the past, the gains from periods of economic expansion have been much more widely distributed. Only 5 percent of the income gains generated from 1954 to 1957 went to the top 1 percent of earners; between 1991 and 2000, 47 percent of the gains went to the top 1 percent. Between 2009 and 2012, 95 percent of the income gains did.[17] In 2018, Oxfam released a report showing that forty-two of the world's richest people hold as much wealth as the bottom half of the world's population combined, some 3.7 billion people.[18]

This explosion of wealth generation and concentration has produced a contemporary philanthropic sector of unprecedented scale and diversity. The speed at which many fortunes have been accumulated, especially in the realms of digital technology and finance, has yielded a crop of major donors distinguished by their relative youth and by their active engagement with their giving. This is a relatively new philanthropic norm; for much of the twentieth century, most wealthy individuals set up foundations or made bequests late in life and somewhat haphazardly (Soskis and Katz 2016; Callahan 2017; Nielsen 1985). Within the last decade, however, the actively engaged living donor has surpassed the legacy institutional foundation as the leading agent of change in the philanthropic sector. That development has reinvigorated long-standing debates about the legitimacy of philanthropy within a democracy and the dangers of concentrated private power, even if putatively directed toward the public good (Reich 2018; Callahan 2017; Soskis 2010).

Harbingers of this "giving while living" trend included Walter Annenberg, who in 1993 donated \$500 million for public schools, and Ted Turner, who in 1997 pledged \$1 billion to support the United Nations. Yet the figure who exemplified the rise of the contemporary

mega-donor is Microsoft founder Bill Gates. Gates and his wife, Melinda, initially established a number of foundations dedicated to supporting libraries and education in the
United States and global health (especially the production and distribution of vaccines).
In 2000, these were merged to create the Bill and Melinda Gates Foundation (BMGF),
which the couple seeded with a gift of nearly $16 billion. It became the world's largest, and
its assets swelled to an even greater size in 2006, when investor Warren Buffett pledged
much of his personal fortune to it, in regular annual installments. By 2015, it held more
than $40 billion in assets, nearly three times as much as the Ford Foundation, the next
largest. In the domestic realm, its main focus has been primary and secondary education,
with decidedly mixed results. More effectively, it has championed work on global health,
spending more than $15 billion on such programs to date. The resources it commands
have elevated the foundation to quasi-state status in its dealings with transnational health
policy organizations such as the World Health Organization (WHO)—for instance, Gates
sits on the board of GAVI, the Vaccine Alliance, to which it has given more than $4 bil-
lion, along with the WHO, the World Bank, and UNICEF (Soskis and Katz 2016; Zunz
2012; Callahan 2017).

Mega-Philanthropy and the Development of Novel Institutional Forms

Gates has provided a model of a bureaucratic and technocratic approach to philanthropy
that has been taken up by other wealthy citizens. It's possible, however, that the Gates
Foundation sits at the high-water mark of the century-long rise of the grantmaking philanthropic foundation. Private foundations have mushroomed in recent decades; from just
over thirty thousand in 1985, there were more than eighty-six thousand by 2015 (Reich
2018). Yet a number of the nation's wealthiest citizens have recently turned to alternative
institutional forms to structure their giving, creating a philanthropic landscape that is
considerably more varied than it was just a quarter century ago. One is the limited liability company, which allows donors to combine grantmaking, political donations, and
for-profit investments in one institution. The model was first developed by the founder
of eBay, Pierre Omidyar, who established a hybrid "philanthropic investment firm," the
Omidyar Network, in 2004.[19] In recent years, Mark Zuckerberg and his wife, Priscilla
Chan, as well as Laurene Powell Jobs, have adopted a similar model in designing their
own philanthropic vehicles.

The other novel institutional form is the donor-advised fund (DAF). Although the
historical roots of DAFs lie earlier in the last century in the informal consultative relationships that developed between donors and the staff of community foundations and charity
federations, the event that triggered DAFs' formal emergence was the Tax Reform Act of
1969. The act widened the split between the tax privileges granted to publicly supported
charities, including community foundations and federations, and private foundations,
which depend for their funding on a single individual or family. During deliberations over
the act, a Cleveland tax lawyer who was advising the city's Jewish charitable federation,
Norman Sugarman, realized that the final bill would unlikely "detail a clear path between
a donor's gift to a public charity and the allocation of those funds."[20] This sparked the idea
that individual donors could contribute to the institution, while making a recommendation of where the gift should be directed; the staff would then follow the donor's advice

and distribute the funds accordingly. Thus, individual donors could enjoy the benefits of control of allocations that private foundations offered, along with the tax privileges of a publicly supported charity. Soon after the passage of the act, Sugarman received a private-letter ruling from the IRS authorizing this arrangement. He began to promote it to other charitable institutions, such as Catholic Charities, community foundations, and Jewish federations, which by the mid-1980s began to refer to it as a "donor-advised fund" (Berman 2015). It was taken up as well by a number of ideologically oriented public charities, such as the progressive Tides Foundation, established in 1976, and the conservative DonorsTrust, established in 1999, which had an interest in shielding donor identity (Callahan 2017).

Most significantly, the DAF model attracted commercial investment firms, who had the personnel, connections to wealthy individuals, and resources to bring in significantly higher levels of contributions. Commercial firms capitalized on the appeal of DAFs to the wealthy, due to their provision of a tax-efficient means of donating appreciated investments and noncash assets. In 1991, the IRS determined Fidelity Charitable Gift Fund to be a public charity. Other commercial firms, like Vanguard, Schwab, and JPMorgan Chase, soon started their own DAFs. Propelled by the explosion of DAFs at commercial sponsoring organizations, the growth of DAFs more generally has been astronomical, exceeding by a factor of four the growth of total charitable giving over the last half decade. According to the *Chronicle of Philanthropy*'s ranking, in 2015, Fidelity Charitable raised more money from private sources than any other charity, bringing in $4.6 billion; it knocked United Way Worldwide from the top spot, where it had sat for all but one year since the *Chronicle* had begun compiling the list in 1991. In 2017, six of the top ten recipients of charitable contributions were DAFs.[21]

The explosive rise of DAFs raises a number of key issues for the sector. Unlike private foundations, DAFs do not entail any payout requirements, and critics have warned that they may encourage a warehousing of charitable resources. Their popularity among the economic elite highlights the extent to which the tax privileges attached to charitable giving often flow disproportionately to the wealthiest citizens.[22] Their spread also signals a weakening of the collectivizing role that institutions such as community foundations have traditionally played in the sector and the corresponding sway of an ethic of charitable individualism. Such a phenomenon can also help explain the rise of peer-to-peer giving through online sites like GoFundMe, which by the end of 2016 had raised more than $3 billion since it started in 2010.[23] The increased popularity of crowdfunding attests to a desire for a direct relationship between giver and receiver, unmediated by institutions like the United Way or national health charities. In a sense, these givers recapitulate the role played by social entrepreneurs within the sector, who have often chosen to work outside existing institutions or social movements.

The charitable sector reflects the economic landscape not merely in the prominence of a corps of mega-donors but in the broader distributional patterns it displays. These suggest that the rise of large-scale giving has been accompanied by a decline in mass giving. Indeed, even as "the share of total itemized giving by those earning $1 million or more per year has nearly tripled" over the last decades, growing from nearly 12 percent in 1995 to 29.8 percent in 2015, "charitable giving deductions from lower income donors have declined significantly. . . . According to one estimate, low-dollar and midrange donors to national public charities have declined by as much as 25 percent over the ten years from 2005 to 2015."[24] Participation rates have declined as well. From 2000 to 2014, the proportion of households giving to charity dropped from 66 percent to 55.5 percent, representing a decline in the engagement of "small" and "medium" donors.

Concerns about the health of mass giving are not new; at the turn of the last century, they spurred the creation of new institutional forms and new fund-raising practices such as community foundations and community chests. It's possible that a century later, they will have a similar galvanizing effect. The maldistribution of charitable giving shapes the contours of the nonprofit sector in other ways as well, since wealthy givers tend to favor certain institutions over others—hospitals and higher education as opposed to human service agencies (Reich 2018). Indeed, of the top one hundred charities that raised the most money in 2017, according to the *Chronicle of Philanthropy*, colleges and hospitals, which make up nearly half the list, saw their charitable support grow 44 percent from 2007 to 2017, even accounting for inflation. The other charities, including social service and health charities that rely less heavily on large donors, saw their charitable support increase by only 4 percent over that period.[25]

Even within particular subsectors, we can see similar patterns of inequality and resource concentration. For instance, "three quarters of the $516 billion in endowment wealth held by U.S. colleges and universities in 2014 was concentrated in the hands of just 11 percent of schools" (Callahan 2017:253). This inequity has led to increased political pressure to impose spending requirements on large endowments; a provision in the 2018 Tax Cuts and Jobs Act, for instance, included an excise tax on investment earnings of private colleges and universities with endowments of over $500,000 per full-time student.[26]

The Increased Prominence of Public–Private Partnerships

If the boundaries between the for-profit and nonprofit realms have continued to blur over the past two decades, so too have those between the nonprofit and governmental domains. Of course, the history of the past two and a half centuries has been a catalog of such blurring: from the commonwealth ideals that animated the early corporate charters, to partnerships like those between the federal government and the private Sanitary Commission during the Civil War, to the close collaboration between the Ford Foundation and the Johnson administration in the implementation of the War on Poverty.

So we must temper claims regarding the absolute novelty of contemporary public–private partnerships. Yet we should also note that they have generated more attention and energy from nonprofit, business, and government leaders in recent years, especially as economic crises and budgetary constraints have placed increased fiscal pressures on local and state governments. In this context, the scope and scale of public–private partnerships have grown, as has their formalization in cooperative arrangements, such as collective impact initiatives, that seek greater integration and collaboration among local public, nonprofit, and for-profit agencies. These partnerships have often imposed more rigorous reporting and evaluation requirements on nonprofits and have involved a complex and varied range of financing instruments, including performance-based contracts (S. Smith 2017; Katz and Nowak 2017; Lemos and Charles 2018). Furthermore, the imperative to pursue cross-sectoral partnerships has recently been more fully incorporated into the formal infrastructure of governance. In 2003, Michigan's governor created the Office of Foundation Liaison, the first cabinet-level office devoted to brokering relationships between a state government and the philanthropic community. Similar institutions soon spread to other locales; a 2010 study identified eighteen examples of local or state governments using a designated office or liaison to foster public–philanthropic partnerships. During the Obama administration, the Departments of Housing and Urban Development and Education created interagency offices to facilitate collaboration with nonprofits and foundations; perhaps the most notable such collaboration was Race to the Top, the $4.3 billion competitive grant program to spur reform in K–12 education (Abramson, Soskis, and Toepler 2014).

This sectoral blurring has taken on other forms as well. In recent years, the nonprofit sector has come to reflect the hyperpolarization that now defines contemporary politics, and, at times, to amplify it. Professionally managed advocacy groups have become skilled at targeting individuals with intense policy preferences (Skocpol 2003). Major donors are increasingly willing to enter into the partisan fray to promote their favored policies (Goss 2016). One recent study, for instance, found that two of the top education funders, the Gates and Broad Foundations, more than doubled their giving to national advocacy groups between 2005 and 2010 (Reckhow and Tompkins-Stange 2015; Callahan 2017).

The conservative counterestablishment, which took root in the 1970s, has grown luxuriantly in the decades since. A rich ecosystem of conservatives and libertarian research and advocacy organizations has developed, funded by many of the same foundations that supported the first generation of institutions, but joined by new funders as well. Many of these have coordinated to leverage their donations, such as the donor network presided over by Charles and the late David Koch (Mayer 2016). Conservatives have made especially impressive gains on the state level, where they have re-created and strengthened the networks of industry-backed think tanks, advocacy organizations, and philanthropy groups that achieved notable policy victories on the national stage (Hertel-Fernandez and Skocpol 2016). Progressives have sought to match conservative advances, with mixed success. They developed, for instance, their own consortium of funders, the Democracy Alliance, and established their own corps of partisan-oriented think tanks, such as the Center for American Progress, founded in the wake of George W. Bush's presidential victory in 2000 (Soskis and Katz 2016).

The Supreme Court's 2010 decision in *Citizens United v. Federal Election Commission*, which found unconstitutional laws limiting the ability of corporations and labor unions to expressively advocate for or against a candidate for political office, unleashed a torrent of corporate funding into 501(c)(4) "social welfare" groups, which could spend on elections without disclosing donors. In 2006, only 2 percent of "outside" political spending (uncoordinated with candidates) came from "dark money" social welfare groups; in 2010, the proportion had risen to 40 percent. In all, election spending by 501(c)(4) organizations grew from slightly more than $1 million in 2006 to nearly $150 million in 2016.[27] The IRS, hampered by budget cuts and tendentious accusations of partisan bias from conservatives, is now even less equipped than in the past to police nonprofit political activity (Colinvaux 2017; Mayer 2016).

The nontransparency of "dark money" nonprofit organizations stands in contrast to the development of a climate of heightened public attention in which nonprofits increasingly operate. Over the last decades, several national print publications have dropped a designated nonprofit beat. Yet targeted journalistic outlets, such as the *Chronicle of Philanthropy*, established in 1988; *Stanford Social Innovation Review* (2003); and the online publication *Inside Philanthropy* (2013) have stepped in to apply scrutiny (and have helped cultivate a shared sectoral identity). Investigative outlets like ProPublica, itself the product of a philanthropic investment (by Herbert and Marion Sandler), have also begun to train a critical spotlight on nonprofit activity and have encouraged mainstream media organizations to enhance their own coverage.[28]

In past decades, public demand for increased scrutiny of nonprofits has been generated by a number of high-profile scandals, such as the one that implicated the long-serving head of the United Way of America, William Aramony, in the mid-1990s; the Catholic Church abuse crisis, investigated by the *Boston Globe*; and, most recently, the controversies surrounding the Trump Foundation, covered assiduously by the *Washington Post*. Additionally, deepening concerns about income and wealth inequality have darkened the reception granted to major philanthropic gifts, focusing attention on their furthering of plutocratic control over public policy (Reich 2018; Callahan 2017).

The increased scrutiny directed toward nonprofits has also stemmed from the shifting expectations of institutional and individual donors. A number of organizations have developed over the last two decades to guide givers and to provide information about nonprofit operation and performance, such as Candid, Charity Navigator, the BBB Wise Giving Alliance, and GiveWell (Abramson and McCarthy 2012). These services have often emphasized monitoring overhead and administrative expenses, though they increasingly seek to develop means of evaluating nonprofit effectiveness and impact as well. Innovations in performance management, impact assessment, and social-outcome measurement, such as the use of randomized-control trials, as well as advances in big data analytics, have ushered in a new evaluative regime. Relatedly, we are now in the midst of a data revolution in nonprofit research. The Taxpayer Bill of Rights, signed by Bill Clinton in 1996, mandated nonprofit disclosure through Form 990, the tax form that nonprofits send to the IRS. A consortium of nonprofit research institutes contracted with the IRS to scan these forms and then digitized them, in order to make the data available online (Brilliant 2000). In 2016, in an important milestone for nonprofit research, the IRS released electronic versions of Form 990 as public, machine-readable data.[29] The sector's capacity to generate information, if not necessarily insights, about its scope, operations, and impact, has never been greater.

The Health of Twenty-First Century Voluntarism
and the Emergence of Networked Social Movements

A range of diagnoses of the health of voluntarism in the United States have emerged over the past decades. In his 2000 book *Bowling Alone*, political scientist Robert Putnam argued that the nation was confronting a serious decline in civic engagement and "social capital," the formal and informal networks and affiliations that create norms of reciprocity and trust, which was evident in Americans' fraying attachments to communal voluntarist organizations. Americans no longer belonged to houses of worship at the rates they once did; they no longer served in parent-teacher associations (PTAs) or joined the Boy Scouts or fraternal leagues in past numbers (Putnam 2000). And they no longer signed up for bowling leagues, and so they "bowled alone." Other scholars have pointed to the dominance of top-down professionalized advocacy organizations, which had supplanted cross-class, participatory membership organizations, as contributing to voluntarism's relative infirmity (Skocpol 2003).

In the wake of the September 11 terror attacks, a brief wave of civic renewal crested. In one survey, 70 percent of respondents reported making a charitable contribution in response to the attacks (Skocpol 2003). Volunteering rates also shot up, reaching a forty-year high soon afterward; but the surge was not sustained, and rates soon subsided, without inaugurating the new age in civic engagement that some had predicted (Dietz and Grimm 2016).

Yet even as some worried that Americans' associational commitments were waning, there were signs of their continued vitality. In a 2003 decision in which the Supreme Court ruled that the Boy Scouts of America were allowed to exclude homosexuals, the Court determined that there was "a right of intimate association," underscoring the significance of the expressive elements of associational life (Hall 2006; Levy 2017). The last decades have also exhibited surges of activism that challenge a narrative of voluntarist declension. If one of the reasons why health care reform failed to pass during the Clinton administration was the lack of grassroots support marshaled on its behalf, the successful passage of the Affordable Care Act in 2010 owed much to precisely such mobilization, coordinated by a host of nonprofits (Kirsch 2011). And marriage equality, the other signal progressive policy victory of the last decade, depended on a similar alliance of professionally managed advocacy nonprofits and local grassroots campaigns (Frank 2017).

The Tea Party protests, Occupy Wall Street, and more recently, the Movement for Black Lives, the Women's March in the aftermath of the election of Donald Trump, and youth-led activism surrounding gun violence and climate change, have all aggressively mobilized citizens to push for policy and social change. They raise important questions about where power and control reside in contemporary social movements, whether in the grassroots or grass-tops. Many of them are clearly characterized by a decentralized, participatory dynamic, with a distributed leadership structure, in which movement content is adapted to fit the needs of varying communities. This networked model of social movements can bypass traditional organizational hierarchies and has been embraced by both progressive and right-wing activists (Heimans and Timms 2018). Older, legacy advocacy organizations, such as the American Civil Liberties Union (ACLU), the NAACP, and the National Council of La Raza (which changed its name to UnidosUS in 2017), have been forced to "rebrand" to tap into and channel these grassroots political enthusiasms.[30]

Many of these mass social movements have made powerful use of social media. Indeed, a sort of millennial promise attached to social media's potential to transform grassroots activism in the first decade of the 2000s, in the aftermath of the "Color" revolutions that swept through Eastern Europe and then at the start of the Arab Spring protests in 2011. Facebook, Twitter, and other social media platforms allowed networked movements to scale up rapidly and to address complex logistical challenges without significant initial

investments in organizational infrastructure. Instead, they could rely on the spontaneous mobilization of activists, what sociologist Zeynep Tufekci has labeled "adhocracy,"
adapting a term first popularized by Alvin Toffler (Tufekci 2017:53). The disappointments
of the Color revolutions and of the Arab Spring have shown the limits of technology in
promoting social change, however, as authoritarian regimes have proved just as capable
of using social media and digital technology to inhibit activism, to manipulate social
discourse, and to inflame and exploit social grievances in service of maintaining the status quo. The possibility that digital protest holds out of accelerating movement building
might carry liabilities to the extent that it obviates the need for the slow, difficult process
of planning mass action that in the past has generated valuable solidarity and strategic
insights (Tufekci 2017).

The impact of digital technology on the nonprofit sector as a whole is similarly profound yet indeterminate. It has transformed how nonprofits assess and promote their work,
attract and interact with clients, and raise funds. Twenty-first-century communication
technologies facilitate the dissemination of information, opinions, and "best practice"
models, and help to create communities of purpose across local, national, and international borders, much as the mail system did in the early nineteenth century. The question
of whether such technologies help democratize the sector, or, because of their significant
costs and training requirements, encourage the concentration of power and resources in
an elite cohort of organizations, will be a vital one to address in the coming years.

Similarly, nonprofits are just beginning to grapple with the extent to which their reliance on digital technology (and likely, in the near future, on artificial intelligence) also
ties them closer to the market and to "the rules and tools of the companies that make the
gadgets and wire the world."[31] There is a measure of empowerment in those bonds, but
also risk and vulnerability. The tension between those two dynamics is not new; it has
characterized voluntary life in the United States for more than two centuries. But it will
surely develop in novel ways in the years ahead.

3   SEEING LIKE A PHILANTHROPIST

From the Business of Benevolence to the Benevolence of Business

Aaron Horvath and Walter W. Powell[1]

OVER THE COURSE OF AMERICAN HISTORY, philanthropists have been both praised and pilloried, depicted as redeemers of democracy and a threat to it. Despite the shifting social terrain in which they have operated, philanthropists—and the organizations they create—have grown in number and influence, acting as a catalytic force in the genesis and development of the modern nonprofit sector. Philanthropic largesse has also played a powerful role in shaping civic life and political affairs. This chapter argues that it is important to understand not only how philanthropists are seen, but also how they see. In narrating the development of American philanthropy from the late nineteenth to the early twenty-first centuries, our aim is to capture changes in what it means to "see like a philanthropist"—that is, to illuminate the meanings and ends of philanthropic wealth. We focus on three core influences on philanthropic visions: (1) the sources of philanthropic wealth, (2) its organizational embodiments, and (3) the criticisms leveled at its outsized influence. We examine the reciprocal dynamic between political challenges to elite power and philanthropic visions. We show that philanthropists have transposed the practices they used to earn their great fortunes into the organizational routines of their philanthropies and turned these into requirements for those who receive their funding. The actions of past philanthropists weigh heavily on future philanthropists. Consequently, the political might of philanthropy both channels and enables the critiques to which its influence is subjected. In narrating this long arc of history, we show how super-rich people's perceptions of themselves and their role in public life have evolved as well as the myriad ways philanthropy has altered civic and political discourse.

Connecting Past and Present

In 1855, a young John D. Rockefeller purchased a ten-cent red notebook he named Ledger A. Following the counsel of Ben Franklin's *Autobiography*, Rockefeller began to track his daily virtues and vices, record acts of thrift, and train impulse into reason. Rockefeller took to personal bookkeeping with zeal, recording his earnings and expenditures with exacting detail. Listed alongside his modest early income as a clerk for Hewitt and Tuttle are many acts of charity, including contributions to Baptist missions, Catholic orphanages, "a poor woman in church," and a black man in Cleveland to "buy his wife" out of slavery in 1859.

Organized charity was only just beginning to take shape. By the end of the nineteenth century, social gospelers and fledgling progressives would seek to ameliorate the social ills of the era. Settlement houses would take root in American cities, and Salvation Army chapters would provide soup, soap, and salvation to the needy. A modern ecumenical form of *noblesse oblige*—detailed in Carnegie's "Gospel of Wealth"—would soon be articulated.[2]

Rockefeller's fortunes—as well as the scale and precision of his beneficence—grew alongside these charitable developments (Chernow 1988:46–51). In 1892, with the aid of a Baptist clergyman, the Reverend Frederick Gates, Rockefeller's penchant for personal and industrial discipline developed into philanthropic discipline. "No longer [was I] groping my way, without sufficient guide or chart, through this ever-widening field of philanthropic endeavor," wrote Rockefeller of Gates's influence (Rockefeller 1909:156). Rockefeller began to practice "scientific giving," which entailed "laying aside retail giving almost wholly, and entering safely and pleasurably into the field of wholesale philanthropy" (Gates 1977:161). The business metaphor was apt. Early efforts in wholesale philanthropy included a $600,000 founding donation to the University of Chicago (a school that, save for the chapel, does not bear his name), the establishment of the General Education Board to fund black and white education in the rural South, and efforts to eradicate hookworm.

Speaking at a small dinner celebrating the tenth anniversary of the University of Chicago, Rockefeller exhorted his fellow businessmen and foreshadowed his philanthropic ambitions:

> Let us be as careful with the money we would spend for the benefit of others as if we were laying it aside for our own family's future use. Directors carry on these affairs [on] your behalf. Let us erect a foundation, a Trust, and engage directors who will make it a life work to manage, without personal cooperation, this business of benevolence properly and effectively. And I beg of you, attend to it *now*, don't wait (Rockefeller 1909:187–188).

Rockefeller did not wait long. In 1909, he signed a deed of trust covering 72,569 shares of Standard Oil—roughly $50,000,000—and entrusted his son, his son-in-law, and Mr. Gates to administer his fortune. As he had done in recent years, he planned to call on businessmen, scientists, and doctors to advise his giving. Seeking legislative approval, he requested a bill of incorporation from the federal government.

Similar trusts had been granted legislative approval before. The American Historical Association had been incorporated by an act of Congress in 1889, and the Carnegie Institution of Washington had been incorporated in 1903—the same year Rockefeller's General Education Board had received its charter. Moreover, Rockefeller did not *need* to receive a congressional charter: his deed of trust was sufficient to establish the Rockefeller Foundation. But a congressional charter would enable Congress to override the foundation, and Rockefeller reasoned that this would insure against improper use of his money by future generations.

Rockefeller's timing could not have been worse. He and his industrial powerhouse were subjected to increasing obloquy over the previous decade. Ida Tarbell, the famous muckraking journalist, sketched a scathing critique of Standard Oil. Regarding Rockefeller, she concluded that "our national life is on every side distinctly poorer, uglier, meaner, for the kind of influence he exercises."[3] In 1908, a jury in Chicago found Standard Oil guilty on 1,903 counts of taking railroad rebates. Before the judge could levy a $29,240,000 fine against the company, U.S. Marshals had to pry Rockefeller away from the Massachusetts hiding place where he had been evading subpoena. Then, amid mounting public enthusiasm for dismantling monopolies, the U.S. Department of Justice sued Standard Oil for violation of the Sherman Antitrust Act. The oilman's image was further blackened when his employee, John Archbold, was caught trying to buy political leniency from senators and a presidential candidate. Endorsement of and association with Standard Oil and its controversial leader had become a liability.

By the time Senate Bill 6888 to incorporate the Rockefeller Foundation was announced, opinions on Rockefeller's charity were mixed. To some, incorporating the foundation meant endorsing "tainted money," "the Trojan horse," and the "kiss of Judas." Others saw it as a redemptive opportunity, arguing that "the public ought to welcome whatever good the money can produce." Recent sins, however, were fresh in political leaders' minds. President William Howard Taft denounced the bill as "an act to incorporate John D. Rockefeller," and Taft's attorney general, George Wickersham, referred to the bill as "an indefinite scheme for perpetuating vast wealth." Was it appropriate, Wickersham argued, that "Congress . . . should assist in the enactment of a law to create and perpetuate in his name an institution to hold and administer a large portion of his vast wealth?"[4]

Opposition to the bill developed in Congress over several years, collecting conditions and limitations[5] before it ultimately collapsed. Rockefeller's reputation was too tarnished, his proposed foundation too big, his vision too broad. In the absence of congressional approval, Rockefeller and his advisors withdrew the bill from Congress and requested a charter from the State of New York instead. The charter was signed into law on May 14, 1913. Mirroring the language of Rockefeller's original deed of trust, it described the foundation's expansive purpose succinctly: ". . . to promote the well-being of mankind throughout the world."[6]

———

Just over a century after the incorporation of the Rockefeller Foundation in New York, a thirty-one-year-old Internet mogul, Mark Zuckerberg, took to his decade-old platform, Facebook, to make an announcement in the form of a letter to his unborn daughter. He and his wife, Priscilla Chan, would commit 99 percent of their company shares—roughly $45 billion—to advances in health care and education. They would think long term, rely on the advice of experts, and leverage modern technologies and business models to improve the world around them.[7] Their mission, though couched in the language of the time, had a familiar ring: ". . . advancing human potential and promoting equality."

The announcement grabbed headlines and was widely lauded by businesspeople and politicians,[8] but, like his robber baron predecessor, Zuckerberg had experimented with other forms of charitable giving before creating his own philanthropic organization. In 2010, Zuckerberg, working alongside Governor Chris Christie and Mayor Cory Booker, had announced on the *Oprah Winfrey Show* a $100 million gift to revamp the public schools of Newark, New Jersey. Although Zuckerberg had never visited the city, he felt confident that he could save it:

> In running a company, the main thing I have to do is find people that are going to be really great leaders and invest in them. And that's what we're doing here. We're setting up a

$100 million challenge grant . . . to implement new programs in Newark and really make a difference and turn Newark into a symbol of educational excellence for the whole nation.[9]

The Newark initiative was widely deemed a failure (Russakoff 2015). Nevertheless, Zuckerberg's business and philanthropic reputation escaped relatively unscathed. Between 2010 and 2015, Zuckerberg and Chan gave nearly $1.6 billion to the Silicon Valley Community Foundation, began a wider and more inclusive school reform initiative in the San Francisco Bay Area, funded the $75 million construction of an acute care building at San Francisco General Hospital (the hospital now bears Zuckerberg's name), and joined the Giving Pledge.[10] Indeed, the Giving Pledge is the *Gospel of Wealth* for the Internet era.[11] By the fall of 2018, in the wake of investigative reports on Facebook's inaction and misdeeds in response to the use of the platform to disrupt the 2016 election, public criticism of Zuckerberg and his sidekick Sheryl Sandberg rivaled Ida Tarbell's 1905 scathing remarks about Rockefeller.

Zuckerberg's Facebook announcement in 2015 signaled an important turn toward a different, more organized form of giving, much like the move Rockefeller had made at the dawn of the twentieth century. Forgoing the philanthropic organizational form that had become increasingly common over the previous century,[12] Zuckerberg and Chan opted to create the Chan Zuckerberg Initiative as a limited liability company (LLC) to pursue their philanthropic interests. As with Rockefeller, their actions provoked many questions. To whom would the company be accountable? Would it be used for the purposes its founders claimed? Was it just another scheme for perpetuating vast wealth? Are investments charity?

There are many parallels between the philanthropic interests of Rockefeller and Zuckerberg. Their charitable organizations shared similarly expansive missions, helped establish and popularize new organizational forms, proclaimed dissatisfaction with past forms of philanthropy, and sought to draw on new ideas to execute their philanthropic visions. There are notable differences as well. When Rockefeller was born, organized philanthropy by the super-rich was not yet routine; when Zuckerberg was born, such philanthropy had become the norm. Rockefeller expressed considerable concern with how the state would regard and shape his beneficence; Zuckerberg's philanthropic pronouncements hardly mention government at all.[13] Rockefeller's image of philanthropy drew on ideas of bureaucratic control, incorporation and concentration, and physicality; Chan and Zuckerberg's draws on ideas of networks, distribution, and virtuality. The two men envisioned seemingly similar philanthropic ends, but each saw the world—what it was, his role within it, its problems, and his ability to change it—in distinctive, sociohistorically specific ways. Both saw like a philanthropist, but the lines of their vision were remarkably different.

———

Rockefeller prophetically noted that "the charities of the twentieth century will not be the charities of the twenty-first century . . . and it is eminently desirable that the dead hand should be removed."[14] In this spirit, this chapter charts the changing outlooks of organized philanthropy. To remove the dead hand from our understanding of organized philanthropy, we survey its landscape as an emergent product of historical legacies and contemporary possibilities. This is a story of not just philanthropic organizations, but also the ideas that underlie these organizations' formation and actions. In telling this story, we illuminate what it means *to see like a philanthropist* and show how the philanthropic field of vision has changed over the past century. Ultimately, this history enables us to better understand the enduring and evolving elements of modern philanthropy, as well as the paths not taken. We view philanthropy not as "mere" acts of generosity by the wealthy, but as reflective signposts that mark collective understandings of democracy, wealth, and the kind of society we have become.

Putting Philanthropic Visions in Their Time and Place

In *Seeing Like a State*, Yale political scientist James Scott (1998) argued that governments approach problems by laying out complicated plans that the politically powerful then approve. Such plans are implemented with little regard for local conditions or knowledge and often wind up as disasters, much like Zuckerberg's Newark school initiative. When states—bureaucrats in offices in a capital—try to assess what is going on, they use maps: maps of territory, people, and laws that attempt to fit human relationships into preconceived categories. But such maps, Scott forcefully argued, are never the real territory, and what is "seen" is only a very small slice of reality. Sociologists Marion Fourcade and Kieran Healy (2017), following in the footsteps of economist Albert Hirschman (1977), have recently written about "seeing like a market." They demonstrate that firms are employing new technologies and practices that sort people, activities, and problems into categories. New tools create new strategies for knowing and acting on the world.

To us, the human vision metaphor[15] suggests the prevailing ideas that help organize and orient a field's activities by providing an ideational order of what philanthropy can and should do—a topology of what is possible and what is appropriate. Like the governments that Scott studied, philanthropists understand social problems and needs through the lenses of their time and elaborate programs and plans to effect change based on the view that those lenses afford. But as experience provokes astigmatisms, such as when philanthropic action encounters obstacles or challenges, lenses are refocused and visions change.

What does it mean to see like a philanthropist? As social critic Dwight Macdonald (1956:3) wryly observed of the Ford Foundation, philanthropy is a "body of money completely surrounded by people who want some." His typification rings with timeless truth. Philanthropists and their organizations have long found themselves overwhelmed on all sides by supplicants.

Building on this, we observe that the "body," "money," and "people" in Macdonald's definition have expanded considerably over the past century. Philanthropic action has long mirrored the origins of philanthropic wealth, and wealth-distributing organizations regularly reflect the forms, people, and routines of their wealth-generating counterparts. The money philanthropists disburse is more than a mere medium of exchange; it also conveys meaning. Alms, contributions, gifts, grants, and investments mark not only distinctive monetary forms but also sharply divergent relationships between benefactor and beneficiary (see Zelizer 1997). Likewise, varying conceptions of recipients (such as the contrasts between the supplicant, the grantee, and the public) imply varying relations and obligations. The interrelations among these mutable components create the philanthropic outlooks of an era. Previously oriented toward the human face of suffering mothers, orphans, and soldiers, modern philanthropy now orients itself to the abstract notions of investment, impact, and scaling.

To see how philanthropic visions have changed over time, we look at them through the lenses of the sociology of knowledge and the sociology of organizations. The sociologist Karl Mannheim (1936 [1997]:97) argued that the "[ideas] of a given time and place must be understood against the background . . . of the society in which they occur." Mannheim's causal arrow points from context to ideas. But the arrow points in the other direction as well. According to Max Weber (1958), fields of rationalized activity are built on deeply held presuppositions that give them purpose and direction—an idea that applies to the analysis of organizations as well. Arthur Stinchcombe (1965:153) tells us that "organizational forms . . . have a history, and that history determines some aspects of the . . . structure of organizations." Organizations bear the imprint of ideas, concepts, values, and understandings that animate the time and place of their founding. Over different time scales, both processes are visible. As John Padgett and Walter Powell (2012:2) assert in the mantra to their book, "in the short run, actors create relations; in the long run, relations create actors." The organizational forms invented in one generation lay the groundwork for subsequent generations, circumscribing and enabling the ideas, choices, and actions that are available later on. Even when later generations contest or reject prior models, the alternatives they promote take shape in the shadow of history.

In our view, changes in philanthropic outlook derive from three focal influences that we discuss in turn. First, we examine how philanthropic efforts come to reflect the interests and industrial practices that generate wealth. When philanthropists look at social problems and needs, they see them through the business lenses that have led to their wealth. When Rockefeller sought to apply his wealth to public matters, for example, the modes of industrial manufacturing that had generated this wealth offered him specific tools and solutions that differ from those afforded to Zuckerberg by the virtual networking that had generated his wealth. Second, we follow the move from donor-centric to organization-centric giving and find that organizational elaboration generates new modes of philanthropic understandings of and interactions with the world. As organizations become routinized and professionalized, they create new persons, spawn new organizations, and provide new ways of thinking and acting. These new categories of thought in turn shape philanthropic directions, sometimes intensifying philanthropists' initial motivations and sometimes undermining them. Third, we consider the evolving criticisms leveled at the actions and influence of philanthropy. We start with the perspective that although philanthropists make contributions to the public, the public decides whether these contributions are seen as reputational repair, tax dodges, risk capital, or plutocratic control. In their relations with government, philanthropists have been variously regulated, feared, criticized, and championed. Such challenges have profoundly shaped the ways philanthropists understand their role in society. Their responses to these influences have fundamentally changed the way they go about their work.

Of these three influences—business influences, organizational influences, and public influences—the second and third have a reciprocal relationship with the practice of philanthropy itself. New philanthropic organizations emerge in the shadow of older ones. Many early foundations still operate today and serve as a powerful template for new

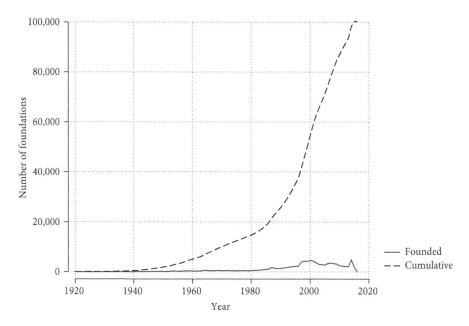

Figure 3.1   Growth in U.S. philanthropic foundations, 1920–2016
Source: Adapted from the National Center on Charitable Statistics, various years.

entrants by shaping what forms of organization and action are thinkable. And even as the new is built in the image of the old, older philanthropic forms are often influenced by new concerns and alternative modes of funding. Similarly, the critiques leveled at philanthropists are themselves subject to change, and this change is often a product of philanthropic influence. So even as philanthropic visions are swayed by public scrutiny, public perspectives are swayed by philanthropy.

These transformations are visible in the historical path between Rockefeller and Zuckerberg. Between these two figures, we delineate five eras of philanthropic outlooks and consider how each emerges from what came before and sets the stage for what comes next. We use important events to mark the turning points in this history of philanthropy, but there's no clean break between each period. Many threads of the past are woven into the future.

Through this history, we trace two broad forms of change: population-level change and changes within philanthropic foundations. To trace population-level change, we map the overall growth and variation in the scale and scope of organized philanthropy and consider novel forms of wealth and philanthropic practice as they emerge. We identify specific mechanisms of change that operate at this level: growth, imprinting, stratification, and categorization. To trace changes within philanthropic foundations, we examine their interconnectedness with and awareness of developments taking place in business, government, and other modes of philanthropy. We find that the growth of philanthropic foundations, as depicted in Figure 3.1, is not simply a change in degree (more foundations, more participants, more money), but also a change in kind (new forms, new practices, new constraints, new opportunities). The growth in number occurs alongside transformations in both visions and routines.

While our immediate focus is on the evolution of philanthropic outlooks in the United States, this chapter also speaks to wider concerns. First, it sheds light on not only the panorama of organized philanthropy in the United States over the past century but also the processes by which central institutions, ideas, and practices of civil society develop over time. This effort is part of a broader project to understand cultural and symbolic emergence and change. Our story is one of neither heroic nor witless actors but rather individuals and organizations collectively making sense of the world around them, using the tools and cognitive models of their times, and seeking to make sense of events and possibilities that current models aren't equipped to help them understand.

The following sections describe five eras of philanthropic foundations, beginning with their initial emergence from a looser set of associations. As these foundations begin to appear, they are simultaneously challenged and elaborated by new entrants and new people in charge of disbursing funds. A period of rapid-fire challenges to their legality, regulation, and control then transforms them from a disparate set of organizations into a self-conscious organizational field with a common identity. As this collective self-consciousness develops, so do internecine ideological struggles for political influence. Most recently, an elaborate set of market-oriented ideas find their way into philanthropic activity, producing disruptive sets of practices and organizational forms.

Many excellent books have been written on these topics—typically with greater awareness of specific periods, foundations, or funding domains (such as education or poverty). We have benefited greatly from these sources in preparing this chapter. Our goal as sociologists is a different appreciation. At the outset of each era's discussion, we summarize it with a table describing seven characteristics of philanthropy in that era: (1) a statement of the era's philanthropic vision, (2) the industry sources of the philanthropists' wealth, (3) the legal forms that philanthropists chose for their organizations, (4) the roles and expertise of staff, (5) common organizational practices, (6) the common themes of philanthropic funding, and (7) the challenges philanthropists faced. Highlighting these characteristics helps us concentrate on how philanthropic vision has evolved in tandem with its organizational forms.

From Retail to Wholesale Philanthropy, pre-1907

It would not be until the end of the nineteenth century that "philanthropy" would connote the private redistribution of wealth, and only later would it become settled into its modern organizational form (see Levy 2016). Table 3.1 highlights the challenges of this first era. Before then, civic organizations—especially those led by aristocratic and ecclesiastical elites—were often viewed as counter to the ideals of the young nation. (See Soskis, Chapter 1, "A History of Associational Life and the Nonprofit Sector in the United States"; also Johnson and Powell, 2017). Moreover, the influence of wealth beyond the grave was thought problematic. Writing to James Madison regarding the influence of past generations on the actions of their successors, Thomas Jefferson asserted that society "belongs in usufruct to the living . . . The portion occupied by any individual ceases to be his when himself ceases to be, and reverts to the society."[16] Nevertheless, patrician influence found

Table 3.1 From retail to wholesale philanthropy, pre-1907

Vision	Money is a gift by the wealthy few to the industrious masses.
Sources of wealth	The first great industrialists and robber barons amass wealth through huge enterprises that extract and refine raw materials and build America's transportation and communication infrastructure (oil, steel, rail, etc.)
Organizational forms	Individual philanthropy predominates the era, and it grows increasingly organized, scientific, and systematic.
Organizational staffing	Personal giving advisors appear at the end of the period (e.g., Frederick Gates for Rockefeller). In newly founded organizations, personal ties matter a great deal.
Organizational practices	Ideas about how to give emanate from organizations promoting scientific approaches to charity. Religious motivations and spontaneous gifts give way to charity sans sentimentality. Charitable investigations are developed as a tool for philanthropy.
Funding	Gifts are made to churches, universities, hospitals, libraries, and parks. Gifts are targeted at people and communities that will help themselves, not those who will become dependent.
Challenges	Social anxieties about the gilded elite becoming a new aristocracy. Philanthropic anxieties about how to dispense with one's wealth before death.

organized outlets. Writing on the *Remains of the Aristocratic Party in the United States,* Tocqueville ([1835] 1969) asserted that although elite influence had been undercut by the new nation's constitution, the explosive growth of eleemosynary endeavors represented a continued elite influence, especially in education and the arts.

These developments did not go unchecked (see detailed discussion in Hilt 2017). The 1820s saw the New York state legislature reserve the legal right to limit the overall size of charitable endowments and the amount of personal property that could be committed to them. Pennsylvania limited the power of its courts to enforce charitable trusts, a number of states banned the creation of charitable organizations, and the Virginia Supreme Court feared that the property of society would be "swallowed up in the insatiable gulph of public charities" (quoted in Hall 1992:23). At a time when the formation of corporations required direct legislative approval, the sanction of an elite-run organization was an uncomfortable surrender of popular sovereignty.[17]

After the Civil War the formation of corporations—previously handled on a case-by-case basis—became routine (Bloch and Lamoreaux, 2017). The Pennsylvania Corporation Act of 1874 created two major classes of corporation: "Corporations for Profit" and "Corporations Not for Profit." The latter included churches, "any benevolent, charitable, educational or missionary undertaking," sciences and fine arts, parks and facilities for "skating, boating, trotting and other innocent athletic sports," clubs for "social enjoyments," cemeteries, mutual benefit societies, fire brigades, trade groups, and the "prevention of cruelty to children and aged persons."[18] (These classifications are mirrored today by the numerous subsections under section 501(c) of the Internal Revenue Code.) In due time, states across the nation liberalized their codes of incorporation.

Even as not-for-profit incorporation swelled, widespread trepidation surrounded acts of charity and the distribution of money to the poor. Citing fears of dependency, legislators in Philadelphia effectively outlawed monetary aid to the poor in the late eighteenth century. In New York, during the Panic of 1837, some claimed that monetary gifts to the poor were to blame for "riot and intoxication," because they pampered "the most detestable and destructive of vices" (Clement 1985:71–72). The Association for Improving the Condition of the Poor equated mendicancy with mendacity and forbade members to make monetary gifts to the poor, insisting instead on gifts of moral restitution. Even during times of economic crisis, the association decried soup kitchens and street handouts (Becker 1961). The Benevolent Societies of Boston discouraged members from giving money or any other form of alms that would "interfere with the necessity of industry, forethought, and a proper self-denial" (Huggins 1971).

Reconstruction-Era Philanthropy

In the throes of civil war, national fraternal orders (such as the Freemasons, the Odd Fellows, the Improved Order of Red Men, and Tammany Societies) and local branches of the American Anti-Slavery Society and other abolitionist groups were joined by organizations practicing increasingly methodical and professionalized forms of voluntary activity. The privately funded, volunteer-led U.S. Sanitary Commission, an outgrowth of the Women's Central Association of Relief in New York, was chartered by Congress to collect supplies and administer medical care to wounded soldiers. It pioneered dispassionate, scientific medical care and helped make charity work professional, systematic, and orderly (Frederickson 1965; Geisberg 2000).

Following in the mold of professional societies founded before the war, wealthy abolitionists founded the American Social Science Association (ASSA) to advance charitable and reformist interests through scientific understandings of society. Shortly after its founding, members of the ASSA created the Conference of Boards of Public Charities to serve as a forum to exchange charity and reform knowledge and experiences, a forerunner to the clearinghouse. Such developments were deeply entwined with those of the social gospel movement, which sought to enact scripture on earth by forging a union between Christianity and social science. Both, according to preachers such as Washington Gladden and Walter Rauschenbush, concerned "laws affecting the welfare of mankind." Though the country was riddled with evils, prior efforts to cure such ills had been "rather uncertainly done" with little effort to "systematize the knowledge" so that "concerted action may be based upon it" (Gladden 1887:223). The settlement movement was the incarnation of social gospel ideas: it simultaneously provided relief to individuals and sought to reform the conditions of society. Participants in the settlement movement would go on to staff early foundations—especially the Russell Sage Foundation (Sealander 2003)—leaving a mark on the shape and purpose of early philanthropic organizations.

Paralleling reformist, social scientific developments, charity organization societies (COSs) crossed the Atlantic from London to Buffalo, New York, subsequently spreading their ideas across the United States. The movement was clothed in the systematizing and scientific ethos of the period: participants sought to provide poor relief in a fashion less sentimental—and in their view more sound—than the settlement movement had done. Evoking an antebellum distrust of the poor, the charity organization movement sought to "sift the helpless poor from the worthless pauper by means of thorough and searching *investigation*—to expose and prosecute imposters and fraudulent charitable societies"

(Gurteen 1882:17, emphasis in original). The professionalization of pauperism, movement proponents concluded, would never have occurred were it not for ill-conceived municipal poor laws and private charity. Yet the indiscriminate abandonment of the poor would not do. There were deserving people among their ranks, and their identification demanded methodical investigation of individuals' conditions and deservingness, or in other words, "scientific organization."[19] Such beliefs threaded a needle between society's collective violation of natural selection and the need for charity conditioned on these grand visions. Such threading, the forerunner to casework, produced a tool that would soon be adopted into philanthropic practice. Gifts of money remained deeply problematic, but methodical study and investigation offered an escape from the quagmire.[20]

Beneficent Robber Barons

The same social and economic conditions that enfeebled scores of Americans (and provoked a plurality of charitable responses) enriched the coffers of the few. Rapid industrial development created immense wealth, endowing a handful of self-made men with vast fortunes. But the Protestant ethic that inspired industriousness disapproved of luxuriating in one's wealth. A good man not only accumulated wealth but also disbursed it through good deeds. Such dualism is found in Rockefeller's oft-quoted belief that "a man should make all he can and give all he can" (Fosdick 1952:6).

The philanthropic interests of a new class of super-rich took shape out of these early theories of charitable organization. Writing in the *North American Review*, Carnegie helped elaborate one form these interests would take. His "Wealth" (1889b)—published as "The Gospel of Wealth" in the British *Pall Mall Gazette*—is as much a paean to capitalism as a directive for philanthropy. The essay opens with the premise that, in accordance with the laws of competition and natural selection, humanity exists in a state of "affairs under which the best interests of the race are promoted, but which inevitably gives wealth to the few" (657). To Carnegie, this situation was not only natural, it was also *proper* if humans, as a race, were to enjoy progress. Efforts to challenge the otherworldly accumulations of wealth were "attacking the foundation upon which civilization itself rests." Indeed, the anarchists and socialists that Carnegie describes *were* calling into question the social order that allowed for untold wealth to amass in the hands of the few, but to Carnegie their charges were in vain. The present conditions, he wrote describing the Gilded Age, were "the best . . . humanity has yet accomplished" (657).

Thus, the great problem of the time was not the immense accumulation of wealth. The problem, Carnegie argued, was that of indiscriminately giving it away. Referencing Herbert Spencer, he asserted that a quarter dollar given to an unknown beggar "will probably work more injury than all the money which its thoughtless donor will ever be able to give in true charity." Passing wealth to progeny would also be injudicious. Inheritance would impair the industriousness of future generations.[21] Carnegie also impugned the practice of giving upon death, even applauding estate taxes because they are the means by which "the state marks its condemnation of the selfish millionaire's unworthy life" (659). It was the rich man's duty to give while he is alive and to administer his funds wisely. The industriousness that equipped him to make money was the same characteristic that equipped him to give it away.

Later in 1889, Carnegie (1889a) again took to the *North American Review* to expound on the proper administration of wealth. In an essay titled "The Best Fields for Philanthropy," he cataloged the laudable ends toward which the rich should administer their funds. First on his list is the university. Indeed, establishing universities was popular in the late nineteenth century. Ezra Cornell, founder of Western Union Telegraph Company, founded his eponymous university in 1865. "The Commodore," Cornelius Vanderbilt, gave $1 million to the Central University of the Methodist Episcopal Church in Nashville in 1873. Though Vanderbilt had never traveled to the state, the school was renamed in his honor. Writing his will in a city ravaged by Civil War and cholera, Johns Hopkins used his wealth to found a series of organizations between 1875 and 1916: an orphanage, a university, a hospital, a nursing school, a medical school, and a school for public health. When California governor and railroad tycoon Leland Stanford's son died of typhoid in 1884, Stanford donated his farm and approximately $40 million to found a university in his honor. In 1890, Rockefeller provided the funds to establish the University of Chicago,[22] and in 1891 merchant and financier William Marsh Rice chartered Rice Institute in Houston (Muir 1972:64–65). The trend continued well into the twentieth century. Carnegie himself founded the Carnegie Technical Schools in Pittsburgh in 1901. In 1968, they merged with the Mellon Institute of Industrial Research, founded in 1913 by another philanthropist, Andrew Mellon.

Second on Carnegie's list was the formation of libraries. With impressive regularity, he created 1,679 local libraries in the United States with $43 million in funds (Van Slyck 1995:217). Third, Carnegie saw the creation of "hospitals, medical colleges, laboratories, and other institutions connected with the alleviation of human suffering" as a worthy charitable end. Fourth, fifth, and sixth, communities needed public parks for recreation, city halls for public meetings, and swimming pools for rejuvenation.

In enumerating the causes toward which the rich should direct their benefactions, Carnegie specified his philosophy of *how* best to give:

> An endowed institution is liable to become the prey of a clique. The public ceases to take interest in it, or, rather, never acquires interest in it. The rule has been violated which requires the recipients to help themselves. Everything has been done for the community [when instead it should be] helped to help itself (Carnegie 1889a:689).

Carnegie's perspective resonated with views that were developing in the various charity movements of the time. Charity should foster self-sufficiency, not indolence. In enacting his vision, Carnegie charged James Bertram, his personal secretary, with managing the day-to-day aspects of administering funds for community libraries. In so doing, Bertram developed an investigatory tool to assess which communities would be best served by and able to sustain a local library.

Carnegie's embrace of philanthropy signaled not a softening, but rather a deepening of the ruthlessness of his business practices. Dedicating a library in Pittsburgh in 1895—three years after one of the bloodiest labor disputes in American history had unfolded at Carnegie's nearby Homestead steel mill—the steelmaker spoke of his decision to distribute his "surplus gains" to new institutions instead of distributing them directly to his employees. To him, raising wages was neither "justifiable or wise." Articulating his vision, he told the gathered crowd that were he to pay his workers "trifling sums" more, it would

Figure 3.2 "Carnegie in his great double role"
Source: *The Saturday Globe*, July 9, 1892.

be "frittered away . . . on things which pertain to the body and not to the spirit; upon richer food and drink, better clothing, more extravagant living." By pooling what could be higher wages into one great sum for the funding of cultural institutions, Carnegie sought to "minister . . . to the divine in man." "Man," he concluded, "does not live by bread alone" (quoted in Nasaw 2006:523).

Carnegie knew well how underpaid his workers were. His common claim that wages were set by the market was true with one hitch: his business controlled the market. But he also was of the view that those worthy of more would quickly transcend their lowly lot, perhaps by availing themselves of the cultural and educational resources he had endowed. The logic of his position was suspect, as depicted by the 1892 cartoon in Figure 3.2. Working daily twelve-hour shifts left as little room for extracurricular self-improvement as meager salaries left for daily bread.

Other wealthy industrialists developed views of methodical philanthropy similar to those espoused by Carnegie.[23] Reflecting on his philanthropy of the 1890s, Rockefeller described his giving as "haphazard . . . giving here and there as appeals presented themselves. I investigated as I could, and worked myself almost to a nervous breakdown."[24] His friend and advisor Gates was frank in recounting his mentee's difficulties. "He was in daily receipt of appeals from individual Baptist missionaries in every region of Baptist missionary endeavor. His office, his house, his table was beset with returned missionaries, each comparatively ignorant of all fields but his own. . . . We cut off every one of these missionary appeals."[25] In Gates's appraisal, Rockefeller's piecemeal approach was unsustainable. Because the philanthropist would be exhausted before his fortunes, Gates counseled Rockefeller to cease his program of one-by-one support and systematically sponsor Baptist missions.[26] Though writing checks became easier, their receipt became more complex. Rockefeller gave $100,000 to the American Board of Commissioners for Foreign Missions, the leading Congregationalist missionary organization. Gladden, a leader of the social gospel movement and a vociferous critic of Standard Oil, decried the gift as "tainted money" and insisted it be returned. "Was the church of Christ to maintain its holy offices with predatory wealth?" he asked (Gates 1977:202; Soskis 2010). Rockefeller's and Gates's giving persisted undeterred.

Philanthropy as Science

Even with increasingly systematic gifts, super-rich industrialists continued to see their wealth accumulate faster than it could be disbursed. Their commitments to organization and efficiency in business came to shape their philanthropic horizons. Commenting on the relatively slow pace of spending Rockefeller's great fortunes, Gates "saw no other course but for Mr. Rockefeller and his son to form a series of great corporate philanthropies for forwarding civilization in all its elements in this land and in all lands" (Gates 1977:207).

In organized philanthropies, three predominant threads were soon woven together: the social obligation of the wealthy, the developing science of philanthropy, and the development of a new organizational form. In the confluence of great fortunes and the belief that charity required careful, deliberate planning and control, the modern idea of philanthropy was born. The interweaving of these threads signaled a broad cultural faith in human meliorism—the belief that it was possible to solve society's problems. It also reflected a more parochial faith—held by the super-rich, who were convinced of their intrinsic brilliance in business dealings—that men of means ought to be the vanguard of social progress.[27] Early philanthropists fostered the economic and cultural conditions that would make a new generation of philanthropic organizations possible. The road they cut, however, would prove to be rutted and unfinished. A new organizational form, the general-purpose foundation, lay just over the horizon, but it would cross paths with mounting criticism of its existence.

Given the business dealings of the industrial titans whose wealth set modern philanthropy in motion, it is tempting to view their charitable dealings as some of the most "gilded" aspects of the Gilded Age. That is, it is easy to view early forays into charity as a sort of golden patina over a lower-grade material—a disingenuous act.[28] But what we see in the actions of men like Carnegie and Rockefeller is not a cynical ploy to win the favor of the masses for the price of a few good deeds but a self-assured confidence in the intrinsic qualities of their industrial genius. Their unmerciful business practices and the magnanimity of their gifts were not inherently contradictory; they were two sides of the same gold coin.

These early philanthropic visions, minted in the image of new social concerns and the myriad ameliorative approaches to their resolution, were (if we take philanthropists at their word) sound and rational solutions to the challenges facing society. Yet when these visions later took shape in new organizations, they did so in a society that chafed at the unchecked accumulation of wealth, no matter how rational its administrators believed they were in disbursing it. The new field of organized philanthropy that emerged was met with an ambivalent and at times hostile social and political environment. Encounters with detractors and a handful of early successes would play a significant role in channeling philanthropic activities and understandings of the public good in the coming years.

Organizing Philanthropy, 1907–1952

The differing philanthropic visions and practices that emerged over the latter half of the nineteenth century were realized in a host of new philanthropic organizations. New York State, which in the 1890s had been torn on the legal status of trusts, became increasingly hospitable to their creation (see Katz, Sullivan, and Beach 1985). At the federal level, too, there was a marked shift in the endorsement of philanthropic organizations aiming to disburse funds for public purposes. The General Education Board, founded by Rockefeller and Gates, received a federal charter in 1903 to expand education without regard to race or sex. In keeping with the scientific mode, Rockefeller committed increasing sums of money to the effort once he was convinced of the board's effectiveness. Carnegie, whose creation of trusts involved a $10 million gift for universities in his native Scotland, received congressional charters in 1902 for the Carnegie Institution of Washington (an organization dedicated to funding basic science), in 1905 for the Carnegie Foundation for the Advancement of Teaching (from which the Teachers Insurance and Annuity Association [TIAA] was born), and in 1910 for the Carnegie Endowment for International Peace, with its ambitious charter to "hasten the abolition of war." Philanthropy was becoming organized and scientific.[29] The ambitions and programs of new organizations are summarized in Table 3.2.

Table 3.2 Organizing philanthropy, 1907–1952

Vision	Money attacks root causes to treat purported evils at their source.
Sources of wealth	Aging robber barons are joined by their families in philanthropic endeavors. Their business enterprises come under fire; trusts are broken up. New philanthropic wealth arrives from retail money and, later, automotive money.
Organizational forms	Individual giving becomes routinized within general purpose foundations. Community foundations attempt to democratize philanthropy. Some bylaws set time horizons for spending wealth.
Organizational staffing	Small staffs are composed of personal advisors with a mix of scholarly and religious backgrounds. Staff rely on experts and social scientists in guiding grantmaking. Heirs take the reins of philanthropic organizations.
Organizational practices	Organizations engage in large-scale funding efforts and demonstration projects, creating new organizations and activities to be taken up by other philanthropists and the state. Grantmakers make early steps toward assessing grants and prospective grantees. Avoiding redundancy becomes an important criterion of philanthropic efficiency. Philanthropic organizations go through a wave of consolidation. Early efforts at limiting the influence of wealth's dead hand commence.
Funding	The concern with addressing root causes drives philanthropic attention toward medical and scientific research with a growing emphasis on the development of social and administrative sciences as well as education. Funding is provided for research institutes and new academic programs.
Challenges	Philanthropists and their organizations are the object of public obloquy and government-led investigations (e.g., the Walsh Commission). Intellectuals critique philanthropists for their heavy influence in the fields they fund, especially in the sciences. Internal dissent among philanthropists centers on how best to pursue public purposes.

Though the new organizations represented the foray of robber barons into the world of organized philanthropy, their foundations were not the first. That distinction goes to a pair of foundations established within a few years of the Civil War. The Peabody Education Fund was founded by George Peabody of Baltimore in 1867 two years before his death, with an initial gift of approximately $3 million. The fund sought to expand education in the Southern states by opening and financially assisting public schools near population centers. Beyond its express purpose, Peabody's organization served as a training ground for many who would go on to be influential figures in American philanthropy. The board was chaired by Robert C. Winthrop and included such Gilded Age luminaries as J. Pierpont Morgan (the son of Peabody's business partner), Theodore Roosevelt, Wickliffe Rose (later a leader of Rockefeller's Sanitary Commission in 1909), and Joseph H. Choate (whose legal challenge to Samuel Tilden's will to establish a free library and reading room would shape the practice of philanthropy and the distinction of gifts from trusts) (Ayres 1911; Taylor 1940).

Inspired by Peabody, a textile manufacturer from Connecticut, John F. Slater, established the Fund for the Education of Freedmen in 1882. Slater, anticipating a discussion that would spur philanthropic debates for decades in the future, sought to distance his money from his control, granting his fund's trustees the "largest liberty of making such changes in the methods of applying the income of the fund as shall seem from time to time best adapted to accomplish the general object herein defined" (Ayres 1911:27). Although Slater and Peabody sought to improve black education, their philanthropy should be understood in context: both philanthropists were accommodating to segregationist Southern politics.

Though trusts and purpose-specific foundations were becoming more common, it was not until 1907 that broad-purpose foundations began to appear, the first being the Russell Sage Foundation, led by Olivia Sage, a seminary-educated reformer and suffragette. Her marriage to Russell Sage—a man so miserly that the *New York Times* ran regular pieces detailing his tightfisted financial schemes[30]—limited her financial contributions. Instead, Sage dedicated herself to "performative philanthropy" (Crocker 2006): she became the first president of the Emma Willard Society and volunteered in the New York Women's Hospital. She published essays as "Mrs. Russell Sage" in the *North American Review*, imploring her fellow woman to be "responsible in proportion to the wealth and time at her command." "While one woman is working for bread and butter," she wrote, "the other must devote her time to the amelioration of the condition of her laboring sister" (Sage 1905).

When her skinflint spouse died in 1906, Sage was able to make good on the moral responsibility she promoted. After consulting with Robert DeForest, an attorney and champion of the charity organization movement (Karl and Katz 1981), Sage secured a charter from New York and established a foundation rooted in the tradition of social work. The Russell Sage Foundation for Social Betterment had a mandate to improve "social and living conditions in the United States." In a letter to trustees in 1907, Sage specified the scope of the foundation's work as "not only national" but also "broad" and emphasized that the foundation was not to replicate work done by other agencies. Instead it was to take on the "larger, more difficult problems; and to take them up so far as possible in such a manner as to secure co-operation and aid in their solution."

The foundation drew staff from social work organizations and settlement houses and eventually turned to social scientists and their research methods to understand and tackle the "root causes" of social ills. Taking a cue from the settlement movement and maps and surveys by Jane Addams and Ellen Gates Starr, the foundation funded a major survey of Pittsburgh to methodically understand the living conditions and needs of people in the city. A team of about eighty researchers documented pressing reform issues such as child labor, work accidents, poor sanitation, and the relations of immigrant enclaves. The results were published in six volumes over the next seven years and served as evidence for the Commission on Industrial Relations as it impugned the legitimacy of major philanthropic gifts (Greenwald and Anderson 1996).

The idea of root causes—"curing evils at their source" (Sealander 2003)—catalyzed other new foundations as well. In 1910, Elihu Root advised Carnegie to put his remaining wealth into a new organization, the Carnegie Corporation, to ensure the efficient administration of his funds. The organization was chartered in New York, but its articles of incorporation revealed a grand goal: "advancement and diffusion of knowledge and understanding." To a degree, the charter represented a concession of Carnegie's personal control over his benefactions. There was too much money to be spent by one man alone. Nevertheless, the foundation remained a creature of Carnegie himself in its early years, its gifts mirroring his personal benefactions and its board rubber-stamping his decisions. Funds flowed to libraries and medical education, but also to Carnegie's other philanthropic organizations. It would be a suspect maneuver by today's standards. Carnegie and the corporation's board were both the makers and takers of his philanthropic gifts.

Rockefeller's foundation, though similar to Carnegie's in inspiration, was molded by the oilman's declining reputation and the protracted legislative scrutiny of his philanthropic activities. Unlike the early years of the Carnegie Corporation, the Rockefeller Foundation drew on the insights of advisors to make distributional decisions. Doctors and Baptist ministers were on call, including the physician Abraham Flexner, who had produced the *Flexner Report* on medical education under the auspices of the Carnegie Foundation for the Advancement of Teaching, and the ministers Wallace Buttrick and Wickliffe Rose, heads of the General Education Board and Rockefeller's Sanitary Commission, respectively.

Great wealth was regularly vilified in the early years of the twentieth century. Theodore Roosevelt, whose progressive stances characterize the era, wrote clearly about the wealthy men who had risen to national prominence:

> There is not in the world a more ignoble character than the mere money-getting American, insensible to every duty, regardless of every principle, bent only on amassing a fortune, and putting his fortune only to the basest uses. . . . Such a man is only the more dangerous if he occasionally does some deed like founding a college or endowing a church, which makes those good people who are also foolish forget his real iniquity. These men are equally careless of the workingmen, whom they oppress, and of the state, whose existence they imperil.[31]

In the public eye, new foundations embodied a broad mandate and a scientific worldview but also represented the calcification of immense wealth and elite influence. Labor-friendly legislators sought to put the new instruments of plutocratic power in dialogue with their own cause. From 1912 through 1915, the Federal Commission on Industrial Relations, known as the Walsh Commission, sought to examine the causes of a wave of labor uprisings. News of the Colorado Coal Wars and the radical unionist bombing of the *Los Angeles Times* building had put the country on edge. Common laborers testified at hearings, and well-known people such as Louis Brandeis and Mother Jones served as witnesses. Economist John R. Commons, who had been involved with the Sage Foundation's Pittsburgh Survey, was on the commission's staff. Men such as Carnegie, Daniel Guggenheim, Henry Ford, and John D. Rockefeller Jr. were called to account for their antilabor actions. The commission's attention turned to the new foundations when it became clear that the Rockefeller Foundation was, independent of government efforts, sponsoring scientific investigations into labor relations.[32] Members of the commission immediately saw a link: the right hand was in the service of the left. Foundations were a tool to whitewash the excesses of business.[33] The depth of the conviction was revealed in the testimony of John Haynes Holmes, a socialist and Unitarian clergyman, who argued that the essence of foundations was "repugnant to the whole idea of the democratic society." In the commission's final report, Rockefeller was called a "menace to the national welfare," and chairman Frank P. Walsh argued for closing the foundation and putting its money toward labor causes (U.S. Congress 1916). Legislation that would have placed foundations under control of Congress was proposed but never passed.[34]

Legislative scrutiny ultimately subsided, but public scrutiny continued. Labor unions in New York City grew sharply critical of Flexner and Raymond Fosdick for serving as commissioners on the city board of education, accusing them of "trying to secure control of public education for the Rockefeller crowd," calling for their resignation, and labeling them agents of a "conspiracy to get control of our education system." By May 1917, both commissioners had resigned from their posts.[35]

Rockefeller's name was toxic elsewhere. Rumors of his association with the fledgling Institute for Government Research (later the Brookings Institution) almost derailed public acceptance of the organization's efforts to be a disinterested expert branch of the federal government. In 1916, rumors swirled in newspapers around the country about the "Rockefeller Inquiry" and "Rockefeller's Probe" and "Rockefeller's Institute," even though, as the foundation itself reported, "not a cent" of Rockefeller money was going to the new institute. Indeed, no Rockefeller money made it to the institute until 1926 by way of the Laura Spelman Rockefeller Memorial. But public alarm was uneven. Fosdick and Robert Woodward, president of the Carnegie Corporation, were early members of the organization's board. The "Silent Partner of Uncle Sam" was buttressed by equally silent philanthropists.[36]

Enlivening Dead Hands

Foundations began to respond to some of the commission's concerns, especially those concerning broad mandates and the perpetuity of perpetual private wealth, and strove to demonstrate their public purpose. With the nation on the brink of joining World War I, Rockefeller Foundation funds increasingly went toward humanitarian war-related efforts: delivering food to Belgium, improving troop morale, and combating meningitis, dysentery, and shell shock in military hospitals.

Some foundations began to carry the scientific ideal to its fullest extent, engaging in demonstration projects to test and prove reform solutions that, in theory, could be taken up by others. The Milbank Memorial Fund began to engage in health demonstrations in an effort to control the spread of tuberculosis in rural communities around the country (Milbank Memorial Fund 1923). The Rockefeller-funded General Education Board worked with the U.S. Department of Agriculture to conduct farming demonstrations that would advance "scientific agriculture" and promote greater yields and profits. The Russell Sage Foundation strove to develop a model community—Forest Hills Gardens in New York—from scratch. With Frederick Law Olmsted as designer, the foundation built a community of Tudor-style suburban homes for working-class families. The neighborhood they created was so well-made that housing prices soon soared, undermining the foundation's intended goals.

In the coming years, some philanthropists began to tinker with the structure and timespan of their foundations. In 1917, Julius Rosenwald, a part owner of Sears, Roebuck, created the Rosenwald Fund to promote the development of black education in the South. The fund's mission—"for the well-being of mankind"—resembled the Rockefeller Foundation's. Unlike the Rockefeller Foundation, however, it placed numerous conditions on its funds. The endowment was *not* to persist in perpetuity; it *could* be dissolved at the discretion of the trustees, and it *must* be dissolved within twenty-five years of Rosenwald's death. Rosenwald spelled out his wishes in a 1928 letter to his trustees:

> I am not in sympathy with [the] policy of perpetuating endowments and believe that more good can accomplished by extending funds as Trustees find opportunities for constructive work. . . . By adopting a policy of using the Fund within this generation we may avoid those tendencies toward bureaucracy and a formal or perfunctory attitude toward the work which almost inevitably develop in organizations which prolong their existence indefinitely. Coming generations can be relied upon to provide for their own needs as they arise. (Quoted in Embree 1936)

Rosenwald's perspective was soon popularized in essays in the *Saturday Evening Post* and the *Atlantic Monthly*. In "Principles of Public Giving" (1929), he argued that "While charity tends to do good, perpetual charities tend to do evil." He reasoned through examples. A perpetual gift to provide meals at a school was senseless in the absence of a food shortage. Previously laudable perpetual contributions to orphanages were now out of step with research suggesting that family homes were a better setting for child development. Short of advocating for the "profligate spending of principal," Rosenwald recommended that trustees spend at least 5 to 10 percent of their capital annually. Foundations should be prepared to change course when new funding needs arise.

About the same time, the creation of the community foundation provided another alternative to philanthropic perpetuity. Established in 1914, the Cleveland Community Foundation focused its attention locally. Under Frederick Goff (made wealthy by Standard Oil), the foundation was to be a "living trust," pooling the funds of Clevelanders. Goff decried the influence of the "dead hand" in an address to the New York Association of Trust Companies at the Hotel Astor in New York City in 1921. "The opinions to which men have attached their property change and become extinct," he argued, making them "the very worst kind of Foundations" (Goff 1921:13). It was therefore important to treat foundations as a living "experiment in benevolence . . . as the usefulness is demonstrated, pass the activity over to the public and continue." Breathing life into the foundations, according to Goff, demanded that philanthropy be democratized to some degree. It would draw on the meager contributions of the many and make appropriations in accordance with committee decisions.

Yet another exemplar of the living hand came in 1922 in the form of the American Fund for Public Service (Garland Fund). The funds came from Charles Garland, an idealistic, communist-sympathizing, twenty-year-old heir to a Wall Street banking fortune who initially refused his $1 million inheritance. Correspondence with journalist Upton Sinclair and Roger Baldwin of the American Civil Liberties Union (ACLU) convinced Garland to direct his spurned inheritance toward "experiments in what it meant to be free in a modern democracy" (Witt 2017:2). Until its closure in 1941, the fund was spent on left-leaning causes such as socialist publications, labor and civil rights organizations, and legal defense for the Scopes Monkey Trial. Most notably, however, the fund was a major supporter of the National Association for the Advancement of Colored People (NAACP), influencing its agenda away from issues of racial violence and toward a campaign against segregated education—a shift that ultimately resulted in the landmark 1954 *Brown* decision (Francis 2019).

As alternative images of the foundation form appeared, some sought a clearer vision of the now scattered philanthropic landscape. Charles F. Thwing, president of Case Western University and the first secretary of the Carnegie Foundation for the Advancement of Teaching (Ris 2017:425), took to the *New York Times* to sketch a set of principles for philanthropic foundations. Following the model of President Woodrow Wilson, his principles were dubbed the Fourteen Points of Philanthropy.[37] Among them were the following statements of proper philanthropy:

> First—To give to undertakings which the government would not be justified in supporting, or would probably not be able to support. . . . Governmental action is necessarily deliberate. It is subject, and properly, to many administrative restrictions. . . .

> Fourth—To give as a demonstration to the community that the usefulness of certain services are so great that the community shall finally assume and perform these services. . . .

> Fifth—To give in order to remove the causes of evils and not to remove the evils themselves. . . .

> Seventh—To give under the advice of wise counselors. . . .

> Ninth—To give in such a way as to quicken others likewise minded to give to the same cause. . . .

> Tenth—To give in such ways and in such amounts as to promote self-help on the part of beneficiaries. . . .

> Fourteenth—To give under conditions that insure supervision by legally constituted authorities . . . [the] public should supervise. . . .

Longstanding philanthropic themes stand alongside emergent ones. For Thwing, the philanthropist must understand the latent needs of his community, pursue root causes, promote self-help, and engage in wholesale philanthropy. Foundations should call upon wise counselors and experts—such as those employed at Russell Sage, Rockefeller, and Carnegie. Thwing suggests that nascent demonstration projects are worthy of contributions from communities and other philanthropists and concludes with an idea sprinkled throughout the writings of post–Walsh Commission donors: *the public should be the ultimate arbiter of good acts.*

Bureaucratization

Major foundations began reorienting their administrative practices. Following Carnegie's death in 1919, his successors—Elihu Root, James Angell, and Henry Pritchett—grew convinced of the need to develop general science as well as the science of government administration. Root, as a former secretary of state and senator, believed that German military might during World War I was a product of Germany's well-funded research apparatus. The United States was disadvantaged because it lacked infrastructure (Root 1919). The Carnegie Corporation subsequently channeled funds toward the development of the National Academy of Sciences, the National Research Council, the Food Research Institute at Stanford University, the National Bureau of Economic Research (NBER), and the Institute for Economics Research (one of the organizations from which the Brookings Institution was later formed).

When Frederick P. Keppel took the Carnegie Corporation's helm in 1923, he insisted on creating a long-term vision for the organization's gifts. Building this long-term vision entailed a consolidated focus on the arts and new forms of adult education, such as classes for prisoners and immigrants. Among Keppel's administrative contributions was an insistence on public accountability. To him, public reporting through annual reports was a duty. In fact, it was only after Andrew Carnegie's death in 1919 that the corporation began to produce an annual president's report.

Keppel elaborated his perspective on the proper organizational characteristics of the foundation in a series of lectures titled *The Foundation: Its Place in American Life* (1930). He emphasized the importance of an administrative staff: though overhead should be kept generally low, he argued, it should "not be so low as to prevent competent administrative direction" (Keppel 1930:66). Similarly, "there is a need for advice of professional competence" (1930:69). In 1925 alone, he explained, the Carnegie Corporation had sought the expertise of "two hundred and eighty-seven [experts] in all, eighty-one in adult education, sixty in the arts, twenty-six in library matters, thirty-eight in connection with modern language study, and twenty-four for other questions."[38] He concluded by arguing that a responsible foundation should be "disinterested" and scientific in its pursuits and possessed with a "moral obligation and practical wisdom." No longer viewing foundations as mere "stewards" of their donor's wealth, Keppel (1930:93–99) recommended they "become clearinghouses of ideas" because, like their "nearest relative," the university, they are "among the best places to find thoughtful men" and an "unbiased critic." In this spirit, Keppel (1944:v) picked Gunnar Myrdal, a Swedish economist, to study the plight of African Americans in the South. The resulting book, *An American Dilemma*, became a central postwar text for the discussion of American race relations. Keppel provided a foreword distilling the foundation's reasons for funding the research: the goal was to "make the facts available and let them speak for themselves."[39]

Similar visions took shape at the Rockefeller Foundation. Acting on the advice of Gates (whose interests were heavily medical), it had hesitated to support the social sciences. The foundation's earlier foray into social science—W. L. Mackenzie King's effort to study labor "unrest and maladjustment" following the Ludlow Massacre in Colorado—had resulted in unwanted congressional attention. But with the development of social science efforts at Carnegie, and with John D. Rockefeller Jr. becoming an advocate, the foundation soon entered into social science funding through the newly created Laura Spelman Rockefeller Memorial. In 1924, the memorial appointed a young psychometrician, Beardsley Ruml, who strongly believed that the foundation should support practical and applied research. It should make clear that its funding was for creating knowledge, not reforming society. Ruml expressed concern with the "controversial nature" of social science problems and thought it would be "wiser to err on the side of conservativism." He recommended grants to "men of competence [working] in a spirit of objectivity and thoroughness."[40] Fears of congressional scrutiny lingered in the language of the memorial's grants. At times, recipients were advised that "the Memorial would appreciate it if no public announcement were made of the gift" (Bulmer and Bulmer 1981:382). Having disbursed more than $40 million, $21 million of which supported social science, the memorial was wound down at the end of the decade, the bulk of its activities were consolidated into the Rockefeller Foundation, and its work developing the field of public administration was carried on by the Spelman Fund of New York. The Rockefeller legacy of the decade includes, along with the founding and funding of many organizations, the creation of the Social Science Research Council, the establishment of the Brookings Institution, and financial sponsorship of President Hoover's landmark Research Committee on Social Trends.

Foundation support for the social sciences was met with sharp rebuke by some. In a series of essays published as *The Dangers of Obedience* (1930), the sharp-tongued political theorist Harold Laski appraised the effect of foundation funding on universities. Describing the archetypal foundation officer, he wrote:

> He travels luxuriously, is amply entertained wherever he goes . . . when you see him at a college . . . it is like . . . the vision of an important customer in a department store. Deferential salesmen surround him on every hand. . . . The effect on him is to make him feel that he in fact is shaping the future of the social sciences. Only a very big man can do that. From which it follows he is a very big man.[41] (Laski 1930:169–170).

Laski's critique notwithstanding, foundations were growing to be more than "big men." Foundations were no longer the incorporation of one man's wealth and image. They were becoming complex bureaucratic creatures. According to Edwin Embree, whose philanthropic résumé included posts at Rockefeller and Rosenwald, "modern philanthropy was the antithesis of traditional almsgiving" and was instead the "business of giving away money." No longer could one "suppose that any social worker or former college professor will work miracles simply because he is in the presence of wealth. Mediocrity, which is the curse of democracies, cannot be transformed merely by millions" (Embree 1930:329).

Embree was candid about the novel difficulties such philanthropic "businesses" faced. There was no method by which philanthropists could weigh the relative merits of the various appeals and requests they received. "Who can say," he asked, "whether the Shady Hill School in Cambridge is more meritorious than a tuberculosis sanitorium in Arizona; a concert singer more valuable to society than an anthropological explorer?" (Embree, 1930:323).

Embree (1930:322) also anticipated some problems emphasized by Laski: "too often the managers and patrons of private organizations become vain and desire to prolong their pet societies long after their usefulness is ended.[42] Later, in an essay in *Harper's*, "Timid Billions" (1949), Embree would charge foundations with lacking vision and purpose, electing to give toward tired ends, instead of "pouring brains and money into frontal attacks on fresh problems." Yet foundations should not overstep their bounds. As he had counseled previously, when private groups enter into rivalry with public agencies, it can hamper the development of essential state services.

New Entrants

As the earliest foundations were finding their footing, a new generation of organizations emerged, built in the image of their prominent predecessors. The new crop included the Commonwealth Fund (established by Anna Harkness, the wife of an early investor in Standard Oil), the Duke Endowment (funded by James Duke's tobacco wealth to focus on projects in North Carolina), and the Kresge Foundation (Sebastian Kresge's retail fortune from what would later become Kmart). As automobiles crossed the country, a new type of wealth drove its way into foundations. The Charles Stewart Mott Foundation was established in 1926 with General Motors money, and the Ford Foundation, Henry Ford's philanthropic endeavor, was founded ten years later. The latter remained relatively quiet—only Ford and Ford Motor Company employees were on the board—until after the war, when Ford stock skyrocketed, taking the foundation from a bit player to a colossus nearly four times the size of Carnegie and Rockefeller (see Sutton 1987).

In the leadup to and amid World War II, the Rockefeller, Carnegie, and other foundations funded efforts to sway American public opinion in support of U.S. intervention in global affairs (Solovey 2013). The move was a turn away from early explorations of a value-free approach to funding science. Men like Keppel and Fosdick had grown frustrated by efforts to slavishly emulate the natural sciences, which they thought distracted from thorny questions of value and morality. According to Fosdick (1952:224), "our social scientists cannot be merely analyzers and computers." Following the war, the Ford Foundation furthered this pro-democracy orientation and began to see its responsibility as advancing democratic values against totalitarian and authoritarian regimes.

Several community foundations opened as well. Among them was the New York Community Trust, which in 1931 was effectively the predecessor to the modern donor-advised funds. Though the early phase of foundation development saw much growth, foundations, too, struggled during the Great Depression. The economic downturn hit community foundations abruptly. The American Bar Association's Committee on Charitable Trusts closed in 1933, and approximately a quarter of all community foundations closed by 1939 (Burlingame 2004:93–94). To fill the void, the newly created National Committee on

Foundations and Trusts for Community Welfare (later renamed the Council on Foundations) sought to strengthen the foundering community trust movement. In the 1950s and 1960s, this collective effort would come to take on new purposes.

Indictment and Coalition, 1952–1977

In 1930, with the memory of the Walsh Commission fading, Embree expressed confidence in the stable legal status of foundations. The question of whether "foundations will subvert democracy [was] pretty well answered," he thought. Foundations, "have neither the money enough nor the brains enough to do it if they wished" (Embree 1930:329).

But confidence had been shaken again in the wake of World War II. In 1951, Rep. E. Eugene Cox, a conservative Democrat from Georgia, charged that foundations' forays into social reform were to blame for the rise of international and domestic communism.[43] In 1952, the congressman's rancor earned him a special committee: the Select Committee to Investigate Tax-Exempt Foundations and Comparable Organizations, also known as the Cox Committee. Hostilities subsided as foundation leaders convinced the committee not only that their activities were *not* communist but also that they *were* engaged in avowedly anti-communist endeavors. As a slate of foundation leaders testified, congressional concern homed in on the scientific merit of Area Studies programs, Sovietology in particular, which had been sponsored by Carnegie, Rockefeller, and Ford. Russell Leffingwell, chair of the Carnegie Corporation board, endured hours of questioning and ultimately affirmed the anti-communist chops of Area Studies. Likening the study of Soviets to that of mosquitoes, he testified, "We could not have built the Panama Canal if we had not studied the evil ways of the mosquito that carried malaria. . . . Communism [is] an infinitely worse disease." We must "vaccinate against it" (U.S. Congress 1952:373).

Leffingwell also made sure to emphasize the exploratory nature of foundation work. "If a foundation 40 years old came to me and said, 'We have made no mistakes . . . isn't that wonderful?' I should say, 'You buried your talent. Surrender your charter'" (U.S. Congress 1952:371, 380). Embree testified that the proper role of foundations was to pursue projects that would not otherwise receive public funding. Fosdick reassured the legislators that foundations were safely "in conservative hands" (U.S. Congress 1952:762). In this spirit, the Cox Committee's final report resolved that foundations were society's "risk or venture capital" (U.S. Congress 1953:3).

Not all were pleased by the committee's about-face. Unconvinced by testimonies to the contrary, Rep. B. Carroll Reese from Tennessee continued to believe that foundations were sponsoring an intellectual network of subversive left-wing radicals. Reese's Select Committee to Investigate Tax-Exempt Foundations and Comparable Organizations opened with more damning assessments than its predecessor, including charging foundations with oversupporting research premised on the "deterioration of moral standards" (Dodd 1954).[44] The report entertained conspiratorial concerns as well: it charged that foundation secretiveness enabled philanthropists to "exercise various forms of patronage which carry with them elements of thought control," and "invisible coercion" (U.S. Congress 1954:17). Worse yet, foundations, via their "informal guild" and interlocked administrators, had fallen prey to the "vices of a bureaucratic system," reserving patronage for friends and kin.

Table 3.3 Indictment and coalition, 1952–1977

Vision	Money expands and extends government goals and seeks to solve major social problems once and for all.
Sources of wealth	Automotive, retail, health care, pharma, and early technology wealth is increasingly represented among prominent philanthropic organizations.
Organizational forms	Foundations grow more bureaucratic, bringing in-house functions previously fulfilled by external advisors and boards. Philanthropic intermediaries, coalitions, and committees begin to appear (e.g., the Council on Foundations, the Foundation Center Library, the Petersen Commission, the Filer Commission).
Organizational staffing	Larger staffs and careers within foundations become more common. Revolving doors between industry and government spin faster.
Organizational practices	Legislative scrutiny sees foundations curtail "controversial" funding and highlight themselves as an extension of public aims. Foundations adopt an increasingly public role as they work to better communicate their activities and contributions to the outside world. The period sees increasing emphasis on value-neutral science, community development, and partnerships. The heavy hands of founding donors recede.
Funding	Giving goes toward supporting government initiatives including urban development, applied science, education, and the extension of civil rights.
Challenges	Legal and legislative challenges aplenty: Cox Committee (1952), Reece Committee (1952), Patman investigation (1961), Treasury Department investigation (1965), Tax Reform Act (1969). All inquire into the activities of foundations, their public value, and their right to the privileges they enjoy. A new corps of conservative intellectuals and philanthropists begin to take issue with what many foundations understood as apolitical.

Foundations bristled at the accusations. Their activities were, according to H. Rowan Gaither of Ford, "totally pro-American and actively anti-subversive" (U.S. Congress 1954:1017). But the committee was unfazed. Ultimately, it proposed new regulatory constraints: limits on perpetuity, the end of tax exemption, restrictions on investments, and restrictions on funding anything that might undermine American values. Rene Wormser, counsel to the committee, popularized its critiques in a book that portrayed foundations as being infiltrated by communists, seeking to expand government, and actively promoting both one-worldism and cultural relativism (Wormser 1958; O'Connor 2007:93). Foundations began to trim potentially controversial programs from their portfolios. The overall profile of foundation in this era changed notably, as stressed in Table 3.3.

Although the committees highlighted public reservations about foundation activities, they also revealed a general lack of information about the scope and scale of organized philanthropy. In 1956, F. Emerson Andrews sought to rectify the dearth of knowledge by establishing the Foundation Library Center. Hoping to preempt future inquiries by making foundations' activities visible, Andrews's center began to collect and publish detailed information on organized philanthropy. Though this information was helpful in disseminating previously opaque information about foundations, more vilification and inquiries were to come.

Yet another congressional investigation was launched in the 1960s. This time, the cause was driven by the Texas populist Wright Patman, who had spent decades doggedly pursuing the financial abuses of millionaires. Though his investigation opened on an amicable note, offering "nothing but praise" for the work of foundations, he ultimately called for further examination of their "feverish growth" (Patman 1961:6560). Patman's investigation represented a departure from preceding ones: he accused foundations of being agents of financial wrongdoing (something for which there was evidence), government-sponsored tax dodges for the rich, and tools for corporate and financial control. With a small investigative staff, Patman proceeded to compile data, conduct surveys, and accuse the Treasury of being overly permissive with foundations. Under pressure, the Treasury released a report in 1965 attending to Patman's concerns. Alongside examples of abuse, the report recommends possible solutions, including prohibitions against self-dealing, foundation ownership of more than 20 percent of any company's stock, and speculating with foundation assets. Foundations would be required to disburse received income annually, postpone realization of charitable deductions until *after* charitable gifts are made, and, after twenty-five years in operation, distinguish foundation management from donors and relatives (U.S. Department of the Treasury 1965). Though reactions to the report were mixed, it helped validate the bulk of Patman's claims (Nielsen 1972:8).[45]

Despite the damning examples in the Treasury report, it took several years for public outcry about tax evasions and the burgeoning political actions of foundations to goad tax reform hearings into action. As the committee's first witness, Patman set the tone. "Philanthropy—one of man's more noble instincts—has been perverted into a vehicle for institutionalized deliberate evasion of fiscal and moral responsibility to the Nation . . . revealing the continuing devotion of some of our millionaires to greed, rather than conversion to graciousness" (Tax Reform 1969:12).

Over the course of the proceedings, foundations and their representatives were berated for frivolity, favoritism, electioneering, and subversive political patronage. Looming regulations provoked a defensive stance. John D. Rockefeller III and Alan Pifer of the Carnegie Corporation convened the Commission on Foundations and Private Philanthropy (the "Peterson Commission") to study foundations and private philanthropy in order to provide policy recommendations. Although the private commission drew a rosier picture than that drawn in the hearings, it advanced regulations that would increase philanthropic accountability without binding foundations in red tape. But the Peterson Commission's report came too late. The year before, in 1969, tax reform had imposed a modern legal regime on foundation governance, including payout rules, reporting and accounting requirements, limits on stock ownership of single companies, restrictions on self-dealing, and weak demands that foundations keep track of the work of the organizations to which they made grants. The imprint of the Treasury report was clear. Foundations were required to pay a 4 percent tax on investment income, cease grantmaking to individuals, disburse funds at a rate equal to or greater than investment income and a threshold set by the IRS, and provide more detailed reporting.

Because the act was a de facto referendum on public regard for foundations, foundation leaders were relieved that its provisions were not more severe. Previously proposed policies—such as the widely disliked lifespan limitations—had not been enacted into law. Anticipation of more spartan regulations instigated a wave of professionalization as organizations such as the Council on Foundations worked to reassert philanthropic legitimacy. The council described foundations as public trusts, rather than private entities. Transparency, responsiveness, and procedural fairness became the bywords of foundation staff.

Having been late with the Peterson Commission, John D. Rockefeller III established a new group, the Commission on Private Philanthropy and Public Needs (known as the "Filer Commission" for its chair, John Filer of Aetna Insurance). Rather than defend philanthropists against the charges of abuse, the commission championed foundations as underwriters of a vibrant civil sector that, through their funding, safeguarded the provision of public goods. The committee sponsored and produced numerous studies, culminating in the 1975 publication of *Giving in America: Toward a Stronger Voluntary Sector*. In its opening pages, the authors are quick to celebrate the American tradition of associational activity, weaving into its history the fundamental role of an ingrained American habit: philanthropy (Commission on Private Philanthropy and Public Needs 1975:9).

The authors did not have to look hard for examples of visible philanthropic contributions. Indeed, the enmity of some politicians toward philanthropic foundations was not embraced by all. While legislative commissions had been debating the role of foundations in America, some funders had been actively bolstering government-led initiatives.[46] The annual reports of the Carnegie, Ford, and Rockefeller Foundations reveal projects reflecting the concerns of Johnson's War on Poverty. Ford, for example, argued that "federal programs often confirm some of the objectives of modern organized philanthropy" and envisioned philanthropists as "supporting experiments and testing ideas that may be applied on a national scale if proven effective" (Ford Foundation 1965:2). To this end, the Ford Foundation supported experimental programs, such as the Gray Areas program, which it billed as "a comprehensive attack (involving other public and private agencies as well as the schools) on the roots of economic and social deprivation and hopelessness" (Ford Foundation 1965:26).

Foundation executives endeavored to craft the meaning of government partnership. In his presidential letter in the Ford Foundation's annual report, Henry Heald argued that the foundation's proper role was to support national objectives. It was, he wrote, "inappropriate to pick leftovers off the government table" (Heald 1965:3). In 1967, the Carnegie Corporation's report reflects on the importance of the public–private partnership and, a year later, lays out a detailed case for the role of foundations in society. The attack on foundations meant that the fate of *all* nonprofit organizations—"religious, educational, medical, and philanthropic"—were now "in serious doubt." Criticisms were framed as attacks on pluralism (Pifer 1982:41).

In the 1970s, the Filer Commission further developed these ideas, arguing that to understand the terrain of philanthropy, the dimensions of a cohesive but poorly understood "third sector" must first be mapped. If philanthropists are critical to the health of such a sector, the question is not how to restrain philanthropic abuses but how to encourage good philanthropy. Overall, the new focus brought greater attention to the processes that foundations used to disburse their funds and the organizations that received them. As the responsibilities of the philanthropic organization were elaborated and program officers became more influential, the imprint of the original donor began to recede.

Not all in the third sector were content with the Filer Commission's priorities. A coalition of public interest, volunteer, and movement groups criticized the commission for its narrow personnel and scope, arguing that it had failed to involve donees and the public in its inquiry. Rather than ignore the antagonistic coalition, however, Chairman

Filer authorized a small grant to formalize the group. The Donee Committee, as it became known, commissioned its own research, even producing a parallel report to that of the Filer Commission, *Private Philanthropy: Vital and Innovative? Or Passive and Irrelevant?* (1975). In *Private Philanthropy*, the Donee group argued that nonprofits should be treated as equal partners in the pursuit of public interests, and grant recipients should be better represented on foundation boards. At the conclusion of the Filer Commission, the Donee group developed into a watchdog organization called the National Committee for Responsive Philanthropy.

Over the previous two decades, critiques of philanthropy had taken several forms. During the period of McCarthyism, scrutiny was virulently anti-communist, accusing foundations, themselves creatures of capitalism, of being shady subversives. At the hands of populists, foundations were charged with being elaborate tax evasions for elites whose claim of public service was a ploy to pad their own pockets. By the time the Tax Reform Act passed in 1969, critics were less concerned with the fundamental existence of foundations and more concerned that they operate properly and become publicly accountable.

Accordingly, foundations sought to clarify their public purposes, and in doing so, heightened their commitment to professionalism and disinterested expertise, which enabled some foundations to operate independently from their founders' watchful gaze. Foundations' administrative overhead costs climbed sharply in the years following the 1969 Act and the professionalizing mandates advocated by the Filer Commission (Frumkin 1998). Whereas staff and trustees had formerly been plucked from industry, academia, and elite social circles, the new staff exhibited a shared sense of purpose and professional identity. Philanthropic ideas flowed as these professionals moved across previously disconnected organizations. The practices of the leading foundations spread to others as new entrants looked for cues on how to behave. Opportunities for such fieldwide communication proliferated. Regional associations of grantmakers, conferences, and professional publications sprang up around the country. Within a few years, a burgeoning academic interest in foundations was reflected in the creation of the Association for Research on Nonprofit Organizations and Voluntary Associations (ARNOVA) in 1971, the *Journal of Voluntary Action Research* in 1972, and the Yale Program on Nonprofit Organizations (PONPO) in 1977. These academic programs helped legitimate the role of philanthropy in propping up a newly defined sector (Barman 2013).

In working out the details of what foundations could and should do within the bounds of regulation and public image, foundations began to consider which political ends they would pursue and how they would pursue them.

Ideology and Advocacy, 1977-2000

Challenges to philanthropic legitimacy in the 1960s left a mark on several prominent foundations. The 1965 Carnegie Corporation Annual Report discussed conditions of inequality for women and African Americans, and its discussion even engaged with C. Wright Mills's *Power Elite*. The Ford Foundation (1967:2) dedicated the first five pages of its 1967 report to discussion of "the first of the Nation's social problems . . . the struggle for Negro equality." "We are far from satisfied about the quality of what we have done so far," the report said, "but we know at least that we are working on the right problem."

Table 3.4 Ideology and advocacy, 1977–2000

Vision	Money challenges and contests government-led public provision, endorses free markets as tool for reform, and lays intellectual tracks for future political developments.
Sources of wealth	Money comes from finance, health care, insurance, and retail, alongside a growing presence of West Coast entrants and technology wealth.
Organizational forms	Newcomer and previously dormant philanthropists rally to shared causes, their interests and gifts linked by political–intellectual philanthropic interme- diaries such as the conservative Philanthropy Roundtable.
Organizational staffing	Conservative intellectuals join up with conservative money. Political opera- tives and professional staffs occupy foundations. Throughout the field, people with extensive postgraduate education forgo academic careers for posts in foundations.
Organizational practices	A spirited defense of the dead hand, donor intent, and markets. Coordinated funding seeks to create a conservative counterintelligentsia and engage in political advocacy. Throughout the field, competition, measurement, and extensive review processes are used to determine and evaluate appropriations.
Funding	Philanthropic gifts help create conservative think tanks and educational institutions that nurture conservative thought (e.g. the law and economics movement, the Federalist Society, school newspapers). Bringing market mech- anisms to bear on education, especially vouchers and charters, becomes an interest across the political spectrum.
Challenges	The role of donor intent—and more largely the public role of philanthropic organizations—is debated within the foundation community. Legal challenges are brought against philanthropic efforts to reform public institutions.

The last quarter of the twentieth century became an era of foundation activism, as sum- marized in Table 3.4.

When McGeorge Bundy, national security advisor under Kennedy and Johnson, moved to the Ford Foundation in 1966, he brought with him the aspirations of the Great Society. The foundation and its resources, as he saw it, were a way to extend public initiatives. With its sights set on policy, the Ford Foundation directed support to an array of civil rights causes. It worked to establish the Council for Public Interest Law and gave support to the NAACP ($1 million in 1967), the Mexican American Legal Defense and Educational Fund ($2.2 million in 1969), the Native American Rights Fund ($1.5 million by 1972), and the Women's Rights Project at the ACLU (led by Ruth Bader Ginsburg). Environmental causes received support as well. Ford bolstered the Natural Resources Defense Council and helped create the Environmental Defense Fund as well as the Sierra Club Legal Defense Fund.

Foundations saw these as *policy* causes more than *political* causes. Because foundations were operating within the mainstream, employing the tools of value-neutral science and reason, and defending the very liberties on which the nation was founded, they believed they could position their endeavors as politically neutral. This belief proved naïve.

To conservatives, support of expansionary state initiatives transgressed against the free market values that occasioned philanthropy in the first place. Equal opportunity in education, employment, human and civil rights, and economic redistribution, especially when pursued through the state, were hallmarks of an expansive state and the legacy of a New Deal order (O'Connor 2010). Henry Ford II's departure from the Ford Foundation in 1977—for which he cited the foundation's flagging support for capitalism—signaled a

coming ideological about-face in the field of philanthropy. A new generation of conservatives sought to redeem philanthropy and public philosophy more generally by offsetting
the intellectual stronghold of liberalism with an intellectual countermovement. A strident,
tendentious, and politically focused philanthropic agenda began to grow in reaction to
the progressivism exhibited at Ford and other foundations. William Simon and Irving
Kristol reached out to new and newly invigorated foundations such as Olin, Bradley,
DeVos, Scaife, Smith Richardson, and Walton, as well as individuals like Joe Coors and
the Koch brothers, and encouraged them to cultivate a base of support for conservative
causes. This countermovement mimicked the modus operandi of more centrist and left
foundations: it funded individuals, research organizations, demonstration projects, and
evaluations in an effort to cultivate knowledge and intelligence. Rather than reject the
weapons of their ideological adversaries, conservatives engaged liberal philanthropic
advocacy in a war of ideas.

Using philanthropic funding to build a conservative intellectual agenda was not altogether new. Founded in the 1930s, the William Volker Fund—initially devoted to combating machine politics and serving community interests in Kansas City—had moved
sharply to the right when Volker (known locally as "Mr. Anonymous" for his quiet generosity) died in 1947. Inspired by Friedrich Hayek's *Road to Serfdom*, Volker's nephew,
Harold Luhnow, rededicated his uncle's wealth to supporting an aggressively pro-capitalist,
anti-communist, and pro-Christian agenda. He immediately funded the creation of the
Mont Pelerin Society to combat the ascendance of Marxist and Keynesian planning in
states around the world, and his efforts helped propel economists such as Milton Friedman
into the mainstream. Luhnow's fervent giving also laid intellectual seeds for the field of
law and economics, which soon began to flourish (Coase 1993; McVicar 2011). Similarly,
the Earhart Foundation patronized a generation of highly influential scholars, including
six Nobel laureates: Hayek, Friedman, George Stigler, James Buchanan, Ronald Coase,
and Gary Becker (Edwards 1999:140).

In the 1970s, chemical and ammunition-manufacturing magnate John M. Olin inherited the conservative philanthropic cause. Olin's eponymous foundation had dabbled in
game management and conservation but had otherwise been largely inactive until Olin,
spurred by the anxieties of the 1960s, Watergate, and the Ford Foundation's liberal turn,
began a philanthropic project to conserve capitalistic values. "My greatest ambition now,"
he told the *New York Times* in 1977 at age eighty-five, "is to see free enterprise re-established
in this country. Business and the public must be awakened to the creeping stranglehold
that socialism has gained here since World War II."[47] Olin passed the reins to William
Simon, recently Richard Nixon's Treasury secretary, who put the funds to work supporting conservative think tanks (including the American Enterprise Institute, the Heritage
Foundation, and the Hoover Institution), developing law and economics programs at
law schools around the country, and funding a conference that spawned the Federalist
Society in 1982. Olin sponsored the work of conservative intellectuals as well. Works by
Milton Friedman, Samuel Huntington, and Michael Novak were created with Olin money.
With the aid of Irving Kristol, the Olin Foundation became the largest supporter of the
Collegiate Network, an organization created to support conservative and libertarian in-
dependent college newspapers. The hundreds of thousands of dollars going to individual

libertarian college newspapers helped elevate the ideas of Ann Coulter at Cornell, Dinesh D'Souza at Dartmouth, and Peter Thiel at Stanford (Teles 2008).

The Olin Foundation was not alone. In 1973, Joe Coors, president of Coors Brewing Company, along with two protagonists of the New Right, Paul Weyrich and Edwin Feulner (a former Relm-Earhart scholar), established the Heritage Foundation as an activist corrective to the cautious, tight-lipped think tanks that dotted the Washington intellectual scene. In the coming years, Coors would help found and fund the pro-business and property rights–focused Mountain States Legal Foundation (1977), the Free Congress Foundation (1977), and the libertarian Independence Institute (1985). Similarly, Charles Koch of Koch Industries helped Ed Crane establish the Cato Institute (1974), which became a torchbearer of American libertarianism. Six years later, Charles and his brother David Koch donated more than $30 million to create the Mercatus Center—an institute housed at a publicly funded university that was nevertheless dedicated to advancing deregulation and free market ideas (Meyer 2010). In 1977, British poultry tycoon Antony Fisher funded what would later be called the Manhattan Institute, an organization as supportive of supply-side economics as it was opposed to welfare policies. It sponsored Charles Murray's *Losing Ground* (1982), a rebuke of the welfare state reminiscent of charity movements from nearly a hundred years earlier: "when reforms finally do occur, they happen not because stingy people have won, but because generous people have stopped kidding themselves" (1982:236). A decade later, surrounded by a conservative chorus singing Murray's tune, President Clinton signaled he would alter government redistribution and in 1996 end "welfare as we know it."

In an earlier era, organizations such as the Brookings Institution had aimed to be "silent partners" to the government. These new organizations were anything but silent: they shrewdly used media exposure and advocacy to change conversations about public concerns. Brookings had previously been accused of—and had vehemently denied—being a mouthpiece for its philanthropic funders. In a twist of history, the new cadre of think tanks were unabashed advocates of their conservative funders' ideological persuasions. The new philanthropic era was enabled by (and in turn enabled) the growing legitimacy of private wealth and initiative for public ends.

Conservative philanthropists worked in concert to advance their new movement. Kristol and Simon established the Philanthropy Roundtable in 1987 to bring ideologically similar organizations together; they cited as motivation their disagreements with the liberal bent of the long-standing Council on Foundations.[48] Much like the Council on Foundations, the organization proclaimed itself a voice for philanthropists. To Kristol and Simon, philanthropy—which depended on the right of individuals to decide how their money is spent—was the utmost expression of individual liberty in a free society.

In the face of assertive conservative moves, moderate and left-leaning philanthropists generally spurned audacious political commitments and instead held steadfast to politically moderate causes. Even the Progressive Policy Institute (PPI), a think tank modeled more on vocal conservative policy shops than on its "silent" progressive predecessors, was avowedly moderate. Founded in in 1989 with philanthropic support from Wall Street financier Michael Steinhardt to support a centrist vision for the Democratic Party, the organization effectively served as the Clinton administration's think tank—hardly a countervailing force to the aggressive philanthropic advocacy on the right.[49]

Other moderate commitments included the growing philanthropic interest in combating global climate change. The Pew Charitable Trusts—a product of Sun Oil money from the 1950s[50]—began funding research on the effect of climate change on temperate forests in the 1980s and established the Pew Center on Global Climate Change (now the Center for Climate and Energy Solutions) in 1998. In 1991, working with the MacArthur, Rockefeller, Packard, and Hewlett Foundations, Pew helped establish the Energy Foundation, which has since advocated for legislation supporting renewable energy and alternatives to fossil fuels.

It is important to contextualize the political tenor of this philanthropy, however progressive it may now seem. Between the 1970s and the 1990s, regulatory environmentalism enjoyed widespread bipartisan support. Remarkably, when the Clean Air Act passed the Senate in 1970, it passed without a single nay vote. By today's timid political standards, President Nixon was an ardent environmentalist. George H.W. Bush campaigned in 1988 on expanding the act, a promise that was fulfilled through another Senate vote in 1990, 89 for to 11 against. Senator Mitch McConnell explained his vote to his local paper: "I had to choose between cleaner air and the status quo. I chose cleaner air."[51]

As conservative philanthropy has shifted further right, moderate philanthropy has toed a centrist line, progressive mostly in relation to its political alters. Some scholars argue that ascendant political conservatism is the product of conservative foundations and wealthy donors patiently supporting a focused group of right-wing think tanks, whereas liberal donors and foundations have distributed their funds widely but have failed to establish an equally powerful network of think tanks spanning the states (see Hertel-Fernandez and Skocpol 2016). Others argue that the transition is best explained by the bipartisan convergence of wealthy donors around certain policy issues, namely education (Reckhow 2016).

Although philanthropic dealings in education are as old as philanthropy itself, the 1980s saw a renewed attention to schooling, couched in the language of free markets and choice. School choice, premised on the idea that public schools should compete for students, became the central object of conservative philanthropic crusades. First conceptualized by Milton Friedman in the 1950s as a system of vouchers, and then proposed by the liberal scholar Christopher Jencks in a conclusion to a 1970s study for the Office of Economic Opportunity, the idea was that parental choice would improve school quality.[52] The first market-oriented philanthropic foray into public education transpired in the early 1980s with the creation of the Educational Excellence Network (now the Thomas B. Fordham Institute), supported by modest sums from by the Olin and Mellon Foundations and later collecting support from Koret, Templeton, Schwab, Carnegie, and Bloomberg, among others (Zinsmeister 2017).

In the coming years, the Bradley Foundation would prove one of the most effective proponents of school choice. The Bradley family had been politically active conservative philanthropists for a long time and had made sizable contributions to the far-right John Birch Society and the *National Review*. Now, with burgeoning assets from the sale of the Allen-Bradley manufacturing equipment company to Rockwell International, the Bradley Foundation sought to deepen its commitment to policy causes and in the mid-1980s spent millions of dollars annually on school reform. The board hired Michael Joyce, formerly president of the Olin Foundation, with the aim of applying the intellectual work Olin had supported to local policy in Wisconsin (O'Connor 2010:139). Wisconsin teachers' unions, the NAACP, and the ACLU filed a lawsuit questioning the constitutionality of diverting public funds for private distribution, but when the program was upheld in Wisconsin courts, the Bradley family hometown of Milwaukee became the leading hub of school choice experimentation.

About the same time, the charter school movement took off in Minnesota with the passage of the country's first charter school law and the first charter school opening in 1992. Wendy Kopp's 1989 undergraduate thesis, "An Argument and Plan for the Creation of the Teachers Corps," led to the creation of Teach for America, which in 1990 secured founding grants from Morgan Stanley, Mobil Corporation, and Union Carbide. Soon, philanthropic funds rolled in: the Walton Family Foundation and later the newly established Broad Foundation both offered financial support for the cause. By posing challenges to teachers' unions and undercutting faith in public education, the organization has helped bring into the mainstream what were once conservative visions of education reform. Over time, the idea that introducing markets and competition into ailing schools would improve performance has been embraced by both sides of the political spectrum.

One of the last major stands for philanthropic support working through extant institutions of public education came with the Annenberg Challenge, which in 1993 gave eighteen sites around the country grants of $1 million to $53 million (for a total of $500 million) to improve the effectiveness of public education. The challenge allowed grantees to implement the reforms they saw as necessary and to do so on their own terms, resulting in a diffuse array of programs and equally variable results. The nationwide initiative was widely deemed a failure and became a rallying point for reform efforts that emphasized grantmaker, not grantee, discretion (Reckhow 2012).

By the late 1990s, various voices had begun to advocate for a new model of philanthropy, drawn more from the worlds of business and venture capital. This model of financial and strategic management quickly gained traction, especially with trustees from the business sector. Ideas about social return on investment, performance metrics, and logic models flowed from these new participants. These ideas challenged the view held in some quarters that foundations were suffocated by layers of bureaucracy, excessive concern for self-presentation (typically reflected in extensive annual reports), and grant support that was tied only to favored projects. Over time, the cachet of ideas from venture capital and publications in the *Harvard Business Review* proved more powerful than the nascent professionalism of the philanthropist world.

A new animating idea was a growing interest in organizational effectiveness. This view came primarily from West Coast foundations such as Hewlett and Packard (Soskis and Katz, 2016). These foundations, based on money from the early computer and tech world, had leaders who eschewed East Coast norms of procedural legitimation. The West Coast foundations actively created a new organizational infrastructure. The Packard Foundation incubated Grantmakers for Effective Organizations, turning this affinity group into an influential voice and a home for foundations concerned about social impact. The Hewlett Foundation was an active participant in the group. The Center for Effective Philanthropy, Social Venture Partners, and eventually Bridgespan began to offer a plethora of consulting services and tools that helped to develop these new norms and practices. Hewlett also helped create the *Stanford Social Innovation Review* at the Stanford Graduate School of Business. Philanthropic consultants transferred practices across the sector, and foundations turned to consultants for help with their operations.

In doing so, they catalyzed a profound shift in the public role of philanthropic influence. Previously, state-centered critiques of philanthropy shaped philanthropic visions, but now, philanthropic ideas increasingly shaped critiques of the state. The long-term effect of this movement was to diminish anxieties over the role that philanthropy, and enormous private wealth more broadly, played in the public sphere.

Moving Fast and Breaking Things, 2000–Present

The professionalism and staffing choices of the major foundations in the late twentieth century were, in part, a response to the push for accountability and greater transparency brought on by midcentury congressional inquiries and the Tax Reform Act of 1969. For the better part of the twentieth century, major foundations recruited heavily from university leaders, especially in the social and behavioral sciences, and from law schools. Consequently, administrative styles associated with academic norms shaped the practices of many leading large foundations. These views were complemented by the more analytical lens brought by the managerially minded employees that increasingly composed foundation staffs by the close of the century.

But just as the late-twentieth-century foundation was becoming more professional and strategic in its orientation, American industry was being reshaped by the technology and finance sectors. Industry moved from manufacturing tangible things to creating ideas, symbols, and algorithms, and this move was accompanied by the marked growth of wealth inequality. Those at the top of the income distribution grew vastly richer, and labor's share grew smaller (Piketty 2014; Saez and Zucman 2016). Risk was shifted to middle-class families and households, an experience the poor and working classes had long known, but now the stratification ladder was much steeper (Hacker 2006). The old financial establishment fractured as vast new fortunes appeared that were untethered to older elite practices (Mizruchi 2013; Chu and Davis 2016). Organizations changed too: they shrank in size as fewer employees were hired and retained, and more tasks were outsourced or accomplished through complex collaborations beyond the boundaries of the firm (Powell 2001; Davis 2009, 2016). The rise of the Internet had dramatic implications as well: start-up companies, appropriating a Schumpeterian mantra of creative destruction for the purposes of "disruption," challenged long-standing industries and generated new forms of business with the possibilities afforded by high-speed, highly networked communication technologies. This dramatic transformation in American business enterprise and in the very nature of modern capitalism had large-scale ramifications for philanthropy, which we underscore in Table 3.5.

One pronounced effect was a shift in the center of philanthropic activity from the East Coast to the West Coast. The Hewlett and Packard Foundations, both founded in the 1960s, were the first big California foundations created out of money made from early tech companies; the Gordon and Betty Moore Foundation, formed at the end of the twentieth century with money from the success of Intel, was another. Pierre Omidyar and Jeff Skoll created new types of philanthropies with their money from eBay, making Silicon Valley

Table 3.5 Moving fast and breaking things, 2000–present

Vision	Philanthropic money seeks to disrupt public institutions and install alternatives.
Sources of wealth	The West Coast becomes the new epicenter of philanthropy. New wealth comes from tech company fortunes and venture finance.
Organizational forms	New legal forms of philanthropic organization emerge. Limited liability companies (LLCs) and donor-advised funds (DAFs) complement large foundations with statelike influence.
Organizational staffing	Young philanthropist couples make for a resurgence in hands-on donors. They work with PhD staffs, data analysts, and networks of experts to advise and evaluate funding activity.
Organizational practices	Practices are simultaneously transparent and secretive as philanthropists put information about their activities in the hands of many but retain control in the hands of a few. Impact, investment, markets, and competitions become commonplace in grantmaking. Randomized controlled trials and evidence-based concerns predominate both funding decisions and evaluations. In contrast to prior eras, philanthropic gifts seek to compete with and provide alternatives to services provided by government.
Funding	Education, environment, health, and international development are focal. Indirect and direct means of advancing philanthropists' policy ideas are normalized.
Challenges	Influence and control by the new gilded elite faces blowback from public and governments.

the epicenter for experiments in philanthropy as well as business. But these influential efforts paled in size compared with the Gates Foundation, formed in Seattle in 2000. Upon its creation, the Bill & Melinda Gates Foundation became the largest foundation in the country. With assets in excess of $40 billion, the foundation has had an enormous impact on American philanthropic practice. The elements of a different approach to philanthropy are visible in both the form and the practices of the Gates Foundation, so we date the beginning of the contemporary era with its founding.[53]

In some respects, the Gates Foundation looks like a traditional twentieth-century foundation. It has a large staff of more than 1,500, many with backgrounds at Microsoft or in university science. Like foundations before it, Gates engages with "wildly disparate" issues. But distinctive to the Gates approach is the use of a common rubric to consider these varying issues. As a matter of policy, funded activities do not commence until the foundation and the grantee have reached an agreement on the "intended results, targets, milestones for reporting deliverables."[54] Indeed, as Melinda Gates said in an interview with Nicholas Kristof, Bill Gates is, in both temperament and practice, a "gear head," someone who "will not accept data that is correlation and not causation." This measurement approach, thanks largely to the foundation's financial and cultural influence, has come to be reflected throughout the nonprofit sector, shaping how many nonprofits—including those not funded by the Gates Foundation—think about their work, understand themselves, and present themselves to others. No money without metrics.

The Gates imprint is evident at other new philanthropic outfits as well, not only in their commitment to measurement but also in the increasing centrality of husband-and-wife teams at the helm and the relative youth of these organizations' founders, which reflects the young age at which tech wealth is being realized.[55] But the young couples leading these organizations grew rich in an era of venture capital and technological solutionism, and their organizations merge the Gates approach with the investment vehicles they know so well. In 2004, Pierre and Pam Omidyar used eBay wealth to create the Omidyar Network, a two-armed "philanthropic investment firm" that issues grants through its tax-exempt foundation and invests through its LLC. Dustin Moskowitz, the co-founder of both Facebook and Asana, and his wife, Cari Tuna, followed a similar path. They opened Good Ventures in 2012 as two different organizations: a private foundation and an LLC focused on impact investing. In 2017, after several years collaborating with the charity evaluator GiveWell, a 501(c)(3) public charity, Moskowitz and Tuna established the Open Philanthropy Project as an LLC to advise a donor-advised fund housed at the Silicon Valley Foundation, recommend and make investments in social enterprises, and support 501(c)(4) political advocacy activities. And perhaps the most notable of the new wave of philanthropic LLCs has been the Chan Zuckerberg Initiative (CZI), announced via Facebook in 2015. The trend shows little sign of abating with the Laura and John Arnold Foundation converting to an LLC in 2019.

Collectively, the most recent generation of philanthropists began rewriting the rules of the field. Their actions and organizations reflect a puzzling paradox of this latest era. On one hand, the new organizations wave the banner of transparency. Their extensive web presence, communications, frequent partnerships, and collaborations all reveal a desire to show the world what they are doing. On the other hand, these new entities represent both the apogee of secretiveness and control concentrated in the hands of the few. The Gates Foundation has one of the most extensive and well-documented philanthropic websites. And in 2015 the foundation launched its Open Access policy, stipulating that published research resulting from its funding should be promptly and broadly disseminated, the data made available, and the articles not hidden behind paywalls. At the same time, the foundation rests in the hands of only three trustees—Bill and Melinda Gates and Warren Buffett—who oversee and direct its activities. And the foundation wields considerable indirect political influence through a diverse network of grantees that "sing from the same hymnbook." That is, Gates is influencing policy—such as the widespread adoption of Common Core State Standards in education—rather opaquely by "calling the tune" (Reckhow and Tompkins-Stange 2015).

Similarly, the Open Philanthropy Project attempts to be radically transparent: it performs openness by publishing analyses of its funding choices in hopes of attracting commentary and enrolling other donors. Hiring decisions, project outcomes, research reports, and conversations with collaborators are also explained publicly, at great length, on its blog. But as an LLC, Open Philanthropy is not required to disclose information, such as staff salaries or annual operating costs, in the manner of a traditional foundation. To the embattled early-twentieth-century foundations the LLC form would have been an unimaginable development: it enables founders to avoid the regulatory requirements that accompany tax-exempt status as a foundation and gives them greater privacy, flexibility, and control than traditional foundations can offer. As with the Gates Foundation, the technocratic model both reveals and conceals.

The new ethos of philanthropy shares a great deal with the origins of the wealth that makes it possible.[56] Donor control is one example: many of the most influential philanthropists of the last two decades have names that are synonymous with the companies that made them rich. Gates, Zuckerberg, and Bloomberg have asserted at least as much control over their philanthropic endeavors as they have over their business endeavors. In spirit, this control is reminiscent of the early days of the Carnegie Corporation, whose organized philanthropy was an extension of the man himself. In the years since Carnegie, the bureaucratization and professionalization of philanthropy has decoupled foundations from the guiding hand of their founders. Yet in recent years, through the efforts of philanthropists who prize "lean" and "agile" companies, we have seen the recoupling of business tycoon and philanthropic organization.

The Giving Pledge illustrates this recoupling. Originating with the commitment of Bill and Melinda Gates of "giving while living," the Giving Pledge began in 2010 with the goal of encouraging billionaires to spend half or more of their wealth on charitable causes by the end of their lives.[57] Moskowitz and Tuna, the pledge's youngest signers, say they intend to disburse nearly all their wealth before they die. Their goal is to "give sooner rather than later" because it will "never be as inexpensive as it is now to help people" (Callahan 2017:121). The movement toward giving as much as possible while alive has attracted many adherents, including Michael Bloomberg as perhaps its most notable proponent. He has quipped that he wants to "bounce a check to his undertaker." The laudability of depleting one's billions for charitable causes aside, the pledge represents a new take on the once-conservative crusade to defend donor intent. As long as philanthropists give while they are alive, they remain in control of how funds are directed. There are no dead hands to worry about. Letters from billionaire signers of the pledge, of which there are currently 187, reflect this sentiment.[58] Although many older donors seek to distribute funds to universities, museums, symphonies, and other long-lasting institutions, the younger cohort's language tends to reveal an autodidactic preparation for a lifetime of giving money away.

Another significant feature of the Giving Pledge letters—which we anticipate being an archival data gold mine for future scholars of philanthropy—is the insight they offer on modern philanthropists' understandings of the problems facing society, the appropriate means for addressing these problems, and the role of the philanthropist in securing their resolution. As of 2016, many of the signers had a philanthropic interest in education, environment, and health (Goss 2016). But the language they use to characterize these concerns is revealing as well. Alongside their celebrations of the philanthropic potential of technology and markets is an expressed frustration with bureaucracy and government. Considering the various ways they could spend their money, Mark and Mary Stevens rank letting "the government take it from you and redistribute it" as the least desirable. Tad Taube sees government policy as ruinous for the capitalistic ethos in that it undermines "work ethic and personal responsibility." Others portray government action as hopelessly incomplete, inadequate, and slow. All share the tacit assumption that philanthropists such as themselves have the right to intervene upon and shape the public sphere. If philanthropists had made such claims so boldly and publicly a century ago, organized philanthropy might have been regulated out of existence. Clearly these are different times.

What, then, are the faiths that undergird the public role that modern philanthropists self-confidently assign themselves? One clue can be found in the pledge letters, which feature ideas such as "investment," "entrepreneurship," "innovation," and "scaling" (Horvath and Powell 2016). Faith in the efficient allocations of markets persists from an earlier era, though with a less explicitly political bent. Zuckerberg, Christie, and Booker's ill-fated plan to salvage Newark Public Schools was heavily couched in the language of start-ups and investments. Proselytizers of impact investing have sought to bring investment tools to bear on philanthropic ends. The growth of social impact bonds and Pay for Success in recent years muddles the distinction between government, philanthropic, and market activities. Investment language has permeated the philanthropic sphere. Sounding more like venture capitalists than like previous philanthropists, Moskowitz and Tuna prefer tractable causes that others have overlooked, such as biosecurity and geoengineering, which have long odds of success but could deliver major breakthroughs. Their policy of "hits-based giving" entails being unafraid of failure.[59]

Contemporary philanthropists also have strong faith in technology. They believe that social problems have technological solutions, as if an app could solve major global problems. Bill and Melinda Gates view themselves as the philanthropic embodiment of computer scientists, but some of their technological hubris wore off when they moved to tackle the challenges of global health, global poverty, and education reform. The challenges of program implementation in the messy terrain of politics, culture, and social structure impeded even their best technical solutions. Still, the foundation continues to be guided by a propensity for taking risks; making large bets on younger, developing grantees with the hope of scaling them; and tolerating failure. While the Gates Foundation has been willing to acknowledge some mistakes, as well as the immense expenditures they've put into failed or marginal experiments, they've offered scant reflection on the long-term costs to students and teachers, most notably in terms of their careers, of participating in experiments that had negligible or negative results.

Zuckerberg's exploits best exemplify this comfort with failure. Facebook's mantra of "move fast and break things" went hand-in-hand with its ambition to digitally connect the world. Likewise, the aspirations of CZI have been described as impossibly ambitious—"help cure all disease in our children's lifetime," "make significant progress in early literacy at scale," and enact "community-driven approaches to build economically vibrant neighborhoods." At CZI, technology is the linchpin that connects these disparate projects. So far, to tackle its goal of eradicating disease, CZI has committed $600 million to create Biohub in San Francisco's Mission Bay medical cluster as an interdisciplinary center that will fund and collaborate with researchers at the Universities of California at San Francisco and Berkeley, Stanford University, and Rockefeller University. CZI is also supporting a data platform called the Human Cell Atlas at Biohub. CZI has invested in a start-up, Andela, that trains software developers in Africa, as well as a video learning app firm in India. In a mix of new and old philanthropy, CZI is collaborating with the Rockefeller Foundation on an initiative called the Communities Thrive Challenge to support economic development in disadvantaged neighborhoods.

Building on these self-confident visions of how to remake the world, the latest era of philanthropy actively seeks to shape policy. This interest appears more widespread and more strident than the activist philanthropy of the 1960s was. Drawing from an original data set of two hundred of the largest philanthropic contributors of the modern era, political scientist Kristin Goss (2016:442) finds that more than half "have serious policy interests and ambitions." Pew Charitable Trusts marked this change in orientation in

2004 by changing its legal form from a foundation to a charity, which freed it to direct a greater portion of its resources toward policy advocacy without violating rules governing nonprofit behavior. In the late twentieth century, foundations were becoming increasingly comfortable advocating for policy change. The Gates Foundation accelerated this process with its vast educational initiatives, from experiments with small schools and support for charter schools to the creation of national Common Core educational standards. The foundation quickly became a force in school reform efforts and the setting of educational policy. Foundations' efforts to set the nation's educational policy have received much scrutiny (Ravitch 2010; Reckhow 2012; Tompkins-Stange 2016). Though Gates may be the "unelected school superintendent of American schools," the foundation has achieved quasi-state status internationally as an influential player in transnational health organizations (Soskis and Katz 2016:21).

These developments come on the heels of diluted campaign finance regulations—epitomized in the *Citizens United* decision of 2010—that have opened pathways for private wealth to more directly and clandestinely shape American politics. Indeed, the lines separating the once-distinctive roles of philanthropist, political patron, and lobbyist have become increasingly blurred. The common governmental embrace of philanthropist-led schemes seems to suggest a breakdown in the healthy tension between state and philanthropic interests. And as political figures increasingly perform both philanthropic and representative roles simultaneously, public expectations of the duties of each role may shift.

The moral imperative of modern philanthropy is to use the fortune one has amassed during one's life to pursue world-changing impacts. In some respects, this moral imperative is not entirely new. It reveals the widespread embrace of commendable practices that have a long history in American philanthropy. But in its pursuit of these visions, the most recent era of philanthropy has witnessed a turn toward new means and new organizational forms. The new legal structures used by tech titans, especially LLCs and donor-advised funds, mean that very big pots of money remain outside the U.S. tax system. As more of the ultra-rich follow these trends, the nation's tax base shrinks, which means a decline in public funds. As a result, fateful decisions about such critical areas as medicine, education, and housing are increasingly made by a small set of techies enacting their visions of the public good.

Wealthy tech billionaires have sought to find gaps and tackle unexplored areas in their philanthropy. They favor visionary or quirky social entrepreneurs over established movements or organizations. They are attracted to new ideas—not established soup kitchens, community centers, or inner-city schools that are flourishing in the face of long odds. The strategy of favoring novelty bears the deep imprint of the technology and venture capital worlds. But this novelty often comes with scaling, tinkering, and displacing the old; it less often involves establishing new-to-the-world institutions. To be fair, our implied comparison with the philanthropy of Rockefeller and Carnegie is incomplete. We have had decades by which to judge the fruits of past philanthropy and seemingly minutes to judge more recent developments.

The enthusiasm for disruption that is so commonplace in the West Coast scene has even influenced the practices of older philanthropies. In the current era, both older foundations and new philanthropists focus on transformative outcomes. Consider the four criteria used to evaluate applications to the MacArthur Foundation's 100&Change competition: proposals must offer solutions that are "meaningful," "verifiable," "feasible," and "durable." The animating vision of this winner-take-most competition, which awarded $100 million to the winning applicant, was that solutions to social problems must have an impact on a very large number of people. Grant applicants were expected to provide extensive evidence—randomized controlled trials, citations, and peer-reviewed scientific articles—that their proposed solutions would effectively address the problems they outlined. The proposed projects were expected to have outcomes that were both durable and lasting. The focus, as interpreted by the competition's finalists, was on children. This attention could be read in two ways. In one, focusing on children is a surefire way to ensure a long-lasting effect. In another, child-focused interventions tend to be some of the most readily measurable (Mueller-Gastell 2019).

We might characterize this recent philanthropic era as a time of impatience, in which hands-on, living donors play an active role and want to see fast results. This restlessness is accompanied by a strong faith that private enterprise can challenge incumbents in a variety of fields, including large business enterprises, standard government practices, and established nonprofits (Horvath and Powell 2016). Belief in the market as a force for social good is reflected in a dizzying array of new tools and organizational forms for philanthropy (Salamon 2014). Although the current era is just two decades old, there are warning signs on the horizon. Donor-advised funds may be popular and viewed by some as a democratizing form of philanthropy, but their tax implications have been loudly criticized (Madoff 2016; Hemel, Chapter 5, "Tangled Up in Tax"). LLC models of philanthropy have also attracted scrutiny. More striking, however, is the cultural shift and the growing view that wealthy philanthropists are loath to challenge the conditions that made them rich (Giridharadas 2018; Reich 2018). Consider the divergent reactions to the effusive publicity surrounding the Giving Pledge and Jeff Bezos's recent announcement of his philanthropic intentions. A *New York Times* commentator quipped that Bezos "should spend his vast fortune pushing for a society where no one can ever become as rich" as he is. Similarly, in the steady stream of revelations about Facebook's inability to protect users' information, and its use to create propaganda sites that influence hundreds of elections around the world, the prestige of Chan and Zuckerberg's giving is dimmed.

Unbridled enthusiasm for all things tech has diminished as well. Top executives from Facebook, Google, and Twitter were brought before Congress to explain their practices in a manner reminiscent of the hearings from the first Gilded Age. The champions of the digital economy are facing blowback about how they use and protect citizens' data and whether their extreme wealth is the source of our current problems. Whereas philanthropists in prior generations were called before Congress to answer for the potential threats their charitable acts posed to democracy, the titans of the current era are being called upon to answer for the damage their businesses have done.

Conclusion

Elite philanthropy, as opposed to mass charitable giving, involves the conversion of personal wealth into private power. That power can be used in different ways, as we have shown. Whether philanthropists attempt to solve social problems or establish notable new institutions, such as public libraries, the modern research university, or medical research centers to eradicate disease, they typically engage in some form of recombination—that is, importing ideas and practices from one domain into another (Padgett and Powell 2012).

Transposition is commonplace; all forms of novelty involve it to some degree (Sandholtz and Powell 2019). Henry Ford and his advisors, for example, appropriated practices from other production industries—flour milling, food canning, breweries, and stockyards—to create the modern automobile assembly line (Hounshell 1984:217–261). The movement of digital technology from computing to photography is a more modern example of an innovative reconfiguration (Tripsas 2009). In both cases, the practices were drawn from "the adjacent possible" (Kauffman 2000), a kind of shadow future that hovers on the edges of the current state of things—a map of the ways the present can reconfigure itself.

Transpositions most frequently occur between domains characterized by cross-traffic and ongoing conversation—that is, across existing channels of interaction. When transpositions occur between domains where traffic is scarce and communication infrequent, new categories of thought and action are created. We can think about transpositions in terms of the distance that the ideas and practices travel. This distance has both cognitive and moral dimensions. On the cognitive side, transposed practices that are not readily recognized seem out of context, off-key, or irrelevant; they do not fit existing mental models. When they come from close by, they are much more readily embraced. On the moral side, distant transpositions may be attacked as inappropriate, outrageous, or even profane. When practices are revered and venerated in one setting and moved to an adjacent domain, they are perceived as appropriate and worthy of emulation.

Elite philanthropy entails two types of transpositions. First, wealthy philanthropists create ostensibly eleemosynary institutions in the mold of the businesses where they earned their fortunes. Not surprisingly, how they earned their money shapes how they give it away. Their stage of life also influences how active they are in creating their philanthropic organizations. These dual considerations—how they operated in business and where they belong in the status order of society—shape their philanthropic practices. This is what we call *the cognitive side of transposition*. There is also a second, perhaps more far-reaching form of transposition that we call *moral reconfiguration*. When philanthropists *impose* their taken-for-granted practices and routines on the recipients of their largesse, they are practicing moral reconfiguration. For example, to attract attention, nonprofits in the most recent era have to act like start-ups or incubators, be prepared to scale, and talk about ambitious plans for growth and impact. This is a transposition of the worldview of tech and venture capital into the community that receives philanthropic support. We think of this requirement as moral because it remakes our understanding of what public purpose should look like, for good or ill.

Over the past century and a half, these changes have also transformed politics. Carnegie and Rockefeller sought to make charity and benevolence more businesslike. They opposed "indiscriminate charity" and created a new model of elite philanthropy as an organized, purposive field of activity. In our language, they wanted benevolence to operate more like an established enterprise by doing things in a systematic, future-oriented manner. In the current era, business is increasingly seen as something that should have a benevolent patina. The boundaries between philanthropy and business have been blurred.

Philanthropy's new organizational forms borrow from those of business and finance. Elsewhere in this volume, scholars analyze the various ways that profit-making activities are now used to pursue ostensibly public benefits (see Ghatak, Chapter 13, "Economic Theories of the Social Sector"; Mair, Chapter 14, "Social Entrepreneurship"; and Delmas, Lyon, and Jackson, Chapter 15, "Nonprofits and the Environment"). With this new vision, businesses should be philanthropic and nonprofits should be entrepreneurial: they should take risks and make big bets.

During the first Gilded Age, there was keen awareness of the contradiction between Andrew Carnegie's philanthropic vision of how to improve "the general condition of the people" and the ruthless way he ran his railroads and steel mills. Both Carnegie and Rockefeller faced strong headwinds as they tried to move business practices into the realm of benevolence. The marriage of monopoly corporate power and elite philanthropy did not sit well with a vision of democracy. Today, in our new Gilded Age powered by an interconnected global economy, the relationship between corporate wealth, elite philanthropy, and political legitimacy has changed. Philanthropy has much greater legitimacy, and the idea that how you make your fortune shapes how you give it away is more accepted and less contested. Political regulation of philanthropy is much less restrictive; indeed, governments welcome and encourage assistance even as their tax revenues decline and we see a creeping privatization of public services. The new vision is to bring benevolence to business, in the hope that corporate enterprise will be less extractive and can be harnessed to solve public problems. This chapter is not the venue for us to comment at length on whether we think such efforts are plausible or salutary, but it is appropriate to end with the observation that philanthropy has undergone a profound shift: where it was once contested, it is now venerated and carries hopes that its legitimacy can rub off on the private sector. That indeed is a remarkable change of vision.

4 THE ORGANIZATIONAL TRANSFORMATION OF CIVIL SOCIETY

Patricia Bromley[1]

DRAMATIC SHIFTS IN RECENT DECADES drive home the need to reevaluate our understanding of the nonprofit sector and why it exists. The sector has expanded massively worldwide in countries that differ in their most elemental features, and within countries nonprofits are increasingly formal and complex organizations that can look very much like their counterparts in business and government sectors. But these developments are not inevitable. Nor are they simply a consequence of functional needs in society to, for example, deliver services more efficiently and effectively.

Starting in the early 1960s, economic explanations for the existence of nonprofit organizations gained momentum and developed into the dominant account of the sector (Hansmann 1980; Salamon 1987). Nonprofits, according to this account, emerged as a result of gaps left by market and government failures. Implicitly or explicitly, these failure-based explanations underpin a great deal of research, practice, and policy related to nonprofits. Yet there are several well-documented reasons to question whether those explanations fully account for the existence of the nonprofit sector. Such arguments fall short of explaining the massive and recent explosion of formal nonprofit organizations across vastly different political, economic, and historical contexts. Moreover, the now-commonplace observation of extensive blurring and cooperation between the business, nonprofit, and government sectors is hard to account for by theories predicting sharp distinctions between actors from those sectors (Ghatak, Chapter 13, "Economic Theories of the Social Sector").

This chapter draws on sociological theories of formal organization to develop an alternative, cultural account of why the nonprofit sector has evolved into its contemporary form. Specifically, it argues that certain features of the sector today—especially its worldwide expansion and its increasingly formal nature—partly reflect the rise and globalization of liberal and neoliberal cultural ideologies. Liberal creeds valorize individuals as a cultural matter on two relevant fronts; first, they celebrate rational, scientific-like action (beyond established evidentiary bases), and second, they celebrate the sacredness of individual human rights and capabilities (despite persistent inequalities). The structures of contemporary formal organization are constituted by these intertwined principles of rational, sciencelike action and human rights. One implication of this argument is that, as a social-structural manifestation of these cultural ideologies, formal nonprofit organization as we know it is likely to weaken if the current liberal world order erodes.

The nonprofit sector has grown massively over the past several decades. This expansion, moreover, is astoundingly widespread: nonprofit organizations have grown in number in countries with very different contexts, they have grown at both domestic and international levels, and they have grown internally by becoming larger and more complex. In the United States the total number of nonprofits exploded from fewer than 13,000 in 1940 to more than 1.5 million by the end of the century (Soskis, Chapter 2, "History of Associational Life and the Nonprofit Sector in the United States"). Prior to the 1930s very few new nonprofits were created per year, but by the late 1960s around 20,000 new organizations were founded per year, and by the 1990s more than 50,000 new nonprofits per year filed for tax-exempt status (Jones 2006). Financially, American nonprofits also show healthy growth. For example, between 2002 and 2012, both revenues and assets grew faster than GDP: after adjusting for inflation, revenues grew 36.2 percent and assets grew 21.5 percent, compared with 19.1 percent growth for GDP (McKeever and Pettijohn 2014). New nonprofits have proliferated outside the United States as well, and this growth has been particularly rapid in countries that lie outside the community of established liberal democracies (Schofer and Longhofer 2011; Schofer and Longhofer, Chapter 27, "The Global Rise of Nongovernmental Organizations"; Dupuy and Prakash, Chapter 28, "Global Backlash Against Foreign Funding to Domestic Nongovernmental Organizations"). In addition, international nongovernmental organizations (INGOs) have skyrocketed in number over time: from 1909 to 2009, INGO growth equates to a shift from roughly 0.1 organization per million people to 8 organizations per million people (Union of International Associations 2018).

A critical feature of these indicators of nonprofit expansion is that they document instances of expanding formal organization. This growth is not simply an artifact of more or better counting; it reflects a fundamental transformation that goes beyond the nonprofit sector. We now live in an "organizational society," as observed by foundational figures in the field of organization theory (Presthus 1962; Coleman 1982; Drucker 1992; Perrow 2009). Organizations are the dominant social structure of our time, reaching into virtually all realms of life. The expansion of registration processes and directories of nonprofits is a central part of the transformation of civil society into a sector marked by increasingly formal organization. These registrations, countings, and accountings of nonprofit activities are substantive indicators of that transformation, rather than a data artifact.

Thus, a striking and central characteristic of the "global associational revolution" (Salamon 1993) is that much of it takes the form of formal organization. An analytical framework that focuses on counting formal organizations does not tell us whether humans are becoming more altruistic, or whether societies are becoming more equal or just. It leaves out many forms of prosocial activity: for example in collectives, such as families, tribes, and diasporas, as well as in looser networks, such as informal social movements and associations. After all, there are multiple ways of conceptualizing and creating civil society, and the formal organizational character of contemporary civil society represents only one such mode. We do not know if there is more "nonprofit" or prosocial activity in the world as a substantive focus, but we do know there is an expansion of "organization" as a structure. This leads to a core question: What does it mean to be a nonprofit "organization"?

This chapter analyzes the organizational transformation of civil society in four parts. First, it sketches the likely sources of this shift. It posits that cultural changes tied to the rise and globalization of Western liberal and neoliberal ideologies generate organizational expansion and formalization of associational life. According to this argument, the liberal valorization of individuals reshapes older forms of social activity, such as loose associations or tight collectivities, making them look more like what we recognize as contemporary formal organizations. Second, it comes to a more complete conceptualization of the unique features of contemporary formal "organization," defining the ideal type of formal organization as an entity constructed to encompass both collective purposes and scientific rationality. Third, it presents a discussion of research directions that emerge from this argument. And fourth, it reflects on potential consequences of the rise of formal organization as a central feature of civil society.

The chapter makes several contributions to research on the nonprofit sector. To begin, it provides a cultural argument for the rise of formal nonprofit organization that explains why this form has emerged and expanded beyond its known functional utility. Prior research on the nonprofit sector has largely focused on understanding the "nonprofit" side of this work (e.g., Frumkin 2002), while other studies of organizational expansion have largely focused on firms and underemphasized the prosocial and nonprofit dimensions of this growth (e.g., Coleman 1982). Next, in presenting this cultural argument, the chapter goes beyond market-based explanations for the blurring between business, nonprofit, and government sectors. A cultural view emphasizes that entities in all sectors are increasingly structured as instances of formal organization; business is becoming nonprofit-like as much as nonprofits are becoming businesslike. Finally, the chapter explores a key implication of this argument: if formal nonprofit organization is associated with contemporary liberal culture, then it is likely to decline if and when liberalism erodes as the core organizing principle of national and world society.

Cultural Bases of Formal Organization[2]

The expansion of formal organization is linked to great cultural shifts that assert the ascendancy of the individual. Conceptions of the hyperempowered individual arise mainly from liberal Western philosophies, although they have spread globally beyond these roots. Two dimensions of expanding individualism are most relevant here. A first core dimension is the reconstruction of all human beings as inherently possessing a sacred status (Elliott 2007). This "cult of the individual" asserts a growing array of rights for more types of people and, related, valorizes human capabilities for rational action (Durkheim 1951, 1961). A second, related dimension is the diffusion of scientific and social scientific thought and method far beyond their traditional areas of focus, constructing social action as more universal, standardized, and orderly.

Following sociological definitions, the term *scientific* and its permutations extend beyond their application to particular disciplines (e.g., chemistry, biology, or medicine) or an actual knowledge base. These terms refer broadly to cultural principles that give authority to systematically developed knowledge and to university-trained experts, rather than to alternative bases of authority such as charisma, tradition, or tacit forms of knowledge (Drori, Meyer, and Ramirez 2003). Moreover, these terms involve a belief in scientific and quasi-scientific methods as a highly legitimate source of authority more than they do an account of the true state of knowledge. In fact, the legitimacy of science as a source of authority, and belief in science as a principle, promote its expansion far beyond reasonable uses. The term *human rights* refers to a multifaceted expansion in the socially defined rights, obligations, interests, and capabilities of all individuals (Meyer and Jepperson 2000; Meyer 2010). Both dimensions are considered part of a cultural belief system because we celebrate scientific action beyond objectively knowable truths, assert human rationality beyond known capability, and valorize the sacredness of individual human rights beyond the realities of persistent global and local inequalities.

These principles provide a new basis for social order and action in which individuals, envisioned as possessing great rational capabilities and expansive human rights, are an increasingly central locus of both change and stability. There are masses of reforms in existing structures, largely in ways that are imagined to reflect and expand individual choice and capacity (e.g., decentralization, privatization, deregulation). But societies embracing these principles are not adequately characterized by imageries of individuals pursuing self-interests in anarchy. The ideals of scientific action and human rights come with strong self-disciplining and self-regulating social controls that provide order and stability (Miller and Rose 1990, 2008). Legitimate action needs to reflect the principles of science and rights (e.g., participatory structures, efficiency and accountability practices like outcomes measurement and evaluation), as do perceptions of self-interest. To use other terminology, *governance* rather than *government* becomes a key source of order and control (Rhodes 1996; Mörth 2004; Osborne 2006, 2010; see also Marwell and Brown, Chapter 9, "Toward a Governance Framework for Government–Nonprofit Relations"). In the following sections, I provide a rough overview of the historical expansion and globalization of these trends before spelling out how they generate formal organization.

Historical Emergence

The cultural shifts related to the global expansion of science and human rights are widely reported (see Price 1961 or Drori et al. 2003 for a general overview on science; see Elliott 2007, Stacy 2009, or Lauren 2011 for an overview on human rights). In many accounts, these shifts are tied to broad political changes related to the evolution of a feudal religious polity with medieval governance structures into the secular, administrative, and legal structures of modern nation-states (Tilly 1990). Enlightenment-era philosophy also helped consolidate and expand secular individualism; realms like education, art, and music became matters of interest to the general public, rather than pastimes for an elite few. To be sure, fully elaborating the exact causes of the massive and complex cultural changes unfolding over hundreds of years are beyond the scope of this paper. But whatever the causes, the clear consequence of these trends was that the scope, scale, and nature of social structure changed dramatically to reflect liberal and neoliberal cultural principles.

Expansion of Science: In the early modern period, an expansion of scientific thinking produced a movement toward administrative reform (M. Weber (1922) 1978). Feudal religious polities with medieval governance structures evolved into the secular, administrative, and legal structures of modern nation-states (Tilly 1990). Early bureaucracies, which included governments, churches, armies, and early corporations, had a rationalized, quasi-scientific form. But they were centralized structures intended to effectively and efficiently carry out the goals of a sovereign or owner; lower levels of these hierarchical structures had little autonomy or empowerment.

Then, in the first part of the twentieth century, an expansion of the social sciences led to the development of scientific approaches to managing businesses (as with Fayol 1949 or Taylor 1914) and generated more systematic approaches to philanthropic giving. Scholars often describe a shift from charity to philanthropy, with the former focusing on religious obligations to alleviate individual suffering and the latter focusing on developing systematic, rationalized, and putatively effective resolutions to social problems (Robbins 2006; Sealander 2003).

In the latter part of the twentieth century, the doctrines and myths of science have become more powerful, and their authority now reaches far into social life (Drori et al. 2003). Today, nearly every domain of natural and social life is analyzable and analyzed. For example, shared scientific principles about the common environment transcend criticisms of cultural relativism and provide a universalistic basis for rules applicable everywhere (Foucault (1978) 1997). In the same way, the expansion of the psychological sciences generates expanded conceptions of the needs of humans, so that any dimension of human development or way of thinking can become a widespread concern. For example, scientific analyses of childhood and its problems grow as children become reconceived as priceless (Zelizer 1994) and provide bases for social organization that now extend to a global level. New organizations arise, and older ones take on new responsibilities, for dealing with various dimensions of childhood—health, education, consumption behavior, protection from abuse by families and firms, and so on.

The extraordinary expansion of scientific authority means that even movements that resist certain kinds of social change—in areas like gay rights or climate change—now sometimes use the language and authority of science, rather than directly invoking alternative cosmologies. And, as a cultural principle, scientific and quasi-scientific endeavors spread into domains that far outpace their actual utility as generalizable Truth, allowing for a great deal of contestation (e.g., about what we know in the "decision-making sciences" or "learning sciences"). Nonprofits and foundations, for instance, are advised to (and sometimes do) build rationalized "theories of change" or "logic models" spelling out their best guess for how to achieve social change using quantified measures and metric (Brest, Chapter 16, "The Outcomes Movement in Philanthropy and the Nonprofit Sector"; Horvath and Powell, Chapter 3, "Seeing Like a Philanthropist").

Expansion of Individual Rights and Capacities: In the eighteenth century, events that culminated in the French and American Revolutions played a central role in the development of individual rights. As new conceptions of justice and equality expanded, they promoted visions of democracy and undermined notions such as the divine right of kings (Bendix 1980). Consequently, highly centralized social structures, like the classic bureaucratic state, lost their charisma. In tandem, ideas of civil society as a distinct social sphere began to flourish. But early voluntary associations were relatively informal expressions of community, unlike the highly structured nonprofit organizations common today.

The new liberal ontology generated a focus on the human individual as the locus of both rights and action. As one indicator, the twentieth century witnessed an explosion of human rights treaties, organizations, and doctrines that spread liberal principles worldwide, and nation-states generally accepted this regime as legitimate at a cultural level (though not always at a practical level) (Elliott 2007, Stacy 2009, Lauren 2011). More rights were constructed and more types of people (e.g., gays and lesbians, disabled people, children, ethnic minorities, women) were almost always seen as individuals rather than corporate groups. And human rights changed focus from entitlements to protection, political standing, and social welfare (T. Marshall 1964): importantly for the expansion of the nonprofit sector, social and cultural matters came to be included. But further, the new human individual was seen as an empowered actor—able and entitled to pursue rights and interests on a global scale (Elliott 2007)—and inherent properties of individual rights and capabilities were seen as universalistic; human rights transcended local polities and their variations. So individuals are now increasingly entitled to choose roles and identities (Frank and Meyer 2002; Jiménez 2010)—but also obligated to respect the rights and capabilities of others.

Globalization

A dramatic cultural shift has thus provided a cosmological frame that imagines social order on a global scale emerging from universalistic principles—a frame that Foucault called "governmentality" ([1978] 1997). This cultural transformation unfolds over hundreds of years, but the end of World War II and the rise of neoliberalism in the 1990s bring notable intensifications of the worldwide expansion of an organizational revolution (e.g., Drori, Meyer, and Hwang 2006; Drori and Meyer 2006). Especially in the wake of World War II, the nation-state lost legitimacy, stigmatized by a half century of horrific evils. In the Western world, corporatist and statist ideas, as well as affiliated communal structures (e.g., traditional professions, the family as a corporate group, and related notions of race and religion as intrinsic properties of nations), lost standing. A positive legal system was not available in the decentralized world system in the wake of World War II, but a social order that would go beyond traditional state-centered mechanisms was widely seen as necessary. The solution, emphasized by the dominant, radically liberal United States, was the construction of forms rooted in the assumptions of rational choice and rights that characterize liberalism (as in de Tocqueville (1836) 2003; see Ruggie 1982). In other words, without the hard laws of a supranational world state, social controls rooted in the assertion of laws of science and human rights have been widely employed.

Throughout the Cold War, the spread of a liberal global order faced resistance from the competing vision of socialism. Following the collapse of the USSR, however, there was no real alternative to liberalism at the global level. Left unchecked, "embedded liberalism" (Ruggie 1982) evolved into its more extreme neoliberal form, and globalization in all forms—social, political, cultural, and economic—became more pronounced. In this context we see the emergence and rapid expansion across all sectors of formal organization. In this neoliberal world order, organizations are not only structured functionally to accomplish goals but also structured to do so as a virtuous citizen of a supranational world that conforms to the principles of science and human rights (Matten and Crane 2005).

Constituting Formal Organization

Overall, the perceived rights, authority, and capabilities of the individual human being grow stronger, and the parts of other social structures—such as nation-states, families, and communities—that are rooted in more communal principles become relatively weaker (Hall and Jacques 1989). Together, the abstract and universalistic principles of scientific rationality and human rights constitute the cultural foundation for the emergence and growth of the social structure that today we call "organization." The rise of ideologies of human rights and scientific capabilities generates the expansion of formal organization in two ways.

First, assertions of human rights and scientific rationality considerably expanded the range of domains in which empowered human initiative seems reasonable (Toulmin 1992). These principles provide a basis for widespread purposive action in a growing array of substantive domains. Underpinned by assertions of rights, purposeful individual activity extends into new domains, such as abolitionism and children's rights. And underpinned by revelations of science, organized activity expands into areas such as environmentalism or animal welfare. Often, these principles—which both stem from expanding individualism—are deeply intertwined. As one example, Oxfam's work began with a predominantly technical vision of international development but increasingly takes on a "rights-based" orientation (Offenheiser and Holcombe 2003). As other examples, environmentalism, educational expansion, and health care are often justified on both scientific and rights-based grounds.

Second, cultural principles of human rights and science provide cultural templates for how activity should be structured. Under human rights principles, decisions and activities should be participatory and respectful of individual rights, and rational, responsible, and organized human action is seen as both possible and necessary. And under scientific principles, means and ends are systematically specified, measured, and monitored, and experts and professionals of all sorts proliferate and are seen as providing legitimate knowledge.

Such long-term changes greatly intensified after World War II and operate in the whole period since, but especially powerfully in the neoliberal era. This generated both increased numbers of organizations in previously unorganized arenas and increased internal elaboration of existing structures as these adapted to expanding external obligations. For example, as cultural pressures to respect a range of rights increase, it now becomes sensible for both Nike (in the business sector) and the Red Cross (in the nonprofit sector) to pursue diversity on their boards, policies for work-life balance, and formal efforts to protect children (by preventing them from making soccer balls or donating blood). Under these new cultural principles, traditional social structures—government agencies, firms, charities, hospitals, and universities—are reconstituted.

As social structures are transformed by these principles of human rights and scientific rationality, they come to look more like what we now recognize as proper, contemporary formal organizations. For instance, an old-fashioned charity responded to some social ill, but a modern nonprofit organization should do so in a way that is accountable, systematic, and effective; a Fordist firm efficiently maximized profits, but a modern corporation should do so while also displaying elements of social responsibility; a traditional government bureaucracy provided public services, but a modern public agency should do so while involving many stakeholders. In all these examples, the latter case illustrates the coming together of rights and scientific rationality through a process that transforms (albeit often partially) an older structure into a contemporary formal organization. These cultural principles are universalistic, envisioned as natural laws that cut across social sectors and extend around the world—although in practice they are not universally shared.

As illustrations, consider the widely reported transformations of two structures that emerged in early modern Western history. Bureaucracy, the first example, was conceived of as a structure serving a sovereign; even in theory individuals throughout its structure were envisioned as passively filling roles rather than empowered actors. Thus, bureaucracy has the scientific rationality of organization but lacks widespread individual empowerment. The transformation (at least partially) of bureaucracy is well recognized (Musolf and Seidman 1980; Osborne 2006, 2010). In both scholarly and public discourses we commonly recognize terms like *postmodern* (Parker 1992; Caporaso 1996), *postindustrial* (Bell 1976; Kumar 2009), and *postbureaucratic* (Heckscher 1994; Kernaghan 2000; Josserand, Teo, and Clegg 2006). These terms indicate a transition from early-modern society, which was dominated by more collective structures like states, family firms, trading empires, and traditional professions, to late-modern society, in which individuals are fundamental units of order (Hall and Jacques 1989). This shift has unfolded throughout the post–World War II period, and especially accelerated globally since the 1990s.

A second key structure that has undergone massive historical change is the voluntary association. Like contemporary organizations, informal associations carry the collective purpose of empowered individuals, but they are weakly rationalized. Well-recognized changes have also occurred in associational life, turning early voluntary associations into more formal organizations. Starting in the nineteenth century, the emergence of incorporation marked an important shift in the structure of voluntary action, with legally incorporated nonprofit entities becoming central components of economies (e.g., professional associations), society and culture (e.g., public good groups), and political systems (e.g., towns and political parties) (Creighton 1990; Kaufman 2008). Early in the twentieth century charitable work developed into a secular full-time career option, and the goals of many associations shifted away from the pursuit of Christian duty, charity, and salvation and toward the pursuit of human rights and scientific approaches to curing social ills (Sealander 2003). In these increasingly bounded, incorporated entities, purposes and goals became an issue of choice and identity, rather than a matter of enacting God's will. Over time, informal associations became increasingly subject to formalization. These changes to associational life are sometimes depicted as creating entities that resemble government bureaucracies (as they increasingly subcontract and take on formal structures), and they do adopt some bureaucratic features (e.g., written policies, full-time career positions). But formal nonprofit organizations are not, by virtue of their collective nature, true bureaucratic hierarchies operating under the authority of an external sovereign.

More recently, observers have also emphasized the commercial transformation of the nonprofit sector and reported on phenomena such as the creation of "hybrid" organiza-

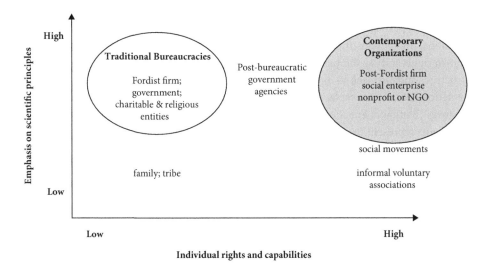

Figure 4.1   The cultural underpinnings of ideal types of social structure
Note: The social structures represented here are roughly classified as ideal types. Empirical research could usefully develop systematic analyses to test the extent to which various types reflect these cultural underpinnings.

tions, social enterprises, and entities led by social entrepreneurs (Dees 1998; Billis 2010; Pache and Santos 2012; Mair, Chapter 14, "Social Entrepreneurship"). Here the rhetoric is that nonprofits are becoming more like businesses because of increased competition (as they take on practices designed to improve efficiency and effectiveness) (Eikenberry and Kluver 2004). Existing explanatory ideas work in part, but they are too narrow to cover the entire scope and scale of the relevant changes. For example, both nonprofits and firms are also becoming attuned to corporate social responsibility practices that extend beyond their core mission or their product-based activities (Pope et al. 2018).

Rather than viewing transformations within the nonprofit, government, and business sectors as independent phenomena, this chapter argues that these transformations arise from common cultural roots. According to this argument, voluntary associations, firms, and government agencies are all simultaneously being reshaped by the emergence of a new metacategory—what is now called organization (Bromley and Meyer 2017). These older forms still exist, of course, but they are increasingly reshaped as instances that, at least in part, fall under the broader category of organization.

Figure 4.1 arrays ideal types of social structure along the dimensions of science and rights. Of course, this depiction reflects ideal theory; in practice things can operate far differently and there is variation within each type. Along the *x*-axis are differences in the extent to which the ideal types reflect assumptions about individual capability for rational decision, choice, and the extent to which individuals possess various rights. Along the *y*-axis are differences in the extent to which the ideal types reflect assumptions about systematic, scientific principles as driving and ordering collective activity.

In the upper right of Figure 4.1 we have the metacategory of contemporary organizations, highly constituted by both rational, scientific principles and assumptions of
human rights and capabilities. For example, post-Fordist firms emphasize inclusive, flatter
structures and also seek to maximize profit (e.g., see Amin 2011); more recently, there are
depictions of the "conversational firm" (Turco 2016) and "democratic organization" in
business (Battilana, Fuerstein, and Lee 2018). Similarly, contemporary, professionalized
nonprofits represent the apex of formal organization in the civil society sphere (e.g., entities that have both a prosocial purpose and rationalized structures like strategic plans,
vision statements, risk management officers, outcomes measurement, and/or diversity
and environmental strategies beyond their own mission). We can also think of ordering
entities within the form of "organization" in terms of their profit motivation. Then, between contemporary firms and nonprofits, we find social enterprises: organizations that
seek both social good and profit.

Importantly, the claim is not that all organizational forms in the upper right of the
figure are exactly alike. We could also emphasize differences between the subforms of
organization along various lines—such as profit or purpose. The core argument here is
that organization has emerged and expanded as a metacategory in society, becoming the
dominant social structure of our time. Entities in the upper right of the figure have more
in common with each other than they do with entities in other quadrants. It becomes
possible to observe that "although there are many differences between collectivities like
factories, prisons, and government agencies, they share one important thing in common:
they are all organizations" (Maguire 2003:1, italics added).

The lower and left sections of the figure capture social structures that do not fit what
we now mean when we think of an ideal or proper contemporary organization. In the
upper left we have another metacategory: traditional bureaucratic structures. Traditional
bureaucracies are qualitatively different from what we now envision as a proper contemporary organization. Specifically, theories of bureaucracy outline their construction as
efficient tools, but with limited individual rights or capabilities involved for roles beyond
the imperative authority of a supreme leader. Ultimate control legitimately resides in a
sovereign. Retrospectively, some apply the label of *organization* to older bureaucracies (e.g.,
Coleman 1982), but this reflects the rise and expansion of the category of organization—
bureaucracies did not receive this label until late in their history (Drucker 1992). Contemporary postbureaucratic public agencies would fall somewhere in between traditional
bureaucracies (upper left) and modern organizations (upper right), as they remain highly
scientized but increasingly incorporate individual empowerment at all levels (Kernaghan
2000; Brunsson and Sahlin-Andersson 2000; Wachhaus 2013).

Moving to the lower sections of the chart, on the right are informal voluntary associations and social movement activities. These reflect a broad vision of universalistic
individual rights and capabilities but have a loose to nonexistent formal structure lacking
emphasis on scientific versions of efficiency or effectiveness (e.g., the recent Occupy Wall
Street movement [Gitlin 2012]). There may be a drift over time as in, for example, the
transition of social movements from being imagined as the utterly irrational "madness
of crowds" (i.e., individual participation is voluntary and rather empowered but unscientific) to their current depiction in a vast literature on contemporary, highly strategic,

social movement organizations (i.e., moving into the upper right area of the figure over time) (Polletta and Jasper 2001; King and Soule 2007; Bringel and McKenna, Chapter 29, "Social Movements in a Global Context"). In the lower left quadrant are collective and sometimes involuntary social structures such as families; participation may be required and involve very limited protection of each individual, but there is also little formal structure delineating rationalized action (e.g., such an organizational chart). Again, however, over time even some families may shift toward operating as proto-organizations with explicitly defined goals, responsibilities, and evaluation, and participation becomes more voluntary with divorce and child emancipation laws.

Institutionalization and Diffusion[3]

Several vehicles institutionalize the cultural principles of scientific rationality and individual rights and capabilities, transmitting the model into concrete settings and transforming older structures. Together, these channels construct and diffuse the model of formal organization within countries and worldwide. Hard law and formal regulation is a key mechanism in this process, but other important mechanisms include expansions in soft law (Mörth 2004), various forms of counting and accounting (Power 1999), and the massification of professionals (Wilensky 1964) largely created by changes in education, especially at higher levels (Schofer and Meyer 2005). Hard law and soft law, counting and accounting, and professionalization are vehicles that transmit cultural ideologies. They constitute "organization" as a legitimate social category, turning this imagined entity into an established "social fact" (Durkheim 1982). Instantiations of this cultural model reshape local settings by producing a continuum of entities that fit the imagined category of "organization" to varying degrees.

Hard and Soft Law

Hard laws represent a high form of rationalized social structure, imagining (and to some degree creating) systems that are subject to standardized, predictable rules (see, for example, Max Weber's discussions of formal bureaucratic rationality [(1922) 1978; see also Kalberg 1980]). Laws powerfully provide an organization with formal boundaries and provide coercive force to the assignment of rights and responsibilities. For example, in the United States, legal developments dating to the nineteenth century granted corporations (including nonprofits, for-profits, and some townships) some of the same rights and protections afforded to individuals (Kaufman 2008). These legal expansions continue through the present; in 2010 the U.S. Supreme Court affirmed the protection of free speech for corporations in a case between the nonprofit organization Citizens United and the Federal Election Commission.

Some assert that corporate personhood creates entities that are a mere "legal fiction" (Fama 1980) or a "nexus of contracts" (Jensen and Meckling 1976). But as a cultural construct, the model of "an organization" expands beyond formal legal status. For example, entire industries and a huge amount of management training are premised on the idea that organizations (with managers and executives enacting their essence) can and do act rationally, can plan and control operations, and can have unique cultures that shape outcomes. As another, in the United States religious entities and those with revenues under

$5,000 do not need to formally register with the Internal Revenue Service (IRS), so in an annual report on the state of the nonprofit sector, the Urban Institute reports that "the total number of nonprofit organizations operating in the United States is unknown" (McKeever 2015:2). In line with the point that legal incorporation alone does not constitute what we mean by "organization," in their path-breaking comparative analysis of the nonprofit sector, Lester Salamon and Helmut Anheier (1998) come to a "structural-operational" definition of a nonprofit organization rather than a legal one. Legal status and compliance represent part of being an organization but not all of it.

Beyond establishing the legal existence of entities, hard and soft laws shape internal structures and spell out where the boundaries of an organization should be drawn. For example, professional norms and laws defining humans as equal and empowered generate formal structures that advance diversity and equality in hiring, promotion, and governance practices (e.g., see Daley 2002 for nonprofit board diversity, or Dobbin 2009 for trends in firms). A similar trend involves the rise of participatory decision making and collaborative governance processes (e.g., see Epstein, Alper, and Quill 2004 for medicine; Kernaghan 2000 for government agencies; or King 1996 for schools).

Counting and Accounting

The emergence and expansion of standardized methods for counting and accounting drive human activities to become more structured as the bounded, formal entities that we recognize as organizations. Quantification creates a basis for making previously distinct social structures comparable (Espeland and Stevens 1998). So, today, charitable work (even the voluntary sort) is no longer seen as unproductive labor; instead, it is seen as analogous to other forms of production, and its contribution to the economy is calculated annually. One recent study, for instance, calculates the contribution of volunteer work as a share of GNP across countries in 1995 (Roy and Ziemek 2000). Relatedly, there are now measures that enable comparisons of organizational performance across different industries, sectors, and countries (see, e.g., a discussion of nonprofit versus for-profit performance in Keller 2011, or the research produced by World Management Survey 2013). We can also now rate and rank organizations on such dimensions as performance, transparency, and account-ability, as well as other forms of social responsibility, thereby enabling the transposition of concern with those dimensions from one domain to another. A number of recent studies examine the creation of charity watchdogs (Lammers 2003; Szper and Prakash 2011) and the rise of measures of social value (see Austin and Seitanidi 2012 for a review).

Professionals

Professionals with university training play a central role in transforming traditional social structures into organizations. Higher education is a key location where socialization into the culture of science and human rights takes place. The worldwide expansion of higher education has reached a level that would have been seen as a massive social problem in any previous period—the fear in earlier times was that overeducation would be a threat to social stability and a waste of resources (Schofer and Meyer 2005). By 2016, nearly 40 percent of the relevant cohort of young people worldwide was enrolled in an institution of higher education—a figure vastly higher than in any previous generation (e.g., in 1970 just 10 percent of the cohort was enrolled [World Development Indicators Online 2018]). This population is no longer concentrated in a few core countries; in peripheral countries, too, the number of university students has increased significantly.

To a large degree, the theory and practice of contemporary formal organization reflects the social behavior of these highly schooled people. In support of this argument, a path-breaking study drawing on a survey of two hundred San Francisco Bay Area nonprofits found that when executives receive managerial training (i.e., in the form of a master of business administration degree, a master of public administration degree, or a certificate in nonprofit management), their nonprofits have more extensive formal structures, such as formal planning, independent financial auditing, quantitative program evaluation, and use of consultants (Hwang and Powell 2009). In the realm of professional training, Roseanne Mirabella and her colleagues have collected detailed data on the growth of nonprofit degree programs over time (Mirabella 2007; Mirabella et al. 2007), and that growth both indicates and facilitates increased formal organization in the nonprofit sector. Overall, evidence of professionalization in the nonprofit sector, often linked narrowly to legitimacy and funding benefits, is widespread (Stone 1989; Alexander 2000; Guo et al. 2011; Suárez 2011).

A brief example, drawn from the expansion of human health concerns inside organizations, helps illustrate these arguments. At one time illness was a mystery to humans, who believed that it was under the control of the fates or gods; poor health was a moral failing, likely punishment for misdeeds in the present life or past ones. Gradually, people came to regard health as something that they could understand and even shape. Eventually, scientific work generated evidence documenting how things invisible to the human eye—microscopic germs, genes, or environmental pollutants—damaged the health of people, animals, and the planet. As individual sacredness expands, ideas of health proliferate further to include new topics such as mood disorders, previously unlabeled mental and physical illnesses, and broad ideas of overall "wellness." These expanding scientized ideas of health, combined with visions of human rights (and health becoming a human right), spawned activist and interest groups that used the normative pressure of hard and soft law. Such efforts sparked the creation of new groups aimed at improving human health, and the creation of formal regulatory structures (such as the Occupational Safety and Health Administration [OSHA] in the United States, along with related policies and laws). Following scientific cultural principles, moreover, both activists and governments tend to use systematic, evidence-based methods—including tools for tracking, rating, and monitoring environmental quality—to protect the environment. There are now many ways to measure attention to health within organizations and countries (such as the World Development Indicators, or the ranking put out by the World Health Organization [WHO]), and various forms of professionalization (such as degrees in health care management and positions for administering a variety of related employee benefits) have emerged to support specialization in these areas. As a result of these developments, any given entity is now likely to include some kind of health-related policies and practices in its formal structures, and is likely to do so in systematic ways that allow for monitoring, reporting, and evaluating progress. In the business world attention to employee health and wellness is sometimes justified as a way to increase productivity or as a response to consumers or shareholders. But those arguments are too narrow as we see this trend in the nonprofit world as well, where productivity is hard to measure, there are no shareholders, and nonprofits are unlikely to be the target of activist or consumer protests. We could imagine similar shifts for other domains, such as environmentalism, where all types of organizations are more likely to have policies and practices related to "being green" and even entities with social missions sign on to environmental agreements like the Global Compact (Pope et al. 2018).

Discussion

Organizational Actors[4]

In relevant sociological and management literatures, the recent emergence of organization as a dominant form of social structure is well recognized (Coleman 1982; Perrow 2009). Although precursors have existed for centuries (e.g., early corporations and bureaucracies), these early structures did not penetrate into as many realms of life and they did not valorize individual rationality and rights to the extent they do now. Today, organizations have become so dominant that their existence is taken for granted and naturalized by casual observers; it seems as though they have always been around. But even in developed liberal democracies much of the expansion of organizations occurred after World War II, and globally it has taken off especially since the 1990s (Drori et al 2006, 2009).

As a definitional matter, what makes organizations distinct from other structures is that they combine (a) the rationalization of bureaucracies (e.g., efforts to clarify lines of accountability with standardized rules and to establish links between means and ends through activities like planning and evaluation) with (b) the collective purpose of voluntary associations of individuals (e.g., the entity itself incorporates the purposes of sovereign individuals and thus has its own legitimate goals and interests, as well as the authority to pursue them). As these characteristics become institutionalized through the legal, accounting, and professional channels described earlier, organizations become envisioned as bounded, rational social actors that carry both rights and responsibilities (Brunsson and Sahlin-Andersson 2000; King, Felin, and Whetten 2010).[5] For instance, conceptions of organized entities as analogous to persons or "fictive individuals," in some phrasings, have long standing in a variety of legal systems (Hansmann and Kraakman 2000). James Coleman classically outlines the legal institutionalization of organizations as bounded entities (1982:14):

> the conception of the corporation as a legal person distinct from natural persons, able to act and be acted upon, and the reorganization of society around corporate bodies made possible a radically different kind of social structure than before. . . . It [the corporation] could act in a unitary way, it could own resources, it could have rights and responsibilities, it could occupy the fixed functional position or estate which had been imposed on natural persons.

Importantly, however, the status of organizations as social actors goes beyond narrowly legal conceptions (Krücken and Meier 2006). Organizations are treated as independent and coherent actors in the media, the theory and practice of management, and the general social imagination. Broadly speaking, to be recognized as an actor of any sort (e.g., a person, an organization, or even a country) means that an entity possesses sovereignty, can pursue its own purposes, and has an identity or "self" (Coleman 1982; Pedersen and Dobbin 1997; King et al. 2010). For example, John Meyer (2010:3), writes: "An actor, compared with a mundane person or group, is understood to have clearer boundaries, more articulated purposes, a more elaborate and rationalized technology. An actor is thus much more agentic—more bounded, autonomous, coherent, purposive and hard-wired." To get counted as an organizational actor indicates broad legitimacy to participate in society as an autonomous creature—one that is reliant on various stakeholder groups but distinct from them.

Decoupling

A core observation is that the evolving cultural model of an organizational actor is just that—a model or an imagined cultural ideal. It is not a ground-up description of what entities actually do or look like. And it is an imagined entity held together by social construction, not a naturally occurring creature. Thus, actual structures differ in how close they come to the vision of "an organization," and empirical studies can explore this variation (see, e.g., Bromley and Sharkey 2017). Organization theory commonly notes significant gaps between models of reality or theories about how things should work and the experienced world (in sociology, see discussions of "decoupling" in Meyer and Rowan 1977 and Bromley and Powell 2012). For instance, we are likely to recognize the Red Cross as more of a "real organization" than a family foundation that exists mainly on paper as a tax shelter; although the two entities may have a similar legal status, one of them has greater sovereignty, purpose, and identity. Organization is often partial, and it can refer to certain activities or ways of thinking that occur within structures that are not themselves complete, formally incorporated entities (Ahrne and Brunsson 2011). Terms like *organizing* and *getting organized* are routinely applied to practices in settings that do not involve official incorporation. Although the archetype of an organization has a defined sovereignty, purpose, and identity, any given organization is likely to be characterized by areas of limited autonomy, multiple views of its identity, and conflicting conceptions of its purpose. But a more sophisticated organization seeks at least to present itself as aligned with the ideal model, and it may at times try various reforms to become more aligned with that model.

As a parallel to the decoupling between the ideal of organization and the practice of it, consider the example of bureaucracy. Actual bureaucracies routinely fail to work according to theory. The chain of command often breaks at some point, as bureaucrats pursue interests of their own (a practice now often called corruption) or reinterpret rules in inventive ways (Dwivedi 1967; Mbaku 1996; Lipsky 2010). Or rules that make no sense in particular local settings are ignored or followed only in ritual (E. Weber 1976). Despite many deviations from practice, the ideology of bureaucratic control, carrying out the will of a sovereign certified by religious, historical, or dynastic authority, has been central to modern societies, often permitting social control on a vast scale. Similarly, organizations that are recognized as more complete actors have sovereignty, purpose, and identity; in practice there is a continuum, and actual entities diverge from the concept.

Beyond the straightforward decoupling of theory or policy from reality or practice, being a proper organizational actor involves a great deal of decoupling between means and ends (Bromley and Powell 2012). Cultural shifts drive an expansion both in the number of organizations and in the range of domains where formal organization takes hold. As a result, there are a growing number of audiences and issues that any given organization must take into account in order to be considered a responsible actor (Bromley and Meyer 2015). As organizations respond to expanding pressures in their environment, they become less coherently structured around their purported goal. Although organizations are depicted as autonomous and rational, they are held together by external definitions that include many inconsistencies and contradictions.

Research Directions

Existence: Fundamental issues related to the existence and nature of nonprofits remain weakly studied, but the rapidly increasing availability of data opens the door for new possibilities. Several research directions emerge from the arguments presented here. As noted at the outset, traditional failure-based theories look to answer questions about when nonprofits, as opposed to for-profit entities, are likely to appear. This chapter takes a different approach, situating the expansion of nonprofits within the expansion of organization in general. Functional explanations rooted in efficiency or effectiveness may explain the rise of formal structures in part, but a cultural view helps explain the timing and accounts for the massive expansion of organization into all areas of life and around the world, beyond known utility. A sophisticated understanding of both functional and cultural arguments reveals that these arguments do not always represent logically discrete worldviews. Rather, they direct attention to somewhat different observations and questions. This chapter urges greater focus on organizational expansion as a key feature shaping the evolution of the nonprofit sector, pointing out that the conceptual utility of for-profit or nonprofit legal status diminishes as sectors blur. In contrast, failure theories seek to explain why organizations take a nonprofit or for-profit legal status, obscuring the historical context of organizational expansion and sector blurring. Empirically, multiple causal forces are likely to be at work, and future studies could work toward understanding the conditions under which settings are likely to be driven more or less by functional efficiency, culture, or alternatives such as elite power. Plausibly, domains with greater technical certainty are less susceptible to being structured by cultural influences because efficiency is self-evident. Thus, domains with greater complexity or uncertainty (slippery concepts, to be sure) may be more easily structured by cultural expectations and thus may experience greater organizational expansion. To the extent that we believe profit goals have more technical certainty than prosocial goals, cultural pressures may drive organizational expansion the most in prosocial areas (including nonprofits and the socially responsible areas of for-profits).

Expansion: This chapter argues that organizations are only partly constructed as a functional response to societal "needs" and that they arise largely because of shifts in underlying cultural conditions. To test this argument, future research could examine where and when the expansion of formal nonprofit activity is most likely to occur. A core hypothesis is that there is likely to be a higher degree of formal organization in settings where liberal principles related to science and human rights flourish (e.g., perhaps in places marked by a growing commitment to education, especially at higher levels). Conversely, on average there is likely to be a lower degree of formal organization in settings marked by alternative bases of authority (e.g., in the form of strong religious belief or a strong centralized government). These hypotheses, which can be tested directly, are in contrast with the view that nonprofits exist solely in order to fill gaps left by the state or the market, although no single explanation need exist alone.

A related hypothesis, emphasizing historical timing, would posit a rapid worldwide expansion of formal nonprofit organization immediately following World War II, when the first steps to create a liberal world order were under way, and again immediately following the collapse of the Soviet Union, which represented the main global alternative to liberalism. Over more than a century, modern history has witnessed an expansion of principles of science and rights. But in the arguments here, there is no theoretical basis for expecting an inevitable march toward liberal modernity in perpetuity; the causes of changing macrohistorical trends are complex and not fully understood, leaving much room for uncertainty about the future. Recent global resurgences of populism, declining democracy, and growing doubt in the neoliberal economic model may indicate an erosion of the liberal cultural model worldwide; if so, nonprofit organization as we know it is likely to be undercut.

Taking a different angle, studies of the extent to which adaptation or selection processes are at work in turning civil society into a formal organizational sector would shed light on the process. We know that the rate at which new nonprofits are founded in the United States has increased markedly in recent decades, but we have little knowledge about the extent to which older structures retain distinctiveness relative to newer ones, or in what ways. Some studies suggest that adaptation also plays a role. Catholic orders, for example, began to reimagine and register formally as INGOs in the 1950s (Wittberg 2006; Gonzalez 2009), and clergy in some denominations have gone into the business of being event planners to adapt to the preferences of their congregation (Putnam and Campbell 2012). Others have looked at the transitions from bureaucratic to postbureaucratic agencies (Josserand et al. 2006). Again, analyses to help understand which domains or dimensions retain distinctiveness or resist pressures toward formal organization and why would be valuable.

Sector Blurring: The blurring of sectors into more standardized contemporary organizations around the world is well documented (Brass 2012; Marshall and Suárez 2014). A cultural view argues that as trends toward scientific rationality and human rights grow, social structures take on the features of what we now call organizations beyond market pressures. For example, organizations seek to become more "professional," and they incorporate broader concerns related to responsibility—such as codes of conduct, whistleblower policies, and strategies for being "green"—regardless of established links to a particular mission or profit. In contrast, economic explanations often take a narrower emphasis on marketization of nonprofits (Billis 1993, 2010; Dees and Anderson 2003; Eikenberry and Kluver 2004), overlooking general professionalization. Economic explanations also tend to locate changes in prior resource dependencies without analyzing why those conditions are themselves altered (e.g., why funders start caring more about measuring the impact of nonprofits or why shareholders start caring more about displays of social responsibility on the part of firms) (Weisbrod 1997). And economic views often focus on a one-way transfer of business practices into the nonprofit world and commercialization (Weisbrod 1998; Young and Salamon 2002; Dart 2004), underemphasizing the extent to which sector blurring is multidirectional. For example, firms have increasingly prosocial and expressive elements as a result of the rise of corporate social responsibility, workplace charity, "social intrapreneurship," and movements to allow greater self-expression in the workplace. Economic and cultural arguments can be tested empirically, for example by generating lists of the organizational structures associated with market pressures versus those associated with being an actor more generally (e.g., as indicators of "identity" perhaps mission or vision statements, or statements of organizational history, or branding activities) and observing diffusion (or not) across various samples of organizations with different resource needs or dependencies.

Variation: Although we should not disregard organizational form or sectoral differences as an important ongoing area of work (Knutsen 2012), the cultural arguments put forth here point toward a different, but equally central, kind of variation: in contemporary organizational society, the differences between more-formal and less-formal entities and sectors may be sharper than the differences between nonprofit and for-profit organizations and sectors. For example, large educational or health care organizations (which can and do take both nonprofit and for-profit forms, located in the upper right of Figure 4.1) may have far more in common with each other than they do with more informal-associational or bureaucratic entities within those fields.

Another form of variation highlighted by cultural arguments is that manifestations of the cultural model of "organization" is expected to vary greatly in real entities. Research could empirically examine gaps between formal models of organization and practical instantiations, and could then develop general arguments about where and why decoupling is likely to occur in the nonprofit sector.

A third important form of variation is persistent cross-national variation, which continues to exist alongside worldwide organizational expansion (in line with Salamon and Anheier's [1998] social origins model; see also Anheier, Lang, and Toepler, Chapter 30, "Comparative Nonprofit Sector Research"); these differences could exist in both the discourse of organization and the practice of it. Indeed, over time growth trajectories that proceed at different rates will lead to greater cross-national differences in absolute terms. As explanatory indicators, ties to a liberal cultural framework or to an alternative social structure (e.g., religious entities, which may remain different from their secular counterparts; see Fulton, Chapter 26, "Religious Organizations") may explain some cross-sectional variation in absolute levels and in growth rates.

Effects: A final set of issues that link the emergence and expansion of formal nonprofit organization involves their instrumental effects. The demand-driven view assumes that these organizations fill a prosocial, functional role, while a cultural view is agnostic about the effects of any particular nonprofit. The arguments put forth here suggest that nonprofit organization may be correlated with other features that are normatively valued in more-liberal societies (e.g., nonprofit organizations and more education or liberal democratic freedoms). But nonprofits themselves may not directly and causally create all of the associated public value (e.g., improved education, health care, democracy, environmentalism). The argument is that an underlying cultural shift unfolding at the macro level may be partly driving related social changes (see Bromley, Schofer, and Longhofer 2018 for a deeper discussion of the relationship between domestic education nonprofits and education outcomes). We still lack causal research that isolates the effects of nonprofit work from the potential influences of broader, contextual trends. Similarly, creative research designs are needed to test beliefs about the effects of particular organizational structures (e.g., "partnerships" or "strategic planning") on desired outcomes across many entities.

Implications and Conclusions

The nonprofit sector has continued to grow in overall size, in the total number of organizations, and in global reach, and it has become increasingly formal, complex, and professionalized. Building on theory from organizational sociology, I argue that this growth is part of a general trend of organizational expansion. The modern system of distinct states, firms, churches, and schools—which prevailed in the early post–World War II period—is transforming into a late-modern system in which these once-diverse entities can become instances under the common frame of "organizations." In becoming organizations, precursors to the nonprofit form take on new features. They shift, for example, from deriving mission and legitimacy from traditional sources (such as God or community) toward operating as autonomous actors that are able and entitled to determine their own goals and purposes (Drori and Meyer 2006; Meyer 2010).

One explanation of this shift is two horrific world wars that undermined government-based control, creating supports for alternative forms of a more global social order. In the postwar period of American dominance, centralized nation-state solutions (including a world state) to social problems became less feasible, and an alternative idea of order rooted in science and in expanded individual rights and capacities took center stage. Following the collapse of the Soviet Union, an even more aggressive celebration of individualism took hold. Social structures worldwide transformed and new ones were created, reflecting these cultural beliefs in scientific rationality and individual rights and capacities. Thus, the growing number and the increasing internal complexity of organizations are driven by a key phenomenon: worldwide cultural change. This argument should not be interpreted as suggesting an inevitable trajectory toward organizational expansion. In fact, I posit the opposite: the worldwide rise of an organizational society rests on the globalization of liberal cultural ideologies of progress and modernization rooted in individualism. Therefore, if these cultural roots shift or are reversed, social structures will change as well. In an alternative world society—for example, one built around central imperial structures—"organization" as we know it would be a less central form of social structure.

One key implication of this argument involves the need to reflect on what is gained and lost as the business, government, and nonprofit sectors blur. Some see the differences between sectors as relatively immaterial and are untroubled by this trend (Dees and Anderson 2003). For instance, in response to a query about business schools that have programs for nonprofits, one scholar responded, "our primary focus is on organizational theory. We believe you can apply it to any type of organization" (Orgtheory.net 2012). Others call for greater attention to the unique elements of public and nonprofit management (Frumkin 2002; Eikenberry and Kluver 2004). A number of excellent studies document how nonprofits try to maintain their expressive (or identity) functions in spite of increasing formalization, or how they reconcile charitable goals with more instrumental pressures (Chen 2009; Knutsen and Brower 2010; Suárez 2010).

This chapter does not argue that organizational expansion and increasing similarity across the sectors creates charities or government agencies or firms that are more (or, for that matter, less) efficient or effective. Nor are the new structures thought to be inherently more (or less) just or socially beneficial or productive than before. At the societal level, it is unclear whether having more nonprofits and government agencies with, for example, systematic performance metrics means that as a whole they are producing better outcomes than before, or whether having more firms with socially responsible structures improves practices.

Several possible concerns arise. Whereas charitable structures in years past could hang much of their legitimacy on tackling a widely shared social purpose or serving a legitimate sovereign, contemporary nonprofit organizations are constructed as autonomous actors and thus increasingly face demands to justify their existence and their work. Pressures for accountability and responsibility arise in the nonprofit sector, along with the related concepts of performance and impact measurement. This parallels the general rise of pressures toward corporate social responsibility in for-profit organizations. Indeed, firms, government agencies, and nonprofits begin to adopt many of the same corporate social responsibility policies and practices (Pope et al. 2018). They all begin to stress their general social responsibilities as organizational actors through things like sustainability reporting, community outreach programs, multistakeholder initiatives, and "good governance" practices such as codes of conduct, whistleblower policies, and risk management procedures. Overall, the legitimacy of charitable structures shifts to reside as much in adopting the trappings of proper organizational actors as in their mission.

The internalization of inconsistencies associated with the expanding responsibilities of being a proper organizational actor can create entities that are rather paradoxical: organizations increasingly claim capacity for autonomous, rational action on many fronts while, at the same time, becoming more enmeshed in a web of responsibilities to diverse stakeholders that limits their actual autonomy. As a result, "responsible" organizational actors may become more accountable but less efficient.

The social controls involved specify that it is less legitimate to overtly pursue narrow self-interests, particularly if they impinge on other actors. In the contemporary organizational world, a great deal of effort goes into displays of accounting for the interests of other stakeholders within a pluralistic society; even powerful actors like foundations seek comply at least in appearance (Brandtner, Bromley, and Tompkins-Stange 2016). But ultimately, social controls are a weakly enforceable mechanism, and displays of responsibility can differ wildly from actual practices, leaving a great deal of leeway for immoral and self-interested action. As Francis Fukuyama writes, "One person's civic engagement is another's rent-seeking; much of what constitutes civil society can be described as interest groups trying to divert public resources to their favoured causes. . . . There is no guarantee that self-styled public interest NGOs represent real public interests. It is entirely possible that too active an NGO sector may represent an excessive politicization of public life, which can either distort public policy or lead to deadlock" (2001:12). Legal oversight of organizations' responsibilities has perhaps not caught up to their rapidly expanding rights, leaving the system vulnerable to corruption and self-interest. Some advocate for a more rigorous corporate criminal justice system—complete with an organizational "death penalty" in egregious cases (Grossman 2016; Ramirez and Ramirez 2017).

A final implication of these arguments is that, as a social-structural manifestation of cultural ideologies rooted in individual empowerment, formal nonprofit organization is likely to be undercut if the liberal world order weakens. Indeed, we see increasing opposition to nonprofit organizations alongside contemporary resurgences of populism, nativism, and nationalism worldwide (Dupuy and Prakash, Chapter 28, "Global Backlash Against Foreign Funding to Domestic Nongovernmental Organizations"). This is of great concern as the world has enjoyed a period of long advancements in human development and expansions in rights. At the same time, many of the benefits we now attribute to nonprofits can and do take other forms that often aren't "counted" in the formal sector—for example, through stronger extended family units or centralized provision of social services by state bureaucracies. Moreover, even accountable organizations can be a source of inequality, as the level of professionalization involved requires high levels of education that exclude vulnerable groups from full participation (see Bloemraad, Gleeson, and de Graauw, Chapter 12, "Immigrant Organizations," for a related discussion of civic invisibility). Observing that nonprofits are increasingly instances of formal organization should draw our attention toward their capacity for both good and evil: they can be vehicles for exclusion and reinforcing elite power—or sources of inclusion and democratization. They can perpetrate corruption—or serve as watchdogs of the public good. They can be sites of dehumanizing conformity—or venues that promote free expression.

5   TANGLED UP IN TAX

The Nonprofit Sector and the Federal Tax System

Daniel J. Hemel[1]

EXEMPTION IS THE TERM MOST OFTEN USED BY scholars, practitioners, and policy makers to describe the relationship between nonprofit organizations and the federal tax system in the United States. But although the term is useful as shorthand to characterize the complicated connections between the nonprofit sector and federal tax law, it also should be recognized as the misnomer that it largely is. The nonprofit sector is subject to a wide range of federal taxes—some of which apply broadly to nonprofit and for-profit entities alike, others of which fall almost exclusively on organizations that are ostensibly "exempt." Insofar as nonprofit entities are excused from payment of federal income tax, exemption comes with a heavy load of compliance burdens, disclosure obligations, and other behavioral restrictions that dictate the day-to-day lives of these organizations. Rather than existing at several steps' remove from the federal tax system, nonprofit entities are, in fact, tangled up in tax.

Indeed, if the relationship between the nonprofit sector and the federal tax system were to be summarized in a single word, *entanglement* rather than *exemption* would be the more appropriate term. Nonprofit organizations in the United States are caught in a complex web of nonprofit-specific code provisions, the most significant of which are summarized and evaluated in previous editions of this book upon which this chapter builds (Simon 1987; Simon, Dale and Chisholm 2006). Even seemingly unrelated tax statutes often tie back to the nonprofit sector in winding ways. There is, moreover, no non-entangling option; even total exemption would result in interactions between tax authorities and nonprofit organizations at exemption's boundaries. Some interactions between the federal tax system and the nonprofit sector are probably desirable. Insofar as the federal tax system seeks to support nonprofit organizations, such support almost inevitably involves a considerable degree of contact. The dominant dilemma in the design of the federal tax rules for nonprofit organizations is how to manage entanglement without releasing all strings.

Before proceeding further, it may help to clarify what exactly "entanglement" entails. The dictionary definition of *entanglement* is straightforward—"the condition of being deeply involved"—but that single definition elides entanglement's many manifestations (Merriam-Webster n.d.). Courts and commentators have drawn a helpful distinction between *administrative entanglement* and *political entanglement* (*Meek v. Pittenger* 1975;

Underwood 1976). Administrative entanglement refers to the involvement of tax authorities in the lives of nonprofit organizations; political entanglement refers to the involvement of nonprofit organizations in the political sphere. Each category can be subdivided further. The clearest form of administrative entanglement is *enforcement entanglement*, which occurs when tax authorities audit the returns of nonprofit organizations or seek to collect taxes from them (e.g., through liens, levies, and foreclosures). Enforcement entanglement can be avoided if nonprofit organizations are exempt from tax, but exemption leads to a second form of administrative entanglement: *borderline entanglement* (i.e., interactions between nonprofit organizations and tax authorities policing exemption's boundaries) (Zelinsky 2012). Meanwhile, political entanglement can occur when nonprofit organizations are *subjects* of political controversy or when they are *participants* in political conflict. The two categories sometimes overlap, as when issues of taxation tug nonprofit organizations into the political sphere. Likewise, the efforts of tax authorities to prevent nonprofit organizations from becoming involved in political conflicts may themselves be a source of administrative entanglement.

Administrative entanglement and political entanglement both refer to the entanglement of the nonprofit sector and the organs of government; a different type of entanglement occurs when nonprofit organizations become involved in the market—for example, by operating profit-seeking enterprises. *Market entanglement* raises several potential concerns. One is a worry about unfair competition between nonprofit organizations that enjoy the benefits of tax exemption and for-profit firms that pay full freight (Rose-Ackerman 1982). A second concern is that excessive entanglement between the nonprofit sector and the market will divert nonprofit organizations from their core missions (Dees 1998). A third is that nonprofit managers will prove ill-equipped to succeed in commercial ventures and that they will squander their organizations' resources when they try (Hansmann 1989). The weight of these concerns is discussed at greater length in other chapters of this book (Mosley, Chapter 10, "Social Service Nonprofits"; Brest, Chapter 16, "The Outcomes Movement in Philanthropy and the Nonprofit Sector"). The key point for purposes of this chapter is that market entanglement is an additional dimension of entanglement between the nonprofit sector and other sectors of society that the tax system seeks to control.

This chapter approaches the phenomenon of entanglement in four sections. The first section sets out the central dilemma in the tax treatment of nonprofit organizations: how to support the nonprofit sector through the tax system while managing administrative, political, and market entanglement. The second section explores the key provisions of the Internal Revenue Code affecting the nonprofit sector and explains how these provisions balance a set of seemingly irreconcilable policy objectives with varying degrees of success. The third section considers recent legislative changes that significantly reduce the tax system's support for the nonprofit sector while generating greater entanglement along several dimensions, and also raising the possibility that some nonprofit entities will opt out of tax-exempt status altogether. A final section offers tentative thoughts on entanglement's future and reflections on possible reforms.

Entanglement in Theory

The notion of entanglement is familiar to lawyers from the First Amendment context, where one element of the Supreme Court's test for whether a provision violates the

Establishment Clause is whether it produces "an excessive government entanglement with religion" (*Lemon v. Kurtzman* 1971, quoting *Walz v. Tax Commission of the City of New York* 1970). Not coincidentally, this oft-cited phrase originates in a case addressing the tax treatment of nonprofit organizations. In that case, Bronx attorney Frederick Walz argued that a New York state statute exempting churches and other nonprofit organizations from property taxes violated the First Amendment's prohibition on any "law respecting an establishment of religion" (Graham 1970). The Supreme Court rejected Walz's argument in a 1970 decision that introduced the concept of entanglement into First Amendment jurisprudence.

The justices' opinions in *Walz* reveal four perspectives on the relationship between exemption and entanglement. Chief Justice Warren Burger, who wrote the majority opinion, posited that exemption minimizes entanglement rather than supporting exempted entities. "Either course, taxation of churches or exemption, occasions some degree of involvement with religion," the chief justice acknowledged, but "elimination of exemption would tend to expand the involvement of government by giving rise to tax valuation of church property, tax liens, tax foreclosures, and the direct confrontations and conflicts that follow in the train of those legal processes" (*Walz v. Tax Commission of the City of New York* 1970:674–675). Justice William Brennan, in a concurring opinion, argued that exemption serves to support "the diversity of association, viewpoint, and enterprise essential to a vigorous, pluralistic society." Although Brennan did not go as far as Burger in arguing that taxation would lead to *greater* government entanglement in church affairs, he said that termination of exemptions would not "quantitatively lessen the extent of state involvement." Exemption, moreover, is "fundamentally different" from—and less entangling than—direct subsidies (i.e., cash grants), according to Brennan, because exemption involves "passive" rather than "affirmative" state involvement (*Walz v. Tax Commission of the City of New York* 1970:690–691). The "symbolism of exemption," he wrote, quoting Harvard Law School professor Paul Freund, is "that organized religion is not expected to support the state" and that "the state is not expected to support the church" (*Walz v. Tax Commission of the City of New York* 1970:691, quoting Freund 1969).

Two members of the court—Justice John Marshall Harlan and Justice William Douglas—both acknowledged the economic equivalence between exemption and subsidy but nonetheless fell on opposite sides of the ultimate 7–1 split.[2] Justice Harlan, in a solo concurrence, said that "sweeping" exemptions like New York's property tax reprieve "need not entangle the government in difficult classifications of what is or is not religious" because the statute covered a broad range of sectarian and secular eleemosynary organizations. He added that exemption is generally less entangling than a direct subsidy because "subsidies, unlike exemptions, must be passed on periodically and thus invite more political controversy" (*Walz v. Tax Commission of the City of New York* 1970:699). The lone dissenter, Justice Douglas, was unmoved by his colleagues' efforts to distinguish exemption from other forms of support. "A tax exemption is a subsidy," plain and simple, he wrote, and he saw little reason to believe that either was less entangling than the other (*Walz v. Tax Commission of the City of New York* 1970:704).

The question presented in *Walz*—whether property tax exemptions for houses of worship result in "excessive government entanglement with religion" or otherwise violate the Establishment Clause—is just one among a constellation of issues surrounding exemption and entanglement. Nonetheless, the justices' opinions in that case illuminate important aspects of the relationship between nonprofit institutions and the tax system. First and foremost, the opinions acknowledge that both taxation and exemption result in some amount of entanglement. As Edward Zelinsky would later write, "In the tax context, there are no disentangling alternatives" (Zelinsky 2017:xv). To use the terminology introduced earlier, exemption trades away enforcement entanglement for greater borderline entanglement. Even if we allow organizations to self-certify that they satisfy the exemption criteria, the process of establishing those criteria still requires lawmakers to decide which organizations do and do not merit the implicit support that exemption provides.

Second, the opinions of Justices Brennan, Harlan, and Douglas highlight some of the most salient similarities and differences between exemptions and subsidies. Exemption is indeed the economic equivalent of taxation coupled with a subsidy equal to the tax liability that the exempt organization otherwise would have to pay. And yet exemptions and subsidies often differ symbolically and programmatically. Exemptions, on the whole, may be less controversial and subject to less frequent reauthorization than subsidies and in this respect may reduce political entanglement. Whether that constitutes an argument in favor of exemptions is contestable. What Justice Harlan refers to negatively as "political controversy" might be cast in a more positive light as "democratic debate."

The comparison between support via exemption and support via subsidy skips over the question of why the tax system should support nonprofit organizations in the first place. One potential answer is that nonprofit organizations produce goods that are quasi-public (i.e., nonrivalrous) or public (i.e., nonrivalrous and nonexcludable), and that market mechanisms tend to underproduce goods of that character. But the public goods account runs into the reality that, for many nonprofit organizations, the production of public goods is not a primary activity. Hospital beds, for example, are both rivalrous and excludable; the same is arguably true for seats in a classroom and in a symphony hall.

A related justification for government support of the nonprofit sector posits that nonprofit institutions tend to redistribute to the poor. This explanation overlaps with the first. We might think of redistribution as a public good because it (possibly) leads to lower crime rates, because it generates greater political and social stability, and because individuals have a moral or aesthetic taste for living in more equal societies (Thurow 1971). In any event, the redistribution rationale—like the public goods account—applies to a relatively small segment of the nonprofit space. While some nonprofit organizations (e.g., soup kitchens and homeless shelters) redistribute, others (e.g., many art museums, operas, K–12 private schools, and business leagues) do not. In some cases, nonprofit organizations that enjoy tax-exempt status actively oppose redistributive efforts (Hendrie 2015; Americans for Tax Reform 2018). Moreover, if the goal is to redistribute wealth from rich to poor, then we might ask why policy makers have chosen to do so indirectly via tax-favored treatment for nonprofit organizations rather than directly through cash assistance, food stamps, housing vouchers, and so on. If the government supports nonprofit institutions through tax exemption in order to advance redistributive objectives, then it is pursuing a far from first-best strategy to achieve that goal.

Three other rationales fare somewhat better in justifying the federal tax system's support for the nonprofit sector. One—which we might call the *Tocquevillian account*—emphasizes the importance of nonprofit organizations as checks on governmental power.

A second—which can be characterized as the *Hayekian account*—highlights the ability of the nonprofit sector to aggregate information and preferences without succumbing to the pathologies of the political process and central planning. A third—which I call the *Pigouvian account*—posits that gifts to nonprofit organizations generate positive externalities (i.e., social benefits that the giver of the gift does not fully capture), and that government subsidies are necessary to ensure that the optimal amount of gift-giving occurs.[3]

Start with the Tocquevillian account. Tocqueville feared that governments in democratic societies would acquire excessive power unless citizens formed and fostered nonprofit associations that organized joint undertakings, generated social capital, and thereby checked governmental growth (Tocqueville [1840] 1899). The implications of Tocqueville's theories for the nonprofit sector have been well rehearsed elsewhere (Clemens 2006; Smith and Grønbjerg 2006); the key point here is that the Tocquevillian account assumes a separation between the nonprofit sector and the state. Government support for the nonprofit sector thus must be designed to avoid excessive administrative entanglement; otherwise the Tocquevillian virtues of nonprofit associations are lost. The implications for political entanglement are more subtle. Separation between the nonprofit sector and the state is a Tocquevillian value, but in order to perform their checking function, nonprofit organizations must interject themselves into political life under certain circumstances.

What I call the Hayekian account differs from the Tocquevillian narrative, but the policy implications are similar. Friedrich Hayek argued that "the peculiar character of the problem of a rational economic order is determined precisely by the fact that the knowledge of the circumstances of which we must make use never exists in concentrated or integrated form, but solely as the dispersed bits of incomplete and frequently contradictory knowledge which all the separate individuals possess" (Hayek 1945:519). Centralized planning is doomed to fail, according to Hayek, because central planners lack the information they need to allocate resources optimally (or even intelligently). Majoritarian electoral processes are unlikely to solve the information problem either. As Saul Levmore puts the point, "Voters across the country are unlikely to be well informed about my local hospital or your university, so a conventional exercise in direct democracy would not delegate decision-making to better informed parties" (Levmore 1998:427). The exemption for nonprofit organizations and its cousin, the deduction for charitable contributions, deliver support based on the resource allocation decisions of individuals who enjoy greater access to information than do legislators and bureaucrats. These individual decisions can be thought of as "ballots" through which individuals cast votes regarding the distribution of public funds.

The Hayekian account, like the Tocquevillian account, counsels against too active a government role in determining the destination and degree of support. After all, the premise underlying the Hayekian account is that individuals know more than the government about which organizations will use funds in the most socially productive ways. The Hayekian account also helps explain why we might opt for exemption and deduction over, say, a several-hundred-dollar voucher that each citizen could allocate to nonprofit organizations of his or her choosing. With exemption and deduction, the size of the subsidy scales with the amount that an organization raises from donors and other constituents. In this respect, as Levmore notes, such subsidies "permit[] intensity of preferences (or knowledge) to be recorded" (Levmore 1998:428).

A purely passive approach to government support for the nonprofit sector would pose obvious problems, however. If any organization could self-certify as tax exempt, then much of the income tax base would wither rapidly. To paraphrase James Madison, if men were angels, no entanglement would be necessary, but given the non-angelic nature of many men and women, the government must establish and enforce some rules to prevent us from transferring all of our assets to exempt entities that exist purely to support our own lifestyles. The Tocquevillian and Hayekian accounts require that nonprofit organizations enjoy a significant degree of freedom from administrative entanglement with government, and yet some strings must remain attached or else the tax base will fall out from under us.

The Pigouvian account (the name being derived from the early- to mid-twentieth century English economist Arthur Cecil Pigou) proceeds quite differently than the Tocquevillian and Hayekian accounts, though some of its implications are similar. It builds on the observation that individuals are imperfect altruists: they derive a personal benefit from giving to others (what might be called "warm glow"), but they do not fully account for the interests of others when allocating resources themselves. The Pigouvian account posits that in some cases, a subsidy for charitable contributions will be needed in order to induce individuals to make gifts that leave society on the whole better off.

Arithmetic may illustrate the point. Imagine that A derives a "warm glow" benefit of 99 from giving 100 to B. A, in other words, is an imperfect altruist: she cares about B, but she still would prefer that resources be allocated to her rather than to B. Thus, absent any intervention, A will fail to make the gift to B even though the total benefit from the gift (A's 99 plus B's 100) is greater than the benefit that A gets from consuming the 100 herself.

Under these circumstances, as Louis Kaplow has explained, total welfare can be enhanced by offering a small subsidy to A for giving to B. Consider, for example, a policy that offers a subsidy of 2 to A for every 100 that she gives to B (Kaplow 1995). The subsidy leads the imperfectly altruistic A to give 100 to B, even though she would not have done so before the subsidy. The reason why is that the benefit of 99 that A derives from giving to B plus the subsidy (worth 2 to her) for doing so exceeds the opportunity cost to A of sacrificing 100. The total benefit in the gift-giving case is 199 as compared to 100 when A declines to give and consumes herself.[4]

Interestingly, nothing in the Pigouvian account is specific to *charitable* giving. The donee (B in the example above) could just as easily be another individual rather than an organization. The Pigouvian justification for subsidizing gifts does depend, though, on the premise that transfers from A to B are bona fide transfers from which A derives utility. If, by contrast, A and B did not care about each other but simply exchanged "gifts" with each other (e.g., A gives 100 to B and B gives 100 to A), then society would have no interest in subsidizing the transfers. Indeed, the back-and-forth transfers would likely reduce social welfare because they entail transaction costs with no benefits. The Pigouvian account thus suggests a need for rules to ensure that subsidized gifts from A to B do not flow back to A.

One important implication of the Pigouvian account is that it suggests that subsidies for charitable giving may enhance social welfare even if charities allocate resources less efficiently than the government. Imagine that C derives a benefit of 60 from giving 100 to a nonprofit organization. Imagine also that the nonprofit organization uses its resources less efficiently than the government would. Assume that the government would generate a benefit of 100 from spending 100, while the nonprofit organization would generate a benefit of only 50 from spending the same amount.

Even though the nonprofit organization will spend its resources less efficiently than the government, there is still a strong welfarist argument in this scenario for offering a subsidy to C to induce her to give to the organization. Say that the government offers C a tax benefit of 40 if she gives 100 to the organization. C is now indifferent between giving 100 to charity (warm glow benefits of 60; tax benefit of 40) and consuming the 100 herself. Thus, by offering a charitable subsidy of 40, the government can induce C to make a charitable gift that leaves C no worse off and society 50 better off, even though the charity is less efficient than the government.

Exactly how large this Pigouvian subsidy for charitable contributions should be is the subject of a robust economics literature.[5] The key point for present purposes is that the Pigouvian account can offer an additional justification for government subsidies to the nonprofit sector that mirrors the Tocquevillian and Hayekian accounts in several important respects and differs in several others. Like the Tocquevillian and Hayekian accounts, the Pigouvian account provides a rationale for a laissez-faire approach to the regulation of the nonprofit sector. Underlying the Pigouvian account is the premise that individuals derive satisfaction from donating to charities that they have chosen; presumably this satisfaction would be squandered if the government commandeered the nonprofit sector and transformed charitable giving into a form of paying taxes.[6] But unlike the Tocquevillian account, the Pigouvian account does not depend on the democratic benefits of nongovernmental organizations and, unlike the Hayekian account, it does not depend on the assumption that the allocation of resources by nongovernmental actors will be more efficient than the allocation of resources by legislators and bureaucrats. To the contrary, the Pigouvian account suggests that legislators and bureaucrats can tolerate a certain amount of inefficiency among nonprofit organizations without sacrificing the welfare benefits of charitable giving.

Finally, note that the decision to support nonprofit organizations through exemption and its cousin, deduction, may reduce administrative and political entanglement relative to direct subsidies, but that decision also raises concerns regarding market entanglement. One concern (discussed at greater length shortly) is that tax-exempt organizations will enjoy an unfair competitive advantage vis-à-vis taxpaying firms that offer similar services. Perhaps a more serious concern is that individuals will seek to claim charitable contribution deductions for transfers to nonprofit organizations that effectively amount to purchases of goods and services—purchases that, in many cases, would not be tax-deductible if they occurred in a more transparent market context. Policy makers may succeed in managing market entanglement through well-designed rules and standards, but the concerns will nonetheless linger. In short, exemption and deduction do not eliminate entanglement altogether but simply trade different types of entanglement for forms that appear to be more tolerable.

Entanglement in Practice

The two main ways in which the federal tax system supports the nonprofit sector are exemption and deduction. Exemption allows nonprofit organizations to earn income without paying entity-level tax; deduction allows donors to a subset of nonprofit organizations to reduce their taxable income by the amount of the gift. But such support comes with strings attached. The federal tax system employs six specific strategies of control over nonprofit organizations that enjoy the benefit of exemption and the subset of those that are also aided through deduction. The six strategies are (1) purpose restrictions, (2) limits on specific activities, (3) nondistribution constraints, (4) transparency requirements, (5) public support conditions, and (6) payout mandates. Not all such strategies are employed with respect to all entities, but all six seek to strike a balance (successfully or not) between support and the various varieties of entanglement.

Purpose Restrictions

Section 501(c) of the Internal Revenue Code provides an exemption from federal income tax for organizations organized and operated for specific purposes. Its sprawling twenty-nine-paragraph list of exempt organizations ranges from congressionally chartered corporations (section 501(c)(1)) to cooperative health insurance issuers (section 501(c)(29)). Most familiarly, section 501(c)(3) allows an exemption for entities organized and operated exclusively for one of nine ends: religious, charitable, scientific, testing for public safety, literary, educational, fostering national or international amateur sports competition, prevention of cruelty to children, and prevention of cruelty to animals. These "(c)(3)" entities include most of the largest nonprofit organizations by assets and revenue. They occupy a privileged position within the nonprofit sector because donors to (c)(3) entities—unlike donors to most other exempt organizations—are eligible to claim charitable contribution deductions for their gifts.[7]

Section 501(c)(3) organizations account for about three quarters of all entities exempt from taxation under section 501, but several other paragraphs are worthy of note. Section 501(c)(4) extends the benefit of exemption (but not deduction) to "organizations not organized for profit but operated exclusively for the promotion of social welfare," including AARP, the American Civil Liberties Union (ACLU), the National Rifle Association (NRA), the Sierra Club, and a number of nonprofit health plans. Section 501(c)(5) reaches labor, agricultural, and horticultural organizations, including the AFL-CIO, the American Farm Bureau Federation, and many of their affiliates.[8] Section 501(c)(6) applies to business leagues, chambers of commerce, real estate boards, boards of trade, and "professional football leagues" (a category that has been extended to include nonfootball athletic associations such as the PGA Tour and the U.S. Tennis Association). Section 501(c)(7) covers "clubs organized for pleasure, recreation, and other nonprofitable purposes." Two separate paragraphs grant exemptions to fraternal societies operating under the lodge system: section 501(c)(8), which applies to societies providing for the payment of life, sick, accident, or other benefits to members or their dependents, and section 501(c)(10), which applies to societies whose net earnings are devoted exclusively to religious, charitable, scientific, literary, educational, and fraternal purposes. Section 501(c)(10) societies are—like section (c)(3)s but unlike most other exempt entities—eligible to receive tax-deductible contributions as long as those gifts are used exclusively for religious, charitable, scientific, literary, and educational (but not fraternal) purposes.

Although the scope of section 501(c)(3) is broad, and the rest of section 501(c) reaches further still, some limits merit mention. First, organizations that engage in illegal activities may be disqualified from exempt status. Thus, in a 1975 ruling, the IRS denied exemption under 501(c)(3) and 501(c)(4) to a nonprofit organization formed to promote world peace that primarily sponsored protests at which it urged demonstrators to engage in civil disobedience.[9] More recently, the IRS in 2013 denied exemption to a nonprofit cooperative association of cannabis producers based on the "well established" principle that "tax deductions and exemptions are not applicable to activities that are illegal."[10] The IRS also has long held that educational institutions seeking exemption under section 501(c)(3) must adopt a "racially nondiscriminatory policy as to students"—a conclusion that it (loosely) derived from section 501(c)(3)'s language regarding permissible purposes.[11] The Supreme Court upheld that position in a controversial 1983 case involving Bob Jones University, which at the time banned interracial dating among its students. "To warrant exemption under § 501(c)(3)," Chief Justice Burger wrote for the court's majority, "an institution . . . must demonstrably serve and be in harmony with the public interest," and its "purpose must not be so at odds with the common community conscience as to undermine any public benefit that might otherwise be conferred" (*Bob Jones University v. United States* 1983:591–592).

Chief Justice Burger's opinion in the *Bob Jones* case drew a sharp rebuke from his colleague Justice Lewis Powell, who found the "element of conformity" in the chief justice's analysis to be "troubling." "Far from representing an effort to reinforce any perceived 'common community conscience,'" Powell wrote, "the provision of tax exemptions to nonprofit groups is one indispensable means of limiting the influence of governmental orthodoxy on important areas of community life" (*Bob Jones University v. United States* 1983:609). The back-and-forth between Burger and Powell illustrates a central challenge for the tax system. On the one hand, the tax system seeks to support the nonprofit sector while avoiding excessive entanglement; on the other hand, few are willing to say that every nonprofit organization is entitled to such support regardless of its purpose. Indeed, even Justice Powell ultimately agreed with the majority's result in *Bob Jones*, though he arrived at that result through different reasoning.

The compromises struck by the IRS, Congress, and the courts are uneasy. The IRS still denies section 501(c)(3) status to educational institutions with racially discriminatory policies toward students, but it grants such status to educational institutions that prohibit students from marrying across religious lines and that bar same-sex relationships.[12] It has denied section 501(c)(3) status to an organization whose primary purpose was to decriminalize sexual activity between "consenting" children and adults—a decision that the Tax Court later upheld—but a number of white supremacist organizations have gained exemption under section 501(c)(3) (*Mysteryboy Inc. v. Commissioner* 2010; Stiffman 2016). Congress, for its part, enacted legislation in 1976 that denied exemption under section 501(c)(7) to social clubs whose written policies discriminate on the basis of race, color, or religion, though it amended that language four years later to reauthorize exemption for clubs that "in good faith" limit their membership to followers of a particular religion "in order to further the teachings or principles of that religion, and not to exclude individuals of a particular race or color."[13] These decisions may or may not be defensible; more importantly for the present discussion, these sorts of legislative and regulatory judgment calls are inevitable whenever the tax system restricts eligibility for exemption and deduction on the basis of purpose.

Limits on Specific Activities

A second way in which the federal tax system regulates nonprofit entities is to limit exemption on the basis of the activities in which organizations engage. These restrictions potentially reduce political entanglement and market entanglement, though at the cost of additional administrative entanglement.

Limits on Political Entanglement: Section 501(c)(3) flatly prohibits organizations that enjoy exemption under that paragraph from engaging in certain political activities. Specifically, it says that a (c)(3) cannot "participate in, or intervene in, . . . any political campaign on behalf of (or in opposition to) any candidate for public office." This restriction is known as the Johnson Amendment, so named for then senator Lyndon B. Johnson, who added it to the code in 1954 after two (c)(3) organizations backed his opponent in the Democratic Party primary for U.S. Senate in Texas (O'Daniel 2001). It has proven to be one of the most controversial features of section 501(c)(3) in the decades since.

Several justifications for the Johnson Amendment are plausible, beyond what was likely the original rationale (i.e., ensuring that Lyndon Johnson retained his Senate seat in 1954). One argument, building on the Pigouvian account, is that political campaigns are zero-sum and so campaign expenditures do not in general lead to positive externalities (or, more precisely, the benefit to the supported candidate is offset by the detriment to her rival). The counterargument is that our democracy functions better with an electorate that is well informed; thus, interventions in political campaigns, insofar as they convey valuable information to voters, do indeed generate positive externalities. Other potential justifications for the Johnson Amendment emphasize its role in reducing political entanglement. The Johnson Amendment arguably shields (c)(3)s from political pressure exerted by elected officials seeking endorsements and other campaign-related support. Partly for this reason, thousands of clergy members and dozens of other (c)(3) leaders spoke out against legislation in 2017 that would have carved out a de minimis exception to the Johnson Amendment (Banks 2017; Taeb 2017). (The proposal passed the House as part of the late 2017 tax reform package but was eliminated from the Senate version and the final legislation for procedural reasons (Aprill and Hemel 2018).) The Johnson Amendment also might be said to preserve a politics- and partisanship-free zone of American life. The argument would be that our polity and our society are stronger and more stable when bonds of friendship and social capital cut across party lines, and that by limiting the benefits of (c)(3) status to organizations that stay out of politics, the Johnson Amendment encourages the sorts of institutions that promote these cross-cutting ties.

Significantly, the Johnson Amendment does not prohibit all political activity on the part of (c)(3) entities. Those organizations still may seek to "influence legislation," as long as those efforts do not become a "substantial part" of the organization's activities. Some (c)(3) entities are eligible to opt out of the substantiality standard and into a quantitative test that allows lobbying expenditures up to a specific dollar limit ($1 million a year for the largest (c)(3) organizations).[14] Educational institutions, hospitals and medical research organizations, and most other public charities can opt into section 501(h); private foundations cannot. Interestingly, Congress in 1976 also excluded churches from eligibility for the section 501(h) quantitative test at the request of religious leaders, who expressed concern that the IRS might be influenced by the test even with respect to churches that did not opt in.[15]

The Johnson Amendment applies only to organizations that are exempt under section 501(c)(3) and section 501(c)(29) (the paragraph for cooperative health insurers). Organizations covered by other code provisions can endorse candidates without losing their exempt status and can engage in lobbying activities without abiding by section 501(c)(3)'s substantiality standard or section 501(h)'s quantitative test. Most controversially, the IRS's interpretation of section 501(c)(4) has allowed organizations exempt under that paragraph to engage in substantial campaign-related activities. Although the statute limits exempt status to organizations that are "operated exclusively for the promotion of social welfare," regulations dating back to 1960 allow organizations to qualify under section 501(c)(4) if they are "primarily engaged" in social welfare promotion. Interventions in political campaigns on behalf of or in opposition to candidates for public office do not qualify as "promotion of social welfare" under those regulations,[16] but the slip from "exclusively" to "primarily" has prompted practitioners to argue and advise clients that section 501(c)(4) organizations can engage in substantial campaign-related efforts—perhaps up to 50 percent of total activity—without running afoul of the primary activity standard (Colvin 2010). The IRS also has said that organizations covered by section 501(c)(5) (labor unions, etc.) and section 501(c)(6) (business leagues, etc.) can engage in political action as long as their primary purpose and activities remain consistent with the code paragraph under which they claim exemption.[17]

The tax treatment of political activity by nonprofit organizations poses challenging normative questions. The key point for present purposes is that whatever approach the tax system takes toward political activity by nonprofit organizations, entanglement of some form is inevitable. The Johnson Amendment's bright-line prohibition on politicking potentially leads to enforcement entanglement, both when the IRS takes away an entity's exempt status and subsequently when the IRS seeks to collect taxes from the now-nonexempt organization. But even that "bright line" is not so bright, as the definition of campaign activity turns out to be fuzzy at the edges.[18] A more permissive regime still requires the tax authority to decide how much is too much and what activities count toward that quantitative or qualitative threshold. The one way to avoid these line-drawing questions would be to give all nonprofit organizations carte blanche to engage in as much political activity as they want without endangering their exempt status, but while that would minimize administrative entanglement over political activity questions, it would only further entangle the nonprofit sector in the political process.

Limits on Market Entanglement: In addition to the limits on political entanglement discussed earlier, the federal tax system seeks to limit market entanglement through the unrelated business income tax, or UBIT. The tax is set at the same rate as the corporate income tax and thus has the effect of treating the "unrelated business income" of an exempt organization as if it were nonexempt income earned by a for-profit firm. It applies both to (c)(3)s and noncharitable exempt organizations. And although total UBIT collections are quite modest (in 2013, less than $500 million for all organizations exempt under section 501(c), or about 0.02 percent of all federal tax collections that year[19]), the UBIT looms large over planning and operations for many nonprofit organizations.

UBIT generally applies to trades and businesses "regularly carried on" by exempt organizations that are "not substantially related" to the organization's exempt purpose,[20] with a number of important exceptions—including for dividends, interest, annuities, royalties, and most rental income.[21] Thus, a university that earns income from an executive master's in business administration program will not pay UBIT on that income stream, because the activity is substantially related to the university's educational purpose, but if the university owns a macaroni factory, then it almost certainly will pay UBIT on its income from that enterprise. The macaroni factory example is not fanciful: the acquisition of a macaroni factory by New York University School of Law in 1947 was one event triggering the passage of the first UBIT statute three years later.[22] Other factual scenarios present more difficult line-drawing challenges. For example, the IRS has ruled that an art museum gift shop's sales of greeting cards that display artwork from the museum's own collection and from other art collections do not constitute "unrelated business income" because those sales "contribute[] importantly to the achievement of the museum's exempt educational purposes by stimulating and enhancing public awareness, interest, and appreciation of art,"[23] but sales of scientific books and city souvenirs by an art museum gift shop are subject to UBIT because those items "have no causal relationship to art or to artistic endeavor."[24]

It is questionable whether the UBIT rules actually protect for-profit firms against competition from nonprofit entities. In the absence of the UBIT rules, nonprofit entities presumably would allocate capital to whatever investments they thought would yield the highest returns. Those investments likely would be spread across sectors, affecting the overall supply of capital and thus the rate of return on capital investment but not necessarily impacting any specific sector disproportionately. To illustrate: imagine that in a world without UBIT, University X enters into book publishing, macaroni manufacturing, and sausage making. Under the UBIT rules, however, University X has the ability to earn tax-exempt income from book publishing but not from macaroni manufacturing or sausage making, and so it may choose to invest in book publishing even when the expected pretax return there is lower than the expected pretax return from macaroni manufacturing and sausage making.[25] The likely result is that with UBIT, for-profit book publishers bear the brunt of competition from universities, whereas without UBIT, the effects of competition would be more evenly distributed. More generally, the UBIT provisions systematically disfavor for-profit firms in sectors such as education and medical care that nonprofit organizations can enter without facing tax (Rose-Ackerman 1982).

The current UBIT regime still can be defended on other grounds. In the absence of the UBIT provisions, nonprofit enterprises would have an incentive to form or acquire active business enterprises in order to take advantage of exemption. Imagine, for example, that the pretax rate of return on capital investment in the corporate sector is 10 percent and the corporate income tax rate is 20 percent. Thus, if a university buys $100 of stock in a for-profit macaroni manufacturing corporation, it can expect to earn after-tax returns of $8 per year. If the university instead buys the macaroni factory and integrates the enterprise into its nonprofit structure, then—absent UBIT—the university's return on the $100 investment would rise from $8 to $10. Indeed, even if the university could not manage the macaroni factory as efficiently as a for-profit corporation could, the university still would be better off buying the factory rather than buying stock in the for-profit macaroni corporation so long as the university could generate greater than an 8 percent return when operating the factory itself. The UBIT rules mitigate this potential distortion by equalizing the tax treatment of the university-owned macaroni factory and the factory owned by a for-profit corporation. This arguably reduces market entanglement, because passive investments in for-profit enterprises are less likely than active investments to divert nonprofit managers from their organizational missions.

The UBIT rules also might be justified on the basis of the Hayekian account outlined earlier.[26] Recall that the argument there was that individuals know more than legislators and bureaucrats about which nonprofit entities ought to receive additional resources. Charitable contributions arguably reflect these individual judgments. So, at least potentially, do decisions to purchase goods and services related to a nonprofit organization's exempt purpose. For example, a student's decision to pay tuition at a particular university, or a patient's decision to pay for treatment at a particular hospital, may reflect the student's or patient's judgment that the university or hospital is effective at achieving its educational or medical mission. Choices by individuals to contribute to charities or to patronize the related businesses of nonprofit organizations can thus be thought of as "ballots" that convey information about which institutions merit the support that deduction and exemption supply. By contrast, a grocery shopper's decision to buy a box of macaroni produced by a university-owned factory potentially tells us less about whether the university is effective at achieving its educational goals, and so—the argument goes—income derived from that sale should not lead to the university receiving any more support from the tax system.[27]

This cursory discussion does not exhaust all of the arguments in favor of UBIT and against. What it does seek to illustrate is that the decision to support the nonprofit sector through income tax exemption—a choice that arguably reduces administrative and political entanglement—potentially leads to greater market entanglement as nonprofit organizations have an incentive to operate unrelated businesses in order to leverage their tax-exempt status. The federal tax system has responded to this outcome through a set of complicated rules that seek to manage market entanglement, but at the cost of additional administrative entanglement.

Nondistribution Constraints

A defining feature of nonprofit organizations—and a central concern of the federal tax regime for nonprofit entities—is the nondistribution constraint: the rule that nonprofit organizations cannot distribute their assets to directors, officers, or others who control the organization. Several provisions embody or reflect this rule. Sections 501(c)(3), 501(c)(4), 501(c)(6), and 501(c)(7) all state that in order for an organization to qualify for exemption under those paragraphs, "no part of the net earnings" of the organization may "inure[]" to the benefit of any private shareholder."[28] Section 501(c)(10) arrives at a similar result through slightly different language.[29] Regulations impose equivalent restrictions with respect to labor unions and agricultural and horticultural organizations exempt under sections 501(c)(5).[30] In addition, section 4958, enacted in 1996, imposes a tax on "excess benefit" transactions between exempt organizations and various "disqualified persons," a category that includes anyone who has been "in a position to exercise substantial influence" over the organization in the previous five years. The tax applies to any transaction between a disqualified person and an exempt organization in which the disqualified person receives an economic benefit that exceeds the value of the consideration that she has provided to the organization. The tax begins at 25 percent of the excess benefit and rises to 200 percent if the transaction is not reversed within the year.[31] Additional penalties for self-dealing apply to private foundations and their contributors and managers.[32]

The relationship between the nondistribution constraint and entanglement is nuanced. Enforcement of the nondistribution constraint and related rules inevitably results in administrative entanglement. For example, section 4958's tax on "excess benefit" transactions requires the IRS to determine whether a nonprofit manager has been paid more than her work is worth—an inquiry that is anything but straightforward (Jones 2000). At the same time, the nondistribution constraint also serves an entanglement management function. To see why, imagine a regime that allowed a deduction for charitable contributions and an income tax exemption for nonprofit organizations but imposed no constraint on distribution. Individuals would have an incentive to hold their assets in nonprofit organizations that they control; whenever an individual desired liquidity, she could direct her organization to distribute its assets back to her. She would, in effect, have an individual retirement account (IRA) with no limits. The tax authority might try to stop this by enforcing purpose restrictions more rigorously and scrutinizing exemption applications more aggressively; otherwise, the consequences for the fisc could be dire. By relying on the nondistribution constraint and similar self-dealing rules, the IRS can reduce the risk of tax arbitrage through exempt organizations without placing too much emphasis on the purpose provisions. These rules related to nondistribution rules are, concededly, crude proxies for whether an organization is pursuing objectives worthy of exemption, but they likely entail fewer difficult value judgments than purpose-focused inquiries might.

The nondistribution constraint has been a topic of considerable scholarly debate over the last several decades.[33] Of particular note, Anup Malani and Eric Posner have proposed that the nondistribution constraint be relaxed so that section 501(c)(3) organizations can raise equity capital and incentivize managers with a share of profits. They acknowledge that this might lead individuals and firms to try to use (c)(3)s as tax shelters, but they respond that nondistribution is a clumsy measure for a (c)(3)'s social value. Instead, they suggest that the IRS could exercise greater judgment in granting (c)(3) status and that Congress could further flesh out the criteria for exemption (Malani and Posner 2007; for a competing view, see Galle 2010). What one thinks of such a reform depends in part on how one weighs entanglement's costs. For Tocquevillians and Hayekians (and possibly to a lesser extent for Pigouvians too), important values are compromised when the tax system's support for the nonprofit sector comes to depend on legislators' and bureaucrats' fine-grained judgments as to which organizational purposes are worthy of public backing. The nondistribution constraint is one way to avoid such fine-grained judgments while also ensuring that nonprofit organizations are not used to extract subsidies from the government for self-benefiting transfers or reciprocal gifts. Advocates of the nondistribution constraint would argue that even if the rule makes it harder for nonprofit organizations to raise capital or incentivize managers, those downsides are preferable to the alternative in which purpose restrictions must be more specifically detailed and policed.

Transparency Requirements

A fourth strategy of control that the federal tax system employs with respect to nonprofit organizations is transparency. Most exempt organizations (other than churches) with gross receipts of $50,000 a year or more—and all private foundations—are required to file annual information returns.[34] Exempt organizations generally must make their information returns available for public inspection.[35] The most familiar of these returns, Form 990, provides a trove of data on the filing organization, including information on its governance structure, principal activities, financial performance, and compensation of directors, officers, and key employees.

Whether or not sunshine is the best disinfectant, it is likely one of the least entangling regulatory strategies. For example, disclosure of officer compensation on Form 990 arguably relieves some of the pressure on the IRS when it comes to enforcement of excess benefit rules. Rather than having to determine whether an organization paid its executive director too much, the IRS can focus on ensuring that the organization accurately disclosed the executive director's compensation and then can rely on donors, the media, and others to judge whether compensation was excessive. Organizations that solicit charitable contributions may have an incentive to disclose some of this information to potential donors regardless of any statutory requirement, but the public inspection mandate facilitates scrutiny by other stakeholders, including beneficiaries, employees, partner organizations, and peer institutions.[36]

Transparency requirements do not, of course, allow policy makers to delegate all difficult value judgments to nongovernmental actors. First, transparency requirements themselves lead to some amount of administrative entanglement, as tax authorities still must enforce those requirements against nonprofit organizations that fail to comply. Second, the design of transparency requirements is not value neutral. For example, deciding whether to require nonprofit organizations to disclose their donors pits transparency values against the associational freedom interests that anonymity protects (*NAACP v. Alabama ex rel. Patterson* 1958). Third, transparency may intensify popular demand for governmental intervention to halt perceived excesses by nonprofit organizations that reporting reveals. For example, Form 990 disclosures that revealed growing university endowments and generous compensation packages for athletic coaches likely added fuel to demands from both sides of the ideological spectrum for regulatory action with respect to the wealthiest educational institutions (Kim 2017; USA Today Editorial 2015). In those cases, transparency led to an increase in political entanglement and—as explored later—an increase in administrative entanglement when Congress enacted taxes aimed at those universities and their highest-paid employees in December 2017.

Public Support Conditions

A fifth way in which the federal tax system regulates exempt organizations—and, in particular, charitable nonprofits—is by tying the most generous tax benefits to some showing of public support. The Internal Revenue Code and accompanying regulations draw a distinction between "public charities" and "private foundations," with public charities receiving the most generous tax treatment. Contributions to public charities now are deductible up to 60 percent of adjusted gross income (versus 30 percent for private foundations);[37] public charities are exempt from 2 percent tax on investment income that applies to private foundations;[38] and—as discussed momentarily—public charities are exempt from payout mandates to which private foundations are subject. Churches, schools, hospitals, and medical research institutions qualify as "per se" public charities, but for other 501(c)(3) organizations, public charity status depends on public support.

The code sets forth three ways for organizations to show that they receive sufficient public support to qualify for public charity status. The first path—the *one third support test*—requires that the organization receive at least one third of its financial support from government grants and contributions from the "general public."[39] (Donors are not considered members of the general public to the extent that they provide more than 2 percent of an organization's support.) A second path—the *facts and circumstances test*—requires that the organization receive at least 10 percent of its support from government and the general public, in which case the test looks to factors such as whether the organization's governing body "represents the broad interests of the public." A third path requires that the organization receive at least one third of its support from contributions from the general public, government grants, and gross receipts from activities related to its exempt purpose, and no more than one third of its support from investments and unrelated business income. A charitable organization that satisfies none of these requirements becomes a private foundation.

The rules regulating the public charity/private foundation distinction are substantially more complicated than the preceding paragraph lets on. The key point is that public charity status depends on some showing that the organization attracts support from beyond a small coterie of donors. The test is not majoritarian. An organization with a few dozen contributors or modest gross receipts can, depending on its other income, qualify as a public charity. Yet an organization that relies exclusively on one individual or one family will generally flunk the public charity test.

The public support conditions broadly conform to the Tocquevillian account of exemption and deduction. Consistent with the Tocquevillian view, the public support conditions ensure that the most generous benefits go toward organizations that build social capital beyond a single family or a small number of families. The public support conditions potentially also incentivize insular organizations to reach out more broadly for members. Thus, the public support conditions subsidize the associational bonds that, in the Tocquevillian view, are democracy's glue. The public support conditions also might be justified on information-aggregation grounds (i.e., the Hayekian view). Only when a number of individuals, each with their distinctive epistemic advantages, come together to support an organization does the organization earn the most robust governmental backing.

The importance of the public support conditions should not be overemphasized. The benefits of being a public charity rather than a private foundation are significant, but the difference between public charity and private foundation status still is slight relative to the difference between section 501(c)(3) status and exemption under the noncharitable paragraphs of section 501(c). Moreover, the remarkable recent rise of donor-advised funds allows philanthropists to obtain the benefits of public charity status while still largely retaining control over the allocation of funds themselves. In short, while conditioning tax-preferred status on public support is one strategy that the federal tax system uses to regulate charitable nonprofits, it is a strategy of which the system makes relatively modest use.

Payout Mandates

One more way in which the federal government sometimes regulates nonprofit organizations is to mandate that they distribute a certain percentage of their assets each year. This strategy is employed sparingly. Only private foundations are subject to payout mandates, and the mandate is modest (5 percent of net assets annually).[40] Private foundations can obtain an exemption from this mandate if they qualify as "operating foundations," which generally means that they must spend at least 85 percent of their net income on the active conduct of charitable activities.[41] By far the largest organization in this latter category is the J. Paul Getty Trust, which runs the eponymously named art museum in Los Angeles (Foundation Center 2014). Congress has at various times considered proposals to apply a payout mandate to the largest university endowments, but it has never enacted such a mandate.[42]

The private foundation payout mandate arguably addresses the concern that foundation managers will seek to stockpile wealth for reasons of self-interest. Managers of wealthier foundations are likely to earn higher compensation (in the form of financial benefits and prestige) than managers of foundations with fewer assets, and a manager who spends down all of the foundation's assets is out of a job (Galle 2016). The 5 percent payout mandate may be understood as a relatively unobtrusive (though arguably insufficient) policy response to these sorts of agency costs. The payout mandate also may reflect a policy judgment that the social value of philanthropic spending is higher today than in the future, though if part of the rationale for exemption and deduction is that dispersed individuals are better able to assess the value of various philanthropic projects than a central government is, one might wonder why that same Hayekian argument would not apply to the *timing* of spending as well (see Klausner 2003 for further discussion).

An alternative justification for the payout mandate builds on Tocquevillian premises. The primary incentive for most 501(c)(3) organizations to retain public charity status is to avoid becoming subject to the private foundation payout mandate. The mandate thus nudges charitable nonprofits toward seeking public support. And when such organizations engender associational bonds, they deliver the greatest benefits to society. In this view, the payout mandate for private foundations is the "stick" half of a carrot-and-stick approach toward encouraging charitable nonprofits to play the role that the Tocquevillian account envisions for them.

Less Support, More Strings

This brief tour through the Internal Revenue Code provisions affecting nonprofit organizations has so far focused on provisions that predate the December 2017 tax law. That law—colloquially (though not formally) known as the Tax Cuts and Jobs Act[43]—altered the tax treatment of the nonprofit sector in several significant ways. The result is that the federal tax system now does less to support and more to constrain nonprofit organizations overall. Beyond the actual provisions of the December 2017 law, the politics surrounding the law's passage suggest potential changes in the relationship between Congress and the nonprofit sector.

The most meaningful change affecting the nonprofit sector in the December 2017 law is one that, on its face, has nothing to do with nonprofits at all: the near-doubling of the standard deduction to $12,000 for single taxpayers ($24,000 for married couples filing jointly). The change is offset by a repeal of the deduction for personal exemptions (and for families with three or more members, the net effect of these two changes is an increase in taxable income). For our purposes, the key consequence is that taxpayers will be much more likely to claim the standard deduction under the new law, and taxpayers who claim the standard deduction cannot claim itemized deductions for charitable contributions.

The impact on 501(c)(3) entities and other organizations eligible to receive deductible contributions is likely to be profound. The Joint Committee on Taxation estimates that the percentage of tax units claiming a charitable contribution deduction will fall from around 21 percent under the old law to roughly 9 percent under the new.[44] The total tax expenditure associated with the charitable contribution deduction will decline by approximately 29 percent, according to the Joint Committee's projections. Notably, this anticipated drop is not the result of any change to the charitable contribution deduction itself. Indeed, the most significant change to section 170—the provision governing charitable contributions—was an increase in the cap on deductions for cash contributions to public charities from 50 percent of an individual's adjusted gross income to 60 percent.[45] The nonprofit sector is so tangled up in tax that changes to altogether separate sections of the code can have multibillion-dollar ramifications for nonprofit organizations.

Other changes in the December 2017 law that will affect nonprofit organizations include the doubling of the estate tax exemption and the dramatic cut in the corporate income tax rate. As for the first, the new law raised the amount that taxpayers can transfer to their heirs at death from approximately $5.5 million ($11 million for a married couple) to $11 million ($22 million for a couple). Since the specter of the estate tax had motivated many high-net-worth individuals to make charitable contributions, this change is likely to lead to less giving. Estimates range from a $4 billion to a $7 billion drop attributable to the estate tax change (National Council of Nonprofits 2018; Rooney 2018). As for the corporate tax cut, the reduction in the top statutory rate from 35 percent to 21 percent is likely to have a negative effect on corporate philanthropy, but perhaps more importantly, it reduces the income tax advantage of exempt status by two fifths. In many cases, because of generous expensing provisions, the effective tax rate on corporate investment is zero or less. As discussed shortly, the lower corporate tax rate may cause some nonprofit organizations to shed exempt status altogether.

At the same time as it (indirectly) reduced the tax system's support for the nonprofit sector, Congress also tied on additional strings. The most significant in dollar terms is a rule that prevents exempt organizations from using losses incurred in one unrelated trade or business to offset taxable income from another. For example, if an art museum loses money on gift shop sales of area maps but earns income subject to UBIT by renting an event space, the organization now cannot deduct its gift shop losses against its event rental gains. Lawmakers articulated no rationale for this new rule, which does not apply to for-profit corporate taxpayers (who can indeed use losses from one trade or business to offset income from another). The most plausible explanation for its inclusion in the law is that it raises a modest amount of revenue ($3.5 billion over the next decade, according to the Joint Committee on Taxation[46]), and sponsors of the December 2017 law knew that they needed revenue from somewhere to finance the law's steep cut in corporate rates.

Two other elements of the December 2017 law appear to be designed to align the tax treatment of nonprofits with that of other employers. The first—and much more significant of the two—imposes a 21 percent excise tax on annual compensation in excess of $1 million paid by an exempt organization to any of its five highest-compensated employees.[47] The measure tracks an existing provision that denies a deduction for amounts in excess of $1 million paid by publicly held corporations to their highest compensated officers.[48] Since the corporate income tax rate is now 21 percent, the excise tax on exempt organizations is economically equivalent to the denial of a deduction for taxable publicly held corporations. The new excise tax on exempt organizations can be thought of as a supplement to the nondistribution constraint, insofar as it deters exempt organizations from distributing earnings to executives in the form of salary rather than dividends. A second, more minor measure applies the UBIT (again, a 21 percent tax) to transportation fringe benefits that an exempt organization grants to its employees.[49] This provision is likewise intended to track the treatment of for-profit employers, who now are denied a deduction for transportation fringes.

Last but not least, the new law imposes a 1.4 percent tax on the net investment income of private colleges and universities whose endowment assets exceed $500,000 per student.[50] The financial impact of the new tax—for universities and for the federal fisc—is limited. For Harvard University, with an endowment exceeding $37 billion, the cost would have been a modest $43 million if the provision had been in effect in 2017 (Guillaume 2018). More disconcerting is what the provision may augur about the relationship between the nonprofit sector and the federal tax system. The new tax specifically targets private colleges and universities while sparing other public charities with vast endowments.[51] As N. Gregory Mankiw, a Harvard economist and former advisor to President George W. Bush, noted in the *New York Times*, the tax has never been justified as anything other than "tribal politics" on the part of conservative lawmakers who view elite universities to be too liberal (Mankiw 2017). An unsympathetic interpretation of the change would be that Congress chose to penalize institutions that were doing too much to provide a Tocquevillian counterweight to the dominant political coalition.

The implications of the new law for the relationship between the federal tax system and the nonprofit sector are likely to be far-reaching. The reduction in support and the addition of new strings raise the question of whether some nonprofit organizations will relinquish the benefits of deduction and/or exemption altogether. For example, a church whose pastor seeks to deliver political endorsements from the pulpit might decide to forgo 501(c)(3) status—and thus free itself from the Johnson Amendment—now that nearly nine tenths of taxpayers claim the standard deduction and thus are indifferent between donating to 501(c)(3)s versus 501(c)(4)s. Likewise, an organization such as the PGA Tour—which has several employees whose compensation exceeds $1 million—might decide that the benefits of exemption no longer outweigh the regulatory costs, especially now that the corporate tax rate is so much lower and the new excise tax on excess compensation applies to the entity.[52]

Indeed, similarly motivated exits from exempt status predate December 2017. Fresh off its initial public offering, Google in 2005 announced the creation of Google.org, a corporate philanthropy that has eschewed exempt status altogether and instead operates as a taxable subsidiary (Vise 2005). Insofar as the parent company can claim business expense deductions for Google.org's costs (as it likely can), the company can more or less match the tax benefits that it would derive from exemption under section 501(c)(3) (Hines, Horwitz and Nichols 2010). In a similar vein, Facebook founder Mark Zuckerberg and his spouse, Priscilla Chan, chose in 2015 to establish a limited liability company (LLC) rather than a tax-exempt private foundation in order to pursue their philanthropic ambitions (Singer and Isaac 2015). Because the LLC's primary asset is non-dividend-paying Facebook stock, the tax advantage of private foundation status would have been marginal, while the use of the LLC form allows the couple to avoid the transparency requirements, payout mandates, and restrictions on political activity that would have accompanied private foundation status. The same year that Zuckerberg and Chan established their philanthropic LLC, the National Football League (NFL)—previously a 501(c)(6) organization—chose to give up that status in part so that it could escape from the transparency requirements that exemption entailed (Belson 2015).

The existence—and increasing attractiveness—of "exit options" such as these limit the potential efficacy of tax law as a tool for regulating the nonprofit sector. Efforts to impose additional activity limits, transparency requirements, and other constraints on exempt organizations run the risk of causing those organizations to opt out of exempt status altogether. To be sure, charitable nonprofits that continue to derive significant revenue from high-income itemizers will almost certainly decide to retain their 501(c)(3) status. And still other organizations may conclude that the reputational benefits of tax-exempt status exceed the regulatory costs. The point remains, though, that as the tax system provides less and less support to the nonprofit sector through exemption and deduction, the ability of policy makers to attach additional strings to exemption and deduction will wane.

Entanglement's Future

The scenario sketched out in the previous paragraph may seem tolerable on first glance. A viable exit option would protect nonprofit organizations from overly intrusive regulatory interventions. But the exit option is viable only insofar as exemption and—especially—deduction cease to deliver the support that they once did. For those who believe that a vibrant democracy requires a robust third sector and that a robust third sector depends in part on the tax system's assistance, a scenario in which nonprofit organizations are nearly indifferent between exempt and nonexempt status is a rather gloomy outcome.

To be clear, such a grim scenario has not yet come to pass. Millions of taxpayers—mostly those with six- and seven-figure incomes—will continue to claim itemized deductions for charitable contributions. Moreover, the changes in the December 2017 tax law most likely to drive a decline in charitable giving—the increase in the standard deduction and the doubling of the estate tax exemption—are set to expire at the end of 2025. Yet even if we revert to the status quo ex ante, the tax incentive for charitable contributions will continue to apply only to the minority of taxpayers who itemize their deductions. The tax incentive for charitable giving has not been broadly participatory for quite some time (Colinvaux 2017).

For precisely this reason, many members of the academic and think-tank communities have long supported replacing the charitable contribution deduction with a credit. All taxpayers who donate to 501(c)(3) organizations (or who donate above a certain percentage of their income to such entities) would claim a credit of somewhere between 12 cents and 25 cents—depending on the particulars of the proposal—for each dollar that they give.[53] Concededly, such a change might distort the decisions of some high-bracket taxpayers as to whether to donate money or volunteer their time. Imagine a lawyer in the 37 percent income tax bracket who can earn $400 an hour but whose time as a volunteer is worth only $300 to a charity. Setting tax considerations aside, the economically efficient decision—if the lawyer wants to donate an hour's worth of work to a charity—would be for the lawyer to work an additional hour and to donate the $400 that she earns. But if she is taxed on that $400 at a 37 percent rate and she receives a credit of only 12 cents on the dollar for contributions, an extra hour of work will finance a cash contribution of less than $300.[54] She may therefore choose to volunteer the extra hour rather than to bill an additional hour as a lawyer and contribute the proceeds. Note, though, that while from a strictly economic perspective this is an inefficient outcome, from a Tocquevillian perspective it may be a feature rather than a bug. Encouraging individuals to engage with nonprofit organizations beyond the simple act of writing a check is consonant with the view that the nonprofit sector strengthens democratic society by building thick and lasting associational bonds.

Perhaps a graver risk is that a charitable contribution credit—by making the fact of government support more transparent—will also break the long-lasting ideological détente among lawmakers with respect to the federal tax system's treatment of the nonprofit sector. Prior to December 2017, politicians had for the most part exhibited remarkable self-restraint in this regard. Neither conservatives nor liberals had sought to use the rules governing exemption and deduction to systematically favor their side or disadvantage the other. The *Bob Jones* case, despite Justice Powell's worries, did not lead the IRS, Congress, or the courts down a slippery slope of deciding which viewpoints would and would not render an organization ineligible for exempt status. Successive Republican administrations cut off federal funding for NGOs that provided abortion counseling, but no administration sought to tear away the tax-exempt status of such groups. A controversy arose in 2013 with respect to allegations that the IRS under the Obama administration had singled out conservative political groups seeking tax-exempt status for special scrutiny, but a subsequent investigation by the Treasury Department's inspector general revealed that the alleged targeting was in fact part of an IRS effort to police the limits on political activities by exempt organizations that affected conservative and liberal groups alike.[55]

In this limited respect, "exemption" may indeed be a reasonably accurate description of the relationship between the nonprofit sector and the federal tax system. This area of law has, for much of our history, remained apart from the ideological wars waged in other tax and nontax fields. The 2013 uproar marked a notable deviation from that norm, and the imposition of the endowment tax in the December 2017 law arguably did as well. The health of the nonprofit sector will depend in no small part on whether these two developments mark the beginning of a broader trend.

In sum, support of the nonprofit sector through exemption and (in some cases) deduction inevitably leads to entanglement of the administrative, political, and market varieties. Yet the Hayekian, Tocquevillian, and Pigouvian rationales for government subsidies to the nonprofit sector require a degree of separation between the nonprofit sector and the state. The six strategies outlined in this chapter seek to strike a balance between excessive entanglement and releasing all strings. Few would defend the existing balance as optimal in all respects, but if and as it is recalibrated, the fundamental trade-off between support and entanglement will remain.

PART II

POLITICS OF
THE PUBLIC SPHERE

THE STUDY OF POLITICS HAS LONG DEVOTED CONSIDERABLE attention to associational life and its role in a democratic society. From Alexis de Tocqueville to Robert Putnam, there is wide engagement with the roles of an autonomous civil society in protecting and strengthening liberal polities. The current chapters attend to this classic theme but bring new issues to the fore. A first recurrent theme across the chapters is that whereas early visions of the nonprofit sector asserted its place as independent from government, it is increasingly problematic to accept the premise that nonprofit organizations operate apart from or outside governing arrangements. Shifts involving privatization have generated more complex combinations of public funding and service provision, bringing increased responsibility and authority. Additional political changes have opened new spaces for nonprofit organizations and associations, leading to greater involvement in advocating for their own causes.

A second theme is that these developments are evident in the rise of new governance arrangements not only in industrialized liberal democratic societies but also in the emerging but contested role of nonprofits in authoritarian or newly democratized regimes, and in the centrality of nonprofit organizations and foundations in steering investments throughout the developing world. The chapters consider the political implications of the nonprofit sector in relatively illiberal times and places, including the massive inequality and rising populism in present-day America.

A third theme is that as a consequence of rising perceptions of nonindependence of the nonprofit sector, the categorical distinctions that justify its special privileges such as tax exemption have themselves become important sources of political contention. This growing contestation over the category of nonprofit organization draws attention to the increasing importance of the formal organizational architecture of civil society as a political matter. In contrast, when weighing the set of political arrangements that is best or socially just, the chapters here call new attention to the intersection of politics and organizational form. Laws governing the protection of private property, contract enforcement, and various corporate forms shape the nature of the nonprofit sector and its implications for justice.

In Chapter 6, Ted Lechterman and Rob Reich use the logic of political theory to appraise and justify social and political arrangements within and around the nonprofit sector. Justification is required because the nonprofit sector plays a role in shaping life outcomes and chances. But emerging challenges unsettle conventional thinking about the ethics of nonprofit enterprise—pervasive and increasing inequality; the erosion of traditional boundaries between market, state, and nonprofit operations; and the globalization of nonprofit activity.

Lechterman and Reich begin by delineating the study of associational life from a purported nonprofit sector, leading to a discussion of why the distinction is important for political theory. The nonprofit sector is that portion of associational life and of civil society that is formally incorporated and faces legal constraints on the distribution of profits along with benefits such as special tax treatment. One concern of a political theory of the nonprofit sector revolves around examining whether limitations on profit-seeking are necessary or sufficient to justify the privileges that typically attach to nonprofits. In coming to an assessment of the nonprofit sector, they contend that normative appraisal benefits from combining philosophical and empirical analysis, illustrating this point with a discussion of the nonprofit sector's responsibilities for poverty relief.

Throughout, Lechterman and Reich defend the family of political theories called liberal democracy. This group of theories spells out how liberal democratic commitments generate a specific set of regulative ideals against which to assess the current nonprofit architecture and identify directions for reform. Specifically, they show ways in which—under liberal democratic ideals—nonprofits can and should promote, respect, or embody principles of justice.

In Chapter 7, Elisabeth S. Clemens explores the political roles of nonprofit organizations, drawing out implications for the politics of choice, mobilization, and arbitrage. Classic economic and political theories of nonprofit organization began from the assumption of individuals with clear preferences. Heterogeneous demand for government services in a democratic system where policies are aimed at the median voter explained why government could not provide for all citizens. And a mistrust of the profit motive in some circumstances explained why markets could also not provide many social goods. In the space between, early theories asserted, we see the rise of nonprofit organizations. But that starting place has been destabilized, both conceptually and historically.

As post–World War II expansions in social policy increasingly relied on forms of contracting out to nonprofit organizations, it has become more difficult for citizens to recognize which programs are publicly funded. The legal status of nonprofit organizations can be a vehicle for gaining competitive advantage between organizations as much as a signal of public-regarding or altruistic organizational behavior. Furthermore, as private entities presumed to have a distinct public mission, nonprofit organizations can extend governmental capabilities in ways that may elude democratic accountability. At the same time, these organizations can enable citizens and private actors to pursue alternative paths to civic mobilization and the production of public goods in situations where government fails to act or even opposes some form of social provision or expression. From the vantage point of political sociology, this linking of private organizations to a mission that is publicly recognized, sometimes subsidized, and often legitimating, creates great potential as a site for innovation and arbitrage between different domains.

In Chapter 8 Sarah Reckhow emphasizes the entanglement of politics and philanthropy in an era of growing income inequality. The number of billionaires in the United States has ballooned since the mid-1990s. Many of these individuals are deeply engaged in philanthropy during their lifetimes, as evidenced by new efforts such as the Giving Pledge, started by Bill and Melinda Gates and Warren Buffett. Philanthropy and politics in the United States have a long and intertwined history; decades-old tax policies enable the creation of private philanthropies and regulate their activities. Yet increasing economic stratification and the concentration of wealth among elites is reshaping the relationship between philanthropy and politics. As public-sector budgets become more constrained by legacy costs and concerns about deficits, funders come to the table in ever-larger numbers and with substantial resources to engage with the political system. Contemporary philanthropists have found many outlets for their ideas and initiatives in the political system—funding policy research and advocacy, piloting programs, and sometimes partnering directly with government.

Reckhow spells out the consequences of expanding philanthropic involvement in politics using data on giving and case studies. The data show that philanthropic giving and political giving by wealthy donors are increasingly linked, and both are expanding. Major living philanthropists support related causes in both charitable work and campaign donations. This overlap occurs in part through the use of organizational vehicles that enable direct supporting for lobbying and political campaigns, which traditional private foundations are barred from funding. She also reveals how philanthropists work in coordination to influence politics—with one another and by convening groups in joint efforts. One form of this coordinated political activity, sometimes called *weaponized philanthropy*, has a "dark" or "undercover" aspect. Whether given as "dark money" or through fully transparent means, the coordinated efforts of very wealthy donors can have far-reaching consequences on the political system in areas such as education, business regulation, and environmental policy.

Overall, the chapters in this section convey a cautious optimism: nonprofits may aim to promote the greater good, but their benefits should not be immediately assumed. There are high stakes to points of political contestation in the nonprofit sector; without care and attention to governing principles, the sector is susceptible to the same dark forces of elitism, inequality, and the pursuit of wealth and power that can corrupt governments. As our recognition of the potential for both good and evil grows, the study of nonprofits, philanthropy, and politics is blossoming. Future inquiries, such as looking at the role of major funders in local and global politics, developing a sharper picture of why and how the wealthy use the nonprofit sector as a vehicle for influence, and normative evaluations of the various possible arrangements, are sure to be of great import.

POLITICAL THEORY AND THE NONPROFIT SECTOR

Ted Lechterman and Rob Reich

POLITICAL THEORY AIMS TO EXAMINE social and political arrangements and asks how these can be appraised and justified. The goal is normative (to evaluate or prescribe) rather than positive (to explain or predict). Social and political arrangements have powerful effects on the life course of anyone subject to them. They define the rules of social cooperation, and different arrangements will distribute society's resources and power in different ways. They are, moreover, not natural facts but human conventions, and thus amenable to change. Political theory asks, therefore, what set of social and political arrangements is best or just? Or, if the best proves to be the enemy of the good, which arrangements are legitimate and deserving of compliance even if less than ideal or fully just?

With this orientation, it is not surprising that political theorists frequently focus their attention on the state and its formal institutions, exploring what makes the exercise of coercive force legitimate and what justice requires in law and public policy. Law and public policy emanate from the state, but they shape social life far beyond formal public institutions. Accordingly, political theorists also examine realms beyond the state.[1] In the past generation, political theorists have given extensive thought to the status of property, markets, and commercial corporations (Anderson 1993, 2017; Murphy and Nagel 2002; Satz 2012; Ciepley 2013), to the status of justice between states (Nagel 2005; Miller 2007; James 2012; Wenar 2016), and to the family and the ethics of the parent-child relationship (Okin 1989; Brighouse and Swift 2014).

Political theorists have also devoted considerable attention to civil society and associational life and their role in a flourishing democratic society. Alexis de Tocqueville (Tocqueville 2012) is the canonical nineteenth-century exemplar, while Robert Putnam (Putnam, Leonardi, and Nanetti 1993; Putnam 2000) is arguably the preeminent twentieth-century scholar. But the corporate form we today call a nonprofit organization did not exist in Tocqueville's day. And Putnam barely makes any mention of nonprofits. This omission is typical of the discipline. Political scientists and theorists alike have paid little attention to the organizational architecture of civil society and the nonprofit sector.

Before proceeding, we propose some conceptual clarification. *Civil society* we take to refer to the myriad associations, formal and informal, enduring and ephemeral, large and small, professional and amateur, that arise in any social order where human freedom is protected to some degree. When afforded individual liberty, the natural sociality of human beings will bring them into diverse affiliations. The associations in civil society stand between the most primordial of associations—the family—and the one that claims a monopoly on coercive power—the state.[2] As we explore in this chapter, civil society associations are a site of mediation between the individual and the state. Within these associations, humans congregate for some common purpose or activity, including religious, educational, cultural, professional, political, and athletic pursuits. For some theorists, civil society encompasses the workplace (Scalet and Schmidtz 2002), and for others even the family counts as a part of civil society (as discussed in Rosenblum 2002). For our purposes, civil society is the associational realm beneath (or in the case of global civil society, above) the state; in this realm, humans assemble into groups to pursue joint projects, independent of any formal, bureaucratic status or incorporation.

Associational life we take to refer to the portion of civil society that is marked by *voluntary membership*. In this respect, the family fits uneasily with associational life insofar as children cannot be said to be voluntary members. Most of civil society is constituted by associations in which people join voluntarily and have freestanding permission to exit. Associational life importantly includes informal associations (the bowling league, the book club, the weekly trivia night at the pub) as well as formal associations (the political party, the religious congregation, the professional society). Some scholars may also regard commercial entities as part of this category.

We follow conventional practice in defining the *nonprofit sector* as the portion of associational life and of civil society that meets two additional criteria. The first is formal incorporation. Within the sector lie organizations that have official standing. It is possible to count—at least in principle—the precise number of nonprofit organizations in each society. It is not possible to count the full number of associations in any society, for too many of them, such as the book club, are unregistered and leave no legal trace. The second criterion is a legal restriction on the distribution of profits that distinguishes nonprofits from business corporations. Nonprofit organizations are limited by law in the way they remunerate their stakeholders, often in return for legal privileges such as tax exemptions. Whether limitations on profit-seeking are necessary or sufficient to justify the privileges that typically attach to nonprofits, and whether "nonprofitness" as such is a useful analytical category, are longstanding questions that course through this chapter.

Do We Need a Political Theory of Nonprofit Enterprise?

Political theory aims to ask—and answer—foundational questions that situate the presence of associational life and the formal organization of a nonprofit sector in relation to a broader political economy that includes the market and the state. These questions include the following: What is the difference, if any, between civil society and the nonprofit sector? Why have a formal nonprofit sector in the first place? If there is to be a nonprofit sector, how should it be organized and governed? Should the nonprofit sector be a society's primary (or secondary) channel for addressing poverty and inequality? Should the set of organizations eligible for nonprofit status be greater or narrower in scope? Should the nonprofit sector welcome commercialization or oppose it? How should power be distributed among donors, managers, and beneficiaries? Which, if any, nonprofit activities deserve public subsidy?

It may seem odd to insist as we do that normative assessment of the nonprofit sector must refer to distinctively political concerns. The nonprofit sector is generally regarded as a natural topic of sociological, economic, or legal inquiry—related to politics, certainly, but not an inherently political matter. This thought rests on a misconception. The nonprofit sector is not an autonomous social phenomenon, spontaneously generated and regulated by an internal logic, as a casual reading of leading economic theories of nonprofit enterprise might suggest (Weisbrod 1975; Hansmann 1987). But neither are civil society and associational life pure conventions of politics, elements of human sociality that disappear if the government were to be swept away in revolution. Consider, for example, the long-standing existence of universities, such as Oxford or Bologna, and religious communities, such as the Catholic Church, that predate the modern state and have survived with considerable organizational stability across centuries and many different governments.

Though it may not be an invention of the state, the nonprofit sector is best understood as *an artifact of the state*, its definition and contours shaped in profound ways by political choices. The sector depends on laws defining property and contracts and codifying various corporate forms, including trusts, foundations, and a multiplicity of nongovernmental organizations. Different configurations of these laws give rise to vastly different specifications of the nonprofit sector—including no formally organized sector at all, but rather a realm of merely informal associational life. This susceptibility to legal stimulus is one powerful reason why the nonprofit sector differs across time and place.

This conceptual discussion sets the stage for considering the more substantive questions for which recourse to political theory is necessary to deliver answers. The design of the nonprofit sector in any society depends on overarching political ideals and accompanying institutional frameworks. Which functions or activities a society allocates to the nonprofit sector reflect fundamental political choices. Political theory is also necessary for justifying and appraising alternative specifications of a society's institutional division of labor. Finally, a central concern of political theory is the exercise of power and how it can be legitimate; insofar as the nonprofit sector involves exercises of power—as it most certainly does—it is an apt topic for political analysis.

Political Theory and the Shape and Purpose of a Nonprofit Sector

Political theorists frequently operate at the level of abstract principle, which is sometimes thought to make such theorizing indulgently utopian at best and utterly irrelevant at worst. But abstraction is unavoidable. The meaning of (e.g.) liberty, equality, security, or diversity, or how these ideals should be ordered in relation to one another, is not self-explanatory; it requires careful normative argumentation. Similarly, people disagree profoundly about the best interpretation and defense of democracy; to defend the value of a democratic society is to take a position on abstract issues such as what constitutes a people, what makes a decision-making process fair, and whether, and if so how, democratic arrangements can produce good outcomes.

Political theory is also productively engaged with empirical phenomena and the work of social scientists. Jeremy Waldron's label for this is "*political* political theory" (Waldron

2016). We share Waldron's aim to map the distinctive *philosophical* tools of normative analysis onto questions of institutional design and performance at multiple levels. Political theory in this mode is distinctive in its attentiveness to the evaluation of institutions in political and social life and in its invitation to dialogue with social scientists and historians. Chapter 7, "Nonprofits as Boundary Markers," by Elisabeth S. Clemens, for example, explores nonprofit organizations as private entities presumed to pursue a public mission. Chapter 2, "History of Associational Life and the Nonprofit Sector in the United States," by Benjamin Soskis, recounts the evolution of nonprofit organizations in the twentieth century. Clemens and Soskis are principally interested in describing; we by contrast aim to identify and prescribe institutional arrangements that better fulfill core political ideals.

To see more plainly how this interdisciplinary engagement can be valuable, take for example the typical concern of political theory with the fair distribution of resources. The nonprofit sector in the United States has historically played a considerable role in addressing poverty and deprivation; less so in social democratic countries. Why is this? Is one model superior to the other? What level of redistribution, if any, should be the responsibility of the nonprofit sector? We take up these questions in the following subsection.

Distributing Justice Through Nonprofit Enterprise

Though modern theories of justice disagree about what forms of equality are morally required, virtually all regard unchosen poverty as deeply objectionable. Most of the philosophical debate about justice over the past three decades has been concerned with specifying what forms of disadvantage are justifiable and, conversely, which forms of disadvantage trigger valid claims for redress. The perspectives that have garnered the most support (arguably, social egalitarianism [Anderson 1999], luck egalitarianism [Dworkin 2000], and neorepublicanism [Pettit 1997]) are united in the idea that justice condemns certain forms of relative deprivation—on some people being worse off than others. By contrast, right-wing theories of justice tend to be more skeptical of equality's purported demands, seeing them as rivals to prized forms of liberty or valuable traditions (Nozick 1974). Even so, leading right-wing theories tend to agree that justice requires robust protections against absolute deprivation—on some people falling below a minimum threshold of opportunity or well-being (Friedman 1962; Gaus 2010; Tomasi 2012). Immiseration is incompatible with justice.

A familiar idea about policies structuring the nonprofit sector is that the state should encourage donations to poverty-relieving organizations and discourage donations for other activities (Cooter 2003; Murphy and Nagel 2002; Fleischer 2009). Proponents of this common position often remind us of the sector's historical connections to almsgiving. The word *charity*, which has now come to represent a technical legal concept, originally referred to a Christian virtue of benevolence. On some readings of the historical record, the direct ancestors of the nonprofit organization were ecclesiastical societies devoted to caring for the sick and destitute. By drawing vivid contrasts between beleaguered soup kitchens and lavish museums and opera houses, traditionalists wish to suggest that the nonprofit sector has betrayed its original moral purpose. But engaging with social science and history exposes this position to some complications and contains helpful lessons.

First, this traditionalist position may be misinformed about the historical relationship of the nonprofit sector to welfare service delivery—at least in the United States. Although nonprofit organizations do provide a significant amount of services to the less advantaged, very little of this activity is financed by donations. And this is by design. As historians of the nonprofit sector point out, the modern nonprofit sector took shape in response to the federal antipoverty initiatives of the 1960s (Hall 1992; Dunning, forthcoming). These initiatives offered substantial federal grants and contracts for the formation of community groups that would deliver social assistance. Many of the organizations in current operation formed directly in response to these incentives, and they derive most of their funding from government grants and contracts, along with fees paid by clients for their services. In other words, most of the nonprofits that conduct social service delivery today are not traditional private charities; these nonprofits are best understood as the face of the American welfare state.

Most observers will still conclude that the poor remain cruelly underserved by current policy. But the evidence suggests that responsibility for this failure does not necessarily lie with the stinginess of American donors or the convolutions of the charitable tax deduction. We can also explain the persistence of poverty as a failure of voters to authorize sufficient state funding to service-delivery groups. Alternatively, we can explain the persistence of poverty as a failure of the state to represent the views of its citizens. (A common finding in political science is that government policies tend to reflect the preferences of the wealthy for limited social spending [Bartels 2016].)

Once we broaden our gaze beyond donations, we confront the further possibility that the persistence of poverty has less to do with policies toward the nonprofit sector and more to do with policy choices in other domains that affect the distribution of wealth and opportunity in general. Suppose that inequities in education, criminal justice, and housing markets provided the best explanation for the persistence of poverty. If this were true, it would mean, perversely, that continuing to define the moral purpose of the nonprofit sector as poverty relief would require the maintenance of unjust institutions so that poverty would persist for nonprofits to address. If certain forms of poverty are an injustice, and redressing injustice requires that we seek in the first instance solutions at the level of the state, clinging to nonprofits as the best mechanisms for poverty relief is to seek a solution in the wrong place (Kymlicka 2001).

The traditionalist position also struggles to make sense of the fact that the nonprofit sector, as we know it today, houses hospitals and universities, sports leagues and book clubs, nature conservancies and identity groups, think tanks and public interest groups, trade associations and insurance cooperatives. The legal definition of the nonprofit sector in the United States classifies organizations into twenty-nine categories, with different tax status and permissions across the range (26 U.S. Code § 501). Depending on how its policy proposals are constructed, a position claiming that welfare service delivery organizations are the only entities worthy of public recognition risks exiling numerous valuable activities and associations that have nothing to do with addressing the gap between rich and poor.

Additionally, some philosophical positions suggest that the responsibility for securing distributive justice is irreducibly collective in nature. Principles of distributive justice apply directly to the formal institutions of the state, and they can only be rightly operationalized through public regulation and administration (Julius 2003; Cordelli 2011; Scheffler 2015; Beerbohm 2016; cf. Murphy 1998). From this perspective, the persistence of poverty is strictly a failure of the collective responsibilities of citizens, discharged through the powers of the state, not of insufficient private generosity. Even if private benefactors could make up the shortfall in funds needed to successfully relieve poverty, we should prefer a collective solution in which we act together as citizens rather than individually as donors in redressing injustice. We explore this idea further in the Emergent Controversies section of this chapter.

This state-centric view of distributive justice faces challenges of its own. Is the state nothing more than a justice machine, and an exclusive provider at that? Suppose that a society appears to be resolutely opposed to discharging duties of justice through taxation and transfer schemes. "Everyday-libertarian" resistance to taxation is a mainstay of American political culture (Murphy and Nagel 2002). Given popular resistance to the policies that justice seems to require, does justice itself recommend a search for second-best options? If so, perhaps applying greater incentives for voluntary responses to poverty and inequality can be justified on grounds of feasibility. To make this case, however, one would have to defend a position that qualifies approaches to justice in relation to popular opinion, a position that accepts limits on the realization of ideals from the very start of theorizing about what ideals might demand of us.

This discussion also highlights the practical limitations of normative theorizing. It would be nice if political theory could provide us with determinate guidance on all questions of institutional design, public policy, and civic obligation. But even political theories developed in close cooperation with insights from social science can rarely offer more than general guidance. There are often a wide range of possible avenues for realizing a given normative principle. Selecting options that are most feasible, expedient, or sustainable in a particular historical setting—especially in the face of opposition—must draw on specialized knowledge and individual judgment. Nonetheless, discussions of political strategy are rudderless and incoherent without the grounding provided by normative principles.

Nonprofits as Democracy's Handmaidens

Taking stock of the various activities that occur within the nonprofit sector has led many social scientists to conclude that voluntary organizations have a special relationship to democracy that cannot be reduced to a function of welfare service-delivery. We note three ways of understanding this relationship (but see Clemens, Chapter 7, "Nonprofits as Boundary Markers," for deeper reflection):

Nonprofit organizations as a bulwark against the state. Civil society organizations can play an important role in maintaining individual rights, such as freedom of conscience, expression, and association. Taken as a whole, the sector can serve as a bulwark against potential invasion of these liberties by an overreaching state. At the same time, civil society depends on a strong legal system of individual civil and political rights. In the absence of the most basic rights guaranteed by the state, including rights to free speech, assembly, and privacy, nothing recognizably like a modern democracy could possibly exist. Of course, civil society in some form or another persists in nondemocratic societies, though as we discuss further shortly, its shape and function is quite different.

In the United States and other liberal-democratic countries, a robust system of general rights has coexisted uneasily with broad denials of rights to specific disadvantaged groups, and nonprofit organizations have been one of the most important mechanisms for confronting these juxtapositions. For example, nonprofit organizations in the United States have been at the forefront of the movements for women's suffrage (National American Woman Suffrage Association, National Woman's Party), civil rights for African Americans (National Association for the Advancement of Colored People, Southern Christian Leadership Conference), and rights for gay and lesbian Americans (Gay and Lesbian Advocates and Defenders, Human Rights Campaign). Associational life and the matrix of nonprofit organizations that partially compose civil society have many times been open to marginalized or disadvantaged groups of citizens who have been denied participation in formal political institutions.

Nonprofits have thus served as one of the primary vehicles by which these denials of rights are resisted. Even when disadvantaged groups have been excluded from specific civil society organizations in addition to the formal political process, they have been able to create their own groups within civil society. In the twentieth century, civil society groups like Amnesty International and, more recently, the Electronic Frontier Foundation have pushed for the expansion and equal application of individual rights. These groups work not just by opposing intrusive government actions but also by working alongside journalists to inform and mobilize public opinion about these issues. Think here of the Charter 77 movement in communist Czechoslovakia that called attention to the failure of the government to respect human rights despite the fact that it had been a signatory to numerous human rights declarations and documents.

We might say that one function nonprofit organizations can serve beyond service delivery is to work as a *counterpublic*, permitting and transmitting the expression of ideas that run counter to official government policy. Nonprofit organizations can do more than help protect individual rights; they are in large measure the way citizens exercise their rights. The rights to association, speech, and religious liberty are all exercised in the context of formal (and informal) groups. It is through participation in these groups that people develop their interests and passions and meet others who share them. As a venue for expressive association, a vibrant nonprofit sector is a crucial part of life in a liberal-democratic society.

Tocqueville made a similar observation in the early nineteenth century when he posited that the many voluntary associations he saw throughout his travels could serve as a "countervailing" power to the federal government (Tocqueville 2012). Much earlier, the Roman historians Polybius and Livy identified the organs of a "contestatory citizenry" as crucial to the health of a republic, a theme that neorepublican political theorists have recently resuscitated (Pettit 1997).

Forming and transmitting political preferences through civil society. A defining characteristic of a liberal-democratic political system is that government is responsive to the preferences and interests of citizens. Civil society organizations can be involved in this defining feature in at least two distinct ways. First, civil society organizations can help citizens discover, develop, and refine their preferences and interests. Second, these preferences and interests can then be transmitted to the formal institutions of government in part through the actions of civil society organizations. As the arena in which citizens discover and refine their preferences and interests, civil society takes on the role that Jürgen Habermas calls "the public sphere" (Habermas [1962] 1991). According to this view, democracy, a system whose goal is to enact the public's vision of the common good, can be meaningful only if there are, outside the formal institutions of the state, mechanisms by which the public can debate and form visions of the common good in the first place. We should not assume that citizen preferences exist in a vacuum or are generated as if by magic. Though democracy's procedural outcomes are the laws and policies enacted by and through formal state institutions, democracy requires a deliberative space outside these formal institutions. In the United States, this vision can be found in both the constitutional provisions guaranteeing freedom of speech and of the press and the widespread worries that perceived declines in the quality and quantity of public discourse are threats to democracy itself.

Civil society organizations as a training ground for democratic life. Tocqueville's *Democracy in America* is a classic statement of the role of civil society organizations in helping Americans learn to be good democratic citizens (Tocqueville 2012). Tocqueville marveled at Americans' habit of solving local problems by forming associations. He saw this tendency as not just an efficient way of getting things done—one that he contrasted with the sclerotic, top-down approach current in much of still-monarchical Europe—but as a crucial way in which the democratic culture of the United States was preserved and reproduced over time. Through institutions like town hall meetings, Americans learned to see themselves as authors of the rules that bound them, and Tocqueville believed that Americans accepted only rules that could plausibly be understood this way.

In the twentieth century, these observations about the importance of civil society for democracy were buttressed by comparative studies of democratic systems that succeeded and failed worldwide. A vigorous civil society exists almost everywhere democracy persists over time. This longstanding view of particular kinds of civil society as necessary supports of democratic governance led to significant anxiety when it was recognized in the late twentieth and early twenty-first centuries that large national membership organizations, which had been some of the most visible and popular civil society institutions, were decreasing in size if not dying out entirely. Drawing on a path-breaking investigation of differences in social conditions between regions of Italy, Robert Putnam popularized the idea of social capital: the value of interpersonal bonds between citizens (Putnam et al. 1993; Putnam 2000). In *Bowling Alone* and other work, he argued that social capital was essential for individual well-being and the health of a democratic regime overall. He also sounded an alarm that social capital in America was declining, potentially putting the democratic system at risk.

Each of the foregoing vignettes reveals how infusing political theory with historical and sociological investigation can broaden our understanding about the roles that the sector might play, along with the different virtues that correspond to these roles. Although welfare service delivery is one potential function of the nonprofit sector, the sector can also perform critical functions in supporting a democratic order.

The Nonprofit Sector and Liberal Democracy

Ideals of freedom of conscience, speech, and association, which individuals can use to explore or realize their own conceptions of the good life (Kymlicka 2002; Sievers 2010), are at the heart of liberalism as a political philosophy. This approach holds that the state should be limited in its reach, that individuals are worthy of equal respect, and that coercively imposed arrangements must be justifiable to each of their subjects (Waldron 1987). Recognition of these liberties is what opens up space for a realm of association that sits between the realms of state and family, mediating between that which is formally public (the state) and that which is thought most private (the family).

Although forms of nonprofit organizational activity exist within many other regime types, they are often at odds with prevailing norms. Strains of communitarian thought and practice deny that a political order should include a realm of association independent from the state (as discussed in Rosenblum and Post 2002). Rather, from this standpoint, human societies succeed only when they operate as organic wholes. Collective control over society ostensibly enables social harmony, economic prosperity, and virtuous living. From this perspective, a realm of free association flourishing between the household and the state threatens to dissolve communal bonds; it paves a road to faction and anomie. Thus, even as nonprofits begin to proliferate in places like China and Singapore, they appear to occupy an unstable position, caught between a desire to assert their independence and the fear of state repression or co-optation (Lin 2015; Lee and Han 2016; Su, Li, and Tao 2018; Clemens, Chapter 7, "Nonprofits as Boundary Markers").

It is also difficult to defend the nonprofit sector without a commitment to democracy. A nonprofit sector and democratic governance are to a great extent mutually reinforcing. The emergence of nonprofit organizations under authoritarian conditions tends to create pressure on the state to respond to popular demands. In Eastern Europe, nonprofit organizations (in cooperation with other elements of civil society) are often credited with helping to dismantle the authoritarian regimes of the Soviet Union.[3]

To defend the idea of a nonprofit sector, therefore, is to defend the ideal of liberal democracy. And this implication is not regrettable. Liberal democracy furnishes an attractive normative ideal for the conditions of modern life. It is an ideal supported by centuries of theory and practice. Until recently, many, if not most, societies either conceived of themselves as liberal democracies or aspired to become so. Despite the rise of illiberal democracies and electoral authoritarianism, the desirability of the liberal-democratic ideal remains unvarnished. Put simply, if we ask on what basis any society should be ordered, the best—or most defensible—answer available is to embrace the ideals of liberal democracy.

What, then, does a liberal-democratic ideal mean for the nonprofit sector? How should the sector fit within this ideal? And how can the liberal-democratic ideal guide societies under social conditions that are hostile to it (a question to which we return in the final section)?

These questions immediately push us back to the question of what exactly liberal democracy means. In the abstract, liberalism describes a political philosophy in which liberty or freedom of the individual is central. Individual liberty is taken to be a default position, a starting presumption, and restrictions on liberty, especially those imposed by the state through coercive means, stand in need of justification. The foundational role of individual liberty delivers a limited government that respects human conscience and religious diversity, with further promises of economic prosperity: in Thomas Jefferson's famous words, "life, liberty, and the pursuit of happiness." In the abstract, democracy describes a method of collective self-governance marked by moral and political equality among its members. Democracy can involve direct participation by all or, in large-scale societies, representative government involving periodic elections.

One can very easily see connections to these elements in the contemporary nonprofit sector. For instance, welfare service-delivery agencies appear to serve equality in some sense; advocacy groups and political parties assist in representation; sports leagues, arts organizations, and religious societies contribute to the sector's pluralism. However, appreciating these connections can also lead to a common fallacy. Some commentators jump to the conclusion that this particular way of structuring civil society exemplifies the requirements of liberal democracy (e.g., Frumkin 2009). However, the presence of liberal-democratic elements in civil society does not on its own argue for the justifiability of their present configuration.

We must beware the temptation to resolve a normative question by consulting public opinion or resorting to survey responses (e.g., Schlesinger, Mitchell, and Gray 2004; Prewitt et al. 2006). This might be called *Weber's fallacy*—mistaking descriptive legitimacy for normative legitimacy.[4] That people comply with or express support for some social standard is no demonstration that the standard is normatively justified or legitimate. Landmark analyses have shown that under certain circumstances there is no way of aggregating majority preferences into a coherent summary position (Arrow 1951). Even if this were possible, a majority opinion can be profoundly mistaken. For instance, political scientists have shown convincingly that majorities have access to limited arrays of facts and fall prey to all sorts of cognitive biases when making political decisions (Achen and Bartels 2017).

In sum, therefore, making normative claims about the nonprofit sector requires a systematic argument about how the different ingredients of the liberal-democratic ideal fit together, and, in turn, how the institutional architecture of the nonprofit sector should be designed to support this ideal.

In what follows, we show how different ways of understanding and ordering the various elements of liberal-democratic principles lead to dramatically different implications for how the nonprofit sector should be organized. We then consider how a society might make legitimate decisions about the nonprofit sector despite abiding disagreement about the ideal architecture for nonprofit activity.

Liberty

We start by focusing on liberty. What is the proper place of liberty in the liberal-democratic ideal, and how does this vision bear on the nonprofit sector? Libertarians rank liberty at the apex of all values and understand it in a specific way: individuals have natural rights to self-ownership, which give them strong claims to private property and against state interference (Nozick 1974). In turn, this position downgrades the value of equality. It holds that while every person is equally free to exercise his or her own natural abilities, no one is entitled to equalized opportunities to participate in economic or political life. Pluralism and efficiency are treated as beneficial by-products of the exercise of natural liberty, but not things to be promoted in themselves.

Libertarians tend to be skeptical about taxation except insofar as it is necessary to protect individual liberty—such as by providing national defense and enforcing laws against theft, murder, assault, trespass, and fraud. The nonprofit sector is best understood as the realm in which individuals exercise their liberty free from coercive interference. Two important institutional implications flow from a libertarian perspective. First, democratic majorities should not subsidize activity in the nonprofit sector, as subsidies necessarily involve taxing individuals for purposes that are not strictly necessary for the preservation of liberty (Fleischer 2015). Second, because nonprofit organizations should be treated as voluntary private associations, governed exclusively by their members, it is impermissible for the state to impose any more extensive constraints on nonprofits, such as nondiscrimination laws. If, for example, the Boy Scouts do not wish to accept gay troop leaders, the state should not force them to do so.

Equality

The libertarian position accounts for certain intuitions about the significance of liberty, but it struggles to account for intuitions we may have about other elements of the liberal-democratic ideal, such as equality.[5] Egalitarians often claim that the benefits and burdens of social cooperation must be justified to each citizen, which entails that institutions ensure a fair distribution of goods and opportunities (Rawls 1971; Dworkin 2000). It seems unfair that some individuals should enjoy the good fortune of a privileged upbringing or luck in the genetic lottery for marketable talents, while others inherit disabilities or the baggage of historical oppression. Correspondingly, these positions tend to conceive the value of liberty as protecting specific interests in expression, conscience, religion, association, and so forth—in a way that allows each citizen fair access to these goods. For egalitarians, opportunities to influence public decisions must be fairly distributed—acknowledging, however, that there is no obligation that citizens be active participants in public life. Pluralism is valuable for these views only insofar as its absence often signals forms of discrimination and economic exclusion. Efficiency, too, enters as a downstream concern: only after we have determined what fairness demands, we ought to take care to spend resources prudently.

Taking equality seriously, therefore, requires a much different approach to the nonprofit sector than that prescribed by libertarianism. It might recommend heavily investing in antipoverty initiatives designed to ensure a fairer distribution of resources (Cohen and Rogers 1995; Murphy 1998). It might support nonprofit organizations devoted to the preservation and expression of specific liberties. And it might seek to intervene in associations that engage in discrimination (Rosenblum 2000). If public institutions cannot discriminate against minorities or women in the workplace, for example, then neither should nonprofit organizations. All-male golf clubs are in this view defective from the standpoint of justice. Racially segregated public *and private* swimming pools are unacceptable. The Catholic Church's historical practice of denying women the opportunity to be priests is suspect. In Nancy Rosenblum's apt phrase, an egalitarian conception of liberal democracy may imply a *logic of congruence* between the norms that govern the state—for example, nondiscrimination and fair equality of opportunity—and the norms that should govern associational life and the nonprofit sector (Rosenblum 2000).

Another implication for egalitarians is a healthy skepticism of big philanthropy (Saunders-Hastings 2018; Reich 2018). Large private foundations are, more or less by definition, a plutocratic element in a democratic society, an effort to direct private assets toward public influence, thereby potentially undermining the value of political equality. We take up these concerns in more detail in the following sections.

Pluralism

Despite the voluminous discussion in civil society literature on pluralism, few political theorists would consider it a first-order or fundamental value. Rather, most regard pluralism as an indicator of other values. When individuals have equal basic liberties, the exercise of their liberty leads them naturally to explore and organize around a panoply of different activities, lifestyles, religious views, and cultural practices. John Stuart Mill famously argued that a society ought to test out various conceptions of the good life through "different experiments of living" (Mill 2015). The absence of pluralism can therefore indicate a troubling restriction of basic liberties, or the objectionable domination of powerful groups. In such cases, it may be appropriate to support pluralism by opening up more opportunities for marginalized groups. This goal could be achieved, for instance, by granting nonprofit status and its associated privileges to a wide array of private associations.

Pluralism also has its limits. Some people will use their liberty to form insular associations to engage in crime, preach theocracy, or trumpet racial hatred. Here enters what some call the "dark side" of civil society. Protecting the liberty of individuals does not lead inexorably to tolerance, civility, and a healthy regard for the dignity of all. It can—and does—lead to intolerance, incivility, and an attempt to exclude or dominate others (Chambers and Kopstein 2001). In these cases, civil society associations may publicly challenge the bedrock principle of equal citizenship; they may also severely restrict the basic liberties of their own members. Although the health of a liberal democracy depends on the flourishing of critical and heterodox perspectives, such a society cannot survive without limits on toleration. Precisely how to strike this balance presents a perpetual challenge. Under what conditions should the intolerant be tolerated?

Prosperity

Another philosophical tradition emphasizes the economic role of nonprofits. This is the outlook of utilitarians who affirm that a society's central aim is to maximize well-being (Goodin 1995). Utilitarians need not embrace liberal democracy; they are democrats only contingently, believing the best form of government is the one that promotes the best outcomes. Although many believe that democratic governance tends to promote better outcomes than alternative processes (Arneson 2009), some utilitarians profess sympathy with technocracy, holding that experts (defined in one way or another) should enjoy a greater share of power than ordinary citizens (Mill 2015). Thus, these positions often lend support to the outsourcing of public functions to nonprofits, entrepreneurs, or so-called philanthrocapitalists (Bishop and Green 2008).

Economistic views of the nonprofit sector tend to envision its role as solving technical problems. Nonprofit organizations can supply "collective goods," such as museums, festivals, churches, parks, and soup kitchens, which are in high demand but undersupplied by markets (Hardin 1982; Steinberg 2006).[6] The state is the collective goods provider par excellence but cannot supply all collective goods well. Conventional wisdom holds that governments are less adept at satisfying the economic preferences of a diverse polity

(Douglas 1983; cf. Elster 1992). Decentralizing the production of certain collective goods helps ensure that citizens' preferences are satisfied efficiently.

One collective good worth emphasizing here is social innovation and problem solving. Nonprofit organizations possess specific virtues that enable various kinds of innovation (Reich 2018). The absence of a profit motive and shelter from electoral pressures allow philanthropic foundations to engage in long-term research and risky experimentation. These activities periodically pay off with new discoveries that benefit great numbers of people.

Legitimacy

What lesson is there to be drawn from this overview of different strains within the ideal of liberal democracy? Laying weight on a given ingredient of the liberal-democratic ideal leads to different implications for the nonprofit sector and the policies that structure it. Libertarians will emphasize the freedom to associate unencumbered by state oversight or limit. They will prize donor discretion, and they will avoid public subsidies for nonprofits. Egalitarians will emphasize equality alongside liberty, placing special weight on the role that nonprofits play in bringing about equality of opportunity and realizing the goals of distributive justice, especially the guarantee of a basic minimum of core goods for all citizens. They will be more likely to endorse congruence between the norms of the state and those that bind nonprofit organizations. Utilitarians will emphasize the economic function of nonprofits and look to the nonprofit sector for its potential role in efficiently delivering goods that neither the market nor the state can or will produce well. Pluralism plays a role in all of these views but not as a first principle.

We need not endorse a particular view of liberal democracy in order to make certain kinds of practical judgments. We can distinguish, for example, between the concept of justice and the concept of legitimacy. Theories of justice are often thought to provide complete answers to the question of what makes a society normatively desirable. Theories of legitimacy, meanwhile, can offer more minimal claims about what states of affairs may be permissible (Rawls 1993; Buchanan 2002; Williams 2005; cf. Simmons 1999). Legitimacy tells us when we are obliged to comply with laws and policies even if we find them wanting by the lights of our favored conception of justice. Legitimacy is an especially helpful concept given the presence of abiding and reasonable disagreement about the details of justice. A society may be able to attain greater consensus on what conditions are minimally acceptable than it can on which conditions are equitable or optimal.

Theories of legitimacy tend to emphasize two essential criteria. For a state of affairs to be legitimate, it must result from reasonably fair procedures and it must respect basic human rights. Reasonably fair procedures include a representative system of government that abides by the rule of law. Basic human rights refer to respecting the dignity of each person. All of the perspectives we considered earlier incorporate these criteria. The conclusion, then, is that a nonprofit sector organized around any of the perspectives we surveyed would be presumptively legitimate. Though it would not necessarily command its citizens' approval, it would at least demand their respect.

Emergent Controversies

Aside from the longstanding debates about what roles (if any) the nonprofit sector should serve and how it should be organized and regulated, a number of emergent trends call out for sustained attention. We examine three: (1) the relationship between the nonprofit sector and persistent economic inequality, (2) the blurring of boundaries between traditional sectoral divisions, and (3) the place of nonprofits in global politics.

Inequality

Widening inequality has combined with several other factors to make the nonprofit sector increasingly controlled by, and responsive to, extremely wealthy individuals. One of these factors is the regressive nature of the system of tax deductions for charitable donations, which creates stronger incentives for donations from higher-income earners (Murphy and Nagel 2002). Another is the legal structure of grant-making foundations, which affords wealthy individuals concentrated and entrenched power over the nonprofit sector (Saunders-Hastings 2018; Reich 2018). Although foundations provide a relatively small proportion of overall funding for the nonprofit sector, their ability to offer large grants on a perpetual basis creates strong incentives for nonprofit organizations to cater their activities to foundation priorities. Whatever function we believe the nonprofit sector ought to serve—be it providing minority collective goods, administering or experimenting with social policy, raising awareness about social issues, and/or contesting the state—it is increasingly doing so on behalf of the wealthiest citizens. These trends prompt us to consider how control over the nonprofit sector ought to be distributed, and the extent to which power should be translatable across different domains of society.

From the standpoint of some of the perspectives we have presented, these trends are either not worrisome or only contingently worrisome. Strands of libertarian thought, for instance, will point out that rising inequality is mainly a by-product of voluntary transactions (Nozick 1974). Even if we find disparities in income and wealth unsettling, introducing new rules or increased taxes to contain inequality will involve objectionable interference with liberty. Strands of utilitarian thought, meanwhile, will want to know the effects of these trends. If increasing control over the nonprofit sector by the wealthy leads to better social outcomes, perhaps this is something citizens should ultimately welcome (Singer 2015). This perspective is implicit in the philanthrocapitalist movement, which heralds the translation of business success into solving social problems and characterizes the approach of many of today's largest foundations (Bishop and Green 2008).

From other standpoints, however, these developments raise the specter of *plutocracy* and thereby reveal a marked tension with democratic principles. The threat of plutocracy is easiest to appreciate when we consider how power within civil society can translate into power over the state. Democracy, according to a familiar view, requires that citizens enjoy equal opportunities for political influence over their common affairs. Some, of course, may think that the demands of democratic equality are satisfied when citizens enjoy the same formal opportunities for influence, such as equally weighted votes and the right to run for elected office. But are equal formal liberties adequate protections against a background of vast inequalities? If electoral campaigns are privately financed, the political agenda becomes overwhelmingly sensitive to the preferences of the wealthy (Gilens 2012; Bonica et al. 2013). Hence the concern among many democratic theorists with campaign finance reform: coercively binding rules cannot be legitimate unless everyone subject to them enjoys substantively fair opportunities to participate in the rule-making process (Beitz 1989; J. Cohen 2009; Kolodny 2014a, 2014b).

Recent developments have revealed that influence over campaigns is just one way in which the wealthy can control political outcomes. Somewhat notoriously, foundations involved in the reform of public education have made grants to cash-strapped government bodies on condition that officials abide by the donors' policy preferences (Reckhow 2013). Less overtly, by funding think tanks, advocacy groups, and leadership-training institutes, wealthy individuals are able to exercise disproportionate influence over the background political culture. Warnings about a "mask of pluralism," "dark money," and an "unheavenly chorus" (all titles of books dramatizing these phenomena) point to the ways in which wealth buys dominance over political debate, apart from its more direct influence over elections (Roelofs 2003; Schlozman, Verba, and Brady 2012; Mayer 2016). These concerns raise the question of whether equality requires limits on the ability to convert wealth into political influence, and how these demands might be met. The countervailing anxiety that regulations on elite influence might objectionably trample on freedom of speech hangs over this controversy.

Worries about plutocracy go beyond the political process. Increasing inequality means that wealthier citizens are also able to exercise disproportionate control over processes and outcomes within civil society (Saunders-Hastings 2018; Reich 2018). This might mean, for instance, that a greater proportion of donations flow toward collective goods preferred by the wealthy, such as high culture and higher education. Such elite dominance of collective goods provision may be objectionable on at least two grounds. First, if we believe that one of the nonprofit sector's main purposes is to provide collective goods preferred by democratic minorities, it may be troubling if the nonprofit sector tends to benefit only the wealthiest people. Second, many of the goods that nonprofits provide help constitute a society's cultural language. By providing institutions for historical preservation, academic inquiry, artistic expression, and social advocacy, the nonprofit sector is instrumental in determining a society's identity and values. Thus, when wealthy individuals enjoy disproportionate influence over the nonprofit sector, they are better able to fashion a society's identity and values in line with their own preferences. (And research shows that the preferences of the wealthy systematically differ from those of the rest of us [Page, Bartels, and Seawright 2013].)

Widening inequality also challenges another democratic function of civil society: its role in fostering civic virtue. The neo-Tocquevillian mantra that voluntary associations are "schools of democracy" seems to presuppose associations with a participatory structure (Putnam 2000). By coming together to discuss challenges and solve problems, citizens are expected to forge social bonds, formulate political identities, and develop capacities for effective political engagement. These benefits do not accrue if citizens do not or cannot actively participate. As Theda Skocpol has shown, the mass membership organizations that dominated the nonprofit sector through much of the twentieth century have been gradually replaced by donor-controlled entities staffed by professional managers (Skocpol 2003). Nowadays, to be a "member" of an organization often means nothing more than having signed up to receive occasional activity updates, while actual organizational decisions reflect negotiations between wealthy donors and hired professionals. The decline in civic participation has several causes, but rising inequality is an important one. Organizations have become more responsive to elites in large part because concentrated wealth has shifted fund-raising incentives away from seeking out small donors. Some scholars have suggested that the solution to this problem lies with new forms of civic engagement made possible by emerging technology (Gimmler 2001). Whether and how the Internet can adequately foster the democratic virtues once located in the nonprofit sector remains to be seen.

Confronting runaway economic inequality is an urgent priority. Recently, some have also suggested ways in which changes to the regulation of the nonprofit sector could work to prevent background inequalities from overwhelming civil society. Some attack the charitable deduction policy regime, arguing for alternative means of subsidizing the nonprofit sector that better serve less wealthy taxpayers (Reich 2011; Pevnick 2013). Others challenge the legitimacy of philanthropic foundations or seek ways to limit their influence (Saunders-Hastings 2018; Reich 2018).

In the absence of regulatory change, nonprofits and their donors also can adopt certain measures voluntarily. Under conditions of enduring injustice and the failure of the state to redress it, perhaps nonprofits and their donors are wrong to focus on providing nonessential goods. Faced with meeting the urgent needs of our fellow citizens who are suffering from homelessness, poverty, systemic racism, or addiction, for example, providing support to the opera or one's alma mater might seem an unseemly indulgence. Several theorists have argued that agents within civil society act wrongly unless they address urgent needs and do so in a cost-effective way (Pogge 2011; Singer 2015; Cordelli 2016). Aside from curbing the discretion that they enjoy over their chosen ends, civil society actors can also take measures to redistribute power in decision-making processes. Instructive examples are the movement among some philanthropists to reject the perpetual life that the foundation form affords them (Soskis 2017), and the movement among nonprofits to include representatives of their beneficiaries on governance boards (McGinnis Johnson 2016).

Hybridity and Shifting Boundaries

The idea of a nonprofit sector seems to presuppose that the political economy should be sharply divided into independent domains, each organized by a different mechanism of transaction: command, in the case of the state; exchange, in the case of the market; gift (or perhaps deliberation), in the case of the nonprofit sector (Young 2000). Each sector, then, would appear to inhabit a distinctive role, which comes along with distinctive regulative ideals. But recent historical developments have initiated considerable blurring of the lines between sectors, with nonprofit organizations acting on behalf of the state and enterprises experimenting with various ways of blending commercial activity with nonprofit goals. Cases of blurred boundaries raise at least three important questions around (1) which set of governing norms ought to apply in hybrid scenarios, (2) whether societies have good reasons to maintain stronger fences between sectors, and (3) whether a three-sector division of institutional labor is ultimately desirable.

Do hybrid forms need hybrid norms? Nonprofits are increasingly taking on governmental or quasi-governmental functions. Consider the growing practice of contracting out government functions to nonprofit agencies, most commonly in the areas of health and human services (Cordelli 2011). Even theorists who draw the line less starkly than libertarians tend to think that different standards of regulation and appraisal apply to governments and private entities. Hybridity challenges this position. Should nonprofit contractors abide by public norms or private norms? If we think that civil society norms should prevail in these cases, we may conclude that these organizations should be at liberty to discriminate between different potential recipients of these services, and that those who believe themselves ill-served or passed over are not entitled to recourse. But if we think that public norms should prevail, we may conclude the opposite: that nonprofit service deliverers must abide by all public norms—including antidiscrimination norms and those that allow citizens to dispute adverse decisions.

The case for stronger fences. Sometimes nonprofits perform or take over presumptively public functions without explicit authorization from the state. Examples include privately funded food banks, homeless shelters, and schools. Private provision offers certain advantages. Government coercion is prima facie objectionable, so initiatives that can accomplish public aims by harnessing freely given resources may seem preferable to those that depend on taxation. Also, private initiatives may be able to innovate and adapt to needs more flexibly than tightly controlled government programs. There are a number of grounds for caution, however.

As we discussed previously, citizens have a moral right to a decent social minimum, and something similar might be said about a basic education. If we think that citizens are owed certain goods as a matter of justice, it may be more important that those goods are provided reliably, on a guaranteed basis, than that they are provided voluntarily or innovatively. Recent advances in political theory have argued that political freedom requires protection against dependence on the goodwill of private benefactors (Pettit 1997; Ripstein 2010). Private provision of essential resources may invite relationships of domination and subordination that are unacceptable among free and equal citizens (Oberman 2011; cf. Taylor 2018).

As we foreshadowed earlier in this chapter, under "Distributing Justice Through Nonprofit Enterprise," another worry is that voluntary efforts to supply essential collective goods deprive the public of the ability to discharge what is in fact a collective responsibility. In this view, realizing conditions of justice is a responsibility that applies to all of us. Welcoming the private provision of essential collective goods allows noncontributors to free-ride on the gratuitous sacrifices of the generous (Beerbohm 2016). From another angle, the voluntary performance of public functions may raise worries about democratic accountability (Lechterman 2018). Arguably, citizens have an interest in opportunities to influence critical policy decisions, whether or not those decisions emanate from traditional state authorities. Private provision may be objectionable insofar as it bypasses democratic deliberation over matters of public concern.

Is the nonprofit sector obsolete? Concerns about privatization seem to favor erecting stronger boundaries between sectors of economic interaction. However, another set of developments forces us to reconsider where these boundaries ought to lie. Recent years have seen for-profit entities incorporating nonprofit objectives, nonprofit entities adopting commercial elements, and fully hybrid "social enterprises" blending both commercial and nonprofit elements in roughly equal parts (Mair, Chapter 14, "Social Entrepreneurship").

Proponents of this hybridity claim that it is a mistake to try to split civil society into acquisitive and altruistic pursuits. Separating civil society into discrete profit-seeking and nonprofit-seeking realms encourages each's distinctive vice: greed in the market and inefficiency in the nonprofit sector. Justice, in this analysis, requires a tighter integration of profit-seeking and beneficence to moderate these risks. Such a view might then recommend a two-sector model comprising a public sector as traditionally understood and a private sector organized around social enterprise. This model naturally comes with several trade-offs that require careful evaluation.

Preliminary evidence suggests that many hybrid organizations face competing pressures from incompatible incentive structures and can be difficult to sustain (Smith, Gonin, and Besharov 2013). The pressure to maintain a bottom line may compromise a social mission, and vice versa. Even if experiments in hybridity can overcome these challenges, more serious concerns remain. Political theorists and philosophers have long argued that market principles are not appropriate in every domain of social life; they undermine the conditions that make certain practices and relationships valuable (Anderson 1993; Satz 2012). Though these studies tend to focus on pure profit-seeking rather than hybrid organizational forms, some of these lessons—such as the transformative influence of the profit motive on value-laden domains like child-rearing and criminal punishment—are instructive. Additionally, as businesses increasingly engage in the provision of collective goods, they encounter some of the problems that we discussed earlier in relation to private provision of public functions. For instance, the fact that social media companies hold oligopolistic control over spheres of democratic deliberation prompts us to consider whether they should be subject to public norms of accessibility and transparency (Rahman 2018; Wu 2018).

Globalism

An increasingly interconnected world has also generated a globalized civil society, one aspect of which features nationally based nonprofits engaged in lobbying international authorities, publicizing global problems, establishing international norms, and delivering goods and services around the world.[7] These phenomena raise challenging questions about the proper role of private actors in global politics.

Certainly, many of the controversies that pertain to the liberal-democratic ideals that inform the regulation of the nonprofit sector in a domestic context also apply in some way to the global context. Consider, for instance, the question of whether and how governmental bodies should share authority with private organizations. In areas of humanitarian and development assistance, many governmental bodies have moved from performing these tasks directly to channeling resources through NGO intermediaries. In what senses is this a desirable shift, and in which areas should it be qualified or resisted? Separately, NGOs are increasingly stepping in to fill gaps in governance, such as in the setting of international environmental and industrial standards (think here of the Forest Stewardship Council and the Institute of Electrical and Electronics Engineers [IEEE], which establishes protocols for communications technology and other industries). Under what conditions can private associations be legitimate providers of global public goods?

Transnational advocacy and its limits. Even as global civil society presents some familiar challenges, many difficulties encountered are notably different in magnitude or kind.

There is, of course, no global government that can charter, protect, and regulate NGOs or the background conditions in which they operate. Disparities in wealth and power between societies are stark and pervasive. And disagreement about fundamental political principles is deep and abiding.

The absence of global government also means that there are no formal institutions of representation to mediate between expressive NGOs and governing bodies. Instead, NGOs press their cases directly to governing bodies, which can afford them formal consultative status and/or administrative authority. Many of these groups claim to be representing perspectives and communities that would otherwise be missing from interstate negotiations. That NGOs make representative claims triggers complaints about their authorization. No one elected Oxfam or Amnesty International, and while they may claim to speak on behalf of common interests or dispossessed communities, their chain of accountability ultimately runs back to their donors (Grant and Keohane 2005; Rubenstein 2015).

The complaint that NGOs lack democratic authorization generates at least two interesting responses. John Dryzek suggests that although international NGOs may not be ideally representative agents from the standpoint of democratic theory, they serve as a considerable counterweight to the more seriously antidemocratic tendencies of global politics (Dryzek 2012: 107): "Compared to other realities in a global order dominated by large corporations, hegemonic states, neoliberal market thinking, secretive and unresponsive international organizations, low-visibility financial networks, and military might, global civil society does rather well."

Another response has been to challenge the conventional understanding of political representation. The traditional view of legitimate representation requires that representatives be authorized and directly accountable to individuals, generally organized into territorially based voting constituencies (Pitkin 1967). Recent discussions in democratic theory have suggested that alternative ways of assessing claims to representation are both possible and necessary. Some scholars propose that without being formally elected, self-appointed representatives may nonetheless exhibit qualities associated with good representation, such as acting on behalf of the interests of the represented and/or responding to their preferences (Saward 2010; Landemore n.d.). Self-appointed representatives may sometimes represent better in these respects than elected representatives do. Others propose that often what matters in political debate is not that everyone's voice is heard, but that all of the relevant positions are put on the table (Dryzek and Niemeyer 2008). Thus, insofar as NGOs help to supplement or challenge dominant discourses, they are legitimate contributors to global political debate. Although these broadened understandings of representation apply most directly to global politics, which lack democratic elections, some argue that nonelectoral representation also has a role to play within states, where the electoral system has become an outmoded mechanism for connecting individuals to decision making (Urbinati and Warren 2008).

Transnational aid and its limits. Disparities in wealth and power across societies generate numerous conflicts. Chief among them is the extent to which rich societies are obliged to provide assistance to poor ones, a question that has received considerable attention from political theorists and philosophers (Singer 1972; Beitz 1979; Rawls 2001; Nagel 2005; Miller 2007; Pogge 2008). Less studied are the duties of and constraints on NGOs that are often called upon to be intermediaries for this assistance (Rubenstein 2015 is one important exception). The traditional practice of state-to-state aid is now supplemented by state-to-NGO and individual-to-NGO models. Bypassing the state may be especially appealing when governments are crippled or kleptocratic. Investing in a variety of small-scale development projects may also help discover innovative solutions to social problems. But these potential benefits must be weighed against the reality that a patchwork of private agencies, even when operating under the best conditions, cannot replicate certain virtues of formal government. They cannot provide universal and equitable access to public goods, and they cannot afford local communities bona fide democratic control over policy decisions (Lechterman, 2020). Even if development NGOs are not meant to replace states but rather to assist societies with the transition to successful self-government, the current evidence indicates that NGOs are most beneficial where governments are already functioning well, while in more fragile contexts NGO activity discourages state development (Cammett and MacLean 2014; Clough 2017; cf. Brass 2016).

The apparent failure of states to supply enough aid, or public disagreement over the direction of aid policy, also leads to a profusion of NGOs supported directly by individual contributions. Although in some cases these initiatives may fill critical gaps or discover innovative alternatives, in others they represent amateurish or parochial efforts that damage development and reinforce power asymmetries (Schnable 2015). Think here of the ill-fated PlayPump water pump (MacAskill 2015), programs that donate used Western clothing to sub-Saharan Africa (de Freytas-Tamura 2017), or the Kony 2012 campaign (de Waal 2015).

Transnational disagreement. Earlier, we noted that principled disagreement about the norms that apply to the nonprofit sector in a domestic setting make it difficult to issue conclusive assertions about how the sector should be justified and appraised. In a global setting, the range and depth of disagreement becomes even more pronounced. Societies with no tradition of an independent civil society, or traditions that look very different from liberal-democratic experiences, nonetheless endeavor to participate in global civic life. To what extent should a globalized nonprofit sector accommodate this diversity?

Even within the liberal-democratic tradition, theorists disagree profoundly on whether and how principles of political morality apply outside the state. Many theorists pair demanding conceptions of justice and democracy within the state with minimalist aspirations outside it (Blake 2001; Nagel 2005; Sangiovanni 2007). NGOs, in this reading, should be predominantly accountable to their donors and beneficiaries, tasked with carrying out their missions—be they religious proselytism, coordinating cottage industries of artisans, or lobbying for the fossil fuel industry. So-called cosmopolitans, meanwhile, endorse demanding ideals of global justice and democracy that may impinge on transnational nonprofit activity (Beitz 1979; Caney 2006; Abizadeh 2008). Cosmopolitans may task NGOs with duties toward democratizing global politics or redistributing global economic gains, either by engaging in these tasks directly or by making their operations consistent with these aims.

Conclusion

In this chapter, we argued for the essential role of political theory in orienting the study and institutional design of civil society, associational life, and the nonprofit sector. We illustrated how philosophical argument and social scientific inquiry can be partners in the design and evaluation of institutional arrangements that structure the nonprofit sector. Registering the intellectual appeal and predominance of liberal-democratic ideals as a framework for social organization, we showed how different ways of understanding these ideals lead to different principles for justifying and appraising the nonprofit sector. We also drew attention to emerging social phenomena that raise new or underappreciated challenges for theory and practice alike.

Our emphasis on liberal democracy may seem peculiar in light of the resurgence of illiberal and nondemocratic regime types in the early decades of the twenty-first century. Electoral authoritarianism has arisen in areas where it was once unimaginable. One-party states that have overseen economic prosperity have proven surprisingly resilient to democratic pressures. The prevalence or apparent success of these models may stoke doubts about the putative superiority of liberal-democratic ideals. And even if we reaffirm those ideals, inhospitable conditions may make applying them seem increasingly difficult.

Of what help are liberal-democratic principles in a world that appears to reject them? The answer is not nearly as mysterious as it may seem. Political ideals provide standards against which to assess current circumstances and identify directions for reform. We have shown various ways in which nonprofits can promote, respect, or embody principles of justice and legitimacy in the face of unfavorable conditions. Nonprofits can lead the charge against economic inequality through advocacy (cf. Walker and Oszkay, Chapter 21, "The Changing Face of Nonprofit Advocacy"), through direct redistribution, and through inclusive management. Nonprofits can monitor and protest abuses of human rights, contest and organize opposition to authoritarian leaders, and model democratic norms in their internal conduct. But these are only a few possibilities. We are optimistic about the creative possibilities of collective action when guided by sound principles.

7 NONPROFITS AS BOUNDARY MARKERS

The Politics of Choice, Mobilization, and Arbitrage

Elisabeth S. Clemens

NONPROFIT ORGANIZATIONS (NPOS) ARE NAMED for what they are not. The same holds true for the closely related category of nongovernmental organizations (NGOs).[1] Both NPOs and NGOs are frequently identified as elements of civil society, itself a term defined in contrast to royal courts and understood as a domain in which private persons could come together to discuss public issues (Habermas [1962] 1991). Given this proliferation of terms, is it possible to identify the specificity of the NPO—or NGO or voluntary association—as a political form? One answer lies in recognizing that, whatever the label, this category of organization is defined by what it is *not*; such organizations are understood in explicit or implicit contrast to some other type of organization. Moreover, as nongovernmental entities with a public mission or privately managed organizations precluded from profit-making, NPOs and NGOs are not simply "not something." They are "not something" in the sense of an anomaly, constituted or operating in ways that diverge from—and perhaps even conflict with—the principles that organize important dimensions of their social context.[2]

From this theoretical vantage point, NPOs should be understood as political constructions that are not themselves part of the formal political system. They are political creations (Novak 2001; Levy 2017), endowed with rights—of legal existence and property holding—but not strictly accountable to the sovereigns or legislatures that bestow these rights (this focus on the legal status of organizations contrasts with the social activities of associating for some purpose that do not require state recognition as a condition of organizational existence). In the U.S. tax code, for example, 501(c)s are defined in contrast to governmental entities on one side and for-profit firms on the other.[3] Within this category, 501(c)(3)s and 501(c)(4)s are distinguished by the somewhat greater—if still substantially constrained—capacity of the latter to engage in explicit political advocacy on issues (but not electoral campaigns; Berry and Arons 2003). As legally recognized and publicly regulated private organizations that often receive privileges (e.g., tax exemptions or subsidies, see Hall 1987), NPOs frequently cluster at the interface of governmental programs and privately managed activities (Mitchell 1991; Clemens 2017). They not only mark but also structure the boundary between state and society, between public and private.

This understanding of NPOs and civic associations as anomalies with respect to state and market has been obscured by the conceptual imagery of an "independent sector" populated by organizations of a distinct kind, with presumably altruistic motives, subject to a separate set of regulatory rules and institutional norms. Starting from such categorical distinctions, scholarship has focused on the distinctive traits of nonprofit and for-profit organizations and the implications of nonprofit status (or "auspice") for a range of behaviors and outcomes (for a discussion of the genealogy of these literatures, see Hansmann 1987). Although the impetus for mobilizing or associating may not originate in politics (see Lechterman and Reich, Chapter 6, "Political Theory and the Nonprofit Sector"), NPOs and NGOs are legally constituted as a distinctive kind of political form that recognizes privately managed and even privately initiated organizations as legitimate vehicles for the advancement of some public good: charity, education, conservation, or the arts, to name only a few.

In this respect, the political creation of such a form by the state represents a mode of delegation—even abdication—of some element of sovereignty. For this reason, rulers throughout much of history have been suspicious of private associations, even those linked to a public-serving mission. Rights-granting charters have been closely held. Even organizations have been required to register, subjected to monitoring and even suppression. Such publicly oriented private organizations represent potential alternatives to government provision, as well as opportunities for mobilizing beyond the limits of the formal political or engaging in arbitrage by leveraging extrapolitical resources for political ends.

By recognizing NPOs as legally constituted at the boundaries of the political, the theoretical project shifts from taxonomy to dynamics, including those that produce boundaries themselves (on "things of boundaries," see Abbott 2001). In England, for example, the Elizabethan Statute of Charitable Uses of 1601 assembled a motley set of activities—including, among others, the repair of bridges, the care of orphans, and the aid of the poor unable to pay their taxes—under the category of charity. Early modern and modern law repeatedly defined categories and promulgated rules that linked categories such as charity to permitted and forbidden activities, liability for taxes, and eligibility for subsidies (Levy 2017; Ware 1989). More recently, legal classification orders have consolidated the concept of a unitary nonprofit or nongovernmental sector and thereby enabled advocates and scholars to make stronger claims for "the sector's" contributions to the public good or national wealth (Barman 2013). Cross-nationally, this accumulation of policies and legal decisions has taken varied forms, more or less approximating the image of an apolitical "independent sector" defined by its differentiation from political conflict and profit making.

Repeatedly contested by private actors and public officials, the boundaries evoked by terms such as *independent sector* have been monitored, revised, and reinforced in response to perceived threats and the potential for disruption. Insofar as the legal status of "nonprofit organization" is tied to the recognition of some public-serving mission, these organizations have the potential to produce public goods and shape civic discourse but are not fully constrained by the rules of democratic politics. Grassroots organizations that emerge as voluntary responses to unaddressed problems may morph into political movements; profit-maximizing actors may embed themselves within nonprofit forms, seeking to channel restricted advantages and revenues into personal coffers. The boundaries established between organizational populations structure the possibilities for such trespasses, subversions, and entrepreneurial reconfigurations. Subsidies and privileges such as tax exemption are piled on one side of a categorical boundary, creating incentives for actors to assume the nonprofit form in order to advance purposes that may be at odds with the legal restrictions on partisanship and profit making.

Just as the nonprofit form may allow citizens and private actors to pursue civic mobilization and the production of public goods in situations where government fails to act or even opposes some form of social provision or expression, the form also enables an extension of governmental capacity in ways that may elude democratic accountability. As private organizations, nonprofits are not necessarily subject to the constraints of civil service hiring, open meetings laws, and requirements for transparency. Although they may claim to represent some community or constituency, they are not subject to accountability through elections (Levine 2016; see also Lechterman and Reich, Chapter 6, "Political Theory and the Nonprofit Sector," on "bypassing deliberation"). From the vantage point of political theory, this linking of private organizations to a mission that is publicly recognized, legitimated, and sometimes subsidized defines the specificity of the nonprofit form and its potential as a site for innovation and arbitrage between different institutional domains.

The political potency of this combination of public-oriented mission and private management explains why many rulers have exercised close control over the authority to grant corporate charters for benevolent organizations as well as the legal battles over the rights of chartered corporations. These were closely held in much of early modern Europe through the eighteenth and even nineteenth centuries. In this respect, the United States set important precedents with its affirmation of freedom of religion (which implied that no ruler or legislature would control the formation of religious corporations), and legislation in many states created the framework for an "open access society" (Lamoreaux and Wallis 2017) in which the right to form religious, civic, and commercial organizations was routinized and made generally available. During the same period, court decisions protected the independence of chartered organizations from legislative interference (on the *Dartmouth College* case in the early United States, see McGarvie 2003). Consequently, the regulatory frameworks for nonprofit activity have often elaborated barriers between these organizations' activities and the explicitly political sphere of campaigns, elections, and policy advocacy (see Part VI, "Advocacy, Engagement, and the Public").

With the United States as the type specimen, this configuration of "nonprofit organization" as an independent sector informed the emergence of the field of nonprofit studies in the 1970s and 1980s (see Soskis, Chapter 2, "History of Associational Life and the Nonprofit Sector in the United States"). But by the late twentieth century, as political challengers and challenged incumbents have attempted to harness these capacities for their own campaigns and agendas, the legal status of the sector itself has been politicized anew. And as the organizational landscape has changed, so have the ways in which theorists have understood NPOs as a specifically political form. In the first edition of this book, James Douglas (1987) focused on the choice to turn to nonprofits, rather than government, as providers of public goods. Here, NPOs are an output of individual choices about the role of government. Many other theorists, before and after, have understood nonprofits as a form of civic or voluntary association that nurtures the political skills and preferences required to be effective in formal political institutions. Here, nonprofits are positioned as an input to democratic politics, generating individuals with organizing skills and groups mobilized for political advocacy.

Although both market models and civic engagement approaches have a long history in research on NPOs, recent developments in both scholarship and contemporary politics have focused attention on the politics of the boundary itself, of the relationship of NPOs to the market and the state. A transnational turn toward public–private partnerships and hybrid forms of social provision has fueled a politics of and by nonprofits across a range of policy domains (see Dupuy and Prakash, Chapter 28, "Global Backlash Against Foreign Funding to Domestic Nongovernmental Organizations"). In combination, these developments call for a political theory of nonprofits that attends to the dynamics of the politicization and depoliticization of this organizational form.

Political Theories of Nonprofit Organization

As nonprofit research consolidated into a recognized field during the 1970s and 1980s, one theory of politics initially claimed pride of place as *the* political theory of NPOs: a market model of democracy. As articulated by Douglas (1987) in the first edition of this book, this account began with individual citizens holding distinctive preferences for public services that are expressed through votes or public opinion polls. Douglas advanced a political analogue to the economic theories of NPOs surveyed by Henry Hansmann in the same volume (1987; on "market failure" models, see Weisbrod 1988). Hansmann focused on "demand-side" responses to the question of why, within a particular industry, "consumers might choose to patronize nonprofit firms in preference to for-profit firms" (1987:37). One influential answer highlighted contract failure and information asymmetries. Where consumers are (or feel themselves to be) unable to evaluate the quality of a good or service—child care or nursing homes, for example—they may choose to patronize providers bound by the "nondistribution constraint" who are presumably less likely to gouge clients or mistreat those under their care in the pursuit of profit.

In a similar spirit, Douglas conceptualized government and nonprofit provision as discrete alternatives, objects of political choice. Public services or goods supported by a majority of constituents would be provided by public agencies; those that are more controversial or preferred by only a minority would be provided by nonprofits (albeit often subsidized by either direct use of public funds or tax expenditures). Deploying the "choice" rhetoric central to much of contemporary economics and political science, these arguments used the traits and preferences of citizens to explain the development of nonprofit sectors and the distribution of activities across states, markets, households, and the variously defined independent or "third sector."

Douglas's model was informed by both the scholarship and the politics of the moment, in which opposition to an expanding, often social democratic welfare state inspired efforts to go beyond conservative critique in order to envision a reenergized charitable sector as an alternative form of public provision supported by redistributive taxation (Douglas 1983; the "third way" and "big society" projects adopted by the Labor government of Tony Blair echoed his arguments). In the decades that followed, this theoretical approach has directly informed policy, reinforcing proposals to inject provisions for choice into domains dominated by public provision such as elementary and secondary education as well as health care for veterans and health insurance for senior citizens (Finn, Manno, and Vanourek 2000; see also Morgan and Campbell 2011; Reckhow 2013).

Whereas Douglas's argument conceptualized nonprofit activities as *alternatives* to government provision, Lester Salamon (1987) documented how the nonprofit sector has grown as a *complement* to government programs in the United States, expanding in parallel with increased flows of public funding (Brown 2018). Cross-nationally, state expansion has involved borrowing capacity from NPOs (Douglas 1987; Frumkin 2002; Smith and Lipsky 1993; Ullman 1998) as well as active sponsorship of the establishment and growth of nonprofit entities that then implement policy (Salamon 1987; Cammett and MacLean 2014).[4] But as social policy has recognized NPOs as providers of publicly funded or mandated services, the crisp imagery of choice between government and the "independent" sector has become more clouded.

In contrast to Douglas's emphasis on the heterogeneity of citizen preferences within a majoritarian polity, recent scholarship has developed more processual accounts—or "feedback models"—of the turn of welfare states toward greater reliance on or collaboration with NPOs. Arguing that policy shapes preferences and therefore politics, these feedback accounts highlight how the expanding partnership between government and nonprofits has reconstructed the political roles of both. During the War on Poverty, for example, the U.S. federal government adopted a "contracting regime" intended to promote innovation and participation as well as to allow a rapid expansion of organizational capacity (Smith and Lipsky 1993). The resulting growth of government funding of nonprofit activities led to claims that these nonprofits were lobbying selfishly for increased funding (Berry and Arons 2003:79–85) and calls to forbid lobbying activity on the part of NPOs receiving public funds (although existing legislation already forbade the use of federal funds to support such political activities). Driven by global waves of neoliberalism and new public management, even highly developed welfare states have experimented with and expanded their reliance on nonprofit agencies and civic associations (as well as, in some cases, for-profit firms) in the private provision of publicly funded social services (Kuhnle and Selle 1992; Suleiman 2003; Ullman 1998; Wijkström and Zimmer 2011).

Although market models began by conceptualizing nonprofits as a discrete source of social provision or clear alternative to government, the policies and projects informed by these arguments have generated an increasingly complex landscape in which public funds and authorizations are delegated to private entities and, in turn, those nonprofit groups may mobilize to demand continuation of government support. But the increasing delivery of publicly funded programs through NPOs may obscure relationships of accountability, distort citizens' understandings of how tax revenues are spent, and allow governments to displace the risks of downsizing and policy shifts onto nongovernmental entities (Morgan and Campbell 2011; Pierson 1994; see also Horvath and Powell 2016). By using public funds to support services that many citizens do not recognize as tax-supported, these arrangements make it difficult—perhaps impossible—to answer that supposedly simple political question of "what are your tax dollars doing for you?" At the same time, the financial dependence of nonprofits, whether on government or donors, may constrain or transform the civic qualities of these organizations.

As a consequence of these policy developments, the expansion of government–nonprofit partnerships has led to the increasing politicization of nonprofits as providers of public services, even as they are increasingly wary of engaging as political actors (on the tendency of nonprofit staff to overestimate the extent to which 501(c)(3)s are restricted from political participation, see Berry and Arons 2003). But if nonprofits are to be understood as important components of civil society, how can this concern with their political engagement be aligned with the repeated celebration of the democratic capacity of voluntary associations to either reinforce or destabilize existing arrangements of rule? With this question, the discussion turns from nonprofits as providers of services to nonprofits as vehicles for political participation. This shift in perspective reveals a different aspect of the politics of the nonprofit form.

Political Socialization and Democratic Participation

In contrast to market models of democracy, many political theories of associations and NPOs begin with strong assumptions about the attributes of these organizations. Civic or voluntary associations are, or should be, embodiments of the organizational forms, social skills, and political virtues required by a liberal democracy.[5] Tocqueville's *Democracy in America* (2004) is the touchstone for a vision in which associational activities are constitutive of citizens as actors, of preferences and interests, and of the capacity to make effective demands on government (Putnam 2000; Verba, Schlozman, and Brady 1995). From this vantage point, associations generate a capacity for collective or political action that may be exercised as an extension of elite power (Hall 1992), as a vehicle for the mobilization of disadvantaged or disgruntled constituencies (Clemens 1997; McCarthy 2003; Small 2009), or as an expression of the diversity of commitments in a pluralist society (Walzer 1984).[6] Yet the odds that NPOs and NGOs will actually meet these strong assumptions concerning organizational character and consequences depend heavily on the specific ways that NPOs are legally constructed in any given time and place.

To the extent that NPOs are equated with civil society (see Lechterman and Reich, Chapter 6, "Political Theory and the Nonprofit Sector," on this point), theorists build on a long tradition in which private voluntary associations are understood as key sites for the political socialization of democratic citizens and for what Jürgen Habermas ([1962] 1991:27) described as "the sphere of private people come together as a public . . . to engage [public authorities] in a debate over the general rules governing relations in the basically privatized but publicly relevant sphere of commodity exchange and social labor." Eagerly appropriating the mantle of Tocqueville and the banner of civil society, such arguments contend that a wide range of formal and informal associations socialize citizens for democratic participation (Fleischacker 1998; Putnam, Leonardi, and Nanetti 1993; Wuthnow 1991, 1998) or that this capacity for democratic socialization should guide the legal regulation of associations (for a critical discussion, see Rosenblum 1998a). Nonpolitical voluntary associations—along with workplaces and religious organizations—are settings in which citizens may practice skills such as writing letters, planning meetings, and making speeches (Verba et al. 1995:310–320) and internalize democratic values and skills (for a critical reflection on this assumption, see Eliasoph 2011).

Such claims for the democratic consequences of voluntary associations inform a rich vein of historical research, particularly although far from exclusively on the United States.

In the telling of American history, the nineteenth century constitutes a "golden age of associationalism" when fraternal lodges and voluntary associations multiplied in cities and towns throughout the nation (Gamm and Putnam 1999; Skocpol 1997; Skocpol, Ganz, and Munson 2000; for a critical discussion, see Kaufman 2002). In addition to providing arenas for political socialization that could then be expressed through political parties and elections, these associations actively collaborated in the provision of public goods (Beito 2000) and served as vehicles for political mobilization outside of the parties themselves (Clemens 1997; Skocpol 2003).

Although the role of voluntarism is central to the literature on American exceptionalism, such civic organizations developed in many societies, often within much more constraining regulatory frameworks (Bermeo and Nord 2000; Hoffman 2003). Indeed, the other great democratic revolution of the eighteenth century featured strong bans on guilds and other voluntary associations, an aversion that marked the trajectory of political development in France well into the twentieth century (Ronsavallon 2007). Nonetheless, the developments that inspired Habermas's theorization of the bourgeois public sphere were evident in many other countries, including Britain (Colley 1992), Russia (Lindenmeyr 1996), and China, where religiously linked voluntary associations served as sites for cultivating the skills and forms of discipline that numerous members then harnessed to the cause of revolution against their faltering empire (Xu 2013).

Such studies of political socialization within voluntary associations provide historical grounding for a long-standing concern in comparative politics. Classic works such as Almond and Verba's *Civic Culture* (1963; see also Fox 1997) addressed the importance of adult socialization in generating the values and practices that sustain democratic polities; associations, not surprisingly, are demonstrated to be important sites of socialization. In an analysis of comparative political stability, Eckstein (1966) underscored the importance of *congruence* between the forms of authority that prevailed within families or associations and the system of formal political authority. The closer the fit, the more stable the regime. Putnam and his collaborators (1993) revived interest in the social foundations of democratic governance and economic development, while Salamon and Anheier (1998) built on comparative-historical accounts of paths to democracy or welfare state regimes (Moore 1966; Esping-Andersen 1990) to develop an account of the social origins of civil society. Recognizing that voluntary associations provide vehicles for political mobilization and sites for civic socialization, these macrosocial accounts explore the political processes that generate spaces and opportunities for political action that is at least partially independent of the organized system of rule.

Whereas the first wave of political theorizing about NPOs focused on the *choice* between governmental and voluntary social provision, the turn to civic engagement generated new questions about political control over the right to organize with all its possible consequences in terms of legal standing, tax status, and even public subsidies. Legal frameworks that allow self-organizing for either civic or economic projects have produced what economic historians describe as "open access societies" (North, Wallis, and Weingast 2009; Lamoreaux and Wallis 2017). In the newly established United States, the principle of religious freedom undercut claims to close political control over the corporate status of religious congregations. A more permissive approach to incorporation was gradually extended to banks, firms, and other voluntary associations. The critical "open access" is to the legal right to form a durable association (Gutmann 1998), precisely the right that was restricted in postrevolutionary France. That limitation of the right of association underscores a point too often lost in celebratory discussions of civil society; some associations may be good for democracy, but others—or perhaps the same ones—may be perceived as threatening to existing political authority. Thus, a key question concerns which kinds of organizations align networks and capacities outside politics with the principles of formal political institutions (on civil society and fascist regimes, see Riley 2010; on civil society and challenges to authoritarian regimes, see Osa 2003).

Even where "open access" societies permit and encourage the formation of legally recognized voluntary associations, the content of regulations may require specific organizational features with implications for the political character of the association. As the legal framework for association developed in the United States, organizational constitutions often required democratic practices such as the election of officers. As associations were increasingly incorporated and regulated by state governments, these political arrangements were required for all but religious associations and benevolent corporations governed by appointed or self-perpetuating trustees. Material conditions might also encourage participatory governance; low budgets, low reserves, and little or no professional staff tended to forestall the logic of Robert Michels's iron law of oligarchy and the corresponding co-optation of activist leaders through their dependence on salary or office holding. Instead, membership served as a political apprenticeship, instilling mastery of skills such as public speaking.

From the nineteenth through the midtwentieth centuries, large membership-based voluntary associations of this type dominated the organizational landscape. Since then, these civic organizations have given way to professionally managed advocacy groups that tend to privilege the already educated and already politicized, rather than serving as schools of citizenship (Skocpol 2003:211–215). Government agencies and private corporations have appropriated the practices of voluntary participation and forged new techniques for generating consent and demobilizing protest (Lee, McQuarrie, and Walker 2015; Walker 2014). As nonprofits become more hierarchical and less likely to engage in participatory governance, they may become less powerful sources of democratic political socialization (Skocpol 2003:234). As nonprofits become more dependent on external funding, they tend to become more bureaucratic and professionalized (Smith and Lipsky 1993:100–108; Grønbjerg 1993:169–198). In a study of advocacy organizations in the peace movement, Bob Edwards (1994:317) found that larger organizations were "more likely than small to be formally organized, have higher levels of procedural formality, prefer to elect their leaders, and have more centralized financial decision making." Yet even in large organizations, specific practices of recruitment and incorporation, including those that build on existing relational networks, may promote greater levels of participation (on campaign organizing, see Han 2016).

Political skills are also cultivated in less obvious settings. Religious organizations may be incubators of political capacities or provide imageries for political action (Verba et al. 1995:317; for historical reviews, see Soskis, Chapter 2, "History of Associational Life and the Nonprofit Sector in the United States"; McCarthy 2003, chaps. 3 and 5; Morone 2003;

Young 2002). In contemporary America, religious associations and networks remain key sites for civic collaboration and even coalitions that cross lines of race, creed, and class (Lichterman 2005; Elisha 2010; see Paxton, Chapter 23, "What Influences Charitable Giving?"). In this way, religious organizing may compensate for obstacles to participation for the poor, minority groups, and women. Thus the pilgrimage, or *peregrenacion*, provided a template for protest mobilization among migrant farmworkers in the 1960s (Ganz 2000) and, through the linking of Catholic parishes to the Industrial Areas Foundation, created opportunities for community residents to develop skills as effective leaders and advocates (M. R. Warren 2001). But this relationship varies across faiths and denominations. Mainline Protestant, Evangelical, and Catholic associations regularly differ in the extent to which religious participation is associated with political participation and skills. Protestantism—whether mainline and evangelical—is more likely to be associated with increased organizational skills and participation, but only mainline Protestantism is consistently linked with increased participation in *nonreligious* associations. Involvement in Catholic associations has weaker political effects than participation in Protestant organizations; this difference, it is argued, reflects the more hierarchical character of Catholic associations and the likelihood that clergy rather than laypeople will be in charge (Verba et al. 1995:245; Wuthnow 1999).

Despite the tremendous appeal of democratic socialization to advocates of the nonprofit sector, these studies suggest that this claim cannot be easily and automatically sustained for all nonprofits or voluntary associations. Even participatory organizations may fail to generate the skills necessary for democratic participation or may cultivate values that are hostile to liberal democracy or contribute to political apathy (Eliasoph 1998, 2011). Other revisionist arguments go further still, contending that voluntary associations may promote separatism, intergroup hostility, and even antidemocratic values (Kaufman 2002). The Klan, the Nazi party, other hate organizations—all have been held up as potent counter-examples to the facile equation of participation with democratic values. As Kathleen Blee writes, "Organized racism is more than the aggregation of individual racist sentiments. It is a social milieu in which venomous ideas . . . take shape. Through networks of groups and activists, it channels personal sentiments of hatred into collective racist acts" (2002:3; see also Fiorina 1999; McVeigh 2009; Rosenblum 1998b; Skocpol et al. 1999:69). Whether challenged by the presence of "nonprofits in disguise" (where self-dealing by management evades the nondistribution constraint) or by NPOs promoting controversial as well as illiberal values, the automatic equation of nonprofit status with civic virtues is brought into question.

Whereas the political variant of a market model began with citizens expressing heterogeneous preferences, civic accounts of associations—including NPOs—highlight how organizational participation cultivates skills, articulates preferences, and constitutes the political selves of citizens. These civic effects are typically envisioned as "upstream" in a democratic system, mobilizing constituencies that will influence the outcomes of elections and the character of policy debates. But such an automatic possibility for democratic input and influence cannot be assumed, given that the legal form for NPOs is a political artifact. As the following section describes, the nexus of nonprofit or civic associations and formal political processes has been fiercely contested and tightly regulated.

Political Frameworks for NPOs

The causal chain from participation to political outcomes is not exhausted by individual socialization and acquisition of civic skills (or even uncivil values). Associations may contribute to democracy by articulating interests, by providing a framework for the careers of those in the political opposition and a "center for action" where associations "form something like a separate nation within the nation and a government within the government" (Tocqueville 2004:216; see also Walzer 1984). Thus, any assessment of the political consequences of voluntary associations and NPOs must directly address the engagement between these private entities and formal political institutions.

Across many varieties of regimes, this connection is shaped by the direct regulation of political participation. The frequent legal decoupling of "charitable" nonprofits from significant political engagement disrupts the assumption—central to so many "civic" arguments about voluntary associations—that the skills and values cultivated in associations are easily transposed to formal politics. The long history of restrictions on association reminds us that voluntary organizations may be potent forces of change and that access to political arenas is itself an object of contestation. In general, the political or advocacy activities of NPOs are treated with care—not least in reports from organizational informants themselves—insofar as direct involvement in electoral politics (as opposed to "education" and advocacy) is circumscribed by nonprofit standing in U.S. law (see Berry and Arons 2003; Boris and Krehely 2003; Wolch 1992:62–76).

In the United States, these distinctions among charity, advocacy, and campaign activities have been articulated through the tax code. But the roots of this system of categories may be found in nineteenth-century jurisprudence. For example, *Jackson v. Phillips*, a case involving a will written before the start of the Civil War but adjudicated after its end, illustrates how philanthropic activity was carefully fenced off from the domain of democratic politics. Unpacking the different clauses of the contested bequest, the judge allowed gifts that would contribute to the "moral education" of now-freed slaves (even through the "fugitive slaves" specified in the will were by then emancipated) but disallowed the portion of the gift intended to support the cause of women's suffrage and, therefore, intended "directly and exclusively to change the laws" (quoted in Zunz 2012:79–80). As governments, both state and federal, added to the exemptions or privileges accorded charities and charitable giving, they simultaneously policed the purposes that could be supported by these resources. Particularly in a democratic polity linked to an economy and society full of inequalities, the giving of gifts and the capacity to volunteer represented points at which extrapolitical advantage might be transposed to electoral activities and decisions reserved for legislatures (Clemens 2020). Although this boundary between charitable giving and the promotion of change through politics was inconsistent, porous, and often violated, the principles elaborated in *Jackson v. Phillips* exemplify one piece of the ongoing construction and reconstruction of a domain for publicly oriented actions carried out by private individuals and organizations.

What were the grounds for such distinctions and such projects of category construction? In a fundamental sense, the lineage of the NPO may be traced to efforts by elites and an emerging bourgeoisie to craft a means to extend their wishes in time (beyond the limits of their own mortal existence) and in scale (beyond the capacities of single individuals).

Given these ambitions, the rights to organizational existence and restrictions on organizational activity were often tightly controlled through such means as the granting of charters. In American history, through the nineteenth century this organizational form functioned as a controversial but effective vehicle for nationalizing projects of northeastern elites such as the expansion of education, religion, and the arts (Hall 1992; Clemens 2020). Well into the twentieth century, the activities and resources of these publicly chartered yet privately governed entities raised political suspicion. State legislation repeatedly enacted trade-offs of authorization or subsidy of private activities in exchange for increases in government oversight (Clemens 2006; Levy 2017; Novak 2001).

In the 1910s, state courts disagreed as to whether associations dedicated to securing legal change through legal means were properly understood as "charitable" and therefore eligible for exemptions from taxation of property and bequests (Zollman 1924:209; Zunz 2012). The 1920s and 1930s brought debates—and ultimately legislation—delineating the rights of corporations to make tax-advantaged contributions to benevolent associations as a means of cultivating community goodwill toward their firms. Only in the 1950s was it determined that these same rights extended to donations made outside a corporation's home community. Throughout these decades, rights to associate came under episodic pressure, particularly as repeated "red scares" made some organizational memberships themselves evidence of criminal conspiracy. As one means of buffering themselves from state repression, some social movements repeatedly anchored themselves in programs that, whether or not they were legally nonprofit corporations, engaged in the kinds of activities closely associated with the nonprofit sector.[7]

The acknowledgment of a freedom to associate did not guarantee the direct translation of associational activity into political engagement. Even in relatively permissive polities such as the United States, these early disagreements foreshadowed a history of legislative oversight in which excessive political activity by foundations or NPOs triggered threats to the exempt status and legal standing of these organizations (Jenkins 1987, 1998; Levy 2017; Wolch 1992:62–69). In the United States, as federal intervention in community and social issues expanded from the 1960s onward, existing community associations and social movement organizations were torn between the appeal of new resources and the perceived threat that engagement with public programs would in time curb their political activities (Andrews 2001; Castells 1983: chap. 13). Similar concerns were prompted by grants from foundations committed to social change (Jenkins 1998:212–215). Tensions also rose between these politically engaged movement organizations and long-established voluntary and service agencies that expected to control any new sources of public largesse (Castells 1983:116). By the end of the decade, both social service and environmental organizations had experienced hostile bouts of regulation in reaction to their advocacy activities (Wolch 1992:63–67).

Through their tax-exempt status and receipt of public funds, both advocacy and service organizations in the United States remain vulnerable to political efforts to use these economic relations as leverage to channel or choke off political activity. In the early 1990s, Congress repeatedly considered—and defeated—a proposal from Oklahoma congressman Ernest Istook "to curtail advocacy by nonprofit groups receiving grants" (Reid 1999:316; see also Berry and Arons 2003:66–92). Although these proposals failed, these regulatory attempts were consequential. Research has repeatedly demonstrated that nonprofits spend fewer funds on political activities than is allowed by law and express considerable wariness and uncertainty about the extent of allowable activity. As Jeffrey Berry observes, "the interest group sector with the strongest disincentive to lobby is 501c3 nonprofits. It is the only interest group sector to whom the government says 'you really shouldn't'" (Berry and Arons 2003:27; Boris and Krehely 2003). Thus, even in liberal democracies, nonprofits may be organized to cultivate civic skills among their members but constrained in their capacity to serve as vehicles for civic politics by the legal restrictions that distance voluntary or charitable activities from electoral engagement.

In contrast to these Anglo-American developments, other European nations and principalities took a less accommodating stance toward associational activity. Fears of conspiracy and restrictions on associations limited the possibilities for organization in some places; in others, civic associations were firmly embedded within the framework of religious authority. In France, democratic revolution was accompanied by laws restricting association and, over the nineteenth century, a pattern of political development that protected the public domain from private organizing—whether corporate, voluntary, or charitable (Huard 2000; Ronsavallon 2007; on charity, see Adams 2007). Along a different trajectory seen in northwestern Europe, associations have developed in tandem with recognized—and often state-endorsed—churches, laying the foundations for the "pillarized" systems of corporatist social provision (Ertman 2000; see also Salamon and Anheier 1998).

By the eighteenth and nineteenth centuries, combinations of growing economic prosperity and institutional reform fueled "the associational mania of midcentury" in much of Europe, a wave that would come to be known as the *Vereinseuphorie* (Nord 2000:xxi). These developments gained early momentum in Britain. As laid out in the Elizabethan Statute of 1601, the law of charities enabled durable and/or collective forms of activity beyond the bounds of the state, so long as that activity was dedicated to purposes approved by the state (Ware 1989). By the eighteenth century, the growing merchant class in London and other cities began to form associations committed to admirable causes, organizations that would also serve as sites for social contact with members of the aristocracy (Colley 1992).

Unlike the Tocquevillian arguments that highlight civil society as a vehicle for democratic participation and a bulwark against the expansion of the administrative state, corporatist models highlight the possibilities of an expansive nonprofit sector that is aligned with or even captured by the state. This is a classic feature of twentieth-century fascist regimes (Riley 2010), but strong ties between factional organizations or parties and nongovernmental social service organizations also characterize mass democracies such as India (Thachil 2011), profoundly contested polities such as Lebanon (Cammett 2014), and contested configurations of electoral politics and neoliberalism in states such as Turkey and Egypt (Tuğal 2017). Comparative research on social provision has documented how many types of regime integrate voluntary and NPOs more closely into the structure of party politics (Cammett and MacLean 2014).

Not surprisingly, the regulation of NPOs—their legal recognition, allowed activities, and relations to state actors as well as donors and volunteers—has been profoundly contested across a range of regimes whether more or less authoritarian, more or less democratic. The persistence of these controversies follows from the basic logic of the Tocquevillian argument: if NPOs are central elements of civil society and promote democratic practices, then we should expect that increasingly authoritarian regimes may diminish the scale, scope, and vitality of the nonprofit sector.[8] Yet the rationale for suppressing voluntary social provision in authoritarian regimes may be offset, at least in some cases, by the recognition that NGOs can generate social provision beyond the capacity of government agencies, thereby contributing to the stability of the regime. The tensions created by these divergent considerations generate intensified politics over the status of NGOs and NPOs.

China exemplifies the resulting dynamics. Between the communist revolution of 1949 and the end of the Cultural Revolution in 1976, the regime suppressed almost all civic associations (Ma 2002:308). Yet in the decades since, political changes have created real, if limited, opportunities for the mobilization of social service and grassroots advocacy groups. The Chinese state has acknowledged a role for NGOs "to help the state reach its constituents, to serve as bridges between the state and society" in ways that would address social problems and allow the government to reduce its budgetary commitments (Ma 2002:310). Yet this move to encourage social organizing without activating the democratizing potential of a growing civil society has led to great ambiguity in the regulatory framework for NGOs. As Anthony Spires (2011) documents for China in the 2000s, grassroots organizations found that "the relatively lax enforcement of law" permitted them space to operate, particularly insofar as they addressed problems beyond the capacity of government officials without attracting media attention.

Within this regulatory framework, nonprofits can provide alternatives or supplements to government social provision, but there are strong barriers to translating the resulting civic capacity into political voice. These "grassroots NGOs survive only insofar as they limit any democratic claims making and help promote the social welfare goals of the state" (Spires 2011:23, 36). Within China, the character and strategy of these organizations varies across locales and issue areas, shaped by patterns of resource dependency and the orientation of local, provincial, and national governments (Dai and Spires 2017; Hsu, Hsu, and Hasmath 2017) as well as by increasing legal constraints on relations between nonprofits and international funders. Chinese foundations, which often resemble operating foundations rather than endowed foundations, have been found to be more transparent when they are less dependent on government funds and more concerned with recruiting and retaining donors (Nie, Liu, and Cheng 2016). The uneven, halting, sometimes reversed regulatory tolerance of NPOs in China is a piece of a more general process of "authoritarian backsliding" from democratic advances (Dresden and Howard 2016).

A related pattern of regulatory tightening is evident in Russia, albeit without the pronounced cultivation of nonprofits as social service providers that marks contemporary Chinese policy. After 1989 and the dissolution of the USSR that followed, many Western governments and foundations sought to enhance the capacity of civil society within Russia and the other former socialist states (Horvath 2013:1–5; Oleinikova 2017; for a related politics over international aid in developing countries, see Dupuy and Prakash, Chapter 28, "Global Backlash Against Foreign Funding to Domestic Nongovernmental Organizations"). The success of these efforts to foster democratically oriented civil society was limited by the legacies of "patronage and personalism" (Spencer 2011; see also Howard 2003:129–136) but nevertheless came to be perceived as a source of threat.

In 2006, additional reporting requirements were adopted out of concerns for both the potential political challenge represented by nonprofits and allegations that the form had been adopted as a front for illicit activity or opportunistic pursuit of international funding (Horvath 2013:123–143; Ljubownikow and Crotty 2014). In 2012, "any NGO receiving funding from abroad" was required "to register as a 'foreign agent,'" a status linked to "crippling financial reporting burdens and prohibitions against working with state agencies" (Hamlett 2017:254). Three years later, Russia adopted the Undesirable NGO Law, under which foreign organizations operating in Russia (including the MacArthur Foundation, Amnesty International, and the National Endowment for Democracy) might be declared "undesirable by the Prosecutor General or the Foreign Ministry" (Hamlett 2017:249; Oleinikova 2017:88). Ambiguity and uncertainty with respect to the enforcement of such laws intensified the incentives for nonprofits to constrain their own activities. Over the same period, other laws targeting the flow of foreign funds to NGOs were adopted in Belarus and Ukraine; the latter did not restrict foreign funding but was particularly focused on constraining groups mobilized against corruption (Oleinikova 2017).

Across centuries, countries, and types of regime, the regulatory framework for nonprofits and civic associations has been repeatedly elaborated and contested. Although the specific actors and stakes in these episodes vary, cumulatively the pattern speaks to the opportunities that follow from the character of these organizations as "not something" and therefore as vehicles for action that is exempt from some of the rules and expectations of other entities in a polity, or a market, or some other domain. As entities that are recognized as anomalous in specific ways—not-for-profit in market systems, nongovernmental in the provision of public goods—NPOs and NGOs also constitute opportunities for forms of arbitrage: the mobilization of resources and efforts across diverse social domains.

Nonprofits as Sites of Arbitrage

If Douglas (1987) asked why social provision is sometimes the responsibility of government and sometimes allocated to nonprofits, a different kind of boundary spanning becomes visible by asking why actors would organize their activities in a nonprofit form rather than some other alternative. One potential answer is that the motives and goals of organizing do not align with the dominant logic of some other domain; this disjuncture between mission and practice has fueled the emergence of new forms of social entrepreneurship. But the choice of a nonprofit form may also be driven by a recognition that the regulatory framework for nonprofits provides distinctive advantages. The presumptions of public-regardingness and altruism that attach to nonprofit activity offer opportunities for rehabilitating reputations, both individual and corporate. Rules allowing for the anonymity of contributions, perhaps adopted to respect the modesty of donors, now allow for the channeling of financial resources to causes without revealing the interests behind such efforts.

The presumption that nonprofits have a distinctively public-serving mission also represents a potential advantage in conflicts over the appropriate scope of public social provision, just as debates over the expansion of the postwar welfare state informed Douglas's initial political theory of NPOs. Arguments in support of increased partnerships with nonprofits have been offered as solutions to the "crisis" of the welfare state. In Europe, well-developed welfare states have turned to expanded collaborations with nonprofits in the face of fiscal crises and "crises of technique" in which traditional bureaucratic methods prove ill-suited to policy problems that require individualized attention rather than the provision of benefits to broad categories of citizens (Ullman 1998). In the late 1990s, Britain's New Labour adopted an essentially communitarian endorsement of government collaboration with nonprofits in part as a means of rejecting the Conservatives' exaltation of the market without requiring New Labour to return to the state-centered policies of their predecessors (Kendall 2000). As has been shown across policy domains, these arrangements of "contracting out" to nonprofits sometimes then become opportunities for nonprofits to make payments to closely related for-profits (e.g., for rent or services), thereby channeling public funding for social provision into market systems (on charter schools, see Reckhow 2013).

Studies of welfare reform suggest how government contracting out to NPOs supplies cover for downsizing programs and shifts risk from public authorities (Austin 2003; Pierson 1994). Insofar as governments turn to extensive collaboration with nonprofit entities, such privatization or contracting-out produces a much more complex situation in which "government accountability to citizens is undermined when responsibility for admission, treatment, and outcomes seem to be in the hands of private organizations" (Smith and Lipsky 1993:209). Insofar as nongovernmental entities are increasingly visible as the providers of social services, the legitimacy of public provision—increasingly restricted to funding rather than implementation—may be undermined. To the extent that publicly funded services are delivered by NGOs, citizens may struggle to answer the question of "what are my tax dollars doing for me?" and may assume that publicly funded services are actually the product of voluntary donations or private enterprise. These arrangements may also provide an opening for patronage politics. If voluntary associations and NPOs are valued, in part, because of their capacity to constitute citizens, then the increasing ties of nonprofits to the state signal an important shift in the relations that constitute and undermine democratic polities.

As NPOs come to resemble professional bureaucratic agencies in all but legal status, then the assumption that this organizational form nurtures democratic participation and organizational skills should be questioned, although not necessarily rejected. Given the extent to which ambiguity about the organizational form pervades research and theorizing on nonprofit entities, any assessment of the political salience of nonprofits must avoid attributing traits or consequences to NPOs simply by virtue of their formal organizational status or auspice. The capacity of NPOs to function as potential sites for the constitution of citizens or vehicles for the expression of articulated interests and values depends on features of organizational structure: the degree of formal hierarchy and professionalism and the opportunities for practicing participation. And, just as the increase in the size and professionalism of nonprofits should prompt reconsideration of their role in political socialization, so the increasing ties between these nongovernmental—as well as not-for-profit—entities and the state raise important questions about the changing relations of the components of civic society to the formal institutions of representation and rule. In the place of a "political theory of nonprofits," the current moment requires close attention to the implication of NPOs in diverse projects of state-building and political mobilization.

If "policy makes politics," the increasingly complex web of relations among government agencies and NPOs will not lead to a simple—or singular—political outcome.

Conclusion

Much research on NPOs has built on an imagery of differentiated domains of social life: the state, the market, and the third or independent sector, which is often equated with the concept of civil society. But just as the nonprofit form is a political creation or artifact, so too is the system of categories that distinguishes regions organized around different models of production and social provision. In the advanced industrial democracies of the postwar decades, the principles informing this division of labor supported general theories of the nonprofit sector: the nondistribution constraint versus the profit motive, government programs supported by majorities versus nonprofits providing public goods desired by minorities.

These influential economic and political theories of NPOs (Hansmann 1987; Douglas 1987) began from individuals with preferences exercising choice. That starting place has been destabilized, both conceptually and historically. As postwar expansions in social policy have increasingly relied on forms of contracting out to NPOs, it has become more difficult for citizens to recognize which programs are publicly funded (Mettler 2011) and to assume that the legal status of NPOs guarantees public-regarding or altruistic organizational behavior. These shifts in the character of the nonprofit sector in the advanced industrial democracies have been paired with the intensified politicization of the nonprofit form in newly democratizing regimes. That same capacity for civic mobilization that has been celebrated in the literature on democratic civil society may easily be perceived as a threat to regime stability just as was the case in postrevolutionary France two centuries earlier. As the framework of postwar liberal democracy comes under pressure around the globe, the legal framework for nonprofit existence and activity is likely to become further politicized. NPOs and voluntary associations constitute vehicles for publicly oriented action that are not entirely contained within formal political institutions and, therefore, they represent potent configurations of possibility and political challenge.

Sarah Reckhow

IN MAY 2017, A 3.3-MILE streetcar line opened in downtown Detroit—a city well known for its lack of public transportation. This project emerged from an unusual financing and management model. The largest single funder was not the U.S. Department of Transportation, the State of Michigan, or the City of Detroit—it was the Kresge Foundation, a private philanthropic organization. A nonprofit, M-1 Rail, operates the streetcar system, known as the QLine (a corporate sponsor, Quicken Loans, purchased the naming rights; other corporations and nonprofit institutions have sponsored stops along the route). No elected public officials sit on the M-1 Rail board of directors, but the group does include Quicken founder and billionaire philanthropist Dan Gilbert, as well as Kresge's CEO and president, Rip Rapson. As a *Next City* article on the project observes: "The city's political class . . . has largely been shut out of the streetcar development project" (Smith 2014). Critics argue that the downtown streetcars were designed for the use of wealthier residents and to attract economic development in the city's core—at the expense of Detroiters from high-poverty neighborhoods who rely on buses.

The debate about the influence of donors on seemingly public-sector projects is much bigger than streetcars in Detroit. The QLine is symptomatic of broader shifts in the role of philanthropy in the provision of public services and public policy. The number of billionaires in the United States has more than doubled since the mid-1990s, and many of these individuals are deeply engaged in philanthropy during their lifetimes. For example, the Giving Pledge, started by Microsoft founder Bill Gates, his wife Melinda, and Berkshire Hathaway CEO Warren Buffett, has inspired 204 high-net-worth individuals or couples to commit to donating the majority of their wealth to philanthropic causes. Meanwhile, as public-sector budgets grow more constrained by legacy costs and concerns about deficits, funders come to the table in ever larger numbers and with substantial resources to engage with the policy process. Sometimes private funders are invited to get involved in supporting public-sector services by public officials seeking aid and support; in other cases, private funders create their own agenda priorities, which may or may not be aligned with the priorities of elected leaders (Lemos and Charles 2018).

I argue that philanthropic efforts in the twenty-first century—particularly those led by the wealthiest individuals and foundations—should be examined not only within their political context but also as an aspect of the political climate. In this regard, my perspective is closely aligned with Aaron Horvath and Walter Powell, who also examine changes in "the institutional environment surround[ing] philanthropy" (2016:89). Only with recognition of this broader context is it possible to fully appreciate the ways that philanthropic power intersects with the political system. As David Callahan explains in his book *The Givers*, "Big philanthropy is arising in an era when the wealthy already seem to control so much territory in America" (2017:8).

The New Gilded Age

The bold steps taken by philanthropists in recent years—such as the QLine project in Detroit, or the 2016 announcement by the Walton Family Foundation to spend $1 billion on charter schools over five years—are somewhat reminiscent of the Gilded Age philanthropists of the early twentieth century. Among the most visible philanthropic gifts of that earlier era was Andrew Carnegie's $60 million to support the construction of 1,689 public libraries across the United States. These libraries have persisted for decades, in many cases still treasured by local communities as public goods. Now, one century later, we are entering an era that many scholars view as a New Gilded Age, with enormous fortunes amassed by the wealthiest members of society and stagnant incomes for most of the workforce (Piketty 2013; Krugman 2014). Just as the first Gilded Age was characterized by the development of major legacy foundations, such as the Carnegie Corporation and the Rockefeller Foundation, a new wave of institution building and philanthropic giving is under way among the corporate titans of the New Gilded Age.

New Gilded Age income distributions show a growing share of income accruing among the top 10 percent of earners since the 1980s, sometimes exceeding the levels of inequality seen in the original Gilded Age. Underlying this pattern, however, is further disparity within the top 10 percent. According to Anthony Atkinson, Thomas Piketty, and Emmanuel Saez, "Most of the changes in the top decile are due to dramatic changes in the top percentile, which rose from 8.9 percent [of total income] in 1976 to 23.5 percent in 2007" (2011:6). Moreover, the share of income amassed by the top 0.1 percent was 12.3 percent by 2007, surpassing the highest level reached during the original Gilded Age (Atkinson et al. 2011). Although the highest earners lost income during the Great Recession, wealth concentration increased and the top 1 percent and top 0.1 percent have retained income shares comparable to Gilded Age levels (Saez and Zucman 2014; Zucman 2019). These economic trends have created massive new fortunes and an extraordinarily wealthy class of plutocrats in the United States.

In addition to economic trends, shifts in the political system have created new and different political opportunities for New Gilded Age philanthropists. First, contemporary philanthropists have considerable flexibility and face relatively little public scrutiny when creating an organization to distribute their wealth. In contrast, the early-twentieth-century philanthropists confronted serious public pushback that framed philanthropy as a threat to democracy, even when simply creating their foundations (Reich 2018; McGooey 2016). When Rockefeller took steps in 1909 to create his foundation and seek a federal charter, the concept of the general-purpose charitable foundation was a novelty, and Rockefeller encountered intense scrutiny and skepticism in Congress (Reich 2018). As Rob Reich explains, reaction against Rockefeller's foundation was so intense, a bill was drafted that would have "limited the size and life span of the foundation and imposed a form of public governance on its operation" (Reich 2018:6). Yet this bill failed, and Rockefeller ultimately turned to the State of New York for a charter, which offered the foundation extensive latitude compared to the oversight and limitations proposed at the federal level. Thus, the general purpose and perpetual private foundation developed in the United States with relatively few restrictions.

According to Reich, the debate over the Rockefeller Foundation "reveals attitudes and reservations about philanthropy virtually never heard in our contemporary era" (2018:136). The private foundation has offered a flexible and advantageous approach for distributing wealth to priorities chosen by the donor—establishing a foundation requires no prior approval from elected officials and comes with favorable tax incentives. Nonetheless, private foundations are increasingly viewed as lacking the flexibility and secrecy that many contemporary donors desire. Many elite donors today route their philanthropic activities through multiple channels; donors are increasingly seeking even more flexible alternatives to the traditional private foundation (such as limited liability corporations and donor-advised funds) and coordinating their philanthropic action with their political giving strategies (Saunders-Hastings 2018).

Second, the rise of think tanks and the interest group explosion of the 1970s has influenced politics, cementing an expansive role for external advocacy groups in the federal policy-making process (Walker 1991; Rich 2004; Grossmann 2012). The growing number of think tanks and interest groups focused on public policy influence has created a target-rich environment for donors seeking grantees with access to policy makers—donors can support organizations that specialize in advocacy, research, and/or specific ideological or issue-oriented perspectives, and even work to coordinate activities across organizations to promote coalitions around specific agenda items (Teles 2008; Medvetz 2012; McDonnell and Weatherford 2013; McDonald 2014).

The most common type of tax status designation among nonprofit organizations is the 501(c)(3) nonprofit, which offers a substantial advantage for fund-raising purposes—tax deductibility for donors (including both individual donors and private foundations). Although 501(c)(3) organizations have some limits on their ability to lobby and are prohibited from electoral campaigning, the (c)(3) status is quite common, particularly among think tanks in the United States. Meanwhile, 501(c)(4) nonprofits, also known as social welfare organizations, are permitted to engage in lobbying and electioneering, and after the 2010 *Citizens United* Supreme Court cases, these organizations gained even broader latitude for providing independent expenditure funds in state and federal elections. As Daniel Chand explains, the "fastest growing, and consequently most scrutinized, type of tax status for nonprofit interest groups is subsection 501(c)(4)" (2014:245). Alongside the growth in 501(c)(4) organizations is the development of complex organizational structures in which nonprofit interest groups partially integrate the activities of 501(c)(3) nonprofits with their 501(c)(4) cousins, along with political action committees (PACs) (Chand 2014; Kerlin and Reid 2010). As Janelle Kerlin and Elizabeth Reid explain in their study of complex nonprofit structures among environmental groups, "Organizations in this structure legally interrelate through overlapping boards, shared finances, and policy agendas with the overall goal of extending their advocacy reach to the farthest extent possible under nonprofit law" (2010:803). In addition to maximizing capacity of advocacy under the existing legal framework, these complex organizational arrangements also create abundant opportunities for wealthy individuals to distribute funds through multiple channels in attempts to influence the political agenda.

Finally, philanthropy in the New Gilded Age is taking place in a climate of public-sector austerity. The Gilded Age philanthropy in the early twentieth century emerged at the outset of a period of extensive state building in the United States, ahead of the New Deal and the Great Society. Government budgets grew considerably during the twentieth century, and public services were added by every level of government. Thus, philanthropic activity in areas like education and relief for the poor was often engulfed later on by a rapidly expanding public sector. Today, the public sector in many places is undergoing a reverse shift. Many state and local governments have contemplated or implemented austerity measures—sometimes in response to steep declines in revenues, at other times in line with the ideological preferences of conservative politicians attempting to shrink government. When public resources are stagnant or declining, donors may find that public officials are particularly interested in projects that are fully funded by private resources. For example, consider the decision by the Baltimore Police Department, following the 2015 protests after Freddie Gray's death and a spike in homicides, to accept private funding for an aerial surveillance program that was not disclosed to the public and was funded by grant money from the Laura and John Arnold Foundation. Baltimore police contracted with Persistent Surveillance Solutions for an airplane to fly eight thousand feet over the city and record hundreds of hours of video for the police (Donovan 2016). Baltimore—a city with well-publicized challenges in criminal justice and entrenched local budget difficulties—may have been particularly susceptible to accepting a privately funded initiative for a controversial project. A weakened public sector could impact the balance of power between private funders and public interests.

Building on these themes, this chapter focuses on the intersection of philanthropy and politics in the twenty-first century and the consequences of expanding philanthropic involvement in politics. Through data on giving and detailed examples, I show that philanthropists are highly engaged in politics as contributors, advocates, and patrons of government programs. First, I discuss prior literature and theoretical perspectives that examine the relationship between philanthropy and politics in a democracy. Second, I show how philanthropic giving and political giving by wealthy donors are linked. I use data on campaign contributions by major living philanthropists to show how philanthropists are often outsized participants in traditional forms of political involvement. Third, I discuss the use of LLCs and 501(c)(4)s among major donors. These vehicles enable direct support for lobbying and political campaigns, which traditional private foundations are barred from funding. Within this discussion, I also consider how philanthropists work in coordination to influence politics—both in one-on-one collaborations and by convening groups in joint efforts. Fourth, I consider philanthropic efforts to directly support activities traditionally viewed as public-sector responsibilities (such as infrastructure and government staffing) in light of the decline of public-sector capacity in some of areas of the United States. Focusing on distressed cities, I address the heightened role of philanthropy in places where government has retreated or lost capacity to respond to major challenges.

I argue that, in combination, these factors make the political system more permeable to various forms of influence from wealthy individuals.

Good Samaritans or Unconstrained Plutocrats?

New philanthropic investments in public priority areas are frequently noted in the media, often with admiring attention. A recent *Wall Street Journal* article, announcing Michael Bloomberg's 2018 pledge of $375 million for education initiatives, follows this playbook. The article notes, "Philanthropists have long sought to improve the country's educational offerings, both as a tool for social mobility and for the sake of the country's economic competitiveness," and concludes by listing other recent major gifts in education philanthropy from Bill and Melinda Gates; Blackstone Group CEO Stephen Schwarzman; and Facebook CEO Mark Zuckerberg and his wife, Priscilla Chan (Korn 2018).

The article approaches philanthropic investments in major areas of public policy (such as education) as supportive and charitable work. We could call this view the "Good Samaritan" perspective: philanthropists seek to improve people's well-being in areas like education, their motives are admirable, and the amounts they have given are impressive. Yet any philanthropic funding that deals with policy issues must inevitably intersect with the political realm. Philanthropists can use their resources, such as large-scale grantmaking and the power to convene organizations and public officials, to impact the direction of public spending, the services offered by governments, the representation of different groups in the political realm, the development of new programs, the structure of partnerships between government and civil society, and many other features of public policy. Given this intersection of public-sector governance and private-sector resources, several perspectives have emerged around a key question: Is philanthropy good or bad for democracy?

Bloomberg's $375 million pledge brings up a broad set of issues related to democracy. Bloomberg is a billionaire and former mayor of New York City whose three mayoral terms featured many prominent and controversial initiatives in educational reform, such as expansion of charter schools and efforts to measure teacher effectiveness. He has been forthright about his intentions to use philanthropy to influence government, and he "focuses much of his giving on leveraging changes in public policy" (Callahan 2017:14). Will Bloomberg, through his new philanthropic investments, pursue policies similar to those highly contested ideas he introduced as mayor? How will the power he amassed through his political career and wealth impact the uptake of his ideas by school districts or states? How will other policy priorities and interests intersect with Bloomberg's initiatives—will other ideas without his financial backing lose out? Moreover, with Bloomberg waging a self-funded campaign for the presidency in 2020, his tangled web of philanthropic and political interests grows even more complex and expansive.

Scholars and journalists focused on philanthropy have considered these types of questions about the role of philanthropists in a democratic society. Often, the concern hinges on whether or how the voice of a philanthropist holds greater sway in a public policy arena compared to the voices of ordinary citizens. In particular, there is some divergence between the perspectives of those who focus on elite philanthropy (billionaire donors and major foundations) and the perspectives of those who look at philanthropy as a broader phenomenon, encompassing ordinary charitable giving by people of more modest means. Since this chapter is focused on elite donors, I primarily discuss those who examine the impact of elite donors in a democracy.

Some proponents of elite philanthropic involvement in policy use the term *philanthro-capitalism* to describe philanthropy as a way to channel the energies of for-profit enterprise to achieve social good (Bishop and Green 2010). From this perspective, the activities of self-proclaimed venture philanthropists, such as Bill Gates, should be celebrated, because venture philanthropists draw on private-sector strategies to advance innovation and effectiveness in philanthropic giving. Furthermore, this type of giving should be encouraged by society, because more social good can be achieved if society promotes the activities of philanthropists who prioritize efficiency and effectiveness. According to Matthew Bishop and Michael Green: "Philanthrocapitalists have a remarkable opportunity to play a leading role in solving the biggest problems facing our world" (2010:278).

Another positive perspective on the relationship between philanthropy and democracy comes from Olivier Zunz (2012), whose history of philanthropy in the United States concludes with the following: "Americans of all classes have invested enormous energy in philanthropy, and . . . the resulting network of foundations and community institutions has enlarged American democracy" (7). It's important to note that Zunz is discussing philanthropy broadly, not just elite philanthropy, to argue that philanthropy has enriched civil society—groups that represent an enormous array of causes and interests would not exist without the significant investments of philanthropists. As Ted Lechterman and Rob Reich observe in Chapter 6, "Political Theory and the Nonprofit Sector," funding civil society can serve a variety of functions that could support a well-functioning democracy, including (1) providing a bulwark for civil liberties against an overreaching state, (2) supporting associational life for the development of public deliberation and preference formation, and (3) providing a training ground for participation in formal democratic institutions. Joel Fleishman, whose book centers on private foundations, offers a similar perspective, arguing that a diverse civil society is the most significant accomplishment of American philanthropy:

> The greatest contribution of America's private foundations, therefore, is in continually empowering widely diverse individuals and groups holding a rainbow of views on every conceivable matter of social policy and civic concern, to organize themselves, to make their views heard, and to transform their ideas and dreams into reality. (Fleishman 2008:50)

Other scholars offer a more conditional set of arguments about philanthropy's relationship to democracy or emphasize critiques. For example, Reich (2016) acknowledges and critiques the plutocratic interests represented by elite philanthropy. Nonetheless, he observes that elite philanthropy can play a distinct role by investing in public priorities that require a long-term time horizon for payoffs (for instance, efforts to mitigate the consequences of climate change). According to Reich, democratic governments tend to have a bias toward the present, discounting the need to invest in policies that would benefit future generations. Foundations are uniquely positioned to invest in experimental and long-range problem-solving ideas that may be too risky or politically infeasible for governments. As Reich explains, "the peculiar institutional form of the foundation can have an important role in democracy in spite of their plutocratic power" (2016:81).

Delving further into the context and priorities of present-day philanthropy, Horvath and Powell (2016) offer a more pessimistic take, arguing that "philanthropy, especially big-money philanthropy, exists in tension—sometimes contributory, sometimes disruptive—with state provision. It alters public conversation, sets agendas, and provides public goods in the absence of public deliberation" (93). In its disruptive form—in which philanthropic-led solutions are an alternative to the public sector, rather than a partner—Horvath and Powell explain that philanthropy can detract from the legitimacy of the public sector and support policy initiatives that bypass public engagement. Emma Saunders-Hastings (2018:152) also argues that contemporary elite philanthropy can be undemocratic, highlighting the "significant, sustained, and structured" influence that elite donors hold over recipient organizations. Furthermore, as Elisabeth Clemens points out in Chapter 7, "Nonprofits as Boundary Markers," increasing nonprofit responsibility for public service provision can undermine government accountability and create confusion among citizens about whether services are publicly or privately provided.

Finally, in *Dissent* magazine, Joanne Barkan offers a full-throated critique of elite philanthropy:

> They [philanthropists] may act with good intentions, but they define "good." The arrangement remains thoroughly plutocratic: it is the exercise of wealth-derived power in the public sphere with minimal democratic controls and civic obligations. . . . Because they are mostly free to do what they want, mega-foundations threaten democratic governance and civil society (defined as the associational life of people outside the market and independent of the state). When a foundation project fails—when, say, high-yield seeds end up forcing farmers off the land or privately operated charter schools displace and then underperform traditional public schools—the subjects of the experiment suffer, as does the general public. Yet the do-gooders can simply move on to their next project. Without countervailing forces, wealth in capitalist societies already translates into political power; big philanthropy reinforces this tendency. Although this plutocratic sector is privately governed, it is publicly subsidized. (Barkan 2013)

As Barkan points out at the end of this passage, an important component of the critique of philanthropic influence in public policy is the fact that it is subsidized by the tax system. In other words, not only can philanthropists fund initiatives that give them a louder voice in policy debates, but their funding choices are publicly incentivized by tax exemptions. Reich (2018) is similarly critical of the charitable tax deduction; as he argues, a tax deduction paired with progressive income tax policy creates "a troubling plutocratic bias in the contours of civil society" (132), since wealthier individuals gain a greater tax benefit for each dollar they donate.

In the remainder of this chapter, I provide further empirical evidence to help the reader weigh the arguments around these varied perspectives. On the whole, I think the evidence aligns more closely with the view that the current shape of democratic governance in the United States gives superwealthy individuals ample opportunity for outsized influence—sometimes in nontransparent ways. Elite philanthropy can be a tool for this influence, and some types of philanthropy are particularly troubling in terms of lack of transparency and use as vehicles for political influence. This is not to say that all philanthropic efforts are antidemocratic, but rather that some forms of elite philanthropy are a means of further concentrating influence and power among the very wealthiest members of society.

Political Benefactors

Political scientists have started to closely examine the relationship between wealth and American politics in the context of growing socioeconomic inequality, often focusing on the behavior, attitudes, and political influence of the affluent (Jacobs and Skocpol 2007; Bartels 2008; Hacker and Pierson 2011; Gilens 2012). Wealthy individuals are known to have high levels of political participation and campaign donation (Schlozman, Verba, and Brady 2012; Gimpel, Lee, and Pearson-Merkowitz 2008). Recent court decisions and Federal Election Commission rulings, most notably *Citizens United v. FEC*, increased awareness among wealthy individuals of the multiple pathways that were legally available for making unlimited contributions to organizations that engage in political campaigning, including 501(c)(4) organizations (Franz 2013). During recent presidential campaigns, ubiquitous media coverage has focused on money in politics, with particular attention to billionaire Super PAC donors like hotel magnate Sheldon Adelson and Charles and David Koch, majority owners of Koch Industries, the second-largest privately held company in the United States. Super PACs are political action committees that can raise unlimited contributions to spend in elections as independent expenditures (in other words, they are not allowed to coordinate with candidate campaign committees).

In an era of growing wealth inequality in the United States, a small class of extremely wealthy individuals is well positioned to play an outsized role in funding political campaigns. Based on research on federal elections, we know that the role of very wealthy contributors is growing. For example, the percentage of campaign contributions from the top 0.01 percent of the voting-age population grew from under 20 percent in the 1980s to 40 percent by the 2012 election cycle (Bonica et al. 2013). Lee Drutman of the Sunlight Institute analyzed the top federal contributors in the 2012 election and showed that 28 percent of all disclosed contributions in that election cycle came from just over thirty thousand people—an extraordinary concentration of political resources among a small group of individuals making up approximately 0.01 percent of the electorate (Bonica et al. 2013).

Given these trends, what is the relationship between major philanthropy and political giving? Do the same donors play an outsized role in both areas? To examine these questions, I begin with data from Kristin Goss (2016) and her analysis of "policy plutocrats," whom Goss defined as major philanthropic donors who focus on policy-oriented giving. Goss began with 194 individual and family donors who either (1) committed to the Giving Pledge; (2) were identified in the Philanthropy 50 (a list of the biggest donors in the United States compiled by the *Chronicle of Philanthropy* annually) for 2012, 2013, or 2014; or (3) led a foundation that made one of the top-100 lists of the Foundation Center (a nonprofit that maintains a comprehensive database on U.S. grantmakers) of largest philanthropies (Goss 2016:444). Goss gathered information about the giving behavior of each individual or family on the list of major donors in order to systematically identify the policy plutocrats. For example, she coded whether the philanthropists had identified policy as one of their stated goals in the Giving Pledge or whether they had given a large grant from their private foundation to support a policy goal (Goss 2016:445). As Goss explained, "These donors are directing not only their money but also their time, ideas, and political leverage toward influencing public policy" (2016:442).

To further extend this line of investigation, I began with Goss's complete list of major donors (both those coded as policy plutocrats and those who were not) and compiled data from the Center for Responsive Politics on each donor or donor household. I gathered every federal political contribution that these individuals made in the 2016 election cycle, including contributions to presidential and congressional candidates, as well as PACs and committees. I used individual names, place of residence, and occupation to match the individual contribution data to Goss's list of donors. For members of the same household or family (spouses, for example) I gathered data on campaign contributions from each person. In total, the 194 major philanthropic donor households gave $396.7 million in federal campaign contributions during the 2016 election cycle. Incredibly, this is 6 percent of all individual contribution dollars in the 2016 election.[1] Consider this observation in light of Drutman's already surprising finding that the top 0.01 percent, or thirty thousand individuals, gave 28 percent of individual contribution dollars. In this case, a much smaller group of people—less than 0.0001 percent—gave 6 percent of the 2016 total.

The significant amount of funding from this group is not altogether surprising, given what we know about major campaign donors. Research has shown that very wealthy people are extraordinarily prolific campaign donors. Goss's list of philanthropists includes some people who are well-known for eye-popping levels of involvement as campaign funders, such as Adelson, David Koch, investor George Soros, and hedge fund manager Tom Steyer. Yet how much overlap exists between the major philanthropists and federal campaign giving? Is campaign funding mostly driven by a handful of individuals giving a lot of money, like Adelson and Steyer, while other philanthropic funders concentrate on philanthropy instead of politics?

The evidence from the campaign finance data that I added to Goss's dataset suggests the opposite—a large share of philanthropic donors are major political donors as well. Overall, 75 percent of the major philanthropists are also federal campaign donors; the median contribution amount is $26,400 and the average amount is $2 million. Although most people do not follow the George Soros model of giving $22.5 million to political campaigns, many wealthy philanthropists do give very large sums. For example, thirty of the philanthropic donor households gave more than $1 million each in 2016. This group includes both well-known individuals, like billionaire technology entrepreneur Sean Parker (founder of Napster), and people with a lower public profile, such as Seth Klarman, a Boston-based hedge fund CEO.

Although wealthy people make a growing share of political contributions, and many of the same wealthy people are also philanthropists, philanthropists can fall into either an extremely high political donation bracket or a comparatively more modest one. Based on Goss's coding for policy plutocrats, 108 of the 194 major donors or donor households demonstrated an interest in policy-oriented giving. I combined this information with the campaign contributions data to see whether the policy plutocrats are more active political campaign contributors than the philanthropists who do not focus on policy. Indeed, there is a significant difference between the groups. The 108 policy plutocrat donors and donor households gave an average of $3.5 million in federal campaign contributions in 2016, while the other 86 major philanthropic donors gave a substantially smaller average of $218,000 in campaign funds.[2] Furthermore, the higher political giving levels among policy plutocrats is present even when controlling for the donor's level of wealth.[3] Thus, policy-oriented philanthropists are also politically oriented in other areas of giving.

These findings show that political giving and philanthropic giving involve many of the same people. Individuals who pledge to give away their wealth or establish large philanthropic foundations—especially those who focus their philanthropy on public policy—are also likely to be major political donors. As large donors, these individuals rarely give exclusively to their own congressional representative. Many give nationally to out-of-state candidates, party committees, and PACs. A recent study by Jesse Rhodes, Brian Schaffner, and Raymond LaRaja (2018) identifies a distinct category of "nationalized donors." According to their research, "what really distinguishes extreme big donors is their . . . interest in spreading their contributions over a wide range of targets and, in particular, [focusing] donations on out-of-jurisdiction House and Senate candidates" (2018:504). They argue that these donors are uniquely well positioned to gain "surrogate" representation from elected officials outside their home states and suggest that this relationship is a key source of political inequality resulting from campaign finance. Thus, many major philanthropists exercise a voice in politics that is greatly amplified by their resources and inserted into out-of-state congressional elections and national politics. To the extent that philanthropy is a subsidized form of voice in public policy, that subsidy is being offered to people who are already exceptionally adept at speaking (through money) in politics.

Strategically Joining Philanthropy and Politics

In addition to directly contributing to campaigns, donors are identifying new strategies for influencing policy outside traditional foundation models. Traditional philanthropy relies on the private foundation, officially recognized by the IRS as a tax-exempt 501(c)(3) organization, as an institutional form for giving. Private foundations must annually file the 990-PF tax form, which reports annual giving and demonstrates that the foundation has met the minimum payout requirement: 5 percent of average market value of net investments each year toward charitable purposes. Thus, to ensure that their spending meets the charitability requirement, foundations generally limit most of their giving to 501(c)(3) nonprofit organizations. They are also restricted from certain types of political activity, such as lobbying, and cannot directly fund political campaigns.

In the last twenty years, some philanthropists have started to develop strategies to work around these restrictions and develop new approaches to organize their charitable giving and other funding activities. An early innovator in this area is billionaire Pierre Omidyar, the founder of eBay. In 2004 he and his wife, Pamela, founded the Omidyar Network, the vehicle they established to distribute their wealth. The Omidyar Network website has a document that describes their approach, called "Building a Philanthropic Investment Firm" (Omidyar Network n.d.) The Omidyars created a hybrid model that combines a limited liability corporation (LLC, taxable) with a tax-exempt 501(c)(3) organization. With the LLC component, the Omidyar Network makes investments in for-profit businesses whose social impacts advance its values. The nonprofit arm makes more traditional nonprofit grants. Unlike with a private foundation, donors who form an LLC receive no upfront tax advantage (just standard charitable deductions when they support nonprofits). The document is also explicit about some ways that the Omidyar Network intends to influence public policy—for example, through the formation of new organizations like the Democracy Fund (which funds bipartisan leadership initiatives and local media platforms) as well as a sister 501(c)(4) organization, Democracy Fund Voice. As a 501(c)(4), Democracy Fund Voice can be involved in activities like lobbying and campaign contributions.

Several of Omidyar's recent investments have involved journalism at both the local and national levels. He founded a nonprofit media organization called First Look Media—in the news arena, the best-known publication associated with First Look is its online news site, The Intercept. One of Omidyar's collaborators is journalist Glenn Greenwald, best known for his articles based on National Security Agency (NSA) documents disclosed by former CIA employee Edward Snowden. The Intercept describes itself as "adversarial journalism," and the publication has followed Greenwald's approach of publishing leaked documents and revealing secret government programs, particularly those related to the military and intelligence. The political orientation of the coverage is liberal. Omidyar's sizable investment in politically oriented media also underscores the sprawling character of his ventures—some transparent, some less so—which involve traditional nonprofits, political organizations with 501(c)(4) status, and media. At least one report on First Look Media, published by Politico, raises concerns about the management of the organization and Omidyar's influence:

> From top to bottom, the company's culture centered on Omidyar, an odd reverence that I thought not only undeserved, but outright embarrassing. This is a guy who got rich mostly through good timing in the tech business, not because he has an outstanding track record in journalism. Now that he's rich, he is surrounded by Yes Men and Women who tell him he's a genius—and while that might be fine in the business world, it's not good for journalism. He was good at staying out of the journalism itself, but a cult of personality existed around him internally that disrupted the whole organization. (Silverstein 2015)

Although Omidyar supports and influences left-leaning media and advocacy, it is not hard to find similar investments in nonprofit media on the conservative side. For example, Charles and the late David Koch (widely known as the Koch brothers) have supported the Reason Foundation, the Daily Caller News Foundation, and American Spectator Foundation. However, media is but one small slice of the Koch funding deployed to influence politics, as the *New York Times* reported: "The Kochs have long tried to shape political discourse through their support of nonprofit organizations, universities, and think tanks" (Ember and Vogel 2017). In a detailed analysis of the organizational strategy of the Koch brothers and their influence on the Republican Party, Theda Skocpol and Alexander Hertel-Fernandez (2016) show how the brothers' influence extends beyond their own resources and through networks to shape the giving of other like-minded donors:

> With Charles in the lead, the brothers have accordingly gone far beyond the tactics of other super-wealthy philanthropists. Not content with scattering donations to disparate institu-

tions and causes run by others, they have moved through phases to build their comprehensive political network—and their latest efforts, the third phase, took shape in the 2000s, when organizations specializing in donor coordination and constituency mobilization were added to the earlier mix of think tanks and advocacy groups. (Skocpol and Hertel-Fernandez 2016:685)

Funding from the Koch brothers and their donor consortium (guided through biannual donor seminars) has supported a wide range of right-leaning organizations, including state and national level think tanks, Americans for Prosperity (a 501(c)(4) organization), and the American Legislative Exchange Council (ALEC) (a 501(c)(3) nonprofit), which drafts model bills for state legislators that reflect donor priorities (Skocpol and Hertel-Fernandez 2016). The donor consortium makes the influence of the Koch brothers' philanthropic activities far more extensive. According to Skocpol and Hertel-Fernandez, "By 2010, more than 200 wealthy invited donors attended the seminars, often in husband-wife pairs, and by now attendance reportedly exceeds 500" (2016:685). Donor seminar guests are required to pledge a minimum of $100,000 per year. Through this channel, the Kochs are able to mobilize an entire network of wealthy conservative donors to support a common set of organizations.

As with media strategies, the donor consortium strategy for gathering philanthropic resources and channeling them into politics is not limited to one side of the political aisle. This approach was also a factor in a policy victory widely celebrated on the Left—the legalization of gay marriage. The Civil Marriage Collaborative (CMC) raised $153 million in philanthropic funding and distributed many grants to state-level organizations. By coordinating the distribution of funds, the CMC made efforts to provide larger grants to fewer states based on their political opportunity contexts. At the state level, groups worked on different strategies including bringing cases to court and supporting voter referendums for marriage equality. The funding collaborative also facilitated a convening that led to the creation of a working group. This working group developed a road map strategy for achieving marriage equality, known as the Roadmap to Victory, which scholars and activists cite as a key moment in unifying both advocates and funders around shared goals to achieve legalization of gay marriage (Freedom to Marry n.d.).

These examples of multi-institutional approaches to giving—practiced by Omidyar through the LLC model as well as the donor consortia—tend to blur the distinctions between political and charitable goals. As nonprofit scholars know well, it can be challenging to separate charitable activity from the political sphere. For those who support the cause of marriage equality, the political advocacy work funded by the CMC could be something to celebrate. Yet similar funding and strategies are also available to opponents of this or any other political movement—and donors can use these strategies without any legal requirements for transparency.

In adopting the LLC model, Omidyar furthers an emerging trend among major donors in Silicon Valley. Two examples of other LLC creations are the Emerson Collective, an LLC started by Laurene Powell Jobs, the widow of Apple co-founder Steve Jobs, and the Chan Zuckerberg Initiative (CZI), founded by Zuckerberg and Chan. The Emerson Collective was founded in 2004, the same year as the Omidyar Network. Powell Jobs has stated that the minimal transparency requirements for LLCs was part of her reason for structuring

Emerson Collective this way: "Doing things anonymously and being nimble and flexible and responsive are all things we value on our team" (Miller 2013). The Emerson Collective is focused on educational policy, environmental issues, and immigration and has started an initiative on economic development in Chicago led by former secretary of education Arne Duncan. Echoing the media-focused activities of other billionaires, Powell Jobs also recently took action through Emerson to become a partial owner of *The Atlantic* magazine, with the expectation of rapidly transitioning to full ownership (Wemple 2017).

The announcement of the CZI drew attention and scrutiny to the LLC model in philanthropy. The sheer size of the gift—at the time of the announcement, the shares that Zuckerberg committed were estimated to be worth $45 billion—naturally garnered significant interest. The LLC's major areas of investment are education, criminal justice, science (focused on health), and San Francisco Bay Area giving. The organization plans to give away roughly $1 billion per year, and the CZI website has recently added a searchable database of grants awarded since 2018 from three funding entities: Chan Zuckerberg Advocacy—a 501(c)4, Chan Zuckerberg Foundation—a 501(c)3, and the Chan Zuckerberg Initiative Donor-Advised Fund. Thus, CZI is moving towards a more transparent approach to grant-making, but so far, Emerson Collective has not."

Even funders who do not adopt the LLC organizational form have strategized ways to align philanthropic giving with more explicitly political forms of involvement. For example, heirs of Walmart founder Sam Walton have created their own 501(c)(4) organization known as the Walton Education Coalition. (It is not clear whether the coalition is supported by any broader membership beyond the Walton family). They hired the former director of another education 501(c)(4), Democrats for Education Reform, to head the coalition. Unlike the Walton Family Foundation, which reports grants on tax returns and maintains a fairly transparent website that profiles their work, the Walton Education Coalition has no website and offers no means of tracking the campaigns and initiatives it supports.

Although the coalition has a low public profile overall, some recent news has emerged that sheds light on its role in educational politics. The Walton Family Foundation is well known for long-standing support of charter schools and school choice. Following the defeat of a high-profile ballot initiative in Massachusetts to expand charter schools in the state, media coverage discussed a report funded by the Walton Education Coalition to explore the reasons that the initiative (known as Question 2) failed (Barnum 2018). As the article explains, the "internal memo was commissioned by the Walton Education Coalition, a political advocacy group that spent heavily in favor of Question 2" (Barnum 2018). The example highlights the ways donor money flows through different vehicles in an attempt to influence issue debates through multiple means. The Walton Family Foundation continues to support new charter schools and associations of charter schools, funding for charter school facilities, and various organizations that provide these schools with teachers and leadership. Meanwhile, the Walton Education Coalition can be involved in political campaigns when charter school issues are at stake. Importantly, the Question 2 example demonstrates how even well-funded initiatives can fail at the ballot box—in this case, likely influenced by heavy union counterspending to defeat the initiative.

Across these organizational forms and strategies, a few patterns emerge. First, as philanthropists engage more directly in politics, they tend to provide less transparent streams of funding. Sometimes, this is the result of the funding vehicle they use, such as an LLC or a 501(c)(4). It is also inherently challenging to trace money that changes hands multiple times through different organizations before arriving at its final destination. Some of the aversion to transparency appears to be intentional—wealthy people are choosing these funding strategies in order to avoid public scrutiny. In other cases, the lack of disclosure could be incidental. After all, 501(c)(4) organizations do not have to disclose their donors, and donors have no reason to disclose contributions that will not provide the benefit of a tax deduction. A lack of transparency does not necessarily imply purposeful secrecy.

A second observation is that donors who are involved in multiple arenas around a policy area often strategize their investments. These are not ad hoc contributions—many very wealthy and politically active donors have an agenda. They support certain policy priorities, certain ideological perspectives, and certain institutional reforms. Their donations wrap around these efforts to put pressure on different aspects of the political system—not only directly through political processes like elections and lobbying, but also by leveraging the more traditional realm of philanthropic policy activity, such as pilot programs, implementation, scaling-up organizations, and funding research, expertise, and human capital.

"A Governmental Vacuum"

In 2016, ten foundations based in Michigan pledged to provide nearly $125 million to Flint's ongoing water crisis efforts as the city begins a long recovery not only from the effects of lead exposure through drinking water but also from the long-term economic and community disinvestment that has plagued the city for many years. The Flint announcement came just over a year after twelve foundations committed $366 million toward Detroit's Grand Bargain—a compromise resulting from the city's bankruptcy proceedings that salvaged the Detroit Institute of Arts and helped fund the city's pension plans. Many of the foundations that contributed to the Grand Bargain also provide millions of dollars to support ongoing community revitalization efforts in Detroit. In both of these Michigan cities facing devastating economic and governmental crises, the philanthropic and nonprofit sector has stepped in to provide substantial capacity and support (Downey and Reckhow 2017).

Scholars across the social sciences have shown how economic, social, and political changes are weakening local governments and contributing to rising philanthropic and nonprofit activity in urban politics (Pill 2018; Levine 2016; Pacewicz 2016; Stone 2015; Anderson 2014; Marwell 2004). "The New Minimal Cities," by Michelle Wilde Anderson, lays important groundwork on the topic of local government austerity. Anderson examines the consequences of local government bankruptcy or financial receivership for urban public services based on analysis of twenty-eight cities that have experienced fiscal crises. According to Anderson, "Local government is shrinking in these and other struggling cities. Years, if not decades, of budget cuts and asset sales have left little beyond a stripped-down version of core service functions like irregular police and fire protection, rudimentary sanitation, and water supply" (2014:1122). Although this extreme form of austerity is not currently widespread in U.S. cities, local governments throughout the country have implemented cuts, partly due to declining federal grants and reductions in revenue sharing in many states (Pew Charitable Trusts 2016).

In Detroit, the reach of philanthropic involvement in propping up or even replacing traditionally public-sector activities is not limited to the famous Grand Bargain from the city's bankruptcy. Redevelopment, land use, and infrastructure in the city have all been shaped by significant philanthropic investments. A 2014 article in *Philanthropy* possibly overstates the case with the headline "Philanthropy Keeps the Lights on in Detroit" (Whyte 2014). Yet there is some justification for the hyperbole, particularly one year after the city had declared bankruptcy. Getting the city's streetlights functioning again was one public investment that emergency manager Kevyn Orr insisted on, even as the city was demonstrating its financial insolvency in bankruptcy proceedings.

One organization featured in the *Philanthropy* article is the nonprofit Midtown Detroit Inc. and its executive director, Sue Mosey. The organization receives broad support from philanthropic funders, mostly based in the Detroit metro area (Reckhow, Downey, and Sapotichne Forthcoming). Mosey is blunt about the ways in which her organization is conducting traditional public functions, including "rezoning the neighborhood, installing streetlights, repaving roads, maintaining parks, picking up trash, planting flowers, paying government salaries, wooing development" (Whyte 2014). In diagnosing the need for this work, Mosey describes a "governmental vacuum":

> "We stepped into a vacuum, especially a governmental vacuum," [Mosey] says, adding that outsiders are shocked at the types of work her group does. She recounts some recent visitors from an Atlanta foundation. "I don't think they could ever really get their head around it. But when you're in a city that has lost so much of its tax base, if you want to move forward you just do what needs to be done." (Whyte 2014)

While the erosion of major public services is an undeniable reality in bankruptcy-era Detroit, the assertion of a "vacuum"—particularly in the governmental and political realm—has some troubling implications.

In fact, the geographic area where Midtown Detroit Inc. is based was not an empty vacuum but rather a neighborhood that has long been known as the Cass Corridor. Yet Midtown Inc.'s influence has been so extensive that the neighborhood is now widely known as Midtown (except by many native Detroiters who stick by the original name). A column in the Detroit *Metro Times* by a local minister describes the Cass Corridor:

> I used to serve as associate to a congregation in the Cass Corridor, somewhat north of Corktown. That was a neighborhood teeming with life and culture, single room occupancy hotels, streetlife in parks and porches and projects, bars where Sixto Rodriguez regularly played. A place where they use to "kick out the jams." The church served the neighborhood, which poured daily in and out the front door. (Wylie-Kellerman 2015)

The Cass Corridor was known as a high-poverty neighborhood with a relatively transient population, as well as a rich cultural life: in other words, not a vacuum. Local activists and leaders in Detroit have criticized the assumption of a "vacuum" or "blank slate" by developers and leaders promoting redevelopment. According to Lauren Hood, founder of a Northwest Detroit nonprofit organization, Live6 Alliance, "to characterize a place that has three quarters of a million people in it as 'blank' is severely shortsighted. The city as 'blank slate' theory negates the cultural contributions and shared life experiences of all of those people" (Hood 2016).

Mosey's comments highlight a "governmental vacuum," which has slightly different implications—more focused on the absence of public services and capacity in a place. In Detroit, nonprofits like Mosey's have risen during a time when government is weakened, taking on authority traditionally reserved for government (such as developing infrastructure). Meanwhile, Detroit's current leadership sees Midtown as a potential model for other neighborhoods. In December 2018, Detroit mayor Mike Duggan announced $35 million in corporate contributions to the city's Strategic Neighborhood Fund targeting community development in seven neighborhoods. As Duggan explained when announcing the grants: "With the help of our partners and this record-breaking commitment, we are taking the strategy that worked in Midtown and scaling it citywide to bring more development to neighborhoods across our city" (DeVito 2018). Thus, in Detroit, the local government sees an opportunity to deploy donors and incorporate them directly into public policy in the city. In this case, the mayor is providing leadership, but in other instances, donors have been the leaders in steering public policy.

Cities like Detroit have enormous challenges in providing public-sector services, but the ways in which philanthropy occupies this space merit scrutiny. The power to shape policies emerges in much bolder form when the public sector comes to the table broke and uncoordinated—if they are invited to the table at all. The light rail line in Detroit, introduced at the beginning of this chapter, provides an example of philanthropy taking the reins in local and regional transportation policy in a manner that excluded elected representatives.

In 2007, a group of Detroit civic elites formed the nonprofit organization M-1 Rail with the goal of relying on private funding to swiftly deliver a small-scale light rail project (Lowe and Grengs, forthcoming). However, simultaneously, the city was developing its own plans, including a longer light rail line along the same corridor, which was later abandoned in favor of a regional bus rapid transit system. All of these municipal plans floundered as the city moved toward financial insolvency. Ultimately, M-1 Rail worked with their congressional delegation to secure federal funding. M-1 Rail leaders were explicit in excluding the city from their streetcar project; as Kate Lowe and Joe Grengs explain, "the city was not initially considered an appropriate lead agency for the streetcar, given its lack of technical capacity and [concerns about] corruption." Meanwhile, decisions related to the planning and construction of the streetcar line tended to put economic development considerations, such as downtown business redevelopment, ahead of plans that would enhance accessibility or integrate the system with the city's other public transportation systems. According to Lowe and Grengs:

> The streetcar does not improve accessibility for transit-dependent populations, who are largely black Detroit residents with needs for connections to regional jobs and opportunities. Not only will it fail to enhance accessibility, it could harm accessibility through displacing some bus service. Even as there could be economic benefits that trickle down to low-income, transit-dependent riders, we contend that transportation public spending should still enhance accessibility for transit-dependent populations and work to address racial and economic disparities in accessibility. (forthcoming)

Financial insolvency created a situation where elected leaders in Detroit had little say in the development of a public transit system. Philanthropic and corporate leaders stepped into this space and designed a transit system along a 3.3-mile route in the downtown core of the city that served the interests of a subset of residents while potentially creating additional barriers to the well-being of others.

Prominent elites stepping forward to reshape a city is not a new phenomenon. Major cities are replete with institutions—hospitals, libraries, museums—that are the product of wealthy donor largesse. Nor is this phenomenon limited to Detroit in the present-day context. The transformation of traditionally public services into partly or wholly nonprofit-delivered activities is visible in many other cases. Among the most prominent recent examples is the conversion of the Orleans Parish public schools (in New Orleans, Louisiana) after Hurricane Katrina into a district composed of nonprofit charter schools. This conversion was heavily supported with a large infusion of philanthropic grant dollars.[4] Considerable debate has ensued on issues ranging from the firing of the majority African American teaching force that had previously worked in the traditional public schools to improvements in academic outcomes under the reorganized school system as well as shifts in political power. For example, Howard Fuller—an African American education professor and strong advocate of choice and charter schools—offered some comments about the politics of reform in New Orleans:

> We need to be clear that there is nothing like New Orleans in the rest of the country . . . the level of financial resources that have gone into New Orleans—there is no comparable level. . . . There are very positive things [in New Orleans] that you cannot deny. . . . But it has also created—amongst certain sectors of that community—a tremendous amount of animosity that worries me in terms of the ability of this to go forward. . . . There's some people in New Orleans who see the education reform stuff as a larger part of black disempowerment, you know, politically. . . . We have got to find a way to make sure that people feel more empowered in this process. (Moran 2015)

Fuller's comments highlight the influence of elites, critiques concerning political empowerment and race, and the far-reaching consequences when overwhelming resources are concentrated on public policy in a single city. New research by Domingo Morel and Sally Nuamah supports Fuller's assessment using public opinion data showing differences between black and white residents' perceptions of the schools in New Orleans (Morel and Nuamah forthcoming).

Furthermore, many advocates have questioned whether elite preferences align with the views held in the broader public—for example, arguing that education reforms like the policies implemented in New Orleans did not involve public input. Some recent research suggests that there are important and systematic differences between the political attitudes of the very wealthy and the views of the broader public (Gilens 2012). For example, Benjamin Page, Larry Bartels, and Jason Seawright's survey of the top 1 percent of earners compares the views of the superwealthy to those of the general public on several aspects of public policy, including education (2013). Their findings show a pattern of greater support for market-oriented education reforms, such as charter schools, among the very rich. The authors conclude:

> Our data suggest that the great enthusiasm of wealthy Americans for improving the US educational system mostly focuses on improving effectiveness through relatively low-budget,

market-oriented reforms, not on spending the very large sums of money that might be necessary to provide high quality public schools, college scholarships, or worker retraining for all Americans. (Page et al. 2013:60)

Interestingly, the preference gap on the issue of charter schools is not very large—while the very wealthy are extremely supportive (90 percent), charter schools also have majority support in the general public (71 percent) (Page et al. 2013:59). However, the very wealthy are far less likely than the general public to support increased public spending for public schools. For example, Page and colleagues find a 52 percent favorability gap on whether the "federal government should spend whatever is necessary to ensure that all children have really good public schools they can go to" (Page et al. 2013:59). Although 87 percent of the general public supports this view, only 35 percent of the top 1 percent agrees.

The influence of philanthropists and wealthy donors in both Detroit and New Orleans points to an erosion of traditional public services and a rise of nonprofit or alternative provision. The public opinion data suggests that the very wealthy are far more supportive of privatizing public services and reducing government spending than the general public. Certainly, philanthropists are not the only proponents of privatization policies. Yet philanthropic investment can introduce an accelerator for implementing these changes in a way that can bypass public debate (Reckhow 2013; Tompkins-Stange 2016).

Meanwhile, the importance of civil society organizations as a bulwark or counterweight to market influence could be heightened in cities with extensive privatization of services and austerity in government, particularly when wealth inequality is growing. In Detroit, an alliance of community organizations led by the Detroit People's Platform produced a report responding to philanthropic influence in the city and recommending a changed approach—the report analyzes patterns of existing grantmaking in the city to show that few funds reach grassroots community organizations and provides twelve specific recommendations to funders for the future (Allied Media 2017). The report states:

A just revitalization of Detroit requires holistic solutions that address . . . racial and economic inequality at their roots. Such solutions address structural inequality head-on, foster wider access to resources and opportunity, and empower individuals and communities. Unfortunately, the philanthropic sector in Detroit has largely not embraced this approach. (Allied Media 2017:5–6)

In the short term, the activists in Detroit have gained some traction, with the formation of the Transforming Power Fund to support social justice philanthropy in the city (Allied Media 2018). There are also important questions about the future of philanthropic investments in more traditional urban nonprofits (at the neighborhood and grassroots levels) and the variation in these investments across different cities (as discussed by Brandtner and Dunning, Chapter 11, "Nonprofits as Urban Infrastructure"). In key instances, nonprofits have worked to expand representation for marginalized groups in cities (de Graauw 2016; Warren and Mapp 2011). Although philanthropists have demonstrated a capacity to influence the redesign of public service provision in cities, they are also major supporters of the urban nonprofit sector engaged with underrepresented groups. Will citizens and their organizational representatives have the capacity to hold increasingly privatized service providers accountable for the public good? Will philanthropic funders support these efforts through their own grantmaking, even if it potentially opens up philanthropically funded policy initiatives to scrutiny or criticism?

Conclusion and Implications

Wealthy donors in the New Gilded Age are active philanthropists and political contributors with strong policy preferences and agendas. This chapter explored how these phenomena intersect with a political system that enables extensive involvement from campaign donors, features complex organizational forms that integrate political and philanthropic giving, and is characterized by government austerity that has reduced public-sector capacity in many areas. Many analysts have argued that philanthropy is essential for U.S. democracy because of its rich contributions to a thriving civil society. But what if many philanthropists foster competing ideological agendas and hidden channels for narrow sets of ideas to influence the policy process and exacerbate inequities in influence? What happens to the less affluent voices that are drowned out by overwhelming resources entering politics from multiple directions? Social scientists have many questions to explore across policy areas and levels of government, seeking to disentangle and gauge the effectiveness of multiple methods used by the affluent to assert their influence. Philanthropy needs to be better understood as a significant mechanism for influence among the most affluent citizens in the American political system.

PART III

GOVERNANCE, CIVIC CAPACITY, AND COMMUNITIES

THE CHAPTERS IN THIS SECTION TACKLE the classic problem of understanding the relationships between government, market, and nonprofits but emphasize new challenges and new arenas of study that make existing approaches less apt. Today, some highly professionalized nonprofits can be almost indistinguishable from for-profit businesses at the ground level. For example, in some cases it can be difficult for clients to see obvious indicators of the form of legal incorporation for some hospitals, schools, or day care facilities based on daily operations. At the same time, nonprofits have increasing power in governance arrangements and a massive role in social service provision. With these changes, nonprofits are often seen as both tools to accomplish a task effectively (often determined by a funder) and an expression of values and commitments (e.g., to promote well-being, community development, civic engagement, or voluntarism). The tension between outcome goals and process goals is particularly fraught in the social services sector as outcome goals have become more and more dominant and process goals are suppressed in lieu of advancing norms regarding professionalization, efficiency, and impact.

In addition to the insights gained by looking at changes in well-developed areas of study, we can develop new knowledge by turning to relatively understudied settings. For example, it is well known that most nonprofits exist in city areas, but the tools and insights of urban studies are only just becoming part of nonprofit research. Using the city as the focus of analyses rather than organizations or sectors reveals the role of nonprofits in constituting what we think of as "a city" and, conversely, the ways in which our thinking about nonprofits is shaped by urban assumptions. Large-scale social transformations also give rise to a host of new issues that call for a reimagining of traditional concepts, such as what we envision as the responsibilities of states and their occupants. One such issue is found in the massive waves of migration moving worldwide. Immigrant communities face a distinct set of challenges that exacerbate their visibility and, thus, equality in the public sphere. As the chapters in this section starkly illustrate, where we look determines what we see, and traditional lenses can lead us to overlook important social problems in which the nonprofit sector is centrally embroiled.

In Chapter 9, Nicole P. Marwell and Maoz Brown develop a framework for thinking about government–nonprofit relations in governance terms. They outline how four decades of rich scholarship have established the importance of nonprofit organizations in government's capacity to deliver public goods—primarily using the conceptual tools of classic failure theories that emphasize sectoral distinctiveness. However, both practitioners and scholars increasingly ask questions about the details of different forms of public–private partnership and their implications for government, nonprofits, communities, and individuals: For example, is relative power between government and nonprofits shifting, and in what ways? Are nonprofits taking over the representative function previously reserved to the state (via regular elections), and what does this mean for citizens? What is happening to government accountability as policy formation and implementation increasingly occur through collaborative governance arrangements?

Marwell and Brown deepen the idea of governance as a conceptual framework for understanding government–nonprofit relations, using the concept to encompass the myriad ways in which nonprofits and governments interact—whether in conflict or in collaboration—to formulate and implement strategies for tackling public problems. They critically analyze existing literature on nonprofit-government relations, focusing on three distinct vantage points that explain how government–nonprofit relations are shaped: (1) institutional conditions, (2) individual motivation and discretion, and (3) interorganizational dynamics. Additionally, they emphasize recurring normative issues of fairness, effectiveness, accountability, and legitimacy that cut across governance discussions.

In Chapter 10, Jennifer E. Mosley provides a fresh take on the conflicting demands placed on social service nonprofits. Most social service nonprofits in the United States depend substantially on governments to sustain their operations and, increasingly, play important roles in policy formulation and implementation. She argues that the sectoral blurring of roles and responsibilities at the government–nonprofit level has also resulted in increased contacts between nonprofit activity and market activity. Notably, concerns regarding accountability and impact regarding the principal–agent relationship between government and nonprofits have led to government-established incentives for social service nonprofits to look, feel, and act increasingly like for-profit businesses. At the same time, these nonprofits have acquired increased power in governance arrangements and as representatives of marginalized populations. Currently, social service nonprofits are challenged to meet the normative expectations many people have for the nonprofit sector with respect to voluntarism, community connections, and independence from government. These organizations have strong incentives to become more professionalized, larger, and more data driven, and to make decisions regarding service provision and advocacy based on resource availability rather than community needs. The resulting tension between expectations and incentives is reflected in the inconsistent policies, practice recommendations, and even scholarship associated with the sector.

Mosley concludes that market-based human services are unlikely to support such characteristics as advocacy, co-production, community representation, civic engagement, and voluntarism, calling into question the ability of the sector to make the contributions to civil society many people expect of nonprofits. When they take on market values, these nonprofits are put in a vulnerable position, as they become subject not only to traditional expectations of the nonprofit sector but also to newer ones associated with for-profit organizations. This entanglement of the nonprofit sector with the corporate order raises issues of accountability and capacity, and thus a growth in demands at the field level to pursue impact and efficiency as central values. Meanwhile, their participation in a growing web of relationships and governance gives nonprofit service providers increasing power and responsibility but limits their ability to maintain meaningful claims of independence from government.

In Chapter 11 Christof Brandtner and Claire Dunning consider how nonprofits constitute civic capacity. Cities are home to a vast array of nonprofit organizations, such as hospitals, universities, tenant unions, and community centers. Research on nonprofit organizations, however, has elided the urban setting of most nonprofits, instead favoring national and organizational levels of analysis. They highlight not only how cities provide an important, immediate social context for nonprofits but also how nonprofits shape cities in important ways. Drawing on nonprofit and urban literatures across several disciplines including sociology and history, Brandtner and Dunning conceptualize nonprofits as urban infrastructure in order to highlight the reciprocal relationship between nonprofits and local communities.

In their view, nonprofits play five key roles as part of a city's urban infrastructure: (1) forges of civic capacity, (2) participants in urban governance, (3) conveners of network interaction, (4) anchors of belonging, and (5) builders of the physical environment. The direct activities of nonprofits shape cities, but the reverse is also true—city settings fundamentally shape nonprofits. Brandtner and Dunning sketch out a broad research agenda that recognizes and further explores the nonprofit sector as a constitutive element of the economic, political, social, and spatial environment of cities. They also call for comparative analyses of cities and neighborhoods to investigate how local nonprofit sectors undergird the city in both constructive and counterproductive ways. The claims are provocative; they envision a vastly different relationship between nonprofits and city government. Nonprofits are co-created with, rather than existing as a substitute for, government agencies and corporations. Cities are the product of organizations and their social, political, and economic networks rather than simply the backdrop of social interactions between people and organizations.

In Chapter 12 Irene Bloemraad, Shannon Gleeson, and Els de Graauw develop the concepts of civic (in)equality and (in)visibility to describe the position of immigrant communities in the nonprofit sector. In Western Europe, North America, and Oceania, at least one in ten residents are foreign-born, and in some countries, over one in four are immigrants. These migrants are highly diverse in their national origins, their ethnoracial backgrounds, their religious affiliations, and their socioeconomic profiles. Attention to immigrants and immigrant organizations at both the individual and organizational levels raises at least three key considerations that call for a move beyond existing theories and analytical frameworks used in the study of nonprofit organizations and associationalism: (1) the additional barriers and opportunities to organizing that come with the multitude of legal statuses migrants hold, as well as the intersection of those statuses with other known barriers to civic equality (e.g., poverty, racial minority status, or language access issues); (2) the influence of immigrants' political socialization in a civic and political system different from the country of residence for third sector participation; and (3) the effect of transnational political and civic engagement for third sector organizing in the homeland or country of residence. As a result, immigrant communities are underrepresented in nonprofit organizations in terms of number, density, breadth, capacity, and visibility. Moreover, migration matters for immigrant civic engagement at the individual and organizational levels, including organizational creation, persistence, and impacts.

Although existing nonprofit organizations could address some immigrant needs or associational desires, research suggests that outreach is rare. In part, this is because existing organizations do not have the capacity or interest to invest in multilingual or multicultural outreach to address immigrants' human service needs or advocacy goals. In addition, immigrant populations bring new social, cultural, and service needs and interests, such as wanting to organize in religious communities distinct from those of the majority and needing specific legal services, activities that existing organizations have trouble identifying or fulfilling. The resulting gap between what existing nonprofits do for immigrants and immigrants' ability to create new associations—a gap that produces civic inequality—can be highly problematic for immigrant communities. For instance, local governments usually allocate grants to community-based organizations to provide human or social services or to subsidize a cultural or sports activity. Absent immigrant-oriented organizations, immigrant communities may fail to secure these resources and experience a curtailed civic life, which in turn has consequences for their ability to foster civic presence and voice in public affairs. Scholars, however, can play a central role in facilitating inclusion through careful attention to civic inequality, a concept that can also be applied to nonimmigrant populations. Civic inequality has extensive implications for immigrants' access to social services, employment, and leadership opportunities as well as their civic voice.

Great social trends, such as urbanization and immigration, create changes in the population that undercut traditional assumptions about the relations between government and individuals. Furthermore, in recent decades there have been increases in consolidation and mergers as big, multiservice organizations are increasingly best situated to compete in the data-driven, professionalized marketplace. Are these large social service nonprofits still associated with close connections to communities? Do nonprofits continue to represent marginalized groups or provide an independent voice that can check government power? There have also been important changes in advocacy norms and a growing awareness of organizations that are functioning more as interest groups for professions or elite preferences than as representatives of marginalized communities. Simultaneously, we see a larger role for nonprofit social service providers in governance, largely through their participation in multistakeholder collaborations. Nonprofits are increasingly asked to participate in such processes in order to help meet accountability challenges at the administrative level, fill in for the "hollow state" associated with contracting regimes, provide needed expertise, and promote coordination across fragmented policy areas. Their participation is also often conceptualized as a proxy for the participation of citizens, and thus a way of advancing democratic norms. These processes are being given increasing power over regulatory, funding, and implementation matters, but the degree to which social service nonprofits are adequately representing the populations they serve is unknown. In the midst of such expansive change, research on the sector is poised for new conceptual and empirical leaps to help explain such complex systems and how they create public good.

9   TOWARD A GOVERNANCE FRAMEWORK FOR GOVERNMENT-NONPROFIT RELATIONS

Nicole P. Marwell and Maoz Brown

MODERN THEORY ON GOVERNMENT–NONPROFIT relations arguably begins with a paper by economist Burton Weisbrod titled "Toward a Theory of the Voluntary Nonprofit Sector in a Three-Sector Economy." Presented in 1972 at the Russell Sage Foundation's Conference on Altruism and Economic Theory, the paper put forward an explanation of the nonprofit sector as an institutional response to unmet demand resulting from limitations on governmental provision of public goods. The paper would later be expanded into a book-length treatise titled *The Voluntary Nonprofit Sector*, a seminal contribution to research on the nonprofit sector.

This historical background is instructive for two reasons. First, as is evident in the title of Weisbrod's 1972 conference paper, theory on government–nonprofit relations is informed heavily by a sector-based model of society, which tends to emphasize similarities among organizations within sectors and distinctions among organizations across sectors. Second, if we start the clock at 1972 with the presentation of Weisbrod's paper, then research on government–nonprofit relations now has nearly half a century of theorizing behind it. During this time there has been ample critique, revision, and expansion of sector-based theories on government–nonprofit relations. We argue in this chapter, however, that sector-based theorization also has obscured larger trends and important details in how government and nonprofit organizations now engage with each other both to provide services and to shape policy. Newer strands of research on this intersection attempt to explain government–nonprofit interaction less by recourse to sectoral distinctions and more by engaging the details of specific social contexts and policy domains. In doing so, this research moves us toward a framework for analyzing government–nonprofit relations most aptly described as *governance*.

Sectoral Analysis of Government-Nonprofit Relations

The sectoral view of government–nonprofit relations has been instrumental in establishing nonprofit organizations as important objects of social scientific analysis. Thanks to the theoretical and empirical work in this tradition, the important roles played by nonprofits in conducting the public's business have been clearly established. Nonprofits engage with government in multiple ways to provide a wide range of public services, as well as to influence and implement new approaches to public policy (Smith and Grønbjerg 2006).

Sector–based approaches to government-nonprofit relations are motivated by a core set of questions. First, pursuing the line of inquiry originated by Weisbrod, if government's function is to solve problems of public goods production, then why do nonprofit organizations exist at all? Answers to this question, which focus on nonprofit service provision, include theories about the sector's role as supplementary, complementary, and competitive to government (e.g., Najam 2000; Young 2000), as well as both supply-side and demand-side explanations of nonprofit service activity (Ben-Ner and Gui 2003). A second question raised by a sectoral framework is whether nonprofits reflect a basic social practice of voluntarism, as distinct from government's uniquely coercive power. Here it is important to acknowledge the common conception of nonprofits as "tangible, significant manifestations of community" (Smith and Lipsky 1993:22), as contrasted with government's reliance on legal mandate and official protocol (Brinkerhoff and Brinkerhoff 2002; Brown 2018). These presumed distinctive sectoral orientations lead to a third fundamental question: What are the unique societal roles played by government versus nonprofit organizations? Although there is certainly evidence that this kind of division of labor exists, a fourth sector-based question begins to trouble this line of thought: What factors make government versus nonprofit auspice matter? This question acknowledges that a sectoral framework may not be useful in all cases, and research has examined possible reasons for deviation from a sector-rooted division of responsibility. This line of inquiry opens a path toward a governance framework for government–nonprofit relations.

A Governance Framework for Analyzing Government–Nonprofit Relations

The term *governance* has enjoyed growing currency in a range of research fields, so much so that Christopher Pollitt and Peter Hupe (2011) dub governance a "magic concept" because of its broad scope, flexibility, and typically positive association. This may seem a charitable way to suggest that the word has been stretched past its useful limits, yet governance has shown impressive persistence in the lexicons of management, public administration, and cognate disciplines. Gerry Stoker (1998) writes that among researchers in these fields there is "baseline agreement that governance refers to the development of governing styles in which boundaries between and within public and private sectors have become blurred" (17). In this sense, the idea of governance has been applied to a broad range of governing contexts, including not only relations between government and the private sector (e.g., Salamon 2002), but also the workings of corporate boards (e.g., Browning and Sparks 2015), the development and monitoring of international multilateral agreements (e.g., Hale and Held 2011), and the exercise of authority over cities (e.g., da Cruz, Rode, and McQuarrie 2019; van den Dool et al. 2015; Pierre 2014) and regions (e.g., Riggirozzi and Wylde 2018).

In a recent synthesis of urban governance research, Nuno da Cruz and colleagues (2019) posit that as an analytical framework, governance "does not require a priori assumptions about the roles of the various actors regarding goal setting, steering, and implementation. Rather, it emphasizes the relationships and interactions between these actors as well as the conditions and rules that frame those relationships and interactions" (1–2). We agree and argue further that this approach to governance is useful beyond the study of cities. Indeed, we draw heavily on da Cruz and colleagues to define a governance framework for government–nonprofit relations as *the relationships and interactions between government and nonprofit organizations, as well as the conditions and rules that frame them, that give rise to goal setting, steering, and implementation regarding public issues* (see da Cruz et al. 2019; Pierre 2014). This definition captures the reality of today's government–nonprofit relations, in which a highly diverse nonprofit sector, engaged in multiple ways with complex state systems, cannot be adequately described with sweeping sectoral claims. Instead, we argue that sectoral distinctions should give way to a scoping of institutional conditions, street-level decisions, and interorganizational relations, thereby yielding a more fruitful empirical accounting of government–nonprofit relations as they occur presently. Although few studies to date have delivered such a complex, multilevel approach, we believe it offers a useful road map for researchers seeking to advance our collective understanding of these issues.

One of the key analytical advantages of a governance framework is that it moves us beyond "reified concepts of the state as a monolithic entity, interest, or actor" (Bevir 2011:1). A governance framework thus takes as given that public and nonprofit organizations are deeply engaged with one another, dynamically creating organizational forms and mechanisms to address public issues. This approach allows researchers to empirically identify the multifaceted practices of a wide variety of state actors, including legislators who produce laws; rule-making bodies that codify statutory implementation; and executive agencies that engage in consultation, contracting, and other collaborative governance procedures. This breaking apart of "the state" into its multiple loci of action illuminates the numerous points of contact between nonprofit organizations and government, including advocacy and lobbying for policy development, as well as more collaborative implementation of a wide range of publicly supported services.

Recent research on service provision, for example, examines how jointly produced services—including public education, child protection, low-income housing, and health care—are planned, funded, delivered, consumed, and evaluated across government and nonprofit organizations (e.g., Boris and Steuerle 2017). Similarly, studies of public policy development examine how legislation and administrative rule making are filtered through and influenced by not only traditional interest groups and lobbyists but also a wealth of nonprofit organizational forms: advocacy groups, social welfare organizations, intermediary agencies, cross-sector coalitions, public-private partnerships, and similar entities (Clemens and Guthrie 2010).

Although many recent studies of both service provision and policy influence explore the pragmatic reality of government–nonprofit relations, only some explicitly invoke the concept of governance. Others take what we see as an implicit governance approach, pursuing a nonessentializing identification of the relevant actors and processes that structure a mode of service provision or policy process. We draw these studies together under our governance framework because they all display an increased attention to specific institutional arrangements that are unique to neither nonprofits nor government, as well as less reliance on a notion of the state as a unitary and discrete actor. These commonalities presage a growing continuity across the multiple disciplinary engagements with government–nonprofit relations. We thus propose governance as a unified analytic framework for these phenomena.

Focused attention to the details of governance raises the possibility of an analytical trade-off between a clearer empirical accounting of the dynamic reality of government–nonprofit relations and the higher-level theoretical propositions offered by a sectoral approach. At the same time, however, a shift to a governance framework allows for consideration of a new set of questions that better illuminates the stakes of ongoing changes in how government and nonprofits engage one another on behalf of the public. Recent research raises and frames these new questions in a largely patchwork fashion. Depending on scholars' disciplinary roots—in law, public administration, sociology, political science, geography, public policy, and so on—there is more or less recognition of certain key aspects of governance. In our review of this work, we draw these somewhat disparate approaches together to identify three different analytical orientations at play in a governance approach to government–nonprofit relations.

First, a number of studies address the *institutional conditions* shaping the possibilities for and prohibitions on how governments and nonprofit organizations engage each other on either service provision or policy development and implementation. Second, some studies illuminate how the *motivations of individuals* at work in government agencies and nonprofit organizations play out in the development and maintenance of governance. And finally, some of the most influential studies of governance examine the *interorganizational relationships* constructed between governments and nonprofits.

The multiplicity and malleability of governance raises a set of normative concerns of which research on this topic should be cognizant. The public–private nature of governance cannot assume clear representation of the public interest, even when the private partner is a nonprofit organization (as opposed to a profit-seeking firm). Indeed, much governance research raises the question of whether diffuse, distributed, and at times emergent arrangements for addressing public issues offer adequate protection for individuals and groups subject to the power of state actors or their empowered nonstate associates. We thus identify four areas of normative inquiry that a governance framework suggests are important for understanding government–nonprofit relations in the present period: fairness, effectiveness, accountability and legitimacy (cf. van den Dool et al 2015).

First, as government and nonprofits interact with each other to co-produce services or policy, how can we understand the level of *fairness* of governance outcomes, that is, who might be advantaged or disadvantaged by them? Second, to what extent does the pursuit of *effectiveness* drive governance? Do these arrangements deliver on their promises? Third, how does governance produce *accountability*, the giving and evaluating of accounts across multiple levels and time scales and in relation to a wide range of audiences? And finally, given that the power of governance stems in part from its perceived *legitimacy*, what are the expectations of various stakeholders for how governance should be carried out?

As we discuss later in the chapter, these normative concerns can appear at any level of analysis in governance research, and all are key to the maintenance of public trust. They are indeed the critical stakes of the move "from government to governance" (Rhodes 1996; Stoker 1998), which diffuses the public's ability to identify, monitor, and weigh in on the ever-more complex decision-making processes carrying the weight of state power. Keeping these normative concerns in focus also should help us maintain sensitivity to our own normative partialities. In particular, we recognize a potentially significant divide between democratic and authoritarian regimes on the interpretation of fairness, effectiveness, accountability, and legitimacy. For example, effectiveness may equate to inclusiveness in one regime and the suppression of dissidence in another; legitimacy may mean democratic mandate in one setting while in another it may mean toeing the party line. Our framework thus declines to set standards for what any of these normative concerns should aspire to, but rather elevates them as issues for investigation in future research.

The chapter proceeds as follows. In the next section, we briefly review the dominant sector-based approaches to government–nonprofit relations. We then touch on recent work that posits the blurring of boundaries across the traditional three-sector model of society (market, state, third sector) in order to contextualize our subsequent discussion of governance. The chapter then develops the governance framework through a review of recent literature that examines government–nonprofit relations at the levels of institutions, individual motivations, and interorganizational relations. We conclude with a call for more deliberate attention to a governance framework, on the grounds that it more accurately represents the present-day empirical reality of government–nonprofit relations than does a sector-based view and also would afford a structure within which cross-disciplinary work on this topic might move toward greater familiarity and coherence.

A Cursory Review of Sector-Based Perspectives

Economic Perspectives on Government–Nonprofit Relations

At the center of sector-based theory on the nonprofit sector is a set of predictions about how certain organizational forms come to occupy market niches according to sector-specific comparative advantages in meeting consumer/citizen demand. The historical point of departure for this line of inquiry is Weisbrod's groundbreaking work on demand-oriented drivers of nonprofit sector formation and growth. In this account, nonprofits fill a gap left by the private and public sectors in the provision of public or quasi-public goods. Profit-driven businesses fail to generate sufficient levels of public goods because these goods are nonexcludable and nonrival, thus incentivizing consumers to avoid paying for services (the well-known free-rider problem) and making it difficult or impossible to charge fees at a level sufficient to cover the costs of production (Weisbrod 1975).

With the advantage of compulsory taxation, government can provide such goods but will remain beholden to median-voter preferences, thus failing to meet heterogeneous or peripheral demand and creating an opportunity for communities and entrepreneurs to meet neglected need through nonprofit enterprise. Thus, under Weisbrod's theory of public goods provision, nonprofits marshal voluntary contributions of money and time to compensate for the joint failure of the private and public sectors to provide optimal levels of collective goods (Kingma 1997).

Henry Hansmann (1980) advanced a complementary view of the nonprofit sector's compensatory function in his theorization of *contract failure*, which occurs when profit-driven businesses exploit information asymmetries by shirking on service quality in order to cut costs. Hence, given certain competitive conditions, the free market is expected to undersupply products and services that are difficult for consumers to evaluate, since consumers will be wary of potentially unscrupulous business owners. Because nonprofit organizations are prohibited by law from distributing profits to owners, they are presumably less incentivized to cut costs and, therefore, less susceptible to contract failure. Accordingly, as Hansmann argues, nonprofit legal status serves as a signal of trustworthiness, thereby reducing transaction costs for vulnerable consumers. Of course, government agencies also face the "nondistribution constraint" and, as a result, may be trusted over for-profit corporations in the face of information asymmetries, but government may not be able to provide adequate levels of service across the demand spectrum, as Weisbrod argued.

Lester Salamon (1987) offered an early and influential innovation on prior theory by questioning the derivative characterization of the nonprofit sector, suggesting that nonprofits do not emerge only to correct for the shortcomings of business and government but rather play a primary role in public service provision. Reversing Weisbrod's theoretical sequence, Salamon argued that nonprofit service provision tends to *precede* government involvement, and that government agencies later enter the arena to correct for "voluntary failure," or the characteristic limitations of nonprofits: insufficiency, particularism, paternalism, and amateurism. A key principle of Salamon's theory of voluntary failure is that the strengths and weaknesses of the public and nonprofit sectors often correspond well, a complementarity that leads to co-production of public goods. Thus, Salamon provides a theoretically grounded explanation for the extensive contracting arrangements between government agencies and nonprofit service providers found in the United States and in other countries with large and developed nonprofit sectors.

Taken together, Weisbrod's elaboration of government failure, Hansmann's of contract failure, and Salamon's of voluntary failure constitute the seminal *three failures theory* of nonprofit emergence and function (Steinberg 2006). These theories traditionally have focused on the ways in which government and nonprofits supplement or complement each other in meeting the demand for public goods.

Civil Society Perspectives on Government–Nonprofit Relations

Between the publications of the first (1987) and second (2006) editions of this volume there was a substantial increase in scholarship on civil society and social capital, much of which valorizes the role of the nonprofit sector in promoting civic vitality and communal fellowship (Barber 1998; Dionne 1998; Putnam 2000). Whereas economic models of the nonprofit sector focus on transaction costs and service provision, civil society models call attention to the "expressive" functions of nonprofits as sites where individuals can pursue their interests and manifest their values through community-building and political engagement (Anheier 2009; Frumkin 2002; Knutsen and Brower 2010). Often labeled *neo-Tocquevillian*, this scholarship evokes and frequently references Alexis de Tocqueville's famous observations of American society in the early nineteenth century, which led the French aristocrat to tout the American propensity for forming associations as a key ingredient in the young democracy's vibrancy and apparent stability.

Unfortunately, much of Tocqueville's emphasis on the critical role of state structures in fostering civil society was lost in the communitarian scholarship of the late 1990s.[1] By arguing that civil society exists "outside the state," authors often overlooked the complex interplay between voluntary association and government (Chambers and Kopstein 2006). Scholars on the conservative end of the political spectrum have been especially inclined to present civil society and government as separate and even antithetical categories, typically suggesting that an expanding state crowds out civic life (Berger and Neuhaus 1996; Olasky 1992; Schambra 1997). Although certain communitarian writers have been more optimistic about the state's role in fostering civil society, their view of government involvement has focused rather narrowly on community service programs and other means of promoting engagement with nonprofits (Baas 2013; Frumkin and Jastrzab 2010). This approach essentially reinforces the idea of the nonprofit sector as a distinct space for civic engagement.

Similarly, scholars writing on social movement nonprofits have generally viewed government circumspectly, often assuming that collaboration with government undermines the advocacy role of nonprofits. In particular, government funding of nonprofits has long drawn critical attention from scholars concerned that such funding may incentivize recipients to soften or scale back contentious political activity in order to maintain contracting relations with public agencies (Nowland-Foreman 1998; Smith and Lipsky 1993; Wuthnow 1991). The reason for such concern is intuitive: the resource dependence resulting from reliance on public-sector funding may alter organizational priorities such that nonprofits are responsive to government objectives rather than to the particular communities they have been established to serve and represent.

State–Society Relations and the "Blurring" Motif

As detailed previously, sector-based perspectives on government–nonprofit relations tend to ascribe distinct roles and purviews to governmental and nonprofit organizations. As Smith and Grønbjerg (2006) summarize, "While the market and civil society approaches recognize that government may impinge on or otherwise undermine the distinctive values of nonprofit organizations, fundamentally, nonprofits are seen as different from government" (236). This presumption of sectoral difference reflects a popular conception of society as a compound of institutional principles embodied in discrete domains: "hierarchical control" in the state, "dispersed competition" in the market, and "spontaneous solidarity" in the community (Streeck and Schmitter 1985). With its origins in Max Weber's pioneering contributions to political sociology, this view of state–society relations is premised on an image of the state as a highly bureaucratic, centralized, and autonomous administrative apparatus. Accordingly, as Jefferey Sellers (2011) remarks, "Analysts in the field have characteristically presumed a sharp analytical distinction, if not always an actual separation, between the state and society" (124).

More recent research casts doubt on the explanatory utility of the conventional state–society dichotomy and the related tripartite classification of business, government, and nonprofit. Scholars increasingly find that sectoral functions and purviews are quite variable, depending largely on political structure, issue area, geography, and other factors. This framing of sector as a politically and culturally contingent category aligns well with a long-running skepticism regarding the usefulness of the sector concept. Indeed, among the original questions in this field of research is whether sectoral affiliation is associated with significant differences in organizational behavior at all (Clarke and Estes 1992; Gray 1986; Krashinsky 1998). Findings on organizational differences by sector have been mixed and highly context-specific; however, even when sector predicts differences, organizations of the same type—for example, hospitals, schools, nursing homes—have many commonalities no matter their sectoral auspice (Kramer 2000:5).

In addition to the difficulty of generalizing about government–nonprofit relations across the many different types of nonprofit organizations, scholars have noted a "blurring of boundaries" whereby organizations in one sector adopt forms and functions typically associated with organizations in another sector (Bromley and Meyer 2017). The growing marketization of government funding (Smith 2012), the entry and proliferation of for-profits in formerly nonprofit-dominated markets (Marwell and McInerney 2005), and the expanding influence of business principles and discourse (Hwang and Powell 2009) have pressured nonprofits to adopt the methods, rhetoric, legal structures, and in some cases goals of for-profit enterprises (Eikenberry and Kluver 2004; Maier, Meyer, and Steinbereithner 2016; Sanders and McClellan 2014; see also Mosley, Chapter 10, "Social Service Nonprofits"). Cross-national comparisons also demonstrate the fuzziness of the nonprofit/business boundary, as profit-returning organizations such as cooperatives and mutual associations make up a central component of the third sector in many countries (Salamon and Sokolowski 2016). At the same time, businesses appear to be adopting features of the nonprofit sector as they face growing accountability pressures (Dobbin 2009), and the global rise of firms that use market mechanisms to pursue social goals also testifies to the growing complexity of "the space between the state and the market" (Knutsen 2016:1563).

Scholars also have paid attention to the porous boundaries between government and nongovernmental organizations (NGOs). The most concrete cases are the so-called GONGO (government-organized nongovernment organization) and QUANGO (quasi-governmental nongovernment organization), nonprofit entities founded by government as a means to devolve official decision-making capacities and/or to garner the legitimacy associated with grassroots, community-based organizations (Cumming 2010). Beyond these kinds of organizations, an extensive record of scholarship documents the scale and importance of "hybrid" or "collaborative" arrangements, in which state policies are formulated and implemented by networks of government and nongovernment actors (Ansell and Gash 2008; Bevir and Rhodes 2011:203; Hall and Kennedy 2008; Heinrich, Lynn, and Milward 2010; Milward and Provan 2000; Stoker 1998). With the apparent rise in such cross-sector collaboration, scholars have put forward more nuanced conceptions of the state and its boundaries, recognizing that "states are not monoliths cleanly divisible from social environments so much as they are complex entities extensively entangled with their broader societies" (Mayrl and Quin 2016:3). Of course, such interpretations of the state do not align well with the image of cleanly separable government and nonprofit sectors.

Although literature on the blurring of sectoral boundaries helps make the case for moving toward a governance framework for understanding government–nonprofit relations, we do not wish to dispense with sector as a useful analytic category. Properly contextualized, sector can remain a useful approach to studying government–nonprofit relations. For example, there is some evidence that sector can explain (albeit imperfectly) important differences in organizational behavior and performance (Rosenau and Linder

2003), and that the nonprofit category may accurately signal social mission orientation (Child, Witesman, and Spencer 2016; Handy et al. 2010; Witesman and Fernandez 2013). We thus put forward the governance framework as a way to shift analytical emphasis toward contextual criteria, thereby making room for nonsectoral analysis as well as potentially enhancing the explanatory value of sectoral affiliation.

As noted earlier in the chapter, only a subset of recent research on government–nonprofit relations explicitly claims the term *governance* as a key orienting principle. In the remainder of this chapter, we attempt to weave together literature evidencing both explicit and implicit connections to a governance framework, thereby providing a more robust review of relevant research findings. We have selected studies for their ability to shed light on at least one analytical orientation in governance research: institutional, individual, or interorganizational. Although specific studies may speak to more than one of these categories, we emphasize only one aspect of any such study. In addition, we note how studies in each of these categories may speak to the four important normative concerns faced by governance researchers.

Neo-Institutionalism and Governance

A governance framework is built in part on the need to address the distinct legal frameworks, cultural milieus, and political environments in which nonprofit organizations exist in order to make sense of how nonprofits cooperate and/or compete with public actors. Among theoretical approaches to this critical task of contextualization, neo-institutionalism stands as an especially fitting strategy, as it concerns itself with what our governance definition refers to as the *rules and conditions surrounding* government–nonprofit relations in specific domains.

Early institutionalist writing focused on intraorganizational structures and processes, with a characteristic emphasis on the interplay of individual interests and strategic decision making (e.g., Selznick 1949). Later institutionalist writing—known as neo-institutionalism—is recognized for shifting focus to broader cultural systems and beliefs that constitute actors and channel their actions (DiMaggio and Powell 1991). Most importantly for the purposes of this chapter, neo-institutionalism is known for its typically "macro, structural perspective," which is oriented to the wider environment in which organizations operate (Hallett and Ventresca 2006:214). Accordingly, a neo-institutionalist approach to governance highlights the ways in which society's cultural and legal prescriptions for political process, public goods provision, and civic activity shape government–nonprofit relations. In particular, a neo-institutionalist analysis of governance addresses the three pillars of institutions (Scott 2014): the *regulative, normative*, and *cultural–cognitive* aspects of social organization. This level of analysis also grants leverage on the following critical normative questions: Regarding *fairness*, what rules and norms exist to ensure that privileges enjoyed by government agencies and nonprofit organizations are balanced by obligations to the public? Do legal regulations and professional best practices promote government and nonprofit transparency and *accountability*? How are criteria for determining the *effectiveness* of governance arrangements established across different national or regional contexts? Finally, how do societal-level expectations for *legitimate* government and nonprofit action enable (or constrain) governance relationships?

Laws and Regulations

Regulative features of institutions comprise rule-setting activities that generate both positive and negative incentives for actors. Notably, W. Richard Scott (2014) observes that "economists, including institutional economists, are particularly likely to view institutions as resting primarily on the regulatory pillar" (60). Despite this predilection, however, a major shortcoming of classic sector-based economic perspectives on the nonprofit sector is that they neglect government's ability to modify regulatory environments in ways that may significantly affect nonprofit behavior and distinctiveness (Faulk 2014).

As an example of how government's regulatory ability can alter the roles and uniqueness of nonprofits, consider the 1965 amendments to the Social Security Act that created Medicare and Medicaid in the United States. This legislation made medical services affordable to millions of poor Americans, "thereby diminishing the redistributive rationale for nonprofits" and setting the stage for substantial growth among for-profit hospitals (James 1998:274). In other words, changes in the U.S. regulatory environment made medical care an entitlement financed by the state rather than a charitable service underwritten by donors, thus rendering nonprofit status less important as a predictor of serving the poor. Furthermore, the 1965 amendments also enacted a variety of "conditions for participation" that service providers must meet in order to take part in these programs, thus reducing the value of nonprofit status as an indication of trustworthiness (as predicted by contract failure theory). For this reason, it is perhaps unsurprising that nonprofit hospitals and nursing homes often do not even bother conveying their legal status to consumers (Malani and David 2008).

A neo-institutionalist governance framework can effectively explain these types of transformations because it eschews broad generalizations about whether or how auspice affects organizational behavior, instead focusing on how specific contextual conditions modulate nonprofit activity and relations with government. A more contemporary example of such contextual conditions can be found in Horwitz, Chapter 17, "Charitable Nonprofits and the Business of Health Care." As Jill Horwitz explains, recent concerns that nonprofit hospitals are no longer providing community benefits at sufficient levels have led to new regulations enforcing a more thoroughgoing charitable orientation among these organizations, including provisions that touch directly on the normative issues highlighted previously. For instance, the introduction of Schedule H to the Form 990 (the tax return that nonprofits file annually with the IRS) routinizes the reporting of community benefits, further institutionalizing accountability protocols. With such regulations in place, nonprofit status may have become a more meaningful point of contrast among hospitals, but such differences should be understood as the product of government's role in shaping regulatory policy rather than as an inherent property of the nonprofit health care sector.

Another example of regulative institutionalization of accountability in government–nonprofit relations is the Government Performance and Results Act (GPRA) of 1993, which was passed amid concerns about the effectiveness and efficiency of government programs. The GPRA required federal agencies to develop mission statements, long-term strategic plans, outcome-oriented performance goals, and performance measurement protocols. However, as Emily Barman (2016) notes, because public services (especially human services) are so often contracted out to nonprofits, these government accountability mandates passed through to nonprofit vendors. Thus, while the GPRA is technically aimed at ensuring *government* performance, the institutional reality of extensive co-production and interdependence with nonprofits resulted in accountability pressures impinging on both sectors in much the same way (Carman 2009).

To summarize, regulative institutionalization influences government–nonprofit relations by configuring the array of incentive structures, political systems, and market opportunities that affect the means of addressing public priorities. A governance framework aims to uncover how the explanatory power and substance of nonprofit status varies under different regulative arrangements, the roles of different actors (especially the government itself) in creating and sustaining these arrangements, and the implications for how organizations cater to public needs and advance political agendas.

Norms, Values, and Meanings

The primacy of social values is, of course, supposed to be a defining characteristic of the nonprofit sector, which is often perceived as "the locus of values" in society (DiMaggio and Anheier 1990:153). As such, nonprofits are normatively charged organizations, making them especially interesting as objects of study under normative and cultural–cognitive neo-institutionalist criteria (Abzug 1999), which center on how prevailing notions of appropriateness, feasibility, and sensibility influence social activity. By normative and cultural–cognitive criteria, the environment molds government–nonprofit relations through the signaling of expectations beyond what laws and regulations permit or proscribe. Taken together, normative and cognitive frames of neo-institutionalist analysis invite not only heightened attention to implicit standards of legitimacy in government–nonprofit relations but also greater scrutiny of how governance arrangements address issues of fairness, accountability, and other priorities related to public service and policy.

A prime example of a sector-based normative rendering of government–nonprofit relations is the portrayal of nonprofits as conduits for voluntarism and community building (Anheier 2009). This communitarian reputation has long been cited as justification for delegating public services to local voluntary agencies (Kissane and Gingerich 2004). Although such rhetoric has been especially pronounced in the United States, it is found in other regions as well. For example, scholars have shown that the Catholic principle of subsidiarity (the idea that social problems should be addressed by the smallest or most decentralized authority possible) has traditionally motivated devolution of state-funded social service provision to local charities in countries such as Germany (Anheier and Seibel 1997), the Netherlands (Brandsen and Pape 2015), and Poland (Nałęcz, Leś, and Pieliński 2015). The normative, sector-based premise behind this devolutionary relationship is that locally rooted nonprofit organizations are the best representatives of their communities and ought to be responsible for catering to local needs and advocating for local interests (LeRoux 2007).

In contrast to this sector-based view of normative roles for nonprofits and government, the empirical purpose of a governance framework is to transcend these sectoral assumptions and instead uncover *how* contextual factors associated with specific regions and policy domains influence the construction, negotiation, and deployment of communitarian credibility and representative legitimacy. For example, through a series of interviews with city officials, community organization staff, neighborhood association members, and other local stakeholders in Boston, Baltimore, and Portland, Robert Chaskin (2003) discovered significant variation in how these groups perceive the relative importance of advocacy, planning, implementation, outreach, and other functions. With respect to how representational legitimacy is constructed, Chaskin found wide agreement among local organizations (including government agencies) on the main antecedents of legitimacy: degree of resident participation, involvement of a diversity of stakeholders, and concrete action leading to a track record of accomplishments. Similar findings also surface in responses from South Side Chicago residents collected by Jennifer Mosley and Colleen Grogan (2013), who found that nonprofit organizations create the trust necessary to achieve nonelected representational legitimacy through building relationships, inclusive and responsive communication, and a record of outcomes related to both policy influence and service provision. Additionally, the authors revealed that residents trust nonprofit community organizations and local public schools equally, contradicting the notion that nonprofits are distinctly legitimate as community representatives (857). We consider these works exemplary of a governance framework because, by identifying and analyzing key contextual criteria affecting local civic ecosystems, they move beyond the reductionist claim that nonprofits naturally embody a "community logic" while government agencies embody a "bureaucratic state logic" (Gray and Purdy 2014).[2]

To summarize, neo-institutionalism has been a remarkably popular paradigm in the study of nonprofit organizations and, more broadly, of government–nonprofit relations. With an expansive frame of reference and a variety of methodological compatibilities (ranging from "large-N" quantitative studies to qualitative archival analysis), this tradition has shed light on how policy regimes drive organizational practices (Edwards 2016), how the valorization of business principles has given rise to increasingly marketized forms of nonprofit service provision and government contracting (Garrow and Hasenfeld 2014), and other areas of interest. By drawing attention to the dynamic regulative, normative, and cultural–cognitive factors driving governance, neo-institutionalism lends itself to the holistic and nuanced understanding of government–nonprofit relations that we advocate here.

Street-Level Theoretical Approaches to Governance

Despite its considerable influence, critics have charged neo-institutionalism with advancing an overly structuralist view of society that downplays the agency of actors. Increasingly influential research agendas on "institutional entrepreneurship," "institutional microfoundations," and "inhabited institutions" evidence a growing awareness that individual decision making works in tandem with cultural and political environments to drive organizational behavior (Binder 2007; Battilana, Leca, and Boxenbaum 2009; Hallett 2010; Powell and Rerup 2017). Street-level bureaucracy theory has long been particularly conducive to the study of how individual decision making affects government–nonprofit relations.

Developed by political scientist Michael Lipsky and colleagues, the original version of street-level bureaucracy theory explained how frontline staff in public agencies (teachers, police officers, caseworkers, etc.) face a combination of goal ambiguity, resource scarcity, and individual discretion that enables (or forces) them to take an active role in policy making. Because much of public policy materializes not in legislation but rather in individual actions at the point of interface with the public (classroom exercises, traffic stops, intake procedures, etc.), frontline staff effectively "make" policy even as they operate within the parameters of protocol (Lipsky 1980:83). Whereas neo-institutionalism focuses on how higher-order political and cultural factors drive organizational processes, street-level theory zeroes in on the deliberations, judgment calls, and compromises of organizational staff (for a review, see Maynard-Moody and Portillo 2010). Lipsky practically ignores the role of nonprofits in public service provision in the original publication of *Street-Level Bureaucracy*, but the thirtieth-anniversary edition of the book (2010) features a new chapter in which he acknowledges government's growing reliance on the nonprofit sector for service delivery (see also Smith and Lipsky 1993). Following Lipsky's recognition of how street-level theory applies to nonprofits as well as government agencies, we aim to incorporate this analytical orientation in our governance framework.

At the street level of analysis, the objective of a governance framework is to probe and explain this mixed-auspice configuration of public policy development and execution, in accordance with aspects of our definition of governance relating specifically to *implementation*. Street-level governance analysis also brings attention to the normative concerns outlined previously: How do government and nonprofit staff tasked with co-production processes become aware of and respond to the range of client or constituent needs and demands, thus ensuring some degree of *fairness* and responsiveness? How are staff incentives structured and aligned to promote *accountability* and *effectiveness* for clients, resource providers, and the public at large? What kinds of behaviors and motivations do public servants and nonprofit professionals perceive as *legitimate* given scarce resources and policy directives?

The reality of worker discretion in government and nonprofits suggests some discrepancy between official policy prescriptions and actual policy outcomes. Arguably the more interesting consideration from a governance perspective, however, is specifically *what workers do* with their discretion (Brodkin 2011). Insofar as a governance framework concerns how governments and nonprofits (whether in cooperation or conflict) conduct the public's business, street-level research in this area should seek to uncover the preferences and predispositions that cause individuals involved in government–nonprofit relations to behave the way they do. For example, a recurring theme in the nonprofit management literature is the concern among frontline staff that government and private funders focus too much on formulaic outcome reporting guidelines (Carman 2007; Hwang and Powell 2009; Maxwell, Rotz, and Garcia 2016). Lehn Benjamin (2012) shows that frontline staff in human service nonprofits approach their work in a deeply relational way, taking time to build connections with clients and fine-tune interventions according to client strengths and limitations. In contrast, outcome measurement frameworks tend to emphasize relatively fixed program models and measurable results rather than worker intuition, flexibility, and qualitative insight. As rigid performance metrics have become more institutionalized, scholars have found that workers struggle to balance their professional inclinations to be flexible and sympathetic with their economic incentives to move clients rapidly through mechanistic service plans (e.g., Soss, Fording, and Schram 2011; Spitzmueller 2016). Appreciating this tension between rule adherence and discretion is integral to a proper understanding of governance systems and how conceptions of effectiveness and legitimacy become contested at the street level.

Unfortunately, scholars studying the motives and value systems among government and nonprofit workers have sometimes been distracted by the sectoral perspective that we wish to de-emphasize. Numerous articles in recent years have claimed to find significant differences in the values, attitudes, and behaviors of public and nonprofit sector workers, such as volunteering (Rotolo and Wilson 2006), civic attitudes (Taylor 2010), career motivations (Lee and Wilkins 2011), positive work sentiment (Chen 2012), and perceptions of red tape (LeRoux and Feeney 2013). Many of these studies, however, do not adequately control for important contextual variables (industry, organizational size, level of government, etc.), thereby inflating the explanatory power of sector.[3]

The utility of a governance framework, then, is to encourage a more creative treatment of how individual discretion animates government–nonprofit relations regardless of actors' sectoral membership. Studies of how personnel differ in their values and motives (and, consequently, in how they exercise discretion) thus need to take into account the structure of public–private relations in which workers operate.

This analytical shift is particularly important in light of the continuing blurring of sectoral boundaries and the potential concomitant shift (at least in liberal democracies) to cross-sectoral and citizen-involved systems of policymaking (see Bryson, Crosby, and Bloomberg 2014). As the setting and implementation of policy agendas become less confined to members of a given sector, it will become more important to redirect our focus from sector to specific roles and responsibilities. To be clear, we are not simply calling on researchers to add more domain-specific control variables to their regressions. Anthony Spires's (2011) qualitative study of grassroots NGOs in China, for example, shows that NGO leaders must navigate a highly antagonistic policy environment and find specific government officials who are sympathetic to their causes. In a telling quote from a Chinese government official friendly to NGOs, Spires demonstrates the importance of analyzing individual discretion in detail rather than simply comparing blocks of undifferentiated sectoral actors:

> The one thing that most NGOs don't understand is that "the government" is not monolithic. There are many different branches to the government, and people within government agencies that have different agendas. NGOs often don't understand the role of the party in the government, either. So I try to help them see the government more clearly—as a complicated thing, not as one simple thing. (2011:15)

Spires's study resembles much of the scholarship on street-level dynamics, which often employs qualitative methods that enable a rich and detailed view of how individuals exercise their volition within the confines of bureaucratic rules (e.g., Binder 2007; Carter 2017; Dai 2014; Kim 2013; Spitzmueller 2016). Another emblematic analysis of street-level governance is an ethnography by Paul Lichterman and Nina Eliasoph (2014), in which the authors demonstrate how different patterns of civic action condition relations between governmental and nongovernmental actors within an affordable housing advocacy coalition composed of housing developers, banks, community advocates, and governmental agencies. According to the authors, the coalition maintains a generally combative approach to the local city government, but it also collaborates closely with supportive city officials who use their discretion to aid the organization's advocacy activity. As the authors point out, "these relations go well with the conceptual definition of civic action that emphasizes collective problem-solving action rather than actors' sectoral affiliations" (821). As with Spires's study of authoritarian China, Lichterman and Eliasoph's study of a cross-sector coalition in the United States illustrates how government–nonprofit relations filter through individuals on the ground.

Interorganizational Approaches to Governance

Some of the most robust studies of government–nonprofit relations that use a governance framework focus on the first part of our definition of governance: *the relationships and interactions between government and nonprofit organizations.* The more general study of interorganizational relations (IOR) traces its roots to Roland Warren, who made one of the earliest calls for the treatment of IOR as a discrete area of study, arguing that the "interorganizational field" (1967:396) poses a necessary object of organizational analysis. Twenty years later, Joseph Galaskiewicz (1985) offered a review of the burgeoning field of IOR, noting the utility of the approach for studies of resource allocation, political advocacy, and legitimacy. Today, the study of IOR has been reconfigured into more discrete theoretical approaches, including resource dependence, population ecology, network analysis, and field analysis, all of which have built on Warren's initial insights.

A governance framework for government–nonprofit relations allows empirical discovery of how institutional forces and individual agency come together in the formation of relationships among organizations. By focusing on the exchanges and conflicts between organizations and the environments in which they operate, research in this vein can begin on either side of the government–nonprofit divide, then trace the relevant connections to other organizations in whichever sector they may be. Scholars in public administration were among the earliest to take this perspective on government–nonprofit relations, given that one of their core audiences—managers working in the public sector—regularly confronted the realities of cross-sector relations in providing welfare state services. Indeed, Salamon (1995, 2002) rightly critiqued the New Public Management vogue of the 1990s (Hood 1991; Osborne and Gaebler 1993) for its caricatured portrayal of government agencies as isolated, hierarchical bureaucracies even as collaboration between government and nonprofit organizations was already well established in the welfare domain.

The core normative questions of governance often feature prominently in studies that take an interorganizational approach. For example, on the issue of *fairness,* how do government agencies and nonprofit organizations negotiate their respective orientations toward clients and constituents? How do different structures of government–nonprofit relations affect the *effectiveness* of governance networks? What formal and informal monitoring and reporting provisions exist between government agencies and nonprofit organizations involved in co-production processes to ensure *accountability*? And how do governance relationships enhance or undermine the *legitimacy* of government agencies and nonprofit organizations, either individually or as collaborators? In this section, we review recent scholarship that examines these and related issues of interorganizational relations, drawing on both resource dependence and network analysis as primary theoretical vantage points.

Interorganizational Relations as Resource Dependence

As mentioned previously, one of the prevalent themes in studies of government–nonprofit relations is that reliance on government funds poses various dangers to the autonomy of nonprofits as voluntary actors. Much of this work has drawn on resource dependence theory (Pfeffer and Salancik 1978) to describe a dominant role for government in its relationship with nonprofits. As the weaker partner, nonprofits allegedly alter their behavior in order to maintain access to government funds—a phenomenon known as *vendorism* (Kramer 1981; Frumkin 2002). Among the concerns about vendorism are that government forces nonprofits to change their approach to client service, causes nonprofits to incur inefficiencies and high transaction costs, reduces private donors' likelihood of contributing to nonprofits, and co-opts nonprofit missions and legitimacy.

Many quantitative studies have attempted to evaluate these claims, including several recent meta-analyses. Whereas early studies offered some support (see Steinberg 1991), the recent empirical evidence is decidedly mixed, though highly dependent on choice of measures (de Wit and Bekkers 2017; Lu 2018; Lu and Xu 2018; Payne 2009). Furthermore, the normative implications of vendorism may depend on perspective; some research shows that increased government funding may press nonprofits to serve more disadvantaged clients, thereby potentially improving nonprofits' responsiveness to community needs (Orden 1973; Morris 2009; Salamon 1995).

We argue that these critical nuances cannot be captured in an oversimplified sectoral image of a coercive, overbearing state and a timid, submissive nonprofit sector. Indeed, some recent research has strongly contested the idea that government holds all the resources while nonprofits depend on its largesse. For example, John Chin (2009) argues that nonprofits—not government agencies—drove the development of HIV/AIDS policy and public resource allocation in New York City. The forceful 1980s movement to bring government attention to HIV/AIDS created a strong set of nonprofits in New York dedicated to this cause, such that by the time government began addressing HIV/AIDS, nonprofit actors already had assembled the substantive expertise and organized constituencies necessary to combat the pandemic. As a result, Chin writes, nonprofits not only provided key services but also "play[ed] an important role in shaping *de facto* local social policy through their participation in community-based planning processes" (2009:432). This case illustrates the potential for variability in how government agencies and nonprofits relate to each other in the emergence of particular governance arrangements (see also, e.g., Levine 2016; Marwell 2004; Suárez and Esparza 2017).

In addition to capturing cases where nonprofits hold resource-dominant positions, a governance framework can allow for more precise descriptions not only of *actors* but of *actions*. For example, rather than simply asking whether nonprofit dependence on government curtails advocacy, we should consider how the nature and meaning of advocacy changes according to governance arrangements. Illustrating this point, Jennifer Mosley (2012) documents how the institutionalization of public–private partnerships in U.S. homeless services has caused some nonprofit directors to take an "insider" approach to advocacy rather than use confrontational tactics. This tactic, however, tends to focus on protecting existing government funding streams rather than pressing for transformative political change. Thus, Mosley argues that "insider, relationship-oriented advocacy is one tool that nonprofit managers use to try to communicate interdependence, build trust, and enhance their reputation as experts" (2012:844). This nuanced depiction of interdependent government–nonprofit relations is a far cry from the oversimplified portrayal of nonprofits kowtowing to public authorities, yet it also raises important questions of how the *quality* (not just the quantity) of advocacy and other activities fluctuates according to governance conditions (for an interesting discussion of relationship-based advocacy in Russia's "managed democracy," see Ljubownikow and Crotty 2016).

Network Governance

In addition to questioning whether government necessarily enjoys a privileged position vis-à-vis nonprofits, a governance framework enables descriptions of government-nonprofit relations as *networks* in dynamic flux, rather than as sectors divided by stark boundaries. Bolstering this idea, Rachel Fyall (2016) draws on a series of semistructured interviews with nonprofit, public, and for-profit professionals, pointing to a variety of advantages for nonprofits that interact with government through cross-sector coalitions. Fyall finds that individuals representing coalitions not only tend to have greater access to elected officials but also are viewed as more persuasive because of their association with a unified and mobilized set of actors. Moreover, coalitions protect nonprofits by shielding individual members from potential government retribution in response to antagonistic advocacy activity (i.e., "strength in numbers"). Fyall's observations reflect a long-standing recognition that groups of interconnected actors, whether in conflict or collaboration, frequently co-produce decisions across the public–private divide (e.g., Laumann, Galaskiewicz, and Marsden 1978).

The governance framework for government–nonprofit relations is perhaps most explicit in studies that take a network approach. Some of these studies are more formal, deploying network analytic methods and emphasizing the structural properties of interorganizational relations, such as density, centrality, embeddedness, and so on (e.g., Knoke 1990). Other studies draw on the idea of networks as a structural metaphor but place more emphasis on the content and meanings of relationships between and among government agencies and nonprofits. This range of approaches aligns well with general trends in network analysis, which has moved from a strong emphasis on the structural dimension (i.e., nodes, ties, equivalence, structural holes) to an appreciation of the importance of examining both network form and content (e.g., Pachucki and Breiger 2010).

In a particularly cogent theoretical exploration of how to incorporate formal network analytical methods into governance research, Keith Provan and Patrick Kenis (2008) argue for conceiving network governance as a variable: "Only by demonstrating that networks with different configurations have different network-level effects can a rationale for developing network-level theories be established" (233). Differentiating network forms by various governance attributes (e.g., goal consensus) and structures (e.g., presence of a lead organization), the authors develop a set of propositions for whether a particular form of network governance is likely to be effective. These propositions are both theoretically derived and based on an impressive record of empirical studies tracing the evolution of nonprofit organizational networks contracted by government to provide a coordinated set of mental health services in several cities (Provan and Milward 1994, 1995; Milward and Provan 2000; Provan, Isett and Milward 2004; Milward et al. 2010).

Drawing on both formal analytic and ethnographic methods to capture network structure and content, Sarah Reckhow (2013) describes how philanthropic organizations such as the Gates Foundation and the Broad Foundation have spent significant resources to develop, test, and implement public school reform strategies. Reckhow delineates the relations among school boards, teachers' unions, public officials, charter schools, and other key players in two cities, persuasively arguing that foundation-funded educational reforms in Los Angeles, with its integrated and consensus-oriented networks, are more stable than in New York, where reforms have been instituted via top-down elite influence and mayoral control. Providing still more evidence of governance variability that depends on context, Ma and DeDeo (2018) use formal methods to examine the structure of interlocking relationships among nonprofit foundation boards in China. Typically, Chinese government officials comprise some proportion of foundation board members, but Ma and DeDeo's analysis shows a partitioning between one group of foundations more closely connected to government officials, and another group centered on business elites. The authors hypothesize that the latter group appears to enjoy greater autonomy from government; however, they note that such a conclusion could be mistaken given that business elites already are closely tied to government. As a result, these foundations may be "act[ing] as an agent of the government itself" (2018:301) despite having no government officials on their boards.

Not all governance studies that invoke network governance use formal network analysis. The concept of collaborative governance (Ansell and Gash 2008) assumes that public service provision typically involves both government agencies and nonprofit organizations and thus requires extensive interorganizational connections to produce consensus-based engagement and decision making among partners from public and private domains (cf. Kettl 2006). David Van Slyke (2007) argues that in the case of public contracting with nonprofits for human services, the governance relationship is likely to shift over time from a principal–agent relationship, characterized by significant mistrust based on presumed shirking by agents and the application of monitoring and sanctions, to a "principal–steward" relationship, where trust and longer-term relations allow for more effective collaborative problem solving under conditions of decreased monitoring. Building on these earlier statements, Kirk Emerson, Tina Nabatchi, and Stephen Balogh (2012) provide a more complex integrative framework for the study of collaborative governance, which they refer to as a collaborative governance regime (CGR) (2). Studying a CGR draws on a number of disciplinary approaches and comprises multiple levels and dynamics of analysis, but at its core lies the tracing of organizational networks involved in collective decision making.

In a similarly conceptual approach, a group of empirical studies examining various aspects of the multisectoral governance of cities embraces the central concept of network analysis—interorganizational relations—without deploying formal network methods. For example, Nicole Marwell's (2004, 2007) study of community-based nonprofit organizations in Brooklyn demonstrates how nonprofits build relationships with government agencies and other nonprofit groups in different fields of action, thereby exercising multiple forms of influence over government deployment of financial resources and regulatory powers to assist low-income neighborhoods. Her ethnographic work illustrates the complex interorganizational networks that develop to implement key decisions that affect the lives of city residents.

Another example of research that provides insight on network dynamics without re-lying on formal network analytic methods is Robert Vargas's (2016) study of violence in Chicago. He shows how political redistricting in that city has affected the ability of non-profits in disadvantaged neighborhoods to build connections with local elected officials and police departments to prevent street violence. His review of local history demonstrates how political party elites took advantage of the decennial redrawing of political district lines to move small areas within the Little Village neighborhood in and out of differ-ent political districts over time. This redistricting undermined nonprofit organizations working to establish connections with local officials and disrupted nonprofits' access to government violence prevention funds. In those areas, Vargas shows that violence contin-ually returns—but in the parts of Little Village where the political district has remained unchanged over time, violence is notably less prevalent.

Finally, in his study of low-income housing development in Cleveland, Michael Mc-Quarrie (2012) shows how changes in governance practice dramatically reconfigured the city's organizational ecology into a "civic monoculture" (75). McQuarrie details how nonprofit intermediary organizations channeled federal low-income housing tax credits to the state public housing authority, which in turn distributed them to neighborhood nonprofit organizations to finance the construction of new homes. Although the nominal purpose of this governance arrangement was to provide capital for low-income hous-ing construction, a second-order effect was that community development corporations (CDCs) were more likely than other community-based nonprofits to survive in Cleveland's low-income neighborhoods. Other types of community organizations—such as civic and protest groups—found themselves delegitimized by the larger governance system, starved for resources and labeled as troublemakers. An end result, argues McQuarrie, was the rise of an extremely limited interorganizational network of CDCs, banks, and tax credit syndicators, which lacked the capacity to respond meaningfully to the foreclosure crisis of the late 2000s.

From Government–Nonprofit Relations to Governance

In this chapter we have argued that sectoral approaches to government–nonprofit relations offer important insights, but that in the fifty years since these approaches were first de-veloped, transformations in both government and nonprofit practice showcase the utility of an alternative perspective: governance. We draw on recent approaches to the idea of governance across multiple fields to make the case that a governance framework is likely to prove more useful for analyzing the future of government–nonprofit relations. We have reviewed research that uses a governance framework—either explicitly or implicitly—at three levels of analysis: institutional conditions, street-level decisions, and interorganiza-tional relations. Most studies examine only one of these levels, but we hope new research will consider how they fit together in an overarching governance framework.

We wish to emphasize that we are not asking researchers to relinquish parsimony by adopting governance as a framework for understanding government-nonprofit rela-tions. We are instead suggesting that researchers who already are engaged in constructive middle-range theory-testing begin to conceptualize their work as part of a larger agenda to recognize and understand the multiplicity of actors involved in policy development and implementation. If theoretical development of governance lags behind empirical investigation of its observable features, then we hope this chapter encourages researchers to push forward more strongly on the former to build a cohesive research agenda.

Constraints on the length of the chapter, as well as this volume's likely dominant audience in North America, necessarily limit the scope of our literature review. In particular, although we have incorporated some international examples, we note the U.S.-centric nature of the chapter. This may seem ironic, given that governance is a more long-standing analytic category for scholars outside the United States. However, one of the main insights of a governance approach is that the details of specific contexts drive our understanding of government–nonprofit relations. We have therefore drawn most extensively on our greater knowledge of the U.S. context. We join R.A.W. Rhodes (2011) in calling for greater discussion across national and regional boundaries moving forward in pursuit of a potentially more integrated theory of governance.

We close with a perhaps tongue-in-cheek suggestion. Should there be a fourth edition of *The Nonprofit Sector: A Research Handbook*, we propose the elimination of a separate chapter on government–nonprofit relations, though one has appeared as a fundamental component of all three existing editions of the volume. Our rationale is the one we have been promoting throughout this chapter: at this point in time, a sectoral perspective obscures more than it illuminates. Instead, we recommend that scholars be ever alert to how the governance of policy domains, places, and other substantively coherent fields of action are shaped by relations between government agencies and nonprofit organizations.

10 SOCIAL SERVICE NONPROFITS

Navigating Conflicting Demands

Jennifer E. Mosley[*]

NONPROFIT ORGANIZATIONS HAVE LONG DOMINATED the social services sector in the United States. Historically, social services provided by nonprofits have often been conceptualized as residual, addressing gaps unfilled by government, but that view is not quite accurate (Salamon 1987a). The growth of the modern welfare state (particularly one that is hesitant and largely privatized) has resulted in a parallel growth in the social service nonprofit sector that functions primarily as a complement to government action and a tool for enacting the safety net. Growth in the social service nonprofit sector has come through shifts in the safety net toward service provision and away from cash-based assistance, and in an ongoing preference toward contracting out government-funded social services to nonprofit organizations. As a result, most social service nonprofits in the United States substantially depend on the government to sustain their operations, and they play increasingly important roles in policy formulation and implementation.

In this chapter I argue that this sectoral blurring between the roles and responsibilities of government and social service nonprofits has also blurred the distinction between nonprofit activity and market activity. Specifically, the concerns regarding accountability and impact found in such a principal–agent relationship has led to government-set incentives for social services nonprofits to look, feel, and act increasingly like for-profit businesses, and the sector has responded affirmatively (Maier, Meyer, and Steinbereithner 2016). Today, except for their funding model, many social service nonprofits are almost indistinguishable from for-profit businesses at the ground level in regard to their attention to the bottom line, level of professionalization, and ambivalence toward their larger civic role. At the same time, they have increasing power in governance arrangements and as representatives of marginalized populations. The resulting tension is reflected in the inconsistent policies, practice recommendations, and even scholarship associated with the sector.

* I thank Nicole Marwell, Walter Powell, Tricia Bromley, Shannon Gleeson, and other participants at the Nonprofit Handbook Author Workshop at the Stanford Center on Philanthropy and Civil Society for their insightful and helpful comments. I also gratefully acknowledge research assistance on the NCCS data from Jade Wong.

Why should we care about this turn toward a market model for social service nonprofits? As Walter W. Powell (Chapter 1, "What Is the Nonprofit Sector?") notes, nonprofits are often seen as tools to accomplish a task (generally determined by a funder) and also as "a medium for the expression of values and commitments" (to promote well-being, community development, civic engagement, voluntarism, etc.). In other words, although they perform an important *instrumental* task in delivering social services, they are also ascribed key *expressive* functions, such as providing community cohesion, advocating for the vulnerable, and promoting ground-level solutions to important social problems. This tension between instrumentality and expressiveness is particularly fraught in the social services sector, as demands to meet outcome goals (related to their instrumental role) have become more dominant and process goals (related to their expressive role) are sacrificed to professionalization, efficiency, and impact.

This "entanglement of the growth of voluntary associations and the nonprofit sector with the development of capitalism and the corporate order" (Soskis, Chapter 2, "History of Associational Life and the Nonprofit Sector in the United States") has led to worries about accountability and capacity, and thus a growth in demands at the field level to pursue *impact* and *efficiency* as central values. These demands are often

- only proven through increased use of data and performance measurement schemes
- framed as proper stewardship of limited resources
- supportive of funding being directed toward measurable programmatic functions rather than civic engagement and advocacy
- co-constitutive with professionalization
- tied to the growth of evidence-based practice and the resulting tensions between that movement and more "traditional" nonprofit notions of person-centered care, co-production of services, and deeper connections to community

The embrace of market values presents a number of challenges for the sector. For example, consolidation and mergers have increased as big, multiservice organizations are increasingly best situated to compete in the data-driven, professionalized marketplace. Although the sector continually generates smaller providers that attempt to recreate or enact a more community-led or community-engaged style, there are few external rewards for that type of work, and competition is fierce. Thus, traditional "economic" theories of the sector (Hansmann 1987; Steinberg 2006; Weisbrod 1988) are called into question. Are social service nonprofits really serving niche needs because of close connections to religious, ethnic, or geographic communities? Do they really inspire more trust?

Additionally, most advocacy by social service nonprofits is now focused primarily on maintaining government financial support in particular industries or subfields (Mosley 2012). This calls into question the ability of the sector to promote substantive social change, as it is in the self-interest of most social service nonprofits to maintain the status quo. Traditional "political" theories of the sector will have to be adjusted if many organizations are functioning more as interest groups supporting an industry than as representatives of marginalized communities (Clemens 2006; Eikenberry and Kluver 2004).

At the same time, we are seeing a larger role for nonprofit social service providers in governance, largely through their participation in collaborative governance processes. Collaborative governance is a term that describes the various ways that nonprofits are involved in multistakeholder decision making about public policy and processes. Non-profits are increasingly asked to participate in such processes—often termed task forces or advisory groups—in order to help meet accountability challenges at the administrative level, fill in for the "hollow state" associated with contracting regimes, provide needed expertise, and promote coordination across fragmented policy areas (Ansell and Gash 2008; Emerson and Nabatchi 2015; Milward and Provan 2000). Their participation is often also conceptualized as a proxy for the participation of citizens, and thus a way of advancing democratic norms (Levine 2016; Mosley and Grogan 2013). These processes are being given increasing power over regulatory, funding, and implementation matters, but the degree to which social service nonprofits are adequately representing the populations they serve is unknown. Given the changes we have seen in advocacy norms and the incen-tives for those running the processes—generally government administrators—to exclude dissenting voices, the democratic impact of their participation is unclear (Dean 2018).

Collaborative governance is not the only way in which social service nonprofits par-ticipate in networks that have community-wide effects, however. Social service nonprofits face strong pressures from funders to participate in both intra- and intersectoral collabo-ration, including signing on to packaged, promoted concepts such as the collective impact model (Kania and Kramer 2011). Strong networks are important for effectiveness in both service provision and advocacy. But the field is currently challenged to create large scale collaborations that don't result in creaming of participants (e.g., selecting clients based on their likelihood of success) and deepening inequities between providers (Wolff et al. 2017).

Private philanthropy is behind some of this push toward increased collaboration, even while it plays a relatively small role in the overall budget of most social service organi-zations. Currently, social service nonprofits are usually more dependent on government dollars than on private philanthropy and often look to individual donors as a secondary source of income. This is based on the common belief that foundation dollars are as diffi-cult to get as government dollars but don't last as long and are generally for lower amounts. Foundations still play important roles in shaping current conditions in the sector, though, by focusing their dollars on "innovation" and in leading the charge toward greater de-mands for impact and output evaluation (Brest and Harvey 2018). By serving as conveners and thought leaders, organized philanthropy has been shown to radically reshape what service technologies are in vogue, what issues are important to address, and even what organizational types are best suited to address them (Dunning 2018; Tompkins-Stange 2016). In this way, philanthropic foundations have a powerful hand in shaping the market for nonprofit social services.

Social service organizations operating according to market principles are unlikely to promote practices such as advocacy, co-production, community representation, civic engagement, and voluntarism. This calls into question the ability of the sector to make the contributions to civil society many people expect of nonprofits (Eikenberry and Kluver 2004). Without these contributions, vulnerable communities could suffer, and residents could potentially become more alienated from the kind of human, social, and political capital needed to improve their lives (Alexander, Nank, and Stivers 1999). Meanwhile, the participation of social service nonprofits in a growing web of collaborative relationships and governance gives them increasing power and responsibility but limits their ability to meaningfully resist market-oriented trends. In the following sections, I review how this tension plays out through the current demographics of the sector, financing trends and tensions arising from government contracting, the relationship between contracting and performance, professionalization, and efficiency demands, and the resulting challenges described above.

Welfare states across the world engage and support third sector organizations in different ways (Esping-Andersen 2013; Salamon and Anheier 1998), and this chapter cannot review all of them; it largely focuses on the United States. There are similar trends elsewhere, however, as documented in work on blurring boundaries between nongovernmental organizations (NGOs) and government in Kenya (Brass 2016), on the marketization of the nonprofit sector in Europe (Bode 2017; Elstub and Poole 2014), and on the growth of social service nonprofit sectors due to increased contracting worldwide (Lu and Dong 2018). Given the already dominant role of government funding in the social service sector in the United States, a key question is whether the social service nonprofit sector can effectively bundle together the moral character that makes it appealing as an alternative to government with the expected cost savings of any outsourcing endeavor. The answer is crucial to the future of social services. Is contracting with social service nonprofits desirable simply because they are "not government"—private, and beholden to market forces—or is there something about the expressive character of nonprofits themselves that it is important to maintain?

Current Demographics and Financing

Social service nonprofits include a broad range of organizations that primarily provide services intended to promote well-being, improve life and living conditions, ameliorate inequalities and disparities, or otherwise assist individuals, families, and communities in need. In practice, they provide services such as mental health and legal aid, job training and employment assistance, food assistance, services for the homeless, child welfare services, and adult day services. Social service nonprofits can be understood as a subset of the larger human services field, which also includes education and health care nonprofits. Those organizations are generally studied separately, however, as they typically have substantially different financial models, operate in fields that are more mixed when it comes to sector (i.e., a stronger role for for-profit and public organizations), and serve a more universal clientele.

Although it is imperfect, the National Taxonomy for Exempt Entities (NTEE) is the dominant system used to categorize nonprofit organizations by their field of practice (Fyall, Moore, and Gugerty 2018; Grønbjerg 1994). In this system, social services are generally operationalized as codes F, I–M, O, and P (including but not limited to mental health, crime and legal services, employment, food and nutrition, housing, disaster relief, and youth development).

As seen at the bottom of Table 10.1, compared to education or health care nonprofits, social service organizations are relatively high in number but small in size. There are over five times as many social service nonprofits in the United States as there are health care nonprofits, but they are, on average, about a twentieth the size of a health care nonprofit (and about half the size of an education nonprofit). From 2006 to 2016, in social services, revenue grew much faster than the number of organizations. Every social service field,

Table 10.1 Size and scope of social service nonprofits in the United States, 2006–2016

	Total number of organizations, 2016	Percent change in number of organizations, 2006–2016	Mean/median revenue, 2016	Percent change in mean/median revenue, 2006–2016
Mental health and crisis intervention (F)	17,106	−0.7%	$3,391,936 / $284,912	74.1% / 114.5%
Crime and legal (I)	20,899	1.5%	$960,272 / $130,497	81.8% / 187.7%
Employment (J)	32,876	−17.3%	$2,418,644 / $260,880	91.5% / 149.7%
Food, agriculture, and nutrition (K)	18,016	22.8%	$1,897,841 / $137,686	143.4% / 127.7%
Housing and shelter (L)	33,618	−1.7%	$1,222,854 / $243,164	76.2% / 102.1%
Public safety, disaster preparedness, and relief (M)	23,150	4.8%	$298,254 / $102,761	64.6% / 89.2%
Youth development (O)	32,795	41.1%	$839,890 / $128,385	64.5% / 144.0%
General human services (P)	98,297	13.5%	$2,764,556 / $241,815	64.0% / 129.7%
ALL SOCIAL SERVICES	276,757	7.1%	$1,972,487 / $190,178	73.5% / 122.3%
In comparison:				
Education (B)	210,559	10.1%	$4,132,595 / $96,246	95.0% / 194.5%
Health care (E)	45,130	1.5%	$38,997,141 / $497,421	92.6% / 90.6%

with the exception of disaster preparedness and relief, saw a doubling (at least) in median revenue over that ten-year period. Revenue is growing even in fields that are declining in number (like employment services), which demonstrates consolidation. In terms of numbers of organizations, broken down by field, we see particular increases during that time in youth development and food, agriculture, and nutrition, and a moderate decrease in the field of employment services.

Financing in Social Service Nonprofits

Social service nonprofits are typically financed through a mixture of government grants and contracts (~65 percent), private foundations and individual donors (~18 percent), insurance payments and fees for services (~6 percent), and other sources of revenue (e.g., investment and business income) (~10 percent) (Morris and Roberts 2018). This mixture varies considerably by field (some fields attract more or less government or private dollars) and region, depending on the pool of public and private funding available in different states and localities. Each type of funding comes with challenges and opportunities for organizational independence, stability, and mission alignment.

The ability to earn money through fees paid for services (either directly or via insurance or Medicaid/Medicare) varies greatly by field. For example, mental health clinics and early childhood programs usually either charge on a sliding scale or are reimbursed by insurance or state programs. Medicaid reimbursements, in particular, make up an increasing proportion of revenue in some fields, especially substance abuse services (Allard and Smith 2014). In other social service fields, income derived directly from clients in the form of fees is typically low, as many social service nonprofits provide services to people with low incomes. Charging fees is either impossible (e.g., services for the homeless), or would compromise who is able to take part in the program (e.g., services for youth or employment-based services). Charging fees can also be controversial. Some argue that it may lead to stronger buy-in by participants, while others argue that it can lead to exclusion of the most vulnerable.[1] Fees, of course, are different than dues. Although rare, membership models of social services (like worker centers or self-help groups) often charge dues and, depending on the scope and cost of services, can achieve considerable financial independence in that way.

Although often lumped together in routine reporting (because of how this income is reported to the IRS), fund-raising from individuals and procuring grants from private foundations require very different organizational practices and have different benefits and challenges from a managerial perspective. First, soliciting individual donations that total a meaningful amount of money is a staff-intensive process. Each donor needs to be solicited individually, and large donors can be demanding in the kind of engagement they expect from the organization. Many small to medium-sized donors are needed to make up for just a few larger grants or contracts. Although individual donors typically do not insist on quantitative assessments of outcomes, they are often very resistant to giving money to "overhead." Websites like Charity Navigator, with their rating systems that punish organizations that invest in infrastructure or capacity needs, underline the concern many donors have regarding efficiency and trustworthiness. This can greatly hamper organizations' ability to grow and to retain flexibility to meet changing conditions on the ground. Individual contributions can also vary widely from year to year and may require substantial board involvement (Hodge and Piccolo 2005). Finally, there is considerable competition for those dollars, as most individual donations in the United States are given to religious organizations and higher education (Giving USA 2018).

Philanthropic dollars are prized to the degree that they provide more opportunity for mission-driven programming and more flexibility than government contracts, while the funding is larger and less capricious than that of individual donors (Froelich 1999). Private foundations value innovation, whereas government funders generally favor already tested programming (Bushouse 2009). This can make foundation funding appealing for organizations trying out new models of service. On the other hand, because most private foundations see their strength as funding innovation, they tend not to fund long-term, safety-net, "charitable" services that many social service nonprofits provide (e.g., community mental health, food pantries, foster care) (Hammack and Anheier 2010). Grants from private foundations also tend to be smaller than government contracts but still require substantial data collection regarding performance and impact. They tend to be more time-limited (e.g., a two-to-three-year grant with a maximum of one renewal) and, like individual donors, sometimes sharply limit funding for general operating expenses. Finally, successfully raising money from private philanthropy depends on establishing connections and requires a high degree of professional skill. For these reasons, grants from private foundations compose a relatively small proportion of the financial portfolio for many social service nonprofits. Despite this, philanthropic foundations play an important role in setting an ideological agenda, which is discussed later in the section on current challenges.

Thus, for many social service nonprofits, the remaining funding category—government funding—is where the action is. Whether state, local, or federal, government funding has become prominent in this sector, and understanding its role and impact is vital to understanding the challenges faced by social service organizations moving forward. As noted previously, government funding comprises approximately 65 percent of the budget of the average social service nonprofit in the United States.

This figure obscures considerable variation, however. In some subfields, like child welfare or homeless services, that average is much higher—closer to 90 percent—whereas in other fields, like legal services for undocumented immigrants, the percentage may be close to zero. Dependence on government funding also varies significantly by state. The federalism of government contracting perhaps matters for no other part of the nonprofit sector more than social services. Government funding can come in multiple forms (e.g., grants, fixed-price contracts, pay-for-performance arrangements, vouchers) and from federal, state, or local sources. The type and the origin of the money matters a lot for how consistent and sufficient it is, who might be eligible for services, and what it can be spent on.

Government funding generally offers the largest dollar figures and is the most consistent (e.g., contracts are generally renewable). In some fields, such as child welfare, a government contract is the only way to access the population of interest. In other fields, such as services for the formerly incarcerated or people who are homeless, donations from individuals or foundations are low relative to the cost of the service provided. Government support may be the only funding available. Shifts in policy that favor providing services in lieu of cash aid,[2] along with the shift toward federal block grants to states, have led to an increase in the types of programs governments fund.

Despite these advantages, however, social service managers are highly critical of government grants and contracts. Applications for funding and the mandated reporting requirements are complex and time-consuming, midstream changes to the contracts occur, and payments are often late—all of which disadvantage smaller organizations with less capacity to weather funding volatility and less professionalized organizations that may be challenged to meet application and reporting requirements (Boris et al 2010). Perhaps the most serious challenge associated with government funding, however, is that it generally does not pay for the full cost of services, which forces organizations to supplement the funding through other means (e.g., taking on debt, increasing private contributions, spending down reserves) (Boris et al. 2010). This "deficit model" of social service financing leads to lower service performance, reduced financial stability, and threats to the social rights of recipients (Marwell and Calabrese 2015).

The 2012 bankruptcy and closure of Hull House, Jane Addams's legendary settlement house, after 123 years of providing social services in Chicago, Illinois, is a prime example of the troubles that can result from overreliance on government funding, given the problematic partnership characteristics described earlier (Clemenson and Sellers 2013). Accounts of Hull House's demise generally note that at the time of its closure, it was more than 90 percent government funded and more than $3 million in debt. This debt is generally attributable to the organization taking out bridge loans to cover late payments[3] for government contracts that didn't cover the full cost of service in the first place. At the time, the state of Illinois had a backlog of about $4 billion in delayed payments to contractors and was taking over six months on average to pay vendors.

Because of the size of many government contracts, organizations easily become overly reliant on them and experience the negative effects of resource dependence (Pfeffer and Salancik 1978). Many contracts include mandates regarding who is eligible for services (e.g., specific ages or diagnoses), what service technologies or program models are appropriate, and what outcomes are preferred. All of these may run counter to an organization's mission, but once dependence has set in, there is little managers can do. In order to promote organizational stability and avoid resource dependence and mission drift, social service nonprofits are typically advised to diversify their funding profiles (Carroll and Stater 2009; Froelich 1999), either across revenue types (donations, grants, contracts, etc.) or within type. To diversify within type, an organization might seek government contracts from different agencies at different levels of government—for example, maintaining federal contracts to deliver Head Start programming while also maintaining state child welfare and early education contracts (typically administered by different agencies with different levels of political support). Some evidence exists that this strategy may be growing, as government funding becomes both more necessary (for maintaining capacity needs) and more precarious (with ongoing state budget crises) (Park and Mosley 2017).

Tensions Involved in Government Contracting

The day-to-day issues that social service nonprofits experience are concerning for many, but they can also obscure a much deeper set of tensions about the role of the sector and how that role may be shifting in response to increased enmeshment with government.

As Ted Lechterman and Rob Reich (Chapter 6, "Political Theory and the Nonprofit Sector") note, political attitudes determine the roles that the nonprofit sector plays. Privately provided social services, funded by government, have become standard partly because this arrangement is appealing to people across the political spectrum. This development reflects the larger adoption of neoliberal thought and the attendant growth of market-oriented interventions in every sphere of life (Birch and Siemiatycki 2016). As suspicion of government's ability to solve social problems grows—and citizens are increasingly being conceptualized as consumers—a nonprofit sector that is governed according to market principles (efficiency, competition, etc.) has emerged as an obvious alternative to government-provided social services. Evidence suggests that in the United States, most people prefer nonprofits to government, trust the sector more, and often do not realize that government funding makes possible such a robust social service nonprofit sector (Mettler 2011; Park, Mosley, and Grogan 2018).

Although in the United States the popular conception of social service nonprofits includes a rhetorical focus on the moral character of the sector, privatization resolves two other, perhaps more central, concerns. These are (1) the deep suspicions many people have of the state interfering with private matters—and almost all social services address such matters—and (2) the desire of the state to save money and outsource responsibility. These concerns suggest that it is indeed the *privateness* of nonprofit organizations that has led to increased privatization (as opposed to their *goodness*). They are "moral" partly because they are private. To that extent, the notion that people prefer them to government because of their moral character is a myth, perpetrated by both sides so as to grow the contracting relationships that both sides have become dependent on.

In the United States, the state has long contracted nonprofits to provide social services (Salamon 1987b; S. R. Smith and Lipsky 1993). Privatized child welfare services date back to the early 1900s. Likewise, many services that we consider privatized were never public in the first place. They were developed after private contracting of public welfare services was established as the default mode of delivery. Examples of these include domestic violence and HIV/AIDS services, both of which came about after long advocacy campaigns by people working in the field. In other words, fields that develop through private funding can work to convince policymakers to take up their causes, encoding them as statutory appropriations. Thus, what we have seen is more aptly described as a growth in government funding of social services—and the mechanism of contracting out to deliver them—rather than privatization per se. There has also been a shift in providing help to the poor and disadvantaged in the form of social services, rather than direct cash aid. Of course, that shift has led to yet more contracting and engagement from private social service nonprofits.

Despite this long history, numerous scholars and critics have decried the effects of contracting on the nature of social services (Alexander et al. 1999; Eikenberry and Kluver 2004; Hasenfeld and Garrow 2012)—some going as far as to label the phenomenon the "nonprofit industrial complex" (A. Smith 2007). Others, however, have praised the relationship as one of "partners in public service," in which nonprofits gain resources and legitimacy while government gains greater flexibility and efficiency (Berger and Neuhaus 1977; Salamon 1995). When assessing this controversy, two issues are conceptually distinct: first, the theoretical and pragmatic rationale for contracting, and second, the nature of how contracts are currently awarded and administered. Although they are often discussed in tandem, they need to be understood separately, as the second is far thornier than the first.

On the first point, contracting is unlikely to slow down for both pragmatic and philosophical reasons. It is baked into the U.S. welfare system in such a way that dismantling the apparatus would be next to impossible, and it is based on arguments harking back to notions of government, market, and voluntary failure that few people disagree with (Steinberg 2006). Wide distrust of the government to provide services sensitive to and targeted at community needs—along with government's reticence to take on the cost—means that it is unlikely to adopt a larger role in directly delivering social services. And despite the growth in social entrepreneurship, it is not feasible to think the for-profit sector will take on a *comprehensive* role in social service provision outside of contracting relationships because there is little money to be earned directly from social service consumers. With private donations constituting only about 20 percent of the total revenue for the sector—and little evidence of crowd-out (Bekkers and Wiepking 2010; Payne 1998)—in order to maintain our current level of social services, government contracting is generally seen as necessary.

The second point—the nature of how those contracts are awarded and administered in practice—is much more controversial. This goes significantly beyond the funding insufficiencies and poor partnership practices engaged in by many public-sector agencies (themselves underfunded). Because competition is embedded in the contracting relationship—it is, in fact, part of its appeal to many—the controversy really stems over beliefs about what that competition is based on: *efficiency* or *effectiveness*.

To social service nonprofits, contract competition often seems to be about blind efficiency—which organization can provide the greatest amount of services for the lowest cost (Boris et al. 2010). Those who see it this way typically believe that cost concerns actually discourage the kind of innovation and investment that may allow for greater effectiveness over the long run. Others, particularly proponents of New Public Management—a movement to make government more "businesslike"—frame contract competition differently. Although they mention efficiency and cost savings as benefits, they present contracting as a way to boost effectiveness by raising performance, promoting innovation, and increasing responsiveness (Heinrich and Choi 2007; Kettl 2011).

Research shows that contracting does not necessarily save money or improve performance—in fact, in health care it has been shown to do the opposite (Duggan 2004). Other research indicates that public–nonprofit partnerships have no effect on efficiency, effectiveness, or equity (Andrews and Entwistle 2010). But either way, if managers of social service nonprofits believe they are being rewarded primarily for efficiency, that is what they will aim for, potentially leading to the perverse outcome of sacrificing effectiveness.

This is troubling because evidence suggests that in social services, competition may actually be more myth than reality (Lamothe and Lamothe 2009; Van Slyke 2003). In many locales, there are not enough providers to create meaningful competition, and lack of capacity in administrative agencies means that contracts are poorly overseen. These findings strengthen the argument that contracting may be less a rational choice than a symbolic and political one. Regardless, as a result of mandates embedded in contracts, social service nonprofits are currently experiencing an uptick in demands for performance measurement, professionalization, and efficiency that many are struggling to adapt to. Furthermore, these demands—drawn from market-oriented thinking but driven by government—are ironically what is leading social service nonprofits to become more businesslike in their practices, potentially threatening the character of the sector that is held up as part of the purpose for contracting in the first place.

Performance, Professionalization, and Efficiency Demands

Critics have long accused social service nonprofits of underperformance and inefficiency, and not without some justification. Thus, growth in contracting has raised significant concerns about accountability, not uncommon in principal–agent relationships. The impression of waste in public agencies and suspicion regarding social welfare participants, who are often constructed to be lazy, dependent, scamming the system, or unable to be rehabilitated (Fraser and Gordon 1994), only heightens these concerns. Given this level of distrust all around, social service nonprofits now widely use quantitative performance measures to demonstrate proper stewardship of limited resources and provide evidence of effectiveness on which future funding can (theoretically) be based. Grounded in principles of New Public Management, a vast international literature describes how the habits and incentives of both individuals and organizations have shifted as a result of a growing audit culture (McLaughlin, Ferlie, and Osborne 2002; Power 2003).

Performance data is requested and used in different ways, with different effects for organizations. Coercive pressures for such data from funders for accountability purposes has led to a growth in shared institutional norms around the value of such data for determining impact. This is a value that social service nonprofits are expected to share and thus produce data that can be used for internal continuous improvement processes, as well as externally oriented accountability (Lynch-Cerullo and Cooney 2011). In addition, although most contracts demand some kind of data regarding performance outcomes, there has also been a growth in performance-based contracting and pay-to-succeed models, in which the nonprofit's payment is based on its ability to meet preset targets (McBeath and Meezan 2010)—a significant step up in accountability expectations.

Social impact bonds are another form of performance contracting attracting substantial attention. Social impact bonds are multiparty contracts between governments, private investors, and social service nonprofits in which the investors provide much of the initial capital for the program but have more say in how it is run and stand to reap profits if the program is successful (Olson and Phillips 2013). These initiatives have been praised for their ability to inject needed capital into the sector and for rigorously evaluating performance. Critics, however, find fault with the notion that private investors benefit from the performance of nonprofits at the expense of taxpayers (and staff salaries), and they do not agree that everything important about a program can be quantifiable as a "social return on investment" (see Brest, Chapter 16, "The Outcomes Movement in Philanthropy and the Nonprofit Sector").

Although performance measurement has grown substantially in both scope and practice, its effectiveness in actually improving services is questionable. For example, Pierre Koning and Carolyn Heinrich (2013) find that as contracts move from partially performance-based to fully performance-based, organizations are more likely to try to game the system through creaming and other strategies for artificially raising performance numbers, but they do not find evidence of improved program outcomes. Instead, they find that although fully performance-based contracts led to increased performance on short-term measures of success (e.g., job placement), they did not lead to improvements on long-term measures (e.g., job duration).

Because we know that performance measurement can lead organizations to unhealthy practices, yet resisting measurement entirely also seems unhealthy—after all, organizations want to be effective, be confident in their approach, and invest in things that work—a large portion of the literature on performance measurement is focused on how to "do it right." People worry about improving indicators, what to measure, connection to mission, how to create a new culture of data use, and more (Janus 2018). At the same time, demands on organizations to "do more with less" and the fact that their survival depends on ever-improving outcomes incentivizes organizations to decouple performance metrics from day-to-day practice (Meyer and Rowan 1977). Organizations may engage in outright falsification or simply take up the common practice of doing case notes and other paperwork at the end of the month (meaning it is not actually used for treatment purposes, merely for auditing, leading to inefficiencies). Social service nonprofits often work with stigmatized and powerless populations and feel stigmatized and powerless themselves, leading to not only decoupling but also the husbanding of resources and a mind-set focused more on short-term survival than long-term impact.

Considerable work exists showing sharp divisions between frontline workers and the data systems with which they are coerced to comply. Workers often perceive a mismatch in beliefs about the nature and goal of the work between their organization and their funder (Meagher and Healy 2003). These divisions lead to staff feeling discredited and alienated, sometimes believing that programmatic decisions do not match long-held priorities (Spitzmueller 2018). Accountability demands are often tied to restrictions on how funding is directed internally, which can change the nature of the services provided or the program mix overall. For example, funding may be restricted to measurable programmatic functions rather than civic engagement and advocacy. From a clinical perspective, funding is often tied to the use of specific evidence-based practices. Such practices, often routinized and with insufficient attention given to cultural or contextual differences between target populations, can conflict with the traditional value that social service practice places on person-centered care and co-production of services.

Lehn Benjamin and colleagues (Benjamin 2012; Benjamin and Campbell 2015) further direct our attention to misalignments between accountability demands, the nature of frontline practice, and the role of clients. They argue that frontline social services generally entail working in partnership with clients in ways that fundamentally resist measurement, because social service practice is nuanced, not replicable, and based on social and professional skill, not routine. In other words, some components of good practice—or some types of practice—cannot be quantitatively measured but are still worth doing, such as helping clients maintain trusting relationships or build confidence, helping communities take ownership of decisions, or building certain kinds of social capital. In this view, social service *programs* are not equivalent to social service *practice*, improvements in which are unlikely to be gained through more rigorous measurement systems.

At the same time, performance measurement, data demands, and reporting requirements all require increased professionalization in the sector (Suárez 2011). They are, in fact, co-constitutive with it, as professional training is often needed to keep up with analytic and strategic trends but also pushes those trends further as leaders and organizations compete. Although professionalization was already on the rise as a response to other types of institutional pressures, the perceived need for professional leadership makes it difficult for some smaller, community-based organizations to maintain ties to the community and internally reflect the client base they serve. It may also be leading to decreased voluntarism. Many social service nonprofits are almost completely professionalized, involving very few volunteers, because of requirements regarding confidentiality, specialized training, and the need for accountability.

Navigating Conflicting Demands

Ultimately, these trends of professionalization, performance measurement, and efficiency demands have led to social service nonprofits looking and acting much like for-profit businesses, largely at the demand of government (and sometimes private philanthropy). Outcome goals are prized over process goals, which creates internal conflict for organizations whose missions rely on a nuanced, indeterminate, nonstandardized process.

Figure 10.1 demonstrates the relationship between government funding, the accountability and performance demands discussed earlier, and the challenges to social service nonprofits' expressive roles (generally seen in a commitment to voluntarism, strong community connections, promotion of civic engagement, and participation in advocacy). Essentially, contracting regimes have raised concerns about accountability, which has led to increased performance assessment and professionalization. Those demands have, in turn, led to an emphasis on instrumental, market-oriented outcome goals and the devaluing of expressive roles and process goals.

Arguments that nonprofits are becoming more like for-profit or market-oriented organizations are not new (Weisbrod 1997), but the recent emergence of hybrid organizations and social entrepreneurship models in the for-profit sector has led to a resurgence of interest in the topic. Using Richard Scott's (2014) theory of the three pillars of institutions (regulatory, normative, and cultural–cognitive), Curtis Child, Eva Witesman, and Robert

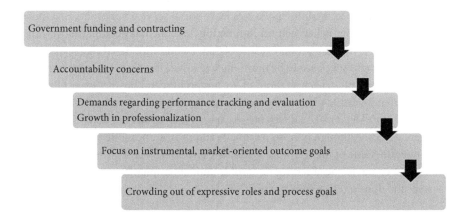

Government funding and contracting

Accountability concerns

Demands regarding performance tracking and evaluation
Growth in professionalization

Focus on instrumental, market-oriented outcome goals

Crowding out of expressive roles and process goals

Figure 10.1 Relationship between increased government funding of social services and crowding out of nonprofits' expressive roles

Spencer (2016) argue that although sectoral convergence is a reality to some extent, strong institutional norms uphold sectoral differences in the minds of practitioners. Over time, however, they find that perceptions of how sectors differ legally (in terms of regulations and funding) are stronger than perceptions of how they differ in their expressive roles.

Patricia Bromley and John Meyer (2017) also take an institutional view of sectoral convergence. They focus our attention, however, on the way that all sectors are changing—not just nonprofits—and note that these changes are generally cultural in nature. It is not that nonprofits are passively responding to pressures put on them by government, but that all three sectors are responding to a larger set of cultural shifts, starting in the wake of World War II, that place a high value on scientific rationality, whereas some practices assumed to be "businesslike" in the nonprofit sector—such as bureaucratic structure and codes of conduct—have their origin in government and higher education.

Thus, although sectoral differences continue to shape regulation (e.g., how organizations are allowed to generate and spend resources, individual vs. board governance), I argue that the normative and cultural–cognitive institutional expectations of the proper expressive role for social service nonprofits may be relaxing. First, normative expectations about the "right" way to behave (either externally or internally imposed) are now largely the same for all sectors—efficient, entrepreneurial, and operating at a professional remove. Second, in the cultural–cognitive sense, it is now taken for granted in the nonprofit sector that a focus on performance (as opposed to expressive functions such as community connection or voluntarism) is needed, that larger grants and contracts demonstrate a more sustainable operation (as opposed to relying more on smaller donations originating from the local context), and that cost-benefit assessments are a valid way of evaluating the worth of a program. Thus, sector matters in that it remains relevant and consequential to the financial viability and revenue model of nonprofit social service organizations. It is less clear that it matters in terms of their internal operations, staffing patterns, program models, and relationship with community members. It is difficult to see how traditional expressive commitments to voluntarism, strong community connections, promotion of civic engagement, and participation in advocacy will be maintained even if those are the things that drew many people to the nonprofit sector in the first place.

Contracting and accountability pressures leave social service nonprofits in a liminal position, as the multiplex beliefs behind contracting fundamentally conflict. Government enters into contracts with nonprofits because of their community-based character but also because contracting is supposed to be more efficient. Thus, it makes sense that nonprofits would be held to traditional expectations of the nonprofit sector but *also* expectations not unlike those that we would place on for-profit organizations (Sanders 2015). We somehow believe that sector *should* make a difference in expressive character but that it should *not* in instrumental roles. Although nonprofit scholars and practitioners often make normative claims about the value of the sector for advancing civil society and promoting the public good, when it comes to social service nonprofits, funders emphasize getting the job done, done well, and done as cheaply as possible.

The Case of Faith-Based Social Services

The case of faith-based social services shows that even when expressive characteristics are prized, the institutionalized nature of social service provision is a powerful force. The faith-based social services subsector received a great deal of attention in the early 2000s for its hypothesized ability to provide better results precisely because of its explicitly "values-based" approach (Kennedy 2003). Faith-based organizations are occasionally pointed to as emblematic of the expressive quality of the nonprofit sector (Olasky 1992).

Although there is initial evidence indicating that, given the right match between organization and consumer, faith-based social services may be more effective (presumably due to the way the service is provided) (Monsma 2006), overall evidence on this point is limited and mixed. For example, Robert Wuthnow, Conrad Hackett, and Becky Hsu (2004) found no differences in recipients' perceptions of the effectiveness and trustworthiness of faith-based versus nonsectarian nonprofits. Most research shows that, ultimately, faith-based nonprofits are not all that different from secular ones (Sosin and Smith 2006; Wuthnow 2004). In general, their openness to a secular world and responsiveness to the same set of institutional pressures is likely as important in shaping the nature and character of their programming as whether they receive government funding or the fact that they are faith-based (for an exception, see Vanderwoerd 2004).

In perhaps the strongest test of this argument, Mark Chaves and William Tsitsos (2001) find unequivocally that the social services that religious congregations provide are not more holistic or intensive than those of other nonprofits, and congregations that collaborate with government are not less likely to provide those kinds of personalized services. They firmly conclude that "religiously based social services are, in general, hardly an alternative to secular nonprofit or government-supported social service delivery. They are, rather, part of that world, likely to rise and fall with it rather than in counterpoint to it. Like the rhetoric portraying nonprofits in general as an alternative to government, the rhetoric portraying religious organizations as carriers of a social service alternative that is peculiarly holistic and transformational obfuscates the empirical reality" (680).

Current Challenges Resulting from Blurring of Roles

The consequences of this blurring of roles between sectors are many. This section reviews three of them: (1) consolidation, (2) changes in advocacy norms and an increased role for social service nonprofits in governance, and (3) new roles for private philanthropy and collaborative efforts.

Consolidation and Mergers

Increased competition for funding, the need for substantial reserves, and demands for performance and accountability data all have put significant pressure on small, community-based social service organizations. At the same time, contemporary social service management has become significantly more professionalized, executive directors are typically rewarded primarily based on organizational growth rather than consumer satisfaction, and board members are often recruited for their connections and ability to broker funds rather than for subject area expertise. These trends have resulted in an increase in mergers and takeovers in the social services nonprofit sector, a consolidation resulting in large, professionalized organizations operating at some remove from the communities they serve. Consolidation also advances institutionalization, as generally the norms and practices of the dominant organization override those of the weaker one in any merger or takeover (Field and Peck 2003).

Because small social service organizations often have at least a few contracts with the state and sometimes own valuable real estate, they have become targets for acquisition by larger social service agencies trying to consolidate their market position. Although an acquisition is sometimes presented as a way of enhancing client services or impact, it generally also stems from the dominant partner's desire to reduce competition and improve visibility, perhaps in a new field or geographic location (Benton and Austin 2010). Such a move is a classic way of managing the external environment (Pfeffer and Salancik 1978).

Consolidation among social service organizations calls into question traditional economic theories of the nonprofit sector (Hansmann 1987). Organizations are caught between (1) traditional expectations of close community and personal connections that facilitate trust in conditions of information asymmetry and (2) the need to make business-oriented decisions to maintain and grow programs that are funded by the state and jettison programs that are not lucrative—a key consequence of most mergers. These conflicting demands often result in decision making based on profit-making calculus—similar in essentially all respects to a for-profit company. In this case, what difference does nonprofitness make? At the same time, the political and civic role of the sector is also challenged; although a merger may increase capacity in the areas of data and performance measurement, marketing, government relations, and fund-raising, it is unlikely to facilitate civic engagement efforts, client involvement in the organization, or more legitimate representation of community needs.

Changes in Advocacy Norms and Increased Role in Governance

Some argue that that the advocacy and representation role that nonprofits have traditionally played on behalf of their constituents is what distinguishes them from the for-profit sector (Berry and Arons 2003). Traditionally, people have pointed to advocacy engagement as evidence of nonprofits' commitment to mission and willingness to stand with and for the communities they serve. Does the advocacy that social service nonprofits carry out really demonstrate this?

Research shows that dependence on government funding is associated with advocacy that largely supports the status quo (Mosley 2012). Instead of focusing on substantive policy change, given the reliance on contracts in the sector, advocacy has become an important way for managers to influence their funding environment and maintain organizational stability (Marwell 2004). Organizations that rely on government funding are strongly incentivized to advocate in order to build support for preferred practice ideologies, increase legitimacy with different stakeholders, and work to support increased public funding in their area of service. This advocacy is largely built on establishing trusting, reciprocal relationships with key administrators and legislators and is focused largely on insider tactics.

To the extent that the sector has become an arm of the state, it cannot effectively present a meaningful counterforce to it (Hasenfeld and Garrow 2012). Rather than helping to modify power imbalances in society by using their own power and legitimacy on behalf of the populations they serve, social service organizations frequently seek to consolidate their power in the system—resembling a traditional interest group rather than an advocate for social justice.

Along with a greater focus on insider tactics and maintenance of government funding, social service nonprofits are increasingly playing an important role in collaborative governance regimes. Defined as a "mode of governance that brings multiple stakeholders together in common forums with public agencies to engage in consensus-oriented decision making" (Ansell and Gash 2008:543), collaborative governance is an essential public management tactic in which public agencies collaborate with private stakeholders, like social service nonprofits, to improve service coordination, implement policy, and promote accountability across sectors. Representatives of government join stakeholders from the community, including representatives of social service nonprofits, to form advisory boards, task forces, or steering committees. These collaborative governance entities are growing in number, and social service organizations in fields like mental health, child welfare, homelessness, and early childhood education are active and involved participants.

Collaborative governance opens up considerable opportunities for social service nonprofits to be involved in the policy process, provide input on crucial decisions, and share expertise because it quite literally gives them a seat at the table. Although perhaps unconventional for those who think of advocacy as standing on the steps of the statehouse with a sign and a microphone, participation in collaborative governance provides a new advocacy venue, and emerging evidence suggests that providers see it as such (Mosley 2014).

This larger role in governance, however, raises a variety of long-standing questions about independence and legitimacy of representation (Levine 2016). Advocacy can be used to improve democratic representation, raising the voices and the interests of those who are not well represented in formal politics. But that can happen in a legitimate way only if clients are involved and have an opportunity to give input—which is rare in an increasingly professionalized social service sector (Mosley and Grogan 2013). Leaders of social service nonprofits are often asked to speak on behalf of their community or clients, but they can end up speaking instead for the interests of their organization or their industry. How different is this from Astroturf advocacy carried out by corporate interest groups (Lyon and Maxwell 2004; Walker 2016)? Granted, participation in a governance role is different from lobbying government (Marwell and Brown, Chapter 9, "Toward a Governance Framework for Government–Nonprofit Relations"), but intentions and the legitimacy of the resulting representation still need to be interrogated. Collaborative governance processes can also lead to exclusivity and divisiveness (Johnston et al. 2011). Which organizations are chosen to participate? If organizations can freely join, which have their voice taken seriously? To what extent are divisions in the field—between larger, professionalized organizations with substantial government funding and more community-based organizations—reflected in those discussions?

Interestingly, social service providers' pursuit of more reciprocal relationships with contract managers—to move those relationship from a principal–agent model to a principal–steward model (Van Slyke 2007)—and growth in collaborative governance has led to increased advocacy opportunities and the potential for greater influence. As a result, advocacy is increasingly part of everyday practice for social service nonprofits. Contrary to some assumptions, government funding incentivizes advocacy engagement rather than suppressing it, and closer relationships with government agents provides increased opportunity and access (Chaves, Stephens, and Galaskiewicz 2004; de Graauw

2016; Mosley 2010). At the same time, advocacy is likely to be more amicable, less oppositional. There are increased opportunities for collaboration and impact through formal
and informal channels, but at the same time, there is an increased risk of co-optation
(Piven and Cloward 1977).

In some ways, social service nonprofits have become "the loyal resistance": advocacy is
present but mostly aims to work within state-sanctioned systems, hoping to gather a larger
slice of the pie—rather than growing the pie for all or challenging basic assumptions about
the social rights of citizens. This clearly calls into question traditional political theories
of the nonprofit sector and its ability to maintain an independent voice (Clemens 2006).

New Roles for Private Philanthropy and Collaborative Efforts

A "hollow" state that lacks internal capacity and is more focused on contracting out
than on program design has led to opportunities for ideological leadership on the part
of private philanthropy. In this way, elite interests are reproduced in the sector, which is
used as a trial ground for new ideas (Reich 2016). Charter schools are the example that
comes to most people's minds (Reckhow 2013), but this phenomenon happens in social
services too, notably in social entrepreneurship models of service and the promotion of
specific intervention models. Social service nonprofits have long been pulled to respond to
multiple stakeholders: community members, consumers of services, activists, board members, individual donors, philanthropic patrons, and others. Often there is alignment—but
when stakeholders' interests, desires, or beliefs conflict, which group is given deference?
In order to maintain both legitimacy and nonprofits' bottom line, it is usually funders or
potential funders (DiMaggio and Powell 1983; Pfeffer and Salancik 1978). In this sense,
although philanthropy does strengthen the innovative capacity of the sector, it is also
channels attention and ultimately likely has a larger impact on social services through its
ideological leadership and investment in concepts and programmatic innovations than
it does through direct donations to social service nonprofits themselves (Bushouse and
Mosley 2018; Reckhow and Tompkins-Stange 2018).

One way we have seen growth in the influence of private philanthropy is through
initiatives to grow collaborative approaches. Collaboration across social service fields is
considered critical to solving wicked problems (like homelessness or substance abuse) by
reducing fragmentation, promoting a holistic approach, and facilitating mutual learning
(Thomson and Perry 2006). Funders value participation in collaborative efforts because
it signals legitimacy, a support system, an understanding of the complexity of problems,
and acknowledgement of risk sharing.

One of the best known of these collaboration efforts is the Collective Impact model, a
structured form of interorganizational collaboration (Kania and Kramer 2011). Generally
funder driven, collective impact takes much of what the scholarly literature on collaboration has been arguing and repackages it in a practitioner-friendly way. It has seen
wide uptake in just a few short years as a tool to bring communities together, coordinate
efforts, and demonstrate outcomes through shared measurement systems. This type of
collaboration comes with a host of warnings and critiques, however. Some questions that
have arisen include the following: Does most of the credit and funding, because of internal
power dynamics, go to the biggest organizations and required "backbone" organizations?

Which organizations are brought to the table? Do they adequately represent the communities concerned? Have issues of equity and racial justice been seriously considered? Does the collaboration channel efforts in a predetermined direction, ultimately stifling the work of ground-level activists (Wolff et al. 2017)?

With independent funding to promote ideas and preferences, philanthropy continues to be able to exercise its expressive role, but social service nonprofits are often seen as philanthropists' instruments—tools or sites in larger schemes for enacting social change. Top-down innovation doesn't generally allow for learning, which could take place from seeing what nonprofits on the ground are doing and what is effective in different communities. It also tends to depend heavily on professional and managerial expertise instead of field-based and localized knowledge and is designed to transcend culture and context (Ganz, Kay, and Spicer 2018). It has a veneer of neutrality, but the rationalized framing usually omits the perspectives and experience of those closest to the problem (Tompkins-Stange 2016). When innovation is seen only when it comes as a high-profile, disruptive force, rather than the resourcefulness and creativity enabled by deep expertise and extensive training, philanthropy becomes more removed from an authentic and democratic understanding of the problems it is trying to solve (Tufekci 2018).

Conclusion

Ultimately, social service nonprofits are not just deliverers of services but part of a much bigger web of governance in their roles as advocates, collaborators, and ground-level innovators. However, there is a real tension in the field as to whether social service nonprofits should be seen as gap fillers responding to market and government failure or as vehicles for strengthening communities and making policy more responsive and equitable. Currently, social service nonprofits are challenged to meet the normative expectations many citizens have for the nonprofit sector regarding voluntarism, community connections, and independence from government. They have strong incentives to become more professionalized, larger, more data driven, and more attentive to resource availability than community needs.

The application of market logic to social service nonprofits emphasizes that attention to the bottom line is simply good management and essential to capacity and quality. What distinguishes the sector is less the nature of the programmatic offerings and more the *personality* or *character* that social service nonprofits bring to their work. The challenge, then, in the face of this logic, is how to stay focused on mission and relational work when the market becomes ever more present in their work.

Optimists assert that robustly defining the outcomes that matter, with funding that is well-aligned to those efforts, could help social service nonprofits meet both instrumental and expressive goals. Certainly, the capacity to use data well will continue to be a skill that separates successful organizations from those who struggle (Janus 2018). One suggestion is for nonprofits to lean into their expressive, value-driven nature and highlight it as a unique strength. Unlike for-profits optimized for instrumentality, nonprofits can leverage community connections and a client-centered approach as strengths, potentially making them more competitive than their for-profit peers in tackling more complex, barrier-rich social issues (Frumkin and Andre-Clark 2000).

Pessimists argue that a healthy civil society is simply incompatible with nonprofit dependence on government funding. In this view, the pursuit of government funding creates perverse incentives for nonprofits that lead them to become ever more focused on meeting the desires of funders rather than the community members they see every day (Dolsak and Prakash 2015). At the same time, the federalized nature of government contracts keeps nonprofits from collectively organizing, as does the fact that the social services are highly siloed by program area (mental health, child welfare, etc.). These aspects of policy design not only make it difficult for nonprofits to have a strong advocacy voice but actively discourage individuals (nonprofit staff and consumers alike) from getting involved or seeing their fates as linked (Michener 2018).

Nonprofit dependence on government funding has notably come about precisely through the rejection of government as a tool to solve problems (and, in fact, sometimes as the source of them) and the embrace of market principles as an alternative. Solutions to social problems are, in turn, seen as technical and knowledge-based rather than political and power-based (Ganz et al. 2018). Recognition of the inequalities baked into our current political system would mandate increased involvement of social service nonprofits in civic engagement and citizen mobilization. Our current focus on innovation, data, and performance measurement, by contrast, privileges the short-term, individual-by-individual approach to meeting social needs and thereby favors the status quo.

Increased enmeshment with government gives social service nonprofits more power and responsibility while limiting their ability to resist marketization trends. This phenomenon can be seen in other fields as well, such as health care and education. Growing austerity and contract competition limit possibilities for dissent and alternative conceptions of the sector (Dodge 2010). Current relationships with government have been conceptualized as principal–agent in nature, implying vertical accountability. If, through changes in collaborative governance and collaborative practices generally, social service nonprofits are to have a larger voice and exercise more control over the social service system, we will need new theorizing of horizontal accountability in the social services (Hill and Lynn 2005; Van Slyke 2007). The future of the social service nonprofit sector is uncertain but could be telling for other parts of the nonprofit sector that are not yet as fully enmeshed with government partners.

11 NONPROFITS AS URBAN INFRASTRUCTURE

Christof Brandtner and Claire Dunning*

CITIES, HISTORIAN AND SOCIOLOGIST LEWIS MUMFORD argued in a speech to urban planners in 1937, are sites of the "urban drama" (Mumford 1937). That is, cities are scenes of the most profound challenges and opportunities for both individuals and collectives. In the twenty-first century, cities are places of rising economic inequality, persistent racial segregation, global migration and displacement, and increasing climate threats. Relatedly, they are also hubs of innovation, creativity, mobilization, and resources; they are places where people come to work, live, join, study, earn, relax, and protest.

Cities are also home to a vast array of nonprofit organizations. Art museums, hospitals, universities, block clubs, advocacy groups, homeless shelters, service providers, and think tanks dot the urban landscape. Nonprofits are the vehicles through which urban residents engage their governments, the spaces in which they meet their neighbors, the educational centers that produce new leaders and knowledge, the anchor institutions that define neighborhoods, and the economic engines that launch regional industries. They care for the sick, preserve the arts, promote causes, occupy real estate, partner with business and government, employ residents, and provide services to those on the top of the economic ladder and those on the bottom. They create public awareness and mobilize resources and people in ways that address and, at times, exacerbate challenges such as exclusion, displacement, and decay.

What is easy to conjure from observing the "urban drama" has been documented in research that analyzes these patterns as products of broad historical and sociological processes. Scholars have demonstrated the necessity of considering cities along numerous axes of analysis, as well as considering the ways nonprofit organizations are (and have been) products of their environments and producers of it. As Richard LeGates and Frederic Stout argue (2015), the city fulfills multiple basic societal functions at once: the citadel (government), the market (economy), and the community (civil society and family). The ways in which nonprofits have become entangled in each of these functions have been the subject of research from a range of disciplines. This chapter traces much of this research

* We thank Luís Bettencourt, Jackie Hwang, Jeremy Levine, Nicole Marwell, Frederic Stout, and the editors of this handbook for their helpful comments. All errors are our own.

throughout a cross-disciplinary literature while highlighting work, in particular, from our respective fields of sociology and history. On balance, we encountered a literature rife with evidence on the urban quality of the nonprofit sector and the centrality of these organizations to the urban drama, but that remains fragmented and lacking a framework for understanding the relationship between cities and their nonprofits.

This chapter synthesizes existing research to argue that nonprofits constitute a form of urban infrastructure that both defines and reflects the city—which we understand as a network of organizations and people in geographically anchored spaces (Laumann, Galaskiewicz, and Marsden 1978). We first discuss the nonprofit sector as a predominantly, though not exclusively, urban phenomenon.[1] We bring together quantitative and qualitative approaches to assess this urban quality. We then consider how the urban environment shapes the behavior of collocated organizations, considering specifically the ways in which urban contexts mold nonprofit organizations such as through shared social, political, and economic institutions (Marquis, Lounsbury, and Greenwood 2011). Nonprofits are not solely a product of their environments, and through their direct and indirect activities they shape the physical, economic, political, and cultural structure of cities. This leads us to outline five key roles that nonprofits play in cities: (1) forges of civic capacity, (2) participants in urban governance, (3) conveners of economic networks, (4) anchors of belonging, and (5) builders of the physical environment. This literature helps us illustrate how nonprofits form an infrastructure that undergirds the city.

Invoking the metaphor of *infrastructure* borrows from the great urbanist Jane Jacobs, who discussed streets and sidewalks as "bound up with circulation" and as part of the lifeblood and functioning of a city (Jacobs 1992:29). Jacobs's use of infrastructure as a metaphor notably refers to both a hard and soft infrastructure—of the physical or material streets and sidewalks that create city grids, and the more amorphous ways that those grids facilitate human interaction. We frame nonprofit organizations and the sector they compose as fulfilling a similar role for cities in both direct and indirect ways. For examples, a homeless shelter provides a direct service but also occupies a physical presence in a neighborhood, receives philanthropic and government resources, and advocates for housing policies; a global nongovernmental organization (NGO) serves a population beyond its headquarters in New York but still has an influence on the neighborhood and city in which it is based through convening meetings, disseminating research, employing staff, and occupying an office building. These nonprofit entities both constitute and reflect the cultural, economic, physical, political, and spatial terrain of the city. They form an urban infrastructure that scholars of cities and of nonprofits ought to acknowledge in order to understand the past, present, and future of cities and the organizations that inhabit them. We conclude the chapter with a research agenda to further this framework and our understanding of the civic life of cities.

The Urban Dimension of the Nonprofit Sector

The nonprofit sector is predominantly, though not exclusively, anchored in cities. In the United States today, more than 80 percent of U.S. nonprofits are in urban agglomerations above twenty-five thousand people. Measures of nonprofit density point to the amount of services and resources provided in a given city (Small and McDermott 2006). Most of these organizations tend to what is happening in front of their door. In a survey of a representative sample of nonprofit organizations in the San Francisco Bay Area, Woody Powell and his colleagues (see Hwang and Powell 2009) found that more than three quarters of surveyed organizations deliver their services or advocacy in the city or county in which they are located. Given that nonprofit organizations deliver a consistent fraction of services on behalf of municipalities (Brandtner and Suárez 2018), differences in the densities of nonprofit organizations between cities may reflect local governance patterns, politics, and need. The relative size or strength of the local nonprofit sector also speaks to other durable properties of the local community such as civic capacity (Lecy and Van Slyke 2012; Rao and Greve 2018) or local governance regimes (Marwell and Brown, Chapter 9, "Toward a Governance Framework for Government–Nonprofit Relations"). Most data on the nonprofit sector as a whole, however, adopt either a national- or organizational-level scale and provide little texture to how cities and their subset of the sector differ.

And yet they do differ, as a brief comparison between cities based on nonprofit tax data, compiled by the National Center for Charitable Statistics, makes clear. Figure 11.1 shows the concentration of nonprofit dollars in cities in the United States and that about a third of overall budgets are tied to nonprofits headquartered in only ten city regions. It also demonstrates, however, that there is stark variation in terms of spending in a given locale—the mean nonprofit dollars spent per year range widely even among the top ten, from around three million in Los Angeles, California, to over twenty-five million in Portland, Oregon. This disparity indicates structural differences between places, although the legal location of national headquarters (e.g., health insurance providers in Portland, Oregon) is distortive. For this reason, comparisons of numbers and densities are more

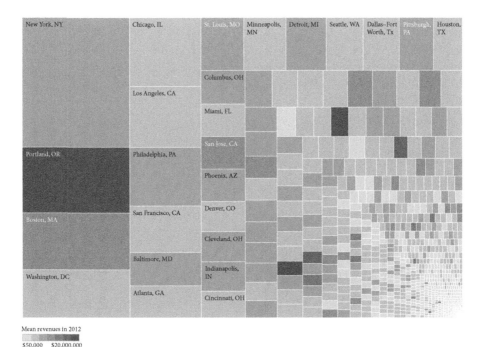

Mean revenues in 2012

$50,000 $20,000,000

Figure 11.1   Where are U.S. nonprofit dollars?

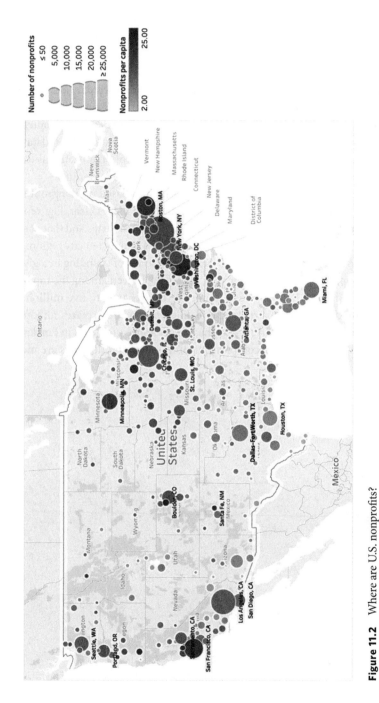

Figure 11.2 Where are U.S. nonprofits?

Note: Nonprofit locations are estimated based on addresses listed on IRS forms 990. Although the city region (i.e., Metropolitan Statistical Area) of these addresses typically aligns with the location of the organization, these locations should be interpreted with care: Not all addresses are correct (e.g., small organizations may list home addresses of a board member), organizations with branches may not file independently but only in the city in which their headquarters are located, and an organization's sphere of activity may not align with its location.

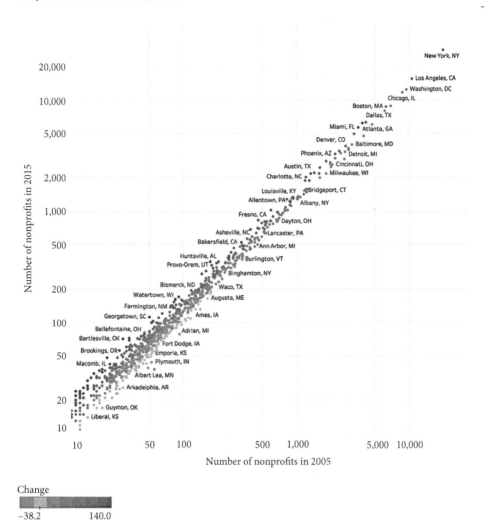

Figure 11.3 How did the number of nonprofits in a given city change from 2005 to 2015?

meaningful. Figure 11.2 shows where the largest local nonprofit sectors are located in terms of the number of organizations, and which cities have the highest numbers of nonprofits per capita. Unsurprisingly, places with national and international NGOs such as Washington, DC, and New York City stand out for both absolute size and the density or ratio of organizations per capita, pointing to some correlation between the two. To hold the position of some large cities constant over time, it helps to look at changing numbers over a discrete period. Figure 11.3 shows that although the growth in the number of nonprofit organizations has been linear, that growth has been uneven. At the same time, it demonstrates a consistency of these differences between cities over a decade. Taken together, these figures underscore great and durable variation in the size of urban nonprofit sectors.

The figures raise questions not only about the causes of such difference between cities and their slice of the nonprofit sector, but also about the local consequences thereof.

Dominant theories of and classic works on nonprofits, however, tend to overlook place in their analyses and thus cannot explain the urban trend as a whole or the local varia-tion. Theories of government failure and contract or market failure (Powell, Chapter 1, "What Is the Nonprofit Sector?") define nonprofits and explain their existence vis-à-vis the absence of the state or market. Research following from these theories tends to rely on national-level data that align with seemingly distinct state or market boundaries (Matsun-aga and Yamauchi 2004; Anheier, Lang, and Toepler, Chapter 30, "Comparative Nonprofit Sector Research"). These findings, particularly from comparative studies of countries or industries in them, have lent support to canonical theories, but research at the city level may tell another story. For example, comparing over three hundred metropolitan statistical areas in the United States, Lecy and Van Slyke (2012) find that higher density of human service nonprofits is associated with more government funding, not with demand het-erogeneity as would have been predicted by Henry Hansmann (1987). This finding adds further weight to the necessity of considering the dimensions of the nonprofit sector at a city level, and of building a theoretical framework for understanding it.

How Cities Shape Nonprofits

Nonprofits are exposed to and shaped by the institutional properties of the city in which they are located on a daily basis: in cities, they share constituents, funders, peers, place, and an understanding of the most pressing problems and how to resolve them (Marquis and Battilana 2009; McQuarrie and Marwell 2009; Marquis et al. 2011). This means that nonprofits are located within a city and influenced by their immediate surroundings, even as those surroundings are themselves filters for external influences beyond the city itself (Self and Sugrue 2002). Broader social and cultural patterns shape and are reflected by nonprofit organizations, as many chapters in this handbook illustrate. As Michael Mc-Quarrie and Nicole P. Marwell (2009:247) argue, "organizations are structured by their geographic, organizational, and institutional environments, and organizations in turn structure their environments." Though they were speaking broadly about organizations, their words hold in particular for the nonprofit sector. In the following discussion, we briefly outline some of the ways in which nonprofits are subject to their discretely local context.

In a city, nonprofits share a demographic, political, and legal environment. Municipal gov-ernments in particular can regulate, direct, and coerce nonprofits, for example, as funders of local organizations or by controlling the process through which a developer can obtain a building permit. As Jesse Lecy and David Van Slyke state, governments "often turned to nonprofit organizations as the street-level implementers" (2012:189–214) of policy in various human service domains. Nonprofits' legal environments have changed over time, as have the policy choices behind which public funds flow into local and private coffers (Katz 1996; Zunz 2012; Levy 2017; Dunning 2018b). Harvey Molotch, William Freudenberg, and Krista Paulsen (2000) argue that cities persist to have different traditions, which are reflected in "connections between local organizations and community social patterns that are perpetuated over time" and reflect the historical and demographic context. For example, Robert Putnam (2000) found social engagement to be higher in the northern U.S.

states, where communitarian Scandinavian groups settled, than in the South. Wesley Long-hofer, Giacomo Negro, and Peter W. Roberts (2018) show that the effectiveness of local civic action—measured as the returns of local campaigns of the UNICEF trick-or-treat program—also depends on the demographic context. According to the study, counties with higher income inequality and greater racial diversity saw more effective mobilizing.

Cultural norms of giving differ from city to city. Networks of organizations within cities and regions can be vital for how nonprofits mobilize resources and collaborate with others. Joseph Galaskiewicz (1985, 1997; Galaskiewicz and Wasserman 1989), with his studies of the social system of philanthropy and corporations in Minnesota's Twin Cities, pioneered this insight on the link between a CEO's embeddedness in local social networks and cor-porate giving. Doug Guthrie and Michael McQuarrie have since built on this with their multicity analysis of the Low-Income Housing Tax Credit, adding that the institutional environment shaped not only how much corporations gave but where and to what causes (2008). For another instance, Michael Lounsbury (2007) describes how mutual associa-tions were structured differently depending on whether they were embedded in the local culture of Boston or New York.

Need for and funding of nonprofit services vary by region. Wolfgang Bielefeld (2000) finds that cities in regions with a strong belief in state intervention have larger nonprofit sectors than those whose emphasis lies on the market or individuals. He also shows that wealthier cities are characterized by more generosity, with support for education and arts organiza-tions more frequent. Demand and supply have complex meanings for nonprofit organi-zations. In a study of organizational practices among nonprofits in the San Francisco Bay Area, Aaron Horvath, Christof Brandtner, and Walter W. Powell (2018) find that certain mind-sets among nonprofit staff—such as strategic outlook and poverty orientation—are related to how organizations perceived and responded to rising demand for their services during the Great Recession. Similarly, András Tilcsik and Christopher Marquis (2013) show that multinational corporations, in the aftermath of small disasters and during mega-events such as the Super Bowl, contribute more financially to the communities in which they are headquartered. The hypothesized effect is that corporations are more likely to interact with nonprofits during such times of heightened attention on the community, for instance through shared board membership (Marquis, Davis, and Glynn 2013).

Competitors and peers are frequently local. The local unit of analysis is often invoked to test models of competition in economic geography and organizational ecology (Marquis and Battilana 2009). For instance, Glenn R. Carroll (1985) studied newspaper competition in U.S. cities to understand the effect of niche width on organizational survival. A study of competition for resources between voluntary organizations in Arkansas inspired much of this work on niches (McPherson 1983). In the nonprofit context, Floris Vermeulen, Debra C. Minkoff, and Tom van der Meer (2016) have investigated how competitive dynamics on the neighborhood level influence the survival of immigrant community organizations. As these cases illustrate, nonprofits compete for resources and influence, which shapes local variation in structures and strategies.

Nonprofit practices are inspired by the practices of their peers. In discussion of community influences on corporate social responsibility, Christopher Marquis, Mary Ann Glynn, and Gerald F. Davis (2007) show that social action of local corporations within regions is relatively homogeneous: the authors report "the average [KLD rating of social responsibility] across the top ten MSAs [metropolitan statistical areas] to be nine times greater than the average of the bottom ten MSAs." In other contexts, geographic spillovers between proximate organizations matter for influencing organizational decision making and the adoption of practices through various mechanisms, including diffusion (Strang and Soule 1998; Czarniawska 2002), migration of skilled workers (Saxenian 1994; Fleming, King, and Juda 2007), and interorganizational collaboration (Whittington, Owen-Smith, and Powell 2009). Although empirical research applying these ideas to the nonprofit sector is scarce, spillover effects resulting from propinquity are likely the same for the adoption of nonprofit practices, such as impact investing or strategic planning, board governance, and staff professionalization.

Scholars of the city and organizations have shown how a range of local influences shaped the behavior of nonprofits over time and place. The causal emphasis lies on how communities alter organizations individually and collectively. Some of these influences are shared among cities and reflect characteristics of cities by nature of their being urban, while others are amplified or muted based on local circumstances. This literature suggests ways that two American cities, Detroit and New York, and their respective nonprofit sectors are both alike and dissimilar, as well as the ways that large and global cities, New York and London, and their respective sectors of nonprofit organizations are both alike and dissimilar. Specifying these influences, their emergence, and their interactions remains an exciting avenue for research. But it is one that prioritizes the understanding of organizational behavior and leaves unexplored how this behavior by individual organizations and their collectives shapes the development of the contexts.

How Nonprofits Shape Cities

The previous section considered how urban context shapes nonprofits. In this section, we explore the reciprocal question of how these organizations shape the places they inhibit. Doing so builds on the important insight from McQuarrie and Marwell that organizations are not empty vessels or mere products of their environments (2009). We add to this literature by emphasizing several causal pathways through which nonprofits shape cities via both direct activities and indirect effects.

We highlight five roles that nonprofits play in cities: (1) forges of civic capacity, (2) participants in urban governance, (3) conveners of economic networks, (4) anchors of belonging, and (5) builders of the physical environment.[2] Table 11.1 summarizes these roles and mechanisms that are not unique, but still common, to nonprofits and then connects these mechanisms to a series of outcomes of interest to social scientists. This table can be read from left to right or from right to left depending on whether a scholarly question is about organizations (e.g., what impacts do community centers have on urban neighborhoods?) or about outcomes (e.g., what increases or decreases democratic participation in cities?). Scholars of different disciplines would likely root themselves in different cells in the table and then, we hope, draw new connections between their research and that of others.

Table 11.1 Five roles of nonprofits in urban environments

Role	Actors	Actions	Outcomes
Forges of civic capacity	CBOs, child care centers, community centers, schools, mutual funds, churches, tenant unions, YMCAs	Bridging and bonding, teaching, convening, mobilizing	Resilience, trust, delinquency, movements, resistance, social change, preservation
Participants of urban governance	Health centers, advocacy groups, schools, churches, CBOs, homeless shelters, block associations, professional intermediaries	Awareness building, providing, advocating, mobilizing, resisting, monitoring, disciplining	Democratic participation, exclusion, representation, (in-)equality of access to resources, policy reform, consolidation and concentration of power
Conveners of economic networks	Chambers of commerce, universities, booster clubs, hospitals, elite clubs, professional associations, foundations	Convening, providing, bridging, transposing, employing, allocating, promoting	Innovation, inertia, jobs, tax revenue, exemption, collaboration, competition, commercial development, marketization
Anchors of identity	Neighborhood groups, INGOs, museums, centers, churches, settlement houses, landmarks, ethnic associations	Branding, proselytizing, mapping, boundary-making, identity-shaping	Reputation, sense of belonging, nativism, boundaries, social control
Builders of physical environments	Universities, hospitals, CDCs, tenant unions, churches	Spending, planning, investing, resisting	Housing, segregation, commercial development, urban renewal, revitalization, gentrification and displacement

Forges of Civic Capacity

Sociologists have long used nonprofits as indicators of functional social networks and, by proxy, of social capital. Whether people know and trust each other, according to Putnam (2000), is a defining characteristic of local communities and how they are governed. Community and neighborhood organizations are not only a product of people joining together. They are also producers of it by offering opportunities for people to congregate and form social ties in spaces including public parks, libraries, squares, community organizations, and sidewalks (Klinenberg 2018). As Mario L. Small's (2009) widely regarded ethnography of New York City child-care centers shows, the relationships that people from distinct backgrounds forge in waiting rooms are the very source of community social capital, which brings a sense of belonging to those who get to know others. Political scientists such as Putnam (2000) have argued that social capital within local communities is a key component of good governance—governments that take citizen participation and transparency seriously.

This ability of nonprofits to foster and create community has had lasting relevance for community-level outcomes in a variety of policy fields. One such outcome is resilience to changes in the natural environment. Eric Klinenberg studied several extreme weather events and found that the social infrastructure—the degree to which people care for each other through community associations, meet in public libraries, and run into each other on sidewalks—is a crucial component of community resilience. In a notable study of the 1995 Chicago heat wave, Klinenberg (2002) found that neighborhoods with practically identical racial and socioeconomic populations had exorbitantly different death tolls. He explained this difference through analyses of organizations and social capital, finding that neighborhoods with more social infrastructure were more likely to protect the elderly from sitting home alone for several days in the extreme heat. Hayagreeva Rao and Henrich R. Greve (2018) make a similar case for community resilience during the Spanish flu and permafrost in Norwegian towns. Relatedly, Patrick Sharkey, Gerard Torrats-Espinosa, and Delaram Takyar (2017) find that the presence of nonprofits in a city leads to lower murder and crime rates because nonprofits facilitate "mobilization from within" communities.

Beyond the creation of trust, nonprofits are associated with the development of civic capacity more generally—social skills that allow recognizing problems and mobilizing and organizing to address these problems (Paxton 2002; Lee, McQuarrie, and Walker 2015). As neo-Tocquevillian scholars argue, nonprofits are schools of democracy by giving people opportunities to express their opinions and practice deliberation and have been shown to bolster civic and organizational skills (Verba, Schlozman, and Brady 1995; Fung 2003; McAdam et al. 2005). The pro-democracy protests in Hong Kong in 2014 serve as a good example for the transposition of organizational capacity from one domain to another. The effective mobilization and organization was a direct result of the vibrant but cooperative community life in local universities, including debate clubs, affinity groups, and student unions. These voluntary groups taught students to design posters, run meetings, and communicate demands that were critical skills in what came to be known as the Umbrella Revolution (Ortmann 2015).

The development of civic capacity and participation is important not only as a result of nonprofit activities in their own right, but because cities then bear the imprint of these past activities or choices. Sven Beckert, for example, links participation in elite social spaces of nonprofits including civic clubs, museums, and cultural institutions to the consolidation of political power among New York elites during the Gilded Age (2001), and Thomas Sugrue considers homeowners associations in Detroit as vehicles for the defense of whiteness and residential segregation (1996). Examples abound in work on the black freedom movement, particularly its manifestations in the urban north, where mobilization by grassroots nonprofit organizations led to more, though often incomplete, equality (Theoharis and Woodward 2003; Countryman 2007; Sugrue 2008). Beyond the social and political, the presence of nonprofit organizations and higher rates of social capital is associated with more business ventures, self-employment, and entrepreneurship (Kwon, Heflin, and Ruef 2013). These community-level effects carry through time, as research using Norwegian mutual organizations and cooperative stores demonstrates (Greve and Rao 2012), and can lead to legacies that shape economic institutions, such as how banking is organized, in the long run (Schneiberg, King, and Smith, 2008).

Participants in Urban Governance

Nonprofits participate in and shape the governance of cities (Marwell and Brown, Chapter 9, "Toward a Governance Framework for Government–Nonprofit Relations"). As part of the formal and informal governing of cities, nonprofits distribute welfare goods and services and mediate between citizens and the state (Salamon 1995; Balogh 2015). According to survey data of U.S. municipal governments from 1992 to 2007 conducted by the International City/County Management Association (ICMA), municipalities consistently deliver a persistent share of their services in collaboration with or outsourced to nonprofit organizations (Brandtner and Suárez 2018). Nonprofits are responsible for homeless shelters in 53 percent of all U.S. municipalities, museums and art programs in 45 percent, and drug treatment in 33 percent. Scholars have profiled the government underwriting of almshouses in early nineteenth-century Baltimore (Rockman 2009), the provision of disaster relief in the interwar period (Clemens 2010), the support of community development under the 1960s-era War on Poverty (Orleck and Hazirjian 2011), the construction of affordable housing in the 1970s (Simon 2001; McQuarrie 2010), and the shift toward fee-for-service models in the 1980s (Smith and Lipsky 1993; Salamon 1995). These analyses highlight the complex and shifting public funding of privately provided safety net services, and how decisions by private providers steered which citizens, what services, and where they received aid. Nonprofits also compensate for the unevenness and discrimination of publicly funded services, often providing services in African American, Latinx, and other marginalized neighborhoods (Higginbotham 1993; Small 2004; S. Lee 2014; Goldstein 2017).

Not merely as the actors delivering services, nonprofits, particularly foundations, have been behind many of the changing patterns of service provision through policy change. In a prominent example, the Ford Foundation's support of community action programs in the 1960s and community development in the 1970s underwrote entire networks of urban nonprofits. These demonstration projects and close relationships between foundation staff and policy makers led to federal policies that furthered such approaches to urban governance, development, and antipoverty programs (O'Connor 1996, 2001; Ferguson 2013; Dunning 2018b; McQuarrie 2010; Guthrie and McQuarrie 2008). More recently, funders interested in urban education have been increasingly using their resources to shape school policy at the local and state levels (Reckhow 2013; Tompkins-Stange 2016; Finger 2018).

Through bottom-up pressures of mobilizing, discerning, and representing the interests of various urban constituencies, nonprofits participate in governance and politics. (Indeed, that we can even talk of a nonprofit as having a "constituency" speaks to the governance roles that nonprofits inhabit.) Sociologists have shown nonprofits to function as new political machines (Marwell 2004, 2007; also Greenstone and Peterson 1973), as lobby groups (Berry and Arons 2003), and as "legitimate representatives of urban neighborhoods" (Levine 2016:1268). Much of the local activism of the black freedom movement—and of the current Black Lives Matter movement—operated through nonprofit organizations to reform local governance practices to desegregate public schools, increase democratic participation, and reduce police violence, among other goals (Theoharis and Woodward 2005; Sugrue 2008). More broadly, Robert Sampson and his colleagues (2005) analyzed data on four thousand public events in Chicago over a forty-year period and attributed displays of civic action to the density of organizations.

Conveners of Economic Networks

Networks play a critical role in structuring the economy and determining flows of resources, ideas, and people between firms (Saxenian 1994; Pflieger and Rozenblat 2010;

Padgett and Powell 2012). Nonprofits have been shown to be brokers of otherwise disconnected parts of these networks (Powell, Koput, and Smith-Doerr 1996; Safford 2009). By forging ties between organizations, they facilitate coordination and innovation through convention and brokerage (Padgett and Powell 2012).

Nonprofits' role in structuring interactions within regions has consequences for development in the civic and economic spheres. In a comparative study on the *Rise and Fall of Urban Economies*, Michael Storper, Thomas Kemeny, Naji Makarem, and Taner Osman (2015) show that the differential development of San Francisco and Los Angeles was intricately tied to the vibrancy of activism, foundations, and community collaboration. The economic geographers start their inquiry with the working hypothesis that "hard" geographic factors must explain why these two cities, which were on a similar economic trajectory in the 1970s, have come to differ so fundamentally by the twenty-first century. Surely, factor costs, industry differences, or the development of technology must explain why 2010 San Francisco wages were a solid third higher than those of Los Angeles. However, the authors find that integrated networks of technologists and dreamers explain the relative rise of the Bay Area to a thriving magnet of innovation and invention. Storper and colleagues particularly credit one business association of local CEOs, the Bay Area Council, which brought together leaders invested in the future of the city region and facilitated conversations about how to become a technology- and skill-based economy. Asking similar questions about regional economic change, historians Margaret P. O'Mara (2005) and Lily Geismer (2015) also point to local booster organizations as promoting the political-economic policies that encouraged the development of the tech industry.

This account mirrors Sean Safford's (2009) findings about the revitalization of two Rust Belt cities: Allentown, Pennsylvania, and Youngstown, Ohio. In Youngstown, the Garden Club was an elite club that brought together members of a select few families; in Allentown, local civic organizations such as the Boy Scouts convened a diverse group of people. The Lehigh Valley Partnership, which emerged from the Boy Scouts, provided opportunities for cross-cutting ties between different social groups and thus fulfilled a similar function in Allentown as the Bay Area Council for Storper. In short, "the realignment of organizational relationships in Allentown has brought different kinds of actors—actors who would not necessarily have been in contact—into a meaningful dialogue, which has in many ways shaped organizational strategies" (Safford 2009:130). The absence of such engagement, Safford argues further, "has led the disintegration of Youngstown's social fabric" (2009:149). These examples show that through their position in networks, nonprofits can have important effects on regional economic development beyond their role as employers (Dunning 2018a) and anchor tenants (Padgett and Powell 2012). Such convening also takes place in many areas of collective action outside economic production, such as neighborhood development (Douglas 2018).

That nonprofits frequently serve as convening bodies that bring together like-minded individuals can have problematic implications for who holds power in a city (Hunter 1953; Domhoff 2014). The activities that might encourage a particular kind of economic development also support the creation of elite networks that can tie firms together (Marquis, Davis, and Glynn 2013). For instance, the presence of upper-class clubs leads to greater local interlocks between corporate boards, which has important implications for firm behavior and economic production (Mizruchi 1996; Strang and Soule 1998).

Anchors of Identity

Through their physical presence and their activities, nonprofits anchor identities of urban neighborhoods and the city as a whole. This sense of belonging to a neighborhood or barrio can lead to inclusion as well as exclusion (Sampson 2012). In the late nineteenth century, settlement houses served as physical spaces that also shaped the reputations and knowledge of neighborhoods in the city. In Chicago, Jane Addams launched ethnographic and social scientific research programs from her famed Hull House to map the social and physical geography of the city that have since supported foundational theories about cities and their residents (1895). Settlement women like Addams altered neighborhood boundaries and public and private space by working in, through, and around settlement houses (Deutsch 2000). In the twentieth century, block clubs and homeowners associations have similarly been vehicles for residents to define their urban space in ways that have produced material gain, excluded based on race or income, created social or political capital, and restructured public transportation (Seligman 2016; Osman 2011; Sugrue 1996; Crockett 2018). Service-provider nonprofits develop and retain territorial attachment to their neighborhoods (Gibbons 2014), as do religious organizations through the invisible geographies of parish boundaries (Gamm 1999) or the creation of a "religious district" (McRoberts 2003). Immigrant and migrant organizations reflect and helped develop ethnic and racial identities for urban neighborhoods in ways that have created community and shaped segregated housing patterns. Nonprofits not only create neighborhood boundaries; they also work to interrupt and reshape them, for instance through working with gang-involved youth to reduce "turf wars" in American cities (Braga, Hureau, and Winship 2008; Vargas 2016). These neighborhood identities serve visitors to cities too, through the creation and branding of "arts districts" or "museum districts" or "innovation districts," which are often anchored by prominent nonprofit institutions (Jones et al. 2016).

If drawing people together in shared identity is a key feature of nonprofit activities, so too is reinforcing separation between different ethnic and social groups. The composition of many membership and voluntary organizations is highly homogeneous, because of homophyly or because organizations are explicitly identity-based (McPherson, Smith-Lovin, and Cook 2001). In some cases, to be sure, homogeneous associations can lead to diversity as well. Matthew Baggetta finds in a study of community choirs in Boston that members live in different neighborhoods, and this diversity in provenance "opens opportunities for members to act as representatives of diverse neighborhoods creating representative bridging ties between groups" (2016:72S). He argues that "the representative bridging mechanism assumes that people in associations talk about their home neighborhoods, 'vouching' for the area and the people who live in it in a way that reduces fears and improves trust."

The urban identities that nonprofits shape also create worldwide linkages between places that exceed the geographic boundaries of neighborhoods or cities. Sharkey and his colleagues (2017:1218) note that nonprofits tap "extra-local networks," which "connect communities to external sources of influence, resources, and political power, all of which strengthen the capacity to achieve common goals and values" (see also Sampson 2012; Vargas 2016). This is true of economic and professional networks that span locales (Boli and Thomas 1997; Sassen 2012; Brandtner 2019). Although many nonprofits are global organizations, they are based locally, and cities around the world are centrally shaped by the presence of nonprofits, constituting them as "global cities" (Sassen 2012; Zukin 2010). Migrant cities are global cities thanks to the influx of people and capital, which have obvious consequences for the founding of certain types of nonprofits. Consider the presence of ethnic and immigration organizations with transnational ties that are the product of globalization and facilitators of it. Networks of global and transnational organizations with headquarters in major cities—such as New York, London, Hong Kong, and Washington, D.C.—reflect the size and weight of the cities in which they are based, further enhance the reputation of their hosts, and attract residents and investment as a result. Even as the activities of many nonprofits promote an identity of global cities, such identity actually masks the local consequences for the places in which organizations are headquartered.

Builders of the Physical Environment

Regardless of the activities they pursue, many nonprofits shape the city by their physical presence as renters of storefronts and office space, and as owners of parks and property. At the same time, they often do not pay taxes on the real estate they occupy and thereby influence the tax revenues of municipalities. In Boston, for example, more than 50 percent of the land is exempt from taxation, but the city relies on property taxes for over two thirds of its revenue (Rackow 2013). These pressures lead to innovations such as voluntary payments in lieu of taxes and policy-based responses to fill municipal coffers.

Nonprofits have also taken active roles in altering the physical infrastructure and layout of cities, both in what they have constructed and in what they have prevented. This was especially true during urban renewal when nonprofits variously participated in, resisted, and benefited from urban renewal. Urban sociologists John Logan and Harvey Molotch identify large nonprofits as "auxiliary players" in their concept of the growth machine but still concede that through construction or support of renewal policies, cultural and educational anchor institutions have been productive development tools (Logan and Molotch 1987:75; Molotch 1976).[3] This argument is supported more recently by examples of the University of Pennsylvania's West Philadelphia Initiatives or Harvard University's expansion into Allston-Brighton, which have produced praise and protest from stakeholders. Nonprofit organizations have similarly shaped the urban built environment by resisting government-planned renewal programs and amplifying the voices of concerned residents (Keyes 1969; Mollenkopf 1983; Hock 2013; Crockett 2018). A significant outcome of those protests was the extent to which grassroots nonprofits won development rights or contracts from the city and took on the tasks of redeveloping their neighborhood housing and commercial spaces themselves in processes that were more participatory and lessened displacement of residents. Scholars have linked these community development initiatives to histories of black power and civil rights, demonstrating how nonprofit community development corporations (CDCs) translated political ideologies into the physical infrastructure of cities (Woodsworth 2016; Rabig 2016; Goldstein 2017). Similarly, Small's

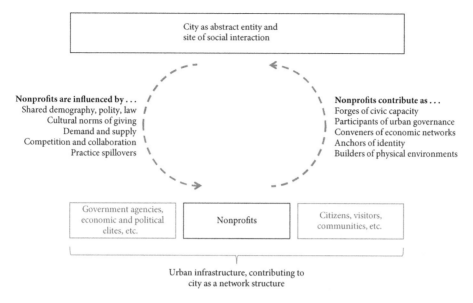

Figure 11.4   Nonprofits and the city: A conceptual framework

account of the Villa Victoria community in Boston connects the Puerto Rican heritage of the nonprofit's leaders to the adoption of Spanish-style architecture and formation of community identity (Small 2004). The outcomes of all of this redevelopment included more affordable housing (McQuarrie 2010), gentrification (Pattillo 2007; Zukin 2010; Arena 2012), and new public transportation (Levine 2017).

In sum, nonprofits fill a variety of roles in the urban drama. To be sure, the degree to which these roles are realized likely differs from city to city. We are not inclined to create a taxonomy of cities describing different classes of cities. More importantly, conceiving of nonprofits as an urban infrastructure highlights that they are rooted in place and shaped by interactions in their dense surroundings. But as McQuarrie and Marwell (2009) stress, organizations are not just derivatives of market, state, and community. The five roles show how nonprofits can be productive of cityscapes as well, as Figure 11.4 illustrates. In the following section, we discuss the theoretical and research implications of this view.

Urban Infrastructure as Analytical Framework

In detailing the physical and social roles of sidewalks in cities, Jane Jacobs (1992:29) observed that "streets serve other purposes besides carrying wheeled traffic in their middles." Our analysis shows that nonprofits—both individually and as a sector—play a similar multitude of roles. As we stated in our structural definition on the city, nonprofits are a constitutive element of many cities in the way that streets make cities through a multitude of uses. The empirical studies of nonprofits and cities cited earlier have established ways in which cities shape nonprofits and the ways in which nonprofits shape cities. We bring those two sides of the literature together and offer a new framework that recognizes the diverse, multi-directional ways in which cities and the nonprofits that inhabit them relate: nonprofits are an urban infrastructure that undergirds the structure of the city. This framework draws metaphorically on both the hard, physical aspects and the soft, cultural aspects of what traditional infrastructure entities like streets, sidewalks, and sewer systems do for cities.[4] What does this metaphor afford us?

First, there is a permanency to infrastructure that is similar to how nonprofits operate in cities, such that choices made in the past about where to site parks or build museums carry forward through time. Once streets are built or nonprofits founded, it is hard, though not impossible, to undo those past choices. We know, for example, that nonprofits rarely "die" or are removed from the Internal Revenue Service (IRS) listings and instead just stop operations, sometimes episodically. Similarly, a city's civic life leaves a lasting imprint that sets the stage for future performances.

Second, like streets, nonprofits have impact as individual entities and as a system; they are things unto themselves and conduits. Infrastructure of any kind is a networked system connecting and moving people, resources, ideas, and activities. Decisions about infrastructure mimic those in the nonprofit sector; questions about who gets served and how, who can and who does participate in decision making, and how financial considerations steer planning and outcomes are central to how streets and nonprofits are built and maintained. Infrastructure includes and draws people and places into the city network and excludes certain people and places. Neither infrastructure of streets nor of nonprofits are in themselves inherently good or bad, but are, in essence, constitutive of city life.

Consequently, as an infrastructure, nonprofits permanently shape the face of today's cities. As Jacobs writes, "if a city's streets look interesting, the city looks interesting; if they look dull, the city looks dull" (Jacobs 1992:29). Even, though a city could exist without streets just as a city could exist without nonprofits, it would look fundamentally different. Infrastructure can be efficient or inefficient in design and function, and can produce a range of positive and adverse effects. As is true of roads and bridges, nonprofits are not unique to cities but, we argue, have amplified direct and indirect effects in cities. Infrastructure, whether of transportation or nonprofits, enable cities to function.[5]

We discussed earlier several—though by no means all—of the roles that nonprofits play in cities and the mechanisms by which they shape the urban environment. Outlining those roles and the literatures on which they draw is, we hope, a contribution of this chapter. At the same time, we want to move beyond any individual role or outcome, row or column in Table 11.1, to consider the table as a whole, as is encapsulated by our concept of nonprofits as urban infrastructure. The mechanisms are linked, overlapping, and simultaneous; a community development corporation may produce housing as a physical alteration to a neighborhood, but that same organization will also have a social impact through the forging of new social ties between neighbors, an economic impact through construction expenditures and the collection of rents, a political impact through the acceptance of public tax credits, and a cultural one through the identification of a neighborhood as undergoing redevelopment or as a low-income community. Through any single activity, a nonprofit plays multiple roles in a city, just as any single street or sidewalk is playing multiple roles, any of which may be deliberate or inadvertent, direct or indirect.

Future Research on Nonprofits as Infrastructure

The infrastructure view on nonprofits emphasizes both the individual organizations and the networks they collectively make. Research could, of course, add more precision to the multitude of roles nonprofits play in cities. Our delineation of five roles earlier reflects what research has considered thus far, but observationally we know that nonprofits do more. Much historical and contemporary work remains to be done, for example, on nonprofit organizations—universities and hospitals in particular—and the rise of the urban service economy. Nonprofits also play a central role in knowledge production through the funding and conducting of research, publishing reports, and organizing convenings to promote findings (see, e.g., Arum and Kepins, Chapter 18, "Education and the Nonprofit Sector," on the roles of universities). Finally, the effects of nonprofits on land value, the sustainability of voluntary action given the skyrocketing real estate prices in many urban centers, and the physical movement of clients between nonprofits are hitherto under-explored (Gans 2002).

This chapter has emphasized indirect local effects of nonprofits. We contend that an overemphasis on direct channels of influence through governance, advocacy, and service provision—while important—risks ignoring the overwhelming importance of indirect channels. The contributions of nonprofits to processes like privatization, gentrification, professionalization, polarization, economic stratification, and racial segregation remain pressing matters for scholarly inquiry. The same is true of geographic variation in recent nonprofit sector trends toward hybrid corporate forms and social enterprise, and the adoption of market solutions to substitute, rather than complement, public services (Mair, Chapter 14, "Social Entrepreneurship"). The ledger on any change is always more complicated than is expected and may look different in the short and long runs. A broader, and therefore stronger, assessment of the myriad roles nonprofits perform as part of the urban infrastructure would move us closer to understanding how nonprofits encourage and/or inhibit healthy, resilient, vital communities.

The fundamental insight of previous research is that the absence of a vivid civil society is associated with a lack of amenities and civic capacity. The causal pathways suggest that, net total and all things constant, cities with livelier nonprofit sectors are expected to see positive effects on their vitality and resilience, net of the economic, demographic, and political conditions that give rise to a thriving nonprofit sector in the first place.[6] Most of the evidence in this chapter stems from places with rich civic lives. (And, relatedly, often in the backyards of places with resource-rich universities). But while the United States as a whole boasts a large and growing nonprofit sector (Hall 2006), many areas in the country are starved for civil society, as Figure 11.1 suggests. Understanding civic deserts, analogously to food deserts, would be an important venue for research. From a policy standpoint, adding an additional nonprofit in a thriving—and possibly even saturated—neighborhood is quite different from founding the first community organization in a previously underserved area. This is particularly true for organizations serving marginalized communities (Bloemraad, Gleeson, and de Graauw, Chapter 12, "Immigrant Organizations"). Part of this inquiry might be about rural nonprofit infrastructure, which we imagine looks similar in some ways to that of urban centers but dissimilar in critical ways.

For social scientists, the concept of nonprofits as urban infrastructure undoubtedly raises questions about the conditions under which nonprofits let the urban drama flourish, or harm and hold back cities and their residents. It is, for instance, reasonable to assume that several city-level conditions moderate the relationship between nonprofits and their environment. In particular, our review suggests that the regime type or governance regime—the degree to which the urban political environment is historically open to the participation of nonprofits—makes a difference. This insight from political sociology is corroborated by network analyses of the biotechnology sector, which has suggested that the role of organizations as generative anchor tenants is in tension with the presence of an "eight hundred-pound gorilla," a large and self-interested organization that dominates the organizational landscape (Padgett and Powell, 2012, Ch. 14).

Although the prospect is tempting, we are nonetheless critical of proposing general conditions under which the entire nonprofit sector influences a city. This is because of the multiple roles we discussed and because of the complexity of "urban vitality" as an outcome. Moreover, simply because a sector or city is doing well, not all people will reap those benefits. On the contrary, the literature repeatedly notes ways in which nonprofit activities improve life for only some and have at times done so at costs to others. The resilience or vitality of a sector or city is linked to measures of equality, equity, and justice but not synonymous with them. Our chapter reveals several basic organizational properties that may curb some of the mechanisms we have discussed. Certain types of nonprofits likely have different positive or negative effects on their environs that depend on the scope of their activities. Clearly, not all nonprofits stimulate their urban environment. Under what condition would we expect a nonprofit *not* to affect its environment in desirable ways?

We argue that a critical organizational-level factor that affects the viability of the roles discussed earlier is community embeddedness. By community embeddedness we mean nonprofits' integration with the local community through face-to-face interaction, the convening of events, and the sharing of information and skills. These activities differ from organization to organization. The growing professionalism of the sector, which has brought an expansion of efforts to scale, migrated services online, and offered intermediary rather than direct services, may be a limiting factor to such embedded activities. Even though professional organizations can have sophisticated programs for outreach and constituent participation, there are likely trade-offs between how process- or impact-oriented a non-profit is, similar to those between instrumental and expressive orientations of nonprofits (see Powell, Chapter 1, "What Is the Nonprofit Sector?").

Much research assumes that nonprofits are aligned either with their constituents or with their funders and professional audiences. We want to suggest that there is a division of labor between nonprofits of different degrees of professionalism, and that an imbalance to one or the other can mitigate collective impact. To give a simple example, if all soup kitchens become highly professionalized intermediaries between food banks and volunteers who distribute meals, these soup kitchens cease to interact with their ultimate beneficiaries.[7] Besides the level of paid and credentialed professionals employed by organizations, the presence, representativeness, and type of members can also influence community embeddedness. A certain level of connectedness of the members of an organization is critical to mechanisms such as brokerage. Also, the ability to bridge diverse groups typically requires heterogeneous membership. A nonprofit sector devoid of members and rich in clients is naturally less inclined to bring together people and organizations.

Nonprofits' integration with the local community also has an economic dimension. We have highlighted that some nonprofits, because of their tax exemption, can have adverse economic effects if they overwhelm a community in numbers. Specifically, if nonprofits do not voluntarily pay taxes and do not employ locals, they may not contribute to the economy at all and instead crowd out taxpaying businesses. Finally, a collaborative relationship with other organizations is a logical condition for many of the positive network externalities that we hypothesized earlier. But the degree to which being integrated with other organizations is beneficial has limits. Dependence on a single institution or funder may lead to cooperation or commercialization, which can inhibit the organization's ability to pursue an independent mission.

These propositions of organizational- and city-level moderators of the effect of local nonprofit sectors are, in specific contexts, empirically testable. To this end, future research on nonprofit infrastructure will need to bridge quantitative and case-based studies that have tended to dominate the nonprofit and urban literature. To date, measures of nonprofit counts and densities have been the primary metrics for empirical analyses of the extent and efficacy of nonprofit activities. This approach has enabled scholars to capture en masse aspects of a large sector and overcomes the mental and financial limitations of doing work across hundreds of cities. These measures, however, are a blunt instrument and derive from either self-reported data on nonprofits registered with the IRS or, in the social capital literature, business establishments that provide amenities and opportunities to meet in local communities such as bowling alleys.

For pragmatic reasons, scholars often arbitrarily limit data sets to 501(c)(3) nonprofits, those with a high enough revenue to file Form 990s, or subsector categories such as human service organizations, but the theoretical basis of such a decision is thin. As Kirsten A. Grønbjerg and Laurie Paarlberg (2001) show, the overlap of density measures based on different data sources is not robust. Nor should the utility of density measures prevent progress on alternate measures that might capture the practices, orientations, and relations of nonprofit organizations in cities. Quantitative measures of efficacy—for instance, on collective impact and the ability to instill civic capacity in the community—pose a particular challenge. The same is true for measures of social movements, informal neighborhood groups, and social enterprises that neither are registered as nonprofits (because they are too small, temporary, or hybrid) nor partake in newsworthy events. Finally, nonprofits have been growing in number linearly for the past couple of decades. As they fulfill redundant tasks and competition for funding and attention becomes tighter, nonlinear effects of nonprofit density on community outcomes may become more salient.

City-level outcomes are difficult to attribute to the presence of nonprofits or any other influence without the specter of endogeneity. Stronger attempts at causal inference such as those advanced by Sharkey and his colleagues (2017) are a way forward. At the same time, it is virtually impossible to specify mechanisms without studying what nonprofits *do* in places with comparable nonprofit density. We know too little about how tactics, tools, and talent differ by region, or about how organizations differ in their receptivity to local politics, historical contexts, and funding environments. Such research could help us recognize how systems of federalism and capitalism create significant variations within and between neighborhoods, cities, and regions, and within and between states and nations. The regional variation of organizational toolkits and mind-sets has implications for promising research designs going forward.

At the other end of the literature, case studies of urban nonprofits capture the complex and dynamic ways in which cities shape and are shaped by nonprofits. Neighborhood or community studies of a single city such as those by Herbert J. Gans and Robert Sampson and those by Jeremy R. Levine, Nicole P. Marwell, Mario L. Small, and Brian D. Goldstein have been a cornerstone of both urban sociology and urban history; this has been particularly true of research on poverty, race, and inequality. Yet only comparative research—or comparative conversations or publications—can map differences and similarities across cities. Broadly, cities share challenges and the dynamics of material constraints. Intricate studies of nonprofit organizations in city regions such as Boston (MacIndoe and Barman 2013) or San Francisco (Hwang and Powell 2009) are a possible avenue but have yet to be expanded to a comparative framework.[8] Comparative studies of nonprofit practices are needed in non-U.S. contexts, and comparing U.S. and non-U.S. cities. On several measures, New York City might share more with global cities such as London, Tel Aviv, and Hong Kong than with Flint and Tallahassee. Framing questions of scale and geography in a comparative lens will also help clarify how much of the nonprofit infrastructure reflects the peculiarities of a city, rather than the ways that both cities and nonprofits are situated in space and time.

Conclusion

Given that nonprofits so strongly reflect and shape the regions in which they are embedded, it is striking that there is no subfield of metropolitan studies within nonprofit research or a section of urban studies dedicated to civil society. Although this chapter alone cannot remedy the lack of such a research program, we have followed in the footsteps of many scholars who have answered questions and pursued research designs that would fall into these domains. Those already engaged in this research might benefit from recognizing the inquiries, conversations, and findings about urban nonprofits in other disciplines. Inter- and cross-disciplinary work can be challenging, but a common interest in cities and nonprofits may unlock the potential rewards of lowering disciplinary walls.[9]

In our survey of the nonprofit and urban literatures, we find that nonprofits play an important role in five interrelated, and sometimes overlapping, domains. As network conveners, they bear on the distribution of economic resources and information by bridging disparate domains. As participants in urban governance, they partake in service delivery, representation of communities, and advocacy of causes. As forges of civic capacity, they generate opportunities for the creation of civic skills, as well as opportunities for mobilization, bridging, and bonding. As anchors of identity, they define local identities and afford global connectedness. And as builders of the physical environment, they provide concrete substance to the shape of the city. Through these roles—and perhaps others—we frame nonprofits and cities as mutually constitutive, as evolving together over time, and as composing a kind of urban infrastructure.

The material in this chapter is empirical, but we are also motivated by normative concerns for the challenges facing the globe and a recognition that cities often contain both extreme versions of those challenges and the resources for their remedy. Nonprofits may be chief among those urban resources by nature of their political, social, and economic capital but may also themselves be part of the problems. We know far too little about how, precisely, nonprofits as individual organizations, subsectors, and a sector as a whole either reduce or reproduce our greatest challenges and how they contribute to or undermine solutions, often in unintended or unrecognized ways. We make no claims about whether nonprofits as urban infrastructure are on balance positive or negative, and we find evidence in the literature that supports both directions. As a result, we urge both nonprofit and urban scholars to better understand the dynamic relationships between the nonprofit sector and the urban. Though intellectually compelling, these research questions are ultimately in service of a need among practitioners and leaders in government, nonprofits, and business to better understand the roles nonprofits play, the networks in which they operate, and the larger-scale direct and indirect consequences of their actions. As cities continue to be places of resources and need, and of capacity and precarity, recognizing which actors can and should fill the leading roles becomes all the more complicated, challenging, and critical.

12 IMMIGRANT ORGANIZATIONS

Civic (In)equality and Civic (In)visibility

Irene Bloemraad, Shannon Gleeson, and Els de Graauw

WHY IS THE STUDY OF IMMIGRANT ORGANIZATIONS a neglected field, and what do we learn in studying such organizations? Scholars of immigration have largely focused on how macro-level phenomena (such as labor markets or ethnoracial hierarchies) influence immigrant incorporation, or on how individual-level attributes (like immigrants' education) shape outcomes such as employment, intermarriage, or voting. They have rarely examined how organizations affect immigrants, or how immigrants create organizations. Conversely, within research on nonprofit organizations and civic associations, attention to immigrant communities has been peripheral at best. We argue that researchers and practitioners need to pay attention to the civic infrastructures of immigrant communities, that is, the set of somewhat formalized and organized groups that are neither public institutions nor for-profit businesses and that serve or advocate for these communities.

Why should we do so? Bringing the study of the third sector into conversation with immigration showcases the challenge of what we call *civic inequality,* that is, a disparity in the number, density, breadth, capacity, and visibility of organized groups in a community. Civic inequality is a cause for concern because it can impede immigrants' access to social services, employment, and leadership opportunities as well as their civic voice in society. Understanding civic inequality also goes beyond the case of immigrants. It should be part of any analysis of nonprofit organizations and marginalized communities.

Still, immigrants deserve specific attention in the nonprofit field. There is a glaring disjunction between the paucity of research and the number of people who are immigrants. As of 2017, around 43 million foreign-born individuals were living in the United States (13 percent of the population), and 7.9 million were living in Canada (21 percent of the population). Additionally, about one in eight residents of France, Germany, Spain, and the United Kingdom, and over one in four residents of Australia and Switzerland, are foreign-born (UNDESA 2017). Although some of the frameworks used to analyze nonprofits and voluntarism can easily extend to immigrants and immigrant organizations, bringing immigration into third sector analysis also raises new questions and demands new explanatory models.

The small but growing body of research on immigrant organizations and immigrants' civic engagement underscores at least two key considerations for researchers and practitioners. First, we must take into account the additional barriers—and, sometimes, opportunities—that migrants' legal status brings to nonprofit organizing and associationalism. This is not just a dichotomy between undocumented status compared to the presumption of citizenship evident in most nonprofit scholarship. It is also about studying and understanding the distinct resources, institutional support, and exclusions that come with the multiple legal statuses that people can hold. Noncitizen legal permanent residents or formally recognized refugees who have a pathway to citizenship are generally less vulnerable to deportation and may enjoy more legitimacy in the eyes of citizens than other foreigners. Migrants who hold a much more precarious status with no permanent residence or access to citizenship—such as temporary workers, international students, migrants given temporary humanitarian protection, or undocumented immigrants—face uncertain time horizons, hold fewer formal rights, have limited access to public services and benefits, and are susceptible to deportation. The challenges presented by one's legal status often overlap with other barriers to civic equality, such as poverty, racial minority status, or limited skills in the majority language.

Second, attention to migration pushes researchers and practitioners to pay attention to transnationalism, both in immigrants' orientation to civic engagement and in nonprofits' activism. Immigrants' prior political socialization—that is, their experiences with a civic and political system different from that of the host country—can shape immigrants' third sector participation in the country of settlement. Such experiences can also lead to new associational forms or organizing strategies. One example is that of *tandas*, or informal loan clubs routinely used by Latinx immigrants to provide community-funded loans. Because migrants have life experiences rooted in more than one country, they may also engage in transnational political and civic activities that connect home and host countries through third sector organizing, volunteerism, and charitable giving. This can generate associational dynamics distinct from the activism of traditional international nongovernmental, development, or advocacy organizations (international nongovermental organizations, or INGOs). For example, how does the work, mission, and administration of an INGO like Amnesty International or Doctors Without Borders compare to the development assistance or donations that immigrants send back to their homeland through hometown associations or private charities? In some cases, migrant remittances and activism are encouraged by the sending state, as is the case for the Mexican *Tres por Uno* (Three for One) matching grant program. In other cases, migrant groups risk surveillance, detention, or even death, in either their home or host country, because of their third sector activities. This is especially the case if their politics, homeland ties, or religion lead them to be labeled subversive or terrorists.

The time is thus ripe for scholars to examine the specificity of immigrant civic engagement and immigrant organizations. We conceptualize an immigrant organization as a civil society or nonprofit organization that serves or advocates on behalf of one or more immigrant communities, promotes their cultural heritage, or engages in transnational relations with countries or regions of origin (de Graauw, Gleeson, and Bloemraad 2013:96). Such organizations may include second- or later-generation individuals of a particular cultural, ethnic, religious, or national-origin background, and even some citizens without immigrant origins. However, a substantial part of the organization's interests or activities should involve issues that tend to distinguish immigrants from native-born citizens, such as legal status barriers, linguistic or cultural obstacles to service, or concern over economic or political development in the country of origin.

Attention to civic and nonprofit organizing is also important for scholars of migration. Much of the migration literature focuses on immigrants' individual- or micro-level integration, including research on civic and political engagement. Less attention has been paid to the meso level of immigrant community life, that is, to the voluntary, civic, and nonprofit groups that are the bread and butter of third sector scholarship. Although mainstream nonprofit organizations—ones that do not focus on immigrants and their children—can address some immigrant needs or associational desires, targeted immigrant outreach is rare. In part, this is because mainstream nonprofits often do not have the capacity or interest to invest in multilingual or multicultural outreach to address immigrants' needs and interests. Sometimes funding sources come with restrictions that prevent nonprofits from helping undocumented residents, as is the case with U.S. federal grants to provide legal aid to poor people. Immigrant populations also have new social and cultural interests or support needs—such as wanting to organize in particular religious communities or needing immigration legal services—that mainstream organizations have trouble identifying, funding, or fulfilling.

Gaps in service delivery and civic organizing feed into what we conceptualize as *civic inequality*. In one version of civic inequality, differences in civic engagement, at the individual level, can lead to unequal aggregate participation between groups of people, such as between people who are immigrants and those who are native-born. However, civic inequality—and its opposite, civic equality—can also be understood as a group-level attribute, distinct from individual- or micro-level immigrant integration measures or large-scale, macro-level socioeconomic and political structures that scholars usually study. In this version, civic inequality at the meso level is a disparity in the number, density, breadth, capacity, and visibility of organized groups in a community. We advocate in particular for such an organization-focused approach. To advance this research agenda, we provide a detailed discussion of how to measure and analyze civic (in)equality.

Distinguishing immigrants' meso-level civic infrastructures from micro-level participation is analytically important and carries real-world consequences. The gap between what existing nonprofits do for immigrants and immigrants' ability to create new associations can be vast and highly problematic for immigrant communities. For instance, local governments often allocate grants to community-based organizations for human or social services, or to subsidize a cultural or sports activity. Absent immigrant-oriented organizations, migrant communities may fail to secure these resources, which can stymie their social integration as well as their ability to have a voice in civic affairs. Conversely, when immigrant communities enjoy a rich infrastructure of third sector organizations, they may benefit from a greater civic presence and voice and faster societal integration. Thus, just as third sector scholars should consider immigrant organizing in their scholarship, migration scholars should better understand how nonprofit organizations and civic engagement shape migration and settlement patterns. More broadly, we believe that the concepts and our proposed empirical measures of civic (in)equality and civic (in)visibility can be extended beyond immigrant populations to study and understand the nonprofit field more generally.

Gaps in Research on Immigrants and the Third Sector
Three distinct academic literatures touch on immigration and the third sector: studies of immigrant integration, research on interest groups and social movements, and scholarship on nonprofit organizations.

Immigrant Integration and Immigrant Organizations
For over a century, U.S.-based social scientists, particularly those in sociology, have studied immigrant integration or assimilation, as it was long called. Their focus has usually centered on measuring and explaining immigrants' economic, social, and cultural integration. Scholars debate whether intergenerational integration proceeds along a straight line, a bumpy one, or distinct pathways that are segmented by immigrants' human capital, racial minority status, and social networks within the community.[1] The focus is generally on the second, U.S.-born generation, who are more removed from the migrant experience.

Political scientists' interest in immigrant incorporation was first articulated through the lens of urban politics and political machines and later in terms of electoral coalition-building, partisanship, and voting.[2] Yet voting—which is limited to citizens in most jurisdictions—is only a small slice of immigrants' political and civic engagement (Martinez 2005). Interest in the political and civic incorporation of foreign-born residents waned as political science shifted to focus on minority politics, with special attention to Black and Latinx politics and growing interest in Asian American political activity. Scholars of minority politics have tended to focus on pan-ethnic solidarity and mobilization, downplaying differences among and within immigrant generations or the unique barriers of noncitizenship.

Across these studies and irrespective of discipline, few scholars adequately consider immigrant communities' civic infrastructures. Rather, in theorizing the determinants of immigrant integration, social scientists focus on how macro-level phenomena such as labor markets, electoral regimes, and ethnoracial hierarchies influence incorporation patterns, or on how individual attributes, like immigrants' education, shape outcomes such as employment, intermarriage, or voting. In its report on the state of immigrant integration in the United States, the National Academy of Sciences concludes that although "the evidence thus far suggests that civil society groups—whether organized by immigrants or predominantly organized by native-born citizens . . .—can facilitate integration," overall "research on the civic and organizational foundations of immigrants' integration is underdeveloped" (NASEM 2015:193).

Immigrant organizations have featured a bit more in historians' work (e.g., Moya 2005). In the nineteenth and early twentieth centuries, immigrant-run private charities and voluntary organizations helped compatriots get a job, obtain a business loan, acquire citizenship, or secure food, clothing, and funeral benefits during tough times. Starting in the late nineteenth century, U.S.-born social reformers became involved, establishing settlement houses, including the famed Hull House in Chicago. Funded by religious groups, charitable associations, and wealthy residents, settlement houses largely targeted the poor, a population that included many immigrants in large Midwestern and northeastern U.S. cities at the time. Today, mainstream nonprofit social service organizations and various levels of governments provide some of the assistance that immigrant associations or settlement houses did a century ago. Yet immigrant-focused nonprofit organizations—including formally incorporated and registered nonprofits as well as more informal groups—still remain important sites for immigrant civic engagement and service provision (de Graauw 2016; Ramakrishnan and Bloemraad 2008).

Beyond the United States, scholars take diverging views of the impact of immigrant organizations on integration trajectories. Most believe that engagement with ethnic organizations reinforces immigrants' ties to each other. Whether this helps or hinders integration is a point of debate. Over fifty years ago, Raymond Breton (1964) coined the term "institutionally complete" to describe immigrant communities where members could conduct most aspects of their lives—work, recreation, religious practice, and social interactions—within ethnic organizations. Studying immigrants in Montreal, Breton concluded that although institutional completeness might prevent interethnic marriage and reinforce an ethnic identity (both considered barriers to immigrant integration), it also facilitated political engagement in the host society (and thus incorporation). Studying immigrant-origin communities in the contemporary Netherlands, Meindert Fennema and Jean Tillie (1999) conclude that immigrant organizations can increase social capital within immigrant communities, thereby increasing social trust and political participation. In these accounts, immigrant organizations may insulate or isolate immigrants in some regards but also promote civic incorporation in other ways. Some also view the biculturalism facilitated by ethnic organizations as psychologically beneficial for immigrants (Berry 2005; Nguyen and Benet-Martínez 2013). Conversely, others claim that excessive intra-immigrant interaction creates "parallel lives," in which immigrants remain isolated from mainstream society.[3] In these accounts, immigrant-run or immigrant-serving organizations tend to be viewed negatively, as slowing or preventing immigrant integration, since they promote bonding social capital over bridging ties.[4]

Interest Groups and Social Movement Organizations

If the immigrant integration literature is characterized by a primary focus on individuals and relatively little attention to organizations, research on advocacy or interest groups and contentious political and civic behavior has the opposite problem: it views organizations as significant, but it largely ignores immigrants.

In the United States, researchers have studied interest and advocacy groups run by or advocating on behalf of ethnoracial minorities (Berry and Arons 2005; Hung 2007; Minkoff 1995), but much of this work fails to distinguish minorities by nativity and immigrant generation. Thus, conclusions about Latinx or Asian American organizations do not distinguish between foreign-born individuals and later generations made up of the children and grandchildren of immigrants. The failure to examine generational differences makes it impossible to carefully consider the implications of migration or citizenship status on the development, mission, or activities of organizations, or to probe the effects of homeland political socialization on immigrant organizing in the host country. It also obscures language access challenges usually felt much more intensely by first-generation immigrants. Similarly, those interested in civic voluntarism and organizational membership have rarely considered the impact of immigrant background on civic engagement, although they have been attentive to ethnoracial background.[5] Only in the last decade or so has U.S.-based organizational scholarship considered immigration status or immigrant background as a key factor shaping civic and political engagement (de Graauw 2016; Marwell 2007; Wong 2006).

The silence around immigration stems from conceptual blind spots as well as data constraints. Many surveys that are used to study civic engagement do not capture immigrant-specific variables such as country of birth, immigration status, citizenship status, or length of residence in the country, making it impossible to identify immigrant civic engagement. And even when such questions are asked, the number of immigrants included in a survey is often too small for nuanced analysis. In the United States, if a nationally representative survey includes one thousand to two thousand respondents, analysts will be lucky to have data on a hundred to two hundred foreign-born people. This group will be highly heterogeneous, hailing from many different countries, holding multiple immigration statuses, and having resided in the United States for just a few years or multiple decades. Teasing out the relative impact of home country, legal status, and length of residence on immigrants' civic engagement becomes almost impossible.

Fortunately, available statistical data are slowly improving, which is critical to document civic inequalities. One analysis of the 2014 Current Population Survey Volunteerism Supplement finds that rates of volunteerism are nearly twice as high for native-born residents of the United States (27 percent) than for foreign-born residents (15 percent), and that volunteerism is higher among naturalized citizens (18 percent) than among noncitizen immigrants (13 percent) (NASEM 2015:191). European data appear to show similar patterns (Voicu and Şerban 2012). Several in-depth organizational ethnographies also provide insights about immigrant civic engagement, though only for select cities and specific immigrant communities (e.g., Chung 2007). When it comes to research on contentious action, scholars in this field have long recognized the importance of social movement organizations (SMOs). By focusing on organizations rather than individual-level participation, this line of research gets closer to our idea of meso-level civic inequality. But researchers in the field have largely been silent on immigrant mobilization.[6] As Irene Bloemraad, Kim Voss, and Taeku Lee argue, "the assumption undergirding most studies of social movements is one of the protesting *citizen*. Protesters might have second-class citizenship.... They can be jailed, attacked, and obstructed ... but they cannot generally be thrown out of the country altogether" (2011:5, emphasis in original). Immigrants' vulnerability to detention and deportation, as well as their often more limited access to resources, public legitimacy, and institutional support, carry important repercussions for immigrants' ability to create and sustain social movement organizations.

The lack of attention to immigrants is unfortunate since it is clear that a robust civic infrastructure can help immigrants advance their issues in the public sphere and engender pro-migrant social movements, despite noncitizenship. The pro-immigration protests of 2006 brought millions of people onto the streets (Voss and Bloemraad 2011). The "DREAMer" movement, which mobilizes undocumented youth to advocate for those without legal status, has built powerful, influential nonprofit organizations (Nicholls 2013). Labor unions, which are longstanding actors in the third sector, have been increasingly involved in immigration issues, partly in response to declining union membership and the growing immigrant workforce (Milkman 2006). Organizations are thus important for understanding immigrant advocacy, and the inclusion of immigrants in existing organizations is significant to understanding organizational capacity, group goals, and change over time.[7]

Nonprofit Organizations and Immigration

Third sector research on the creation, persistence, and disbanding of nonprofit organizations has rarely considered the specificity of immigrant communities. Yet nonprofits intersect with immigrants in multiple ways. Religious institutions, often a first point of contact for immigrants in their new environs, are a vital component of the newcomer community and the integration process (Foley and Hoge 2007; Kivisto 2014). Following World War II, the U.S. government increasingly worked with voluntary resettlement agencies (VOLAGs) to help displaced people and refugees secure housing, find jobs, and get established in the United States (de Graauw and Bloemraad 2017). These agencies, some with religious roots and others of secular origin, now constitute the backbone of the refugee resettlement process, working in partnership with federal, state, and county agencies through public grants and private giving (Bruno 2015). Beyond refugees, nonprofit organizations provide other immigrants with health and legal services, counseling, and emergency food or housing assistance, especially in cases where migrants are explicitly or effectively barred from public programs because of their immigration status (Cordero-Guzmán 2005; de Graauw 2016; Marwell 2007). The small but growing literature on immigrant-serving organizations underscores the important work that the third sector does for immigrant and refugee communities.

Classic theories of the nonprofit sector contend that the creation of nonprofit organizations is motivated by failures of the market or of government (e.g., Grønbjerg 1998; Hansmann 1987). These theories may well apply to nonprofits serving immigrants. In most places, immigrants constitute a minority of the population, and hence profit-driven businesses may be less willing or able to provide goods and services specific to an immigrant minority, producing market failure. Similarly, governments may be less likely to serve immigrant populations, given public opposition, immigrants' lack of voting power, and the inability of large government bureaucracies to respond efficiently to the evolving needs of changing migrant populations, thereby producing government failure. These market and government shortcomings create needs and opportunities for nonprofit organizations to provide goods and services to the newcomer community.

Existing nonprofit scholarship does not, however, offer a good theoretical framework for understanding when, why, and how nonprofits focus on immigrants and whether immigrants are better served through mainstream or immigrant organizations. Immigrants do not necessarily have to establish their own nonprofits; nonprofit organizations rarely make membership or service provision contingent on nativity. Thus, in some cases, immigrants derive the same benefits from the human and social services, advocacy, and social, cultural, or recreational activities of existing nonprofits as nonimmigrants. Mainstream baseball leagues, animal rights organizations, and food pantries can all include immigrants. Nonprofit scholars have not investigated the relative benefits or trade-offs of involvement in immigrant versus mainstream organizations. Immigration and civil society researchers have paid more attention, debating whether bonding (within-group) organizations or bridging (mainstream) organizations better advance immigrant integration and community social capital. There is no clear verdict, in part because of methodological difficulties in identifying what drives an organization's impact on integration.

We suspect that the effects of immigrant organizations tend to be positive. Indeed, concerns about "too much" immigrant organizing rest on the unquestioned and problematic assumption that immigrants have the option of participating in a mainstream organization as compared to setting up their own. A more likely alternative is that, absent immigrant organizations, there is a lack of nonprofit support for immigrants. For example, mainstream organizations may not have services germane or easily accessible to immigrants, and they often lack translators or multilingual staff, culturally appropriate human services, or immigrant-related legal services (de Graauw et al. 2013). Mainstream organizations also often engage in inadequate outreach to immigrant communities (e.g., de Leon et al. 2009; LaFrance Associates 2005). This creates barriers for elderly immigrants or immigrant parents who may wish to join a senior center or parent-teacher organization, respectively, but who struggle with English or do not know that such organizations exist. Existing research shows that immigrant-oriented community-based organizations provide bilingual and bicultural human services (Cordero-Guzmán 2005; Marwell 2007), flag immigrants' unique needs to decision makers (de Graauw 2016), mobilize immigrants' political participation (Wong 2006), help low-income and precarious immigrant workers, including those without legal status (Fine 2006; Gleeson 2012), and promote cultural vitality (Hung 2007). The activities that mainstream organizations provide, such as football or ballet, may differ from immigrant interests and passions, such as cricket or Mexican folkloric dance.

In these cases, there is a community need for immigrant nonprofit organizations. Based on 501(c)(3) nonprofit data for organizations in four cities in the San Francisco Bay Area, we found that between 2004 and 2007, the proportion of immigrant nonprofits, at 17 percent of the total of all registered nonprofit organizations, was much smaller than the immigrant share of the total population, which stood at 38 percent (de Graauw et al. 2013). We also found that although a longstanding immigrant gateway city such as San Francisco allocated public money to immigrant nonprofits in rough proportion to the percentage of immigrants in the city's population, newer gateways such as San Jose or immigrant-rich suburbs in Silicon Valley did not, even as foreign-born residents constituted about half of the region's poor population. These data raise the possibility of significant civic inequality for immigrant communities, even in cities and metro areas with large immigrant communities.

Bringing Immigrants and Immigration into the Nonprofit Conversation

The historic neglect of scholarship on immigration and nonprofit organizations has been rapidly changing over the past decade. As Figure 12.1 shows, through the 1980s and 1990s, Google Scholar counts fewer than ten items per year with titles that include the word "organization" or "organisation" combined with "immigrant," "migrant," or "refugee." But whereas the average number of items was barely three per year in the 1980s, since 2010, Google Scholar counts over fifty-six items per year, an almost twenty-fold increase.[8] This burgeoning literature provides an emergent map of key findings, as well as intriguing paths that need to be explored.

How should we bring immigrants and migration into the nonprofit conversation? In what follows, we primarily focus on legal status, usually the factor that most sharply

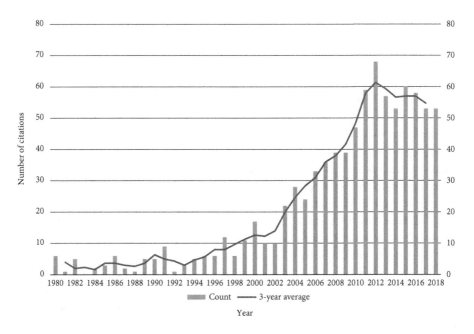

Figure 12.1 Citations in Google Scholar with "(im)migrant" or "refugee" and "organization(s)" or "organisation(s)" in the title, 1980–2018

Note: There has been a fifteen-fold increase in the number of articles, from four in 1981 (three-year average) to a high of sixty in 2012. Because Google Scholar can be behind in finding publications issued in the last one to two years, it is likely that the average of fifty-five to sixty citations per year has held constant.

Source: Authors' calculation from Google Scholar. See note 8 for methodology.

distinguishes migrants from others in a society. But we also underscore the need for more research on the consequences of migrants' cross-border experiences and ties, for example, in transforming existing associational practices and organizational forms. To illustrate the importance of legal status and a transnational lens, we draw predominantly on U.S.-based scholarship and secondarily on research in Western Europe and Canada. Although this reflects the geographical focus of existing scholarship, future research and theorizing should engage with dynamics in other settings, such as the organizational efforts of migrant workers in the oil-rich Gulf states or of refugees outside traditional immigrant-receiving countries in the West.

Immigrant Civic Engagement: The Individual Level

Attention to immigrant populations raises new issues of individual-level civic inequality: Who is able to participate and who actually engages in the nonprofit sphere? The limited survey data suggest that, in the United States, foreign-born individuals participate in canonical civic activities less than native-born citizens (NASEM 2015; Ramakrishnan and Baldassare 2004). In Europe, too, immigrants are less likely to be members of an organization and belong to fewer associations than the native born, although differences decrease with length of residence and often disappear by the second generation (Voicu and Şerban 2012).

Intersectional identities also matter. For example, within immigrant communities, some research suggests that women may be more involved, perhaps because of their frequent role as children's primary caregivers, which requires interfacing with schools, health care services, and government bureaucracies (Jones-Correa 1998; Milkman and Terriquez 2012). Such interactions can build civic skills and political consciousness that motivate engagement. Race, class, and sexuality can also shape immigrant civic activity.

Part—but not all—of the gap between foreign-born and native-born populations' engagement can be understood through existing explanatory frameworks. As among the native born, strong predictors of immigrants' civic engagement include education, employment, and trust in others (Morales and Giugni 2011; Sundeen, Garcia, and Raskoff 2009; Voicu 2014; Voicu and Şerban 2012). To the extent that immigrants may have more modest levels of education (e.g., because of limited educational opportunities in their homeland) or are more likely to live in poverty or economic insecurity (because of language barriers or discrimination), these known obstacles to participation greatly impact certain immigrant communities. In the United States, whereas 15 percent of native-born citizens live below the federal poverty level, the proportion rises to 18 percent among the foreign born.[9] The latter estimate obscures the impact of immigration status and the particular advantage of citizenship: of immigrants who report being naturalized citizens, only 11 percent fall below the poverty line, but 25 percent of noncitizens are poor by federal standards. Citizenship status also intersects with other attributes to stratify civic participation. Although 35 percent of naturalized immigrants hold a four-year college degree or higher—a slightly higher percentage than the native-born population at 31 percent—only 23 percent of noncitizens enjoy high levels of education, and 39 percent have no high school diploma.

We need, however, additional, immigrant-specific explanations for individual-level variation in civic participation. These include the impact of language skills, national origin, and immigration status. Immigrants must demonstrate a working knowledge of English to become a U.S. citizen, and thus lack of citizenship can reflect linguistic barriers to mainstream civic participation. But lack of U.S. citizenship may also signal that a person is undocumented or holds a temporary or precarious legal status. Fear of deportation can reduce civic participation and limit the pool of leaders or alter the civic activities that undocumented residents are willing to take on (Gast and Okamoto 2016). For example, although undocumented workers are no longer considered unorganizable, unions and worker centers must address unique barriers to immigrants' participation (Milkman 2006). Evidence also suggests that temporary residency status can discourage immigrants from claiming their rights and possibly stymie their civic engagement more generally (Griffith and Gleeson 2017). Shifting political winds regarding immigration, such as during the administration of President Trump, can result in new anti-immigrant policies that make it more challenging or dangerous for undocumented immigrants to engage in the civic sphere. Lack of permanent legal residency clearly hurts third sector involvement, even if it is not an absolute barrier to it.[10]

Even for immigrants who are legally allowed to reside in the host country, lack of citizenship can be a barrier to creating, leading, or being a member of a nonprofit organization or civic association. Formal restrictions prohibit noncitizens from joining a political party or founding a political association in all eleven Central European countries of the European Union and in Turkey.[11] Until 1981, France forbade foreign nationals from forming an association. Given xenophobic or anti-immigrant sentiments among the public, as well as government surveillance of Muslim immigrants for involvement with purported terrorist cells, some immigrants may not participate in a nonprofit or charitable organization, even where the law does not prohibit it, out of fear of drawing the attention of hate groups or government authorities (Chaudhary and Guarnizo 2016).

To understand individual-level civic integration, researchers can extend existing arguments about immigrant integration, either as a process of more or less straight-line assimilation across generations, or as a differentiated process of segmented assimilation by socioeconomic and racial minority status. Alternatively, especially in the first generation, we may need to view immigrants' civic participation as embedded in a transnational field that is affected by both the context in the country of origin and the country of residence, contexts that vary in their social, economic, and political institutions (Levitt and Glick Schiller 2004). Immigrants can sometimes vote in homeland elections, even if they become naturalized citizens in the country where they live. The outreach efforts of political parties and consular institutions that coordinate with diaspora organizations—in the origin and host countries—may produce unique opportunities for immigrant civic engagement. In general, scholars studying the U.S. case have been more optimistic about the positive effect of homeland mobilization for domestic engagement, whereas the research in Europe is more mixed and raises the question of whether outreach by homeland groups might insulate or isolate migrants.

The experience of having lived in at least two distinct civic and political environments adds complexity to immigrants' participation in the third sector. Researchers find that associational norms and social or political trust in both the sending and receiving countries help predict civic membership (Aleksynska 2011; Just and Anderson 2012; Voicu 2014). Transnational experience can be a benefit: homeland civic engagement (such as union organizing or participation in political movements) can provide leadership skills, unique viewpoints on associationalism, or organizing strategies that migrants tap in their new country of residence (Hagan 1994). Conversely, prior political socialization can also generate barriers. Especially for those from nondemocratic nations or countries rife with political corruption, migrants may hold different norms about voluntarism and charitable giving and be more suspicious or fearful of civic engagement. Still, home-country effects should not be overstated: the impact of host-society civic norms appears to be a stronger predictor of engagement than those of the homeland, especially as length of stay increases and immigrants become citizens.

Indeed, the willingness of a receiving country to extend citizenship to immigrants affects levels and processes of civic and political integration. Across nineteen European democracies, Aida Just and Christopher J. Anderson (2012) find that acquisition of citizenship increases noninstitutionalized political and civic engagement, especially among immigrants from nondemocratic countries. They suggest that migrants from nondemocratic countries may initially have fewer civic skills, less political knowledge, and weaker political trust or participation norms, but they may develop these norms and skills during the naturalization process, along with reassurances that participation is a right, or even a responsibility, of citizenship. Similarly, Bloemraad (2006) argues that Canada's strong investments in settlement and multicultural policies help immigrants build community organizations and participate in the public sphere more than immigrants from the same homeland who must navigate the U.S. *laissez-faire* system of immigrant integration. In this sense, whether a receiving country has a relatively open and liberal citizenship policy—with support for integration—or whether it provides a more hostile reception affects immigrants' civic engagement.

Local variation within a country also shapes nonprofit activity in immigrant communities. Local political culture, density of existing civic organizations, and demography can determine who is given a seat at the table for organizing (de Graauw and Vermeulen 2016). For example, in San Francisco—a city known for its progressive politics and long history of community involvement in addressing social and political issues—immigrants have created and participate in many nonprofit organizations that advocate for immigrant rights and routinely work with city agencies to provide services to immigrant communities. In Houston, a city more politically divided between Democrats and Republicans, we see notably less of this (de Graauw and Gleeson 2017). Differences between urban, rural, and suburban settings can also shape the evolution and persistence of immigrant organizations.

Immigrant Civic Engagement: The Organizational Level

Researchers must also consider civic inequality at the organizational level. Such civic inequality involves disparities in the number, density, breadth, capacity, and visibility of organized groups in a community (Ramakrishnan and Bloemraad 2008). Rather than focus only on individuals' organizational membership, voluntarism, and civic activities—the primary focus of research on immigrants and the third sector to date—we argue that immigrant organizations merit study and analysis as a distinct unit of analysis.

As with most measures of inequality, we start from an assumption that communities should, all else equal, have roughly similar motivations, interests, and abilities for civic organizing. If some communities have greater organizational presence than others, we can speak of civic inequality. Inequalities may stem from different interests (some communities feel a greater need to organize than others), differential resources and skills to engage in associational life, or structural factors (such as immigration and settlement policy or immigration and citizenship status) that impede organizing for some while facilitating it for others. When organizational inequalities become large and durable over time, we can even speak of civic stratification. Conversely, where governments and foundations invest in immigrant communities, we may see patterns of organizational parity. Once established, immigrant organizations can be important vehicles for mobilizing resources and enacting and implementing laws that support immigrant needs (de Graauw 2016). At this organizational level, how does an analytical lens that pays attention to immigrants and immigration change what we know about the third sector?

One lesson is that policies quite removed from third sector scholarship, such as immigration and refugee law and their attendant programs, can affect third sector organizing. Existing debates over the founding and persistence of nonprofit organizations often focus on supply or demand arguments (e.g., Grønbjerg and Paarlberg 2001). A demand-side view privileges purpose: nonprofits emerge when they fill a need or interest not met by the business sector (market failure) or by the public sector (government failure), spurring formation of immigrant-run groups such as a Bollywood dance group or an immigrant advocacy organization. Consistent with demand arguments, some researchers find more immigrant organizations in communities with a greater concentration of poorer and more recent immigrants, who face high integration barriers because of limited language skills or lack of citizenship (Chan 2014; Hung 2007; Joassart-Marcelli 2013). Nonprofits located in these places fill an important demand for language-accessible and culturally appropriate services.

Supply-side accounts argue, in contrast, that many needs and interests exist, but organizational creation and survival require a sufficient supply of material resources, such as private giving (by individuals or foundations) or public funding (through government contracting), as well as human capital, such as community members' leadership skills and connections. In line with such arguments, researchers find differences in nonprofit formation among immigrants from different national or ethnic backgrounds, variation that appears tied—at least in part—to the material and human resources internal to the community (Chaudhary and Guarnizo 2016; Joassart-Marcelli 2013).[12] At a policy level, state welfare spending and municipal funding for antipoverty or urban development efforts also affect nonprofit creation and survival, including the vitality of immigrant organizations (de Graauw 2016; de Graauw et al. 2013).

But existing research also suggests that immigrant-specific factors matter. The concept of political opportunity structure, developed in research on social movements, is germane here: immigrant civic infrastructures can vary across countries and within them, depending on whether and how immigration law and migrant-targeted policies affect them. Scholars have demonstrated how the material resources and logistical support of U.S. refugee resettlement programs and Canadian government grants for immigrant integration and multiculturalism affect the number, density, and type of nonprofit organizations that serve distinct immigrant communities or bring immigrants together for social, religious, or recreational purposes (Bloemraad 2005, 2006; Chan 2014; Chaudhary and Guarnizo 2016; Hein 1997; Joassart-Marcelli 2013). Conversely, since undocumented immigrants in the United States are ineligible for most federally funded services, certain public grants or contracts are not available to help organizations that serve these migrant populations (de Graauw and Gleeson 2018). Law and policies can thus supply critical material resources, as with federally and philanthropically funded refugee resettlement, but they can also impede or block integration efforts. When policies change, the impact on immigrant organizations can be significant. President Trump's decision to drastically downsize the U.S. refugee program in 2018 led dozens of refugee resettlement organizations reliant on U.S. State Department funding to close their doors (Vongkiatkajorn 2018). Bringing migration and immigrant organizations into the nonprofit scholarship thus requires researchers to consider how policy areas unconnected to the third sector nevertheless have an impact on the creation, persistence, and success of nonprofit and community organizations.

The dynamics of private funding can also play out differently for immigrant organizations. Beyond public grants or contracts, nonprofits also regularly garner revenue from membership dues, philanthropic gifts, corporate sponsorship, and fees for services.

Immigrant-serving organizations can face disadvantages in attracting such private funding. Economic hardship within immigrant populations can reduce organizations' ability to charge membership or service fees. The perceived illegitimacy of immigrants as deserving recipients of funds—because of their legal status or more generally their "foreignness"—can have an impact, as with the reluctance among some philanthropic funders to support immigrant organizations in politically conservative regions. Even when philanthropic donors specifically target immigrant communities, certain activities—such as citizenship assistance, fraud prevention, and get-out-the-vote campaigns—may garner more backing than other immigrant needs, such as deportation defense or criminal defense for incarcerated immigrants, because the former are deemed less politically controversial (de Graauw and Gleeson 2018). Overall, given the growing anti-immigrant sentiment in the United States and elsewhere, immigrant organizations operate in a more challenging environment than most mainstream organizations.

Measuring Immigrant Organizations, Civic (In)equality, and Civic (In)visibility

What would a research program that examines immigrant nonprofit organizations look like? How should researchers measure concepts such as civic (in)equality and civic (in) visibility?

Identifying the Universe of Immigrant Nonprofits

First, scholars need a sense of the universe of immigrant nonprofits. One tactic is to leverage formal data on incorporated nonprofit organizations. In the United States, this includes data from the Internal Revenue Service (IRS), which captures the tax filings of most incorporated nonprofit organizations (de Graauw 2016; de Graauw et al. 2013; Gleeson and Bloemraad 2012). Researchers interested in immigrant communities have used similar registries in other countries, such as financial data on registered charitable organizations in Canada (Chan 2014) and business association records in the Netherlands (Vermeulen 2006). Government administrative data offer important benefits in data uniformity and scope, especially when the process of building original databases would require tallying thousands, if not millions, of organizations.

Despite advantages, these data also come with challenges. Official statistics such as 501(c) (3) IRS filings in the United States do not represent the full universe of community-based groups, producing organizational undercounts (Grønbjerg and Paarlberg 2002; Lampkin and Boris 2002). U.S. nonprofit registration data miss organizations with limited revenues and religious organizations, both of which are not legally required to register with the government. Germane to immigrant communities, these databases also exclude groups formed by people who do not know about registration requirements, find them onerous or antithetical to their mission, or put off formalizing or incorporating an organization, perhaps out of fear of surveillance by the government or by hate groups. Researchers estimate that federal IRS listings cover only about 60 percent of all civic organizations, an undercount also found among immigrant organizations in the San Francisco Bay Area (Gleeson and Bloemraad 2012; Grønbjerg and Paarlberg 2002). All in all, official databases are incomplete in listing formal immigrant organizations, and they do not tally the small and informal groups active in immigrant communities.

A second problem is that it is difficult to identify immigrant organizations in non-profit registries. One strategy in the United States is to rely on existing codes that identify minority-oriented organizations. Certain National Taxonomy of Exempt Entities (NTEE) codes that organizations enter on IRS Form 990 signal that a group engages in activities geared toward ethnoracial minorities. However, these codes can be imprecise for research on immigrants. Not all organizations that target ethnoracial minorities focus on immigrant-origin populations, and not all immigrant-serving organizations label themselves as ethnoracial. Additionally, the NTEE code developed specifically for organizations that provide immigrant/ethnic services (code P84) is not widely used by immigrant nonprofits that also engage in other activities. As an alternative to such codes, some researchers use computer keyword searches for particular labels or strings of words in organizational names, such as *Mexican* or *Korean* (Chan 2014; Cortés 1998), or they identify organizations by the ethnic-specific surnames of board members and other leaders (Hung 2007) or by board members' country of birth (Vermeulen 2006). Such strategies are entirely reasonable but can lead to significant omissions or erroneous inclusion of nonimmigrant organizations.

Another approach, albeit far more tedious and labor intensive, is to hand-code hundreds or thousands of organizations in official databases to identify immigrant-serving organizations. Using a combination of NTEE codes, organizational names, and information collected during fieldwork, we individually coded immigrant organizations after we confirmed (via websites, directories, and interviews) that the organization had a mission or activities that addressed the aspirations or problems of people with immigrant origins (de Graauw 2016; Gleeson and Bloemraad 2012). Other scholars employ similar intensive coding strategies but categorize organizations by the proportion of a group's clientele or membership that is foreign-born (Cordero-Guzmán 2005; de Graauw 2016). Researchers can also consider organizational activities: for example, whether programming, meetings, and social and recreational activities are offered or conducted in multiple languages.

Given the limits of existing databases, such lists can be supplemented by other sources of information such as directories of social and human services and historically specialized "ethnic" phone directories that listed community groups. In their ongoing research, Els de Graauw and Erwin de Leon are triangulating various directories—including those maintained by immigrant organizations themselves, city officials whose purpose is to serve immigrant communities, and local foundations that invest in immigrant communities—to identify immigrant-serving nonprofits in New York City and to determine how visible these organizations are to government and philanthropic leaders.

Beyond Simple Counts: Comprehensive Organizational Data and Civic (In)visibility

Administrative data frequently suffer from a lack of depth about organizational features important to nonprofit scholars. To collect more comprehensive data, researchers can draw on formal organizational lists to create a list of all immigrant organizations in a particular place, then conduct an original survey of (a sample of) these organizations (e.g., de Graauw 2016). Such a survey can ask about budgets, services, clientele, workforce, membership structure, advocacy activities, and so forth. This method is more time-consuming than relying on existing datasets and requires diligence in securing a strong response rate to the survey, but it offers the important advantage of collecting data unavailable in formal registries.

A persistent challenge—in using either administrative or survey data—is how to define and confirm the prevalence of immigrant-focused activities and programming. Organizations can be very entrepreneurial in attracting new funding streams, without fundamentally reorienting their leadership or building lasting structures that make them more immigrant-friendly. A low- or no-cost health clinic might translate some materials into immigrant languages or employ a bilingual nurse who works a few hours a week but otherwise conducts business as usual. Conversely, some mainstream organizations may go to great lengths to mask the extent to which they serve immigrant populations to avoid criticism from risk-averse funders or xenophobic critics. Finally, it can be difficult to identify whether organizations serve multiple immigrant generations. An existential (and empirical) question arises as to whether later-generation organizations are appropriately considered "immigrant," or whether they should be conceptualized differently, such as an ethnoracial organization or a mainstream organization. A handful of scholars use ethnography to probe the day-to-day work environment, decision making, and conflicts within immigrant organizations that serve multiple generations (e.g., Chung 2007). Providing important insight that complements large-N data studies, ethnographies reveal the challenge of categorizing individuals and organizations as immigrant or not. At the same time, as with ethnographic work of all sorts, researchers must weigh the trade-off between the depth of knowledge gained versus the breadth of knowledge lost when studying only a few organizations.

Between a strategy of trying to study all organizations or just a handful, some researchers use field methods—including semi-structured interviews with community members and some ethnography—to identify "publicly present" or "civically visible" immigrant organizations (Chaudhary and Guarnizo 2016; Gleeson and Bloemraad 2012). In one study, researchers identified "all groups known to local officials, to ethnic or mainstream media, or to key leaders and volunteers working in the nonprofit sector" as a measure of civic visibility (Gleeson and Bloemraad 2012:348; Bloemraad and Gleeson 2012). The goal is to measure the extent to which decision makers or others outside the immigrant community recognize organizations run by and catering to immigrant residents. A reputational tally was created using semi-structured interviews that asked officials to list all the community organizations in their city, with subsequent probing for organizational sector (e.g., housing, recreation) and demographic groups. In another study, researchers examined what they term "socio-political legitimacy" by focusing on the perspectives of elected and nonelected local officials who make decisions about policy, resources, and services (Gnes and Vermeulen 2018).[13] Yet another approach analyzes how mainstream media report on local immigrant communities, including their coverage of organizations (Bloemraad, de Graauw, and Hamlin 2015).

When using reputational data, scholars recognize that journalists and decision makers have imperfect information and do not always have good recall, capturing only a slice of immigrant organizational life. They argue, however, that this civic visibility, or lack thereof, is in itself telling. Understanding which organizations are known beyond the immigrant community carries consequences for organizational survival as well as political decision making, resource allocation, and public attitudes about immigration. For example, in examining immigrant and ethnic organizations in Amsterdam, researchers found that the degree to which organizations are known and legitimate in the eyes of the immigrant constituency and external actors is more important to organizational survival than neighborhood context (Vermeulen, Minkoff, and van der Meer 2016). A drawback, however, is that field-based techniques are time-consuming and often temporally and geographically restricted. Tellingly, almost all hand-coded and field-based research on immigrant organizations focuses on one city or metropolitan region within a manageable but relatively narrow window of time.

Measuring Civic (In)equality

As outlined earlier, we conceptualize civic inequality at the meso level as disparities in the number, density, breadth, capacity, and visibility of organized groups in a community. Making claims about inequality requires some standardized measure of comparison. Against whom or what should immigrant nonprofits be measured?

A straightforward approach compares organizations serving immigrants to those serving the native-born or overall population. Researchers can also compare communities based on national origin, religious affiliation, racial minority background, or some other demographic characteristic.[14] One technique is to create a density score, calculating the number of immigrant nonprofit organizations identified in an administrative dataset per 1,000 immigrants in the population, and then to compare that figure to the density of all nonprofits in the general population. Using this approach, we found that around 2006, there were 5.5 registered nonprofit organizations per 1,000 city residents in San Francisco, but only 2.2 immigrant organizations per 1,000 foreign-born residents (de Graauw et al. 2013:99). We also found a roughly two-to-one ratio in nonprofit density for all city residents compared to foreign-born residents in San Jose and two nearby Silicon Valley suburbs.

Alternatively, the proportion of all organizations that serve immigrants (or a particular immigrant community) within the full universe of nonprofit organizations can be compared to immigrants' share of the total population. Dividing one by the other generates a civic inequality index where a value close to one suggests that a group's demographic presence in an area is on par with its share of registered nonprofits. Values close to zero suggest significant underrepresentation. Values above one indicate a share of nonprofit organizations larger than a community's demographic weight. Such a proportionality measure can be extended to consider the number of grants or the dollar amount of public or foundation funding that go to immigrant organizations as a proportion of total nonprofit grants or other funding (de Graauw 2016; de Graauw et al. 2013).

Rather than compile aggregate counts, scholars can also investigate the size of nonprofit organizations, as measured by the number of members, clients, staff, or volunteers, or by the financial resources and activities of the group. Such data provide information on whether immigrant organizations have fewer financial and human resources than mainstream nonprofits. Researchers can further investigate the range of organizational types in a community, to see whether nonprofit activity is concentrated in a particular domain (e.g., religious organizations vs. arts organizations vs. sports organizations). One can also investigate the range of nonprofit activity, for example to identify groups that focus on services or advocacy, or groups whose programming is oriented to more domestic, home-land/transnational, or international activities (see Chan 2014; Chaudhary and Guarnizo 2016). The breadth of organizational types can be a measure of whether an immigrant community is institutionally complete (e.g., Bloemraad 2005; Breton 1964; Chaudhary and Guarnizo 2016). When these measures—be it numbers, funding, domain of activity, or something else—differ substantially for immigrant communities as compared to a majority or native-born reference group, civic inequality may exist.

Why Civic (In)equality Matters for Immigrants

Although little research has examined civic (in)equality in immigrant communities, what has been done suggests that the current number and density of immigrant nonprofit organizations lags compared to demographic benchmarks. Research also shows that the geographic dispersal of these organizations does not necessarily match immigrant settlement patterns, with suburban and rural areas contending with fewer nonprofit re-sources (de Graauw et al. 2013; Joassart-Marcelli 2013; Roth, Gonzales, and Lesniewski 2015; Truelove 2000).

But why should we be concerned if there are fewer immigrant organizations or if there is less public funding for them? Mainstream nonprofit organizations may serve immigrants well. As we noted earlier, some observers worry that excessive immigrant or ethnic organizing self-segregates a community and impedes immigrant integration. Yet the general literature on the third sector, interest groups, and social movements suggests that civic inequality diminishes democratic voice and service provision, and it reduces access to sports, recreation, and the arts, or to other organizations set up to bring together people who share an affinity or interests. It is thus logical to presume that immigrants and immigrant communities bear negative consequences from civic inequality, with broader implications for how democracy functions in society. Surprisingly, however, there is very little empirical research probing the possible harms or repercussions of civic inequality for immigrant communities, in large part because immigrant organizations have featured so little in scholarship to date. We end the chapter by considering some of those reper-cussions, as well as avenues for future research.

Underserved: The Hardships of Limited Nonprofit Service Providers

A few studies suggest that in the absence of immigrant organizations, foreign-born resi-dents access fewer human and social services. Immigrants in Silicon Valley, for example, were estimated to have two to four times the social service needs of native-born residents, but they are about half as likely to receive help (Santa Clara County Office of Human Relations 2000). To the extent that immigrants in this region need to turn to nonprofits for help, those that primarily serve communities of color—almost all of which are largely immigrant-serving organizations—had smaller staffs and 40 percent less income than other nonprofits (LaFrance Associates 2005). Similarly, examining Chicago suburbs with substantial Mexican-origin populations, Benjamin J. Roth and his colleagues (2015) found that immigrant organizations were more likely to report low revenues and complain of insufficient funding compared to mainstream nonprofit service providers.

Smaller staff and limited funding could be a reflection of less effective organizations. However, there is reason to believe that the problem instead lies with the lion's share of resources going to mainstream organizations that are still not adequately addressing immigrant needs. In the Chicago study, despite low revenue, immigrant organizations had a larger percentage of bilingual staff (paid and volunteer), and they offered more immigrant-specific services such as English as a Second Language (ESL) classes, cultural programming, or legal services like citizenship assistance than mainstream organizations (Roth et al. 2015). Similarly, the history of Southeast Asian refugee resettlement in North America in the late 1970s and 1980s suggests that mainstream organizations were ill-equipped to help these newcomers, even when an organization had experience serving displaced people. As a result, earlier-arrived compatriots or citizen co-ethnics established Southeast Asian mutual aid associations and ethnic-specific organizations, often helped by federal government resources, to offer targeted, language-accessible and culturally appropriate services (Bloemraad 2006; Hein 1997).[15]

An area for future research is to evaluate the impact of nonprofit service provision on immigrant integration over time. Based on the refugee resettlement experience, immigrant organizations may be essential early on, providing immigrants with a safe space for companionship, support, and immigrant-tailored services. We know less about long-term effects—that is, whether immigrants living in nonprofit-rich environments are more successful in their economic, social, and political incorporation. Alternatively, immigrant organizations may be effective in the short term but could isolate immigrants from mainstream society over the long term. Adjudicating between these possibilities will require both large-N empirical studies that map variation in the universe of immigrant civil society, as well as in-depth qualitative research that pinpoints the mechanisms by which organizations affect immigrant populations.

Jobs and Leadership: Nonprofits as Employers and Schools of Civic Learning

Third sector scholarship considers nonprofits as job generators. In the United States in 2012, the nonprofit sector offered paid work to 11.4 million people, or 10.3 percent of private sector workers (Friesenhahn 2016). Research in immigrant communities also identifies the third sector as a source of employment and economic mobility, especially for those who face barriers entering the general labor market because of limited majority language skills, foreign credentials not recognized in the host country, or employment discrimination (Bauder and Jayaraman 2014; Bloemraad 2006). Immigrant advocacy organizations have even become a source of employment for young undocumented immigrants, although differences in job access are observed across nationality groups and types of nonprofits (e.g., Cho 2017). Thus, in line with existing scholarship, the nonprofit sector offers employment and perhaps upward mobility for the foreign born, but the particular legal situation of immigrants—especially the lack of official employment rights—limits who can find jobs in the third sector, and whether they can be salaried with benefits or must resort to contract or stipend positions that forestall employer-sponsored benefits such as health care. Scholars need to develop more nuanced ways of thinking about nonprofit sector employment, especially for undocumented immigrants whose work is legally and structurally precarious.

Beyond employment, nonprofit organizations have also long been identified in the literature as potential "schools" that teach leadership and civic skills, via either traditional civic associations (Verba, Schlozman, and Brady 1995) or change-oriented social movement organizations (McAdam 1988). There are good reasons to believe that third sector groups can play a similar role for immigrants, especially those who might be unfamiliar with the political and civic norms of the host country, and who feel intimidated to speak out because of linguistic and educational barriers. For example, in Kathleen Coll's (2010) study of immigrant Latinas in San Francisco, participation in a feminist workers' organization led to greater claims-making and sense of political efficacy, even among undocumented women. Studying the impact of grassroots youth organizing groups, Veronica Terriquez (2012) reports increased civic and political engagement among immigrant-origin alumni of these groups, leading her to draw parallels between the youth organizations and civil rights groups from the 1960s. And de Graauw (2016) discusses how many elected and nonelected city officials with immigrant backgrounds in San Francisco started their careers in the city's immigrant nonprofit sector, suggesting that immigrant nonprofits can serve as valuable training grounds and pipelines for immigrant and minority government leaders. Taking organizational inequality seriously raises another hypothesis to explain gaps in foreign- and native-born associationalism: if fewer immigrant-oriented organizations exist in a region, the chances for employment, leadership development, and acquisition of civic skills are reduced.

This is not to say that third sector organizations are a panacea to tackling inequalities in civic engagement. Studying Latinx janitors who are members of what she labels a "social movement union," Terriquez (2011) finds that impacts can be unequal and differentiated. Comparing union participants and nonparticipants, she finds no differences in parent workers' engagement with their children's schools in routine activities like volunteering or attending a parent-teacher organization meeting. However, union participation does lead to more change-oriented activities, such as mobilizing others to attend public meetings and challenging school officials to change institutional practices. In these cases, union training in public speaking, step-by-step organizing, and negotiation provide parents with the skills and confidence to engage school authorities.

Negative public discourse that stigmatizes immigrants' service use can also hinder nonprofits' ability to act as "civic schools" or leverage service provision as a mobilizing tool. Melanie Jones Gast and Dina G. Okamoto (2016) did fieldwork in two nonprofits that combine service provision and advocacy. The organizations paired service provision with requests for participation in political education and advocacy work. This led some women to feel that they could ask for help only if they paid the organization back with volunteer hours. Although a reciprocity norm may also exist in nonprofits catering to citizen clients, Gast and Okamoto argue that the feeling of obligation may be amplified for immigrants because of a national public discourse that stigmatizes immigrants' welfare use and labels the undocumented as particularly undeserving. Some immigrant mothers became reluctant to ask for help, even when their families desperately needed assistance, because they had little time to volunteer or they wanted to avoid public engagement out of fear of immigration enforcement. Here, again, immigrant background is salient to understanding the extent to which third sector groups can act as civic schools for immigrants.

Advocacy and Civic Voice

On balance, existing scholarship suggests that third sector organizations have positive effects on individual civic and political engagement, though researchers face a problem of causal identification: the types of individuals who join or participate in those organizations may just be more civically and politically minded to begin with. Theoretically, there is good reason to believe that positive civic effects also apply to immigrants, and a small number of studies support this argument empirically. Fennema and Tillie (1999) argue that immigrant communities with a denser civic infrastructure of organizations and overlapping board memberships experience increased solidarity, which in turn increases the level of mainstream political participation and generalized trust exhibited by immigrants. However, legal status constraints erect high hurdles for immigrants, and anti-immigrant discourses may do so, too.

A separate question is whether third sector organizations, as independent actors, can produce far-reaching structural social change. In the case of formal nonprofits, third sector scholarship tends to be pessimistic about advocacy and what nonprofits can achieve in politics, often concluding that they do little (e.g., Andrews and Edwards 2004; Berry and Arons 2003; Taylor, Craig, and Wilkinson 2002). In the United States, nonprofits with 501(c)(3) tax-exempt status are limited in the amount of lobbying they can do, and they are barred from partisan electioneering. Nonprofits operating with few staff and on shoestring budgets may not have the resources to invest in advocacy, while those with government contracts may be fearful that their advocacy bites the hand that feeds them. Immigrant organizations have the added challenge of advocating for marginalized and vulnerable communities against a backdrop of increasingly aggressive immigration enforcement and a highly politicized environment with fractured public support for immigrant rights.

Still, given many immigrants' exclusion from formal politics, nonprofits may play a critical role in civic and political voice for immigrant communities. Recent research shows that immigrant nonprofits have secured important advances in immigrant rights policies (de Graauw 2015, 2016). Not only do they articulate the needs of immigrants often shut out of formal politics because they are denied a vote, but once policies are enacted, they can be especially effective in pushing government bureaucracies to implement new policies, transforming rights and services on the books into reality on the ground. More broadly, social movement organizations in the United States have worked hard to keep the dream of comprehensive immigration reform, including a path to citizenship for undocumented immigrants, on the political agenda and in the media spotlight. "DREAMer" organizations—immigrant rights groups often led by young undocumented or immigrant-origin activists—are credited with pushing former president Barack Obama to create the Deferred Action for Childhood Arrivals program in 2012, temporarily shielding undocumented youth from deportation and providing work authorization (Nicholls 2013).

Advocacy organizations that speak out on behalf of marginalized communities have, in past scholarship, been criticized for primarily articulating the interests of the most privileged in a minority community, such as white women's grievances in the feminist movement, rather than intersectional identities and issues (Strolovitch 2007). Scholars studying the pro-immigrant movement have similarly critiqued organizations and leaders for initially privileging the most sympathetic in the undocumented community, high-lighting the plight of those who came to the United States as children and who achieved extraordinary success in school or selfless service in the community and military (Yukich 2013). More recently, some observers underscore the broad, intersectional approach to social justice embraced by young immigrant activists who seek coalitions across legal status, sexual identity, race, and class backgrounds (Terriquez 2015). Thus far, the literature on interest and advocacy groups in political science and social movements scholarship has largely ignored immigrants and migration issues. Future research needs to investigate whether existing concepts prevalent in these fields, such as framing, political opportunity structure, and resource mobilization, apply equally to noncitizens, especially those who are formally barred from key rights, who may be seen as illegitimate by voters and decision makers, and who are at risk of deportation.

In short, third sector scholarship needs to take better account of the diverse communities and constituents that nonprofit organizations serve and represent. One core group are immigrants, who may face unique challenges due to precarious documentation status or lack of citizenship, or other reasons linked to migration, such as language barriers or lack of experience with local civic norms. Immigrants may also be a source of innovation for the third sector, as they bring with them unique associational traditions from their country of origin and possible transnational orientations. We also spotlight the way that immigration law and either inclusive pro-immigrant or exclusionary anti-immigrant policies help scholars understand patterns of civic inequality, whereby some immigrant communities remain underrepresented and underserved by third sector organizations across a range of arenas. This civic inequality carries significant implications for resource distribution, employment mobility, and civic voice. Unaddressed, disparities can become solidified into patterns of durable civic stratification with negative implications for immigrants' long-term societal integration and the overall health of democratic societies.

PART IV

NONPROFITS, MISSION, AND THE MARKET

FOR MUCH OF THE TWENTIETH CENTURY, the nonprofit domain was seen as a sphere that was distinct from the state or the market. The very idea of a third sector reflected the assumption that civil society organizations exist as alternatives to business and governmental organizations. But over the past few decades the market model has grown in appeal, losing negative connotations associated with greed and supplanting earlier assumptions about the possible strategies that civil society organizations should pursue. This new orientation comes in many shapes and operates under a variety of labels, and there are still debates about whether the embrace of an outcomes orientation comes at the expense of mission. Nevertheless, the general theme of nonprofit organizations as separate from the sphere of enterprises no longer captures the full spectrum of activities in the sector.

The chapters in this section approach this transformation through a variety of lenses. Maitreesh Ghatak assesses economic theories of the social sector, with an eye toward explaining the circumstances in which both social value and financial opportunities may be combined. Johanna Mair examines research on social entrepreneurship, a burgeoning subfield that includes various kinds of organizations that combine a social purpose and an entrepreneurial bent. Magali Delmas, Thomas P. Lyon, and Sean Jackson look at the many ways in which market forces are being used to support social causes, most notably with regard to issues concerning the environment. Paul Brest traces how foundations and philanthropists have moved to become more strategic and focused on the outcomes of their giving.

In Chapter 13, Maitreesh Ghatak both reviews existing economic theories of the non-profit sector and amends and extends them to include new types of organizations that combine features of nonprofit and for-profit forms. Economists, of course, are model builders, and the best models are simple ones with interesting implications. Other disciplines tend to want to make things more complex and add in context and other factors, but such efforts are at odds with good model building. Perhaps it is best to think of model building as like furnishing a house one room at a time, and getting it done well, rather than trying to furnish an entire house all at once. A simple model represents a central tendency, with room for deviation that has interesting implications for the model. For scholars of the economy, the significant presence of nonprofit organizations in nations across the world, in terms of both employment and contributions to GDP, poses an interesting puzzle—why are there organizations that do not seek to maximize profits?

In the 1980s, economists Henry Hansmann, Burton Weisbrod, and Dennis Young developed arguments that explained the presence of nonprofits as a response to market and government failures. Their insight was that the nondistribution constraint on non-profits was a mechanism that disciplined nonprofits not to compromise on quality in the delivery of services. This model yielded a host of interesting implications about the trade-offs between costs and quality. To be sure, the nondistribution constraint did not eliminate opportunistic behaviors, as perks and salaries can substitute for profits. But it did point to an important insight—perhaps there are employees who are attracted to organizations because of their mission or cause. This idea has been paired with a more general recognition in the economics literature that calls into question the assumption of narrow self-interest and wrestles with developing models that incorporate commitments, whether to a cause, an identity, or a reputation or to various social norms.

In his chapter, Ghatak seeks to build a model of enterprises that balance a social mission with entrepreneurial intentions. Simply put, how can an enterprise pursue both social and financial objectives, without one goal working in opposition to the other? There is an emerging lexicon for such efforts, and Johanna Mair discusses them in her chapter. Ghatak goes further and recognizes that some traditional for-profit firms may assign social mission a high priority. These efforts could be seen, he argues, on a continuum. For-profits operate under market discipline, but while prioritizing profit maximization they may also respect a minimum threshold for meeting certain social objectives. Similarly, we can view nonprofits as working to enhance a social objective, subject to break-even constraints. Social enterprises, he argues, have more flexibility. In some circumstances, they maximize the social objective, subject to financial constraints; in other circumstances they may maximize a financial objective, subject to social constraints. The challenge, in Ghatak's view, is the mission-integrity problem. With both illustrative examples and the tools of formal modeling, he works out an argument for the conditions under which a social enterprise might be preferable to either a nonprofit or for-profit alternative, un-derscoring the crucial importance of selecting employees who are motivated by an or-ganization's mission.

In Chapter 14 Johanna Mair takes a naturalist approach to social enterprises, drawing on a unique, large-scale interview study of more than one thousand such organizations in nine countries. She examines social enterprise in different national contexts, with the assumption that the meaning of social purpose may vary across locales. To be included in the survey, an organization had to (1) have a social mission, (2) engage in revenue-generating activity involving the sale of products or services, and (3) employ at least one full-time-equivalent (FTE) employee. The virtue of casting such a wide net is capturing heterogeneity in forms, practices, and challenges. Yet despite the diversity among survey respondents, a common metric is number of people, whether in terms of number served, number who volunteer, or number empowered. Size is clearly a *lingua franca* in terms of accomplishment. There is also commonality in terms of groups who are served, most notably the elderly, children, and those left behind. There are marked differences, however, with regard to whether the actions have any influence on domestic public policy; in some countries there is impact, whereas in others none at all.

One arena in which social enterprises are very active is environmental causes. From cap-and-trade climate policies to fair trade consumer products, market solutions have found fertile soil here. In Chapter 15 Magali Delmas, Thomas P. Lyon, and Sean Jackson examine an array of approaches that promote environmental sustainability. Most notably, they examine the use of information disclosure strategies in a variety of guises such as aiding stockholders, favoring companies that use green practices, and signaling to consumers which companies engage in sustainable production. These efforts reflect a change in the repertoire of many environmental advocates, from opposition to collaboration. Transparency is a low-cost and effective means to rally consumers to environmental causes, making green practices something consumers want and, consequently, a standard that firms must provide.

Delmas, Lyon, and Jackson review three strategies of certification—product labeling, performance assessment, and governance practices. Information disclosure entails four attributes. The first is codification, making information that was formerly secret or tacit explicit to the public. A second feature is the creation of standards for environmental performance. Once in place, advocates can push for them to be ratcheted up while opponents can seek to lower them, but they become guidelines by which to judge performance. Third, certification brings outside third parties, typically nonprofits, that do the monitoring work to ensure that standards are upheld. The certifiers make standards more credible. The fourth element is communication, which entails conveying information so that a label or display makes green practices transparent to the consumer. Thus, whether they codify, standardize, certify, or communicate, these strategies provide potent tools for nonprofits seeking sustainability goals. Their efficacy, of course, depends on whether governments and corporations join forces with nonprofits or resist them. As in other domains of nonprofit activity, complex multistakeholder coalitions are forming that blend market metrics and a commitment to environmental causes.

Just as environmental progress has been tethered to information disclosure efforts, the outcomes movement in philanthropy has been aimed at analyzing and making visible critical aspects of nonprofit performance. In Chapter 16, Paul Brest takes us on a "personal" journey, charting both the history and his own involvement in efforts to make philanthropy more strategic by focusing on the deliverables that nonprofits provide. Because of the wide array of nonprofit activities, such as service delivery, policy advocacy, and cultural and environmental preservation, a single common approach to making philanthropy strategic is unlikely. Nevertheless, Brest has been a champion of the results-oriented focus across a variety of philanthropic endeavors. His conception of an outcomes framework is deceptively simple—clear goals, data-based strategies for achieving those goals, monitoring to permit course corrections, and evaluation of efforts. In his view, lack of progress toward this approach is as much the fault of philanthropists as it is of recipients. He closes with thoughts that echo Chapter 15; some form of transparent certification would be invaluable in fostering mutual learning between donors and recipients. But he is not optimistic that such openness is in the cards.

The chapters in this section reflect the uneven movement toward the use of market criteria to gauge nonprofit goals and performance. In some domains, such as the environment, there is a collective willingness to embrace metrics that signal progress toward goals of sustainability. In other realms, neither donors, politicians, nor nonprofit leaders are on the same page. But such challenges are not unique to the world of practice. As Ghatak illustrates, building a theory that combines both social purpose and competitive dynamics is challenging indeed.

13 ECONOMIC THEORIES OF THE SOCIAL SECTOR

From Nonprofits to Social Enterprise

Maitreesh Ghatak[*]

ACCORDING TO THE U.S. BUREAU OF LABOR STATISTICS, in 2016, employment in nonprofit organizations represented 10.2 percent of total U.S. private sector employment.[1] Internationally, nongovernmental organizations (NGOs), a subset of organizations in the nonprofit sector that engage specifically in international development, have been supplementing and sometimes replacing government agencies in the provision of relief and welfare, social services, and various projects in developing countries. The number of international NGOs rose from less than two hundred in 1909 to nearly one thousand in 1956 to more than twenty thousand in 2005 (Werker and Ahmed 2008).

This substantial presence of nonprofits in the economy presents several conceptual challenges to economists. First, if a private organization does not seek to maximize profits, modeling its behavior becomes a challenge. After all, financial incentives are an important engine of economic activity in a market economy. If the objective of a nonprofit is not profit, then what exactly is it, and how do we know that this supposed objective is not profit maximization by another name? If the objective is some form of social welfare, how can we be sure that the rational, utility-maximizing agent of economics textbooks (often referred to as *homo economicus*) will in fact pursue it? How can we be sure that such an agent will not pursue a selfish objective, such as capturing rents? How can an organization that does not maximize profits survive competition from for-profit organizations, particularly in markets where there are no entry barriers?

Second, the existence of nonprofits calls into question the neat division of economic activity into two spheres: the market sphere and the government sphere. It points to a gray zone in the black-and-white picture of the economy that divides all economic activity into (a) a profit-driven private sector that produces private goods efficiently and (b) a public

* I would like to thank Tim Besley for many helpful discussions on this topic. Indeed, the chapter draws a fair bit on our joint work. I would also like to thank Jonathan de Quidt, Patrick François, Robert Gertner, and Hannes Mueller for helpful discussions on this topic, Linchuan Xu for research assistance, and Johanna Mair, Walter W. Powell, and other participants at the Stanford Nonprofit Handbook conference for helpful feedback. The responsibility for all errors and omissions is mine.

sector that corrects market failures, provides public goods, and carries out redistribution to serve equity objectives.

Even within the framework of mainstream economics, some scholars are questioning these traditional views related to the motivation of economic agents. They are also questioning the simplistic model that equates for-profit firms with the production of private goods and government entities with the provision of public goods.

A large body of empirical work, especially within the field of experimental economics, has increasingly called into question the view of individuals as being driven by narrow self-interest.[2] In light of this growing body of empirical evidence, recent theoretical work in economics has moved beyond stylized models of motivation based on a narrow view of *homo economicus*—an archetypal figure that cares only about money and leisure—and has embraced a wider perspective on motivation.[3] Broadly speaking, this work has focused on different approaches to prosocial motivation, such as commitment to a mission, commitment to an identity (being a "good" or "responsible" person, a good teacher or doctor or friend or parent), commitment to an "in-group" (e.g., family, community, tribe), intrinsic rewards, reputational concerns and social norms, status rewards, and pure altruism.[4]

At the same time, a large body of evidence has accumulated on varieties of government failure related to, for example, corruption, waste, absenteeism, and poor service quality. A related development involves the rising importance of private social sector organizations, including not only nonprofits but also hybrid organizational forms such as social enterprises, public–private partnerships, and contracting-out of public service provision to private providers. The rising importance of this sector highlights the limitation of equating the provision of public goods and services with provision through government agencies.[5]

A central research objective of modern microeconomic theory has been to understand how the economic institutions that underlie the "invisible hand" of the market actually work. The starting point of modern organizational theory in economics is to understand the boundaries of the firm—that is, the classic "make or buy" decision—how much to produce in-house and how much to procure from outside. The literature that has emerged has advanced our understanding of how the scope, size, and organizational form of a firm and how it manages workers or raises capital depends on the nature of the production process, various contracting frictions, transactions costs, and informational asymmetries.[6]

A large literature on the economics of nonprofits has emerged since the early 1970s (see Hansmann 1987 for a review), and this literature addresses alternative theories of nonprofits that I review in the next section. I argue that although this literature has provided a convincing explanation of why the nonprofit form may be a constrained efficient solution to certain underlying contracting problems, it does not provide a clear framework to explain the rise of hybrid organizational forms—social enterprises, in particular—that flexibly combine features of both nonprofit and for-profit organizations. Next, I discuss the rise of social enterprises and provide some examples. After that, I discuss a new agency problem that I call the "mission-integrity problem." This concept is an extension of the multitasking problem that has been a primary focus of the literature on nonprofits, and it has the potential to provide a theoretical framework to explain nonprofits, for-profit firms, and social enterprises. A key part of my analysis focuses on the interaction between the selection of prosocial individuals in the social sector and the mission-integrity problem.

In the next section, I discuss the self-selection of motivated managers into social enterprises. Finally, I offer some concluding observations on the emerging research agenda in the economic theory of social sector organizations.

Existing Theories of Nonprofits

Many of the leading theories of nonprofits can be traced to the core insight of the multi-tasking literature (Holmström and Milgrom 1991) in contract theory. The term *multitasking* refers to a situation where a job involves multiple tasks and the performances of each task are not all equally measurable. In such situations, providing incentives has to strike a balance across these different dimensions. For example, if the manager of an organization is entrusted with both cutting costs and maintaining quality, which is not easily monitorable, then providing sharp financial incentives to the manager will not be optimal as that may lead to excessive cost cutting at the expense of quality. The general lesson from this literature is that if an organization has multiple outputs and its nonpecuniary outputs are difficult to measure, then a muting of financial incentives may be necessary. Moreover, if the social outputs of an organization are of great value to its owner or principal or stakeholders, then they may opt for the nonprofit form to decrease managers' incentive to pursue financial profits by sacrificing social objectives.

The existing literature on nonprofits, building on the work of Henry B. Hansmann (1980) and Burton A. Weisbrod (1988), with more recent contributions by Edward Glaeser and Andrei Shleifer (2001), identifies the nonprofit sector as a residual sector that arises to overcome market and government failure in the provision of some goods and services. According to this work, a nondistribution constraint (NDC) serves as a mechanism to overcome certain contractual problems, which Hansmann calls *contract failure*. The NDC (Hansmann 1980) used by nonprofits stipulates that nonprofits can earn revenues or generate a financial surplus, so long as they are retained for future spending, distributed to beneficiaries in some form, or given to employees who lack control rights.

This literature shows that an NDC may be a constrained optimal choice in the presence of agency problems. Motivating an agent on a contractible task (effort in increasing output or reducing costs) may produce undesirable outcomes because it leads to neglect of a noncontractible task (effort in improving quality). Given this cost-quality trade-off, for-profit entities will tend to lower costs at the expense of product or service quality, whereas nonprofits have little incentive to compromise quality in that way (see Glaeser and Shleifer 2001). This logic reflects the core insight of the multitasking model (Holmström and Milgrom 1991), since an NDC is a form of "flat" incentive. The choice of organizational form thus depends on how much the principal of an organization values quality (or any other nonpecuniary aspects of production) as opposed to profits. Here I provide a simple illustration of the logic of this theory.

Suppose the quality of a service can be high or low, namely, $q = q_h$ or $q = q_l$, but it is not directly measurable or observable to the consumer. To produce higher quality, a firm must incur higher costs. In particular, suppose the costs of producing a service of high and low quality are c_h and c_l, respectively, with $c_h > c_l$. As quality cannot be directly observed or measured, only a single price can be charged for this service, which is denoted by p. In a for-profit firm, choosing low quality would yield a profit of $p - c_l$ (denoted by π), which is higher than the profit yielded by choosing high quality, namely, $p - c_h$ (which we set to 0 for simplicity). In a nonprofit organization, the manager or owner does not directly benefit from the cost savings that arise from the low-quality choice and will therefore have no incentive not to provide higher quality.

This is a simple illustration of a cost-quality trade-off, which is an example of contract failure. A more general version of this trade-off occurs when a firm chooses an action that can be of two types, a prosocial one and a commercial one. The former type has a potential social benefit but is also costly, while the latter type has no social benefit but is low in cost. A nonprofit organization has no financial incentive to take a commercial action, while a for-profit firm has no incentive to take a social action.

A clarifying remark about using simple models like the one just presented to illustrate different economic theories may be helpful. A simple model is meant to focus attention on one particular force (e.g., the cost-quality trade-off) whose variation will determine whether a specific organizational form will emerge. However, several other variables are being held constant (the ceteris paribus assumption). For example, a simple theory of the nonprofit form may posit that this form is merely a means to attract a motivated workforce that will work at lower wages (e.g., Preston 1989; Weisbrod 1988) or a means to get tax benefits. Alternatively, where a cost-quality trade-off exists, something other than a pure nonprofit or a pure for-profit firm may emerge. For example, a profit-sharing partnership may be optimal when it is hard to assess service quality (see Levin and Tadelis 2005), and such partnerships are common in professional service industries—such as law, accounting, medicine, investment banking, architecture, advertising, and consulting—but not elsewhere. In other words, a cost-quality trade-off is neither necessary nor sufficient for the emergence of nonprofits. Unlike a general theory, a simple model indicates a likely association or a central tendency but allows for a range of possibilities that may deviate from that tendency and yet be consistent with it.

A variant of this argument suggests that charities should take a nonprofit form in order to assure donors that their money will indeed reach beneficiaries and not be pocketed by the managers of a donee organization. Contract failure arises in situations where the quality of a good or a service cannot be ascertained before (or sometimes even after) its consumption—a situation that leaves considerable scope for opportunism. Common examples of this situation include plumbing, car repair, health care, education, and child or elder care. An NDC is said to protect against opportunism; managers have a reduced incentive to compromise quality since they cannot pocket financial profits directly.[7]

It is not clear that having an NDC will eliminate opportunistic behavior. The fact that profits cannot be directly distributed does constrain the way that surplus can be extracted from a nonprofit, but salaries and perks provide a mechanism through which nonprofit managers can extract surplus. Indeed, the starting point of the work of Glaeser and Shleifer (2001) is that nonprofit managers extract surplus in an indirect and possibly inefficient way: for every dollar they extract in the form of perks or benefits, they receive only a fraction of that value, and this effect mutes their incentive to compromise quality. After all, direct cash is preferable to perquisites in the form of goods and services. The same effect reduces their incentive to maximize revenues. The literature correctly notes the downside of nonprofits that is implied by this logic: if nonprofit managers have little incentive to pursue profits at the expense of noncontractible quality, they also have little incentive to cut costs in socially productive ways. In this respect, for-profit firms are preferable.[8]

Barring a few exceptions, the economics literature on nonprofits has placed little focus on the motivation of those who manage or work in those organizations (Handy 1995; Preston 1989; and Weisbrod 1988 are exceptions). It is often remarked that these individuals systematically differ from the rest of the population in terms of their prosocial motivation.[9] A key factor in the effectiveness of nonprofits may well be their ability to attract employees who are committed to a cause, as noted by Anne E. Preston (1989), Weisbrod (1988), and Timothy Besley and Maitreesh Ghatak (2005). This factor may in turn influence the choice of organizational form in the provision of experience and credence goods. The two-way interaction between employee selection and incentives has received little attention and will be a major focus of the next section of this chapter.

Emergence of Social Enterprise

Because of the rise of social enterprises in the last few decades, the classification of all organizations as discrete nonprofit, for-profit, or government entities is no longer possible. This development points to a basic limitation of the contract failure literature, which assumes that the choice of organizational form is between for-profit and nonprofit entities only. Social enterprises belong to a set of organizations that are neither traditional profit-maximizing firms, nonprofit organizations, nor publicly owned and controlled government agencies. These hybrid forms of organization are often referred to as *social enterprises* even though, as Roger L. Martin and Sally Osberg (2007) acknowledge, many other types of firms operate under that banner.[10]

The defining goal of a social enterprise is to balance making profits with pursuing a social mission (Katz and Page 2010). As J. Gregory Dees (1998) puts it, social enterprises combine "the passion of a social mission with an image of business-like discipline, innovation, and determination commonly associated with, for instance, the high-tech pioneers of Silicon Valley" (1). They aim to bring entrepreneurial approaches to social problems, thereby providing an alternative to the perceived rigidity and inefficiency of existing institutions in the government and philanthropic sectors.

In the economics literature, *mission* is not a widely used term, and instead individuals or organizations are said to pursue *objectives*, which can be financial (e.g., profit maximization) or social (e.g., a cleaner environment). In the management literature, *mission* involves an overall vision, while *objectives* refers to specific and concrete goals that are part of a broader strategy to achieve the mission. I will stick to the terminology of *mission*, but given that my framework here is somewhat abstract, I could substitute the term *objectives* or *goals*.

I should also clarify that many organizations—including for-profit firms—have multiple objectives, including social and commercial ones. What matters is which objectives have priority. We can think of for-profit firms as operating under strict market discipline, which requires them to prioritize profit maximization while respecting a minimum threshold for meeting certain social objectives (e.g., environmental standards). Likewise, we can view nonprofits as working to maximize a social objective, subject to a break-even constraint and an NDC. In contrast, social enterprises have a flexible approach: in some circumstances they maximize a social objective, subject to a break-even constraint; in other circumstances they maximize a financial objective, subject to the constraint that their actions do not fall short of a minimum threshold for meeting their social objective.

Indeed, in the management literature, social enterprises are viewed as aiming to balance making profits with advancing a social mission (see Katz and Page 2010) and as avoiding the rigidity of either a nonprofit or a for-profit form. They are viewed as pursuing profit and social good in tandem, in part by making considered choices to pursue one over the other at any given time (Reiser 2010). The underlying premise is that there is a trade-off between these objectives and that both nonprofit and for-profit entities face constraints that make resolving this trade-off difficult. Because nonprofits cannot distribute profits, the nonprofit form is not an option for entrepreneurs who intend to blend equity finance with the pursuit of social goals. Managers of a for-profit firm, meanwhile, have a legal obligation to maximize profits for the firm's owners. Also, market forces push them to give priority to profit maximization over social objectives; otherwise, they risk losing both market share and investor confidence.[11]

Like most nonprofits, social enterprises are allowed to earn revenue, but unlike nonprofits, they face no equivalent of an NDC that restricts the distribution of residual earnings—no constraint, that is, other than the requirement that its activities align with its social mission. However, as Dees (1998) points out, "For social entrepreneurs, the social mission is explicit and central. This obviously affects how social entrepreneurs perceive and assess opportunities. Mission-related impact becomes the central criterion, not wealth creation" (2).

The role of social enterprises in the economy has attracted increasing attention in recent years, partly in response to the growing number of real-world examples of social enterprises in both the developed and developing worlds (see Porter and Kramer 2011). The management literature presents many interesting case studies. For example, LendStreet Financial helps reduce indebtedness among low-income people by delivering financial literacy programs and providing incentives that encourage responsible repayment (see Lee and Battilana 2013). Prior to delivering these services to a new client, LendStreet purchases the client's debt from one or more institutional investors. When clients increase their rate of repayment, LendStreet earns revenue that enables it to sustain its operations.

Consider the following examples:

In Africa, where children frequently die of diarrhea from bad sanitation, Dignified Mobile Toilets (DMT), founded by Isaac Durojaiye (who died in 2012), runs a franchise system for public toilets. He supplies mobile toilets to slum areas, where previously unemployed young people operate the toilets and charge a small fee for their use. These operators keep 60 percent of the income and pass the rest to DMT which uses the money to buy new toilets.

Nic Frances runs a group that aims to cut carbon emissions in 70 percent of Australian households over ten years. His group, Easy Being Green, gives low-energy light bulbs and low-flow shower heads to households that agree to sign over the rights to the carbon-emission credits that use of the equipment will earn. The group then sells those credits to companies and used the proceeds to finance its activities. Easy Being Green now aims to expand globally.[12]

Altrushare Securities is a brokerage firm that engages in the sorts of activities that one might expect of a Wall Street outfit, such as buying and selling stock and providing research on companies. Unlike its peers, however, Altrushare is majority-owned by a pair of charities, each of which controls about one-third of the firm. "We're a for-profit institutional brokerage, and we have to compete on execution and commissions and do so with the same technology and talent you would expect from a top-tier firm," said Peter Drasher, a co-founder of Altrushare, which is based in Bridgeport, Connecticut. "What makes us different is our non-profit ownership and our mission, which is to support struggling communities with our profits."[13]

A common theme in the literature on social enterprises is the tension between their commercial and social missions. In the commercial microfinance sector, for example, the social mission of relaxing borrowing constraints on the poor comes head-to-head with profit-seeking that may occur at the expense of the poor, raising the specter of "mission drift" (see Yunus 2011). Ben and Jerry's, an ice cream brand that was established to follow strong ethical norms (e.g., using hormone-free milk sourced from local farms) while pursuing commercial ends, was sold to Unilever at the behest of shareholders, raising questions about its future as a social enterprise (see Page and Katz 2012).

The Mission-Integrity Problem

What nonprofits, social enterprises, and the kinds of hybrid organizations discussed in the previous section have in common is that they are all mission-driven organizations that operate in settings where principals or agents may have nonpecuniary motivations and where outputs cannot be measured well enough to make standard incentive contracts useful. In some cases, these outputs are purely private goods (e.g., health care with no externalities, such as cosmetic surgery, or commercial research). In other cases, the outputs also have a public-good component, either because the goods deliver positive externalities in the form of nonexcludable or nonrival benefits (e.g., environmental protection), as one sees in standard public economics, or because society cares about directly ensuring a minimum provision of certain goods (e.g., basic health care, education, helping the poor).

The dual mission framework of social enterprises raises new agency problems for mission-oriented organizations, since the objectives of profit-making and advancing social good are often at odds in the social sector (as with the cost-quality trade-off). If we know that social goals will usually override commercial goals, then a nonprofit form will work best. Similarly, if we know that commercial goals will usually override social goals, then a for-profit firm is the appropriate organizational form. But given that social enterprises claim to be flexible in balancing social and commercial objectives, they require a mechanism that can balance those objectives in a way that is consistent with a broad mission. Besley and Ghatak (2017a) call this challenge the "mission-integrity" problem. I will illustrate this problem with a simple example.

For this purpose, I will adapt the illustration provided in the preceding section. Suppose a firm chooses an action x that can be one of two types, which I denote by 0 and 1. Earlier I equated these types with providing high quality and low quality, respectively, but here I will allow for alternative interpretations. The first type of action (denoted by 0) has a potential social benefit but is also costly, while the second type of action (denoted by 1) has no social benefit but is low in cost. The former is a prosocial action, while the latter is a commercial action.

Suppose it is possible to verify whether a manager has undertaken the prosocial action or the commercial action. Now suppose that there are two types of situations that can arise. In one, social considerations outweigh financial considerations, and so taking the prosocial action is the right thing to do. In the other, financial considerations outweigh social considerations, and so the commercial action is the appropriate one to undertake.

However, only the manager can observe the true facts of the situation, and therefore we cannot figure out whether the manager is doing the right thing merely by observing his or her actions. What matters is that the production or distribution of a good entails a potential conflict between social and commercial objectives, and yet the underlying reason for taking an action is not observable by outsiders, including the owners or principals of an enterprise.

Several applications would fit this scenario.

Think of situations in which the goal is to widen access to certain goods or services; education, health care, and legal services are important examples. The prosocial action can be interpreted as providing access to "deserving" beneficiaries on preferential terms (e.g., free treatment for the poor), while the commercial action involves offering no special access or concessions. The manager may observe an individual who is to be served (say, a patient or a student or a potential beneficiary of a targeted welfare program) and decide what action to choose.

The social objective may also be related to externalities associated with the good's production. For example, environmental externalities may arise requiring firms to balance cost efficiency against the social costs of pollution. Suppose the commercial action is to use a standard technology, while the prosocial action is to use a costlier but more environmentally sound technology. The manager's choice is to decide whether it is worth giving up profits by choosing the latter technology if the environmental benefits that are external to the firm are substantial enough.

Situations, or *states*, are denoted by σ Like actions, they are of two types, and I will denote them by 0 or 1 as well. In state $\sigma = 0$ the prosocial action $x = 0$ is the right one from the social welfare point of view, while in state $\sigma = 1$ the commercial action $x = 1$ is the right one from that point of view. How, then, do we ensure that the manager will make the right choice—the choice that is consistent with the mission of the organization? This is the mission-integrity problem.

In Table 13.1, I provide details regarding the financial and social payoffs under the four possible combinations of actions and states. In a prosocial state, taking a prosocial action leads to a social payoff of $S = \bar{S}$ and a financial payoff of $\pi = \underline{\pi}$. However, if a commercial action is taken, the social payoff is zero, while the financial payoff is $\pi = \bar{\pi}$ irrespective of the state. In a commercial state, if a prosocial action is taken, then the social payoff is $S = \underline{S}$ while the financial payoff is $\pi = \underline{\pi}$. Here, I assume that $\bar{S} > \underline{S}$ and $\bar{\pi} > \underline{\pi}$. Moreover, I assume that in the prosocial state, it is more efficient to take the prosocial action, namely, $S + \underline{\pi} > \bar{\pi}$. In contrast, in the commercial state, it is more efficient to take the commercial action, namely, $\bar{\pi} > \underline{S} + \underline{\pi}$. This poses a sharp dilemma: How do we ensure that the right action is taken in the right state?

Table 13.1 Social and financial payoffs for various states and actions

	$\sigma = 0$	$\sigma = 1$
$x = 0$	$S = \bar{S}, \pi = \underline{\pi}$	$S = \underline{S}, \pi = \underline{\pi}$
$x = 1$	$S = 0, \pi = \bar{\pi}$	$S = 0, \pi = \bar{\pi}$

One way to ensure mission integrity is to impose a rigid mission on an organization. Nonprofit organizations, for example, are designed to protect mission integrity by following a clear social mission. Many sectors of the economy—in particular, health, education, and poverty relief—rely heavily on such organizations. Here, by design, commercial considerations are set aside, and the manager is expected to choose $x = 0$ irrespective of whether $s = 0$ or 1. The downside of this arrangement is that from a social welfare point of view, there may be times when commercial considerations outweigh social considerations. In this scenario, nonprofits are inefficient.

For-profit firms also have a rigid mission—to maximize profit. External shareholders can invest in a for-profit firm knowing that it has a legal obligation to pursue that goal. In this case, any deviation from profit maximization would pose an agency problem, even though this deviation may be carried out for the most worthy of social goals (see Friedman 1970 for a statement of this position). The downside of this arrangement is that social considerations sometimes outweigh commercial considerations. In this scenario, for-profit firms generate a negative externality.

In the existing framework, which I discussed earlier, the separation of for-profit and nonprofit entities may seem like an efficient division of labor between the provision of private goods and the provision of public goods. But the rigidity that characterizes both nonprofit and for-profit entities has a downside. From a social welfare point of view, there are times when engaging in profit-oriented activities is most desirable and times when pursuing other ends is most desirable. Thus, it makes sense to seek a more nuanced way to balance those two types of activity. That is indeed one of the claimed advantages of social enterprises: they eschew the rigidity of both nonprofit and for-profit forms. The question is, how do they guarantee mission integrity? To be effective, in other words, social enterprises have to solve the problem of achieving the right trade-off between profit and purpose.

In the absence of contractual solutions, the mission-integrity problem creates a role for what Katz and Page (2010) call "mission-sympathetic parties," who are appointed to achieve an optimal trade-off between commercial and social considerations. Selection on the basis of motivation can thus become a mechanism to achieve mission integrity. When individuals care about the mission of an organization, they will care about whether the organization is indeed committed to that mission.

Besley and Ghatak (2017a) formalize this argument and show that one key mechanism through which social enterprises can achieve mission integrity while eschewing the rigid approach of nonprofit and for-profit forms is the selection of managers who are motivated by a social mission. In that case, managers can be given a financial stake in their organization, and this incentive structure will ensure that they will "do the right thing" depending on the situation—namely, maximizing profits when that is appropriate but deviating from that practice when social objectives are more important. However, external monitoring by stakeholders offers another option to make sure that the performance of social enterprises conforms to their social objectives.

Consider all three organizational forms: for-profit, nonprofit, and social enterprise. With a for-profit firm or a social enterprise, the manager is a full residual claimant on profits, whereas the manager of a nonprofit earns only a flat wage. For-profit and nonprofit entities curb the autonomy of managers by stipulating a rigid mission. In a social enterprise, the manager has discretion over the balance between profit and purpose.

If managers are sufficiently motivated (that is, if they put sufficiently high weight on a social payoff), nonprofits and social enterprise are equivalent, as managers of this type will always put more weight on social objectives than on profits. However, for moderately motivated managers, the flexibility of social enterprises mitigates the mission-profit trade-off, and giving them discretion over action is more efficient than the rigid approach followed by either nonprofits or for-profit firms. That is because they will always choose $x = s$, i.e., $x = 1$ when $s = 1$ and $x = 0$ when $s = 0$. In contrast, managers of for-profit firms will always choose $x = 1$ while managers of nonprofits will always choose $x = 0$.

However, this effect has to be balanced against the fact that if the social payoff is very valuable to a principal or owner (or if the social state is much more frequent than the commercial one), then the nonprofit form should be chosen over both for-profit and social enterprise forms. Similarly, if the commercial payoff is more valuable to a principal or owner (or if the commercial state is much more frequent than the social one), then the for-profit form is the correct option.

This framework allows us to move beyond the for-profit-versus-nonprofit trade-off, which has been a primary focus of the existing literature on social enterprises. Another interesting implication of this framework is that when owners or principals do not like a social payoff (when, for example, they put a negative weight on it because of ideological considerations), they face a problem that resembles a standard agency problem, with the social payoff functioning like a private benefit to a firm's manager. Thus, for-profit firms that prohibit taking a prosocial action will be the preferred organizational form among owners or principals who object to a social payoff. This insight is in keeping with the well-known claim by Friedman (1970) that the only social responsibility of business is to make profits.

Selection of Socially Motivated Managers

The approach taken in the previous section challenges a central tenet of standard economic design, in which the assumption of *homo economicus* restricts attention to agents with narrowly self-interested goals. The sustainability of social enterprises actually rests on the selection of agents with appropriate motivations to achieve the right trade-off between commercial and social goals. Even though, as I noted earlier, the potential role of nonprofits in attracting motivated managers is recognized (see, for example, Weisbrod 1988), the formal theoretical literature on nonprofits has not explicitly considered the role of intrinsically motivated managers, and in particular, how their presence interacts with underlying agency problems. A key insight of the Besley and Ghatak (2017a) framework is to show that once the heterogeneity of manager motivation and self-selection is taken into account, social enterprises emerge as a natural alternative that allows the social sector to go beyond the standard for-profit versus nonprofit trade-off.

This insight provides an interesting contrast with certain assumptions that prevail in the existing literature on nonprofits. In that literature, it is assumed that managers have no nonpecuniary motivation and care only about money and their disutility of effort. As a result, nonprofit status is seen as necessary to manage the cost-quality trade-off. Once we allow for managers who have nonpecuniary motivation, nonprofit status ceases to be a necessary condition for aligning commercial and social objectives. Allowing for prosocial motivation therefore opens the door for more flexible organizational forms, such as social enterprise.

However, a key question then emerges: How do social enterprises select for socially motivated managers? Motivation, like ability or conscientiousness, is not readily observable, and one must have mechanisms in place to ensure selection of the right kinds of individuals. The selection can take the form of direct screening. An empirical implication of this argument is that social enterprises will spend much more time and effort on recruiting managers who are committed to a social mission than for-profit firms do. In for-profit firms, by contrast, ability and other standard labor market characteristics will play a larger role in recruitment screening.

There is ample empirical evidence that nonprofit and public-sector organizations recruit individuals who have more "public-service motivation" (see Cassar and Meier 2018 for a recent review). There is also some evidence that social enterprises tend to hire workers who are highly motivated to achieve an organization's mission and who fit with the values espoused by the organization (Brolis 2017).

There is a more subtle conceptual issue to consider: if the motivation or commitment level of workers and managers is not observable, what mechanisms can social enterprises use to screen for the right kinds of people? Let's extend the model to allow for two types of potential managers: selfish and motivated. Selfish managers are driven only by financial goals, while motivated managers put a weight θ on the social payoff. With respect to selfish managers, achieving mission integrity requires use of a pure nonprofit form, since only that form will remove financial calculations from their decision making. (The model assumes that in this case, selfish managers do not mind choosing the right state-contingent action, since they are indifferent to the social consequences of their decisions.).

With respect to motivated managers, achieving mission integrity requires allocating a share of profits as a bonus to make sure that they do not always choose prosocial actions at the expense of pursuing an appropriate financial payoff. In particular, let w_H be the flat wage offered in a hybrid organization and λ be the share of profits offered as a bonus. For a motivated manager to choose the right course of action in both states of the world, the following two constraints must be satisfied:

$$\theta \overline{S} + w_H \geq \lambda \overline{\pi} + w_H$$
$$\lambda \overline{\pi} + w_H \geq \theta \underline{S} + w_H.$$

The first constraint indicates that in the state where the social payoff is high, the manager will take a prosocial action. The second constraint indicates that in the state where the financial payoff is high, the manager will take a commercial action. These inequalities give a range of values for λ that will achieve mission integrity:

$$\frac{\theta \overline{S}}{\overline{\pi}} \geq \lambda \geq \frac{\theta \underline{S}}{\overline{\pi}}.$$

Thus, in nonprofits the incentives are right for selfish managers, while in hybrids the incentives are right for motivated managers. Put differently, the selection of workers and managers for nonprofits and the choice of the nonprofit form are not independent, as it would appear from the existing literature, in which one strand of research (e.g., Weisbrod 1988) focuses on the selection aspect while another strand (e.g., Hansmann 1980) focuses on the role of the NDC in curbing incentives for managers to let commercial considerations override prosocial considerations. The main argument for nonprofits—namely, that it removes commercial considerations from decision making—is reinforced if there are grounds to believe that not every decision maker fully agrees with the mission of his or her organization. Likewise, if decision makers are indeed committed to the mission, then contract failure is less likely and one can consider relaxing the rigidities of the NDC (e.g., if the NDC limits an organization's ability to access capital).

However, a key question remains: How do organizations solve the selection problem? If individuals are heterogenous in terms of their commitment to the mission of an organization and if information on their commitment level is not observable, how can the organization make sure that it selects the right managers? This is the classic problem of self-selection: If the quality of an applicant is subject to private information, is it possible to design a compensation package that will select for the "right" kind of applicant?

Suppose two types of organizations are in place, a nonprofit and a hybrid, and the former offers a flat wage w_N and the latter offers both a flat wage w_H and a share of profits λ as a bonus. Is it possible to set these values in a way that satisfies the mission-integrity constraints of both organizations *and* in a way that leads selfish agents to self-select for the nonprofit and motivated agents to self-select for the hybrid organization? A distinctive aspect of the problem, as it turns out, is that meeting those conditions is not possible. In standard problems that involve asymmetric information, we typically worry about the self-selection constraint on one type of agent but not both. Yet here, we have to worry about the self-selection constraints on both types of agents. To make the nonprofit attractive to selfish agents, the flat wage has to be high, but in that case motivated agents will also be attracted to the nonprofit: they get the social payoff by choosing the prosocial action in both states of the world. To make the hybrid attractive to motivated agents, the bonus has to be set high (as high as the mission-integrity constraint will permit) to offset the lower flat wage, but in that case the hybrid becomes attractive to selfish agents as well!

Let $\hat{\pi} = q\underline{\pi} + (1-q)\bar{\pi}$ be the average profit when a commercial action is chosen in both states of the world, and $\hat{S} = q\bar{S} + (1-q)\underline{S}$ be the average social payoff when a prosocial action is chosen in both states of the world. Then the self-selection constraint for selfish agents to prefer a nonprofit is

$$w_N \geq \lambda\hat{\pi} + w_H.$$

The corresponding self-selection constraint for motivated agents to prefer a hybrid is

$$q\theta\bar{S} + (1-q)\lambda\bar{\pi} + w_H \geq \theta\hat{S} + w_N.$$

Intuitively, the flat wage differences must be such that (a) selfish agents would not want to work in a hybrid organization, and (b) motivated agents would not want to work in a nonprofit. The trouble is, there is only one instrument—the wage difference—to achieve both goals, and using that instrument turns out not to be possible.

Formally, $\lambda\hat{\pi} > q\theta\overline{S} + (1-q)\lambda\overline{\pi} - \theta\hat{S}$, as this is equivalent to $\lambda q\underline{\pi} > -(1-q)\underline{S}$, which is always true. Thus, both parts of this dual requirement—that the nonprofit wage premium $w_N - w_H$ must be greater than $\lambda\hat{\pi}$ to attract selfish agents to the nonprofit sector, and that it must be smaller than $q\theta\overline{S} + (1-q)\lambda\overline{\pi} - \theta\hat{S}$ to prevent motivated agents from joining the nonprofit sector—cannot simultaneously hold.

That means there are two possible options. First, one can set the wage in hybrid organizations so low that selfish agents will not join them, while motivated agents will opt to join nonprofits instead. Second, one can set the nonprofit wage at a level that is unattractive to motivated agents, but in that case selfish agents will be drawn to hybrid organizations. Both options have downsides; a selfish agent in a hybrid organization will pursue only financial objectives since he or she gets a share of the profits as a bonus and does not value the social objectives by the assumption of being selfish, while a motivated agent in a nonprofit will pursue only social objectives since financial incentives are absent.

Two factors suggest that the former is likely to be the preferred "second-best" option. First, there is a paucity of motivated agents relative to selfish agents in the population. Screening out selfish agents, therefore, is a much bigger concern than screening in motivated agents. Second, within the social sector, the loss from pursuing a commercial objective when a social objective should receive priority is likely to be of greater concern than the loss from pursuing a social objective when a commercial objective should receive priority.

We do not have direct evidence to support the model outlined here. However, existing work on nonprofit wage differentials suggests that it should be possible to carry out similar work with respect to social enterprises. For example, there is some evidence that at the same qualification level, nonprofit workers earn less on average than for-profit workers. However, when the labor market is tight and for-profit and nonprofit employers compete, a wage gap between the two sectors may not be observed. Recent work shows that if one controls for this demand-side factor, the relationship between that wage gap and the share of labor demanded by nonprofits is driven by "motivated types" sorting into nonprofit jobs who are willing to take a wage cut (Jones 2015). There is also evidence that those who work in the nonprofit sector believe they are underpaid but choose to continue to work in the sector for reasons that are value-based and because they find certain job characteristics appealing (Handy et al. 2007). There is also evidence that measures of prosocial motivation predict the decision to work in the nonprofit sector, and that workers in the sector accept a wage discount for that reason (Serra et al. 2011).

Concluding Remarks

An emerging research area seeks to understand the social sector from an economic point of view and to integrate the sector either into a standard economic framework that applies to for-profit firms producing private goods (e.g., economics of contracts and organizations, industrial organization, finance, labor) or into a standard framework that applies to government entities providing public goods (e.g., standard public economics).

Much of the economic reasoning that underpins the standard understanding of resource allocation in the private sector does not quite apply to the social sector. To start with, the quality of goods and services provided in the social sector—which include experience goods to credence goods—is typically non-contractible. Also, many of these goods and services have externalities: that is, their benefits or costs are partly external to the organization that provides them. According to Ronald Coase (1960), the inefficiencies that arise from externalities have to do with the difficulty of creating property rights. In the standard economic framework for private goods, making the decision maker in a firm the residual claimant on property rights leads to efficient outcomes. In fact, "creating property rights" and "contractibility" are very similar concepts. If output is hard to measure and/or attribute to a given agent (e.g., in the moral hazard problem that applies to teams), then how do you pay people appropriately for their marginal product? If quality is noncontractible, then how do you charge buyers a price that reflects the value that they place on it? The core issue in the kinds of problems that I have discussed—the kinds of problems that have traditionally been the focus of public economics—is noncontractibility, namely, when the output is difficult to measure and price. If noncontractibility is not the issue and output is measurable, then nonrivalry (namely, one person's consumption not reducing another person's consumption, as is the case with standard private goods like apples) simply changes the pricing formula (e.g., subscription or rental rates for cable TV) from that of standard private goods, without requiring any major change in the analytical framework. Naturally, the emerging research agenda draws on insights and tools both from the economics of contracts and organizations and from public economics.

There are several important potential areas of research in this emerging literature. Of particular interest is the financing of social enterprises. For example, one advantage of social enterprises over nonprofits is that the former can raise equity while the latter can only incur debt. More generally, there are several fascinating areas of future research related to the continuum of organizations that spans from for-profit firms to social enterprises of various kinds to nonprofits. With respect to social enterprises, topics for future research include organization design (e.g., delegation, ownership structure) and the implicit and explicit incentive mechanisms (e.g., reputation, career advancement, incentive pay) that these organizations use; quality, performance, and impact assessment of the outputs of these organizations; how these organizations interact at an industry level and how they interact with other types of organizations; and government regulatory policy regarding these organizations.

14 SOCIAL ENTREPRENEURSHIP

Research as Disciplined Exploration

Johanna Mair[*]

SOCIAL ENTREPRENEURSHIP—THE PRACTICE of addressing social problems by means of markets—has become an increasingly prominent approach to engaging in private action for public purpose. In this chapter, I will refer to a *social enterprise* as an organization that practices social entrepreneurship. Social enterprises—broadly understood as organizing tools to address a wide range of social problems (including homelessness, integration of refugees, elderly care, cyberbullying, and mental health) by relying on market-based activities—have become a recognized community of organizations across geographies. Over the last decade, social enterprises have attracted new forms of capital in the form of impact investment or venture philanthropy (Letts, Ryan, and Grossman 1997; Hehenberger, Mair, and Seganti 2018; Brest, Chapter 16, "The Outcomes Movement in Philanthropy and the Nonprofit Sector"); they have become partners or competitors of businesses in creating and addressing new markets (Seelos and Mair 2007); and they have been courted by policy makers as cost-effective providers of social services (Teasdale 2012; Grohs, Schneiders, and Heinze 2017).

To understand the global enthusiasm for social enterprises, it is helpful to revisit how social entrepreneurship as a field of practice has evolved over the last two decades. First, although hardly anyone has argued that social enterprises constitute a new phenomenon, early writings portrayed them as blurring the boundaries between the public, private, and social sectors and as being more effective than existing approaches within each of those

* This chapter builds on a large-scale research project—SEFORÏS—that has benefited from financial support provided by the European Union through the Seventh Framework Programme for research, technological development, and demonstration under grant agreement 613500. I would like to thank my fellow travelers on the SEFORÏS journey, especially Marieke Huysentruyt, Ute Stephan, and Tomislav Rimac. Nikolas Rathert helped explore the data presented in this chapter and has provided valuable insights. Woody Powell reminded me of the beauty and richness in Alexander von Humboldt's work. Patricia Bromley, Magali Delmas, and other participants in the workshop that led to this volume provided very helpful comments.

sectors (Dees 1994, 1998). Second, associating social enterprises with innovation (Dees and Anderson 2006) and with the ability to address newly emergent or stubbornly persisting social problems in novel or unconventional ways (Seelos and Mair 2005) fueled hopes and sparked interest among stakeholders who previously focused on charity or corporate social responsibility (CSR) as the private form of tackling social problems and on welfare as the public form of tackling such problems. And third, the systematic scouting and celebrating of social enterprises by intermediary organizations such as Ashoka and Echoing Green, along with the addition of courses on social entrepreneurship in business schools and schools of public policy, shaped a distinct professional identity and a set of career paths for social entrepreneurs.

The trajectory of social entrepreneurship as a field of practice has been marked by debates over the meaning of social entrepreneurship—debates that often take the form of open contestation and ideological conflict. These debates have resulted in a tacit agreement to use the label in ways that leave room for ambiguity (Chliova, Mair, and Vernis forthcoming). For some observers, social enterprises heroically step in where governments and markets have failed to address social problems. These observers regard social entrepreneurs as change makers equipped with a unique ethical fiber (Drayton 2006) or as leaders who courageously alter an "unpleasant equilibrium" in society (Martin and Osberg 2007:33). Others interpret the rise of social enterprises as the triumph of a strain of neoliberal thought that idealizes markets and business as drivers of social change (Dey and Steyaert 2010). These observers believe that social enterprises not only threaten the legitimacy of government and organized civil society as the most effective providers of social services but also pose a threat to democratic principles (Ganz, Kay and Spicer 2018).

Research on social enterprises has not been shielded from these debates. Early research efforts have devoted ample ink and substantial effort to clarifying definitions (Zahra et al. 2009; Light 2008; Austin, Stevenson, and Wei-Skillern 2006; Mair, Robinson, and Hockerts 2006) and to arguing for or against a unifying theory of *the* social enterprise (Santos 2012; Dacin, Dacin, and Tracey 2011). An unintended consequence of these efforts is that scholars have lost sight of the need to situate social enterprises and the problems they address in space, time, and institutional context. My colleagues and I joined this conversation by proposing a pathway for research that explicitly builds on the embeddedness of social enterprises in societal and institutional realities as "a source of explanation, prediction and delight" (Mair and Martí 2006:36) and advocates for a deeply contextualized study of those enterprises (Seelos et al. 2011). We portrayed social enterprises as organized efforts to address social problems by combining and recombining various institutional and organizational features in novel and unconventional ways (Mair and Martí 2009). The theoretical potential inherent in the study of social enterprises, we argued, lies in examining the process by which they address social problems *in* context and not devoid of context (Mair 2010; Mair and Rathert forthcoming). Scholars, we further argued, can harness this potential most productively not by developing a grand theory of social entrepreneurship but rather by developing midrange theories that refine, adapt, and recast existing theories.

Over the last decade, research on social enterprises has attracted interest from scholars across multiple disciplines, including law (Brakman Reiser 2013), history (Hall 2013), sociology (Vasi 2009; Galaskiewicz and Barringer 2012), and economics (Besley and Ghatak 2017). Management journals in particular have become a popular outlet for studies of social enterprises. In-depth case studies have helped unpack the unconventional ways in which social enterprises create impact with respect to a broad range of social problems (Seelos and Mair 2017), including poverty (Mair, Martí, and Ventresca 2012), inequality (Mair, Wolf, and Seelos 2016), and drug addiction (Lawrence and Dover 2015). Studies focusing on specific problem domains such as work integration (Pache and Santos 2013; Crucke and Knockaert 2016) and microfinance (Battilana and Dorado 2010; Zhao and Wry 2016) have helped clarify realities in those domains. Most work in this field, however, has focused less on the challenges or problems that social enterprises address than on how social enterprises are organized (Battilana and Lee 2014; Ebrahim, Battilana, and Mair 2014). Case studies on individual enterprises, for example, have exposed organizational challenges, struggles, and failures (Smith and Besharov 2019; Tracey and Jarvis 2006). This productive stream of work has predominantly deployed perspectives and concepts related to different institutional logics, and it has portrayed social enterprises as organizations that combine a welfare logic and a commercial logic while pursuing both social and commercial goals (Battilana et al. 2015; Pache and Santos 2013; Besharov and Smith 2014; Wry and York 2017). This emphasis has forcefully directed attention to conflicts arising from a duality in logics and has foregrounded the need to achieve balance in the pursuit of social and business goals. For example, in a thoughtful case study on Digital Divide Data, a digital outsourcing company that offers training and employment to disadvantaged youth in developing countries, Wendy K. Smith and Marya L. Besharov (2019) portray social and business goals as guardrails for social enterprises. These guardrails demarcate a confined space for maneuvering that is filled with paradox and tension—a space where social enterprises experiment with practices, shape and reshape their identity, and confront demands from external stakeholders. Work of this kind has helped bring the study of social enterprises into the academic mainstream and position it as a legitimate topic for management research. However, this trend has limited organizational scholars' interest in this field to a narrow set of theoretical questions about how social enterprises cope with dual logics.

In seminal studies on organizations (Blau and Scott 1962), the pursuit of multiple and potentially conflicting goals has been identified as a defining characteristic of organizations in general. Seeing social enterprises merely as sites where dual goals are at play may therefore prevent us from clarifying whether and how they are distinct from other organizational forms. The duality of social and commercial goals, moreover, is not unique to social enterprises but is intrinsic to organizing in almost all institutional domains that entail a public purpose, such as health, education, and the arts. Finally, limiting the scope of social enterprises to the pursuit of commercial and unspecified social goals may prevent the development of a more comprehensive understanding of the role that social enterprises play in society and the economy—a role that can vary in time and space. Relying on common or widely accepted perspectives can limit theorizing as disciplined imagination (Weick 1989) because it constrains the approach that scholars take to *seeing* and potentially limits the creativity that they bring to *looking*—to their choice of methods to use in the search for explanation and truth (Abbott 2004; Schneiberg and Clemens 2006).

The objective of this chapter is to inspire theorizing by revealing the organizational realities of social enterprises across different geographies, given that the meaning of public purpose varies across problem domains and local context. Until recently, systematic and comparative analysis of how institutional context affects and is affected by social enterprises has been stalled by a dearth of available data. Existing comparative studies are often based on datasets collected for different purposes, as in the case of the Global Entrepreneurship Monitor (GEM) database (Stephan, Uhlaner and Stride 2015; Kibler et al. 2018), or are designed to fit well-rehearsed theories that originated in political science or the study of civil society organizations. Janelle A. Kerlin (2010, 2013), for example, studies the emergence and prevalence of social enterprises as a by-product of the specific welfare regime (Esping-Andersen 1990) or the social origin (Salamon and Anheier 1998) of the country in which they operate. Although both of those approaches have helped advance a comparative research agenda, they can be limiting. The former approach limits the range of questions that scholars can meaningfully and validly address and prevents scholars from accurately capturing the organizational realities of social enterprises; the latter approach prevents them from detecting meaningful differences among social enterprises within the same country context.[1]

In this chapter, I report on insights and patterns emerging from data collected in a large-scale study of more than one thousand social enterprises in nine countries. (Joining me in carrying out this study was a group of scholars that included Marieke Huysentruyt, Ute Stephan, Tomislav Rimac, and others. See the following text for more information on this study.) Inspired by Alexander von Humboldt and Aimé Bonpland's exploration of the geography of plants, in this chapter I seek to uncover features that social enterprises have in common and to understand how they vary when they "grow in a different habitat" (Humboldt and Bonpland 1807). My argument is that embracing rather than taming the diversity among social enterprises facilitates future theorizing. A disciplined approach to exploring whether and how social enterprises vary across context helps identify features of a social enterprise archetype and to inspire the search for real-types that complement ideal-type schemes to categorize social enterprises. This approach also helps clarify the role that social enterprises play in the economy and society and how this role differs across contexts. Finally, disciplined exploration generates empirical evidence that can inform and refine ideological debates on social enterprises as well as popular images of those organizations.

The Scope of Exploration

From April 2015 to December 2015, I was part of a consortium of scholars that undertook a journey to explore the variety of social enterprises across different geographical and institutional contexts. The objective of our study on Social Entrepreneurship as a Force for More Inclusive and Innovative Societies (SEFORÏS) was to advance research and to inform policy by developing comparative knowledge on social enterprises. In total, we surveyed directors or managing directors from 1,045 social enterprises in China, Germany, Hungary, Portugal, Romania, Russia, Spain, Sweden, and the United Kingdom. In addition, we collected qualitative data and conducted a comparative case study project that covered three social enterprises in each country. (See http://www.seforis.eu for detailed reports on all nine countries.)

The choice of sampling method was critical to our study. Because official and comparable registrars for social enterprises or tax codes in and across countries are largely missing, we opted to employ respondent-driven sampling (RDS), an approach used in public health and sociology (Heckathorn 1997) to identify social enterprises and to obtain a representative sample of them in each country. We kept the selection criteria for the sample to a minimum, thereby ensuring comparability across context without compromising our ability to explore heterogeneity. To qualify for the study, an organization had to (1) have a social mission crosschecked in multiple ways by our trained interviewers; (2) engage in revenue-generating activity involving the sale of products or services, with the proceeds of that activity accounting for at least 5 percent of total revenue; and (3) employ at least one full-time-equivalent (FTE) employee. We used validated scales as well as tailored and open-ended questions in the interview and survey instruments we built. Interviews with the director of each social enterprise lasted an average of ninety minutes and were complemented by a thirty-minute online survey. We trained and coached about thirty interviewers, who conducted interviews in a local language and followed strict rules of back-translation.[2] More than 30 percent of the interviews were cross-checked and independently coded by a second rater. To triangulate interview data, we also collected data on matters such as mission, employment, and finances. For a more extensive discussion of our methods and how we applied RDS, see Marieke Huystentruyt and colleagues (2017).

In hindsight, many of the choices we made in studying the organizational and local realities of social enterprises resemble the approach that Humboldt and Bonpland followed in their landmark study of the geography of plants. In particular, our approach was informed but not constrained by existing categorization schemes for institutional context and organizational form. By starting from, but not limiting ourselves to, a set of three characteristics that defined qualifying social enterprises, we enhanced our ability to uncover emerging features, forms, and patterns. Through this way of *looking*, we tried to mitigate (even if we could not completely avoid) biases that could stem from the theories that scholars typically use (Schneiberg and Clemens 2006), and we opened up an opportunity to *see* differently—and to see different things.

The Landscape of Social Enterprises—Emerging Patterns

Evidence from our study helps to reveal the economic and societal role of social enterprises. In 2014, the social enterprises that we surveyed jointly served more than eight hundred million beneficiaries, generated more than €6 billion in revenue, earned nearly €70 million in surplus/profits, and employed slightly more than half a million people. (See Huysentruyt, Mair, and Stephan 2016 for a more detailed summary of our high-level findings.)

One size does not fit all for the social enterprises in our sample. Social enterprises across but also within countries differed considerably in terms of revenues and numbers of employees. Although in Germany, Portugal, Spain, and the United Kingdom more than 40 percent of all social enterprises had revenues of more than €1 million, in China and Russia more than half of all social enterprises had revenues of less than €80,000.[3] The median count for FTE employees ranged from 7 in Sweden to 24 in the United Kingdom. The median count for volunteers varied substantially across countries as well, ranging from 3 to 3.5 in Russia and Sweden to 15 in China and Romania. One third of social enterprises in the survey did not involve volunteers in their work.[4]

Similarly, *one form does not fit all* for the social enterprises we surveyed. We found that social enterprises use a variety of legal forms and are not bound by the legal form that they adopt. The roles that they play in the economy or society are equally diverse. They are active participants in the *market for public purpose*, but how they engage in this market varies considerably across problem domain and country context. They are *inherently social* with regard to what they do and how they operate. This social footprint in turn reflects a local imprint; it is shaped by social, economic, and political realities and by historical institutional legacies. Social enterprises also take an active role in *shaping their institutional environment* in ways that go beyond the delivery of goods and services. Finally, their decision to pursue a social mission by commercial means does not turn them into battlefields of competing logics or sites of unresolvable paradox. However, our research on social enterprise does show that multiple mandates can create *conflict*.

In the following sections, I further unpack these findings. In doing so, I refer to existing research on nonprofit organizations in an effort to inform and inspire future theorizing.

Legal Form as Choice

For researchers on nonprofit organizations, legal form is the defining feature of the organizations they study. Yet legal form is neither a uniform nor a defining characteristic of social enterprises, and the choice of form depends on a number of factors, including both institutional aspects (such as the repertoire of available forms and the legitimacy associated with those forms) and pragmatic aspects (such as beneficiaries' ability to pay for services and the ability of an organization to access funds that may be legally restricted to a specific form).

Our project allowed us to systematically investigate patterns in the legal forms that social enterprises chose across nine countries and to explore the factors that determined such choices. From our case studies, we learned that legal form strongly influences the nature of these organizations. Apart from questions of personal liability, risk, and taxation, the legal form of a social enterprise affects how outside parties perceive the organization, the funding sources it can tap, and the stakeholder groups with which it can and must engage (Mair, Wolf, and Ioan 2020; Wolf and Mair 2019). As Figure 14.1 shows, the social enterprises in our sample adopted legal forms associated with different tax regimes. Nonprofit forms (50.14 percent)[5] and for-profit forms (26.70 percent)[6] accounted for most of the organizations in the sample. In addition, 5 percent of social enterprises adopted forms associated with cooperatives, and a smaller share of them adopted hybrid forms such as the community interest company (CIC), a legal form introduced in the United Kingdom in 2005 that requires reinvestment of profits for the public good. However, 13 percent of organizations in the sample did not rely on a single legal form but instead chose a dual arrangement that allowed them to combine legal forms within and across nonprofit and for-profit legal statuses.

The dominance of nonprofit legal forms in our sample masks important differences across countries. Figure 14.2, which shows the distribution of legal forms within and across countries, reveals patterns that call for a detailed inquiry into the role that institutional context and historical legacies play in the choice of legal form among social enterprises. In

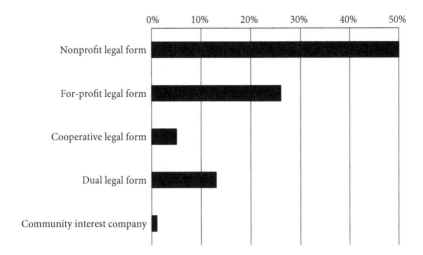

Figure 14.1 The spectrum of legal forms: Share of different legal forms of social enterprises across nine countries (*N* = 1,045)

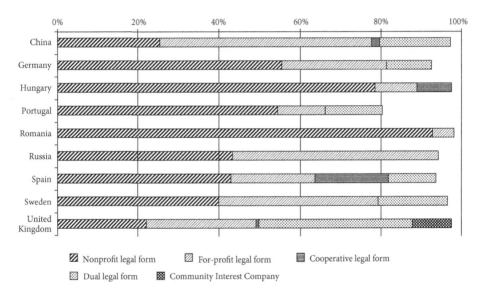

Figure 14.2 Patterns of legal forms: Share of different legal forms of social enterprise by country (*N* = 1,045; empty categories not shown)

China and Russia, the majority of organizations adopted a for-profit legal form, whereas in Germany, Hungary, Portugal, Romania, Spain, and Sweden, nonprofit legal forms predominated. In Portugal and Spain, a comparatively higher percentage of social enterprises opted for historically available forms, such as cooperatives. The United Kingdom stands apart from other countries because the majority of social enterprises there combined different legal forms.

In countries other than the United Kingdom, a relatively small share of social enterprises combined legal forms. In China (17.6 percent), Germany (12 percent), Portugal (14.2 percent), Spain (11.2 percent), and Sweden (24.3 percent), a modest portion of social enterprises adopted a second legal form. Qualitative insights from our case studies suggest that social enterprises take this step in order to harness the legal opportunities and advantages associated with different legal forms. Combining legal forms allows social enterprises to increase access to resources and to align internal operations with outside expectations. For example, although a for-profit legal form may allow an organization to successfully operate in a market environment and to increase and diversify its revenues, a nonprofit legal form signals its commitment to a social mission. As a founder of a social enterprise in Germany explained:

> We did this [combining legal forms] so that people take us seriously. We do not really need this legal form for our work. But people think only a nonprofit is appropriate for this. If we say we are a for-profit, they think we want to make money out of it.

Auticon, a social enterprise in Germany offering IT service delivered by people with autism, operates as a business (GmbH) but set up a nonprofit sister organization (gGmbH) to offer training services for people on the broader autism spectrum. Auticon uses the for-profit form to signal competitiveness in its service delivery, and it uses the nonprofit form in order to remain a respected player among organizations that serve people with autism.

Social enterprises seem to *make do* with the legal forms available in their country and to adopt formal arrangements that are suitable to the pursuit their goals. When asked about priorities for legal change in their country, only 11 percent of survey respondents cited the creation of a specific legal status for social enterprises as a priority. In countries like the United Kingdom, where special legal forms are readily available, social enterprises seem to prefer combining widely recognized forms that are already in common use. One potential explanation for this preference is that combining traditional legal forms gives social enterprises more flexibility to add activities that either rely on donations or have the potential to generate revenues.[7]

We also detected a correlation between the age of a social enterprise and its choice of legal form. Younger organizations seem to be more likely to adopt a for-profit legal form. In our sample, nonprofit organizations were on average twenty-one years old, and for-profit organizations were on average fifteen years old.

Participating in the Market for Public Purpose

Our project allowed us to uncover patterns in how social enterprises participate in the market for public purpose and how they define their role in that space. (I define "market for public purpose" as a social space and area of exchange that encompasses both private and public efforts to address social problems of public interest.) Next I will use data on sources of finance, interaction with governments, and competitive dynamics to describe these patterns.

Financing Social Enterprises

Seventy percent of the social enterprises in our sample relied on selling products or services as their primary mode of financing operations. In all nine countries, that activity was the most important mode of financing operations and the most important source of liquidity for social enterprises. On average, social enterprises financed 57 percent of their activities this way—a level far above our selection cutoff point of 5 percent. Of all countries in our study, Spain was the one in which social enterprises were most reliant on this form of financing; that source accounted for almost 70 percent of total financing in that country. Grants, meanwhile, represented the second most important source of financing (26 percent of total financing, on average) for social enterprises in our sample. In Romania, financing through grants was nearly as important as sales. Financing through equity investments played only a minor role in all countries: the cross-country average for that source was less than 4 percent of total financing. Only in China did investments in the form of equity from a founder make up a considerable portion (17 percent) of financing for social enterprises. Donations constituted a notable source of financing (between 10 percent and 11 percent) in three countries: Germany, Romania, and Russia. Loans and membership fees played a negligible role in social enterprise financing, except in Sweden, where 4 percent of social enterprises deployed loans, and in Hungary, where 3 percent of social enterprises relied on membership fees. Figure 14.3 provides a comparison of financing sources across countries.

Interacting with the Public and Private Sectors

The research on nonprofit organizations documented in the first and second editions of this handbook focused on understanding what distinguishes nonprofit organizations from other forms of organized action for the public good—particularly forms that exist in the business and government sectors. Implicit in these research efforts was the assumption that nonprofit organizations constitute a "third" or "social," sector. Social enterprises have been portrayed as entities that blur the boundaries between the three sectors (Dees and Anderson 2002). More recently, commentators have made the case that social enterprises form, and should be seen as, a fourth sector (Sabeti 2011). Our project offers empirical insights that suggest an alternative or complementary perspective. In this perspective, social enterprises constitute a community of organizations that pragmatically navigate markets for public purpose in ways that reflect the context in which they address social problems.

Figure 14.4 shows patterns of sales by and grants to social enterprises across countries. An analysis of these two dominant forms of social enterprise financing illuminates how social enterprises interact and transact with the public and private sectors.

In China, Portugal, Romania, Russia, Spain, and the United Kingdom, social enterprises mainly sell to private organizations or individuals. Sweden is the only country where the government is the dominant buyer of products and services offered by social enterprises. An analysis of grants received by social enterprises complements the analysis of sales and helps clarify the realities of the markets for public purpose in which social enterprises operate. Figure 14.4 shows how patterns of grantmaking to social enterprises vary considerably across countries. In Hungary, Portugal, Spain, Sweden, and the United Kingdom, grants from government sources accounted for 15 percent to 32 percent of financing and outweighed grants from the private sector. Such favorable grant schemes appeared to be absent in China, Germany, Hungary, and Romania, where grants from private sources outweighed grants from public sources.

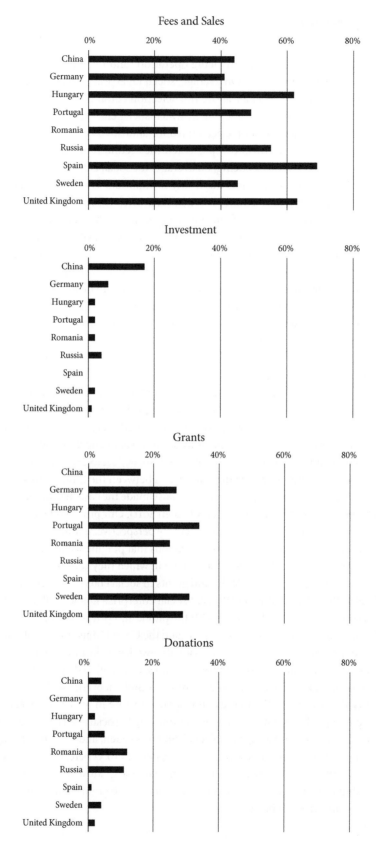

Figure 14.3 Comparison of sources of financing across countries

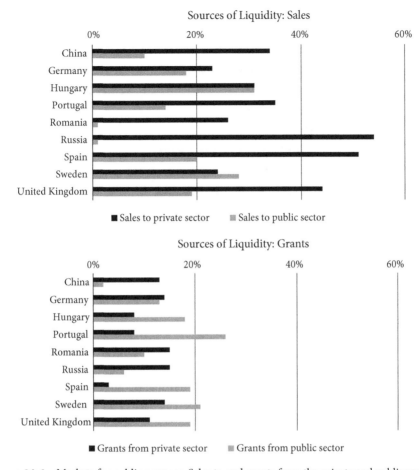

Figure 14.4 Markets for public purpose: Sales to and grants from the private and public sectors

Analyzing patterns of sales to and grants from private and public sources may help explain how social enterprises navigate the space between the public and private sectors and how this relationship changes over time.

An examination of how social enterprises interact and transact with government is especially revealing. See Figure 14.5 for an analysis of sales to and grants from governments across countries.

We found striking cross-country differences in the role that government plays in the life of social enterprises. In Hungary and Sweden, the government played a dominant role both as a buyer of social goods and services and as a provider of grants. In China and Russia, governments played a considerably reduced role. But we also found notable differences between those two countries. In China, selling to the government was more prevalent than receiving grants, whereas in Russia, the opposite pattern was evident.

Such patterns reflect not only the context in which social enterprises operate but also the priorities of governments and the range of private organizations that pursue public and social purposes. Exploring these patterns systematically and over time will help clarify

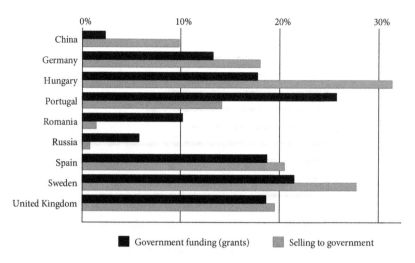

Figure 14.5   Markets for public purpose: Sales to and grants from government

the extent to which governments "use" social enterprises to outsource their obligation to address social problems. Further exploration of this kind will also help clarify the effect of austerity programs and financial crises on how social enterprises interact with governments.

Finally, these patterns need to be viewed not in isolation but in the context of how other public or private organizations address the same social problem or operate in the same problem domain.

Competing on Public Purpose

In all countries covered by our study, a variety of private and public organizations are active in social problem domains. To probe for patterns of competition among those organizations, we asked social enterprises to specify entities that provide products or services that are similar to their offering. In China, Russia, and the United Kingdom, social enterprises identified businesses as the most dominant type of competitor; in Germany, Hungary, Portugal, Romania, and Sweden, they identified nonprofit organizations; and in Spain, they identified other social enterprises. A large majority of social enterprises across all countries indicated that they did not regard government or public sector service providers as a competitor. On average, 20 percent of surveyed social enterprises reported that they did not face competition at all. This finding corroborates the view that social entrepreneurship can be understood as an activity that addresses newly arising or stubbornly persistent social problems in novel ways and by relying on unconventional business or organizing models (Seelos and Mair 2007; Mair, Battilana, and Cardenas 2012). Overall, these findings suggest the need for a more systematic assessment of the relationship between context, problem domain, and the extent of novelty or unconventionality in social enterprises (Mair, Rathert, and Huysentruyt 2018).

Seminal work by Max Weber ([1922] 1978) and Paul J. DiMaggio and Walter W. Powell (1983) identified competition as a force that fosters homogeneity among organizations that share the same purpose or operate in the same field. How do patterns of competition affect the likelihood that social enterprises will adopt the same legal form? In our sample, we detected a clear difference between social enterprises that face competition from non-profits and those that do not. When social enterprises operate in a competitive context dominated by nonprofits, they tend to be very homogenous in their choice of legal form. That context, in short, seems to create a strong bias for the adoption of a nonprofit form. Contexts marked by a high degree of competition from government are also associated with more homogeneity in the choice of legal form. When social enterprises perceive no direct competition, or when their competitive landscape is populated by organizations with a dual legal form, by for-profit entities, or by other social enterprises, the likelihood that two social enterprises will have the same legal form is much lower than it is when they operate in a nonprofit-dominated context.

Collaborating for Public Purpose

Social enterprises not only compete but also collaborate as they tackle social problems. Data from our survey reveals that collaboration with other entities is a widely shared feature of social enterprises across countries. Only 1.1 percent of social enterprises in our sample (11 out of 1,045) reported that they did not collaborate with another organization in the last twelve months. Social enterprises in Hungary and Russia reported the highest rates of collaboration. Table 14.1 shows the entities with which social enterprises collaborated in each country in our survey and indicates patterns of collaboration with the five most frequently cited partners. These patterns vary considerably across countries. In China and Russia, partnering with for-profit organizations is the preferred mode of collaborations. In Spain and the United Kingdom, social enterprises collaborate most extensively with other social enterprises. In Portugal and Sweden, partnering with local authorities is widespread.

The Social Footprint of Social Enterprises

Social enterprises are inherently social in how they work; they collaborate with other entities. Their social nature, however, is typically associated with how much impact they create—how much progress they make in addressing a specific social problem. Not surprisingly, therefore, a shared characteristic of social enterprises is that they systematically measure and report on their social performance. About 65 percent of the social enterprises in our survey track social performance, with country-level scores on this characteristic ranging from a high of 97 percent in Portugal to a low of 48 percent in Spain. The most widely used indicator to assess social performance was *number of beneficiaries or clients served*, with the exception of Sweden, where measuring *satisfaction of beneficiaries or clients* was the most prevalent indicator. The use of specific indicators also varied across countries; in China, for example, *number of volunteers* was a popular indicator, while in Portugal *number of people empowered* was used extensively. In other countries, such as Germany, most social enterprises seemed to have settled using on a repertoire of indicators that has become standard within their country.

Although recent scholarship has started to investigate social performance in different countries, including Japan and the United Kingdom (Liu, Eng, and Takeda 2015) and

Table 14.1 Patterns of collaboration by social enterprises across countries

Countries	Collaboration partner						
	Other social enterprises	Nonprofits	For-profits	Local authorities	National government	Universities	Organizational networks/alliances
China	11%	30%	34%	11%		5%	
Germany	23%	19%	17%	8%	13%		
Hungary	11%	48%	21%	11%	13%		
Portugal		38%	27%	28%		14%	13%
Romania	6%	53%	9%	17%	3%		
Russia	4%	27%	42%	14%	5%		
Spain	33%	21%	9%	12%			9%
Sweden	12%	21%	19%	22%			13%
United Kingdom	30%	24%	19%	15%			7%

Sample sizes: China: N = 102, Germany: N = 107, Hungary: N = 122, Portugal: N = 111, Romania: N = 109, Russia: N = 104, Spain: N = 125, Sweden: N = 106, United Kingdom: N = 135

France (Battilana et al. 2015), we still lack a systematic account of the range of social problems that social enterprises address as a community of organizations and how the problem domains they inhabit vary across geographies. We also have no systematic account or mapping of people and communities that benefit from social entrepreneurship. An analysis of the problem domains in which social enterprises are active and of the beneficiary patterns in different countries, therefore, can provide empirical insights that will advance our theorizing on the relationship between social enterprises and the market of public purpose.

Mapping Social Problem Domains

I concur with Howard S. Becker that it may be impossible to define what a social problem is (Becker 1966). Scholars, however, have succeeded in bringing some clarity to this question. Social problems involve harmful conditions and the people exposed to these conditions (Loseke 2003). They "have to be seen in an historical context and in a structural dimension interacting with cultural interpretations of experience" (Gusfield 1989:431). Social problems are defined collectively (Blumer 1971). The work of defining social problems occurs in public arenas "where social problems are discussed, selected, defined, framed, dramatized, packaged and presented" (Hilgartner and Bosk 1988:59). Participants in those arenas and the patterns that characterize their participation vary across cultural contexts and can include public agencies, media, courts, civil society, social movements, and religious institutions. By taking an active part in these arenas, social enterprises identify and specify social problems (Mair, Battilana, and Cardenas, 2012). Through this process, they attach meaning to social problems, make social problems salient, and amplify or diminish the halo around social problems (Mair and Rathert forthcoming).

We found that social enterprises are active in a diverse array of problem domains and that these domains vary across countries. Applying the categorization scheme of problem domains widely used by scholars to compare nonprofit organizations across countries—the

Table 14.2 Distribution of problem domains for social enterprises across countries

Countries	Culture and recreation	Education and research	Health	Social services	Environment	Development and housing
China		17%	15%		20%	
Germany		21%	15%			27%
Hungary			12%	27%		24%
Portugal		15%		22%		30%
Romania		11%		50%		20%
Russia		17%		25%	23%	
Spain	11%				22%	42%
Sweden	15%		14%			42%
United Kingdom		12%		12%		54%

Sample sizes: China: $N = 102$, Germany: $N = 107$, Hungary: $N = 122$, Portugal: $N = 111$, Romania: $N = 109$, Russia: $N = 104$, Spain: $N = 125$, Sweden: $N = 106$, United Kingdom: $N = 135$

International Classification of Nonprofit Organizations (ICNPO) (Salamon and Anheier 1997; see also Anheier, Lang, and Toepler, Chapter 30, "Comparative Nonprofit Sector Research," for a review and critique)—we observed certain domains that social enterprises inhabit in almost all countries and other domains that constituted a natural habitat for social enterprises in specific countries. Table 14.2 shows the distribution of the three most cited problem domains in each country.

Development and housing represented a prominent domain in all countries except China and Russia. Among social enterprises in Germany, Portugal, Spain, Sweden, and the United Kingdom, it constituted the most cited category. *Education and research* and *social services* were also widely cited domains in several countries. A focus on education was most pronounced in Germany, and a focus on social services was most pronounced in Romania. A focus on social services was much less pronounced in Germany, where the provision of social services is largely in the hands of six publicly funded social welfare organizations (*Wohlfahrtsverbände*) (Anheier and Salamon 2006). We found that *environment* constituted an important problem domain for social enterprises in China, Russia, and Spain but not in other countries. In all countries we studied, *health* constituted a popular domain. However, only in China, Germany, Hungary, and Sweden did *health* appear as one of the three most cited domains for social entrepreneurship. *Culture and recreation* constituted a salient domain for social enterprises only in Spain and Sweden.

Slightly more than 5 percent of the social enterprises in our sample operated in more than one of the domains identified by ICNPO. Within a given domain, however, social enterprises typically engaged in multiple activities, which in turn often involved different beneficiary groups. On average, social enterprises in our sample engaged in three to four activities. Thus, although social enterprises may not be diversified at the domain level, they are diversified in how they operate within a domain. Simply relying on domains to categorize social enterprises may mask important nuances in what they do—in particular, how they address a social problem and for whom they create impact—and thus prevent scholars from *seeing* how novel or unconventional they are. Relying solely on existing and well-vetted classification schemes such as ICNPO may also prevent scholars from advancing their knowledge base regarding the variety of private action for public purpose. In Chapter 30, "Comparative Nonprofit Sector Research," Helmut K. Anheier, Markus Lang, and Stefan Toepler make a similar point and argue for taking other perspectives on categorization—such as those promoted by schools of comparative capitalism (Hall and Soskice 2001)—more seriously. This point is important because social enterprises do not operate in a social, economic, or political vacuum. Another way to enhance comparative understanding of social enterprises is to incorporate beneficiaries into this analysis.

Identifying Beneficiaries

Research on social entrepreneurship has dedicated surprisingly little attention to the people affected by social problems. We asked social enterprises about the beneficiary groups that they target with their activities. The results show that they rarely focus on a single beneficiary group. On average, the social enterprises in our sample targeted approximately three beneficiary groups at the same time. Table 14.3 shows the distribution of the five most salient beneficiary groups in each country.

We uncovered similarities as well as important differences with respect to targeted beneficiaries across countries. *Children and youth* and *citizens* were among the top five beneficiary groups in all countries. The popularity of citizens as a target group suggests that social enterprises should be viewed as part of the "troubled persons" professions—occupations that help shape "the process by which publics experience social problems, interpret and imbue them with meaning, and create and administer public policies" (Gusfield 1989:432). This finding also suggests the need to undertake a more dedicated exploration of how social enterprises address social problems in new ways or how they identify new problems to address—in other words, how their activities are novel or unconventional.

People with disabilities constituted the most salient beneficiary group in Hungary, Romania, and Russia and were ranked as important in all countries with the exception of Germany. In Germany, almost half of all social enterprises identified either *other social organizations or enterprises* (40 percent) or *social sector practitioners* (9 percent) as an important beneficiary group. These findings highlight the importance of taking into account the historical legacy of how the provision of public goods and social welfare is organized. In Germany, social welfare provision is highly institutionalized; it is organized around six social welfare agencies that are associated with specific political and religious constituencies and are financed primarily through public funding, and these agencies are widely seen as the main or sole legitimate providers of social goods and services (see Grohs et al. 2017 for a more extensive discussion). Social enterprises in Germany therefore often become evangelists for an alternative approach to addressing social problems, and—as our findings show—they act as intermediaries (in the form of incubators for social ventures, for example) that deliberately position themselves as field builders.

Our analysis reveals several context-specific patterns that highlight the importance of situating social entrepreneurship in time and space. In China, for example, 12 percent of social enterprises targeted *left-behind/rural communities*; Russia, meanwhile, was the only country where *women* and *elderly* constituted salient target groups. In 2015, the year that

Table 14.3 Distribution of primary beneficiaries of social enterprises across countries

| | | | | | | Beneficiaries | | | | | | |
Countries	Children and youth	Citizens	Unemployed	People with disabilities	Families, parents	Other social organizations or enterprises	Social sector practitioners	People in low-income households	Women	Elderly	Migrants	Left-behind/ rural communities
China	24%	24%		11%		21%						12%
Germany	24%	23%				40%	9%	10%				
Hungary	18%	35%		36%	16%						9%	
Portugal	24%	32%		16%		18%	10%					
Romania	22%	20%		31%	9%			17%				
Russia	13%	33%		37%					3%	4%		
Spain	10%	29%	11%	21%		20%						
Sweden	33%	23%	20%	16%		12%						
United Kingdom	13%	20%		11%		25%		10%				

Sample sizes: China: N = 102, Germany: N = 107, Hungary: N = 122, Portugal: N = 111, Romania: N = 109, Russia: N = 104, Spain: N = 125, Sweden: N = 106, United Kingdom: N = 135 we conducted our survey and the year that the refugee crisis in Europe started to unfold, 9 percent of social enterprises in Hungary (an entry point to Europe for refugees who took the so-called Balkan route in 2014) cited *migrants* as an important beneficiary group. In Germany (the preferred destiny of many refugees), 6.5 percent of social enterprises cited *asylum seekers* as an important beneficiary group. Asylum seekers are not listed in Table 14.3 as they are not among the five most salient groups in Germany.

Paying close attention to beneficiaries can also help scholars analyze the impact of social enterprises as a community of organizations. In many cases, we found that beneficiaries are integrated into the service delivery of a social enterprise. As noted previously, Auticon in Germany offers IT specialist services provided by people with autism. That organization and many others in our sample create direct value for a group of disadvantaged people, but their work also has systemic implications. Around one quarter of the social enterprises in the sample train and/or employ disadvantaged or marginalized individuals and/or help them find new employment opportunities. Social enterprises that engaged in activities related to *employment and training* (14 percent of the total) served 5.66 million beneficiaries (Huysentruyt and Stephan 2017). Our data thus corroborates anecdotal evidence that suggests that social entrepreneurship can be a tool to make labor markets more inclusive (Mair 2018).

Aligning Mission and Mandate

A social mission and the pursuit of social goals are defining characteristics of organized private action for public purposes. An important discussion in the nonprofit literature focuses on when and under which conditions a social mission is compromised to a degree that results in mission drift, mission creep, or mission displacement (Weisbrod 1998). The general assumption has been that when nonprofit organizations engage in commercial activity, the likelihood that they will drift from their social mission increases (Skloot 1987; Weisbrod 2004). More recent research on social enterprises has adopted this theme and has emphasized the difficulty of pursuing social and commercial goals in parallel. The gist of this argument is that mission drift is likely to occur when a social enterprise seeks to pursue goals associated with incompatible institutional logics—a welfare logic and a business logic, for example (Besharov and Smith 2014; Pache and Santos 2013; Mair, Mayer, and Lutz 2015). Studies have shown that this tension is present in microfinance and potentially leads social enterprises in that field to drift from their social mission (Battilana and Dorado 2010).

Although current research on social enterprises identifies the duality of social and commercial goals as a source of conflict, our data suggests that social goals are not fatally compromised by commercial activity. We used three markers to assess the relationship between commercial activity and social goals. First, scores related to the pursuit of economic and social goals—which we based on interview data and on secondary reports by our research analysts—revealed that in all countries social goals were prioritized over economic goals.[8] Second, responses to one question in our survey—"If you only run your revenue generating activity, to what extent would you also generate social impact?"—yielded scores that show a strong alignment between commercial and social activities across all countries, albeit with slightly lower average scores in Hungary and Romania. And third, the fee-for-service model, which represents an integrated approach to pursuing a social goal

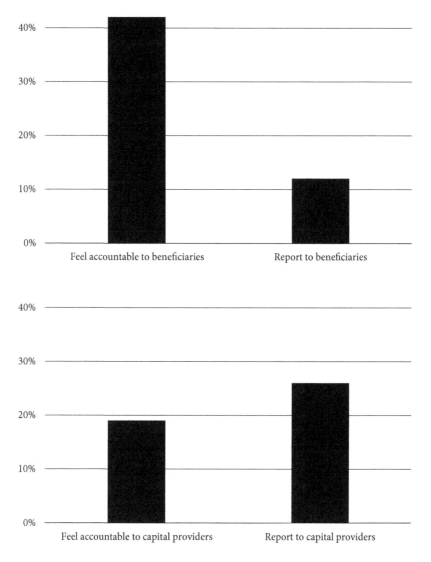

Figure 14.6 Locating sources of conflict: Accountability and reporting among social enterprises (*N* = 1,030; missing data)

while engaging in commercial activity, was the dominant model in almost every country in our survey. Only in Sweden was the service-subsidizing model (in which commercial activities are differentiated from social activities and used to finance the pursuit of social goals) slightly more prevalent than the fee-for-service model.

Although we did not discover patterns of mission drift of the kind often cited in the current literature on social enterprises, we did find that social enterprises hardly operate in a conflict-free zone. Instead of a battle between institutional logics, we detected an incongruence between mission and mandate. While the mission of a social enterprise centers on pursuing social goals and achieving impact for a specific target group, a mandate is "imposed by external bodies, be they funders, governments, or standard-setting or accreditation agencies. Such organizations frequently dictate the 'musts' a nonprofit is required to observe or practice in order to receive funding, approval, or certification" (Minkoff and Powell 2006:593). Analyzing the entities to which social enterprises must report and to which they feel accountable (Ebrahim et al. 2014) can enable scholars to capture internal and external pressures more accurately and to detect sources of misalignment between mission and mandate. Figure 14.6 illustrates this pattern of misalignment with respect to accountability and reporting relationships.

We asked social enterprises to specify the entities to which they feel accountable and the entities to which they report. Forty-two percent of the social enterprises in our sample indicated that they feel accountable to beneficiaries, and *beneficiaries* was by far the most frequently stated accountability group. Yet only 11 percent of social enterprises indicated that they report their activities to beneficiaries. The opposite pattern holds for *capital providers*; only 18 percent of social enterprises feel accountable to this group, yet 26 percent of them indicated that they report to capital providers.

External pressures from powerful resource providers seem to prevail over internal desires and shared understandings of the parties that social enterprises exist to serve. This insight holds particular interest in the context of another finding from our research; when asked which stakeholder groups were most supportive of them, social enterprises across all countries ranked *investors* as the lowest group (while ranking *community* as the highest group, followed by *media* and *authorities*). A theoretical and empirical focus on mandates may help to interrogate the role of capital provider and to bring renewed attention to power as a crucial factor in theorizing about social enterprises.

Social Enterprises as Institutional Change Agents

As I have demonstrated, our data supports the pervasive image of social enterprises as providers of goods and services to address a social problem. However, our data also sheds light on the role that social enterprises play in institutional change. Although previous qualitative work has shown how social enterprises alter formal and institutional arrangements locally (Lawrence, Hardy and Philipps 2002; Mair, Martí, and Ventresca, 2012; Lawrence and Dover 2015; Mair et al. 2016), the role of social enterprises in affecting the institutional context in which they (and the problems they tackle) are embedded has received limited systematic attention.

We asked the social enterprises in our sample about their involvement in changing legislation or influencing policy making. More specifically, we asked (1) whether their organization has changed or helped to change legislation over the past year, and (2) whether their organization has influenced or helped influence policy making over the past year. Figure 14.7 shows the result of this inquiry.

Overall, 33 percent of social enterprises claimed to have changed or helped to change legislation over the past year. (Of that group, 56 percent targeted national legislation, 21 percent targeted regional legislation, and 16 percent targeted local legislation.) In addition, 47 percent of social enterprises reported that they had influenced or helped influence policy making over the past year. (Of that group, 55 percent influenced national policy making, 24 percent influenced regional policy making, and 15 percent influenced local policy making.)

Figure 14.7 Institutional change: Social enterprises' involvement in changing legislation and influencing policy making

Our analysis revealed important differences across countries in whether and how social enterprises pursue institutional change efforts. We detected very high levels of policy-making influence in Germany and the United Kingdom but no influence at all in China. However, China, along with Hungary and Romania, scored high on effecting change in legislation. This involvement in changing legislation was particularly prevalent in certain countries with an authoritarian legacy—China, Romania, and Hungary—though not in Russia. We also found that data on involvement in legislative change is sensitive to contemporary events. In 2016, for example, China implemented the Charity Law, and this legislation allowed social organizations to move from a quasi-legal framework to a legitimate and regulated space. The social enterprises in China that we surveyed seemed to be actively involved in this process.

Our data supports perspectives that treat institutional change efforts as an integral aspect of the work of social enterprises (Mair and Ganly 2008; Dover and Lawrence 2012). The pervasiveness of such efforts among organizations in our sample runs counter to claims by commentators who exclude advocacy from the repertoire of activities that define social entrepreneurship (Martin and Osberg 2007). Interestingly, research on institutional change or social movements that focuses on organizations whose primary objective is to change the law or influence policy has largely failed to recognize the role of social enterprises as advocates of policy and legal change. Paying more attention to the latent goals (Mair et al. 2016) or hidden transcripts of social enterprises (Scott 1990) may help researchers compare and reconcile the institutional change and social delivery efforts of social enterprises. Such an approach helps forge a productive conversation about social change and is less prone to deepen ideological divides.

Continuing Research on Social Enterprises as Disciplined Exploration

The data generated by our exploration demonstrates clearly that social enterprises do not operate in an institutional vacuum. Societal, economic, and political aspects of the environment in which they operate matter for how they function, which legal form they adopt, which problems they address, and their potential to create impact. The aim of this chapter is to advance the study of social enterprises: to provide room for imaginative theorizing based on disciplined exploration and to foster dialogue across disciplinary lines. As with the ambition of Humboldt and Bonpland in their study of plants, the objective here is to embrace the diversity inherent in the phenomena under review—social enterprises, in this case—as a starting point to detect patterns (*Verflechtungen*) and possible features of a global archetype. Going forward, I see two foci of exploration that present especially promising opportunities to advance this agenda.

First, future research can investigate in more detail the relationship between legal form, problem domain, and institutional context. The outer form matters for organizations (Weber [1922] 1978), just as it does for plants (Humboldt and Bonpland 1807). For example, an examination of how legal forms are used offers an analytical framework for assessing how institutional context affects social enterprises; for revisiting the relationship between social enterprises, the market, and the state; and for generating new insights on how problem domains are governed (Seibel 2015). Using data from our study, we analyzed the likelihood that two social enterprises will adopt the same legal form if they operate in the same country and in the same problem domain. The results of that analysis, as shown in Figure 14.8, reveal the level of homogeneity in the choice of legal form across countries and problem domains.[9]

In the United Kingdom, social enterprise legal forms are fairly heterogeneous across problem domains, as indicated by the low likelihood that any two social enterprises in a domain will choose the same legal form from the range of options identified in Figure 14.1 (for-profit, nonprofit, dual, cooperative, and community interest company). In other countries, we identified important intracountry differences. In Portugal, for example, social enterprises in *health* are likely to assume the same legal form as their peer social enterprises, whereas social enterprises in *housing and development* vary more widely in their choice of legal form. Our data reveals dominant governing patterns in specific problem domains; in Hungary almost all social enterprises in *education and research* share the same legal form, and a similar pattern applies in Romania to social enterprises in *health* and (to a slightly lesser degree) to social enterprises in *social services*. How problem domains are governed differs across countries, and that difference affects the choice of legal form in ways that reflect a variety of factors, including historical legacies, the salience of a problem domain in society, political debates and party politics, and the perceived and actual magnitude of the underlying problem. Future research can probe these factors in greater detail and thereby put the study of social enterprises in active dialogue with prominent work on classifying social welfare regimes and different varieties of capitalism. The data shown in this chapter is cross-sectional, but the analysis offered here can inform future longitudinal studies that place social enterprises in the context of how societies, welfare regimes, and systems of economic order—along with their respective institutional arrangements—evolve over time (Anheier and Krlev 2014; Deeg and Jackson 2007).

Second, future research can continue the search for features that social enterprises hold in common in order to identify a global "social enterprise" archetype. Our dataset is limited to nine countries; it does not cover the United States or any other country in the Americas, nor does it cover any developing countries. However, the analysis presented

Figure 14.8 Legal form homogeneity among social enterprises across countries and problem domains

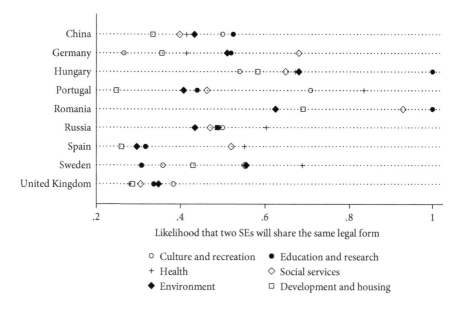

Likelihood that two SEs will share the same legal form

- ○ Culture and recreation
- ● Education and research
- + Health
- ◇ Social services
- ◆ Environment
- □ Development and housing

Table 1 Patterns of collaboration by social enterprises across countries

Countries	Collaboration partner						
	Other social enterprises	Nonprofits	For-profits	Local authorities	National government	Universities	Organizational networks/alliances
China	11%	30%	34%	11%		5%	
Germany	23%	19%	17%	8%	13%		
Hungary	11%	48%	21%	11%	13%		
Portugal		38%	27%	28%		14%	13%
Romania	6%	53%	9%	17%	3%		
Russia	4%	27%	42%	14%	5%		
Spain	33%	21%	9%	12%			9%
Sweden	12%	21%	19%	22%			13%
UK	30%	24%	19%	15%			7%

Sample sizes: China: N=102, Germany: N=107, Hungary: N=122, Portugal: N=111, Romania: N=109, Russia: N=104, Spain: N=125, Sweden: N=106, UK: N=135

(continued)

Figure 14.8 (*continued*)

Table 2 Distribution of problem domains for social enterprises across countries

	Social problem domain					
Countries	Culture and recreation	Education and research	Health	Social services	Environment	Development and housing
China		17%	15%		20%	
Germany		21%	15%			27%
Hungary			12%	27%		24%
Portugal		15%		22%		30%
Romania		11%		50%		20%
Russia		17%		25%	23%	
Spain	11%				22%	42%
Sweden	15%		14%			42%
UK		12%		12%		54%

Sample sizes: China: N=102, Germany: N=107, Hungary: N=122, Portugal: N=111, Romania: N=109, Russia: N=104, Spain: N=125, Sweden: N=106, UK: N=135

Table 3 Distribution of primary beneficiaries of social enterprises across countries

	Beneficiaries											
Countries	Children and youth	Citizens	Unemployed	People with disabilities	Families, parents	Other social organizations or enterprises	Social sector practitioners	People in low-income households	Women	Elderly	Migrants	Left-behind/rural communities
China	24%	24%		11%		21%						12%
Germany	24%	23%				40%	9%	10%				
Hungary	18%	35%		36%	16%						9%	
Portugal	24%	32%		16%		18%	10%					
Romania	22%	20%		31%	9%			17%				
Russia	13%	33%		37%					3%	4%		
Spain	10%	29%	11%	21%		20%						
Sweden	33%	23%	20%	16%		12%						
UK	13%	20%		11%		25%		10%				

Sample sizes: China: N=102, Germany: N=107, Hungary: N=122, Portugal: N=111, Romania: N=109, Russia: N=104, Spain: N=125, Sweden: N=106, UK: N=135 in this chapter reveals a number of features that characterize social enterprises across geographies. Along with a focus on social mission and the practice of revenue generation through commercial activity, our study identified the measurement of social performance and collaboration in the pursuit of public purpose as defining characteristics. Complementing the study of the outer (legal) form of social enterprises with research on internal organizational features will help identify the features of a global archetype and examine variations of that archetype more explicitly.

Humboldt and Bonpland distinguish between species of plants that grow only in certain geographies and "social species" that grow in multiple habitats. Similarly, future studies examining the repertoire of organizational features of social enterprises may detect different species of social enterprises. Research in this area will also help uncover how such species, or particular features of a species, travel across different contexts or take root only in specific contexts. Finally, combining an analysis of organizational features with a systematic analysis of problem domains and country contexts will allow for a disciplined exploration of novelty and unconventionality in the study of social enterprises. Opportunities for the empirical and theoretical study of social enterprises are numerous. The greatest potential may lie less in developing a grand theory of social enterprise than in pursuing disciplined exploration that thoroughly deploys the tools we have at hand.

15 NONPROFITS AND THE ENVIRONMENT

Using Market Forces for Social Good

Magali A. Delmas, Thomas P. Lyon, and Sean Jackson

THE ENVIRONMENT HAS TRADITIONALLY BEEN the domain of nonprofit organizations. For decades, nonprofit organizations have worked to reduce the negative impact of market-based activity on the environment. However, more recently nonprofits have started to adopt the methods and values of the market to achieve sustainability goals. One of the primary strategies that nonprofits use is to disclose, or pressure corporations to disclose, information about the environmental impact of their products and processes. These information disclosure strategies seek to help stakeholders make green purchases or invest in corporations that use green practices, thus incentivizing corporations to reduce their negative environmental impact. In this chapter, we review the benefits and the challenges encountered by nonprofits in their attempt to use information disclosure strategies.

In the United States, the end of the nineteenth century and the beginning of the twentieth century saw the creation of several environmental non-governmental organizations (NGOs).[1] For example, the Sierra Club was founded in 1892, and the Audubon Society was founded in 1905. These NGOs launched important conservation campaigns and participated in the movement that led to the creation of the U.S. National Park Service in 1916. The 1970s saw the rise of NGOs that actively mobilize citizens to take action at the state and federal levels and urge policy makers to adopt and implement strong environmental protection policies. The Environmental Defense Fund was created in 1967, the Natural Resources Defense Council was formed in 1970, and Greenpeace was founded in 1971. The birth of these NGOs coincided with the passage of important environmental legislation, including the National Environmental Policy Act, the Safe Drinking Water Act, and the Endangered Species Act, as well as the creation of the Environmental Protection Agency (EPA) and the Occupational Safety and Health Administration (OSHA). The regulatory framework that emerged from these developments allowed NGOs to lead the fight against industrial pollution by using litigation to press for enforcement. At the time, the relationship between companies and NGOs was typically one of tension and mutual distrust.

However, since then some NGOs have radically changed their strategies (Kong et al. 2002). As Michael E. Kraft (2001:141) writes, "the role of NGOs in the United States has changed significantly over the past thirty years as environmental advocacy groups moved from a posture of confrontation and adversarial relations with government and industry to one characterized by professionalism and cooperation." For example, NGOs now routinely engage in strategic collaborations with corporations to help them reduce their environmental impact (Rondinelli and London 2003). A notable example of this trend is the collaboration between McDonald's and the Environmental Defense Fund to develop more sustainable packaging (Peloza and Falkenberg 2009). This collaboration drew on complementary expertise from both the private sector and the nonprofit world to reduce the environmental footprint of packaging for McDonald's sandwiches.

NGOs are also increasing their use of information disclosure strategies as a low-cost way to exert market and legal pressure on companies. These strategies aim to inform consumers, investors, and other NGOs about the environmental attributes of products or processes in order to help these stakeholders make more-responsible market decisions. Some approaches, such as those pursued by confrontational NGOs such as Greenpeace and Rainforest Action Network (RAN) (Lyon 2012), emphasize the "naming and shaming" of heavy polluters. Other approaches set environmental performance standards and certify their achievement, often with support from third-party certification entities (Delmas and Colgan 2018). Perhaps the most prominent example of this strategy is the attempt by nonprofit organizations to influence consumptions patterns through the development of product eco-labels (Fischer and Lyon 2014).

NGOs use information disclosure strategies not only to promote green products but also to promote green practices within companies. They use investing tactics, such as shareholder resolutions (Graves, Waddock, and Rehbein 2001) and socially responsible investments (Guay, Doh, and Sinclair 2004; Delmas, Etzion, and Nairn-Birch 2013), to encourage or pressure corporations to increase their transparency and to become more environmentally sustainable. In addition, nonprofit organizations are increasingly using information disclosure strategies to support the creation of hybrid models (Delmas and Young 2009; Boyd et al. 2017) or "atypical" organizational forms (Brés, Raufflet, and Boghossian 2018) that incorporate approaches and values of the for-profit marketplace. For example, the B Corporation is a certification created by B Lab, a 501(c) nonprofit. B Lab awards B Corp status to companies that operate in a socially and environmentally responsible manner (Honeyman 2014).

Some scholars have argued that this trend toward marketization may harm democracy and citizenship by undermining nonprofit organizations' ability to create and maintain a strong civil society (Eikenberry and Kluver 2004). Others applaud this development, arguing that many governmental and philanthropic efforts have fallen short of expectations (Dees 1998) and that leveraging market forces can achieve social change on a larger scale than traditional nonprofits have been able to muster (Crutchfield and Grant 2012).

In this chapter, we review how nonprofits are using information disclosure strategies to influence corporations. These strategies differ in terms of whether they focus on individual products or on firms, and in terms of their prescriptiveness. More specifically, we discuss three types of information disclosure strategies: certification of green or socially responsible products, also called eco-labeling; codification and certification of corporate disclosure of environmental performance; and certification of different types of firm governance structure.

What Are Information Disclosure Strategies?

Information disclosure strategies have four main elements, as depicted in Figure 15.1: codification, standardization, certification, and communication. Each element pertains to information about the environmental or social impact of corporate products or practices.

First, *codification* represents the conversion of tacit knowledge into explicit knowledge. Codification of information about environmental and social performance is important because that information involves a complex phenomenon that can be interpreted and evaluated in many ways (Delmas, Etzion, and Nairn-Birch, 2013). Perhaps the best-known codification scheme is the Toxic Release Inventory, which the EPA has operated since 1988; it requires firms that emit more than a threshold level of toxic chemicals to report such emissions according to a structured process. More recently, voluntary schemes operated by NGOs have emerged, including the Global Reporting Initiative, which provides a structured process for corporate sustainability reporting, and CDP (formerly called the Carbon Disclosure Project), which provides a structured process for corporate reporting of greenhouse gas emissions and strategic responses to climate change.

Second, *standardization* involves setting environmental performance standards for participating products or organizations. Standards reflect explicitly formulated and explicitly adopted rules and thus differ from social norms, which are implicit (Brunsson, Rasche, and Seidl 2012). The International Organization for Standardization (ISO) defines a standard as a "document, established by consensus, and approved by a recognized body, that provides for common and repeated use, rules, guidelines, or characteristics for activities or their results, aimed at the achievement of the optimum degree of order in a given context" (International Organization for Standardization 2001:8). Two prominent examples of standards are those created for coffee farming by Fairtrade Labelling Organizations International (hereinafter Fairtrade) and those created for forest management by the Forest Stewardship Council (FSC).

Third, *certification* occurs when a recognized entity attests that a product or organization has met a certain standard or level of achievement. Third-party certification lends credibility to an information disclosure strategy because it provides independent monitoring that eliminates potential conflicts of interest (Delmas 2002; D'Souza, Taghian, and Lamb 2006; Jahn, Schramm, and Spiller 2005; Leire and Thidell 2005; Nilsson, Tunçer, and Thidell 2004). Most, but not all, standards set by NGOs include a certification process to ensure compliance.

Fourth, *communication* takes the form of a labeling system that conveys information to stakeholders. Labeling is typically applied to products and helps solve problems related

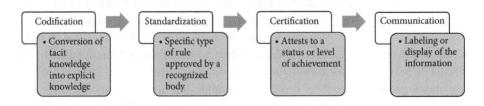

Figure 15.1   The four elements of information disclosure strategies

to information asymmetry between corporations and consumers at the point of sale (Delmas and Grant 2014.)

One typical example of an information disclosure strategy is the use of eco-labels, which signal to consumers the environmental attributes of a product. The goal of eco-labels is to provide easily interpretable information and thereby elicit increased demand for products perceived as environmentally favorable (Delmas and Grant 2014). Examples of eco-labels developed by nonprofits include the FSC label for lumber, the Marine Stewardship Council (MSC) label for food products that come from sustainable fisheries, and the Leadership in Energy and Environmental Design (LEED) label for green buildings. Although information disclosure strategies often include all four elements, nonprofits sometimes choose to use only some of them. For example, some eco-labels do not include third-party certification. And as we discuss shortly, CDP includes codification and certification but not standardization or communication (labeling).

Information disclosure strategies may include both a positive and a negative aspect—in other words, a "carrot" and a "stick" (Fleckinger, Glachant, and Moineville 2017). Such a strategy can focus on praising companies whose products or practices rise above the standard established by a nonprofit, or it can focus on shaming companies that fall below the standard. Although shaming bad performers was traditionally the more widely used tool, nonprofits now rely increasingly on praising good performers. For example, nonprofits such as Greenpeace and RAN gained renown for their aggressive media-based strategies to shame companies that engage in rainforest deforestation or that use nonsustainable palm oil (Coombs 2014; Copeland and Smith 2014). In these cases, the objective was to boycott products or practices that nonprofits judged to be undesirable. Praising good performance proves to be a little more challenging, because praise can increase demand and hence increase the total environmental footprint associated with that performance (Feddersen and Gilligan 2001; Baron and Diermeier 2007). In addition, it is easier to screen out unacceptable practices than to decide on which practices are acceptable.

Information disclosure strategies can be defined as a type of governance, or as "a social function centered on efforts to guide or steer societies toward collectively beneficial outcomes and away from outcomes that are collectively harmful" (Delmas and Young 2009:6). These strategies can be useful for addressing environmental problems that are difficult to solve in a regulatory context—for example, because they involve international externalities that cross jurisdictional boundaries. Theory and empirical evidence both suggest that information disclosure strategies can lead to improved environmental performance by increasing (1) consumer awareness of a firm's environmental performance, (2) a firm's liability under legal statutes, (3) pressure from investors and/or employees to report a firm's pollution abatement, and (4) a firm's susceptibility to community coercion (Delmas, Montes-Sancho, and Shimshack 2010; Kirchhoff 2000; Maxwell, Lyon, and Hackett 2000; Reid and Toffel 2009; Roe et al. 2001).

Nonprofits are not the only entities to develop information disclosure strategies. Governments and industry or trade associations use these strategies as well, either independently or in collaboration with nonprofits. Governments have traditionally been the main source of information about the environmental or social performance of firms or products. For example, the EPA publishes information on chemical and toxic substances that are manufactured in, or imported into, the United States (Hamilton 1995). However, nonprofits are now increasingly taking the lead in performing such functions (Vandenbergh and Raker 2017), either independently or through multistakeholder organizations. For example, the MSC is an organization that brings together actors from the for-profit sector, civil society, and the public (Chiroleu-Assouline and Wijen, forthcoming).

Because NGO-led certification systems do not rely on government for rule-making authority but instead derive their authority from stakeholders who choose whether to demand products that receive certification, Benjamin Cashore (2002), together with his colleagues Graeme Auld and Deanna Newsom (2004a), refers to these systems as *non-state market driven* (NSMD). Others refer to these systems as a form of *private regulation*: in other words, they are a governance system formed by a coalition of nongovernment actors to codify and monitor the conduct of private entities (Bartley 2007; Büthe 2010, Mayer and Gereffi 2010).

Although policies for corporate disclosure or product labeling backed by government coercion require compliance by all market actors, systems of product labeling developed by nonprofits are voluntary and allow market actors to adopt or ignore labeling requirements as they see fit. This distinction raises questions about the effectiveness of voluntary disclosure strategies, and we will address these questions more fully in the following sections. For now, we note that in principle, voluntary disclosure can be sufficient to induce full disclosure of information if the receivers of information (such as consumers or investors) assume that a failure to disclose indicates poor performance (Milgrom and Roberts 1986). However, a failure to disclose may not be perceived as dispositive if disclosure is costly (Verrecchia 1983) or if there is a possibility that the sender of information (such as a certification body) is not fully informed (Shin 2003). Thus, one should expect that voluntary disclosure will generally be less effective than mandatory disclosure.

We turn now to a discussion of specific nonprofit-led information disclosure strategies, beginning with product eco-labels.

Information Disclosure Strategies to Influence Product Environmental Impact

Over the past two decades, product eco-labels have become increasingly common. Eco-labeling is a voluntary method of codification, standard setting, certification, and communication that focuses on the environmental or social performance of products. The objective of eco-labels is to reduce an information asymmetry between producers and consumers of green products by providing credible information about a product's environmentally responsible attributes (Crespi and Marette 2005). Typically, consumers have limited access to information that would help them accurately assess invisible product attributes such as social and environmental performance. Eco-labels can prompt informed purchasing choices by environmentally responsible consumers (Leire and Thidell 2005:1062) without resorting to regulation.

For example, the FSC, an international multistakeholder nonprofit organization, issues an eco-label for wood products that have met FSC criteria.[2] Products bearing this label originate from a forest that an independent, third-party organization has determined to be well managed. The FSC requires a chain-of-custody certification before a product can be labeled as FSC-certified. This certification mandates the tracking of a wood product

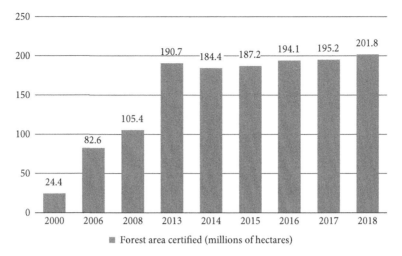

Figure 15.2 Forest area certified by the FSC, 2000–2018
Source: https://ic.fsc.org/en/facts-and-figures.

from forest to consumer, providing an audit trail to ensure that the product came from a sustainably managed forest. As of January 2018, some two hundred million hectares in eighty-six countries were certified as compliant with the FSC's Principles and Criteria—an amount that marked a 200 percent increase over the preceding ten years. (See Figure 15.2.)[3]

Another example is Fairtrade coffee. Scholars have shown that the Fairtrade eco-label contributes direct and indirect benefits to small-scale farmers, their families, and their communities by improving children's education and home quality and by lowering debt (Murray, Raynolds, and Taylor 2003; Jaffee 2007; Bacon et al. 2008; Utting-Chamorro 2005). By 2007, Fairtrade had certified 62,219 metric tons of coffee and had attained the biggest market share for a socially responsible coffee standard. By the end of 2016, there were 1,411 Fairtrade-certified producer organizations in 73 countries, representing more than 1.66 million Fairtrade farmers and workers (Fairtrade International, 2016).[4] In 2016, Fairtrade-certified sales amounted to approximately €7.88 billion worldwide, a total that represented a 485 percent increase from 2006. (See Figure 15.3.)[5]

According to the Ecolabel Index directory, the number of eco-label programs has grown from a mere dozen worldwide in the 1990s to more than 460 today. Moreover, these programs now span 199 countries and 25 industry sectors.[6] But this growth has been accompanied by consumer confusion and organizational skepticism. For example, consumers have admitted to difficulties in recognizing the differences among eco-labels for coffee, of which there are now at least six (Delmas and Clements 2017). In early 2012, the British supermarket chain Tesco PLC dropped the United Kingdom's Carbon Trust label, citing the label's prohibitively high costs and minimal consumer recognition (Quinn 2012). However, there is no denying that both the overall value of eco-products and the recognition of certain eco-labels are growing. For example, in the United States, retail sales of organic foods increased from $3.8 billion in 1997 to $40 billion in 2017.[7] Moreover, nearly four out of five U.S. households recognize the Energy Star label, which is a joint project

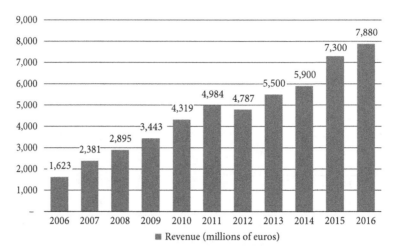

Figure 15.3 Revenue of Fairtrade International products worldwide, 2006–2016
Source: https://www.statista.com/statistics/271354/revenue-of-fair-trade-products-worldwide-since-2004/.

of the EPA and the U.S. Department of Energy (EPA 2010). In fact, American consumers have purchased more than one billion Energy Star–labeled products (EPA 2012). What might explain such variations in value and recognition? Why are consumers drawn to certain eco-labels more than others?

The efficacy of eco-labels as a policy tool to achieve environmental and social objectives has been the subject of considerable scholarly research. This literature has focused on single eco-labels (Albersmeier, Schulze, and Spiller 2009), on how eco-labels are perceived by consumers (Botanaki et al. 2005; Batte et al. 2007, Loureiro and Lotade 2005; Leire and Thidell 2005), on consumers' inclination to change their purchasing behavior in favor of eco-labels (Loureiro 2003; Blamey et al. 2000), on the environmental and social benefits of eco-labels (Blackman and Rivera 2011), and on how institutional context facilitates or hinders the effectiveness of eco-labels (Utting-Chamorro 2005; Utting 2009). Broadly speaking, this research shows that consumer awareness and understanding of eco-labels, the credibility in those labels, and consumer willingness to pay for an eco-labeled product all favor the diffusion of eco-labels (Leire and Thidell 2005; Delmas, Nairn-Birch, and Balzarova 2013). It also shows that these strategies do not operate in an institutional vacuum. We review these elements in more detail in the following sections.

Consumer Awareness and Understanding

Environmental products are credence goods, which means that it is difficult for consumers to assess the validity of certain claims made about their environmental quality. Eco-labels are a tool for conveying information about environmental or social impact (Anderson and Hansen 2004) and, in particular, for reducing the search costs related to that information (Teisl, Roe, and Hicks 2002). If an eco-label is to successfully reduce information search costs, consumers need to have awareness and understanding of the eco-label. Awareness involves the extent to which consumers know about the existence of an eco-label program (Banerjee and Solomon 2003:109). Understanding involves consumers' ability to interpret the connection between an environmental issue, a label's meaning, and the actions taken by the eco-label program to mitigate the issue (Banerjee and Solomon 2003:109).

For example, by 2004, public awareness of the Fairtrade label was reported to be at 63 percent in Luxembourg, 50 percent in the United Kingdom, 44 percent in Ireland, and 39 percent in Sweden (Krier 2007). A phone survey in 2008 found that 48 percent of Canadian respondents and 36 percent of U.S. respondents were somewhat or very familiar with the Fairtrade label. The same survey found that 71 percent of Canadians and 62 percent of Americans were somewhat or very familiar with organic labels (Feinberg et al. 2008). Taken as a whole, this data indicates that Fairtrade has done well in raising awareness among consumers (Auld 2010).

Consumer awareness is a necessary factor in the success of an eco-label scheme, but consumers must also be able to understand the environmental information conveyed by each label and how this information may vary across certification programs. Research shows that only 20 percent of coffee consumers have a good understanding of the organic coffee eco-label, and a much smaller share of consumers have a good understanding of competing coffee eco-labels, including those provided by RAN, Bird Friendly, Fairtrade, and UTZ (Delmas and Clements 2017).

Credibility

The credibility of the eco-labeling process is also essential to facilitating consumer confidence in eco-labels and consumers' willingness to purchase eco-labeled products. Credibility can be defined as the perception, or assumption, that the operations of an actor or agent are trustworthy, responsible, desirable, and appropriate (Cashore et al. 2004b).[8]

Eco-labels take different forms. In some cases, they are issued by independent organizations that develop transparent environmental criteria and use third-party verification. In other cases, they merely represent claims by manufacturers to be environmentally friendly in some way (Ibanez and Grolleau 2008). The presence of the second type of eco-label may produce confusion about credibility in the minds of consumers. Unsubstantiated claims can result in adverse selection; if producers provide false or misleading information about environmental attributes and underlying production practices, consumers may choose products that do not, in fact, have the attributes claimed by that type of eco-label (Grodsky 1993; Ibanez and Grolleau 2008).

There is some evidence that the profusion of eco-labels creates confusion among customers about the goals, credibility, and expected benefits of an eco-label, and that this confusion has an adverse impact on the success or adoption rate of an eco-label (Leire and Thidell 2005; Delmas and Lessem 2017; Harbaugh, Maxwell, and Roussillon 2011). This confusion can inhibit the benefits that the eco-labels seek to achieve.

To be credible, eco-label programs should be transparent, nondeceptive, free from conflicts of interest, accepted by stakeholders, and based on reliable assessment procedures (Bass and Simula 1999). This set of attributes can be achieved for any given eco-label standard by satisfying the following elements of standard governance: stringency, stakeholder involvement, third-party certification, and transparency.

Stringency. An eco-label's credibility depends on whether its standard is stringent enough to signal exemplary environmental performance. Consumers will quickly lose confidence in a label that fails to differentiate poor performance from good performance. The contrast between the labeling schemes implemented by the Programme for the Endorsement of Forest Certification (PEFC), the Sustainable Forestry Initiative (SFI), and the FSC helps illustrate the concept of stringency. PEFC and SFI are widespread schemes that do not require a minimum level of performance among participants. The FSC, meanwhile, mandates specific levels of performance.[9] In 2001, an environmental organization called Forest-Ethics attacked SFI for its lack of stringency and described the label as a "green façade."[10] As a consequence, seven companies—including four Fortune 500 corporations (Aetna, Allstate, Office Depot, and Symantec)—said they would phase out their use of the label.

Stakeholder involvement. Stakeholder involvement is a key component of the credibility of eco-labels (Leire and Thidell 2005). For example, this element has been a fundamental principle of the development of FSC standards. The FSC claims that its process for developing standards is clear and accessible, that no stakeholder interest dominates that process, and that all interested stakeholders take part in the process (FSC 2007). The FSC board of directors includes representatives from environmental NGOs, rural development agencies, human rights and worker organizations, and industry groups, as well as consumers of forest products (Gerez Fernández and Alatorre Guzman 2003). The FSC's global standards are developed and modified through a participatory process involving environmental, social, and economic stakeholders, and those standards provide a framework for developing specific standards for different regions, countries, or ecosystems (Counsell and Loraas 2002; Freris and Laschefeski 2001).

When an eco-label scheme does not involve all representative stakeholders in its design and operations, it can be criticized for its lack of independence from a specific group of stakeholders. For example, the MSC was launched as a collaboration between Unilever, the world's largest purchaser of frozen food, and the World Wide Fund for Nature (WWF), an international conservation organization. This exclusive relationship caused much controversy because it failed to involve a wide range of stakeholders in the design and implementation of the label (Constance and Bonanno 2000). To strengthen its independence and fend off assertions that it was a puppet of WWF and Unilever, the MSC was restructured as a fully independent nonprofit organization in 1999 (Cummins 2004).

Third-party certification. Third-party certification is "a procedure by which a third party provides written assurance that a product, process or service conforms to specified standards, on the basis of an audit conducted to agreed procedures" (Bass, Markopoulous, and Grah 2001). For example, the MSC certification program accredits independent entities that assess fisheries against the standard that the MSC has developed (Potts and Howard 2007). Third-party certification has been shown to be the most effective mechanism for guaranteeing not only improved environmental or social performance (Blackman and Rivera 2011) but also credibility in the eyes of consumers (Leire and Thidell 2005).

Transparency. Transparency represents the ability of external parties to access information regarding the sustainability and governance practices adopted by an eco-label scheme. For example, consumers should be able to trace green products through a *transparent chain of custody*. The FSC standard maintains a chain-of-custody system that tracks timber from an original FSC-certified forest to its purchase by consumers. It requires certification bodies to make their reports on forest management audits and their risk assessments of Controlled Wood publicly available on the Internet. In contrast, PEFC only provides public summaries of audit reports and suffers from weaknesses in its reporting and auditing process (Auld and Gulbrandsen 2009).

In conclusion, consumer confidence in the credibility of an eco-label can be enhanced by stringency in the use of environmental or social criteria, involvement of representative stakeholders, third-party certification, and transparency about the certification process. Yet even with high levels of consumer awareness and understanding, credibility may not be enough to ensure that a label will increase sales of product. Another important challenge for an eco-label involves the willingness of consumers to pay a premium for eco-labeled products.

Willingness to Pay

Eco-labeled products often carry a price premium because of the additional cost associated with meeting environmental or social standards. This price premium represents both the cost of certification to an eco-label and the cost of changes associated with improved performance. For example, studies show that these additional costs range between 15 percent and 30 percent for organic wine certification (Delmas, Doctori, and Shuster 2006). Consumers must be willing to pay such costs in order for the eco-label to thrive.

Some research suggests that few people are willing to pay a premium to advance the environmental or social impact of a product (Vogel 2005). For example, in the ten years since forest certification first emerged, many producers of certified wood have failed to receive a price premium for their products (Wilson, Takahashi, and Vertinsky 2001; Anderson and Hansen 2004). In some cases, to be sure, altruistic customers may purchase eco-labeled products as a substitute for donations to an environmental organization (Kotchen 2005). However, such altruistic customers may represent only a small percentage of all consumers. Indeed, research shows that genuinely altruistic, "true blue green" customers represent just 9 percent of the population (Roper Organization and Johnson Wax 1990).

Recent research indicates that consumers are more likely to purchase green products if those products provide additional private benefits (Delmas and Colgan 2018). Green products have been defined as an "impure public good" because they yield both public and private benefits (Cornes and Sandler 1996; Ferraro, Uchida, and Conrad 2005; Kotchen 2005). Maria K. Magnusson and her colleagues (2001) found that the most important purchasing criteria for organic products were related to private benefits, such as quality, rather than environmental attributes.

Another private benefit commonly associated with green products concerns their health attributes. Many consumers assume that organic foods not only taste better but also provide greater health benefits than their conventionally grown counterparts (Huang 1996; Huang and Lin 2007; Jolly and Norris 1991). In some cases, that assumption is valid. Cows that produce milk certified as organic by the U.S. Department of Agriculture, for example, are not exposed to the kinds of carcinogenic hormones, antibiotics, and pesticides that are used in conventional dairy practices.[11] Several studies show that health concerns, along with environmental concerns, are a major reason why people choose organic food products (Davies, Titterington, and Cochrane 1995; Tregear, Dent, and McGregor 1994; Wandel and Bugge 1997).

Additional motivations to purchase green products include conspicuous consumption and peer pressure. Research shows that visibly prosocial actions act as a signal of virtue, creating a positive reputation for those who take such actions. Psychologists have found that having such a reputation allows consumers to obtain a number of nonmarket goods, such as trust (Barclay 2004), friends, allies, romantic partners (Griskevicius et al 2007; Miller 2009), and leadership positions (Hardy and Van Vugt 2006). In a context where purchasing green products or exhibiting green behavior is the norm, social pressure can reinforce an individual's desire to purchase a green vehicle (Kahn 2007) or an eco-labeled product. Similarly, Charles J. Corbett and Suresh Muthulingam (2007) show that the adoption of LEED certification is related to signaling behavior; an organization that pursues that label aims to communicate something about its practices to other parties, including regulators, customers, and the public.

In summary, although consumers may wish to buy green products, the price premium for doing do is a strong deterrent. Their willingness to pay for green products is typically rooted not in altruism but in the private benefits that these products provide or in the status that comes with purchasing such products (Delmas and Colgan 2018).

In addition, the effectiveness of eco-labels will vary according to the institutional and economic environment in which they operate. For example, Karla Utting-Chamorro (2005) studied the effectiveness of Fairtrade in Nicaragua and concluded that the ability of that eco-label scheme to significantly raise living standards for small coffee producers was limited by factors such as the debt problems faced by cooperatives, a lack of government support, and volatile international coffee prices. We will address this point in more detail in the conclusion.

Summary
In this section, we have reviewed the literature on eco-labels to evaluate the efficacy of eco-label schemes with respect to three elements: consumer awareness and understanding, credibility, and willingness to pay. These elements vary widely across eco-labels, and even the most prominent eco-labels have achieved only limited consumer awareness and acceptance. Thus, they are no substitute for government regulation. Still, they can help promote environmental improvement efforts that go beyond the level required by regulation. (In some cases, of course, regulation is absent.)

Information Disclosure Strategies to Influence Corporate Practices
Nonprofits also use information disclosure strategies to encourage socially responsible practices at the firm level. For example, the Global Reporting Initiative (GRI) offers guidelines to assist firms with reporting systems. GRI is an international, independent organization that helps businesses, governments, and other organizations understand—and communicate information about—their performance in areas such as climate change, human rights, and corruption. Like the international environmental management standard ISO 14001, the GRI framework enables third parties to assess the environmental impact

of a company's direct activities, as well as activities in its supply chain. The GRI guidelines include reporting criteria on energy, biodiversity, and emissions. Over nine thousand organizations currently report with GRI.[12]

Another example is CDP (formerly the Carbon Disclosure Project), a nonprofit organization that aims to induce companies to disclose their exposure to risks associated with climate change and to improve their preparedness for such risks. In this section, we describe how CDP has become a prominent and influential institution that shapes the ways corporations report on their carbon emissions. We review the literature to understand the drivers of participation in CDP, the quality of the information disclosed through CDP, and the effectiveness of the CDP program. This example allows us to contrast the design of firm-level disclosure strategies with that of product-level disclosure strategies.

Although it is a nonprofit, CDP has secured primary support from a group of more than eight hundred institutional investors with more than $100 trillion in assets as of 2018. These investors include Bank of America, BlackRock, California Public Employees' Retirement System (CalPERS), Goldman Sachs, and Morgan Stanley, among others. Since 2002, CDP has asked the world's largest companies every year to complete a detailed questionnaire that covers their greenhouse gas (GHG) emissions, along with the risks, opportunities, and management strategies associated with those emissions. CDP publicly discloses company responses on its website, presumably in the hope that publicizing this information will affect investment behavior.

Investors have expressed concern over the financial risks to which companies might be exposed because of climate change. Two types of financial risk contribute to this concern. One type involves the direct effects of changing weather patterns and rising sea levels. The other type involves the effects of regulation, such as increased exposure to abatement and liability costs.

In addition, there are important philosophical issues related to defining the emissions that a firm must report. So-called Scope 1 emissions come directly from a firm's own facilities, and there is no dispute that these emissions can be attributed to the producing firm. Scope 2 emissions are indirectly associated with production processes; the most common example involves emissions generated from the electricity used by a manufacturing firm. There is some controversy over whether these emissions should be attributed to the manufacturer, or whether they should be attributed solely to the electricity producer. Scope 3 emissions emerge during the use of a product itself, as when a consumer drives an emission-producing vehicle. These emissions also engender considerable controversy over proper attribution (Matisoff, Noonan, and O'Brien 2013). CDP only requires that Scope 1 emissions be reported, although it encourages reporting of other types of emissions as well.

Participation in CDP has grown rapidly. The first cycle of the project (CDP1) was endorsed by 35 institutional investors with $4.5 trillion in assets, and results were made public on February 17 2003. Among companies on the FT Global 500 list, 71 percent responded to the CDP1 questionnaire and 45 percent answered it in full. Since then, both the number of institutional investors who have endorsed CDP and the questionnaire response rate have steadily increased. By the fourth cycle (CDP4), the project had been endorsed by 225 institutional investors with more than $31 trillion in assets. The CDP4 results, which were made public on September 18, 2006, showed that among FT Global

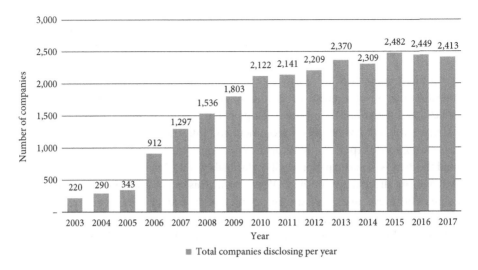

Figure 15.4 Number of companies disclosing to CDP, 2003–2017
Source: https://www.cdp.net/en/scores-2017.

500 companies, 91 percent responded to the questionnaire and 72 percent answered it in full (Kim and Lyon 2011b). By 2017, more than 2,500 unique companies were participating in CDP. (See Figure 15.4.)[13]

Researchers have explored four main questions about CDP. First, they have studied the factors that make one firm more likely than another to participate in CDP. Second, they have studied the impact of CDP participation on share prices using event study methods. Third, they have studied the impact of CDP participation on environmental performance. Fourth, they have studied the quality of the disclosures made to CDP and the usefulness of information in CDP reports.

Drivers of Participation

Participation in CDP is voluntary, in that it is not mandated by law. Still, pressure from activists, investors, and other stakeholders, as well as media coverage, may influence which firms decide to participate. Moreover, internal characteristics of firms, such as the nature of their leadership team, might influence decisions to participate.

Erin M. Reid and Michael W. Toffel (2009) found that firms were more likely to participate in CDP if they or others in their industry faced shareholder resolutions or threats of state regulation. Ben W. Lewis, Judith L. Walls, and Glen W. S. Dowell (2014) found that firms led by newly appointed CEOs or by CEOs with MBA degrees are more likely to respond to CDP, while those led by CEOs with law degrees are less likely to respond. Walid Ben-Amar, Millicent Chang, and Philip McIlkenny (2017) found that for a sample of publicly listed Canadian firms over the period 2008–2014, the likelihood of CDP participation increased with the percentage of women serving on a firm's board of directors. Dayuan Li and his colleagues (2018) found that Chinese firms are more likely to participate in CDP if they are large, if they have received more-favorable media treatment on environmental issues, and if they hold environment-related patents.

Stock Market Impact of Participation

One would expect firms' voluntary participation in CDP to be associated with higher share prices. Such participation, in other words, functions as a signal of superior environmental performance, and hence would be expected to positively affect a firm's stock price—relative to the stock prices of nonparticipants—around the date of CDP disclosure.

Beyond the direct effect of disclosure, one might also expect CDP participation to have an indirect effect on shareholder value by moderating the impact of external shocks. Indeed, the empirical literature suggests that investors view firms with more-extensive prior disclosures as being better prepared for possible future environmental regulations. Rationality-based stock valuation models suggest that a firm's share price is the present value of expected cash flows, discounted at the appropriate rate of return. A regulatory threat has a potentially negative effect on a firm's expected cash flows because it raises the possibility of future regulatory costs associated with compliance, payment of penalties, or liability. Those costs, in turn, would decrease the firm's expected future cash flows. Thus, when the threat of regulation increases, investors may take a more favorable view of firms that are better prepared to cope with environmental regulation.

Kim and Lyon (2011b) found no systematic evidence that CDP participation during the period 2003–2006, in and of itself, directly increased share prices. Consistent with the work of Reid and Toffel (2009), this finding suggests that participation was not entirely voluntary but was the result of pressure from shareholders, regulators, and institutional investors involved in CDP. (Profit-maximizing firms normally take actions to increase profits. If participation was a voluntary decision, presumably it would increase profits, but this did not occur.) However, Kim and Lyon also examine indirect effects of CDP participation—that is, the possibility that CDP participation buffered the firm from the impact of exogenous events on share prices. In particular, the share prices of CDP participants were less affected by exogenous events (e.g., Russia's ratification of the Kyoto Protocol on October 22 2004) that caused the likelihood of environmental regulation to rise. The authors estimate that this buffering effect had a value of $8.6 billion, or about 86 percent of the size of the carbon market in 2005.

Su-Yol Lee and colleagues (2015) studied a sample of Korean firms that participated in CDP in 2008 and 2009, and they found that participants saw their share prices drop. However, this effect was mitigated if a firm had released its carbon news periodically through the media in advance of its CDP disclosure. These findings are consistent with several other studies, which show that voluntary disclosure of carbon emission reductions lowers share prices (Jacobs, Singhal, and Subramanian 2010; Fisher-Vanden and Thorburn 2011; Lyon et al. 2013).

However, Ella Mae Matsumura, Rachna Prakash, and Sandra C. Vera-Muñoz (2014) studied CDP data from 2006 to 2008 and found that participants saw their share prices rise, although this benefit decreased as the level of reported emissions increased. Patrick J. Callery and Jessica Perkins (2017) found evidence that among firms that choose to disclose carbon management strategy and their carbon emissions performance, those that achieve higher performance scores from CDP attain higher capital market value.

Overall, the evidence suggests that firms receive little direct financial benefit from participating in CDP. Evidence is stronger that CDP participation can buffer a firm against losses from increased regulatory threats. Moreover, exactly how a firm reports its CDP disclosure makes a difference in how the market responds. Reporting regularly on performance via the media and providing details on a firm's carbon management strategy enhance investors' response to a firm's carbon disclosure.

Environmental Impact of Participation

Models of voluntary disclosure suggest that CDP participants are most likely to be firms that already have better environmental performance than nonparticipants (Milgrom 1981; Verrecchia 1983; Shin 2003). However, if participation is not voluntary—if it results from pressure by concerned stakeholders—firms with poorer environmental performance may be more likely to participate than those with better performance. One might also expect that participation in CDP would have a direct effect on environmental performance, because participation makes it easier for external stakeholders to obtain data about firm performance and hence to apply pressure for improvement.

The environmental impact of participation is obviously important but has received little research attention. However, Daniel C. Matisoff (2013) studied the first four years of CDP 2003–2007, and found that corporate participation in the project had no impact on plant-level carbon emissions, emissions intensity, or industrial output.

Quality of Disclosures

Although CDP provides participants with a structured questionnaire, it may be possible for a firm to manipulate its reporting so as to greenwash its image—to make its performance look greener than it really is (Delmas and Montes-Sancho 2010; Lyon and Maxwell 2011). One way a firm can improve its appearance is by limiting its reporting to cover only Scope 1 emissions. Another way is by manipulating how it responds to the portion of the CDP questionnaire that allows for unstructured, long-form answers.

Matisoff and his colleagues (2013) found that over the period 2003–2010, reporting of Scope 2 emissions had improved but the transparency and quality of reporting on direct (Scope 1) emissions and Scope 3 emissions had not. During that period, Japanese and European Union firms had increased transparency, while American firms had decreased transparency. Energy-intensive industries had either increased transparency or remained the same, while less energy-intensive industries had become less transparent. Chonnikarn Jira and Michael W. Toffel (2013) studied Scope 2 emissions and found that suppliers are more likely to share climate impact information when buyers' requests for such information are more prevalent, when buyers appear to be committed to using such information, when suppliers belong to more-profitable industries, and when suppliers are located in countries with greenhouse gas regulations.

Kira Fabrizio and Eun-Hee Kim (2016) found that firms vary widely in terms of the readability of the open-ended section of their CDP reports. These researchers also found that on average, the performance score awarded by CDP does not predict subsequent environmental performance, at least as measured by a firm's Scope 1 emissions. However, in the case of reports with higher readability scores, the CDP performance score does predict subsequent performance. Callery and Perkins (2017) studied ways in which participants can manipulate the structured portions of the CDP questionnaire and found that many participants provide misleading disclosures in an attempt to maximize scores while avoiding substantive performance improvements. The most egregious form of this practice occurs when firms claim reduced emissions over time, even though the absolute level of emissions they report is higher than the level they reported in previous years. (This is the same type of strategic disclosure behavior identified by Kim and Lyon (2011a), who also show that many firms claimed emissions reductions even when their actual level of emissions increased over time.) This type of manipulation is less common among firms that obtained third-party assurance of their reports. Happily, there is evidence that CDP's evaluation of firm performance is usually not distorted by greenwashing techniques of this kind.

Summary

CDP has become a prominent and influential nonprofit institution that shapes how corporations report on their carbon emissions. Most large companies now feel compelled to report to CDP on their emissions, the risks that climate change poses for their financial performance, and the steps they are taking to minimize those risks. This development has certainly increased awareness of the importance of climate change within the business sector. In addition, since "what gets measured gets managed," one would expect CDP participation to result in better management of greenhouse gas emissions. Research shows that participation in CDP is driven by both external stakeholder pressures and internal corporate characteristics. Participation does not appear to have strong direct financial benefits, but it may help buffer a firm against external shocks that increase the risk of regulation. Unfortunately, participation alone does not appear to lead to improved environmental performance. However, companies that provide higher-quality reports to CDP do appear to reduce their emissions in subsequent years.

Information Disclosure Strategies to Influence Firm Governance Structures

Nonprofits have begun to use information disclosure strategies to change the governance of for-profit organizations in order to encourage them to internalize environmental and social costs. In particular, they are fostering the adoption of hybrid organizational forms that embed social purpose within a business enterprise (Doherty, Haugh, and Lyon 2014). Like other information disclosure strategies, this approach involves standard setting, certification, and labeling. However, it applies those practices not to a single product but to an entire organization—which is a much more complex undertaking.

Social enterprises are a prominent example of a hybrid form. They combine the kind of purpose-driven organizing that characterizes nonprofits with a revenue-generating mechanism that can enable financial independence and scalability. In doing so, they incorporate two potentially conflicting logics: that of the for-profit corporation, which seeks to capitalize on market opportunities to maximize profit, and that of the nonprofit, which seeks to harness financial resources to achieve social or environmental benefits. Social enterprises belong to what some refer to as the "social economy" and represent a departure from a purely capitalistic model. Some observers argue that hybrid social enterprises have the potential to achieve social change on a grander scale than nonprofits can achieve because they have a looser constraint on attracting resources than nonprofits do (Crutchfield and Grant 2012).

Benefit corporations are the most common legal structure for social enterprise in the United States, and they are growing significantly in number (Cooney et al. 2014). The structure was initially developed by B Lab, a Philadelphia-based nonprofit that was founded in 2008. B Lab oversees the Certified B Corp certification for socially minded corporations. The certification was crafted in the style of LEED or Fairtrade, but it applies to companies that operate in a socially and environmentally responsible manner (Honeyman 2014). B Lab assesses a company's net social and environmental impact using an extensive evaluation framework called the B Impact Assessment. Organizations receiving an overall score of 80 or more are eligible for the certification. As part of its advocacy of social enterprise, B Lab has lobbied for legislation to form a legal structure that fills a niche between 501(c) nonprofit designation and the traditional C corporation. As of 2018, thirty-three U.S. states offered legal "benefit corporation" status.

B Lab has a standardized certification process that allows for comparison across sectors. Indeed, all B Corps are audited through a somewhat similar process. Although the version of B Impact Assessment that a company uses depends on its region, industry, and size, most of the questions on the assessment are common to all versions. This similarity across industry, region, and size allows researchers to examine the social performance of B Corps across a broad cross-section of the economy. B Corp certification is transparent and gives researchers access to a wide range of information. B Lab has posted most of its impact reports on its website, thereby enabling site visitors to evaluate the performance of any B Corp. B Lab also recently open-sourced a dataset of assessment scores on the website https://data.world (an open-data resource that focuses on B Corps).

Much of the current empirical research on social enterprise domains focuses on B Corps. In the introduction to a 2018 special edition of the *Journal of Business Venturing* that focuses on this structure, Peter W. Moroz and his colleagues (2018) lay out several reasons for the growing research interest in B Corps: "[B Corps] provide a rich backdrop in the field of entrepreneurship with respect to how prosocial opportunities are formed, and the factors that moderate how they endure and change over time" (Moroz et al. 2018).

The original nineteen B Corps were certified in May 2007. As of May 2018, the B Corp community had grown to encompass more than 2,250 companies. (See Figure 15.5.)

Growth in the number of B Corps has been driven by a few factors. For one thing, B Corps have received an increasing amount of media attention (Cao, Gehman, and Grimes 2017). Additionally, as industry-leading companies like Patagonia and Ben and Jerry's have continued to renew their B Corp status, they have lent authenticity to the certification. Additionally, the passage of benefit corporation legislation in many jurisdictions has conferred social and cultural legitimacy on the brand. These factors in combination create a positive feedback loop around B Corp certification, and given a decrease in the availability of alternative hybrid forms (Cooney et al. 2014), B Corp certification is increasingly becoming a "focal point" for socially minded entrepreneurs (Robson 2015).

B Lab has grown in part by tapping into existing communities of social enterprises that enable it to expand into new regions. As of 2018, seven B Lab partners were operating in fifty-eight countries. These partners included Sistema B in Latin America, B Lab Europe

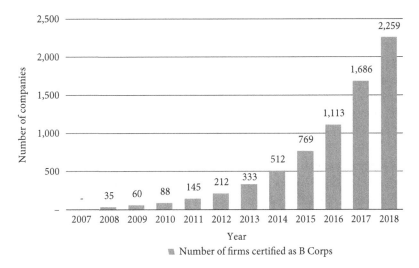

Figure 15.5   Number of companies certified as B Corps, 2007–2018
Source: https://data.world/blab/b-corp-impact-data, as of May 13th, 2018

(headquartered in the Netherlands), and B Lab East Africa (headquartered in Kenya). Notably, B Lab has limited offerings in Asia, with B Corp Asia claiming only eighty B Corporations.

Almost half (47 percent) of all B Corps are based in the United States, and 82 percent of them are based in Western nations. The prominence of this form in Western nations is partly due to the absence of B Lab infrastructure in other regions. This regional variance has consequences for how the certification is seen and how it fits into the social enterprise landscape. Given that the genesis of the social enterprise model can be traced partly to microfinance organizations and other commercial organizations in emerging markets, B Corps might be seen as an imperfect fit for the model as a whole.

One non-Western region that has seen a notable growth in B Corp certification is Latin America, where the B Lab partner Sistema B has certified 329 B-Corps, including top scorers in both the environmental category and the community category. Several notable research papers on social enterprises focus on Latin America (Battilana and Dorado 2010), and some of these papers focus specifically on B Corps in that region (Munoz, Cacciotti, and Cohen 2018).

Within the United States, researchers have found a strong link between the characteristics of a state and the density of B Corps in that state. As one might guess, B Corp density is higher in states with more-liberal, higher-educated, and more health-conscious populations (Hickman, Byrd, and Hickman 2014). The regional context in which a B Corp operates plays a significant role in how it uses the certification. For example, the industry-region configuration has a strong effect on whether an organization sees value in promoting its B Corp category membership through use of the B Corp logo on its products or its web presence (Gehman and Grimes 2017). Industry-region configuration also affects the rate at which women-owned businesses choose to obtain B Corp certification after passing the assessment (Grimes, Gehman, and Cao 2018).

B Corps operate predominantly in white-collar and consumer-facing industries, in which the value of certification for the purposes of employee recruitment and consumer marketing is greatest and in which the assessment process may be easiest to complete and pass. In particular, 24.1 percent of B Corps are in professional and technical services; 9.4 percent are in financial and insurance services; 8.5 percent are in information technology, communication, and technology; 9.2 percent are in manufactured goods; 8.4 percent are in retail; and 8 percent are in wholesale.

The Challenge of Measuring Social and Environmental Impacts

The primary challenge that social enterprises face is to balance the logic of achieving financial sustainability with the logic of creating social impact. Tension arises around the uncertainty regarding how an organization should weight these two logics. Without a well-defined model of governance and operations, hybrid organizations may drift toward either a traditional for-profit model or a nonprofit model (Pache and Santos 2010). For example, some socially minded founders focus on social values at the expense of operations, causing their firm's economic productivity (and consequently its net social impact) to suffer (Battilana et al. 2015). Others experience "mission drift" and reduce or abandon their commitment to social goals over time (Pache and Santos 2010). Even with good intentions and an awareness of the challenges they face, the leaders of hybrid organizations need to make difficult trade-off decisions.

A significant aspect of this challenge concerns the difficulty of measuring social impact. Unlike economic value, which can be measured using specific monetary units, social value cannot be so easily quantified. This is one reason why the literature on nonprofit impact evaluation remains limited (Werker and Ahmed 2008). Another aspect of this challenge is methodological: it is often difficult to devise a counterfactual to use in evaluating what would have happened in the absence of a nonprofit or of specific nonprofit program. Some academic studies have estimated the effect of individual projects through randomized evaluations. For example, evaluations of certain projects in Kenya and India found that they improved educational outcomes (Banerjee et al. 2007; Kremer 2003). Not all randomized evaluations of NGO programs, however, find positive outcomes; some of them find that a program has made no difference (Duflo and Kremer 2005). Additionally, there is no commonly accepted rate of exchange for comparing social value and economic value. Therefore, managers must intuitively decide between maximizing an organization's financial security and increasing its social impact. If the organization is considering an investment of current profits in expanding future social value, this decision can become even more complicated.

At the core of B Corp certification is the B Impact Assessment. This assessment aggregates two hundred individual questions, each weighted uniquely by B Lab and the Standards Advisory Council, a group made up of representative figures from the social enterprise field and academia. These entities specify the weighting of each question based on the industry and size of a company. Companies that receive 80 points or more are allowed to certify as B Corps. To help break down the assessment, B Lab assembles the questions into five categories: Governance, Community, Workers, Environment, and Customers. (Table 15.1 provides B Lab's description of the categories and a sample question

Table 15.1   B Corp categories

	Description	Sample Question
Governance	The Governance Impact Area evaluates a company's overall mission, ethics, accountability, and transparency.	What portion of your management is evaluated in writing on their performance with regard to corporate social environmental targets?
Community	The Community Impact Area evaluates the company's community engagement and impact, including topics related to diversity, job creation, supplier relations, charitable giving/community service, and local involvement. In addition, this section also includes options for companies whose business model is designed to address specific community-oriented problems, such as workforce development for underserved groups and poverty alleviation through fair trade supply chains.	During the last fiscal year, how much did your company source (in currency terms) from local, independent suppliers?
Workers	The Worker Impact Area evaluates the company's contribution to employee well-being, including topics related to compensation and benefits, training, health and safety, and job flexibility.	What percentage of full-time workers were reimbursed for continuing education opportunities in the last fiscal year?
Environment	The Environment Impact Area evaluates a company's overall environmental stewardship including its facilities, resource use, emissions, and (when applicable) its supply chain and distribution channels. This section also includes options for companies whose product or service is designed to address a specific environmental problem, for instance by redesigning traditional manufacturing practices or by producing products that create renewable energy, reduce consumption or waste, conserve land or wildlife, or educate about environmental problems.	What percentage of energy used is from renewable onsite energy production for corporate facilities?
Customers	The Customers Impact Area evaluates companies whose products or services are designed to address a particular social problem for or through their customers, such as health or educational products. The section focuses on the impact of the product/service and the extent to which it benefits underserved communities. For many companies this section will not apply.	If relevant, how many customers/clients served in the last twelve months qualify as poor or very poor, with incomes below \$2/day? Do not double-count. Estimates within +/–5% acceptable.

Source: https://b-lab.uservoice.com/knowledgebase/articles/864318-impact-areas-governance
-workers-community-envi   and   https://bimpactassessment.net/how-it-works/frequently-asked
-questions/%EF%BB%BF, accessed February 19, 2019.

from each category.) Because scoring on the assessment varies question by question, the categories differ significantly in the distribution of points that they allot to companies.

Additionally, the B Impact Assessment includes a Disclosure Questionnaire that covers child labor violations, adverse regulatory history, use of banned pesticides, and other disqualifying characteristics. Notably, points for various areas of performance are weighted according to the social value that B Lab and the Standards Advisory Council place on them, not on their difficulty of attainment. As a result, companies regard some areas covered by the questionnaire as low-hanging fruit, and they work to improve performance in those areas in order to catch up to their peers (Sharma, Beveridge, and Haigh 2018).

One issue that often arises in discussions of B Corp certification is whether companies have an incentive to surpass the 80-point minimum score. One reason is to qualify for B Lab's Best for the World list, which celebrates companies whose score places them in the top 10 percent of all certified B Corps either in their overall ranking or in one of the five categories. Given that B Lab and the B Corp model have relatively low brand recognition, it is unlikely that consumers will reward higher B Impact scores. However, a score above the 80-point baseline may influence investors looking to incorporate the B Impact Assessment into their rating for ESG (environmental, social, and governance) performance. More commonly, companies work to achieve a higher-than-baseline score as part of an effort to audit and improve internal operations (Gehman and Grimes 2017). Researchers have found that an organization's overall score has a limited relationship with its financial success (Chen and Kelly 2015) and with whether a company chooses to recertify as a B Corp (Cao et al. 2017). Still, companies often use B Impact scores as a way to compare their performance with that of their industry peers.

Finally, there is the question of whether hybrid social enterprises in general, and B-Corps in particular, can advance large-scale change in support the social economy. Beyond merely promoting the growth of hybrid models in the marketplace, social enterprises can have an outsized impact by influencing other firms in their industries. In a study that focused on a social enterprise in the Scandinavian energy market, Sandra Olofsson, Maya Hoveskog, and Fawzi Halila (2018) found that social enterprises introduced key practices "that are now standard in the industry."

Summary

In conclusion, B Corps are quickly becoming the most prominent hybrid organizational form in the United States and are making substantial inroads abroad. B Corps, as we have noted, are a diverse group of organizations that are still seeking legitimacy. The prominence and diversity of B Corps makes the B Corp certification process an exciting area of research.

One of our primary findings relates to the efficacy of B Corps as an eco-label. We identify a dilemma at the heart of B Corp certification. Although the broad applicability of the certification across industries and regions makes it a promising source of social enterprise research, that quality also limits its real-world efficacy as an eco-label. Because of the breadth of the B Impact Assessment, B Corp certification does not guarantee any specific outcome beyond an extremely general form of positive social impact. In that respect, it differs from FairTrade or LEED certification, which guarantees a more specific form of impact.

Conclusion

Information disclosure strategies are increasingly used by nonprofits and can be divided into three categories based on whether they aim to provide information about product-level environmental and social performance, firm-level environmental and social practices, or firm-level governance. Information disclosure strategies in these three categories bear some similarities. They codify, standardize, certify, and communicate (label) information. However, there are important differences among these strategies in terms of design quality and effectiveness.

Information Disclosure Strategies and Their Institutional Environment

As we have discussed, information disclosure strategies are often designed by nonprofits in coordination with other actors, including firms and government.

First, although the focus of this chapter is on nonprofits, it is clear that information disclosure strategies do not operate in a political vacuum and that government plays an important role, directly or indirectly, in facilitating their emergence. For example, in the case of the CDP disclosure process, participation in the program may be more relevant or valuable to firms that operate in an environment where climate regulation is more likely. This is consistent with research that shows that corporate environmental behavior is strongly influenced by political forces—in particular, the perceived threat of regulation (Segerson and Micelli 1998; Maxwell et al. 2000; Delmas and Terlaak 2001; Kim and Lyon 2011a). Governments also support or endorse NGO certification schemes by, for example, specifying particular schemes (such as FSC or Fairtrade) in their procurement guidelines (Prag, Lyon, and Russillo 2016). This partly explains why about 64 percent of environmental labeling schemes are nominally present in only one country and why the diffusion of such schemes varies significantly across the globe (Gulbrandsen 2006; Horne 2009; Prag et al. 2016). Further research can identify more specifically the elements of the institutional environment that explain this variation.

Second, although MSC, FSC, and CDP are often described as nonprofits, they are better seen as multistakeholder organizations that represent actors from the business world, civil society, and, to some extent, government (Boström and Hallström 2010). As we discussed with respect to eco-labels, standard setting that relies on compromise or consensus among a diverse set of stakeholders is more likely to be perceived as credible by consumers and more likely to be adopted. Yet researchers have raised questions as to how such multistakeholder organizing can affect the participation and power of nonprofits (Boström and Hallström 2010). In the same vein, the emergence of the B Corporation illustrates that the boundaries between the nonprofit sector and the market economy are becoming less clear. This development raises important questions about the governance of such hybrid organizational models and about their effectiveness in addressing sustainability concerns.

How Effective Are Information Disclosure Strategies?

Product eco-labels provide consumers with otherwise unavailable information on a product's environmental sustainability characteristics. By filling this information gap, eco-label schemes enable socially and environmentally aware consumers to make informed purchasing decisions that help the planet. From a corporate perspective, eco-labels can be a tool to advance strategic goals, such as product differentiation, relief from regulatory pressure, and compliance with green procurement policies of large retailers and government. However, eco-labels have proliferated in recent years and have done so with relatively little quality assurance; although some labels achieve widespread recognition, credibility, and demand, others are associated with greenwashing, consumer confusion, and compromised product quality (Delmas and Burbano 2011). Questions linger about whether information disclosure strategies implemented by nonprofits can effectively resolve tensions between the demands of the marketplace and the pursuit of public good. For example, a decade ago, some scientists criticized MSC for its lack of stringency, claiming that market incentives had led the MSC certification scheme away from its original goal and toward the promotion of ever-larger capital-intensive operations (Jacquet et al. 2010).

With the rapid growth of eco-label schemes, several questions have arisen. Increased competition between eco-labels has led to some confusion for producers and consumers regarding the differences between eco-labels and what they all stand for (Delmas and Lessem 2017). In the food market, for example, it is unclear whether eco-labels reinforce each other in "greening" that market, or whether the existence of competing eco-labels creates confusion that discredits eco-labels as a whole. More research is needed on what motivates customers to seek green products (Delmas and Colgan 2018). Do these "green" consumers occupy a small fringe of the population, or do specific attributes of green products make them attractive to a larger population?

One challenge associated with the study of the empirical effectiveness of information disclosure programs involves the difficulty of attributing program-induced changes to agent preferences (Blackman and Rivera 2011). Indeed, products offered under the aegis of such programs may provide additional quality attributes that complicate this issue. For example, if organic-labeled products gain market share, it is difficult to establish whether consumers who buy those products are expressing a preference for environmental improvement or for other aspects of product quality (such as health, safety, and taste). Do consumers value the public benefit provided by green products (reduced environmental impact) or only the private benefit associated with these products (improved personal health or higher product quality)?

We also need to better understand the limitations of information disclosure strategies. Are these approaches capable only of capturing a marginal share of consumers, or can they be effective in transforming an entire market? Experience to date suggests that even the most widely recognized eco-labels capture only about 10 percent to 20 percent of a given market. How can such market penetration be leveraged to create wider social change?

Although information disclosure strategies have grown exponentially in recent years, more research on their effectiveness is necessary. When is a policy of shaming laggards more effective than one that focuses on rewarding leaders? How does competition between eco-labels affect their effectiveness? How severe is the problem of consumer confusion that may result from the proliferation of eco-labels? Do information disclosure strategies function as substitutes for traditional regulation or as complements to it? How do these approaches interact? Do standards and certification systems simply recognize firms that are already performing well, or do they incentivize weaker performers to improve? Although much progress has been made in understanding how nonprofits attempt to protect the environment, plenty of opportunities for future research remain.

16   THE OUTCOMES MOVEMENT IN PHILANTHROPY AND THE NONPROFIT SECTOR

Paul Brest[*]

IN JANUARY 2000, THROUGH A SET of happy coincidences, I assumed the role of president of the William and Flora Hewlett Foundation, one of the largest foundations in the world. As a former dean of Stanford Law School and grantee, I appreciated Hewlett's practice of providing general operating support (GOS) wherever possible, rather than just supporting particular projects. After arriving at the foundation, however, I soon learned that its board and program staff treated GOS almost as an end in itself, rather than as an effective means to achieve the foundation's and grantees' shared goals. Most of the foundation's programs did not have overarching strategies, nor did they ask applicants to articulate their intended outcomes and plans for achieving them.

Two early moments remain vivid for me. First, shortly after my arrival, we were asked to renew a multimillion-dollar grant to improve public schools in the San Francisco Bay Area. The intended outcomes were vague, and the theory of change for achieving them was opaque and so convoluted as to make a Rube Goldberg contraption seem simple by comparison.

The second involved my inquiry into the rationale for a series of grants that brought Western ranchers, farmers, and environmentalists together in mediated conversations. The environment program staff convened a group of experts and evaluators to address my questions. When I pressed the participants to describe the program's intended outcomes and how the conversations would lead to them, their responses focused on the intrinsic value of the dialogue. The evaluators were concerned not with tracking outcomes but with reviewing the conversation process. Even as a newcomer to philanthropy, I thought that we need something more substantive.

As an inveterate academic, I read everything I could find on foundation strategy, but the literature was sparse. Although peer foundations, including the venerable Rockefeller

[*] I am grateful to Nicholas Kristof Branigan and Isabella Fu for research assistance; to Jeff Bradach, Phil Buchanan, Jed Emerson, Jacob Harold, Carla Javits, Mark Kramer, Mario Morino, Thomas Tierney, Michael Weinstein, and Lowell Weiss for their comments on the manuscript as well as their contributions to the sector; and to Iris Brest, as always, for her incisive edits.

and Ford Foundations, offered some striking examples of strategic initiatives, few had an overall strategic approach in their DNA.

So my new colleagues and I began what turned out to be a decade-long do-it-yourself project. To use an evocative cliché, we started building the outcomes boat while sailing it. In the process, we lost some of the crew and accidentally threw a few grantees overboard as well.

More about the journey later. But let me begin with where we landed. In 2012, near the end of my tenure, the Hewlett Foundation published *Outcome Focused Grantmaking: A Hard-Headed Approach to Soft-Hearted Goals*, a guidebook that set out ten elements of the foundation's evolving approach to grantmaking (Hewlett Foundation 2012a). Four of those elements constitute what I shall call an *outcomes framework*:

1. clearly defined goals
2. evidence-informed strategies for achieving those goals
3. monitoring progress in order to make appropriate course corrections
4. evaluating ultimate success

The Hewlett Foundation continues to lie at the self-consciously outcome-oriented end of a continuum of practice. However, the past several decades have seen an acceleration of a trend toward the use of evidence-informed strategies among large U.S. foundations—including many that have only come into being since the turn of the twenty-first century, such as the Laura and John Arnold Foundation, the Bill & Melinda Gates Foundation, and the Open Philanthropy Project—and some nonprofit organizations such as the youth-serving groups supported by Blue Meridian Partners.

This chapter chronicles the rise of the contemporary outcomes movement and its components, benefits, hazards, and limits. Common synonyms for *outcome-oriented* include *strategic*, *results-oriented*, and *effective* (Brest 2015; Meehan and Jonker 2018). I write in the first person because I was a participant-observer while at the Hewlett Foundation and remain an active advocate, teacher, scholar, cheerleader, and occasional scold. Although the outcomes movement is global in nature—exemplified by New Philanthropy Capital in the United Kingdom—I focus on the United States, which has been its main locus.

Although it may seem obvious to many readers, it is worth being explicit about the rationale for basing philanthropy and nonprofit management on outcomes. During 2016, Americans made a total of $390 billion in charitable donations to nonprofit organizations in such areas as religion (32 percent) and education (15 percent); human services (12 percent) and health (8 percent); arts, culture, and humanities (5 percent); and environment and animals (3 percent). Individuals (including bequests) accounted for 80 percent of the total, foundations for 15 percent, and corporations for 5 percent (Giving USA 2017).

Even granting the huge subsidy that the income tax deduction provides to many donors, one might say that it's their money and they can do what they wish with it, whether they seek to maximize outcomes, burnish their reputations, or just feel good. Or one might be concerned that too narrow a focus on outcomes thwarts experimentation and risk taking—an argument that I will return to later in this chapter. But society surely is better off when organizations that provide essential services to the sick or needy or advocate for social change deploy their resources to serve their intended beneficiaries effectively.

Early Antecedents

The roots of the contemporary outcomes movement lie not in the nonprofit sector but in business and government. Their emerging interest in efficient management was facilitated by improved accounting and budgeting methods, cost-benefit analysis, and, eventually, the computer. New tools and concepts were adopted by self-consciously professionalized government employees and transmitted across domains by an emerging management consulting industry as well as by executives who moved between business and government.

- *Business.* The scientific management movement, founded by Frederick Taylor at the turn of the twentieth century, aimed to improve efficiency and labor productivity (Drucker 1999). Taylor focused on the quantity of outcomes. In the 1980s, W. Edward Deming shifted attention to the quality of outcomes and laid the foundation for an approach called Total Quality Management (Waddington 1995). In the 1990s, Robert Kaplan and David Norton's Balanced Scorecard extended this evolving framework to track data on nonfinancial phenomena, including customer satisfaction, internal processes, and an organization's ability to learn and improve (Kaplan 1992).
- *Municipal government.* In the early 1900s, municipalities began serious efforts to improve efficiency (Horvath 2018). For example, the New York City Bureau of Efficiency was formed to study "the principles governing successful commercial organizations, and then to apply those principles to the conduct of municipal departments" (M. Lee 2008). As the twentieth century drew to a close, David Osborne and Ted Gaebler published *Reinventing Government,* an influential book that reflected a continuing interest in improving local governments performance (Osborne and Gaebler 1992).
- *The national government.* The roots of modern data-informed decision making by the national government lie in a multivolume report commissioned by President Herbert Hoover on environmental, demographic, economic, organizational, and religious trends (President's Research Committee on Social Trends 1933). The latter part of the twentieth century saw rising interest in performance measurement and productivity improvement. When Robert McNamara, formerly president of Ford Motor Company, became President John F. Kennedy's secretary of defense, he imported business performance practices into his department. With the help of the RAND Corporation, the U.S. Department of Defense developed a planning-programming-budgeting system that tied budget items to program objectives (West 2011). This initiated a succession of outcomes-oriented budgeting processes, culminating in the Government Performance and Results Act of 1993 (GPRA) and the GPRA Modernization Act of 2010, which mandated performance measurement and program evaluation by federal agencies (Hatry 2013).
- *Nonprofit organizations.* The management and measurement of nonprofit performance emerged after World War II as governments began to provide large-scale support to nonprofit programs in areas such as juvenile delinquency prevention, urban development, occupational training, and preventive health (Freeman, Rossi, and Wright 1979). This focus on outcomes accelerated during President Lyndon B. Johnson's War on

Poverty, which provided massive federal funding to organizations that delivered social services to the poor (Dunning forthcoming). The assessment of those services created an urgent need for robust methods of performance measurement and evaluation (Suchman 1967).

- *Think tanks and public policy schools.* Many of the developments described above were facilitated by new academic and quasi-academic institutions: the Brookings Institution (1916), the Social Science Research Council (1923), the National Bureau of Economic Research (1920), and the RAND Corporation (1948). Syracuse University's Maxwell School of Citizenship and Public Affairs, the nation's first public policy school, was founded in 1924.

Early Foundation Work

Much of John D. Rockefeller's philanthropy at the beginning of the twentieth century was guided by Frederick T. Gates. When the Rockefeller Foundation was established in 1913, Gates arguably became the first foundation program officer in history. But his work for Rockefeller preceded that development. Influenced by the Progressive Era values of rationality and empiricism, Gates explained that he "gradually developed and introduced into all [of Rockefeller's] charities the principle of scientific giving" (Gates 1977:161).

Among other things, Gates was distressed by the unscientific state of U.S. medicine and disease control (Gates, 1977). This concern led to the founding of the Rockefeller Institute for Medical Research (RIMR) in 1901 and the Rockefeller Sanitary Commission (RSC) in 1909 (Rockefeller Archive Center n.d.c). RIMR sought to develop a better understanding of infectious diseases such as tuberculosis, diphtheria, and typhoid fever (Rockefeller Archive Center n.d.c). RSC had the particular goal of eradicating hookworm, which it accomplished by pursuing (in today's parlance) a well-thought-out theory of change: First estimate disease prevalence in particular areas. Then cure the infected populations in those areas. Follow up by educating communities to use sanitary outhouses to prevent reinfection (Rockefeller Archive Center n.d.f).

In the following decades, the Rockefeller Foundation continued to address global health problems (Rockefeller Archive Center n.d.a). It responded to an epidemic of tuberculosis in post–World War I France by training doctors and nurses and educating the public (Rockefeller Archive Center n.d.d). It dealt with yellow fever by working in the field to destroy mosquito breeding grounds and in the lab to develop what remains the primary vaccine for the disease (Rockefeller Archive Center n.d.e). Rockefeller's antimalaria work involved efforts by scientists to test different methods for controlling that disease and by field workers to eradicate specific species of malaria-carrying mosquitoes (Rockefeller Archive Center n.d.b).

The Ford Foundation was established in 1936. Within a decade it had developed five program areas: the establishment of peace, the strengthening of democracy, the strengthening of the economy, education in a democratic society, and individual behavior and human relations (Ford Foundation 1949). Later, it recognized that these objectives were so broad as to allow for "a near-infinity of laudable subgoals" and made efforts to define its objectives with greater specificity (Magat 1979:19).

Among Ford's most noteworthy outcome-oriented projects was its mid-twentieth-century collaboration with Rockefeller to fund agricultural technologies to develop high-yield cereals in the developing world—an effort that became known as the Green Revolution (Toenniessen, Adesina, and DeVries 2008).[1] Together with Rockefeller and other foundations, Ford also played a major role in global population stabilization (Influence Watch n.d.). Domestically, it was a significant funder of the civil rights movement and addressed (not always successfully) issues of urban education and poverty (Influence Watch n.d.).

In 1975, an internal study found that Ford's approach to evaluation was "intuitive" and "perfunctory" (Magat 1979:39). As a program officer noted, "evaluation is very time-demanding and costly. Individual projects were monitored, but they weren't independently or scientifically evaluated" (MacFarquhar 2016: para. 12). Around that time, however, the foundation helped establish the Manpower Development Research Corporation (MDRC), a nonprofit social policy research organization that mounts large-scale demonstration projects and evaluations of policies and programs targeted to low-income people (MDRC n.d.). MDRC pioneered the use of random assignment in program evaluations (MDRC n.d.).

New Concepts and Tools

Paralleling and subsequent to some of the phenomena just mentioned, new concepts and tools played an essential role in the development of the outcomes movement.

Impact Evaluation

A signal moment in the history of impact evaluation came in 1963, with the publication of Donald T. Campbell and Julian C. Stanley's *Experimental and Quasi-Experimental Designs for Research*, which championed the use of experimental methods to evaluate social policies. Carol H. Weiss's *Evaluation Research: Methods for Assessing Program Effectiveness* (1972) championed the evaluation of programs based on the elements of their theories of change. Through his tellingly titled *Utilization-Focused Evaluation* (4th ed., 2008), Michael Quinn Patton brought program evaluation into the nonprofit mainstream.

Evaluation subsequently became a growth industry, with for-profit and nonprofit groups as well as universities competing for contracts and grants to evaluate government and nonprofit programs (Freeman, Rossi, and Wright 1979). Later, at the turn of the twenty-first century, the launch of two major organizations concerned with evaluating global poverty interventions further broadened the scope of program evaluation: the Abdul Latif Jameel Poverty Action Lab (J-PAL) and Innovations for Poverty Action (IPA).

Cost-Benefit Analysis

The use of cost-benefit analysis (CBA) to evaluate government programs traces its origins to the Flood Control Act of 1936, which required CBA for proposed federal waterway infrastructure projects (Quade 1971). The Flood Control Act of 1939 went a step further by requiring that for any given project, "the benefits to whomever they accrue [be] in excess of the estimated costs" (Farnham and Guess 2000:304–308).

In the 1980s, the administration of President Ronald Reagan began to mandate that all federal regulations be subject to CBA—mainly as a means of curbing the federal government's regulatory reach—and consequently CBA was applied to a wide variety of social and environmental programs (Executive Order No. 12866 1993).[2] As the environmental law scholars Richard L. Revesz and Michael A. Livermore (2011) have argued, however, CBA is not an intrinsically conservative tool but one that is valuable for any outcome-oriented policy maker. Indeed, it lies at the core of contemporary pay-for-success programs (to be discussed later).

The Logic Model, or Theory of Change

The *logic model* dates to a 1970 study commissioned by the U.S. Agency for International Development (USAID) to help improve its assessment of foreign aid projects. Fry Consultants (1970:iii) proposed a "logical framework for evaluation" with four categories—inputs, outputs, project purpose, and sector or programming goal—that were designed to assist the agency in the "careful and objective sorting of evidence" (IV-5).

Use of the logic model as a framework for program design as well as assessment soon spread to other development agencies (Practical Concepts n.d.:3). In 1996, United Way of America (UWA) published a 170-page manual, *Measuring Program Outcomes: A Practical Approach* (United Way of America 1996), whose four-part logic model—inputs, activities, outputs, and participant outcomes—was adopted by many of its own members and by other nonprofits.[3] In 2004, the W. K. Kellogg Foundation published its *Logic Model Development Guide* (W. K. Kellogg Foundation 2004).

Today, the logic model concept is regarded as a core part of any outcomes framework for program planning and assessment (Funnell and Rogers 2011). An increasingly common term for this concept is *theory of change*. Efforts to distinguish the two terms are more confusing than helpful. I prefer *theory of change* because that term reflects the need for change as a predicate to achieving outcomes more clearly than the term *logic*.

The Computer

It is worth reminding readers who grew up with personal computers that the digital computer emerged only in the 1950s. As with most other developments chronicled in this section, computer use migrated from business to government and eventually to the nonprofit sector.

Although computers facilitate real-time feedback on organizations' activities, their value depends on the data they are fed as well as how that data is analyzed and used. The New York Police Department's pioneering development of CompStat in the 1990s is emblematic of this point. CompStat mapped indicators such as the frequency and location of various crimes, and police commanders were held accountable for CompStat scores in their jurisdictions (Police Executive Research Forum 2013).[4] For both better and worse, however, CompStat exemplified the aphorism that what gets measured gets managed. The commanders' weekly CompStat reports tracked crime statistics, including arrests, but not stop-and-frisk episodes—even as the design of the CompStat system created incentives for the police to rely on the stop-and-frisk tactic (Smith 2018). The profligate use of this tactic and its discriminatory effect on minority residents eventually led to an injunction restricting its employment (Smith 2018).

Emergence of the Contemporary Movement

The preceding discussion suggests a general progression toward the practice of tracking outcomes. Although no particular event marks the start of the contemporary outcomes movement, I would situate its origins in the last decade or so of the twentieth century.

Before coming to specific examples, I should note that between 1984 and 2002, under the leadership of Harvey Dale and then Joel Fleishman, the Bermuda-based Atlantic Philanthropies made more than $200 million in grants to support the infrastructure of the nonprofit sector (Proscio 2003). In so doing, Atlantic joined a small number of foundations making such grants, but the outsize scale of its effort gave it an outsize influence. Over time, Atlantic developed a strategy that responded to "three overriding problems facing the not-for-profit sector today: a lack of reliable data and analysis on what the not-for-profit sector is and does with what impact; inadequate human, financial, and intellectual capital to discharge its responsibilities effectively and efficiently; and the weakening of social capital in the U.S." (Proscio 2003:23). Atlantic's overall goal was "to improve the effectiveness, enhance the impact, and strengthen the accountability of the nonprofit sector" (Proscio 2003:23). Toward that end, Atlantic funded many of the infrastructure organizations and research centers described later in this chapter (Proscio 2003).

Most activities during this phase of the outcomes movement originated in foundations rather than the nonprofit organizations they support. Unlike operating nonprofits, which typically have major commitments to particular activities, foundations can change course quite readily (perhaps sometimes too readily). Moreover, they can exercise considerable influence over their grantees for the reason suggested in Dwight Macdonald's description of the Ford Foundation as "a large body of money completely surrounded by people who want some" (Macdonald 1989:3).

Influential Academic Writings

As was the case a century earlier, advances in philanthropy during this period have a lineage in the business sector. Two important articles in *Harvard Business Review* exemplified this influence.

Michael E. Porter, a prominent professor of business strategy at Harvard Business School (HBS), and Mark R. Kramer, a venture capital investor, begin "Philanthropy's New Agenda: Creating Value" (Porter and Kramer 1999) with the observation that foundations impose costs on the social sector. In addition to their own administrative costs, they impose administrative burdens on grantees. They also pay out only a fraction of their endowments annually (often just the 5 percent minimum required by the U.S. Internal Revenue Code), rather than making all of their charitable funds immediately available to grantees. These costs, the article argues, are socially justified only if foundations create net benefits. They can do so by selecting capable grantees and improving their performance, attracting other funders, and advancing knowledge and practice within a given field. "A foundation creates value when it achieves an equivalent social benefit with fewer dollars or creates greater social benefit for comparable cost" (Porter and Kramer 1999:126).

In "Virtuous Capital: What Foundations Can Learn from Venture Capitalists," Christine W. Letts, William P. Ryan, and Allen S. Grossman (1997), who were affiliated with HBS, the John F. Kennedy School of Government at Harvard University, and the Hauser Center for Nonprofit Organizations at Harvard University, respectively, argue that foundations compromise an organization's effectiveness when they fund its individual programs rather than providing general support for its core needs. The authors describe venture capital practices that foundations should emulate: risk management, learning from experience, performance measurement, a focus on partnership rather than oversight, adequate funding, long-term relationships, and plans for exit. The article concludes:

> The venture capital model emerged from years of practice and competition. It is now a comprehensive investment approach that sets clear performance objectives, manages risk through close monitoring and frequent assistance, and plans the next stage of funding well in advance. Foundations, although they excel in supporting R&D, have yet to find ways to support their grantees in longer-term, sustainable ways. Because organizational underpinnings were not in place, many innovative programs have not lived up to their initial promise. The venture capital model can act as a starting point for foundations that want to help nonprofits develop the organizational capacity to sustain and expand successful programs. (Letts et al. 1997:44)

Conventional Foundations

Porter and Kramer described the practice of the best foundations and sought to provide a nudge to others. In the two decades since their article appeared, the number of U.S.-based foundations grew from fifty thousand to about ninety thousand (Statista n.d.). Most of these entities have no staff and are essentially tax-advantaged extensions of individual donors' or families' checkbooks. But this period also saw the creation of amply staffed foundations such as the Gates Foundation, which joined well-established predecessors like the Rockefeller, Ford, and Hewlett Foundations.

An old saw in philanthropy goes, "If you've seen one foundation, you've seen one foundation" (Gunther 2018: para. 1). Nonetheless, large foundations have much in common. Most of them are conglomerates, with a variety of programs that focus on different substantive areas and with a staff of program officers who have at least some expertise in those areas. The commitment to an outcomes orientation varies among foundations and even among programs within the same foundation but has almost surely grown in recent years. Joel Fleishman's *The Foundation: A Great American Secret; How Private Wealth Is Changing the World* (2009) provides a good overview of the sector.

Venture Philanthropy

Most grantmaking foundations support programs in service delivery, research, education, the arts, and (increasingly) advocacy. Venture philanthropy funders tend to support the incubation and scaling of service delivery organizations.

Even before Letts, Ryan, and Grossman's article, George Roberts, a founding partner of the global investing firm KKR & Co., had launched a venture philanthropy program with the goal of supporting homeless individuals in the San Francisco Bay Area. In 1990, Roberts hired Jed Emerson to run the Homeless Enterprise Development Fund, which four years later broadened its mission to cover other destitute and difficult-to-employ individuals (J. Emerson, personal communication, April 13, 2018). The Roberts Enterprise Development Fund (later known as REDF) invested in a portfolio of social enterprises that provide job training and employment opportunities (REDF n.d.a). A prototypical example from its current portfolio is Cara:

> Cara has helped people affected by poverty (and often the challenges of recovery, domestic violence, episodic homelessness, and incarceration) to get and keep quality jobs and, more

importantly, rebuild hope, self-esteem, and opportunity for themselves and their families in the process. Cara operates two social enterprises: Cleanslate, a community beautification and maintenance company, and Cara Connects, a staffing agency. These market-competitive businesses create gateway jobs for those they serve and produce a significant [social] return on investment—nearly $6.00 in societal benefits for every dollar invested. (REDF n.d.b)

The estimate of Cara's social return on investment (SROI) reflects REDF's innovative and ambitious effort to monetize the social value created by its investees. From the start, REDF measured what it termed "socio-economic value"—"cost savings and revenues [that] may be realized in decreased public dollar expenditures and in increased revenues to the public sector through additional taxes collected" (Gair 2002:4). With support from private foundations, REDF developed a comprehensive data-tracking system, OASIS (Ongoing Assessment of Social Impacts). Like many early-stage efforts to measure social impact, OASIS was complex and imposed significant burdens on REDF's grantees; REDF has greatly simplified it over time (C. Javits, personal communication, August 9, 2018).

Several other venture philanthropy organizations emerged during this period. Venture Philanthropy Partners, founded by Mario Morino and others, focuses on vulnerable children and youth in the Greater Washington, D.C., area. NewSchools Venture Fund, founded by Kim Smith and the venture capitalists John Doerr and Brook Byers, invests in programs and organizations related to public education.

In 2000, under the leadership of Michael Bailin, the Edna McConnell Clark Foundation (EMCF) changed from a conventional grantmaking foundation to, in effect, a venture philanthropy organization that uses unrestricted funding and technical assistance to incubate and scale organizations serving disadvantaged youth (Grossman and Sesia 2011). In the words of a Harvard Business School case study co-authored by Allen Grossman (also a co-author of the "Virtuous Capital" article), "EMCF brought an investor's mentality to grantmaking" (Grossman and Sesia 2011:3). It retained the Bridgespan Group, a then-new philanthropic consulting firm (see the following section), to engage in a due diligence process that assessed the services, financial health, operational viability, leadership and management, and evidentiary basis of each potential grantee (Grossman and Sesia 2011). Grants from EMCF were contingent on an organization's ability to meet performance milestones during three stages: "early," "growth ready," and "sustainable growth" (Grossman and Sesia 2011:4). EMCF subsequently solicited external philanthropic funds to scale its investments in youth-serving organizations (Grossman and Sesia 2011).

Infrastructure Organizations

In 1999, Bain & Company launched an independent, nonprofit consulting firm named the Bridgespan Group. Thomas Tierney, CEO of Bain & Company, and Jeffrey Bradach, then an associate professor at HBS, co-founded the entity, whose aim (to quote its current mission statement) was to "[strengthen] the ability of mission-driven organizations and philanthropists to achieve breakthrough results in addressing society's most important challenges and opportunities" (Bridgespan n.d.: para. 1).

Tierney and Bradach were motivated by an insufficient supply of data-driven, analytical strategy consulting services for the nonprofit sector.[5] Bridgespan—so named because it provides a bridge between the business and nonprofit sectors—was designed to draw on

Bain's funding, talent, knowledge, and infrastructure to improve the performance of non-profit organizations and foundations. Bain's motivations were to increase its community impact, to burnish its brand and reputation, and—by allowing its staff to rotate in and out of Bridgespan—to improve recruiting and retention. (Over time, Bridgespan came to rely mainly on its own staff.) Along with support from Bain, Bridgespan was launched with grants from the Atlantic Philanthropies and other foundations, and it continues to rely on foundation support as well as fees from its clients.

Bridgespan engages in direct consulting, leadership development, and research and publishing.[6] Over time, the firm developed a particular focus on issues related to poverty. Appropriately for an organization with that mission, Bridgespan has a theory of change in which its activities aim to increase its clients' and others' impact in improving the lives of disadvantaged populations. As a staff member noted, however, "anecdotal evidence and client feedback aside, it's difficult to assess the long-term impact of the work given the multiplicity of factors affecting an organization's results and the fact that we are consulting to the organization, not doing the work" (Grossman, Greckol-Herlich, and Ross 2009:10).

Also during this period, Porter and Kramer (co-authors of the *HBR* article on foundations) launched what soon became two organizations. Together with Phil Buchanan, they established the Center for Effective Philanthropy (CEP), whose current mission, stated on its home page at https://cep.org, is "to provide data and create insight so philanthropic funders can better define, assess, and improve their effectiveness—and, as a result, their intended impact." CEP's tools, including its Grantee Perception Report, are used by many large foundations. Porter and Kramer also created FSG (originally Foundation Strategy Group), which consults with foundations, nonprofit organizations, and corporations on strategic planning and evaluation.

At the turn of the twenty-first century, philanthropists were served by a plethora of membership organizations, including the Council on Foundations, the Philanthropy Roundtable (founded as a conservative alternative to the Council on Foundations), the National Committee for Responsive Philanthropy (which has a progressive orientation), the National Center for Family Philanthropy, and various issue-oriented and regional grantmaker associations. Independent Sector, founded by John Gardner, was unique in having a membership of nonprofit organizations as well as funders. Although all of these organizations have some programming focused on maximizing outcomes, none of them defines itself in terms of that principle. A significant addition to the philanthropic infrastructure was Grantmakers for Effective Organizations (GEO), a membership organization that consists of funders committed to improving nonprofit organizations' performance by pressing for general operating support as well as capacity building support.

Research, Writing, and Teaching

These years also saw the launch of HBS's Social Enterprise Initiative, the first MBA program of its kind; a half-dozen university-based research centers on philanthropy and the nonprofit sector; two university-based publications, *Stanford Social Innovation Review* and *The Foundation Review*; and a practitioner-oriented publication, *Nonprofit Quarterly*. New books that prescribe good practices for foundations included Laura Arrillaga-Andreessen (2011), *Giving 2.0: Transform Your Giving and Our World*; Paul Brest and Hal Harvey

(2018), *Money Well Spent: A Strategic Plan for Smart Philanthropy*; William F. Meehan III and Kim Starkey Jonker (2017), *Engine of Impact: Essentials of Strategic Leadership in the Nonprofit Sector*; Mario Morino (2011), *Leap of Reason: Managing to Outcomes in an Era of Scarcity*; and Robert Penna (2011), *The Nonprofit Outcomes Toolbox: A Complete Guide to Program Effectiveness, Performance Management, and Results*. An increase in university-based courses concerning the social sector was accompanied by the emergence of executive education programs and online courses that targeted philanthropists and nonprofit leaders.

Critics of the Outcomes Movement

Resistance to the developments chronicled in the preceding sections was largely passive. The outcomes movement did engender several vocal critics, however. William Schambra, former director of the Bradley Center for Philanthropy and Civic Renewal at the Hudson Institute, has been a persistent critic, arguing that the focus on outcomes is anathema to civil society:

> We need a vital local civil society, right in front of our faces, to draw us out of that individualistic isolation, to engage us in the affairs of our own immediate communities, wherein we learn through direct, daily interaction with others to become responsible, self-governing citizens. Our vast, bewildering, and ever-growing profusion of nonprofits—in all their naïve, amateurish, bumbling, redundant glory—may appall those who want to see social services delivered in a neat, orderly, rationalized and centralized way. But Tocqueville would have said that this is a small price to pay for the education in democratic self-government provided by our thick, organic, local network of civic associations. (Schambra 2014: "The Centrality of Local Giving," para. 14–15)

While Schambra opposed strategic philanthropy from a conservative perspective, Bill Somerville, former head of the Peninsula Community Foundation (which was absorbed into the Silicon Valley Community Foundation in 2006), echoed his sentiments from a progressive point of view, arguing that philanthropists should not question the intuitions of the staff of community organizations (Somerville and Setterberg 2008).

Dennis Collins, former president of the James Irvine Foundation, raised cognate concerns in *Just Money: A Critique of Contemporary American Philanthropy*:

> "Hyperrationalism" and "managerialism" are taking over the nonprofit sector, including philanthropy. These new "isms" appear to be crowding out a more values-driven, mission-centered approach to philanthropy and replacing it with technically-based, efficiency-driven, outcome-centered processes. In short, supplanting art with a pseudo-science that imagines metrics and matrices are reality rather than a set of useful but limited tools. (Collins 2004:64)

In the same book, Bruce Sievers, former director of the Walter & Elise Haas Fund, similarly complained about contemporary philanthropy's adoption of a business-inspired framework that focuses on "methods to increase leverage, grow return on investment, enhance effectiveness, improve evaluation, measure outcomes, strengthen organizational development, and so on" (Sievers 2004:130). Use of that framework, he wrote, "suggests that human action can be understood in terms of linear, sequential steps that can be orchestrated in predictable ways to arrive at a goal" (Sievers 2004:135).

I return to these criticisms later. But first, let's look at the framework that underlies an outcomes orientation.

Managing to Outcomes

Virtually every activity engaged in by a nonprofit organization is at least implicitly intended to achieve a social or environmental (hereafter, simply social) outcome. Depending on its mission, an organization's intended outcomes may include improving individuals' material well-being, creating and preserving knowledge and culture, or protecting the environment. All things considered, managing to outcomes allows for the most effective use of an organization's resources—and redounds to the advantage of both beneficiaries and funders.

As mentioned earlier, the four essential elements of the framework for managing to outcomes are clearly defined goals (or outcomes), evidence-informed strategies, monitoring progress, and evaluating success. These elements are largely manifest in the structure of a theory of change (or logic model). Strategies for providing social services to individual beneficiaries can neatly satisfy all four elements. Other strategies—such as those related to advocating for policy change, supporting basic research, and promoting nascent fields and movements—fit the framework less tightly but can benefit from an outcome orientation nonetheless.

The Choice of Outcomes Precedes an Outcomes Framework

Let's return to the Hewlett Foundation's manual, *A Hard-Headed Approach to Soft-Hearted Goals*, and begin with the goals. Philanthropists pursue a virtually infinite number of goals (Foundation Center n.d.). Their choice may be affected by religious, political, or moral beliefs—for instance, by the ethical theory of the effective altruism movement, which demands that one give to alleviate as much distress as possible (MacAskill 2016). An outcomes framework has nothing to say about the choice of goals, however. It comes into play only after that choice has been made. For better or worse, the framework is value-neutral—as useful to National Right to Life as to NARAL Pro-Choice America; as useful to the Brady Campaign to Prevent Gun Violence as to the National Rifle Association.

When a decision maker is motivated by a particular value, such as reducing mortality, it may be possible to compare the outcomes of different approaches and organizations. GiveWell, for example, rates health-related charities in developing countries based on their cost-effectiveness in increasing "disability-adjusted life years" (GiveWell 2017a). But many, if not most, outcomes are not commensurable. To invoke Jeremy Bentham's quip, one cannot compare the value of push-pin (a popular game of his time) with that of poetry (Bentham 1830:206–207).

The recognition that the choice of outcomes precedes an outcomes framework dissolves the supposed tension between philanthropy based on "the head" and philanthropy based on "the heart" (Cantor and Gunther 2018). The choice of philanthropic goals is essentially a matter for your heart. Only after making that choice does the head come in to determine whether an organization that promises to fulfill your heart's desire actually has a plan and the capacity to do so. Of course, nonprofit organizations, no less than retail sellers, use clever marketing techniques—the teary-eyed child, the polar bear on an isolated ice floe—to short-circuit donors' rational processes. But the donor who cares about results and yet succumbs to these techniques will be left with a broken heart.

The Paradigm of Service Delivery

Service-delivery programs aim to improve individuals' lives by, for example, reducing obesity, teen pregnancy, opioid addiction, and homelessness, or by improving educational outcomes or workforce participation. I use as an example a program designed to reduce recidivism among young men who have been released from prison.

Outcome: A recidivism-reduction program has a specific outcome—preventing participants from returning to prison. Whether, and to what extent, an outcome has occurred is not always self-evident but must be determined based on certain indicators. Some recidivism-reduction programs use data from prison systems; others use judicial sentencing data.

In some cases, different indicators may reflect quite different intended outcomes. For example, although the Robin Hood Foundation and REDF both seek to reduce poverty, the former uses improvement in individuals' earnings as an indicator, whereas the latter uses individuals' tax payments (and does so mainly as a proxy for government cost savings). Other organizations with a similar goal might use a region's overall poverty rate. Similarly, indicators concerning global human rights, gender violence, and sex trafficking may reflect very different intended outcomes (Merry 2016).

Strategy: The interventions that make up most recidivism-prevention programs involve three basic components: psychological counseling to help beneficiaries cope with daily problems, job training, and assistance in job placement and retention. One typical way of describing a program strategy is through its theory of change. Leaving aside *inputs* (such as adequate resources, competent staff, and good relationships), a simple theory of change might look like Figure 16.1.

Activities and outputs (hereafter, just activities) are what the program does and delivers to its clients. *Intermediate outcomes* are changes in the clients' behavior (e.g., getting and retaining a job) that result from the activities. The *ultimate outcome* is the desired result (e.g., not returning to prison) that stems from the intermediate outcomes. Between each step in the theory of change are causal links (indicated here by arrows).

To say that a strategy is informed by evidence is to claim an empirical basis for these causal links. In this example, as in the case of many service-delivery programs, the sources of such evidence may range from randomized controlled experiments to well-designed observational studies of similar programs.

Monitoring Progress: An outcome-based process includes feedback to learn how a program is doing in order to make necessary course corrections. By hypothesis, if a service provider does not engage in the prescribed activities, the intermediate outcomes will not occur, and if the intermediate outcomes do not occur, the ultimate outcome will not occur.

Activities and outputs	Intermediate outcomes	Ultimate outcome
Provide counseling ➡	Client learns to cope	
Provide job training ➡	Client is prepared for employment	➡ Client does not recidivate
Provide job placement assistance ➡	Client is placed in and retains job	

Figure 16.1   Illustrative theory of change

Therefore, the service provider will develop metrics and, ideally, targets for each activity, for each intermediate outcome, and for the ultimate outcome.

Evaluating Success: What ultimately matters is the ultimate outcome—in this case, avoidance of recidivism. The success rate for most service-delivery programs will seldom be 100 percent; often it will be considerably lower. A liminal question is: Success as compared to what? A rough starting point is the baseline for the population of similarly situated people. But there are many problems with so simple a metric—not the least of which might be a service provider's inclination to select clients who are the most likely to succeed in attaining the ultimate outcome.

And that problem points to the fundamental question of a program's *impact*: Did the program *cause*, or at least contribute to, the ultimate outcome (assuming that this outcome has occurred)? The goal of evaluation is to determine whether and to what extent the outcome would *not* have occurred without the program. The recidivism-prevention program's apparent success might be due not just to cherry-picking participants but to self-selection by ex-offenders who are likely not to recidivate, or perhaps to demographic changes that reduced recidivism within the targeted population more generally.

Why take the trouble and incur the expense to assess the program's contribution to the outcome? From a service provider's point of view: to improve, expand, revise, or abandon the program depending on the results. From a funder's point of view: to extend, withdraw, or set conditions for further support. And from the broader field's point of view: to improve other recidivism-prevention programs.

The More Complicated Case of Policy Advocacy

The typical service-delivery program checks all of the boxes of the outcomes framework. Advocacy for policy change—for example, increasing the availability of national health insurance or reducing the availability of firearms—is more complicated.[7] Consider, for example, an advocacy campaign for legislation that raises the age at which an individual can own a gun to twenty-one.

Every advocacy effort involves two theories of change. The first typically bears close resemblance to the paradigmatic theory of change: It posits that a policy, if adopted, will lead to specified results. In our example, this theory of change would address the causal links between a minimum age for gun ownership and the ultimate outcome of a reduction in shootings. We'll assume that sound evidence supports those causal links. Now let's look at the second theory of change, which concerns the strategy underlying the proposed advocacy campaign.

Outcome: The outcome is clearly defined: enactment (including the executive's signature) of legislation prohibiting individuals under age twenty-one from owning a gun.

Strategy: In "The Elusive Craft of Evaluating Advocacy," Steven Teles and Mark Schmitt suggest that the paradigmatic theory of change does not readily apply to political advocacy:

> Advocacy . . . is inherently political, and it's the nature of politics that events evolve rapidly and in a nonlinear fashion, so an effort that doesn't seem to be working might suddenly bear fruit, or one that seemed to be on track can suddenly lose momentum. Because of these peculiar features of politics, few if any best practices can be identified through the sophisticated methods that have been developed to evaluate the delivery of services. . . . Tactics that may have worked in one instance are not necessarily more likely to succeed in another. What matters is whether advocates can choose the tactic appropriate to a particular conflict and adapt to the shifting moves of the opposition. . . . Successful advocates know that such plans are at best loose guides, and the path to change may branch off in any number of directions. . . . Successful advocacy efforts are characterized not by their ability to proceed along a predefined track, but by their capacity to adapt to changing circumstances. (Teles and Schmitt 2001:39–40)

Although Teles and Schmitt are absolutely correct on the macro level, they overlook the fact that every specific implementation of an advocacy strategy involves a micro theory of change. For example, every lobbyist—and policy advocacy often involves lobbying—knows to focus efforts not on legislators who are safely on your side or hopelessly against you, but on those who might be swayed to your side. And an experienced lobbyist pursues a bespoke set of tactics (in effect, a theory of change) for each swayable legislator. Those tactics may include persuasive argument, promises to support other legislation, or threats verging on extortion.

Monitoring Progress: For each legislator who must be swayed to vote for the legislation, the policy advocate's activities involve designing and implementing a strategy custom-tailored to that legislator's particular interests. The intermediate outcomes are the legislator's change of attitude with respect to the bill and his or her voting behavior. The ultimate outcome is the bill's enactment. This is not a fanciful analogy to monitoring the progress of a social program; it is how real-life policy advocates keep track of how they're doing.

Evaluating Success: As with the recidivism-prevention program, the fact that the intended outcome occurred does not mean that your particular effort was responsible for it. A school shooting might have led to a widespread public outcry that swayed many legislative votes, regardless of your advocacy. In contrast to a service-delivery program, in which many participants' outcomes can be aggregated and contrasted with those of a comparison group, the one-off nature of advocacy efforts makes the attribution of outcomes difficult. Difficult, but not impossible. In case studies done for the Open Philanthropy Project, historian Benjamin Soskis assessed the contributions that particular philanthropic efforts had likely made to (respectively) smoking reduction in the United States and enactment of the Affordable Care Act (Soskis 2013, 2015). In each case, he was able to conclude, with appropriate caution, that an advocacy campaign had made a positive difference.

Indeterminate Outcomes: Early-Stage Advocacy and Field Building

In the preceding example, the intended outcome was clear: a twenty-one-year-old age limit for the ownership of guns. But advocacy efforts often do not begin with such clear outcomes. For example, Soskis's case study of the Affordable Care Act indicates that for many years, several foundations advocated broadening health insurance without having a particular approach in mind. They sought certain outcomes but were waiting for social and political forces to converge before engaging in an intensive strategy focused on a particular solution. The same pattern applies to the early stages of many civil rights movements that culminated in landmark victories.

Outcomes are even less determinate in efforts to build new fields. By *field*, I mean a common set of issues, theories, and practices in which theorists and practitioners share a vocabulary and a set of norms, values, and basic texts. Examples of fields developed within the past half century include bioethics, geriatrics, and end-of-life care.

Let's examine the Hewlett Foundation's twenty-year initiative to build the field of conflict resolution. As of 1984, when the initiative was launched, mediation and arbitration were well-established practices in labor law and civil litigation but had not significantly touched disputes involving the environment, family, community, and many other areas of potential conflict (Kovick 2005). The foundation believed that there was great potential in expanding these practices but that the field needed development in depth as well as breadth:

> Conflict resolution had been practiced for generations according to "rules of thumb," developed through experience and passed down to future practitioners through an apprenticeship model. The field had no efficient means either for developing new knowledge about conflict resolution or conveying it to the world of practice. As a result, there was only limited insight into the dynamics of conflict, and only limited capacity for innovation in the form of new, more effective models of practice. The Foundation's vision for the field, expressed through its field-building strategy, was a field of conflict resolution eventually coming to resemble other fields such as medicine or law—practiced by professionals, who were trained in academic institutions, based on theory that understood the dynamics of conflict and how to resolve it most effectively, and supported by professional associations that would continue to promote advancements in practice. (Kovick 2005:9)

To advance that vision, the foundation undertook a three-pronged field-building initiative: (1) developing conflict resolution theory through support for interdisciplinary research centers, (2) supporting organizations of conflict resolution practitioners, and (3) strengthening the field's infrastructure through support for organizations such as the National Institute for Dispute Resolution, which promotes the field and supports innovation (Kovick 2005). These three prongs were, in effect, the initiative's activities and intermediate outcomes.

The foundation's approach was to make unrestricted multiyear grants and to follow a generally hands-off policy, intervening only when organizations were underperforming or at risk of fragmenting into unsustainable small entities. In 2002, in the belief that the field of conflict resolution had matured to a point where it no longer needed philanthropic support, the Hewlett Foundation decided to exit the field (Kovick 2005).

Should the foundation's grants in building the field of conflict resolution be characterized as outcome oriented? I believe that the answer is yes. Although it was impossible to specify the intended outcomes in detail, the initiative was designed from the start to improve the processes and increase the availability of conflict resolution and to extend that practice to new domains. The foundation identified three areas in which to make its initial set of grants in the belief that support for conflict resolution theory, practitioner organizations, and infrastructure—along with efforts to link those elements—was essential to building and sustaining the field.

This was the foundation's theory of change. The individual grants were made with mutual expectations about the grantee organizations' activities and hoped-for outcomes. The foundation assessed the achievements of individual grantees and made midcourse corrections accordingly.

Complex Problems and Emergent Strategies

In "Eyes Wide Open: Learning as Strategy Under Conditions of Complexity and Uncertainty," Patricia Patrizi, Elizabeth H. Thompson, Julia Coffman, and Tanya Beer (2013) build on the work of Henry Mintzberg to note that "foundations engage many large and extraordinarily difficult and complex problems. . . . Yet [they] . . . have downplayed the complexity of their work and in many cases ignored the uncertainties surrounding their strategic enterprises. . . . The failure to learn during strategy is a serious problem" (Patrizi et al. 2013:56).

While Patrizi and her colleagues (2013) emphasize the importance of using feedback to make strategic course corrections, in "Strategic Philanthropy for a Complex World," John Kania, Mark Kramer, and Patty Russell (2014) go further to suggest that the causal models reflected in conventional theories of change are not applicable to complex challenges such as advocacy, field building, and systems change. They argue that, in contrast to a "rigid and predictive model of strategy," these challenges require "a more nuanced model of emergent strategy that better aligns with the complex nature of social progress" (Kania et al. 2014:26):

> Emergent strategy still requires that a clear strategic intent guide the funder's actions, but it acknowledges that specific outcomes cannot be predicted. Emergent strategic philanthropists will continually strive to react to changing circumstances, so flexible and textured frameworks such as system maps must replace the linear and one-dimensional logic model as the primary means of clarifying strategy. (Kania et al.:29)

For all of the complexities of large-scale change, however, virtually every emergent strategy must eventually be implemented through a set of predictive strategies. At any given time, a policy advocate must make predictive decisions; for example, "We should devote resources to persuading Senator Jones about the merits of our policy proposal because he has great influence with his peers; and based on our observations, Senator Jones is most open to the following arguments: . . ." Field building is no less complex. Yet as difficult as it may be to predict the interactions among the various organizations that constitute a field, at any given time a field builder must support a set of particular organizations, each of which has its own relatively narrow predictive strategy.

All of this said, Kania and his colleagues' effort to extend the framework of strategic philanthropy beyond a narrow focus on conventional theories of change reflects how far the outcomes movement has come in just a few decades.

Can Organizations and Philanthropists *Not* Be Outcome Oriented?

In light of the generous scope that I've given to what counts as an outcomes orientation, a reader may wonder what does *not* meet that standard. Like many other human activities, charitable donations can have multiple simultaneous motivations. They can be designed to achieve social outcomes and, at the same time, be motivated by reciprocity, gratitude, a desire for personal recognition, a quest for financial gain, or the "warm glow" (Andreoni 1990:464) that accompanies virtually every act of generosity. But sometimes the latter motivations supplant rather than supplement an outcomes orientation. In *Strategic Giving: The Art and Science of Philanthropy*, Peter Frumkin argues that the "expressive function" provides an independent rationale for philanthropy:

> The private consumptive and expressive function of philanthropy is directed at meeting the psychic and social needs of donors. . . . Both the private and personal benefits of giving are important ends in their own right. . . . [Philanthropy supports] the self-actualization of donors by. . . . allowing individuals to find meaning and purpose in their lives. . . . Although giving may generate benefits that accrue to communities and seeing those benefits may actually be part of the satisfaction realized by a donor, philanthropy has a rationale that is distinctly personal and private: to give the donor some measure of satisfaction and psychic reward. (Frumkin 2008:18–19)

Donations made with emotional motivations but without any due diligence about a recipient organization's capacity to achieve outcomes are not outcome oriented. Nor are donations to organizations whose putative theories of change are based on willful ignorance of available evidence, as in the cases of the Drug Abuse Resistance Education (DARE) program (Clayton, Cattarello, and Johnstone 1996; Ringwalt, Ennett, and Holt 1991); the Scared Straight delinquency-prevention programs (Petrosino et al. 2013); and abstinence-only teen pregnancy prevention programs (Mathematica n.d.).[8]

Does an Outcomes Orientation Actually Improve Impact?

The outcomes movement does not underrate the value of expertise, which plays an important role in virtually every professional field or calling (Brest and Krieger 2010). Rather, it is premised on the belief that expertise guided by evidence will lead to better outcomes than expert intuitions alone. Unfortunately, many intuitively obvious strategies fail not because they involve thoughtful long-shot bets but for want of thoughtful planning. An outcomes orientation is essentially a commitment to the value of rational decision making.

Of course, strategic planning and evaluation take more time and cost more than an approach based on pure intuition. But an outcome-oriented process takes account of this reality; it incorporates a rough cost-benefit analysis, in which strategy and evaluation are costs that are justified only to the extent that they are outweighed by their potential benefits.

The Movement Today

What is the situation today? In addition to considerable research and writing, new organizations have been created. An increasing number of nonprofit organizations are using terms like "social return on investment" (L. Lee 2015: para. 9) and "strategic philanthropy" (L. Lee 2015: para. 9; Korff 2015). Let's examine how, and to what extent, these concepts are actually being implemented.

The Interest in Evidence-Informed Strategies and Measurable Outcomes

The outcomes movement is undergirded by evaluation techniques that have enabled governments and nonprofit organizations to pursue strategies that are informed by evidence.[9] Arnold Ventures, whose "core objective is to maximize opportunity and minimize injustice (Arnold Ventures 2019), is perhaps the single largest funder of efforts to promote evidence-informed policies.

The Value and Limits of Metrics

I return here to Dennis Collins's and Bruce Sievers's criticisms of the outcomes movement's managerialism and metrics orientation. Measuring the outcomes of service-delivery organizations is critically important to their beneficiaries, their funders, and the organizations themselves. Yet, as Albert Einstein is said to have written, "Not everything that counts can be counted, and not everything that can be counted counts." However dubious its attribution may be (Quote Investigator 2011), the aphorism makes two good points.

To begin with the second point, nonprofit organizations engage in a considerable amount of unnecessary counting, much of it demanded by philanthropic and government funders. But this is not a consequence of an outcomes framework. On the contrary, that framework determines what's worth counting (outcome indicators that reflect an organization's theory of change) and what's not (most other things). The use of an outcomes framework as a learning mechanism to improve organizations' performance would eliminate vast amounts of useless data collection and analysis.

Even within an outcomes framework, organizations sometimes seek more precision than is useful. REDF's initial measurement system proved to be unnecessarily detailed and complex, and the organization moved to adopt much simpler approaches to helping its grantees measure their social value added. The Hewlett Foundation, in its initial efforts to compare the value of alternative program strategies, sought far more precision than the wide margins of error permitted. Both of these cases are good examples of going too far, hitting a wall, and backing up. But until you hit the wall, you may never know how far you can reasonably go.

Turning to the first point in the Einstein quotation, surely it's true that not everything that counts can be counted. Even putting aside the extreme case of trying to measure a church's contribution to its congregation's salvation, it is often implausible to measure the spiritual and cultural outcomes of religious activities, museum exhibits, orchestral performances, or liberal arts educations.

Still, even in these cases, the use of wisely chosen indicators and smart survey techniques can inform operational and funding decisions. For example, the Hewlett Foundation's performing arts program combines qualitative indicators based on site visits, performance reviews, and the like with quantitative criteria such as paid and free attendance at grantee events, attendance by diverse demographic groups, and rates of participation in grantees' education and community-based programs. In the foundation's words, these indicators help "program staff make their assumptions explicit and bring to the surface aspects of grantee performance that might otherwise have gone unrecognized" (Hewlett Foundation 2012b:21).

Combining different sorts of data can be difficult, however. In emphasizing REDF's efforts to integrate qualitative and quantitative information, Jed Emerson invoked the metaphor of "a constellation of numbers connected by the dark matter of narrative" (J. Emerson, personal communication, April 13, 2018). Michael Weinstein, former chief program officer of the highly metric-driven Robin Hood Foundation, emphasized that "smart funders would no more make grant decisions based solely on the arithmetic of benefit/cost ratios than smart admissions officers at competitive undergraduate colleges would make decisions based solely on the arithmetic of SAT scores" (Weinstein and Bradburd 2013:86–87). But a Robin Hood Foundation staff member observed that "there's a power in the simplicity of a benefit-cost ratio. And it's hard, once [the numbers] are out there, to argue with them" (Ebrahim and Ross 2012:13). On the one hand, numbers can have a strong anchoring effect even when one knows that they are estimates with large margins of error. On the other hand, a reliance on the intuitions of experts unguided by data seems no less dangerous than a reliance on data unmediated by intuition.

In any event, advocacy for policy and system change is seldom amenable to anything like the kind of outcome evaluation that works for service-delivery organizations. Here, an outcomes-oriented approach calls for a well-thought-out theory of change, supported by evidence of its plausibility and coupled with an awareness of the huge risks or uncertainties that attend these efforts. In most such cases, even trying to quantify the likelihood of success is a fool's errand.

Pay-for-Success Programs—When Outcomes Count

Evidence-informed strategies, evaluation, and metrics come together in the emerging practice of pay-for-success (PFS) funding. Government agencies frequently contract with both nonprofit and for-profit organizations to provide services to improve the well-being of individuals—for example, by reducing recidivism, homelessness, or drug use. Although governments have traditionally paid service providers based on their activities in treating clients, the past decade has seen the emergence of PFS, or results-based, financing programs, in which providers are paid not for activities but for outcomes. For example, rather than paying a service provider for the hours spent counseling clients after their release from prison, a PFS contract pays for reducing the clients' rate of recidivism. Because government agencies often lack the experience to contract for outcomes, several intermediary organizations have emerged to assist in putting together these deals (Kodali, Grossman, and Overholser 2014; Khare 2017).

At a minimum, PFS programs must be premised on evidence of the success rate of the intervention for the client population—ideally established by randomized controlled trials (RCTs). Many PFS programs also incorporate RCTs to determine payments: for example, a service provider will be paid only to the extent that its treatment cohort had lower recidivism rates than a control group. In some recent PFS programs, however, payments are made merely on proof that a service provider has achieved specified outcomes that are better than the estimated outcomes in the absence of an intervention. This so-called rate card method of payment reduces both the costs involved in calculating the payment and the period between service delivery and payment. Its major downside is that it does not contribute evidence about whether the program actually achieves impact; without some form of evaluation, one cannot know what would have happened in the absence of the intervention.

These programs are just one manifestation of contemporary efforts to pay for performance—in areas ranging from medicine to law enforcement to education. The success of these efforts has been mixed, to say the least (Muller 2018). The unanticipated effects of the federal No Child Left Behind Act of 2001 (NCLB) illustrate some of the hazards of this approach. First, payment based on certain outcomes may divert attention from other valuable outcomes. In the case of NCLB, an emphasis on math and reading scores led schools to deemphasize arts and sciences (Lynch 2007).

Second, NCLB produced phenomena of the sort described by Campbell's Law, posited by Donald Campbell, a major figure in the modern evaluation movement: "The more any quantitative social indicator is used for social decision-making, the more subject it will be to corruption pressures and the more apt it will be to distort and corrupt the social processes it is intended to monitor" (Campbell 1979:85). (The American comedian W. C. Fields captured the same sentiment in his 1939 film *You Can't Cheat an Honest Man*, when he said, "If a thing's worth winning, it's worth cheating for" (Marshall 1939).) Under NCLB, schools sometimes removed or declined to admit students who would bring down the school's aggregate scores, or they focused attention on so-called bubble kids, whose slight improvement would significantly improve those scores (Hart 2010). Similarly, some observers of the CompStat system in New York City (mentioned earlier) voiced concern that it may have discouraged police officers from recording crimes in order to create a false appearance of lower crime rates (Chen 2010; Levitt 2003; Moses 2005).

Third—granted that the social science literature shows that the effects of rewards on motivation are highly situation-specific—payment for outcomes under NCLB created a system of extrinsic motivation that might have crowded out teachers' intrinsic motivation to do well for their students (Muller 2018).

These are not reasons for rejecting programs that reward outcomes. After all, programs that pay service providers on the basis of time spent rendering services have their own motivational hazards; they create incentives for providers to spend excessive time with clients or simply to inflate their reported hours.[10] But PFS programs should be designed to curtail counterproductive strategic behavior. For example, they should bar service providers from choosing only the clients who are most likely to succeed in a program.

Outcome-Oriented Strategies in Conditions of Risk and Uncertainty

PFS programs offer just one example of the value of CBA in developing and evaluating service-delivery programs aimed at improving social outcomes. As mentioned earlier, REDF assesses its programs' cost savings for local governments. The Robin Hood Foundation assesses grantee organizations based on CBA calculations that use estimates of beneficiaries' projected increase in lifetime earnings (Weinstein and Bradburd 2013).

The outcomes of programs of these sorts tend to be pretty stable from one year to the next. The cost per participant is known, and the benefits correspond to the number of participants in a cohort who achieve the program's outcomes, such as getting and keeping a job. By contrast, policy-advocacy and system-change strategies—efforts involving issues such as criminal justice, climate change, firearms regulation, and marriage equality—are fraught with incalculable uncertainties. Sievers (2004) provides examples of philanthropic support for social change efforts that were not subject to accounting rules:

> The environmental movement, the rise of the conservative agenda in American political life, and the movement toward equality for the gay and lesbian communities, all aided by significant philanthropic support, have transformed American life in ways that lie beyond any calculations of "return on investment." . . . Commitment of philanthropic resources to these issues was not merely a matter of analyzing increments of inputs and output; it was a moral engagement with wooly, unpredictable issues that called for deeply transformational action. (Sievers 2004:138)

And Collins (2004), another critic of the outcomes movement, observes that "one of the most pernicious consequences of this rush to proficiency is the impulse to avoid, if not eliminate, funding to address big, complicated, messy, seemingly insoluble problems, problems rife with uncertainty, risk, and inefficiency, and projects whose potential for failure is high. . . . The reluctance or inability of foundations to 'swing for the fences' is discouraging" (Collins 2004:65–67).

Sievers and Collins are surely right that ambitious social change efforts are not amenable to the sorts of calculations appropriate for service-delivery programs. Fifteen years after they mounted their critiques, however, their fears have yet to be realized. On the contrary, the intervening years have seen an unprecedented amount of philanthropic resources flow to long-shot, system-changing initiatives, many of them supported by the most outcome-oriented foundations in existence—funders such as the Arnold Foundation, the Hewlett Foundation, and the Open Philanthropy Project. These efforts reflect the fundamental insight of an expected-return mind-set: adopting a strategy with high costs and a low probability of success is justified, if not morally compelled, when the benefits are extraordinarily great—even in cases where the probability of success may be unquantifiable.

Charity Ratings: Supply and Demand

In 2007, the Hewlett Foundation launched the Nonprofit Marketplace Initiative (NMI), with the goal that within eight years, "10 percent of individual philanthropic donations in the United States (approximately $20 billion per year), would be influenced by high-quality performance information" (Arabella Advisors 2012). As I was leaving the foundation in

2012, we commissioned an evaluation of NMI. As it turned out, the initiative fell far short of its ambitious goal. In retrospect, we neither appreciated the costs of obtaining reliable outcome information nor understood donors' lack of motivation for using it.

Nonetheless, NMI did help launch several charity-evaluation websites. In addition, it solidified GuideStar as a major source of information about nonprofit organizations, and it enabled Charity Navigator to begin its first, albeit unsuccessful, foray into providing outcome data. NMI may also have had a role in driving a notable trend; the proportion of donors using performance data to choose among multiple nonprofits increased from 3 percent in 2010 (Hope Consulting 2010) to 9 percent in 2015 (Camber Collective 2015).

Other than lost opportunity costs, the initiative did no harm. Well, *almost* none. I recall working closely with one social entrepreneur who thought he could develop a cost-effective charity evaluation system based on expert and beneficiary reviews. After we rejected one idea after another as not sufficiently valid or reliable, he gave up and moved to Australia to open a bed-and-breakfast.

Today, two charity-rating organizations, GiveWell and ImpactMatters, focus on the evaluation of outcomes. Because of the difficulties of assessing impact, however, each has rated just a handful of charities. GiveWell rates only organizations that provide direct services like distributing malaria-preventing bed nets or providing pills to treat intestinal parasites. Its website explains: "We believe there have been many efforts to find and address the root causes of poverty, and that they haven't generated strong conclusions or successful programs" (GiveWell 2017b: "Why the focus on direct aid," para. 1). Most of the charities that receive its top ratings fight diseases such as malaria and schistosomiasis (parasitic worms) or improve the economic well-being of the world's poorest people. GiveWell doesn't merely assess whether organizations achieve results but also compares their cost-effectiveness in doing so—based, for example, on the cost per life saved.

ImpactMatters issues ratings of the impact of nonprofits that "directly deliver services to achieve a specific health, anti-poverty, education or similar outcome." The methodology adopted by ImpactMatters is highly similar to GiveWell's, as it bases its quantitative outcome variable on rigorous studies that use RCTs or pre-post surveys that are properly controlled for.

A relatively new organization, Mission Measurement, is developing the Impact Genome Project, which aggregates various sources of information about a particular program and uses the techniques of big-data analysis to predict the "likelihood a program will achieve a particular outcome, the average expected cost for a program to produce a single 'unit' of impact, and the total number of people served by a program that are projected to achieve a particular outcome" (Ashoka 2014: para. 3).

GuideStar, in collaboration with Independent Sector and the BBB Wise Giving Alliance, has taken a different approach. Rather than rating organizations or their strategies, its five Charting Impact questions invite nonprofits to state in their own words their goals, strategies, capabilities, measures of progress, and accomplishments to date (GuideStar n.d.). Although a charity's ability to answer these questions persuasively may only indicate that it has a good public relations staff, its refusal or inability to answer them persuasively should at least make a donor think twice about supporting it.

Whatever its limitations may be, Charting Impact has the potential to help assess advocacy and other strategies that are not subject to quantitative evaluation. Though it hasn't yet happened, an independent organization with expertise in the relevant subject matter could assist individual philanthropists in assessing an organization's strategy (i.e., theory of change) and its progress toward intermediate and ultimate goals.

Delivering information about an organization's effectiveness is only half the task, however. As the saying goes, you can lead a horse to water, but you can't make it drink. Research indicates that a large majority of donors aren't willing to put much effort into learning about the impact of the organizations they support—and they remain uninterested in impact data even when it's placed in front of them (Camber Collective 2015).

Measuring the Impact of Impact Investments

Impact investing consists of actively placing capital in enterprises that generate social or environmental goods, services, or ancillary benefits, with expected returns ranging from the highly concessionary (below-market) to above-market. Impact investments may take the form of equity investments, loans, or guarantees. They have been made in areas including education, environment, energy, health, and global poverty alleviation.

By contrast to mainstream, socially neutral investors, who seek only financial returns, impact investors also seek to achieve social impact. Nonconcessionary impact investors expect to achieve risk-adjusted market-rate returns as well as social impact. Concessionary impact investors are willing to sacrifice some return. Program-related investments (PRIs) are concessionary investments made by U.S. private foundations; the Internal Revenue Code treats these investments like grants in many respects (Brest 2016).

Impact investing involves two quite different kinds of impact: the impact of the investee enterprise and the impact of an investment on that enterprise's outputs.

With respect to the first kind of impact, the outcomes framework described earlier applies to the social strategies of impact investees in precisely the same way that it does to nonprofits. To date, the performance measures developed for the impact investing sector—the Impact Reporting and Investment Standards (IRIS) and the related Global Impact Investing Rating System (GIIRS)—have mainly concerned activities and outputs rather than outcomes. But a new initiative called Rise Labs, a collaboration between the private equity firm TPG Growth in collaboration with the Bridgespan Group, has developed an outcomes-based evaluation framework that will measure impact and also take account of negative externalities (Addy et al. 2018).

The second kind of impact involves a question that seldom arises in the purely philanthropic financing of nonprofits: when and to what extent does an investment enable an enterprise to produce more of its value-added outputs? The answer to this question indicates the "investment impact," or "additionality," of an investment—the degree to which it enables the enterprise to create social outcomes *in addition to* the outcomes that it would have created with capital provided by ordinary, socially neutral investors. There are several possible ways that impact investors can create additionality, the most obvious of which is to provide capital at lower cost or on more flexible terms than the enterprise could otherwise get in financial markets (Brest, Gilson, and Wolfson 2016). Impact investors in private equity markets also can provide enterprises with technical assistance in achieving social as well as financial goals (Impact Management Project 2018).

The impact investing industry has at best ignored, and at worst resisted, the question of additionality. There are several possible explanations. First, causal inference is difficult in any event, and this question calls for such inference on a secondary level. Second, many socially motivated investors are satisfied with an investment portfolio that aligns with their values—by investing in companies that produce good things (health products in the developing world) or produce things in good ways (by creating jobs) and not in companies that produce bad things (cigarettes) or produce things in bad ways (by polluting)—whether or not their investments create impact.

Third, and quite simply, it is difficult to achieve social impact and simultaneously expect risk-adjusted market returns. PRIs and other impact investments that explicitly sacrifice financial returns almost always have additionality—more or less by definition. But other forms of impact investment, particularly those that promise market-rate returns, face a challenge in this regard. Much of the growth of the impact investing industry is fueled by commercial institutions seeking to get more wealth under management, and an assessment of additionality does not necessarily promote this objective.

Whose Voices Matter in Determining Outcomes, Indicators, and Strategies, and in Assessing Progress and Success?

The outcomes movement has been accompanied by considerable attention to the relationships among funders, nonprofit organizations, and their shared beneficiaries. For the most part, the main point of focus has involved the tension that may occur between funders and their grantees.

One cannot determine, a priori, whether a funder or a grantee is the better strategist. Although a grantee organization often has more on-the-ground knowledge and expertise, a staffed foundation may have a broader overview of a given field than any single organization in that field. But philanthropists should beware of the dangers of hubris, and, when they do develop their own strategies, they should engage key grantees in that effort. Patrizi and Thompson (2010) note that strategic plans are "often developed in isolation from those doing the work—the grantees supported to execute the strategy. . . . Even when grantees are included in planning, they're rarely seen as full partners in the process. . . . A frequent result is weak strategy. . . . Grantees need to be treated as the central partners that they ultimately are in the strategy process" (Patrizi and Thompson 2010:55).

Strategic philanthropists often insist on monitoring progress and evaluating outcomes according to metrics they specify, and grantees often prefer to retain control over monitoring and evaluation—and some grantees, of course, prefer to avoid monitoring and evaluation altogether. The most effective way to reconcile these differences and improve outcomes lies in pursuing conversations between funders and grantees along the lines suggested by Patrizi and Thompson.

Although the power dynamics between funders and grantees is a perennial issue, the importance of "constituent voice" (Keystone Accountability n.d.: "Constituent Voice," para. 1) or "listening to those who matter most, the beneficiaries"—to quote the title of an important article by Fay Twersky, Phil Buchanan, and Valerie Threlfall (Twersky, Buchanan, and Threlfall 2013: "Early Rumblings," para. 4)—has come to the fore only in the past decade. A new organization, the Fund for Shared Insight, founded by Twersky from the Hewlett Foundation, and Hilary Pennington from the Ford Foundation, among others, seeks to improve foundations' practices regarding beneficiary feedback and their own transparency.

Especially with the recent resurgence of grassroots social justice movements, beneficiary voices will likely become louder and more pervasive in the coming years. Heeding these voices would enable philanthropists to respond at least partially to growing concerns about the threat that large-scale philanthropy poses to democratic decision making. (See Tompkins-Stange 2016; Callahan 2017; Reich 2018; cf. Giridharadas 2018.)

The State of the Outcomes Movement and Its Path Forward

At the very least, the past several decades have seen the continuation of a century-long lumpy trend toward increasing nonprofit organizations' ability to achieve social outcomes. The developments chronicled in the preceding pages, however, suggest that something more is under way—something that we might call a movement. Philanthropists, nonprofit leaders, and academics have self-consciously worked to improve the social sector's effectiveness. In so doing, they have collaborated, moved among each other's organizations, and kept each other on their toes through argument and competition.

Yet for all of the activities described, only a fraction of wealthy philanthropists and family foundations—and only a fraction of the organizations they support—have adopted anything close to an outcomes orientation. Mario Morino, a savvy participant-observer in the sector, writes:

> I'd like to believe that this progress is a sign of pervasive disruptive transformation throughout the social sector. I'd like to believe that the majority of nonprofits are now poised to materially improve their impact by being more analytical about causal relationships and how they assess their performance. I'd like to believe that the majority of funders are poised to make decisions based on evidence and merit rather than loyalty, stories, and relationships. Yet the reality—in absolute terms—is that the promising developments . . . still touch only a small minority of nonprofits, foundations, and donors. (Morino 2011:39)

What are the barriers to further progress? Although the concepts underlying an outcome-based program strategy are not intrinsically difficult, they are not intuitive for many nonprofit leaders and philanthropists (Brest 2003). Developing a theory of change requires a degree of intellectual discipline that seems in short supply. And the task of using evidence to assess the strength of the causal links in a theory of change is equally challenging, if not more so.

Many staff and board members of nonprofit organizations are unfamiliar with an outcomes framework and often feel so pressed to attend to day-to-day operations and fund-raising that they pay scant attention to strategic planning. Also, many nonprofit organizations do not have demonstrable impact and may be better off not disclosing outcome data.

Many philanthropists are satisfied with the "warm glow" (Andreoni 1990:464) of charitable giving. Indeed, knowledge about their grantees' mixed results may reduce their motivation to give (Niehaus 2014). Moreover, many funders are averse to paying indirect costs (or overhead expenses) for their grantees' strategic planning, monitoring, and evaluation efforts. They may be subject to the psychological phenomenon of "overhead aversion" (Gneezy, Keenan, and Gneezy 2014:633), or perhaps they just want a free ride. Beyond compromising an outcomes approach, the failure to pay overhead expenses pushes organizations into a "nonprofit starvation cycle" (Gregory and Howard 2009: "Funders' Unrealistic Expectations," para. 1) that undermines the sector's overall effectiveness.

What could help move beyond these barriers? The availability of robust impact data will likely improve over time. But the most persistent challenge lies in philanthropists' and nonprofit organizations' reluctance to adopt an outcomes framework that can make use of available data. Meeting that challenge will require the broad diffusion of, and adherence to, professional norms that favor an outcomes orientation.

The norms of most professions or callings are undergirded by accountability to peers, other stakeholders, or regulatory authorities. As yet, there is no movement toward meaningful peer review. And although philanthropists are subject to regulations that cover certain organizational, procedural, and ethical issues, they are not regulated with respect to outcomes. On the whole, that's a good thing, given the costs that regulatory incompetence and political interference would impose on the valuable diversity of American philanthropy and civil society. Yet in the absence of regulation, only a small minority of donors adhere to norms that focus on effectiveness.

How might the sector continue to move toward an outcomes orientation in the absence of regulations? Here are some relevant factors that may advance that goal:

- *Common principles and practices.* Whatever their differences, the books and journal articles mentioned in this chapter converge on a general set of outcome-oriented norms. The Impact-Driven Philanthropy (IDP) initiative has succinctly captured a set of principles and practices that have been developed in recent years by a group of funders, donor educators, and nonprofit leaders (Giving Compass n.d.).
- *Education in outcomes frameworks.* An increasing number of courses at the undergraduate, postgraduate, and professional-school levels—including free online courses—cover core aspects of an outcomes framework. Unfortunately, however, donor education programs aimed at high-net-worth philanthropists have not been able to gain interest and support from their target audience.
- *Giving circles and learning communities.* In contrast to their unwillingness to learn from donor education programs, philanthropists are often willing to participate in giving circles that combine grantmaking with peer-to-peer education. Examples include Social Venture Partners International and Silicon Valley Social Venture Fund. Efforts to expand such opportunities would be welcome.
- *Certification of competency.* At present, anyone can print the words *philanthropic advisor* on a business card. But for every advisor who actually contributes to a philanthropist's outcomes, dozens lack the capacity to provide any help at all. The existence of the National Network of Consultants to Grantmakers indicates that there may be some demand for certification that philanthropists could require of advisors, consultants, and staff members. But a robust certification process must be rooted in a curriculum that includes a core set of principles and practices like those that IDP has formulated.
- *Transparency.* Transparency about an organization's strategies opens its work to scrutiny by various external stakeholders. As noted earlier, CEP offers foundations the

opportunity to obtain grantees' feedback from a Grantee Perception Report. Most of the questions used in the report do not directly pertain to effectiveness, however, and most foundations do not make their reports public. GrantAdvisor, a Yelp-like service for grantees that does not require a foundation's cooperation, focuses more on relationships and accessibility than effectiveness. Unfortunately, the growth of donor-advised funds and limited liability corporations in lieu of foundations reduces what modest transparency currently exists. I don't see a ready solution to this problem.

In *Good Work: Where Excellence and Ethics Meet,* Howard Gardner, Mihaly Csikszentmihalyi, and William Damon (2001) describe journalism as a domain that has developed professional practices concerning accuracy and fairness—practices that journalists tend to follow even though accountability is weak (granted that some journalists have no standards at all). The authors suggest that although journalists have developed these practices mostly on their own or with peers or mentors, such practices can be taught and shared.

In my most hopeful vision for the future, philanthropists and nonprofit leaders—like journalists—would identify as members of a calling with common standards of excellence. Perhaps we're already on this path, but the movement could be accelerated by a concerted field-building effort along the lines of successful efforts to build the fields of bioethics, end-of-life care, and conflict resolution.

Those fields have benefited from the emergence of practitioners who identify themselves as professionals. Although an increasing number of nonprofit staff members have cultivated such an identity, many high-net-worth donors who make their own philanthropic decisions do not approach their giving with a professional ethos. The challenge for the next decade will be to imbue donors with an outcomes orientation while, at the same time, acknowledging the legitimacy of their diverse substantive goals.

PART V

BALANCING ACCESS AND INCLUSION

THE TRIO OF CHAPTERS IN THIS section focus on some of the largest subfields in the nonprofit sector—health care, education, and the arts. These are, not surprisingly, the domains associated with very large donors and high-profile organizations that attract considerable public attention. Examples come easily; consider the huge gifts of Michael Bloomberg to Johns Hopkins University, or the gift of Marc and Lynne Benioff to the UCSF Benioff Children's Hospital, or the dozens of museums named after their famous donors, such as The Getty, The Gardner, The Whitney, The Broad, etc. Precisely because there are so many large, well-funded organizations in these domains, questions of access and inclusion arise. Who gets into these elite schools, hospitals, and museums? As soon as Bloomberg made his gift to ensure need-blind admissions in perpetuity at Johns Hopkins, critics wondered if social mobility would have been better enhanced if the gift had gone to community colleges. Similarly, one could ask who has access to the world-class care at well-funded children's hospitals, and whether museums are bastions of elite privilege?

Moreover, these are domains where there is both competition among nonprofits, between large and small ones and those with a national profile and those that are local, as well as with public institutions, be they schools, hospitals, or cultural organizations. In addition, because of the size of these domains, for-profit firms enter these markets, albeit selectively. Moreover, many nonprofits in these domains depend on earned income activities that lead to engagement with for-profits. Thus, even though health care, schooling, and the arts are fundamentally different, there are intriguing organizational parallels across them in that they are fields in which nonprofits, for-profits, and public sector organizations interact, compete, and collaborate. Consequently, the boundaries between the different institutional forms are often blurry and these lines of demarcation have shifted notably over time.

In Chapter 17, Jill R. Horwitz examines both the roles that nonprofits play in the health sector and those that health care entities play in the nonprofit sector. The promotion of health has been recognized as a valid charitable purpose for centuries, at least dating back to the earliest years of the seventeenth century in England. The entities that provide health care have been recognized as charitable nonprofits in the United States, entitled to associated tax exemptions and related benefits, since the relevant taxes were imposed. Despite their dominance and lengthy pedigree as charities under the law, health care has presented a challenge to popular, legal, and aspirational understandings of nonprofits. In part, this may be due to the status of health care charities as financial giants in the contemporary nonprofit sector. Representing only slightly more than 10 percent of all charities, health care nonprofits account for the largest part of the sector's revenues, expenses, and assets.

To further spell out the position of health care in the nonprofit sector and vice versa, Horwitz presents data regarding the number, types, and finances of U.S. health care charities. She revisits the history of nonprofit health care, challenging a widely held belief that health care charities historically provided care to the needy free of charge but have lost their way from their donative roots. She also surveys the recent, voluminous research on the role of ownership in health care provision and reviews recent and proposed regulation of health care nonprofits. Horwitz observes that nonprofit health care organizations are treated differently both from other charities and from other health care organizations. She concludes with a suggestion that despite copious research on health care nonprofits, much of the value that nonprofits bring to health care may well have been overlooked because that value may be hidden in the restraint it imposes on decisions to offer services and in the disciplining influences it has on competitors.

In Chapter 18 Richard Arum and Jacob L. Kepins provide a landscape of the U.S. education system, which has been conceptualized as differing by sector (nonprofit, public, for-profit) and level (K–12, sub-baccalaureate, and four-year colleges and universities). They examine the extent to which institutional characteristics vary along these dimensions, but they also note how—similar to the trends in other nonprofit sectors—recent scholarship has challenged the extent to which nonprofit schools are unique. Economic, social, and technological changes have led to the adoption of organizational practices that have produced schools that are increasingly hybrid with respect to organizational form, particularly with marketization in higher education. Boundaries across sector and level have become more permeable, with schools delivering new forms of education (such as online education) and serving student bodies that have become increasingly broad, diverse, and diffuse.

Arum and Kepins extend a traditional sectoral analysis of nonprofit schooling by arguing that we need to recognize the fundamental importance of nonprofit intermediaries in structuring and legitimating the basic features of the education system in the United States. Intermediaries are entities that occupy the space in between at least two other parties, operate independently of these two parties, and provide distinct value beyond what the parties alone would be able to develop or to amass by themselves. For example, in education many testing agencies, accreditation bodies, and ratings or watchdog groups are nonprofit intermediaries. In the context of a weak centralized state, such organizations can have great influence. In particular, many of the core aspects of organizational processes associated with public, nonprofit, and for-profit schools—such as regulation, quality assurance, resource acquisition, and the selection and credentialing of students—are institutional functions that are carried out by and dependent on nonprofit intermediaries.

In Chapter 19, Francie Ostrower focuses on the sustainability of the nonprofit arts subsector. The arts today face significant challenges, such as declining attendance across multiple art forms, financial difficulties, and the possibility that the supply of nonprofit arts organizations has outstripped demand for them. One former National Endowment for the Arts chair has gone so far as to propose that the nonprofit model of support for the arts in the United States has reached the limits of its capacity and needs to be rethought. This raises the question, however, of potential models for adaptation and change, such as adoption of for-profit business approaches, hybrid models, and greater engagement with, and responsiveness to, the wider community.

Analyses of the prospects for sustainability raise the normative question of whether and why arts should be supported. Ostrower examines policy rationales for support of the nonprofit arts, attending to debates over their value and legitimacy. Some have argued, for example, that the tax deduction for donations to nonprofit arts organizations should be limited or eliminated on the grounds that arts organizations do not serve the poor. Others argue that the arts provide wider public value that extends beyond their immediate clientele to the wider community, and thus warrant public support directly or indirectly through structures that sustain nonprofit organizations.

A common argument pits questions of financial sustainability against those of inappropriate commercialism in the nonprofit sector. The chapters here provide several other approaches that move beyond this debate. First, evaluating substantively similar organizations in similar ways may be more appropriate than imagining a sectoral divide. For example, it is likely in the interests of patients that charitable health organizations are structured—at least in some ways—in highly rationalized ways like their for-profit counterparts rather than becoming more like disaster funds, churches, or community theater groups. Second, a loss of nonprofitness on some dimensions is emerging alongside an expansion on others; more work is needed to articulate and theorize the growing role of nonprofit intermediaries and advocacy organizations in systematically structuring and defining organizational fields, public policies, and governance more broadly. Third, as the case of the arts aptly illustrates, in many instances the fundamental issue at stake is less about commercialization and more about the need for a public conversation about what types of charitable and associational activity merit active government support.

As these chapters show, issues of nonprofit sustainability are tied to broader debates about the feasibility and desirability of maintaining a distinct nonprofit sector. To some degree, financial self-sustainability has become a moral imperative as much as an instrumental one. Should public policy support nonprofits that cannot raise enough funding from the public and cannot exist without government? The question affects small entities, like local theater or dance groups, and large ones, like health care or education providers. In addition, the ability to create a sustainable nonprofit likely varies by the mission and intended beneficiaries of activities, with those aimed at wealthier individuals and where there is a larger audience having greater likelihood of success. But a tension arises because nonprofits that are highly successful financially face criticisms of becoming too businesslike, undermining trust in the organization. In health care, and to an extent also in education, the legitimacy of some nonprofit service providers is undercut by the size of their endowments and revenues. Moreover, in these fields a distinctive governance role is emerging with nonprofit intermediary and advocacy organizations, who further create a private regulatory process that has major ramifications for the public at large. These chapters cover distinct domains that nevertheless reflect common underlying debates and tensions.

17   CHARITABLE NONPROFITS AND
THE BUSINESS OF HEALTH CARE

Jill R. Horwitz[*]

NOT ONLY DO HEALTH CARE ORGANIZATIONS play an outsized role in government spending and the U.S. economy generally, they also play an outsized role in the nonprofit sector. Health care nonprofits make up about 13 percent of all public charities, yet account for the majority of the nonprofit sector's revenues and expenses, and almost half of its assets (McKeever 2015, tables 1 and 2). Because of this extensive economic presence, politicians, scholars, journalists, and others have criticized these giants of the nonprofit world as insufficiently charitable. They find nonprofit health care organizations so dissimilar from their image of conventional charities that they often question whether health care organizations should be considered charities at all.

There are many possible explanations for why the types of charitable health care entities discussed in this chapter—hospitals, insurers, nursing homes, and similar businesses that provide front-line medical care and/or insurance—seem to fit uneasily within the sector. Perhaps some unease has to do with their financing model; nonprofit health care organizations are largely self-sustaining, raising revenues from payments for services rather than from donations. Another potential explanation may be their role in markets; they compete with for-profit and government organizations in the same markets and operate in a manner that is hard for some observers to distinguish from commercial businesses. In fact, patients and insurance beneficiaries often don't know whether the health care organization with which they are interacting is a nonprofit or for-profit. Given the widespread use of for-profit management companies among all types of hospitals, even sophisticated observers may have a hard time identifying the ownership of an entity.

Another source of discomfort could stem from the fact that the larger health care industry is filled with people and organizations that are virtually all for-profit. For example,

[*] The author thanks Woody Powell, William Sage, and participants at a conference on this volume sponsored by and in a doctoral student seminar of the Stanford Center on Philanthropy and Civil Society for insightful comments; Allison Borsheim, Rebeca Fordon, Lynn McClelland, and Joshua Parson for excellent research assistance; and the University of Victoria Department of Economics for the time and space to write.

pharmaceutical companies, medical product manufacturers, and medical equipment providers are typically for-profit corporations. In this context, nonprofit health care seems to be only a small part of the medical-industrial complex. Through complex corporate structures and management agreements, lines among nonprofit and for-profit organizations may become blurred.

Furthermore, the members of the medical profession—whether organized in the form of sole proprietors, partnerships, or professional corporations—traditionally have operated as or in for-profit entities. Although observers have not thought of these actors as strictly profit-maximizing, the medical profession has played a principal role in determining the activities of nonprofit health care organizations, such as hospitals, thus raising questions about whether those activities are conducted to benefit physicians at a cost to patients or society at large. As more physicians are directly employed by nonprofit hospitals, questions related to the significance of ownership have loomed even larger.

The common thread among these many arguments for questioning the appropriateness of the nonprofit designation for health care entities is some variant of inappropriate commercialism. Rationalizing the role of health care organizations in the sector, however, may be easier if one considers charitable, nonprofit health care organizations on their own terms rather than in comparison to other types of charities. This chapter attempts to do so. Charitable health organizations do not have to be more like disaster funds, churches, or community theater groups to be appropriately organized as charitable nonprofits and enjoy the related benefits under the law. If one evaluates them as health care organizations, the degree of commercialization no longer seems so inappropriate. Rather, modern health care charities fit into a long charitable tradition, one that is quite different from their for-profit counterparts. This chapter suggests that treating health care charities as legitimate charities would be the wise course.

The health care entities addressed in this chapter are primarily those that (1) are organized as corporations (although some are charitable trusts), (2) consist of big provider organizations (i.e., mainly hospitals, nursing homes, and insurers), and (3) attract the attention of regulators and scholars (unlike more conventional health charities such as those that fund disease research or relieve the suffering of sick children and their families). Importantly, the discussion is limited to legally recognized public charities.

The legal definition of *charity* emerged as a part of the law of trusts during the development of the common law in England, and its formal content can be traced to the 1601 Statute of Charitable Uses (also known as the Statute of Elizabeth), which itself shares striking similarities to passages from William Langland's fourteenth-century poem *Vision of Piers Plowman*. These early definitions of charity include some forms of care for the sick. Ideas from these sources have found their way into modern U.S. tax law (Horwitz 2009).

Modern public charities, including health care charities, have two critical attributes. First, they are private, meaning that they are not owned by the public. Support from the government in the form of tax exemptions and other benefits does not make charities public entities. Second, unlike for-profit entities, they cannot be owned by private owners nor can they adopt the purpose of pursuing profits. Instead, they must have purposes benefiting the public, broadly defined, and these benefits must be identified by founders in a charity's organizing documents. Following convention and the bulk of social science research on health care charities, this chapter uses the terms *charity* and *nonprofit* interchangeably except when the argument requires that a distinction be made.

This chapter focuses on charities rather than nonprofits more generally for several reasons. First, nonprofit health entities are predominantly public charities, organized as nonprofits under state law and eligible for extensive tax benefits under Section 501(c)(3) of the Internal Revenue Code (i.e., they have enough public support to escape classification as a private foundation). In fact, public charities constitute about two thirds of all registered nonprofits (McKeever 2015: table 1). Second, most of the modern complaints about health care nonprofits stem from the concern that they do not deserve the benefits of charitable status under the law, such as preferential tax treatment. Finally, the general public's understanding of *nonprofit* typically refers to the category of organizations that are public charities (and not noncharitable nonprofits such as country clubs). Nonetheless, because they play such an important role in the health care sector, the chapter also discusses nonprofit insurers, even though they are generally not organized as public charities.

Following this introduction, the next section provides an overview of nonprofit health care in the United States in relation to its for-profit and government counterparts. The section outlines the scale and market share of nonprofit providers, including hospitals, nursing homes, and insurance companies. The section summarizes the number of organizations; revenues, assets, and expenses; utilization; and employment. This discussion illustrates that there is a great deal of variation in the ownership mix of different types of health care organizations.

The third section investigates the history of nonprofit health care entities in the United States and questions the frequently repeated assertion that nonprofit health care organizations, particularly hospitals, have lost their way by changing from fully charitable almshouses providing free care for those in need into fee-charging, ruthless big businesses. Although there is some evidence for a fall from this particular vision of charity, the historical record is more complicated than commonly represented. There is also a long history of nonprofit health care organizations as settings in which physicians used poor patients for training and as fee-charging providers. In short, even the earliest nonprofit health care entities were both charities in good standing and inextricably involved in commercial activity. That some degree of commercialization was built into the model from the beginning is a historical fact that we must recognize and should work to understand.

The fourth section reviews scholarly research about nonprofit/for-profit distinctions among health care entities. Because there are several existing literature reviews on the subject, including in previous editions of this volume, it cites only recent research. It also surveys research concerning a wider range of providers than is commonly addressed in reviews, such as dialysis providers and hospices. The section is organized around the two sets of questions that scholars most commonly address: (1) How do nonprofit, for-profit, and (less commonly) government-owned health care organizations differ? (2) Do nonprofit health care organizations merit federal and state tax exemptions? The scholarship that answers the first question frames nonprofit organizations as a form of health care organization—finding mainly favorable results when compared to other ownership forms. The scholarship that addresses the second question thinks of nonprofit health care organizations primarily as nonprofits, and from that perspective finds them wanting.

The fifth section turns to the legal and policy landscape. It observes that nonprofit health care organizations are treated quite differently—sometimes more favorably and other times less favorably—from both other nonprofit organizations and other health organizations. Drawing on previous work (Horwitz 2016), the section highlights a few salient examples and considers the justifications, sometimes explicit and at other times implicit, for the disparate treatment. It finds no consistent justification, and often no justification at all, for the variable treatment of nonprofit health providers, by either health law or nonprofit law. Indeed, their treatment often seems to operate at cross purposes, with the law sometimes favoring and at other times disfavoring the same entities for the same expected behavior.

The chapter concludes that there is a strong case to be made for contemporary nonprofit health care entities as charities in good standing, in light of both their current behavior and their history. The conclusion suggests that the critiques of charitable health care entities are misplaced and that, given both the history of health care entities and their modern context, we have much to gain by treating them as fully legitimate charities.

Ownership Landscape[†]

Health Care Nonprofits as Nonprofits

Depending on which measure one assesses, health care organizations play either a small or a large role in the nonprofit charity landscape. In several respects, they are quite small. As can be seen in Table 17.1, between 2000 and 2013, health care organizations have accounted for a high of 14.4 percent and a low of 12.1 percent of all charities. In fact, hospitals and primary care facilities have ranged from only 1.0 to 2.8 percent of charities. They also account for only a small percentage of total contributions received by charities. For example, in 2009, they received 7.4 percent of all charitable contributions, and in 2014 they accounted for 8.5 percent of all charitable contributions (McKeever 2015: table 5).

In other respects, they are the giants of the sector. In terms of finances, health care nonprofits dwarf other types of nonprofits. As can be seen in Table 17.2, between 2000 and 2013, they accounted for between 55 and 60 percent of total revenues, about 60 percent of expenses, and between 39 and 43 percent of all assets in the nonprofit sector. Hospitals and primary care facilities alone, despite representing such a small number of charities, account for most of the revenues (as can be seen in Figure 17.1), expenses, and assets of all health charities. To give a sense of scale, in terms of finances, educational institutions—including higher education and all others—come in second on these measures. However, as can be seen in Figure 17.2, despite these high levels of revenues and assets, on average, nonprofit hospitals' operating margins are negative in a given year.

Nonprofit health care organizations are also major employers in the health care sector. In 2012, they constituted 46 percent of private employment in the health care and social assistance industries, and those industries capture 68 percent of all nonprofit employment

† The author estimated all statistics that are presented without a citation. The underlying data are from the American Hospital Association's Annual Survey of Hospitals for the year reported. Percentages in this section may not total 100 because of rounding.

Table 17.1 Number and percentage of nonprofit health care organizations (selected years, 2013–2000)

Type of charity	2013	2011	2010	2009	2007	2005	2004	2000
					Number of charities			
Health	37,732	41,619	44,128	44,130	42,880	41,243	38,633	36,057
Hospitals and primary care facilities	7,062	7,308	7,657	7,526	7,360	5,045	3,139	6,929
Other health	30,670	34,111	36,471	36,604	35,520	36,198	35,494	29,128
All public charities	293,103	335,037	366,086	362,926	342,995	310,683	299,033	249,859
					Percentage of charities			
Health	12.90%	12.40%	12.10%	12.20%	12.50%	13.30%	12.90%	14.40%
Hospitals and primary care facilities	2.40%	2.20%	2.10%	2.10%	2.10%	1.60%	1.00%	2.80%
Other health charities	10.50%	10.20%	10.00%	10.10%	10.40%	11.70%	11.90%	11.70%
Other public charities	87.10%	87.60%	87.90%	87.80%	87.50%	86.70%	87.10%	85.60%

Notes: These data are from Urban Institute reports that contain summary information from the National Center for Charitable Statistics, Core files. They include information only from public charities that reported to the IRS on Form 990 and were required to do so based on gross receipts. Organizations that had their tax-exempt status revoked for failing to file were not included. Virtually all of the charities discussed in this chapter should be included in these data.

Sources: Data for 2013 from McKeever 2015, table 2, p. 51. Data for 2011 data Pettijohn 2013, table 2. Data for 2010 and 2000 from Blackwood, Roeger, and Pettijohn, table 3. Data for 2009 from Roeger, Blackwood, and Pettijohn 2011, table 2. Data for 2007 from Wing, Roeger, and Pollak 2009, table 2. Data for 2005 from Blackwood, Wing and Pollak 2008, table 2. Data for 2004 from Urban Institute 2007, table 3, p. 49.

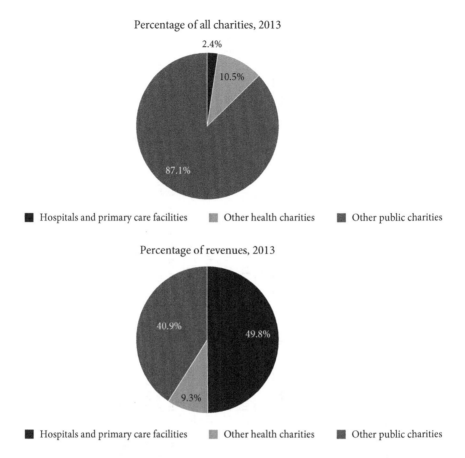

Figure 17.1   Health care charities: percentage of all charities and percentage of revenues, 2013
Notes: These data are from Urban Institute reports that contain summary information from the
National Center for charitable statistics, Core files. They include information only from public
charities that reported to IRS on a form 990 and were required to do so based on gross receipts.
Organizations that had their tax-exempt status revoked for failing to file were not included. Virtually
all of the charities discussed in this chapter should be included in these data.
Source: Data from McKeever 2015, table 2, p. 51.

in 2012 (Friesenhahn 2016). Hospitals alone accounted for 4 million jobs—35 percent of
nonprofit employment—with nursing and residential care adding another 1.2 million
jobs (Friesenhahn 2016).

Ownership and Division of Labor in the Health Care Industry

There is less of a clear division of labor among ownership types in the production of health
care than in other areas of endeavor in which nonprofits are prominent. For example,
producers of activities conventionally thought to be the high arts—ballet and modern
dance companies, orchestras, operas, chamber music organizations, and art museums—are
almost all nonprofits. On the other hand, dinner theaters, jazz ensembles, circuses, and

dance schools are almost all for-profit (DiMaggio 2006). Although nonprofit schools exist at all levels—from preschool through postgraduate school—there is some specialization. More than half of child care centers are for-profit (Sosinsky, Lord, and Zigler 2007). From fall 1999 through fall 2015, between 9.6 percent and 11.7 percent of elementary and secondary students were enrolled in private schools (National Center for Education Statistics 2018: fig. 1). Among four-year-degree-granting institutions with first-year undergraduates, there were more private nonprofits (1,295) than public schools (698) or for-profits (402) during 2016–2017 (Institute of Education Sciences 2018:178). However, public (885) and for-profit (518) schools dominated two-year institutions, with only 97 nonprofits in 2016–2017 (Institute of Education Sciences 2018).

In contrast, nonprofit, for-profit, and government health care organizations tend to compete directly against each other in the same markets, and to a great extent they offer the same general types of services such as hospital services, hospice, or nursing home residences.

Hospitals. Among general medical and surgical hospitals, excluding federal hospitals (e.g., military, Department of Justice [prisons], Bureau of Indian Affairs, and veterans'

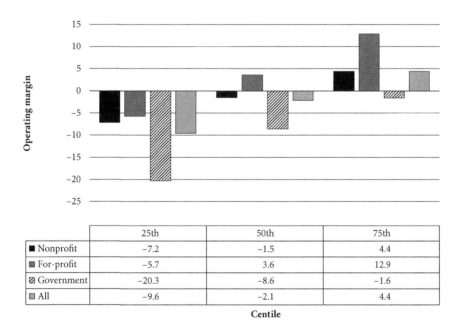

	25th	50th	75th
■ Nonprofit	−7.2	−1.5	4.4
■ For-profit	−5.7	3.6	12.9
▨ Government	−20.3	−8.6	−1.6
▨ All	−9.6	−2.1	4.4

Centile

Figure 17.2 Hospital operating margins, 2012
Notes: Data include all general medical and surgical hospitals excluding military and federal Department of Justice hospitals. Operating margins defined as (Total Patient Revenues–Contractual Allowances–Total Operating Expenses)/(Total Patient Revenues–Contractual Allowances).
Source: Author's analysis of data from the American Hospital Association Annual Survey 2012 and the Centers for Medicare & Medicaid Services Health Care Cost Reports 2012.

Table 17.2 Revenues, expenses, and assets of health care charities and all public charities (selected years, 2013–2000)

	2013	2011	2010	2009	2007	2005	2004	2000
Revenue (in billions $)								
Health	1,025.30	942.4	907.7	842.7	788.7	672.131	616.449	459.4
Hospital and primary care	864	798.5	773.4	716	663.5	492.498	446.433	383.2
Other health	161.3	143.8	134.3	126.7	125.2	179.633	170.016	76.2
Total public charities	1734.1	1593.6	1514.2	1399.3	1399.7	1144.022	1050.134	836.9
Expenses (in billions $)								
Health	975.8	895.3	missing	827.5	739.4	637.323	588.299	missing
Hospital and primary care	823.9	758.4		698.7	626.4	468	426.672	
Other health	151.9	136.9		128.8	113	169.323	161.627	
Total public charities	1623.8	1498.2		1399.9	1251.9	1053.487	981.271	
Assets (in billions $)								
Health	1392.8	1202.6	1141.8	1046	1003.2	826.159	748.34	606.9
Hospital and primary care	1133.5	973.3	926.9	844	792.8	608.836	539.604	468.2
Other health	259.3	229.3	214.9	202	210.4	217.323	208.736	138.7
Total public charities	3225	2856	2708.9	2533.6	2576.8	1975.792	1819.32	1500.2

Notes: These data are from Urban Institute reports that contain summary information from the National Center for Charitable Statistics, Core files. They include information only from public charities that reported to IRS on Form 990 and were required to do so based on gross receipts. Organizations that had their tax-exempt status revoked for failing to file were not included. Virtually all of the charities discussed in this chapter should be included in these data. $ billion are reported in each year's dollar value, unadjusted.

Sources: Data for 2013 from McKeever 2015, table 2. Data for 2011 from Pettijohn 2013, table 2. Data for 2010 and 2000 from Blackwood, Roeger, and Pettijohn, table 3. Data for 2009 from Roeger, Blackwood, and Pettijohn 2011, table 2. Data for 2007 from Wing, Roeger, and Pollak 2009, table 2. Data for 2005 from Blackwood, Wing, and Pollak 2008, table 2. Data for 2004 from https://www.hplct.org/assets/uploads/files/Nonprofit%20Almanac.pdf Pp. 50

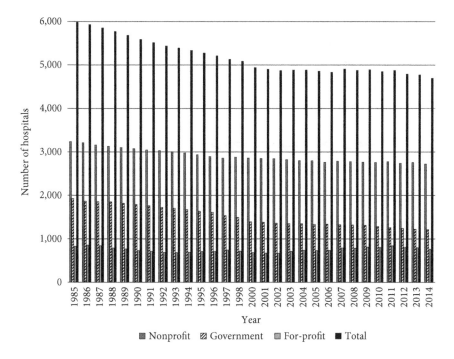

Figure 17.3 Number of general medical and surgical hospitals by ownership type, 1985–2014
Source: Author's estimates based on all hospitals reporting to the American Hospital Association's
Annual Survey 2014.

hospitals), in 2014 about 58 percent were nonprofit, 26 percent were government, and
16 percent were for-profit owned. A great deal of ink has been spilled discussing the
rise of for-profit health care, particularly in the hospital sector. And, indeed, there has
been some for-profit growth even though the total number of hospitals has been falling.
However, because of closures and conversions to and from nonprofit and government
ownership, as can be seen in Figure 17.3, the distribution has been remarkably stable over
time. Among all general medical and surgical hospitals, urban and rural, there was about
a 2.24 percentage point increase in the number of for-profit hospitals from 1985 to 2014,
although the number of nonprofit hospitals increased by about double that amount over
the same period.

More substantial growth in for-profit hospital care can be seen if one measures total
admissions by ownership form rather than by the number of hospitals. For example, in
1985 only 9 percent of admissions were to for-profit hospitals, with 67 percent at nonprofits
and 23 percent at government-owned hospitals; by 2014, these admission levels were 15
percent, 70 percent, and 15 percent respectively.[1]

As with education, the ownership mix of hospitals differs by specialty. For example,
as can be seen in Figure 17.4, in 2014, most children's hospitals were nonprofit (over 90
percent). In contrast, over 82 percent of both heart and orthopedic specialty hospitals,
which tend to be very profitable, were for-profit. Even within types of specialties, hospitals of different ownership further specialize. Nonprofit hospitals make up the bulk of

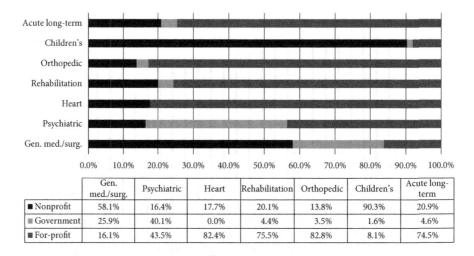

	Gen. med./surg.	Psychiatric	Heart	Rehabilitation	Orthopedic	Children's	Acute long-term
■ Nonprofit	58.1%	16.4%	17.7%	20.1%	13.8%	90.3%	20.9%
▪ Government	25.9%	40.1%	0.0%	4.4%	3.5%	1.6%	4.6%
■ For-profit	16.1%	43.5%	82.4%	75.5%	82.8%	8.1%	74.5%

Figure 17.4 Percentage of hospitals by ownership type, 2014

Source: Author's calculations from all hospitals reporting to the American Hospital Association's Annual Survey 2014.

all teaching hospitals, which constitute about 6 percent of general medical and surgical hospitals; in 2014, 62 percent were nonprofit, 35 percent were government-owned, and 3 percent were for-profit.[2] Among general medical and surgical hospitals, nonprofit hospitals are also by far the most likely to run an American Medical Association–approved residency program; in 2014, 67 percent were nonprofit, 21 percent were government-owned, and 12 percent were for-profit.[3]

The mix of hospital types also varies by whether an area is densely or sparsely populated. In the most populated areas (metropolitan divisions), with some variation over time, nonprofits account for just under two thirds of hospitals (62 percent in 2014), government-owned hospitals account for 18 percent, and for-profit hospitals make up around 20 percent. The more rural[4] the area, the more likely a hospital is to be government-owned (in 2014, 43 percent of rural hospitals) or nonprofit (48 percent) and the less likely a hospital is to be for-profit (9 percent).[5]

Nursing homes. In 1983, Bruce Vladeck wrote that "Nursing Homes are the most numerous health-care institutions in the United States, though hardly the most visible or best understood" (Vladeck 1983:352). Although scholars have substantially increased the attention they give to nursing homes, they are still understudied in relation to hospitals. As can be seen in Table 17.3 and Figure 17.5, nursing homes are largely for-profit, with nonprofits a far second, and government nursing homes a distant third. Between 2004 and 2014, the number of nursing homes declined slightly. Over the same period, for-profit nursing homes increased their market share (from 61.5 percent in 2004 to 69.8 percent in 2014), while the market shares of nonprofit and government nursing homes declined (nonprofit from 31.1 percent to 24.0 percent; government from 7.5 percent to 6.2 percent).

Table 17.3 Number of nursing homes by ownership type, 2004–2014

	For-profit	Nonprofit	Government	Total
2004	9,900	5,000	1,200	16,100
2005	10,582	4,495	955	16,032
2006	10,578	4,381	964	15,923
2007	10,639	4,278	940	15,857
2008	10,621	4,167	914	15,702
2009	10,644	4,143	915	15,702
2010	10,741	4,009	896	15,646
2011	10,824	3,951	898	15,673
2012	10,814	3,897	919	15,630
2013	10,887	3,815	936	15,638
2014	10,913	3,756	971	15,640

Sources: Data for 2004 are from "Nursing Home Facilities: December 2006." *Centers for Disease Control and Prevention*, table 1, p. 1. Data for 2005–2014 are from "Nursing Home Data Compendium 2015 Edition." *Centers for Medicaid & Medicare Services*, 2015, figure 1.3, p. 11.

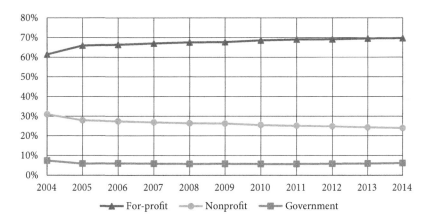

Figure 17.5 Percentage of nursing homes by ownership type, 2004–2014
Sources: Data for 2004 are from Centers for Disease Control 2006, table 1. Data for 2005–2014 are from Centers for Medicare & Medicaid Services, 2015, figure 1.3.

Other health care providers. A mix of owners can also be found among other types of providers. The hospice industry has seen a dramatic change in ownership (Stevenson et al. 2016; Thompson, Carlson, and Bradley 2012). For-profit share grew from 5 percent to about 51 percent of the hospice industry from 1990 to 2011 (Aldridge et al. 2014). Since then, the share of for-profits has climbed to well over 60 percent, with year to year variation. In 2016, 67 percent of Medicare-certified hospice facilities were for-profit, 29 percent were nonprofit, and the remaining 3.9 percent were government (National Hospice and Palliative Care Organization 2017).

Home health care providers are even more likely to be for-profit. In 2014, 80 percent were for-profit, 15 percent were nonprofit, and the remaining 5 percent were government-owned (Centers for Disease Control and Prevention 2017).

Health Insurers. As with other subsectors in the health care sector, nonprofits are only part of the insurance landscape. Americans with health insurance are covered by for-profit, nonprofit, and government-sponsored plans. In 2016, 35 percent of Americans had government insurance through Medicare, Medicaid, or other public systems (Kaiser Family Foundation 2016). Fifty-six percent of Americans were covered by employer or nongroup plans, and these included a mix of nonprofit and for-profit insurers.

As with recipients of services from other organizations in the health care field, many insurance beneficiaries do not know whether they are insured by the government, for-profit companies, or nonprofit companies. Some beneficiaries of government-sponsored insurance receive some or all of their coverage through private insurance contractors. Many people who are covered by employer-sponsored insurance interact with a commercial (nonprofit or for-profit) insurance company for customer service, but their underlying insurance is provided by their employer, not the insurance company that contracts with the employer for administrative services such as processing claims and performing utilization review or gatekeeping functions.

Nonetheless, among the large health plans in the United States (i.e., those with at least 100,000 enrollees) in 2012, 63 percent (97 plans) were nonprofit and 27 percent (41 plans) were for-profit, with the remaining 10 percent (16 plans) being government-owned (Alliance for Advancing Nonprofit Health Care 2012). For-profit companies, however, are larger. Therefore, about half of enrollees were covered by nonprofits and slightly fewer by for-profits in 2012; nonprofits covered 50 percent of fully insured beneficiaries and 45 to 53 percent of total beneficiaries, including those insured by their employers, while for-profits covered 47 percent of fully insured beneficiaries and 53 percent of total beneficiaries, including those insured by their employers (Alliance for Advancing Nonprofit Health Care, 2012).

Among nonprofits, the landscape is also complicated. Nonprofit insurers may be legally organized as charities under state incorporation law. However, the bulk of them are not eligible for the extensive tax benefits associated with I.R.C. 501(c)(3) or I.R.C. 501(c)(4). Rather, since 1986, they have been governed by I.R.C. 501(m) as providing "commercial type insurance," which roughly includes all insurers that provide indemnity insurance, such as traditional Blue Cross and Blue Shield plans. Moreover, many nonprofit insurance companies are organized as mutual nonprofits, entities owned by policyholders; any excess premiums are reinvested in the insurer or given to the members through dividends or reductions in premiums. Under the Internal Revenue Code, mutual insurers—that is, 501(c)(15)s—are tax-exempt but receive fewer tax benefits than public charities under 501(c)(3).

Finally, health maintenance organizations (HMOs), which are a hybrid of medical provider and insurer, may be organized as nonprofits under state law. Their history of tax exemption has been volatile. Although 501(m) did not apply to them as they did not provide commercial insurance, the tax exemptions of HMOs—some under 501(c)(3), but mostly under 501(c)(4)—have been increasingly challenged by the IRS.

The preceding discussion highlights the central and enduring role of health care entities among charities and of charities among health care entities. At the same time, it documents some of variation among these entities.

Nonprofits and Commercialization in Historical Context

The distorting effects of profit-seeking among nonprofits—museums generating more revenue from gift shops, restaurants, and parking than from admissions, and megachurches with onsite Starbucks franchises and gyms—have long troubled scholars (see, e.g., Colombo 2002, 2007b; Weisbrod 1998). Nonprofit hospitals, however, are frequently identified as the canonical example of charities that have taken an impermissible commercial turn.[6] In some respects, their reputation has been earned. For example, today many nonprofit hospitals use complex corporate structures, often involving collaborations and formal affiliations with for-profit entities (e.g., Colombo 2002). Indeed, among nonprofits that have some taxable revenues, health care nonprofits are second only to housing nonprofits in their propensity to use taxable subsidiaries. Their for-profit partners account for over 60 percent of all taxable subsidiaries of nonprofits (Yetman and Yetman 2008). Moreover, health care nonprofits' commercial behavior, including profit-seeking, tends to increase with increased competition with for-profits (Horwitz and Nichols 2009; Levitt 1986).

Among the most prominent and disapproving charges made against modern nonprofit health care organizations, particularly hospitals, is that they have lost their way from their charitable roots as almshouses, where care was once freely given to those in need. David Rosner's (1982) classic study of hospitals in New York dates the shift from a paternalistic service orientation to a bureaucratic, medical, and business orientation to the late nineteenth and early twentieth century. Daniel M. Fox (2013:102) observes that "the values and principles of governance embraced by leaders of non-profit organizations, and especially of hospitals, have contributed to the growing commercialization of the health sector during the past half-century." Relying on Rosner's account, Fox (2015) also identifies the beginning of commercialization as the late nineteenth century and traces what he sees as a paradox—a history of health policy incentives that led to both the expansion of nonprofit health enterprise and its commercialization. However, according to Fox, a move away from commercialization began in 2010 when the ACA "encourage[d] tax-exempt organizations to contribute to the public good" (Fox 2015:180).

Others speak more generally about the long-term trend. For example, according to Adam Reich (2014b:10), "early hospitals in the United States were indistinguishable from almshouses, and guaranteed the poor a basic (if limited) right to care." Although he recognizes that almshouses need to be understood in their historical context, he is one of many writers who paint a glorified picture of almshouses and early hospitals in comparison to which modern entities fall short. He explains that hospitals are losing the struggle to maintain local ties because they operate in an "increasingly market-driven institutional environment" (Reich 2014a:1578). Cecilia McGregor (2007) traces her overview of charity back to Egypt in service of an argument that charities should provide free care for uninsured and inadequately insured patients.

More boldly, Kerry O'Halloran (2012:4) claims that "'Profit' and 'charity' are not readily reconciled." Her definition of charity leans heavily on Richard Titmuss's (1970) concept of gifts and altruism, which argued that charity becomes tainted (literally in his study documenting inferior blood donations) when mixed with commerce. According to O'Halloran's account, although charities have had business interests in the past, the focus on business has increased dramatically (O'Halloran 2012:123). Health care in the United States is offered as a prime example, in large part because the United States does not have universal public health insurance or a government-owned hospital system. Quoting congressional testimony on nursing home shortages from 1965, she endorses the story of the fall of health care charities: "The image of a voluntary institution as a charitable organization, financing its care of patients to a substantial degree through philanthropy . . . is largely anachronistic" (O'Halloran 2012:265).

Although it is beyond the scope of this chapter to address the comparative claims about national health care systems, observers often fail to acknowledge that (1) a great deal of health care in the United States is covered by public payers and (2) other national systems substantially involve nongovernmental actors (e.g., pharmaceutical insurance in Canada). Nonetheless, there is a strong argument to be made that patients in the U.S. system, which relies on a greater share of private care provision (both for-profit and charitable) than other systems, are likely to benefit from more of those providers being charitable since charities are less likely to prioritize profit-making than are for-profits. This observation does not mean that all providers should be charities. Given the massive cost of modern medicine, even subtracting generous estimates of overhead and profits in the current system, there is simply no possibility that charities could meet the health care needs of the U.S. population. And, as this section explains, they never fully did.

The historical record of nonprofit health care organizations in America (and elsewhere) does not support the story of a linear transformation from early providers of free care for the needy to modern charitable nonprofits degraded by commercialization.[7] At a minimum, the early history shows that if nonprofit status and commercialization of health care is an American paradox, it began with colonial health care endeavors. Some early hospitals were charitable in the popular sense of the word, but (1) many did not grow out of almshouses but in fact treated inmates from neighboring almshouses for payment; (2) there is considerable evidence of commercialization among charities, beginning with almshouses themselves and the earliest hospitals (which were largely self-supporting); and (3) nonprofit health care organizations have always, at times to a greater and lesser degree, operated in a system of private markets. This section takes each of these observations in turn.

Did Modern Health Care Entities Have Their Roots in Almshouses?

Evidence that hospitals grew out of almshouses is mixed. In some cases, doctors treated inmates in almshouses, and almshouses sometimes had infirmaries to treat inmates who could not be treated in the living quarters of the poorhouse. For example, the infirmary in the Philadelphia Almshouse was known as the Philadelphia Hospital (Packard 1963). Some hospitals that were affiliated with the almshouses subsequently separated from them or took them over entirely, transforming them into hospitals (Dowling 1982). A government almshouse could transform into a government hospital, as in the case of the Baltimore City Hospital, which did not separate from the Baltimore City Department of Public Welfare until 1964 (Kerson 1981).

In other places, hospitals were always separate institutions (Dowling 1982). For example, early colonial almshouses, such as those established in the 1600s in Virginia, New Amsterdam, and Boston, did not become hospitals even though they cared for the sick (Dowling 1982). The example of the country's first true hospital, founded in 1751, is illustrative. According to its founder, Benjamin Franklin, the Pennsylvania Hospital was established as an independent charity for the poor and sick, funded mostly by private subscription but, because donations were insufficient, with additional funding from the Pennsylvania Assembly (Cohen 1954). Unlike the Philadelphia infirmary, it did not limit treatment to a group of residents (Price 1985).

In fact, it is not modern hospitals but nursing homes that most directly emerged from almshouses. Sidney Watson's (2010) detailed account of the history of the nursing home industry traces the development of nursing homes from almshouses, which were originally used only when home care was unavailable. She describes how "the feeble elderly, chronically ill, physically disabled, and those with mental retardation" remained in county and municipal almshouses into the early twentieth century (Watson 2010:941). For example, a report from the 1930s about Missouri almshouses describes rural almshouses as farms, run by farmers who received pay to keep inmates. The report criticized these facilities, stating that they were "ill adapted to care for all the types of cases which they receive, have little or no hospital facilities or special provisions for the care of mental cases and are likely to be managed by unqualified and incompetent personnel" (Pihlblad 1938:204). The growth of public payment systems, with inadequate budgets, led to the creation of rest, nursing, and convalescent homes in which frail, elderly, and disabled poor people could receive housing and some care, albeit often substandard (Watson 2010). Thus, the organizational heirs to the almshouse are, and have always been, predominantly for-profit rather than nonprofit entities.

Almshouses, Hospitals, and Payment by Poor Patients

There is plenty of evidence to verify that charity—in the form of giving help without expectation of monetary reward—has been provided by some almshouses and nonprofit health care organizations since their earliest appearance in the United States. Almshouses were founded to help the poor, vagrant, and sick who could not find housing or sustenance elsewhere. Similarly, the charter of the Massachusetts General Hospital, founded in 1811, required it "to support thirty sick and lunatic persons who were charges of the state," although later the requirement was changed to depend on the income available to the hospital from sales of property donated by the Commonwealth (Commission on Hospital Care 1947:439). The petition to the Pennsylvania legislature to found the Pennsylvania Hospital portrays precisely the vision of charity contemporary critics imagine modern hospitals should fulfill:

> The kind Care of our Assemblies have heretofore taken for the Relief of sick and distempered Strangers, by providing a Place for their Reception and Accommodation, leaves us no Room to doubt an equal tender Concern for the Inhabitants. And we hope they will be of Opinion with us, that a small Provincial Hospital, erected and put under proper Regulations, in the Care of Persons to be appointed by this House, or otherwise, as they shall think meet, with Power to receive and apply the charitable Benefactions of good People towards

enlarging and supporting the same, and some other Provisions in a Law for the Purposes above mentioned, will be a good work, acceptable to God and to all the good People they represent." (Packard 1963:182).

However, the operations of the almshouses and hospitals were always more commercial than this aspirational language would suggest. Some inmates in almshouses were so sick, old, or physically or mentally disabled that they could not work—but everyone else did. At a minimum, inmates helped run the almshouse. For example, poor women were busy "preparing food, making and washing clothing and bedding, birthing and raising children, nursing the sick, tending the handicapped, laying out the dead" (Herndon 2012:351). In 1835, Philadelphia's Board of Guardians of the Poor—the entity with the authority to collect a poor tax and distribute it to the indigent—prioritized admission to the almshouse for female inmates according to whether they were aged and helpless women in bad health; could sew and knit; or were good sewers, spinners, scrubbers, and washerwomen (Rosenberg 1977). Sewing appears to have been important. Those who refused to work were compelled by force. "Although the Maryland almshouse was supported through taxes, those poor who were able to work could be compelled to do so by the overseer in the almshouse or workhouse; refusal subjected the person to no more than thirty-nine lashes" (Quigley 1997:126).

The almshouses were themselves workhouses or attached to workhouses, or they contracted out inmates as workers. Inmates farmed, whitewashed buildings, and maintained and repaired the grounds and buildings (Bourque 2012). In fact, during the antebellum period, the Philadelphia almshouse established a manufactory to produce textiles, hoping to compete with British imports (Bourque 2012). Some inmates worked for their keep; some were paid cash for their work; some worked in exchange for "goods, liquor, and the approval of supervisors" (Bourque 2012:388). Some also held paid jobs offsite. In worse cases, for example in Maryland, "the Trustees of the Poor were given the right to bind out, or indenture, any poor child or orphan under their care in the poor house" (Kerson 1981:204).

Lest one believe that these activities were conducted exclusively for the purpose of developing job skills for the benefit of the residents, rather than reflecting a commercial orientation among almshouse or hospital boards, consider how those unable to work were treated. In response to the increasingly unmanageable crowds that came to stare at patients through the windows to their cells, in 1767 the board imposed a fee on those who wished to observe patients who were in the hospital because of lunacy—essentially transforming them into a sideshow—and only removed it twenty-four years later because of injury to the patients (Packard 1963).

As the earliest hospitals emerged—either in conjunction with or separately from almshouses, as discussed previously—they were largely self-supporting and, therefore, engaged in commercial endeavors. During the late eighteenth century, the Pennsylvania Hospital imported medicine and sold it at a profit; it also ran working farms that, in addition to supplying the hospital with milk and produce, brought in revenues through external sales (Dorner 2016).

The earliest hospitals also charged for treatment of some poor patients. There are records of the managers of the Philadelphia Hospital negotiating its rates with the Pennsylvania Almshouse to admit sick almshouse inmates to the hospital. The hospital sometimes reduced its fees to settle the debts of the almshouse and, at least in the spring of 1799, admitted six patients without pay; at other times the hospital refused to treat almshouse patients for free because of the expense (Packard 1963) Even poor patients who were admitted for free treatment were required to bring a security deposit from the local overseer of the poor as indemnification, so that the hospital would not be stuck paying for the transport or burial of the patient's dead body. The security was required "in case they die, or to defray the expense of carrying them back to their place of abode, and that they may not become a charge of the city" (Packard 1963:196).

Perhaps more costly to patients than compelled labor, being ogled, or paying for services were the payments they made with their bodies as objects of experimentation and medical study. As Gert H. Brieger noted, "As early as 1769, Samuel Bard of New York remarked that 'the nature of diseases, and the practice of medicine cannot be taught but in a public hospital" (1972:233). The role of nonpaying patients as teaching material has persisted in charitable health care organizations from their earliest days and into the modern context (e.g., Dowling 1982; Brieger 1972; Vogel 1978:174). In some cases, recognition of the opportunity for training subjects inspired the shift from almshouse to hospital. For example, the Maryland almshouse began transforming itself into a medical institution when "the potential of the Almshouse as a teaching facility for a medical school began to be appreciated" (Kerson 1981:205).

Medical residents paid the almshouses and hospitals to hone their practice, which appears to have involved treating most complaints with "bleeding, purging, and puking" (Price 1985:387). This use of patients as subjects caused John Jones, physician to Benjamin Franklin and George Washington, to remark, "Among the variety of public errors and abuses to be met with in huyman affairs there is not one, perhaps, which more loudly calls for a speedy effectual reformation than the misapplied benevolence of hospitals for the sick and wounded" (Brieger 1972:238).

Given this long history of inmates and patients' payment for health care in the form of money, labor, and their bodies, it is a stretch to characterize almshouses and early hospitals as providing services as gifts to the needy. These relationships included some forms of conventional charity, but they can nonetheless be accurately characterized as commercial. The history does not suggest that contemporary health care nonprofits that charge fees and limit free services have strayed far from their roots.

Medicine for the Non-Indigent

Until the end of the nineteenth century, people who were sick entered hospitals only if they had no other options. At that time, you would stay at a hospital only "if you could not afford care at home, had no relatives to help provide nursing, or lived in such crowded tenement quarters that there was no room for a sick person" (Brieger 1972:235). Countless descriptions of the fetid and dangerous conditions, such as one story from a newspaper in 1860 of rats devouring a newborn's face, make clear why these environments were avoided by anyone with the means to do so (Brieger 1972; Dowling 1982).

Therefore, most people received care outside the hospital. Moreover, the care that they received was as inescapably commercial as it is today, and perhaps even more so.

First, throughout the history of the United States, sick people and their families have paid physicians out of pocket for their care, only very recently via insurance. For example, in the nineteenth century, people diagnosed themselves and determined when to find a physician and pay for treatment.

> As a result, medical practice developed as a form of self-employment, in which the physician received his earnings from fees obtained for services rendered on a voluntary case-by-case basis. Physicians in the nineteenth century competed for the patient's dollar not only with other physicians, but also with lay and part-time practitioners, who frequently charged less than physicians and provided serious competition for them during much of the period. (Rothstein 1972:13).

The transformation of nineteenth-century to twentieth-century medicine has been one of increasing protection from these markets through regulation—licensing, basing medicine on what looks like modern science, raising educational standards, and improving medical schools (Kett 1968).

Second, hospitals did not take all comers. They chose patients based on their social status, often accepting only those recommended by the hospital's patrons (Dowling 1982). They selected patients based on the potential profitability of treating their ailments. Yet courts did not refrain from classifying a charitable hospital "as an eleemosynary institution, even though it may limit its services and benefits to certain classes of society or to patients suffering from certain types of ailments" (Commission on Hospital Care 1947:587).

Both government and nonprofit hospitals always charged fees, although the former were typically lower. (For fee tables from the nineteenth and early twentieth centuries, see Dowling 1982:77, table 17.5). From their earliest days in America, nonprofit hospitals have accepted "patients able to pay a part or all of the cost of their care" (Commission on Hospital Care 1947:537). Of course, those fees were considerably more affordable than they are today.

Throughout the twentieth century, expensive hospital charges have raised policy concerns. A report issued in 1932 by the Committee on the Costs of Medical Care, a self-organized committee of prominent physicians supported by one million dollars of foundation funding that issued fifteen separate reports over five years (Gore 2013), noted that hospital care was out of reach for patient of moderate means (Committee on the Costs of Medical Care 1932). The report describes how "a number of voluntary hospitals in this country are now developing special plans for the so-called 'patient of moderate means,'" including fixed-maximum fee schedules, bill adjustments, and various cost controls such as flat-rate maternity services (these ring to modern ears as something like capitation) (Committee on the Costs of Medical Care 1932:83). Sometimes the government helped poor patients take advantage of these programs through subsidizing treatment, but it left most poor patients behind (Gore 2013). The report's call for insurance was condemned in an accompanying minority report as exploiting medical men and representing "a further step in the commercialization of medicine" and later deemed an incitement to revolution by the editor of the *Journal of the American Medical Association* (Committee on the Costs of Medical Care 1932:175.)

A few years later, a 1947 report from the Commission on Hospital Care, an independent committee formed by the American Hospital Association, made clear that nonprofit hospitals were not meant for the indigent, distinguishing them from those "maintained by government mainly for indigent patients" (Commission on Hospital Care 1947:168). The report stated, "Independence of operation and the need of attracting wide public interest in the establishment and maintenance of voluntary hospitals have influenced their location in areas offering the greatest prospects for their financial solvency." (Commission on Hospital Care 1947:170).

Nonetheless, charging fees that were high enough to be self-sustaining yet low enough for patients to afford has posed a challenge for nonprofit hospitals from their beginnings. Eventually, prepaid plans started appearing and then indemnity insurance covered health care costs, including at nonprofit hospitals. "By 1940, 10 percent of the U.S. population had insurance. By 1957 . . . 72 percent of the U.S. population had health insurance" (Kinney 2010:409).

As is the case today, profits from relatively high-paying patients subsidized lower-paying or indigent patients in various ways, such as to purchase capital equipment used for all patients or to subsidize care itself. Using profits in this way—reinvesting them in the hospital—is different from the practice of actively cost-shifting, which involves raising private-pay prices to make up for cuts by public payers. Upon investigation, cost-shifting appears to be less common than frequently assumed (Frakt 2011), particularly given evidence that private payers copy pricing strategies of public payers (see, e.g., Clemens and Gottlieb 2017). Even at the founding of the Pennsylvania Hospital, poor patients were admitted up to the level that they could be accommodated by revenues from interest on the hospital's stock, and then "the managers shall have the liberty of taking in other patients, at such reasonable rates as they can agree for; and the profits arising from boarding and nursing such patients, shall be appropriated to the same uses as the interest-money of publick stock" (Packard 1963:196).

Nonprofit hospitals have always treated poor people, subsidizing some care to a greater or lesser degree, but they never were exclusively or even primarily organized to provide free care to the indigent. Today, as before, some patients must rely on the provision of free treatment. But if one is to argue that contemporary health care charities are undeserving of their charitable status, it should not be on the grounds that they have strayed too far from their roots in the exclusive provision of free care, as there was no such foundation.

Scholarship on Nonprofit Health Care Organizations

Several literature reviews and metastudies survey research on ownership of nonprofit health care organizations, particularly hospitals (e.g., Herrera et al. 2014; Eggleston et al. 2008; Shen et al. 2007; Schlesinger and Gray 2006a; Rosenau and Linder 2003; Sloan 2000; Gaynor, Ho, and Town 2015). There are also a number of thorough reviews of research on nursing home ownership (e.g., Hillmer et al. 2005; Comondore et al. 2009). Other reviews address ownership and outcomes. For example, Mark Schlesinger and Bradford H. Gray (2006b) categorize studies of hospitals, nursing homes, and managed care organizations by nonprofit or for-profit advantage, finding that nonprofits most often perform better than, although sometimes equal to, for-profits according to several measures of quality, cost, and access. Lisa R. Shugarman, Nancy Nicosia, and Cynthia R. Schuster (2007) provide a limited review of papers studying differences in health care provider costs, demonstrating mixed results. Given the availability of these resources, this section provides only a broad overview of prior research, mainly citing studies published after the previous edition of this book was released in 2006, except when citing an older study provides context for discussing new areas of attention.

Scholarship on nonprofit health care organizations has concentrated on two sets of questions. First, there is a large and long-standing body of research, particularly quantitative empirical research, asking whether and how nonprofit, for-profit, and (less commonly) government-owned health care organizations differ. Most recently, scholars have considered how nonprofits respond to market conditions, including ownership mixes in the market. Second, scholars have asked whether nonprofits merit federal and state tax exemptions. Most recently, scholars have investigated the relationship between the Affordable Care Act (ACA) and the activities of nonprofit health providers, as well as addressing questions concerning whether nonprofits provide sufficient community benefits to localities.

Although it is beyond the scope of this chapter to address divisions within charitable health care entities, there are important distinctions among them. Indeed, "the Catholic Church owns or oversees the national's largest group of not-for-profit health care sponsors, systems, and facilities, comprising nearly 12.4% of hospitals in the United States" (Kutney-Lee et al. 2014:135). Whether a provider has a church affiliation may make a meaningful difference for a provider's community and its patients. For example, religious hospitals are more likely to report to the American Hospital Association that they provide certain listed community benefits than are other nonprofits (Ferdinand, Epané, and Menachemi 2014). Some religious hospitals, particularly Catholic hospitals, limit access to services such as abortion, in vitro fertilization, tubal ligations, or vasectomies in many circumstances. Even within Catholic hospitals there are differences. Kenneth R. White and Roberto Dandi (2009) recently examined the mission statements of Catholic health systems and, although they found tremendous similarities in the statements, they also found that different systems prioritized values differently and some expressed different values altogether. However, if differences among nonprofits (e.g., between religious and secular nonprofit hospitals) were greater than the differences among nonprofit, for-profit, and government entities, the scholars would not have found the outcomes reported in this section. Moreover, there is some evidence that patients do not perceive much of a difference between religious and secular health care nonprofits: "patients treated in Catholic hospitals appear to rate their hospital experience similar to patients treated in non-Catholic hospitals" (Kutney-Lee et al. 2014:140).

Differences Among Nonprofit, For-Profit, and Government Health Care Organizations

Although they have generated mixed findings, in part because they focus on different outcomes and use different datasets, most of the studies on quality of care and service mix find that nonprofits tend to outperform comparable for-profits on service. However, there are fewer differences in studies that concentrate more directly on financial behavior, such as providing free care.

Hospitals. As research reviews suggest, the bulk of analyses focus on hospital behavior. Most recently, a few studies take novel approaches to quality measurement. For example,

Hanadi Hamadi and colleagues (2018) consider the effects of ownership on health in hospital markets, rather than only among hospital patients; they find that hospital referral regions with the greatest number of nonprofits had better affordability, access to care, and prevention and treatment outcomes than government and for-profit hospitals. In a survey of nonprofit hospital board chairs, Ashish Jha and Arnold Epstein (2010) found that board chairs of high-performing nonprofits chose quality as one of their top two priorities, suggesting that hospital performance can be improved through interventions with their boards.

There is considerable recent evidence that nonprofit hospitals offer different services than for-profits. For example, Jill R. Horwitz (2003, 2005, 2007) shows that among urban hospitals, nonprofits are more likely than for-profits to offer relatively unprofitable services, less likely to offer relatively profitable services, and less responsive to financial incentives when profitability changes. The same results hold for rural hospitals (Horwitz and Nichols 2011). Analyzing a 20 percent sample of U.S. community hospitals, Marco A. Castaneda and Dino Falaschetti (2008) find that although nonprofit, government, and for-profit hospitals differ in the quantity of different types of services provided, those differences should not be attributed to ownership itself but rather to the fact that different types of hospitals decide to locate in different types of markets; they conclude that observed differences in care provision likely reflect differences in objectives of the hospitals rather than noncontractible quality and asymmetric information hypotheses. Tom Chang and Mirielle Jacobson (2012) show that financial pressure increases the probability that a nonprofit hospital provides profitable services—a finding inconsistent with both the view that nonprofits are merely "profits in disguise" and the view that they are "purely altruistic," instead supporting the idea that they maximize output of health services or perquisites for medical staff. In another study, David Dranove, Craig Garthwaite, and Christopher Ody (2017) demonstrate that, on average, nonprofit hospitals responded to reductions in assets related to the 2008 stock market collapse by reducing their offerings of relatively unprofitable services, but not by raising prices, cutting operating costs, or decreasing free care for indigent patients. Theresa Morris, Kelly McNamara, and Christine H. Morton (2017) find that women who give birth in for-profit hospitals are much more likely to have cesareans than women with similar patient-level characteristics in nonprofit hospitals.

In terms of relations with patients, nonprofits "appear more trustworthy in delivering services, being less likely to make misleading claims, to have complaints lodged against them by patients, and to treat vulnerable patients differently from other clientele" (Schlesinger and Gray 2006a:W291). However, Michael Vlassopoulos (2009) has argued that if an organization can establish and sustain an accurate reputation regarding its quality of care, for-profit rather than nonprofit is the preferred form because the for-profit will more efficiently seek to provide high-quality care.

Several studies focus more specifically on financial behavior. Researchers have shown that nonprofits provide considerably more uncompensated care than for-profits, but when adjusted for hospital characteristics, the differences are small (Bazzoli et al. 2006; Congressional Budget Office 2006). That the adjusted difference is not more pronounced has been a topic of great concern to policy makers. However, for-profits are more likely to exit markets, likely in response to financial pressure, than are nonprofits (Miller and Wilson 2018).

Another topic of interest is upcoding, in which hospitals assign an inaccurate billing code to increase reimbursements. All hospitals upcode. However, for-profits are generally more likely than nonprofits and government hospitals to do so (Silverman and Skinner 2004), especially when opportunities to deploy this strategy increase (Dafny 2005), such as when for-profit systems take over the management of hospitals that offer the greatest opportunity to upcode (Dafny and Dranove 2009). Moreover, Paul Gertler and Jennifer Kuan (2009) find that nonprofits and for-profits pay a similar price when buying a for-profit hospital, but nonprofits pay less when buying a similar nonprofit (e.g., a religious nonprofit buying a religious hospital would pay less than a for-profit for the same hospital), suggesting that nonprofits are driven by different objectives, such as aligning the missions of the acquiring and target hospital, than are for-profits.

Yet the behavior of nonprofits is not utterly at odds with that of for-profits. Nonprofits pursue profits, and they engage in accrual-based and real earnings manipulations to reach predetermined targets, particularly to avoid reporting high incomes (Brickley and Van Horn 2002; Leone and Van Horn 2005; Eldenburg et al. 2011; Vansant 2016). Nonetheless, on the whole, the evidence regarding service offerings and financial behavior of nonprofits undermines claims that "all types of enterprise in health care, regardless of type of corporate control, engage in practices to maximize revenues and profits." (Kinney 2010:424).

The bulk of research on ownership in health care markets focuses on the direct effects of ownership on an organization. However, the indirect effects, through the mix of owners within a market, may be extremely important as well. For example, Jill R. Horwitz and Austin Nichols (2009) find that nonprofits with more for-profits in their markets behave like for-profits by offering more profitable services and fewer unprofitable services and changing their service mix in response to changes in financial incentives. Nonprofit hospitals in markets with relatively high for-profit penetration are also more likely to upcode (Silverman and Skinner 2004). Finally, although hospitals in areas with relatively high HMO penetration have lower cost growth than hospitals in areas with lower HMO penetration, hospitals in areas with high for-profit HMO penetration have even lower cost growth than those in markets with low for-profit HMO penetration (Shen and Melnick 2004).

Another study considered the factors associated with the competitiveness of nonprofit hospital markets, finding that higher donations and levels of Medicare population are positively correlated and median income is negatively correlated with market concentration (Paul, Quosigk, and MacDonald 2017). Finally, Rune Stenbacka and Mikhel Tombak (2018) argue that because a for-profit monopoly selects a lower quality than a nonprofit supplier, the socially optimal reimbursement rate with a nonprofit monopoly exceeds that with a for-profit monopoly.

Nursing homes. Several reviews and meta-analyses on ownership in the nursing home industry find significant evidence of higher quality in nonprofit nursing homes compared to their for-profit counterparts (Ronald et al. 2016; Comondore et al. 2009; Hillmer et al. 2005). Measures of higher quality included lower overall probability of a nursing home resident being hospitalized (Hirth et al. 2014), lower probability of being hospitalized for suspected pneumonia (Konetzka, Specter, and Shaffer 2004), fewer thirty-day hospitalizations and greater improvement in mobility, pain, and functioning after post-acute care (Grabowski et al. 2013), and more autonomy of nurses (Ben-Ner and Ren 2015). Anna A. Amirkhanyan, Hyun Joon Kim, and Kristina T. Lambright (2008) find that public and nonprofit nursing homes have equal quality, but that public nursing homes have a higher share of Medicaid recipients and, therefore, may provide greater public service. Moreover, among nursing homes in Maryland, facilities owned by for-profit chains (small, medium, and large) have lower quality of care as reported by families than independent nonprofits, facilities in nonprofit chains (which were all small in Maryland), and independent for-profits (You et al. 2016).

Analyses of nursing homes that convert ownership status have also shed light on differences among forms. For example, David C. Grabowski and David G. Stevenson (2008) show that nursing homes converting from nonprofit to for-profit status generally exhibit deterioration in their performance, while nursing homes converting from for-profit to nonprofit status generally exhibit improvement. Anna Amirkhanyan (2008) shows that among nursing homes that converted from government (county) ownership to private ownership, those that converted to nonprofit form did not reduce quality and those that converted to for-profit home reduced quality.

Scholars have also considered the effects of market mix in the nursing home industry, finding that nonprofit market share improves quality among for-profit nursing homes (Grabowski and Hirth 2003).

A recent strand of studies that asks whether nonprofit managers use their organization's status to signal quality rather than to provide high quality is less favorable to nonprofits. For example, Daniel B. Jones, Carol Propper, and Sarah Smith presented evidence that the more that patients have access to information about quality of care, the less likely a provider will choose to be nonprofit status, concluding that nonprofit nursing homes used their nonprofit status for marketing purposes (i.e., as an inaccurate signal of quality to prospective patients) but not to provide quality (Jones, Propper, and Smith 2017).

Other providers: insurers, dialysis companies, home health, and hospice. There is comparatively little research on ownership in the health insurance industry. Much of the existing scholarship has used conversions from nonprofit to for-profit ownership to identify differences among the forms. For example, Ethan M. J. Lieber (2018) finds evidence that when nonprofit insurers convert to for-profit status, the coverage rates of the population in their markets increase, suggesting expanded access to insurance; however, Lieber also found evidence of increased risk selection, suggesting that people who were bad insurance risks may have been worse off after a conversion from nonprofit to for-profit. Leemore S. Dafny (2019) finds that in areas in which the converting insurer commanded substantial market share, the insurer and its competitors all raised premiums and Medicaid enrollment rates increased, suggesting that former beneficiaries of these private insurance plans could no longer afford them. One other study shows no short-term effects of conversion from nonprofit to for-profit status on HMO prices, profit margins, hospital days or ambulatory visits, or the provision of Medicare and Medicaid insured products (Town, Feldman, and Wholey 2004). Others find mixed results on the affordability of coverage and overall spending in states with conversions (Conover, Hall, and

Ostermann 2005) but argue that policy makers should be cautious in relying on early results (Hall and Conover 2006).

Several recent papers have examined nonprofit ownership in the dialysis industry. There is mixed evidence on mortality, with some studies finding a large effect after controlling for risk of patients but no difference when using a different econometric method (i.e., an instrumental variables approach) (Brooks et al. 2006). Other papers conclude that there are higher mortality rates among for-profits (Szczech et al. 2006). Nonprofit dialysis centers appear to outperform for-profits in many other respects. For example, nonprofit dialysis centers are more likely than for-profits to adopt technology to improve quality rather than amenities (Hirth, Chernew, and Orzol 2000), have considerably lower hospital admissions rates (Dalrymple et al. 2014; Lee, Chertow, and Zenios 2010) and complication rates (Straube 2014) than for-profits, are less likely to use EPO (a profitable drug used to treat anemia resulting from kidney disease) than for-profits (Thamer et al. 2007), and are more likely to list patients for transplants and to provide education about transplants with a nephrologist (Balhara et al. 2012) than for-profits. Another recent paper demonstrates that for-profits have financial advantages (Wilson 2016).

Very recently, both the popular press and scholars have focused on ownership in the hospice business. David G. Stevenson and his colleagues (2016) found that for-profit hospice providers were more likely than comparable nonprofits to treat patients for longer periods of time and discharge them alive, suggesting both market segmentation in terms of the patients treated and greater responsiveness on the part of for-profits to profit-making incentives. The authors also found that factors such as organizational size and being a member of a chain of facilities independently contributed to differences. Other scholars have found that for-profits admit more profitable patients than religious nonprofits (Lindrooth and Weisbrod 2007), such as long-term patients and those with particular diagnoses (Wachterman et al. 2011; Aldridge et al. 2014); provide fewer community benefits such as serving as training sites, conducting research, and providing free care (Aldridge et al. 2014); and employ a less professionalized staff (Cherlin et al. 2010). Patients in for-profit hospice also receive a narrower range of services (Carlson, Gallo, and Bradley 2004), as do their families in terms of bereavement services (Barry et al. 2012).

Finally, lower quality of care has also been found among for-profit home health care organizations in terms of the risk of hospitalizations (Decker 2011:202) and the likelihood of discharge within thirty days (Grabowski et al. 2009:140).

Tax Exemption and Community Benefit

The creation of a nonprofit healthcare organization is generally a matter of state statutory and common law, although some organizations are federally chartered charities. Whether a nonprofit enjoys the various benefits often associated with state-designated nonprofit status, including state and federal tax exemptions, is a distinct question of federal and state law. Scholars have done a great deal of writing examining the requirements for nonprofit hospitals and insurers to obtain income tax exemption, arguing over whether those exemptions are justified, and proposing alternative requirements for exemption.

Many of the articles, particularly recently, concern whether nonprofit hospitals provide sufficient benefits to their communities. As Sara Rosenbaum (2016) explains, this focus stems from growing attention to the social determinants of health, the convergence of business and health interests following Medicare payment reforms penalizing readmissions to the hospital, and new tax exemption requirements, some of which are implied by changes to the form that hospitals must file annually with the IRS and others of which are stipulated under the ACA.

Several scholars have cataloged state laws that require nonprofit hospitals to report the benefits these hospitals provide to their communities (e.g., Hellinger 2009; Gray and Schlesinger 2009a, 2009b; Young et al. 2013). They have also attempted to quantify the value of hospital tax exemptions as well as the amount of different types of community benefit provided. In a 2008 report, the Government Accountability Office estimated the federal income tax exemption of nonprofit hospitals at $13 billion annually starting from 2002 (U.S. Government Accountability Office 2008). Rosenbaum and her colleagues (2015) placed the value for 2011 at almost double that amount when accounting for state income, state and local sales taxes, and local property tax exemptions.

Others have examined the types and value of community benefits provided by exempt hospitals. Gary J. Young and his colleagues (2013) estimate that in 2009, nonprofit hospitals spent an average of 7.5 percent of their operating expenses on community benefits. Importantly, this percentage varied a great deal among hospitals, ranging from about 1 percent to 20 percent of operating expenses. The vast majority of community benefit expenses went to free care for indigent patients and other patient care services; only a small amount went to direct community health improvement. Susanna C. Tahk (2015) has similarly demonstrated that the bulk of community benefit goes to providing relief for the poor. Other scholars have shown community benefit requirements to be positively associated with spending on free care (Singh et al. 2018, Lamboy-Ruiz, Cannon, and Watanabe 2017).

A large number of scholars suggest that these benefits provided by nonprofit hospitals are inadequate or do not justify the tax exemptions (e.g., Rosenbaum et al. 2015; Rubin, Singh, and Jacobson et al. 2015; Colombo 2007a; Schneider 2007; McGregor 2007). David A. Hyman and William M. Sage (2006) have argued that the wrong hospitals get the largest reward from tax exemption and propose that those rewards should be provided on a graduated basis linked to quantifiable measures of community benefit, broadly and locally defined. It follows from their argument that some community benefits may be more valuable than others. For example, contributing to the public good by improving community health may be more valued by the community than redistributing resources in the form of expensive, high-end medical care.

Many scholars have proposed that more specific or stricter standards than those imposed under the current system should be adopted as requirements for exemptions (e.g., Rubin, Singh, and Young 2015; Rubin et al. 2013; Schirra 2011; Folkerts 2009; Alexander et al. 2008; Kane 2006; Bloche 2006; Colombo 2005). Most recently, some argue that exemptions would no longer be needed given the increase in the percentage of Americans insured in the wake of the ACA (Corbett 2015:153–156).

However, whether community benefits provided are adequate to justify exemption depends a great deal on how they are defined, particularly regarding the treatment of money owed to the hospital that cannot be recovered, known as bad debt (Bazzoli, Clement, and Hsieh 2010). There is a strong argument to be made that critics have focused too narrowly on the provision of free care for indigent patients. Hospitals make many choices related to community in addition to how much free care to provide (Gray and Schlesinger 2009a). Proposals to condition exemption on free care for indigent patients (as well as any other particular type of benefit) risk unintended consequences, such as a hospital changing its service mix to make up lost revenues. These risks have not been acknowledged in present public debates (Molk 2012; Tyrrell 2010; Singer 2008; Horwitz 2006, 2007).

Even if the ACA had succeeded in insuring almost all Americans—which it did not— exemptions would likely remain valuable. On the one hand, there is strong evidence that insured patients use more, not less care; when people lose coverage, admissions to nonprofit hospitals go down (less than at for-profit hospitals), suggesting that patients with insurance are more attractive to nonprofit hospitals than other patients (Anderson, Dobkin, and Gross 2012) and insurance may reduce the need for subsidies tied to free care. However,

> not all insurance will be equally attractive to providers, and nonprofit and government pro-viders are more likely than for-profits to offer services needed by the poor. Moreover, as has always been the case, all patients, regardless of their wealth, are poorly situated to evaluate the care they receive. They need not only to access care, but to trust their providers not to provide too little, too much, or the wrong kind of care. (Horwitz 2016:555).

For example, compared to similar for-profits, nonprofit hospitals were less likely to offer invasive cardiac procedures, including various types of stenting (Horwitz 2005), some of which recently have been shown to have little or no benefit over placebo treatment for many patients (Lancet Editorial 2017). In medical circles the chance findings that come from unnecessary testing are often called *incidentalomas*, and their consequences can be grave when patients are given more unnecessary testing and sometimes dangerous treatment when the patient would have remained healthy without any testing or treat-ment at all. Although forgoing unnecessary testing and treatment may be worth a great deal in terms of patient health and financial savings for the state, identifying and valuing overtreatment that did not occur is like hearing the dog that didn't bark. It's hard to hear.

Researchers have also turned their attention to state property tax exemptions for chari-ties. They discuss trends in local governments challenging exemption, with some extremely strict applications of tests that involve, for example, requirements for the exclusive use of property for charitable purpose being violated by common arrangements such as the use of contract physicians or an organization of physicians in a manner that leads to collab-orative care (Smith and Woodhull 2017; Swogier 2017; Brody 2016; Stewart 2009). State and local taxing authorities have increasingly used various types of payments in lieu of taxes (PILOTs) to raise revenues from nonprofits, particularly targeting hospitals because of their financial resources and their tendency to provide services to people who do not live within the jurisdiction of the local tax area (Fei et al. 2016).

In sum, there is an enormous body of research regarding the significance of nonprof-its in the health care sector. Even so, there is room for more. In particular, evidence on nonfinancial outcomes and also on the effects of ownership on markets and the providers in them have been understudied.

The bulk of the research has focused on hospitals and, more recently, on nursing homes. Recently, scholars have expanded their efforts to include insurers, dialysis centers, hospice providers, and other entities. Given the wide variation in specific subjects studied, generalizing across studies can be difficult. Nonetheless, nonprofit providers more likely perform better on a range of important outcomes than do their for-profit counterparts.

Nonprofit and Health Law: The Special Treatment of Health Care Charities

Both of the legal topics centrally implicated in this chapter—health law and nonprofit law—have been subject to the critique that they aren't distinctive areas of law at all, but are unrelated collections of different areas of law that happen to apply to certain kinds of relationships or entities. In the case of health law, scholars have debated at length about whether the subject has a core set of concerns that form a coherent field or is instead an example of the law of the horse, a collection of general laws that are applied in a specific area (Bloche 2009, Hall, Schneider, and Shepherd 2006). Nonprofit law similarly brings together disparate areas such as trust, corporation, tax, and property law; only now is the American Law Institute drafting its first "Restatement of the Law, Charitable Nonprofit Organizations" to clarify a single law of charities. It is, therefore, unsurprising to find that inconsistencies and even incoherence run throughout the law as it is applied to nonprofit health care organizations.

This section, drawing extensively from Horwitz (2016), considers a few of the major legal and policy areas in which nonprofit healthcare organizations are treated differently from analogous for-profits, and in which nonprofit health providers are treated differently from other types of nonprofits. On the one hand, it addresses tax law as an example of how nonprofit law treats health care organizations *more* restrictively than other types of nonprofits. On the other hand, it addresses antitrust law as an example of how other areas of law treat nonprofit health care providers *less* restrictively than other types of health care providers. These two examples, as well as others, illustrate how sometimes the law treats nonprofits as more suspect and at other times as more trustworthy than comparable organizations. There is no consistent justification for the differences in treatment across legal issues. Indeed, the explanations for the special treatment of nonprofit health care organizations are often contradictory—with more restrictive application of nonprofit law being applied to health care organizations because of their relative commerciality in terms of insufficient efforts to relieve poverty and forgo charging fees, and less restrictive application of other laws being justified because of their relative lack of profit-seeking behavior.

Stricter Requirements Under Nonprofit Law: Tax Exemption

For some time, federal and state laws regarding tax exemption have placed stricter requirements in terms of community benefits on nonprofit health care providers, particularly hospitals, than on other types of nonprofits. In the mid-twentieth century, a series of revenue rulings imposed particular requirements on nonprofit hospitals and insurers seeking federal income tax exemptions and related benefits available to other nonprofits—including income tax exemption, the receipt of tax-deductible donations, the ability to issue tax-exempt debt, and other benefits—that they did not impose on other charities such as museums or schools. From 1956 to 1969, nonprofit hospitals were required to be "operated to the extent of [their] financial ability for those not able to pay for the services rendered" (Rev Rul. 56-185 1956-1 C.B. 202). Since 1969, the IRS has had no explicit charity care requirement for tax-exempt status. Instead, a nonprofit hospital could secure exemption by either (1) providing free or subsidized care to the extent of its financial ability or (2) meeting an alternative community benefit test, involving treating all patients who were able to pay or were insured, and operating an emergency room where needed (Rev. Rul. 69-545 1969-2 C.B. 117). Federal regulators have interpreted the term *community benefit* broadly.

In response to concern that nonprofit hospitals were not sufficiently charitable in their activities—such as in their aggressive billing policies, particularly billing uninsured patients list rates and insured patients much lower rates (Brooks 2008; Colombo 2007a)—Congress conducted a series of hearings and commissioned studies (IRS 2014; Senate Finance Committee 2006; House Committee on Ways and Means 2005). The IRS created a new schedule (Schedule H) for hospitals to file as part of their IRS Form 990, the federal information return. Although the schedule does not explicitly require the relief of poverty, the relief of poverty figures so prominently in the document that hospitals understand they must provide free care to obtain exemption. It is not surprising, therefore, that a recent analysis finds that hospitals largely spend their community benefit dollars on activities related to poverty relief (Tahk 2014).

In addition, in the early 2000s, plaintiffs' lawyers brought a series of claims against hospitals for inflated billing based on supposed violations of the hospitals' tax exemptions. They lost virtually all of these cases, sometimes based on not having standing and other times more substantively. As Mark Hall (2013) explains, it wasn't that the complaints about unconscionable billing didn't have merit. They did. But the lawyers focused on the wrong legal theory—"they concocted a legal theory based on the federal requirements for maintaining charitable tax exemption"—when what was really at issue was "conventional consumer protection and contract-based claims" under state law (Hall 2013:8). By trying to extend the requirements for tax exemption to even higher standards, the lawyers and the courts missed the opportunity to enforce general laws that apply to all hospitals (Hall and Schneider 2008).

Most recently, the ACA included provisions adding conditions to existing rules for federal tax exemption and related benefits that apply to charitable hospitals otherwise eligible for exemption under § 501(c)(3) (I.R.C. § 501[r] [2015]; Additional Requirements for Charitable Hospitals, 79 Fed. Reg. 78954-01 [December 31 2014]; Crossley 2016). Hospitals that are charities must (1) establish financial assistance and emergency medical care policies, (2) limit charges to patients eligible for assistance under those policies, and (3) make reasonable efforts to identify eligible patients before engaging in extraordinary collection actions against them. Hospitals must also conduct community health needs assessments and adopt implementation strategies to meet those needs at least once every three years. Hospitals that do not report on and comply with the requirements face a $50,000 tax and risk losing their tax exemptions altogether.

The tax treatment of health insurance companies similarly has varied over time. Many nonprofit insurers were fully exempt until 1986, when the Tax Reform Act made insurers that provide "commercial-type" insurance as a substantial part of their activities ineligible for exemption (Hill and Mancino 2002; Supp. 2014-2 at 22.06). Certain insurers were still able to qualify for preferential tax treatment in the form of special deductions as long as they met certain requirements, such as maintaining high-risk and small-group coverage plans (I.R.C. § 833 [2015]).

There also has been considerable activity at the state level, largely regarding the exemption from local property taxes. States typically grant income tax exemption to entities that are eligible for federal income tax exemption, although some state statutes and constitutions contain provisions that include different, usually more stringent, requirements for exemption. Because many nonprofit health care entities do not earn significant profits but do own real property, property tax exemptions can be more valuable to these organizations than income tax exemptions. Because local governments have been under financial strain in recent years, they have turned to nonprofits—especially hospitals but also large universities—to help produce revenue to cover these shortfalls.

These local government strategies include increasing restrictions on property tax exemptions. Some states have imposed or increased community benefit requirements linked to these exemptions (Klebes 2015; Stewart 2009; Goodman 2009; Hellinger 2009). For example, Pennsylvania hospitals can meet the requirement by providing uncompensated care in an amount equivalent to at least 5 percent of net patient revenue (10 Pa. Stat. § 375[d][1][iii] [1997]); applicants for a hospital license (or any subsequent successor or acquirer) in Massachusetts must agree to maintain or increase the percentage of patient revenue allocated to uncompensated care (Mass. Gen. Laws 111 §51G[3] [2000]) Many localities have negotiated for donated services (Brody 2007) and PILOTs (Fei et al. 2016). At the extreme, some local governments have denied hospitals' claims for property tax exemptions altogether (e.g., *Provena Covenant Med. Ctr. v. Dep't of Revenue*, 236 Ill.2d 368 [2010]; *AHS Hospital Corp. v. Town of Morristown* 28 N.J.Tax 456 [2015]).

The underlying message is that nonprofit hospitals are not sufficiently charitable because they don't do enough to relieve poverty. Of course, the relief of poverty is important and these heightened requirements for nonprofit health entities may increase the provision of free care for indigent patients, but doing so may well come at the expense of other patients and other charitable obligations such as providing high-quality care, providing unprofitable services, or forgoing the provision of some profitable services (Horwitz and Cutler 2015). Although there is political pressure on other types of charities to address problems associated with poverty, such as encouraging universities to grant admission and provide benefits to first-generation students, no other type of charity is required to relieve poverty to qualify for property tax exemption.

Lenient Requirements Under Health Law

There are many examples of health and related laws treating nonprofit health care providers more leniently than analogous for-profits, and various justifications have been advanced for this leniency. Most are based on some version of the idea that nonprofits are more trustworthy than for-profits because they are not (or are not as) motivated by seeking profits as are otherwise comparable for-profits or, less plausibly, because they are thought not to compete at all. Having their focus on something other than seeking profits, so the justification goes, will lead nonprofits to more readily act in the interest of their patients and, therefore, nonprofit health care organizations don't need to be so tightly regulated. These justifications are often at odds with the calls for restricting or removing tax exemption discussed earlier.

This section addresses the favorable treatment of nonprofits under the corporate practice of medicine doctrine. However, this is not the only example of readily favorable treatment of nonprofits by health or related law. Horwitz (2016) discusses other examples in detail: the ACA's extensive reliance on nonprofits, the (changing) history of courts applying antitrust law so as to allow nonprofit hospitals to merge because of an assumption that nonprofits do not compete on prices or would not raise prices after a merger, charitable immunity in tort law, and the different treatment of hospital and insurer conversions depending on whether they are converting to or from nonprofit form.

The corporate practice of medicine doctrine typically forbids corporations from directly employing physicians to provide medical services. These restrictions can be found in state statutes, common law, and medical licensing rules that imply that only human professionals and not legal persons, such as corporations, can practice medicine (Axelrod 1997). Although the law is strictly observed only in some states, it remains on the books in many others and influenced the development of what are now customs in corporate structure (Sage 2016; Hall 1988). For example, it explains why hospitals tend to have contractual arrangements with their medical staff rather than employing them directly, and why insurers do not technically pay doctors for care; rather, beneficiaries assign payments to their doctors by contract.

The rules are mainly meant to protect patients by insulating the independent judgment of physicians from commercial pressure and, according to some scholars, such rules are also meant to protect the status and income of physicians (e.g., Fichter 2006). The law presumes that contractual relationships do not raise these same risks.

States tend to exempt certain entities, frequently nonprofits, from corporate practice rules (Mars 1997; Axelrod 1997; *Berlin v. Sarah Bush* 1997 at 11–12; *Grp. Health Ass'n v. Moor* 1938 at 446–447). The exemption for nonprofits generally rests on the idea that because they aren't motivated by profits, nonprofits can avoid "the principal evils attendant upon corporate practice of medicine [that] spring from the conflict between professional standards and obligations of doctors and the profit motive of the corporate employer" (Michigan Attorney General 1993, quoting *People ex. rel. State Bd. of Medical Examiners v. Pac. Health Corp. Inc.* 1938 at 431; Hansmann 1981:580–585). The California Court of Appeals similarly concluded that "concerns about for-profit corporations have nothing to do with non-profit teaching hospitals" (California Med. Ass'n, Inc. v. Regents of Univ. of California 2000 at 550).

As with developments regarding the charitable income tax exemptions, states have begun limiting the exemption from corporate doctrine practice for nonprofits. California now exempts only charities that do not charge patients and various community clinics (Cal. Bus. & Prof. Code § 2400). The justification for applying the doctrine to nonprofits is that the dangers of lay control over physician practice are not limited to profit-seeking and, therefore, even if nonprofit lay owners would not steer physicians toward profit-seeking to the same degree as for-profits, they might nonetheless jeopardize independent caregiving by encouraging some profit making or try to direct care for other institutional and non-medical purposes (*California Physicians' Serv. v. Aoki Diabetes Research Inst.* 2008 at 1515–1516). In Illinois, which has been the leader in challenging nonprofit hospital property tax exemptions, the state supreme court maintained that nonprofits, like for-profits, can disrupt the "safeguarding [of] the physician's professional judgment from lay interference or protecting the public's general health and welfare" (*Carter-Shields v. Alton Health Inst.* 2002 at 460).

As with the application of other laws, such as antitrust, the history of exemption for nonprofits from the corporate practice doctrine highlights the presumption that non-profit status insulates organizations from a degree of profit-seeking that would interfere with the practice of medicine and, therefore, protects patient welfare. On the other hand, perhaps they shouldn't be trusted given the finding that nonprofit health care employees have been found to demonstrate what researchers have identified as Machiavellian tendencies, such as acting in an impersonal, rational, and strategy-oriented manner rather than person-oriented (Richmond and Smith 2005).

In sum, the way the law treats nonprofit health care entities seems to depend not on the behavior or characteristics of those entities themselves but rather on those of the organizations to which they are being compared.

Conclusion

The charitable sector encompasses a striking diversity of organizations. That these organizations vary tremendously in size, age, scope, financing, and purposes makes it impossible to define the sector precisely. Nonetheless, a conventional image of "charity" persists and is challenged by the presence of health care nonprofits of the sort discussed in this chapter. Rosemary Stevens's observation that hospitals "carry the burden of unresolved, perhaps unresolvable contradictions," continues to be true (Stevens 1989:361).

Considered in the context of health care and of their history, however, their rightful claim to charity status becomes clear. There was no golden age when health providers acted entirely outside commercial markets, serving those in need without compensation. Neither government nor donors have ever been willing to provide resources sufficient for health care charities to deliver all the care patients need. Therefore, health care charities have always had to be self-sustaining, which has meant charging for services and finding various other avenues for generating revenues. The need to find revenues has grown as health care has become more effective and more expensive. We should not bemoan the necessary commercialization. At least some commercial activities have allowed health care charities to cross-subsidize in terms of both underwriting care for poor patients and, as importantly, refraining from oversupply of profitable services.

Nonprofit health providers, in fact, do well when compared to existing for-profits rather than to folklore about nonprofit medical providers in olden times. Although this advantage may not be expressed in every dimension, by important measures nonprofit health care providers outperform their for-profit competitors. The evidence suggests they have different goals than for-profits, particularly being less profit-seeking than otherwise comparable for-profits. Whether these differences are sufficient to justify tax benefits is a separate and, particularly at the local level, a somewhat difficult question. But asserting that they are not charitable because they are unlike other types of charities in terms of relying on donations or relieving poverty is at a minimum ahistorical and in a larger sense discounts their enormously important role in the sector.

Indeed, a more sympathetic eye might find that nonprofit health care providers are players in good standing in the sector and offer the potential to solve some of the pressing health policy challenges we face. In fact, Schlesinger and Gray (2006a), the co-authors of an earlier version of this chapter, advocated for a recommitment to nonprofit providers as one way of fulfilling the increased need for trust in the health care sector as policy makers take an evidence-based turn that risks neglecting harder-to-measure values. Protecting community benefits that aren't readily captured in economic figures is precisely the kind of role that a good charity ought to play.

Finally, in describing the role of nonprofits in health care markets, their commercial history, and how they differ from other health care providers, this chapter should not be mistaken for a full-throated embrace of commercialism. Many thoughtful scholars have highlighted the social significance of health care institutions operating in commercial contexts, particularly the hospitals in which many of us are born and die. Such studies have found these institutions coming up short. For example, Rosemary Stevens's *In Sickness and in Wealth: American Hospitals in the Twentieth Century* remains an apt analysis of the ways in which hospitals reflect and contribute to power dynamics in American society and should still serve as a call for improvement. On a larger scale, we have been unable to harness the political will to provide universal insurance or to take adequate steps for cost control.

Nonetheless, nonprofits play a unique, often positive, role in contemporary health care provision. Setting up historical straw men against which to judge them or overestimating their similarities to other providers risks misunderstanding their contribution and potential.

18 EDUCATION AND THE NONPROFIT SECTOR

Schools and Organizational Intermediaries

Richard Arum and Jacob L. Kepins

WITH THE DECLINE OF ORGANIZED RELIGION and a broad set of sociocultural challenges to the primacy of the family, education has emerged as a critical institution for socialization and the larger organization of modern society. The functions of education are broad and diffuse—schools serve as a mechanism for social reproduction and social mobility, a site for human development and socialization, a source for knowledge production and dissemination, and a vehicle for connecting individuals and institutions to the larger society (Stevens, Armstrong, and Arum 2008). Education is not only recognized by individuals as a mechanism for human development and social mobility but also lionized and championed by politicians and pundits as a panacea for social ills. "We may all gossip privately about the uselessness of education," John Meyer (1977:75–76) noted several decades ago, "but in hiring and promoting, in consulting the various magi of our time, and in ordering our lives around contemporary rationality, we carry out our parts in a drama in which education is authority."

In the United States, since at least the nineteenth century, education has been "heavily freighted with ideological meaning and administered locally" as if it were a "fourth branch" of government (Tyack and James 1986:69). Education has dramatically expanded worldwide and—setting aside recent illiberal threats and reversals to the long-term cultural hegemony of science and rationality—is embraced as an elixir and functions for society as, sieve, incubator, temple, and hub (Stevens et al. 2008). This chapter discusses how nonprofit organizations have benefited from and played a prominent role in creating the conditions that have enabled the United States education system to fulfill these functions.

Nonprofit organizations can be defined as that portion of associational life and of civil society that is legally codified and formally incorporated (see Lechterman and Reich, Chapter 6, "Political Theory and the Nonprofit Sector"). This definition generally follows Lester M. Salamon and Helmut K. Anheier's (1992:268) logic that nonprofit organizations are distinguished by five structural/operational characteristics: they are "formally constituted, non-governmental in basic structure, self-governing, non-profit-distributing, and voluntary to some meaningful extent." Adopting this definition, schools comprise a significant share of the nonprofit sector. Salamon (2012) estimates that 18 percent of nonprofit organizations that report to the Internal Revenue Service (IRS) are focused on education or research, and 21 percent of revenues in the nonprofit sector are generated by education- or research-focused entities. Moreover, more than ten million students are served by nonprofit educational institutions each year (Stewart, Kane, and Scruggs 2012).

Nonprofit institutions are especially prominent in U.S. higher education, particularly at the level of four-year colleges and universities that offer bachelor and graduate-level degrees. Approximately 40 percent of all higher education institutions and 56 percent of four-year colleges and universities are private, nonprofit organizations (Salamon 2012). Nonprofit higher-education institutions rely on philanthropy for a significantly larger share of their revenue than do public institutions: 11.1 percent compared to 3.4 percent (Salamon 2012). These institutions include some of the oldest existing nonprofit organizations; many colleges and universities were legally codified and incorporated centuries ago (Soskis, Chapter 2, "History of Associational Life and the Nonprofit Sector in the United States"). More recently, colleges and universities have also played a significant role in creating and disseminating normative models that apply more generally to nonprofit organizations. Nonprofit staff and consultants, for example, are increasingly trained in higher-education academic programs that specialize in nonprofit management, leadership, administration, development, communication, and public administration.

Background

The U.S. field of education has traditionally been conceptualized as varying along two principal dimensions: institutional level (i.e., K–12 or higher education) and organizational sector (i.e., public, nonprofit, and for-profit). It is worth noting that U.S. public schools historically were established, organized, and administered locally, with centralized state and federal involvement only appearing as a more recent phenomenon. Alexis de Tocqueville ([1836] 2003), for example, recognized *public* schools as the epitome of an American penchant for *voluntary* forms of association; he noted, "it is by the attention it pays to Public Education that the original character of American civilization is at once placed in the clearest light (Tocqueville [1836] 2003:60)." Tocqueville further pointed out that while the state mandates the existence of a school, "the township builds, pays, and superintends it" ([1836] 2003:83) with local "committee-men . . . appointed to attend to the schools and to public instruction" ([1836] 2003:81). This voluntary, associational character of the origins of K–12 schooling in the United States has elements that share features in common with nonprofit forms of organization.

Distinctions among organizational forms are equally complex in the for-profit sector. For example, for-profit colleges and universities vary in terms of their ownership stakes being held privately, controlled through private equity firms, or publicly traded; among these forms, shareholder-value-oriented organizational behavior is most pronounced in publicly traded entities (Eaton et al. 2016).

Recent scholarship has further challenged the extent to which nonprofit school practices consistently embrace nonprofit institutional logics. Economic, social, and technological changes have led to the adoption of organizational practices that have produced schools that are increasingly hybrid with respect to organizational form, particularly in higher education. For example, scholars have lamented the extent to which public higher education has embraced "academic capitalism" and become "commercialized" and "corporate" (Slaughter and Rhoades 2004; Kirp 2003). K–12, given its more stable public funding support, has faced fewer organizational pressures than higher education to change (Stevens and Kirst 2015) but nevertheless has witnessed the growth of accountability demands and school-choice-related reforms (such as charter schools). In addition, boundaries across sector and level have become more permeable, with schools delivering new forms of education (such as online education) and serving student bodies that have become increasingly broad, diverse, and diffuse. These changes have been augmented in part by technological developments, such as the growth of computer-assisted administration, advisement, and instruction (Kamenetz 2010; Carey 2016).

This chapter will review literature that has focused on the emergence of hybrid school organizational forms, which manifest only limited deference to previously defined boundaries. However, we argue here for the need to move past school-centric scholarship on nonprofit education. Instead, we embrace a conceptual recognition that schools are embedded in institutional fields that, at a more fundamental level, are organized and structured by nonprofit entities. For scholars of nonprofits, the field of education is particularly interesting, and not simply because large numbers of schools in the United States are nonprofits (albeit often with for-profit elements). Rather, what is analytically compelling and worthy of consideration is the extent to which many of the core aspects of organizational processes associated with public, nonprofit, and for-profit schools—such as regulation, quality assurance, resource acquisition, and the selection and credentialing of students—are institutional functions that are carried out by and dependent on *nonprofit intermediaries*. Organizational intermediaries are defined by Benson Honig (2004:267) as "organizations that occupy the space in between at least two other parties . . . operate independently of these two parties and provide distinct value beyond what the parties alone would be able to develop or to amass by themselves. At the same time, intermediary organizations depend on those parties to perform their essential functions." This dynamic is particularly prevalent in higher education, which will receive greater focus and analytical attention in this discussion.

The prominent position of nonprofit entities in the institutional field is the product of the self-organization (and self-interest) of schools as organizations as well as the state's reliance on third-party, nonprofit intermediaries to deliver and regulate social welfare services, including education, in the United States (Balogh 2015; Mettler 2011, 2014; Howard 1999). As Mitchell L. Stevens and Ben Gebre-Medhin (2016:124) have argued, the United States is characterized by "an extraordinarily wide range of organizational systems blending public and private purposes, funds and personnel." Elisabeth S. Clemens (2006) has aptly applied the metaphor of a Rube Goldberg machine to characterize the extent to which social welfare and education are cobbled together organizationally by state actors to deliver services to the public. The unique character of education and welfare provisioning in the United States has deep historical roots going back to the associational character of the republic (Tocqueville [1836] 2003) and a political institutional structure that reflects Americans' "insatiable demands for collective action while assuaging their enduring fears of big government" (Balogh 2015:2). The predominance of nonprofit intermediary institutions discussed in this chapter should therefore be understood as a phenomenon consistent with the larger American tendency toward the use of extragovernmental mechanisms to deliver and promote social welfare.

In the discussion that follows, the relationship of nonprofit organizations to education is explored in terms of (1) variation in institutional characteristics of schools by organizational type in K–12 and higher education, (2) the emergence in education of hybrid organizational forms and the blurring of institutional boundaries, and (3) the prominent role of nonprofit intermediaries in the complex apparatus that delivers education in the United States. Implications for future research of the nonprofit character of education are discussed in the chapter's conclusion.

Variation in Institutional Characteristics

A reasonable starting point for understanding the nature of nonprofit organizations in education is to identify both the prevalence and institutional distinctiveness of nonprofit schools in K–12 and higher education. In terms of institutional differences, we focus on institutional characteristics related to demographics of faculty and students served; resources, operationalized either as tuition or as student/teacher ratios; and, for colleges and universities, historic changes in sources of research and development (R&D) funding. The data analysis reveals that although K–12 and postsecondary institutions may be distinct entities at the organizational level, a great deal of isomorphism exists across public, nonprofit, and for-profit educational sectors.

Our analysis proceeds by distinguishing K–12 schools across four categories: "traditional" public schools, charter public schools, private secular schools, and private religious schools. Data are drawn from various surveys implemented by the U.S. Department of Education's National Center for Education Statistics and reflect the 2015–2016 academic year (Snyder, de Brey, and Dillow 2019). Although for-profit schools are active providers in both early-childhood preschool and higher-education marketplaces, we do not include them in our analysis because of their relative scarcity. A report on education management organizations indicates that for-profit charter schools represent fewer than 850 total schools operating in thirty-five states and the District of Columbia (Miron and Gulosino 2013) while the number of other for-profit K–12 schools is also negligible. Figure 18.1 illustrates the proportion of K–12 enrollments that are distributed across these four organizational school types. Eighty-six percent of students attend traditional public schools, while 5 percent attend public charter schools. The percentage of students attending private schools has in recent decades hovered around 9 percent, with 7 percent in private, religious schools and 2 percent in private, secular schools in 2015–2016.

At the higher-education level, we distinguish between four-year colleges and universities that offer baccalaureate and graduate degrees and sub-baccalaureate institutions that provide two-year associate degrees, vocational certificates, and other credentials. Within the four-year and sub-baccalaureate population of schools, we also distinguish among public, nonprofit, and for-profit institutions. Figure 18.2 identifies the distribution of higher-education enrollments by organizational level and sector. Most higher-education students attend public institutions, with 40 percent of student enrollments in public four-year and 31 percent in public sub-baccalaureate institutions. Nonprofit four-year institutions enroll 20 percent of higher-education students, while nonprofit sub-baccalaureate

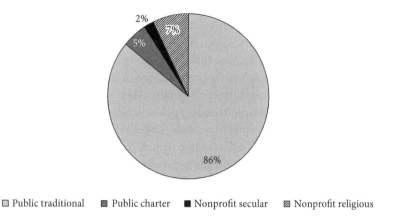

Figure 18.1 Composition of K–12 schools by sector

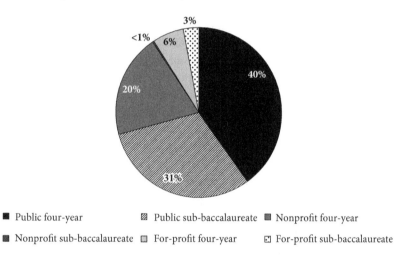

Figure 18.2 Higher education enrollment by sector and level

institutions enroll only 0.4 percent of higher education students. The for-profit sector enrolls less than 10 percent of students (6 percent in four-year institutions and 3 percent in sub-baccalaureate institutions).

K-12 Schools

Despite the tendency toward normative and coercive isomorphism across K–12 organizational sectors and types (DiMaggio and Powell 1983), there are persistent differences in organizational characteristics of K–12 schools across sectors and with respect to organizational forms. Table 18.1 identifies characteristics of K–12 schools for the four distinct organizational forms we have identified: traditional public, charter public, private secular, and private religious schools. Most schools across organizational forms are at the elementary level, which are smaller on average than secondary schools, with the exception of charter schools (average enrollment in traditional public elementary schools is 492; in traditional public secondary schools, 700; elementary charter schools, 379; secondary charter schools, 306). Although traditional public schools are rarely a combination of elementary and secondary schools, 20 percent to 30 percent of charter and private schools are some combination of the two. Enrollments at combined charter schools are similar to traditional secondary schools with approximately 630 students on average. Religious private nonprofit schools are considerably larger than their secular counterparts, with the exception of combined elementary/secondary private schools, which are similar in terms of enrollments regardless of the presence or absence of religious affiliation.

Approximately 50 percent of both traditional public and charter schools are classified as low-income—more than half of students receive free/reduced-price lunches. However, a higher proportion of charter schools have student bodies where more than 75 percent of students receive free/reduced-price lunches. Conversely, most private schools do not participate in the National School Lunch Program (NSLP). Of the private schools that do participate in the NSLP, religious schools are more likely than secular schools to have high poverty levels.

Regarding the racial/ethnic composition of public schools, as Table 18.1 shows, charter schools are less likely to be majority-white and significantly more likely to be either majority-black or majority-Hispanic. Moreover, charter schools are more likely than traditional public schools to have student compositions in which more than 90 percent of students are black or more than 90 percent of students are Hispanic. These statistics underlie a body of literature suggesting that school choice, driven by charter school availability, may be a driving force in maintaining racial school segregation (Perry 2017). Research along these lines indicates that charter schools may tend to be more racially segregated than their surrounding public school zones (Gulosino and d'Entremont 2011; Frankenberg, Siegel-Hawley, and Wang 2011). In contrast, the private nonprofit sector is much more likely to serve primarily white students: 77 percent of nonprofit religious schools and 55 percent of nonprofit secular schools are majority-white; 41 percent of nonprofit religious schools and 22 percent of nonprofit secular schools are more than 90 percent white.

With regard to faculty, teachers in public schools have higher levels of educational attainment than those in the nonprofit sector; private-school teachers are approximately four times as likely to have less than a bachelor's degree than their public-school counterparts. However, the private sector, across organizational forms, is marked by considerably lower student–teacher ratios. Traditional public schools have twice as many students per teacher as nonprofit secular schools. Charter schools have the highest ratio of students to teachers—more than traditional public schools and nearly double that of nonprofit religious schools.

Postsecondary Institutions

Postsecondary institutions are varied in terms of organizational type and environments, both within and across the public, nonprofit, and for-profit sectors. Table 18.2 presents characteristics of postsecondary institutions, and Table 18.3 presents the composition of faculty at these institutions. Within four-year organizations, we disaggregated by public, nonprofit, and for-profit institutions and included baccalaureate and postbaccalaureate enrollments and programs. Sub-baccalaureate institutions are broken down by sector in the same manner as four-year institutions, but they also include organizations that offer degree and certification programs requiring less than two years of instruction.

Table 18.1   Characteristics of public and private K–12 schools, 2015–2016

	Public schools		Private schools	
	Traditional	*Charter*	*Secular*	*Religious*
Elementary	68.8%	56.2%	64.0%	63.1%
Secondary	24.6%	23.0%	8.5%	8.5%
Combined	5.9%	20.5%	27.5%	28.4%
Other	0.7%	0.3%	-	-
% Free/reduced-price lunch				
0%–25%	19.6%	22.2%	5.9%	9.3%
25.1%–50%	27.4%	18.0%	2.6%	4.1%
50.1%–75%	26.9%	18.6%	1.2%	2.0%
>75%	23.9%	32.6%	1.9%	5.8%
Missing/school does not participate	2.3%	8.7%	88.5%	78.9%
Average enrollment	522.4	417.0	102.3%	176.9%
	(439.2)	(547.2)	(207.4%)	(224.4%)
Students by gender				
Male	51.5%	49.6%	53.5%	51.3%
Female	48.5%	50.4%	46.5%	48.6%
School racial composition				
Majority white	53.5%	34.5%	72.7%	77.3%
Majority black	8.3%	23.5%	6.7%	7.7%
Majority Hispanic	16.2%	25.4%	4.7%	5.5%
> 90% white	15.8%	3.9%	21.9%	40.6%
> 90% black	2.2%	10.2%	2.5%	4.5%
> 90% Hispanic	4.6%	7.3%	1.4%	1.6%
Faculty*				
% < Bachelor's	2.4%		8.4%	
% BA/BS	40.5%		48.5%	
% > Bachelor's	57.0%		43.1%	
Student/teacher ratio	16.1	22.1	8.3	11.8
	(16.4)	(75.3)	(20.2)	(12.1)
N =	101514	6855	7015	15413

Note: Standard deviations are in parentheses. Public school numbers include all schools that are not classified as charter schools. Public and private school data are derived from the Common Core of Data, the Private School Universe Survey and the Digest of Education Statistics: 2017 (Snyder, de Brey and Dillow, 2019). Private school faculty data are from the 2011-2012 school year. Average enrollment is average across school levels in each sector.

Tuition to four-year and sub-baccalaureate institutions is quite varied by organizational forms. Public schools, on average, cost less than both for-profit and nonprofit schools at the same organizational level. In addition, for-profit four-year institutions are less expensive, on average, than nonprofit four-year institutions—perhaps due, in part, to large average salary differences between nonprofit and for-profit colleges and universities. This

Table 18.2 Characteristics of college student bodies by organizational sector and level, fall 2015

	Full sample	Four-year institutions			Sub-baccalaureate institutions		
		Public	Nonprofit	For-profit	Public	Nonprofit	For-profit
	Mean	Mean	Mean	Mean	Mean	Mean	Mean
Total enrollment (fall)	2,891.7	11,702.4	2,476.5	1,643.8	5,035.7	279.4	201.5
	(6,880.3)	(11,856.8)	(5,107.0)	(8,201.4)	(7,067.3)	(852.9)	(302.2)
In-state tuition	$33,054.77	$22,611.97	$41,891.27	$33,996.59	$14,777.60	$28,325.26	$33,725.82
	(15,142.92)	(4,425.27)	(13,850.20)	(5,455.07)	(3,104.95)	(11,166.68)	(16,283.63)
Out-of-state tuition	$36,272.74	$33,233.97	$41,895.91	$33,996.59	$17,475.15	$28,325.26	$33,725.82
	(13,935.61)	(8,475.54)	(13,842.67)	(5,455.07)	(4,357.07)	(11,166.68)	(16,283.63)
% Awarded financial aid	86.0%	86.3%	91.4%	89.2%	80.2%	82.6%	85.7
	(16.7)	(10.5)	(16.8)	(18.9)	(15.6)	(22.7)	(16.4)
% Female	64.6%	55.9%	54.8%	58.7%	58.6%	67.2%	77.7%
	(24.1)	(9.6)	(19.9)	(23.2)	(14.6)	(27.1)	(27.0)
% White	51.8%	57.8%	58.7%	42.4%	59.4%	50.6%	44.6%
	(27.5)	(22.8)	(23.7)	(23.1)	(25.3)	(32.4)	(29.9)
% Black	18.5%	13.1%	13.1%	25.0%	13.7%	21.0%	24.0%
	(22.1)	(18.6)	(18.7)	(21.1)	(16.2)	(24.6)	(25.4)
% Hispanic	14.1%	10.9%	8.1%	13.8%	14.2%	15.3%	19.0%
	(18.7)	(13.2)	(9.5)	(16.0)	(17.5)	(23.8)	(23.2)

% Asian	3.8%	4.8%	4.4%	4.4%	3.0%	3.9%	3.3%
	(7.6)	(6.2)	(6.5)	(7.7)	(5.2)	(7.9)	(9.3)
% Other/multiple race/ethnicity	4.1%	4.9%	3.4%	4.2	5.6%	4.8%	3.6%
	(7.8)	(10.0)	(5.8)	(4.5)	(11.9)	(11.6)	(5.5)
% Ages 25–64	45.0%	30.3%	41.2%	67.8%	36.9%	51.0%	49.0%
	(23.4)	(16.8)	(30.1)	(20.4)	(14.3)	(22.5)	(18.0)
SAT Critical Reading 25th percentile	468.0	460.3	474.7	431.9	405.6	436.8	-
	(70.8)	(56.5)	(78.1)	(62.7)	(40.0)	(83.9)	
SAT Critical Reading 75th percentile	577.0	567.7	585.0	549.7	503.9	535.5	-
	(72.0)	(59.3)	(77.8)	(78.4)	(49.9)	(98.3)	
SAT Math 25th percentile	474.4	472.7	477.5	424.9	405.9	428.6	-
	(75.0)	(62.4)	(81.6)	(73.7)	(53.8)	(91.8)	
SAT Math 75th percentile	583.2	580.5	587.4	540.7	501.1	523.6	-
	(75.2)	(66.1)	(79.7)	(82.8)	(61.1)	(86.3)	
Student loan 3-year default rate	13.3%	7.5%	7.0%	14.6%	17.6%	18.1%	17.2%
$N =$	7116	714	1639	701	1259	261	2542

Note: Standard deviations are in parentheses. Data were gathered from the Integrated Postsecondary Data System (IPEDS), fall 2015. Tuition is in constant 2015 dollars. Observations are based on cases with full responses to variables of interest. Enrollment totals include all students enrolled in the institution as of the fall 2015 term. Loan default rates were gathered from the Federal Student Aid office of the U.S. Department of Education (2017); numbers of reporting institutions are slightly lower than those in IPEDS because of differing surveys and methods.

Table 18.3 Mean faculty composition of post-secondary institutions by sector, rank, and tenure status, fall 2015

	Four-year institutions			Sub-baccalaureate institutions		
	Public	*Private*	*Private (for-profit)*	*Public*	*Private*	*Private (for-profit)*
Tenured/tenure-track faculty total	179.0	77.0	8.8	55.3	10.1	3.0
	(242.6)	(151.6)	(5.8)	(59.4)	(10.3)	-
Nontenured/Non-tenure-track faculty total	165.8	66.7	26.8	66.9	30.9	17.2
	(291.8)	(190.1)	(62.8)	(106.1)	(65.7)	(18.0)
Tenured/tenure-track						
% Full professors	23.0%	17.0%	0.4%	9.7%	0.8%	0.0%
% Associate professors	22.5%	14.9%	0.5%	5.8%	0.7%	0.0%
% Assistant professors	19.5%	12.1%	0.2%	6.0%	0.9%	0.0%
% Instructors	2.0%	0.5%	0.1%	22.2%	0.1%	0.2%
% Lecturers	0.3%	0.0%	0.0%	0.1%	0.0%	0.0%
% No-rank faculty	2.7%	0.3%	0.0%	6.6%	0.8%	0.0%
Nontenured/non-tenure-track						
% Full professors	1.3%	11.0%	7.4%	4.1%	2.7%	2.4%
% Associate professors	2.3%	9.3%	5.0%	3.2%	4.7%	0.4%
% Assistant professors	6.4%	15.6%	7.6%	4.1%	4.6%	0.3%
% Instructors	9.2%	9.5%	60.1%	19.1%	42.3%	58.1%
% Lecturers	6.8%	1.8%	0.5%	1.0%	0.3%	1.0%
% No-rank faculty	4.0	8.0%	18.1%	18.0%	42.0%	37.8%
Student-to-faculty ratio	17.3	12.3	14.2	16.9%	14.4	15.4
	(4.3)	(7.8)	(6.7)	(6.6)	(8.9)	(8.2)
N =	706	1,444	499	907	80	410

Note: Standard deviations are in parentheses. Data are derived from the Integrated Postsecondary Education Data System (IPEDS), 2015. Observations are based on institutional responses. Sub-baccalaureate institutions include trade schools and certificate only schools. Faculty rank categories are options on the IPEDS survey, and the categorization of faculty is dependent on each institution's classification scheme. Numbers of institutions are based on institutions that provided faculty classifications. Faculty averages and student-faculty ratios are based on numbers derived in Table 18.2 sample from IPEDS.

relationship, however, is in the opposite direction for sub-baccalaureate institutions; for-profit sub-baccalaureate institutions offer more expensive degrees than their nonprofit counterparts. We also observe that a slightly higher percentage of students receive some type of financial aid in nonprofit and for-profit schools than public schools at both the four-year and sub-baccalaureate level.

Related to financial aid is student loans and student loan debt, both private and federally subsidized. The second-to-last line of Table 18.2 presents the three-year federal loan default rate for the 2014 cohort of students attending public, nonprofit, and for-profit institutions. The official U.S. Department of Education statistics indicate that the overall default rate is 11.5 percent. This average rate is skewed upward by the high default rates at for-profit institutions. The average default rate at four-year for-profit institutions is approximately double that of other four-year institutions. Interestingly, though, default rates across the sub-baccalaureate sector are similar across institutional forms. The rates are appreciably higher when five-year default rates are measured for higher education institutions, as colleges and universities often encourage students to apply for short-term debt deferment or forbearance: student five-year default rates for nonprofit schools are at 8.5 percent; for public schools, 14.5 percent; and for for-profit schools, 24.9 percent (Miller 2018).

Examining variation in student demographic characteristics across postsecondary organizational sectors and levels, we find that female students outnumber male students nearly 2 to 1, but this discrepancy is especially noticeable in for-profit sub-baccalaureate institutions, where female students outnumber male students at a rate of more than 3 to 1. Moreover, white students compose more than 50 percent of all students across sectors, types, and forms, except in for-profit institutions, where they constitute less than half of the total enrollment. Conversely, black and Hispanic students are typically overrepresented in for-profit institutions, relative to their representation in higher education overall. This is particularly the case in sub-baccalaureate institutions. Finally, similar to black and Hispanic students, older students—age twenty-five to sixty-four—are overrepresented in for-profit and in sub-baccalaureate nonprofit institutions.

With the exception of for-profit sub-baccalaureate institutions—which did not report or typically require scores—data are reported for the SAT scores of the incoming first-year class at postsecondary institutions. The data indicate that students attending sub-baccalaureate and for-profit institutions score considerably lower than their peers attending public and nonprofit four-year institutions. This applies to both verbal and math portions of the entry exams. Although not reported, ACT scores suggest the same differences across institutions and sectors.

Table 18.3 extends the analysis of the organizational characteristics of postsecondary institutions by examining the composition of faculty across organizational sectors and levels. The plurality of faculty at public four-year institutions are tenured or tenure-track faculty, including full, associate, and assistant professors. However, there is a considerable contingent of non-tenured/non-tenure-tracked faculty at these same institutions. Whether tenure-track or not, faculty at postsecondary institutions are classified by their academic rank/status from full professors at the very top and instructors and nonclassified faculty at the bottom. Nonprofit four-year institutions have a similar distribution of faculty, albeit with considerably more non-tenured faculty. For-profit four-year institutions, on the other hand, are radically different from their public and nonprofit counterparts. Most for-profit four-year faculty are non-tenured instructors, with only around 1 percent of their faculty at any rank being tenured or tenure-track.

Sub-baccalaureate institutions vary more across public and nonprofit sectors than for-profit and nonprofit sectors with regard to faculty tenure. Nonprofit institutions employ larger proportions of non-tenured faculty than public institutions. However, the largest portion of faculty at all three forms of sub-baccalaureate organizations are categorized as instructors. Tenured faculty at public sub-baccalaureate institutions are more likely classified as instructors rather than employed in professorial positions. However, the largest share of faculty at public sub-baccalaureate institutions are either non-tenured or non-tenure-track.

In coverage of the topic of nonprofit education in a prior edition of this volume, Patricia J. Gumport and Stuart K. Snydman (2006) argued that the increasing hybridization of postsecondary institutions explained trends in post-secondary R&D funding support through 1997. We extend their analysis, reporting in Table 18.4 the amount and sources of R&D expenditures by public and private nonprofit postsecondary institutions from 1977 through 2016, in inflation-adjusted 2018 dollars. Public universities have consistently spent approximately twice as much on R&D as nonprofit universities; however, the sources of those funds have changed over time.

In 1977, approximately 77 percent of R&D funds for nonprofit institutions came from the federal government, compared to nearly 61 percent for public universities. In 2016, 60 percent of nonprofit institutions' R&D funds originated with the federal government, compared to approximately 50 percent for public universities. Over that interim period, the portion of R&D funds for public and nonprofit institutions attributed to the federal government not only decreased but also converged slightly—the difference between four-year nonprofit and public institutions shrank from 16 percentage points to 10.

What is not evident from the preceding observations is that federal funds for R&D actually grew significantly from 1977 through 2006 (Gumport and Snydman 2006) but then leveled off—as a proportion of total R&D funds—after 2006. Academic institutions themselves have increasingly contributed their own resources, often in the form of required matching funds for grant eligibility. In 1977, public universities provided approximately 16 percent of their own R&D budget, and nonprofit institutions provided a mere 6 percent. However, by 2016, reported public and nonprofit institutional outlays had grown considerably, representing 27 percent and 21 percent of postsecondary R&D budgets, respectively. This increase is due in part to changes in long-standing funding policies implemented by the federal government. As the former provost of Columbia University, Jonathan R. Cole, observes, "[the] federal government was actually making universities pay for government grants and contracts" (2016:306). Other sources of funds, such as those from private industry or state/local sources, have not matched the pace of academic institutional self-investment. In fact, state and local funds account for proportionally less of R&D budgets in 2016 than they did in 1977.

Institutional Isomorphism and Hybrid Organizational Forms

In recent decades, economic, social, and technological changes have undermined the organizational distinctiveness of nonprofit educational institutions. For example, the

Table 18.4 Sources of R&D funds at public and private institutions, 1997–2016

Year and institution type	Total	Federal government	State or local government	Industry	Academic institution	Other sources
			1977			
Private	$2,294.98	$1,774.65	$53.70	$90.60	$146.67	$229.51
Public	$4,146.77	$2,543.50	$538.54	$129.25	$667.95	$267.53
			1987			
Private	$6,734.79	$5,010.82	$153.48	$468.53	$579.41	$522.70
Public	$12,514.61	$6,620.27	$1,467.53	$782.95	$2,855.22	$788.49
			1997			
Private	$12,603.78	$9,107.70	$265.15	$879.09	$1,277.93	$1,073.92
Public	$25,962.80	$13,863.02	$2,707.76	$1,834.37	$5,919.37	$1,638.28
			2006			
Private	$19,570.81	$14,678.11	$391.42	$978.54	$2,152.79	$1,174.25
Public	$41,174.96	$23,469.73	$3,294.00	$2,058.75	$9,470.24	$2,882.25
			2016			
Private	$26,257.79	$15,780.93	$367.61	$1,759.27	$5,592.91	$2,757.07
Public	$50,150.82	$25,476.62	$3,911.76	$2,708.14	$13,540.72	$4,513.57

Note: All figures are in millions of 2018 dollars. Data for 1977, 1987, and 1997 were gathered from Gumport & Snydman (2006); other data were gathered from National Science Foundation reports (2010; 2018). Inflation adjusted to constant 2018 dollars using the Consumer Price Index calculator available from the Bureau of Labor Statistics. National Science Board. (2010). *Science & engineering indicators 2010.* Alexandria, VA: National Science Foundation. National Science Board. (2018). *Science & engineering indicators 2018.* Alexandria, VA: National Science Foundation.

growth of hybrid organizational forms has been fostered by third-party entities—including for-profit firms—that provide administrative, instructional, counseling, and other institutional services to schools. The growing reach of these firms has partially been driven by technological changes that have provided opportunities to provide a broad array of education-related services, growth in the perceived value and need for managerial consulting expertise, and declining organizational capacity of public sector institutions related to diminished funding support.

Charter Schools

The emergence and growth of charter schools is a prominent and significant example of the appearance of new hybrid forms of organizations in education. In 1991, Minnesota passed the first charter school legislation that supported the establishment of specialized schools, which would be exempt from certain statutory regulations, an approach that quickly spread to other states (Henig 2008). Charter school legislation and institutions were able to attract political support from a diverse set of constituencies, families, and students, particularly in urban areas that were eager for alternatives to traditional public-school options perceived as failing. By 1996, more than half of the states had charter school laws approved; ten years later, "the number of states was up to forty, the number of schools to just under 4,000 and the number of students to somewhere around 1.1 million" (Henig 2008:47).

Charter schools in many ways exemplify the extent to which organizational school forms have been blurred. Although charter schools rely on public funding, they take a wide variety of organizational forms across and within states with respect to governance and management. Authorization for a charter school can be held by a nonprofit entity, a school district, a university, or, in some states, a for-profit entity. Although administrative oversight typically is subject to public meeting, accountability, and transparency requirements, some charter schools outsource management functions to either a for-profit or a nonprofit education management organization (Bulkley 2004). Charter schools can be stand-alone entities or connected to a larger network with shared administrative oversight. Nationally, about 16 percent of charter school operations are run by nonprofit charter school management organizations, which operate four or more schools (Furgeson et al. 2012). In some states, the charter school could also be run as or by a for-profit entity. Given the diversity of charter school organizational configurations, clear distinctions between public, nonprofit, and for-profit school types are challenging to identify. For example, if a nonprofit university holds the charter authorization for a local school, is the charter school a public or nonprofit entity? What if a local school district holds the charter authorization, but the school is managed and operated by a nonprofit charter school management organization? These varying configurations likely have implications for organizational behavior and educational experiences.

Higher Education

Higher education has also faced external pressures that have led to institutional isomorphism and hybridization. Postsecondary institutions—regardless of whether they are public, nonprofit, or for-profit entities—have become increasingly reliant on student tuition, debt markets, and federal funding support in the form of Pell grants, guaranteed student loans, and tax credits. State and local funding of public higher education has stagnated in recent years, despite increased enrollments. Local and state funding for higher education in constant 2015 dollars was $82 billion in the 2000–2001 academic year and $81 billion in 2014–2015. Because of expanded higher-education enrollments (which increased from 8.3 million to 10.7 million during this period), this stagnation of overall state and local funding support has led to a significant drop in state and local support on a per-student basis, from $9,910 in the 2000–2001 academic year to $7,570 in 2014–2015 (Baum and Johnson 2015). Conversely, the share of public higher-education funding covered by tuition has increased from 29 percent in 2000 to 47 percent in 2015. However, state funding support for public higher education varies dramatically across states; tuition is needed to cover only 15 percent of costs in Wyoming compared to 87 percent in Vermont (State Higher Education Executive Officers 2018). Public universities also typically have independent boards of regents or trustees that are set up to run the institutions and allow a degree of quasi-autonomy from state governors and legislators in many locales.

Postsecondary institutions have worked to identify a diversity of funding streams, including private philanthropy, alumni support, and partnerships with private firms. Higher-education institutions have organized themselves to pursue external funding to undertake and subsidize research activities—enterprises that are often at the core of their institutional identities and their quests for prestige, status, and legitimacy. Although private colleges and universities (excluding for-profit institutions) are formally classified as nonprofit organizations, public colleges and universities have also established parallel partnering nonprofit foundations in the form of 501(c)(3) "supporting organizations" that hold millions and sometimes billions of dollars of endowment funds targeted for the support of specific higher-education institutions. As the sociologist Charlie Eaton (2018) has documented, college and university endowments have grown tremendously in recent decades. These endowments have benefited both from access to the increasing wealth held by institutional patrons in the context of rising societal economic inequality and from continued tax exemption. If indirect tax arbitrage is included in estimations (where construction is financed through tax-exempt mutual bonds, rather than through accumulated assets), the tax subsidy benefiting higher-education endowments can be valued at approximately $20 billion annually. Tracking total endowment assets for the wealthiest 5 percent of nonprofit colleges and universities, Eaton (2018) documents that endowment assets increased (in constant 2012 dollars) from $17.8 billion in 1977 to $126.2 billion in 2012.

Rather than use increased endowment income to provide educational opportunities by significantly expanding enrollments or access for economically disadvantaged students, elite institutions instead are investing these resources in further enriching educational experiences. Enrollments in wealthy nonprofit colleges and universities increased only modestly during this period, while the percentage of Pell grant recipients from 2000 to 2012 increased slightly in liberal arts colleges and was flat at research universities. Meanwhile, these institutions doubled instructional spending per student (Eaton 2018).

The hybridization of higher education has also been promoted by legislative encouragement for corporate-university partnerships. Following the 1980 Bayh-Dole Act, which allowed colleges and universities to file for patents on discoveries funded by federal grant dollars, higher-education institutions also expanded public–private partnerships and investment in biotech, engineering, and related fields (Owen-Smith and Powell 2003). Although funds from these sources typically make up only a small part of school budgets, the nonrestricted, discretionary character of these resources gives patent-generating activity exceptional weight in shaping organizational behavior.

Prior scholarship on the nonprofit sector has documented the extent to which finance, mission, and governance of higher education in the United States has "shown an increasing trend toward commercialization and related hybridization such that the boundaries between non-profits and for-profits in that domain have become indistinct" (Gumport and Snydman 2006:462). For example,

> public and private non-profit institutions have begun to adopt more market-oriented curriculum and business practices that resemble characteristics of the for-profit form . . . conversely, proprietary institutions have increased efforts to appear more traditional, or mainstream, by applying for accreditation and expanding their curricula and degree offerings to include more general education and transferable credits." (Gumport and Snydman 2006:465)

Along with financial resources, students are distributed unevenly and through varying mechanisms across educational sectors and institutional levels. Whether through neighborhood affiliation or through gerrymandered districts, public schools traditionally draw their student bodies from within a given geographic locale. Postsecondary institutions, with the exception of a small, elite set of institutions, draw most of their students from within state or local communities. The place-based character of much of education persists and has enduring implications for schools as organizations (Stevens and Gebre-Medhin 2016). However, as types and choices of schools expand, and technological changes create new opportunities for online instructional delivery, the choice set for individuals deciding among nonprofit, for-profit, and public institutions is expanding to include not only local institutions but also a number of online options to which students can apply for consideration. Historically, nonprofit and public four-year colleges have served students with relatively similar characteristics that are distinct from those attending public two-year colleges (Gumport and Snydman 2006). From an organizational perspective, it is worth exploring the extent to which student flows and enrollment in different forms of schooling are stable or changing, as well as the extent to which markets are segmented or overlapping.

In order to understand pools of applicants to various forms of schooling, we must examine how student and family expectations factor into school choice, at both the K–12 and postsecondary levels. Indeed, the legitimized structures and processes of schools are so deeply ingrained that one could hardly imagine a high school without periods dividing the day or a college without a humanities department. Exceptions to the normative character of educational organizations exist, but they are few and far between. Differences across organizational types often reside more in symbolic and superficial differentiation among organizations, which attract families and students, rather than substantive differences in organizational structures or practices. At the K–12 level, for instance, parents and families may choose between nonprofit religious and secular schools largely on the basis of the social characteristics of students enrolled there, or they may apply to any number of public charter schools with varied emphases, while still receiving forms of education that are aligned with similar collegiately oriented public-school curriculum standards in all other ways. In higher education, consumers are known to choose colleges based on emotional sentiments and familial affiliation. Fit, feel, and style are put forth as legitimate criteria, although they may not be connected to instructional differentiation.

Student expectations of educational organizations are particularly pronounced at the postsecondary level. As previously mentioned, stagnating state investment in higher education has led to increases in tuition and fees at many public colleges and universities. Although college-bound high school students feel pressure to compete for a limited number of spaces in elite institutions of higher education, colleges and universities are simultaneously competing with each other for tuition dollars. Normative isomorphic pressures on colleges and universities to attract students, as consumers or inputs claimed on college ranking scorecards, lead to a shift in the taken-for-granted understanding of what it means to be a college student and how colleges should interact with them (Arum and Roksa 2011). For example, despite funding cuts, institutional investment in amenities and student services continues to increase. Isomorphism is pronounced across educational sectors as a result of these normative pressures. The social amenities included in a consumer-driven residential model promoted by elite nonprofit colleges—and supported to a significant extent by federal subsidies—is often replicated not only at flagship public research universities but also at regional state campuses, through leveraged debt (Eaton et al. 2016). College campuses often compete for students based on the quality of their student centers, athletic facilities, dining halls, and residential accommodations. Research suggests that most college-bound students choose schools that prioritize investment in social amenities over academics (Jacob, McCall, and Stange 2013).

Boundaries associated with educational level and mission are also given little institutional deference. Colleges and universities are eager to cater to nontraditional students, whether they are older adults seeking additional education and training, adolescents enrolled in dual-degree coursework during high school, or residents of other countries. Community colleges expand to offer four-year degrees; elite colleges grow their schools of continuing studies; public universities acquire or develop online degrees to compete in national and international markets. Indeed, innovations in technology have led to the emergence of firms focused on digital courseware, learning management systems, student advisement, and administrative management systems that have been developed, packaged, and widely deployed in education (Carey 2016). These educational products and services often involve for-profit entities that have been capitalized not directly by the government but often by venture capitalists, U.S. foundations, or other sources of private sector funding (Stevens and Kirst 2015).

Although the shifting and blurring organizational forms of schools are one important trend in contemporary education, another aspect of nonprofits' involvement in the education field has been largely overlooked. We highlight in the following section the extent to which schools are embedded in organizational fields that are dependent on the state, but with nonprofit intermediaries empowered to take on significant functions. To illustrate the central role of nonprofit intermediaries in U.S. education, we highlight the role of foundations and professional associations; discuss how quality assurance is primarily accomplished through nonprofit accreditation agencies; and examine how sorting, selecting, and reifying student ability levels occurs through the efforts of nonprofit assessment firms.

Nonprofit Intermediaries and the Educational Field

Schools' institutional practices are strongly shaped by the organizations with which they interact in larger institutional fields. In particular, we assert that to appreciate the extent to which the nonprofit sector is implicated in U.S. education, it is necessary to move beyond a school-centric approach to emphasize the role of nonprofit intermediaries in education. Nonprofit intermediaries, which include providers of standardized testing and accreditation organizations, have played prominent roles in organizational governance, structure, and operations and have generated widespread legitimacy for education. This dynamic has been particularly evident with colleges and universities, where nonprofit intermediaries have taken on myriad functions.

Nonprofit intermediaries have featured prominently in the organization of higher education for more than a century. The prominence of nonprofit entities in the U.S. education field emerged in the context of a weak federal government that preferred the use of less visible mechanisms to support social welfare and education. Stretching back to the nineteenth century, Brian Balogh (2015:23) noted that U.S. citizens preferred "national governance that was inconspicuous" in character. Distrust of centralized forms of authority led to the successful emergence of "politically acceptable alliance(s) of institutions and professionals in civil society and the private sector to deliver these public benefits"(Balogh 2015:21). In education, nonprofit intermediaries were developed and embraced to solve myriad organizational problems including the organization of the professoriate, quality assurance, and processes to allocate students to schools. Schools were assisted in conducting these efforts, each of which focused in some way on organizational structure and legitimacy, not just by the state, but often more directly by private foundations, which catalyzed, organized, and provided financial backing to put in place these intermediaries, systems, and processes.

Private foundations played a prominent role in shaping the U.S. education system, in many ways filling a vacuum created by the relative absence of federal government centralized oversight and authority for system governance, operation, and direction. In recent years, as economic inequality has reached levels similar to that found during the beginning of the twentieth century, private foundations have been established with extraordinary resources and capacity to shape the field of education (Reckhow and Snyder 2014). For example, the Bill & Melinda Gates Foundation, which includes resources pledged from Warren Buffett, will in the near future have resources approaching $80 billion. The foundation employs thousands of personnel and designates U.S. education as one of its primary targets. New forms of philanthropy have emerged that have undermined distinctions between nonprofit and for-profit organization. Mark Zuckerberg and Priscilla Chan, for example, have chosen to forgo the tax advantages of nonprofit status to avoid disclosure requirements and political constraints, establishing their philanthropic organization as a privately held limited liability corporation. Irrespective of organizational forms, philanthropic entities, more often than not, focus to some extent on schooling, as education receives a significant portion of both corporate and private philanthropy (Guthrie et al. 2008; Foundation Center 2015).

Private philanthropic organizations, such as the Bill & Melinda Gates, Eli Broad, Kellogg, and Ford Foundations, have in recent years been at the forefront of actively promoting educational reforms (Tompkins-Stange 2016). Such actions echo similar initiatives dating back to the nineteenth century. Recent scholarship has highlighted the extent to which reforms are not simply imposed by private foundations onto passive local stakeholders but throughout history have rather been jointly designed and enacted within "action spaces" (McDonald et al. 2014) that allow for "interstitial collaboration" (Malczewski 2017). Given that the educational system in a democratic society requires social actors with divergent interests to work together, private foundations "often relied on an associational synthesis, in which national policymaking was promoted by using public and private resources, and through cooperative action by voluntary and private organizations at the state and local level" (Malczewski 2017:239). For example, the General Education Board partnered with white supremacist state governments and rural black communities to create public schools for black students in the South during the Jim Crow era (Malczewski 2016). The Carnegie Foundation created a mechanism—the credit hour—that harmonized and structured higher-education instruction and enrollment, making possible not only a retirement system that needed to distinguish between full-time and part-time employment (Lagemann 1992; Tyack and Tobin 1994) but also a mechanism to develop a coherent system of higher education in the absence of a strong centralized federal government.

The involvement of private foundations in education often takes the form of public–private partnerships; philanthropic resources serve as a catalyst for developments and innovations in the educational system, but the educational initiatives that are typically advanced ultimately rely on public funding for sustainability. Julius Rosenwald, for example, provided funding for the construction of thousands of schools in the South but required local communities to provide matching funding for the actual construction as well as evidence of long-term public support for school maintenance and staffing (Malczewski 2016). The Carnegie Foundation's support for the faculty retirement system included initial seed funding, but higher education institutions and faculty ultimately were responsible for funding the system. The character of private foundation involvement in education is thus often fleeting in terms of the duration of specific initiatives but with lasting implications for the development of educational structure and practices.

Private foundations were also instrumental in supporting the emergence of professional disciplinary associations, which provided the basis for organizing much of the research, teaching (i.e., undergraduate majors and PhD programs), service commitments, and orientation of faculty. Not only did foundations support disciplinary associations directly but they also supported nonprofit organizations that could strengthen their role in the field. For example, the Social Science Research Council, given the perceived connection between the social sciences and democratic forms of government, received critical support from the Ford, Rockefeller, Carnegie, and Russell Sage Foundations (Worcester and Sibley 2001). Although these professional disciplinary associations avoided direct efforts to negotiate compensation and other terms of employment (unlike K–12 teacher and postsecondary faculty unions, which have focused on those matters), they have played a significant role in structuring a system of education and defining faculty identity, expectations, and norms about professional activities and careers.

Colleges and universities have also self-organized through nonprofit entities to advance their own institutional interests vis-à-vis the state. Six prominent higher education associations (the American Association of Community Colleges, the American Association of State Colleges and Universities, the American Council on Education, the Association of American Universities, the Association of Public Land-grant Universities, and the National Association of Independent Colleges and Universities) have played an effective and defining role in enacting the regulatory environment in which colleges and universities operate. These associations have worked effectively to ensure that the business of higher education is stable, secure, and satisfactorily supported by the state.

In addition to the role that voluntary associations have played in the professional organization of educators and the institutional self-organization of colleges and universities, nonprofit entities have taken on responsibilities of quality assurance and the allocation of resources between state actors, institutions, and consumers (Davies and Mehta 2018). Nonprofit organizations serving these functions have provided a means for educational organizations to maintain legitimacy by conforming and performing institutionalized ceremonies and rituals, such as periodic accreditation reviews, while simultaneously decoupling the technical process of schools from direct oversight (Meyer and Rowan 1977; DiMaggio and Powell 1983). Regulation and oversight of an expanding educational system represented problems for the state, institutions of higher education, and the general public, which were readily solved by solutions provided by nonprofit intermediaries. These nonprofit intermediaries, particularly in higher education fields, buffered institutions from more intrusive inspection while generating the necessary legitimacy required for organizations to extract resources from the state and consumers.

Regulation of educational institutions in the United States is often diffuse and indirect, with schools only loosely coupled with larger administrative structures (Weick 1976). Although this degree of relative autonomy varies across schools based on factors such as organizational legitimacy and resource dependence, local, state, and federal regulation exist in a manner that often intentionally builds in ambiguity around interpretation and implementation. In the context of this regulatory complexity and uncertainty, government authorities have empowered third-party accreditation agencies to implement reviews of comparable character and familiar form across public, nonprofit, and for-profit settings. Normative and mimetic forces are pronounced in accreditation processes of this character.

The state, being ill-equipped and disinclined to inspect the institutional performance and quality of schools seeking resource allocations, has relied on third-party entities to perform this task. Higher-education accrediting agencies, which predate the government mandate for accrediting, became repurposed as an intermediary between the state and educational organizations, allowing them to demonstrate quality assurance ceremonially. Accreditation began as a way of legitimizing exchange between higher-education actors and defining which organizations were included in the institutional field. Two pieces of legislation inserted government authority into the process of accreditation: the Veterans Readjustment Assistance Act of 1952 and the Higher Education Act of 1965. These two pieces of legislation were crafted to serve different purposes, but each also required organizations receiving federal funds to be accredited in accordance with federally instituted rules for accreditation. The federal government did not establish accrediting agencies; rather, it legitimized and empowered them by authorizing and relying on their activities.

Currently, accrediting agencies are dually positioned as both gatekeepers of organizational resources (i.e., access to public funding) as well as legitimators of knowledge and processes (i.e., normative definitions of appropriate educational activities). That this task is taken on by nonprofit intermediaries is not without significance. Jeffrey Pfeffer and Gerald R. Salancik (2003) write that the role of accreditation is an exercise of control of one organization over another. However, this description presupposes that one organization has some legitimate claim to control another organization. In reality, the activities of higher-education accrediting agencies are co-created and constructed by organizations and their members that are being accredited. Their constituent members pay for the service of accreditation, which consists of a mix of self-appraisal and peer review (J. Eaton 2012). Accrediting agencies are not detached, independent authorities wielding unilateral control over educational organizations. Rather, they are a part of a field-level system of rituals and ceremonies that offer legitimacy to activities while, simultaneously, decoupling their activities from close inspection (Scott 2015).

Admissions testing in higher education is another ritualized process that decouples higher-education organizations from inspection activity. Although the history and original purpose of admission testing is debated (for discussion, see Calvin 2000 and Lemann 2000), it is worth highlighting the extent to which nonprofit colleges and educational foundations, such as the Carnegie Foundation, invested in the establishment and organization of the field through the use of nonprofit entities such as the Educational Testing Service, American College Testing, and the College Board (Lagemann 1992). These nonprofit intermediaries designed, propagated, and administered the organizational infrastructure that has subsequently governed the allocation of students to colleges and universities. Although not required by law, particularly after World War II, standardized testing became a ubiquitous part of the admissions process despite ongoing criticisms (Crouse and Trusheim 1988; Calvin 2000; Sedlacek 2003).

The institutional willingness to allocate scarce educational opportunities on the basis of testing routines is explained not solely by the technical efficiency of identifying which students are most likely to succeed in undergraduate studies, but rather by adherence to a system of symbolic exchanges that legitimize and sanctify the process. For higher-education organizations, the testing process solves a key legitimation problem by minimizing inspection of the technical process related to the selection of students (Meyer and Rowan 1977). In turn, the nonprofit intermediaries providing the examination are legitimated by the continued acceptance of test scores by higher-education organizations. The process itself becomes a part of the taken-for-granted frame not just of secondary and postsecondary education but of contemporary understandings of human development and social privilege (Stevens 2007). Schools host testing in their facilities in a ceremony that has developed its own rites and rituals. The sanctity and silent reverence found during an admission test rivals that of the most devout congregation's silent meditation for redemption from their sins.

Nonprofit intermediaries have taken on significant roles in shaping the field of education. The activities they are involved in—lobbying the federal and state governments on behalf of institutional members, organizing the professoriate into disciplinary areas represented by professional associations, and arranging for accreditation and assessment—are core to the survival, stability, and legitimacy of the education system. The nonprofit character of U.S. education thus goes well beyond school-level characteristics and differences.

Conclusion

The expansion of higher education in the mid-twentieth century did not happen in a vacuum. As Robert Fiala and Audri Gordon-Lanford (1987) show, public sentiment viewing education as a means of national human capital development was prevalent during this period. Higher education was increasingly recognized not as an elite status symbol but rather as a necessity for citizens in societies that were becoming increasingly democratic and dependent on technologically advanced forms of production (Schofer and Meyer 2005). The passage of the Higher Education Act of 1965 cemented the legitimacy of higher education in contemporary society as the federal government—part of Lyndon Johnson's Great Society initiative—began to subsidize the education of citizens who had traditionally not had access to college (Martin 1994).

Nonprofit entities historically have played a significant role not just in delivering education but in structuring and defining the organizational field. Nonprofit intermediaries worked together with colleges and universities to co-create and enact a stable organizational field that generated institutional processes to manage and legitimate the flows of people and resources. Nonprofit intermediaries, including foundations, assessment firms, professional associations, and accreditation agencies played a prominent role in defining the organizational field. Accrediting agencies, created to standardize degree requirements and admission criteria across organizations, were empowered by federal legislation to legitimate institutional access to federal financial resources. These voluntary associations of organizations were responsible to each other for demarcating the minimum acceptable limits for institutional performance as well as admitted students and graduates. The standardized limits enacted formally create legitimate barriers to both access to institutions and resources. Furthermore, higher-education organizations used the highly rationalized and ceremonial process of admissions testing to create a buffer between their own activities and direct inspection. Testing was legitimated by its presumed reliance on scientific construction and diffused widely across the educational field. Testing firms effectively legitimated the allocation of students to stratified tiers of higher education.

John W. Meyer, Richard Scott, and Terrence E. Deal (1981) discuss the necessity of fragmented systems of organizational coupling to deal with the needs and wants of competing constituencies. Accreditation, which is enacted by individuals from organizations that are the simultaneous subject and object of inspection, ensures that the expected structural components (departments, student services, etc.) are maintained, largely irrespective of student outcomes. Testing companies, through a similarly legitimized process, buffer higher-education organizations from constituencies who may seek to inspect or scrutinize their admissions.

In the context of a broad expansion of education in the twentieth century, nonprofit entities played a critical role in facilitating public and state support for education and institutionally structured and insulated the educational system from organizational challenges. An appreciation of the role of nonprofit intermediaries bolsters the claims of early institutional theorists regarding the decoupling of activities and the reliance on good-faith shows of compliance with socially accepted rituals and myths to secure legitimacy.

Nonprofit scholars can contribute to education research by encouraging scholarship to move beyond school-centric approaches to appreciate the role of the state and nonprofit intermediaries in structuring the larger organizational field of education.

Despite the expanse of knowledge and research into educational organizations, there are still considerable avenues worthy of further exploration. Examining school choice, Mark Berends and Genevieve Zottola (2009) note the lack of scholarship examining the bureaucratic structures and organizational practices across schools and sectors with respect to differences in state laws regarding school choice and charter school regulation. Researchers in particular could explore the role that nonprofit and for-profit school management organization plays in how charter schools are organized and how they relate to each other. For example, does whether charter schools are governed by public, for-profit, or nonprofit entities relate to isomorphic pressures and organizational arrangements across the sector?

More research could also be directed toward understanding how external influences, such as accreditation or testing, affect organizational processes. Research could examine how differences in regulatory requirements across sectors and states alters organizational behavior. Furthermore, the use of standardized testing in accountability systems in recent years increases the level of inspection on educational organizations. However, not all schools, grades, or curricula are subject to these testing regimes. This inconsistency implies that educators are subject to varying testing and accountability pressures within organizations. Furthermore, research could extend work on how independent educational foundations and other nonprofit intermediaries influence organizational change. Nonprofit organizations continuously seek to implement or influence school reform efforts; however, more research is needed to articulate and theorize how nonprofit intermediaries systematically structure and define the organizational field in which individual schools operate.

19   NONPROFIT ARTS ORGANIZATIONS

Sustainability and Rationales for Support

Francie Ostrower[*]

NONPROFIT ORGANIZATIONS HAVE PLAYED an important role in the arts and cultural life of the United States. Today, however, nonprofit arts organizations face significant challenges, and their viability and significance is a subject of debate. Examples include declining or stagnant attendance across multiple art forms (NEA 2015), financial difficulties (see, e.g., Keating and Pradhan 2012; Nelson et al. 2014; Pompe and Tamburri 2016), and the possibility that the supply of nonprofit arts organizations has outstripped demand for them (Tepper 2008; Zakaras and Lowell 2008). These challenges raise questions about the rationales for the nonprofit arts sector in its current form and the significance and sustainability of nonprofit arts organizations. This chapter focuses on these issues in discussing the recent research and policy literature on the nonprofit arts sector.

In some cases, questions and challenges signify a further evolution of longstanding themes and tensions in the nonprofit arts field, notably between exclusivity and inclusivity, an issue that runs throughout much of the literature. Tensions between exclusivity and inclusivity have been associated with established arts organizations from their inception (DiMaggio 1986a) and expressed themselves in evolving ways (Accominotti, Khan, and Storer 2018; McDonnell and Tepper 2014; Ostrower 2002). From the perspective of this chapter, those tensions offer one useful lens through which to view some of the major developments, challenges, and responses that we see in the nonprofit arts field today.

More of the literature is about large and established nonprofit arts organizations, and that is reflected in this chapter. This is shifting, however, as research encompasses a wider portion of the nonprofit arts world, and strands of the cultural policy literature question the current distribution of support within the nonprofit arts (see, e.g., Sidford and Frasz 2017; Rosenstein 2018). As the chapter discusses, the nonprofit arts sector is not homogeneous, and challenges and opportunities may vary among different types of nonprofit arts organizations.

[*] The author thanks Patricia Bromley, Paul J. DiMaggio, and Walter W. Powell for their helpful comments.

Much of the recent discussion of nonprofit arts organizations takes place in literature that is focused on arts policy and arts participation, rather than on nonprofit organizations per se. One prominent theme is that nonprofit organizations should be seen as part of a larger and interconnected arts sector. Some emphasize interconnectedness among different sectors within the arts, some argue that arts policy has relied too much on nonprofits, and some question assumptions about the distinctiveness and centrality of nonprofit organizations' role in the arts (see, e.g., Cherbo, Vogel, and Wyszomirski 2008; Ivey 2005, 2008; Rushton 2015; Tepper 2008). Although these literatures sometimes point to the interconnectedness of nonprofit and other sectors, they also raise questions about the contemporary relevance and centrality of the nonprofit sector in the arts as it stands today.

As this introduction suggests, current issues of sustainability, and policy rationales for it, are closely interconnected. Pressures facing nonprofit arts organizations call on them to consider and advocate their value, expand their constituencies, and reflect on the scope of their missions and the possibilities for achieving these under shifting circumstances. Historically, debates over the value of the nonprofit arts have reflected different opinions about the value of and public interest in the arts themselves (Smith 2010). What is striking today is the extent to which questions about nonprofit arts organizations are being expressed by those who concur with the public value of the arts but question the preeminence of nonprofit organizations as vehicles for promoting that value.

From the perspective of this chapter the nonprofit form remains of considerable relevance and importance for the expressions of a variety of mission-driven artistic endeavors that will not be sustained through government support or the marketplace and are extensive enough to require some type of formal organizational structure. At the same time, the preeminence of the nonprofit form in the arts is not being taken for granted in the literature, and traditional hierarchies and ways of operating are being questioned.

Demographic, technological, social and economic shifts are creating considerable pressures for change and adaptation on individual organizations to maintain their sustainability. We do not mean to suggest that the nonprofit arts have not faced challenges in the past. Nonprofits' role and prominence in the arts has evolved in the past, and we should expect it to continue to evolve in the future. That includes arts nonprofits' relationship with other nonprofits, and organizations in other sectors. This chapter discusses some of those pressures and developments that may influence that evolution.

One significant topic that has not been a focus of research since the last edition of this volume is the intersectoral division of labor in the arts. This diminished interest is consistent with recent emphases on interconnectedness, similarities rather than differences among organizational forms, and perceptions that the nonprofit form is overused. This chapter suggests, however, that rather than turning research away from considering intersectoral divisions of labor, these trends should prompt renewed attention to the circumstances under which nonprofits become more advantageous or less advantageous options, to typologizing and analyzing cross-sector relations, and to comparing both similarities and differences between nonprofits and a seemingly growing array of alternatives.

The chapter begins with an overview of major characteristics of the nonprofit arts sector described in the literature, including sources of support and sectoral growth. Next, the chapter discusses prominent explanations for the nonprofit form in the arts, recent perspectives on the distinctiveness of the nonprofit form, and potential hybrid alternatives. The chapter then turns to major challenges to sustainability, discussing patterns of attendance at multiple art forms in which nonprofit organizations are prominent. It concludes by outlining some areas for future research.

The Nonprofit Arts Sector: An Overview

This section provides an overview of some major characteristics of the nonprofit arts sector (for detailed statistical descriptions of the nonprofit art sector, see Kushner and Cohen 2016; McKeever, Dietz, and Fyffe 2016; Toepler and Wyszomirski 2012). The *National Arts Index*, based on data from the Internal Revenue Service (IRS) Business Master files at the Urban Institute's National Center for Charitable Statistics,[1] reports that in 2013, there were ninety-five thousand nonprofit arts organizations in the United States (Kushner and Cohen 2016:iii, 43). Of these, we know far more about organizations with gross receipts of $50,000 or more, from publicly available information the organizations are required to report on IRS Form 990. There were about twenty-nine thousand such public reporting charities in the arts, culture, and humanities in 2013. Nonprofit arts organizations represent a relatively small portion (10 percent) of the number of reporting public charities (McKeever et al. 2016:165), and an even smaller portion of nonprofit revenues (2 percent) (2016:190). By subfield, the twenty-nine thousand arts nonprofits broke down as follows: performing arts (35 percent); historical societies (13 percent); museums and museum activities (11 percent);[2] and other types of organizations (41 percent), such as media and communications organizations, arts service organizations, and arts education organizations (McKeever et al. 2016 197).

Many arts programs are embedded within other (non-arts-specific) nonprofit organizations, such as universities and community centers, which are not captured by these statistics. Accordingly, the nonprofit organizational presence in the arts extends beyond the numbers of arts-specific nonprofit organizations.

There is considerable variability among nonprofit arts organizations in terms of size, professionalization, mission, purpose, and forms of community engagement. Nonprofit arts organizations differ in more ways, however, than these organizational attributes. Kevin F. McCarthy and Kimberly Jinnett (2001) differentiate between arts organizations focused on presenting the canons of a particular art form, those that promote art as an avenue for community improvement, and those that focus on training artists and promoting engagement in creative processes (see also Grams 2008). Terence E. McDonnell and Steven J. Tepper (2014) distinguish between high-culture-focused nonprofit arts organizations (such as art museums, theaters, and ballets) and popular-culture-oriented organizations (such as cultural and ethnic festivals and indie/college radio stations).

The number of for-profit arts establishments in the United States (650,000) far exceeds the number of nonprofit organizations (Kushner and Cohen 2016:iii). However, nonprofits predominate in several disciplines (DiMaggio 2006; Kushner and Cohen, 2016, Toepler and Wyszomirski 2012). Nonprofit organizations constitute almost 90 percent of museums and visual arts institutions, 75 percent of dance companies, and 60 percent of theaters. By contrast, nonprofits make up only one third of music organizations. Nonprofits do constitute the majority of organizations in classical music fields, including opera, chamber music, and symphony orchestras (DiMaggio 2006; Toepler and Wyszomirski 2012:231–234). As these statistics indicate, nonprofits predominate in high-culture forms (DiMaggio 2006). Research is also revealing nonprofit prominence in other arts fields, such as outdoor arts festivals. In a survey of over 1,400 such festivals, Carole Rosenstein found that most were under the auspices of nonprofit, generally small organizations (2010:41). Some nonprofit organizations are among the most well known arts organizations, both nationally and internationally (Toepler and Wyszomirski 2012), such as Alvin Ailey American Dance Theater, Carnegie Hall, the Los Angeles Philharmonic, and the Metropolitan Museum of Art.

In the second edition of this volume, Paul J. DiMaggio (2006) pointed to an emerging trend whereby the nonprofit form was expanding to a wider variety of arts programs and organizations that look quite different from the early high-culture nonprofits created by local urban elites. Thus, the Metropolitan Museum of Art (founded in 1870) offers an example of the preeminence of the nonprofit form among arts organizations of international renown cited in one discussion (Toepler and Wyszomirski 2012:231); the Los Angeles Poverty Department (a performance group composed mainly of homeless people, founded in 1985)[3] provides an example of an arts institution with "direct social relevance" in another (Borwick 2012:40). Using data from the National Center for Charitable Statistics for 2001, Carole Rosenstein and Amy Brimer (2005:192) estimate that approximately 20 percent of organizations in the arts, culture, and humanities field were "producing, promoting, or supporting non-Western classical, ethnic, traditional, folk and noncommercial popular expressive forms." Zannie Giraud Voss and her colleagues conclude that "arts and cultural organizations in the U.S. are well distributed across the country, serving communities both poor and affluent, rural and urban, not just on the coasts and not just in major metropolitan markets" (Voss et al. 2018:2; see also Voss and Voss 2017).

Another question concerns the geographical distribution of nonprofit arts organizations in the United States. Although no statistics on this distribution were identified in the current literature, the National Center for Arts Research Vibrancy Index (Voss et al. 2018) ranks "arts vibrant" communities, based partly on the presence of nonprofit arts organizations but also on other measures (such as the presence of freelance artists and levels of government support). Ranking the most arts-vibrant communities separately for large, medium, and small communities, Voss and her colleagues find the first two categories represented throughout the country, whereas western states predominate in their list of the most vibrant small communities (Voss et al. 2018:3; see also Voss and Voss 2017 for a map of nonprofit arts locations).

Growth and Expansion of the Nonprofit Form

The previous section describes the current breadth of the nonprofit arts sector, but the nonprofit presence in the arts was not always large. Stefan Toepler and Margaret J. Wyszomirski (2012) note that until the end of World War II, high-culture institutions were the nonprofit exceptions in a mainly commercial arts field. Philanthropy has played a significant role in expanding the nonprofit presence in the arts. Early creation of nonprofit arts organizations was intimately bound to the efforts of urban elites (DiMaggio 1986a, 1986b, 2006). Later, institutional funders (foundations and, following the creation of the National Endowment for the Arts [NEA], government) fueled substantial increases in the number of nonprofit arts organizations in the arts in the latter half of the twentieth century.

The advent of foundation and government funding during the 1960s and 1970s, initiated by the Ford Foundation's extensive program of institution building in the arts, had a profound impact on the development of the modern nonprofit arts sector. Prior to the 1950s, the arts were not a major area of foundation interest (Smith 2010). In 1957, the Ford Foundation initiated a program that would invest hundreds of millions of dollars into supporting the arts, frequently through matching grants to nonprofit arts organizations that leveraged additional donations (Anderson 2007; DiMaggio 1986b; Ivey 2005; Smith 2010). At the governmental level, the NEA was created in 1965 along with state arts agencies around the same period (DiMaggio 1986b:4). Prior to the creation of the NEA, only twenty-three states had state arts agencies. The NEA was required to allocate funds to any state with a state arts agency, however, and thus within a few years almost every state had established such an agency (NEA 2012:6). By the 1990s, 90 percent of large foundations were making grants to the arts (Smith 2010:276). Much of this funding was aimed at increasing the geographical distribution of access to the fine arts through nonprofit organizations. For instance, John Kreidler (1996) notes that a major purpose of Ford Foundation funding was to increase access to the fine arts through creation of regional arts nonprofits outside New York City, especially in dance and theater. As geographical disparities lessened, government and large foundation arts supporters prompted greater attention to participation by minority groups (DiMaggio and Ostrower 1992), but the types of arts supported still tended to be nonprofits presenting Euro-American high culture (DiMaggio 1986c; Lewis 2000).

These newly available sources of support from institutional funders created incentives for arts groups to adopt the nonprofit form, a requirement for receiving grants (Anderson 2007; DiMaggio 2006; Ivey 2005; Smith 2010; Toepler and Wyszomirski 2012). Sheila Anderson (2007) observes that prior to the Ford Foundation's programs in theater, artists would not necessarily create a tax-exempt organization intended to survive the artist. Similarly, DiMaggio (2006) observes that prior to the 1970s, small presses were generally proprietary, but those created later frequently chose the nonprofit form. Toepler and Wyszomirski (2012) note that some previously commercial and proprietary firms, such as in the dance field, converted to nonprofit status. This apparent adoption of the nonprofit form in response to new funding opportunities suggests that an important issue for future research is to examine the conditions under which the nonprofit form becomes a more or less advantageous option.

The nonprofit presence in the arts increased dramatically by the end of the twentieth century. The number of art museums, theaters, symphonies, opera, dance companies, and other performing arts organizations increased by 59 percent between 1990 and 2001 (Tepper 2008:364–365). The number of reporting arts, culture, and humanities organizations further grew from 24,013 to 29,301 between 2003 and 2008, declining slightly to 29,137 in 2013 (McKeever et al. 2016:171).[4] For the larger universe of arts nonprofits, including those with gross receipts below the reporting threshold, the National Arts Index reports growth from 84,000 in 2002 to 113,200 in 2010 (Kushner and Cohen 2016:43). In 2011, there was a sharp (20 percent) drop in the numbers. The authors observe, however, that this drop largely reflects the removal from the records of thousands of nonprofits that had not filed returns with the IRS for three years, as well as some closures resulting from the recession. After 2012 the numbers increased again, to 95,000 (Kushner and Cohen 2016:43).

The Significance of Philanthropic Sources of Support

The nonprofit arts sector differs from the nonprofit sector as a whole with respect to sources of funding, relying to a greater extent on private philanthropy. Private giving constitutes 44 percent of revenues for arts, culture, and humanities organizations (McKeever et al. 2016:196) as compared with 13 percent of revenues for public charities as a whole, or 24 percent when higher education and hospitals are excluded from calculations (2016:166–167). Still, arts and cultural nonprofits also rely on fees for services and goods from private sources for a substantial portion of their income (32 percent). Another 10 percent of funding comes from government grants, and less than 2 percent in fees for services from government (McKeever et al. 2016:196). Arts and cultural organizations are distinctive in this low level of reliance on government fees, which is at 24 percent for the sector as a whole (McKeever et al. 2016:166).

Although they are highly reliant on private funding, the area of arts, culture, and humanities receives only 5 percent of total philanthropic donations (Giving USA 2018:32). Mark Ottoni-Wilhelm (2009:4), analyzing Philanthropy Panel Study survey data, reports that 8 percent of households gave to arts and culture in 2008. This percentage rises considerably with household income, from 4.1 percent among those with incomes $50,000 or under, to 8.7 percent among those with between $50,000 and $100,000, and reaching 15.7 percent among those with household incomes over $100,000 (Ottoni-Wilhelm 2009:7). Differences in rates of giving to arts and culture organizations are even more pronounced when broken down by the head of household's level of education. Although less than 2 percent of those with a high school degree or less donated to an arts or cultural organization, the figure steadily climbs to a high of 24.8 percent among those with some graduate coursework or more (Ottoni-Wilhelm 2009:11).

The preceding study did not break down the percentage of overall donations going to arts and culture by household income. That breakdown is reported in the *U.S. Trust Study of High Net Worth Philanthropy* (U.S. Trust and Lilly Family School of Philanthropy 2018), which examines households with incomes over $200,000 and/or net worth over $1 million (excluding the value of primary residence). This study also finds a high percentage of households (27 percent and 24 percent in 2015 and 2017, respectively) donating to arts and culture. However, only 5 percent and 2 percent of the share of total dollars contributed went to arts and culture in 2015 and 2017, respectively (U.S. Trust and Lilly Family School of Philanthropy 2018:16), a figure that is not higher than the overall 5 percent of total philanthropic donations that go to the arts cited earlier (Giving USA 2018:32).

Wealthy elites were instrumental in creating and sustaining many arts organizations, but reliance on elite philanthropy has privileged organizations that can attract funding from wealthy donors and foundations. This reliance also promotes the predominance of affluent individuals as members of nonprofit arts boards, service on which is frequently connected to the ability to raise or contribute funds. Further, nonprofit arts boards are quite homogeneous with respect to race and ethnicity (see, e.g., Abzug and Galaskiewicz 2001; Ostrower 2002, 2013; Rosenstein 2018; Sidford and Frasz 2017).

Online giving to the arts has been on the increase, a development that has been characterized as facilitating "democratized engagement," whereby individual artists and smaller organizations can connect directly to donors (Giving USA 2018:308). The NEA reported that $280 million had been raised for the arts through the crowd-funding platform Kickstarter since 2009 (NEA 2012). Much remains to be learned about whether such technological developments are engaging new donors and whether and how patterns of support through these platforms differ from individual philanthropy through other means. It also remains to be determined how much online giving goes to nonprofit arts organizations.

Some research indicates that revenue sources are associated with variations in nonprofit arts organizations' behavior (Alexander 1996; DiMaggio 1986a; Kim, Pandey, and Pandey 2018; Powell and Friedkin 1986). Victoria Alexander (1996) concludes that a shift to greater institutional support (corporate and governmental, as compared with individual) had a broadening impact on museums. These institutional funders, she found, preferred to support exhibitions that appeal to large audiences. By favoring certain types of exhibits the museums already offered, the funders shifted the overall mix of museum exhibitions. More recently, using data on performing arts organizations from DataArts, Mirae Kim and her colleagues (2018) concluded that higher funding from foundations, local governments, and corporations was positively associated with performing arts organizations' offering more free programs (measured as a ratio of free to total attendance at organizational offerings, such as performances, lectures, and workshops). Giving from individuals and the federal government were unrelated to free programming. Revenue generated by what the authors classify as "private benefits" (including earned income sources such as admission fees, tuition for classes, and parking garages) were mixed (Kim et al. 2018:142, 146).

Additional research is needed to systematically understand how, and how much, different sources of funding and different funding mixes influence programmatic and other choices among nonprofit arts organizations. Equally important is to understand the mechanisms through which such impact occurs and how funder choices and priorities interact with those of recipient nonprofit arts institutions.

Many countries have subsidized the arts through direct government support, but the United States has generally eschewed that route (Mulcahy 2000; Throsby 2010). However, government policies do result in considerable indirect support, including through the tax deduction for charitable donations that arts and cultural nonprofits, like other nonprofits, may receive. According to one estimate, the U.S. government forgoes 33 to 35 cents for every $1 donated to a tax-exempt arts organization by individuals with larger incomes who itemize contributions on their tax returns (NEA 2012:18). By virtue of their nonprofit status, nonprofit arts organizations are also tax-exempt themselves (subject to exceptions applying to them as well as other nonprofits).

Arguments for such indirect support through the tax system rest on claims that the tax deduction results in more private giving than would otherwise take place and allows for more varied and decentralized decision making by shifting decisions from government to private individuals (Throsby 2010; see also Cowen 2010). On the other hand, this approach has been criticized as skewing the nonprofit arts sector toward the tastes of affluent donors who are more likely to itemize and thus be in a position to take advantage of the deduction (Rosenstein 2018; Throsby 2010). This line of thinking has led some to oppose the charitable tax deduction for philanthropic giving (Reich 2011). In the nonprofit sector, some, including arts advocates, have by contrast called for an expansion of the tax deduction so as to make it available to non-itemizers (see Americans for the Arts 2017a, 2017b).

Some raise issues of equity related to race, ethnicity, and different cultural traditions in the distribution of cultural support. Holly Sidford and Alexis Frasz (2017) conclude that most contributed income goes to a small group of large cultural institutions that largely focus on Western European fine arts and include few organizations with missions focused on artistic traditions from Africa, Asia, Latin America, the Middle East, or Native America (Sidford and Frasz 2017). By contrast, they find that although smaller nonprofits (with budgets under $1 million) constitute the vast majority of arts and cultural organizations, and many of these do focus on such artistic traditions (or other indigenous and folkloric traditions), they received only 21 percent of all giving (Sidford and Frasz 2017:6). They also point to disparities in funding for cultural groups in rural communities, who received less than 2 percent of foundation arts funding (Sidford and Frasz 2017:7), and groups whose main mission is serving communities of color, who received 4 percent of foundation arts funding (2017:7). Examining ten cities with high levels of giving to the arts, they generally find similar patterns at the local level, with giving concentrated in a small number of large institutions (Sidford and Frasz 2017:7).

Nonprofit Presence in the Arts: Rationales

Whereas the previous section described the prevalence of nonprofit organizations in the arts, this section explores the question of why arts organizations adopt the nonprofit form. The topic of rationales for creating certain types of organizations as nonprofits and the intersectoral division of labor in the arts in general have not been prominent foci of research since the last edition of this volume, which offered detailed discussion of these issues. As mentioned earlier, this lack of scholarly attention may partly reflect a number of trends in the arts policy literature: a tendency to emphasize interconnectedness rather than difference among organizational forms in the arts, a questioning of perceived assumptions about the distinctiveness of nonprofits versus for-profits in the arts, and suggestions that the nonprofit form has been used too frequently. The following is a brief review of what continue to be major explanations for the nonprofit presence in the arts.

From an economic perspective, Henry B. Hansmann (1980, 1986) argues that nonprofit status permits nonprofit organizations to function in parts of the arts market that cannot be sustained by market forces. In this view, there is no ticket price at which organizations in these areas can recoup their actual costs of operations. However, the high ratio of fixed to variable costs in mounting productions results in a low marginal cost of adding a performance or one more audience member once the show is mounted. Pricing tickets at the marginal cost would not cover full expenses, but insufficient demand exists to price tickets high enough to cover full expenses. In his view, price discrimination, or charging patrons different amounts, offers a solution. Although price discrimination can partly be implemented through charging different prices for different seats, Hansmann contends that an adequate system of price discrimination would be too difficult to implement through ticket sales alone. Instead, the nonprofit form enables organizations to implement a system of voluntary price discrimination, whereby some individuals voluntarily pay more by making donations. Individuals are willing to donate to nonprofit arts organizations because the legal prohibition preventing nonprofits from distributing surplus earnings to private parties permits donors to trust that their contributions will be used to support the organization's artistic services (Hansmann 1986). Although this argument is developed further in the case of performing arts organizations, Hansmann (1980) also believes that it is applicable to museums.

William J. Baumol and William G. Bowen's influential "cost disease" theory (1965, 1966) also contends that subsidies, in the form of donations or government support, are critical for performing arts institutions, because performing arts organizations are inherently subject to ever-widening gaps between revenues and expenses. They argue that performing arts organizations must spend a considerable part of their budget on labor costs, which increase over time, but lack ways to contain or reduce rising costs by increasing productivity (e.g., through technology). In their words (Baumol and Bowen 1965:500), "it is fairly difficult to reduce the number of actors necessary for a performance of *Henry IV, Part II*." Baumol and Bowen's theory remains widely influential in economic studies of the arts with a line of research focused on assessing various components of their claims about the cost disease. Results have been mixed, with different research variously supporting or failing to support the presence of a cost disease in the arts, and some questioning the inevitability of a widening gap between earned income and expenses and the impossibility of achieving productivity gains (see Ostrower and Calabrese 2019 for a review).

A different, historically based account is offered by DiMaggio (1986a, 1986b), who attributes the creation of early nonprofit arts organizations to nineteenth-century urban upper classes. In his view, the nonprofit form was not a reaction to marketplace forces but represented a deliberate effort to insulate certain types of art from the marketplace. The nonprofit form was well suited to the project of creating and institutionalizing a distinction between "high" and "popular" culture, removing the former from market influences, and keeping institutions under the authority of their elite patrons, who served as trustees. Thus, using the nonprofit form, they created a prestigious status culture to which they had special access. The nonprofit form eventually spread to smaller cities and other arts forms that had previously been organized as commercial endeavors (DiMaggio 1986a, 1986b, 2006).

The tensions between forces promoting exclusivity and pressures for greater openness provide one useful lens through which to view developments within the nonprofit arts sector. DiMaggio's account places status interests, rather than economic concerns, at the core of the nonprofit endeavor in the arts. Yet even at their inception, these high-culture institutions included educational efforts and have embodied evolving tensions between exclusivity and other factors, including efforts at legitimation of the special status of high-culture arts and revenue generation needs (DiMaggio 1986a, 1986b; see also Accominotti et al. 2018; McDonnell and Tepper 2014). Furthermore, these organizations were never fully shielded from the market and have had to generate earned income. Thus, established arts organizations have variously incorporated other constituencies, even as elite groups carved out exclusive niches for themselves in relation to the organizations (Accominotti et al. 2018; Ostrower 2002). As organizational needs (e.g., for funds) call for greater openness and change, elites have adapted, becoming more open with regard to organizational accessibility and operations but perpetuating the board itself as an exclusive elite enclave (Ostrower 2002).

Likewise, McDonnell and Tepper (2014) contend that high-culture nonprofits have historically embodied dual conceptions of their role and mission. They fostered the elevation of fine art as sacred and unique and cultivated elite audiences, while also promoting access to the arts, community service, and education. They note that the public-serving rationale for nonprofit status and the interests in gaining widespread legitimacy for the status of high culture referenced by DiMaggio also meant that arts institutions had to be more than exclusive clubs.

While situating the historical development of established high-culture nonprofit arts organizations in the class-based projects of nineteenth-century elites, this account does not assert an inherent link between the nonprofit form and high culture or any particular class. To the contrary, DiMaggio (2006) notes that others, such as immigrant groups, also used the nonprofit form and that in the twentieth century the groups making use of the nonprofit form in the arts became significantly more diverse. He concludes that "the nonprofit legal form is to some extent an empty shell that can be employed for an almost unlimited range of noncommercial (and some commercial) purposes, depending on who has the motivation and capacity to use it" (DiMaggio 2006:440). Still, as he also notes, "the ability for artistic communities to take advantage of the nonprofit form depends on power and influence as much as on need" (DiMaggio 2006:439).

From this perspective, understanding the rationales for the use of the nonprofit form cannot be an abstract exercise or one that looks solely to properties of the nonprofit form itself but must attend to who creates and uses these organizations, under what circumstances, and for what purposes. This view is consistent with the increasing variety of nonprofit arts organizations one finds in the field today. This approach also cautions against viewing organizations as static, and advises being attentive to how they respond to shifts in environmental circumstances. At the same time, as DiMaggio (2006:439) also notes, artistic communities' ability to use the nonprofit form does not depend solely on need but also on power and influence. Therefore, research attention also needs to be given to barriers to the use of the nonprofit form, for whom such barriers are higher, and how this influences the contours of the nonprofit arts landscape.

If nonprofit arts organizations cannot sustain themselves on the market through earned income, then they must garner support elsewhere. In order to do so, they need to be seen as meriting support. As James A. Smith (2010) notes, there has long been an ambivalence in the United States as to whether the arts represent a private or public good and therefore whether the arts should be able to sustain themselves in the market (or not at all). Such debates continue, and are likely to endure because the arts are "mixed" or "merit" goods that provide both private and public benefits (DiMaggio 2006; Smith 2010; Throsby 2010).

The literature proposes a variety of ways that the arts benefit individuals that experience them, as well as wider benefits that extend beyond the direct artistic experience. With respect to individuals, studies suggest a variety of behavioral, cognitive, and health benefits, such as improved grades. With respect to benefits that go beyond the individual, the arts have been seen as fostering civic engagement, economic growth, and expression and preservation of cultural identity (for a review of the literature and critiques of it, see McCarthy et al. 2005; Throsby 2010). Mark Stern and Susan Seifert (2017) find that in low-income areas, the presence of cultural resources is associated with measures of social well-being, including measures related to health, schooling, and personal security. They propose that neighborhood cultural assets facilitate social connections, which in turn foster social well-being. Various studies find relationships between arts participation and civic engagement, such as Kelly LeRoux and Anna Bernadska's (2014) observation that audience-based engagement is associated with civic engagement even after controlling for variables such as age and income. Additionally, a number of surveys have found that individuals perceive the arts as being of value to themselves and their communities. Mark Hager and Mary Kopczynski (2003), for instance, found that in each of five communities studied, individuals placed a higher value on the arts for their communities than for themselves. Furthermore, many respondents that did not themselves attend arts events still saw a high value of the arts in their communities. Among the reasons cited were the value of the arts for children and preserving cultural heritage.

The Nonprofit Form: Recent Assessments of Its Distinctiveness

A question of interest for nonprofit research has been the extent to which nonprofit form per se matters, with studies comparing the behavior of organizations delivering the same services or products but with different organizational status (e.g., provision of services by for-profit versus nonprofit hospitals). Such comparisons are not readily available in the nonprofit arts field, however, because nonprofit arts organizations tend to occupy different niches than commercial firms (DiMaggio 2006; Toepler and Wyszomirski 2012:231–233).

Some recent literature contends that institutional differences associated with form in the arts have been overstated. Bill Ivey (2005, 2008), past chairman of the NEA, argues that nonprofits have incorrectly been assumed to be very distinctive from, and superior to, commercial forms as a vehicle for advancing the public interest as it pertains to the arts. He argues that both for-profits and nonprofits pursue the multiple goals of art, financial success, and some sense of public interest (Ivey 2005). He further suggests that cultural policy aimed at supporting the arts has focused too narrowly on the nonprofit arts as the sole vehicle for promoting the public interest (Ivey 2008). Note that Ivey is not questioning the public value of or interest in the arts. His argument illustrates how the preeminence and distinctiveness of the nonprofit form is being questioned by those who regard the arts as having a public value, as discussed in the introduction to this chapter.

Likewise, Joni Maya Cherbo and her colleagues (Cherbo et al. 2008) argue that nonprofits must rely on earned income for a significant part of their revenues, and commercial arts organizations often are concerned about their product's quality and social impact. They contend that a distinction based on one being reliant on generating profits and the other being committed to an educational or charitable mission is overly simplistic. Economist Michael Rushton (2015) argues that nonprofit arts organizations and commercial firms use many similar business methods, including multiple forms of price discrimination. He observes that major trends in cultural policy, such as thinking about cultural districts, are not confined to nonprofits, and he argues that when thinking about the arts, "focusing on nonprofits with the exclusion from consideration of other sorts of organizations no longer makes sense, if it ever did" (2015: para. 16).

Much of the literature questioning nonprofit/for-profit distinctions in the arts is conceptual, and sometimes anecdotal, in nature. Tim Donahue and Jim Patterson (2010), however, offer one empirically based comparison of nonprofit and for-profit forms and find significant distinctions. As part of their study of professional theaters, they compare for-profit professional and nonprofit professional theaters and assess the relationship between the two. First, they emphasize the different organization of endeavors in the two arenas. Commercial theaters are generally formed as a partnership or company to produce a single play and disband, with open-ended production runs and closure dates being determined by ticket sales. By contrast, nonprofit theaters generally intend an indefinite organizational life, typically have preset end dates for productions, often own or lease their own venue, and rely only partially on box office returns (Donahue and Patterson 2010:2).

Substantively, Donahue and Patterson (2010:2–3) find that nonprofits do play a distinctive role in theater in the United States, serving as a major source of new play and musical development, producing more varied types of work, and in many locales serving as the primary source of theater available. In fact, they find that substantial numbers of new commercial productions (on Broadway) originate in nonprofit theaters. Likewise, they find that a substantial portion of Tony awards for Broadway shows were for plays that originated in nonprofit theaters.

This example calls attention to the fact that extensive interaction between organizations in different sectors may well co-exist with (or even stem from) differences in the organizations associated with sector, a topic warranting additional research. The results illustrate why, as argued at the start of this chapter, an acknowledgment of interconnectedness and commonalities among arts organizations in different sectors should not deter, but prompt and inform, research on the intersectoral division of labor and cross-sector relationships.

Hybrid Alternatives and Cross-Sector Relations

In recent years, much attention has been given to the hybrid organizational forms that incorporate features of organizations from two or more of the nonprofit, for-profit, and public sectors. This topic includes the emergence of legally recognized categories of organizations with missions that combine profit generation for owners and social goals (for a discussion of such forms that have been enacted by a number of state governments, see Reiser 2012). Given the challenges faced by nonprofit arts organizations (discussed in the next section), some have suggested such new legal forms may offer a viable alternative to the nonprofit form in the arts in some instances (see Undercofler 2012). However, and after an initial spate of enthusiasm for this idea, there is little evidence that such forms have been adopted by arts organizations to any significant extent.

One example of these new legally recognized hybrid forms is the benefit corporation. Ellen Berrey (2018) finds that at least 7,704 benefit corporations have been formed since 2010. Yet in a random sample of 570 of them, she found that only 3, or less than 1 percent, were in the arts (E. Berry, personal communication, September 17, 2018).

Rushton (2014) considers the applicability of the hybrid form in the arts, focusing on another type of legal hybrid, low-profit limited liability companies (L3Cs). He concludes that the hybrid form is unlikely to have much usefulness for nonprofit arts groups. He argues that hybrids offer no advantages to compensate for giving up the tax exemption or tax-deductible donations permitted with nonprofit status. He likewise concludes that hybrid forms do not offer advantages over traditional for-profit forms in the arts for organizations that can generate profits solely through earned income.

Creating a legal hybrid organization is not, of course, the only alternative to creating a nonprofit organization. One option still involves the nonprofit form—by using an already incorporated nonprofit to serve as a fiscal sponsor. This approach permits an artist or unincorporated association to solicit and receive grants (under the sponsor's umbrella) without creating a new organization. An example of one well-known national organization that serves as a fiscal sponsor for arts projects is Fractured Atlas, whose mission includes "eliminating practical barriers to artistic expression" (https://www.fracturedatlas.org/site/about/). For those who believe nonprofit status is too often adopted as a default option, fiscal sponsorship is seen as a more effective alternative in some circumstances (Undercofler 2012). Fiscal sponsorship, however, is not necessarily a permanent alternative to creating a new nonprofit. Entrepreneurs can also use fiscal sponsorship in the early stages of new undertakings that later incorporate nonprofits (Andersson and Neely 2017). Examining a sample of 184 nonprofits that serve as fiscal sponsors, Fredrik O. Andersson and Daniel G. Neely (2017) found that the largest percentage (34 percent) were in the field of arts, culture, and humanities (494).

More common than the use of legal hybrid forms (and by some accounts increasingly common) are collaborations that cross sectors. A case in point is the growth of collaborations between nonprofit theaters and commercial producers (Cox 2014; Donahue and Patterson 2010). Nonprofits may develop new plays that are later picked up by a commercial producer; a producer can go to a nonprofit with a play to develop; and a nonprofit can solicit financial support to produce a new show in exchange for an option to produce it (Cox 2014). In one scenario, commercial producers provide "enhancement money" to nonprofit theaters to increase the budget for a show produced by the nonprofit (which can mount the show at a lower cost), with the right to bring the show to a commercial run (if successful), while the nonprofit may be entitled to a share of future earnings (Donahue and Patterson 2010). Such collaborations still involve a fairly small number of theaters, and these arrangements have been a source of some controversy and charges of mission drift (Cox 2014; Donahue and Patterson 2010). Still, a recent *American Theatre* article observes that the wall separating commercial and nonprofit theaters has been "felled" over the past thirty years, and "Today the overlap between the two sectors is a fact of life" (Cox 2014: para. 3).

Varied and complicated collaborations also exist between nonprofit arts organizations and public sector entities, apart from direct funding and indirect support through the tax system (DiMaggio 2006). For instance, a number of nonprofit museums, performing arts centers, and other types of institutions are located on public sector land, and some arts nonprofits have governance structures involving both private and public sectors (DiMaggio 2006; Rosenstein 2018). One example of such a governance structure is found among the "large minority of important art museums," where the public sector has authority over the organization's physical plant, but a nonprofit organization controls the art collections and endowment (DiMaggio 2006:444). Chris N. Burgess and David B. Pankratz (2008) offer various examples of multisector collaborations, such as a national project to expand arts education for children and youth in public housing, which involved the National Guild of Community Schools of the Arts, the NEA, and the U.S. Department of Housing and Urban Development.

A growing theme in recent literature has been that the nonprofit arts are one facet of a larger arts industry (akin to agriculture or education) composed of activities and organizations from multiple sectors, including the nonprofit, corporate, public, and informal sectors. This perspective has been proposed as a broader lens through which to view the arts, in contrast to a more exclusive focus on nonprofit organizations (Cherbo et al. 2008). From this perspective, an increase in for-profit and nonprofit collaborations has been observed. More research is needed, however, to theoretically and empirically understand these cross-sector relations and assess their outcomes (Burgess and Pankratz 2008; DiMaggio 2006).

The Nonprofit Arts Sector: Challenges to Sustainability

Nonprofit arts organizations face a number of challenges related to their sustainability and relevance, including declining or stagnant attendance and financial difficulties. Changes in how people attend, notably declines in purchase of subscriptions, have implications for long-standing business models.[5] Some of these challenges raise questions about the capacity of established arts organizations to adapt in a world with shifting demographics, leisure patterns, and technological options. In the context of the present discussion, one key question is whether established arts organizations are now paying a price for their historical association with cultural and status hierarchies.

Attendance Patterns

Although the supply of nonprofit arts organizations continued to increase until recent years, different patterns emerge when it comes to demand. The NEA's Survey of Public Participation in the Arts (SPPA) indicates declining or stagnant attendance rates at multiple art forms in which nonprofit organizations are prominent (NEA 2015). Furthermore, those who do attend are doing so less frequently, and declines are occurring across multiple demographic groups, including those with high levels of education, who are most likely to attend (NEA 2015:5). One concern has been generational shifts in attendance, with declining attendance among younger audiences. An often-heard assumption is that generational shifts are driving audience declines. In an analysis of SPPA data, however, Mark Stern (2011) concludes that age and generational cohort actually explain little about changes in arts participation. He points instead to broader changes in people's lives and preferences, including a more personal and flexible approach to cultural engagement.

In the performing arts, previous SPPA analyses reveal declines in attendance at opera, classical music, theater, musical theater, and ballet, generally between 2002 and 2008, although attendance at plays also declined between 2008 and 2012 (NEA 2015:7-9, 2018). Preliminary findings from the most recent survey in 2017 show attendance stabilizing for each of these performing arts forms (NEA 2018). Attendance at outdoor performing arts festivals, an area that also has a strong nonprofit presence (Rosenstein 2010:41), actually increased between 2008 and 2017. Since attendance at outdoor performing arts festivals was not tracked until 2008, it is not known whether declines occurred previously. Attendance at this form grew from 21 percent in 2008 and 2012 to 24 percent of the adult population in 2017 (NEA 2018:6).[6]

Turning to the visual arts, attendance at art museums and galleries declined between 2002 and 2012. Attendance then increased from 21 percent in 2012 to 24 percent in 2017, though it remained below the 27 percent attending in 2002 (NEA 2015, 2018:7). The percentage of adults touring parks, monuments, buildings, or neighborhoods for historic or design value also increased between 2012 and 2017 (from 24 percent to 28 percent). In this case as well, 2017 attendance did not exceed the 2002 figure (32 percent).

Earlier we noted that in the context of the present discussion, one relevant question is whether established nonprofit arts organizations may be paying a price for their historical association with hierarchy and exclusivity. Significantly, the few increases in attendance since 2012 mentioned earlier occurred in activities (such as outdoor performing arts festivals) that "have drawn a broader cross-section of the U.S. adult population—one that is demographically more diverse—than have some other types of arts events" (NEA 2018:2).

Supply and Demand

Expansion in supply coupled with declining or stagnant demand poses a major challenge to the nonprofit arts field. When asked to comment on declining attendance figures, one former head of the NEA famously—and controversially—replied, "There are too many theaters" (see Marks 2011). Many analysts propose that the supply of nonprofit arts organizations has exceeded demand for what they offer (Borwick 2012; Ivey 2008; Kreidler 1996; Tepper 2008; McCarthy, Ondaatje, and Novak 2007; Zakaras and Lowell 2008). The issue is not just about competition for attendees but increased competition for funding resulting from the large number of organizations (Ivey 2008; McCarthy et al. 2007; Nelson et al. 2014). For instance, some observers have argued that the matching-grant model of support for nonprofit arts, developed by the Ford Foundation and then diffused to governmental funders and other foundation funders, has reached the limits of its ability to expand (Ivey 2008; Kreidler 1996).

Still, one study of births and mortality of arts and cultural nonprofits in six cities found considerable levels of new organizations being created (Dietz et al. 2013:1). Sixty percent of organizations reporting in 1990 were still reporting by 2010, but for every one that closed another 2.6 were created (Dietz et al. 2013). Larger organizations were more likely to survive with some variations by discipline. Although some argue that too many nonprofit organizations are being created, Susan Nelson and her colleagues (Nelson et al. 2014) contend that the problem is not in the number of new creations (which they see as a sign of artistic vitality) but in the failure of financially weak nonprofits to exit the field.

Different parts of the nonprofit arts sector may be more or less impacted by these developments. Kevin McCarthy, Arthur C. Brooks, Julia Lowell, and Laura Zakaras (2001) predict that large performing arts organizations will increasingly adopt practices akin to their for-profit counterparts (e.g., increasing earned income through merchandising), while small ones will target niche audiences. They argue that neither of these strategies is available to medium-sized organizations, leaving them at particular risk of failure. Writing about the performing arts, they predict that the distinction between large and small organizations will become more significant than that between for-profit and nonprofit organizations. The study of births and mortality referenced earlier, however, found that survival was positively associated with size (Dietz et al. 2013).

Organizational Responses and Contemporary Relevance

Audience declines are a cause of wide concern in the field and one of the main pressures on nonprofit arts organizations noted in the literature. One response has been organizational efforts to expand and engage audiences. As noted, low levels of attendance by younger audiences are of particular concern in the field, and the predominantly white audiences, boards, and staff of many established arts organizations contrasts markedly with the composition of their geographical communities. Furthermore, declines are being experienced among audiences that are traditionally most likely to attend. It goes beyond the scope of this chapter to discuss the array of audience-building efforts that have been undertaken and studied (for a review and discussion of the literature on audience building among nonprofit performing arts organizations, see Ostrower and Calabrese 2019). Some types of efforts under way include providing more opportunities for socializing and social interactions (e.g., parties connected with performances, occasions for performer–audience interactions such as postperformance discussions), experimenting with technology, performing in nontraditional venues, providing opportunities for more active audience engagement (believed to be attractive to younger audiences), using market research to better understand current and potential audiences, and creating more welcoming, informal, and/or social environments. The success of various audience-building efforts in attracting and engaging new audiences, particularly over the long term, however, remains inconclusive and in need of further research (Ostrower and Calabrese 2019).

Interestingly, some measures being taken are designed to overcome barriers attributed to perceptions of the exclusivity that, as this chapter has discussed, has been a characteristic of many high-culture institutions. Likewise, although separating high culture from popular culture was part of the project of early nonprofit arts creation (DiMaggio 1986a, 1986b), some organizations are incorporating elements of both in efforts to increase audiences. For instance, the New World Symphony performed in a late-night club format that combined live classical music with a DJ playing electronic dance music (Brown and Ratkin 2013). As this example illustrates, some organizations are experimenting with dispensing with traditional expectations of audience comportment, such as by allowing people to move around freely during a performance.

Another effort, also aimed at attracting younger audiences, is the Isabella Stewart Gardner Museum's Gardner After Hours, which offered a social event. Here, the museum offered informal activities, brief talks, games promoting exploration of the collections, and a bar and live music in the courtyard. The events aimed to bring younger audiences to the museum to explore the galleries, while responding to their perceived desire for a social event (Harlow 2014).

A question raised by some of the literature is whether declining or stagnant patterns of attendance indicate a fundamental loss of relevance faced by established nonprofit arts organizations. Jeffrey Nytch (2013:89–90) writes that classical music organizations "continue to present concerts in a paradigm that was established in the 19th century—and then wonder why 21st century audiences are less and less interested in what they have to offer" (see also Borwick 2012). Doug Borwick (2012) argues that nonprofit arts organizations are too insular and need to rethink the nature of their obligations to the public as nonprofits. In his view, they will not overcome problems of declining audiences by focusing on audience building for their own institutions but instead need to engage in community building and focus on becoming more deeply ingrained in their communities. He argues that this will require a shift in attitude to see themselves as doing things "with" rather than "for" the larger community.

One line of research has called for attention to arts participation that goes on outside formal nonprofit arts organizations. In this view, attendance at some art forms may be declining, but arts participation itself is flourishing—outside formal arts organizations and in ways other than attendance, such as creation (Novak-Leonard and Brown 2011; Pulh, Marteaux, and Mencarelli 2008; Reidy 2014; Tepper 2008; Wali, Severson, and Longoni 2002; Walker, Scott-Melnyk, and Sherwood 2002; for reviews see Novak-Leonard et al. 2014; Stallings and Mauldin 2016).

For the purposes of this discussion, the relevant point is the implication is that declining attendance figures do not equate to a declining interest in arts engagement per se. Instead, they raise questions about potential shifts in the prominence and relevance of nonprofit organizations as vehicles for that arts engagement. Other research, however, has pointed out that the informal arts sector and the nonprofit sector are also interconnected. Thus, Rosenstein and Brimer (2005) argue that nonprofit organizations, such as the nonprofit ethnic, cultural, and folk organizations they studied, play an important role in structuring and sustaining informal and community-oriented expressive activities.

One theme in the current arts participation literature is that people today seek more active forms of arts engagement than offered by attending arts events in the role of passive spectator (see, e.g., Brown and Novak-Leonard 2011; Conner 2013). For instance, Alan S. Brown and Jennifer L. Novak-Leonard forecast that arts organizations that depend exclusively on a "consumption model of program delivery will slowly lose ground in a competitive marketplace" (2011:4). Some examples of opportunities that permit more active engagement include classical music concerts including both professional and amateurs and projects involving audiences in creating theater programs (Brown and Novak-Leonard 2011). Although the need to provide opportunities for active engagement is a prominent theme in the audience-building literature (Ostrower and Calabrese 2019) this can involve quite varied efforts, ranging from restructuring postperformance discussions to providing opportunities for audiences to influence artistic programming.

This discussion has summarized some of the prominent ideas about the sources of and responses to challenges facing nonprofit arts organizations. As noted earlier, for the purposes of this chapter, one significant development is a line of discussion that challenges the hierarchies and exclusivity incorporated into the creation of high-culture arts institutions. DiMaggio (2006) argues that these hierarchical models of culture and sharp boundaries between high and popular culture have been eroding—the distinction proposed as central to the identity of nonprofit arts organizations. What impact does this development have on these organizations, their identities, and how they think about their mission? Having adapted in the past, what adaptations will they make in the future?

Canon-focused arts organizations have greater difficulty implementing projects to build broader audience participation than organizations such as community cultural centers that incorporate such goals into the core of their mission (Farrell 2008; Joynes and Grams 2008). McDonnell and Tepper (2014) find that during periods of crisis, high-culture organizations fall back on traditional narratives that appeal to rationales for their existence in terms of wealth, excellence, and distinction but do not serve them well under contemporary circumstances. Instead, such language limits their ability to mobilize broad support and demonstrate their relevance, creating an attitude that inhibits the development of new relationships and forms of community engagement. Ivey (2008:170) makes a related observation when he argues that orchestras' claims to music "with a unique spiritual and intellectual value" served them well in seeking philanthropic and governmental support, while simultaneously alienating audiences and isolating classical music organizations from their contemporary context.

As noted at the outset of this chapter, arts organizations are not homogenous, and the pressures they face also vary. Several challenges discussed in the preceding section relate to established, large canon-focused arts organizations. As discussed earlier, other arts organizations, such as smaller and rural organizations, face challenges related to the current distribution of funding in the arts (Sidford and Frasz 2017:6). Additional research is needed to understand the similarities and differences in the challenges and opportunities faced by arts organizations that vary along a number of dimensions, such as size, discipline, goal, geographical location, and audiences served.

Conclusion

The nonprofit form has played a key role in the arts and cultural life of the United States. The literature also points to the ongoing significance that nonprofits play in the arts, but one that may well be in transition. If, as discussed, rationales for the use of the nonprofit form cannot be an abstract exercise or one that looks solely to properties of the nonprofit form itself, then additional research is needed to understand who is creating and using these organizations, under what circumstances, and for what purposes, both artistic and otherwise. This line of research would include a consideration of current incentives and disincentives for the use of the nonprofit form, and of its alternatives. Much of the literature, as seen in this chapter, advocates going beyond a focus on nonprofit organizations. It calls for a perspective that views nonprofits as part of a wider and interconnected arts field. Although that may be true, such insights invite further attention, both theoretically and empirically, to systematically explore similarities and differences between nonprofit and commercial firms, and the relationships between the nonprofit, commercial, public, and informal sectors. Although multiple examples of interactions have been cited, much remains to be done to classify such instances into larger patterns of relationships and outcomes.

The nonprofit arts offer a wealth of future research possibilities. To what extent are broadening definitions of the arts and arts participation reflected/incorporated into nonprofit arts organizations? How are the dynamics between inclusivity and exclusivity evolving? How is the nonprofit form in the arts being used today by different groups and to what ends? In what ways are current philanthropic priorities influencing the nonprofit arts? What options for organizational form are more or less available to different types of artistic endeavors? How do nonprofit arts interact with organizations in other sectors—and cross boundaries within the nonprofit sector? Which areas of the nonprofit arts are being more or less impacted by contemporary challenges? What opportunities and/or pressures does the need to attract both earned income and philanthropy create for nonprofit arts organizations, and how do they handle these? How are nonprofit arts organizations seeking to expand and engage new audiences—and with what results? Will new business models emerge? How is technology impacting arts organizations? Virtually every topic addressed in this chapter is in need of future research. The nonprofit arts did not always look the way they do today—and there is every reason to believe that they will continue to evolve.

PART VI

ADVOCACY, ENGAGEMENT, AND THE PUBLIC

THE NONPROFIT SECTOR IS A NOISY WORLD, as organizations rally for particular causes, mobilize constituents, and press for certain policies. Nonprofits both advocate for their interests and are used by others as a venue for causes. As the chapters in this section show, advocacy efforts shape public policies at multiple levels of government. Nonprofits are also crucial in shaping public opinion and in sustaining the envisioned role of the public in society. These chapters emphasize the growing advocacy efforts by traditional public charities, the more aggressive social movement activism and lobbying of political nonprofits, and the role of the nonprofit media in building conceptions of the public. Across these diverse settings, several themes recur, harking back to the conceptual threads in the volume's earlier section on the politics of the public sphere. Most dramatically, the world of advocacy and public opinion is a highly political one, fraught with tensions between competing political ideologies. We again see that resources carry weight as wealthy donors push their agendas and preferences through advocacy and the media. Together, the chapters analyze changes in how constituencies or publics can be organized, issues of representation and authenticity, the relationship between business elites and purportedly public good organizations, and broader questions of democratic deficits and civic capacity.

In Chapter 20, David Suárez highlights the social change activity of organizations that have received comparatively little attention in the broader literature on advocacy—those that are formally chartered as traditional service-providing public charities. Suárez outlines how advocacy is developing into a core component of the tactical repertoire of 501(c)(3) public charities, becoming a legitimate tool for pursuing mission. His starting point is a large and distinctive body of work on the influence of private organizations on civic participation. The tendency of individuals to form and become members of voluntary associations was a central focus of Tocqueville's authoritative investigation into democracy in early nineteenth-century America. These foundational observations inspired much subsequent academic inquiry, demonstrating that traditional membership organizations often model democratic processes and participatory practices. Besides reinforcing democracy by acting as "laboratories for citizenship," many membership organizations mediate the relationship between individuals and their government by fostering a commitment to civic engagement.

Suárez argues that their history of civic engagement puts public charities in an increasingly strong position to engage in advocacy at the organizational level, a dynamic and powerful approach for achieving social change. He builds a framework for systematically studying features of organizations and their environments that influence the advocacy outcomes of charitable nonprofits. The framework emphasizes the inputs that shape nonprofit advocacy, but he goes further to end with a discussion of the opportunities and challenges associated with investigating outcomes. Suárez highlights salient, underexplored research questions on the role of private organizations in social change, drawing primarily from sociology, political science, and interdisciplinary fields such as public policy, public management, international relations, and nonprofit studies.

In Chapter 21, Edward T. Walker and Yotala Oszkay take stock of broad trends in nonprofit advocacy in the twenty-first century, focusing on the U.S. experience. Whereas the previous chapter focused on the role of 501(c)(3) public charities, their focus is on a rise of nonmembership advocacy organizations (NMAOs), such as policy planning organizations, think tanks, and advocacy-driven operations focused on deploying professional skills to advance particular causes. Trade associations have become central vehicles for advancing the interests of firms and industries in broader political discourse. Think tanks are a growing site for deploying knowledge and science in the service of politics. And formally organized social movement and political entities have come to play a critical role in advocating for social, economic, and political change. In a context marked by the rising prominence of NMAOs, they provide a rethinking of many enduring assumptions about the political role of the third sector.

Walker and Oszkay underscore the tension between the democratizing potential of nonprofit advocacy organizations versus the features of contemporary advocacy nonprofits that either reinforce "de-democratizing" tendencies or reflect a broader democratic recession. They unpack these tensions along six key dimensions: (1) features of advocacy nonprofit organizational structures that may support or challenge democratic outcomes; (2) pressures toward accountability by third-party monitors, which often deploy metrics that may disadvantage advocacy nonprofits, particularly those that engage in grassroots organizing; (3) questions of whether nonprofits challenge versus reinforce inequalities; (4) the rising use of nonprofits as political intermediaries for corporations or other interests—including concerns about the practice of "astroturfing" and the rise of "dark money" social welfare organizations; (5) practices of advocacy nonprofits that, separate from their structure, may limit democratizing potentials; and (6) the role of information and communication technologies (ICTs) in reshaping the practices of advocacy nonprofits. These factors are used as the basis for drawing tentative conclusions regarding the prospects for nonprofits as sources of democratic civic and political action in light of a challenging external sociopolitical environment.

In Chapter 22, Mike Ananny draws our attention to the role of nonprofit media in helping envision and create conditions for collective, communicative self-governance. Starting with a tour of U.S. journalism's historical orientations to news organizations and proceeding through a discussion of the financial and technological forces shaping contemporary nonprofit news, he introduces a typology that maps press funding techniques onto normative models of the public. The typology provides a tool for scholars and reflective practitioners alike to think about how nonprofit funding gives rise to networked publics, demonstrating how choices about the institutional design of nonprofit news have consequences for the kind of democratic self-governance that media systems can support.

Ananny reveals the intersection between the types of publics that emerge from different media systems and, in particular, from nonprofit media, through a three-part structure. First, he traces the institutional forces that have historically driven the nonprofit news sector, examining several canonical examples for evidence of how the nonprofit understood its institutional conditions and what it saw as its public responsibilities. Second, he inspects a recent expansion in the nonprofit news sector. He observes not only the appearance of not-for-profit news publishers creating original stories, but also of a new set of actors including philanthropists driving news experimentation, research organizations guiding best practice, and digital crowd-funding platforms transforming individuals into donors and participants. Today's nonprofit news sector is a mix of patrons, publishers, and platforms pursuing sharply different images of public service, media accountability, and civic participation. Finally, Ananny explores how historical forces and contemporary dynamics point to persistent, cross-cutting normative themes in nonprofit news. The intersections, compliments, and frictions of yesterday's and today's news sector come together to create a rich picture of how institutional dynamics shape broader ideals of journalistic trust, participation, and accountability.

The role of nonprofit organizations in advocating for public policies is well established, as nonprofit organizations have long sought to provide representation for particular interests, communities, and geographic regions. But in a period of rising inequality and civic transformation, the character of such advocacy has changed markedly. A growing array of private organizations contribute to social change by advocating for "their" causes. More indirectly, these actions contribute to involvement in community activity by shaping definitions of the public. Nonprofits increasingly act as intermediaries between corporations and policy makers, ranging from transparent and aboveboard partnerships all the way to covert "astroturf" campaigns. Most notably, nonprofits play a vital role in shaping flows of knowledge and authoritative information, defining public views on key issues of the day. With the growing influence of nonprofit advocacy and shifting vehicles for pursuing change, questions about how and when private organizations drive social change take on renewed urgency and centrality.

20 ADVOCACY, CIVIC ENGAGEMENT, AND SOCIAL CHANGE

David Suárez[*]

PRIVATE ORGANIZATIONS, FORMAL AND INFORMAL, always have played an integral role in social change. In the United States, recognition of the power of private organizations to advocate for causes and shape public policy informed the establishment of the Republic itself. In Federalist Paper number 10, written in 1787, James Madison defended the proposed regulatory framework of the Constitution as a safeguard against private organizations acting as "mischiefs of faction" that could undermine democratic governance (Cohen and Rogers 1992). Respect for personal liberty and freedom of association nevertheless limited federal restrictions on such organizations, and in his 1835 book *Democracy in America*, Alexis de Tocqueville emphasized that private organizations also could serve as bulwarks against the "tyranny of the majority." Whether viewed as supporting or weakening democracy, private organizations clearly could exert considerable influence in the nascent democratic polity. Echoes of these competing perspectives persist in the contemporary context. Questions associated with how, when, and why private organizations shape social change have generated an extensive body of empirical research across multiple disciplines. The expansive breadth of studies on this topic makes it difficult to establish boundaries for a review of the literature (Jenkins 1987, 2006; Burstein 1998; Andrews and Edwards 2004).

The challenge of synthesis is compounded by the presence of a relatively separate body of work on the influence of private organizations on public (civic and political) engagement (Campbell 2008; Grønbjerg and Prakash 2017). In addition to spurring change directly, some private organizations contribute to social transformations indirectly by fostering commitment to community activism and broader public policy reform (Han 2016). The tendency of individuals to form and become members of voluntary associations was a

* This work was supported by the Ministry of Education of the Republic of Korea and the National Research Foundation of Korea (NRF-2016S1A3A2925085). I would like to thank Hokyu Hwang for the extensive research collaborations on advocacy that serve as the foundation for this chapter. Tricia Bromley, Liz Clemens, Brad Fulton, Aaron Horvath, Nicole Marwell, Jennifer Mosley, Woody Powell, Ted Lechterman, and Ed Walker provided insightful comments on the draft.

central focus of Tocqueville's authoritative investigation into democracy in early America, a pattern so extensive and noteworthy that the United States became characterized as a "Nation of Joiners" (Schlesinger 1944). These foundational observations inspired substantial academic inquiry, demonstrating that membership organizations often model democratic processes and participatory practices (Clemens 2006). Besides reinforcing democracy by acting as "laboratories for citizenship," many membership organizations also mediate the relationship between individuals and their government by driving political engagement (Han 2016; Minkoff 2016). Much like the scholarship on direct social change activity by private organizations, questions about how, when, and why these groups foster public engagement have generated long-standing, multidisciplinary lines of research (Knoke 1986; McFarland 2010; Theiss-Morse and Hibbing 2005).

Drawing on both of these domains of academic inquiry, for the purposes of the chapters on advocacy in this book, organizational advocacy is defined as "public interest claims either promoting or resisting social change that, if implemented, would conflict with the social, cultural political, or economic interests or values of other constituencies or groups" (Andrews and Edwards 2004:481). This chapter specifically examines the social change activity of organizations that are formally chartered as tax-exempt 501(c)(3) organizations—that is, service-providing public charities (Burstein 1998; Andrews and Edwards 2004; Jenkins 2006; Hojnacki et al. 2012; Almog-Bar and Schmid 2014). These organizations have received comparatively little attention in the literature on organizational advocacy, presumably because they are perceived as having limited influence on public policy. Nonprofits that explicitly prioritize social change activity must incorporate under other designations such as 501(c)(4) (social welfare organizations), 501(c)(5) (labor unions), 501(c)(6) (business leagues and chambers of commerce), or 527 (political groups). Given that the primary purpose of public charities must be service provision—not advocacy—what justifies a focus on their social change activity?

I argue that advocacy is developing into a core component of the tactical repertoire of 501(c)(3) public charities and becoming a legitimate tool or strategy for pursuing mission in the nonprofit sector (Avner 2010; Crutchfield and Grant 2012; Fyall 2016a, 2016b; Suárez and Esparza 2017; Hwang and Suárez 2019). In addition, I suggest that public charities are increasingly well positioned to blend organizational advocacy with civic engagement, a dynamic and powerful approach for achieving social change (Marwell 2004, 2007; Baumgartner et al. 2009; Han 2014; Levine 2016). Finally, although many studies find that organizational characteristics influence advocacy outcomes, the topic has not been explored systematically (Salamon 2002a; Child and Grønbjerg 2007; Suárez and Hwang 2008; Leroux and Goerdel 2009; Guo and Saxton 2010; Mosley 2010; Almog-Bar and Schmid 2014; Han and Argyle 2016; Lu 2018a, 2018b). As a means of facilitating such an undertaking, this chapter presents a novel theoretical framework for investigating advocacy by charitable nonprofits. The framework specifies five aspects of public charities that, in addition to institutional context, inform advocacy outcomes: external operational environment, managerialism, collaboration and relational embeddedness, funding model, and mission and organizational field.

In order to develop the main arguments, the following section situates the roles and activities of social change organizations in historical and legal context. Besides documenting key regulatory changes that have shaped the historical trajectory of advocacy organizations in the United States, the section highlights three trends that inform advocacy by public charities today: the transformation of public engagement, the advocacy group explosion, and the tremendous growth of public sector contracting and collaboration (Berry 1977, 1999; Clemens 1993, 1997; Smith and Lipsky 1993; Grønbjerg and Salamon 2002; Minkoff 2002; Skocpol 2003; Frumkin 2005; Hwang and Powell 2009; Bromley and Meyer 2017). Building on these observations, the next section develops the arguments and elaborates the conceptual frame. The focus of the framework is on the inputs or independent variables (organizational characteristics and features of the organizational environment) that shape advocacy outcomes. The concluding section attends to the opportunities and challenges associated with investigating those advocacy outcomes.

The Contemporary Landscape for Nonprofit Advocacy

The current conditions of U.S. nonprofit advocacy have their roots in the early republic. A striking feature of the United States in the nineteenth century was its large number of voluntary associations (Tocqueville [1835] 1969). Although active associations during the colonial period were primarily religious organizations, the number of other voluntary groups grew rapidly after independence was declared—most notably in the period following the Civil War (Schlesinger 1944). Many of these groups were established in response to local needs or unique community conditions, yet associations grew at least as rapidly in rural areas as in urban areas, and much of the increase was attributable to the expansion of membership federations that drew on the Constitution as a model for their structure (Gamm and Putnam 1999; Skocpol, Ganz, and Munson 2000; Hall 2006). These patterns indicate that growth in associations was influenced not only by modernization and demographic pressures from urbanization and immigration but also by the consolidation of the nation-state and the growth of the federal government, such as the establishment of the U.S. Post Office (Weir and Ganz 1997; Gamm and Putnam 1999; Skocpol et al. 2000; Crowley and Skocpol 2001).

Though not all early associations were active in promoting social change, they are relevant for understanding contemporary advocacy organizations because they provided citizens "with their greatest school of self-government," according to Schlesinger (1944), who noted that citizens "have been trained from youth to take common counsel, choose leaders, harmonize differences, and obey the expressed will of the majority. In mastering the associative way they have mastered the democratic way" (Schlesinger 1944:24). The growth of associations began to plateau around 1940, an important shift given their important role in political socialization (Verba and Nie 1972; Gamm and Putnam 1999). The dwindling number of individual memberships and interpersonal interactions in associations since the 1960s marks another significant recent change, signaling a broader transformation away from involvement in associations and a weakening of traditional forms of public engagement (Putnam 1995, 2000; Gamm and Putnam 1999; Skocpol and Fiorina 1999; Skocpol 2003, 2004).

Despite the historical significance of membership associations as venues and vehicles for civic and political participation, the transformation of public engagement is relevant for understanding current organizational advocacy dynamics because declining participation in associations suggests that these groups have become less central as social change actors. The transformation of public engagement, however, is not just a simple story of decline and decay; at least some evidence suggests that new forms of participation have emerged (Paxton 1999; Guo and Saxton 2014). Although public engagement (as well as typical measures of social capital) does seem to be diminishing overall, the means by which individuals participate—for instance, through social media campaigns and other "virtual" modalities promoted by many types of organizations—have not remained static over time. Furthermore, for-profit organizations have started to become more adept at, and interested in, building support for their causes by outsourcing public engagement initiatives to consulting firms (Walker 2014). Undoubtedly very different from conventional participation in associations, efforts of this nature nevertheless do constitute public engagement, further shaping the present landscape for nonprofit advocacy.

The same period that saw decreased individual participation in associations and the emergence of new forms of public engagement also marked the beginning of an advocacy group "explosion" (Berry 1977; J. Walker 1991; Clemens 1993; Minkoff 1994, 1999, 2002; Strolovich 2007). The civil rights movement, which contributed to the passage of the Civil Rights Act in 1964 and many other reforms, spurred the dramatic growth of advocacy organizations. Many of the advocacy organizations that emerged during this time were informal social movement groups that mobilized people for protests and demonstrations in support of civil rights, but others were formal nonprofits that relied entirely on professional staff to achieve their missions (Berry 1977, 1999; McFarland 1984; Jenkins and Eckert 1986; Staggenborg 1988). Unlike participation in social movement groups or membership associations that promote public engagement, participation in these new public interest groups often was achieved exclusively through financial donations—critiqued as "checkbook advocacy" (Skocpol and Fiorina 1999; Skocpol 2003, 2004).

The advocacy group explosion that began decades ago is consequential for understanding current organizational advocacy dynamics not only because it contributed to the current number and variety of advocacy groups but also because this phenomenon initiated the dramatic rise of professionally staffed rather than member-driven advocacy organizations. These staff-focused citizen lobbies have not necessarily replaced membership groups, nor is the field of advocacy limited to these two basic types of organizations, yet professional groups that represent public interests have become increasingly visible and consequential players in policy reform (Berry 1977, 1999; Skocpol 2003; Minkoff, Aisenbrey, and Agnone 2008; Walker, McCarthy, and Baumgartner 2011). Moreover, the dramatic expansion of advocacy organizations that began during the civil rights era contributed to the legitimation of advocacy among identity-based charities (e.g., women, ethnic and racial minority groups) (Clemens 1993; Minkoff 1994, 2002). These groups, which had focused on service provision before the 1960s, began to integrate advocacy into their organizational repertoire during this period. Additionally, many social movement organizations incorporated formally as charitable nonprofits while maintaining their interest in policy reform, indicating that this nascent blending of services and advocacy was not driven entirely by identity-based charities (Edwards 1994; Cress 1997).

These integrative developments are surprising when viewed in light of the long-standing and divisive regulatory debates concerning political activity by charitable nonprofits. For example, tax-exempt status for Margaret Sanger's American Birth Control League was denied in 1930 based on the argument that providing a tax break for an organization lobbying the legislature for greater access to birth control constituted a public subsidy for political advocacy (Jenkins 2006). Because of lack of consensus, limitations on charities' advocacy were not defined precisely even after the establishment of the 501(c) designation in 1954 (Hall 1992, 2006; Reid 1999; Boris and Krehely 2002; Jenkins 1987, 2006). During the 1950s and the 1960s, organizations such as the NAACP and the Sierra Club were deemed excessively political and had their status as public charities revoked; they were forced to become 501(c)(4) social welfare organizations (Berry and Arons 2003; Jenkins 1987, 2006). These enforcement actions by the federal government had their legal basis in an undefined "substantial expenditure test" for lobbying, to which all charitable nonprofits were subject until the Tax Reform Act of 1976. Even today, this vague regulation is the default test for 501(c)(3) status upon incorporation (see Table 20.1 for a brief overview of advocacy regulations for 501(c)(3), 501(c)(3)-PF, 501(c)(4), and 527 nonprofits).

The growth of public sector contracting also informs the current environment for advocacy by charitable nonprofits (Frumkin 2005; Marwell 2004, 2007, 2010; Barman 2006; Hwang and Powell 2009; MacIndoe 2010; Mosley 2012; Levine 2016). The public sector in the United States has a long history of contracting with nonprofits and participating in other types of public–private partnerships. The triumph of neoliberalism and New Public Management during the 1980s led to extensive decentralization and devolution of government—to the point that some scholars began to describe the federal government as a "hollow state" (Smith and Lipsky 1993; Salamon 1995; Kettl 1997; Milward and Provan 2000; Grønbjerg and Salamon 2002). Much of the initial research on government contracting anticipated that public sector revenue would dampen nonprofit advocacy because it was assumed that contracted organizations would not want to "bite the hand that feeds" (Smith and Lipsky 1993; Berry and Arons 2003).

Contrary to expectations, most studies instead find a positive relationship between government contracting with nonprofits and nonprofit advocacy for social change (Chaves, Stephens, and Galaskiewicz 2004; Leech 2006; Leroux and Goerdel 2009; Mosley 2012; Almog-Bar and Schmid 2014; Lu 2018a). Rather than "buying silence" from nonprofits through co-optation and resource dependence, greater government funding has brought nonprofits into regular contact with government, providing public charities with opportunities to advocate for greater resources, establish patronage relationships with elected officials, and act as nonelected neighborhood representatives (Marwell 2004, 2007, 2010; Kelleher and Yackee 2009; Mosley 2012; Levine 2016). Meanwhile, the earlier emphasis on "arm's length" or transactional contracts in public management has declined, giving way to networks of service provision and collaborative forms of governance as strategies for mitigating intractable social problems (Ansell and Gash 2008; Osborne 2010; Suárez 2011; Bryson, Crosby, and Stone 2015). These collaborative arrangements have provided new channels for nonprofits to engage with public agencies, often complementing the opportunities provided by contractual ties (Mosley 2010, 2011; Fyall 2016a, 2016b; Suárez and Esparza 2017). Like the transformation of public engagement and the advocacy group explosion, public management reform clearly is relevant to the contemporary context for nonprofit advocacy.

Table 20.1 Advocacy-relevant federal regulations: 501(c)(3), 501(c)(3)-PF, 501(c)(4), and 527 nonprofits*

	501(c)(3) Public charities	501(c)(3)-PF Private foundations	501(c)(4) Social welfare organizations	527 Political Organizations
Tax status	Tax-exempt; contributions are tax-deductible	Tax-exempt; contributions are tax-deductible	Tax-exempt; contributions are not tax-deductible	Tax-exempt; contributions are not tax-deductible
Disclosure of donors	No	Yes	No	Yes
Lobbying activities	Permitted, as long as expenditures are "insubstantial"; (h) electors have more clearly defined expenditure limits	Prohibited, though grants for general operating support may be used for lobbying	Permitted, no limit on expenditures	Permitted, as long as expenditures are "insubstantial"; may be taxable if not furthering political purposes
Political activities	Prohibited from engaging in partisan political activities; nonpartisan voter registration is permitted	Prohibited from engaging in partisan political activities; grantmaking for nonpartisan voter registration is restricted but permitted	Permitted, but must be secondary activity (generally less than half of expenditures)	Permitted, no limit on expenditures
Other advocacy activities	Unlimited mission-related public education, policy research, litigation, rulemaking, community mobilization and/or organization	Unlimited, may engage in all (non-lobbying) activities permitted for a 501(c)(3)	Unlimited, may engage in all activities permitted for a 501(c)(3)	Limited, may engage in all activities permitted for a 501(c)(3)—for influencing the outcomes of elections to public office
Advocacy targets	Government, business (for-profit), nonprofit	Government, business (for-profit), nonprofit	Government, business (for-profit), nonprofit	Government

Note: This table should not be treated as a substitute for legal advice.

* Regulations for 501(c)(5) and 501(c)(6) nonprofits most closely resemble those of 501(c)(4) nonprofits.

Sources: Reid 1999; Avner 2010; Lyon 2014; Alliance for Justice 2015; Schadler 2018.

In summary, three key trends or processes have played a critical role in shaping the nonprofit advocacy landscape: the transformation of public engagement, the advocacy group explosion, and the growth of public sector contracting and collaboration. In the section that follows, I link this overview to the main arguments and present a conceptual frame for future research examining advocacy among charitable nonprofits.

Service-Providing (Charitable) Nonprofits as Advocates

In this section, I argue that advocacy is becoming a legitimate component of the toolkit that charitable nonprofits use to pursue mission. I further suggest that opportunities are growing for public charities to blend organizational advocacy with civic engagement. These conclusions run counter to some scholarly expectations; many studies indicate that service-providing nonprofits are reluctant to engage in advocacy (Boris and Krehely 2002; Berry and Arons 2003; Bass et al. 2007; Avner 2010). Considerable evidence demonstrates that few charitable nonprofits lobby, even though it is legal for them to do so. Because many nonprofit leaders are uncertain about restrictions, they eschew advocacy altogether in order to avoid jeopardizing their organizations' tax-exempt status (Reid 1999; Berry 2005; Bass et al. 2007; Suárez and Hwang 2008; Mosley 2013). Despite their reluctance to lobby and clear restrictions against electioneering (endorsing or aiding candidates for elective office), there are some indications that nonprofit advocacy is becoming increasingly prevalent.

As noted earlier, many identity-based public charities began to engage in advocacy during the civil rights movement. Moreover, incorporating social change activity into their repertoire bolstered the likelihood of organizational survival (Clemens 1993, 1997; Minkoff 1994, 1999, 2002). Although there is not yet longitudinal research exploring the extent to which the blending of services and advocacy has expanded beyond identity-based nonprofits, cross-sectional studies and research focused on specific fields (i.e., civil/human rights, environment, human services) indicate that involvement in some form of advocacy is now rather common (Sampson et al. 2005; Child and Grønbjerg 2007; Leroux 2007, 2009, 2011; Kelleher and Yackee 2009; Nicholson-Crotty 2007, 2011; MacIndoe and Whalen 2013; Fyall 2016a, 2016b; Hwang and Suárez 2019). Moreover, the body of research on public sector contracting and collaboration shows that (a) interdependence between government and nonprofits continues to grow and (b) as discussed in the previous section, this interdependence facilitates and even spurs advocacy (Chaves et al. 2004; Mosley 2012; Pekkanen, Smith, and Tsujinaka 2014; Suárez and Esparza 2017; Lu 2018b). These findings suggest that advocacy expands in fields with public–nonprofit ties—and because public agencies interact regularly with public charities in a broad array of fields (i.e., education, health, human services), the opportunities for this expansion are many and varied.

The argument that nonprofit advocacy is becoming more pervasive is also strengthened by recent research on a related but unique type of nonprofit organization—philanthropic foundations (see Reckhow, Chapter 8, "Politics, Philanthropy, and Inequality"). Private foundations, which are public charities whose primary purpose is to distribute grants to nonprofits, have a distinctive designation that prohibits any lobbying or electioneering (501(c)(3)-PF). Even though foundations are permitted to provide grants for advocacy, and although they can engage in advocacy directly as long as they do not support or oppose legislation, considerable evidence indicates that philanthropic institutions historically have had just modest involvement in policy activity (Jenkins and Eckert 1986; Jenkins 1987, 1998; Suárez 2012). Nevertheless, recent evidence suggests that foundations have become emboldened in their social change agendas, acting as institutional entrepreneurs by using their voices and philanthropic resources to pursue policy reform (Rich 2004; Bartley 2007; Reckhow 2013; Quinn, Tompkins-Stange, and Meyerson 2014; Goss 2016; Tompkins-Stange 2016; Suárez, Husted, and Casas 2018). Given that philanthropic institutions face greater restrictions on advocacy than the public charities they support, their growing willingness to pursue social change sends a strong positive signal to other nonprofits about the legitimacy of the activity.

In light of these emerging trends, it appears that although many public charities have been reluctant to embrace advocacy, this pattern is shifting toward greater social change engagement. There are also indications that public charities are increasingly well positioned to blend direct organizational advocacy with political forms of public engagement—a trend that could have important implications for the power of service-providing nonprofits to influence social change (Marwell 2004; Han 2014; Han and Argyle 2016; Levine 2016). Although individual involvement in civic groups and membership in associations are declining in the United States, many conventional service-providing nonprofits promote public engagement (Putnam 1995; Skocpol and Fiorina 1999; Skocpol 2003; Campbell 2008). Often, the types of public engagement these public charities encourage are nonpolitical, such as volunteering, and those that do promote activism undoubtedly differ in their effectiveness (Theiss-Morse and Hibbing 2005; Guo and Musso 2007; Baggetta 2009; Lichterman and Eliasoph 2014; Minkoff 2016; Longhofer, Negro, and Roberts 2018). Nevertheless, a growing body of research finds that common civic events like festivals, fund-raisers, and efforts to clean up or restore local landmarks (such as parks) increasingly incorporate social change elements—or "blended social action" (Meyer and Tarrow 1998; McAdam et al. 2005; Sampson et al. 2005).

The implication of these findings is that many public charities no longer draw sharp distinctions among different forms of public engagement. Increasingly, nonprofits that foster nonpolitical civic participation are extending those activities in political directions. Service-providing nonprofits have thus become a locus of collective social change activity, and public sector reforms may enable these organizations to leverage their public engagement for policy influence. In other words, the growth of public sector contracting and public–private collaboration provides avenues for service-providing nonprofits to exert direct policy influence, and these reforms also reinforce the potential for public engagement to serve as a tool for indirect policy change. As an example, Nicole P. Marwell (2004, 2007, 2010) demonstrates that some public charities have developed "reliable voting constituencies" for elected officials by mobilizing their stakeholders to support candidates that protect their services—which the elected officials then reward with ongoing public sector funding for those nonprofits. As the breadth and depth of the public services that charities provide has expanded in this era of public sector devolution, some public charities have even superseded elected politicians as representatives of their communities, granting them considerable informal authority over the distribution of public resources and input into policy (Levine 2016).

A recent review of the literature on civic engagement concluded that a key to strengthening the influence of public participation is to "invest in organizations, and focus especially on organizations that a) can link authentic grassroots power with elite lobbying relationships, and b) have strategic capacities" (Han and Argyle 2016:5). Public charities, which are constrained by vague yet persistent lobbying regulations, face far greater obstacles in developing "elite lobbying relationships" than corporations or social welfare groups (i.e., AARP, Planned Parenthood). Nevertheless, the transformation of public engagement has led some service-providing nonprofits to develop their grassroots power and strategic capacities, not only by becoming more active in policy engagement but also by investing in new technologies (like social media) as a means to pursue change (Guo and Saxton 2014). Just as important, contemporary approaches to public management have created novel opportunities for nonprofits to combine organizational advocacy with public engagement in the pursuit of social change (Schlozman, Verba, and Brady 2012; Lyon 2014; E. Walker 2014). Taken together, these observations suggest that nonprofit advocacy is becoming more prevalent among public charities, but no systematic evidence exists to support or refute this argument or to examine whether nonprofits are becoming more influential as social change actors.

A conceptual framework is therefore needed to test these arguments, demonstrate change in the sector over time, and explain variation in social change activity among nonprofits. The discussion of the contemporary landscape for nonprofit advocacy established the current institutional environment and political opportunity structure that public charities face in pursuing their missions (DiMaggio and Powell 1983; McAdam, McCarthy, and Zald 1996). This landscape can change over time, becoming more or less favorable for nonprofit social change activity. This landscape is not the only consequential context for public charities, however. The conceptual frame I propose, presented visually in simplified form in Figure 20.1, prioritizes five aspects or dimensions of public charities that, besides institutional context, inform advocacy outcomes: the external operational

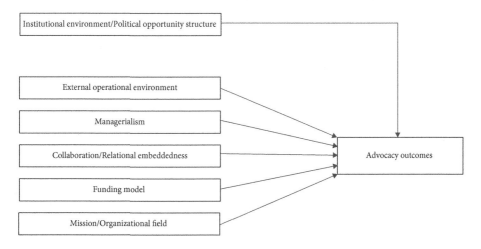

Figure 20.1 Conceptual framework for the drivers and determinants of nonprofit advocacy

environment, managerialism (professionalization and rationalization), collaboration and relational embeddedness, funding model, and mission and organizational field. These five elements are presented here as the key drivers and determinants of nonprofit advocacy; however, which factors are most salient in a particular situation likely depends on the advocacy outcomes under consideration. Although the concluding section attends to some of the advocacy outcomes that merit greater research attention, the following section concentrates primarily on the inputs or independent variables that matter for advocacy outcomes.

The Drivers and Determinants of Nonprofit Advocacy

External Operational Environment: In contrast to institutional effects, which have a sweeping and pervasive influence on organizations, the influence of the external operational environment works at a more local level (Bromley and Meyer 2017; Bromley, Chapter 4, "The Organizational Transformation of Civil Society"). As an example, Christof Brandtner and Claire Dunning (Chapter 11, "Nonprofits as Urban Infrastructure") emphasize cities as an important context for nonprofits—which nonprofits shape and also by which nonprofits are shaped. Nonprofits contribute to civic capacity, to urban governance, and to many other aspects of city life, and those nonprofits similarly are influenced by local regulations, by the spatial or geographic layout of the cities in which they provide services, and by many additional features of cities. Viewed in this manner, the external operational environment is nested within the broader institutional environment, both of which can have consequential and independent effects on the behavior of organizations—in this instance in relation to public charities and advocacy outcomes.

Another aspect of the external operational environment for nonprofits is competition—for clients and other resources—which several studies indicate influences advocacy outcomes such as lobbying, the advocacy tactics that nonprofits adopt, and the resources that nonprofits dedicate to advocacy (Suárez and Hwang 2008; Guo and Saxton 2010; MacIndoe 2010, 2014). Urban–rural distinctions often are consequential for advocacy outcomes as well, as are specific characteristics of the communities and clients that public charities serve, such as wealth, political orientation, and ethnic or racial diversity (Leroux and Goerdel 2009; Mosley and Galaskiewicz 2015; Kim and Mason 2018; Suárez et al. 2019). These indicators by no means constitute an exhaustive list; many aspects of context are substantively relevant to public charities' advocacy. Indeed, a recent review of the literature emphasized that concerted attention to context is necessary for advancing the field of research on organizational advocacy, implying that a comprehensive conceptual frame should take many aspects of the external operational environment into account (Hojnacki et al. 2012).

Managerialism: Several relevant concepts and indicators are encapsulated under the umbrella label of *managerialism*, which refers to ideologies that structure nonprofit attention to the technical or "businesslike" aspects of their work (Maier and Meyer 2011; Maier, Mayer, and Steinbereithner 2016). Professionalization is one aspect of managerialism, which refers to the reliance on formally trained (credentialed) and/or paid staff for service delivery. Over the past few decades, charitable nonprofits have become much more professionalized, favoring paid staff with academic credentials over volunteers and "amateurs" (Smith and Lipsky 1993; Karl 1998; Frumkin 2005; Hwang and Powell 2009; Suárez 2011). Professionalization appears to have a positive effect on nonprofit advocacy, but many aspects of professionalization have not been explored in great depth (Mosley 2010; Marshall and Suárez 2014; Lu 2018a). The effects of distinctive types of formal training for staff (managerial versus substantive) on advocacy have not received much attention, for instance, nor have the relative effects of formal training and reliance on paid staff (Hwang and Powell 2009).

Rationalization is another component of managerialism, which refers to the formal "construction of charitable organizations as 'actors' with clear identities" (Hwang and Powell 2009:272). As with professionalization, nonprofits have become more rationalized over time, incorporating policies and practices that are presumed to strengthen organizational accountability, efficiency, and effectiveness (Barman and MacIndoe 2012; Meyer et al. 2013; Marshall and Suárez 2014; Maier, Buber, and Aghamanoukjan 2016; Bromley and Meyer 2017; Hwang and Suárez 2019). Rationalization has been posited to drive engagement in advocacy, based on the premise that advocacy is becoming an accepted "best practice," much like performance evaluation or strategic planning, yet little research has explored the idea (Hwang and Suárez 2019).

A holistic conceptual frame for the study of nonprofit advocacy should incorporate measures of managerialism because research has demonstrated their explanatory power, but attention to professionalization and rationalization may also clarify one of the most consistent findings in the literature: organizational size has a positive effect on public charity engagement in advocacy (Child and Grønbjerg 2007; Lu 2018a). Organizational size tends to be used as a proxy for capacity, suggesting that larger public charities are more likely to engage in advocacy because they have the requisite skills to do so, yet this measure provides no information about what organizations actually do. In contrast, managerialism attunes research on advocacy to the human resources within nonprofits and to the operational tools, rules, and routines that nonprofits embrace (Maier et al. 2016; Bromley and Meyer 2017). Though managerialism is not necessarily a better synonym for capacity than organizational size, the incorporation of measures of professionalization and rationalization should help specify the underlying mechanisms driving size's consistent positive effect.

Collaboration and Relational Embeddedness: Collaboration and relational embeddedness refer to the diverse social ties and networks that nonprofits develop with actors beyond their organizational boundaries (Powell 1990; Galaskiewicz, Bielefeld, and Dowell 2006; Small 2006; Baumgartner et al. 2009; Clemens and Guthrie 2010). Collaboration entails interorganizational cooperation to achieve a common goal by sharing information, resources, programs, or expertise (Bryson et al. 2015). Such partnerships demonstrate a willingness to engage external audiences to pursue mission, which could provide skills that are useful for advocacy—especially in coalitions (Hojnacki 1997; Fyall and McGuire 2015). Consistent with this argument, a growing body of research finds that collaboration has a positive effect on nonprofit advocacy (Leroux and Goerdel 2009; Mosley 2010; Hwang and Suárez 2019). However, this research could benefit from becoming more nuanced. Public charities can collaborate in numerous ways with other nonprofits, for-profit businesses, government agencies, and actors from multiple sectors, yet it remains unclear how the characteristics of these ties shape advocacy outcomes.

Relational embeddedness entails ties between public charities and other actors that are not limited to formal interorganizational collaborations, such as social relationships with legislators. As with collaboration, these ties can be formed with actors in the nonprofit, for-profit, or government sector and tend to have a positive effect on advocacy outcomes (Baumgartner et al. 2009; Marshall and Suárez 2014; Han and Argyle 2016; Lu 2018a). For instance, a study examining influences on outcomes of policy debates found that the organizational constituency or alliance (i.e., pro, con) with more high-level government allies won on the policy issue 78 percent of the time, and the side with more midlevel government allies won 60 percent of the time—percentages that were among the highest of the indicators they considered (Baumgartner et al. 2009). Relational embeddedness also refers to informal (i.e., noncontractual) community bonds, ties to civil society and community stakeholders that can be activated for public engagement. As with linkages to individuals in government, evidence suggests that nonprofits that involve constituents in activities and have more extensive links to the local communities they serve tend to have a positive effect on advocacy involvement (Han 2014; Marshall and Suárez 2014; Lu 2018a). Collaboration and relational embeddedness are therefore integral components to examine in research on advocacy by public charities.

Funding Model: Although the consistent, positive effect of government funding on nonprofit advocacy has been discussed already, nonprofits have a variety of other potential sources of revenue that could inform advocacy outcomes (Leroux and Goerdel 2009; Mosley 2010, 2012). Foundations, for example, are powerful patrons that exert coercive, normative, and mimetic pressure on the behavior of nonprofit organizations (Hwang and Powell 2009). Research on foundation grants for advocacy indicates that this source of revenue deters organizations from engaging in contentious or transgressive social movement activity—though it may increase the likelihood of organizational survival and even bolster nonprofit capacity for achieving a moderate social change agenda (Jenkins 1998, 2006). With the recent evidence of greater foundation involvement in advocacy, however, the persistence of these patterns is unclear (Quinn et al. 2014; Goss 2016; Suárez et al. 2019).

Another source of revenue that some have found consequential for advocacy is earned income, or market-based revenue (Eikenberry and Kluver 2004; Meyer et al. 2013; Maier et al. 2016). Whereas government funding (grants and contracts) tends to generate advocacy by public charities, and foundation funding often channels nonprofits away from contentious tactics, several studies have found that market revenue decreases the likelihood of nonprofit advocacy (Galaskiewicz et al. 2006; Hwang and Suárez 2019). Nonprofits that pursue market revenue may decrease their organizational advocacy for a number of reasons. They may have concerns about alienating clients and customers, market-based activities may be time-consuming and "crowd out" opportunities for advocacy, or extensive earned income activity may foster a transactional relationship with clients and lead nonprofits to become less involved in their communities (Galaskiewicz et al. 2006; Hwang and Suárez 2019). Whatever the explanation, earned income appears to have substantive importance for organizational advocacy.

In addition to attending to nonprofit revenue sources, research on nonprofit advocacy should also consider funding diversity. The important distinctions here are between specific sources of revenue (i.e., foundations, government agencies, earned income), the extent to which an organization relies on any particular source of revenue, and the overall breadth of revenue sources on which a nonprofit relies. Though there are some studies on how the presence of a given source of nonprofit revenue (i.e., a dichotomous indicator for foundation grants) affects advocacy outcomes, much less research exists on how the dependence on specific revenue sources or the total number of funding sources drive advocacy. An extensive body of research nevertheless emphasizes the effects of resource dependence on organizational strategy, reinforcing the value of attending to funding models in research on nonprofit advocacy (Leroux and Goerdel 2009; Mosley 2010).

Mission and Organizational Fields: An organizational field is a set of organizations within a recognized domain, which in nonprofit research is often defined as the primary industry or subsector to which a nonprofit is dedicated (i.e., education, arts, human services, health) (Scott 2001). Many studies have demonstrated that organizational fields structure nonprofit involvement in advocacy, typically finding that environmental organizations and human services organizations are more engaged in advocacy than organizations in other fields (Child and Grønbjerg 2007; Suárez and Hwang 2008; Guo and Saxton 2010). Although organizational fields capture one dimension of the nonprofit work that informs advocacy outcomes, organizations within fields have distinctive missions that are also relevant to advocacy outcomes (Minkoff and Powell 2006). For instance, all arts organizations are part of the same broad organizational field, but the mission and identity of the organizations within that field contribute to variation in advocacy involvement (Kim 2017; Kim and Mason 2018).

More concretely, some service-providing nonprofits specify a commitment to social justice, social change, or rights (i.e., civil, political, human), and organizations that adopt this discourse tend to be substantially involved in advocacy (Suárez 2012, Suárez et al. 2019). Though the mission of an organization can be specified narrowly on its website or in Internal Revenue Service (IRS) documents, mission statements can be loosely coupled with the work that nonprofits actually undertake, implying that a clear understanding of nonprofit programs and activity is critical for elucidating the role of nonprofits in advocacy (Bromley and Powell 2012; Powell, Horvath, and Brandtner 2016). Some organizations have a long history of engaging in advocacy as institutional entrepreneurs, for instance, and prior involvement in social change activity undoubtedly matters for a host of advocacy outcomes (Mintrom and Vergari 1996; Suárez 2009, 2012; Quinn et al. 2014). This operational or enacted mission manifests in other ways as well, some of which are relevant for research on nonprofit advocacy—such as hiring management staff with lobbying experience or pursuing the 501(h) election (an opt-in alternative to the ambiguous "substantial expenditure" test for lobbying) (Leroux and Goerdel 2009; MacIndoe and Whalen 2013; Lu 2018a).

These five aspects or dimensions of public charities—when considered along with the institutional environment—constitute a holistic conceptual frame for the study of advocacy by public charities. Propositions and hypotheses were not elaborated because there was no expectation that each element of the conceptual frame would have the same effect regardless of the advocacy outcome, although the framework did strive to identify and build on previous empirical findings. Moreover, no effort was made to produce a comprehensive list of indicators and measures that align with each aspect of the conceptual frame. The primary purpose in introducing this framework was to establish a basic theoretical model for the organizational behavior of public charities that could be applied to cross-sectional and longitudinal data on a broad range of advocacy outcomes. The following section reprises the arguments made in the chapter and discusses some of the advocacy outcomes that, with sufficient empirical testing that builds from a consistent conceptual frame, have the potential to strengthen core knowledge in the field.

Discussion

Advocacy research explores consequential questions about the roles, representativeness, and relevance of advocacy organizations—as well as the influence of diverse social forces on public (civic and political) engagement—yet reviews of the literature consistently uncover few empirical generalizations (Jenkins 1987, 2006; Baumgartner and Leech 1998; Andrews and Edwards 2004; Baumgartner et al. 2009; McFarland 2010; Hojnacki et al. 2012; de Figueiredo and Richter 2014). The conclusion from a widely cited review is typical: "The research reviewed here presents promising leads but few conclusive patterns" (Andrews and Edwards 2004:491). Part of the difficulty in generalizing from available research stems from the breadth of advocacy outcomes that get explored in this body of work. Simply defining advocacy as a concept is not a trivial task, as associated activities can be direct or indirect as well as social or political (Reid 2000; Jenkins 2006). An additional obstacle to identifying consistent patterns in the literature is that conceptual frames differ across studies, even within disciplines. This chapter has concentrated on addressing this latter problem in relation to public charities.

Although the lack of a consistent conceptual frame, definitional ambiguity, and the diversity of possible outcomes all inhibit broad inferences about nonprofit advocacy, innovative research on many questions would contribute to the literature. This chapter has argued that advocacy is becoming a more socially acceptable and common tool for pursuing mission among public charities and that these service-providing nonprofits are increasingly well positioned to combine organizational advocacy with civic engagement in the pursuit of social change. These arguments merit attention because public charities play diverse, underappreciated roles as political actors, and institutional change could be amplifying their involvement and power (Sampson et al. 2005; Marwell 2010; Han 2014; Han and Argyle 2016; Levine 2016). Other emerging avenues of productive inquiry include research on the tactics that nonprofits utilize for advocacy (i.e., insider, outsider), the venues they select (i.e., local, state, federal, international), the targets they pursue (i.e., nonprofit, for-profit, government), and the scope and intensity of their social change efforts (Guo and Saxton 2010; Mosley 2011, 2012; Walker et al. 2011; MacIndoe and Whalen 2013; Buffardi, Pekkanen, and Smith 2015; Fyall 2016a).

There is no shortage of advocacy outcomes worth investigating in relation to public charities, and this chapter did not even attempt to address the limited literature on the organizational consequences of engagement in advocacy, such as whether advocacy leads to an increase in fund-raising, growth in volunteer recruitment, or success in program implementation. Considerable work also remains to be done in establishing a convincing link between public charities' advocacy activities and policy outcomes of interest. For example, lobbying outcomes are studied frequently in research on advocacy organizations, demonstrating that corporations and trade groups are responsible for the preponderance of lobbying expenditures and that organizations with considerable resources are more likely to lobby independently than smaller groups (de Figueiredo and Richter 2014). At the same time, "numerous studies have attempted to estimate the effects of lobbying on policy outcomes. However, the validity of their results depends on the dataset and econometric methods employed to identify and isolate the causal effect of lobbying" (de Figueiredo and Richter 2014:168–169).

When researching the effects of advocacy organizations on the policy process, causal attribution is equally difficult and faces significant barriers. Public charities contribute to many aspects of the policy process, from setting the policy agenda to policy enactment, implementation, and monitoring, yet only limited progress has been made in identifying the conditions under which advocacy organizations are likely to be successful in any component of their policy reform efforts (Andrews and Edwards 2004; Jenkins 2006; Hojnacki et al. 2012). The chapter on advocacy in the previous edition of this volume offered a trenchant summary, concluding that research on policy impacts "has been limited in its coverage of multiple types of impact, time sequences, and the range of relevant factors that might condition the effectiveness of nonprofit advocacy. Few studies are multivariate, and few capture the political context that may influence the effectiveness of different types of advocacy work" (Jenkins 2006:324). Given that advocacy nonprofits are pervasive and widely viewed as consequential political actors, discerning their effects on policy outcomes remains a critical research topic (Sampson et al. 2005; Hojnacki et al. 2012; Bushouse 2016).

Finally, novel research on advocacy by public charities needs to be undertaken in relation to the policy efforts of other types of organizations. Even though the chapter has claimed that advocacy among public charities is increasing and that public charities are increasingly well positioned to blend public engagement with direct organizational advocacy, their overall influence may not be growing despite these developments. As a result of the Citizens United case, decided by the U.S. Supreme Court in 2010, restrictions on political campaign expenditures were eased for for-profit corporations and other types of politically active groups. For-profit corporations have always had a financial advantage in the world of special interests, contributing to the observation that democracy in the United States is sustained by unequal voice—an "unheavenly chorus" of actors—and the lifting of restrictions could exacerbate these inequalities (Schlozman et al. 2012; see also recent research on efforts by for-profits to manufacture civic participation (E. Walker 2014; Walker and Oszkay, Chapter 21, "The Changing Face of Nonprofit Advocacy").

In conclusion, this chapter has highlighted the social change activity of service-providing nonprofits, an organizational form that has not received much attention in the broader literature on advocacy. The chapter elaborated two arguments, positing growth in the prevalence of advocacy among public charities and an increase in their power as they take advantage of opportunities to blend advocacy with civic engagement. Applying a common conceptual frame is critical for testing these and many other arguments effectively, yet extensive variation in the application of theory has limited the comparability of results across studies. Though many features of organizations and their environments influence the work they undertake, the five dimensions put forth in the proposed conceptual frame can be applied to a wide variety of advocacy outcomes. Ultimately, research that consistently implements a robust conceptual frame will advance the field and contribute to demonstrating the effects of nonprofit advocacy on policy, inequality, democracy, and other meaningful societal outcomes.

21 THE CHANGING FACE OF NONPROFIT ADVOCACY

Democratizing Potentials and Risks in an Unequal Context

Edward T. Walker and Yotala Oszkay

DIVERSE ANALYSTS, GOING BACK AT least to Alexis de Tocqueville ([1835] 2003), have pointed to the critical role that advocacy groups play in supporting a healthy and vibrant civic enterprise, the social integration of communities, and the responsiveness of policy makers to the diverse needs and interests of their constituents (Barber 1984; R. Putnam 2000; Lichterman 2006; Sampson et al. 2005). Substantial literatures document how nonprofit advocacy groups help expand civic engagement, call attention to underrepresented constituencies, and foster democracy more broadly (for reviews, see Fung 2003; J. Jenkins 2006; E. Walker 2013b). In recent decades, this idea has been reinforced by those who hold out hope for advocacy groups as sources of meaningful civic integration and public participation but also contested by others who worry that the changing features of organized civil society are preventing these groups from effective action. These concerns point to polarization, inequality, and interactions among increasingly politicized corporations, democratically challenged governments, and wealthy individuals as factors limiting the potential for advocates to foster democratic outcomes (Lee, McQuarrie, and Walker 2015; Skocpol 2003, 2004; Skocpol and Williamson 2016; Skocpol and Hertel-Fernandez 2016; Soss and Jacobs 2009; Norris 2011; E. Walker 2014; I. Martin 2013). As we discuss in this chapter, although the assumption is often that more advocacy will mean stronger democratic representation, that is not always the case.

This mixed combination of factors has generated a palpable ambivalence among scholars about the prospects for nonprofit advocates to compensate not only for deep and serious democratic deficits in many contemporary societies (Norris 2011; Wolin 2017) but also for a crisis in institutional trust, particularly among young people (e.g., Bonikowski and DiMaggio 2016). In the United States, for instance, many analysts suggest that political advocacy groups tend to reinforce the unequal context in which they operate (Lee et al. 2015). Others have noted that wealthy constituencies have found novel means by which to mobilize mass advocacy on their behalf (E. Walker 2014; I. Martin 2013; Phillips-Fein 2009). Additionally, the largely donor-driven push toward standardization and commensuration for nonprofits may be having negative consequences for the advocacy sector, as advocacy groups typically do not offer easily quantifiable deliverables (Teles and Schmitt 2011). Lastly, new information and communication technologies (ICTs), initially envisioned as tools of broad-based collective empowerment, may be reinforcing communicative and participatory echo chambers. Users of ICTs in civic contexts may be less likely to encounter opposing views or alternative perspectives (e.g., Boutyline and Willer 2016; Sunstein 2018) and more likely to engage primarily in transactional rather than substantial styles of participation (e.g., Shulman 2009; but see Karpf 2010).

In this chapter, we examine general trends in nonprofit advocacy with respect to democracy in the twenty-first century. We focus our investigations primarily on the United States. Following Charles Tilly (see Tilly and Wood 2013), we understand democracy to be "relatively broad and equal citizenship" tied to binding consultation of citizens with regard to state personnel and policies, along with the protection of citizens from arbitrary state action (and without severe restrictions on access to citizenship itself). We perceive a tension between the potential for nonprofit advocacy groups to serve as sources of democratic engagement and their tendency toward reinforcing a broader context in which democracy appears to be receding (see Levitsky and Ziblatt 2018). We examine six key areas in which scholars have made substantial contributions to understanding the prospects for (de-)democratizing activity by nonprofit advocates: (1) structural features of advocacy nonprofit organizations; (2) pressures toward accountability by third-party monitors; (3) inequalities in the broader social context; (4) the rising use of nonprofits as political intermediaries for corporations or other interests; (5) practices of advocacy nonprofits that may limit democratizing potential by prioritizing mobilizing over organizing; and (6) the role of ICTs in reshaping the practices of advocacy nonprofits.

As in the previous chapter, we understand advocacy organizations to be associations that "make public interest claims either promoting or resisting social change that, if implemented, would conflict with the social, cultural, political, or economic interests or values of other constituencies and groups" (Andrews and Edwards 2004:481; Suárez, Chapter 20, "Advocacy, Civic Engagement, and Social Change"). The scope of our investigation is focused on nonprofits, including those incorporated as conventional charities (under code 501(c)(3)), social welfare organizations (under code 501(c)(4)), and private foundations that engage in advocacy. We do, however, note that not all advocacy organizations are incorporated as nonprofits, and indeed most associations are informal, grassroots, and unchartered; David Horton Smith (1997) appropriately labeled such associations the "dark matter" of the nonprofit sector. Diverse and influential contemporary social movements—including many that have become very prominent, such as Black Lives Matter, #MeToo, and Never Again—are not, in large part, centrally organized around nonprofit structures (although some have become established in response to these movements, such as Stand with Parkland, Time's Up Legal Defense Fund, and Black Lives Matter Foundation). This lack of formal incorporation poses a challenge for scholars, who may need to rely on domain-specific censuses of organizations within particular issue areas (for an illustrative example regarding local environmental associations, see Andrews et al. 2016). We return to these considerations later in the chapter, especially as they relate to shifting nonprofit structures and new uses of communications technologies in organizing.

Changing Nonprofit Organizational Structures

As the previous chapter observed, in recent years the nonprofit sector has become increasingly professionalized. Similar to other organizational fields that have witnessed increasing "marketization" (Kraatz and Zajac 1996; Berman 2011), increased participation in higher education and pressures for greater efficiency and accountability have led to a new class of nonprofit and advocacy professionals who, with their credentialed expertise, help nonprofit organizations become more "businesslike" (Dart 2004; Hwang and Powell 2009; King 2017; Jordan and Maloney 1997; Bosso 2005; McInerney 2014). Such trends can be observed in the field of advocacy and civic engagement, where paid professionals and business elites have taken on the advocacy tasks typically associated with social movement activists (a trend harking back to the classic arguments of John D. McCarthy and Mayer N. Zald (1973, 1977). This professionalization has influenced changes in the organizational structures of nonprofit advocacy groups that may limit their potential democratizing benefits.[1]

One such emergent nonprofit advocacy structure, the nonmembership advocacy organization (NMAO), has drawn particular attention along these lines. NMAOs are entirely staff-driven, functioning as a pure form of professionalized advocacy group. In a study of Washington, D.C.–based organizations, Debra Minkoff, Silke Aisenbrey, and Jon Agnone (2008) found that NMAOs made up about 25 percent of advocacy organizations, with an additional 10 percent of the sector comprising organizations that form a decentralized nonmembership advocacy network. NMAOs—often self-described as institutes, centers, funds, projects, or task forces (Walker, McCarthy, and Baumgartner 2011)—vary in their advocacy activities and the extent to which these activities are seen as overtly political.

For example, one well-researched NMAO is the Children's Defense Fund (Skocpol 2003), directed by the charismatic former civil rights movement leader Marion Wright Edelman, which works to advance antipoverty policy and focuses on prototypical forms of nonmembership advocacy such as direct-mail fund-raising, lobbying, research, media outreach, and coalition building (Minkoff et al. 2008; Skocpol 1999; Walker, McCarthy, and Baumgartner 2011). Public interest legal advocacy groups are another important type of NMAO, emerging out of the "cause lawyering" of the 1960s (see Sarat and Scheingold 1998). Such groups deploy legal expertise to advance litigation and provide defense for individuals and activist teams in the name of a specified movement (Scheingold and Sarat 2004). Although groups working on civil rights issues—such as the NAACP Legal Defense and Educational Fund and the American Civil Liberties Union—were typically associated with this form of professional advocacy, the years that followed involved a major expansion of conservative legal advocacy organizations (Southworth 2004; Teles 2008).

Think tanks, as nonmembership professional organizations comprising experts who specialize in forms of knowledge production, were also put to highly politicized uses. Both popular and scholarly discourse vacillate between (1) characterizing think tanks as organizations that explicitly work to advance (often elite) political goals (Peschek 1987), in which case they are often described as "policy planning organizations," and (2) portraying them as autonomous entities whose research and analyses remain largely independent of political and economic interests (McGann and Weaver 2002). Thomas Medvetz, in his study of think tanks (2012), traces the emergence of the contemporary think tank to the progressive and conservative politics of the 1960s and 1970s. Activists on both the left and right, he argues, were skeptical of the technocratic experts affiliated with government. In order to challenge these experts' conclusions, they formed organizations like the Institute for Policy Studies (on the political left) and the Heritage Foundation (on the right), thereby occupying an "interstitial" space between academic, political, business, and media fields (see also Rich 2005; Himmelstein 1992). Although progressive organizations initially inhabited a substantial part of this space, their relative influence has receded. Conservative think tanks have come to dominate the field because of higher levels of support from big business and greater autonomy from academic institutions (Medvetz 2012).

The emergence of the think tank field, as Medvetz and other scholars have suggested, took place alongside a larger conservative project of launching nonmembership organizations that work to advance free enterprise policy. The 1960s also saw the rise of business associations like Business Roundtable and the U.S. Chamber of Commerce (Gross, Medvetz, and Russell 2011; Medvetz 2012; Mizruchi 2013; Vogel 1996). Through such organizations, business elites mobilized to scale back government regulation, taxes, and union power, arguing that the social safety net could be replaced with private support and institutions (Mizruchi 2013). Although, as Mark Mizruchi notes (2013), these changes were seen as victories by conservatives, they ultimately led the corporate elite, once able to collectively organize for policies that benefited both business and society (e.g., supporting full employment, civil rights, poverty measures, and environmental policies), to become victims of their own successes: more fragmented and less collectively effectual (even if individual firms and industries are quite powerful today).

Other important transitions in advocacy structures are reflected in the recent prominence of "philanthrocapitalism" (Bishop and Green 2010), in which the private donations of individual economic elites are becoming more central to nonprofit advocacy. On both the left and right, highly successful business entrepreneurs like Bill Gates, Mark Zuckerberg, Oprah Winfrey, and the (far more partisan) Koch brothers have established private foundations that fund think tanks, advocacy organizations, and other nonprofits. Analysts that celebrate these efforts suggest that such individuals can transfer the skills that brought them success in the market to achieving important social goals (Bishop and Green 2010). However, some argue that the logic of philanthrocapitalism—that is, an individualistic, market-based approach to philanthropy—runs counter to the spirit of civil society, therefore undermining any collective forms of advocacy (Edwards 2008). As Garry W. Jenkins (2010) argues, through large donations and the increasing use of limited-purpose grants, such foundations have generated disproportionate control over nonprofit advocacy efforts.

Indeed, these trends toward the professionalization and personalization of advocacy have prompted many scholars to contemplate the implications for broader questions of democracy and representation. The most popular of these arguments have been advanced by Robert D. Putnam (2000) and Theda Skocpol (1999, 2004; see also Fiorina 1999), who note that such trends correspond with declines in civic engagement and increasing inequalities in representation and political participation. Although it would not be reasonable to attribute these changes solely to nonmembership groups—indeed, there was no proportional increase in the prevalence of NMAOs relative to membership associations in the closing decades of the twentieth century (Walker, McCarthy, and Baumgartner 2011), shifts in participatory practices of both membership and nonmembership groups—such as less reliance on bottom-up processes of representation and greater attention to outside donors—reflect the increasingly unequal and polarized social and political environment in which they now operate.

Accountability Pressures

The increased professionalization of nonprofit advocacy is taking place concurrently with the development of evaluation tools and metrics to assess the social impact of nonprofits (Polonsky and Grau 2010; Sloan 2009; Cordery and Sinclair 2013; Berghmans, Simons, and Vandenabeele 2017; Jepson 2005). Although this change is not uniformly negative— and, as we describe, may improve some aspects of organizational performance—there is also evidence that this shift may restrict the capacity for advocacy nonprofits to advance democratic practices. This is the case because these metrics generally reward organizations that focus on providing direct services rather than organizing constituencies.

As advocacy nonprofits are becoming more professionalized and driven by the interests of paid staff, stakeholders are concerned about whether their contributions are being put to good use. Such concerns, and documented cases of nonprofit managers misappropriating organizational resources (Gibelman and Gelman 2004), have prompted new methods for transparency and the emergence of third-party monitors and raters, often called "charity watchdogs" (Szper and Prakash 2011). However, the effects of such quantification (and the commensuration of practices they likely encourage) are unclear. Many scholars are now asking how best to measure the messy world of advocacy and whether such metrics can be applied fairly or will inevitably discourage certain types of efforts that do not easily lend themselves to quantitative analysis.

Nonprofit assessment is typically conducted for the benefit of institutional and/or individual donors (Cunningham and Ricks 2004), both of which make contributions to nonprofits in the hope of advancing some cause. Although foundations (institutional donors) often have paid professionals on staff to manage evaluation, individual donors, despite providing the bulk of charitable giving, are rarely as cognizant about whether an organization is "efficacious" (Cunningham and Ricks 2004). Third-party rating agencies— such as Charity Navigator, GuideStar, and the Better Business Bureau's Wise Giving Alliance—attempt to close this knowledge gap by providing assessments of nonprofits based on financial health and annual reports. Although some agencies use qualitative measures to assess a nonprofit's performance, these organizations tend to rely heavily on financial data provided by IRS Form 990 and financial statements (Lowell, Trelstad, and Meehan 2005; Polonsky and Grau 2010). Ratings are based on how a nonprofit allocates funds to particular activities such as fund-raising and charitable services (Cordery and Sinclair 2013; Polonsky and Grau 2010).

These quantified financial metrics to assess nonprofits pose a number of concerns for the advocacy sector. Most directly, such metrics tend to account for all staffing expenses as part of associations' administrative overhead costs, which penalizes advocacy groups that focus on grassroots organizing rather than service provision. Such metrics may disincentivize donations to groups that engage in democratic organizing and reward those who put more of their effort into programs and services. Such notions are consistent with research on "reactivity" in organizational fields (Espeland and Sauder 2007), which suggests that organizations often revise their activities when they are being measured on a particular performance metric. Accountability metrics may present advocacy as a "bureaucratic drag" on resources, thereby constraining efforts to advance social causes (Jepson 2005:517).

Further, some scholars argue that the performance of nonprofits cannot be captured by a singular efficiency metric that examines inputs and outputs (Cordery and Sinclair 2013). This argument is especially salient for advocacy nonprofits given their general and not easily measurable goals of empowering constituencies and engendering sociopolitical change. Relatedly, advocacy efforts rarely follow a linear path (Gill and Freedman 2014). As Steven Teles and Mark Schmitt (2011) point out, advocacy groups frustrate standardized evaluation because the use of one tactic may be effective in one time and place and ineffective in another; campaigns must be continuously adapted to their context and failure is frequent, usually resulting in a "very long slog" toward change (Teles and Schmitt 2011:40). Performance metrics based on the allocation of donor contributions do not adequately account for this complex advocacy environment.

It is not clear, however, whether accountability metrics and ratings agencies are truly consequential for organizational outcomes. For example, in a study of Charity Navigator, Rebecca Szper and Aseem Prakash (2011) found that charity ratings did not have an effect on donors' support of nonprofit organizations. Margaret F. Sloan (2009), on the other hand, found that nonprofits that were marked "did not pass" on an accountability scale did not see a significant change in donations. Survey research (Van Iwaarden et al. 2009) and interviews with donors (Cunningham and Ricks 2004) suggest that donors do not find much use for the current metrics and that such metrics may actually stand in the way of the perceived efficacy of an organization, in part because it may not be worth devoting scarce resources to such extensive data gathering and measurement.[2] Many respondents in Kate Cunningham and Marc Ricks's study (2004) expressed that focusing on evaluation metrics would detract from more important goals and hinder donor–nonprofit relations.

Some scholars conclude that evaluation metrics must move beyond crude measures of outcomes to consider more complicated processes of social change. Teles and Schmitt (2011) argue that donors should ignore metrics altogether and instead evaluate advocacy groups more holistically. Such an approach might involve "spread betting"—funding various organizations, strategies, and issues and focusing on long-term portfolios of advocates. Others recommend the involvement of stakeholders in evaluation and an ongoing dialogue about missions and values (Jepson 2005). This involvement approach may allow advocacy organizations to adapt their strategies to better represent their constituents and donors, ultimately becoming more efficacious in navigating the "slog" of social change.

Negotiating Inequalities: Beyond Social Capital

Social change is understood to be a central goal of nonprofit activity. The prevailing image of the nonprofit sector, particularly with respect to nonprofits that provide social services, depicts organizations providing social supports that compensate for the limitations of public welfare programs and failures of the marketplace (Weisbrod 1977). These efforts, and the philanthropy that makes them possible, are believed to help ameliorate social inequalities (in intention, if not always in outcome; see Prewitt 2006). Advocacy nonprofits are also expected to provide redress against social inequalities: they help galvanize political pressure to generate changes in government programs or other redistributive efforts (McCarthy and Walker 2004), procure funds to support social service nonprofits (J. Jenkins 1998), and support private efforts by firms or industries to assist vulnerable communities (Hall 2006). Indeed, it is telling that McCarthy and Zald's (1977) definitive paper, which shaped more than a generation of scholarship on social movements and advocacy, described a social movement as "a set of opinions and beliefs in a population which represents preferences for changing some elements of the social structure *and/or reward distribution of a society*" (McCarthy & Zald 1977:1217–1218, italics added). There is, then, some expectation that nonprofit advocates support efforts to generate a more equitable distribution of societal resources.

A related expectation, rooted in neo-Tocquevillian ideas (R. Putnam 2000), holds that civic associations help build social capital. This connective process provides numerous benefits to communities, one of which is increasing the potential for equity and inclusivity (Portes 1998). However, this form of "positive" or "bridging" social capital is not the only relational feature that can emerge out of civic engagement and associated networking. "Negative" or "bonding" social capital serves primarily to reinforce exclusive ties based on homophily (Portes 1998; Portes and Landolt 2000). Because the bridging form has received the lion's share of scholarly attention, there is a widespread expectation that civic participation will help challenge social inequalities through the formation of broad-based social networks that cut across divides of party, race, class, and other key social cleavages. Empirical findings on social capital, diversity, and interpersonal trust, however, do not always support this hopeful narrative (Costa and Kahn 2003; Portes and Vickstrom 2011; E. Walker and Stepick 2014; R. Putnam 2007).

A variety of critiques have begun to emerge, pointing out that although many social advocacy nonprofits are focused on challenging inequality, they are nonetheless operating in an environment in which social inequalities are rapidly proliferating, and they are not immune from the problems that manifest in such a context (see Lee et al. 2015). Skocpol (2003) highlighted how widening political polarization and income inequality have coincided with the advocacy landscape shifting from broad associations that integrate members across social classes toward single-issue associations with less internal diversity. Other scholars have described shifts toward "protest businesses" (Jordan and Maloney 1997) or similarly supply-side-focused advocacy efforts (Bosso 2005; Brady, Schlozman, and Verba 1999) that focus heavily on the interests of particular donors, rather than organizing constituencies across a broader range of demographic backgrounds. These shifts are also reflected in the changing membership structures of associations and the rise of philanthrocapitalism described earlier in this chapter.

Further, as a variety of critiques have begun to point out, the participatory engagement that nonprofit advocacy groups facilitate may help reinforce broader social inequalities rather than challenge them. Public consultation and facilitation of participation is often used by political and business elites to generate buy-in for programs that exacerbate inequalities (Lee, McNulty, and Shaffer 2013; I. Martin 2015). For example, this concern has been expressed regarding World Bank programs that have participatory features, which may limit and constrain the political power of deliberative processes (Ganuza and Baiocchi 2012). Similarly, in many participatory settings, people with the highest levels of income and education tend to be significantly overrepresented because advocacy organizations and other political recruiters selectively target these groups, knowing they are most likely to contribute their time (Brady et al. 1999; E. Walker 2008, 2014). Further, in a politically polarized environment, political organizers are likely to seek out those who agree on highly charged issues rather than actively work across those divides. Finally, as we discuss in the next section, there are also strong tendencies toward using nonprofits as agents of outside interests, particularly by political and economic elites.

The Rise of Nonprofits as Political Intermediaries for Elite Interests

The question of whether nonprofits serve as intermediaries for outside interests predates the current context. For instance, the first U.S. political consulting firm, Campaigns Inc., effectively mobilized third-party advocates to defend their corporate clients in the 1930s (Sheingate 2016). There have always been some concerns that nonprofits are used by outside interests to advance their agendas. Consider how trade associations advance business interests (Aldrich and Fiol 1994), service-providing nonprofits often carry out the tasks called for by government principals (Marwell 2004), and other nonprofits act as proxies for the preferences of wealthy donors and foundations (see Prewitt 2006). This issue has taken on new meaning and significance, however, in the twenty-first century. New technologies, changes in U.S. electoral spending laws, and the increasing political mobilization of the business sector have combined to provide a fertile environment for using nonprofits as mediators between well-resourced third parties and policy makers.

We note three phenomena in the present rise of nonprofits as political intermediaries for elite interests. The first is the expanding practice of business "astroturfing." Contrasting with community-driven grassroots organizing, astroturfing artificially creates or prompts nonprofit intermediaries to (often covertly) advance the interests of a firm or industry (E. Walker 2014; see also Walker and Rea, 2014). The second phenomenon, "dark money," uses nonprofits to surreptitiously influence political campaigns and elections (see Hansen, Rocca, and Ortiz 2015). Third, strategic political philanthropic efforts are used to fund allied nonprofits that advocate for policy changes that benefit the economic interests of a business or powerful individual (see, e.g., Rothman et al. 2011). Although each of these undertakings is distinct, these uses of nonprofits as political intermediaries raise similar questions about the trustworthiness of nonprofits and challenge expectations that nonprofits can be assumed to be significant forces for broader societal democratization. We unpack each of these phenomena next.

Astroturfing can be characterized as advocacy activities that involve (1) heavy (often material) incentives for participants (for instance, "paid protesting"), (2) efforts by the sponsor to distance itself from these political activities by masquerading the nonprofit as an independent effort by civil society groups, and/or (3) forms of fraud (e.g., forged letters, communications shared without consent). For example, after facing major controversies over its store openings and substandard employee benefits practices in 2005, Walmart created the Working Families for Walmart organization to defend the company against its critics and lobby legislators (E. Walker 2014). Airbnb, which has faced challenges from labor unions, incumbent hotel industry interests, and local housing activists, created an advocacy organization to help press for the company's interests against its opponents

(Steinmetz 2016). Tobacco company Altria created Citizens for Tobacco Rights, similar to earlier tobacco-funded organizations such as the National Smokers Alliance (Givel 2007). These third-party organizations, sometimes called corporate "front groups" (E. Walker 2014), are often structured as nonprofit organizations and designed to appear, in most respects, as noncorporate civil society organizations.

The practice of establishing such entities has expanded considerably given the growing field of professional consultants who provide these services to firms (E. Walker 2009, 2014), the reputational sensitivity of firms and the interest they have in signaling the support of civil society organizations, and the interests of the sponsored or partnering nonprofits in expanding their funding base in a period of shifting priorities for foundations, government funders, and other outside patrons. However, because of the heavy funding, infrastructural support and staffing, and ultimate political aims behind such campaigns, public audiences often view such groups with considerable skepticism (E. Walker 2009, 2014). There are substantial risks for both nonprofits and the business interests that strategically use them to gain political advantages; in some respects, these partnership-related risks are similar to those that were described by Joseph Galaskiewicz and Michelle S. Colman (2006) in an earlier edition of this volume.

Dark money refers to campaign contributions made through nonprofit organizations, the sources of which need not be disclosed. Changes in U.S. election laws following the Supreme Court's ruling in *Citizens United v. Federal Election Commission* (2010)—which allowed corporations and labor unions to make unlimited contributions for "express advocacy" and "electioneering communications" out of their general treasury funds—effectively increased the funding and eventual political campaign expenditures of "social welfare" organizations incorporated under Internal Revenue Code section 501(c)(4) (as well as 501(c)(6) trade associations). Such social welfare nonprofits spent $257 million on federal elections in the 2012 election cycle, compared to $86 million in the 2008 cycle (Bass 2016). Given that these organizations are not required to disclose their donations or donors, a broad set of concerns have been raised about how this dark money is unaccountable to citizens, government, or other critical public audiences (Mayer 2016). Although disclosure was not required prior to *Citizens United*, the ruling unlocked new avenues of spending directly out of corporate treasuries (Winkler 2018). 501(c)(4) social welfare organizations are not, under U.S. law, permitted to have political activities as their "primary purpose," but the IRS's capacity for enforcement of this rule has been limited in recent years, the rules are not always clear about how "primary purpose" is defined, and efforts to enforce these rules have faced major backlash when attempted (e.g., Bump 2015).

The use of such nonprofits to advance the political interests of corporations and wealthy individuals, conducted in a way that obscures the ties between these donors and the nonprofits they support, has raised critical questions about the role of such nonprofits in American democracy (Mayer 2016). Although the highly political 501(c)(4) organizations represent only a small fraction of all such social welfare organizations, their use in this fashion prompts analysts to consider (1) whether citizens and policy makers will become less trusting of other social welfare nonprofits, even those that are not serving as political pass-through vehicles for firms and wealthy individuals; (2) whether the political uses of this nonprofit form are exacerbating inequalities in political representation and augmenting problems of democratic deficits and heightened political polarization; and (3) the extent to which the lack of IRS enforcement of the political activities of such groups may have spillover or signaling effects, leading other types of nonprofits to test many kinds of limits on political activities. These areas all have significant potential for future research.

A third way that nonprofits can serve as political intermediaries is through strategic philanthropic efforts by firms, industry groups, or wealthy individuals that benefit the patrons indirectly by funding associations allied with their political or economic interests. A recent study, for instance, found that corporate philanthropic contributions tend to follow similar patterns as other kinds of corporate political engagement, in that "grants given to charitable organizations located in a congressional district increase when its representative obtains seats on committees that are of policy relevance to the firm associated with the foundation" (Bertrand et al. 2018). This would indicate that philanthropy serves as a sort of covert mechanism of corporate political influence. Similarly, Edward Walker (2013a) found that when examining all corporate foundations linked to S&P 500 health firms, contributions from these foundations to charitable causes tended to increase significantly in the year following major corporate controversies, suggesting that philanthropy may play some role in managing firms' political threats and help to engage in corporate face-saving.

Similarly, patient advocacy organizations often serve as key political intermediaries linking firms and industry groups to policy makers, particularly when a health-related firm or industry is facing a major controversy or regulatory threat (on patient advocacy groups more generally, see Best 2012). Such was the case when pharmaceutical firm Mylan, engulfed in a major scandal over steep increases in the price of its EpiPens, partnered with the nonprofit Allergy and Asthma Network—alongside the American Latex Allergy Association, the Food Allergy and Anaphylaxis Connection Team, and the Asthma and Allergy Foundation of America—requesting that the government reimburse more of the cost of the treatment (Lipton and Abrams 2016). Similarly, there is evidence that pharmaceutical firms like Eli Lilly strategically fund patient advocacy groups such as the National Alliance on Mental Illness, which is known for its advocacy of drug-based treatments for mental illness in lieu of conventional psychotherapy (Rothman et al. 2011). Medical device manufacturer Medtronic is also known for its strategic donations to heart advocacy groups; the firm is a leader in implantable defibrillator technologies (E. Walker 2013a).

As is clear in many of the preceding cases, there is often a transactional relationship between nonprofits and the patrons who fund them to act as their intermediaries. The distinction between transactional and deeper relational organizing is further explored in the next section.

Mobilizing Versus Organizing: Questions of How Advocacy Nonprofits Engage Mass Participants

In much prior research that considers how advocacy organizations (and social movements more broadly) engage their mass participants, *mobilization* was used as a covering term for nearly all actions that mass activists take both backstage and in public view in order to advance a social cause or raise a grievance. However, more recent work has encouraged a clearer distinction between *mobilizing* as the specific public actions that activists take (e.g., protesting, petitioning, writing letters to legislators) and *organizing* as the backstage work of organization and infrastructure building that helps build long-term capacity for advocacy nonprofits (Han 2014; Brown 2016). Organizing, as understood here, is often underappreciated by both scholars and activists themselves, as such practices normally take place outside public view and do not draw the same attention as (especially more dramatic forms of) public protesting. Organizing is difficult to study, for instance, using the standard tool of protest event analysis—newspaper reports of public protests (see Earl et al. 2004). Newspaper reports typically capture only the mobilization and not the organization building that precedes and/or accompanies it. To study organizing and related internal processes sufficiently, scholars have instead turned to ethnography (e.g., Blee 2012), in-depth interviewing (Han 2014), field experiments (Han 2016), and internal surveys of activist leaders (Andrews et al. 2010). Collectively, these studies provide a much richer understanding of how organizing complements mobilizing, delivering certain benefits that mobilizing alone cannot.

In a groundbreaking study, Hahrie Han (2014) further developed the distinction between mobilizing and organizing (see also Weir and Ganz 1997), highlighting the more "transactional" nature of mobilizing compared to the more durable value of organizing. Consistent with the model of interfaith grassroots community organizing (Walker and McCarthy 2004, 2010; Wood 2002; Warren 2001), organizing practices of the type envisioned by Han (2014) result from the understanding that collective interests often emerge out of the participatory process (rather than playing a strong role a priori; see Munson 2008). In her 2014 study, Han observed that high-engagement organizational chapters—those that performed more long-term organizing and infrastructure building—were much more effective at building long-term engagement and developing grassroots leaders; low-engagement chapters focused on transactional mobilizing, casting a wide net to draw in individuals to take specific actions without meaningfully enrolling them as democratic participants.

The distinction between mobilizing and organizing has clear implications for whether advocacy nonprofits reinforce or overcome democratic deficits in modern societies. Nonprofit advocacy campaigns that focus only on transactional mobilizing run the risk of limiting their democratic potential. A substantial literature has shown that short-term participation does not build the participatory skills that result from meaningful long-term engagement (see Verba, Schlozman, and Brady 1995), nor does it reliably build greater collective capacity (Han 2014). Organizing efforts may also be more effective at bridging various social divides, whether around religion (Braunstein, Fulton, and Wood 2014), race/ethnicity, social class, or other political cleavages (for a review, see E. Walker and Stepick 2014).

There are numerous countervailing tendencies in contemporary advocacy nonprofits' organizing and mobilizing efforts. On the one hand, there is evidence that organizations focused on low-income communities such as Faith in Action (formerly known as the PICO National Network) are developing substantial campaigns focused on developing thick relational ties in local communities, and that these efforts are having political impacts (see Swarts 2011). We have also seen significant efforts since the 2016 election to develop substantial long-term organizing efforts, such as Indivisible and Organizing for Action, which are currently working on building long-term social infrastructures for electing female candidates (L. Putnam and Skocpol 2018). Yet alongside this trend toward intensive organizing is the appeal of large-scale communications technologies and social media, described in greater depth next, which facilitate the ease of short-term mobilization. The growth of these platforms has raised widespread concerns about transactional participation via "slacktivism" or "clicktivism" (e.g., Shulman 2009). These terms describe short-term actions that neither develop participants' civic skills nor influence policy, as legislators may discount prompted communications or those that appear to follow a standard script (E. Walker 2014). The ineffectiveness of these practices may, in part, be driving the present search for authenticity in social movement practices (E. Walker and Stepick forthcoming), as well as the interest in building up organizing over mobilizing.

The Changing Technological Environment

Technology is an increasingly prevalent part of citizens' daily lives, not only in social networks but also on the many online platforms for work, leisure, purchasing, and political participation in which users' experiences are shaped by algorithm-based decision making and data-driven analytic practices. A ubiquitous question across numerous fields concerns the extent to which technologies are replacing traditional ways of interacting. This trend may lead nonprofit advocacy groups to favor mobilizing over organizing in the contemporary context. Consistent with the private sector's embrace of social media and other Internet technologies, nonprofits are also now turning to online tools as means for generating attention for and participation in their causes (Asencio and Sun 2015; Guo and Saxton 2014; Kanter and Fine 2010; Young 2017; Bail, Brown, and Mann 2017). The use of such technologies, despite radically lowering the costs of collective action (Bennett and Segerberg 2013), has nonetheless increased anxiety about ICTs' democratic implications for nonprofit advocacy groups.

Scholars have identified numerous ways in which advocates and social movements more generally turn to technology tools to advance particular causes (e.g., Gainous and Wagner 2013). Despite popular commentator Malcolm Gladwell's (2010) prediction that the "revolution will not be tweeted," a hotbed of research has provided substantial evidence to the contrary, especially with respect to the Arab Spring and Turkey's Gezi Park uprising (see Tufekci 2017). Studies have shown that platforms like Facebook and Twitter facilitate the coordination of protest, with spikes in online activity corresponding to increases in protest turnout (Steinert-Threlkeld 2017; Tufekci and Wilson 2012).

Other work has highlighted how ICTs have constituted new kinds of social movement repertoires. Jennifer Earl, for instance, has extensively examined different forms of Internet activism, such as online-petition signing, email campaigns, and virtual sit-ins (Earl 2006; Earl and Kimport 2011; Earl and Schussman 2008). She and her colleagues identify a typology based on different advocacy purposes including information distribution, facilitating offline protest, generating participation online, and campaigning online (Earl et al. 2010). Similarly, Jeroen Van Laer and Peter Van Aelst (2010) categorize recent social movements involving technology as either "Internet-supported" or "Internet-based," arguing that social movements that are Internet-based such as online petitions and hacktivism—in which activists hack websites for political purposes—constitute entirely new forms of collective action. David Karpf (2012) documents the "MoveOn effect," a reference to the policy advocacy group MoveOn.org, describing the rise of new organizations designed around these emerging forms of political advocacy. In this research, scholars show that online technologies are not just channels through which activists communicate and protest is coordinated but also the actual sites of social movement activity. In a recent book, Karpf (2016) describes the practices of these organizations as "analytic activism" using technology and data to listen, monitor, and test alternative strategic approaches in political campaigns.

It is important to resist engaging in technological determinism by overstating the role of ICTs as a politically disruptive force (Howard and Hussain 2013). Such technologies have the potential to reduce participation costs, increase the scale of protest, and help coordinate action, particularly in repressive regimes (Earl et al. 2013; Little 2015). However, scholars are also adamant about pointing out that the traditional means of organizing identified in early social movement scholarship are still consequential for political change (Tufekci 2014). Furthermore, these scholars emphasize that access to such Internet technologies is still stratified, as there is still a meaningful digital divide between those who have easy and regular access to, and feel comfortable using, ICTs and those who do not (Ananny and Kreiss 2011).

Concurrent with this discourse is a discussion about the role of advocacy organizations in the context of such changes. Although research has shown that Internet technologies can serve as powerful organizing tools, studies on nonprofit advocacy and traditional social movement organizations' use of such technologies illustrate that such organizations largely use them for information distribution and generating attention (i.e., publicizing events and fund-raising unrelated to advocacy) rather than for mobilization (Guo and Saxton 2014; Stein 2009; Young 2017). This work is consistent both with Earl's findings (2006) that most online mobilization tactics are used by "warehouse sites" (e.g., Change. org or PetitionOnline.org) that are independent from any specific causes or social movement organizations and Karpf's argument (2012) about the rise of "activity-based" (i.e., user-generated and more open-ended) rather than "issue-based" forms of organizing.

This research points to an "organizational digital divide" (McNutt 2008:2), wherein organizations with limited resources and staff are unable to engage in online advocacy efforts. For instance, Lauri Goldkind (2014) found that younger organizations with the financial and human capital to support technology were more likely to engage in e-advocacy. Exploring nonprofits that serve immigrant communities, Heath Brown (2015) found that more than 50 percent of these organizations do not use social media; furthermore, adoption rates are lowest among Asian American and Middle Eastern American organizations. Brown argues that this institutional divide could translate to a broader digital divide, as social media serves as a primary means through which contemporary voters and activists access political, policy, and electoral information. Together, this research shows that the inequalities permeating organizational structures become reflected in access to these advanced social movement repertoires.

Such changes suggest, at the very least, a division of labor between the new "warehouse" (Earl 2006) or "netroots" (i.e., online-organized; Karpf 2012) organizations and traditional advocacy organizations such that they take on responsibility for different stages of social movement processes. Research has indicated that the newer, online organizational forms may be more useful in the earlier stages, coordinating otherwise disparate activists at scale to generate enough disruption to bring awareness to a cause. The latter organizations, on the other hand, through both traditional means of organizing and the use of technology, may be more effective in the later stages of advocacy, facilitating offline mobilization and sustaining the long-term ties needed to produce more durable social change (Earl 2015).

Conclusions

Nonprofit advocacy organizations play a critical role in American democracy. There are many reasons to hold out the Tocquevillian ([1835] 2003) hope that such associations can continue to serve as a source of voice for underrepresented communities, a force for more equitable representation, and as a means toward broader civic and political cohesion. They may, in the longstanding tradition of research on nonprofits, also help compensate for the problems that emerge from the limitations of government programs and failures of the marketplace.

At the same time, however, a number of critical challenges to advocacy associations may limit their democratic benefits. Shifting membership structures may not as effectively enroll participants in meaningful ways, opting instead for more distant and transactional forms of engagement. Pressures from third-party monitors may incentivize nonprofits to do less organizing and more service provision. Broader social inequalities may encourage nonprofit advocacy groups to engage in supply-side recruitment and resource development strategies that further privilege the most educated and well-resourced. Advocacy organizations may increasingly be deployed as strategic intermediaries to advance the interests of elite patrons or capitalist firms or industries. As a consequence of these changes, advocacy groups may favor transactional mobilizing over deeper and more long-term forms of organizing and movement infrastructure building. Similarly, transitions linked to the rising use of ICTs may lower advocacy groups' costs of collective action yet facilitate forms of engagement that are less durable and less capable of building broader support.

We are left with a mixed picture of the potential for nonprofit advocates to promote broader democratization in the modern era. We may be reaching a point in which the nonprofit field is relatively saturated without an accompanying growth of civic engagement. Although contemporary society may valorize public engagement, the dominant forms of participation may reinforce tendencies that are either negative or neutral toward democracy. The challenge for twenty-first-century advocacy nonprofits is to find novel strategies for harnessing resources, technologies, social networks, alliances, and broader cultural supports to overcome the significant constraints they face today in promoting a more democratic society.

ADVOCATING FOR WHAT?

The Nonprofit Press and Models of the Public

Mike Ananny

IT MAY SEEM STRANGE TO PLACE a chapter on journalism in a handbook section focused on advocacy. Especially in American press traditions—steeped in tropes of objectivity, the disinterested pursuit of truth, and a faith in journalism's ability to separate facts and values—journalists are supposed to be anything *but* advocates. In the popular imagination and many journalists' self-conceptions, the press is independent. It doesn't advocate for anything. It simply investigates, observes, describes, and disseminates information, disclaiming investment in any particular outcome.

There are at least three problems with this narrative. First, journalists *do* have interests. Publishers, editors, and reporters carry with them their own ideas about what's right and wrong, what counts as good evidence, and what's relevant and newsworthy. Decades of scholarship in communication and sociology have traced the rituals, routines, habits, and assumptions driving journalism. Second, the press is never truly independent. Historically, it has always been intertwined with market expectations, government sources, editorial boards, audience demands, new technologies, and cultural norms. Some journalists and armchair political theorists may celebrate the press as a disinterested arbiter of timeless notions of truth, but research and journalists' own self-reflections suggest otherwise. Press freedom has always been a reflection of each era's social, political, economic, and technological forces. At different times in history, the press has been closer to or further away from markets, states, audiences, and technologies, but the press has never been a completely autonomous institution. Finally, the press *can* advocate for something: the public. If the idealized press is interested in anything, it is the public interest: issues and challenges that need to be understood and acted on collectively, separate from whatever markets and states might say. In eras of deep partisan division, technological upheaval, and economic crisis, it may sound quaint to assert this kind of public interest, but if the press should advocate for anything, it is common goods and a civic life beyond whatever a given era commodifies or a particular government defines as a state interest (Ananny 2018).

Exactly *how* the press defines and pursues this public interest is a perennial debate. What motivates journalists, how they act, where news circulates, which outcomes journalism produces, and how owners, audiences, and states direct their resources—these all constantly shift. Depending on your perspective, they add up to a press that is broken or well tuned. But historical and structural patterns can help us better understand *how* each era's press advocates, and how notions of the public interest both emerge from and challenge assumptions about press advocacy. This chapter considers how one domain of journalism—the nonprofit press—advocates for the public interest, by navigating and often explicitly opposing the commercial, market-driven forces that dominate American journalism. Indeed, the continued existence of the nonprofit press shows that free markets are not the same thing as a free press. The nonprofit press imagines—and advocates for—its own ideal of press freedom, its own image of the public interest.

In his foundational study of media concentration and the influence of ownership, C. Edwin Baker (2007) argued that different democracies need different types of media. This deceptively simple claim questioned the idea that the media are a single institutional entity serving a shared and uniform ideal of democracy. It reframed the question of the media–democracy relationship as a two-sided conversation between organizational and institutional forces that configure the media—who owns the media, how journalists practice, which stories emerge, how audiences interpret and act on the news—and normative evaluations of the self-governance that such forces make possible. In characterizing both ideals of democracy and operations of the media as contingent and contestable, Baker highlights the need to consider simultaneously two dimensions of the press: (1) the institutional dynamics that give rise to news production, circulation, and interpretation, and (2) the normative criteria by which to judge those dynamics, take stock of their public significance, and potentially demand new configurations of the press and democracy.

Journalism scholars tend to organize the study of news into three broad themes. The first focuses on the production of news:

- the often unstated, institutionally situated nature of journalistic practices and values, and journalists' roles as gatekeepers of what qualifies as newsworthy people, places, and events;
- the acquisition of skills and attitudes through curricula, appeals to public service, and norms of professionalization; the role of organizational form, ownership models, and labor markets in determining which events and topics are covered and defined as news; and
- the regulatory forces and legal regimes that constrain and sanction journalists and influence their senses of professional autonomy both real and imagined (Berkowitz 1992; Boczkowski 2009; Carlson 2015a; Christin forthcoming; Gans 1979; Schudson 2000; Tuchman 1978).

The second broad area of scholarship focuses on audiences' relationships to news:

- how news helps people learn about people and events, change or retrench their opinions, and make and defend identities, and how it drives some actions over others;
- differences among news audiences, with some consumers perceived as more commercially or politically valuable than others;

- advertisers' roles as intermediaries between journalists and audiences, with the power to influence the kind of news journalists see as commercially viable and publishers' obligations to distinguish between the kind of news they want to produce and the kind of news advertisers want to support; and
- increasingly, the role that "active audiences" and platform intermediaries play in news: interpreting news differently, driving aspects of news production and circulation, and demanding from journalists and advertisers alike changes aligned with their (dis)pleasure with the news landscapes that have been created for them (Bell and Owen 2017; Braun and Gillespie 2011; Napoli 2011; Prior 2007; Stroud 2011; Wahl-Jorgensen 2007).

Finally, recognizing that the press is the only commercial institutional explicitly mentioned in many constitutions, journalism scholarship asks normative questions about the following:

- the role that journalism and news plays—or *should* play—in creating the imagined communities of democratic societies;
- the ideological orientations of supposedly autonomous journalists with the power to shape news narratives;
- the kinds of issues that journalists have historically seen as core or peripheral to their democratic roles, and the kinds of people, places, or events that are seen as conventional versus taboo; and
- the underlying conceptions of democracy, freedom, and speech that drive many of the press's technological infrastructures, regulatory and legal regimes, and professional cultures (Ananny 2018; Anderson 1983; Baker 1998; Christians et al. 2009; Curran and Seaton 2009; Zelizer 2017).

How might we trace through nonprofit news the relationships between journalism's practices, audiences' relationships to news, and the press's institutional power to envision and instrumentally construct self-governing collectives? How do these forces appear in historical and contemporary approaches to press funding, with particular focus on how nonprofit news is supported? Most broadly, how do different types of publics arise from different types of nonprofit funding models?

This chapter offers ways to think about these questions. I suggest that although they have roots in longstanding sociologies of journalism and the news, these questions can be posed anew for a contemporary era in which the press lives not in any single set of news organizations, professional communities, or information genres; rather, it is distributed across a fragmented, loosely coordinated set of sociotechnical conditions that structure news production, circulation, and interpretation. These conditions—which I call the "networked press"—depend not only on journalistic judgment and editorial standards but also on increasingly intertwined relationships with technology companies, algorithmic processes, and the somewhat limited and unstable patterns of online audiences.

In this chapter, I focus on how the networked press is funded and argue that its funding dynamics lead to different types of publics. After historically situating networked press funding dynamics, I sketch a typology that relates these dynamics to types of publics and conclude with some thoughts on how to further investigate the normative patterns of public making that underlie the networked press. Recalling my earlier assertion that the nonprofit press advocates for a particular vision of the public interest and Baker's call to think about how different types of democracy need different types of media, I show how the nonprofit press both depends on and gives rise to particular types of publics.

U.S. Journalism's Public Responsibilities as Organizational Form and Ownership

U.S. news organizations' understandings of their public responsibilities have always been intertwined with their organizational forms and ownership models. Starting in the Revolutionary War era, state actors and government officials openly sponsored particular printers. These patron-backed printers dominated markets with explicitly partisan messages that made no pretense of editorial fairness, content neutrality, or what would eventually be called journalistic objectivity. Newspapers were party instruments; the jobs of writer, editor, and publisher were explicitly combined (the role of reporter not yet having been invented); and publication owners were rewarded with generous government contracts precisely because they could be relied on to print material that helped party interests (John 1998, 2012; Schudson 1998).

In the early years of the Republic, before the idea of press freedom had undergone judicial review, state officials routinely vetted printers' publications, speech perceived as treasonous was banned, and the government's censorship power was codified in legislation (although the Alien and Sedition Acts were subsequently overturned) (Halperin 2016). The modern notion of press freedom did not yet exist in principle, let alone practice. The institutional press was synonymous with the printing and distribution of publishers' opinions that often simply echoed those of political parties.

Although this partisan-fueled, state-funded, "party press" era of U.S. news continued through the nineteenth century, it gradually shifted form. Newspapers began to earn revenue through a mix of advertising revenue, newsstand sales, subscriptions, and political patronage. The foundations of the "penny press" era were laid in the 1840s—spurred on by a mix of low-cost printing, population growth, increased literacy rates in multiple languages, and larger urban populations (Schiller 1979; Schudson 1978)—yet many newspapers kept their political affiliations and sponsorships. By 1870, "Republican papers accounted for 54% of all metropolitan dailies and gathered 43% of the total circulation in these cities. Democratic papers comprised 33% of daily newspapers and 31% of circulation" (Hamilton 2006:37). However, as marketplace models rewarded newspapers that appealed to broader audiences and increasingly apolitical advertisers, journalistic independence emerged not from ideals but economic necessity. Rather than functioning as party mouthpieces, publishers like Joseph Pulitzer and William Randolph Hearst discovered that they could refashion newspapers into vehicles for their own images of the public, using the social, technological, and economic underpinnings of the penny press to engage in a kind of editorial trade-off or utilitarian moralism. They could on one hand cheaply produce apolitical news that audiences wanted to read and advertisers wanted to sponsor (murders, love affairs, scandals) with images that attracted attention (Barnhurst and Nerone 2001), and on the other use the proceeds to fund the journalism that *they* wanted to produce—that they thought audiences *needed* to be publics. The role of the reporter and the genre of the interview were invented as ways for news organizations to show their audiences and advertising markets that the news was not coming from partisan sponsorship or publishers with agendas but from independent, fact-driven research about the societies within which audiences lived (Schudson 1995). A commercial press emerged from this idea that news was about *people's* lives and that newspapers should reflect what printers, journalists, and publishers understood to be *public* interests (Nerone 2015). The foundations of the contemporary press thus began to appear: by 1900, "independent newspapers accounted for 47% of metropolitan dailies" (Hamilton 2006:38). Muckrakers and investigative reporters like Ida B. Wells, Upton Sinclair, and Nellie Bly mixed social justice missions with gripping narrative styles (Protess et al. 1991). In 1922, Walter Lippmann published his seminal book *Public Opinion*, in which he lamented how easily the public could be manipulated, coined the word *stereotype*, and called for a "scientization of journalism" (Hallin 1985). Lippmann's vision focused the press on independently reporting objective, verifiable facts that could fight government censorship, public relations spin, market subservience, and audiences' tendencies toward passionate, moblike rule (Butsch 2008). Indeed, this era saw the beginning of modern journalism's belief that both its financial health and its moral mission lie in the belief of objectivity as "a faith in 'facts,' and distrust of 'values' and a commitment to their segregation" (Schudson 1978:6).

In a short period of time, the press showed how it could earn financial support not only through state sponsorship and partisan control but also through a variety of alternative means: commercial models, the patronage of wealthy individuals, social justice appeals, engaging and sensationalist narratives, and a commitment to professionalized objectivity. The twentieth century would see an attendant growth of ownership models with commensurate and diverse understandings of editorial judgment and public service. For example, private news companies headed by families (the most common type of news organizations) were often closely affiliated with the public priorities of elite policy makers and industry leaders. Publicly traded companies, in contrast, had fiduciary responsibilities to stock owners and marketplace metrics of success. Foundation-funded trusts and charities supported both short-term reporting projects and long-term institutional investments that aligned with their strategic interests. Nonprofit news corporations aimed for marketplace success, not to pay dividends or build financial dominance but rather for the purpose of reinvesting into coverage and attracting journalists driven by social justice missions. Employee-owned cooperatives arose to give journalists more control over not only their daily work routines and editorial decisions but also what Murdock (1982:122) calls the "allocative" decisions about policy, strategy, hiring, and financing that structure the conditions under which journalists work (Bezanson 2003; Bradlee 1975; Chomsky 2006; Graham 1998; Levy and Picard 2012; Picard and van Weezel 2008; Villalonga and Amit 2006). Indeed, the dominant model of press freedom began to be seen as journalism's ability, through its financial and ownership models, to separate itself from anything that interfered with *its* vision of public life.

As Baker suggested, different visions of public life required different types of media—and thus different types of press freedom (Ananny 2018). By the 1920s, many of the economic dimensions of contemporary debates over press freedom and public life had become evident. Several disparate perspectives and motivations that arose in this period persist today. For example, if journalists think that healthy public life requires partisan contests and that their mission is to surface different political positions, they may see anything that interferes with the partisan press as an attack on (their version of) press freedom. If they think that a free press is akin to free markets, they may see journalism's commercial successes and failures as indicative of the press's ability to support a market-place of ideas. If journalists eschew partisanship and commercialism in favor of social justice missions, they may perceive a need for financial investments from civil society actors (e.g., foundations and wealthy patrons) who share their progressive agendas and can insulate them from parties and markets. If they see audience preferences and attention economies as their primary channels, they will seek access to the media and genres that will attract attention and render compelling narratives (e.g., akin to the images, stunts, and investigations that helped nineteenth-century news earn mass appeal). Lastly, if they see their profession grounded in objectivity, they will strive for separation from parties, audiences, markets, social agendas, and sensationalism—a distance from the worlds they report on that lets them separate facts and values.

This latter focus on distancing journalists from the social worlds they aimed to describe manifested throughout the twentieth century in a set of increasingly intricate "rituals of objectivity" (Tuchman 1978). These practices rested on the belief that "the news" existed independent of journalists' reporting. "Good journalism" (Gardner, Csikszentmihalyi, and Damon 2002) manifested as journalists' ability to accurately report the words of "bureaucratically credible sources" stationed at predictable locations (Tuchman 1978). They reported on scientific public opinion polls (Herbst 1995) and analyzed documents from official sources (Neff 2015). They scoped their stories within newspapers' thematic sections and avoided thinking too much about a large and abstract public they could never directly know (Darnton 1975). They subtly tried to reflect the wishes of their publishers (Beam 1993; Chomsky 2006; Wagner and Collins 2014) while claiming independence to choose their sources and defend their ledes (Murdock 1977). They learned how to inflect their writing with their own perspectives through subtle word choices that showed so-phisticated readers that they were more than simply disinterested scribes (Glasser and Ettema 1993; Lipari 1996). Professional journalists tried to be both deeply embedded within social worlds and independent of them.

By the late twentieth century, several perennial questions of the press and press freedom had been posed: How is a news organization's image and execution of its public mission influenced by its owners? How does its organizational form influence how it understands its audience? Where does its revenue come from and how does this influence news pro-duction and circulation?

New Nonprofit Actors Broaden Journalism's
Institutional Field and Challenge Public Dynamics

This history has often been told though studies of individual news organizations, particu-lar publishers, or case studies of events. Scholars traced the behaviors of canonical, often predictable sources of news work, with little appreciation for how journalism operates as an *institution* whose "loosely coupled arrays of standardized elements" (DiMaggio and Powell 1991:14) combine to both reveal and shape the conditions under which news is produced, circulated, and interpreted. A full review of these neo-institutional and field-based understandings of journalism is beyond the scope of this chapter, but more recent scholars have conceptualized contemporary journalism not as a monolithic practice but as manifold field-level, multi-organizational processes that live across a set of human and computational actors that, together, create news and its public meanings (Ananny 2014; Benson 2006; Benson and Neveu 2005; Boczkowski 2004; Carlson 2015a).

This field increasingly contains a distinct space of *nonprofit* journalism. It seems to have distinct normative logics that explicitly reject the commercial nature of mainstream journalism. These logics appear not only in how "nonprofit journalists" (Konieczna and Powers 2017) work but also in a new array of nonprofit and foundation-funded organizations that have arisen to support nonprofit news production (Benson 2017). Their goals are premised on assumptions about how previous news markets have failed journalists, audiences, and ideals of democratic self-governance (Konieczna 2018).

This field is beginning to take stable shape, as described in Konieczna (2018) and summarized in Table 22.1's overview of a 2018 study of the U.S. nonprofit journalism field by the Institute for Nonprofit News (McLellan and Holcomb 2018).[1]

Although this snapshot of the field has methodological limitations—self-reports, no longitudinal picture, a lack of cross-tab information that would provide greater specificity—it sketches dimensions along which the field is progressing. Nonprofit news organizations tend to focus on one or two topics, often centered on investigative projects that they see as core to a public interest mission. Nonprofit news organizations are also relatively young, with the median organization eight years old and nearly half the organizations founded between 2009 and 2011. Foundations provide the bulk of revenue to nonprofit news organizations, with most of this money used for editorial expenses. Most staff are white, suggesting that the field of nonprofit news lacks racial and ethnic diversity, much like its commercial, for-profit counterparts (American Society of Newspaper Editors 2017). Finally, unlike their for-profit counterparts—which have increasingly moved audience engagement to social media platforms and discontinued their site comments—nonprofit news organizations seem to keep audiences close by hosting comments and fund-raising through crowdsourcing campaigns on their own websites, running community events and meetings, and holding online chats.

Nonprofit news organizations rely heavily on foundations and are often offshoots of other nonprofit organizations. The Omidyar Foundation, the Sandler Family Foundation, the Kaiser Family Foundation, the Nieman Foundation, and the Columbia Journalism School have all founded news organizations explicitly designed to be freer from commercial revenue pressures than for-profit counterparts. They claim that their funding models, ownership structures, and organizational forms let them pursue public missions and make editorial judgments that are more flexible and responsive to fast-changing conditions of online news. Similarly, though not publishers per se, nonprofit research organizations like the Institute for Nonprofit News, the Pew Research Center, the Knight Foundation, the Reynolds Journalism Institute, and Columbia's Tow Center for Digital Journalism and Brown Institute for Media Innovation have arisen as powerful nonprofit journalistic actors. They fund reporting projects, develop new experimental digital tools, define best practices, disseminate research, sponsor academics, convene public forums, publicly

Table 22.1   Self-stated dimensions of nonprofit news organizations

Primary mission			
Investigative journalism (39%)	Explanatory/analysis journalism (23%)	News and events (19%)	Mix (19%)

Geography of coverage focus				
State (33%)	National (25%)	Local (23%)	Regional (10%)	Global (9%)

Publishing frequencies		
Daily (56%)	Weekly (27%)	Less than weekly (17%)

Topics covered						
Government policy (74%)	Environment (66%)	Government oversight/ watchdog (66%)	Politics (65%)	Education/ schools (61%)	Social justice/ inequality (58%)	Crime and justice (53%)

Total revenue (in US$, 2017)				
< $250,000 (74%)	$250,000–$500,000 (20%)	$500,000– $1 million (16%)	$1 million– $2 million (17%)	> $2 million (20%)

Revenue diversity			
4 or more sources (34%)	2 sources (25%)	3 sources (24%)	1 source (17%)

Revenue streams				
Foundations (57%)	Individual giving and memberships (33%)	Events (3%)	Advertising/sponsorship (3%)	Other (4%)

Operating expenses (% of total nonprofit spending on. . .)			
Editorial (67%)	Administration (16%)	Revenue generation (10%)	Technology (6%)

Staff race/ethnicity (% of staff who identify as . . .)				
White (73%)	Asian (9%)	Hispanic (8%)	Black (7%)	Other (3%)

Audience engagement (% of organizations that use . . .)									
Comments (84%)	Crowd- sourcing (47%)	Events (47%)	Tip line (42%)	Meetings (40%)	Opinion pages (32%)	Live online chats (23%)	Other (23%)	Engagement platforms (14%)	Ombudsman/ public editor (2%)

Source: Adapted from McLellan and Holcomb 2018.

pressure both news organizations and technology companies, and heavily influence what it means to be a public, mission-driven news organization (Lewis 2011).

The nonprofit journalism space is also characterized by new ways of earning revenue that mix philanthropic, crowdfunded, and membership-supported funds, often blurring lines between for-profit and nonprofit publishing. For example, the *New York Times* recently created a new philanthropic division to allow it to partner with foundations and universities (*New York Times* 2017). For-profit news organizations Vox and Vice News regularly partner with nonprofits ProPublica and Marshall Project to gain access to original, high-quality content that they believe their commercial readers want but would not otherwise encounter (Owen 2017). Further, many local news organizations switch between nonprofit and for-profit status (Schmidt 2018; Wang 2016) as they experiment with implementing paywalls, crowdfunding resources for particular stories, renaming subscribers as "members," and otherwise trying to identify business models that let them be revenue neutral (Aitamurto 2016; Ananny and Bighash 2016; Lee 2017). Indeed, some confusion over official status and form has played out in prolonged IRS deliberations over how to determine the tax-exempt status of news organizations with shifting missions and business models (Chittum 2011; Nonprofit Media Working Group 2013).

It is increasingly hard to talk about *nonprofit news* as a static or stable category neatly defined by an official organizational form or consistent ownership model. Rather, the term seems to have a broader meaning, indicating a changeable organizational status, invoked as a rhetorical device used to attract revenue, signal editorial independence, and serve as the basis for partnering with a variety of institutional actors. Understanding the field of nonprofit news requires investigating not only the actions of not-for-profit publishers but also the influence of a mix of patrons, publishers, platforms, and discourses that together portray varied images of public service, accountability, and participation.

"We're Not a Media Company": How New Technological Actors Help Create the Networked Press and Complicate Its Funding

The nonprofit news sector should thus be understood not only in terms of ownership control and organizational form but also in light of institutional and normative forces jockeying for public power, professional legitimacy, and financial security amid a set of private, for-profit commercially driven media technology platforms that increasingly dominate the conditions under which news circulates (Bell and Owen 2017; Chadwick 2013; Deuze and Witschge 2017; Nielsen and Ganter 2017). Indeed, the earlier reconceptualization of journalism beyond the domain of single organizations and field-level actors is now further complicated by technology companies, many of whom do not see themselves as media companies and do not want to become media companies. Facebook, for example, has repeatedly insisted that it makes technology, not media (Napoli and Caplan 2017). Despite their reluctance to self-identify as media entities, technology companies are creating with news organizations a field of journalism that is distributed across journalists, advertisers, and state regulators, and increasingly shaped by the influence of algorithm makers, data providers, and artificial intelligence creators.

This field—inhabited by technology companies like Facebook, Google, Twitter, and Amazon—shows itself not only in journalists' practices and media distribution channels but also in subtler *infrastructural* dynamics. The "networked press" is an often invisible and always intertwined set of sociotechnical structures that determine the conditions under which news is produced, circulated, and interpreted (Ananny 2018). News audiences increasingly live on social media platforms; proprietary algorithmic systems surface some news over others; and user interface designs control how audience members can see, react to, share, and comment on news. Journalists see social network sites not only as publishing channels but as beats in themselves that are worthy of coverage. Moreover, most online news advertising flows through marketplaces that are almost completely controlled by Google and Facebook. The very definition of *journalist* is changing as increasingly hybrid labor markets emerge for technology "product managers" who can move seamlessly between news organizations and technology companies, shifting between human–computer interaction design and editorial judgment. Just as the press is no longer easily separable into for-profit or nonprofit sectors, it is also increasingly difficult to talk about the press as something that lives only or even mostly within news organizations. The power of technology companies to influence news production, distribution, and sensemaking must be acknowledged.

Amid these dynamics, news organizations seem to be trying to *use* nonprofit status as a tool for experimentation. This status may function as a potential means toward economic stability among fickle advertising dynamics, as a cultural marker of independence from for-profit technology companies, or an existential, ideological response to an increasingly commercialized, advertising-driven publishing space—an arena that is dominated by actors who, despite their power, do not see themselves as media companies with editorial missions or public responsibilities. For analysts concerned with how organizational forms and ownership structures relate to the press's public mission, empirical and normative challenges have shifted; they now require seeing "the press" as a relational, *networked* object of study distributed across sociotechnical infrastructures.

The networked press is simultaneously instrumental and symbolic. It lives in messy, intertwined dynamics between technologists and journalists vying for control over powerful, privately controlled communication infrastructures. It also exists as an ideal—an autonomous institution imagined as a counter to mis- and disinformation, serving as the guarantor of collective, self-determining, democratic publics.

Accordingly, we are at an empirical and normative crossroads. We need to examine the sociotechnical dynamics underpinning the funding of the networked press, including the increasingly blurred lines between for- and nonprofit dimensions. We also need to ask what *kind* of publics such dynamics assume and create. Recalling Baker's argument that different democracies need different media, how do different kinds of publics emerge from different types of networked press funding dynamics, especially those playing out in the space between for- and nonprofit journalism?

Different Funding Makes Different Publics

Expanding on earlier work on networked press funding dynamics (Ananny 2018), this section sketches out questions for moments when networked press funding dynamics meet ideals of the public. Specifically, based on an analysis of seven years of trade press discourse (2010–2016) about how the networked press funds itself—what Matt Carlson (2015b) calls the "metajournalistic discourse" that shows how journalism thinks about its institutional dynamics—I first identify seven dimensions of networked press funding. I then propose a set of questions that scholars of both journalism and the nonprofit sector might ask about how funding connects to publics. Although the literature on publics is expansive and broader than what can be discussed here,[2] I briefly discuss eight ideals of the public to support this discussion.

Dimensions of Networked Press Funding

- **Paywalls.** A paywall is a virtual "barrier between an internet user and a news organization's online content" (Pickard and Williams 2014:195) that can be crossed only by paying money. Some paywalls are always in place, making content available only to subscribers, while others come into effect after users have exceeded the number of articles to which the news organization allows free access.

- **Commodified readers.** News organizations often sell to advertisers and marketing firms the data they collect on readers' demographic details and Internet patterns. They also model readers in categories that signal to advertisers their values as consumers or ask readers to answer survey questions in exchange for access to stories. Often without informed consent, readers are commodified into revenue sources for companies other than news organizations. Readers do not overtly pay for the news they consume—it appears to be "free"—but their seemingly private behavioral patterns and demographic characterizations are modeled and sold by both news organizations and technology companies.

- **Crowdfunding.** Conceptualizing readers as investors, some news organizations raise money from site visitors, asking them to sponsor stories in progress, to support free-lancers who make appealing pitches, and to provide feedback on potential coverage by pledging support for topics and coverage areas. Although some news-specific crowdfunding sites have appeared, news organizations and freelance journalists also use all-purpose crowdfunding sites like GoFundMe.com and Kickstarter.com, tailoring their marketing and campaigns to those platforms (Jian and Shin 2015; Jian and Usher 2014).

- **Commodified expertise.** Some news organizations commodify their journalists' labor and create price-discriminated access to their products. For example, they earn revenue by selling access to member-only events, to raw data that their journalists have gathered and/or vetted, and to tiered levels of content through application programming interfaces. News organizations increasingly see themselves as curators of people, data, legitimacy, and interpretation, selling access to this trusted expertise (ProPublica n.d.).

- **Sponsored content.** Variously called native advertising, paid content, or promoted stories, some news organizations explicitly mix commercial and editorial content, creating advertisements that look like stories and subcontracting out staff to advertisers willing to buy journalistically produced marketing materials. Such blurring appears in hybrid genres—ads that look like stories and vice versa—and shared labor pools between advertising and editorial departments (Wojdynski 2016).

- **Organizational partnerships.** Several news organizations create strategic alliances with other news organizations and technology companies, agreeing to share sourcing and credit, creating platform-specific versions of stories, exclusively sequestering some news within platform-created mobile apps and data formats, and training staff on how best to prepare stories for particular platforms. The terms of such partnership are usually proprietary secrets, but news organizations make such deals as ways to share labor, data, online traffic, or privileged positions within algorithmically determined news feeds (Center for Collaborative Media 2018; Stonbely 2017).

- **Research sponsorship.** Although not publishers per se, some journalism researchers—both independent think tanks and university academics—enter into strategic partnerships with technology companies, accept sponsorship from platform companies, and receive funding from foundations, all of which have programmatic interests in better understanding the networked press.

Each of these dimensions is relevant to the practices of a range of news organizations and technology companies, and many publishers and platforms engage in more than one of the strategies described. Together, these dimensions illustrate a diversity of revenue dynamics used by both for-profit and nonprofit news organizations.

Ideals of the Public

Since publics are constructed through complex and intertwined normative, sociological, cultural, and technological forces—that is, they are always made, never found—it becomes evident that different publics are possible, depending on different communicative conditions. Though the list is not exhaustive, the following ideal types of publics often appear as assumptions or goals of the networked press.

- **Deliberation and consensus-based.** Most closely aligned with Jürgen Habermas's notion of the public sphere (Habermas 1989), this type of public privileges the rational, information-based exchange of private perspectives among equal, private individuals who discover public consensus on topics of shared interest through deliberation that endures until decisions are made.
- **Participatory social good.** Grounded in an ideal of civic life as experiencing and sharing a wide variety of cultural perspectives through engagement with a diverse set of people, social positions, media practices, and communicative settings, this model shapes the public good through mutual exchange and experimentation with perspective taking.
- **Aggregated opinions.** Driven by the development of techniques for modeling, sampling, and representing social groups through individual surveys and statistical methods, this image of the public rationalizes people and public opinion into demographic and quantitative patterns (Salmon and Glasser 1995).
- **Shared consequences.** Often associated with John Dewey (1954) and American pragmatism, this type of public arises from the discovery of social conditions and material impacts that individuals cannot escape, with the idea of "public" emerging only when people see which aspects of their lives are inextricably linked.
- **Sustained differences.** Eschewing the ideal of consensus or shared identity, this type of public aims to be a "decentered" space inhabited by people of different languages, identities, and ideological positions who can speak "across their difference" while remaining accountable to each other (Young 2000:107).
- **Agonism and contestation.** Expanding further on the scope of diversity, this type of public explicitly rejects a goal of consensus, deliberation, or even mutual acceptance of difference; instead it calls for a "sphere of contestation where different hegemonic political projects can be confronted" (Mouffe 2005:3–4).
- **Enclaves.** Recognizing the harm that visibility can do to historically disempowered groups who need time and space to discover their shared conditions and plan for resistance against dominant social forces, this public calls for private communication

within and among groups that need "to survive and avoid sanctions, while internally producing lively debate and planning" (Squires 2002:448).

- **Recursive.** Inspired by observations of hacking cultures concerned with maintaining the technological ability to control the conditions under which they communicate and convene (Kelty 2008), this public is concerned with having the power to define and manage itself, according to the associative criteria it chooses.

In Table 22.2, I present critical questions at the intersections of funding instruments and public types. Though it is certainly not comprehensive in light of the myriad questions that could be asked—nor does it indicate which questions may be more or less important—the table illustrates how, for any given approach to funding, key questions can be posed around whether, or how, particular publics can emerge from that support.

Starting with a funding instrument, the chart can be read as follows: *If this approach to funding is taken, and this type of public is desired, then this question needs to be addressed.*

In terms of advocacy, the press is constantly struggling with whether to represent or amplify their own interests and those of others, or to eschew all interests and retreat into objectivity and neutrality, letting events and sources guide their storytelling. Advocacy begins to look complicated.

Sometimes, journalists openly champion interests and values that a given era defines as obviously right and worthy of public mobilization. Though people may differ about policy interventions and remedies, it is largely uncontroversial for journalists to investigate and write about the eradication of poverty, disease, and various social inequalities. Journalists may not get the money and time they need from their editors to pursue the topics in great depth, but few publishers would see a story pitch on links between structural racism and health outcomes as fringe or unprofessional advocacy. This is what James S. Ettema and Theodore L. Glasser (1998) mean when they describe most investigative reporting as fundamentally conservative. Though many investigative journalists courageously pursue stories that challenge power and put themselves at risk, they follow largely uncontroversial commonsense assumptions about what is right and wrong, what is worth advocating for, and what mainstream norms champion. No one questions the values of an investigative reporter exposing government fraud or unjust incarceration; such things are plainly wrong. But when Ida B. Wells wrote her exposés of lynching cultures in the U.S. South, she was criticized by both politicians and journalists for attacking the region's historical traditions and pursuing her *own* ethical interests, not broadly shared values. And when, in his investigative novel *The Jungle*, Upton Sinclair advocated for labor rights by uncovering the unsafe working conditions in meat-packing plants, public officials responded by reforming the plants' unsanitary food preparation practices; his interests in workers' unsafe environments and long hours were seen as his personal missions, not widely shared calls to action.

The press usually advocates in ways that people expect. Journalists resist taboo, controversial topics and instead largely work within what Daniel C. Hallin (1986) calls the "sphere of legitimate controversy." This is the sphere where debate is encouraged, where healthy democratic discourse is thought to live. But debate and discourse are limited to perspectives and opinions that are *already* seen as acceptable, that align with other people's

Table 22.2 Sample critical questions at the intersection of networked press funding dimensions and types of publics

Funded by . . .	Publics as . . .							
	Deliberation and consensus	*Participatory social goods*	*Aggregated opinions*	*Shared consequences*	*Sustained differences*	*Agonism and contestation*	*Enclaves*	*Recursive*
Paywalls	Is the information required for full argumentation available to all, regardless of cost?	Can a rich range of diverse participants afford access to news?	Do invitations to participate in and see the results polls and surveys require payment?	How does the ability to pay for news impact surfacing shared conditions?	How is an ability to pay for news correlated with kinds of difference?	Can challengers of entrenched power afford the news that strong challenges need?	Can disempowered groups earn revenue from private forums?	How are paywalls configured and changed, and who has power to do so?
Commodified readers	How can readers be commercially targeted while ignoring their identities?	Are readers with low commercial value less likely to participate?	How can opinions of those without commercial value motivate surveys and polls?	How can shared experiences be reconciled with personalized marketing?	How do online ad systems variously ignore or leverage personal differences?	Can power challenges come from those with low commercial value?	Can people be modeled and targeted without harming their privacy?	What signals are used to surveil users and value their information?
Crowdfunding	How do fund-raising and marketing campaigns align with rational debate?	Are some participants more or less accessible through different crowdfunding campaigns?	What kind of populations and issues are surveyed through crowdfunding?	Are revenues earned and shared among impacted groups?	Can diversity be supported by crowdfunding, or do such campaigns need uniform appeal?	Are some types of power difficult to challenge in highly visible participatory marketing?	How do public campaigns for financial support impact the need for privacy?	How available is knowledge about crowdfunding systems and success metrics?

Commodified expertise	Can commercialized data and labor be uninvested in outcomes?	Do self-valuations of labor and data create different participation styles?	How do commercially valued data drive some aggregates over others?	Do news data and labor surface a range of shared consequences?	Can differences surface that lack support from commodified data or labor?	How financially valuable are controversial data sets and labor?	Can enclaves influence the types of data and labor that are seen as valuable?	Can news organizations create and value new forms of labor?
Sponsored content	Can advertisers make sustained, long-term investments in highly rational debate?	Are audiences equally cognizant of differences between editorial and sponsored content?	Do advertisers sponsor polls/surveys, and how widespread is knowledge of the sponsorship?	Can shared social conditions appear that have little commercial value or individual appeal?	How can differences other than those with commercial appeal be supported?	Will advertisers sponsor controversial topics and commercial challenges?	Is a group's commercial value limited because of its need for privacy and lack of power?	Can people distinguish between sponsored and unsponsored content?
Organizational partnerships	Are partnership terms arrived at equitably and transparently?	Can groups other than partner constituents participate?	How do partners collaborate on questions and poll techniques?	How do partners' conditions diverge or intersect?	Do partnerships sustain or collapse partner differences?	Can partners create individual perspectives on controversies?	Which power struggles should organizations align with?	How do partners understand how the partnership works?
Research sponsorships	Will funders support long-term, open-ended consensus building with no initial interest?	What standards of participation do sponsors value in grantmaking and program evaluation?	How do funders' preferences (questions, techniques) impact aggregations?	Do funders invest in outcomes and social conditions beyond their own interests?	Do funders sustain a suite of initiatives, some of which may be contradictory?	Will funders support research that challenges entrenched power, including their own?	Can funders let groups be small, private, and exclusive?	Are sponsorship conditions known and changeable?

commonsense expectations of advocacy. Most news coverage exists in this sphere—such as pro-choice versus pro-life, the death penalty, tax policy, health care, social programs.

In contrast, two other spheres receive little attention, but both teach us something about how the press understands advocacy. The *sphere of consensus* is filled with topics that journalists do not think need advocacy. For example, human trafficking rings may need to be investigated and there are legitimate debates about what to do about it, but no one openly debates the merits of slavery. Mainstream society has reached a consensus that there are not two legitimate sides to slavery. Environmental coverage is a kind of crossover category between the sphere of consensus and the sphere of legitimate controversy. Some politicians persist in seeing the human cause of climate change as debatable, and some news organizations continue to tell "both sides" of the climate change story. But other news organizations have moved the topic into the sphere of consensus. For example, in 2013 the *Los Angeles Times* declared that it would no longer print letters to the editor that questioned the existence of human-caused climate change (Thornton 2013). To the *Times*, the debate was over, there was no legitimate controversy, and consensus had been reached. To the extent that the *Times* was advocating for a particular cause of climate change, it did so by declaring that part of the climate change story to be over.

Conversely, the *sphere of deviance* contains issues that are considered too far outside mainstream concern to warrant journalistic attention. For a long time, transgender rights, same-sex marriage, and single-payer health care were all considered too deviant to cover. And for years, the mainstream U.S. press largely ignored the HIV/AIDS epidemic, leaving coverage to the gay press until the issue was seen as sufficiently important to overcome enterprise journalists' hesitation to cover the gay community (Rogers, Dearing, and Chang 1991).

The press advocates, but it does so in subtle ways. By adopting widely held, commonsense classifications of topics as debatable, taboo, or lacking controversy, it essentially advocates for a conservative system of values, the system that dominates the cultures and eras it operates within. For journalists to do otherwise—to overtly inject their *own* sense of what *they* think should be covered separate from what dominant social forces imply—would be to acknowledge that they have points of view, and that those perspectives can and should guide coverage. This is usually a bridge too far for U.S. journalists steeped in rituals and routines of objectivity. In this case, the public is presumed to be a deliberative, consensus-building public that needs journalists to provide disinterested, unbiased information that tells the stories of advocates representing viewpoints seen in acceptable, predictable tension.

Journalistic advocacy can also come from publishers' interests—from the perspectives of those with the power and resources to inject their own values into coverage. Although they rarely overtly direct their newsrooms, evidence suggests that reporters and editors are aware of their publishers' interests and will tailor coverage to align with what they perceive their boss's perspectives to be (Bezanson 2003; Chomsky 2006; Wagner and Collins 2014). To the extent that such a news organization advocates, it does so subtly and through the influence of its owner. Advocacy—or the perception of interests—can also take the form of subtle organizational norms. A news organization that caters to what it sees as its readers' interests may declare itself independent, but it is, in fact, beholden to market interests. Put differently, such a news organization advocates for *its* ideas of what *markets* see as readers' interests. It becomes a second-order advocate driven by what commercial interests see as audience desires. Such market-driven logics—even those that go unstated but underpin newsroom cultures—may skew coverage away from topics that may be of great public significance but little overt audience interest. Such a newsroom is driven more by customer service than public advocacy.

Relationships between funding and advocacy can also be seen in organizations that focus on particular beats. The Kaiser Family Foundation's funding of health care reporting is a type of advocacy in that it supports news organizations that cover its broad themes; journalists' individual reporting may be independent of the foundation's editorial oversight, but the foundation defines the general scope of coverage. Similarly, the newly funded news organization The Markup—founded by former Wikimedia head Sue Gardner and former ProPublica journalists Jeff Larson and Julia Angwin—is underwritten by Craigslist founder Craig Newmark, as well as the Ford, Knight, and MacArthur Foundations. To the extent that The Markup practices advocacy (in its case, focused on investigative reporting designed to hold technology companies publicly accountable), it does so in ways that are consistent with its funders' expectations of the beats and debates it will cover.

Many types of advocacy may appear throughout news organizations and journalists' reporting. Some are overt and appear in choices like whom to interview and what language to use. Others are more structural, embedded in subtle relationships between publishers and editors, journalists and audiences, social norms and habits of reporting. The aim of Table 22.2 is to trace these sources of power and public making through particular funding arrangements and to pose normative questions of those arrangements. Journalism and its funders are under no obligations to pursue any particular vision of the public, but in their choices to accept or pursue some funding over others, they leave clues about which publics they value and advocate for and which are seen as unacceptable or biased. The questions at the intersections of revenue sources and types of publics are meant to help scholars and practitioners alike better appreciate the kind of publics nonprofit news creates.

Conclusion

What kind of publics can different configurations of the press support? Recalling Baker's claim that different democracies need different media, this chapter argues that the U.S. press has always grappled with how to both ensure and resist intertwined senses of financial success and public service. Striving to be distinct from other forms of publishing, how can news organizations render their organizational missions and senses of public service in their financial models? How do news organizations' ownership models and financial relationships to markets, states, benefactors, audiences, advertisers, and organizational partners empower or interfere with the kinds of publics they can create?

Though not without historical antecedents, these questions are being posed anew as the core configuration of the press is changing. New entrants have appeared as journalistic partners, new types of fund-raising are now possible, and new understandings about the role of information in public life are in flux as more people than ever, for lower cost than ever, can *look* like the press. Journalism is faced with the critical question of how it differs from media and technology platforms, and how its public service is like or unlike other information providers.

One way to understand these differences is to examine closely not only how the networked press funds itself but also how different approaches to funding lead to different types of publics. I have tried to argue in this chapter that the press may better be thought of as the *networked* press—a distributed set of intertwined sociotechnical forces through which news is produced, circulated, and interpreted—and that this networked press is experimenting with a variety of ways of funding itself. Some of these funding techniques make the press seem like a new type of public service—affinities for crowdsourcing, online advertising, and philanthropic support can make journalism seem more accessible than ever. Other approaches show the press to be a deeply commercial enterprise that is highly dependent on online surveillance, subservience to technology platform preferences, and commodification of its labor and data. Although many nonprofit news organizations can be classified according to their official tax status or organizational mission, the degree to which the networked press intertwines commercial and noncommercial forms and for-profit and nonprofit interests makes it difficult to say exactly where the nonprofit press starts and stops.

The nonprofit press represents a kind of advocacy journalism. Its advocacy is not linked to a particular issue, position, or outcome but rather to an ideal of the public. In contrast to a state-driven media system that may confuse government interests with journalistic mission, or a market-driven media system that equates audience desires with public interest, the nonprofit press carves out a third space that is arguably better equipped to advocate for an image of the common good that is free(r) from politics and commerce. The challenge, though, is to identify this third space and advocate for *it* by thoughtfully and purposefully ensuring the financial health of nonprofit journalism.

MOTIVATION, MEANING, AND PROSOCIAL BEHAVIOR

The chapters in this section reflect on a set of intersecting questions about who supports and participates in nonprofit organizations and why. Beyond these empirical questions, the authors reflect on what the concepts mean. A prominent theme is that the answers are conditioned by how we define an act of giving. To some degree, the challenges of such definitions are technical; we would like to know the monetary donations of all households, but information from tax returns excludes all non-itemizers. Beyond the need for better data, the authors drive home the point that decisions about what counts are constitutive and draw the boundaries of the nonprofit sector. Analyses of how much people give or volunteer and why are tied to normative and ethical debates about different understandings of secular and religious commitments, public value, and the public benefit. Furthermore, how we understand and measure particular acts of giving have downstream implications for what we find when we analyze the broader social and organizational factors that promote or inhibit charitable acts. What we find then plays a role in shaping consequential policies such as nonprofit evaluations by intermediary organizations or tax preferences. Thus, questions of what we mean by giving or volunteering can have substantial effects that spill over to shape the sustainability of different types of nonprofits.

In Chapter 23, Pamela Paxton reviews core findings and discusses the challenges related to research on charitable giving, interrogating the questions of who gives, to what causes, why, and to what effect. One classic finding in the literature on giving indicates that the greatest giving occurs among the poorest and wealthiest households. Another well-known result points to significant differences in giving priorities between wealthy and nonwealthy donors, with the former giving more to education and the latter more to religion. Problematizing this accepted "knowledge," she underscores how different kinds of measurement matter greatly for understanding giving behavior. For example, a focus on formal giving typically underestimates total giving, and formal giving may be higher among the wealthy. Acts of generosity such as remittances among immigrant communities, helping extended family members, or giving immediate cash donations to the homeless are not counted in most giving estimates. Estimated household giving levels are typically calculated from itemized tax returns, but only a small proportion of the poorest families submit itemized tax returns. We do not know if non-itemizers give more or less of their household income to charity.

Paxton argues that a charitable gift is fundamentally a relationship between a donor and a nonprofit. As a relational construct, a gift cannot be distilled down to either just the amount given or the amount received. In order to understand charitable giving more fully, we must examine three influences capturing all sides of the relationship between donor and recipient: (1) the traits and motivations of individual donors (the supply side); (2) the characteristics and activities of nonprofits (the demand side), and (3) the social, economic, and political forces that are external to but influence the individual–nonprofit relationship. As noted in earlier parts of the volume, the relationship between donor and recipient is changing in part because of a growing movement to focus on gifts that show instrumental effectiveness more than focusing on a warm glow or sense of well-being for the giver. Paxton closes by discussing the movement toward effective philanthropy, raising the question of whether donors can truly be expected to privilege dispassionate calculations over subjective preferences.

In Chapter 24 Laura K. Gee and Jonathan Meer consider whether activities that increase donations to one nonprofit (or donations made through one specific method) come at the expense of others. Much of the research on charitable giving has concentrated on how to increase monetary donations to a single organization, often looking at whether donors respond to self-interest or the instrumental effectiveness of their gift. We know there are, in some years, massive fluctuations into (or away from) certain organizations, such as the Red Cross's increase in donations following a disaster (or decrease following scandal). Despite well-recognized organizational fluctuations, overall giving has remained relatively constant as a proportion of GDP for many years. Thus, Gee and Meer ask, do donors have a fixed budget of altruistic acts, or is the overall altruism budget expandable?

They explore the answer to this question by first discussing whether an act needs to be totally unselfish to be counted in the altruism budget. Gee and Meer assess the various components of the altruism budget, including but not limited to monetary donations, volunteering of time, and in-kind gifts. The bulk of their chapter analyzes current research on how changes in one type of giving affect others, both over time and contemporaneously. The findings of shifts over time are consistent if somewhat counterintuitive; future giving does not seem to be reduced by current giving, suggesting that the altruism budget is expandable across time. However, the impact of an act of giving on contemporaneous gifts to other charities or on other forms of giving is more difficult to summarize. These questions are of fundamental importance to broader issues about philanthropy. The implications of fund-raising activities are very different for society if fund-raising is a zero-sum game, in which donations given to one cause crowd out donations to another. If resources spent on fund-raising merely cannibalize donations from elsewhere, then many of these efforts may be wasteful.

In Chapter 25 Nina Eliasoph reveals how an emphasis on the voluntariness of donating time generates misleading ideas about volunteering. "Voluntariness" is, she argues, a placeholder for something we value: volunteering potentially offers free labor, camaraderie, altruism, and job training. Volunteers propagate cultural identities, create social capital, and fight for social change. Volunteer settings can give people a chance to learn how to make decisions together and think about the bigger social picture. Getting to the most fundamental issues in the study of volunteering requires an explicit focus on which actions are actually valued rather than relying on voluntariness as an abstraction that allows the underlying purpose to be assumed rather than stated directly.

Eliasoph problematizes three common ways of distinguishing volunteering from other kinds of activities: the presence or absence of state coercion, payment, and customary moral obligation. She shows that these three common definitions obscure much of the reason why we care about volunteering: its ability to provide a range of social goods. She makes the case for shifting our focus from voluntariness to the social goods the person who is examining volunteer work actually cares about, be they providing needed free labor, creating "schools for democracy," or something else. Although distinguishing volunteering from other kinds of work is not easy, the borders between the voluntary sector and other sectors are often where the most interesting action takes place.

In Chapter 26, Brad R. Fulton outlines the significant and pervasive influence of religious organizations in the U.S. nonprofit sector. Congregations continue to be the most ubiquitous voluntary organization in the United States, and other types of faith-based organizations maintain a substantial presence in every major domain of the nonprofit sector. They are distinct in many ways, from the meaning they can bring lives of individuals and families to the special protections afforded solely to religious organizations to guarantee their separation from the state. Perhaps most importantly, Americans "choose" their congregations, that is, we do not have a national religion. Thus, American voluntarism and religious commitment are intertwined.

At the same time, in response to broader social changes, religious organizations are experiencing some of the same shifts of organizational structure, culture, and identity, such as growing concerns about inequality and diversity, as well as pressures of financial sustainability. Some have taken on new corporate-style management structures and use social entrepreneurship as a tool for sustainability, while others blend secular and religious elements. Pursuing such research can broaden our understanding of who participates in the sector and how different types of organizations define, run, and adapt themselves in a complex institutional environment amid shifting social, political, and economic conditions.

Fulton begins by defining the field of religious nonprofit organizations and estimating the distribution of religious organizations in the major nonreligious domains of the nonprofit sector—a task far less straightforward than it may first appear. Like Eliasoph in the previous chapter, he reflects on the categorization challenges that are involved. He identifies religious nonprofits' distinctive characteristics and examines how they are similar to their secular counterparts, illustrating that in the contemporary world the activities and goals of many religious organizations are often closely aligned with those of secular nonprofit organizations. Given this alignment, the chapter then explores various research avenues for approaching religious nonprofits as formal organizations. Examining religious entities brings the limits of current organization theories into sharp relief, helping to shed light on trends toward rationalization and professionalization in the religious sphere.

The landscape of charitable giving has changed markedly over the past few decades, particularly with increasing emphases on measurement of effectiveness and efficiency on multiple fronts becoming of greater consequence. We can now talk about the effectiveness of congregations almost as routinely as we talk about school or hospital effectiveness. In part, emphases on categorization and measurement stem from a growing movement advocating for philanthropy that is motivated by proof of impact. Although effective altruism remains a small part of the field, it has influential champions and is having widespread impact. There are several reasons to be cautious, however. Scientific information can turn off positive emotions and remind donors of the uncertainty of measuring outcomes, thus reducing giving. Measures of giving or volunteering and their effects are also often reductionist; indicators hide contested normative assumptions about the boundaries of the sector, ethical justifications for why we want to measure a particular outcome, and multiple reasonable perspectives involved. A partial solution is to be explicit and targeted in establishing boundaries. For example, proponents of effective altruism may get more traction with other donors if they abandon cause neutrality and allow people to donate passionately across causes but effectively within causes. Broadly, understanding the nonprofit–individual relationship, how external forces shape that relationship, and how giving can be improved will allow both donors and nonprofits to increase charitable giving, plan for negative external shocks, and better allocate charitable gifts to produce the most consequential outcomes.

23   WHAT INFLUENCES CHARITABLE GIVING?

Pamela Paxton

CHARITABLE GIVING IS CENTRAL TO NONPROFITS. In 2017, $410 billion was contributed to nonprofit organizations, and 70 percent of that giving came from individuals (Giving USA 2018a). Charitable giving is an important source of revenue for nonprofits. Although on average, only 13 percent of nonprofit organizations' income comes from charitable donations (Salamon, Sokolowski, and List 2004), this average conceals substantial variation. Some nonprofits use donations to supplement fees they charge or government support they receive, but others rely on donations almost entirely (Rose-Ackerman 1996). Charitable giving is strongly supported by and subsidized through the U.S. tax system (Clotfelter 1985; Reich 2010).

In this chapter, I begin by describing the extent of charitable giving, noting differences in giving priorities between wealthy and nonwealthy donors. I also explain that a focus on formal giving typically underestimates total giving. I then discuss three influences on charitable giving. A charitable gift is fundamentally a relationship between a donor and a nonprofit. To understand charitable giving, therefore, we must examine the traits and motivations of individual donors (the supply side), the characteristics and activities of nonprofits (the demand side), and the social, economic, and political forces that are external to but influence the individual–nonprofit relationship. I close by introducing the new movement to make charitable giving more effective, discuss the ways that giving can be improved, and ask whether donors can truly be expected to privilege dispassionate calculations over subjective preferences.

What Are Rates of Charitable Giving in the United States and Where Does the Money Go?

According to the Philanthropy Panel Study through the Panel Study of Income Dynamics, about 55 percent of households donated at least $25 to charity in 2014 (Ottoni-Wilhelm 2017). This percentage has changed over time, rising from 61 percent in 2000 to a high around 65 percent in 2008 and then dropping to 55 percent in 2012 (Meer 2017). The average household donation is $2,514, while the median is $900 (Ottoni-Wilhelm 2017).

These numbers matter because individual giving is by far the dominant source of contributions to nonprofit organizations. In 2017, individual donations made up 70 percent of total giving to charities. If bequests (giving after death as directed in a will) are included, this percentage rises to 79 percent. Apart from dips during recession years, the total amount of giving has steadily increased over time, reaching $410 billion in 2017. (As a percent of the nation's gross domestic product (GDP), giving remains steady at about 2 percent of GDP (Giving USA 2018a; see also Havens, O'Herlihy, and Schervish 2006:543).) Altogether, individual giving was responsible for $287 billion in contributions to nonprofits in 2017.

These numbers actually underestimate total giving, because they reflect only formal giving and do not consider a wide range of informal giving. Impulsive gifts to a charity cash box or five dollars thrown in a collection plate are not counted. Person-to-person donations to homeless individuals are excluded too. Nondeductible contributions to political or 501(c)(4) organizations are not typically included, and crowd-funded donations are often missed (Soskis 2017). When informal giving is included, estimates of the incidence of giving and the total amount given increase substantially (O'Neill 2001; Rooney, Steinberg, and Schervish 2004; Hall 2001; Soskis 2017). A focus on formal giving may particularly underestimate giving by immigrant communities, some racial and ethnic groups, and those at lower income levels. For example, remittances from immigrants or their descendants to family outside the United States, along with other forms of diaspora giving, can outstrip official development aid (Newland, Terrazas, and Munster 2010; Adelman, Schwartz, and Riskin 2016). And gifts to extended, nonhousehold family members make up a large part of the giving of some communities of color (Stack 1997; Smith et al. 1999). Indeed, an ethnographic study of eight communities of color found that members of these communities expressed a preference for terms such as *sharing* rather than *charity* or *philanthropy* (Smith et al. 1999).

Where do people give? Figure 23.1 shows what percentage of total contributions go to different types of nonprofits using data from Giving USA (2018a). Religious organizations receive the largest proportion at 31 percent of all contributions. The second largest category is education at 14 percent of all contributions. These percentages have changed over time; although the percentage of gifts to education has increased, giving to religion has decreased. Figure 23.2 shows how giving to religion has changed over the last sixty years. From 1955 to 1965, giving to religion was about 50 percent of total giving. This decreased slightly in the 1970s to about 45 percent and remained steady at around that level through 1995. Between 1995 and 2017, the percent of giving to religion dropped to 31 percent. Benjamin Soskis (2017) explains, "Such figures clearly reflect deep-seated cultural trends. For example, much of the early decline in religious giving stemmed from a drop in enrollment in Catholic parochial schools, which had constituted as much as one-tenth of all private philanthropic contributions in 1950. More recently, increased secularization and a declining attachment to religious institutions have likely contributed as well" (see Fulton, Chapter 26, "Religious Organizations," for an extended discussion of giving to religious organizations).

Wealthy and nonwealthy people give to different kinds of organizations. Although religious organizations receive one third of all donors' contributions, they receive only 12 percent of contributions from high-net-worth donors.[1] Generally, the higher a household's income, the smaller the share of its donations that goes to religion (Rooney et al.

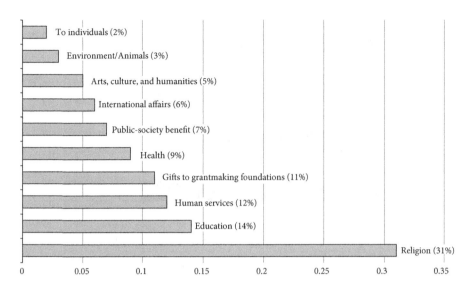

Figure 23.1   Percentage of total contributions by recipient category
Source: Data from Giving USA 2018a.

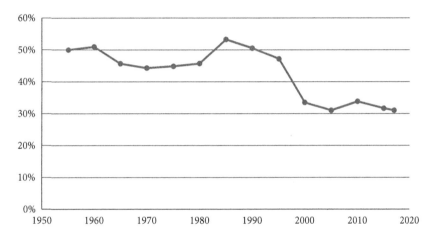

Figure 23.2   Change in the percentage of total contributions to religious groups, 1955–2017
Source: Data from Giving USA (various years).

2007). High-net-worth donors are far more likely to give to education, especially higher education (U.S. Trust 2014); this group gave 27 percent of its donations to education. Figure 23.3 shows how different income groups allocated their donations to different categories of nonprofits. Differences in priorities are immediately apparent. For example, higher-income groups give a far larger percentage of their donations to arts and health organizations than other groups do.

Wealthy donors' different priorities appear again in donor-advised funds. Only 11 percent of donations from donor-advised funds go to religious organizations, while 29 percent

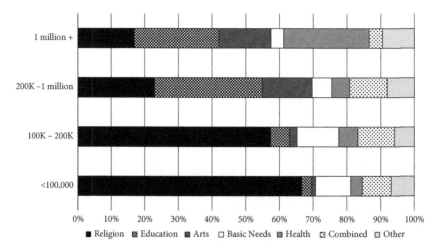

Figure 23.3 Percentage of total contributions going to recipient categories by income group, 2005

Source: Rooney et al. 2007.

go to education (Giving USA 2018b). Different giving preferences across income levels matters to the nonprofit sector. Rob Reich (2010) argues that since the U.S. tax code provides greater rewards for giving by the wealthy, it creates a "plutocratic bias" where the interests of the wealthy prevail.

High-net-worth donors are also more likely to give to foundations, charitable trusts, and donor-advised funds. In 2013, 28 percent of all giving from high-net-worth households went into these kinds of holdings (U.S. Trust 2014). Since 1978, foundations have tripled their percentage of total giving from 5 percent to 16 percent of total giving, while individual giving has declined as a percentage of total giving from 83 percent to 71 percent (Giving USA 2018a). A focus on funding future giving vehicles such as foundations solidifies the influence of wealthy donors on the direction of giving over time and generations (Reich 2016).

What Influences Charitable Giving?

A charitable gift is essentially a relationship between a donor and a nonprofit. So to understand charitable giving, we need to examine the traits and motivations of individual donors (the supply side), the characteristics and activities of nonprofits (the demand side), and the external social, economic, and political forces that influence the individual–nonprofit relationship. In this section we address each of these explanations in turn.

Supply Side: Donor Traits and Motivations

Why does an individual choose to make a donation to a nonprofit? Individuals may donate to receive some sort of private benefit from their donation. When people donate, they can receive rewards ranging from concert tickets to schooling for their child to a building named after them. They may also receive social acclaim (Becker 1974), entrée to an elite gathering (Rose-Ackerman 1996), or renown for their wealth (Glazer and Konrad 1996;

Harbaugh 1998). As Lise Vesterlund (2006:573) explains, "At the most extreme level the private benefit of donating is no different from that of purchasing any other private good."

But what about those who give to achieve more than private gain? Researchers ask whether people donate from altruism—a desire to increase others' well-being or the public good (Kolm 1969; Sen 1977)—or because they want to achieve a "warm glow"—a sense of satisfaction just from making the gift (Andreoni 1990; Arrow 1972). Neuro-imaging studies suggest that both motivations exist. The same neural pathways are activated when people make payments to themselves, when they see a charity receive money, and when they choose to donate money to a charity. So people get both altruistic and warm-glow satisfaction from giving to charity (Harbaugh, Mayr, and Burghart 2007). But motivations still vary: some people experience a stronger neural response when they see a charity receive money than when they receive money themselves (Harbaugh et al. 2007). Altruism versus warm glow is a useful way to distinguish two different motivations that both result in charitable giving.[2]

The most proximate cause of a charitable gift is being asked to give. So when we ask what characteristics make some people more likely to donate than others, the answer is often about which characteristics make it more or less likely that the person will be asked to donate in the first place. In the simplest sense, the larger a person's network, the more likely it is that he or she will be solicited. But it isn't just ego-to-alter-network ties that increase solicitation chances: memberships in voluntary associations, religious groups, or other "communities of participation" (Schervish and Havens 1997) embed people in recruitment networks that make them more aware of opportunities to donate and nurture the social connections that facilitate solicitation. And when other people in one's network are giving, there is social pressure to contribute as well (Frey and Meier 2004; Shang and Croson 2009; Meer 2011; Croson and Shang 2013).

Take involvement in religious organizations. Belonging to a religious organization, attending religious services, and participating in smaller religious gatherings are all associated with higher rates of charitable giving (Independent Sector 2002; see Bekkers and Wiepking 2011b for an extensive review). Although all major religions instruct on morality and teach adherents to care for others, it is not this "conviction" aspect of religion that matters for charitable giving (Wuthnow 1991). More important is that religious groups provide "community"—the organizational context where giving is mobilized (Wuthnow 1990, 1991; Hodgkinson 1990; Jackson et al. 1995). Religious organizations provide "a place to hear about needs in the community, social networks that can be used to recruit volunteers, and subgroups that plan helping activities" (Wuthnow 1990:12). And participating in religious groups isn't just associated with giving to religious organizations and causes; it's also associated with secular giving. But it's not simple attendance that's associated with secular giving—it's deeper participation in groups within the church and the networks those groups create (Jackson et al. 1995). A similar dynamic helps explain the often-reported association between participating in voluntary associations and charitable giving (Jackson et al. 1995; Brown and Ferris 2007). Or consider education, which is strongly linked to charitable giving (see Bekkers and Wiepking 2011b for a review). Education increases awareness of need and can lead to increases in income. But more importantly, education also draws people into group memberships that increase the likelihood that they'll be asked to donate (Brown and Ferris 2007).

Charitable giving generally increases with income. This relationship is often described as a U; giving is highest among both lower- and higher-income people as a proportion of their income. As John A. List (2011) says, "Households with incomes between $20,000 and $40,000 give 5 percent of their income to charity. As incomes grow to about $75,000, gifts fall to 2 percent of income, but then rise slightly to 3 percent." Studies of high-net-worth donors (incomes greater than $200,000 or net worth more than $1,000,000) suggest that they give more: 7 percent to 8 percent of their income (U.S. Trust 2014). There are several explanations for this U shape. First, as Figure 23.3 shows, lower-income households tend to give a higher proportion of their donations to religious organizations, which may expect their members to give a certain percentage of their income (e.g., 10 percent). Second, income is not the same as wealth. If some "low-income" people are actually wealthy (e.g., retired with high assets), they're actually donating not from their income but from their accumulated wealth (James and Sharpe 2007). However, John J. Havens and his colleagues (2006) argue that the observed U-shaped relationship between charitable giving and income is a myth generated by survey methodologies that leave out of their calculations the large proportions of low-income households that contribute nothing. They argue, "When these 'zeros' are included and the percentage of income is calculated for all households in the sample, the left-hand side of the U virtually disappears. What remains of the uptick at the lower end of the income spectrum can be explained by taking into account household wealth in addition to income" (Havens et al. 2006:545).

Some studies have found a gender difference in giving (e.g., Andreoni, Brown, and Rischall 2003; Mesch et al. 2006); women are more likely to donate then men. Because charitable giving is recorded at the household level, it can be difficult to disentangle gender from other factors. For example, as income and educational level are included in a model, observed gender differences in charitable giving tend to decrease (Wiepking and Bekkers 2012). Men and women may also prefer to give their money to different causes (see Wiepking and Bekkers 2012 for a review). In married couples, men and women make different decisions about how to allocate charitable gifts (Andreoni et al. 2003).

Demand Side: Nonprofit Characteristics and Activities

Nonprofits differ in ways that may make them more or less appealing to different donors. Further, nonprofits actively work to attract donations and retain donors. What kinds of characteristics and activities of nonprofits attract donations?

To begin, a substantial body of research spanning public administration, organizational studies, and accounting has asked which organizational characteristics help nonprofits attract private donations. This largely financial literature predicts nonprofit donations with organizational elements such as administrative expenses, organizational wealth and asset hoarding, and executive compensation (e.g., Weisbrod and Dominguez 1986; Tuckman and Chang 1991; Tinkelman and Mankaney 2007; Calabrese 2011). Occasionally, studies also assess more unusual factors, such as whether a nonprofit is endorsed by a celebrity (Harris and Ruth 2015) or signals an attachment to a community (Ressler et al. 2018). This research is typically based on data that nonprofit organizations submit to the Internal Revenue Service. The key document is Form 990, an annual return that the IRS requires from many nonprofit organizations that contains detailed financial information.

This research has found a number of connections between the characteristics of non-profits and their donations. Consider employee compensation. Some donors express discomfort with high executive salaries, apparently seeing intrinsic rather than extrinsic motivations as a prerequisite for working in the nonprofit sector (Charity Navigator 2010; see Pallotta 2009 for an impassioned rebuttal to this perspective). Steven Balsam and Erica E. Harris (2013), for example, find that high executive compensation dissuades donors from contributing. Sophisticated donors actively seek out information about executive salaries by looking at Form 990s, whereas small donors respond only when a nonprofit's compensation levels attract media attention. The response from donors was robust: Balsam and Harris observe that two years after organizations were mentioned in media articles about compensation, they experienced 15 percent lower growth in donations, and growth decreased even more for nonprofits with explicitly charitable missions. And donors aren't looking only at executive compensation: Wenli Yan and Margaret F. Sloan (2016) find that median employee compensation also suppresses donations.

Consider also nonprofit efficiency—the ratio of program expenses to total expenses. This ratio has been heavily publicized by charity watchdogs such as Charity Navigator and the Better Business Bureau's Wise Giving Alliance, which criticize nonprofits with high overhead (management and fund-raising expenses). At issue is "the use of efficiency measures by donors in determining which organizations receive individual contributions" (Calabrese 2011: 860). Donors do penalize nonprofit organizations that display less efficiency (i.e., have high overhead costs) with decreased contributions (e.g., Weisbrod and Dominguez 1986; Jacobs and Marudas 2009).

Nonprofits are not passive players in their Form 990 reporting; many have lowered their reported overhead ratios below the guidelines recommended by charity watchdogs. But nonprofits have some choice in which expenses they classify as related to program services, and some may also be responding to efficiency pressures by underreporting their administrative or fund-raising expenses on their Form 990s. Ranjani Krishnan, Michelle H. Yetman, and Robert J. Yetman (2006) examine nonprofits that report zero fund-raising expenses and find that 50 percent of these nonprofits' websites and 38 percent of their audit statements show evidence of fund-raising activities that they should have reported on the Form 990. They also find that underreporting fund-raising expenses is positively associated with managerial incentives such as higher compensation.

Nonprofits have more strategies available to them. Many nonprofits actively fund-raise; they find potential donors through prospect research, build a solid base of annual contributors, cultivate relationships with major gift prospects, and steward their donors to deepen the relationship after a gift (Sargeant and Shang 2010). Every year, nonprofits spend an average of $100,000 in fund-raising to raise over $750,000 in gifts (Andreoni and Payne 2011). At its core, fund-raising is an attempt by a nonprofit to influence an individual's decision making about giving.

For decades, nonprofits had only the vague recommendations of professional fund-raisers to advise them about what techniques work to increase charitable donations. But in the past twenty years, a growing body of research is providing concrete data about how donors respond to different fund-raising techniques. Consider a matching grant—a pledge from a lead donor to match other donors' contributions dollar for dollar or by some other ratio. Intuition might tell us that larger matches (2:1 or 3:1 versus 1:1) would provoke a larger response from donors, but this turns out not to be the case. In a study by Dean Karlan and John A. List (2007), having a match increased the donation rate by 20 percent, but donors who were offered a 1:1 match gave as often and as much as those offered higher match rates. Other studies have confirmed this result (e.g., Karlan, List, and Shafir 2011; Eckel and Grossman 2008; Martin and Randal 2009). Laura K. Gee and Michael J. Schreck (2018) find that threshold matches that require a certain number of donors to be awarded are more effective at raising the donation rate than a 1:1 match. Importantly, using data from the website donorschoose.org, Jonathan Meer (2017) finds that matching money for one project does not crowd out donations to other projects.

Acquiring seed money is another fund-raising technique: nonprofits can announce that one or more lead donors have already contributed some funds. Seed money sends a message to potential donors that the charity is high quality and pre-vetted by experienced donors. Field experiments suggest that seed money can be extremely effective. John A. List and David Lucking-Reiley (2002) told potential donors that 10 percent, 33 percent, or 67 percent of the total needed for the goal had already been raised. More seed money led to both higher donation rates and a higher average size of the gift. Moving from the 10 percent to the 67 percent condition resulted in a sixfold increase in contributions (see also Rondeau and List 2008; Verhaert and van den Poel 2012). Seed money is most effective if donors are told that the seed money will be used to cover administrative expenses so that any additional gift will go entirely to programming (Gneezy, Keenan, and Gneezy 2014).

The findings on matching grants and seed money suggest that donors compare themselves with other donors when they're deciding whether and how much to give—and that's exactly what a series of field experiments have found. For example, Bruno S. Frey and Stephan Meier (2004) find that students are more likely to donate to a charitable fund when they're told that a high proportion of other students have already donated. Hearing about other donors influences not only donation rates but also the amount donated. During a public radio station's fund-raising drive, Jen Shang and Rachel Croson (2009) told some callers making a pledge about other donations. Callers who were told that a prior donor had given a median-size gift to the station ($75) gave no more than callers who were not told about a prior donor. But when callers were told that a prior donor had given a $300 gift, they gave on average $13 more. Apparently, receiving information about a larger-than-average gift by a prior donor inspired or shamed donors into making larger donations themselves (see also Smith, Windmeijer, and Wright 2015). Social distance matters here; matching the gender of the caller and the prior donor led to higher contributions than when the reference donor and caller were gender-mismatched (Shang, Reed, and Croson 2008). And in a study of alumni giving, being asked to give by a former acquaintance (especially a former roommate) increased both the likelihood of a donation and the size of the gift (Meer 2011).

These field experimental studies provide useful information for nonprofits. Nonprofits can generate higher levels of giving by securing private funds early for seed money or matching grants. But in the case of matching, there is no need to waste the lead donation with an overly generous match. In contrast, securing a seed grant that covers the largest possible percentage of the total need will reap significant benefits. And by making donors aware of other donor choices, nonprofits can create social pressure that will yield higher donation rates and higher returns.

External Forces: Government, Economy, and Social Change

While the characteristics and motivations of each side of the individual–nonprofit partnership are critical to understanding charitable giving, so too are a range of social, economic, and political forces that are external to but influence the individual–nonprofit relationship. To begin with, government regulations and policies may change an individual's calculus about charitable gifts.

Nonprofits enjoy a favored U.S. tax status—they are exempt from taxes themselves, and most can also receive tax-deductible gifts—because they are thought to be public serving (Frumkin 2002; Hopkins 2011).[3] The justification for state subsidization of this sector is that the forgone tax revenue stimulates the production of public goods—that it "produces greater social value than what the state could have produced on its own" (Reich 2010:182). The centerpiece of this state subsidization is the charitable donation tax deduction, first enacted in 1917, that can reduce a taxpayer's tax burden (Clotfelter 1985).

Economists describe the charitable donation tax deduction as "reducing the price" of a charitable gift. Consider a taxpayer in the 24 percent marginal tax bracket who itemizes deductions. The "price" of a one-dollar donation for this taxpayer is actually only 76 cents because the charitable gift is tax deductible. This makes governmental tax policy quite important for charitable giving. If the government raises marginal tax brackets so that the taxpayer's marginal bracket changes to 32 percent, the taxpayer now faces a lower "price"—68 cents for a $1 donation instead of the original 76 cents. On one hand, this change in tax policy may increase charitable gifts, since the price of the gift is lower. On the other hand, the taxpayer has just paid more taxes and may therefore feel that he or she has less money to give.

So how do changes in the price of giving affect donations? Findings are quite mixed, both within and across observational and experimental studies (see Vesterlund 2006 for a review). Economists care about the effect of changes in the price because it determines whether charitable contributions should be tax deductible at all. In particular, they are concerned with whether charitable giving is "price elastic." That is, for the charitable donation tax deduction to be effective, the deduction must increase contributions by more than the government's cost of providing the deduction. If charitable giving is *not* price elastic, then the government should not offer the tax deduction and should instead just transfer the tax money it collects to charities itself.

Is charitable giving price elastic? List (2011:169–172) reviews the existing evidence and concludes, "Combining the totality of the evidence . . . I am left with the thought that there is a fair amount of evidence, although not universal agreement, that charitable giving is at least unitary price elastic if not price elastic, especially amongst the high-income classes. This result suggests that if one were interested in stimulating the charitable sector, one avenue is to enhance the tax deductibility of individual charitable contributions" (2011:172).

Another way a government can influence the individual-nonprofit relationship is by providing supplementary funding to some nonprofits.[4] Individual giving is not the only source of revenue for nonprofits—government grants are important to many. Of concern, however, is whether government grants "crowd out" giving by individuals. Remember the basic motivations that individuals could have about giving: individuals may donate from "altruism"—the desire to increase others' well-being (Kolm 1969; Sen 1977)—or they may donate to achieve a "warm glow"—a sense of satisfaction just from making the gift (Andreoni 1990; Arrow 1972). If people are only looking for increases in the public good (altruism) then government grants to nonprofits should crowd out (possibly even dollar for dollar) charitable gifts (Bergstrom, Blume, and Varian 1986). But if donating also gives people a "warm glow," we should not see crowd-out from government grants.

Although some experiments show crowding out, research that draws on tax or donation data suggests that government grants do not crowd out private giving, or crowd it out at very low levels (e.g., Clotfelter 1985, Kingma and McClelland 1995; de Wit and Bekkers 2016; see Gee and Meer, Chapter 24, "The Altruism Budget," for a review).[5] Evidence that a warm-glow benefit overcomes any crowding out also comes from neural imaging studies. William T. Harbaugh and his colleagues (2007) found that people had a stronger neural response to giving voluntarily than to having money taken from them and given to charity (a taxlike transfer). This suggests that people do feel a "warm glow" when they give. But these neural pathways were also activated in the taxlike transfer, suggesting that altruism also motivates people to give.

Beyond government regulations or policies, the general economic climate is likely to influence the individual–nonprofit relationship. Using a simple regression of the percentage change in charitable giving on the percentage change in the S&P 500, List (2011) finds that 40 percent of the variation in charitable giving can be explained just by changes in the stock market. He finds that a 1 percent increase in the S&P 500 correlates with a 0.19 increase in giving the following year. So, good economic times lead to more charitable gifts. On the flip side, during economic recessions demand for services increases and nonprofits need donations more than ever, but individuals feel constrained in their ability to give (Salamon 2003). Giving USA tracks overall giving to nonprofits over time and finds that giving either levels off or declines during recession periods (Giving USA 2018a:42). However, using the same data, List (2011:161) finds that charitable giving is generally "sticky downwards": it does not decline as rapidly under poor economic conditions as it increases during good conditions. He speculates that this is due to the social pressure on donors to maintain past levels of giving. Certainly, nonprofits are not passive actors and may step up their fund-raising and stewardship to maintain donor gifts. List's analysis ends in 2008. In contrast, new research that uses individual panel data to analyze the Great Recession that began in 2008 finds sharp declines in giving during that recessionary period, most likely due to increased economic uncertainty on the part of donors (Meer, Miller, and Wulfsberg 2017).

In addition to governmental and economic forces, a variety of other external forces can influence charitable giving. For example, many observers have noted generational change in giving behaviors, with younger generations giving differently than older ones. In the past, people tended to give to umbrella organizations such as the United Way or Catholic Charities, which decided for them how the funds should be spent. Today, donor advisors argue that new generations wish to pursue "strategic" or "venture" philanthropy, sometimes called the "new philanthropy" (Cobb 2002; Bick 2007; Frumkin 2008; Moody 2008). These donors are more engaged and likely to adopt business principles in making donations. They choose for themselves the recipients of their gifts and monitor the effects of the gift. The rise of new philanthropy has gone hand-in-hand with the rise and increased use of charity aggregator and evaluation sites such as Charity Navigator or GiveWell (but see Szper and Prakash 2011). It also corresponds to the rise of an organizational norm for more metrics, efficiency, and effectiveness (Espeland and Stevens 2008; Barman 2016; Bromley, Chapter 4, "The Organizational Transformation of Civil Society"). On one hand, these new philanthropy donors are empowered, directed, and engaged in their giving. They may be more comfortable with failure and support riskier projects. On the other hand, nonprofits are now being asked to expend time and money demonstrating effectiveness in ways they did not traditionally have to (Snibbe 2006; Brest, Chapter 16, "The Outcomes Movement in Philanthropy and the Nonprofit Sector").

Another change that nonprofits confront is the growing importance of technology and increasing use of social media. Technology is transforming the sector. A range of smartphone apps and websites now market easy fund-raising to nonprofits, while advocacy organizations use social media to raise awareness and incite public discussion about their issues. The combination of social media attention and online ease of donation can be incredibly powerful for a nonprofit. Consider two recent charitable giving "moments": the 2014 ALS ice bucket challenge and the 2018 RAICES Facebook viral fund-raising campaign. During August 2014, the "ice bucket challenge" allowed friends to challenge others through social media to dump a bucket of ice water over their heads and donate to the Amyotrophic Lateral Sclerosis (ALS) Association. The challenge helped the ALS Association raise over $115 million in just a few months and increased awareness dramatically. "Over 6 million videos were shared on YouTube, and the videos of celebrities such as Bill Gates received over 20 million views. . . . the Wikipedia page on ALS went from around 3,000 daily views to a surge of traffic peaking on August 21st with over 450,000 views in a single day" (Wicks 2014:479). Similarly, in June 2018, nationwide outrage over the Trump administration's forced separation of more than 2,500 migrant children from their parents found an outlet: a Facebook fund-raising page set up by a couple in California. Over a two-week period, the recipient of the Facebook fund-raiser, the Refugee and Immigrant Center for Education and Legal Services (RAICES) received $20.5 million in donations and another $5 million through their official website (which crashed briefly because of the increased traffic). This amount was three times their annual budget and more than forty times what the nonprofit raised in the entirety of 2017 (Yaffe-Bellany 2018).

These were impressive viral fund-raising success stories in which social media helped create what we might call a "charitable giving moment." But many nonprofits make appeals over social media, where competition for attention is intense. Why do some appeals result in a "moment" while others do not? An initial assessment of the ice bucket challenge was that it combined "authenticity, vanity, and a brilliant made-to-go-viral design" (Tucker 2014). RAICES likely benefited from a "first mover" advantage; in other words, its fund-raiser provided an early outlet for an upset and angry citizenry. The power of social networks is on display in both examples. The Facebook fund-raiser automatically linked to existing social networks, while the ice-bucket challenges worked through nominations of friends. In each case, not only did donors' Facebook friends and Twitter followers see the video or donation, but their social network's social network saw it too.

Researchers and observers are only beginning to understand how new forms of memetic communication matter for nonprofits. When does an appeal culturally resonate? As Christopher A. Bail (2016b:281) explains, "cultural resonance" is the idea that "organizations will be more likely to generate the momentum necessary for a social movement if they produce discourses that fit, or resonate, with the way people understand the world around them." Advocacy organizations that find ways to resonate or bridge to other issue areas create social media conversations that bring in more people (Bail 2016a, 2016b). Incentives matter too in encouraging donors to share such appeals (Castillo, Petrie, and Wardell 2014). Emotional language and images resonate powerfully for donors (Paxton, Velasco, and Ressler 2019), especially when prior conversation has lacked emotion (Bail, Brown, and Mann 2017). Much remains to be understood before nonprofits can harness the power of technology and social media. However, the enormous text data created by social media, the millions of newly available Form 990 records, and the new analytic tools provided by computational social science suggest more information to come, very soon.

Is Charitable Giving Effective?

Some charitable giving is wasted. Individual donors, foundations, and corporations can make bad choices and fund nonprofits that spend little on programming or that have good intentions but ineffective programs. The most egregious nonprofits can make the news for diverting 96 percent or more of the funds they raise to their for-profit solicitors (often with a name such as "Wishing Well" that closely resembles a legitimate charity like "Make-A-Wish"). But other nonprofits operate under good financials but with programs that do not collect outcome data and have never been evaluated for effectiveness (Molino 2011; Brest, Chapter 16, "The Outcomes Movement in Philanthropy and the Nonprofit Sector"). It's crucial, therefore, to ask whether donors should try to be more effective in their giving and whether it's possible for them to do so.

The effective altruism movement was pioneered by Peter Singer (1972, 2010) and argues that donors should take a utilitarian approach to donating; in other words, they should try to produce the most good for the most people with each dollar. Departing from a traditional approach, which advises donors to identify and then fund their passion (e.g., Bronfman and Solomon 2010), effective altruism requests that potential donors be dispassionate, consider every possible cause, and fund those that will do the greatest good (MacAskill 2015). Singer (2010) stresses international giving, using the joined arguments that all lives are equal and that donations are more cost effective in less developed countries.[6] Effective altruism, in short, tries to move donors away from "warm glow" or "donor-focused giving" to "recipient-focused giving" (Friedman 2013). A number of nonprofits, websites, and funds have been developed to help donors make better decisions about where to direct their gifts (see Brest, Chapter 16, "The Outcomes Movement in Philanthropy and the Nonprofit Sector").

How can donors make their giving more effective? There are a wide range of options, each with its own proponents. To begin with, donors are often advised to investigate a charity's financials, especially its Form 990—the annual return required by the IRS for many nonprofit organizations. In the early days, advice stressed overhead, or the ratio of administrative expenses plus fund-raising to total expenses. Advisors recommended that donors avoid nonprofits with high overhead, variously defined as greater than 10 percent or 25 percent of expenses. But many observers have since argued that a strict focus on overhead causes nonprofits to underfund staff and leadership, avoid evaluating their programs, and put off infrastructure repairs and updates (Gregory and Howard 2009; Pallotta 2009). Better advice is for donors to make use of resources that show how to read a Form 990 (e.g., Institute for Local Government 2010) and one of the many new sites that provide searchable e-filed Form 990s (e.g., ProPublica's Nonprofit Explorer). With a twelve-page base form (not including additional schedules), the Form 990 is an incredible source of data on nonprofits, including their finances, expenditures, governance, compliance with federal requirements, compensation paid to certain people, and numbers of staff and volunteers.

Another suggested strategy is to consider a gift's social return on investment. This approach stresses an investment model of philanthropy and works to calculate the ratio of the cost of a nonprofit's inputs to the value of their outcomes or impact. This can be simple in some cases: If one soup kitchen feeds people for $6.85 per person while another manages $4.25 a person, then, all other things equal, donors may want to maximize their social return on investment by funding the second soup kitchen. Akin to a traditional monetary return on investment, the second soup kitchen produces a greater social return (people fed) for an investment (donation). But in many cases, the benefit is not guaranteed, which makes calculating the benefit/cost ratio far more difficult (Brest and Harvey 2018). For example, a nonprofit that provides job coaching cannot guarantee it will produce a full-time job. So any calculation of benefit would have to include an estimate of the probability of getting a job. The Robin Hood Foundation attempts to "monetize everything" so that social returns on investment can be compared across disparate nonprofit categories. For example, they have calculated the lifetime value of a high school graduation to be $190,000 and of each additional year of college to be $40,000 (M. M. Weinstein and Bradburd 2013). These numbers allow them to compare nonprofits working in quite different areas of education. In the area of health or international development, proponents of maximizing the social return on investment tout the notion of a quality-adjusted life year (QALY), in which a value of 1 represents one year in perfect health. Disparate health interventions can be compared by their costs of creating a QALY (QALY/$).[7]

Donors can also pay close attention to outcomes and evaluation data provided by nonprofits. At the most basic level, a nonprofit should provide information on its activities and the outputs of those activities. A donor can obtain information about a nonprofit's activities through written reports, websites, phone conversations, or site visits. For example, the nonprofit that provides job coaching could report the number of people enrolled in coaching and the number of coaching sessions per person. This is a minimum level of reporting that should be expected of most nonprofits (Brest and Harvey 2018). Next-level reporting would include some attention to progress in indicators of outcomes (e.g., short-term effects of activities on recipients' behaviors, knowledge, or perception) or impact (long-term and aggregate effects of a sustained program, service, or intervention on an overall target population) (see Brest, Chapter 16, "The Outcomes Movement in Philanthropy and the Nonprofit Sector"). For example, a nonprofit may keep records showing that job coaching led to 90 percent of their clients finding and keeping a job for at least six months. A nonprofit may also report declines in unemployment in the community in which they operate to attempt to demonstrate impact.

Unfortunately, however, few nonprofits appreciate the issues of selection that loom large in much of their programming. And many conflate metrics with actual causal impact. Take job coaching: is the fact that 90 percent of a nonprofit's clients found and kept a job due to the nonprofit's programming? Or is it due to the social position or motivation of the clients themselves? Is a tutoring nonprofit that reports higher grades for its students the reason for student success, or is it the personal or family characteristics of the students? Though many nonprofit observers have noted these selection issues, few nonprofits take them seriously. Instead, they tend to take credit for all recipient success without considering any counterfactuals. Proponents of effective giving argue that nonprofits must demonstrate cause: that their program *caused* an observed outcome. They recommend randomized controlled trials (RCTs) as the best method to demonstrate cause. By randomly dividing people into an intervention group (those who participated in some program) and a control group (those who did not participate), nonprofits can argue that any differences between the two groups are due to their programming.

But not every nonprofit can or should undertake RCTs to demonstrate causality, especially those engaged in direct service provision. Does a soup kitchen or clothing closet really need an RCT to demonstrate that it feeds or clothes people?[8] Even in the area of direct service provision, however, new approaches are emerging. Some donors are arguing for direct giving based on the success of conditional and unconditional cash transfers in government provision of social welfare (Arnold, Conway, and Greenslade 2011; Hanlon, Barrientos, and Hulme 2010). This approach empowers recipients to choose how to spend donated funds themselves and increases their consumption, food security, and psychological well-being (Haushofer and Shapiro 2016).

So, should donors approach charitable giving dispassionately—maximizing social return or funding only nonprofits with successful RCTs? Can we expect them to? Although a dispassionate observer may direct charitable dollars to do the most good regardless of personal preference, research suggests that donors do not always respond favorably to this approach. Dean Karlan and Daniel Wood (2017) used a field experiment to investigate donor response to information about a charity's effectiveness. Partnering with Freedom from Hunger, they sent solicitation letters to potential donors. Some recipients got the standard fund-raising letter, which featured a story focused on a beneficiary. Others got that story plus scientific information about the program's impact. The addition of scientific information had no overall effect on whether people donated or the amount they donated. This information did, however, make an important difference across large prior donors and small prior donors. Large prior donors gave more when they received the scientific impact information, suggesting that they were willing to consider evidence in accord with suggestions from the effective altruism movement. However, small prior donors gave *less* when they received additional scientific information. Karlan and Wood argue that these smaller donors were motivated largely by warm-glow giving. The scientific information, they speculate, "turned off" these positive emotions by reminding the donors that the effectiveness of charitable giving is inherently uncertain. Without the warm glow, the donors weren't motivated to give.

Donors simply believe in subjective choice themselves and more than effective altruists do. Jonathan Z. Berman and his colleagues (2018) find that when given the choice to donate across charitable fields, individuals feel that donors have subjective preferences that can override evaluations of effectiveness. People choose less effective charitable options in favor of their subjectively preferred category and also judge others who also choose subjectively less harshly. But *within* charitable cause areas, people do respond to effectiveness (Caviola et al. 2014). Because effective altruism can be powerful within charitable cause areas and among large donors, it's an important direction for the field, even if it remains a small part of charitable giving. Meanwhile, proponents of effective altruism may get more traction with other donors if they abandon cause neutrality and allow people to donate passionately across causes but effectively within causes.

The landscape of charitable giving has changed over the past few decades and will continue to change going forward. Understanding the nonprofit–donor relationship, how external forces shape that relationship, and how giving can be improved will allow both donors and nonprofits to increase charitable giving, plan for negative external shocks, and better allocate charitable gifts to produce the most effective outcomes.

24   THE ALTRUISM BUDGET

Measuring and Encouraging Charitable Giving

Laura K. Gee and Jonathan Meer

IN RECENT YEARS, SOME CHARITIES HAVE seen huge increases in their receipts—for example, the viral Ice Bucket Challenge in 2014 coincided with an increase of over 200 percent in donations to the ALS Association (Steel 2014). Yet between 2012 and 2017, overall monetary donations to U.S. nonprofits held steady at around 2 percent of GDP (Giving USA 2018). Patterns like this inspire questions about the limits of the overall budget for the nonprofit field in general—what we will refer to as the *altruism budget*. When donations increase to one recipient, do they decrease for others? When they increase now, will they decrease later? And if people give more of one kind of donation—for example, money—do they give less of another—for example, time? In short, do donors have a fixed budget of altruistic acts? Or, conversely, is the overall altruism budget expandable? These questions are of fundamental importance to broader issues about philanthropy. The implications of fund-raising activities are very different for society if fund-raising is a zero-sum game, in which donations given to one cause fully offset donations to another. If resources spent on fund-raising merely cannibalize donations from elsewhere, then many of these efforts may be wasteful.

This chapter reviews the state of the research on the nature of the altruism budget. After a discussion of the definition of an altruistic act, we describe the different kinds of altruistic acts that we include in our concept of the altruism budget. The bulk of the paper reviews the state of the research on how changes in one type of giving affect others, both over time and contemporaneously. The findings of shifts over time are consistent, if somewhat counterintuitive: future giving does not seem to be reduced by current giving, suggesting that the altruism budget is expandable across time. In other respects, the nascent research in this challenging field of inquiry does not yet offer much beyond suggestive answers. We detail the difficulties with estimating causal effects of competition between recipients of altruism later in the chapter. In order to fully examine the nature of the altruism budget, researchers would need to observe all of the altruistic acts an individual engages in over their lifetime. This is infeasible. Precise answers can be found for more narrowly defined questions, like how increases in giving to one cause on a specific online platform affect giving to other causes on that platform at a certain time. But this does not truly answer the question of how the altruism budget shifts more broadly. We offer directions for further research into how increased giving to one recipient affects giving to others.

What Is Altruism?

Social scientists have yet to agree on a single definition of *altruism*. Indeed, it is quite difficult to establish a firm definition of the concept. The dictionary definition of *altruism* is "unselfish regard for or devotion to the welfare of others," and the attendant example of the word used in context is "charitable acts motivated purely by altruism" (Merriam-Webster n.d.).

This example highlights the difficulty of offering a scientific definition of altruism: charitable acts are generally observable, but their motivations are less knowable. Donating money to a charity is generally accepted as an altruistic act, but is it always purely "unselfish"? Indeed, Rene Bekkers and Pamala Wiepking (2011) list altruism as only one of the eight mechanisms for making a charitable donation.

Often there are explicit benefits to a donor from making a donation. In the United States, donors can deduct monetary and in-kind gifts from their income taxes, thus lowering their tax bill.[1] Even without this preferential tax treatment, acts that are generally considered altruistic offer many private—or one might go as far as to say selfish—benefits. Examples abound: when parents volunteer at a child's school, they believe they have more control over their child's class placement (Gee 2011). People donate more to their alma maters as their children approach college age, and they expect those donations to buy their children favorable treatment in the admissions process (Meer and Rosen 2009). Someone may make a person-to-person gift of time, such as babysitting for a neighbor in need, with the expectation that they will be owed a favor. The frequent use of "donor premiums," or gifts from the charity to donors (either before making a donation, as an inducement to give, or afterward as a token of appreciation) suggests that a more explicit exchange of consumption goods for donations plays a role in giving (Alpizar, Carlsson, and Johansson-Stenman 2008; Eckel, Herberich, and Meer 2018; Falk 2007; Meer and Rosen 2012). The Internal Revenue Service (IRS) explicitly recognizes that donations are not fully altruistic: it offers charities guidance on how to make "good faith estimates of the fair market value" of the goods and services (e.g., an invitation to a gala) they provide to donors and uses these estimates to reduce the amount that itemizing taxpayers can deduct on their income tax returns.[2]

In addition to explicit benefits that result from donations, how someone *appears* when they donate is of utmost importance. The increase in donations when someone is able to appear more generous from donating is one of the most robust findings in the literature (Andreoni and Bernheim 2009). A related desire to acquire "status" can also motivate giving (Blumkin and Sadka 2007; Glazer and Konrad 1996; Harbaugh 1998a, 1998b; Kumru and Vesterlund 2010). The benefits to charities and donors of observable donations can multiply when the donation sets an example for others or provides information about the most effective or worthy charities, particularly if the individual making the donation is well known (Andreoni 2006a; Karlan and List 2012; List and Rondeau 2003; Potters, Sefton, and Vesterlund 2005, 2007; Vesterlund 2003; Kessler 2017). Evidence suggests that when gifts are made publicly, prospective donors are influenced not only by others' giving patterns but also by knowing that they are being observed themselves (Castillo, Petrie, and Wardell 2014; Gee and Schreck 2018; Shang and Croson 2009; Smith, Windmeijer, and Wright 2015). A complementary mechanism is that people may donate because they want to avoid shame or explicit punishments for not contributing.[3]

Making donation decisions more observable is not always helpful, however. For instance, if donors are promised some explicit benefit when they donate—such as some highly valued gift—they may be concerned that donating will make them appear selfish instead of generous (Ariely, Bracha, and Meier 2009). Such a backlash to explicit benefits because of image concerns may be particularly likely among individuals with less established or known reputations (Exley 2017). Other, related image concerns may also arise, such as when donations signal not only one's generosity but also one's income (Bracha and Vesterlund 2017).

Most of the private benefits described here are available only if the donor's identity is known. It may seem, then, that anonymous donations are purely altruistic. But even anonymous donors may experience giving's implicit benefits. For example, donating can be an act of self-signaling that allows donors to think of themselves as good and generous people (Bénabou and Tirole 2006). Donors may also receive a "warm glow"—a personal feeling of well-being—from saying yes to requests for donations. And the amount of warm glow may vary by how the charity plans to use the donation.[4]

There is a well-established correlation between being asked for a donation and actually making a gift of time or money. But it can be difficult to ascribe causality to correlations between being asked and being a donor, since the former may also influence the latter. Using a variety of approaches, including both field and natural experiments, researchers have found substantial evidence in favor of "the power of the ask" (Andreoni and Rao 2011; Meer and Rosen 2011).[5] Nonetheless, there are several ways to make asks more effective, and these strategies may work because they make the donor enjoy the act of giving more, or the act of declining to give less. First, asks should be in person and trigger empathy (Jason et al. 1984; Small and Loewenstein 2003). Second, asks are more effective when the solicitors are more physically attractive or have a personal connection with the prospective donor (Meer 2011; Price 2008; Raihani and Smith 2015).[6] Third, asks are more effective if there will be future interactions between a donor and the recipient (Rand and Nowak 2013). Fourth, asks are more effective when they cannot be avoided (Andreoni, Rao, and Trachtman 2017; DellaVigna, List, and Malmendier 2012). Fifth, asks are more effective when they come as a surprise (Exley and Petrie 2018).

As the use of premiums makes clear, nonprofits themselves don't care as much as Merriam-Webster does about whether donations are purely selfless. For the nonprofit, understanding the motivations behind donating is helpful only to the extent that it helps increase donations. Broader society too may care less about the psychology of altruism than about using resources for positive actions. We adopt this more use-based definition: the altruism budget, in our view, includes but is not limited to all donations, no matter what their motivation. This use-based definition is the most expansive view—an upper bound—on the items in the altruism budget. This approach allows us to remain agnostic on donors' motivations and avoid making often arbitrary decisions about the underlying motivation for various actions.

What Is in the Altruism Budget?

The most common measure of total charitable giving is simply the total amount of money given to nonprofit organizations—although from 1929 to 1959, the National Bureau of Economic Research (NBER) included in its measures of total charitable giving both government spending on social welfare programs and person-to-person gifts, such as remittances sent overseas (Soskis 2017).[7] These kinds of monetary gifts are relatively easy to measure, but focusing solely on them may lead us to miss the bigger picture.[8]

Recent years have seen a burgeoning interest in measuring other forms of charitable giving. The most frequent focus is on gifts of time—that is, volunteering.[9] Hybrid gifts, such as donating blood or an organ, which take up time but also involve literally giving up part of one's self, could form yet another category. Or consider a highly educated lawyer who turns down a well-paid law firm job to work at the nonprofit Innocence Project, or even at a public defender's office, for a much lower salary. Is this lawyer making a charitable donation of some kind? Are their actions altruistic? To what extent are they personally beneficial? It can be difficult to categorize many of these actions.[10]

Beyond time and money, many other gifts could be included in the overall altruism budget, but the value of these gifts is often difficult to quantify. A donation of $500 to the local YMCA is most likely valued at $500, but what about a donation of a couch worth $500 to the donor but only $300 to the charity?[11] In a similar vein, when actor Ethan Hawke appears in a video campaign for the YMCA, he gives not only his time but also his reputation (Look to the Stars 2018). How can the latter be measured? How does the value of Ethan Hawke's appearance compare with celebrity chef Marcus Samuelsson's in the same video?[12]

Paying a premium for charity-linked goods—for example, outdoor gear with a charity's logo, from which the charity receives a portion of the profits—may be another form of charitable donation (Elfenbein and McManus 2010). One could also add donations to politicians whose views one believes would benefit society. Intrafamily altruism can play a role as well, though an act may be thought of as less selfless if the beneficiary is one's own kin. From a purely evolutionary perspective, a parent sacrificing his life for his child still gains the private benefit of passing along his genes (Samuelson 1993). None of these actions falls under the traditional notion of "charitable giving," yet they may be motivated by altruism nonetheless.

Arguably, the altruism budget should include but not be limited to gifts of money, time, material goods, and reputation. And since the altruism budget includes so many different kinds of gifts, it is impossible to measure with any accuracy for any individual or group of people. It may, then, not truly be possible to answer questions about the altruism budget's flexibility with complete accuracy. What we can do, though, is look at the relationships between some of its components for hints about any trade-offs between them.

In the next section, we discuss selected findings on whether changes in one type of charitable giving lead to changes in others. We will not summarize the rather large literature on whether donations from one party crowd out donations from another party, as in the case of government spending crowding out individual giving (see Vesterlund 2006; Andreoni 2006b; Ottoni-Wilhelm, Vesterlund, and Xie 2017).

Is the Altruism Budget Fixed?

To grasp the difficulty of measuring the altruism budget's flexibility, it's helpful to imagine the ideal experiment that would fully measure it. The ideal experiment would allow for the collection of granular data on every aspect of the altruism budget, including formal giving to a charity, informal giving (say, to panhandlers), volunteering, purchases of charity-linked goods, and intrafamily altruism. But even a snapshot of every type of altruistic act would be insufficient. Donations may crowd out others intertemporally: an inducement to make a donation today may reduce giving next year, or even in one's bequest.[13] If all of this data were available, a researcher could randomly assign perturbations to one type of giving or another (through, say, providing incentives to give to a specific charity or in a specific manner). By observing these incentives' ripple effects on donations both within and across time periods and comparing the behavior of incentivized donors with those who did not receive those incentives, we could definitively answer the question of whether gifts at different times, to different sources, and of different forms are substitutes or complements. For obvious reasons, this kind of experiment is impossible. This level of detail and intrusiveness in data collection over a span of decades is simply unachievable. But by examining subsets of this question, researchers can begin to sketch the outlines of these relationships.

When Donors Increase Their Gifts to One Recipient, Do They Decrease Their Gifts to Others?

Perhaps the most natural place to begin is with different recipients. Does giving to one recipient result in fewer gifts to another recipient? Do efforts to raise money for one recipient cannibalize donations to others, or do they increase total giving?

Laboratory experiments offer the advantage of a controlled environment and examine how much substitution results from increasing incentives to donate to one recipient in a set of choices and from expanding the set of choices itself. Some laboratory studies find that increased giving to one recipient decreases giving to others (Corazzini, Cotton, and Valbonesi 2015; Harwell et al. 2015; Deck and Murphy 2018). Other laboratory studies, however, find that increased giving to one recipient increases total giving (Krieg and Samek 2017; Filiz-Ozbay and Uler 2018). Although concerns about the validity of applying findings from laboratory experiments to real-life situations are not unfounded, the unparalleled control they offer allows researchers to examine these questions with minimal interference from other, unobserved influences. Therefore, the mixed evidence in the lab settings suggests that this is a particularly difficult and perhaps context-specific question to answer. As an example of how this answer can vary depending on the type of competition, an increase in the number of charities available increases aggregate giving (though giving to each individual charity falls somewhat), while the availability of matches for some charities shifts donations toward them while leaving overall individual giving unchanged (Schmitz 2018).

Outside the laboratory, natural disasters are commonly used as an unexpected shock to giving to one type of charity. Somewhat surprisingly, most of these studies find that increased giving in response to a natural disaster is positively associated with other giving both at the time of disaster and following it (Brown, Harris, and Taylor 2012; Deryugina and Marx 2015; Scharf, Smith, and Wilhelm 2017). Similarly, when a matching grant induces giving to one project on the Donorschoose.org platform, giving does not decline to similar projects (Meer 2017). However, David Reinstein (2011) finds that when controlling for an individual's time-invariant attributes (like innate altruism), giving to one type of charity is correlated with less giving to other types of charities.

Research on directed giving, in which donors can target their donations toward specific functions within a charity, also sheds some light on this question. Judd Kessler, Katherine Milkman, and C. Yiwei Zhang (2017) and Catherine Eckel, David Herberich, and Jonathan Meer (2017) find that allowing donors to express their preferences results in higher donations among those who give, but Mackenzie Alston and her colleagues (2018) find no strong effects. Altogether, the evidence on this particular question is mixed, and additional research would be fruitful.

When Donors Give More of One Kind of Gift, Do They Give Less of Another Kind?

Most of the previous work looking solely at gifts of time and gifts of money finds that an increase in gifts of time is correlated with an increase in gifts of money (Andreoni, Gale, and Scholz 1996), so at first glance one might take this as evidence that giving money causes an increase in gifts of time, and vice versa.[14] However, generous people are likely to give in multiple ways, so finding a correlation does not imply such a causal relationship. Merely observing that someone who makes significant monetary donations also volunteers a relatively large amount of time does not mean that making the monetary donations caused the volunteerism (or vice versa). Understanding the causal, rather than correlational, relationship is necessary to answer the question of whether the altruism budget is fixed across gifts in different forms.

Early studies using survey data found evidence in favor of the idea that increasing one form of giving would increase other forms (Brown and Lankford 1992), but later studies find that the relationship may be more complicated (Andreoni et al. 1996; Feldman 2010; Yeomans and Al-Ubaydli 2018). For example, a person who is induced to give more money because of a tax break may learn about worthy causes when making those monetary donations and then start to volunteer more. Here one would observe a positive correlation between gifts of money and time, but the gift of money did not directly cause the increase in gifts of time. This distinction matters because the early evidence implied that inducing donors (or volunteers) to give (or volunteer) more would lead them to engage in the other activity more, whereas the later evidence implies that the altruism budget may be more fixed.

Beyond studies of observational data, a number of laboratory experiments have investigated the relationship between gifts of time and gifts of money. The results from these studies imply that gifts of time and money tend to offset each other, suggesting a relatively fixed altruism budget (Andreoni et al. 1996; Lilley and Slonim 2014; Brown, Meer, and Williams 2018).

As discussed earlier, the altruism budget includes many kinds of donations beyond time and money. Unfortunately, there is little research on choices involving two or more of these other types of gifts, most likely because relatively little data has been collected about these other forms of giving. Daniel W. Elfenbein, Raymond Fisman, and Brian Mc-Manus (2012) examined how charity-linked goods affect purchasing behavior but did not gather data about the interplay between the purchase of these goods and other donative behavior. More broadly, however, some research indicates that people may substitute one moral act for another; for example, people are more likely to donate money after they have lied (Blanken, van de Ven, and Zeelenberg 2015; Gneezy, Imas, and Madarász 2014). This finding suggests that the altruistic act of giving money is sometimes a substitute for other "moral" behavior.

Taken together, these studies indicate that although donations of time and money tend to increase together, that doesn't necessarily mean the altruism budget is expandable, and the few controlled laboratory studies imply that the altruism budget is fixed. Yet researchers have at most focused on two forms (usually time and money), though the altruism budget is far more diversified. A promising approach for future research would be to expand the number of forms across which prospective donors can substitute.

When Donors Give More Now, Do They Give Less Later?

Finding ways to increase giving today is less meaningful if it simply reduces giving in the future. Generous people are likely to give throughout their lives, so merely observing that certain people give generously at multiple points in time doesn't tell us whether current giving affects later giving in general. By using random assignment in field experiments or natural experiments that create shocks to giving, researchers can better ascertain whether giving today crowds out giving tomorrow.

A few articles imply that gifts today may lead to fewer gifts tomorrow (Meier 2007; Van Diepen, Donkers, and Franses 2009). Donors may become "fatigued" by multiple or frequent solicitations and simply tune out or even actively avoid these requests (Damgaard and Gravert 2018). However, the preponderance of the evidence finds that gifts today do not cannibalize gifts tomorrow. Jen Shang and Rachel Croson (2009), Maja Adena and Steffen Huck (2019), and Marco Castillo, Ragan Petrie, and Anya Samek (2017) find that donors induced to give more by a certain message do not give less in subsequent donation drives. Jason Cairns and Robert Slonim (2011) find that total donations at Catholic masses increased with an additional collection, with only about a fifth of the amount of the second round coming from reductions in the first round. Meer (2017) finds that matching-driven increases in giving to certain types of charities do not reduce future giving to related charities. Craig E. Landry and his colleagues (2010) similarly find that donors induced to give by a lottery give more in future solicitations that don't include the lottery incentive. Bekkers (2015) finds that those offered a match do not give less in response to a natural disaster months later. Kimberley A. Scharf and her colleagues (2017) use high-frequency data on donations following natural disasters and similarly find that giving is not offset by lower donations later.

All of these articles focus on donations of money, but Nicola Lacetera and his colleagues (2012) find similar patterns in blood donations: providing material incentives at a blood drive increases the number of people donating blood and has no negative effect on future blood drives at the same location without incentives. Taken together, these results dovetail with the evidence on habit formation in charitable giving, which suggests that creating a habit of giving when young can lead to greater generosity later in life (Meer 2013; Rosen and Sims 2011). Well-specified research on short-term substitution (over, say, a matter of months) can add to this body of knowledge. But investigating substitution over the longer run and even into bequest giving would provide a fuller picture.

Conclusion

Increasing donations to a single recipient may be a worthy endeavor. But society at large is more concerned about overall charitable giving. Therefore, we must go beyond a focus on increasing a particular type of altruistic act, at a specific time, to a particular recipient. Instead, we must strive to understand the potential for increases in one kind of donation to one recipient at a particular time to be offset by decreases in other kinds of donations to other recipients later on. Obstacles to this understanding include the difficulty of defining altruistic acts and measuring the many kinds of altruistic acts.

Overall, the evidence is decidedly mixed on whether the altruism budget is fixed or flexible. Perhaps surprisingly, gifts at one point in time do not seem to be neutralized by lower giving later. But the impact on contemporaneous gifts to other recipients or through other forms of giving is more difficult to summarize. This is still a fairly new area of research that suffers from a relative lack of data. A truly comprehensive data set would provide information about the total amount of all possible types of gifts a person gives to all possible recipients at all the possible times.

A complementary question to this discussion considers what might lead individuals to make a conscious decision not to give. For instance, preventing the ask from being avoided or making surprise asks may be effective because individuals have difficulty finding excuses not to give.[15] Indeed, one provocative finding from the literature is that it can be profit maximizing for a charity to allow prospective donors to opt out of being solicited (Kamdar et al. 2015). Even when the ask is not directly avoided, individuals often search for excuses—such as some chance that their donation will not have an impact or charity performance metrics—as a reason not to give (Exley 2015, 2018). But understanding why people *don't give* is even more difficult than understanding why people *do give*. Lack of response to a solicitation may arise from inattention, lack of interest, procrastination, or active distaste. As a counterpart to questions about what underlies altruistic behavior, understanding the complexity of motives for not giving is an important avenue for future work.

25 WHAT DO VOLUNTEERS DO?

Nina Eliasoph

WHY DO WE CARE ABOUT VOLUNTEERS and the voluntary sector? Many reasons are possible: volunteers potentially offer free labor, convivial sociability, and a selfless spirit of altruism. Volunteering can provide a healthful distraction for potentially delinquent youth, job training for the unemployed, or professional training toward a career. Volunteers can propagate cultural identities, form recreational clubs, fight for vast social change, and win small victories for their neighborhoods. When volunteer settings give people a chance to learn how to make decisions together and think about the bigger social picture, they can operate like small schools of democracy. The everyday experience of volunteering can embody any of these values.

All of them are worthwhile. Many nonprofits try to make them all happen at once. But not all volunteers do all these things, and none can do them all at the same moment (Eliasoph 2016; Garrow and Hasenfeld 2014; Mosley 2012).

This chapter's goal is to clear away some seemingly obvious but misleading ideas about volunteering. In common sense, as well as much scholarship, what is good about volunteering is, unsurprisingly, based on . . . its voluntariness! But what if the focus on voluntariness distracts us from focusing on whatever it is that we really value in volunteering? I argue that when we assume that voluntariness is the defining feature, we are using voluntariness as a vague placeholder for something we value. It might be anything on the preceding list or something else, but if you want to study nonprofit volunteers, it makes more sense to focus on whatever you actually value about volunteering than to rely on voluntariness as a vague placeholder.

The bulk of the chapter discusses and problematizes three common ways of distinguishing volunteering from other kinds of activities: the presence or absence of state coercion, payment, and customary moral obligation. I show that these three common definitions obscure much of the reason we care about volunteering: its ability to provide a range of social goods that we often lump together and gloss with the label *volunteering*. I then make the case for shifting our focus from voluntariness to whichever social goods the person who is examining volunteer work actually cares about, be they providing needed free labor, creating schools for democracy, or something else. I offer five examples of alternative focuses that can help researchers more clearly see how volunteers pursue social goods, both in everyday interaction with one another in nonprofits and also within larger economic, political, and cultural structures. In the end, I argue that although distinguishing volunteering from other kinds of work is not easy, the borders between the voluntary sector and other sectors are often where the most interesting action takes place (Alexander 2006).

What Is Volunteering? Work Without State Coercion, Customary Obligation, or Pay?

Crossnational surveys of volunteering require precise definitions of "the nonprofit volunteer," but their precision cannot fix a nagging empirical problem. To begin with, the boundaries between *nonprofit* and other things, and between *volunteer* and other things, are porous. In addition, naming itself does a lot of work for whoever is doing the naming: boundaries are often in the eyes of the beholders, and beholders often argue about what counts as "real" volunteering in a "real" nonprofit. Internally, many volunteers question their own motives. This chapter argues that for some kinds of research, it makes more sense to ask why you, or whoever is doing the naming, wanted to name someone a volunteer and why you or they care about nonprofit volunteering.

Others in this volume have already discussed the important question of how to define *nonprofit* (Bromley, Chapter 4, "The Organizational Transformation of Civil Society"; Powell, Chapter 1, "What Is the Nonprofit Sector?"). I will only note in passing that according to its most influential, formal, legal definition, the nonprofit sector includes Greenpeace, the National Hot Rod Association, the Emily Dickinson International Society, the Moose Club, many of the world's soup kitchens and ballet studios, the parent association at your local elementary school, and most American hospitals and museums (but not most French hospitals or museums, since they are almost all state-sponsored). Some are hundred-year-old, giant, international NGOs with directors and recipients of aid on opposite sides of the globe; others are tiny, local groups whose ten members all see each other weekly for a year before the group folds.

The usual approach to defining the nonprofit sector (also called the third sector, voluntary sector, or civic sphere) is to define it by what it is not: nonstate, nonmarket, and nonfamily (e.g., Wolfe 1989). Often, scholars name each sector and assume that action inside it fits the sector's boundaries the way wine fits into a bottle. The problem is that the action may not conform to the bottle's shape; the action can change the bottle's shape, if volunteers challenge their own position in relation to the state or the market, for example. And the bottles are scrambled together in the first place, since many nonprofits blend funding from nonprofits, governments, private individual donors, foundations, and corporations, and since "the nonprofit" exists only because governments have made nonprofits possible.

Defining "the volunteer" is just as hard as defining "the nonprofit." On the one hand, many people who are called volunteers do not feel like volunteers. They often feel compelled by the market, or by the state, or by custom. Some people volunteer because they must plump up a résumé to show future college admissions offices and potential employers that they are good, caring, selfless people (Handy et al. 2010; Eliasoph 2011, Bonetti and Riccardo 2015). Many have to work for free in their chosen field so that they can eventually get a job in it (Swidler and Watkins 2009). Many have to do volunteer work to pass a college class. Some are called "volunteers" but are paid—such as Peace Corps and AmeriCorps volunteers, who get paid enough for a person from a wealthy nation to live on (which would seem like a fortune for someone from most of the world). And what about the millions of American teens who do volunteer work because "community service" is a graduation requirement in their high schools (Wilson 2012)? What about employees who go to a protest that their company "suggests" they should attend and who may fear that if they do not attend, they will get fired or their jobs will move to another country (Walker 2014)? What about job trainees who have to do volunteer work to get welfare benefits? Do they all count as volunteers?

On the other hand, many people who do not get called volunteers, such as paid social workers, work long hours after work for free, taking care of the same people they serve at work. Are they *not* volunteers before 5:00 p.m., but volunteers after 5:00, even if they are doing the same thing they did from 9:00 to 5:00? What about people who live in villages in which it is customary to pitch in to help repair roads every spring, without pay, when these villagers know that if they don't pitch in, they'll be socially ostracized (Helander and Sundback 1998)?

In the end, defining nonprofit volunteering by its voluntariness may be missing the point: what matters is *why you care* about separating out nonprofit volunteers' activities from other activities. If the main reason that you care about volunteers is that they provide beneficial goods and services, then you should count the number of hours volunteers contribute to a nation per year and find a way to measure volunteers' skills at providing those goods and services, so you can measure the voluntary sector's contribution, perhaps counting it as hidden labor, that measures of the GDP should take into account (e.g., Salamon et al. 2003). If you care about increasing volunteers' chances for upward mobility and self-improvement, measure that. If you care about the voluntary sector because you have an idea of volunteering's unique contribution to democracy, then you should examine volunteering in ways that highlight this particular social good.

Formulating the question this way follows the "pragmatist" logic that John Dewey describes in an essay on the logic of scientific inquiry (1920:153): if you are evaluating a cherry orchard, you implicitly have a "for what?" in mind. If you want to harvest the fruit, your question is "How sweet are the cherries?" If you want to build cabinets, your question is "How many feet of good timber?" If you are kids interested in climbing trees, you wonder how solid each limb is. If you are teenagers looking for a secret place to kiss, you look for shady spots to hide under the boughs.

One good way to see a word's definition, in everyday usage, is to ask "as opposed to what?" Sometimes, people talk as if the opposite of *voluntary* is *coerced by the state*. Others implicitly define *voluntary* as the opposite of *paid*. According to this definition, working for money is implicitly another form of coerced labor, in addition to state coercion. The cultural power of this definition is why a nonprofit has to include some volunteers, as opposed to including only paid employees: not being paid makes their work seem more voluntary.

A third typical opposite of *voluntary* is *unquestioned*, like the customary mutual aid that people in precapitalist societies consider simply natural and normal and that still is in play in some places (Kropotkin [1892] 2006). It has its own kind of coercive power that comes from custom. In many touching studies of the transition to industrial capitalism in England, E. P. Thompson (1969) showed that when helping neighbors was not optional but was socially required, making a profit when others were in need was called *usury* and was considered a sin. Tocqueville implicitly adopts this definition of volunteering as the opposite of *natural and unquestioned* in *Democracy in America*. "Aristocracy links everyone in one long chain from peasant to king," he says. When democracy comes along, it "breaks the chain and frees each link" ([1835] 1969:508); as a result, feelings of solidarity are "reduced almost to nothing in democratic countries; they must therefore be *artificially created*, and only associations can do that" (515; italics added). To fit this definition, nonprofit volunteers should be joining on purpose, not just simply because they are bowing to an unquestioned moral order.

So now we have three possible definitions of volunteering: one that opposes it to government coercion, one that opposes it to market coercion, and one that opposes it to unquestioned moral obligation. But all three of these definitions present us with a challenge when we try to locate its defining feature: locating government coercion is hard; locating market coercion is hard; and distinguishing between customary, unquestioned moral obligations and voluntary ones also is hard. And once we do locate these different kinds of coercion, we see that they may or may not matter, or may matter differently, for the social action that made us care so much about volunteering in the first place.

Coerced or Controlled Versus Autonomous

According to our first common definition, nonprofit volunteering should be neither imposed nor politically controlled by the state. A usual illustration of state coercion is the Soviet-era's mandatory, so-called voluntary, unpaid Saturday work brigades, the *subbotniki*, in the Soviet Union and Eastern Europe. But the *subbotniki* present us with a puzzle: however coerced that volunteering was, it also provided the workers with many of the traditional benefits of volunteering. Many participants relished working shoulder-to-shoulder for the common good, cleaning parks, planting trees, and repairing shared buildings. Many Russians have been pining for those work brigades since the Soviet Union collapsed; they mourn that after that collapse, everyone had to start competing all the time (Clément 2015, 2017). The collapse of the stifling but secure and sociable Soviet order was followed by decades of chaos, enforced competition, emotional isolation, and lack of solidarity. Interviewees waxed nostalgic about the feeling of togetherness, shared work for the common good, and sociability that the *subbotniki* provided. This is the point: if the main value you hope to find in volunteering is the feeling of togetherness it produces, or if you value it because it's providing useful labor for the good of all, and if you are not focusing on whether the volunteering can easily become a school for democracy, then it does not matter if volunteering is government-controlled.

Even if a "school for democracy" is indeed a big part of what makes you care about volunteering, there is still a reason to doubt that volunteering that is sponsored by the state will be different from volunteering that is not. The sponsorship may not matter, because even in organizations that are completely state initiated and funded, the state may not exert control. The issue is about control, not sponsorship or funding. How do we know if the state is controlling the nonprofit volunteers? In some cases, it's fairly easy to tell. Many Chinese NGOs are not just funded by the government but also organized and strictly controlled by the government. These nonprofits are called, with only a small bit of sarcasm, GONGOs: government-organized non-government organizations. Volunteers in these GONGOs cannot easily oppose the government about issues such as human rights, labor, or environmental planning. They can help the government provide beneficial services, such as caregiving, but they can't easily question the government's policies (Xu 2017; Spires 2011). In France, in contrast, where about 43 percent of associations get government funding, even NGOs that openly defy the government get funding. So if the main reason you care about volunteering is its potential to be a "school of democracy," then the Chinese NGOs would not count but the French ones would. By contrast, if you're interested in the free labor that volunteers contribute to society or the feelings of fellowship that volunteering can produce, then both the French and the Chinese NGOs could count.

Figuring out what to count as government control is even harder than this example makes it look. If, as in some NGOs in authoritarian countries, volunteers clearly express an opinion or idea and the government explicitly prevents them from publicizing the opinion or acting on the idea, then the government is controlling the group. That is clear enough. But what if volunteers *preemptively* silence themselves? Many studies (Clément 2017; Eliasoph 1998; Gaventa 1980; Hamidi 2010; Norgaard 2011; Elsayed 2018; Talpin 2011; Luhtakallio 2012; Hustinx and De Waele 2015; among others) find volunteers silencing *themselves*, even without being aware of doing so, and without consciously noticing much state control. If they do so because they know they are powerless, fear that they are powerless, or firmly expect to be silenced, then how do we decide whether subtle forms of state control are in play?

If control is the issue, then it would be up to the researcher to decide whether those volunteers' fears and expectations were correct. This is the implicit logic behind various large-scale measures of democracy, such as the Varieties of Democracy database (Varieties of Democracy Project 2018): by examining laws, political parties, elections, social conditions, and over a hundred other variables, researchers should, in theory, be able to demonstrate how realistic the fears would be. If the fears are realistic, then the volunteers are under state control; if the researcher deems any fears unrealistic but the volunteers sound like they have no political concerns anyway, then the researcher would have to assume that the volunteers don't care about politics. In principal, a researcher could spend a lot of time with volunteers to see if they are actively narrowing their circle of concern because they assume that caring about politics would be futile or dangerous. But that would require watching the volunteers interact with each other in various settings over time and would require a great deal of interpretive work.

In my own ethnographic research (Eliasoph 1998), I heard school volunteers, while speaking in their group, avoiding questions that occasional visitors and newcomers brought to the group about the lack of government funding that caused their kids' school's roof to cave in, lack of money for computers, environmental problems, racism in the school, and other potentially "political" issues. The volunteers tried to avoid having to treat anything as a political issue. Instead, the long-term, loyal volunteers devoted lavish attention to topics such as building the throne for the homecoming queen, raising funds for the school, or their proud acquisition of the Royal Dog Steamer, which could roast twenty hot dogs at a time at school sports events, including Polish dogs, brats, wieners, foot-longs, and more! But the same volunteers who avoided politics in the group meetings revealed concern about these same issues when they were talking to each other in other situations, outside their group meetings. In their meetings, they tried only to talk about what they felt they could realistically do, often congratulating each other for being so effective at fund-raising and doing the tasks they set for themselves. When newcomers brought up conflict, funding, and more seemingly distant political issues, the long-standing volunteers ignored them, to focus with glee on the logistics of what they assumed that they could realistically do. Focusing on what they assumed they could not fix would have undermined their upbeat, can-do spirit.

Political scientist Camille Hamidi heard something similar in an NGO for minority youth in France. When speaking with the youth volunteers about their job-hunting woes, even the paid adult organizers who were members of the radical Green Party avoided making the connection between the misery of job-hunting and broader political issues. When speaking to members of the minority youth group, the organizers wanted to encourage the kids to try hard and have a can-do spirit and not to focus on long-term problems of anti-Muslim discrimination and structural unemployment that they could not immediately fix. But in other contexts, the same organizers indignantly decried the discrimination immigrant youth faced, and capitalism in general (Hamidi 2010).

If volunteers explicitly say that they don't care about big political problems and that they're freely choosing only to focus on what they can do realistically, which to them includes figuring out how to use the Royal Dog Steamer but does not include pressuring the government to fix the school's roof, then it can look as if the group is not controlled. In this and many other ways, it is often hard to distinguish between government control and its absence, even within one person, even within one's own self.

Unquestioned and Customary Versus Optional

If what you value in volunteering is volunteers' consciously, freely choosing to band together, then you might focus on the distinction between work that is unquestioned versus work that is optional. Consciously choosing to work together, as in Tocqueville's "artificially created" associations, means recognizing that what you are doing is not simply natural or God-given but rather something that ordinary humans have made and can control. This distinction presents a big puzzle for cross-national surveys of the voluntary sector. In many rural Finnish villages, for example, residents would be socially ostracized if they didn't take part in road building, barn raisings, or other shared activities like America's "quilting bees" of yore. In these Finnish "bees," like the many forms of mutual aid in most precapitalist societies (Kropotkin [1892] 2006), sharing does not feel like a choice. It seems simply natural, and if some quirky outlier in the village does not experience it as natural, then social acceptance demands participation anyway (Helander and Sundback 1998:18). This puzzle about how voluntary a shared activity has to be to count as volunteering also appears in debates about whether to include religious volunteering as truly voluntary, or whether this is even the right question (Tugal 2017). Identifying volunteering by looking for action that isn't mandated by custom has another problem: the sharp distinction between "inside" and "outside" is, itself, a modernist, Western concept in the first place (Elias [1939] 1982; Tugal 2017). For much of history, distinguishing private, inner feelings from social obligation was hard, if not impossible; some languages have neither the word nor the concept for that interior world of private, unspoken intentions (Rosaldo 1982).

Distinguishing obligatory obligation from voluntary obligation is not easy—not in one's own mind, and much less in someone else's. As many nations dismantle their welfare services, making volunteers do the work that paid social service providers once did to care for elders, disabled people, and youth (Smith and Lipsky 1993; Lichterman 2005; Eliasoph 2011), many studies describe volunteers' feelings waffling, moment by moment, as they ask themselves, "Am I voluntarily serving? If I am a decent, moral being, do I have a choice? What if my volunteering is ineffective because the state and its paid professionals *should* do this work?"

In *The Moral Neoliberal*, for example, Italian volunteers and employees of charity nonprofits say in some moments that they feel glad to help, grateful that they can serve humbly, and filled with mercy and lovingkindness. They really *hope to feel* that they don't have a choice, not because they're coerced, but because they *want* to feel, "This is who I am, I can do no other."

On the other hand, the same volunteers and employees sometimes speak of despair, resentment, and righteous indignation over the impossibly large task of making volunteers provide services that volunteers cannot realistically provide and that they wish the state would provide (Muelebach 2012; Verhoeven and Tonkens 2013; Grootegoed 2013; Grootegoed, Bröer, and Duyvendak 2013). Although they want to feel like the kind of person who freely helps, they also see that they often cannot realistically help the people they aim to help, and they resent being set up for failure. They can see that real help would be too time-consuming or expensive for volunteers to do, or would require too much expertise for volunteers to provide, and that the state needs to provide the service. To summarize their complex internal dialogues as "volunteering" would miss this mixture of wishing to be helpful, trying to avoid feeling helpless, and indignantly thinking that they are doing a job that the state should do.

Paid Versus Unpaid

Just as it is hard to see whether control is coming from the state, so is it also often hard to know whether control is coming mainly from a profit-making company. If you Google almost any corporation and add the word *volunteer* or *civic*, you'll find a web page that describes the company's volunteer projects. ExxonMobil, BP, Georgia-Pacific—many do it (Shachar and Hustinx 2019). Usually, they organize apolitical projects. BP, for example, asked employees in 2011 to donate old business-formal dresses to female job seekers and to clean up beaches (though not the same beaches that their company had destroyed in a massive oil spill the year before).

Some corporations go further toward politics by enlisting "volunteer" employees to picket on behalf of a cause that will benefit the corporation (Stauber and Rampton 1996; Walker 2014). Some corporations coerce volunteers; employees who do not contribute risk being fired. Other companies do not coerce so directly. In those cases, it's hard to draw a line between freedom and market-based coercion, because companies can threaten not just to fire the specific individuals who do not "voluntarily" go to city hall to defend the company but also to shut down whole industries and move away. In the 1990s, for example, timber companies threatened to move to other countries to avoid environmental regulation, and the companies lavishly funded campaigns to convinced some loggers in the Pacific Northwest that clear-cutting forests was the only way for the loggers to avoid unemployment. As a result, some loggers joined their employers to fight against environmental regulation (Stauber and Rampton 1996). Theoretically, it could be possible to decide what the balance was between coercion and persuasion here, but as in the question of "government control," the researcher would need to do a great deal of interpretive work to locate this balance. Theories of political conversation would guide us to listen to the volunteers' backstage jokes, songs, complaints, and whispers, to see if the volunteers resisted the corporation's way of bringing the market and voluntary sector together (e.g., Scott 1990; Bayat 2010; Eliasoph 1998).[1]

Money matters here—more than it should if it's purely part of "the voluntary sector." The timber industry induced loggers to picket on its behalf not only by threatening them with individual firings and mass layoffs but also by winning them over ideologically, and that victory depended, in part, on the timber industry's having more money than the environmentalists had to spend on funding ad campaigns; scientific research to highlight logging's benefits for flora, fauna, and waterways; social groups and meetings; lobbyists; market research to figure out how to sell its ideas to voters; and other ways of spreading ideas and influencing policy. The organizers that corporations hire to plan their volunteering efforts often invoke multiple, competing justifications of their work (Shachar et al. 2016), so it makes sense that the volunteers would, too.

There's yet another problem if *voluntary* means *unpaid*: often, the substantive distinction between paid and unpaid staff can be insignificant. Many social service workers' dizzy careers career between sectors as fast as the grants appear and disappear. A volunteer might quickly move to a paid job in which she works eighty hours a week while being paid for only forty, then to a paid position in another nonprofit while volunteering in a third nonprofit, and then to a city-funded job that feels nearly identical to the job in the nonprofit, round and round, with not much difference in the work, and within all the same social networks (Hamidi 2010; Eliasoph 2011; Swidler and Watkins 2009). John Krinsky and Maud Simonet (2016) portray a New York City parks manager who has a two-faced business card: on one side, he is an administrator with the New York City Department of Parks and Recreation; his name is displayed with the Parks Department logo and a .gov address. On the card's other side, he is an executive director of a nonprofit parks conservancy; his name is displayed with the nonprofit's logo and a .org address. So would we say that some hours of the day, he's under government control, and others, he's in the nonprofit sector? The same confusion might hit the job trainee who works under him, mandated by a welfare agency to clean parks. The job trainees are sometimes called volunteers. Are they volunteers for a city agency or a nonprofit? Since their volunteer work allows them access to needed welfare benefits, should we not consider it paid labor? Like the directors, the job trainee may have difficulty deciding which half of herself is in play at any particular moment.

The distinction between paid and unpaid presents still another puzzle: even if volunteers are not getting paid, often someone else is getting paid a lot because of their work. For example, when state or nonprofit volunteers replaced many of the unionized city employees who used to maintain New York City's parks, the nonprofit sector grew at the expense of the unionized, municipal government sector. When they beautify parks, these unpaid workers become part of a city's real estate speculation, fueling a growth machine that sometimes increases rents to the point that they get squeezed out of their own homes (McQuarrie 2011). The volunteers are inadvertently generating profits for landlords and real estate speculators, so, by some definitions, they are "workers" in a citywide, profit-making enterprise: they are generating profits. Volunteers and their labor are not separate from the market system—they're an important part of it.

To Study Mixed Motives, Don't Try to Unscramble Them

If what makes people nonprofit volunteers hinges on whether they're controlled by the market or the state or an unquestioned moral order, we have a general problem: usually, the volunteer has many motives at once. Volunteers often internally interrogate themselves about their own motives (see also Hustinx and Lammertyn 2003 and Eliasoph 2011 on this self-questioning). And as Femida Handy and her colleagues (2010) observe, somewhat in passing, when teen volunteers tell an interviewer that they're motivated by altruism, they may just be saying what they guess is the right thing to tell an interviewer. Nonprofit volunteers often argue with one another about which motive is really in play. Helping others is supposed to be an avenue for self-improvement and morally uplifting for the volunteer. It's also often supposed to help the volunteer test out a career and learn job skills. Volunteering is supposed to be good for one's health, preventing colds, heart attacks, and mental illness. If a volunteer experiences the activity as a choice in some moments of the day but not others, should we check the box marked voluntary, half voluntary, or not voluntary? Figuring out what to count as voluntary could require peering deep into actors' souls and imagining that there, in the deepest place within, the actor actually *can* distinguish between voluntary and involuntary.

But when we listen to volunteers talk about their motivations, we should expect to find layers upon layers upon layers of feelings, hopes about feelings, and fears about feelings. The Italian volunteers *hope to feel* that they have no choice because their integrity demands that they act; while they also secretly suspect that they might just leave at any moment to do something more rewarding; while they also see that as volunteers, they cannot do their job well; while they also resent the state for offloading an impossible job onto volunteers. In other studies, volunteers express internal doubts, worrying that they're just volunteering as a way to stuff their résumé for selfishly instrumental purposes in the face of grave social problems—asking oppressed people to "pimp their poverty" so privileged people can get grants and lines on their résumés (Eliasoph 2011). Among all these internal suspicions, hopes, fears, and other feelings *about* feelings, which would the researcher take the most seriously?

Similar layers of feelings, and feeling about feelings, appear in many ethnographies. To take another example from my own work: when a teen civic engagement project in the American Midwest got money to do volunteer projects, the disadvantaged teens in the group suggested having parties for themselves, since giving teens like them (who knew they were in prevention programs for at-risk youth) something to do that would be good for society. The teens who were *not* disadvantaged disagreed, saying that the group members were not the problem; they were supposed to be fixing other people's problems (Eliasoph 2011). But those same nondisadvantaged teens who thought that they were volunteering to fix other people's problems secretly suspected one another and themselves of just wanting to fluff up their résumés so they could brag about how caring they are on college applications.

Similarly, when disadvantaged French teens went to refurbish a hospital in Madagascar, they were ostensibly going to help others, but the organizers considered the trip to be also, or mainly, an educational project for the volunteers, and some volunteers accused others of treating it more as a vacation than a work brigade (Hamidi 2010). As Laura K. Gee and Jonathan Meer argued in this volume's previous chapter, if our understanding of volunteering (donating time) to a nonprofit depends on our assessment of how altruistic the volunteers' motives truly are, we get lost in an endless series of questions about what constitutes true altruism.

Some researchers try to get around these questions by focusing not on volunteers' motives but on who benefits from their work: are their actions "member benefiting" or "other benefiting"? The idea is that although both a soccer club and a free clinic rely on volunteers, the soccer club doesn't aim to help others whereas the clinic does. The problem with this distinction is that many nonprofits explicitly aim to do both, like the Midwestern teen civic engagement groups and the French group that went to Madagascar. To help others *is* to help yourself, in this approach.

Microlending programs blend self-help and help of others in yet another way. In one study of microlending in rural India (Sanyal 2014), the female recipients do everything that a Tocquevillean would hope: they develop fellow feeling, they learn to organize a group, and they develop a bit of social awareness. They do everything except the main thing that the microlending organization promises: make money. So they are helping themselves but not the way the program promises. When the World Bank promotes volunteering worldwide, in the interests of promoting economic development, do similar tangles arise, or different ones (World Bank 2012)? Seeing how the various missions tangle is more useful than trying to untangle them.

When We Don't Spotlight Voluntariness, What Else Comes to Light?
Focusing on voluntariness blinds the researcher to some of the most important differences between ordinary citizens' engagements. Furthermore, it may not be possible to distinguish between volunteering and not volunteering. Where does that leave researchers? I offer five ways of focusing research on volunteering differently.

First, as I suggested earlier, researchers can focus on what it is they value about volunteer: civic action, democratic participation, social solidarity and a spirit of connection, or whatever other social good that they habitually use the convenient and ennobling but distracting label *volunteering* to signal. Shifting the spotlight this way can open up new questions about how paid or unpaid, coerced or uncoerced, controlled or uncontrolled volunteers are creating that particular social good.

Second, scholars of volunteering might highlight institutional control itself and identifying its consequences. These scholars might borrow from John Gaventa's (1980) study of Appalachian miners. In this study, institutional control of the miners became most

visible when it came to an end. Miners who were members of a corrupt, undemocrati-
cally run union in the 1970s initially insisted to an interviewer that they did not care a bit
about politics. They professed utter apathy . . . *until* they got a "democratic union" that
gave union members real voice (Gaventa 1980). Soon, their apathy started to vanish!
They started becoming eager not just to participate in the union but also, remarkably, to
vote, talk about politics, watch the news, have meetings, and pay attention to politics in
all sorts of new ways. Now that they assumed they could do something about political
problems, they said they *did* care about politics. They became eager to challenge the
mining company's power and to name it as coercive and unjust. The union had changed
its way of connecting its own action to market and state action. The political scope of
miners' conversations widened.

Likewise, researchers may gain new insight into the nature of volunteering when there
is a shift in the institutional forces that contextualize it and give it meaning. What happened, for example, when local associations became legal in Russia (Zhuravlev, Yerpyleva,
and Saveleva 2017)? What happened when they become illegal in Egypt (Elsayed 2018)?
Then the "volunteers" begin either doing something new or giving new meanings to old
activities.

Third, scholars of volunteering might shine their intellectual beams on nonprofits'
interactional styles, asking how, or whether, the organization's habitual styles foster the
social good the researcher cares about (Eliasoph and Lichterman 2003; Lichterman and
Eliasoph 2014). For example, consider three organizations organized to help immigrants
and refugees in Denmark. The first, Friendly Danes, tries to convince citizens that immigrants and refugees are decent, nondangerous people and that citizens should make
immigrants and refugees feel welcome and at home. A second helps individual refugees
or families, one at a time, with things like finding housing and processing citizenship
papers. And a third fights the laws that make immigration so dangerous (Toubøl 2017;
Carlsen 2019; see Ramirez 2016, for a similar pattern in the United States). Internally, each
group has a different interactional style. For example, in the third, talking about social
conflict is required, but in the first, it's taboo—Friendly Danes just wanted to be friendly
and welcoming and not highlight conflict. As in these examples, interactional styles can
highlight or downplay conflict; they can also encourage long-term or short-term social
bonds, encourage or discourage discussions of systemic social change, and encourage
group members to speak for the vast majority or for a segment of the population. This
constellation of factors composes a group style. Some styles are better for enlisting volunteers at providing free labor; other styles are more likely to become schools for democracy,
and others provide other goods.

By focusing on a group's interactional style, researchers can see how a group collectively
imagines volunteering in relation to the various forms of coercion I have described. In
doing so, the group is shaping the market, the state, and the customary moral order, as
well as other institutionalized spheres, in relation to one another. Different societies have
different laws and historically solid ways of balancing the market, the state, the voluntary
sector, religion, and other spheres. These laws and histories are powerful, but there is also
always some motion, partly generated by actors themselves, maintaining or transforming
a society's way of balancing the spheres. A focus on style shows the actors' role in creating

this motion; it shows "the welfare mix" *in the making* (Henriksen et al. 2015; Hustinx and De Waele 2015; Meilvang, Carlsen, and Blok 2018; Meriluoto 2018).

A fourth distinction that this approach should make researchers notice is between volunteering with living beings versus volunteering with inanimate objects. Short-term, sporadic volunteers who crave bonding with human (or even animal) recipients of aid can often do more harm than good. In contrast, people who are picking up trash on the beach do not have to get to know the beach. If you value volunteering for the free labor it provides, then it is crucial to distinguish between the kinds of volunteering that require no long-term engagement with a live recipient versus the kinds that do.

In the after-school programs I studied, some volunteers aimed for a transformational experience of deep emotional bonding. They hoped to achieve this instant intimacy by conducting rowdy snowball fights on the street with the kids at dusk, for example. But these short-term, sporadic volunteers' relationship with the kids had to happen quickly, before the volunteer stopped coming. Distracting kids from doing their homework did more harm than good. Once in a great while, a volunteer succeeded in "bonding" quickly, usually with a lonely or fragile kid who was desperate for a bond; the short-term volunteer's sudden ripping of the bond then did more harm than good, especially with kids who had dared to risk bonding and who most needed a reliable bond.

Fifth, and perhaps most surprisingly and urgently, this approach repeatedly reveals a reliably important distinction: actors' time spent onsite. The main distinction may well not be between volunteers and staff but between those who have been working for many years—paid or unpaid—versus the plug-in, short-term employees or volunteers who help one day a week for a few weeks. Paid employees in social service jobs like those after-school programs can get to know their clients, whereas plug-in volunteers cannot.

This point requires a long illustration: in the after-school programs I studied, some long-term paid employees had deep knowledge of their kids. These employees were there every day, for years at a time, learning about the kids' lives. I spent the most time with Emily. She usually had fifteen or so kids in her program over the course of the four and a half years I spent in her program with them. She had long-standing inside jokes with them; knew the kids' teachers, parents, and neighbors; knew what their home life was like; knew more about the teens' love lives than the teens' parents knew; knew what each kid was learning in school; and even knew how fast some kids' hair grew! When Emily would get together with paid staff from other nonprofit and state-sponsored after-school programs, they would have long, reflective discussions with each other, both about their own working conditions and about the kids' living situations. These employees, in a loose network of youth programs around town, were nearly all white, and most of them had grown up in nearly all-white rural villages in the northern Midwest of the United States. After having repeated experiences of being trailed by security guards while shopping with their mostly African American program participants, these white adult employees now could joke and commiserate with each other about what "shopping while black" is like. When the adults were together, they critiqued their own programs, joking, for example, about a grant application's demand that the applicants document how many crimes, drug addictions, and pregnancies their programs' Friday night pizza parties had averted. These staff members were getting a good education in the schools of democracy that they were creating for one another. What made it possible was "quantity time" with the youth: its duration and rhythm both mattered (Mische 2009).

Conversely, plug-in volunteers would come to the programs for a few months at a stretch at most, for an hour or two a week. Some adult volunteers were students from the nearby university who had to do volunteer work for a semester, starting in late September and ending in mid-November. Often, today's volunteer would give advice that contradicted yesterday's volunteer's advice about how to do the homework. Once I was helping a girl with her homework who had been given contradictory advice each afternoon for three weeks on a long-term project. Now it was due in two days, and I was adding to the mess by saying that it looked to me like yesterday's volunteer had encouraged her to ignore the teacher's assignment. I went off to make a phone call, and when I came back, another volunteer had already undone my advice. I often heard kids lying to new volunteers (as most usually were new) about what they had been taught at school (the Pythagorean theorem? Conjugate *to be* in Spanish?) so they could weasel out of doing their homework. After a session or two like this, most adult volunteers gave up trying to offer homework help.

Clearing the overgrown underbrush of common sense pays off: common sense would have us focus on voluntary, unpaid labor, not voluntary, paid labor. But when we focus on what we value about volunteering, it becomes possible to see that the paid/unpaid distinction may matter less than, for example, time spent onsite. With this theoretical clarity, we can dive back into our field and notice something new: since employees typically spend more time onsite than sporadic, plug-in volunteers do, employees also have a better chance of creating those schools for democracy in these social service nonprofits than volunteers do. The historical dimension of volunteering becomes clear, then: in other historical moments, volunteers stayed onsite for decades, developing "invisible careers" working with the people they served (Daniels 1988; Hillman 1960). "Time spent onsite" becomes a distinction that the commonsense lens would have made impossible to see.

Conclusion

Yes, it is hard to draw a clear line between *volunteer* and *coerced*—to distinguish between volunteers who are controlled by the market, the state, or the moral order and those who are free. But this chapter ultimately argues that the borders between market, state, custom, and voluntary sector are often precisely where the most interesting action is: in that narrow, perhaps nonexistent space, for example, between the front and the back of that nonprofit/government New York park manager's business card.

Instead of focusing on identifying voluntariness, then, we can focus on what it is we value about what volunteers are doing and on how they're doing those things in relation to their organization and larger social structures. Whatever their possibly fleeting, probably mixed motives are, volunteers have to coordinate action in some patterned way. And by focusing on the varied forms of volunteering instead of trying to define them out of the picture, we can see the patterns in activities that people call volunteering and in organizations that people call nonprofits.

Crosscutting the Nonprofit Sector

Brad R. Fulton

AS THE OTHER CHAPTERS IN THIS SECTION MAKE clear, religious organizations are a significant and pervasive component of the U.S. nonprofit sector. They receive more charitable dollars than any other category of nonprofit organization—more than one third of all giving (Giving USA 2019). Religious organizations also mobilize more volunteers than any other type of nonprofit: three fourths of adult volunteers regularly attend religious services, and one third of adult volunteers learn about service opportunities through their congregation (Grønbjerg and Never 2004; Urban Institute 2004). Religious organizations are also the most prevalent type of organization in the nonprofit sector, encompassing not only congregations but also a wide variety of other faith-based organizations that provide a vast array of products and services (Ressler, Fulton, and Paxton 2019). Religious organizations operate in every major domain of the nonprofit sector and include religious media companies, faith-based prisons, "creation care" environmental movements, and Christian biker clubs.

Given the scope and scale of religious organizations in the nonprofit sector, it is critical to understand what characterizes these organizations, how they are different from and similar to secular nonprofit organizations, and how religion influences the nonprofit sector more broadly. However, nonprofit scholars have dedicated relatively little attention to religious organizations and still less to religion within the nonprofit sector. Indeed, the first edition of this handbook (Powell 1987) did not include a chapter on religious organizations, and the role of religion in the nonprofit sector in general has been understudied (J. Wood 1989; see also DiMaggio and Anheier 1990). A chapter in the second edition of this volume incorporated the sociology of religion but did not consider religious nonprofits through an organizational lens (Cadge and Wuthnow 2006). Organizational scholars have largely ignored religion in their study of organizations, neglecting both the study of religious organizations and the examination of religion in organizations (Tracey, Phillips, and Lounsbury 2014). As a result, little is known about the impact of religion and religious affiliation on nonprofits' characteristics, practices, and outcomes.

Existing research across a range of fields indicates that (1) participating in collective religious practices such as praying or singing together can facilitate social bonding among members of a socially diverse organization (Braunstein, Fulton, and Wood 2014), (2) religious beliefs can be a powerful and sustaining motivator for participating in a wide range of voluntary and charitable activity (Lim and MacGregor 2012), (3) religion and religious organizations play a central role undergirding democratic life in the United States (Fulton and Wood 2018), and (4) religiously rooted calls for justice and equality can provide a broad-based foundation for sustained civic action and advocacy (R. Wood and Fulton 2015). These findings illustrate the relevance of religion and religious organizations in the nonprofit sector and the importance of understanding the mechanisms underlying their impact.

It is also imperative to critically examine the assumed dichotomy between religious and secular nonprofits. The role of religion in the nonprofit sector is relevant to not only religious organizations but also secular organizations that incorporate religious elements or include faith-oriented participants. At the same time, some religious organizations operating in nonreligious domains of the nonprofit sector downplay their religious affiliation, making them functionally indistinguishable from their secular counterparts. In contrast, some religious organizations differentiate themselves from their secular counterparts by adopting an explicitly religious identity and incorporating religious practices into their activities. Despite the substantial overlap in activities and wide variation in approaches to religion, attempts to discern differences and similarities between religious and secular organizations and to understand how religion impacts the nonprofit sector have been inhibited by the dearth of research on religious organizations and religion within nonprofit and organizational scholarship.

This chapter begins by defining the field of religious nonprofit organizations—a task far less straightforward than it may first appear—and estimating the distribution of religious organizations in the major nonreligious domains of the nonprofit sector. The next section identifies religious nonprofits' distinctive characteristics and examines how they are similar to their secular counterparts, illustrating that the activities and goals of many religious organizations are often closely aligned with those of secular nonprofit organizations. Given this alignment, the chapter then explores various research avenues for approaching religious nonprofits. Finally, the chapter looks ahead to a strategic site for future research: hybrid organizations, specifically those that embody both religious and secular characteristics and pursue both nonprofit and for-profit aims. The research directions suggested in this chapter can not only generate insights about the field of religious nonprofits but also lead to greater understanding of the organizational life of the nonprofit sector as a whole.

Defining the Field of Religious Nonprofit Organizations

What defines a religious nonprofit organization in contrast to other types of nonprofits? Understanding the characteristics and activities of religious nonprofit organizations requires a clear definition of this organizational field, but achieving such clarity has vexed scholars for decades (Jeavons 1998). Most scholars agree on the general boundary demarcating secular and religious organizations: secular organizations have no explicit affiliation with religion, whereas religious organizations declare some such affiliation (Bielefeld and Cleveland 2013a). However, on the margins are nonprofits such as Habitat for Humanity and Charity: Water that have faith-inspired origins but provide entirely secular products and services and are perceived by the general public to be secular organizations (Baggett 2000). Similarly marginal are nonprofits such as the American Humanist Association that reject belief in the supernatural but resemble religious organizations in many ways, for example by having chaplains, hosting weekly gatherings, and performing life-cycle ceremonies such as weddings and funerals (Cimino and Smith 2014).

Another key question to address is how different types of religious organizations are classified. Although scholars generally agree on the definitional distinction between religious and secular organizations, they disagree about how to define, demarcate, and designate subsets of religious organizations. Although all religious organizations are considered nonprofits, most scholars recognize congregations as a distinct subset, commonly defining them as local organizations (e.g., churches, synagogues, mosques, and temples) whose primary purpose is to facilitate regular corporate religious worship among their adherents (Cnaan and Curtis 2013). Even religious traditions that are typically not organized as congregations in most parts of the world (e.g., Buddhism, Hinduism, and Sikhism) tend to adopt a congregational form when operating in the United States (Warner 1993, 1994). But although every congregation is a religious organization, not every religious organization is a congregation. And beyond congregations, the differentiations and designations of religious nonprofits become murky (for examples, see Bielefeld and Cleveland 2013a; Chaves 2002; Ebaugh, Chafetz, and Pipes 2006; Jeavons 2004; Scheitle 2010; Torry 2017).

For conceptual simplicity and analytical clarity, this chapter divides the field of religious nonprofits into two major subcategories—congregations and faith-based organizations (FBOs). The FBO subcategory includes all nonprofit organizations, apart from congregations, that include religion as part of their identity, such as (1) nonprofits directly affiliated with congregations (e.g., denominational offices, councils of churches, and mission agencies); (2) nonprofits focused primarily on promoting religious beliefs and practices (e.g., community prayer groups, prison ministries, and religious media producers), which are sometimes referred to as parachurch organizations (Scheitle and McCarthy 2018); and (3) nonprofits that are faith-based but whose core activity is something other than explicitly promoting religion (e.g., education, health care, or human services).

Despite the prevalence and pervasiveness of FBOs throughout the nonprofit sector, the total number and distribution of FBOs in the sector is not known, because the Internal Revenue Service (IRS) classifies an organization as "religious" only if its core activity is related to religion.[1] Organizations that are faith-based but engage primarily in nonreligious activities are classified according to their core activity, such as education or human services. Consequently, there are no data indicating whether an organization engaged primarily in nonreligious activities is faith-based, making it infeasible to calculate the number of FBOs operating in the various domains of the nonprofit sector.

In 2016, however, the IRS made electronically filed Form 990 data publicly available in machine-readable format. Form 990 asks organizations to describe their mission or most significant activities, and in one analysis, Robert Ressler, Pamela Paxton, and I searched these organizations' names and mission statements for key words related to religion in an attempt to identify faith-based nonprofits that are engaged primarily in non-religious activities.[2] Table 26.1 displays the results of that analysis: we found that

Table 26.1 The distribution of religious organizations in the major nonreligious domains of the U.S. nonprofit sector

Major NTEE category (code)	Number of organizations analyzed	Percentage identified as religious organizations
Arts, culture, and humanities (AR)	15,884	7%
Education (ED)	27,379	18%
Environment (EN)	7,660	3%
Health (HE)	26,419	15%
Human services (HU)	63,170	16%
International (IN)	3,658	30%
Mutual/Membership benefit (MU)	418	27%
Public and societal benefit (PU)	20,194	12%
All nonreligious domains combined	164,782	15%

Note: Results based on a "religious" keyword search of the names and mission statements of all 501(c)(3) organizations that e-filed Form 990 in 2015.

among the nonprofit organizations whose core activity is something other than religion, 15 percent include religious language in their name or mission statement. Each major domain of the nonprofit sector has organizations that appear to be faith-based, and in the education, health, human services, international, and mutual/membership benefit domains, 15 percent or more of the organizations appear to be faith-based. This analysis provides the first estimate of the distribution of FBOs in the major nonreligious domains of the nonprofit sector and indicates that the presence of FBOs is substantial and widespread. Additional calculations indicate that approximately 150,000 FBOs are operating in the nonreligious domains. This estimate does not include the approximately 350,000 FBOs and congregations whose primary activity is to promote religion, resulting in a total of approximately 500,000 religious nonprofit organizations in the United States.[3]

Crosscutting the broad range of activities in which FBOs engage is the wide variation in their levels of religiosity. The religiosity of an organization is the extent to which religion is a part of its identity, affiliations, and activities, ranging from being deeply infused with religion to exhibiting only its vestiges. Characteristics used to assess an FBO's religiosity include its mission statement; sources of funding and affiliations with specific religious traditions; the religious commitments of its board, staff, and volunteers; and the amount of religious referencing in its facilities, materials, programs, and goals (Bielefeld and Cleveland 2013a; Ebaugh et al. 2006; Fu, Cooper, and Shumate 2017; Jeavons 1998; Monsma 2009; Sider and Unruh 2004; S. R. Smith and Sosin 2001). These characteristics, however, can fail to uncover religious beliefs and motivations that are not explicitly stated but deeply influence a nonprofit organization's activity (Cameron 2004), especially when the products or services the nonprofit provides appear to be entirely secular (Austin et al. 2018).

In addition, because the measures used to assess organizations' religiosity tend to be more relevant and observable among Christian organizations, focusing on these metrics can hinder researchers' ability to assess the religiosity of nonprofits based in other religious traditions (Bielefeld and Cleveland 2013a; Hugen and Venema 2009; Jeavons 2004; Netting, O'Connor, and Yancey 2006; Schneider and Wittberg 2011). In the United States, the percentage of people identifying as Christian is declining, while the percentage of people who are religiously unaffiliated or affiliated with a non-Christian religious tradition is increasing (Johnson and Grim 2013; Pew Research Center 2015). Similarly, the number of non-Christian congregations in the United States is also growing (Grammich et al. 2012).

Extensive research in the field of religious studies examines differences between religious traditions (H. Smith and Marranca 2009), but relatively little research has examined differences between religious traditions' congregations (Dyck et al. 2005), and still fewer studies have examined how FBOs grounded in different religious traditions resemble or differ from one another (Fulton 2017; Netting et al. 2006). In fact, most research on FBOs has been limited to Christian-based organizations (Torry 2017). Given the variety of religious traditions represented in the faith-based sector (Fulton and Wood 2017) as well as the substantial policy interest in the role of religion in FBOs (Bielefeld and Cleveland 2013b)[4], examining differences across nonprofit organizations with disparate religious affiliations, forms of religious expression, and levels of religiosity is an important area for future research.

The legal definitions used to delineate religious nonprofits introduce a further element of complexity. Despite the increasing religious diversity in the United States, the IRS continues to exhibit a Christian-centric orientation. Its policies and documents use the term *church* to refer to congregations of any religious tradition, even though the term's use is typically limited to Christian congregations. Likewise, the IRS often uses the term *minister* when referencing the leaders of congregations, yet only Protestant Christian congregations use that term to refer to their leaders.

Government entities (e.g., courts, legislatures, and agencies), however, have generally avoided specifying what qualifies as a church (Hopkins and Middlebrook 2008). The IRS states that the term *church* includes any organization claiming to be a church, association of churches, or integrated auxiliary (U.S. Department of the Treasury 2015). Although the IRS does have a list of criteria it uses to assess whether an organization qualifies as a church, these criteria are only guidelines, and organizations claiming church status are not required to fulfill them. In effect, if an organization declares itself to be a church, it will be treated as such by the IRS and will enjoy all the associated privileges and exemptions (assuming that the organization does not violate the other conditions of exempt status, for example by distributing net earnings to individuals or shareholders or campaigning for or against political candidates). For example, in 2005 the IRS allowed the religious organization Young Life, which is generally viewed as a parachurch organization, to be recognized as a church (Bostwick 2007; Scheitle 2010). However, because Young Life was already registered with the IRS and continued to file annual returns, it is unclear what the organization gained (from a legal perspective) by claiming church status. Campus Crusade for Christ, another large parachurch organization claiming church status, does not file annual returns (GuideStar 2018a). Nonetheless, its annual reports, which are audited by independent certified public accountants, are publicly available. The Christian relief organization World Vision International also claims church status and follows a similar reporting model (GuideStar 2018b).

Despite the transparency of these particular organizations, evidence suggests that the ability to avoid disclosing their financial activity motivates some FBOs to claim church status (Barbee 2004; Barnes 2014; Charity Navigator 2018). Given the lack of restrictions on qualifying as a church, it is not surprising that a nontrivial number of FBOs make this claim. In a 2010 study that analyzed two thousand of the largest Christian nonprofit organizations (excluding traditional churches), approximately 6 percent claimed church status (Scheitle 2010). This statistic underestimates the actual percentage of FBOs that claim church status, because it does not include non-Christian organizations, smaller organizations, or, problematically, organizations that have not registered with the IRS because they are not required to do so because of their church status. As a result, the distinction between congregations and FBOs becomes blurred in a range of instances that cannot reliably be quantified.

This discussion demonstrates that although the idea of a religious organization may seem conceptually simple, delineating and distinguishing among religious organizations is practically challenging. Religious affiliation is not always all-or-nothing; it may appear in different forms and degrees. Moreover, although nonprofits that are influenced by religion need not disclose such affiliation, organizations claiming to be churches are not required to qualify for this status in any formal way. More research is needed to better understand the basic scope and scale of the field of religious nonprofit organizations as well as the varied roles religion plays in these organizations.

Differences Between Religious and Secular Nonprofit Organizations

What does existing research tell us about the differences between religious and secular nonprofit organizations? How are they treated differently under the law, and how does the organizational performance of religious nonprofits compare to that of their secular counterparts?

Legal Status

Religious nonprofits' constitutionally protected status distinguishes them legally from secular nonprofits. Although scholars may differ on how best to assess the religiosity of religious organizations, the U.S. government views all religious organizations equivalently under the religion clauses of the First Amendment. These clauses forbid the government from privileging religion (e.g., supporting religious organizations) and from prohibiting its free exercise (e.g., restricting religious expression). This status imparts both challenges and benefits. Compared with secular nonprofits, religious organizations are less able to procure federal funding to provide social services because of the restrictions on government support for religious organizations. On the other hand, although secular nonprofits must follow all federal employment laws, religious nonprofits are exempt from laws that impose on their religious beliefs such as some antidiscrimination employment laws and the Affordable Care Act mandate to provide health care benefits that cover birth control (Bielefeld and Cleveland 2013b).

The subset of religious nonprofits designated as congregations enjoy further freedoms that are not accorded to secular nonprofits. Although the constitutional nonestablishment and religious freedom laws apply to all religious organizations, the IRS grants special privileges and exemptions that apply only to congregations (and select associated entities such as integrated auxiliaries, associations of congregations, and affiliates of congregations). Notably, as mentioned earlier, congregations are not required to register with the IRS; they are automatically presumed to be tax exempt, their contributors' donations are tax deductible, and they need not file annual tax returns or report their financial activity (Hopkins 2016).[5] Church status also exempts congregations' "ministers" (i.e., staff who perform ministerial services) from paying self-employment, social security, and Medicare taxes and allows them to exclude housing expenses from their taxable income via the ministers' housing allowance (U.S. Department of the Treasury 2017).[6]

In contrast, none of these exemptions are given to employees of FBOs or secular nonprofits, even though the services they provide are often similar to those provided by ministers of congregations. FBOs receive no special privileges and exemptions from the IRS beyond the general exemptions that other, secular 501(c)(3) nonprofit organizations enjoy, such as (1) donations being tax deductible, (2) relaxed restrictions on the use of copyrighted material, (3) eligibility for special nonprofit postal rates and tax-exempt financing, (4) exemption from nondiscriminatory pricing laws, and (5) exemption from paying income tax and federal unemployment tax as well as property tax and, in some states, sales tax.

With their distinct legal status, congregations in the United States come closest to achieving the ideal type of an independent sector organization. Compared with all other types of nonprofit organizations, congregations operate with the greatest degree of independence from the government. The vast majority of congregations receive no financial support from the government; less than 2 percent receive government funding to provide social services (Fulton 2016b). Congregations also face the least amount of government regulation, intervention, and oversight, and their finances and activities are generally free from government entanglement. Congregations' autonomy is most apparent in their functional exemption from certain federal laws. Although no federal statute allows congregations to provide sanctuary to immigrants facing deportation, the government considers congregations to be "sensitive locations," meaning that under most circumstances federal immigration enforcement officers will avoid arresting people in congregations. Consequently, congregations can provide sanctuary knowing that federal agents are unlikely to carry out arrests inside their premises. In addition, congregations are the only organizations exempt from gender antidiscrimination laws, and they can refuse to recognize a same-sex marriage without consequence.

Furthermore, although the Johnson Amendment—a law that prohibits 501(c)(3) nonprofits from endorsing and financially supporting political candidates—applies to both religious and secular nonprofits, if efforts to repeal this amendment succeed, the repeal will affect religious nonprofits in distinct ways. Most significantly, repealing the Johnson Amendment would effectively make contributions to political candidates via 501(c)(3)s tax deductible, and such contributions made via congregations would not be subject to the IRS reporting requirements. The ability to shepherd tax-deductible political contributions without attendant reporting requirements may make claiming church status—a status not available to secular nonprofits—even more attractive to FBOs.

Clearly, U.S. laws grant religious organizations a heightened degree of autonomy. However, only congregations benefit from exemptions from taxes and reporting requirements. Although faith-based nonprofits enjoy some freedoms that secular nonprofits do not—

such as the ability to decline to subsidize employees' birth control—they are otherwise indistinguishable from secular organizations in terms of their treatment under the law. Future research could examine the degree to which tax advantages and other legal distinctions factor into organizations' decisions to identify as FBOs or claim church status.

Organizational Effectiveness

A core function of nonprofit voluntary associations is bringing people together around a shared interest, and congregations gather more people more regularly than any other type of association, faith-based or secular (Chaves 2004). Congregations' effectiveness as conveners is due primarily to their distinct role as facilitators of regular corporate religious worship. However, apart from conducting religious rituals, most of congregations' nonritual activities are similar to those offered by FBOs and secular nonprofits. For example, all three types of nonprofits have organizations involved in educating participants, facilitating artistic activity, hosting social events, raising funds, mobilizing volunteers, offering humanitarian aid, deploying disaster relief efforts, providing social services, and advocating for issues or groups. The main difference between organizational types is that congregations' involvement in these activities is secondary to their primary function of gathering people for religious worship, whereas FBOs' and secular nonprofits' involvement in a particular activity tends to be its primary function (Clerkin and Grønbjerg 2007). As a result, FBOs and secular nonprofits tend to be more specialized than congregations, but congregations are likely to have a larger, more committed, and more cohesive corps of volunteers (Graddy and Ye 2006).

Despite their myriad shared endeavors, most research comparing the activities of congregations, FBOs, and secular nonprofits has focused on similarities and differences in their provision of social services—assessing the quality, characteristics, and types of services provided—and the comparisons tend to be primarily between FBOs and secular human service organizations. Although no study has systematically compared the functioning and effectiveness of FBOs with those of secular organizations, comparisons of specific types of programs indicate that faith-based nonprofits tend to provide equivalent or superior services compared with their secular counterparts (Bielefeld and Cleveland 2013b). The comparisons include examinations of prisoner reform programs (LaVigne, Brazzell, and Small 2007), international development organizations (Clarke and Ware 2015), nursing homes (Amirkhanyan, Kim, and Lambright 2008), refugee resettlement agencies (Eby et al. 2011), and poverty relief programs (Kissane 2008).

Faith-based and secular human service nonprofits often have similar functional characteristics with regard to the services they provide, yet many FBOs have additional features as well as ties to congregations that can facilitate service provision, such as (1) free meeting space at partner congregations, which reduces operating costs (Ammerman 2005); (2) clergy referral systems, which can help connect new clients with the appropriate services (Yamada, Lee, and Kim 2012); (3) spiritual intervention methods, which offer a wider array of therapeutic strategies (Hodge 2011); (4) broad social support systems, which can facilitate recovery and social stability (Levin 2014); and (5) a large volunteer base, which can enable the provision of services on a larger scale (Leviton et al. 2006).

On the other hand, faith-based human service organizations address fewer types of needs (often limited to immediate needs and emergency assistance) (Boddie and Cnaan

2012), offer a narrower range of services (providing primarily food, clothing, shelter, and basic health care) (Clerkin and Grønbjerg 2007), and are less likely to employ certified professionals than secular nonprofits. The differences in the service provision focuses of faith-based and secular nonprofits, however, are often complementary (Graddy and Ye 2006). Secular nonprofits provide primary services such as substance abuse and mental health treatment, while FBOs offer supplemental services such as informal counseling, mentoring, and support groups (Wong, Fulton, and Derose 2018). Consequently, it is common for faith-based and secular nonprofits to collaborate in providing services (Ebaugh et al. 2007; Fulton 2016a). Some secular mental health care providers enlist faith-based collaborators to create a continuum of care for the client and the client's family. For example, a faith-based foster care and placement program may collaborate with a secular nonprofit agency that is licensed to certify foster parents (Thomas 2009). Such collaborations enable the respective organizations to leverage their assets to more effectively accomplish their shared goals.

These findings show that when religious organizations are compared to secular organizations performing equivalent functions, the faith-based organizations appear to do so marginally more effectively, likely because of the additional resources available to FBOs through their close associations with congregations. However, because FBOs and secular organizations tend to provide slightly different services in overlapping realms, they need not be approached as competitors. Although more comprehensive comparisons of the organizational performance of religious and secular organizations would be valuable, the ways in which these classes of organizations collaborate is also an important area for further study.

Similarities Between Religious and Secular Nonprofit Organizations

Having discussed some of the ways in which religious and secular organizations differ, this section asks how they are similar. An often overlooked similarity between religious and secular nonprofits is that both types of organizations can be influenced by religion. The religious–secular dichotomy among nonprofit organizations oversimplifies religion's place in the nonprofit sector. Secular nonprofits are not necessarily entirely nonreligious (Cadge and Konieczny 2014). Religion can be present in and influence secular nonprofits through the religious beliefs, commitments, and practices of an organization's founders, staff, or volunteers (Tracey et al. 2014). In both religious and secular nonprofits, religion can influence attitudes toward work and volunteering as well as approaches to making decisions, setting goals, and resolving conflict (Weaver and Stansbury 2014). Religion's role in an organization is not limited to only prosocial outcomes; it can also fuel prejudice, undermine cohesion, and provoke conflict (Chan-Serafin, Brief, and George 2013). Despite religion's capacity to influence organizational life, research on the role of religion in nonprofit organizations has been limited, especially among secular nonprofits. Religion's persistence and pervasiveness in U.S. society warrants exploration of its impact on the nonprofit sector.

Additionally, every major domain of the nonprofit sector has a distinct faith-based (often Christian) organizational presence, from traditional poverty relief efforts to mental health, education, and the arts. These organizations and their secular counterparts often operate in similar spheres, either in cooperation or in direct competition. Likewise, they face similar operational, management, and personnel concerns and are subjected to the same legal requirements. Despite FBOs' religious basis, these organizations tend to mimic the form of their secular counterparts with regard to authority, governance, and hierarchy, as well as processes such as bureaucratization and professionalization (Hinings and Raynard 2014). Indeed, when congregations are excluded from the discussion, faith-based and secular nonprofits tend to be much more similar than different.

This resemblance, however, has not always been so apparent. Amid the general rise of formal organization as a central feature of civil society (see Bromley, Chapter 4, "The Organizational Transformation of Civil Society"), research that examined religious organizations tended to focus on their distinctly religious nature and sacred characteristics (Beckford 1985). Following the widespread onset of secularization in the 1960s, however, the line between the sacred and the secular within religious organizations has been blurred substantially (Chaves 1993), as has the line between religious and secular nonprofits.

The distinctiveness of religious organizations has been eclipsed by expectations that they perform like secular organizations (Hinings and Raynard 2014). All organizations face pressures to adopt legitimate forms and practices, and because many board members of nonprofit organizations (faith-based and secular) work in the for-profit sector, they bring templates for how effective organizations should look and function. These templates include formal organizational structures, standardized administrative processes, and specialization among staff and volunteers. Despite being predominantly secular in their origins, these models are embraced equally by faith-based and secular nonprofits (Hinings and Raynard 2014). Likewise, religious and secular organizations encounter similar challenges related to scaling activities, managing resource flows, and sustaining a stable base of volunteers. Although having an affiliation with religion distinguishes faith-based nonprofits from their secular counterparts, both types of organizations face these common institutional pressures and organizational demands.

These observations illustrate that religious and secular organizations share not only similar structural characteristics and organizational challenges but also, in the United States at least, religious influence through participants and leadership. Because faith-based and secular nonprofits operate alongside each other in many of the same activity domains and operate similarly as organizations, comparative analyses across all domains are certain to advance understanding of both types of nonprofits as well as the nonprofit sector in general. The following section considers some relevant organizational theory approaches that could be used to engage such lines of inquiry.

Religious Organizations and Organizational Theory

What can studies of religious organizations tell us about organizations more generally and nonprofit organizations in particular? What theories can be applied to these investigations to further our understanding of the nonprofit sector? Noting the relative dearth of research at the intersection of religion and organizations, this section examines three prominent organizational theories that could be used to inform understanding of religious nonprofits and how they are different from and similar to their secular counterparts: organizational identity, organizational culture, and institutional theory. By describing these theories' relevance and application to a wide array of religious organizations, this section demonstrates how examining religious organizations can advance understanding of nonprofit organizations as a whole. The section underscores the importance of examining religion in nonprofit organizations that may not be explicitly religious. In doing so, it further illustrates the myriad types of religious organizations whose activities extend beyond religion to engage other domains of the nonprofit sector, including immigrant rights advocacy, microfinance, higher education, and environmental activism.

Organizational Identity

The concept of organizational identity is prominent in organizational research, and its relevance and significance for understanding the function and distinctiveness of religious nonprofits cannot be overstated. The identity of a religious organization is central to its existence and purpose. An organization's identity is based on characteristics that are both projected and perceived as being central, enduring, and distinct to the organization (Albert and Whetten 1985). Because claims on an organization's identity can come from multiple sources, an organization can have multiple, often competing or contradicting identities (Pratt and Foreman 2000). Religious nonprofits typically have a diverse array of constituents, stakeholders, and critics and often must compete with one another and their secular counterparts. Consequently, religious organizations face unique and significant challenges in establishing organizational identities that appeal to their diverse audiences and enable them to maintain their competitive advantage.

An organization's projected and perceived identity is shaped by its objective features, the subjective experiences of its participants, and its surrounding environment (He and Brown 2013). Among religious nonprofits, the identity-shaping process is complicated by each organization's need to manage both a religious identity and an identity related to its functional purpose, which is often not explicitly religious—for instance, Jewish Family Services offers programs for seniors, Catholic Charities provides support to refugees, and Jobs for Life helps formerly incarcerated people obtain jobs. Consequently, religious nonprofits must often determine how much they want to claim religion as part of their identity. Some religious nonprofits, especially those aligned with conservative religious movements (e.g., Bob Jones University, Mercaz USA, and the Catholic League), emphasize their religious identity to appeal to their base and distinguish themselves from their secular or "less religious" competitors (Emerson and Hartman 2006). In contrast, other religious nonprofit organizations—often those operating outside the United States, such as World Relief and International Justice Mission—downplay their religious roots because they believe that their affiliations with religion may impede their ability to accomplish their objectives (Berger 2003).

Because a nonprofit organization's religious identity and functional identity compete with each other for prominence, on occasion one identity must surrender to the other. For example, over time the Young Men's Christian Association adopted its acronym *YMCA* as its primary identity, and in 2010 began referring to itself simply as *the Y*, effectively masking its association with Christianity. Interestingly, though, the Y remains registered with the IRS as a religious organization. In contrast, most of the general public perceives the Y to be a secular health and fitness center. To further complicate this case, local Y chapters operate with a high level of autonomy and vary tremendously in how much they emphasize their Christian identity. The degree to which these chapters explicitly highlight Christianity depends on the priorities and orientations of the chapter's executive director, board members, and surrounding community (Herzog 2016).

As this example highlights, given religious organizations' often complex structural arrangements, competing priorities, diverse stakeholders, and varied surrounding environments, they provide excellent cases for examining differences between an organization's projected and perceived identity as well as the relationship between those identities—topics that organizational theorists continue to debate (Brown et al. 2006; Ravasi 2016). Research that shows how religious nonprofits manage competing identities can inform nonprofit scholarship in general—for example, by illuminating how nonprofits address conflicts between their social mission and financial sustainability (Jäger and Beyes 2010) or how they resolve tensions between volunteers' and employees' differing perceptions of their organization's identity (Kreutzer and Jäger 2011).

Research on organizational identity formation can also help explain how religious nonprofits develop an identity that enables them to engage and retain a socially diverse base of participants. For example, Dennis A. Gioia and his colleagues (2010) analyze how a new organization with a diverse group of constituents forges its identity and find that the organization moves through a sequential four-stage process to ultimately converge on a consensual identity. They also identify recurrent processes, such as negotiating identity claims and assimilating legitimizing feedback, that cross-cut the stages and can disrupt or facilitate identity consensus. If a nonprofit organization regularly runs aground when negotiating claims between competing identities, it can struggle to coalesce around a consensual identity. On the other hand, if an organization can effectively generate and incorporate legitimizing feedback from external stakeholders, this practice can bolster the organization's efforts to forge a consensual identity. Such research, which highlights the interaction between internal resources and external influences in the identity formation process, is critical for understanding how religious nonprofits form their identity (Gioia et al. 2013). More broadly, scholars can draw on organizational identity research to examine how the nonprofit sector, with its diverse collection of subsectors, stakeholders, social purposes, and civic aspirations, forges a cohesive identity.

Recent research applies organizational identity theories to the Episcopal Church and the identify transformation it is experiencing in the wake of electing its first openly gay bishop (Kreiner et al. 2015). This decision has generated both harsh criticism and exuberant praise from the denomination's members as competing subgroups concurrently seek to change and preserve their organization's identity. The authors use the case of the church's "identity crisis" to refine the concept of organizational identity work—the processes by which participants transform an organization's identity (Sveningsson and Alvesson 2003). The authors develop the construct of *identity elasticity*—tensions that simultaneously stretch and hold together social constructions of identity—to explain how an organization's identity is produced through ongoing dialectic tensions that both stretch and strengthen it. This concept of identity elasticity, developed through research on a religious organization, also advances understanding of identity change processes in organizations in general. Research on organizational identity transformation is particularly relevant to nonprofit organizations because they operate in social, political, and economic contexts that are often shifting, which requires them to adapt their identities in order to remain relevant and competitive.

Although organizational identity has become a core component of organization theory, relatively few examinations of religious organizations use an organizational identity frame (Tracey 2012). Religious nonprofits provide a rich empirical context in which to study the formation, maintenance, and transformation of organizational identities for several reasons. To begin with, new religious nonprofits often develop distinct organizational identities. Many long-standing religious nonprofits, meanwhile, have strong and enduring identities, while others are undergoing significant identity transformations. Moreover, because religious organizations operate in every major domain of the nonprofit sector, they provide a natural comparison group when analyzing the identities of secular nonprofits.

Organizational Culture

Closely related to but distinct from organizational identity is organizational culture (Whetten 2006). Early research on organizational culture focused on an organization's values, norms, and practices and tended to be oriented around three major perspectives: integration, differentiation, and fragmentation (Alvesson 2012; Martin and Frost 2011; Schein 2010). Integration focuses on efforts to create a unified organizational culture; differentiation focuses on the dynamics of competing subcultures within an organization; and fragmentation focuses on the ambiguities, contradictions, and paradoxes found within most organizational cultures.

A recent development in organizational culture research draws from sociological analyses of groups and focuses on the patterns, styles, and modes of interaction between group participants (Fine 2012). Building on the concept of inhabited institutions (i.e., recognizing that institutions are inhabited by people doing things together), this research reveals how an organization's culture is developed through its members' interactions (Fine and Hallett 2014). For example, examinations of socially diverse nonprofit organizations reveal the variety of competing cultures they contain and illustrate how interactions among members from diverse backgrounds shape the organizations' distinctly intersectional cultures (Walker and Stepick 2014). Such meso-level analyses, which examine aggregations of people characterized by a shared place and social network, are well suited for research on the complex organizational cultures that often characterize religious organizations and other types of nonprofits.

Although many religious nonprofits, especially congregations, tend to be socially homogenous, an increasing number are actively seeking to become more diverse along multiple social dimensions (Edwards, Christerson, and Emerson 2013). However, their often-entrenched organizational cultures related to gender, race, and class can hinder advances in diversity (Fulton, Oyakawa, and Wood forthcoming). For example, an analysis of evangelical parachurch organizations reveals that although they espouse egalitarian views on gender, traditional gender norms persist within the organizations and adversely affect female employees' fund-raising efforts and leadership prospects (Perry 2013). Research on multiracial congregations indicates that despite their racial diversity, such congregations often need to privilege white members' religiocultural preferences to keep these members involved (Edwards 2008). Betsy Leondar-Wright (2014) shows how leaders' inability to

understand and bridge different class cultures within class-diverse, faith-based organizations can undermine their capacity to address common organizational problems.

As this body of research shows, socially diverse religious nonprofits face challenges in
their efforts to create inclusive, cohesive organizational cultures. But as other studies show,
religion can be a resource in this effort as a bridge between social differences. A study of
faith-based community organizing organizations indicates that religious practices, such
as collective prayer, can function as cultural bridges that enable these organizations to
foster bonds across racial and socioeconomic differences (Braunstein et al. 2014). Related
research on cultures of interaction among faith-based housing advocates offers insight
into how an organization's group style can influence its ability to involve a diverse base of
constituents (Eliasoph and Lichterman 2003; Lichterman 2012). Group styles are routine
ways of talking and acting that shape the everyday interactions of a set of people. This
cultural-interactionist framework highlights the importance of creating an inclusive group
culture within which all parties in a diverse organization feel comfortable and represented
(Leondar-Wright 2014; Lichterman 1995). Cultural practices that can help bridge social
differences extend beyond religious practices to include activities such as playing games,
sharing a meal, and singing together. Such practices are not restricted to religious nonprofits; they can be observed—and studied—in secular nonprofits as well.

A recent study of faith-based immigrant rights organizations extends this line of research by analyzing how an organization's group style influences constituent involvement
(Yukich, Fulton, and Wood 2019). The study examines the conditions that produce substantial organizational involvement across lines of difference. The authors highlight the
notion of a *representative* group style—that is, a style that incorporates preferred practices
of the full spectrum of constituents an organization seeks to involve. The authors find that
a representative group style can enable organizations to achieve and sustain greater levels
of social diversity than nonrepresentative group styles enable. Such research leverages the
complex internal dynamics of religious nonprofits to better understand an organization's
culture and how it influences participants' involvement. These insights can be applied
to any organization that aspires to be more socially diverse, a common goal for many
nonprofit organizations.

Institutional Theory

Institutional theory, which focuses on how institutional environments shape organizations'
structures and practices, is another broad framework that nonprofit scholars can use to
examine religious organizations (Meyer and Rowan 1977). To date, however, their use of
this theoretical framework to analyze religious nonprofits has been limited (Tracey 2012).
Among the few examples is a study that examines the diffusion of organizational innovation among Christian denominations with respect to the practice of ordaining women
(Chaves 1996). Another study demonstrates how concerns about institutional legitimacy
influenced the votes of leaders who participated in the Second Vatican Council (Wilde et
al. 2010). A third study illustrates how isomorphic pressures can influence black churches'
likelihood of sponsoring HIV/AIDS programs (Fulton 2011). Although these sociologists
of religion have used institutional theory to better understand religious organizations,
rarely have religious organizations been used to further develop institutional theory. Given

the pervasiveness of religious nonprofit organizations, this gap represents an opportunity to pursue more robust theoretical frameworks.

Recent developments in institutional theory, specifically related to institutional logics and institutional work, are particularly relevant to research on religious organizations and nonprofits more broadly (Gümüsay 2017). Institutional logics are systems of cultural elements and practices that individuals and organizations use to structure their activity and provide meaning (Thornton and Ocasio 1999). Although religion is recognized as a core societal institution with an associated logic (Friedland and Alford 1991), organizational scholars rarely incorporate the logic of religion into their analyses of secular organizations. Indeed, among the core societal institutions defined by institutional logics, religion is the least examined by organizational scholars, and among the core logics, the logic of religion is the least used (Tracey et al. 2014). Although these metrics suggest a general bias against religion among organizational scholars, they also reveal gaps in the literature waiting to be filled. At the same time, research on religious organizations rarely incorporates the other core logics (e.g., the state, market, professions, and community) (Tracey 2012). If more nonprofit scholars were to make an analytical shift to include the logic of religion in their analyses of secular nonprofits and incorporate other core logics in their analyses of religious nonprofits, this research would both facilitate comparisons between religious and secular nonprofits and generate broader insights about the logics driving the nonprofit sector.

Religious nonprofits provide fertile terrain for understanding how organizations leverage complementing logics and negotiate competing logics. Recent research demonstrates how the different forms of religious nonprofits incorporate the logic of religion and combine it with other logics. For example, religious universities seeking to compete athletically with secular universities confront competing logics in defining success as an organization based on religious mission, educational commitments, and athletic ambitions (Nite, Singer, and Cunningham. 2013). Similarly, Islamic banks face the oppositional logics of Islamic religion and the market (Syakhroza, Paolella, and Munir 2018). These opposing logics can influence the banks' hiring practices (Boone and Özcan 2016) and lead to innovative adaptations such as microfinance programs that target families and incorporate religious work incentives (Gümüsay 2015).

In another example from the nonprofit sector, faith-based humanitarian organizations that are headquartered in the United States and provide services in other countries encounter distinct institutional logics that span multiple societal contexts and involve actors from different institutional arenas (Burchardt 2013). The new meanings and practices emerging at the interface of the distinct institutional logics can influence an organization's form, dynamics, and performance. Similarly, interfaith social change organizations involved in the religious-environmental movement employ a strategic combination of moral, communal, and economic logics when encouraging faith communities to adopt energy-saving technologies and behaviors (Biscotti and Biggart 2014).

Examining the logic of religion and its intersection with other logics is critical for understanding religious nonprofits that are engaged with broader aspects of society, including their secular counterparts. In addition, understanding how religious organizations manage competing logics and respond to pressures from secular organizations could help advance scholarship on the contemporary issues of institutional complexity and pluralism (Greenwood et al. 2011). Overall, the logic of religion merits more attention from not only nonprofit scholars but also organizational theorists. Such research could help advance institutional theory by creating more opportunities to explore compatibilities between logics.

Institutional work, which examines how individual and organizational actors affect institutions, is another strand of institutional theory that is relevant for religious nonprofits and the broader nonprofit sector (Lawrence and Suddaby 2006). Most institutional approaches to understanding organizations focus on the convergence and reproduction of organizational norms and practices, rather than on efforts to resist isomorphic pressures (Battilana and D'Aunno 2009). A growing literature on institutional work, however, has been filling this gap by highlighting the role of individuals and organizations in creating, maintaining, and disrupting institutions (Lawrence and Suddaby 2006; Lawrence, Suddaby, and Leca 2009; Lawrence, Leca, and Zilber 2013).

Research that applies an institutional work lens to its examination of religion and religious organizations has helped explain the emergence of new organizational forms, the maintenance of precarious inter-institutional arrangements, and the disruption of organizational fields. For example, studies of the Emerging Church, a nascent Christian movement known for its anti-institutional orientation, explain how the movement's affiliated nonprofit organizations engage in institutional work to resist normative pressures that value reliance on formally trained and credentialed professionals (Marti and Ganiel 2014; Packard 2011). Some of these organizations resist institutionalization by adopting an inverted labor structure; they fill full-time positions with lay workers and employ religious professionals on a part-time basis. This practice leverages the intimate knowledge that homegrown leaders possess and reduces opportunities for religious professionals to implement institutional processes.

Other research examines the challenges that evangelical Christian colleges face in straddling the institutional fields of conservative theology and higher education, which exert conflicting pressures (Taylor 2015). Taylor's analysis reveals that some of these colleges successfully navigate this tension and maintain viability by engaging in creative institutional work that appeases one set of stakeholders without alienating another (Taylor 2015). A study of the religious nonprofit The Fellowship—a low-profile prayer group for government, corporate, and religious elites—describes how the organization combines institutional and anti-institutional elements to resist the push to bureaucratization (Lindsay 2010). This intentional organizing strategy enables The Fellowship to locate itself at the interstices of multiple institutional arenas, which allows it to draw from multiple resource streams and maintain a desired level of anonymity. Each of these examples illustrates the utility and promise of incorporating an institutional work framework to better understand the role actors play in shaping religious nonprofits—an approach that clearly applies to other nonprofit organizations as well.

The myriad types of religious organizations mentioned in this section highlight their broad range and presence in every major domain of the nonprofit sector. As a field, religious organizations offer a variety of contexts that both resemble and differ from their secular counterparts; applying organizational theories to the novel contexts of religious organizations may help refine these theoretical constructs in ways that further our understanding of nonprofit organizations as a whole. The combination of nonprofit scholars' minimal attention to religion, sociology of religion scholars' minimal contributions to organizational theory, and organizational scholars' minimal engagement with religious organizations has resulted in limited knowledge about the dynamics of religion in the nonprofit sector. In recent years, however, these fields have revived appeals to advance research at the intersection of religion and organizations. Such research promises to increase the relevance and scope of organizational theory as well as our understanding of religious organizations and the role of religion in the nonprofit sector.

Hybridity Among Religious Organizations

I have argued that one promising route to advancing our understanding of the nonprofit sector is to bring the sociology of religion and organizational scholarship together in two ways: by integrating research on religious nonprofits with organizational scholarship and by examining religion in organizations. To illustrate the prospects of this integration of fields, this chapter concludes with a discussion of hybridity and hybrid organizational forms. It addresses questions of what hybrid organizations are, how they emerge, what forms they take on within the nonprofit sector, and what types of hybridity are presently seen among religious nonprofits.

Hybridity refers to the combination of disparate elements to form distinct entities. Hybrid organizations draw from multiple institutional logics to create novel organizational forms that span institutional boundaries and operate at the intersection of multiple logics (Jay 2013). Some scholars assert that the entire nonprofit sector is a collection of hybrid organizations that variously combine elements of the market, state, and community logics (Brandsen, Van de Donk, and Putters 2005).

Although many nonprofit scholars use the concept of hybridity merely to describe blended organizational forms, some scholars have begun to theorize how hybrid forms emerge (Skelcher and Smith 2015). Institutional theory, specifically the institutional logics perspective described in the previous section, provides a helpful theoretical foundation for explaining the emergence of hybrid organizations (Pache and Santos 2013). Scholars claim that hybrid organizational forms develop in contexts of overlapping institutional logics (Skelcher and Smith 2015). For example, the Delancey Street Foundation simultaneously engages multiple logics through its residential self-help organization. This organization employs participants to work in its social enterprise ventures and uses the profits, along with private donations and government grants, to provide new residents with free housing, food, clothing, and job development training. The plurality of competing and contradicting institutional logics in play prompts the creation of novel organizational forms that can accommodate these logics, and the various combinations of logics produce a variety of hybrid forms.

The nonprofit sector is particularly suited for developing theories of hybridization, because nonprofit organizations often operate under a plurality of logics (Pache and Santos 2013). They respond to these multiple logics by adapting their organizational forms to accommodate their embedded position in multiple institutional arenas (Kraatz and Block 2008). An early example of research on hybridity in the nonprofit sector examines the development of the service/advocacy organizational form, which integrates political advocacy with service provision in response to competing institutional pressures to relieve immediate needs and provide long-term solutions (Minkoff 2002). More recently, social enterprise organizations, which straddle the logics of the market and community, emerged in response to competing pressures to both meet social needs and be financially self-sustaining (Doherty, Haugh, and Lyon 2014; Gidron and Hasenfeld 2012).

Religious nonprofit organizations offer an even richer context for theorizing about hybrids, because many such organizations operate by default at the intersection of more than one logic. As *religious* organizations, they are influenced by the logic of religion, and those whose primary activity is something other than religion are also influenced by the logic associated with that arena of activity. Consequently, religious nonprofits can provide excellent cases for examining the mechanisms underlying the formation and sustainability of hybrid organizations.

Faith-based philanthropy is one arena in which elements from multiple institutional logics can be combined to create innovative organizational forms and leveraged to accomplish organizational objectives. For example, the Israel bond project, which solicits gift investments from the Jewish-American diaspora, combines elements of the market, state, community, and religion logics to create a program for generating financial resources that overcomes limitations associated with transnational bond markets and conventional philanthropy (Lainer-Vos 2012).

Another example relates to the professionalization of the nonprofit sector (Hwang and Powell 2009) and the emergence of hybrid professions in religious organizations (Torry 2017). As congregations adopt businesslike models and require greater managerial oversight, the position of executive pastor (i.e., the congregation's chief operating officer) has emerged and grown in prominence (Powell 2009). This development has altered the training and credentialing expectations of religious leaders such that many seminaries and divinity schools have begun offering management courses (Cornwell 2017), and some nonprofit management programs are marketing to religious professionals (Ebrahim 2012). Similarly, many of the leadership skills needed to lead FBOs are now more likely to be obtained from a public affairs or business school than a seminary or divinity school (Torry 2014).

Finally, social entrepreneurial activity is becoming more prevalent among religious organizations and individuals acting on their religious beliefs (Spear 2010). Some religious organizations form social enterprises that sell secular products and services to fund their charity work (Starling 2010). Other faith-based social enterprises have been established to help start congregations and supplement the salaries of bi-vocational pastors (Picardo 2015) or to partner with government agencies to support community development initiatives (Fitzgerald 2009). Despite religious organizations' and individuals' increased involvement with social entrepreneurship, the relationship between religion and social entrepreneurship remains underexamined (Tracey 2012). Analyzing this relationship could reveal more about why certain organizations and individuals engage in social entrepreneurial activity.

More broadly, including religion and religious nonprofits in research on hybridity can help scholars better understand who is innovating in the nonprofit sector and why particular hybrid organizational forms emerge. The variety and complexity of newly emergent forms present a ripe opportunity for examining the evolving role of religion in the nonprofit sector.

Conclusion

Defying the predictions of secularization theory (Berger 1967), religious organizations remain an integral aspect of contemporary society. Congregations continue to be the most ubiquitous voluntary organization in the United States, and FBOs maintain a substantial presence in every major domain of the nonprofit sector. Many religious organizations have exhibited shifting identities, cultures, and logics, often in response to broader social changes and pressures, and some have taken on new hybrid forms by incorporating corporate-style management structures and social entrepreneurship. Despite the unique status of congregations in the United States, the many similarities (as well as notable differences) between FBOs and secular nonprofits indicate that research on religious organizations can yield new advancements in our overall understanding of the nonprofit sector. At present, the limited research on religious organizations and religion in the nonprofit sector leaves a substantial gap in our knowledge of the sector. Pursuing such research can broaden our understanding of who participates in the sector and how different types of organizations define, run, and adapt themselves in a complex institutional environment amid shifting social, political, and economic conditions.

PART VIII

GLOBAL AND COMPARATIVE PERSPECTIVES

THE CURRENTS OF GLOBALIZATION FLOW throughout the volume. At times, this is relatively obvious, as with the rise of immigrant organizations. Other times, global pressures are rather subtle, as with the spread of the organizational form of a nonprofit or NGO and evolution of various best practices of governance and accountability for these entities. The chapters in this concluding section bring the complex global forces that shape nonprofit sectors around the world to the fore. Reflecting the multidimensional nature of globalization itself, the chapters approach the matter in very different ways. Several key tensions emerge. First, there has been a massive expansion of nonprofit activity worldwide and an explosion of advocacy activity including social movements, especially since the 1990s. All the chapters point to this growth, shedding light on its multiple causes and forms. At the same time, there is a rising countertrend, perhaps suggesting the explosion of nonprofit activity in the late twentieth century is unlikely to continue indefinitely. Thus, as civil society gains in power and authority, it becomes subject to increasing criticism and a backlash from a growing number of governments and members of society—a process reminiscent of Karl Polanyi's "double movement" describing the reciprocal process of growing marketization alongside increasing protections against it.

In Chapter 27, Evan Schofer and Wesley Longhofer reflect on the character, causes, and consequences of a global "boom" of NGOs, especially since the 1990s. They argue that the growth of domestic nonprofit sectors stems from global cultural forces. In particular, the NGO emerged as a preferred organizational template in the international community, emblematic of the dominant liberal ideologies that generally favor and legitimate private organizing. International organizations and donors increasingly supported NGOs, and the template of the NGO provided a global category and model that subsumed much existing organization. As a manifestation of cultural preferences, rather than a functional response to contextualized needs developed from the ground up, there is less reason to expect NGOs to be superior service providers relative to government or business. Indeed, as the authors note, the literature is mixed: much research is largely optimistic about the positive benefits of NGOs, but there are also sharply critical voices that observe instances of dysfunction and failure.

The global cultural character of NGOs helps account for divergent views in existing research on their benefits and drawbacks. That is, increased transnational association is distinct from normative assertions of the sector's value. Setting claims of good and evil aside, what becomes clear is that human capacity for transnational associational forms and interaction is greatly augmented as NGOs become increasingly structured in standardized global forms and categories, operating as an integrated organizational field. However, current populist and nationalist attacks on liberal ideologies could portend the stagnation of global organizing. Whereas earlier fears about the decline of civil society are rooted in atomizing modernity, technology, or various sources of corruption (e.g., narrow self-interest and rent-seeking, or capture by powerful donors and elites), Schofer and Longhofer suggest that NGOs may come under attack from a different source: illiberal movements and regimes.

In Chapter 28, Kendra Dupuy and Aseem Prakash take up the issue of the global backlash against civil society. As in other chapters, the authors observe that civil society grew rapidly in the Global South and former communist countries after the Cold War, contributing to a push for global democratization and improved service delivery. But a puzzle emerges soon after. Foreign aid was essential to the growth of domestic nonprofit sectors, and as a result of huge influxes of funding, the numbers of domestic and international organizations operating in resource-strapped countries boomed in the 1990s. Later in that decade, however, a curious trend began to emerge: low-income countries increasingly started to restrict the operational abilities of civil society organizations (both foreign and domestic), including their access to and use of funds raised from foreign sources.

Dupuy and Prakash empirically explore the causes of this increase in legal restrictions in poor countries and investigate the impact of the legal backlash on civil society organizations. The restrictions these laws impose are coming in all sorts of different forms. In some places, government authorization is now required for locally operating NGOs to receive funding from international sources, while others have started requiring organizations to report receipt of internationally sourced funds to the government. Some governments set specific limits on the amounts of international financing organizations can receive; others restrict the types of organizations that can receive foreign funding. These legal restrictions reflect two ways in which the state is seeking to reassert its sovereignty. First, states want to control the ability of foreign donors, private or governmental, to influence their domestic politics though financial support to NGOs. Second, states are limiting the domestic political and economic space available to NGOs to function effectively. This clampdown on civil society is part of a wider pushback against key democratic rights and freedoms that has swept the globe in the past decade.

In Chapter 29, Breno Bringel and Elizabeth McKenna consider the global context of social movement organizing. The late 1980s heralded a sudden succession of protests around the world—in cities as diverse as Cairo, São Paulo, Lisbon, Hong Kong, and New York, city streets were awash with activists. Although this wave of unrest was remarkable, the wider phenomenon of global protest diffusion has a long history. Long predating the rise and spread of digital networks, the history of transnational social movement activism encompasses religious uprisings, abolitionism, anticolonial independence movements, and the anti-globalization protests that marked the turn of the twenty-first century. Guided by a historical view, they have two main aims. In the first section, they situate global social movements in a *longue-durée* perspective, outlining patterns in how transnational collective action has both taken shape in the real world and been studied by social scientists. They draw on a select review of research that speaks to the multiple levels and scales at which social movements operate, identifying three genres of scholarship: (a) labor internationalism (and the antiracist and anticolonial movement studies that similarly address how activists confront global capitalism); (b) polity studies, which takes the nation-state as the primary movement target; and finally (c) a postmodern and postcolonial turn to the universal dynamics of social contestation.

The diverse paradigms for studying global social movement activity come with distinct strengths and weaknesses. In the second half of the chapter, Bringel and McKenna draw lessons from what was gained and lost in the transition from one approach to the next by considering the content, form, and temporality of global social movements. There is a puzzling development in the body of research on global social movements. Despite an upsurge in scholarly interest in the topic and widespread coverage of multicountry mass demonstrations like the Arab Spring, recent levels of transnational activism do not appear to have kept pace with late-twentieth-century predictions. In part, the surprisingly low levels of activism come from a mutual neglect of research on political context and content and research on the organizational forms, practices, and routines that constitute social movements.

In Chapter 30, Helmut K. Anheier, Markus Lang, and Stefan Toepler critically assess the state of comparative nonprofit sector research. Whereas other chapters in the volume speak to macroprocesses that are assumed to operate more or less worldwide, comparative research emphasizes the distinctiveness across countries. The two approaches, global and comparative, are related but generate different insights. Over the past three decades, as the sector itself has gained policy salience globally, comparative nonprofit research has also made significant strides. Observing this associational revolution, in the 1990s, scholars at the Johns Hopkins Comparative Nonprofit Sector Project launched an ambitious empirical and conceptual initiative to deepen our understanding of nonprofit sectors around the world, which provided the foundations for much of our contemporary comparative knowledge. The research project developed definitions and classifications for comparative research, presented data to position the sector economically, and introduced a conceptual framework for understanding variations in nonprofit sector size and scope: namely, the social origins theory.

Twenty years after its first formulation, Anheier and his colleagues revisit the social origins theory as well as underlying basics of comparative nonprofit sector research to date. They suggest that there is a need to rethink the definition and classification of nonprofits and to reexamine the overall analytic approach, including nonprofits' institutional embeddedness in the three institutional complexes of market, state, and civil society. Given the context of perceptions of a shrinking or closing space for civil society, efforts to align nonprofit and civil society research agendas should become a core task of comparative, crossnational research in this field in the near future, ideally linked to other, broader research efforts in the social sciences.

As a whole, the section addresses the interplay of national and global dynamics in nonprofit organizing. The two levels—national and global—are linked, in that the emergence of the NGO as a dominant cultural model for organizing is associated with new global forces that propel the formation of NGOs, over and above national-level organizational and political factors. But global trends interact with domestic legacies and distinctive political, economic, and social conditions, creating distinct cross-national arrangements in each country. Recognizing both variation around the world and the diffusion of global trends to vastly different national settings exposes the contextual assumptions of early theories. For example, ideas of market and government failure presume liberal market economies with decentralized, competitive electoral systems and heterogeneous demand for public goods; they were not necessarily meant to have international applicability. One consequence is that research on the sector tends to emphasize times and places that fit existing theoretical assumptions. Another is that we have focused on politically left-leaning issues, leaving us with little analytical leverage on understanding antiliberal or illiberal movements and associations. In an era of growing backlash against liberal democracy, market capitalism, and free association worldwide, there is an urgent need for data and theory to explain global changes and solve the most pressing social problems.

27 THE GLOBAL RISE OF NONGOVERNMENTAL ORGANIZATIONS

Evan Schofer and Wesley Longhofer

THE WORLD IS AWASH IN NONGOVERNMENTAL ORGANIZATIONS (NGOs). In 1989, economist Kenneth Boulding (1989:244) observed that the rise of the NGO "is perhaps one of the most spectacular developments of the twentieth century, although it has happened so quickly that it is seldom noticed." A similar sentiment was expressed by Harvard historian Akira Iriye, who wrote that to ignore the NGO is to "misread the history of the twentieth-century world" (Iriye 1999:424). Greeted with much fanfare in the 1990s, NGOs were often seen as "magic bullets" or "favored children" of international development. In the years since, the excitement has tempered (Edwards and Hulme 1996; Werker and Ahmed 2008); nevertheless, NGOs have become such a fixed part of social and political life in much of the world that to question their purpose or longevity seems absurd.

The pervasiveness of the NGO is reflected in their sheer numbers, which are staggering, even though precise figures remain elusive. A 2014 analysis by the Central Bureau of Investigation estimated that more than two million NGOs were operating in India alone.[1] Up to ten thousand NGOs have reportedly been active in Haiti in recent years, leading to its reputation as a "republic of NGOs" (Katz 2013). The Moroccan Ministry of Interior reports more than 130,000 civil society organizations currently in operation (or, for those counting, roughly one for every 270 people; USAID 2016). Between 80 and 90 percent of villages in Bangladesh are home to at least one NGO (Gauri and Galef 2005; Rahman 2006), which seems plausible given that more than 250,000 are registered with the Bangladesh Department of Social Services and other governmental agencies (USAID 2016). And at the global level, the Union of International Associations lists more than seventy-five thousand active and dormant international nongovernmental nonprofit and voluntary organizations. These include both well-known organizations, like Amnesty International and Oxfam, as well as hundreds of professional associations, such as Belgium's International Federation of Landscape Architects (Union of International Associations 2019). As a point of comparison, the United Nations estimated that there were roughly eighty thousand multinational corporations in 2006, suggesting, at least in quantity, a rough one-to-one correspondence with international NGOs (UNCTAD 2007).

What is more, the number of NGOs around the world is expanding. In our previous work (Schofer and Longhofer 2011), we documented cross-national variation and growth trends of NGOs and other societal organizations. Figure 27.1 shows the global distribution of NGOs. Most are found in the affluent societies of Western Europe and North America, while much fewer organizations are found in parts of sub-Saharan Africa and Southeast Asia. Figure 27.2 illustrates the growth of organizations over the period from 1991 to 2006. Growth occurs essentially everywhere in this period, generally at very high rates. Particularly rapid expansion can be seen in Eastern Europe and Central Asia, which makes sense given the dissolution of the Soviet Union. But moderate or high rates of growth can be found elsewhere across Europe, Asia, the Middle East, and sub-Saharan Africa. As Patricia Bromley (Chapter 4, "The Organizational Transformation of Civil Society") and others have noted, organizational expansion has taken place across countries despite widely varying levels of economic development and severity of local problems.

Similarly, the number of *international* nongovernmental organizations (INGOs) rose dramatically over the much of the twentieth century. They now constitute a primary infrastructure of global civil society (see Figure 27.3; also Boli and Thomas 1999; Kaldor, Moore, and Selchow 2012). Growth may have slowed a bit in recent years (Kaldor, Moore, and Selchow 2012), though John Boli and George Thomas (1999) note substantial lags before newly founded organizations are included in conventional data sources, which makes it hard to fully assess the extent of the change.

The international community has heavily supported the expansion of NGOs at the local level, especially in recent decades. The United Nations first established its Committee on NGOs in 1946 to report to the Economic and Social Council (Otto 1996). Although the UN engaged NGOs directly in some programs, such as refugee assistance, as early as the 1950s, it was not until the 1980s that NGOs became a central focus of the organization. By the 1990s, the UN was spending more than $2 billion per year on various NGO conferences, as well as training and capacity-building programs (Reimann 2006). Today, more than five thousand NGOs hold formal consultative status with the UN.[2] Rapid growth of NGOs can be found in many sectors, including environment (Longhofer and Schofer 2010), education (Bromley, Schofer, and Longhofer 2018), and human security (Murdie 2014), among others.

The growth of NGOs is often assumed to yield widespread benefits. Its champions herald the role of NGOs in expanding democratic governance, alleviating poverty, and delivering key services when states are unable or unwilling to do so (Brass 2016; Bratton 1989; Fowler 1991). As a result, much of the discussion of NGOs is explicitly normative and, at times, even triumphalist. Proselytizers sing the virtues of local organizations as vehicles for empowering vulnerable populations and contributing to collective goods, from building wells and providing microloans to performing critical advocacy and watchdog roles in the wider political system. Similarly, Amanda Murdie (2014) describes how much of the literature in international relations assumes that international NGOs embody a set of "shared values" and "moral authority" to advocate on behalf of citizens under repressive regimes and others seeking justice (Risse 1999; Keck and Sikkink 1998).

Yet NGOs have their critics. Their effects on development and other outcomes are often impeded by their dependence on donors, technocratic approaches, and weak ties to local constituencies or stakeholders; in some cases, the activities of NGOs may perpetuate inequalities or make them worse (Banks, Hulme, and Edwards 2015; Edwards and Hulme 1996; Campbell 2003; Mosse and Lewis 2005).

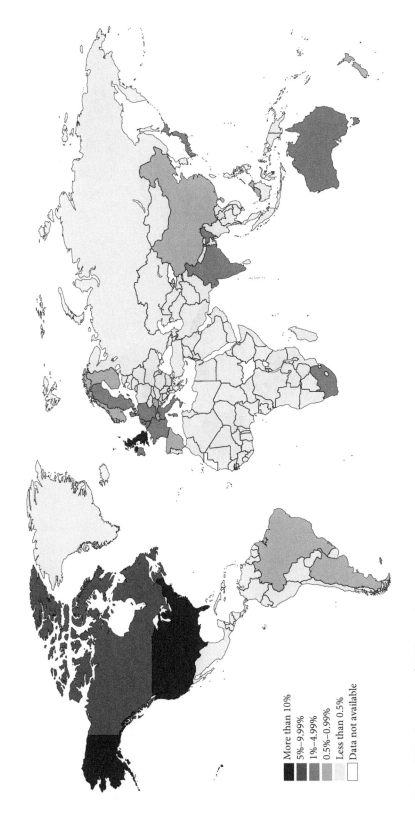

Figure 27.1 Percentage of NGOs, 2006

More than 10%
5%–9.99%
1%–4.99%
0.5%–0.99%
Less than 0.5%
Data not available

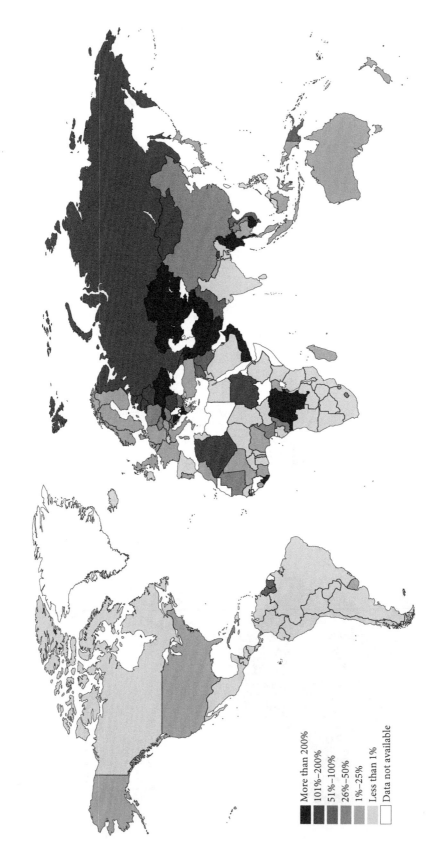

Figure 27.2   Percentage change in NGO density (per 100,000 people), 2006

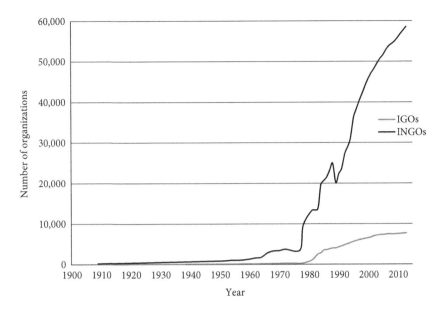

Figure 27.3 Number of organizations in the *Yearbook of International Organizations*, 1909–2011
Source: Union of International Associations 2013, https://uia.org/yearbook

In this chapter, we set aside the normative question of whether NGOs have fulfilled their promises. Instead, we focus on a more fundamental question: How can we explain the emergence and expansion of the NGO as a dominant model for organizing social activity? The issue gets less attention than one might expect, perhaps because, for proponents of NGOs, their existence requires little explanation: NGOs arise because they are beneficial. Scholarly attention consequently shifts toward the question of why there aren't more NGOs, given the pressing needs of communities around the globe.

We examine a broader range of possible explanations for the growth of NGOs by viewing them as *organizations* embedded in global culture, as Sarah Stroup (2012), Susan Cotts Watkins, Ann Swidler, and Thomas Hannan (2012), and others have done. We suggest that the laudatory voices in the academic and policy literatures are emblematic of broader liberal ideologies that have become entrenched in the contemporary international community and that have propelled the rapid expansion of NGOs. However, recent global events should cause us to reconsider whether the growth of NGOs will continue indefinitely, or whether current populist and nationalist attacks on liberal ideologies may signal the decline of these organizations (see Dupuy and Prakash, Chapter 28, "Global Backlash Against Foreign Funding to Domestic Nongovernmental Organizations"). Put simply, if the past century was indeed the "Century of NGOs" described by Akira Iriye (1999), what does the present one hold?

What Is an NGO?

The term *NGO* carries multiple meanings. First, *NGO* can be used very generally, as a near-synonym for the "third sector" that encompasses nonprofit organizations, membership associations, civil society organizations, and advocacy groups that are part of neither the state nor a for-profit firm. Thus, NGOs are a subset of a much broader civil society that encompasses all extrastate organizations, from "business organizations to unions to book clubs to dance companies to congregations" (Kallman and Clark 2016:37).

Alternatively, *NGO* can refer more specifically to donor-funded international development or humanitarian organizations working in the Global South. For example, Eric Werker and Faisal Z. Ahmed (2008:74) borrow from the World Bank's Operational Directive 14.70 to define NGOs as "private organizations 'characterized primarily by humanitarian or cooperative, rather than commercial objectives . . . that pursue activities to relieve suffering, promote the interests of the poor, protect the environment, provide basic social services, or undertake community development' in developing countries." Similarly, Jennifer Brass and her colleagues (2018) characterize an NGO as "any nonprofit, non-governmental organization that works in the development, humanitarian, advocacy, or civil society sector." This line of thinking often (though not always) distinguishes NGOs from related organizational forms, such as community-based organizations (CBOs), which may have greater local participation and work to the benefit of their own members rather than other external parties.

Finally, some definitions of the term *NGO* blur the distinction between international and domestic organizations, whereas others refer exclusively to domestic ones. Development and humanitarian circles, for instance, routinely use it to denote organizations that operate in several countries or are broadly transnational in scope. In other contexts, for instance among scholars interested in disentangling transnational and domestic civil society, a distinction is made between NGOs and INGOs that separates organizations that are international in scope or membership from those that have purely domestic or local members and stakeholders.

In this chapter, we are interested in the general expansion that is occurring across many types of organizations that get classified as NGOs, and our arguments transcend fine distinctions (e.g., between NGOs, NPOs, and CBOs). Consequently, we use the term *nongovernmental organization* broadly to indicate any nonstate, nonprofit organization formed for the purpose of pursing collective goals, such as—but not limited to—those related to humanitarian assistance and broad-based development. Like the nonprofits described in the introduction to this volume, NGOs are formal, voluntary, nondistributive, and typically tax-exempt entities (in most legal contexts) that operate at multiple levels, ranging from local, community-based development organizations to large, professionalized international NGOs (see Powell, Chapter 1, "What Is the Nonprofit Sector?"). We will use the term *INGO* when referring specifically to NGOs that function transnationally.

What Is the NGO Boom?

Speaking broadly, the NGO boom is the widespread establishment of new organizations that could—by one or another definition—be labeled NGOs. The boom reflects a historical moment of global enthusiasm for many kinds of voluntary, civic, and nonprofit organizing. But we suggest that the NGO boom involves a more profound change. It is the emergence of a truly global category and organizational template for structuring nonprofit, voluntary, and civic organizing. The NGO reimagines these activities as part of a global field, rendering them more consistent across societies and facilitating global coordination. It is an abstract and universalizing concept and technology that provides a grammar for organizing private activities within the international system. Just as the emergence of nation was linked to the imagined community of modern states and citizens, the rise of the NGO is part and parcel of an imagined global community of states and private action.

We are increasingly accustomed to a common global frame of reference for describing and coordinating nonprofit, voluntaristic, and charitable activities. Anyone anywhere can create an NGO with or for anyone anywhere (though this is often true more in theory than in practice) (e.g., Schnable 2015). It is easy to forget how heterogeneous such activities can be. Historically, nonprofit, civic, and charitable activities were extremely diverse, reflecting distinct national, political, organizational, cultural, and legal contexts. Indeed, nonprofit sectors were organized so differently that it has taken decades of work to figure out how to compare them systematically (see Anheier, Lang, and Toepler, Chapter 30, "Comparative Nonprofit Sector Research").

The NGO boom does not erase this earlier plurality of national and local organizational forms, but it overlays older structures and sometimes reshapes them. For instance, older entities such as missionary schools or traditional farm cooperatives have often reconstituted themselves as NGOs in recent years. Brass (2016) describes the dramatic growth of NGOs in Kenya, many of which remain or grew out of the precolonial self-help *harambee* groups as well as colonial-era missionary institutions. Nor is the NGO the first or only globalized category or form. International religious orders, for example, propelled missionary organizations in earlier centuries. And the nonprofit form and related legal frameworks spread to many countries in the twentieth century. However, the NGO is *essentially* universalistic in its conception, linked to fantasies of seamless worldwide coordination and representation. Its rise in the 1980s and 1990s represents a significant step toward globalization of activities that formerly manifested themselves in a variety of local forms.

Explaining the Global NGO Boom

To understand the growth of NGOs, we begin with a range of conventional arguments from sociology and political science that speak to societal variation of civic, voluntary, and nonprofit organizations. Then we focus on the rise of the NGO as a dominant global paradigm for organizing.

Classic work on civil society viewed societal organizations as the product of modernization and political development (e.g., Almond and Verba 1963). It assumed that many functional benefits arose from collective organizing. Schools would be enhanced by active parent organizations to do fund-raising; communities would benefit from development organizations that produced essential collective goods like wells; local political organizations would contribute to effective representation; and so on. So the real question is: which people have the capacity to organize effectively and reap these gains? The empirical answer was that people with resources, education, and skills tend to be most involved in civic life and voluntary organizations (e.g., Brady, Verba, and Schlozman 1995).

These classic arguments largely focused on explaining individual variation in organizational participation, but their logic has been extended to explain aggregate societal differences and change over time. Economic development, for instance, brings affluence and leisure time, which are key resources for civic involvement and the establishment of organizations. Modernization and political development also bring mass schooling, which provides critical skills for participation in civil society. According to these theories, the spread of NGOs is therefore a consequence of national economic development trajectories.

A second set of arguments, more focused on understanding comparative variations than historical expansion, argues that national political institutions, laws, and norms shape political participation and societal organizing (e.g., Fourcade and Schofer 2016; Schofer and Fourcade-Gourinchas 2001; Skocpol and Fiorina 1999; see Anheier, Lang, and Toepler, Chapter 30, "Comparative Nonprofit Sector Research," for a more extensive treatment). For instance, democratic political institutions allow for organizations to influence political decision making and institutionalize societal norms of participation, which support civic involvement and nongovernmental organizing (e.g., Kerrissey and Schofer 2018). Other structural features create different results. For instance, corporatist governance arrangements are associated with increased societal organizing, while state bureaucratic centralization is associated with less (Fourcade and Schofer 2016). And national legal frameworks and tax laws may create incentives for the creation of nonprofit organizations (Anheier, Lang, and Toepler, Chapter 30, "Comparative Nonprofit Sector Research"). These arguments mostly concern comparative variations in civic organization and NGOs, but some address trends in organization expansion. For instance, if NGOs flourish in democratic societies, then the global NGO boom can be explained in terms of the third wave of democratization.

A central point of contention in these debates is the role of the modern state. American political conservatives have generally cast the state as an enemy of civil society: for them, a large and presumably overbearing state crowds out voluntary organizing (e.g., Joyce and Shambra 1996). Only by cutting back the state can private associations flourish. By contrast, political sociologists are more likely to see the state as a source of support for civil society, for example through social policy that relies on private service providers. The latter argument seems rather obvious when one takes a comparative and historical view. The twentieth century saw huge growth in national states as well as civil organizations and NGOs. Also, the large states of the world—such as the welfare states of Scandinavia—coexist with very high numbers of domestic organizations (see Figure 27.1). The expansion of the state spurs brings new domains and public undertakings into the civic sphere, legitimating the formation of and providing resources directly to NGOs in the pursuit of shared public problems (Schofer and Longhofer 2011:540; Skocpol 2003; Tarrow 1998). For example, most environmental NGOs in the United States emerged *after* the establishment of the Environmental Protection Agency (EPA) and related legal frameworks (Hironaka 2014; Longhofer and Schofer 2010).

This role of the state also comes up in discussions of development NGOs in the Global South. A common narrative casts the emergence of NGOs as a demand-side response to the state's failure to promote economic and societal development (e.g., Hansmann 1987; Weisbrod, 1977, 1978). Early economic development efforts, sponsored by international development agencies and donor countries, were largely state-led. According to this account, decades of failed development projects prompted both citizens and international donors to seek alternatives to corrupt and inefficient states (Salamon 1994). Consequently, NGOs exploded onto the scene in the 1980s in what scholars have characterized as a paradigm shift from state-centered to privately led development (Brass 2016; Kamat 2004). We do not disagree that such a transformation took place, but we would question whether state failure, which has occurred frequently throughout history, is a sufficient explanation. And we would note again that NGOs also proliferate in many countries with robust and effective states.

Conventional perspectives emphasize local or national-level factors and struggle to explain the rapid growth of NGOs that has occurred across a range of countries since the 1980s. We offer an alternative account, which treats this growth as a global phenomenon.

The NGO in Liberal World Society

Our explanation for the overall expansion of NGOs draws on sociological neo-institutionalism, world society theory, and parallel streams of research in international relations. These approaches attend to global and normative dimensions of contemporary organizing. We maintain that liberal ideologies that extol the importance of private organizing have become central in global discourse and are now fully institutionalized in the policies of international organizations and development banks. The diffusion of these ideas propels the spread of the NGO and related organizational forms on a global scale. It also suggests that modern NGOs are elements of a global organizational field (Meyer and Scott 1983; Fligstein and McAdam 2015), which helps make sense of them—and their flaws.

Sociological neoinstitutionalism explains social life as the consequence of cultural models and understandings that become institutionalized in custom or governance. Classic work argues that organizational structures reflect their environment, which may include rules and regulatory structures but also shared cultural myths and ideologies. One often-noticed consequence of this phenomenon is that organizations are surprisingly uniform in their formal structure (Meyer and Rowan 1977; DiMaggio and Powell 1983).

Several lines of argument from the neo-institutional literature are relevant for our purposes here.

Institutionalized Models of Organization: Institutionalized cultural frameworks shape the underlying grammar of organizing in a society (Jepperson and Meyer 1991; Jepperson 2002; Bromley and Meyer 2016). Organizational forms such as the membership association, labor union, or craft guild are not natural but reflect historically specific assumptions. Societies in which liberal ideologies and institutions take hold—such as Anglo countries—tend to organize around private associations like NGOs (Jepperson 2002).

Hyper-Organization: Liberal ideologies involve a culture of empowered actorhood, which leads to increased organizing. We have entered an era of "hyper-organization" (Bromley and Meyer 2016), of which the NGO boom is a primary manifestation.

World Society and Diffusion: Neo-institutional scholars have argued that the international sphere now has global institutions and cultural models of its own, which create isomorphism across nation-states. This approach to globalization, referred to as *world polity theory* or *world society theory* (Meyer et al. 1997), provides useful purchase on the question of how NGOs multiplied rapidly around the world in a fairly short period of time. These core insights provide the foundation for a general explanation for the NGO boom.

Institutionalized Models of Organization in the Liberal Era

The post-1945 period was marked by the ascendance of liberalism, as manifested in increased faith in markets, individualism, democratization, and expansive globalism. The reasons why are beyond the scope of this chapter, but this shift was in no small part due to the emergence of a liberal power—the United States—as both a principal architect of postwar international institutions and an exemplar that was widely emulated (Meyer et al. 1997; Hironaka 2017). Post–World War II liberalism was consequential in two ways. First, liberalism brought a distinctive grammar of organizing, which differs markedly from other types like continental statism and corporatism (Jepperson and Meyer 1991). In liberal models of governance, political authority ultimately lies in empowered individuals who participate in society directly or via mediating associations, rather than in a bureaucratic state or "functional" collectivities such as labor and the business sector (Jepperson 2002; Jepperson and Meyer 1991). The propensity for people to behave as "actors" is not a natural feature of modern individuals; rather, it reflects particular institutionalized cultural understandings and imperatives that prevail in the contemporary world (Meyer 2010). As liberal norms became central in postwar global culture, INGOs grew rapidly in the international sphere, turning a previously state-centric world polity into an organizationally diverse world society (Boli and Thomas 1999; Cole 2017).

Second, the postwar era brought rapid expansion of international institutions. These were concerned not just with conventional international issues of trade and security but also with broader liberal visions of social progress. These institutions became involved with education, development, and, later, environmentalism and human rights. This period was typified by waves of global diffusion, as newly independent regimes around the globe rapidly conformed to dominant international policy models (Meyer et al. 1997).

Some predicted that the rapidly growing states of this period would crowd out private association, but the result was quite the opposite: nongovernmental organizing surged. As states extended their purview to new domains—ever more aspects of the economy, health and sanitation, environment—citizen and industry organizations followed. For instance, the number of environmental NGOs increased after states began to regulate environmental problems, not before (Longhofer and Schofer 2010). This pattern can be understood in terms of conventional political opportunities and incentives. Environmental impact assessment legislation, for example, created important new opportunities for citizen influence via lawsuits. In addition, international and state attention to new issues had an important legitimating effect. They constructed environmental issues as social problems, which spurred organizing (Hironaka 2014; Schofer and Longhofer 2011).

Hyper-Organization: The Neoliberal Era in World Society

The liberalism that flourished in the international community intensified following the demise of Soviet communism, liberalism's main ideological competitor in the postwar era. With the United States as the sole superpower and dominant economy, midcentury "embedded liberalism" gave way to neoliberalism (Ruggie 1998). The international development regime, previously focused on large state-centric development projects, shifted as extreme liberal ideology provided a new vocabulary for development planning (Hwang 2006). Individuals would now serve as the engines of development in a decentralized fashion, coordinated by markets and civil society.

Parallel trends of rationalized organizing occurred across many sectors, a process that Patricia Bromley and John W. Meyer call hyper-organization (Bromley and Meyer 2016). Traditional forms like universities, family businesses, and charities were transformed into rationalized, formal, and greatly expanded organizational actors managed by MBA-wielding personnel (e.g., Hwang and Powell 2009).

Especially after the 2008 global financial crisis, the 1990s-era faith in the magic of markets and private organization seems naïve. It would almost be quaint if not for the many destructive policy legacies that ensued, such as the World Bank's "structural adjustment" programs. It is hard to overstate the enthusiasm for neoliberal ideas about private action as a source of democratic progress that gripped this period. Much as economists helped carry liberal market ideologies around the world, scholars such as Robert Putnam touted a romanticized vision of community involvement. Such ideas were taken up by major organizations like the UN and the World Bank as well as national elites, establishing private organizing as a solution to a wide range of social and political concerns (Fourcade-Gourinchas and Babb 2002; Schofer and Longhofer 2011).

In short, the NGO emerged as the panacea for pressing global problems, such as poverty and sustainable development (Schofer and Longhofer 2011). Murdie (2014) describes this process as the emergence of new pro-NGO norms in the international community. Thus, throughout the 1990s, we see key international organizations, such as the UN and the World Bank, championing and funding voluntary organizations and NGOs. For example, as early as 1981, the World Bank began developing guidelines for working with NGOs in its projects. Its aim was both to fill in gaps created by state and market failures and to increase public participation in World Bank–financed activities (Shihata 1992). Today, nearly 90 percent of World Bank–financed projects involve the participation of NGOs in some capacity (World Bank 2018). Similarly, USAID supports NGOs through programs like its Democracy, Human Rights and Governance initiative, which supported sixty Sri Lankan organizations in the months leading to the 2015 presidential and parliamentary elections. Roughly 20 percent of official development assistance from the OECD flows to or through NGOs (OECD Development Assistance Committee 2015). In 2005, only 0.10 percent and 0.68 percent of Canadian and Irish aid, respectively, was channeled through NGOs; in 2012, the respective shares were 18.68 percent and 38.64 percent.

This increased emphasis creates tremendous pressure across the globe to organize as an NGO. First of all, the material incentives are huge. Many types of funding explicitly require NGO status. Local religious missions and community groups now routinely incorporate themselves as formal NGOs to obtain backing. What is more, the NGO is now the primary vehicle for stakeholder participation in international venues, such as the UN. The increasing dominance of the form means that people will think to organize in terms of NGOs by default—it is now just "the way things are done." Not only does this produce a profusion of NGOs, but we will suggest that there are second-order effects as nonprofit, civic, and charitable organizations come to be organized around common global models and templates.

Rethinking the Consequences of NGOs

What is the impact of the NGO boom? As we have seen, the proponents of NGOs take it as a matter of faith that they create positive change. They point to exemplars that provide critical services, orchestrate successful development projects, represent the voices of marginalized peoples, and act as effective watchdogs or advocacy groups. This celebration of NGOs is characteristic of the liberal period, in which private actors of all kinds have been charged with pursuing democratic governance and economic development. As the sector swells, the organizations gain authority and legitimacy, thus potentially amplifying their capacity to transform societies in ways beyond mere service delivery. Yet in spite of great hopes attributed to these organizations, one can find many failures. Perhaps not surprisingly, critics observe examples of incompetence, waste, and ineffectiveness. They also suggest that NGOs may be particularistic, unaccountable, or distorted by economic incentives or organizational interests.

Systematic studies of NGO effects are rare. Virtually no research compares the impact of NGOs to that of alternative organizational forms with comparable resources—for instance, how aid projects involving NGOs perform relative to projects involving state agencies or religious groups. The conventional view, which has strong functionalist overtones, sees voluntary associations and NGOs as a source of social capital that enhances democratic participation and produces collective goods. If these claims are true, NGOs should have a variety of observable effects that would be recorded in case studies of development projects, policy evaluation studies, and aggregate studies of developmental and policy outcomes.

And, indeed, that is what research often reports. In a recent systematic review of more than three thousand articles on NGOs and international development, Brass and her colleagues (2018) find that whether NGOs affect development outcomes is the most common research question in the current scholarship. More than half of the empirical studies on NGOs in the health and governance sectors report that when NGOs act as service deliverers or advocacy organizations, they produce a positive outcome. When NGOs act as substitutes or complements to state services, positive outcomes are reported on a range of health issues, including contraceptive use, HIV transmission, vaccine uptakes, legal reforms, and the detection and treatment of cholera, tuberculosis, and cataracts. Similarly, NGOs were effective in persuading the Pakistani government to enforce the Convention on the Elimination of All Forms of Discrimination Against Women (Afsharipour 1999).

However, the authors also note important potential sources of bias in prior research, including bias against reporting null effects and the overlooking of some sectors and geographies. And perhaps more surprising is that nearly half of the published research reports either negative findings or no findings at all, challenging more functional accounts of NGOs. Critical studies of NGOs explore a range of themes and arguments. First and foremost, a large literature chronicles NGO dysfunction and failure. Just as state agencies often find themselves unable to solve complex social problems, NGOs fail in their efforts to generate collective goods or produce social change. The reasons are many and varied.

Planning may be inadequate; project goals may be unrealistic; local stakeholders may not have been sufficiently consulted; resources may fall short; and so on. Beyond general planning and organizational failures, critical analyses point to a series of systemic issues that bedevil the NGO sector (Banks et al. 2015). Specifically, NGOs are private organizations, whose interests may not align fully with the communities they represent. They may become corrupt or vehicles of rent-seeking, rather than truly working for collective benefit (Dill 2009). And, as private organizations, they may lack accountability.

These issues are exacerbated in the international development sector, where NGOs often serve as intermediaries in a larger social system (Swidler and Watkins 2017; Schuller 2009). Rather than responding to local needs, NGO agendas may be shaped by the whims of international donors. One consequence of this disconnect is that internationally funded NGOs focus on results-based projects with very short time horizons, rather than making the kinds of long-term investments needed to effectively resolve entrenched social problems (Swidler and Watkins 2017). For example, Schuller (2012) provides an account of two nongovernmental organizations—Sové Lavi and Famn Tet Ansanm—active in Haiti prior to and during the 2010 earthquake. The effectiveness of both NGOs was shaped largely by the interests of international donors, namely USAID and the European Union, which, in the case of the former, pressured Sové Lavi to promote abstinence-based HIV/AIDS campaigns over its own condom programs during the George W. Bush administration. The relationship between donors and NGOs became more fraught in the aftermath of the earthquake, including the deadly cholera outbreak that brought global attention to the failures of many NGOs and humanitarian agencies.

The world society perspective suggests that NGOs are succeeding as part of a global liberal mythology, structuring a global field of organizing whose participants are linked through shared frameworks. This idea suggests another disconnect observed by critics of NGOs: namely, that NGOs are creatures of a global system and thus may not always be well suited to addressing the concrete needs of local stakeholders. Neo-institutional scholars expect that such systems may produce a great deal of loose coupling (Bromley and Powell 2012). The grandiose plans of international donors and the NGO activities they give rise to may create tension with complex local realities (much like the global development regime, generally; see Ferguson 1990).

However, institutionalized myths can produce real-world consequences, prompting tighter coupling over time or even large-scale social change (e.g., Schofer and Hironaka 2005; Hironaka 2014). As the resources devoted to NGOs grow, they may become more effective. And if donors require NGO participation, then NGOs become a necessary condition for success. Localities unable to mobilize or attract NGOs will lose out on resources and projects. As NGOs become more and more taken for granted, the claims made on their behalf sometimes become self-fulfilling.

The key point is that the NGO boom isn't just an increase in numbers of organizations but a structuring of organizations in a common global field with shared ideas and organizational templates. This shift facilitates many kinds of international coordination. A world of NGOs is a world in which international organizations can more easily organize with local stakeholders, while local groups can form international networks with each other and link up to governance structures (e.g., via consultative status). NGOs tend to think of themselves as part of such a global field. For instance, they routinely adopt strategies and forms from their counterparts in other localities. Again, the contrast is to the historically heterogeneous and sometimes incommensurable domestic nonprofit and civil society sectors, which involve diverse organizational forms and models.

Thus the impact of globally sponsored and globally legitimated NGOs comes from their mediating role, which allows them to link global and local. In the extreme case, NGOs reflect world society "on the ground"; that is, they carry international organizational models, cultural frames, and discourses into national contexts. For instance, countries rife with local NGOs can connect with international institutions and obtain development aid and financing more easily (Bromley et al. 2018). Whether this is good or bad may be in the eye of the beholder. Those who envision NGOs as a vehicle for "authentic" grassroots or indigenous mobilization may be disappointed. The NGO sector tends to be guided by global ideologies, which may not correspond to those of indigenous communities and their understandings of success. The NGOs that thrive in the current world environment are more "glocal" than local: rationalized, professionalized, and organized in terms of globally recognized themes and technologies (Robertson 1992). However, the increased funneling of resources and attention into NGOs working with the environment, human rights, and development—as part of the liberal world society—may seem preferable to some alternative ideological programs, which we discuss shortly.

It is also possible that while the consequences of the NGO boom have been diffuse, they have also been transformative. In our previous work on the origins of voluntary associations, we proposed that organizational expansion produces distinct typologies of civil society writ large (Schofer and Longhofer 2011). We classified Sweden, for example, as a classic type of civil society with an NGO sector that is highly educated, democratic, and diverse. Thus, we see all kinds of NGOs active in Sweden, such as industry associations, recreational clubs, and advocacy organizations. In contrast, other civil societies are more state-driven, such as Korea (which has a high proportion of industry associations). Many others are development-centric and (we argue) largely exogenous. Tanzania, for instance, has many associations devoted to development agendas in areas like public health (especially HIV/AIDS), women's rights, and sustainable development. Finally, we recognized that the NGO boom did not happen everywhere and some civil societies are still repressed with a sparse number of associations generally, and especially few addressing social and political advocacy.

NGOs in a Post-Liberal Global Order?

The global liberal order has come under increased criticism and attack in the past decade (Guillén 2018). The specific reasons are still being debated, but scholars suggest that the 2008 global financial crisis fractured neoliberal fantasies regarding the miraculous benefits of markets and financialization. And economic and political strains produced by global trade and economic integration may have contributed to the resurgence of far-right and nationalist parties. Democracy and press freedom have begun to decline, and explicitly illiberal regimes are on the rise (Freedom House 2018).

According to the conventional standpoint, there is no obvious reason that the international order would have much of an effect on NGOs. To the extent that NGOs are mainly about addressing local needs and concerns, their fate should be independent of global turmoil. If anything, the recent changes in the global system may generate greater organizing, as communities step up to fill the gaping voids left by postcrisis austerity across Europe and elsewhere.

By contrast, we suggest that recent attacks on liberalism have important implications for the NGO boom. NGOs are an offshoot of the liberal international order. If the neoliberal ideologies underlying NGOs are attacked and lose legitimacy, the logic of organizing is undercut and criticisms of NGOs may take on greater force (Bromley, Schofer, and Longhofer forthcoming). For instance, in a world of resurgent nationalism and antiglobalism, international and even domestic NGOs may be reimagined as a threat to national sovereignty.

Indeed, we see evidence of this (see Dupuy and Prakash, Chapter 28, "Global Backlash Against Foreign Funding to Domestic Nongovernmental Organizations"). Illiberal leaders like Hungary's Viktor Orbán have attacked some NGOs as part of Western efforts to undermine national sovereignty. A number of states have become more vocal in their criticisms of NGOs as potentially illegitimate actors in local politics. And these criticisms have resulted in new policy initiatives to restrict NGO activities in a number of countries—from Azerbaijan to Equatorial Guinea to Vietnam (Dupuy, Ron, and Prakash 2016; Bromley, Schofer, and Longhofer forthcoming; Schofer, Meyer, and Lerch 2018). More recently, in the United States, prominent NGOs like the Natural Resources Defense Council and InterAction are facing increasing pressure to register as foreign agents.[3]

Scholars perennially announce the decline of civil society. A common fear is the atomizing effects of modernity or technology (e.g., Putnam 2000). Others worry about various sources of corruption: parochial self-interest, the political economy of donors, or the machinations of powerful interests or elites. We suggest that NGOs may come under attack from a different source: illiberal movements and regimes. To the extent that these grow and challenge the existing international order—or fracture it, like Brexit—we expect greater rhetorical, legal, or even physical attacks on NGOs. The age of liberalism is certainly not over: the core international institutions of the world, such as the United Nations, continue to sustain liberal ideologies and support NGOs. Illiberal populist and nationalist movements remain sporadic and have not coalesced into a coherent alternative to the existing global order. Thus, it is premature to make apocalyptic predictions. But the era of unbounded and unchallenged faith in NGOs may have already passed. NGOs may continue to expand but likely at slower rates. With the ascent of populist and nationalist mobilizations that challenge international institutions, it becomes easier to foresee a world with fewer NGOs.

28 GLOBAL BACKLASH AGAINST FOREIGN FUNDING TO DOMESTIC NONGOVERNMENTAL ORGANIZATIONS

Kendra Dupuy and Aseem Prakash

AFTER THE COLD WAR, CIVIL SOCIETY ORGANIZATIONS, or nongovernmental organizations (NGOs), grew rapidly in the Global South and former communist countries as part of Western countries' push for democratization, economic development, and improved effectiveness of foreign aid. For example, in Kenya, the number of non-church foreign NGOs grew from 37 to 134 between 1978 and 1987, and the number of local NGOs grew from 57 to 133 during the same time period (Fowler 1991). Today, the number of foreign and local NGOs active in Kenya is estimated to number over 7,200, in addition to more than three hundred thousand community-based organizations (USAID 2015). Other countries follow a similar pattern, with foreign aid influxes partially fueling the NGO boom.

But in the mid- to late 1990s, a curious countertrend emerged: several developing countries began enacting laws that restricted the ability of NGOs (both foreign and domestic) to operate in their territories (Dupuy, Ron, and Prakash 2015, 2016). Of particular interest, many laws restricted NGOs' access to foreign funding. Moreover, in recent years, some developed countries such as Canada, Norway, and Israel have imposed restrictions on NGOs as well.[1]

The restrictions these laws impose are of different types (Dupuy et al. 2016). In Equatorial Guinea and Angola, government authorization is required for locally operating NGOs to receive funding from international sources, whereas Azerbaijan and Belarus require organizations to report receipt of internationally sourced funds to the government. Vietnam forbids the receipt of international funds that will negatively affect political order. Some governments set specific limits on the amounts of international financing organizations can receive; for instance, the Algerian government has discretionary power to set a cap on how much foreign money NGOs can legally receive, whereas Ethiopia has determined that human rights organizations cannot receive more than 10 percent foreign funding. In terms of restrictions on the use of foreign funding, Zimbabwe prohibits such funding from being used on voter education, whereas Rwanda allows only 20 percent of funds to be used on administrative expenses. Several governments require regular and extensive reporting on the receipt and use of foreign funds, such as Indonesia, Burundi, and India.

These legal restrictions reflect two ways in which the state is seeking to reassert its sovereignty (Dupuy et al. 2016). First, states want to control the ability of foreign donors, private or governmental, to influence their domestic politics though financial support to NGOs. We view these as "border control" measures that protect the external sovereignty of the state (Andreas 2000). Second, states are limiting the domestic political and economic space available to NGOs to function effectively. We view these as "within-border" actions that defend the internal sovereignty of the state in relation to nonstate actors—namely, by constraining the political opposition. These can include measures such as new registration laws and restrictions on lobbying that do not have a direct connection with border control measures.

This chapter focuses on the new foreign funding laws. These have elements of both border control and within-border controls (Dupuy et al. 2016). Through these laws, governments seek to insulate domestic politics from outside influence exercised by foreign funders while also denying resources to domestic political opponents. Arguably, governments would be less worried about external funding if NGOs functioned in a depoliticized way. With the rise of rights-based approaches, however, NGOs often become aligned with opposition groups. Consequently, the new foreign funding laws have a within-border dimension because they reflect the attempt by governments to deny resources to their political rivals. This chapter reports on the literature examining the confluence of domestic and international considerations that motivate governments to enact foreign funding laws.

This chapter also engages with the debate on the alleged obsolescence of the state. Since the 1970s, scholars have claimed the emergence of a world polity or a "global society" steeped in Western norms (Chandhoke 2002), with NGOs as their chief conveyor belts (Meyer et al. 1997). States are supposed to face tremendous isomorphic pressures to conform to these customs. In the 1990s, scholars interpreted the rising prominence of NGOs as heralding an era of "politics beyond states" (Wapner 1995). There was almost giddiness about the emergence of a global civil society operating independently of the interstate system (Lipschutz 1992).

Democracy promotion and holding of competitive elections are important global norms championed by key global institutions such as the United Nations and the World Bank. But the emergence of NGO laws across countries is a stark reminder of the continued role of the state in shaping the rules of domestic politics, its ability to enforce border controls and within-border measures, and its willingness to defy global consensuses. These regulatory developments suggest that international efforts to promote civil society in developing countries function within the parameters established by states. That is, they require approval (explicit or implicit) of the nation in whose territory NGOs operate. Global norms about civil society promotion have not constrained governments from cracking down in the NGO sector. Thus, the "global" dimension of the global society is operative only if domestic governments want it to be.

This chapter also challenges social scientists to reexamine their theories about NGOs. Scholars suggest that NGOs (especially ones that deliver services, often called nonprofits) emerge as a response to both government and market failures (Weisbrod 1977; Salamon and Anheier 1998; Young 2000). Because states are the guarantors of property rights, market failure accompanies state failure. Indeed, in fragile and poor failed states, NGOs are the major provider of public services.[2] But this does not explain why NGOs should emerge in developed countries. In these places, the notion of market failure takes on a new dimension; it is rooted in information asymmetries between buyers and sellers. Henry B. Hansmann (1980) suggested that NGOs take hold in these countries because they are deemed trustworthy by consumers as a result of the nondistributional constraint under which they function. That is, although NGOs can generate profits (as nonprofit hospitals do), they cannot distribute them to their owners. On this count, firms are less trustworthy. This sort of argument is echoed in advocacy literature. These scholars claim that NGOs are "principled actors" that are not motivated (unlike firms) by instrumental concerns (Keck and Sikkink 1998).[3] Thus there are two dimensions of the same NGO narrative. In the agentic (principled-actor) perspective, NGOs are virtuous because they do not pursue profits, whereas in the institutional (nondistributional-constraint) perspective, NGOs are trustworthy because their owners do not receive profits.

These theoretical claims about the virtues of the NGO sector raise an interesting question.[4] Why are some governments rejecting this narrative, when Western policy elites continue to hail the NGO sector as the "third way" to solve societal problems? One quick answer may be that NGOs are collateral damage in the rise of populist, right-wing ideologies. These ideas challenge elite consensus on free trade, civil society promotion, and international/regional institutions. The 2009 Eurozone crisis (and the austerity policies that followed it), and more recently the ongoing refugee crisis,[5] are noted as triggers of the backlash against probably the most notable regional institution of the recent era, the European Union. In this "blame populism" view, governments restrict foreign funding to NGOs in response to populist demands.

Yet few EU countries (with the exception of Hungary,[6] Poland,[7] and Austria[8]) have cracked down on the NGO sector. Even countries such as Italy that have recently voted in right-wing governments have not intervened in civil society. We suggest that attributing the suppression of NGOs to populism misses the bigger picture. First, most countries that have enacted restrictive laws are in the developing world, particularly in Africa, and not in the EU. Second, this crackdown began well before the two crises that mark the rise of populist politics. As the literature suggests, the barriers placed on NGOs reflect the confluence of Western donors' funneling of increased levels of foreign aid through NGOs as opposed to recipient governments, the rise of rights-based approaches in advocacy that invariably pit development NGOs against local governments, the lack of domestic support for NGOs, and regimes' political vulnerability as reflected in the closeness of previous elections (Dupuy et al. 2015, 2016).

We recognize that some countries might have stemmed foreign funding to NGOs in the wake of the 9/11 terror attacks. We also acknowledge that the measures taken against NGOs reflect a larger trend in the global recession of democracy, with partially and fully democratic states repressing various civil and political liberties, including the freedoms of association, assembly, information, and expression (Diamond 2015; Plattner 2015; but see Levitsky and Way 2015). However, it is critical to remember that the suppression of NGOs predates the democracy recession narrative that emerged after the failure of the Arab Spring.[9]

So if populism and democracy recession are not to blame, what motivates governments to crack down on civil society organizations? After all, NGOs are supposed to promote development, bridge deficits in public-goods provision, and help the underprivileged. Furthermore, anti-NGO initiatives have important fiscal implications: our work suggests that the adoption of a restrictive NGO finance law is associated with a 32 percent reduction in bilateral aid flows (Dupuy and Prakash 2018). This chapter outlines a political explanation. Advocacy NGOs that promote democratization or human rights are often critical of the domestic government. But with the rise in the rights-based approach to development that promotes equal provision of public goods and services (Hamm 2001; Cornwall and Nyamu-Musembi 2004), even nonadvocacy NGOs (nonprofits) focused on providing merit goods and services are directly drawn into local politics. A key reason is that most governments in developing countries are unable to provide the requisite quality and quantity of public services. Although NGOs have historically provided public goods, the rights-based approaches have transformed them into critics of government. For example, several NGOs hitherto devoted to supplying health services to the underserved now suggest that health care is a right and therefore demand that governments supply health care to all people. Of course, governments probably cannot do so; this is why NGOs were supplying it in the first place. What is crucial for this chapter is that this new advocacy role implicates them in domestic politics because they seem to be allied with dissidents. Because NGOs tend to depend on foreign funding, governments believe or claim that political dissent is instigated by foreign powers (call it the "Soros effect").

As actors seeking regime survival, we expect governments to act against their critics. And because much of foreign funding for NGOs is routed through the formal banking[10] sector, governments have a low-cost and reliable administrative means to deny them access to these resources. Governments' anxiety about the foreign-funded NGO sector increases because they recognize that they gain legitimacy, in part, by providing public goods. When the NGO sector replaces the state as the key supplier of these goods, governments feel politically insecure. Not surprisingly, they have compelling political incentives to crack down on the NGO sector.

But are governments' actions against these organizations costless? For example, suppose these actions lead to citizen outrage, and people flood the streets. After all, NGOs are supposed to have deep connections with people. NGOs supply them with merit goods and services or advocate on their behalf. Yet few such sustained protests have taken place in countries that have cracked down on civil society. Perhaps this is where the corrosive effects of foreign aid on the health of civil society can best be discerned. Governments are emboldened to target NGOs because they anticipate little domestic backlash. They believe that internationally funded NGOs are not well rooted in the local community. And in many cases, NGOs do not have a vocal domestic constituency that feels ownership, rises up in support of them, and imposes political costs on governments.

Why this disconnect? A common criticism is that NGOs are more responsive to donors' concerns than those of the communities they serve. This means that NGOs are advocating for issues that are important to Western audiences, not to the people with whom they are working. Second, even the public goods they supply may not be of the appropriate type, an accusation that is often leveled against foreign aid. Finally, there is arguably a reputational problem (D. Smith 2012). NGOs are sometimes viewed as a part of the "aid establishment" that is disconnected from the groups they try to help. NGO scandals, such as the recent Oxfam case, provide credence to the view that even internationally acclaimed humanitarian organizations sometimes behave in unprincipled ways and show little respect for the countries in which they function (Scurlow, Dolsak, and Prakash 2019).[11] However, there are exceptions such as Greenpeace, "the only global environmental charity that accepts no corporate or government donations so we can maintain a much needed independent voice."[12]

Thus, while the crackdown on NGOs reflects a larger trend in democracy recession, it also raises serious questions about the legitimacy of the Western-funded NGO model, the wisdom of funneling foreign aid through NGOs that also delegitimize local governments, and NGOs' insistence on portraying all sorts of issues as "rights." Fundamentally, it forces scholars to confront an important issue: can Western funding purchase the NGO sector abroad? Or, does a viable and political resilient NGO sector need to be endogenous, homegrown, and rooted in the local community?

NGOs and the Washington Consensus

There is some confusion about the definition of NGOs (Vakil 1997; Johnson and Prakash 2007). Scholars tend to define them by what they are not: actors not part of government. Given this open-ended definition, scholars debate how NGOs are distinct from social movements, civil society, or the nonprofit sector more generally (Vakil 1997; Lewis and Wallace 2000). In this chapter, we view NGOs as organizations that are not formally a part of the government or the for-profit sector. Ideally, if they are indeed the "third sector," they should be financially independent of both the state and the corporate sector. This is not often the case, especially for the large visible international NGOs engaged in humanitarian and advocacy work. For example, in 2017, governmental funding accounted for 43 percent of Oxfam's £409 million income.[13]

NGOs often have a legal persona, a status offering distinct benefits, such as the right (in some cases) to issue tax-deductible receipts. In contrast to the formal NGO sector, local, grassroots civic organizations sometimes do not have a legal status. They are therefore not included in the definition of NGOs, even though they may have an important role in social mobilization, service delivery, or generating social capital more generally. Similarly, local organizations as described by Robert Putnam (1995) that supply public or club goods, and communitarian organizations such as those described by Elinor Ostrom (1990), engaged in sustainable use of common-pool resources, may not be formally registered as NGOs.

As mentioned earlier, the NGO sector saw dramatic growth worldwide after the Cold War. NGOs proliferated in the Global South and former communist countries largely because of patronage from Western donors and institutions. There was a massive infusion of funds for NGO promotion by Western powers and the multilateral institutions they dominate (Reimann 2006). The policy expectation was that the NGO sector would become the vehicle to spread liberal norms, encourage democratization, and foster market-based development. Furthermore, Western donors probably assumed that NGOs would find it difficult to raise resources within resource-poor countries and therefore viewed their financial support as an appropriate way to establish and strengthen these organizations.

But the NGO sector also grew because it emerged as a subcontractor for the delivery of public services that were previously supplied by governmental agencies. This trend was ideologically rooted in the domestically oriented "reinventing government" agenda

(Osborne 1993) and the internationally oriented "Washington Consensus" (Williamson 1993). Internally, during the 1980s, Western governments began relying more heavily on NGOs to deliver public services, instead of their own agencies. This reflected the Reagan-Thatcher philosophy of reducing government's footprint across policy spheres. In the 1990s, the "reinventing government" approach also encouraged governments to outsource service provision to NGOs. This led to the emergence of NGOs as governmental contractors, something that has been replicated abroad in the context of aid delivery. In this sense, government has played a strong role in the emergence and growth of NGOs worldwide, as Evan Schofer and Wesley Longhofer (2011; Chapter 27, "The Global Rise of Nongovernmental Organizations") argue.

It is difficult to find accurate estimates of the level of contractorization of foreign aid through NGOs (Burger, Owen, and Prakash 2018). By some estimates, the share of foreign aid to Africa channeled through NGOs rose from just 1 percent in 1990 to about 20 percent in the late 2000s (Englebert and Tull 2008). In part, this growth in NGO funding reflected the "aid fatigue" among Western donors that led them to devise new mechanisms to deliver funds besides governmental bureaucracies. This cohered with the Washington Consensus's project to dismantle governmental control over the economy, which began in the 1980s as developing countries sought structural adjustment aid from the World Bank and the International Monetary Fund (Nelson 1995; Levine 2002). Aid ineffectiveness found an obvious culprit: the governments of aid recipient countries. These were regarded as corrupt, incompetent, and captured by local power structures. In contrast, donors believed that NGOs had the expertise, grassroots knowledge, and incentives to identify appropriate aid projects and beneficiaries, as well as the human infrastructure to deliver aid (Edwards and Hulme 1996; Dietrich 2013). By some estimates, about one fifth of bilateral aid is routed through NGOs: the OECD puts the number at 19 percent for the United Kingdom, 23 percent for the United States, 25 percent for Norway, and 40 percent for Ireland (OECD Development Assistance Committee 2015).

Yet the emergence of a donor-funded NGO sector has had unexpected consequences, both in developing countries with communist legacies (Cooley and Ron 2002; Henderson 2003; Sundstrom 2006) and in those without them (Chahim and Prakash 2014). In these settings, NGOs had little prior experience of (and opportunities for) systemically engaging the local population for support, resources, and legitimacy. Citizens, too, had no frame of reference with which to assess the role of nonstate actors in their social, economic, and political lives. Simply put, NGOs lacked local connections that donors imagined that they had or could acquire quickly.

Foreign funding created other problems as well. Despite their good intentions, Western donors have created a perverse incentive structure for both local NGOs that want to become clients of global ones (Hearn 2007) and global NGOs that compete to attract funds (Bob 2002; Cooley and Ron 2002). Whereas NGOs were celebrated for their non-hierarchical, horizontally networked relationships, foreign aid has created hierarchical patron–client ties between Western donors and NGOs. Without debating whether NGOs have fundamentally different organizational DNA from firms, competition for donor funds compel NGOs to function essentially in the same way as them (Sell and Prakash 2004; Prakash and Gugerty 2010).

Arguably, NGOs could work with traditional grassroots organizations to form bonds with the local community. This strategy could allow NGOs to marry their expertise in generating external funds with becoming established locally. Yet this sort of synergy faces challenges. Foreign funding tends to create distance, not connectedness, between donor-funded and local civic organizations. For one, the two types of organizations operate very differently. NGOs tend to employ professional staff operating in offices located in major cities. These managers have degrees from foreign universities. Their success is often measured by their ability to work the media as well as attract grants. NGO professionals often see progress in terms of moving from smaller to larger organizations (and eventually, getting into the "multinationals"), not in building relationships with local communities. Consequently, NGO professionals have few incentives to engage as equals with less sophisticated, sometimes poorly educated, local actors.

Another difficulty is that maintaining the steady flow of foreign money requires following the donors' agenda. This includes governmental and intergovernmental funders as well as private foundations. Scholars note the role of the big three American foundations—Carnegie, Ford, and Rockefeller—in promoting U.S. norms during the Cold War through their foreign aid programs (Parmar 2012). In the current epoch, there is a concern about the "Gates Effect" in public health due to the vast resources at the command of the Gates Foundation (Roberts and Enserink 2007). Resource dependency leads NGOs to reproduce norms rooted in donor-inspired development discourse (Chandhoke 2002). NGOs may well become an integral part of the world society (Meyer et al. 1997), but sometimes they have little connection with the local community in which they are supposed to function.

Costs and Benefits of the NGO Crackdown

The restrictions on NGOs that governments have enacted typically do one or more of the following: limit NGOs' ability to obtain foreign money; specify the amounts of foreign money NGOs may legally receive; determine the mechanisms through which NGOs may access foreign aid; prescribe if, and how, NGOs can use foreign funds, including the issues on which they can work; and specify foreign aid reporting and tax requirements. With few exceptions, these laws are not aimed at specific categories of NGOs, such as human rights organizations or health groups. Furthermore, these restrictive laws do not distinguish between types of foreign funding, including money from private foundations, or money from bilateral or multilateral aid agencies.

Are these restrictive laws simply symbolic, or are governments serious about their enforcement? After all, governments in developing countries are notorious for enacting laws but not enforcing them. This discrepancy could be due to resource scarcity, lack of technical capacity, corruption, and so on. Sometimes governments have the resources and the capacities but no intention of enforcing laws. In such cases, implementation gaps reflect a symbolic approach to politics. Indeed, there is some evidence that states seek the reputational benefits of enacting specific types of laws but avoid the costs of enforcing them. There is an audience, domestic or international, that champions such laws and rewards states when they are enacted. Many human rights treaties have been criticized on these grounds: autocracies sign but do not enforce them (Hathaway 2007).

Conceptually, such implementation gaps are not likely to hold for strict NGO funding laws. Powerful international actors do *not* want developing countries to establish these laws. International media is harshly critical of countries that do so.

For example, when the Ethiopian government proposed its new restrictive NGO law in 2008, Human Rights Watch, Amnesty International, UN agencies, and others condemned the proposed law, and the international media published multiple negative articles about it (Dupuy et al. 2015: 443). Thus, instead of garnering benefits, the governments of developing countries face the risk of incurring substantial reputational loss and monetary damage in the form of aid reductions (Dupuy and Prakash 2018). Ultimately, laws that limit NGO funding are enacted by governments in spite of (not because of) international pressure. This suggests that they have strong incentives to implement them as well.

What, then, motivates governments to face the potential consequences of implementing of such laws? Our work offers a political explanation for both their incidence and timing. As we have reported elsewhere (Dupuy et al. 2016), governments have a higher probability of enacting such laws when they are politically insecure, typically just after they have faced competitive elections.

Consider these examples. In 2005, Ethiopian prime minister Meles Zenawi's government permitted opposition parties, for the first time, to fully campaign in national parliamentary elections. Contrary to the government's expectations, however, "the opposition swept seats in Addis Ababa and finished strongly in other urban areas" (Lacey 2005). Fearful for its political survival, the government claimed that its rivals had won only 176 of 546 parliamentary seats—far fewer than likely—and passed new rules designed to bolster its legislative powers. Opposition groups, including the Coalition of Unity and Development, responded with furious demonstrations, which government forces harshly suppressed (Human Rights Watch 2010). Officials later claimed these protests had been spurred by outside actors and funds. In 2009, they passed a law dramatically restricting foreign funding to locally operating NGOs (international or domestic) explicitly working on human rights and other politically sensitive issues. These groups are now required to raise 90 percent of funds locally. Such laws are not just paper tigers; instead, they have been seriously enforced. As a result, the organized Ethiopian human rights sector has all but shut down (Dupuy et al. 2015).

Something similar happened in Zimbabwe in 2008, when then-president Robert Mugabe grudgingly permitted semifree national elections. Political challenger Morgan Tsvangirai's Movement for Democratic Change performed better than expected, prompting Mugabe to declare that foreign aid was being "channeled through nongovernmental organizations to opposition political parties, which are a creation of the West" (Dugger 2008). Shortly thereafter, Mugabe's government enacted laws curbing the flow of overseas funds to locally operating NGOs (Human Rights Watch 2008; International Crisis Group 2009).

Likewise, in Ecuador, the government of left-leaning president Rafael Correa was rocked by a political crisis in 2010, followed by a national referendum in May 2011. Soon afterward, Correa's government passed new regulations for foreign-sponsored domestic NGOs, outlawing activities "incompatible with public security and security" and banning over a dozen INGOs from the country. Foreign-funded NGOs, Correa said, were undermining his government at the behest of right-wing groups (Freedom House 2012; Reyes

2011). A year later, Correa passed even tighter NGO rules, granting the president wide discretion to shut down civil society groups (Human Rights Watch 2013).

The governments in each of these examples believed that if they did not act against foreign-funded NGOs, they would face an emboldened opposition and heightened public criticism of their policies. Aid recipient countries must balance several conflicting imperatives: the political imperative of regulating NGOs to ensure regime durability, the economic imperative of securing larger aid inflows, and the reputational imperative of being viewed as cooperative with international norms. We find that in a large number of such countries, political exigencies have crowded out economic and reputational ones.

These governments' fears of foreign-supported NGOs are well founded because this type of organization has the ability to influence politics. NGOs can deploy their infrastructure to organize antigovernment protests at home (Murdie and Bhasin 2011), or to damage a country's reputation abroad. Governments wait until after competitive national elections to crack down on foreign-funded NGOs because the losing side typically contests the results by organizing protests. Emotions run high and governments simply cannot afford to let these go unchecked. Hence, they have the incentive to weaken this opposition, and NGO restrictions are one route to achieve this political goal. After an election, governments may also feel they have gained room and legitimacy for political maneuvering. Prior to elections, they felt obliged to tread lightly, fearing backlash if they press too hard on NGOs. Afterward, however, governments perceive a (limited) window of opportunity to crush their opponents.

How Have Donors Responded?

Western donors tend to view this crackdown in one of two ways. First, they can view it as developing countries rejecting Western norms about democracy and civil society promotion. Given that Western countries have vocal domestic constituencies devoted to these issues, these nations may feel compelled to punish governments enacting anti-NGO laws. They could issue condemnatory statements, or impose some sort of sanction.

Second, regulatory crackdown could undermine aid effectiveness and invite backlash against foreign aid at home. Viewed in this way, donors have "skin in the game" (Taleb and Sandis 2014). Thus, there are two explanations as to why Western donors might cut aid in response to strict NGO laws. These aid reductions could be motivated by the desire to punish democracy recession and/or to the impediments to aid delivery.

Foreign aid is a critical component of global public policy and contributes to about 10 percent of the gross domestic product (GDP) of developing countries. Yet the effectiveness of aid to promote economic development continues to be a topic of passionate debate (Easterly 2006; Kaufman 1992; Sachs 2006; Vernon 1957). Some suggest that if aid is provided to the "wrong" countries for the "wrong" reasons, it is likely to be ineffective. Therefore, how donors disburse aid among recipient countries has attracted considerable scholarly attention. Broadly, the literature identifies two types of donor motivations: donor interest versus recipient characteristics (Lewis 2003; Maizels and Nissanke 1984; McKinley and Little 1979; Neumayer 2003; Schraeder, Hook, and Taylor 1998). The former emphasizes donors' instrumental motives, whereas the latter highlights their altruistic ones.

Regarding the reputational costs mentioned earlier, because foreign aid is such an important issue, governments are probably aware that the international outrage that cracking down on it provokes has real, material consequences. For example, whether in their annual country reports or in press briefings, the U.S. State Department is seldom shy about condemning such countries. International NGOs (such as Amnesty International and Human Rights Watch), prominent think tanks, and foundations have also expressed alarm over these developments. The Carnegie Endowment issued a report titled "Closing Space" on this subject.[14] Transparency International has spoken out against new foreign funding laws. A prominent German NGO, the Heinrich Boll Foundation, publicly and with some fanfare, pulled out of Ethiopia after the country enacted its restrictive NGO funding law in 2009.

There are several implications of this concerted international outcry. First, it will undermine a government's reputation for supporting democracy. Because democracy is often viewed as a proxy for rule of law and good governance, the government could see a decline in its international standing on these counts as well. Foreign investors who fear erosion in the rule of law may decide to move their money to other locations that still welcome NGOs. And because many of these governments are resource poor, a reduction in foreign aid can pose serious problems for the delivery of basic public services. Thus, developing-country governments likely recognize that their actions will have concrete material and reputational consequences.

The new laws also create a dilemma for donors. On the one hand, they may decide to maintain aid levels for multiple reasons. First, they are probably motivated to provide aid to promote economic development and public health, or to reduce poverty. Because developing countries continue to face problems in these areas, and given the commitment of donor countries to the Sustainable Development Goals (Sachs 2006), donors may decide to revert to routing funds through governments. After all, they want to come across as respectful of national sovereignty, including how the country in question seeks to regulate foreign resource inflows, lest they are accused of neocolonialism. Second, donors may fear that aid reductions could lead to state failure, thereby inducing global terrorist groups to establish operations in the territory (and, in the contemporary context, lead to outmigration).

On the other hand, donors may decide to reduce their aid. They may believe that their aid will be ineffective without appropriate NGOs to deliver it. As we have seen, the decision to deliver foreign aid to NGOs was partially motivated by the belief that developing country governments probably do not have the motivations and capacities to use aid effectively. With "aid fatigue" in donor countries (Bräutigam and Knack 2004; Lancaster 2008), donors may fear negative publicity if they continue to provide funds to countries with restrictive civil society laws. Besides wanting to preserve their own commitment to democratic norms, they may seek to reduce aid lest they face a political backlash at home for coddling dictators. The possibility of this backlash is high because NGOs that are disadvantaged by the new laws in recipient countries will have strong incentives to mobilize against them through their transnational advocacy networks (Keck and Sikkink 1998).

Why is foreign aid ineffective, why the aid fatigue, and where do NGOs fit into this puzzle? Scholars suggest that aid is ineffective because donors provide it to serve their aims, not the needs of the recipients (Lundsgaarde, Breunig, and Prakash, 2010). Of course, both motivations can cohere, but often they do not. Many donors do not provide aid with the goal of lifting recipient countries out of poverty. They do not take into account the appropriateness of the aid, recipient need, the quality of delivery systems, or the country's absorptive capacity. Instead, donors have been (and are) guided by considerations such as slowing the spread of communism, fighting against terror, rewarding military allies, promoting the economic interests of their firms, or rewarding political support.

Some aid critics favor strategies that reduce donations but create incentives for developing countries to engage in international trade and commerce. For instance, Uganda's former trade minister, Edward Rugumayo (2004), noted that "economic growth in Africa depends on donor funds and this is like building an economy on a pack of cards or shifting sand. Export trade should be the solid ground on which economies should be built." In his congressional testimony on the African Growth and Opportunity Act in 1997, Benjamin Kipkorir, the Kenyan ambassador to the United States, noted that "Africans have come to realize that trade not aid is the way to the future" (Kipkorir 1997). In this line of thinking, then, for aid to be effective, it must address and fuel the more immediate drivers of economic growth—export-oriented trade—rather than factors with a more distant relationship to growth, namely strengthening the pillars of democratic governance (such as civil society) and public service delivery.

Another category of critics believes that aid can have its desired results only if it is delivered effectively. For them, the problem lies not in to which country or for what reason aid is given, but in how it is put to use. The culprit in this narrative is the recipient government, the assumption being that state bureaucracies have neither the capabilities nor the incentives to deliver aid effectively. Hence, these critics recommend minimizing the role of governments in the provision of aid, and perhaps even cutting them out altogether.

This is where NGOs enter the aid puzzle. Given the hype about civil society, donors tend to (or may even want to) believe that NGOs have the expertise and the infrastructure to deliver aid appropriately. Consequently, donors hope that aid will promote democracy, development, and other goals if channeled through NGOs instead of governments (Banks, Hulme, and Edwards 2015; Edwards and Hulme 1996; Mitlink, Hickey, and Bebbington 2007; Van Rooy 1998). If NGOs are the critical vehicles for effective delivery of aid, the enactment of laws that restrict aid flows to them should pose serious problems for donors. After all, donors confront "aid fatigue" (Bauhr, Charron, and Nasiritousi 2013) at home. Aid critics (including a surprisingly large section of population in some countries, especially the United States) accuse governments of neglecting domestic needs and spending large budgetary resources abroad. Periodic media exposés about corruption in the "foreign aid industry" and the lavish lifestyles of rulers of impoverished but aid-supported countries accentuates the domestic backlash against aid.

Restrictive NGO laws have, indeed, impacted negatively on donors by influencing aid allocations to law-adopting countries. In our previous work (Dupuy and Prakash 2018), we analyzed a panel of 134 countries receiving aid from 29 donor countries for the years 1993 to 2012. These donor countries belonged to the OECD's Development Assistance Committee (DAC). In our main model, we focused on civilian bilateral aid only. We found that the adoption of a restrictive NGO finance law is associated with a large reduction in bilateral aid inflows: on average, bilateral aid inflows reduce by 32 percent (depending on the model specification) after a country enacts such a law. Our finding holds even after we control for levels of democracy and civil liberties, which suggests that aid reductions are motivated not by democracy recession but by the removal of NGOs from delivery chains. In real terms, developing countries in the sample receive an average of US$307 million in foreign aid, a 32 percent (one third) reduction that represents nearly US$100 million less in aid—a substantial cut for many aid-receiving countries.

Conclusion and Future Research

In the 1990s, scholars declared the onset of a global "associational revolution" and viewed it as analogous to the rise of the modern nation state (Salamon 1994). Yet even as this revolution was spreading, it was also being rolled back. One might even suggest that this diffusion-rollback dialectic is akin to Karl Polanyi's (1944) "double movement," but in a different context: the process of Western-funded NGOization that disembedded civil society from its local roots and violated the sanctity of national borders created a counterpush by states to reclaim their sovereignty. Unfortunately, democratic consolidation in these countries became collateral damage because states sought to roll back foreign-funded NGOs. They did this not out of concern about NGOs' effects on civil society, but because states began viewing foreign-funded NGOs as allies of their political opponents.

This chapter has offered a political explanation for why states enact these legal restrictions despite the anticipation of negative repercussions for doing so. The broader message is that scholars need to bring the state back into the study of the NGO sector because the state retains the ability to create and deny political opportunities and resources to it. This should not come as a surprise; after all, with the contractorization of the NGO sector, states have become important resource providers to this sector. Our chapter suggests that the characterization of the rise of the NGO sector as laying the foundation of politics beyond states (Wapner 1995) is unfounded. The "nongovernmental" character of NGOs should be questioned because states continue to control the rules under which NGOs operate—and, more importantly, the conditions under which they receive financial support from abroad. States govern NGOs' access to territories and populations and grant NGOs permission to operate in specific issue areas (Bratton 1989; Jalali 2008, 2013; Henderson 2011). The N in NGO should not lead scholars to prematurely declare the death or obsolescence of the state. As our chapter shows, such rumors are vastly exaggerated.

This chapter also provides important cautionary lessons for the study of the diffusion of institutional blueprints and ideas across countries. The Washington Consensus assumed that Western institutions could be easily transplanted to other settings, whether creating markets via the "shock therapy" of privatizing governmental-owned firms (Mishler and Rose 1997), or by creating a modern NGO sector through the infusion of foreign funding and political facilitation by Western-dominated global institutions (Reimann 2006). Although the merits of shock therapy continue to be debated, there are visible signs that a large number of developing countries have not accepted the Western framework for the NGO sector, particularly where its ability to receive foreign monies is concerned.

Broadly, the NGO crackdown shows the fragility of Western norms about civil society promotion. Instead of a global society (Meyer at al. 1997) steeped in Western norms, we see developing countries violating these norms. This rollback is surprising because it imposes a significant material cost for these countries, given how much they rely on international aid. Interestingly, our work suggests that donor response seems to be guided by concerns about NGOs no longer being available to deliver foreign aid. Concerns about democracy recession do not seem to drive aid reductions, which raises important questions about the commitment of Western donors to democracy promotion.

This chapter hopefully also raises theoretical questions about the modern concept of civil society. In *Democracy in America*, Alexis de Tocqueville noted the important role of self-organized civic associations in the American polity, writing: "In democratic countries the science of association is the mother science; the progress of all the others depends on the progress of that one."[15] NGOs are supposed to represent the power of communities to self-organize so that they can provide for local public goods. Indeed, NGOs are expected to serve as the buffer between the individual and the state. When NGOs mobilize resources locally, they become accountable to local communities. And when the state seeks to suppress NGOs, communities could be expected to rise to their defense. Unfortunately, NGOs in the developing world have turned into subcontractors for overseas donors, dependent on foreign resources instead of raising funds locally. This has eroded their downward accountability to the communities they serve. This contractorization of NGOs provides the political cover for governments to crack down on NGOs without fear of retaliation. These concerns are not new. Even in the 1990s, scholars had warned of the perils of NGOs becoming governmental subcontractors (Edwards and Hulme 1996; S. Smith and Lipsky 1993). But Western donors and NGOs seem to have ignored it. In some ways, the emergence of laws leading to decreased donor funding may actually be a blessing in disguise. This decline will drive home the message that foreign monies cannot purchase the NGO sector abroad. Legitimate NGOs must emerge endogenously and have roots in the communities they serve.

History, Content, and Form

Breno Bringel and Elizabeth McKenna

ON DECEMBER 17, 2010, A TWENTY-SIX-YEAR-OLD fruit seller named Mohamed Bouazizi poured paint thinner over his body and struck a match. Bouazizi's public self-immolation set off street protests that toppled an autocratic regime in Tunisia and catalyzed a wave of protests known as the Arab Spring. During this same period, anti-austerity demonstrations swept Portugal, Spain, and Greece. Across the Atlantic Ocean, protesters inspired by Madrid's *indignados* pitched tents in lower Manhattan, a symbolic occupation of Wall Street that spread to more than two hundred cities throughout the United States (Adams 2015). Other countries in both the Global North and the Global South experienced protests with similar characteristics during the same period. Fueled by indignation and rapid-fire communication technology, this cycle of protest seemed to signal a sea change in the scope, scale, and dynamics of social struggle around the world (Castells 2013; Howard and Hussain 2011; Piven and Shefner 2014; Tufekci 2017).

It is tempting to interpret the sudden succession of protests on the streets of Cairo, Lisbon, New York, São Paulo, Hong Kong, and elsewhere as absolutely new or as a unique set of events linked to the political and economic conditions of the late-aughts. Remarkable as this wave of unrest was, the phenomenon of global protest diffusion long predates the rise and spread of digital networks. Its history stretches from religious uprisings to abolitionism, from anti-colonial independence movements to the anti-globalization protests that marked the turn of the twenty-first century.

Guided by this historical view, this chapter has two main aims. In the first section, our goal is to situate global social movements in a *longue-durée* perspective, outlining what we see as three patterns in how transnational collective action has both taken shape in the real world and been studied by social scientists. Following the proposal and scope of a handbook, we offer a select review of research that speaks to the multiple levels and scales at which social movements operate. Within the vast literature on transnational activism, we identify three genres of scholarship: (1) labor internationalism (and the anti-racist and anti-colonial movement studies that similarly address how activists confront global capitalism); (2) polity studies, which takes the nation-state as the primary movement target; and finally (3) a postmodern and postcolonial turn to the universal dynamics of social contestation. In our survey of this literature, we aim to identify what was gained and what was lost in the transition from one paradigm to the next. In the second half of the chapter, we outline a research agenda that takes these lessons into account by considering the content, form, and temporality of global social movements.

The terms *transnational activism* and *global social movements* are often used interchangeably (e.g., Bennett 2005; Fisher et al. 2005). We consider them to be both theoretically and practically distinct and use them to mean different things throughout this chapter. *Activism* refers to the use of direct action methods to bring about desired social and political change. It can involve disruptive tactics (or *contentious politics* in the social movement nomenclature), such as protesting, rioting, or bird-dogging a decision maker. Activism can also entail less confrontational activity, like circulating a petition, launching a social media campaign, or attending a committee hearing.[1] In repressive contexts, activism is often necessarily more subtle (Chen and Moss 2018); some forms it can assume include dissident writings (Glasius 2013), subversive faith-based displays (Levine 1988), or neighborhood-level associational activity (Lin 2020). Diaspora communities that raise money for humanitarian assistance—as, for example, Myanmar's exiled populations did for borderland refugees (Simpson 2013)—or a mobilization in which thousands of people around the globe simultaneously post social media messages in support of climate justice (Padawangi 2013) are examples of transborder activism.

By contrast, a transnational social movement involves "mobilized groups with constituents in at least two states, engaged in *sustained* contentious interaction with power-holders in at least one state other than their own, or against an international institution, or a multinational economic actor" (Tarrow 2001:11, emphasis added).[2] One such movement is La Vía Campesina, an international peasant movement founded in 1993 and made up of 182 organizations in 81 countries, and which makes claims on states for sustainable agriculture, food sovereignty, and gender equity. Examples of the kinds of transnational actors that are often the subject of research in the subfield include international government institutions like the International Monetary Fund, the World Bank, international NGOs, global human rights organizations, and international ethnic, social, or religious movements.[3]

Trends in Contemporary Global Movements: Research and Social Practice

Although any attempt to classify and periodize a body of work as large and diverse as global social movement studies is a reductive endeavor, our goal is to sketch the outlines of the field's intellectual history in relationship to the best available evidence of how this sort of activism unfolded. Thus this section will not be an exhaustive inventory of all global movements ever recorded; instead, we use this selective literature review to demonstrate why more historical grounding is needed as scholars turn their attention to the global dynamics of contentious politics. And scholarly interest in the topic does appear to be on the rise: the number of dissertations archived in ProQuest that relate to transnational activism or global social movements increased from just 4 dissertations in 1989 to 106 in 2016.[4] As reflected in Figure 29.1, as a percentage of all dissertations archived in the database that include *social movements* or *activism* in the abstract or keywords ($N = 7,733$), those incorporating a global dimension of analysis increased from less than 5 percent in 1989 to a peak of 29 percent in 2007.

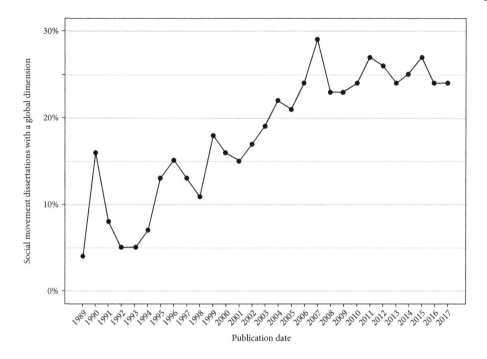

Figure 29.1 Evolution of dissertations related to global social movements, 1989–2017
Source: ProQuest Theses and Dissertation Database, https://www.proquest.com/libraries/academic/dissertations-theses/

Did this upswing in transnational social movement scholarship mirror patterns of contention in real world, as many scholars predicted it would? Shortly after the Iraq War protests of 2003—thought to be the largest international demonstrations in history—Sidney Tarrow wrote, "We are witnessing, if not a full-blown global civil society or an integrated transnational polity, at least a trend toward new forms and new levels of transnational contention" (2005:xii). One way to assess the hypothesis that globally oriented activism has increased as the world "flattens" (Friedman 2005) or "shrinks" (Herod 2003) is by testing this proposition against data from one of the increasingly comprehensive large-N databases of contentious political events.

Two such databases, the Global Database of Events, Language, and Tone (GDELT) and the Worldwide Integrated Crisis Early Warning System (ICEWS), monitor the world's news in print, web, and broadcast media in over 100 languages. The power of these databases derives from their ability to aggregate large amounts of events through automated coding procedures. As social researchers gain access to vast quantities of textual data, machine learning techniques are now being used to detect patterns in large corpora, including newspaper articles (DiMaggio, Nag, and Blei 2013; Newman and Block 2006), meeting transcripts (Fligstein, Brundage, and Schultz 2017), and patents (Kaplan and Vakili 2015).

At the time of this writing, coded output of the ICEWS database is publicly available via the Harvard Dataverse, and includes more than seventy million rows of text-based data spanning the years 1995 to 2016.[5] Events are automatically identified from international, regional, national, and local sources, partially mitigating one of the common critiques of

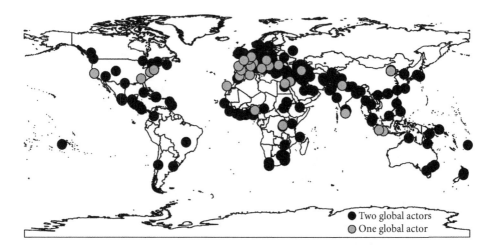

Figure 29.2 Transnational activism and contentious political events, 1995

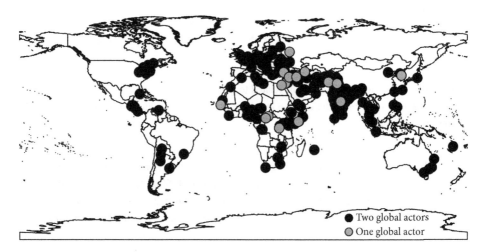

Figure 29.3 Transnational activism and contentious political events, 2016

newspaper data: namely, that not all contentious political events are covered in canonical media sources like the *New York Times*, much less earn international coverage (Ortiz et al. 2005). ICEWS events are coded as triplets. Each consists of an initiating actor, an event type, and a target actor. Purely U.S. domestic events are excluded and geographical-temporal metadata are extracted and associated with the events reported in the news article (Boschee et al. 2018).

Filtering for sociopolitical interactions that are both collective and contentious, and which involve one or more transnational actor, allows us to track changes in real-world instances of transnational activism over time.

The map points shown in Figures 29.2 and 29.3 indicate the location of a contentious political event as reported in more than 170 media sources that were coded as involving a transnational actor as either a target or initiator of the action. As a percentage of all contentious political events detected in the database, there were 62 percent *fewer* protest events involving one or more global actors in 2016 as compared to 1995. The percentage was similar for 2011, the year of the Arab Spring and the major anti-austerity protests in southern Europe, with 60 percent fewer such events as compared to 1995.

In a purely quantitative sense, this finding runs counter to the assumption that the "rooted cosmopolitans" (Tarrow 2002), "transnational advocacy networks" (Keck and Sikkink 1998), and "global non-state" actors (Sassen 2002) that emerged in the 1990s inexorably increased (or at least intensified) their contentious political activity. After the emergence of anti-globalization activism in the late 1990s, the growing capacity of nonstate actors to organize across borders while agitating both state and international institutions showed no signs of abating (Boli and Thomas 1999; Sikkink and Smith 2002).[6] In her study of the Battle of Seattle, Jackie Smith demonstrated how that "protest of the century" adapted local repertoires of action to the international stage (2001). Smith and her colleagues later extended this line of research to examine how transnational coalitions of citizen groups responded to the deleterious effects of globalization (2008), with a focus on one particular form of transnational activism: the World Social Forum. Smith and her colleagues argue that the forums, which began in 2001 in Porto Alegre, Brazil, were an important precursor to the mass protests that swept the globe in the early 2010s (Smith et al. 2014). Curiously, however, the ICEWS data suggest that globalization did not ipso facto trigger more instances of transnational activism so defined. Nevertheless, the possibility should be considered that global social movements have become so powerful as to "restructure world politics" (Khagram, Riker, and Sikkink 2002) in ways that are simply not detected in these large-N event databases. This includes their importance in everyday spaces and submerged networks related more to experiences than to protest events (Bringel and Pleyers 2017).

Moreover, event-based protest research does what much social movement scholarship tends to do: privilege disruptive tactics at the expense of the more prosaic kinds of action on which successful social struggle inevitably depends. The phrase "the long march through the institutions," popularized by German New Leftist Rudi Dutschke (and often attributed to Antonio Gramsci) signified "working against the established institutions while working in them" (Marcuse 1972:55). According to this strategy, it is by way of "insinuation and infiltration rather than confrontation" that radicalism succeeds (Kimball 2000). In addition, the automated coding of political data is far from flawless (Schrodt and Van Brackle 2013). The systems are still vulnerable to missing, duplicative, or misclassified events.[7] "If something doesn't get reported in a newspaper or a similar outlet," notes political and computer scientist David Lazer, "it will not appear in any of these databases, no matter how important it really is" (Singer 2016).

Faced with this confluence of increased scholarly attention (Figure 29.1) in transnational activism and an apparent stasis in its contentious manifestations (Figures 29.2 and 29.3), we propose three paths that would enrich research on contemporary social movements. First, we think that the subfield would benefit from a historical orientation that recovers the political content of activism, the analytical concern that dominated studies of the anti-colonial, anti-capitalist, and anti-racist movements of the seventeenth through the nineteenth centuries. Second, it should retain but complicate the polity model's focus on the institutional dynamics of movement activism. Finally, we suggest that research should integrate these perspectives with the field's relatively recent fascination with the new organizational forms of activism observed in the early years of the twenty-first century. In the following sections, we review some of the lessons bequeathed by these prior literatures.

Placing Cross-Border Collective Action in Historical Context
Anti-Capitalist, Anti-Colonial, and Anti-Racist Global Movements

We start from the same point as early scholars of social movements: with self-consciously global social movements that resisted three interrelated systems of worldwide exploitation: capitalism, colonialism, and slavery. We classify the first of these bodies of research, a "resolutely pro-Marxian" strand (Tilly 1978:48), as *labor internationalism*. Classic works in this vein placed the international struggle of the proletariat at the center of the theory of history. Marx and Engels's famous 1848 injunction—"Workers of the world, unite!" ([1848] 1978)—became the rallying cry of radical labor movements for the next 150 years (Löwy 1998). According to Marx, industrial society is not the design of any one nation-state; rather, it is the product of the dynamics of capitalism. Therefore, the grievances inherent in different class situations transcend borders. Social movement research in the Marxist tradition insists on the primacy of shared positions in the organization of production. Key works of scholarship investigated peasant revolutions in Algeria, Angola, China, Cuba, Mexico, Peru, Russia, and Vietnam (Paige 1975; Wolf 1969); as well as the historically specific relationships among agrarian classes, landlords, and bureaucrats in Britain, China, France, Germany, India, Japan, and Russia (Moore 1966). There was also Charles Tilly's analysis of the history of collective action in Western Europe and North America (Tilly 1978:48).

A launch point for much of this work was the rise and fall of the International Working Men's Association (IWMA), also known as the First International: a political organization founded amid the labor union revival of the 1860s to resist capitalism on a global scale. It illustrates some of the contradictions that would plague Marx's elusive worldwide proletarian revolution and the scholarship that attended to it. In his inaugural address to the IWMA at St. Martin's Hall in central London, Marx described the dire conditions of the British laboring classes. "With local colors changed," he said, "the English facts [of poverty and increasingly obscene wealth concentration] . . . reproduce themselves in all the industrious and progressive countries of the Continent" (Marx [1864] 2000). The only antidote, he proclaimed, was for workers of different countries to link arms in universal, emancipatory struggle. As is well known, Marx predicted that as the rate of profit declined to zero, widespread worker rebellions would beget the dissolution of the capitalist world system. Even though, as Giovanni Arrighi showed in his analysis of evolutionary patterns of world capitalism (2009), systemic cycles of accumulation are progressively shortening, the mass uprisings predicted by Marx did not come to fruition. Asked whether a second proletariat revolution would be possible, labor scholar Peter Waterman dismissed it as an impossibility, given that "there was no first coming of this mythical creature" (1998:349).

Paul DiMaggio (2001) offers an account of the reasons why Marx's predictions of imminent worldwide revolution did not materialize. The six explanations he reviews can be reduced to two broader ones. First, advanced capitalist nations and firms used offensive practices that forestalled the declining rate of profit, such as outsourcing exploitation to peripheral countries and exploiting ever more vulnerable populations, including immigrants and ethnic minorities (Sassen 1983; Schoenberger 1988). Second, monopolists and oligopolists employed defensive (or class conciliatory) tactics. These included distributing profits among professional salaried managers (Galbraith [1967] 2007), bureaucratizing the enemy (Edwards 1979), and using the spoils of monopoly pricing to pacify the workforce (Baran and Sweezy 1966). Most political economists agree that these two sets of practices had anesthetizing effects on the trade unions and undercut the potentially revolutionary ambitions of the underclasses.

Historians identified other explanations for the First International's inability to forge a global solidarity movement. Drawing on primary documents, Henry Collins showed that the varied development of national labor movements across Europe meant that British trade unionists, by far the most well established, saw no point in collaborating with the "technically and organizationally backward" workers on the continent (1962:412). Collins observed that whereas "in Switzerland, strikes were treated as abnormalities; in Belgium as acts of war," England's trade unions were "within their accepted limits, powerful" (1962:412). Contrary to Marx's proclamation, some laborers felt that the workers of the world needn't unite after all—at least if they wanted to secure incremental gains—so long as their bargaining partner was a reform-oriented government. Corroborating this research, Edward Shorter and Charles Tilly later showed that workers have historically secured rights by making claims on the nation-state rather appealing to a supranational body (1974).[8] Meanwhile, as Boaventura de Sousa Santos and Hermes Augusto Costa note, capital—and not the laboring underclass or minority movements—managed to internationalize with far more success (2005:18).

In contrast to the relatively bloodless domestic labor reforms covered in this research, a parallel body of work examines contemporaneous—and more militant—global uprisings, including indigenous struggles, slave revolts, anti-colonial wars of independence, and attempts at Pan-African revolutions (Aptheker 1937; Du Bois 2007; Tarrow 2007). In his foreword to Cedric Robinson's influential book *Black Marxism* ([1983] 2000), Robin Kelley explains this coincidence: "At the very same moment European labor was being thrown off the land and herded into a newly formed industrial order, [A]frican labor was being drawn into the orbit of the world system through the transatlantic slave trade" (xiv). According to Robinson, many slave-led rebellions took inspiration not from Western Marxism's formulation of the transnational and transhistorical proletariat but from West and Central African culture, merging different influences. The same holds true for Latin America, where the political language of social movements is the result of situational changes and an available "political and conceptual repertoire" that is reinvented and redefined over time, assigning new meanings to classic themes and transformative political action in the region, as evidenced by, for example, the anti-imperial and decolonization movements (Bringel 2019).

The relationship between abolitionism and anticapitalism remains the subject of much scholarly debate (e.g., Ashworth [1995] 2007; Bender et al. 1992). Undeniable, however, is that Marxist thinking—if not Marx himself—was present in many of these revolutionary movements (Cabral [1964] 2010; Fanon [1963] 2004).[9] The abolitionist movement itself, which peaked in the late eighteenth and early nineteenth centuries, was a significant early instance of cross-border struggle (Drescher [1977] 2010). Scholars have examined the networks that structured the slave trade and the abolition movement (Ingram and Silverman 2016), the overlooked role of female antislavery activists (Jeffrey 1998), and the strategic use of pressure tactics like the "carrot of British financial aid" and the "stick of the possible boycott of colonial produces" (Murray 1980:53).[10] Richard Blackett's work (1983, 2000, 2013) draws attention to the ways in which black Americans' role in the struggle for emancipation is often excised from popular and scholarly discourse, as well as how transatlantic connections strengthened the movement. Instead, it is the changing normative regime—found in the work of Enlightenment philosophers like John Locke and Montesquieu—that emphasized constructs like "moral capital" (Brown 2006) and the "rhetoric of sensibility" (Carey 2005) that received the most attention among scholars of abolitionism in the Global North. Black radical scholarship provided a trenchant critique of this discourse and literature (e.g., Robinson [1983] 2000).[11]

Distinct from many movement studies that came later, what the literature on the anti-capitalist, anti-colonial, and anti-racist global movements briefly outlined earlier have in common is their concern with the dynamics of politics, power, and structural oppressions (Hetland and Goodwin 2013; Walder 2009). This scholarly preoccupation with movement claims and content, however, receded as critiques of orthodox Marxism's failure to explain country-by-country patterns of social struggle gained prominence. As Jeff Goodwin and Theda Skocpol observed the year the Berlin Wall fell, the Marxist hypothesis that "misery breeds revolt" could not explain why and where protests and revolutions occur (1989:490). Critics note that even at their peak popularity, materialist analyses could not explain, for example, the strike waves of the 1930s. The French sit-down strikes, the United States' mass automobile and steelworkers' strikes, and the Arab revolt in Palestine all suggest that rebellions do not depend on some threshold level of hunger, oppression, or immiseration. Instead, scholars have shown that global levels of protest sometimes increase, sometimes decrease, and sometimes stay the same when material well-being improves (Gould 2005:239).

The Polity Model

Acknowledging these limitations, a second school of social movement research placed collective action struggles squarely within the bounds of the territorial nation-state. This shift coincided with the academic institutionalization of social movement studies in the 1960s and 1970s, after which *political process* and *resource mobilization* theories emerged as the dominant theoretical paradigms. Most work in this intellectual lineage used what Elizabeth Armstrong and Mary Bernstein called the polity model, a "state-centered view of power" (2008:77), which generally ignored the nonstate and suprastate institutions in which power also inheres.[12] What is more, for much movement scholarship originating in the Global North, analysis of the world beyond the United States or Western Europe is the exception rather than the rule (Bringel 2011; Mariátegui 2005).[13]

Instead, many seminal works in the polity tradition were written in the long afterglow of the American civil rights movement, whose successes justified its usage as the primary case from which new theoretical insights emerged (e.g., Andrews 2004; McAdam [1982]

1999; Morris 1984). Among these scholars' interventions was the call to reenter human agency in social movement studies, rejecting both the mass society theorists' model of collective action as extreme and irrational crowd behavior, as well as collective behavior theorists' analysis that "system strain" results in the normative ambiguity and alienation that in turn produces social movements (Buechler 2000). Although political process theory is sometimes criticized for its structural bias (Goodwin and Jasper 2004), many polity model researchers call attention to the fundamental sources of human agency of social movement leaders, the institutional forms they create, and the tactical repertoires they creatively employ to mobilize their constituents.

At the same time, the polity model's tendency toward methodological nationalism has been thoroughly critiqued (e.g., Oommen 2012)—and, in some cases, partially corrected. In Doug McAdam's introduction to the second edition of *Political Process and the Development of Black Insurgency*, for example, he notes that "scholars in the political process tradition have generally failed to fully appreciate the multiple embeddings that shape the interpenetrations and actions of political actors" ([1982] 1999:xxxi). Civil rights leaders, McAdam argued, recognized that they could strategically leverage the geopolitical context of the Cold War when making their demands. So long as black citizens at home were denied the right to vote, the national political establishment lost the veneer of moral superiority that it relied on while fighting communist regimes abroad. Tarrow, another originator of the political process model, later made it his project to examine the processes and mechanisms that explain transnational activism, the fusion of international and domestic contentious politics, and whether "new" forms of movement organization are "simply producing old local wine in new global bottles" (2005:214). Michael Mann (1984, 1997), among others, offers a skeptical answer to Tarrow's line of inquiry, qualifying the effects of globalization. Mann argues against declaring the death of the nation-state, noting the uneven effects of transnational interactions on domestic sources of power, in the realm of both the material ("hard geopolitics") and the ideological or normative ("soft geopolitics").

The Third Phase of Modernity

Finally, in what sociologist José Maurício Domingues (2012) named the "third phase of modernity" (and several others called "flexible modernity" or "postmodernity"), scholars and activists interrogated the taken-for-grantedness of the Westphalian political order in movement studies. Research on transnational movements proliferated after the fall of the Berlin Wall. These included studies of indigenous movements like the Zapatistas (Inclán 2008; Stavenhagen 2003), land reform struggles connected to La Vía Campesina (Martínez-Torres and Rosset 2010), feminist movements (Dufour, Masson, and Caouette 2011), anti-globalization mobilizations culminating in the 1999 Seattle protests (Levi and Murphy 2006; Smith 2001), the international environmental movement (Longhofer and Schofer 2010), and global human rights campaigns (Gohn 2011; Sikkink 1993), among others.

This marked scale-shift away from the framework of the polity model reflected a "decentering of the nation-state as a hegemonic reference for protests" (Bringel 2015:123). But many of these studies still hewed to the theoretical and methodological assumptions of earlier decades. For example, even as Margaret Keck and Kathryn Sikkink acknowledge the increasingly blurred boundary between the international and national realms (1998:4), the boomerang pattern they propose—a metaphor used to refer to the risks nation-states face from increasingly powerful transnational alliances—has been criticized for reifying the global–local dualism of the earlier scholarly order.

Recent work, such as Tianna Paschel's comparative investigation of black movements in Brazil and Colombia, shows that the improbable gains of ethnoracial justice struggles were not the result of the boomerang of international pressure "echo[ing] back" against a domestic setting in which decision makers were "deaf" to movements "too weak to advance their own claims" (Tarrow 2005:200). Instead, these victories emerged from the *alignment* of global and local openings (Paschel 2016:227). Similar to McAdam's analysis of civil rights leaders' strategic use of the Cold War geopolitical rhetoric, Paschel showed that the "Afro-Brazilian movement was able to leverage [unprecedented international openings] effectively because the Brazilian state had invested decades in projecting its image as a racial paradise abroad" (2016:236) at the same time as the domestic Afro-Brazilian movement strengthened its internal capacities. Adding still more complexity to the boomerang model is Yan Long's research on international AIDS activism in China, which showed that transnational interventions can birth new forms of domestic or "diplomatic repression" rather than new human rights advances. Long's longitudinal case study showed that transnational interventions mainstreamed AIDS and, in the process, created "new repressive actors" (with new repressive repertoires) out of social health organizations (2018).

The body of scholarship that emerged in this third phase of modernity sparked original and much-needed discussions about the cross-national dimensions of social contestation, articulating territories, networks, and scales in a more flexible and dynamic way. As Paschel's and Long's research makes clear, there is no absolute contradiction between the local and the global, as the widely used boomerang metaphor tends to suggest. International dynamics interpenetrate domestic politics in vital ways—the two are not completely separate spheres of political action. Moreover, although a wide literature has demonstrated the efficacy of legalistic international pressure on human rights concerns, the extent to which such interventions are similarly effective on questions related to global capitalism and the political economy of extractivism—where we first began with Marx—is less clear (Caren, Gaby, and Herrold 2017; Thomas and Mitra 2017).

Critical Reflections and New Research Directions

Such an oversight is not uncommon. Many accounts of global activism examine the variety of transnational social movement organizations (TSMOs), but don't address their political content, much less the material forces that so preoccupied the labor internationalists, decolonial thinkers, and anti-racist scholars referenced earlier. This omission may be due, in part, to the longstanding and growing specialization of fields of study with close proximity, such as labor studies and social movement research (Ferguson, Dudley, and Soule 2017). The split is reflected in the semantic emptying of terms like *activist*. As Jonathan Smucker observes, social movement adherents were historically classified as "*abolitionists, populists, suffragettes, unionists,* or *socialists*" (2017:18), all terms that referenced specific political context and content. The more modern term "activist, on the other hand, is an apparently 'contentless' label that now traverses political issues and social movements," he notes (Smucker 2017:18). Part of what makes sociology distinctive is its attention to the social and material bases of politics as reflected in the terms Smucker enumerates.

Rethinking Power and Capitalism

Careful analysis of the ways in which economic power translates into other kinds of power is one of the central contributions of the discipline of sociology (Bourdieu [1979] 1984; Weber [1922] 1946). And yet scholars have noted that class has receded to the background in much research (Manza and McCarthy 2011), despite renewed interest in the issue after the 2008 crisis (Barker et al. 2013). Mainstream studies of social movements have often been criticized for bracketing out the distribution of power (and its oft-utilized proxies, like wealth, income, ideology, and education) in attempts to identify the microprocesses of mobilization. For much of this line of inquiry, whether protesters seek to topple a dictator or torch a McDonald's—and whether the protagonists of protests are elites or marginalized members of an aggrieved population—is of secondary concern. Instead, the emphasis is on discerning which collective-action frames are operative; how well attended protests are and how often they occurred; and the causal effects of communication, recruitment, and tactical diffusion (e.g., Baldassarri and Bearman 2007; Bearman and Everett 1993; Ketelaars 2016; Wang and Soule 2012).

   Andrew Walder (2009:398) in particular has argued against this turn, claiming that the field's focus on framing processes and the ways in which networks catalyze collective action while eschewing political economy "radically narrows the intellectual horizons of the field" (398). In a similar critique of this trend, Gabe Hetland and Jeff Goodwin (2013) observe that social movement scholars have increasingly—and inexplicably—ignored how inequality and capitalism affect protest and political contestation. They write:

> The more recent scholarship tends to ignore not only the direct and proximate effects of capitalist institutions on collective action, but also the ways in which capitalist dynamics indirectly shape the possibilities for protest, sometimes over many years or even decades, by, for example, influencing political institutions, political alliances, social ties, and cultural idioms. Instead, recent scholarship tends to focus on short-term shifts in "cultural framings," social networks, and especially "political opportunities," rarely examining the deeper causes of such shifts (Hetland and Goodwin 2013:86)

The political content of social movements—if addressed at all—is often reduced to *either* material claims (such as wage disputes, welfare reform, or other redistributive issues) on the one hand, or identity-based recognition claims on the other (Fraser 2009). The artificial separation between capitalist dynamics and what the new social movements literature called "post-material" claims (referring to the women's, ecology, LGBT, and peace movements, among others) was never wholeheartedly accepted in Latin America and in other peripheral regions of the world.[14] For example, Brazil's *Movimento dos Trabalhadores Sem Terra*, widely known as the Landless Movement, or MST, combines the struggle for land and agrarian reform (a traditional material and structural claim) with more "identity-based" or transversal claims regarding race, gender, and environmental politics (Bringel 2013). In this and many other cases, the intrinsic relation between culture, nature, and territory makes it impossible to separate the "cultural" from the "material," since both are interwoven in the defense of movement participants' lives and livelihoods.

Some research on the protests that erupted in the wake of the 2008 global financial crisis—with which we began this chapter—emphasizes this intersection of structure and culture. Examining the anti-austerity protests in Portugal, borne of "contagion" and "communication," Elísio Estanque, Hermes Augusto Costa, and José Soeiro argue that, in contrast to other cycles marked by postmaterialist values, economic issues have gained a new centrality in both global protests and the research that studies them (2013). Donatella della Porta's *Social Movements in Times of Austerity* praises this new trend, arguing that "there is much to gain from bringing reflection on [social class] cleavages back into social movement studies" (2015:12). We are encouraged by both the epistemological and political learnings that are emerging from movement experiences rooted in the Global South—and by increased attention by scholars in the Global North to the constraining and enabling conditions of capitalism—and expect it to continue.

Another Kind of Right Censoring

Another consideration is that much of the research in the three epistemological traditions surveyed earlier examines movements from the perspective of minority challenger groups and progressive left-wing movements. Characteristic of this tendency is Charles Tilly's definition of a social movement: "the sustained, organized challenge to existing authority in the name of [a] deprived, excluded, or wronged population" (1995:37). Scholars rarely subject reactionary countercurrents or elite-led contentious politics to the same level of scrutiny. Similarly, a great deal of the research on global social movements that took place in the third phase of modernity referred exclusively to the action of advocacy groups acting in the name of "principled issues" (Sikkink 1993; Keck and Sikkink 1998; Finnemore and Sikkink 1998). What of groups rallying around unprincipled causes? Few scholars take Al Qaeda, the right-wing Atlas Network, the spread of neo-Pentecostalism, or even contemporary fringe right-wing groups as research objects, even though they arguably meet the empirical and analytic criteria for social movements outlined in the literature.

Across these three paradigms, we observe a tendency for scholars to study movements with left-leaning political content, making them overrepresented in the canon. Returning to the ProQuest dissertation database, we used a random-number generator to select a 10 percent subsample ($N = 313$) of dissertations on transnational activism archived between 1989 and 2016, which we then read and coded for a specific claim, a meta claim, and an ideology claim (left, right, mixed, or unknown).[15]

The coded output, depicted in Figure 29.4, reveals a new meaning for the phrase "right censoring." Most dissertations focused on topics closely associated with progressive causes. For every dissertation related to a conservative, reactionary, or regressive global movement, five are written on causes more closely associated with left politics. Although there always tends to be a lag and overcorrection in the study of world events, we suggest that our tendency to study emancipatory movements helps explain the inadequacy of existing frameworks to explain the revival of anti-democratic, nativist, anti-globalist, and white supremacist movements in Europe and the United States, the rise of religious

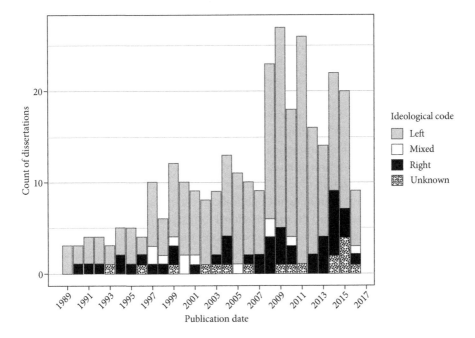

Figure 29.4 Political content of dissertations on global social movements, 1989–2017
Source: ProQuest Theses and Dissertation Database, https://www.proquest.com/libraries/academic/dissertations-theses/

fundamentalism in parts of the Middle East, and the ebbing of the so-called Pink Tide in Latin America.

Kathleen Blee and Kimberly Creasap (2010) note that there is indeed a growing literature related to rightist causes, and right populism in Europe in particular (see Toscano 2019). They point to a robust body of research on the role of women, websites, and white supremacists in scholarship on conservative activism; however, they note that scholarship on the global connections among right-wing movements and their relationships to institutional politics is limited. With this in mind, one avenue for future research might examine whether and how the mechanism of diffusion (or contagion), widely studied in the literature on leftist transnational activism, might be operative for right-wing movements as well.

An especially fruitful research direction might examine these rightist movements in a Polanyian sense by attempting to understand the sort of double movements of which they are a part.[16] The emerging right-wing social movements in the world in recent years cannot be understood in isolation. On the contrary, we need relational interpretations that analyze the history, emergence, and dynamics of these movements, taking into account a broader field of contention that includes diverse actors, targets, and spaces. Yet studies that analyze movement-countermovement interactions are still scarce (Meyer and Staggenborg 1996). Examining these dynamics may help us understand how, for example, the unprecedented successes of the civil rights, women's, and environmental movements of the 1960s relate to the anti-government, right-wing movement that wrested control of the Republican Party (Ganz 2018). We would do well to be less left "movement-centric" (McAdam and Tarrow 2010), pay more attention to activists' enemies and targets (Luders 2010), and sharpen our analysis of how conservative and reactionary activists make the long march through institutions as well (Skocpol and Hertel-Fernandez 2016).

Organizational Forms and Temporality of Global Social Movements

Another less trodden path in global social movement studies rescues some of the polity literature's concern with organizational forms and repertoires. In the previous edition of this volume, Elisabeth Clemens analyzed how organizational structures and practices shape political socialization (2006). If this is the case, than scholars of transnational activism cannot stop at examining the political content of social movements. They must also turn a critical eye toward the organizational forms, practices, and routines of which they are composed, as well as how they change over time.

One of the most incisive reminders of the link between the content and form of associational activity comes from Sheri Berman's (1997) study of the Weimar Republic, in which she showed that civil society activity based on bonding rather than bridging ties can aid the rise of fascism. This led her to observe that "political institutionalization may be less chic a topic these days than civil society, but it is logically prior and historically more important" (1997:401). Her account shows that activism is not an unalloyed good. Nor is charity. Clifford Bob's research (2002, 2009, 2010), for example, shows how many INGO funding practices can be characterized as Darwinian: groups engage in fierce competition with each other to appeal to international donors for scarce resources—sometimes to the detriment of the needs and interests of their own constituencies. In the United States, this culprit for this dynamic was named "the nonprofit industrial complex" (Rodríguez 2007), a reference to the ways in which funders sometimes reinforce the power dynamics they purport to fix. This research suggests that the politics of social movement funding practices merit investigation as well.

Building from this body of research, we propose two further research topics that bear on the organizational dimensions of global social movements: the time horizons of protest cycles and the formal structures and diffuse platforms that link them together (or not). With regard to the first dimension, our effort to distinguish activism from movements at the outset of this chapter is also a comment on the temporal lenses through which scholars analyze social movements. The medium-term political consequences of many of the post-2008 protest movements demonstrate that large numbers of people in the streets are perhaps neither a necessary nor sufficient condition for movement success.

In some cases, amorphous masses can inspire powerful countermovements. In 2011 in Egypt, for example, the 10-million-person mobilizations that toppled a feckless Mubarak ultimately led to a military-judicial seizure of power (Tuğal 2014). That same month, in Brazil, diverse individuals from across the ideological spectrum took part in mass mobilizations in more than 350 cities across the country. After the initial outpouring, however, the democratizing demand that had sparked the protests—a call for free public transportation—receded. The protests' progressive elements were outmatched by a subsequent wave of reactionary demonstrations that grew into a full-blown authoritarian movement. With help from the traditional purveyors of power like the media, the judiciary, and economic power elite, Brazil's authoritarian movement overtook all levels of government in both the 2016 and 2018 elections (Bringel 2016; Bringel and Pleyers 2019; McKenna 2019). In Turkey, the Gezi protests that relied on a digital infrastructure, but no internally legitimated leadership, were easily and forcibly dispersed (Tufekci 2014:14). Almost ten years after the beginning of this global cycle of protests, the world appears to have moved from indignation to polarization and, in simple terms, from democratization to authoritarianism. We can draw some lessons from these cases about the tension inherent in the temporal choices scholars must make in the study of social movements.

Doug McAdam and William Sewell note that much social movement research avoids this choice, "betray[ing] no temporality whatsoever" (2001:90). The framing literature and cross-sectional surveys of movement activists in particular seems to have "no particular conception of time" (2001: 90). McAdam and Sewell identify two temporal rhythms that have dominated in the study of social movements and revolutions: long-term processual change and the protest cycle. By contrast, they lament the lack of focus on "the precise sequencing of actions over the course of a few hours or days . . . [which] may have structuring effects over a very long run" (2001:102). Sewell's analysis of the storming of the Bastille—which, he argued, catalyzed the French Revolution and invented the very category of revolution itself—exemplifies what the authors term event-based sociology (1996a, 1996b). Since this intervention, some studies have focused on the momentary and contingent choices that actors make in high-stakes moments and their short and long-term effects (Seguin 2016). One noteworthy example is David Snow and Dana Moss's (2014) retheorization of spontaneity. Snow and Moss argue that the importance of unplanned actions that take place as protests unfold militates against what they call the "overly-organized" conception of how movements operate.[17]

At the same time, as Max Weber famously observed, "Politics is a strong and slow boring of hard boards." Street protests, strikes, boycotts, and critical elections represent only the most visible forms of struggle over the distribution of power, as Alberto Melucci insisted in all his work. Although event-based sociology can be key to understanding conjunctural dynamics, a focus on open political conflict alone obscures how power relations also operate through nondecisions, agenda control, and other structures that allocate authority over what issues are even up for debate (Lukes [1974] 2005; Pierson 2015). Analyses restricted to the first face of power, typical of the kinds of studies that use newspaper data (as we did in Figures 29.2 and 29.3), often fail to examine what Theda Skocpol and Alexander Hertel-Fernandez call the "organizational universes" that structure long-term political shifts (2016:681).

This limitation opens new possibilities for future research. The first is related to the continuities and ruptures that take place between protest cycles. Excessive focus on protest waves—and on the sensational newspaper coverage they often generate—often makes us overlook what happens in between cycles. The intercycle lens can be provide a useful analytical approach with which to examine the continuities, ruptures, and innovations that take place over time. The cadence of protest cycles and the mechanisms that link the peaks to the troughs mean that what happens after and between the "moments of madness—when all is possible" (Tarrow 1993) may be as important as the collective-action events themselves.

A second possibility relates to the temporalities of protest cycle analyses. There is a kind of division of intellectual labor in the social sciences among the analysts of these cycles. Those linked to political economy and historical sociology tend to approach them from a *longue-durée* perspective, focusing mainly on the dynamics of capitalism (e.g., Arrighi 2009; Braudel 1977; Wallerstein 1974). These authors have developed sophisticated elaborations of economic cycles but maintain a problematic relationship with what they call "anti-systemic movements" because of their sometimes deterministic emphasis on immutable structural and historical forces. A second way of interpreting protest cycles is associated primarily with political sociology and historical institutionalism, schools of thought that have helped us understand political cycles in the medium term, such as the periods that scholars sometimes refer to as "waves of democratization" (Huntington 1991). In this case, social movements are also often considered a consequence—but not a creator—of suprapolitical and institutional dynamics. Finally, within this division of intellectual labor in the social sciences, social movement scholars tend to study protest cycles in the short term, which often narrows the scope of the scholarly contribution. The length of a given cycle of protest is often just a few weeks or, at best, a few months. Far too few studies integrate these different temporalities (short, medium, and long-term) into coherent analytical frameworks.

Given this challenge, how might future scholars of transnational activism and social movements theorize the relationship between protest events, their cultural and material content, and the broader political cycles of which they are a part? How can a more complex, dynamic, and contingent understanding of the impacts of global protest help us understand the current moment characterized by democratic setbacks? To what extent can an analysis of the temporalities of social movements contribute to our understanding of changes in organizational forms? Time-based analyses are fundamental to any assessment of social movements and their myriad organizational forms. The answer to these questions, we argue, would significantly advance the state of the art of social movement research and praxis.

Final Words

In 1897, Albion Small wrote a short essay in one of the *American Journal of Sociology*'s earliest issues. He argued that the term *social movement* "once had dignity," which it had lost, because of the confusion surrounding what, exactly, it means. "Let us try to represent the social movement candidly," he wrote:

> So long as men have lived they have at times showed two opposite dispositions; first, to calmly take life as they found it; second, to try to better themselves. It would be altogether distorted to represent past times as controlled by the former impulse, and to assert that the latter is peculiar to our day. The migrations of Semites and Mongols and Teutons would disprove that. The history of industry and commerce and war and science would disprove it. The study of every great nation would disprove it. Men have always tried to improve their condition. (Small 1897:340–341)

We have attempted to make three interventions that could strengthen future research on the perennial phenomenon that is the social movement. First, as Small observed more than a century ago, transnational activism and global social movements are hardly "peculiar to our day." In much of the research we surveyed, the overwhelming tendency is for social movement scholars to study transnational activism and movements as though they were historically novel phenomena. Second, theoretical and empirical research that bridges the *content* (political and cultural) and *form* (organizational, tactical, and temporal) of transnational movements would represent a welcome intellectual contribution to the field. Finally, scholarship that rescues capitalism and power and moves beyond the tendency to study single temporalities and movements that are left-leaning in their politics (and that operate primarily within the bounds of the nation-state) would help address systematic biases in the dominant theoretical frameworks of the subfield.

Despite our focus on history throughout this chapter, we would be remiss to ignore the deep transformations taking place in contemporary activism today. Around the world, there is something of a consensus that we are living through the change of an era. The actors and their respective practices and grammars of action have changed considerably vis-à-vis the broader shifts in societies. Deciphering these transformations requires transcending rigid frameworks, short-termism, and even the fierce urgency of the present. It also requires thinking globally and in an open and dynamic way, learning from the participants of social movements and synthesizing accumulated knowledge. This chapter was an attempt to map a few possible steps in that direction. Many more must also be taken.

A Critical Assessment

Helmut K. Anheier, Markus Lang, and Stefan Toepler

THIS CHAPTER OFFERS A CRITICAL REVIEW of comparative, cross-national research on the nonprofit sector. It argues for a need to revisit the fundamental assumptions
underlying comparative research in this area. Specifically, we suggest a reexamination of
the definition and classification of nonprofit organizations; a review of the institutional
embeddedness of nonprofit organizations and their relationship with the three institutional
complexes of market, state, and civil society; and the field's analytic approach, in particular
the social origins theory. We ultimately call for the field's connection to a wider social
science research agenda. The outcome of this would be a comparative-historical research
agenda informed by political science and sociology to complement the macroeconomic
approach, largely based on national income accounting, that has characterized the field
for nearly three decades.

Since the first edition of this book (Powell 1987), the field of nonprofit studies has come
of age in many countries. Conceptual issues seem more settled; there is a set of mostly
complementary theories about the existence and the behavior of nonprofits in market
economies; and the empirical base of the field has improved in both quality and quantity.
The academic infrastructure has expanded, too. Teaching programs in a growing number
of countries have responded to student demands at both undergraduate and master's levels
(Mirabella and McDonald 2012; Mirabella, Hvenmark, and Larsson 2015); the number of
PhD students entering the field has increased (Jackson, Guerrero, and Appe 2014; Shier
and Handy 2014); academic journals with respectable impact factors were launched, as
were scholarly associations (D. Smith 2013); and textbooks, dictionaries, encyclopedias
and handbooks addressing an international audience have been published (e.g., Anheier
2014, Anheier and List 2005; Anheier, Toepler, and List 2010; Wiepking and Handy 2016;
D. Smith, Stebbins, and Grotz 2017).

What is more, the policy relevance of nonprofit organizations seems to have increased
(Suárez, Chapter 20, "Advocacy, Civic Engagement, and Social Change"; Walker and
Oszkay, Chapter 21, "The Changing Face of Nonprofit Advocacy"), leading to greater
recognition at both national (e.g., Almog-Bar and Young 2016; S. Smith and Grønbjerg
2015) and international levels (Schofer and Longhofer, Chapter 27, "The Global Rise of

Nongovernmental Organizations"; Dupuy and Prakash, Chapter 28, "Global Backlash Against Foreign Funding to Domestic Nongovernmental Organizations"), as reflected in the UN's Cardoso Report (Cardoso 2004). Independent research institutes and think tanks have sprung up in many countries. So have consultancies specializing in nonprofit organizations or specific topics (such as philanthropy or NGOs), which have proliferated in the political and economic capitals of the world. Being an expert on nonprofit organizations is no longer as unusual as it may have been a generation ago. Indeed, a certain acceptance into the academic and political mainstream marks the field today—something that was certainly absent in the 1980s.

A Field Evolving

At the risk of oversimplification, three major periods characterize the international development of nonprofit research. The 1970s and 1980s saw the field emerge in the context of the American economy and society at a time of extended economic recession and subsequent retrenchment of welfare programs; in the 1990s, international efforts gathered momentum; and the 2000s onward brought a focus on civil society and the advocacy role of nonprofit organizations.

The 1980s were largely a decade of theory building shaped by the U.S. experience, as presented in the first edition of this book (Powell 1987). The research agenda at that time set forth three main questions (DiMaggio and Anheier 1990): why do nonprofit organizations exist in market economies, what is their organizational behavior, and what is their impact? The major theories introduced during that period still provide the foundations for the field, and, indeed, subsequent developments build on them (see Steinberg 2006; Anheier 2014: chap. 8).

Of particular importance here were the heterogeneity theory or government failure theory, which suggested that when unsatisfied demand for public and quasi-public goods occurs in situations of demand heterogeneity and limited public budgets, nonprofit providers form (Weisbrod 1975, 1988; Kingma 2003; Slivinski 2003). The trust theory or market failure theory proposed that the nondistribution constraint makes nonprofits more trustworthy under conditions of information asymmetry, which makes monitoring expensive and profiteering likely (Hansmann 1987; Ortmann and Schlesinger 2003). The stakeholder theory argued that given profound information asymmetries between provider and consumer, which imply significant transaction costs, stakeholders decide to exercise control over delivery of club goods (Ben-Ner and Van Hoomissen 1991; Krashinsky 2003). The interdependence theory posited that because of initial collective-action advantages, nonprofit organizations precede government in providing public goods; however, because of "voluntary failures," they are likely to develop synergistic relations with the public sector over time (Salamon 1995).

What these theories had in common was that they were based on the "American case" of a liberal market economy with a decentralized, competitive electoral system and heterogeneous demand for quasi-public goods. They were not necessarily meant to have cross-national applicability. Nonetheless, in the late 1980s, the first comparative studies began to appear.[1] Estelle James (1983, 1987, 1989) pioneered the field with her empirical work on the supply and demand conditions of nonprofit service provision in developing countries. She argued that they differed from developed market economies mainly in the chronic scarcity of quasi-public goods, such as education and health care, irrespective of demand heterogeneity or trustworthiness considerations. In most cases, such shortages were due to limited state capacities to deliver these goods; in others, it was indicative of elite capture.

Insights from these and other studies formed the basis of entrepreneurship theory (James 1987), which argues that nonprofit organizations are created by entrepreneurs seeking to maximize nonmonetary returns. The entrepreneurs in James's theory are political, religious, cultural, and humanitarian activists driven by values (including worldviews, moral dispositions, beliefs, and opinions) and normative dispositions. They use the nonprofit form for product bundling and co-production—for example, services such as teaching, caring, or healing that take place in a value-based context. Their hope is that infusing service provision with values would make recipients more susceptible to the organization's ultimate purpose. Religious schools or hospices are perhaps the clearest examples.

At the same time, economists also picked up the notion of product bundling to understand the revenue generation strategies of nonprofit organizations. They differentiated between preferred quasi-public goods, preferred private goods, and nonpreferred private goods (Schiff and Weisbrod 1991). For example, in a religious context, the preferred quasi-public good is the value to be spread in order to create a community of faith, such as the Christian gospel or the Qur'an. Alternately, the preferred private good, which nonprofits aim to optimize, is the education delivered in parochial schools or madrassas. Finally, the nonpreferred private good, which nonprofits use opportunistically, would be sales of religious symbols, pamphlets, or relics.

The co-production concept similarly emerged during that period and received the attention of public administration scholars (Brudney and England 1983) and economists (Ostrom 1975). It refers to situations where the consumers or beneficiaries of a service, often a quasi-public good, collaborate with providers on its design and delivery. For example, patients co-design treatment plans with their health care providers; residents organize neighborhood watches to improve public safety; and nonprofit housing organizations require tenants to help with the construction and maintenance of their future homes (Brandsen, Steen, and Verschuere forthcoming). In addition to individual utility considerations, co-production includes a commitment to a common good and some level of communal trust, which made the concept attractive to social welfare scholars and urban planners.

The noneconomic motivations highlighted by James became a preoccupation of a body of comparative research that looked at how nonprofits combine services with value dispositions (see Anheier and Seibel 1990; Wuthnow, Hodgkinson, and Associates 1990). This approach focused on instances of institutional patterns that rest on deep-seated social, religious, or political foundations. Examples are the principle of subsidiarity in Germany (Anheier and Seibel 2001), pillarization in the Netherlands (Burger et al. 1999), the social economy in France (Archambault 1997), the British tradition of charity (Kendall and Knapp 1997), popular movements in Scandinavia (Lundström and Wijkström 1997; Tranvik and Selle 2007), or concepts of the public sphere in Japan (Amenomori 1998).

The main insight of this research was that embedded institutional patterns and the underlying values they express—that either challenged or supported the political system in place—shaped not only the size and composition of the nonprofit sector but also the basic orientation of its organizations.[2]

Comparative Nonprofit Sector Research: Looking Back, Looking Forward

This upswell of research in the 1980s left students of the nonprofit sector conceptually richer, but poorer in evidence that could be used to test the cross-national applicability of these theories. The 1990s corrected some of that imbalance. It was a decade of establishing the methodological and empirical foundations of comparative research. Of these efforts,[3] the most impactful was the Johns Hopkins Comparative Nonprofit Sector Project (CNP) (Salamon and Anheier 1996). CNP addressed major challenges that had long frustrated students of comparative nonprofit sector research. It introduced a definition, a classification system, and ways of measuring nonprofit activity. Most importantly, CNP succeeded in meeting two major objectives. First, it was instrumental in establishing a satellite account on nonprofit organizations as part of the international System of National Accounts, or SNA (United Nations 2003). Its work on this front allowed for the increased collection of comparable data on different nonprofit sectors across time. Second, CNP aided the creation of initial attempts to understand cross-national variations in nonprofit sector size and scale through the social origins theory.

While systematic comparative nonprofit research, heavily driven by CNP efforts, was taking shape, the early 1990s saw the simultaneous revival of the concept of civil society that often overlapped with nonprofit-focused research but remained distinct in its emphases and intellectual orientations. *Civil society* rather than *nonprofit* became the predominant label for more activist and political forms of voluntary action. The civic resistance against the military juntas of Latin America and then the totalitarian state socialism in Central and Eastern Europe patterned interests in Gramscian notions of civil society as a protective sphere guarding society against an overpowering state and emphasizing the potential for conflict.

Central European intellectuals and dissidents like Adam Michnik and Vaclav Havel as well as Western intellectuals like Ralf Dahrendorf and Timothy Garton Ash were prominent voices in the revival of the idea of civil society after the fall of the Berlin Wall in 1989 (e.g., Kumar 1993).

The concept soon gathered considerable political acceptance and was quickly co-opted by influential U.S. foundations (Quigley 1997; Aksartova 2009), which provided additional currency to the policy proliferation of the field as a whole (Lewis 2014). But it also created conceptual confusion as to how the notions of a nonprofit sector and civil society differ: for some, the nonprofit sector and civil society were basically synonymous, exemplified by CNP, which changed its labels from nonprofit to civil society in the late 1990s, while leaving the basic approach described earlier untouched.[4] For John Keane (2005:26), CNP was accordingly among the "various research projects that suppose that civil society is equivalent to the not-for-profit 'third sector.'" In the field of international development, Thomas Carothers (1999) similarly held that civil society often gets equated with NGOs, albeit inappropriately. For others (Dahrendorf 1997; Kaldor 2003), civil society is distinct from the organizational focus of nonprofits and reflected more individual dispositions on the one hand, even reaching into aspects of civility, and institutional characteristics on the other, as exemplified by Jürgen Habermas's public sphere (1989).

Clearly, the decisions CNP made in the 1990s had, and continue to have, major consequences for the development of comparative nonprofit sector research.[5] It is therefore worthwhile to review them in some detail, and in particular so that they may inform a future research agenda. However, as seen, CNP and comparative nonprofit research do not perfectly align with the full breadth of the international civil society discourse. In the following, we will therefore first reexamine the cross-national definition, classification, and theorizing of nonprofit sector research and then discuss the implications of the nonprofit versus civil society dimension before providing a concluding outlook.

Defining Nonprofits

First, there is the question of definition. Although defining what a nonprofit organization was relatively straightforward in the U.S. context,[6] it was more complex internationally for two reasons. First, international data systems, most prominently the SNA, defined nonprofit organizations in ways that were unsuitable for comparative research (see special issue of *Voluntas* 4(2), 1993; Anheier, Rudney, and Salamon 1994). The SNA (2009) uses a standard revenue approach, according to which nonprofits do not price their goods and services to cover the cost of production, are not financed predominantly through taxation, and are not primarily consuming entities. In other words, they are defined as a residual category: they are not market producers, government organizations, or households. Specifically, nonprofit organizations that receive more than half of their revenue through fees, charges, and sales are treated as market producers and allocated to the business sector; those that receive more than half of their revenue from government are treated as part of the public sector; and those that do not offer goods and services are treated as households. The resulting sector of "nonprofit institutions serving households" received little attention by statistical agencies; at the time CNP commenced in 1990, just a handful of the nearly two hundred countries providing SNA statistics reported any data on the nonprofit sector. As a result, available official data on the nonprofit sector were sparse, distorted, and inconsistent (Anheier et al. 1994). Second, with viable approaches lacking for comparative purposes, relying on national definitions and ways of measuring the sector turned out to be a major challenge.

Faced with these issues, CNP turned to the national level. It found that different legal systems, institutional patterns, cultural traditions, and levels of development accounted for a great diversity of organizational forms located between the state, the market, and the family.[7] The challenge CNP faced went well beyond seemingly merely semantic issues. For example, the British call public schools what the Americans call private schools; similarly, in Europe, different national definitions of foundations are difficult to reconcile (Toepler 2016, 2018b). Underneath these differences are often deeply rooted institutional histories and cultural patterns—even for close cousins like the American and British charities that share origins in the English Poor Laws of 1601.

In confronting such an immense terminological tangle, CNP chose to focus neither on how nonprofits are defined by respective legal systems nor on their functions, such as charity or public benefit, as defined in different national or cultural contexts. The former would have generated confusion that would have stifled comparative research; the latter would have invited normative debates about what constitutes these functions, how to assess their contributions, and who gets to define the public good. Consider the definitional challenge: what do American nonprofit universities like Yale or Stanford, Japanese industry associations like Keidanren, Catholic schools in France, a network of homes for the elderly run by the social services branch of a Protestant Church in Germany, village associations in Ghana, urban improvement organizations in Brazil, Amnesty International, Greenpeace, a sports club in Denmark, a village hall in England, Islamic endowments in Egypt (*waqfs*), and the Ford Foundation have in common?

As a way forward, CNP introduced a structural-operational definition (Salamon and Anheier 1992a, 1997) as a common denominator cutting across different functional conceptualizations, legal systems, levels of development, and national traditions. According to this definition, nonprofit organizations are organized, private legal, and self-governing entities that are nonprofit-distributing and voluntary. The sum of entities so defined constitutes the nonprofit sector of a given country.

Taking nonprofits out of their particular legal, cultural, and national contexts was bold. This conceptual maneuver is of critical importance, as it establishes a nonprofit "sector" as the totality of organizations fitting the preceding definition. The CNP approach does not ask if a country has some notion of a distinct sector for organizations set apart from the market and the state, or if the sector fits into the cultural, political, or social context of the country's institutions. Instead, it identifies the sum of nonprofit organizations based on an operational criterion. Then it estimates the size of the sector using an essentially SNA-like approach to GDP measurement based on employment indicators.

Figure 30.1 shows the relative size of the nonprofit sector measured as a share of the economically active population in all forty-one countries covered by the CNP database as of 2016.[8] The sector's size varies between 15.9 percent in the Netherlands and 0.7 percent in Romania. To arrive at these percentages, CNP sums up the share of both full-time equivalent paid employees and volunteers working in the nonprofit sector relative to the economically active population (e.g., 10.1% + 5.8% in the case of the Netherlands; 0.3% + 0.4% in Romania).

The forty-one-country average of this central measure of economic size is 5.6 percent. There are a few countries in the sample whose sector comprises less than 1 percent of the economically active population (e.g., Romania, Poland, and Slovakia). By contrast, there are some countries whose sector's size exceeds 10 percent (e.g., the Netherlands, Israel, and Belgium). Figure 30.2 shows that in most countries, the nonprofit sector constitutes less than 5 percent of the working population, with 1 to 3 percent as the modal category. Countries with large nonprofit employment share are clearly the exception. The distribution is positively skewed, which means that the median at 4.6 percent is below the average of 5.6 percent. In other words, smaller nonprofit sectors are more common than larger ones.

However, the sector aggregations displayed in Figures 30.1 and 30.2 may not necessarily fit the broader institutional reality of a country. Some of the countries included may not have known that they had a nonprofit sector of this sort, linguistic differences set aside. Countries may have a range of organizations located between the state and the market,

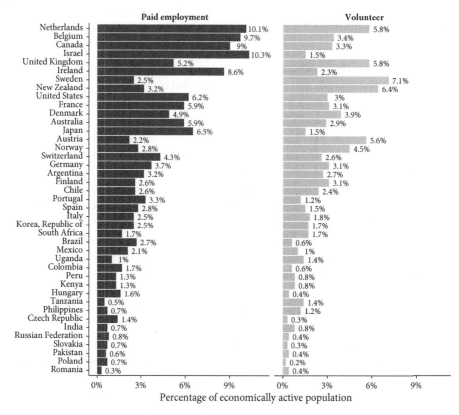

Figure 30.1 Size of nonprofit sector paid vs. volunteer workforce, by country

Source: Author; based on data reported in Salamon et al. 2017, pp. 276–279.

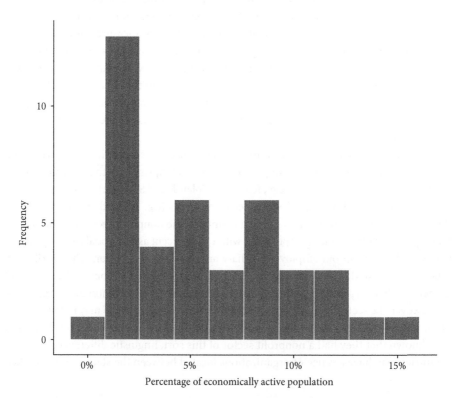

Figure 30.2 Histogram of nonprofit sector size by country

Source: Author; based on data reported in Salamon et al. 2017, pp. 276–279.

their institutional patterns perhaps only weakly organized around the nondistribution constraint and the other features of the structural-operational definition. Even if they can be grouped together along these lines, they may not be thought of as a coherent "sector."

Three brief examples from Europe illustrate these differing conceptions. In France, the overall institutional concept is the social economy, which includes voluntary associations, cooperatives, and mutual corporations (Archambault 1997). In Germany, on the other hand, the notion of public utility largely serves as the overarching concept that covers service providers, associations, and foundations (Anheier and Seibel 2001). Finally, in Britain, there are two parallel notions, charities and voluntary organizations (Kendall and Knapp 1997). These countries use neither CNP's definition of a "nonprofit organization" nor the concept of a nonprofit sector.

In essence, CNP did for cross-national research what Peter Hall (1992) argued that initiatives like the Yale Program on Nonprofit Organizations did in the United States: it invented the nonprofit sector. Hall criticized the cryptonormative stance of nonprofit research in the United States, which he saw as caught between two opposing "projects"—a liberal approach to increase social participation and a conservative approach to limit the size of government. By contrast, CNP's intent was more methodological when it established the definition of nonprofit organizations and sectors.

Let's reexamine the CNP definition in the context of a conceptual mapping of the nonprofit sector and its institutional proximities (Figure 30.3). Recall that the structural operational definition established five core characteristics for nonprofits independent of their basic form, governance structure, or purpose. This is appropriate for national accounts purposes, as such distinctions need not enter SNA logic. Thus stock corporations, for-profit cooperatives, limited liability companies, and joint proprietorships are all market producers despite their differences. Similarly, all types of public agencies and quasi nongovernmental organizations (*quangos*) are treated as government entities irrespective of their actual form or purpose. Lastly, different types of nonprofit organizations are treated the same under SNA guidelines. Yet the three basic categories of nonprofits (and the many hybrids that exist[9]) imply not only different types of governance but also different purposes and activities that arise from different institutional contexts. Specifically:

- In the case of nonprofits as membership associations, members and their shared interests provide the raison d'etre for the very existence of the organization; they constitute some kind of internal democracy. Members typically have a decisive role in leadership formation and representation in governing bodies. Membership associations therefore require some degree of freedom of association and a capacity for self-organization. In many countries, freedom of association was a politically contested issue and part of a struggle to establish a realm of citizen engagement independent of direct state supervision. As a result, a country's degree of self-organization is contingent on state–society relations, as well as factors like religion, education, socioeconomic status, class mobilization, and regionalism.
- For nonprofits as corporations based on set capital and limited liability, a self-perpetuating board substitutes for owners and publicly represents the organization. Such corporations are typically service providers. They operate mostly in the fields of

education, social services, health care, and, to a lesser degree, housing. Their emergence is linked to the development of the modern corporation, the rise of the service economy, and the welfare needs of modernizing societies. Unlike associations, they require significant capital and regular revenue. Reforms in recent decades across both advanced and developing countries increasingly see such corporations as part of new public management and quasi-market arrangements.

- Nonprofits as asset-based foundations feature a governing board that holds and operates an endowment in trust for a dedicated charitable purpose. They are among the freest institutions of modern society, in that they can operate independent of short-term expectations of market returns or political support. Unlike associations, they have no internal demos (i.e., membership). In contrast to corporations, they rarely provide a service to customers. Their setup requires not only accumulated capital but also a license or guarantee from government to operate with significant freedom.

As Figure 30.3 illustrates, nonprofit organizations do not exist in isolation from the three institutional complexes of state, market, and civil society. In fact, the nonprofit sector emerged over time in ways that involved complex and conflictual interactions with other institutions. In many cases, it created overlaps with them: markets with social enterprises or cooperatives; the state with public authorities, quangos, and public–private partnerships; and civil society with social movements and forms of civic engagement.

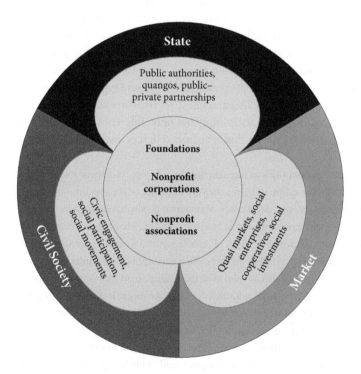

Figure 30.3   Mapping nonprofit organizations and institutional proximities

We now turn to three historical examples that illustrate the embeddedness of nonprofit organizations.

In France, the state had for prolonged periods of time suppressed most forms of private, voluntary initiative. Although the Ancien Régime had already abolished foundations in order to contain the power of the Catholic Church, the Loi Le Chapelier, established shortly after the revolution in 1791, also forbade all intermediary associations between the citizen and the state. The idea was that the state was to serve as the arbiter of the public will. Although a social economy was gradually developing out of the workers' movement, organized civic activity remained limited over the following century. It was not until the Law on Associations in 1901 that this type of voluntary organization was relegitimized. The law reintroduced it as a legal form under the tutelage of a central government. The relationship between the market economy and social economy on the one hand, and the association movement and sociability on the other, were part of the emerging nonprofit sector. Whereas the social economy was championed by the workers' movement, the association movement's ranks came from the urban middle class. Foundations continued to face a very restrictive political-legal environment throughout most of the twentieth century and were only allowed to operate under state tutelage until the 1980s (Barthélémy 2000; Worms 2002; Archambault 1997). In other words, the French nonprofit sector has historically involved the corporate form of nonprofit service providers closely linked to the social economy. It is less concerned with associations as social self-organization and hardly at all with independent assets.

In the Scandinavian countries, the state also played an important role in shaping the nonprofit sector. During the nineteenth century, broad-based popular movements emerged that connected local members with national politics. These movements provided professional services, political representation, and recreational activities for their membership. The emergence of the welfare state was thus met with a membership-based organizational infrastructure that continued to flank it, even as the actual service provision fell to state institutions (Wollebæk and Selle 2008). In Sweden, the public status of the state church (which lasted until the 1990s) facilitated the transition of nineteenth-century charitable institutions to state responsibility (Lundström and Wijkström 1997). The Swedish nonprofit sector consists mostly of associations developing mutually supportive relations with the state; it is neither a sector of corporate service providers nor of asset-based foundations.

In Germany, unlike France and Scandinavia, all forms assumed importance. The *principle of self-administration*, or self-governance, originated in the nineteenth century as part of a conflict settlement between the expanding Prussian state administration and the rising urban middle class. Under an autocratic regime, it allowed for the development of a specific kind of civil society that emphasized the role of the state as grantor of freedom for the regulated self-organization of municipalities, as well as trades and professions. It also allowed both associations and foundations to flourish in a controlled way. Elsewhere, the *principle of subsidiarity* provided a framework for settling secular-religious tensions, especially those involving the Catholic Church. After World War II, this principle developed into a policy pattern that prioritized nonprofit over public administration of social services (Sachße 1994), which led to a significant expansion of nonprofit corporations. Finally, the *principle of communal economics*, linked to the workers' movement, led to the cooperative movement and the social economy. This principle assumed significant importance during the reconstruction era of the 1950s and 1960s, especially in housing. Many communal organizations later transformed to for-profit entities.

In none of the cases do we see the sort of nonprofit sector conceptualized as by CNP per se. It overlaps with other institutional complexes but in ways that are different in France as they are in Germany or Sweden. What is more, the institutional space that nonprofit organizations occupy can contract, sometimes radically. The introduction of the National Health Service in postwar Britain meant that many hospitals and health-related entities that were organized and registered as charities were nationalized and thereby became public corporations and trusts (Kendall and Knapp 1997). This significantly reduced the economic size of the nonprofit sector. In the United States, Henry Hansmann (1990) showed that nonprofit credit and savings associations, thrift societies, and mutual insurance companies gradually declined as more effective government regulation of the financial sector took hold after the Great Depression. More recently, the conversion of many nonprofit institutions into for-profit entities increased commercial competition and reduced the number of U.S. nonprofit hospitals considerably between the 1980s and late 2000s (Goddeeris and Weisbrod 1998; Gray and Schlesinger 2012).

As with the Scandinavian example, the orientation of the nonprofit sector can change as well. The incorporation of most church-related charities into the public sector, with the parallel proliferation of popular social movements resulting in a civic culture of participation and voluntarism, left only a limited role in terms of service provision for the sector (Lundström and Wijkström 1997). An emerging hallmark of many hybrid and authoritarian regimes, like Russia and China (Benevolenski and Toepler 2017; Teets 2014), is efforts to suppress Western-funded social justice NGOs that are heavily engaged in advocacy activities. At the same time, these governments are creating incentives to enlist more apolitical, service-focused nonprofits in what represents a neoliberal turn away from the statist welfare regimes of the past (Tarasenko 2018).

In short, the institutional positioning of the nonprofit sector illustrated in Figure 30.3 can shift over time, which suggests the notion of co-evolution of institutional analysis (Mahoney and Thelen 2010). The structural operational definition, by contrast, cannot accommodate this phenomenon. Using examples from housing and health care in Victorian England, Susannah Morris (2000) raised this issue. For example, companies constructed social housing on a commercial basis, paying investors dividends, but pursued a fundamentally social mission. Because such organizations would fail a core criterion of the nondistribution constraint, a temporal application of the structural operational definition would lead to a distorted view of the Victorian (quasi) nonprofit sector. Morris accordingly questioned the viability of any conclusions drawn from empirical work based on the CNP definition.

However, the CNP definition's inability to take historical shifts into account is not necessarily a shortcoming. The CNP definition was first and foremost designed to measure the current economic scale of the nonprofit sector, and to enable cross-national comparisons.[10] Variations in scale and composition of the sector at any given point in time are a baseline for assessing larger institutional shifts in the conception of public and private responsibilities and the resulting interplay of the public, market, and nonprofit sectors. For example, in some places, cooperatives and mutuals remain more firmly in the nonprofit realm of solidarity and mutual help, whereas elsewhere they have largely become heavily commercialized and transitioned into the market. The emergence of social enterprise is another sector-straddling phenomenon, where an application of the CNP definition can lay bare different choices in the way that the public and the private are balanced in different contexts.

Yet to gain a better understanding of the field, in particular in view of theory development, it may be time to look at the state, market, and civil society adjacent and their relationships with the nonprofit sector.[11] These factors, in turn, are closely related to the functions that researchers like Ralph M. Kramer (1981, 1987) and others have long associated with nonprofit forms:

- Service provider role, often as nonprofit corporations: these organizations take on or complement services offered by government and businesses. They often cater to minority demands and provide trust goods (high information asymmetries and high transaction costs), thereby achieving an overall more optimal level of supply.
- Vanguard role, typically as nonprofit corporations and foundations: as mentioned before, these are less beholden than businesses to owner expectations of return of investment and are not subject to the exigencies of shorter-term political success. They are closer to the front lines of many social problems and, because they can take risks and experiment, they foster innovation in service provision and increase the problem-solving capacity of society as a whole.
- Value-guardian role, as product bundling service providers, but also as associations and foundations: these organizations help express different values (religious, ideological, cultural, etc.) across a population and within particular groups when governments are constrained by either majority will or autocratically set preferences. They thereby contribute to cultural diversity and ease potential tensions.
- Advocacy role, mostly as associations but also as foundations: when governments fail to serve all members of the population equally well, and when prevailing interests and social structures disadvantage certain groups while giving unjust preference to others, nonprofits can serve as public critics and become advocates. They thereby give voice to grievances, reduce conflict, and possibly create policy change.

In other words, we propose that a future research agenda revisit the question of definition. We suggest this not to advocate for the replacement of the structural-operational definition, but in order to enshrine functions or objectives as crucial factors that set nonprofits apart from both governmental agencies and businesses (Toepler and Anheier 2004). The new question that orients research would be this: what organizational forms, based in what institutional sectors, provide quasi-public goods and services and act as vanguards, value-guardians, and advocates? Such questions will lead researchers to examine the interfaces between the nonprofit sector and the state, market, and civil society, including hybrid forms.

Classifying Nonprofit Activities

There is also the issue of the classification of nonprofit activities. Available national and international classifications of economic activities from the SNA[12] lump many nonprofit

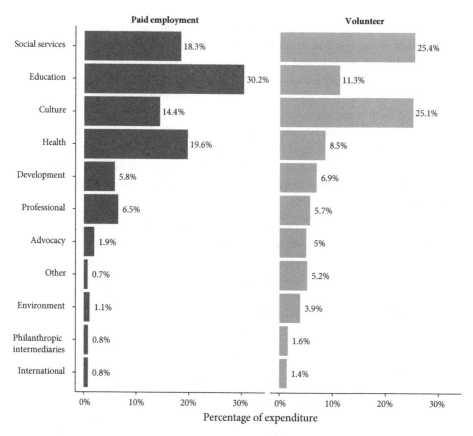

Figure 30.4 Nonprofit sector workforce, paid vs. volunteers, in 22 countries by field of expenditure

Source: Based on data reported in Salamon et al. 1999, pp. 478–482.

activities into few general categories; they do not provide the specificity needed for measuring sector composition. Bespoke classification systems like the American National Taxonomy of Exempt Entities (NTEE) prove too country-specific (Salamon and Anheier 1997). In response, CNP developed the International Classification of Nonprofit Organizations, or ICNPO (Salamon and Anheier 1992b). This system was used to show the distribution of employment, expenditure, and revenue data, with the goal of measuring the composition of nonprofit sectors internationally (see Salamon et al. 1999).

The ICNPO follows the classification guidelines of SNA-related systems. It is based on the majority expenditure rule, according to which the activity that accounts for the largest share of an entity's total operating expenditures determines its classification (Salamon and Anheier 1992b). For example, a nonprofit entity spending 51 percent of its operating budget on providing social services, 40 percent on housing, and 9 percent on advocacy would be classified under "social services." Hence, the ICNPO is an expenditure-based system, not an activity-based one. Consequently, it likely overemphasizes the three fields that make up about two thirds of total nonprofit sector spending: education, social services, and health care (see Figure 30.4). At the same time, it probably downplays activities that are less expenditures intensive, like advocacy, culture, environment, and philanthropy. In other words, service-providing nonprofit corporations that are engaged in endeavors that require large expenditures dominate the resulting measurement of the sector composition, while other activities in fields disproportionately populated with less service-focused nonprofits, including associations and foundations (most of them without employment), figure less prominently.

Figure 30.4 shows the distribution of nonprofit activity across different fields. The graph distinguishes between paid and volunteer work with dark and light gray bars. The dark gray bars indicate that expenditure-intensive fields like education and research, health, and social services make up the largest share of paid nonprofit activity (68 percent); all other fields make up only 31 percent. The light gray bars include the estimates for the substitution value of volunteer activity. Expenditure on culture, which mostly consists of recreational activities and amateur sports, turns out to be substantially higher with volunteers included (25 percent) than without (14 percent).

Two aspects of this graph are relevant for future research. First, given its emphasis on employment, which concentrates in education, health care, and social services, the picture of the nonprofit sector that emerges seems like a close approximation of the welfare regimes of a given country, and hence its level of economic and institutional development. This points to the importance of nonprofit corporations and their regulation and governance, as entities in these three fields (e.g., schools, universities, hospitals, homes for the elderly) are typically larger and capital- as well as labor-intensive. We will return to the implication of this finding when we consider the possibility that variations in nonprofit sector size and composition reflect broader social, economic, and political forces.

Second, as a result of the SNA rule, the ICNPO's classifications subordinate an organization's secondary activities to its primary one. Clearly, this can introduce distortions. For example, a nonprofit that provides mostly social services but also some health care and advocacy would have all of its expenditures classified under "social services." In the SNA, this is a well-known problem. It is tolerated because multiproduct corporations that reach sufficient size tend to split off into separate entities, which are then classified individually.

However, in the case of nonprofit organizations, product bundling is not only common but close to their very raison d'etre. The primary expenditure rule therefore poses a major conceptual problem, since it disregards product bundling and co-production. This oversight makes it impossible to test a core facet of both nonprofit theorizing (James 1987; Weisbrod 1988) and the rationale for the existence of these organizations in market economies.

A future research agenda could correct these shortcomings by extending the classification of nonprofit activities. As with the CNP definition, the proposal here is not to replace the ICNPO, as it represents a crucial tool for measuring the economic size and composition of the sector following SNA rules. Rather, the goal would be to develop activity measures that combine service delivery with other functions. These would complement the current expenditure approach for measuring the nonprofit sector. Ideally, a conceptually grounded and extended classification system would mirror the functions of nonprofit organizations mentioned earlier.[13]

Comparative Nonprofit Theory

Definitions and classifications serve descriptive purposes, yet their main task is to assist in building theories that enhance our understanding of differences among nonprofit sectors around the world. Indeed, using the nation-state as the unit of analysis, CNP developed a much-needed infrastructure for this project.

The social origin theory, initially proposed by Lester M. Salamon and Helmut K. Anheier (1998) and further developed by Anheier (2014:220–223) and by Salamon and his colleagues (2017), remains the main outcome of CNP theory building. It explains the size of a given nonprofit sector by emphasizing the factors responsible for variations in workforce size and its revenue base. The core idea behind this approach is that these variations can be traced back to the institutional embeddedness of the nonprofit sector in familial and community structures, as well as religious, political, and economic systems. Speaking broadly, the decisions of individuals and nonprofit entrepreneurs to rely on the market, the state, or the nonprofit sector for quasi-public goods and services is necessarily influenced by pre-existing supply and demand conditions. These reflect existing power constellations within state–society relations.

Unlike the more microeconomic theories mentioned earlier, the social-origin approach is comparative-historical in nature. It views the nonprofit sector today as a product of past conditions and developments. Rather than having just one deciding factor (e.g., degree of heterogeneity), the theory lays out diverse institutional trajectories that account for cross-national variations among nonprofit sectors. For example, some countries have relatively large nonprofit sectors because their governments pay for a substantial share of the services nonprofits provide. Under these circumstances, the nonprofit sector either could be the extension of a government seeking to limit its active role in service-provision (e.g., Britain) or could be powerful enough to extract significant funds from government (e.g., Germany). Other countries may have large nonprofit sectors because governments spend fairly little on welfare programs (United States), and nonprofit organizations rely on fees and charges rather than government subsidies. By contrast, countries with smaller nonprofit sectors may have a government that delivers adequate quasi-public services directly (e.g., Sweden), or a government that does not but nonetheless restricts nonprofit activities (e.g., Russia).

According to the social origin theory, such outcomes are the result of complex developments stemming from long-term social and cultural "moorings," as well as conflicts and their settlements among a range of actors and groups with varying power. These might include governments and state authorities, landed elites, urban middle classes, professions, peasants, working-class movements, organized religions, colonial administrations, among others. Even though the outcomes of the interaction of these factors can seem random and context-specific at times, overarching patterns emerge. These invite theoretical expectations that can be further refined (see the discussion of clustering later in this chapter).

In short, origin theory assumes that long-term constellations among actors and groups shape nonprofit sector scale, scope, and institutional embeddedness (Table 30.1). This approach focuses on the *longue durée* to examine change along two dimensions: the extent to which governments spend directly on the kinds of activities nonprofits provide (i.e., the direct substitution pattern), and the degree to which governments cofinance the nonprofit sector (i.e., the third-party government or complementarity pattern). These two dimensions can be expanded by a fourfold classification system of nonprofit regime types (Table 30.2), drawing on a welfare typology constructed by Gøsta Esping-Andersen (1990):

- In the *liberal type*, represented by the United Kingdom, a lower level of government social welfare spending is associated with a relatively high degree of government cofinancing of the nonprofit sector.
- The *social democratic type* is very much located at the opposite extreme. In this model, exemplified by Sweden, state-sponsored and -delivered social welfare protections are extensive; the room left for service-providing nonprofit organizations is therefore quite constrained.
- In between these two types are two additional ones, both of which are characterized by strong states:
- In the *corporatist* type, represented by France and Germany, the expanding welfare state has been induced to make common cause with powerful nonprofit institutions linked to established religious and political interests. As a result, the state pays for a significant share of nonprofit service-delivery expenditures.
- In the *statist type*, the state retains the upper hand in a wide range of social policies. It exercises power on its own behalf, or on behalf of business and economic elites. In such settings—historically Japan has been an example, as are present-day Russia and Mexico—limited government social welfare programs do not translate into high levels of government cofinanced nonprofit activity, as in liberal regimes. Rather, both government welfare initiatives and government sponsorship of nonprofits remain highly constrained.

Advancing the social origins approach beyond its initial formulation requires three steps. The first of these is a proposed conceptual typology with countries grouped under one of the four regime types (Tables 30.1 and 30.2). The second is employing model-based clustering, as suggested by John S. Ahlquist and Christian Breunig (2012), to identify the existence of the regime typology in "the real world" using CNP data. Typology conformation, however, is an intermediate step. The third task, therefore, is to link country clusters corresponding to the four regime types to different characteristics of the social moorings: the role of elites, class relations and social divisions, the power of religions, the strength of various political ideologies, and so on.

Such a recursive approach to theory construction brings up several fundamental issues. First, because of the long time frame and complexity of the factors it identifies as

Table 30.1 Nonprofit sector size and government social spending

	Nonprofit sector size *Small*	Nonprofit sector size *Large*
Government social spending Small	**Statist** Russia	**Liberal** United Kingdom
Government social spending High	**Social democratic** Sweden	**Corporatist** Germany

Source: Adapted from Anheier 2014; Salamon and Anheier 1998.

Table 30.2 Government social spending and government cofinancing of the nonprofit sector

	Government social welfare spending Low	*Government social welfare spending High*
Government cofinancing Small	**Statist** Russia	**Social democratic** Sweden
Government cofinancing High	**Liberal** United Kingdom	**Corporatist** Germany

Source: Adapted from Anheier 2014; Salamon and Anheier 1998.

important, the social origins theory is difficult to test empirically. This difficulty is of a different sort than the economic theories mentioned earlier. The social origins theory lacks the parsimony of economic theories and calls for difficult qualitative judgments about the relative power of broad social groups, actors, and ideologies over time. Moreover, the focus on the *longue durée* of social moorings entails a certain imprecision in determining which historical factors shape the present and which do not.

Second, model-based clustering of countries does not necessarily lead to empirical results that fall neatly into one regime type or another (Ahlquist and Breunig 2012; Breunig and Ahlquist 2014). If this is the case, the clusters have to be reevaluated to find out why the expected types cannot be found, and why countries do not match. That said, model-based clustering is less likely to generate fewer diverging clusters than explorative and descriptive methods. Yet it cannot relieve researchers from the task of interpreting the identified clusters and checking the reliability of the variables and samples chosen.

Third, we should recall that the CNP definition measures nonprofits divorced from their institutional environment. In allocating countries to a particular regime type, however, social origins theory brings in institutional factors rooted in a country's social moorings and its broader historical development. In other words, it imputes institutional meaning. For example, the three principles of subsidiarity, self-administration, and communal economy are employed to make a case for the corporatist nature of Germany's nonprofit sector. Yet these principles are responsible for only limited segments of the sector as delineated by CNP and the ICNPO: social services in the case of subsidiarity, professional associations and chambers when it comes to self-administration, and housing for the communal economy. The other segments of the sector are not implicated, but organizational forms outside the scope of the CNP definition are quangos and their many variants in the case of self-administration, and cooperative societies and mutual associations in the case of the communal economy (see Figure 30.3).

France, too, is classified as corporatist, but the social foundations of its nonprofit sector are completely different from the German case. They include the long-term impact of Jacobine ideology, the workers' movement, and late-twentieth-century associationism. From a comparative perspective, this suggests that the characteristics of the social moorings are neither necessary nor sufficient across cases, and that they reflect developments specific to a country rather than more general factors associated with the nonprofit regime type in question. In other words, we have a proposed typology (Tables 30.1 and 30.2) but no systematic and parsimonious set of factors associated with particular regime types.

Fourth, the social origins theory can lead to a certain circularity. France, as a corporatist country, developed a corporatist nonprofit sector; Sweden, as a social democratic country, established a social democratic one. But is France corporatist because of its nonprofit sector, or vice versa? Is Sweden social democratic because of its nonprofit sector, or vice versa? In other words, the explanation for grouping countries under particular nonprofit regime types would have to stress the larger institutional forces and patterns that made the French and Swedish nonprofit sectors what they are.

For example, Dag Wollebæk and Per Selle (2008; Selle and Wollebæk 2010) doubt the existence of a social-democratic nonprofit regime. Using the case of Norway, they argue that the institutional characteristics of Scandinavian nonprofit sectors existed long before the emergence of social democracy. Associating the contours of the sector with a social-democratic regime masks key factors of the *longue durée*, such as historically strong linkages between the local and the national level, the close association between volunteering and organizational membership, and the role of Protestant churches. Together, these factors account for the unique nature of the Scandinavian nonprofit experience.

Fifth, perhaps because Salamon and Anheier (1998) introduced the social origins theory as a heuristic that neither explicitly addresses causality nor clearly identifies its central variables, its applications are too varied for a systematic assessment. Table 30.3 lists over twenty studies applying the social origins theory that have been published between 2000 and 2018. Some studies use the four nonprofit regime types as a dependent variable (*explanandum*), some as the independent variable (*explanans*), and for others the explanatory positioning seems unclear. Some studies are qualitative case studies of specific countries, while others employ cross-national quantitative data. Seok Eun Kim and You Hyun Kim (2016) offer the most comprehensive quantitative study to date, yet they use a different dependent variable (a size variable based on SNA and not CNP data) and a different independent variable (government social protection spending instead of government social spending).[14] Generally, the studies reveal a great diversity in the operationalization of characteristics and factors associated with the social moorings and developments involved.

In essence, the social origins theory faces challenges that are common to comparative-historical approaches that track long-term institutional shifts to make causal inferences about the present. In many instances, co-evolutionary patterns are at work over the *longue durée* (Mahoney and Thelen 2010). Sometimes these are triggered or taken into a different direction by epoch-making events, critical junctures, or less fundamental but nonetheless influential developments. So when Wollebæk and Selle (2008) question the applicability of the social democratic model to Norway, they are pointing to co-evolution. James Mahoney and Kathleen Thelen's (2010) insight was that institutions, once created, do not only change in subtle, gradual ways; they also influence adjacent institutions and organizational fields. Their idea applies to the nonprofit sector as well. Wollebæk and Selle (2008), for instance, point to global trends such as individualization and marketization that have begun to reduce the uniqueness of the Scandinavian model through the gradual and subtle ways Mahoney and Thelen (2010) suggest.

These reflections ultimately challenge the explanatory power of regime theories generally. Is the U.S. nonprofit sector a liberal regime because of factors specific to its

Table 30.3 Studies using social origins theory

#	Original study	Number of countries	Regime types as explanandum	Regime types as explanans
1	Acheson, Harvey, and Williamson 2005	1	No	Yes
2	Archambault 2017	1	No	Yes
3	Archambault, Priller, and Zimmer 2014	2	No	Yes
4	Clarke 2013	1	Yes	Yes
5	Einolf 2015	207	No	Yes
6	Haddad 2017	1	No	Yes
7	Hustinx, Handy, and Cnaan 2010	6	No	Yes
8	Hustinx et al. 2012	2	No	Yes
9	Ju and Tang 2011	1	No	Yes
10	Kabalo 2009	2	Yes	Yes
11	Kala 2008	1	No	Yes
12	Kamerāde, Crotty, and Ljubownikow 2016	6	No	Yes
13	Kerlin 2010	36	No	Yes
14	Kim and Kim 2015	1	No	Yes
15	Kim and Kim 2016	20	No	Yes
16	Lajevardi et al. 2018	4	Yes	Yes
17	Lecy and Van Slyke 2013	1	No	Yes
18	Lee 2005	1	Yes	No
19	Lehner 2011	1	Yes	No
20	Nissan, Castaño, and Carrasco 2012	38	No	No
21	Principi et al. 2012	3	No	No
22	Salamon, Sokolowski, and Haddock 2017	41	Yes	Yes
23	Suleiman 2013	-	No	No
24	Svidroňová, Vaceková, and Valentinov 2016	1	No	Yes
25	Wagner 2000	6	Yes	No

development as part of American society, or because the United States is a liberal market economy, or because American society is prototypical of a more general Western pattern of modernity with a high degree of individualism and a preference of self-organization over state authority? Could it be that all three somehow apply, and along complex lines suggested by co-evolution? So it should not surprise us that two central features of the social origins theory remain an open issue more than two decades after it was introduced. The first is whether the discernible clusters of countries that the theory supposes can actually be found. The second is whether an emphasis on sector moorings has led to parsimonious sets of explanatory factors that vary more across regime types than within them, and that show idiosyncratic, regime-specific combinations.

What is more, we should expect such a clustering to reveal more than a split between developed economies on the one hand and developing or transition ones on the other. Otherwise, variations would be the result of different levels of economic development (note that in Figure 30.1 most countries with small nonprofit sectors were less-developed countries or transitioning at the time). Results should also show clusters other than those based on the varieties-of-capitalism approach (Hall and Soskice 2001); we see in Figure 30.1 that most of the countries with a large nonprofit sector are coordinated market economies. Clearly, because the social origin theory covers complex explanatory terrain, it has set itself the difficult task of finding patterns and structures that other theories and typologies tend to ignore.

Clustering

Figure 30.5 presents results from model-based clustering for forty-one countries using the variables "government social spending" and "government cofinancing of the nonprofit sector."[15] The model that best fits the most recent CNP data identifies three components with different variance and ellipselike shapes.[16] Roughly speaking, the shapes indicate the reliability of the identified clusters. For instance, one can be rather certain that Mexico (MEX) is part of a different cluster than the United States (USA) given that both countries are placed within different shapes. The placement of Austria (AUT) and Hungary (HUN) in the same cluster as the United States (USA)—as indicated by the triangular symbols—is, by contrast, less certain. Slight changes might lead to the placement of Austria (AUT) and Hungary (HUN) in the same cluster as the Czech Republic (CZE). The shapes are thus used to illustrate the underlying model's certainty about key clusters, whereas the circular, triangular, and square symbols denote general cluster memberships.

Alternately, Figure 30.5 uses a scatterplot to plot the variable government social spending against government cofinancing of the nonprofit sector using most recent CNP data (Salamon et al. 2017:276–279). The data points of France and Germany, for example, are close together because the two chosen variables have similar values for both countries.

The first clustering suggests two main findings. First, there seem to be only three clusters, with the social democratic one missing. Second, many countries are in between clusters.

Specifically:

- The countries expected to fall into the statist cluster, such as Russia and Mexico, clearly appear to cluster together. Japan is nowadays outside this cluster, as suggested earlier. All countries in the statist cluster are characterized by low government social spending and low cofinancing of the nonprofit sector.
- The second cluster, by contrast, groups countries expected to fall within liberal and social democratic clusters. Although the United States, as a prototypical liberal country, is grouped with Australia as predicted, it also shares the same cluster as the typically social democratic Norway. Even though the placements of other social democratic countries such as Sweden and Denmark are less clear, these countries are grouped surprisingly close to liberal ones. Government social spending is visibly higher in Norway than in the United States. Still, using government cofinancing of the nonprofit sector as a second measure, the United States and Norway are closer than the United States and Mexico, or Norway and Mexico.

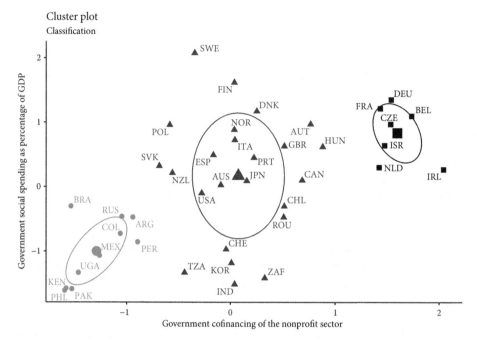

Figure 30.5 Model-based clustering of nonprofit sectors
Source: Based on data reported in Salamon, Sokolowski, and Haddock 2017. pp. 276–279.
Note: Figure uses ISO3 country abbreviations. See table 30.4 for further details.

- The third cluster contains European countries that have traditionally been described as corporatist, with high government social spending and high cofinancing of the nonprofit sector.

Although this three-cluster model best suits the data, there are several models with one to five components that are not considerably worse in terms of fit. One way to respond to difficulties in the identification of clusters is to refine theory building and to assemble data that contain more clustering information. This is what Salamon and his colleagues (2017) attempted by adding a fifth type to the social origins typology: the traditional type. According to Salamon and his colleagues (2017:84–85), this type is characterized by a large number of volunteers and an equally large amount of revenue contributed by philanthropy. In other words, Salamon and his colleagues (2017) argue that the statist type really consists of two types: the original statist type described earlier, and the new traditional type associated with countries like the Philippines and Peru. Table 30.4 lists all countries by hypothesized clusters.

The clustering in Figure 30.5 suggests that Salamon and his colleagues (2017) have a point: a number of countries at the lower end of the statist cluster are grouped very closely together. They expect those countries to form a cluster because they do not just have low levels of government social spending and cofinancing of the nonprofit sector but also depend to a larger extent than traditional statist countries on volunteers and philanthropic giving. To demonstrate the value of the expanded typology, they introduce two

Table 30.4 Countries by regime type hypothesized

#	Country	Iso3c	Social origins
1	Australia	AUS	Liberal
2	New Zealand	NZL	Liberal
3	Switzerland	CHE	Liberal
4	United Kingdom	GBR	Liberal
5	United States	USA	Liberal
6	Argentina	ARG	Outlier
7	Czech Republic	CZE	Outlier
8	Denmark	DNK	Outlier
9	Hungary	HUN	Outlier
10	Italy	ITA	Outlier
11	Japan	JPN	Outlier
12	Portugal	PRT	Outlier
13	South Africa	ZAF	Outlier
14	Austria	AUT	Social democratic
15	Finland	FIN	Social democratic
16	Norway	NOR	Social democratic
17	Sweden	SWE	Social democratic
18	Brazil	BRA	Statist
19	Colombia	COL	Statist
20	Korea	KOR	Statist
21	Mexico	MEX	Statist
22	Poland	POL	Statist
23	Romania	ROU	Statist
24	Russian Federation	RUS	Statist
25	Slovakia	SVK	Statist
26	Spain	ESP	Statist
27	India	IND	Traditional
28	Kenya	KEN	Traditional
29	Pakistan	PAK	Traditional
30	Peru	PER	Traditional
31	Philippines	PHL	Traditional
32	Tanzania	TZA	Traditional
33	Uganda	UGA	Traditional
34	Belgium	BEL	Welfare
35	Canada	CAN	Welfare
36	Chile	CHL	Welfare
37	France	FRA	Welfare
38	Germany	DEU	Welfare
39	Ireland	IRL	Welfare
40	Israel	ISR	Welfare
41	Netherlands	NLD	Welfare

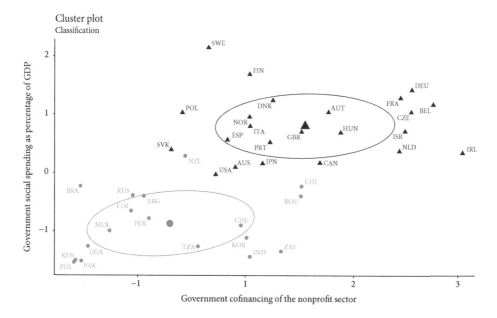

Figure 30.6 Model-based clustering using an expended set of variables
Note: Figure uses ISO3 country abbreviations. See table 30.4 for further details.
Source: Data reported in Salamon, Sokolowski, and Haddock 2017, pp. 276–279.

additional variables: "volunteer share of the nonprofit workforce" and the "philanthropy share of nonprofit revenue."

Will we find five clusters if we rely on more measures than government social spending and cofinancing of the nonprofit sector? Figure 30.6 shows the results from model-based clustering using the same measures from Figure 30.5 plus measures for the volunteer share of the nonprofit workforce and the philanthropy share of nonprofit revenue. The model with the best fit for the extended dataset identifies two components with differing variance and ellipsoidal shape. In order to facilitate comparison between both plots, we use the same plot as in Figure 30.5 but add updated cluster information.

The statist cluster does look different from the previous model, yet not in the expected way. Countries such as Korea (KOR) and Tanzania (TZA) are now placed in the statist cluster, whereas the Philippines (PHL) and Peru (PER) do not appear in a new cluster. Interestingly, the selected model no longer distinguishes between the social democratic, liberal, and corporatist clusters. Instead, it suggests a two-cluster solution that could be interpreted as a split between a statist and a nonstatist cluster. Just as with the previous three-cluster model, we cannot claim that the two-cluster model is substantially better than possible alternatives: models ranging from one to four components are not far off.[17]

Note that the identification of cluster groupings is not the same as a test of the social origin theory. To test whether the social origin theory can account for variations in the size of different nonprofit sectors, we would first of all have to find clearer groupings. Then we would have to design appropriate measures for the factors with which the theory is concerned: the influence of governments and state authorities, landed elites, urban middle classes, and so on. The task would also involve accounting for settlements between these social actors on regime types, and of regime types on nonprofit sector size. Unfortunately, this will only be possible once comprehensive time series data are available.

The model-based clustering solutions we have presented thus far do suggest, however, that theory building based on regime typologies could be approached from a different angle. Instead of drawing distinctions among ever more fine-grained types and subtypes of nonprofit regimes, both case study researchers and quantitative analysts in the social origin tradition might profit from pondering the question of whether there are actual constraints on theoretical generalization. For instance, can we really claim that differences in volunteering and philanthropic giving are large enough to set the nonprofit sectors of countries apart? Or are such differences likely to disappear when economic development increases or other macro factors change?

What is more, why are the nonprofit sectors of countries with growth trajectories like those of Korea, Russia, and Mexico still substantially different from countries with similar levels of economic development in Europe? It might be that two underlying and consistent clusters emerge. The first would be a cluster of countries where family- and kinship-based networks and autocratic conventions result in lower capacities for self-organization; the second would be a cluster with more "organized democratic publics" (Dewey 1927:98–100), whose ability to form institutions across society is relatively more pronounced. Within these two clusters, different histories of power struggles among social groups become "encoded" in the cultural and structural memory of a given society (Abbott 2016:13–14). Such struggles appear to be akin to the more political dimensions of the civil society concept. Thus we argue that an important step in extending the social origin theory is to tie it more closely to civil society research.

Enter Civil Society

What is civil society, and how does it differ from the nonprofit sector? Clearly, like the nonprofit sector, civil society is at some level an ensemble of many different kinds of organizations, ranging from small community-based associations to large international NGOs like Amnesty International or Greenpeace. But it is more than that. What separates civil society and the nonprofit sector is less what organizations fall under which category than the location of each within the wider society (see Figure 30.1). This implies that the two are differentiated by functions, such as interest mediation and advocacy, as well as individual behaviors, such as civility, civic engagement, and participation in society. Civil society is an arena for the self-organization of citizens and established interests seeking voice and influence, as two prominent definitions by Ernest Gellner (1994) and Keane (1998) make clear.

Located between the state and the market, civil society, according to Gellner (1994:5), is a "set of non-governmental institutions, which is strong enough to counter-balance the state, and, whilst not preventing the state from fulfilling its role of keeper of peace and arbitrator between major interests, can, nevertheless, prevent the state from dominating and atomizing the rest of society." These institutions may not necessarily be organized. Rather, they express themselves through individual behaviors and value dispositions as well as cultural traditions. Charity, the rule of law, civility, and civic mindedness are institutions, but they may not manifest themselves in a distinct organizational form.

On the other hand, the organizational form that most closely fosters the ideal civil society of the neo-Tocquevillean tradition (e.g., Putnam 1994, 2000), which places importance on creating trusting relations among people, is the membership association. Through the facilitation of face-to-face interactions among individuals, associations serve as the schools of democracy imagined by Alexis de Tocqueville (2003) and Robert Putnam's creators of trust and norms of reciprocity. Earlier we suggested incorporating the three main forms that nonprofits typically take into definitional approaches. This also has considerable bearings here, as nonprofit corporations and foundations may be less conducive to creating trust and the norms and democratic practices often associated with civil society. Although philanthropic foundations can leverage their grantmaking to support citizen associations and convene communities, the role of nonprofit corporations in the neo-Tocquevillean perspective is less clear. Rightly or wrongly, Putnam (2000) accordingly did not see the post–World War II rise of the nonprofit sector as contradicting his claim of a decline of social capital, the analysis of which was based on mass membership associations rather than corporate nonprofit service providers.

For Keane (1998:6), civil society is an "ensemble of legally protected non-governmental institutions that tend to be non-violent, self-organizing, self-reflexive, and permanently in tension with each other and with the state institutions that 'frame,' constrict and enable their activities." Taken together, civil society expresses the societal capacity for self-organization and the potential for the contested but ultimately peaceful settlement of divergent private interests. Civil society for Keane is therefore a broader notion. It is less about delivering a service or organizations and more about how to advance causes that may or may not be deemed as in the public benefit by particular governments, political parties, and businesses and nonprofits. Yet self-organization certainly doesn't preclude service provision. For example, voluntary associations engaged in mutual support activities over time develop increasingly professionalized services.

However we define the term, merging the nonprofit and civil society research agendas could get in the way of greater conceptual clarity and hinder theory construction. At the same time, both are concerned with questions around the functions of advocacy and value guardianship in particular. What is more, some of the more significant contemporary research trends in the field suggest a growing intersection. More specifically, civil society is arguably under significant threats from two sides. First, many scholars, as well as policy makers and funders, are increasingly concerned about the "closing space" for civil society internationally. This circumscribes the tendency of mostly authoritarian-leaning governments to restrict the more political, claims-making parts of civil society, primarily composed of human rights, democratization, and environmental advocacy NGOs that seek the promotion of (Western) values, often with substantial international donor support (Christensen and Weinstein 2013; Carothers and Brechenmacher 2014; Carothers 2015; Rutzen 2015; Dupuy, Ron, and Prakash 2016; Poppe and Wolff 2017; Dupuy and Prakash, Chapter 28, "Global Backlash Against Foreign Funding to Domestic Nongovernmental Organizations").

However, there has been a growing sense recently that the space for civil society may be changing rather than closing entirely (Alscher et al. 2017; Anheier, Lang, and Toepler 2019). Space is constricting for certain advocacy organizations but expanding for others.

As we mentioned earlier, democratic and authoritarian governments alike are attempting to build relationships with more apolitical parts of nonprofit sectors in efforts to improve the quality and availability of public services (Salamon and Toepler 2015). The push to involve nonprofits into social service contracting has come into view in countries like China (Teets 2014; Zhao, Wu, and Tao 2016) and Russia (Benevolenski and Toepler 2017; Skokova, Pape, and Krasnopolskaya 2018), raising significant concerns about governmental co-optation and reduced self-organization of society. This shift suggests that the relationship and balance between civil society and the nonprofit sector is changing.

Within this changing space, the second threat emerges: a marketization of civil society. As Keane (2005) reminded us, the philosophical development of the concept of civil society in the eighteenth century inexorably linked it to the market. In the post-1989 revival of the idea, however, a "purist" view of civil society took hold that separated it entirely from the market and market influences. Instead, it focused on civil society's democratization potential and its protective function against both state and market excesses. With the rise of neoliberalism, Keane (2005:27) maintains that "market presumptions" have nevertheless tacitly infiltrated civil society thinking. Putnam-style, neo-Tocquevillean arguments buttressed the notion that a strong civil society leads to better economic performance and governance (Lewis 2014). From this perspective, civil society improves markets and creates good governance by building the trust that functioning markets require; however, other views on civil society take a more critical perspective, arguing that "markets and civil society are structured by mutually exclusive logics" (Keane 2005:27).

Analysts following the latter perspective perceive nonprofits not as constitutive of, but as significant contributors to, civil society development and democracy. Nonprofits do so through the fulfillment of Kramer's four functions (1987), discussed earlier. Their ability to perform these functions is potentially undermined by marketization that derives from market incentives and practices being pushed on them through New Public Management and similar neoliberal government reform measures (Eikenberry and Kluver 2004; Yu and Chen 2018). As the social contracting space is widening, even in otherwise restrictive political regimes, civil society faces the risk of losing the core functions that nonprofits contribute—although, as Jianxing Yu and Keijian Chen (2018) caution, the dynamics of this change may play out differently in non-Western contexts.

Whether the marketization concerns of nonprofit researchers closely correlate with the co-optation concerns of civil society researchers remains to be seen, but it is clear that the "changing space" for civil society is an area where the research agendas overlap. A comparative research focus on the expressive dimension and the functions of nonprofits is significant here in both nonprofit and civil society research, but it is also important to differentiate among the main nonprofit forms in this respect. The associations of individual citizens banding together in the Tocquevillean notion of civil society may cause political difficulties for the state when they act as value guardians or advocates, thereby risking the contraction of their space. But there are no serious concerns about marketization because service delivery is typically not the core function of these organizations.[18]

In hybrid and authoritarian regimes, it is typically membership groups engaging in advocacy on rights issues that are the target of repressive state action (e.g., Daucé 2014). However, membership often remains too small to support sustained advocacy efforts at the national level, which creates dependencies on foreign donors that make cutting off international support a key element of the authoritarian suppression of NGOs (see Dupuy and Prakash, Chapter 28, "Global Backlash Against Foreign Funding to Domestic Nongovernmental Organizations"). Although some of these organizations were able to survive in Russia through regional support networks, the forced withdrawal of foreign funds virtually wiped out rights-based NGOs in some parts of the country (Toepler et al. 2019). As membership associations are classically subject to the free rider problem (Olson 1965), funding is a perennial concern for these organizations independent of the political environment in which they operate. The so-called NGOization concern from the social movement literature (Choudry and Kapoor 2013) also applies to associative civil society, as public and private donors prefer to support discreet services rather than advocacy. Another concern for associations is declining membership and active involvement due to individualization trends and the emergence of social media that allow participation in advocacy activity without necessarily corresponding organizational participation (Guo and Saxton 2014; Mosley, Weiner-Davis, and Anasti forthcoming).

By contrast, marketization is an issue of primary importance for the nonprofit corporations that are benefiting from the quickly expanding space for social service contracting in authoritarian countries. Besides religious organizations, the charitable part of the U.S. nonprofit sector is heavily dominated by the corporate form. In Europe, social service providers that historically had the legal form of association converted to corporation/company status, for reasons having to do with liability and expedience in decision making. But in doing so, nonprofits run the risk of losing some of their unique features, such as their value base. Research efforts could therefore usefully focus on identifying opportunities to imbue more of a civil ethos into the delivery of nonprofit services through the leveraging of street-level service delivery expertise. Ideally, this would allow for an increase in political voice and the public contestation of values.

For foundations, the situation is different still. Endowment assets insulate foundations economically from market pressures, but these organizations are not immune from political ones (Toepler 2018a). As quasi-autonomous institutions not accountable to voters, members, or clients, their difficult fit into liberal democratic societies has long been noted (Nielsen 1972; Prewitt 2006), which poses significant questions about their basic democratic legitimacy (Heydemann and Toepler 2006). Accordingly, much research has focused on exploring core foundation roles as a justification of the privileges afforded to them, including innovation, social change, preservation, and complementing or substituting for the state (Anheier and Toepler 1999; Anheier and Daly 2007; Anheier and Hammack 2010; Hammack and Anheier 2013; Anheier 2018). Partly in response to incentives created by government eager to mobilize private resources for public purposes, and partly in response to the creation of new wealth, foundations have begun to proliferate over the past three decades in most parts of the world (Toepler 2018b). At the same time, concerns about elite control over public agendas, the ability of these institutions to address social inequality, and the effects of their administration of social functions have also been proliferating (Anheier and Leat 2018; Anheier, Leat, and Toepler 2018).

Although the twain of civil society and nonprofit research may never fully meet, a stronger focus on civil society could allow nonprofit researchers to identify independent variables to help advance the social origins theory and cross-national nonprofit research more generally. The capacity of self-organization can lead to larger nonprofit sectors but also to greater roles for governments or the expansion of the social economy. The way self-organization manifests itself and becomes institutionalized depends on the forces the social origins theory has begun to identify but may do so more systematically by reminding itself "that certain parts of the past are continuously (re)encoded into the present synchronic social structure, in the sense of thereby acquiring historicality—the appearance of endurance in time" (Abbott 2016:14). The challenge for both nonprofit and civil society research is to figure out how this (re)encoding process works and whether its outcomes explain important phenomena in the nonprofit sectors of the present.

Toward a New Research Agenda
The purpose of this chapter is to advance the research agenda by offering a critical review of comparative, cross-national research on the nonprofit sector. It suggests a comparative-historical research agenda informed by political science and sociology to complement the macroeconomic approach, based on national income accounting, that has dominated the field for nearly three decades. Such a future agenda would look at the development and embeddedness of nonprofit organizations and sectors in the context of three other institutional complexes: state, market, and civil society (see Figure 30.3).

Specifically, we propose to revisit the methodological approach by (1) reopening questions of definition and developing a comparative terminology that captures the different functions of and forms of nonprofit organizations (associations, corporations, foundations) and (2) developing a classification system that reflects core features of nonprofit organizations, namely product bundling and co-production.

We also propose the reexamination of the analytic approach of the social origins theory by clarifying cause and effect, in the sense of dependent and independent constructs, and watching for co-evolutionary patterns. Only a more systematic and theory-guided approach can clarify what is inside the typology (as either a dependent or independent variable) and what is outside (as either antecedent or consequential factors). Otherwise, problems of endogeneity will remain, even if better data coverage and time series become available.

Finally, we see a need to connect the field of comparative nonprofit sector research to the wider social science research agenda; we fear that otherwise a certain isolation from mainstream scholarship could set in. Although there may well be others, two avenues suggest themselves immediately, both of which offer the possibility of showing where the distinctive added value of comparative nonprofit sector research lies relative to sociopolitical and economic developments. These are the Varieties of Democracy (or V-Dem) and the Varieties of Capitalism approaches.

V-Dem (Coppedge et al. 2018) has established long-term data series surveying key aspects of civil society and social self-organization in the context of government and governance characteristics. Exploring the possibility of a nonprofit research agenda with the V-Dem approach would offer a fruitful way forward, as would linking CNP nonprofit sector data with V-Dem data. We should recall that a full test of the social origins approach requires longer time series, which is precisely what CNP cannot offer. In other words,

V-Dem could help improve the nonprofit–civil society and the nonprofit–state sections of Figure 30.3. For example, Helmut K. Anheier, Markus Lang, and Stefan Toepler (2019) used V-Dem data for an initial exploration of the changing space for civil society among G20 countries.

The Varieties of Capitalism approach (Hall and Soskice 2001) postulates that two main types of capitalism exist among developed countries: liberal market economies and co-ordinated market economies. In coordinated market economies, governments are more proactive and assume a greater regulatory stance vis-à-vis the private sector, in which actors show a significant degree of self-organization (Schneider and Paunescu 2012:732). In between both types are regimes that show some of the characteristics of each, or exist in some hybrid form. The empirical base established by the Varieties of Capitalism approach could help shed light on the nonprofit-for-profit relation in Figure 30.3, especially with regard to the key concept of market and nonmarket coordination.

Both projects, and the concepts and data they provide, ultimately offer important yardsticks for assessing the relative contributions of both nonprofit sector regime types and comparative nonprofit sector research generally. Comparative research in this field has made much progress since the first edition of this book appeared. It is now time to broaden analytic lenses and to sharpen methodological approaches.

NOTES

Chapter 1

I greatly appreciate comments from Elisabeth Andrews, Aaron Horvath, and Ted Lechterman on earlier drafts.

1. To be sure, profit or surplus is not precluded, but it may not be given to officers, employees, or anyone who exercises control over it.

2. The U.S. tax code specifies that charitable purposes include the relief of poverty; the advancement of knowledge or education; the advancement of religion; the promotion of health, government or municipal purposes; and other purposes that are beneficial to the community.

3. Of course, many for-profits have all manner of affinity groups, but they are usually peripheral to the core activities of firms. Socially responsible initiatives may be championed inside businesses (Davis and White 2015), but such efforts may be aimed more at employee retention and marketing than real substance (Turco 2012).

4. But it is useful to remember Max Weber's (1947) comment, "The quantitative spread of organizational life does not always go hand in hand with its qualitative significance."

5. To be sure, this argument suggests that people working in the nonprofit sector are less motivated by opportunism, and that their career interests and the needs of their clients align. Both assumptions are debatable, as we saw with the Oxfam scandals in Haiti.

6. Initiated by Bill and Melinda Gates and Warren Buffett, the Giving Pledge is a public commitment by super-high-net-worth individuals to dedicate the majority of their wealth to philanthropy.

7. Kaisa Snellman and her colleagues (2015) observe that in the United States, participation in high school clubs and sporting activities has a notable effect on educational attainment and future earnings. But they also note that there is a large "engagement gap," as the financial costs and parental time involvement of such participation keep them out of reach of many families.

Chapter 2

1. Steven R. Weisman, *The Great Tax Wars* (New York: Simon and Schuster, 2002), 258.

2. See also Darren Walker, "Old Money, New Order," *Foreign Affairs* 97, no. 6 (November 2018): 158–166.

3. Joseph B. Lynch, "The 'Charities' Provisions of the Internal Revenue Code," *Fordham Law Review* 234, no. 10 (1941): 235.

4. Robert Cameron Mitchell, Angela G. Mertig, and Riley E. Dunlap, "Twenty Years of Environmental Mobilization: Trends Among National Environmental Organizations," *Society and Natural Resources* 4, no. 3 (1991): 228.

5. David Pozen, "The Tax-Code Shift That's Changing Liberal Activism," *The Atlantic*, November 27, 2018, https://www.theatlantic.com/ideas/archive/2018/11/501c3-501c4-activists-and-tax-code/576364/.

6. William Schambra, "The Man Who Named the 'Independent Sector': The Legacy of Richard Cornuelle," *Chronicle of Philanthropy*, May 5, 2011.

7. Peter Dobkin Hall, quoted in "Panel Discussion: Where You Stand Depends on Where You Sit," *Public Performance and Management Review* 25, no. 1 (September 2001): 78.

8. Ihsan Bagby, "Mosques in the United States," in *The Oxford Handbook of American Islam*, ed. Yvonne Y. Haddad and Jane I. Smith (New York: Oxford University Press, 2014), 231.

9. See Daniel W. Drezner, *The Ideas Industry: How Pessimists, Partisans, and Plutocrats Are Transforming the Marketplace of Ideas* (New York: Oxford University Press, 2017); Tevi Troy, "Devaluing the Think Tank," *National Affairs* (Winter 2012): 80; and Jonathan Mahler, "How One Conservative Think Tank Is Stocking Trump's Government," *New York Times Magazine*, June 20, 2018.

10. See also Randall Balmer, "The Real Origins of the Religious Right," Politico, May 27, 2014, https://www.politico.com/magazine/story/2014/05/religious-right-real-origins-107133?o=0.

11. See Marvin Olasky, "The Tragedies of Compassionate Conservative," *World*, April 4, 2018, https://world.wng.org/content/the_tragedies_of_compassionate_conservatism.

12. Melissa Brown, Brice McKeever, Nathan Dietz, Jeremy Koulish, and Tom Pollak, "The Impact of the Great Recession on the Number of Charities," Urban Institute National Center for Charitable Statistics, 2013, https://www.urban.org/sites/default/files/publication/24046/412924-The-Impact-of-the-Great-Recession -on-the-Number-of-Charities.PDF; Rob Reich and Christopher Wimer, "Charitable Giving and the Great Recession," Russell Sage Foundation and the Stanford Center on Poverty and Inequality, October 2012, https://inequality.stanford.edu/sites/default/files/CharitableGiving_fact_sheet.pdf.

13. Brice McKeever, "The Nonprofit Sector in Brief 2018: Public Charities, Giving, and Volunteering," Urban Institute, 2018, https://nccs.urban.org/publication/nonprofit-sector-brief-2018#the-nonprofit-sector-in -brief-2018-public-charites-giving-and-volunteering.

14. Carol J. De Vita and Katie L. Roeger, "Measuring Racial-Ethnic Diversity in California's Nonprofit Sector," Urban Institute, 2009, https://www.urban.org/sites/default/files/publication/30726/411977-Measuring -Racial-Ethnic-Diversity-in-California-s-Nonprofit-Sector.PDF; "Leading with Intent: 2017 National Index of Nonprofit Board Practices," BoardSource, 2017, https://leadingwithintent.org/wp-content/uploads/2017/11/ LWI-2017.pdf.

15. Alex Daniels and Rebecca Koenig, "How New Forms of Philanthropy Are Squeezing Traditional Charities," *Chronicle of Philanthropy*, December 5, 2017.

16. Alex Daniels, "Ford Foundation to Put $1 Billion from Endowment into Social Investments," *Chronicle of Philanthropy*, April 5, 2017; Marc Gunter, "Doing Good and Doing Well," *Chronicle of Philanthropy*, January 8, 2019.

17. Neil Irwin, "The Benefits of Economic Expansions Are Increasingly Going to the Richest Americans," *New York Times*, September 26, 2014, https://www.nytimes.com/2014/09/27/upshot/the-benefits-of -economic-expansions-are-increasingly-going-to-the-richest-americans.html?rref=upshot&_r=0&abt= 0002&abg=1.

18. Oxfam International, *Reward Work, Not Wealth*, January 2018, https://d1tn3vj7xz9fdh.cloudfront.net/ s3fs-public/file_attachments/bp-reward-work-not-wealth-220118-en.pdf.

19. Pierre Omidyar, "How I Did It: eBay's Founder on Innovating the Business Model of Social Change," *Harvard Business Review*, September 2011, https://hbr.org/2011/09/ebays-founder-on-innovating-the-business -model-of-social-change.

20. Lila Corwin Berman, "How Norman Sugarman Became $50B Godfather of Charitable Funds," *Forward*, November 14, 2015.

21. Chuck Collins, Helen Flannery, and Josh Hoxie, *Warehousing Wealth: Donor-Advised Charity Funds Sequestering Billions in the Face of Growing Inequality*, Institute for Policy Studies, 2018, https://ips-dc.org/wp -content/uploads/2018/07/Warehousing-Wealth-IPS-Report-1.pdf.

22. See Lewis B. Cullman and Ray Madoff, "The Undermining of American Charity," *New York Review of Books*, July 14, 2016.

23. Katie Rogers, "GoFundMe Says It Has Helped Campaigns Raise $3 Billion," *New York Times*, December 14, 2016.

24. Patrick Rooney, "The Growth in Total Household Giving Is Camouflaging a Decline in Giving by Small and Medium Donors: What Can We Do About It?," *Nonprofit Quarterly*, Fall 2018, accessed online at https://nonprofitquarterly.org/2018/11/21/total-household-growth-decline-small-medium-donors/; Chuck Collins, Helen Flannery, and Josh Hoxie, *Gilded Giving: Top-Heavy Philanthropy in an Age of Extreme Inequality* (2016), accessed online at https://ips-dc.org/wp-content/uploads/2016/11/Gilded-Giving-Final-pdf.pdf.

25. Drew Lindsey, "Who's Raising the Most: The 100 Charities That Are America's Favorite," *Chronicle of Philanthropy*, November 2018.

26. Moriah Balingit and Danielle Douglas-Gabriel, "Here's What the GOP's Proposal to Overhaul the Tax Code Means for Schools, Students and Parents," *Washington Post*, December 18, 2017.

27. See data from the Center for Responsive Politics, "Political Nonprofits (Dark Money)," https://www.opensecrets.org/outsidespending/nonprof_summ.php.

28. Benjamin Soskis, "Nonprofit Boosters or Muckrakers—Can't the Press Be Both?" *Chronicle of Philanthropy*, March 1, 2015.

29. Peter Olsen-Phillips, "IRS Unleashes Flood of Searchable Charity Data," *Chronicle of Philanthropy*, June 15, 2016.

30. See, for instance, Benjamin Wallace-Wells, "The A.C.L.U. is Getting Involved in Elections—and Reinventing Itself for the Trump Era," *New Yorker*, June 8, 2018, https://www.newyorker.com/news/news-desk/the-aclu-is-getting-involved-in-elections-and-reinventing-itself-for-the-trump-era?reload=true; Jacey Fortin, "N.A.A.C.P., Seeking a New Voice, Names Derrick Johnson as President," *New York Times*, October 21, 2017; "The Largest U.S. Latino Advocacy Group Changes Its Name, Sparking Debate," NPR, July 21, 2017, https://www.npr.org/sections/codeswitch/2017/07/21/538381366/the-largest-latino-advocacy-group-changes-their-name-sparking-debate.

31. Lucy Bernholz, *Blueprint 2018. Philanthropy and Digital Civil Society: The Annual Industry Forecast* (*Stanford Social Innovation Review*/Stanford Center on Philanthropy and Civil Society, 2018), 7. https://pacscenter.stanford.edu/publication/philanthropy-and-digital-civil-society-blueprint-2018/.

Chapter 3

1. We are grateful to Kelly Besecke, Paul DiMaggio, Claire Dunning, Stan Katz, Kathleen Much, Rob Reich, Jim Smith, and Ben Soskis for their thoughtful comments. Audiences at the Stanford Networks and Organizations Workshop, the SCANCOR workshop, and the PACS Nonprofit Sector Handbook Conference provided valuable feedback and comments on earlier drafts.

2. Carnegie's essay "Wealth" appeared in the 1889 *North American Review*; he proclaimed that "the man who dies rich dies disgraced . . . unwept, unhonored and unsung." Rockefeller wrote to Carnegie to express wholehearted agreement with the argument: "be assured, your example will bear fruits, and the time will come when men of wealth will more generally be willing to use it for the good of others" (Fosdick 1952:6).

3. Ida Tarbell, "John D. Rockefeller: A Character Study, Part Two," *McClure's Magazine* 25 (1905): 397.

4. For these and other contemptuous statements about Rockefeller's efforts, see Fosdick 1952:19–20; Bremmer 1988:113; and Pringle 1939:661-663.

5. Most of these were readily accepted by Rockefeller and his advisors. Had the bill ultimately passed, one might imagine a radically different trajectory for American philanthropy. Fosdick enumerates these conditions: (1) The foundation would be limited to $100 million in assets. (2) The foundation's income was to be currently applied to the purposes for which it was created. (3) After fifty years, the foundation might distribute the principal as well as the income. This was to become mandatory after one hundred years. (4) Foundation trustees were subject to approval by the majority of nine people: the president of the United States; the

chief justice of the Supreme Court; the president of the Senate; the speaker of the House; and the presidents of Harvard University, Yale University, Columbia University, Johns Hopkins University, and the University of Chicago. (5) No more than 10 percent of the foundation's assets could be invested in a single corporation.

6. New York Chap. 488, Jan 23, 1913, *An Act to Incorporate the Rockefeller Foundation*.

7. Chan and Zuckerberg used their open letter to their newborn daughter ("A letter to our daughter," December 1, 2015, https://www.facebook.com/notes/mark-zuckerberg/a-letter-to-our-daughter/10153375081581634/) to express frustration with common charitable time horizons: "the greatest challenges . . . cannot be solved by short term thinking," they wrote, and "partnering with experts is more effective for the mission than trying to lead efforts ourselves."

8. The "comments" section following Zuckerberg's Facebook post reads like a Who's Who snapshot of Silicon Valley and national politics circa 2015.

9. *The Oprah Winfrey Show*, "Mark Zuckerberg Announces $100 Million Grant," September 24, 2010.

10. The *Giving Pledge* is an initiative created by Bill and Melinda Gates and Warren Buffett to encourage the world's wealthiest individuals and couples to commit more than half their wealth to philanthropy. It began in 2010 with 40 signees, and, as of 2018, includes 175 signees from twenty-two countries.

11. There are notable differences between the pledge and the "Gospel." Carnegie would be outraged to learn that many giving pledge signers look to give via bequest. To him, to die rich was to die disgraced.

12. See Dana Brakman Reiser, "Is the Chan Zuckerberg Initiative the Future of Philanthropy?" *Stanford Social Innovation Review* (Summer 2018), https://ssir.org/articles/entry/the_rise_of_philanthropy_llcs.

13. Zuckerberg sees the state as a target of reform, particularly in regard to immigration, but he demonstrates little concern for how the state may reform his philanthropy.

14. As quoted by Starr J. Murphy, Rockefeller's attorney, to the Senate Committee on the District of Columbia on March 12, 1910.

15. "Seeing like a philanthropist" need not connote 'seeing like a person.' We mean it to connote the social role of the philanthropist. Sometimes this role is inhabited by an individual, but it is often inhabited by philanthropic organizations. At present, even the lone philanthropist is embedded in a network of organizations and professionals that shape his or her philanthropic interests and actions.

16. J. P. McClure, *The Papers of Thomas Jefferson*, vol. 15, March 1789 to November 1789 (Princeton, NJ: Princeton University Press, 1958), 392.

17. For example, in 1829, James Smithson, an enigmatic Brit, made a bequest of gold sovereigns to the U.S. government for the "increase and diffusion of knowledge." The gift was received with nearly a decade of congressional debate and indecision as to whether and how the funds should be used. Senator William Preston, a Whig from South Carolina, saw Smithson's will as an effort to immortalize a foreigner, concluding that it was "too cheap a way of conferring immortality" (Preston 1836). Similarly revealing was the case of Dorothea Dix, a Jackson-era advocate for the mentally ill. She had enrolled numerous state legislatures and both houses of Congress in support of a bill to make a grant of public lands for the benefit of indigent persons. Though the effort was supported in spirit, it stood on unfamiliar legal ground. President Franklin Pierce vetoed the bill, writing, "I . . . feelingly acknowledge the duty incumbent on us all as men and citizens, and as among the highest and holiest of our duties, to provide for those who, in the mysterious order of Providence, are subject to want and to disease of body or mind; but I cannot find any authority in the Constitution for making the Federal Government the great almoner of public charity throughout the United States" (Pierce 1854).

18. Pennsylvania Corporation Act, 1874, First-Class—"Corporations Not for Profit," 10.

19. Not all were keen on a Darwinian model of charity: some mockingly described the COS movement as "cringe or starve" (Ziliak 2004).

20. The model was adopted in cities around the country. In Denver, the financial coordination of COS efforts eventually gave rise to the United Way (United Way Denver, n.d.).

21. This condemnation of inheritance was common among several titans of the time. Vanderbilt saw "inherited wealth as a big handicap to happiness . . . as certain death to ambition as cocaine is to morality"

(Goff 1921:25). Vanderbilt's words proved prophetic. His son Cornelius Jeremiah Vanderbilt killed himself five years after his father's death. His other son, William Vanderbilt, who had inherited nearly $100 million, lived only another seven years to enjoy it.

22. Rockefeller's gifts to Chicago exemplify the mixed religious and scientific philanthropic mode of the era. According to Nielsen (1972:49), whenever Rockefeller visited the university's president, William Rainey Harper, he was encouraged to genuflect and join in a prayer that they would have a good conversation. Once they had taken their seats, Harper would appeal for Rockefeller's financial support.

23. Rockefeller's regard for Carnegie's philanthropy wavered between contempt and praise. At times Rockefeller and Gates were weary of what they considered to be Carnegie's profligate and ostentatious benefactions. In 1903, however, Rockefeller wrote to Carnegie with adulation and respect: "Keep right on with your grant work of giving away money, regardless of the criticisms of cranks and fools. You have already given away more money than any man living" (quoted in Nasaw 2006:518).

24. Rockefeller 1909.

25. Gates 1977:162.

26. Gates's advice to Rockefeller should be viewed through his intellectual and spiritual commitments, which were emblematic of the interwoven threads of the era. He described his views as a "religion of Jesus, of science, and of evolution alike" (Gates 1977:205).

27. According to Karl and Katz (1987:6), the emergence of organized philanthropy depended on "a recognition of progress and choice" that made "the eradication of poverty possible, not through divine intervention but through human endeavor."

28. Indeed, the lives of men like Carnegie are bound with seeming contradictions that inspire cynicism. His steel plants developed armor for naval warships, but his Endowment for International Peace called for the abolition of naval war. David Nasaw, Carnegie's biographer, is clear on this matter: Carnegie "never intended or considered his philanthropy as expiation for his sins as an industrialist, he was surprised, then dismayed, when others did" (Nasaw 2006:461).

29. Even unorganized, personal philanthropy was being placed under the scientific lens. In 1912, a study by William Allen of the New York City Bureau of Municipal Research examined "philanthropy's mail bag." Specifically, Allen categorized the six thousand philanthropic appeals sent to Mary Harriman, wife of recently deceased Ed Harriman (of railroad wealth), and treated them as a sample of the nation's needs as well as fodder for understanding how best to construct an appeal. In his extensive treatment of the data, Allen provides "A Magna Carta for Givers," explores the idea of a charity clearinghouse as well as standards and schools for good giving practices, and advises that ultimately, "philanthropy, no matter how lavish and wise, cannot take the place of efficient government" (Allen 1912).

30. Russell Sage was cheap with life too. In the 1890s, a man who felt cheated by Sage entered the tycoon's office and threatened to detonate a bag of dynamite if Sage didn't give him the money he owed him. Sage apparently used William Laidlaw, his clerk, as a human shield. A paralyzed Laidlaw later sued Sage for damages of at least $25,000, but Sage appealed the decision and never paid a dime.

31. Theodore Roosevelt, "True American Ideals," *The Forum* 18 (1895): 748.

32. One of the bloodiest moments in the Coal Wars was the Ludlow Massacre. In 1914 the Colorado National Guard was called in to pacify striking workers and their families at the Rockefeller-owned Colorado Fuel and Iron Company. The militia opened fire, killing nearly thirty laborers and family members. The Rockefeller Foundation hired W. L. Mackenzie King, a political scientist and later a prime minister of Canada, to investigate the causes of the unrest.

33. Charges of whitewashing predate those of tax evasion. The passage of the Revenue Act of 1913 and the Sixteenth Amendment, ratified that same year, enabled Congress to levy income taxes and, in the same move, provide a tax exemption to philanthropic activities. This incentive was spurred further by the Revenue Act of 1935, which progressively taxed incomes across the nation.

34. About the same time as the foundation form was under fire, charitable giving was being legislatively endorsed. The War Income Tax Revenue Act of 1917—adopted upon U.S. entrance into World

War I—provided that "contributions or gifts actually made within the year to corporations or associations organized and operated exclusively for religious, charitable, scientific, or educational purposes, or to societies for the prevention of cruelty to children or animals," would be "allowable as deductions." The aim of the now-familiar tax deduction was to encourage private philanthropy.

35. The narrative is captured well in a series of *New York Times* reports. See "Labor Renews Its Attack on Flexner. Charge Rockefeller Ties," February 6, 1916; and "Dr. Flexner Quits Education Board. His Connection with Rockefeller Organization Aroused a Storm of Criticism," May 18, 1917.

36. "Probe of U.S. Offices: Rockefeller Institute to Make Widest Inquiry in History," *Washington Post*, July 23, 1916; "Rockefeller's Probe Aimed at Efficiency," *Washington Herald*, July 24, 1916; "Lawmakers Hint at Coming Attacks on Rockefeller Inquiry," *Washington Times*, July 25, 1916; "Rockefeller Not in National Research," *New York Times*, July 25, 1916; "Investigate the Government," *Saturday Evening Post*, August 26, 1916; and "Silent Partner of Uncle Sam," *Washington Star*, August 19, 1928. Sources found in "Clippings Relative to Institute for Government Research, 1916–1929," Box 1, Entry 98, Brookings Institution Archives, Washington, DC.

37. C. F. Thwing, "Thwing Gives Fourteen Points of Philanthropy—Ohio Educator Considers the Principles That He Believes Should Rule in the Making of Great Gifts—How Waste Can Be Prevented," *New York Times*, February 15, 1924.

38. Which, inexplicably, adds up to only 229 experts.

39. The Carnegie Corporation's endorsement of the book grew tepid in the 1950s. During the congressional investigations of the 1950s, Myrdal's work was viewed as a tendentious socialistic polemic against the segregationist status quo—the sort of "moral relativism" from which Carnegie would seek to distance itself (see O'Connor 2007: 85-86).

40. Beardsley Ruml, "Memorandum: Conditions Affecting the Memorial's Participation in Projects in Social Science," 1924, Folder 31, Box 2, Series 2, Laura Spelman Rockefeller Memorial Records, Rockefeller Archive Center, Sleepy Hollow, NY.

41. In emphasizing the man's size, it is likely that Laski was obliquely and crudely identifying Ruml as the epitome of the problem. Ruml was particularly rotund (Sealander 1997:85).

42. Indeed, Rockefeller was going through such a period of vanity. With hopes that good management could resolve staff problems and intraorganizational factionalism, the board hired Chester I. Barnard, a celebrated business executive and management scholar, as the foundation's president.

43. He blamed the rise of Chinese communism, for example, on Rockefeller's philanthropic initiatives. Rockefeller was indeed operating in China, beginning with the China Medical Commission in 1914, but its focus was medical education.

44. Indeed, this debate was something foundations were struggling with internally. Ironically, the Dodd Report itself was the product of an empirical research endeavor that had been understood as an effort "to gather and weigh the facts" (Dodd 1954:15). Indeed, Dodd's testimony delves into the methods of data collection and analysis for his report.

45. Prominent foundations can be found on both sides of the "for" and "against" divide in the Joint Committee on Internal Revenue Taxation's Digest of Statements submitted to the Committee on Ways and Means with Respect to the Treasury Report on Private Foundation, published in 1965 (U.S. Department of the Treasury, 1965). Notably, not one foundation favored conversion to independent management after twenty-five years.

46. However questionable philanthropists' actions had been to some in government and the public, there is no question they had played an influential public role and shaped the processes and concerns of government at least since Wilson created his War Industries Board. Hoover, for example, backed by Rockefeller money, sponsored an extensive study of the social challenges facing the country. Later, Kennedy and Johnson embraced philanthropic funding and a similar technocratic ethos in seeking to advance federal administration. Indeed, the growing number of think tanks working to improve government processes and

policies—among them the Brookings Institution, NBER, the Social Science Research Council, and RAND Corporation—were creatures of philanthropic funding. Beyond public–private partnerships, philanthropists could claim to have made numerous contributions on other fronts. The Carnegie Corporation effectively underwrote the creation of PBS and *Sesame Street* in an effort to advance educational television.

47. T. E. Mullaney, "Olin: Staunch Fighter for Free Enterprise," *New York Times*, April 29, 1977.

48. See W. King and I. Molotsky, "Washington Talk: Briefing, Alternative Umbrella," *New York Times*, February 1, 1987, for a report.

49. To be sure, there were a handful of ardently left-leaning foundations. One example is the Haymarket People's Fund, created in 1974 by an antiwar activist and Pillsbury heir. Befitting its politics, it was named in reference to the 1886 Haymarket affair. The longstanding aim of the foundation has been to change the conditions that endowed its contributors with wealth to spare.

50. Pew's evolving political tendencies demonstrate how progeny and professionals spur departures from initial donor interests. J. Howard Pew was—along with the Volker and Relm-Earhart funds—an early devotee of the pro-capitalistic cause, with a particular concern for the erosion of Christian values in America. Pew was one of the early supporters of the Foundation for Economic Freedom, the oldest libertarian think tank in the United States.

51. S. Thomma, "Senate Backs Overhauling Clean Air Act; Kentucky Senators Join 89–11 Vote Despite Problems for Coal Miners," *Lexington (KY) Herald-Leader*, April 4, 1990: A1.

52. See Milton Friedman, "The Role of Government in Education," in *Economics and the Public Interest: Essays Written in Honor of Eugene Ewald Agger*, ed. Robert A. Solow (New Brunswick, NJ: Rutgers University Press, 1955); and Christopher Jencks, "Giving Parents Money for Schooling: Education Vouchers," *Phi Delta Kappan* 52, no. 1 (1970): 49–52.

53. The history of the foundation is rather complicated. Its origins date back to 1994, when it was created by Bill and Melinda Gates as the William H. Gates Foundation and run by Bill Gates's father with a focus on global health. In 1997, the Gates Library Foundation was created to bring Internet access to U.S. public libraries. It became the Gates Learning Foundation in 1999 and expanded its vision to include college readiness. In 2000, all these activities were merged into the Bill & Melinda Gates Foundation. In 2006, investor Warren Buffett made a lifetime pledge to the foundation of Berkshire Hathaway stock valued at $30 billion. The gift is paid in yearly installments. Subsequently, the foundation restructured, and it created a trust to hold donated investment assets from Bill and Melinda Gates and annual contributions from Buffett.

54. Such policies are detailed extensively on the Gates Foundation website at https://www.gatesfoundation.org/How-We-Work.

55. Previously many spousal philanthropic partnerships developed after one partner's death, either distributing the deceased's fortunes or distributing fortunes in the name of the deceased (consider the creation of the Russell Sage Foundation and the family of Rockefeller philanthropies circa 1920).

56. In the same vein, new philanthropic ventures often mirror some of the well-known problems of Silicon Valley. Open Philanthropy's small staff is not particularly diverse, which is not surprising since the effective philanthropy movement has attracted adherents from a narrow demographic—in the words of *The Economist*, "young, white men with degrees in science and philosophy" ("Faith, Hope and Clarity," June 2, 2018, p. 54). And in a move that mirrors Silicon Valley's "vaporware" trope, some members of the tech elite have loudly announced a turn to philanthropy but have apparently never given a dime. Jack Dorsey, CEO of Twitter, and Nicholas Woodman, CEO of GoPro, both garnered acclaim for their generosity after making high-profile announcements that they were starting big foundations. But four years after their announcements, there are no visible signs of any foundation or charitable activity. The monies were parked in donor-advised funds at the Silicon Valley Community Foundation, creating tax advantages for the CEOs but exhibiting no generosity. (David Gelles, "A Trendy Tax Loophole," *New York Times*, August 5, 2018; Owen Thomas, "Twitter CEO's Charity Work a Mystery," *San Francisco Chronicle*, December 17, 2018. See also A. Semuels, "The Black Hole That Sucks Up Silicon Valley's Money," *The Atlantic*, May 14, 2018.)

57. Mirroring the commitments of the Rosenwald Fund of the 1920s—and Julius Rosenwald's belief that perpetual charity would be an evil—the Gateses plan for their foundation to disband within twenty years of their deaths.

58. There are some notably absent names on the Giving Pledge. Steve Jobs, long circumspect on philanthropy, did not sign. According to his biographer, he was "contemptuous of people who made a display of philanthropy or thinking they could reinvent it" (Isaacson 2011:106), and his long-running rivalry with Gates could not have helped the matter. His views are striking in contrast to the actions of his wife, Laurene Powell Jobs, who founded the Emerson Collective, a philanthropic LLC, in 2004. Like Jobs, Oprah Winfrey did not sign the pledge. Unlike Jobs, however, Winfrey is philanthropically quite active. Remarkably, though she attended the original meeting of the Giving Pledge, she has yet to sign it (Dalzell 2013).

59. M. Gunther, "Giving in the Light of Reason," *Stanford Social Innovation Review* (Summer 2018): 23. Notably, one of the organizations most closely associated with Moskowitz and Tuna, GiveWell, is the product of two former hedge fund analysts. But the investor orientation comes with a philosophical twist. GiveWell rates charities on the basis of cost per life saved, following the ideas of Princeton philosopher Peter Singer (2009).

Chapter 4

1. Thanks to comments from Maoz Brown, Curtis Child, Michelle Reddy, and audiences at the 2018 ARNOVA conference and the workshop for authors of this volume hosted by the Center for Philanthropy and Civil Society. This chapter builds on a line of research on the ways organizations are constituted by their environment called institutional and neoinstitutional theory. It is indebted to foundational work by John W. Meyer, Walter W. Powell, and Richard W. Scott. It builds directly on recent contributions related to organizational actorhood by Christof Brandtner, Nils Brunsson, Jeannette Colyvas, Frank Dobbin, Gili Drori, David Frank, Hokyu Hwang, Georg Krücken, Ron Jepperson, Alwyn Lim, Wes Longhofer, Shawn Pope, Kirstin Sahlin-Andersson, Evan Schofer, David Suárez, and Francisco Ramirez. Parts of this chapter build on Meyer and Bromley 2013; Bromley and Meyer 2015, 2017; Bromley and Sharkey 2017; Bromley, Schofer, and Longhofer 2018; and Pope et al. 2018.

2. This section adapted from Meyer and Bromley 2013 and Bromley and Meyer 2017.

3. Adapted from Bromley and Meyer 2015, 2017. Classic concepts related to these ideas of "vehicles" for transmitting cultural content include Paul DiMaggio and Walter Powell's (1983) mechanisms of institutional isomorphism and Richard Scott's pillars of institutionalization (2008). In recent formulations, institutionalization and diffusion are conceptualized as distinct processes; this approach offers a promising path for future work (Colyvas and Jonsson 2011).

4. Parts of this section adapted from Bromley and Sharkey 2017.

5. The view of an organization as an actor stands in contrast to theories in which an organization is simply a context for action or an instrument for achieving another actor's goals and interests (e.g., the "principals" of agency theory [Jensen and Meckling 1976], the "sovereign" of a bureaucracy [M. Weber (1922) 1978, or a straightforward vehicle for efficient transactions [Williamson 1979]). Organizations are of course not natural persons, but over time they are increasingly constructed in a way that is more similar to individual actors (Meyer and Jepperson 2000; Bromley and Meyer 2015). Overall, the meaning of *organization* has evolved from a description of a patterned social structure (e.g., the organization of society in eighteenth-century France) into a creature unto itself (e.g., "an organization").

Chapter 5

1. For helpful comments, I thank Ethan Ames, Ellen Aprill, Joseph Bankman, Paul Brest, Patricia Bromley, Jacob Goldin, Walter Powell, and participants in the Nonprofit Handbook Author Workshop at the Stanford Center on Philanthropy and Civil Society.

2. The ninth seat was vacant at the time of the decision. It would be filled days later when the Senate voted to confirm Harry Blackmun to the court (Weaver 1970).

3. Neither Tocqueville nor Hayek had much to say about the federal tax system's treatment of the non-profit sector. Tocqueville died three years before the first federal income tax took effect. Hayek's treatment of the "independent sector" is limited to three pages of the third volume of *Law, Legislation, and Liberty* (Hayek 1982:49–51). Nonetheless, ideas immanent in the writing of Tocqueville and Hayek can be (and to some extent already have been) developed into reasonably robust justifications for the federal tax system's general attitude toward the nonprofit sector. Pigou, for his part, *did* write (at some length) about charitable giving and related issues (Pigou 1907). The Pigouvian account here, however, is derived from later authors writing in the welfare economics tradition, whose work is influenced by Pigou but does not follow directly from Pigou's prescriptions (Andreoni 1990).

4. A's benefit is 99 of warm glow plus 2 from the subsidy, but the benefit of 2 from the subsidy should not be counted because it comes at a cost of 2 to taxpayers.

5. For one important contribution, see Saez (2004). For an impressively clear overview that is accessible to non–economically trained audiences, see Bakija (2013).

6. On the disutility that individuals associate with paying taxes, see Sussman and Olivola (2011).

7. Organizations whose purpose is testing for public safety are—curiously, unlike other section 501(c)(3) entities—ineligible to receive tax-deductible contributions.

8. The American Horticultural Society and state-level horticultural groups tend to seek and obtain exemption under section 501(c)(3), thus enabling them to receive deductible contributions.

9. Rev. Rul. 75-384, 1975-2 C.B. 204.

10. I.R.S. Priv. Ltr. Rul. 201333014 (May 20, 2013).

11. Rev. Rul. 71-447, 1971-2 C.B. 230.

12. See, for example, Hebrew Union College–Jewish Institute of Religion (n.d.) ("At this time applicants who are married to or in committed relationships with non-Jews will not be considered for acceptance to the Rabbinical, Cantorial or Masters in Education programs. . . ."); Pulliam Bailey (2015).

13. See Act of Oct. 20, 1976, Pub. L. No. 94-568, 90 Stat. 2697; Act of Dec. 24, 1980, Pub. L. No. 96-601, § 3, 94 Stat. 3495, 3496 (codified as amended at § 501(i)).

14. See I.R.C. § 501(h); Staff of the Joint Committee on Taxation, JSC-5-87, Lobbying and Political Activities of Tax-Exempt Organizations 5 (1987).

15. Staff of the Joint Committee on Taxation, JCS-33-76, General Explanation of the Tax Reform Act of 1976, at 415 (Dec. 29, 1976).

16. See 25 Fed. Reg. 11,741 (1960) (codified as amended at Treas. Reg. § 1.501(c)(4)-1(a)(2)).

17. See General Counsel Memorandum 34233 (December 30, 1969). For a comprehensive treatment of these issues, see Aprill (2011).

18. The IRS sought to address this fuzziness in 2007 with a revenue ruling that addresses twenty-one different factual situations involving varying degrees of political involvement. See Rev. Rul. 2007-41, 2007-25 I.R.B. The judgment calls embodied in the revenue ruling are themselves a form of borderline entanglement.

19. See Internal Revenue Service, Statistics of Income Division, Unrelated Business Income Tax Returns, Tax Year 2013, tbl. 1 (October 2016), https://www.irs.gov/pub/irs-soi/13eo01ub.xls; Internal Revenue Service, 2013 Internal Revenue Service Data Book 3 (2014).

20. I.R.C. §§ 512(a)(1), 513(a).

21. I.R.C. § 512(b).

22. See *C.F. Mueller Co. v. Commissioner* (1951:120–121); Note (1968); see also Hearings of the Revenue Revision of 1950 Before the House Committee on Ways and Means, 81st Cong., 2d Sess. 579–580 (1950) (statement of Rep. Dingell) ("From the purely competitive standpoint . . . the advantage of a tax-exempt organization . . . is so great that, if something is not done to level it off, the macaroni monopoly will be in the hands of the universities.").

23. Rev. Rul. 73-104, 1973-1 C.B. 263.

24. Rev. Rul. 73-105, 1973-1 C.B. 264.

25. On the treatment of university presses under the UBIT rules, see Harding (2008:112–114).

26. Hayek himself said that "it is most important for a healthy society that we preserve between the commercial and the governmental a third, *independent sector.*" Hayek (1982:391). While his reasons for wanting to preserve the nonprofit sector's independence from the government are clear, his reasons for wanting to preserve its independence from the market are less so.

27. To be sure, consumers might make macaroni-buying decisions based on their assessment of the macaroni maker's charitable good works. For example, charitable activities are an integral element of the branding of Newman's Own, a maker of pasta sauces, salad dressings, and other food items.

28. See I.R.C. §§ 501(c)(3), (4), (6).

29. See I.R.C. § 501(c)(10) (allowing exemption only if "the net earnings of [the organization] are devoted exclusively to religious, charitable, scientific, literary, educational, and fraternal purposes").

30. See Treas. Reg. § 1.501(c)(5)-1(a)(1).

31. See I.R.C. § 4958.

32. See I.R.C. § 4941.

33. For the seminal article on the subject, see Hansmann (1980).

34. I.R.C. § 6033.

35. I.R.C. § 6104.

36. Regarding "outrage constraints" on executive compensation at nonprofit institutions, see Galle and Walker (2014).

37. See I.R.C. § 170(b)(1)(B), (G). The 60-percent-of-AGI cap for contributions to public charities applies from 2018 to 2025, after which the cap falls back to 50 percent.

38. See I.R.C. § 4940.

39. See Treas. Reg. § 1.509(a)-3.

40. I.R.C. § 4942.

41. Treas. Reg. § 53.4942(b)-1(c).

42. For a summary of such proposals, see Wolf (2011).

43. The legislation lost its name after the Senate parliamentarian ruled that the section setting forth the bill's short title violated a procedural restriction on provisions in budget reconciliation bills that do not affect revenues or outlays. See Aprill and Hemel (2018:125).

44. Staff of the Joint Committee on Taxation, JCX-34-18, Estimates of Federal Tax Expenditures for Fiscal Years 2017–2021, at 49 tbl. 4 (May 25, 2018); Staff of the Joint Committee on Taxation, JCX-3-17, Estimates of Federal Tax Expenditures for Fiscal Years 2016–2020, at 45 tbl. 3 (January 30, 2017).

45. The new law also repealed the charitable contribution deduction for amounts paid in exchange for college athletic event seating rights and strengthened the substantiation requirement for certain contributions.

46. Staff of the Joint Committee on Taxation, JCX-67-17, Estimated Budget Effects of the Conference Agreement for H.R. 1, the "Tax Cuts and Jobs Act"—Fiscal Years 2018–2027 (December 18, 2017), https://www.jct.gov/publications.html?func=startdown&id=5053.

47. I.R.C. § 4960.

48. I.R.C. § 162(m).

49. I.R.C. § 512(a)(7).

50. I.R.C. § 4960.

51. See, for example, Kaiser Foundation Hospitals, Form 990, at 11 (2016) (reporting securities holdings of more than $22 billion).

52. See PGA Tour, Inc., Form 990 (2016).

53. For a summary of such proposals, see Colinvaux, Galle, and Steuerle (2012).

54. After earning $400 and paying the 37 percent tax, the lawyer would be left with $252. If she contributed the $252 to charity, she would receive a credit of $30.24 (i.e., 12 percent of $252). If she contributed the $30.24, she would receive an additional credit of $3.63 (i.e., 12 percent of $30.24). If she continued to contrib-

ute her credits and to claim credits on those contributions ad infinitum, the resulting amount would be $252/
(1–0.12), or $286.36.

55. See Treasury Inspector General for Tax Administration, "Review of Selected Criteria Used to Identify
Tax-Exempt Applications for Review" (September 28, 2017), https://www.treasury.gov/tigta/auditreports/
2017reports/201710054fr.pdf.

Chapter 6

1. Many theorists believe, however, that the existence of a state is not necessary for motivating research
questions in political theory, and that orienting our thinking around the state can inhibit scrutiny of oppres-
sive social relationships (Phillips 1992; G. A. Cohen 1997).

2. Though common today, this definition breaks with a long tradition in the history of political thought
(Taylor 1990). For early modern writers, "civil society" was used to distinguish a law-governed condition
from a lawless state of nature. Thus, for many years, "civil society" included the state as well as nonstate
organizations.

3. This trend has important exceptions. Nonprofits have sometimes served to fragment societies and
provide social infrastructure for authoritarian rule, as in Weimar Germany (Berman 1997).

4. Our claim is not that Max Weber himself was guilty of this mistake. Rather, the fallacy inheres in reading Weber's powerful claims about descriptive legitimacy as normative claims (Weber [1922] 1978).

5. Indeed, some commentators argue that libertarianism is not ultimately compatible with liberal democracy and instead works to support an anarchistic ideal (Freeman 2001).

6. "Collective goods" include the traditional category of "public goods," along with the often neglected
but critically important categories of "club goods" and "merit goods" (Steinberg 2006).

7. Conventionally, nonprofits that operate outside the state are called nongovernmental organizations
(NGOs). Some scholars reserve the term *NGO* for well-established organizations that engage in advocacy
and/or humanitarian assistance, such as Human Rights Watch or Save the Children. This terminological
choice leaves us without language to discuss the surfeit of nonprofit groups that perform other functions,
such as the Fédération Internationale de Football Association (FIFA), People to People International, and the
International Society for Third-Sector Research.

Chapter 7

1. For their insightful and challenging comments, I am grateful to Marta Reuter and all the participants
in the track on civil society organizations at the 2019 meetings of the European Group for Organization
Studies.

2. Although related to the understanding of nonprofits as mediating between state and society (see
Lechterman and Reich, Chapter 6, "Political Theory and the Nonprofit Sector"), the argument here highlights
the tensions and dynamics created by private organizations with public-serving missions.

3. 501(c)(1)s, however, are "government instrumentalities" created by Congress (Barman 2013:126).

4. There are also important historical examples of support that flowed in the opposite direction as foundations subsidized the expansion of government capacity. In the case of education for African Americans in the
American South after the Civil War, foundations and voluntary associations not only contributed to the provision of public education but also subsidized the development of new state-level agencies (Malczewski 2016).

5. These arguments often combine a number of distinct claims: that participation in associations contributes to the development or maintenance of a sense of community, to the preservation of freedom, or to the
capacity for self-governance (M. E. Warren 2001:17).

6. These arguments concur in viewing the role of associations and formal politics as complementing one
another in a democratic polity, a line of argument that has provoked a corresponding critique of the "dark
side" of civil society (Chambers and Kopstein 2001; Fiorina 1999).

7. The Black Panthers, for example, organized "the Free Breakfast for Children Program, liberation
schools, free health clinics, the Free Food Distribution Program, the Free Clothing Program, child develop-

ment centers, the Free Shoe Program, the Free Busing to Prison Program, the Sickle Cell Anemia Research Foundation, free housing cooperatives, the Free Pest Control Program, the Free Plumbing and Maintenance Program, renter's assistance, legal aid, the Seniors Escorts Program, and the Free Ambulance Program" (Bloom and Martin 2010:184).

8. As Dupuy and Prakash discuss in Chapter 28, "Global Backlash Against Foreign Funding to Domestic Nongovernmental Organizations," governments in developing countries are more likely to impose restrictive regulations on NGOs, whether foreign or domestic, in times of political threat or vulnerability.

Chapter 8

1. This is based on the total amount of contributions from individuals in 2016 reported by the Center for Responsive Politics, which was $6.7 billion.

2. This difference in means is statistically significant based on a two-sample comparison-of-means test.

3. I ran a simple regression model predicting federal campaign contributions with two dummy variables—policy plutocrats and membership on the Forbes 400 list of wealthiest Americans. Only the policy plutocrat variable was both positive and statistically significant.

4. New Orleans schools received an estimated $250 million in philanthropic dollars and competitive grants during a ten-year period from 2005 to 2015 (Holly et al. 2015).

Chapter 9

1. Tocqueville attributes the energy of American associational life to the "administrative decentralization" of the American political system. Although he makes clear that this system of dispersed power inevitably entails a variety of inefficiencies in government, Tocqueville also insists that it promotes a sense of personal investment in local and national policy making, with the result of encouraging civic participation: "In the United States the native country makes itself felt everywhere. It is an object of solicitude from the village to the entire Union" (Tocqueville 2000:90).

2. Indeed, in certain cases scholars have found that nonprofits are acting more like policy-setting elected bodies than as derivative service providers. For instance, Jeremy Levine (2016) argues through an extensive ethnographic analysis of a community development initiative in Boston that nonprofit leaders superseded elected officials as community representatives, appropriating the discourse and practices of electoral representation. David Suárez and Nicole Esparza (2017) draw on dozens of interviews from a public–nonprofit partnership within a local division of the National Park Service to show that the nonprofit organization in question wielded considerable decision-making power in relation to its public partner. Reviewing their evidence, Suárez and Esparza propose that growing rationalization and managerialism in the nonprofit sector "will diminish public sector control (increase nonprofit discretion) in public-nonprofit partnerships" (656).

3. Unsurprisingly, studies that attempt to control for relevant domain characteristics such as region and service area tend to arrive at less significant differences (see, e.g., Miller-Stevens, Taylor, and Morris, 2015; Peng, Pandey, and Pandey, 2015; Lee, 2012).

Chapter 10

1. For an interesting history of fee-charging in the social services, see Brown 2018.

2. For example, instead of a monthly welfare check, participants may be offered job placement assistance, child care vouchers, and/or a referral for mental health services.

3. Bridge loans are needed when payments are late in order to cover the cost of providing services, for example, rent and payroll.

Chapter 11

1. These organizations and the activities they pursue are not unique to some legal definition of a city (as opposed to a town or village). Rural areas, of course, are also home to museums, health centers, and food

pantries. Even in rural places, nonprofits can be rooted to local communities. That being said, most of the work reviewed here and the arguments derived from it applies most to places that are also dense. Because density increases the likelihood of social interaction in a network, it amplifies some of our arguments.

2. These are by no means the only roles that nonprofits play—for example, we might have discussed nonprofits as employers, patrons of the arts, or knowledge producers—but those covered here are particularly well documented.

3. Carolyn Addams argues that many of these growth machine actors in fact live in the suburbs, not the city (2014).

4. Likening nonprofits to infrastructure should not portray them as static in ways that contrast with the dynamism of nonprofits. Nor do we want the metaphor of infrastructure misunderstood as more top-down and centrally planned than is necessarily true of the nonprofit sector, which, in general, is regarded as bottom-up and not coordinated by some command center. It is worth noting the ways in which streets are shaped from the bottom up and nonprofits are steered from the top down as well.

5. There are disciplinary differences over whether organizations, including nonprofit organizations, have "agency." Sociologists may take nonprofits as entities unto themselves, whereas historians typically frame nonprofits as vehicles through which people act and express themselves. We each follow our disciplinary norms but see great value in taking seriously the approaches of the other field. For that matter, perhaps an architect, planner, or engineer might take issue with our characterization of streets as lacking agency.

6. As Figure 11.3 suggests, the biggest predictor of the civic life of cities is their past civic life.

7. Apart from this factor, however, we abstain from the idea that some form of natural "diversity" or "multiplicity" of types of organizations is inherently beneficial to nonprofits' impact, although it is possible that such a relationship exists.

8. Exceptions include Guthrie and McQuarrie's work on Seattle, Cleveland, and Atlanta (2008).

9. Our view is informed by fundamental principles in our respective disciplines: history and sociology. For sociologists, individual actions are embedded in social structure; this relationship is reciprocal, as wider social structures are created and sustained by the individuals that are bound by it (Granovetter 1985; Sewell 1992; Martin 2009). Organizational behavior—such as that of nonprofit and voluntary organizations—is determined by their embeddedness in social structure *and* the fact that organizations mold and make these structures (Powell and Brandtner 2016). As Padgett and Powell (2012) argue, in the short run actors make networks; in the long run, structures make actors. The permanency and entanglement of city structure and nonprofit infrastructure thus suggest that, with time, these two evolve alongside each other. Historians emphasize that nothing about the past, current, or future configuration of the nonprofit infrastructure of cities is or was inevitable. It was the product of choices made in the past and so in looking ahead to the future, understanding how and why something was built, is valuable for those who seek to change it. As this relates to nonprofits and cities, historians have noted how changing legal regimes, political ideologies, policy packages, and governing strategies have shaped nonprofits and their urban operations. A core insight has been that the neutral or nonpartisan face of nonprofit organizations has been a tool for segregation, racial discrimination and the consolidation of power among urban elites, as well as a tool for community empowerment, mobilization, and expanding rights. The urban environment is thus not a passive backdrop for nonprofit activity but made up of a host of social structures that are centrally defined by their constituents, which include nonprofits. As new categories of organizations emerge and evolve, the constellation and relative interests of these actors adapt accordingly.

Chapter 12

1. This literature is vast. Foundational works include Gordon 1964, Gans 1992, Portes and Zhou 1993, and Alba and Nee 2003; also see Waters and Jiménez 2005.

2. See, for example, Dahl 1961, Jones-Correa 1998, Ramakrishnan and Espenshade 2001, and Wong 2006.

3. In the United Kingdom, the concept of "parallel lives" was articulated in the 2001 Cantor report (CCRT 2001). In Germany, similar concerns were expressed starting in the 1990s as *Parallelgesellschaften* (parallel societies) (Vertovec and Wessendorf 2010:8).

4. Spurred by Robert Putnam's contention that immigrant-generated diversity might undermine social capital, there is a small cottage industry assessing the relationship, if any, between diversity and generalized trust, social ties, membership in organizations, and so forth (for one review, see van der Meer and Tolsma 2014). Almost none of this work assesses whether immigrant *organizations* affect such outcomes (but see Fennema and Tillie 1999) or the consequences—for immigrants and the native majority—of membership in immigrant organizations as compared to mainstream ones.

5. For example, in their widely cited work on civic engagement, Sidney Verba and his colleagues (1995) examine how socioeconomic background, education, ethnoracial minority status, and even religious affiliation affect participation. They do not consider immigrant background in depth.

6. The inattention to immigration by social movement scholars was, up to about a decade ago, more pronounced among American scholars than those in Europe. For example, Ruud Koopmans and his colleagues (2005) produced influential work on immigrants' claims making using social movement concepts. European research on immigrants' political incorporation has also long used the social movement concept of political opportunity structure (Bloemraad and Vermeulen 2014). This research was not, however, primarily interested in organizations.

7. From a social movements perspective, the rise of pro-immigrant or pro-refugee social movement organizations can generate countermovement dynamics, which we do not address here because of space limitations.

8. These calculations were made using Google Scholar between December 6 and 12, 2018. The search string identified all items with the terms "immigrant" or "refugee" or "migrant" and the word "organization(s)" or "organisation(s)" in the title. The total count returned by Google Scholar was adjusted by first eliminating multiple counts of the same item in the same year, and then further adjusted by eliminating items that contained the search terms but did not concern the study of immigrant organizations. Thus, items about migrating animals were dropped, as were items about the organization of work for migrants that did not deal with nonprofits. Items in which "organization" or "organisation" was part of an official name for an international, intergovernmental institution were also eliminated (e.g., titles that referenced the International Labour Organization, the Organization of African States, or the World Health Organization). The authors underscore that these calculations are illustrative, not definitive. We are happy to share coding rules and the precise search string upon request.

9. These statistics are from the U.S. Census Bureau, 2012–2016 American Community Survey 5-Year Estimates, Table S0501, https://factfinder.census.gov.

10. On the civic engagement of undocumented immigrants, see for example Coll 2010, de Graauw 2016, Gleeson 2012, Terriquez 2012, and Voss and Bloemraad 2011.

11. This is according to the "political participation" policy indicators enumerated by the Migrant Integration Policy Index. See http://www.mipex.eu/political-participation, accessed December 10, 2018.

12. A few scholars have also adopted an organizational ecology approach, arguing that when the number and density of organizations increase substantially, some organizations will fail because of resource competition (Vermeulen et al. 2016).

13. Some researchers also draw on techniques for studying interlocking directorates to examine the degree to which members of nonprofit boards span immigrant and mainstream communities, which could be conceptualized as bridging social capital. Alternatively, if the board memberships of immigrant and mainstream organizations are distinct networks, this may generate bonding social capital within the community (Fennema and Tillie 1999; Vermeulen et al. 2016).

14. In comparing immigrant communities, a researcher must decide whether to focus exclusively on those born abroad (first generation) or to include in a population, reputational, or media count anyone reporting a particular ethnicity (e.g., anyone who identifies as Mexican or Mexican American, so including the second generation and beyond). The chosen strategy may differ depending on the outcome of interest.

15. Earlier migrants can, and often do, help new arrivals. Yet new arrivals cannot always rely on organizations started by earlier cohorts of compatriots, especially when migrant waves differ by social class, region of origin, religious or ethnic background, political ideology, or other internal divisions.

Chapter 13

1. A study of eight OECD countries from roughly a decade ago (Salamon et al. 2007) shows that nonprofit organizations contributed 8 percent to GDP on average (7.2 percent in the United States). Health, education, and social services accounted for 61 percent of the contribution of nonprofits to GDP on average in those eight countries. More recent estimates suggest that the contribution of the nonprofit sector to the GDP of the United States has declined slightly to 5.4 percent in 2015 (see McKeever 2018).

2. See Besley and Ghatak 2018 for a recent review of this literature.

3. See Akerlof and Kranton 2005, Benabou and Tirole 2006, and Besley and Ghatak 2005.

4. This work can be separated from behavioral economics, which studies departures from certain consistency axioms in a rational choice framework. One can have many objectives other than maximizing private wealth or consumption of private goods and yet be strictly rational. Even in standard public economics models, people care about public goods and services. In this literature, the premise is that there is some failure in government provision of public goods, regulations, and private voluntary actions by individuals (e.g., models of voluntary charitable contributions).

5. See Besley and Ghatak 2017b for a discussion.

6. See Gibbons and Roberts 2013.

7. More generally, reputation can be an important incentive mechanism when the quality of a good is intangible, as in the case of experience goods.

8. This is a modified version of the multitasking argument of Holmström and Milgrom 1991.

9. See Ortmann 1996 for a discussion.

10. Terms like *public benefit corporations* (Shiller 2012) or *B corporation* (Reiser 2010), *social enterprise* (Dees 1998; Bornstein 2004), *social business* (Yunus 2007), and *community interest company* (Reiser 2010) are part of an emerging lexicon, but all stand for somewhat different organizational forms.

11. See Reiser 2010 for a discussion from a law and economics perspective. The legal framework for hybrid organizations is evolving, and there are many unresolved questions. For example, as Rachel Culley and Jill R. Horwitz (2015) note, a key question focuses on how to solve legal disputes that occur when profit making and social purpose conflict.

12. See Kristof 2007.

13. See Strom 2007.

Chapter 14

1. For an insightful conceptual attempt to examine variety within country contexts, see Defourny and Nyssens 2017.

2. All interviewers participated in an on-site training week before conducting the survey and participated in biweekly coaching and reflection sessions during the interview period.

3. In Germany and Portugal, a few social enterprises have very large revenues—revenues of more than €100 million and €10 million, respectively.

4. Employment and volunteering seemed to be weakly positively and significantly correlated, suggesting that these two activities can be understood as weak complements to, rather than substitutes for, the social enterprises in our sample (Huysentruyt and Stephan, 2017).

5. Examples of nonprofit legal forms include charities, associations, federations, foundations, community interest companies, social solidarity institutes, limited liability companies with public benefit status, and private nonenterprise entities (China-specific).

6. Examples of for-profit legal forms include limited liability companies, general partnerships, limited companies with shares, partnerships organized under the civil code, and unincorporated businesses (China-specific).

7. Once it registers as a CIC, a social enterprise cannot receive donations. Another reason why social enterprises that are eligible for other for-profit forms may not adopt the CIC form is that CIC regulation imposes a cap on dividends that they can distribute.

8. Details of this analysis are shared in the cross-country report at http://www.seforis.edu.

9. We created a measure of heterogeneity/homogeneity using a Herfindahl-Hirschman index for legal forms in each country/domain. The formula is $HHI = \Sigma_{i=1}^{N} S2i$, where i is any given legal form and s is the share of that legal form out of all social enterprises (per country and problem domain).

Chapter 15

1. This chapter uses Kerstin Martens's (2002) definition of NGO: "NGOs are formal (professionalized) independent societal organizations whose primary aim is to promote common goals at the national or the international level" (282).

2. http://us.fsc.org, accessed July 11, 2019.

3. https://ic.fsc.org/en/facts-and-figures, accessed September 19, 2018.

4. https://annualreport16-17.fairtrade.net/en/, accessed October 20, 2019.

5. https://annualreport16-17.fairtrade.net/en/, accessed October 20, 2019.

6. http://www.ecolabelindex.com, accessed September 9, 2018.

7. https://www.statista.com/statistics/235805/us-retail-sales-of-natural-and-organic-food/, accessed September 12, 2018.

8. Adapted from a similar definition of legitimacy (Cashore et al. 2004b:188).

9. https://us.fsc.org/en-us/certification/forest-management-certification, accessed October 20, 2019.

10. http://www.greenbiz.com/blog/2011/03/30/whos-peddling-pulp-fiction-sfi-vs-fsc-forestry-wars, accessed July 11, 2019.

11. http://www.organicfacts.net/organic-animal-products/organic-milk/health-benefits-of-organic-milk.html, accessed July 11, 2019.

12. Global Reporting Initiative 2016.

13. https://www.cdp.net/en/info/about-us, accessed July 11, 2019.

Chapter 16

1. Like many large-scale development projects, the Green Revolution may have had unintended adverse consequences (Hazell 2009).

2. For a detailed example of the application of CBA to tobacco regulations, see Brest 2017.

3. The publication of this manual may have been motivated, in part, by UWA's need to document outcomes in the aftermath of its president's highly publicized fraudulent use of the organization's funds (Hendricks, Plantz, and Pritchard 2008:14).

4. See also Ash Center for Democratic Governance and Innovation n.d.

5. The following paragraphs are based on my interview with Tierney and Bradach, May 23, 2018, and two HBS case studies (Grossman, Greckol-Herlich, and Ross 2009; Grossman and Kalafatas 2000). I am on Bridgespan's board of directors.

6. For a time, Bridgespan had a fourth area of operations—serving as a talent scout for nonprofit organizations—which it abandoned after work in that area pulled the organization too far away from its core mission.

7. In the following examples, I'll assume that the organization doing the advocacy is not subject to any significant limits on lobbying.

8. The Scared Straight program continued operating in the face of evidence that it actually increased delinquency (Petrosino et al. 2013).

9. See, for example, the Pew-MacArthur Results First Initiative, the U.S. Department of Education's What Works Clearinghouse, and the congressionally established Commission on Evidence-Based Policymaking.

10. This explains in part why Oklahoma's replacement of its pay-for-service vocational rehabilitation program with a pay-for-performance program both reduced the state's costs and improved clients' outcomes (Better Government Corporation 1997; Rosegrant 1998; O'Brien and Revell 2005).

Chapter 17

1. The author's calculations are based on the AHA's Annual Survey of Hospitals 1985 and 2014.

2. The author's calculations are based on the AHA's Annual Survey of Hospitals 2014, survey question asking whether the hospital is a member of the Council of Teaching Hospitals and Health Systems (COTH) of the Association of American Medical Colleges."

3. The author's calculations are based on the AHA's Annual Survey of Hospitals 2014, survey question asking whether the hospital offers residency training approval by the Accreditation Council for Graduate Medical Education.

4. The measures of urban and rural locations have changed over time, so precise comparisons to years earlier than 2004 are not possible. Nonetheless, among hospitals in metropolitan statistical areas with populations equal to or greater than 100,000 people in 1985, about 61 percent were nonprofit, 21 percent were government, and 18 percent were for-profit owned.

5. The author's calculations are based on the AHA's Annual Survey of Hospitals 2004–2014. Metropolitan divisions and rural areas are based on census definitions related to core-based statistical areas, at county level designations. The census definitions are as follows: (1) Metropolitan Divisions are smaller groupings of counties or equivalent entities defined within a metropolitan statistical area containing a single core with a population of at least 2.5 million. Not all metropolitan statistical areas with urbanized areas of this size will contain metropolitan divisions. A metropolitan division consists of one or more main/secondary counties that represent an employment center or centers, plus adjacent counties associated with the main/secondary county or counties through commuting ties. (2) Rural counties are those with no place in them designated as an urbanized area or having an urban cluster. For more detail, see Kathy Miller, "Urban/Rural Areas and CBSAs," http://www.rupri.org/Forms/WP2.pdf.

6. Health care insurers also are frequently criticized as rapacious profit-seekers. I do not address this argument in detail both because of space constraints and because nonprofit insurers are typically treated as noncharitable nonprofits under state and federal law and, therefore, are not eligible for many of the benefits that critics wish to forbid health charities from accessing. Nonetheless, their history is instructive. They had their roots in fraternal societies, which were based on mutual aid and not public charity, making the contemporary mutual form the successor to these earlier institutions. As the Blue Cross plans grew in scope in the mid-twentieth century, states enacted enabling legislation that allowed them to form as nonprofits and to enjoy tax-exemption (Thomasson 2002). Over time, many of the benefits were withdrawn, in part because of the commercialization of the industry. As Deborah Stone (1993) explains, the business strategy of actuarial fairness rather than solidarity exemplifies the American private health insurance industry.

7. In an article explaining the value of the nonprofit form, I observed that early-twentieth-century nonprofits were essentially almshouses for the poor who were deemed worthy, and not agents of business (Horwitz 2006).

Chapter 19

1. The IRS Business Master File includes organizations registered for tax-exempt status with the IRS (see https://nccs.urban.org/database/overview-nccs-data-files).

2. Note that the "Museums and Museum Activities" category in the National Taxonomy of Exempt Entities used in the analysis comprises a variety of types of museums, including natural history and science museums as well as art museums.

3. For founding dates, see https://www.metmuseum.org/about-the-met and https://www.lapovertydept .org/lapd-history/.

4. The threshold for reporting to the IRS was raised in 2010 from $25,000 to $50,000, making comparisons before and after that period difficult. These figures are drawn from McKeever, Dietz, and Fyffe 2016, which presents comparisons only for organizations that had over $50,000 in receipts for all periods.

5. We discuss attendance trends shortly. For a review of the research on nonprofit arts financial state, see Ostrower and Calabrese (2019).

6. As of 2012, the SPPA also asked about attendance at "other" performing arts events (i.e., performing arts not specifically queried in other SPPA questions), which showed increases in 2017 (NEA 2018:7), but there is no way to know if any significant portion of these events were associated with nonprofit arts organizations.

Chapter 21

1. As noted earlier, however, we are often seeing more flexible structures among associations and networks that are not formally incorporated as nonprofits. Although we lack systematic evidence that can speak to this directly, many of the constraints we describe here may be causing a shift away from nonprofit incorporation for many advocacy causes (just as restrictions on foundations may be encouraging the rise of donor-advised funds; see Steuerle 1999).

2. Still, donors who are themselves more involved in advocacy tend to be more likely to rely on the ratings of watchdog sites (Cnaan et al. 2011).

Chapter 22

1. The study is based on surveys with 88 news organizations and secondary data provided by the 180 institutional members of the Institute for Nonprofit News network. All organizations are registered as 501(c)(3), representing a combined staff of approximately 2,200 people and a combined annual revenue of approximately $350 million USD.

2. For broad discussion of different types of publics, see Breese 2011; Calhoun 1998; Christians et al. 2009; Downey, Mihelj, and König 2012; Fung 2003; and Held 2006.

Chapter 23

1. High-net-worth households are those whose net worth (excluding their home) is more than $1,000,000 or whose income is greater than $200,000.

2. There are other ways to "slice" the motivations that drive charitable giving. For example, Adrian Sargeant (1999) describes five types of utility that people might get from making a gift: emotional (warm glow), familial (family benefits such as schooling or an in memoriam medical research gift), demonstrable (seeing their gift make a difference), practical (buying concert seats or a named building), and spiritual (giving as an expression or requirement of faith). René Bekkers and Pamala Wiepking (2011a) provide eight mechanisms.

3. Religious nonprofits enjoy an especially favored status and are exempt from many reporting requirements.

4. In fact, by providing some services itself, the government influences the distribution of the entire nonprofit sector. Market failure theory proposes that the private sector's inability or unwillingness to provide much-needed collective goods, coupled with government's limitations in satisfying the public demand for these goods, leads to the need for a private, voluntary sector to provide these goods (Salamon 1987; Weisbrod 1977). The nonprofit sector therefore acts as a compensatory force against market failure and the failure of government to adequately serve citizens in need; it fills particular voids with volunteered time and charitable contributions (Ott and Dicke 2012).

5. Crowding out individual giving is not the only possible effect of a government grant. Andreoni and Payne (2003, 2011) show that nonprofits sometimes respond to a government grant by reducing fund-raising.

6. Singer's (2010) book makes a moral argument about giving. Although on the surface, a utilitarian philosophical approach seems difficult to refute, some scholars have taken issue with the ethics outlined in this approach (Woodruff 2018). See also Lechterman and Reich, Chapter 6, "Political Theory and the Nonprofit Sector," for a discussion of a range of values that can be elevated in the nonprofit sector.

7. The Robin Hood Foundation attempted to monetize a QALY and decided on $50,000 (M. M. Weinstein and Bradburd 2013:35).

8. In cases where there is no scarcity—where everyone who wants an intervention can receive it—it may be unethical to withhold the intervention from some. In cases where there is scarcity, however, one could argue that it is most ethical to provide the programming randomly.

Chapter 24

1. Myriad scholars discuss the sensitivity of charitable giving to its tax treatment (e.g., Steinberg 1990; Clotfelter 1985; Andreoni 2006b; Bakija and Heim 2011).

2. See "Charitable Contributions—Quid Pro Quo Contributions," https://www.irs.gov/charities-non-profits/charitable-organizations/charitable-contributions-quid-pro-quo-contributions.

3 An extensive literature shows that in laboratory experiments, punishments increase contributions to public goods. See Chaudhuri 2011 and Ledyard 1995 for formal surveys of the literature, and see DeAngelo and Gee 2018 and Andreoni and Gee 2012 for more recent additions.

4. The warm glow a donor experiences may vary by the charity's use of the donation. For example, donors seem to have a distaste for seeing their money used toward administrative overhead costs, despite the necessity of such costs to operate a nonprofit (Gneezy, Keenan, and Gneezy 2014; Meer 2014).

5. Barış K. Yörük (2009) links several data sets and uses an instrumental variables approach to show that being solicited increases the likelihood of making a gift by nearly twenty percentage points. Michael Sanders and Sarah Smith (2016) show that a prompt to give to charity during the will-making process significantly increases the likelihood that a will includes a charitable bequest. Gee (2011) uses survey data to show that the importance of the ask may also apply to gifts of time by documenting a positive correlation between being made aware of volunteer opportunities and actual volunteering. For a more detailed discussion, see Paxton, Chapter 23, "What Influences Charitable Giving?"

6. John A. List and Michael K. Price (2009) show that minority solicitors are less likely to receive donations from both nonminority and minority households.

7. For more details on the history of charitable giving, see Soskis, Chapter 2, "History of Associational Life and the Nonprofit Sector in the United States."

8. In fact, measuring all monetary charitable gifts is not as easy as it may seem. In the United States, donations that are itemized on tax forms can be measured, but only about 26 percent of households itemized their deductions in 2017 (Council of Economic Advisers 2017). Giving USA devotes twenty pages to explaining how it estimates monetary gifts in its 2018 report on annual giving. For example, in its 2018 report, Giving USA estimates gifts by individuals by separately using IRS data for those who itemize and the Philanthropy Panel Study for those who do not itemize. Additional data are used to estimate gifts in response to disasters and for "mega-gifts" over $300 million. Adjustments are made using stock market returns and estimated responses to changes in the tax code. Other methods are used to measure the gifts from bequests, foundations, and corporations. Suffice it to say that even the relatively simple measurement of monetary donations is far from trivial.

9. See Eliasoph, Chapter 25, "What Do Volunteers Do?" for a more detailed discussion of what should count as a donation of time.

10. See Jones 2015 and Ruhm and Borkoski 2003 for a discussion of wage differentials in the nonprofit sector.

11. The answer to this question may depend on how self-serving it is to identify a particular gift as a donation (Dahl and Ransom 1999).

12. The answer to this question may depend on whether you are the booking agent for Ethan Hawke or for Marcus Samuelsson.

13. For discussions of issues related to donations at the end of life and through bequests, see Joulfaian 2001, 2005, and Meer and Rosen 2013.

14. An exception is the work of Naomi E. Feldman (2010), who documents the same positive relationship between gifts of time and money but goes on to show that the time and money are substitutes in an economic sense, yet increased consumption of one actually changes the costs of the other (e.g., a person who gives money to a charity often experiences a fall in the costs of donating time because that charity now asks them to volunteer).

15. See Andreoni and colleagues (2017) and DellaVigna and colleagues (2012) for a discussion on avoidance behavior by potential donors.

Chapter 25

1. Democratic theory usually suggests looking for verbal expressions, since we use words to make plans and offer alternatives, but people also use nonverbal expression to resist domination For example, "When the great lord passes, the wise peasant bows deeply and silently farts" (Scott 1990).

Chapter 26

1. The classification system the IRS uses to classify nonprofit organizations based on their core activity is the National Taxonomy of Exempt Entities (NTEE).

2. In this analysis, we used the code developed by Robert W. Ressler and his colleagues (2018) to parse the unstructured XML data and convert them to a structured format.

3. The calculations are based on results from our analysis in this study and nonprofit sector estimates provided in Brauer 2017, Candid 2019, McKeever 2018, and Scheitle, Dollhopf, and McCarthy 2016.

4. An ongoing debate concerns the White House Faith-Based Initiative and whether the federal government should give money (via grants and contracts) to faith-based social service organizations. Some opponents of the initiative argue that FBOs subject their clients to religion and therefore the government giving such organizations money violates the separation of church and state. Proponents counter that FBOs are providing needed services and that the organizations' religious beliefs and practices should not be a factor in the decision. A relatively underexamined topic in this debate is the functional role that religion plays in FBOs (Ebaugh et al. 2006; Sinha 2013).

5. Because congregations are not required to report their financial activity to the IRS, publicly available data on the finances and economic practices of congregations is scant (Mundey, King, and Fulton 2019).

6. In 2017, the U.S. District Court for the Western District of Wisconsin declared the ministers' housing allowance unconstitutional (*Gaylor v. Mnuchin*, No. 16-cv-215). As this chapter went to press, the court's decision on this case was under appeal.

Chapter 27

1. Dhananjay Mahapatra, "India Witnessing NGO Boom, There Is 1 for Every 600 People," *Times of India*, February 22, 2014. https://timesofindia.indiatimes.com/india/India-witnessing-NGO-boom-there-is-1-for -every-600-people/articleshow/30871406.cms.

2. United Nations Department of Economic and Social Affairs, "NGO Branch," NGO Branch, August 28, 2019. http://csonet.org/.

3. Evan Halper, "Is That Environmental Group a Pawn of Beijing? Nonprofits Wary of Being Branded 'Foreign Agents,'" *Los Angeles Times*, June 14, 2018. http://www.latimes.com/politics/la-na-pol-foreign-agents -20180614-story.html.

Chapter 28

1. http://carnegieendowment.org/2015/11/02/closing-space-challenge-how-are-funders-responding-pub -61808.

2. For instance, faith-based NGOs provide an estimated 50 percent of health services in the Democratic Republic of Congo. International and local NGOs provide 75 percent of health services in Sudan's North

Darfur state and nearly 100 percent of all social services in southern Somalia (Olivier et al 2015; Yagub and Mtshali 2015; UNICEF 2016).

3. The principled-actor narrative is probably also predicated on the assumption that the NGO sector attracts individuals who are devoted to pursuing the social good and are beyond instrumental temptations.

4. The ongoing Oxfam scandal poses problems for the principled-actor narrative and reminds us that even globally renowned principled actors are susceptible to systematic governance failures. This chapter is not making the case that the NGO crackdown is a direct response to such scandals, although such scandals undermine NGOs' credibility among both aid donors and aid recipient countries and perhaps even mute the backlash against the regulatory crackdown.

5. This crisis began in 2014 as refugees from war-torn countries such as Syria along with economic refugees from other countries began arriving in southern Europe, often with the intention to travel to Germany or Austria via the southern and central European countries. The EU refugee policy was deeply unpopular in many countries, and this led them to adopt policies that were in violation of their EU commitments. Because some liberal NGOs are actively involved in helping refugees in both their travel and resettlement, the populists often demanded a crackdown on NGOs.

6. Hungary has justified its crackdown by linking NGOs to George Soros's attempts to interfere in its domestic politics. Hungary has also proclaimed its intentions to crack down on NGOs that are working in the area of refugee relief, an issue championed by the EU.

7. https://www.politico.eu/article/pis-polish-ngos-fear-the-governments-embrace/.

8. A 2015 law prohibits Muslim religious organizations from receiving foreign funding.

9. However, political commentators such as Fareed Zakaria (1997) had pointed out the rise of illiberal democracy a decade earlier.

10. Twenty countries have specific regulations in place that require NGO foreign funding to be routed through the formal banking sector.

11. https://www.washingtonpost.com/news/monkey-cage/wp/2018/02/19/the-oxfam-scandal-shows-that -yes-nonprofits-can-behave-badly-so-why-arent-they-overseen-like-for-profits/. See also http://www.bbc .com/news/uk-43031911.

12. https://donate.greenpeace.org/hpp/pay.shtml.

13. http://www.bbc.com/news/uk-43031911.

14. http://carnegieendowment.org/2016/10/04/closing-space-and-fragility-pub-64774.

15. https://www.atlasnetwork.org/news/article/alexis-de-tocquevilles-legacy-in-the-early-21st-century.

Chapter 29

1. A large literature addresses the difference between "doing activism" and "being an activist" (Bobel 2007). Pamela Oliver and Gerald Marwell define activist as "someone who care[s] enough about some issue that they are prepared to incur significant costs and act to achieve their goals" (Oliver and Marwell 1992:252). Bert Klandermans (1994), Francesca Polletta and James M. Jasper (2001), and Ziad W. Munson (2008) show that movement participants change the way they see themselves (as well as the world) through activism. This chapter addresses the practice rather than the microsocial characteristics of the person.

2. Verta Taylor's theory of abeyance (1989) articulates the conceptual relationship between activism and movements. Social movement structures can serve as the organizational and ideological sinews that connect the inevitable peaks and troughs of activism. Activism is event-centric and time-delimited and may or may not be part of a more sustained political struggle, whereas social movements take place over longer time horizons and draw on the collective capacities of identifiable constituencies. Activism therefore refers more narrowly to the repertoires used in claims making; movements, on the other hand, are the cultural and organizational settings in which those claims are embedded.

3. The specific legal and organizational contours of groups engaged in these global struggles vary widely. Transnational activists may be linked to domestic or international NGOs, networks (online or offline), labor

movements, or autonomous movement organizations. The concept of *social movement organizations* (SMOs), used in the U.S. scholarship to refer to the "complex, or formal organization which identifies its goals with the preferences of a social movement . . . and attempts to implement these goals" (McCarthy and Zald 1977), was expanded in the 1990s with the term *TSMO* (also *TSMI*, for *transnational social movement industry*), which refers to the same phenomenon on a global scale (Smith, Chatfield, and Pagnucco 1997).

4. This analysis is based on a keyword search for terms related to transnational social movements in ProQuest Dissertation and Theses Global (PQDT), a collection of dissertations and theses with four million entries (roughly ninety thousand added each year). A search for "social movement" or "activism" and "transnational" or "global" or "international" in the abstract of uploaded manuscripts for the period 1989–2017 retrieved 1,578 results. Nearly 90 percent of theses retrieved were in English, followed by 9 percent in Chinese, and much smaller percentages in Spanish, Swedish, French, German, and others. In Figure 29.1, data are normalized to reflect the total number of dissertations related to social movements that were uploaded each year to ProQuest ($N = 7,733$).

5. To access the original data, visit https://dataverse.harvard.edu/dataset.xhtml?persistentId=doi:10.7910/DVN/28075.

6. John Boli and George Thomas use counts of the cumulative number of INGOs in existence as a proxy measure for activity levels (1999:261).

7. The ICEWS algorithms monitor events in multiple languages, which clearly enhances the generalizability of movement studies that use this kind of data (as compared to studies restricted to English-language media). But this feature also has drawbacks, notably for the potential misclassification of words. In Portuguese, for example, the word for *protest* is frequently used in its singular verb form, that is, as an expression of dissatisfaction—as opposed to the substantive version more often used in English to refer to a contentious repertoire. In Wei Wang and his colleagues' set of experiments designed to test the validity and reliability of GDELT and ICEWS, they found that the latter system was more robust, with roughly 80 percent of keyword-filtered events correctly classified as protest events (2016:1503). The authors note that the system was, however, still vulnerable to reporting duplicate events, with roughly 20 percent of the recorded events appearing more than once.

8. Charles Tilly (1995) later warned that because globalization undermines state capacity, workers must invent new strategies that take into account the international dynamics of capitalism if they are to win back some of the many rights they've lost after the assault on organized labor that has taken place since the 1980s (French 2000).

9. Although history continues to defy predictions of global, united, and revolutionary worker action (Schlossberg 1935), scholars have noted that few major political and social movements since the French Revolution were *not* responses to Marxism (e.g., Landauer 1959). Marxism, "a scientific creed, if this contradiction in terms is permissible," wrote Ernst Borinski, "became the gospel of social and political protest movements and revolutions, and in turn did ignite the counter-gospel of as many counterrevolutions" (Borinski 1961:269).

10. Clare Midgley (1996) has argued against one consensus that boycotts of slave produce represented a "minor and unsuccessful aspect of the popular campaign against slavery" (137). Her research suggests that the effect of slave sugar boycotts that took place in Britain in 1791 and 1825 on anti-slavery policy and public support has been underestimated.

11. Nancy Stepan (1982) also pointed out this paradox about the abolition movement: "A fundamental question about the history of racism in the first half of the nineteenth century," she wrote, "is why it was that, just as the battle against slavery was being won by abolitionists, the war against racism in European thought was being lost. The Negro was legally freed by the Emancipation Act of 1833, but in the British mind he was still mentally, morally and physically a slave" (1).

12. As Alexander Wendt (1999) observes, however, criticizing political theory for being "state-centric" is like criticizing a theory of forests for being "tree-centric" (9). We argue that the problem, however, is more

complex: it is about how this perspective limits our understanding of the multiscalar dynamics of activism in contemporary social movements, many of which do not always take the nation-state as the central referent.

13. Given the profoundly asymmetrical nature of global power relations, it is perhaps unsurprising that there was never a time in which scholars of and from the Global South disregarded the international dynamics of contentious politics, even when the movements they studied operated in what appeared to be purely domestic arenas (e.g., Borras, Edelman, and Kay 2009; Bringel and Cairo, 2019; Mamdani 1995; Ray and Katzenstein 2005).

14. Outside the social movement subfield, beginning with Kimberlé Crenshaw's seminal work on intersectionality published more than twenty-five years ago (1991)—though the precise history of the founding of the term is disputed (Nash 2017)—a robust literature has documented the interconnectedness of social categories like class, gender, and race (Hancock 2016).

15. Raw and coded data available upon request.

16. Karl Polanyi's argument is that economic liberalism became a "secular religion" in the late nineteenth century, whereas the New Deal and welfare state interventionism signaled its relative death. He argues that social legislation (e.g. safety standards, worker's compensation, and protections against child labor) were reactions to the deadliness of unregulated markets. Paradoxically, according to Polanyi, this double movement allows laissez-faire liberalism to survive.

17. An analysis that links content and form with this temporal dimension might examine whether rightists have a tendency to slow build, whereas leftists or emancipatory movements follow a trajectory that resembles more of a punctuated equilibrium.

Chapter 30

1. At about the same time, a literature on nongovernmental organizations (NGOs) began to emerge in parallel and mostly focused on the role of Western nonprofit organizations in a developing country context (e.g., Edwards and Hulme 1996; Hulme and Edwards 1997; Fischer 1998; Lewis 2014). Much of this literature, however, had an applied focus and sought a greater understanding of the role of NGOs in humanitarian assistance, development projects, and international relations. What is more, opportunities for international meetings and exchanges between nonprofit scholars began to increase in the 1990s, greatly facilitated by the International Society for Third-Sector Research (ISTR), founded in 1993.

2. See the discussion around Figure 30.3 in the context of the nonprofit sector definition and classification.

3. The 1990s saw other cross-national projects probing different aspects of the broad nonprofit theme, especially across Europe. These included, inter alia, the emergent phenomenon of social enterprises (Borzaga and Santuari n.d.); funding sources (Doyle 1996); volunteering (Gaskin and Smith 1995), and foundations (Schlüter, Then, and Walkenhorst 2001). However, none had CNP's scale, scope, and impact.

4. For example, the first summary publication of CNP results was titled "The Emerging Nonprofit Sector" (Salamon and Anheier 1996), and the second was titled "Global Civil Society" (Salamon et al. 1999), even though it was essentially the same project.

5. The structural-operational definition is widely used by researchers in the field, as is the classification system; *Global Civil Society* (Salamon et al. 1999), the volume that presented findings from the twenty-plus-country expansion of CNP, continues to be frequently cited as a general reference, despite the fact that the data are now more than two decades old; satellite accounts following the CNP approach were established in more than a dozen countries (Salamon et al. 2012).

6. This is so because researchers commonly accept federal tax law designations to demarcate the kinds of nonprofit organizations that are the subject of research. For the most part, U.S. research is focused on just two of the more than two dozen types of tax-exempt entities (Anheier 2014: table 3.1). On the one hand, these are the so-called charities regulated under Section 501(c)(3) of the Internal Revenue Code, which exempts religious, educational, charitable, and other broadly public-serving purposes. 501(c)(3) status comes with

the added benefit of deductibility of donations for donors, but the additional cost of sharp restrictions on political campaign and lobbying activities. The second category of exempt organizations typically included are Section 501(c)(4) social welfare organizations, which are also public-serving, cannot offer deductibility of donations, but are less restrained in their political activities.

7. Indeed, there is great profusion of terms in the English language alone: *nonprofit sector, charities, third sector, independent sector, voluntary sector, tax-exempt sector, nongovernmental organizations, associational sector,* and *philanthropy* (Salamon and Anheier 1997). Other languages have their own, and typically as diverse, nomenclature.

8. The compilation of these figures followed the SNA approach, based on available employment and wage statistics to which estimates of the volunteer component was added. The economically active population comprises the population between ages sixteen and sixty-five performing economic activities outside the household and irrespective of formal work contracts—a modification necessary to take the informal economic sector into account that in many countries represents a significant share of the economy.

9. The concept of hybridity is gaining considerable analytic attention. Although there is no firm consensus as of yet, hybrid organizations are currently primarily conceived of as organizations that intermingle the social missions of nonprofits with the commercial logic of the business sector (see Abramson and Billings, forthcoming; Anheier and Krlev 2015).

10. Note that similar approaches are found elsewhere in the social sciences: intelligence is defined by the IQ, an operational measure based on a test, although many expressions of intelligence exist; similarly, in comparative political science, democracy is defined by a limited number of structural-operational characteristics, even though many variants of democracies exist, including their institutional embeddedness in society. Yet for such fields to develop further, more refined and context specific definitions are needed.

11. The recent EU-funded Third Sector Impact (TSI) project began to move in this direction. While firming up the boundary between the organizational and the individual, TSI proposed expanding the core definition to better capture social enterprises and social economy organizations at the institutional proximity to the market by softening the nondistribution criterium (Salamon and Sokolowski 2016). Although this is a useful step, Kirsten Grønbjerg (in Defourny, Grønbjerg, and Meijs 2016) correctly points out that the approach stops short of addressing similar boundary issues between public and private at the nonprofit sectors' proximity to the state.

12. Most prominently, the UN's International Standard Industrial Classification of All Economic Activities (ISIC), the EU's NACE (Nomenclature Statistique des Activités Économiques dans la Communauté Européenne) and the North American Industry Classification System (NAICS).

13. So far analysts had to use activity fields as rough proxies to differentiate between service provision (e.g., health, education, social services) and expressive functions (e.g., culture and recreation, advocacy).

14. Kim and Kim (2016) examine the growth of expenditures of nonprofit institutions serving households in twenty OECD countries over a twenty-one-year period. Their results suggest that private philanthropy and government social protection both have a strong effect on nonprofit sector size. Unfortunately, their results are not directly comparable, as they use a different dependent variable based on the SNA definition that, as we have seen, explicitly excludes nonprofits substantially financed by the government as well as market-producing nonprofits. Also, the key independent variable differs in that Kim and Kim measure government social protection instead of government social spending.

15. Unlike traditional cluster analysis, model-based clustering based on mixture models is not merely a tool for exploratory and descriptive purposes but can be relied on to assess cluster solutions based on statistical theory (Ahlquist and Breunig 2012; Breunig and Ahlquist 2014). There are established conventions on the number of clusters and groupings that are to be expected given a set of parameters. Moreover, statisticians have developed a measure of uncertainty that allows more precise judgments about the placement of countries, and there are restraints on possible geometrical arrangements (Banfield and Raftery 1993; Fraley and Raftery 1998). As mentioned before, none of these calculative devices replaces substantive interpretation.

Yet model-based clustering is much less dependent on qualitative judgments, and therefore the clustering process itself is more reproducible.

16. We rely for the fitting procedure on the model with the highest Bayesian information criterion (BIC). According to statistical convention, models with a BIC difference of 2 or less are difficult to distinguish. Yet a BIC difference of 10 or greater can be considered strong evidence for a specific model (Ahlquist and Breuning 2012:99). Figure 30.7 shows that model VII can be easily distinguished from other models given its high relative BIC values (y-axis). It also shows that the optimal number of clusters is 3 (x-axis).

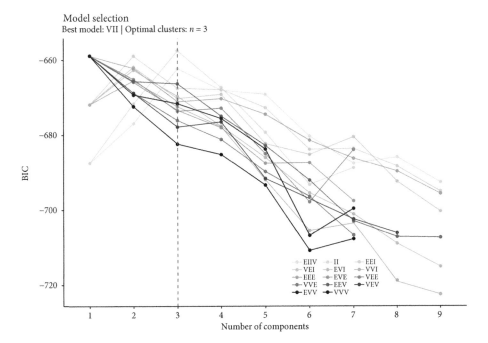

Figure 30.7 Bayesian information criterion (BIC) for the model presented in Figure 30.5
Note: Figure uses ISO3 country abbreviations. See table 30.4 for further details.

17. Figure 30.8 shows, however, that there is a ten-point difference between the best-fitting model and the proposed five-component solution. Although the overall clustering solution remains uncertain, we can confidentially rule out a five-or-more-components solution.

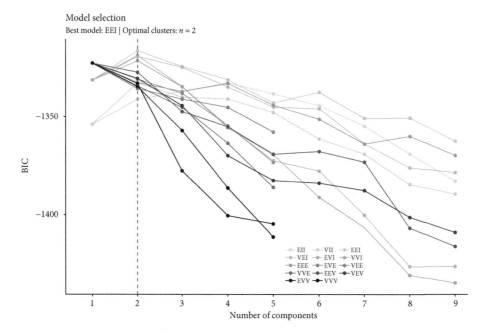

Figure 30.8   Bayesian information criterion (BIC) for the model presented in Figure 30.6
Note: Figure uses ISO3 country abbreviations. See table 30.4 for further details.

18. Of course, voluntary associations can take on some service delivery on behalf of their members or constituents and eventually grow into service providers that lose their community and voluntary ethos, roots, and functions because of the influence of government funders (Smith and Lipsky 1993).

REFERENCES

Introduction

Chapter 1. What Is the Nonprofit Sector?

Acemoglu, Daron. 2017. "We Are the Last Defense Against Trump." *Foreign Policy*, January 18. http://foreignpolicy.com/2017/01/18/we-are-the -last-defense-against-trump-institutions/.

Anheier, Helmut. 2009. "What Kind of Nonprofit Sector, What Kind of Society? Comparative Policy Reflections." *American Behavioral Scientist* 52(7): 1082–1094.

———. 2014. *Nonprofit Organizations: Theory, Management, Policy*, 2nd ed. London: Routledge.

Anheier, Helmut, and Lester Salamon. 2006. "The Nonprofit Sector in Comparative Perspective." In *The Nonprofit Sector: A Research Handbook*, 2nd ed., ed. Walter W. Powell and Richard Steinberg, 89–114. New Haven, CT: Yale University Press.

Barman, Emily. 2013. "Classificatory Struggles in the Nonprofit Sector: The Formation of the National Taxonomy of Exempt Entities, 1969–1987." *Social Science History* 37(1): 103–141.

Berman, Sheri. 1997. "Civil Society and the Collapse of the Weimar Republic." *World Politics* 49(3): 401–429.

Berry, Jeffrey M. 1999. *The New Liberalism: The Rising Power of Citizen Groups*. Washington, DC: Brookings Institution Press.

———. 2016. "Negative Returns: The Impact of Impact Investing on Empowerment and Advocacy." *PS: Political Science and Politics* 49(3): 437–441.

Bloch, Ruth H., and Naomi R. Lamoreaux. 2017. "Voluntary Associations, Corporate Rights, and the State: Legal Constraints on Development of American Civil Society, 1750–1900." In *Organizations, Civil Society, and the Roots of Development*, ed. Naomi R. Lamoreaux and John J. Wallis, 231–270. Chicago: University of Chicago Press.

Boris, Elizabeth T., and C. Eugene Steuerle. 2006. "The Scope and Dimensions of the Nonprofit Sector." In *The Nonprofit Sector*, 2nd ed., ed. Walter W. Powell and Richard Steinberg, 66–88. New Haven, CT: Yale University Press.

Brandtner, Christof. 2019. "Cities in Action: City Climate Action, Civil Society, and the Organization of Cities." PhD diss., Stanford University.

Brilliant, Eleanor. 2000. *Private Charity and Public Inquiry: A History of the Filer and Peterson Commissions*. Bloomington: Indiana University Press.

Brooks, Richard, and Timothy W. Guinnane. 2017. "The Right to Associate and the Rights of Associations: Civil Society Organizations in Prussia, 1794–1908." In *Organizations, Civil Society, and the Roots of Development*, ed. Naomi R. Lamoreaux and John J. Wallis, 291–330. Chicago: University of Chicago Press.

Clemens, Elisabeth S. 2006. "The Constitution of Citizens: Political Theories of Nonprofit Organizations." In *The Nonprofit Sector: A Research Handbook*, 2nd ed., ed. Walter W. Powell and Richard Steinberg, 207–220. New Haven, CT: Yale University Press.

Cohen, Joshua, and A. Arato. 1992. *Civil Society and Political Theory.* Cambridge, MA: MIT Press.

Davis, Gerald, and Christopher White. 2015. *Changing Your Company from the Inside Out.* Boston: Harvard Business School Press.

Eig, J. 2016. *The Birth of the Pill: How Four Pioneers Reinvented Sex and Launched a Revolution.* Basingstoke, UK: Macmillan.

Esping-Anderson, Gosta. 1990. *Three Worlds of Welfare Capitalism.* Princeton, NJ: Princeton University Press.

Fiorina, Morris P. 1999. "Extreme Voices: A Dark Side of Civic Engagement." In *Civic Engagement in American Democracy*, ed. Theda Skocpol and Morris P. Fiorina, 395–425. Washington, DC: Brookings Institution Press.

Frumkin, Peter. 2002. *On Being Nonprofit: A Conceptual and Policy Primer.* Cambridge, MA: Harvard University Press.

Gilens, Martin. 2012. *Affluence and Influence: Economic Inequality and Political Power in America.* Princeton, NJ: Princeton University Press.

Habermas, Jürgen. 1989. *The Structural Transformation of the Public Sphere: An Inquiry into a Category of Bourgeois Society.* Cambridge, MA: MIT Press.

Hall, Peter D. 1987. "A Historical Overview of the Private Nonprofit Sector." In *The Nonprofit Sector: A Research Handbook*, ed. Walter W. Powell, 32–65. New Haven, CT: Yale University Press.

———. 1992. *"Inventing the Nonprofit Sector" and Other Essays on Philanthropy, Voluntarism, and Nonprofit Organizations.* Baltimore: Johns Hopkins University Press.

———. 2006. "A Historical Overview of Philanthropy, Voluntary Associations, and Nonprofit Organizations in the United States, 1600–2000." In *The Nonprofit Sector: A Research Handbook*, 2nd ed., ed. Walter W. Powell and Richard Steinberg, 32–65. New Haven, CT: Yale University Press.

Han, Hahrie. 2016. "The Organizational Roots of Political Activism: Field Experiments on Creating a Relational Context." *American Political Science Review* 110(2): 296–307.

Hansmann, Henry. 1987. "Economic Theories of Nonprofit Organizations." In *The Nonprofit Sector: A Research Handbook*, ed. Walter W. Powell, 27–42. New Haven, CT: Yale University Press.

Hart, Oliver, Andrei Shleifer, and Robert W. Vishny. 1997. "The Proper Scope of Government: Theory and an Application to Prisons." *Quarterly Journal of Economics* 112(4): 1127–1161.

Hertel-Fernandez, A. 2016. "Explaining Liberal Policy Woes in the States: The Role of Donors." *PS: Political Science and Politics* 49(3): 461–465.

Hertel-Fernandez, Alex, Theda Skocpol, and Jason Sclar. 2018. "When Political Mega-Donors Join Forces: How the Koch Network and the Democracy Alliance Influence Organized U.S. Politics on the Right and Left." Working paper.

Hilt, Eric. 2017. "Corporation Law and the Shift Toward Open Access in the Antebellum United States." In *Organizations, Civil Society, and the Roots of Development*, ed. Naomi R. Lamoreaux and John J. Wallis, 147–179. Chicago: University of Chicago Press.

Hood, Christopher. 1995. "Contemporary Public Management: A New Global Paradigm?" *Public Policy and Administration* 10(2): 104–117.

Horvath, Aaron, and W. W. Powell. 2016. "Contributory or Disruptive: Do New Forms of Philanthropy Erode Democracy?" In *Philanthropy in Democratic Societies: History, Institutions, Values*, ed. Rob Reich, Chiara Cordelli, and Lucy Bernholz, 87–122. Chicago: University of Chicago Press.

Hwang, Hokyu, and Walter W. Powell. 2009. "The Rationalization of Charity: The Influences of Professionalism in the Nonprofit Sector." *Administrative Science Quarterly* 54(2): 268–298.

James, Estelle. 1987. "The Nonprofit Sector in Comparative Perspective." In *The Nonprofit Sector: A Research Handbook*, ed. Walter W. Powell, 397–415. New Haven, CT: Yale University Press.

Johnson, Paula D. 2018. *Global Philanthropy Report: Perspectives on the Global Foundation Sector.* Cambridge, MA: Harvard Kennedy School.

Karl, Barry. 1987. "Nonprofit Institutions." *Science* 236: 984–985.

Krashinsky, Michael. 1998. "Does Auspice Matter? The Case of Day Care for Children in Canada." In *Private Action and the Public Good*, ed. Walter W. Powell and Elisabeth S. Clemens, 114–123. New Haven, CT: Yale University Press.

Lamoreaux, Naomi R., and John J. Wallis, eds. 2017. *Organizations, Civil Society, and the Roots of Development.* Chicago: University of Chicago Press.

Lei, Ya-Wen. 2018. *The Contentious Public Sphere: Law, Media, and Authoritarian Rule in China.* Princeton, NJ: Princeton University Press.

Levy, Jonathan. 2016. "Altruism and the Origins of Nonprofit Philanthropy." In *Philanthropy in Democratic Societies: History, Institutions, Values*, ed. Rob Reich, Chiara Cordelli, and Lucy Bernholz, 19–43. Chicago: University of Chicago Press.

Lin, Jean. 2020. *A Spark in the Smokestacks: Environmental Organizing in Beijing Middle-Class Communities.* New York: Columbia University Press.

Longhofer, Wesley, Giacomo Negro, and Peter W. Roberts. 2018. "The Changing Effectiveness of Local Civic Action: The Critical Nexus of Community and Organization." *Administrative Science Quarterly* 63, https://doi.org/10.1177/0001839218762403.

Mauer, Elizabeth. 1998. "The Importance of Organizational Form: Parent Perceptions Versus Reality in the Day Care Industry." In *Private Action and the Public Good*, ed. Walter W. Powell and Elisabeth S. Clemens, 124–136. New Haven, CT: Yale University Press.

McFarland, Daniel, and Reuben Thomas. 2006. "Bowling Young: How Youth Voluntary Associations Influence Adult Political Participation." *American Sociological Review* 71: 401–425.

Nelson, Richard R., and Michael Krashinsky. 1973. "Public Control and Organization of Day Care for Young Children." *Public Policy* 22(1): 53–75.

Pollitt, Christopher, and Geert Bouckaert. 2011. *Public Management Reform: A Comparative Analysis—New Public Management, Governance, and the Neo-Weberian State.* Oxford, UK: Oxford University Press.

Powell, Walter W., Aaron Horvath, and Christof Brandtner. 2016. "Click and Mortar: Organizations on the Web." *Research in Organizational Behavior* 36: 101–120.

Powell, Walter W., and Jason Owen-Smith. 2012. "An Open Elite." In John F. Padgett and Walter W. Powell, *The Emergence of Organizations and Markets*, 466–495. Princeton, NJ: Princeton University Press.

Powell, Walter W., and Kurt Sandholtz. 2012. "Chance, Necessite, et Naivete: Ingredients to Create a New Organizational Form." In John F. Padgett and Walter W. Powell, *The Emergence of Organizations and Markets*, 370–433. Princeton, NJ: Princeton University Press.

Putnam, Robert D. 2000. *Bowling Alone: The Collapse and Revival of American Community.* New York: Simon and Schuster.

Putnam, Robert D., Robert Leonardi, and Raffaella Y. Nanetti. 1993. *Making Democracy Work: Civic Traditions in Modern Italy.* Princeton, NJ: Princeton University Press.

Riley, Dylan. 2010. *The Civic Foundations of Fascism in Europe: Italy, Spain, and Romania, 1870–1945.* Baltimore: Johns Hopkins University Press.

Rosenblum, Nancy L., and Robert C. Post. 2002. *Civil Society and Government.* Princeton, NJ: Princeton University Press.

Rudney, Gabriel. 1987. "The Scope and Dimensions of Non-Profit Activity." In *The Nonprofit Sector*, ed. Walter W. Powell. New Haven, CT: Yale University Press.

Salamon, Lester M. 1987. "Partners in Public Service: The Scope and Theory of Government-Nonprofit Relations." In *The Nonprofit Sector*, ed. Walter W. Powell, 99–117. New Haven, CT: Yale University Press.

———. 2012. "The Resilient Sector: The Future of Nonprofit America." In *The State of Nonprofit America*, 2nd ed., ed. Lester M. Salamon, 3–86. Washington, DC: Brookings Institution Press.

Salamon, Lester, S. Wojciech Sokolowski, Megan A. Haddock, and Helen S. Tice. 2012. *The State of Global Civil Society and Volunteering: Latest Findings from the Implementation of the UN Nonprofit Handbook.* Working Paper No. 49. Baltimore: Johns Hopkins Center for Civil Society Studies.

Sampson, Robert J., Doug McAdam, Heather MacIndoe, and Simon Weffer-Elizondo. 2005. "Civil Society Reconsidered: The Durable Nature and Community Structure of Collective Civic Action." *American Journal of Sociology* 111 (3): 673–714.

Schlesinger, Mark, and Bradford H. Gray. 2006. "Nonprofit Organizations and Health Care: Some Paradoxes of Persistent Scrutiny." In *The Nonprofit Sector: A Research Handbook*, 2nd ed., ed. Walter W. Powell and Richard Steinberg, 378–414. New Haven, CT: Yale University Press.

Scott, W. Richard, Martin Ruef, Peter Mendell, and Carol Caronna. 2000. *Institutional Change and Healthcare Organizations: From Professional Dominance to Managed Care*. Chicago: University of Chicago Press.

Simon, John G. 1987. "The Tax Treatment of Nonprofit Organizations: A Review of Federal and State Policies." In *The Nonprofit Sector*, ed. Walter W. Powell, 67–98. New Haven, CT: Yale University Press.

Skocpol, Theda. 2011. "Civil Society in the United States." In *The Oxford Handbook of Civil Society*, ed. Michael Edwards, 109–121. Oxford, UK: Oxford University Press.

———. 2003. *Diminished Democracy: From Membership to Management in American Civic Life*. Norman: University of Oklahoma Press.

———. 2016. "Why Political Scientists Should Study Organized Philanthropy." *PS: Political Science and Politics* 49(3): 433–436.

Skocpol, Theda, Marshall Ganz, and Ziad Munson. 2000. "A Nation of Organizers: The Institutional Origins of Civic Voluntarism in the United States." *American Political Science Review* 94(3): 527–546.

Snellman, Kaisa, Jennifer Silva, Carl Frederick, and Robert Putnam. 2015. "The Engagement Gap: Social Mobility and Extracurricular Participation Among American Youth." *Annals of the American Academy of Political and Social Science* 10(1): 194–207.

Spires, Anthony J. 2011. "Contingent Symbiosis and Civil Society in an Authoritarian State: Understanding the Survival of China's Grassroots NGOs." *American Journal of Sociology* 117(1): 1–45.

Starr, Paul. 1982. *The Social Transformation of American Medicine*. New York: Basic Books.

Stinchcombe, Arthur L. 1965. "Social Structure and Organizations." In *Handbook of Organizations*, ed. James G. March, 142–193. Chicago: Rand McNally.

Taylor, Verta. 1989. "Social Movement Continuity: The Women's Movement in Abeyance," *American Sociological Review* 54(5): 761–775.

Teles, Steven. 2008. *The Rise of the Conservative Legal Movement: The Battle for Control of the Law*. Princeton, NJ: Princeton University Press.

———. 2016. "Foundations, Organizational Maintenance, and Partisan Asymmetry." *PS: Political Science and Politics* 49(3): 455–460.

Tufekci, Zeynep. 2017. *Twitter and Tear Gas: The Power and Fragility of Networked Protest*. New Haven, CT: Yale University Press.

Turco, Catherine. 2012. "Difficult Decoupling: Employee Resistance to the Commercialization of Personal Settings," *American Journal of Sociology* 118(2): 380–419.

Useem, Michael. 1984. *The Inner Circle: Large Corporations and the Rise of Business Political Activity in the U.S. and U.K.* New York: Oxford University Press.

Walker, Edward T., John D. McCarthy, and Frank Baumgartner. 2011. "Replacing Members with Managers? Mutualism Among Membership and Nonmembership Advocacy Organizations in the United States." *American Journal of Sociology* 116(4): 1284–1337.

Weber, Max. 1947. *The Theory of Social and Economic Organization*, trans. A. M. Henderson and Talcott Parsons, ed. with an introduction by Talcott Parsons. Glencoe, IL: Free Press.

Weisbrod, Burton A. 1975. "Toward a Theory of the Voluntary Nonprofit Sector in a Three-Sector Economy." In *Altruism, Morality, and Economic Theory*, ed. Edmund S. Phelps, 171–195. New York: Russell Sage Foundation.

———. 1988. *The Nonprofit Economy*. Cambridge, MA: Harvard University Press.

———. 1989. "Rewarding Performance That Is Hard to Measure," *Science* 5(May): 541–545.

Weisbrod, Burton A., with S. Long. 1977. "The Size of the Voluntary Non-Profit Sector: Concepts and Measures." Research paper sponsored by the Commission on Private Philanthropy and Public Needs. Washington, DC: U.S. Government Printing Office.

Part I. Emergence, Transformation, and Regulation

Chapter 2. A History of Associational Life and the Nonprofit Sector in the United States

Abramson, A., and R. McCarthy. 2012. "Infrastructure Organizations." In *The State of Nonprofit America*, ed. L. M. Salamon, 423–458. Washington, DC: Brookings Institution Press.

Abramson, A., B. Soskis, and S. Toepler. 2014. "Public-Philanthropic Partnerships: A Review of Recent Trends." *Foundation Review* 6(2): 52–66.

Adam, T. 2002. "Transatlantic Trading: The Transfer of Philanthropic Models Between European and North American Cities During the Nineteenth and Early Twentieth Centuries." *Journal of Urban History* 28(3): 328–351.

Anderson, E., and A. Moss Jr. 1999. *Dangerous Donations: Northern Philanthropy and Southern Black Education, 1902–1930*. Columbia: University of Missouri Press.

Attie, J. 1998. *Patriotic Toil: Northern Women and the American Civil War*. Ithaca, NY: Cornell University Press.

Barman, E. 2006. *Contesting Communities: The Transformation of Workplace Charity*. Stanford, CA: Stanford University Press.

Barnett, M. 2011. *Empire of Humanity: A History of Humanitarianism*. Ithaca, NY: Cornell University Press.

Berman, L. 2015. "Donor Advised Funds in Historical Perspective." *Boston College Law School Forum on Philanthropy and the Public Good* 1: 5–27.

Bernard, J. 1998. "Original Themes of Voluntary Moralism: The Anglo-American Reformation of Manners." In *Moral Problems in American Life: New Perspectives on Cultural History*, ed. L. Halttunen and L. Perry, 15–40. Ithaca, NY: Cornell University Press.

Berry, J. M. 1997. *The Interest Group Society*, 3rd ed. New York: Longman.

Bishop, M., and M. Green. 2008. *Philanthrocapitalism: How the Rich Can Save the World*. New York: Bloomsbury Press.

Bornstein, D., and S. Davis. 2010. *Social Entrepreneurship: What Everyone Needs to Know*. New York: Oxford University Press.

Boyer, P. 1978. *Urban Masses and Moral Order in America, 1820–1920*. Cambridge, MA: Harvard University Press.

Bremner, R. 1988. *American Philanthropy*, 2nd ed. Chicago: University of Chicago Press.

Brilliant, E. 1990. *The United Way: Dilemmas of Organized Charity*. New York: Columbia University Press.

———. 2000. *Private Charity and Public Inquiry: A History of the Filer and Peterson Commissions*. Bloomington: Indiana University Press.

Brown, D., and E. McKeown. 1997. *The Poor Belong to Us: Catholic Charities and American Welfare*. Cambridge, MA: Harvard University Press.

Brown, M. 2018. "The Moralization of Commercialization: Uncovering the History of Fee-Charging in the U.S. Nonprofit Human Services Sector." *Nonprofit and Voluntary Sector Quarterly* 47(5): 960–983.

Butterfield, K. 2015. *The Making of Tocqueville's America: Law and Association in the Early United States*. Chicago: University of Chicago Press.

Cabanes, B. 2014. *The Great War and the Origins of Humanitarianism, 1918–1924*. New York: Cambridge University Press.

Callahan, D. 2017. *The Givers: Wealth, Power, and Philanthropy in a New Gilded Age*. New York: Knopf.

Camarillo, A. 1991 "Mexican-Americans and Nonprofit Organizations: An Historical Overview." In *Hispanics and the Nonprofit Sector*, ed. H. Gallegos and M. O'Neill, 15–32. New York: Foundation Center.

Carnegie, A. 2006. "The Gospel of Wealth and The Best Fields for Philanthropy." In *The "Gospel of Wealth" Essays and Other Writings*, ed. D. Nasaw, 1–30. New York: Penguin.

Carson, E. 1999. "The Roles of Indigenous and Institutional Philanthropy in Advancing Social Justice." In *Philanthropy and the Nonprofit Sector in a Changing America*, ed. C. Clotfelter and T. Ehrlich, 248–274. Bloomington: Indiana University Press.

Casey, J. 2016. *The Nonprofit World: Civil Society and the Rise of the Nonprofit Sector*. Boulder, CO: Kumarian Press.

Chafe, W. 1991. *The Paradox of Change: American Women in the Twentieth Century*. New York: Oxford University Press.

Chaves, M. 2003. "Debunking Charitable Choice." *Stanford Social Service Review* 1(2): 28–36.

Clemens, E. 2010. "In the Shadow of the New Deal: Reconfiguring the Roles of Government and Charity, 1928–1940." In *Politics and Partnerships: The Role of Voluntary Associations in America's Political Past and Present*, ed. E. Clemens and D. Guthrie, 79–115. Chicago: University of Chicago Press.

Colinvaux, R. 2017. "Nonprofits and Advocacy." In *Nonprofits and Government: Collaboration and Conflict*, 3rd ed., ed. E. Boris and C. E. Steuerle, 191–215. Lanham, MD: Rowman and Littlefield.

Collier-Thomas, B. 2010. *Jesus, Jobs, and Justice: African American Women and Religion*. New York: Knopf.

Coquillette, D., and B. Kimball. 2015. *On the Battlefield of Merit: Harvard Law School, the First Century*. Cambridge, MA: Harvard University Press.

Cortés, M. 1998. "Counting Latino Nonprofits: A New Strategy for Finding Data." *Nonprofit and Voluntary Sector Quarterly* 27(4): 437–458.

Cott, N. 1977. *The Bonds of Womanhood: "Woman's Sphere" in New England, 1780–1835*. New Haven, CT: Yale University Press.

Covington, S. 1997. *Moving a Public Policy Agenda: The Strategic Philanthropy of Conservative Foundations*. Washington, DC: National Committee for Responsive Philanthropy.

Crocker, R. 2006. *Mrs. Russell Sage: Women's Activism and Philanthropy in Gilded Age and Progressive Era America*. Bloomington: Indiana University Press.

Curti, M. 1961. "Tradition and Innovation in American Philanthropy." *Proceedings of the American Philosophical Society* 105(2): 146–156.

Cutlip, S. 1965. *Fund Raising in the United States: Its Role in America's Philanthropy*. New Brunswick, NJ: Rutgers University Press.

Dalzell, R. F. Jr. 2013. *The Good Rich and What They Cost Us*. New Haven, CT: Yale University Press.

Dawson, H. 1998. "'Christian Charitie' as Colonial Discourse: Rereading Winthrop's Sermon in Its English Context." *Early American Literature* 33(2): 117–148.

Diaz, W. 1999. "Philanthropy and the Case of the Latino Communities in America." In *Philanthropy and the Nonprofit Sector in a Changing America*, ed. C. Clotfelter and T. Ehrlich, 275–292. Bloomington: Indiana University Press.

Dietz, N., and R. Grimm Jr. 2016. "Doing Good by the Young and Old: Forty Years of American Volunteering." *Nonprofit Quarterly* 23(3): 42–49.

Dighe, A. 2012. "Demographic and Technological Imperatives." In *The State of Nonprofit America*, ed. L. M. Salamon, 616–638. Washington, DC: Brookings Institution Press.

Diner, H. 1992. *A Time for Gathering: The Second Migration, 1820–1880*. Baltimore: Johns Hopkins University Press.

Dobson, S. 2014. *Freedom Funders: Philanthropy and the Civil Rights Movement, 1955–1965*. Washington, DC: National Committee for Responsive Philanthropy.

Dolan, J. 1985. *The American Catholic Experience: A History from Colonial Times to the Present*. Garden City, NY: Doubleday.

Fea, J. 2016. *The Bible Cause: A History of the American Bible Society*. New York: Oxford University Press.

Ferguson, K. 2013. *Top Down: The Ford Foundation, Black Power, and the Reinvention of Racial Liberalism*. Philadelphia: University of Pennsylvania Press.

Ferris, J., and E. Graddy. 1989. "Fading Distinctions Among the Nonprofit, Government, and For-Profit Sectors." In *The Future of the Nonprofit Sector: Challenges, Changes, and Policy Considerations*, ed. V. Hodgkinson, 123–139. San Francisco: Jossey-Bass.

Finkenbine, R. 2003. "Law, Reconstruction, and African American Education in the Post-Emancipation South." In *Charity, Philanthropy, and Civility in American History*, ed. L. Friedman and M. McGarvie, 161–178. New York: Cambridge University Press.

Fitzgerald, M. 2006. *Habits of Compassion: Irish Catholic Nuns and the Origins of New York's Welfare System, 1830–1920*. Urbana: University of Illinois Press.

Foner, E. 1988. *Reconstruction: America's Unfinished Revolution, 1863–1877.* New York: Harper and Row.

Fosdick, R. 1952. *The Story of the Rockefeller Foundation.* New York: Harper and Row.

Frank, N. 2017. *Awakening: How Gays and Lesbians Brought Marriage Equality to America.* Cambridge, MA: Harvard University Press.

Fremont-Smith, M. 2004. *Governing Nonprofit Organizations: Federal and State Law Regulation.* Cambridge, MA: Belknap Press.

Frumkin, P. 1998. "The Long Recoil from Regulation: Private Philanthropic Foundations and the Tax Reform Act of 1969." *American Review of Public Administration* 28(3): 266–286.

———. 1999. "Private Foundations as Public Institutions: Regulation, Professionalization, and the Redefinition of Organized Philanthropy." In *Philanthropic Foundations: New Scholarship, New Possibilities*, ed. E. Lagemann, 69–98. Bloomington: Indiana University Press.

Furner, M. 1975. *Advocacy and Objectivity: A Crisis in the Professionalziation of American Social Science, 1865–1905.* Lexington: University Press of Kentucky.

Gamm, G., and R. Putnam. 1999. "The Growth of Voluntary Associations in America, 1840–1940." *Journal of Interdisciplinary History* 29(4): 511–557.

Geiger, R. 1993. *Research and Relevant Knowledge: American Research Universities Since World War II.* New York: Oxford University Press.

Ginzberg, L. 1990. *Women and the Work of Benevolence: Morality, Politics, and Class in the Nineteenth-Century United States.* New Haven, CT: Yale University Press.

Goen, C. C. 1985. *Broken Churches, Broken Nation: Denominational Schisms and the Coming of the American Civil War.* Macon, GA: Mercer University Press.

Gordon, L. 2017. *The Second Coming of the KKK: the Ku Klux Klan of the 1920s and the American Political Tradition.* New York: Norton.

Goss, K. A. 2016. Policy Plutocrats: How America's Wealthy Seek to Influence Governance. *PS: Political Science and Politics* 49(3): 442–448.

Green, E. 2003. *This Business of Relief: Confronting Poverty in a Southern City, 1740–1940.* Athens: University of Georgia Press.

Gross, R. 2003. "Giving in America: From Charity to Philanthropy." In *Charity, Philanthropy, and Civility in American History*, L. Friedman and M. McGarvie, 29–48. New York: Cambridge University Press.

Hall, P. D. 1992. *Inventing the Nonprofit Sector and Other Essays on Philanthropy, Voluntarism, and Nonprofit Organizations.* Baltimore: Johns Hopkins University Press.

———. 2003. "Philanthropy, the Welfare State, and the Careers of Public and Private Institutions Since 1945." In *Charity, Philanthropy, and Civility in American History*, ed. L. Friedman and M. McGarvie, 363–383. New York: Cambridge University Press.

———. 2004. "A Historical Perspective on Evaluation in Foundations." In *Foundations and Evaluation: Contexts and Practices for Effective Philanthropy*, ed. M. Braverman, N. Constantine, and J. Slater, 27–50. San Francisco: Jossey-Bass.

———. 2006. "A Historical Overview of Philanthropy, Voluntary Associations, and Nonprofit Organizations in the United States, 1600–2000." In *The Nonprofit Sector: A Research Handbook*, 2nd ed., ed. W. W. Powell and R. Steinberg, 32–65. New Haven, CT: Yale University Press.

Hammack, D., ed. 1998. *Making the Nonprofit Sector in the United States: A Reader.* Bloomington: Indiana University Press.

———. 1999. "Foundations in the American Polity, 1900–1950." In *Philanthropic Foundations: New Scholarship, New Possibilities*, ed. E. Lagemann, 43–68. Bloomington: Indiana University Press.

Hammack, D., and H. Anheier. 2013. *A Versatile American Institution: The Changing Ideals and Realities of Philanthropy Foundations.* Washington, DC: Brookings Institution Press.

Harmon, E. 2017. "The Transformation of American Philanthropy: From Public Trust to Private Foundation, 1785–1917." Doctoral diss., University of Michigan.

Haskell, T. 1985. "Capitalism and the Origins of the Humanitarian Sensibility, Part 1." *American Historical Review* 90(2): 339–361.

Hawley, E. 1974. "Herbert Hoover, the Commerce Secretariat, and the Vision of an 'Associative State,' 1921–1928." *Journal of American History* 61(1): 116–140.

———. 1998. "Herbert Hoover, Associationalism, and the Great Depression Crisis of 1930–1933." In *With Us Always: A History of Private Charity and Public Welfare*, ed. D. Critchlow and C. Parker, 161–190. Lanham, MD: Rowman and Littlefield.

Heimans, J., and H. Timms. 2018. *New Power: How Power Works in Our Hyperconnected World—and How to Make It Work for You*. New York: Doubleday.

Hertel-Fernandez, A., and T. Skocpol. 2016. "Why the States Turned Right." *Democracy: A Journal of Ideas* 39: 46–59.

Heyrman, C. 1977. "A Model of Christian Charity: The Rich and Poor in New England, 1630–1730." Doctoral diss., Yale University.

Hofstadter, R., and W. Metzger. 1955. *The Development of Academic Freedom in the United States*. New York: Columbia University Press.

Huyssen, D. 2014. *Progressive Inequality: Rich and Poor in New York, 1890–1920*. Cambridge, MA: Harvard University Press.

Iriye, A. 1999. "A Century of NGOs." *Diplomatic History* 23(3): 421–435.

———. 2009. "Nongovernmental Organizations and the Making of the International Community." In *Globalization, Philanthropy, and Civil Society: Projecting Institutional Logics Abroad*, ed. D. Hammack and S. Heydemann, 32–43. Bloomington: Indiana University Press.

Irwin, J. 2013. *Making the World Safe: The American Red Cross and a Nation's Humanitarian Awakening*. New York: Oxford University Press.

Jenkins, C. 1998. "Channeling Social Protest: Foundation Patronage of Contemporary Social Movements." In *Private Actions and the Public Good*, ed. W. Powell and E. Clemens, 206–216. New Haven, CT: Yale University Press.

John, R. 1990. "Taking Sabbatarianism Seriously: The Postal System, the Sabbath, and the Transformation of American Political Culture." *Journal of the Early Republic* 10(4): 517–567.

Jones, M. M. 2013. *The American Red Cross from Clara Barton to the New Deal*. Baltimore: Johns Hopkins University Press.

Karl, B. D. and S. N. Katz. 1981. "The American Private Philanthropic Foundation and the Public Sphere 1890–1930." *Minerva* 19(2): 236–270.

———. 1987. "Foundations and Ruling Class Elites." *Daedalus* 116(1): 1–40.

Katz, B., and J. Nowak. 2017. *The New Localism: How Cities Can Thrive in the Age of Populism*. Washington, DC: Brookings Institution Press.

Kauffman, L. A. 2017. *Direct Action: Protest and the Reinvention of American Radicalism*. New York: Verso.

Kaufman, J. 2002. *For the Common Good? American Civic Life and the Golden Age of Fraternity*. New York: Oxford University Press.

Kirsch, R. 2011. *Fighting for Our Health: The Epic Battle to Make Health Care a Right in the United States*. Albany, NY: Rockefeller Institute Press.

Kimball, B. 2014. "The First Campaign and the Paradoxical Transformation of Fundraising in American Higher Education, 1915–1925." *Teachers College Record* 116(7): 1–44.

———. 2015. "'Democratizing' Fundraising at Elite Universities: The Discursive Legitimation of Mass Giving at Yale and Harvard, 1890–1920." *History of Education Quarterly* 55(2): 164–189.

Kloppenberg, J. 1998. "Life Everlasting: Tocqueville in America." In *The Virtues of Liberalism*, 71–81. New York: Oxford University Press.

Knauer, N. 1994. "The Paradox of Corporate Giving: Tax Expenditures, the Nature of the Corporation, and the Social Construction of Charity." *DePaul Law Review* 44(1): 1–97.

Kohl-Arenas, E. 2016. *The Self-Help Myth: How Philanthropy Fails to Alleviate Poverty*. Oakland: University of California Press.

Lagemann, E. C. 1983. *Private Power for the Public Good: A History of the Carnegie Foundation for the Advancement of Teaching*. Middletown, CT: Wesleyan University Press.

———. 1989. *The Politics of Knowledge: The Carnegie Corporation, Philanthropy, and Public Policy*. Middletown, CT: Wesleyan University Press.

Lankford, J. 1964. *Congress and the Foundations in the Twentieth Century*. River Falls: Wisconsin State University Press.

Laurie, B. 1989. *Artisans into Workers: Labor in Nineteenth-Century America*. New York: Hill and Wang.

Lawson, M. 2002. *Patriot Fires: Forging a New American Nationalism in the Civil War North*. Lawrence: University Press of Kansas.

Lemos, M., and G. Charles. 2018. "Patriotic Philanthropy? Financing the State with Gifts to Government." *California Law Review* 106: 1129–1193.

Levy, J. 2016. "Altruism and the Origins of Nonprofit Philanthropy." In *Philanthropy in Democratic Societies: History, Institutions, Values*, ed. R. Reich, C. Cordelli, and L. Bernholz, 19–43. Chicago: University of Chicago Press.

———. 2017. "From Fiscal Triangle to Passing Through: Rise of the Nonprofit Corporation." In *Corporations and American Democracy*, ed. N. Lamoreaux and W. Novak, 213–244. Cambridge, MA: Harvard University Press.

Lubove, R. 1965. *The Professional Altruist: The Emergence of Social Work as a Career, 1880–1930*. Cambridge, MA: Harvard University Press.

Lyman, R. 1989. "Reagan Among the Corinthians." *Nonprofit and Voluntary Sector Quarterly* 18(3): 203–210.

Marsden, G. 1994. *The Soul of the American University: From Protestant Establishment to Established Nonbelief*. New York: Oxford University Press.

Martin, W. 1996. *With God on Our Side: The Rise of the Religious Right in America*. New York: Broadway Books.

May, H. 1949. *Protestant Churches and Industrial America*. New York: Harper.

Mayer, J. 2016. *Dark Money: The Hidden History of the Billionaires Behind the Rise of the Radical Right*. New York: Doubleday.

McCarthy, K. 2003. *American Creed: Philanthropy and the Rise of Civil Society, 1700–1865*. Chicago: University of Chicago Press.

McGarvie, M. D. 2003. "The *Dartmouth College* Case and the Legal Design of Civil Society." In *Charity, Philanthropy, and Civility in American History*, ed. L. Friedman and M. McGarvie, 91–105. New York: Cambridge University Press.

McGirr, L. 2001. *Suburban Warriors: The Origins of the New American Right*. Princeton, NJ: Princeton University Press.

McKeever, B., N. Dietz, and S. Fyffe. 2016. *The Nonprofit Almanac 2016*. Lanham, MD: Rowman and Littlefield.

Mirabella, R., and N. Wish. 2001. "University-Based Education Programs in the Management of Nonprofit Organizations: An Updated Census of

U.S. Programs." *Public Performance and Management Review* 25(1): 30–41.

Moniz, A. 2016. *From Empire to Humanity: The American Revolution and the Origins of Humanitarianism*. New York: Oxford University Press.

Morgan, E. 2002. *Benjamin Franklin*. New Haven, CT: Yale University Press.

Morris, A. 2009. *The Limits of Voluntarism: Charity and Welfare from the New Deal Through the Great Society*. New York: Cambridge University Press.

Nasaw, D. 2006. *Andrew Carnegie*. New York: Penguin.

Nash, G. 1988. *The Life of Herbert Hoover: The Humanitarian 1914–1917*. New York: Norton.

———. Smith, B., ed. 2004. "Poverty and Politics in Early American History." In *Down and Out in Early America*, ed. B. Smith, 1–38. University Park: Pennsylvania State University Press.

Neem, J. 2008. *Creating a Nation of Joiners: Democracy and Civil Society in Early National Massachusetts*. Cambridge, MA: Harvard University Press.

Nielsen, W. A. 1972. *The Big Foundations*. New York: Columbia University Press.

———. 1985. *The Golden Donors: A New Anatomy of the Great Foundations*. New York: Dutton.

Oates, M. 1995. *The Catholic Philanthropic Tradition in America*. Bloomington: Indiana University Press.

O'Connor, A. 1996. "Community Action, Urban Reform, and the Fight Against Poverty: The Ford Foundation's Gray Areas Program." *Journal of Urban History* 22(5): 586–625.

———. 1999. "The Ford Foundation and Philanthropic Activism in the 1960s." In *Philanthropic Foundations: New Scholarship, New Possibilities*, ed. E. Lagemann, 169–194. Bloomington: Indiana University Press.

———. 2008. "Financing the Counterrevolution." In *Rightward Bound, Making American Conservative in the 1970s*, ed. B. Schulman and J. Zelizer, 148–168. Cambridge, MA: Harvard University Press.

———. 2010. "Foundations, Social Movements, and the Contradictions of Liberal Philanthropy." In *American Foundations: Roles and Contributions*, ed. H. Anheier and D. Hammack, 328–346. Washington, DC: Brookings Institution Press.

O'Neill, M. 1989. *The Third America: The Emergence of the Nonprofit Sector in the United States*. San Francisco: Jossey-Bass.

Putnam, R. D. 2000. *Bowling Alone: The Collapse and Revival of American Community*. New York: Simon and Schuster.

Reckhow, S., and M. Tompkins-Stange. 2015. "Singing from the Same Hymnbook at Gates and Broad." In *The New Education Philanthropy: Politics, Policy, and Reform*, ed. F. Hess and J. Henig, 55–77. Cambridge, MA: Harvard Education Press.

Reich, R. 2018. *Just Giving: Why Philanthropy Is Failing Democracy and How It Can Do Better*. Princeton, NJ: Princeton University Press.

Rodgers, D. T. 1998. *Atlantic Crossings: Social Politics in a Progressive Age*. Cambridge, MA: Belknap Press.

Rosner, D. 1987. *A Once Charitable Enterprise: Hospitals and Health Care in Brooklyn and New York, 1885–1915*. Princeton, NJ: Princeton University Press.

Rothman, D. 1971. *The Discovery of the Asylum: Social Order and Disorder in the New Republic*. Boston: Little, Brown.

Ruswick, B. 2013. *Almost Worthy: The Poor, Paupers, and the Science of Charity in America, 1877–1917*. Bloomington: Indiana University Press.

Salamon, L. 1987. "Of Market Failure, Voluntary Failure, and Third-Party Government: Toward a Theory of Government-Nonprofit Relations in the Modern Welfare State." *Nonprofit and Voluntary Sector Quarterly* 16(1): 29–49.

———. 1989. "The Changing Partnership Between the Voluntary Sector and the Welfare State." In *The Future of the Nonprofit Sector: Challenges, Changes, and Policy Considerations*, ed. V. Hodgkinson, 41–60. San Francisco: Jossey-Bass.

———. 1994. "The Rise of the Nonprofit Sector." *Foreign Affairs* 73(4): 109–122.

———. 1995. *Partners in Public Service: Government-Nonprofit Relations in the Modern Welfare State*. Baltimore: Johns Hopkins University Press.

———. 2012a. "The Resilient Sector: The Future of Nonprofit America." In *The State of Nonprofit America*, ed. L. M. Salamon, 3–86. Washington, DC: Brookings Institution Press.

———. 2012b. *America's Nonprofit Sector: A Primer*, 3rd ed. New York: Foundation Center.

Schaffer, R. 1991. *America in the Great War: The Rise of the War Welfare State*. New York: Oxford University Press.

Sealander, J. 1997. *Private Wealth and Public Life: Foundation Philanthropy and the Reshaping of American Social Policy from the Progressive Era to the New Deal*. Baltimore: Johns Hopkins University Press.

Sinha, M. 2016. *The Slave's Cause: A History of Abolition*. New Haven, CT: Yale University Press.

Skocpol, T. 1997. "The Tocqueville Problem: Civic Engagement in American Demcracy." *Social Science History* 21(4): 455–479.

———. 2003. *Diminished Democracy: From Membership to Management in American Civil Life*. Norman: University of Oklahoma Press.

Smith, D. 1993. "The Field of Nonprofit and Voluntary Action Research: Then and Now." *Nonprofit and Voluntary Sector Quarterly* 22(3): 197–200.

Smith, J. 1991. *The Idea Brokers: Think Tanks and the Rise of the New Policy Elite*. New York: Free Press.

Smith, S. 2017. "The Future of Nonprofit Human Services." *Nonprofit Policy Forum* 8(4): 369–389.

Soskis, B. 2010. "The Problem of Charity in Industrial America, 1873–1915." Doctoral diss., Columbia University.

Soskis B., and S. Katz. 2016. *Looking Back at 50 Years of U.S. Philanthropy*. Menlo Park, CA: William and Flora Hewlett Foundation.

Sullivan, B., S. Katz, and P. Beach. 1985. "Legal Change and Legal Autonomy: Charitable Trusts in New York, 1777–1893." *Law and History* 3(1): 51–89.

Teles, S. 2008. *The Rise of the Conservative Legal Movement: The Battle for Control of the Law*. Princeton, NJ: Princeton University Press.

Thelin, J. 2011. *A History of Higher Education*, 2nd ed. Baltimore: Johns Hopkins University Press.

Thelin, J., and R. Trollinger. 2014. *Philanthropy and American Higher Education*. New York: Palgrave Macmillan.

Thomas, J. 1983. *Alternative America: Henry George, Edward Bellamy, Henry Demarest Lloyd and the Adversary Tradition.* Cambridge, MA: Belknap Press.

Troyer, T. 2000. "The 1969 Private Foundation Law: Historical Perspectives on its Origins and Underpinnings." *Exempt Organization Tax Review* 27(1): 52–65.

Tufekci, Z. 2017. *Twitter and Tear Gas: The Power and Fragility of Networked Protest.* New Haven, CT: Yale University Press.

Wall, J. 1970. *Andrew Carnegie.* New York: Oxford University Press.

Walters, R. 1976. *The Antislavery Appeal: American Abolitionism After 1830.* Baltimore: Johns Hopkins University Press.

Winston, D. 1999. *Red-Hot and Righteous: The Urban Religion of the Salvation Army.* Cambridge, MA: Harvard University Press.

Wright, C. 1992. *The Transformation of Charity in Postrevolutionary New England.* Boston: Northeastern University Press.

Wyllie, I. 1959. "The Search for an American Law of Charities, 1776–1844." *Mississippi Valley Historical Review* 46(2): 203–221.

Young, D., and J. Casey. 2017. "Supplementary, Complementary, or Adversarial? Nonprofit-Government Relations." In *Nonprofits and Government: Collaboration and Conflict*, 3rd ed., ed. E. Boris and C. E. Steuerle, 37–70. Lanham, MD: Rowman and Littlefield.

Young, D., L. Salamon, and M. C. Grinsfelder. 2012. "Commercialization, Social Ventures, and For-Profit Competition." In *The State of Nonprofit America*, ed. L. M. Salamon, 521–548. Washington, DC: Brookings Institution Press.

Zunz, O. 2012. *Philanthropy in America: A History.* Princeton, NJ: Princeton University Press.

Chapter 3. Seeing Like a Philanthropist: From the Business of Benevolence to the Benevolence of Business

Allen, W. H. 1912. *Modern Philanthropy: A Study of Efficient Appealing and Giving.* New York: Dodd, Mead.

Ayres, L. P. 1911. *Second Great Foundations.* New York: Russell Sage Foundation.

Barman, E. 2013. "Classificatory Struggles in the Nonprofit Sector: The Formation of the National Taxonomy of Exempt Entities, 1969–1987." *Social Science History* 37(1): 103–141.

Becker, D. G. 1961. "The Visitor to the New York City Poor, 1843–1920." *Social Service Review* 35(4): 382–396.

Bloch, R. H., and N. R. Lamoreaux. 2017. "Voluntary Associations, Corporate Rights, and the State: Legal Constraints on Development of American Civil Society, 1750–1900." In *Organizations, Civil Society, and the Roots of Development*, ed. Naomi R. Lamoreaux and John J. Wallis, 231–270. Chicago: University of Chicago Press.

Bremner, R. H. 1988. *American Philanthropy.* Chicago: University of Chicago Press.

Bulmer, M., and J. Bulmer 1981. "Philanthropy and Social Science in the 1920s: Beardsley Ruml and the Laura Spelman Rockefeller Memorial, 1922–29." *Minerva* 19(3): 347–407.

Burlingame, D. 2004. *Philanthropy in America: A Comprehensive Historical Encyclopedia, Volume 1.* Santa Barbara, CA: ABC-Clio.

Callahan, D. 2017. *The Givers: Wealth, Power, and Philanthropy in a New Gilded Age.* New York: Knopf.

Carnegie, A. 1889a. "The Best Fields for Philanthropy." *North American Review* 149(397): 682–698.

———. 1889b. "Wealth." *North American Review* 148(391): 653–664.

Chernow, R. 1988. *Titan: The Life of John D. Rockefeller, Sr.* New York: Vintage Books.

Chu, J., and Davis, G. F. 2016. "Who Killed the Inner Circle? The Decline of the American Corporate Interlock Network." *American Journal of Sociology* 122: 714–754.

Clement, P. F. 1985. *Welfare and the Poor in the Nineteenth-Century City: Philadelphia 1800–1854.* Teaneck, NJ: Fairleigh Dickinson University Press.

Coase, R. H. 1993. "Law and Economics at Chicago." *Journal of Law and Economics* 36(1): 239–254.

Commission on Private Philanthropy and Public Needs. 1975. *Giving in America: Toward a Stronger Voluntary Sector.* Washington, DC: Report of the Commission on Private Philanthropy and Public Needs.

Crocker, R. 2006. *Mrs. Russell Sage: Women's Activism and Philanthropy in Gilded Age and Progressive Era America.* Bloomington: Indiana University Press.

Dalzell, R. F. Jr. 2013. *The Good Rich and What They Cost Us.* New Haven, CT: Yale University Press.

Davis, G. F. 2009. *Managed by the Markets.* New York: Oxford University Press.

———. 2016. *The Vanishing American Corporation.* Oakland, CA: Berrett-Koehler.

Dodd, N. 1954. *The Dodd Report to the Reese Committee on Foundations.* New York: Long House.

Edwards, L. 1999. *The Conservative Revolution: The Movement That Remade America.* New York: Free Press.

Embree, E. 1930. "The Business of Giving Away Money: The Problem Facing the American Foundations." *Harper's Monthly Magazine* (August): 320–329.

———. 1936. *Julius Rosenwald Fund: The Review of Two Decades, 1917–1936.* Chicago: Julius Rosenwald Fund.

Ford Foundation. 1965. *Annual Report.* New York: Ford Foundation.

———. 1967. *Annual Report.* New York: Ford Foundation.

Fosdick, R. B. 1952. *The Story of the Rockefeller Foundation.* New York: Harper and Brothers.

Fourcade, M., and K. Healy. 2017. "Seeing Like a Market." *Socio-Economic Review* 15(1): 9–29.

Francis, M. M. 2019. "The Price of Civil Rights: Black Lives, White Funding, and Movement Capture." *Law and Society Review* 53(1): 275–309.

Frederickson, G. M. 1965. *The Inner Civil War: Northern Intellectuals and the Crisis of the Union.* Champaign-Urbana: University of Illinois Press.

Frumkin, P. 1998. "The Long Recoil from Regulation: Private Philanthropic Foundations and the Tax Reform Act of 1969." *American Review of Public Administration* 28(3): 266–286.

Gates, F. 1977. *Chapters in My Life.* New York: Free Press.

Geisberg, J. A. 2000. *Civil War Sisterhood: The U.S. Sanitary Commission and Women's Politics in Transition.* Boston: Northeastern University Press.

Giridharadas, A. 2018. *Winners Take All: The Elite Charade of Changing the World.* New York: Penguin Random House.

Gladden, W. 1887. *Applied Christianity: Moral Aspects of Social Questions.* New York: Houghton Mifflin.

Goff, F. H. 1921. *The Dead Hand.* Cleveland, OH: Cleveland Trust.

Goss, K. A. 2016. "Policy Plutocrats: How America's Wealthy Seek to Influence Governance." *PS: Political Science and Politics* 49(3): 442–448.

Greenwald, M. W., and M. Anderson. 1996. *Pittsburgh Surveyed: Social Science and Reform in the Early 20th Century.* Pittsburgh, PA: University of Pittsburgh Press.

Gurteen, S. H. 1882. *A Handbook of Charity Organization.* Buffalo, NY: Author.

Hacker, J. 2006. *The Great Risk Shift: The New Economic Insecurity and the Decline of the American Dream.* New York: Oxford University Press.

Hall, P. D. 1992. *Inventing the Nonprofit Sector and Other Essays on Philanthropy, Voluntarism, and Nonprofit Organizations.* Baltimore: Johns Hopkins University Press.

Heald, H. 1965. "To Secure the Blessings . . ." *Ford Foundation Annual Report, 1965.* New York: Ford Foundation.

Hertel-Fernandez, A., and T. Skocpol. 2016. "Explaining Liberal Policy Woes in the States: The Role of Donors." *PS: Political Science and Politics* 49(3): 461–465.

Hilt, E. 2017. "Corporation Law and the Shift Toward Open Access in the Antebellum United States." In *Organizations, Civil Society, and the Roots of Development,* ed. N. R. Lamoreaux and J. J. Wallis, 147–179. Chicago: University of Chicago Press.

Hirschman, A. 1977. *The Passions and the Interests.* Princeton, NJ: Princeton University Press.

Horvath, A., and W. W. Powell. 2016. "Contributory or Disruptive: Do New Forms of Philanthropy Erode Democracy?" In *Philanthropy in Democratic Societies: History, Institutions, Values,* ed. R. Reich, C. Cordelli, and L. Bernholz., 87–122. Chicago: University of Chicago Press.

Hounshell, D. 1984. *From the American System to Mass Production, 1800–1932.* Baltimore: Johns Hopkins University Press.

Huggins, N. I. 1971. *Protestants Against Poverty: Boston's Charities, 1870–1900*. Westport, CT: Greenwood.

Isaacson, W. 2011. *Steve Jobs*. New York: Simon and Schuster.

Johnson, V., and W. W. Powell. 2017. "Organizational Poisedness and the Transformation of Civic Order in Nineteenth-Century New York City." In *Organizations, Civil Society and the Roots of Development*, ed. N. R. Lamoreaux and J. J. Wallis, 179–230. Chicago: University of Chicago Press.

Karl, B. D., and S. N. Katz 1981. "The American Private Philanthropic Foundation and the Public Sphere 1890–1930." *Minerva* 19(2): 236–270.

———. 1987. "Foundations and Ruling Class Elites." *Daedalus* 116(1): 1–40.

Katz, S. N., B. Sullivan, and C. P. Beach. 1985. "Legal Change and Legal Autonomy: Charitable Trusts in New York, 1777–1893." *Law and History Review* 3(1): 51–89.

Kauffman, S. 2000. *Investigations*. New York: Oxford University Press.

Keppel, F. P. 1930. *The Foundation: Its Place in American Life*. New York: Macmillan.

———. 1944. "Foreword." In *An American Dilemma: The Negro Problem and Modern Democracy*, ed. G. Myrdal, v–viii. New York: Harper and Brothers.

Laski, H. J. 1930. *The Dangers of Obedience and Other Essays*. New York: Harper and Brothers.

Levy, J. 2016. "Altruism and the Origins of Nonprofit Philanthropy." In *Philanthropy in Democratic Societies: History, Institutions, Values*, ed. R. Reich, C. Cordelli, and L. Bernholz. Chicago: University of Chicago Press.

Macdonald, D. 1956. *The Ford Foundation: The Men and the Millions*. New York: Reynal.

Madoff, R. 2016. "When Is Philanthropy? How the Tax Code's Answer to This Question Has Given Rise to the Growth of Donor-Advised Funds and Why It's a Problem." In *Philanthropy in Democratic Societies: History, Institutions, Values*, ed. R. Reich, C. Cordelli, and L. Bernholz. Chicago: University of Chicago Press.

Mannheim, K. (1936) 1997. *Ideology and Utopia*. London: Routledge.

McVicar, M. J. 2011. "Aggressive Philanthropy: Progressivisms, Conservatism, and the William Volker Charities Fund." *Missouri Historical Review* 105(4): 191–212.

Meyer, J. 2010. "Covert Operations: The Billionaire Brothers Who Are Waging a War Against Obama." *New Yorker*, August 30.

Milbank Memorial Fund. 1923. "Progress of Demonstration Units." *Milbank Memorial Fund Quarterly Bulletin* 1(1): 2–9.

Mizruchi, M. S. 2013. *The Fracturing of the American Corporate Elite*. Cambridge, MA: Harvard University Press.

Mueller-Gastell, K. 2019. "The Value of Measurability: Evaluating Charitable Organizations." Working paper, Stanford University.

Muir, A. F. 1972. *William Marsh Rice and His Institute*. Houston, TX: Rice University.

Murray, C. 1984. *Losing Ground: American Social Policy 1950–1980*. New York: Basic Books.

Nasaw, D. 2006. *Andrew Carnegie*. New York: Penguin.

Nielsen, W. A. 1972. *The Big Foundations*. New York: Columbia University Press.

O'Connor, A. 2007. *Social Science for What?* New York: Russell Sage Foundation.

———. 2010. "Bringing the Market Back In: Philanthropic Activism and Conservative Reform." In *Politics and Partnerships: The Role of Voluntary Associations in America's Political Past and Present*, ed. E. S. Clemens and D. Guthrie, 121–150. Chicago: University of Chicago Press.

Padgett, J., and W. W. Powell. 2012. "The Problem of Emergence." In *The Emergence of Organizations and Markets*, ed. J. Padgett and W. W. Powell. Princeton, NJ: Princeton University Press.

Patman, W. 1961. *Congressional Record*, 107(73).

Pierce, F. 1854. "Veto Message." UCSB American Presidency Project.

Pifer, A. 1982. *Annual Report Essays: 1966–1982*. New York: Carnegie Corporation.

Piketty, T. 2014. *Capital in the 21st Century*. Cambridge, MA: Harvard University Press.

Powell, W. W. 2001. "The Capitalist Firm in the 21st Century: Emerging Patterns in Western Enterprise." In *The Twenty-First Century Firm: Changing Economic Organization in International Perspective*, ed. Paul DiMaggio, 33–68. Princeton, NJ: Princeton University Press.

Preston, W. C. 1836. "Smithson Legacy." *Gales & Seaton's Register of Debates in Congress* 12(65): 1374–1375.

Pringle, H. F. 1939. *The Life and Times of William Howard Taft.* New York: Farrar and Rinehart.

Ravitch, D. 2010. *The Death and Life of the Great American School System: How Testing and Choice Are Undermining Education.* New York: Basic Books.

Reckhow, S. 2012. *Follow the Money: How Foundation Dollars Change Public School Politics.* Oxford, UK: Oxford University Press.

———. 2016. "More Than Patrons: How Foundations Fuel Policy Change and Backlash." *PS: Political Science and Politics* 49(3): 449–454.

Reckhow, S., and M. Tompkins-Stange. 2015. "Singing from the Same Hymnbook at Gates and Broad." In *The New Education Philanthropy: Politics, Policy, and Reform*, ed. F. Hess and J. Henig, 55–77. Cambridge, MA: Harvard Education Press.

Reich, R. 2018. *Just Giving: Why Philanthropy Is Failing Democracy and How It Can Do Better.* Princeton, NJ: Princeton University Press.

Ris, E. W. 2017. "The Education of Andrew Carnegie: Strategic Philanthropy in American Higher Education, 1880–1919." *Journal of Higher Education* 88(3): 401–429.

Rockefeller, J. D. Sr. 1909. *Random Reminiscences of Men and Events.* New York: Doubleday, Page.

Root, E. 1919. "The Need for Organization in Scientific Research." *Bulletin of the National Research Council*, 1.

Rosenwald, J. 1929. "Principles of Public Giving." *Atlantic Monthly* 143: 599–606.

Russakoff, D. 2015. *The Prize: Who's in Charge of America's Schools?* New York: Houghton Mifflin.

Saez, E., and Zucman, G. 2016. "Wealth Inequality in the United States Since 1913: Evidence from Capitalized Income Tax Data." *Quarterly Journal of Economics* 131(2): 519–578.

Sage, M. O. 1905. "Opportunities and Responsibilities of Leisured Women." *North American Review* 181(588): 712–721.

Salamon, L. 2014. *New Frontiers of Philanthropy.* New York: Oxford University Press.

Sandholtz, K., and W. W. Powell. 2019 "Amphibious Entrepreneurs and the Origins of Invention." In *Oxford Handbook on Entrepreneurship and Collaboration*, ed. J. Reuer and S. Matusik. New York: Oxford University Press.

Scott, J. C. 1998. *Seeing Like a State: How Certain Schemes to Improve the Human Condition Have Failed.* New Haven, CT: Yale University Press.

Sealander, J. 1997. *Private Wealth and Public Life: Foundation Philanthropy and the Reshaping of American Social Policy from the Progressive Era to the New Deal.* Baltimore: Johns Hopkins University Press.

———. 2003. "Curing Evils at Their Source: The Arrival of Scientific Giving." In *Charity, Philanthropy, and Civility in American History*, ed. L. J. Friedman and M. D. McGarvie, 217–240. New York: Cambridge University Press.

Singer, P. 2009. *The Life You Can Save.* New York: Penguin.

Solovey, M. 2013. *Shaky Foundations: The Politics-Patronage-Social Science Nexus in Cold War America.* New Brunswick, NJ: Rutgers University Press.

Soskis, B. 2010. "The Problem of Charity in Industrial America, 1873–1915." PhD diss., Columbia University.

Soskis, B., and S. Katz. 2016. *Looking Back at 50 Years of U.S. Philanthropy.* Menlo Park, CA: William and Flora Hewlett Foundation.

Stinchcombe, A. L. 1965. "Social Structure and Organizations." In *Handbook of Organizations*, ed. J. G. March, 142–193. Chicago: Rand McNally.

Sutton, F. X. 1987. "The Ford Foundation: The Early Years." *Daedalus* 116(1): 41–92.

Tax Reform. 1969. *Hearings Before the United States House Committee on Ways and Means*, 91st Congress, 1st sess., February 18–20.

Taylor, J. F. 1940. "New Chapter in the New York Law of Charitable Corporations." *Cornell Law Review* 25(3): 382–400.

Teles, S. 2008. *The Rise of the Conservative Legal Movement: The Battle for Control of the Law.* Princeton, NJ: Princeton University Press.

Tocqueville, A. de. (1835–1840) 1969. *Democracy in America*, ed. J. P. Mayer. Garden City, NY: Anchor Books.

Tompkins-Stange, M. E. 2016. *Policy Patrons: Philanthropy, Education Reform, and the Politics of Influence.* Cambridge, MA: Harvard Education Press.

Tripsas, M. 2009. "Technology, Identity, and Inertia Through the Lens of the Digital Photography Company." *Organization Science* 20(2): 441–460.

United Way Denver. n.d. "History." Who We Are, United Way Denver. https://www.unitedwaydenver.org/who-we-are, accessed June 1, 2018.

U.S. Congress. 1916. "Final Report." Commission on Industrial Relations. Washington, DC: U.S. Government Printing Office.

———. 1952. "Hearings." House Select Committee to Investigate Foundations and Other Organizations. Washington, DC: U.S. Government Printing Office.

———. 1953. "Final Report." House Select Committee to Investigate Foundations and Other Organizations. Washington, DC: U.S. Government Printing Office.

———. 1954. "Hearings, Tax-Exempt Foundations." House Special Committee to Investigate Tax-Exempt Foundations and Comparable Organizations. Washington, DC: U.S. Government Printing Office.

U.S. Department of the Treasury. 1965. *Treasury Department Report on Private Foundations.* Washington, DC: U.S. Government Printing Office.

Van Slyck, A. A. 1995. *Free to All: Carnegie Libraries and American Culture, 1890–1920.* Chicago: University of Chicago Press.

Weber, M. 1958. *Protestant Ethic and the Spirit of Capitalism.* New York: Scribner.

Witt, J. F. 2017. *The Fund: A Story of Money and Politics in America.* Unpublished manuscript.

Wormser, R. 1958. *Foundations: Their Power and Influence.* New York: Devin-Adair.

Zelizer, V. A. 1997. *The Social Meaning of Money.* Princeton, NJ: Princeton University Press.

Ziliak, S. T. 2004. "Self-Reliance Before the Welfare State: Evidence from the Charity Organization Movement in the United States." *Journal of Economic History* 64(2).

Zinsmeister, K. 2017. *The Almanac of American Philanthropy.* Washington, DC: Philanthropy Roundtable.

Chapter 4. The Organizational Transformation of Civil Society

Ahrne, G., and N. Brunsson. 2011. "Organization Outside Organizations: The Significance of Partial Organization." *Organization* 18(1): 83–104.

Alexander, J. 2000. "Adaptive Strategies of Nonprofit Human Service Organizations in an Era of Devolution and New Public Management." *Nonprofit Management and Leadership* 10: 287–303.

Amin, A., ed. 2011. *Post-Fordism: A Reader.* Oxford, UK: Blackwell.

Austin, J. E., and M. M. Seitanidi. 2012. "Collaborative Value Creation: A Review of Partnering Between Nonprofits and Businesses. Part 2: Partnership Processes and Outcomes." *Nonprofit and Voluntary Sector Quarterly* 41: 929–968.

Battilana, J., M. Fuerstein, and M. Lee. 2018. "New Prospects for Organizational Democracy? How the Joint Pursuit of Social and Financial Goals Challenges Traditional Organizational Designs." In *Capitalism Beyond Mutuality? Perspectives Integrating Philosophy and Social Science*, ed. R. Subramanian, 257–288. Oxford, UK: Oxford University Press.

Bell, D. 1976. "The Coming of the Post-Industrial Society." *Educational Forum* 40(4): 574–579.

Bendix, R. 1980. *Kings or People: Power and the Mandate to Rule.* Berkeley: University of California Press.

Billis, D. 1993. "Sector Blurring and Nonprofit Centers: The Case of the United Kingdom." *Nonprofit and Voluntary Sector Quarterly* 22: 241–257.

———. 2010. *Hybrid Organizations and the Third Sector: Challenges for Practice, Theory and Policy.* Hampshire, UK: Palgrave Macmillan.

Brandtner, C., P. Bromley, and M. Tompkins-Stange. 2016. "'Walk the Line': How Institutional Influences Constrain Elites." In *How Institutions Matter! Research in the Sociology of Organizations*, vol. 48B, ed. J. Gehman, M. Lounsbury, and R. Greenwood, 281–309. Bingley, UK: Emerald.

Brass, J. N. 2012. "Blurring Boundaries: The Integration of NGOs into Governance in Kenya."

Governance: An International Journal of Policy, Administration, and Institutions 25: 209–235.

Bromley, P., and J. W. Meyer. 2015. *Hyper-Organization: Global Organizational Expansion.* Oxford, UK: Oxford University Press.

———. 2017. "'They Are All Organizations': The Cultural Roots of Blurring Between the Nonprofit, Business, and Government Sectors." *Administration and Society* 49(7): 939–966.

Bromley, P., and W. W. Powell. 2012. "From Smoke and Mirrors to Walking the Talk: Decoupling in the Contemporary World." *Academy of Management Annals* 6(1): 483–530.

Bromley, P., E. Schofer, and W. Longhofer. 2018. "Organizing for Education: A Cross-National, Longitudinal Study of Civil Society Organizations and Education Outcomes." *Voluntas: International Journal of Voluntary and Nonprofit Organizations* 29(3): 526–540.

Bromley, P., and A. Sharkey. 2017. "Casting Call: The Expanding Nature of Actorhood in US Firms, 1960–2010." *Accounting, Organizations and Society* 59: 3–20.

Brunsson, N., and K. Sahlin-Andersson. 2000. "Constructing Organizations: The Example of Public Sector Reform." *Organization Studies* 21: 721–746.

Caporaso, J. A. 1996. "The European Union and Forms of State: Westphalian, Regulatory or Post-Modern?" *Journal of Common Market Studies* 34(1): 29–52.

Chen, K. K. 2009. *Enabling Creative Chaos: The Organization Behind the Burning Man Event.* Chicago: University of Chicago Press.

Coleman, J. S. 1982. *The Asymmetric Society.* Syracuse, NY: Syracuse University Press.

Colyvas, J. A., and S. Jonsson. 2011. "Ubiquity and Legitimacy: Disentangling Diffusion and Institutionalization." *Sociological Theory* 29(1): 27–53.

Creighton, A. L. 1990. *The Emergence of Incorporation as a Legal Form for Organizations.* Doctoral diss., Stanford University.

Daley, J. M. 2002. "An Action Guide for Nonprofit Board Diversity." *Journal of Community Practice* 10(1): 33–54.

Dart, R. 2004. "Being 'Business-like' in a Nonprofit Organization: A Grounded and Inductive Typology." *Nonprofit and Voluntary Sector Quarterly* 33(2): 290–310.

Dees, J. G. 1998. "Enterprising Nonprofits." *Harvard Business Review* (January–February): 55–67.

Dees, J. G., and B. B. Anderson. 2003. "Sector-Bending: Blurring Lines Between Nonprofit and For-Profit." *Society* 40(4): 16–27.

DiMaggio, P. J., and W. W. Powell. 1983. "The Iron Cage Revisited: Institutional Isomorphism and Collective Rationality in Organizational Fields." *American Sociological Review* 48(2): 147–160.

Dobbin, F. 2009. *Inventing Equal Opportunity.* Princeton, NJ: Princeton University Press.

Drori, G. S., and J. W. Meyer. 2006. "Scientization: Making a World Safe for Organizing." In *Transnational Governance: Institutional Dynamics of Regulation*, ed. M.-L. Djelic and K. Sahlin-Andersson, 32–52. New York: Cambridge University Press.

Drori, G. S., J. W. Meyer, and H. Hwang, eds. 2006. "Globalization and Organization: World Society and Organizational Change." Oxford, UK: Oxford University Press.

———. 2009. "Global Organization: Rationalization and Actorhood as Dominant Scripts." *Research in the Sociology of Organizations* 27: 17–43.

Drori, G. S., J. W. Meyer, F. Ramirez, and E. Schofer, eds. 2003. *Science in the Modern World Polity: Institutionalization and Globalization.* Stanford, CA: Stanford University Press.

Drucker, P. F. 1992. "The New Society of Organizations." *Harvard Business Review* (September–October): 95–104.

Durkheim, E. 1951. *Suicide*, trans. J. Spaulding and G. Simpson. Glencoe, IL: Free Press.

———. 1961. *Moral Education*, trans. E. K. Wilson and H. Schnurer. Glencoe, IL: Free Press.

———. 1982. "What Is a Social Fact?" In *The Rules of Sociological Method*, 50–59. London: Palgrave.

Dwivedi, O. P. 1967. "Bureaucratic Corruption in Developing Countries." *Asian Survey* 7(4): 245–253.

Eikenberry, A. M., and J. D. Kluver. 2004. "The Marketization of the Nonprofit Sector: Civil Society at Risk?" *Public Administration Review* 64(2): 132–140.

Elliott, M. A. 2007. "Human Rights and the Triumph of the Individual in World Culture." *Cultural Sociology* 1: 343–363.

Epstein, R. M., B. S. Alper, and T. E. Quill 2004. "Communicating Evidence for Participatory Decision Making." *Journal of the American Medical Association* 291: 2359–2366.

Espeland, W. N., and M. L. Stevens. 1998. "Commensuration as a Social Process." *Annual Review of Sociology* 24: 313–343.

Fama, E. F. 1980. "Agency Problems and the Theory of the Firm." *Journal of Political Economy* 88(2): 288–307.

Fayol, H. 1949. *General and Industrial Management*. London: Pitman.

Foucault, M. (1978) 1997. "Security, Territory, and Population." In *Michel Foucault, Ethics: Subjectivity and Truth*, ed. Paul Rabinow, 67–71. New York: New Press.

Frank, D. J., and J. W. Meyer. 2002. "The Profusion of Individual Roles and Identities in the Postwar Period." *Sociological Theory* 20(1): 86–105.

Frumkin, P. 2002. *On Being Nonprofit: A Conceptual and Policy Primer*. Cambridge, MA: Harvard University Press.

Fukuyama, F. 2001. "Social Capital, Civil Society and Development." *Third World Quarterly* 22(1): 7–20.

Gitlin, T. 2012. *Occupy Nation: The Roots, the Spirit, and the Promise of Occupy Wall Street*. New York: HarperCollins.

Gonzalez, M. 2009. *Organizational Expansion and Change in the Roman Catholic Church: 1950–2000*. Doctoral diss., Stanford University.

Grossman, D. I. 2016. "Would a Corporate Death Penalty Be Cruel and Unusual Punishment." *Cornell Journal of Law and Public Policy* 25(3): article 4. http://scholarship.law.cornell.edu/cjlpp/vol25/iss3/4.

Guo, C., W. A. Brown, R. F. Ashcraft, C. F. Yoshioka, and H. K. D. Dong. 2011. "Strategic Human Resources Management in Nonprofit Organizations." *Review of Public Personnel Administration* 31: 248–269.

Hall, S., and M. Jacques. 1989. *New Times: The Changing Face of Politics in the 1990s*. New York: NYU Press.

Hansmann, H. B. 1980. "The Role of Nonprofit Enterprise." *Yale Law Journal* 89(5): 835–901.

Hansmann, H., and R. Kraakman. 2000. "The Essential Role of Organizational Law." *Yale Law Journal* 110(3): 387–440.

Heckscher, C. 1994. "Defining the Post-Bureaucratic Type." In *Sociology of Organizations: Structures and Relationships*, ed. M. Godwyn and J. H. Gittell, 98–106. Thousand Oaks, CA: SAGE.

Hwang, H., and W. W. Powell. 2009. "The Rationalization of Charity: The Influences of Professionalism in the Nonprofit Sector." *Administrative Science Quarterly* 54(2): 268–298.

Jensen, M. C., and W. H. Meckling. 1976. "Theory of the Firm: Managerial Behavior, Agency Costs and Ownership Structure." *Journal of Financial Economics* 3(4): 305–360.

Jiménez, T. R. 2010. "Affiliative Ethnic Identity: A More Elastic Link Between Ethnic Ancestry and Culture." *Ethnic and Racial Studies* 33(10): 1756–1775.

Jones, M. L. 2006. "The Growth of Nonprofits." *Bridgewater Review* 25(1): 13–17. http://vc.bridgew.edu/br_rev/vol25/iss1/8.

Josserand, E., S. Teo, and S. Clegg. 2006. "From Bureaucratic to Post-Bureaucratic: The Difficulties of Transition." *Journal of Organizational Change Management* 19(1): 54–64.

Kalberg, S. 1980. "Max Weber's Types of Rationality: Cornerstones for the Analysis of Rationalization Processes in History." *American Journal of Sociology* 85(5): 1145–1179.

Kaufman, J. 2008. "Corporate Law and the Sovereignty of States." *American Sociological Review* 73: 402–425.

Keller, G. 2011. "Comparing the Effects of Management Practices on Organizational Performance Between For-Profit and Not-for-Profit Corporations in Southeast Wisconsin." *Journal of Business and Economics Research* 9(3): 29–38.

Kernaghan, K. 2000. "The Post-Bureaucratic Organization and Public Service Values." *International Review of Administrative Sciences* 66: 91–104.

King, B. G., T. Felin, and D. A. Whetten. 2010. "Perspective—Finding the Organization in Organizational Theory: A Meta-Theory of the Organization as a Social Actor." *Organization Science* 21(1): 290–305.

King, B. G., and S. A. Soule. 2007. "Social Movements as Extra-Institutional Entrepreneurs: The Effect of Protests on Stock Price Returns." *Administrative Science Quarterly* 52(3): 413–442.

King, M. B. 1996. "Participatory Decision Making." In *Restructuring for Authentic Student Achievement: The Impact of Culture and Structure in 24 Schools*, ed. F. M. Newmann and Associates, 245–263. San Francisco: Jossey-Bass.

Knutsen, W. L. 2012. "Value as a Self-Sustaining Mechanism: Why Some Nonprofit Organizations Are Different from and Similar to Private and Public Organizations." *Nonprofit and Voluntary Sector Quarterly.* http://nvs.sagepub.com/content/early/2012/09/03/0899764012457244.abstract.

Knutsen, W. L., and R. S. Brower. 2010. "Managing Expressive and Instrumental Accountabilities in Nonprofit and Voluntary Organizations: A Qualitative Investigation." *Nonprofit and Voluntary Sector Quarterly* 39: 588–610.

Krücken, G., and F. Meier. 2006. "Turning the University into an Organizational Actor." In *Globalization and Organization: World Society and Organizational Change*, ed. G. S. Drori, J. W. Meyer, and H. Hwang, 241–257. Oxford, UK: Oxford University Press.

Kumar, K. 2009. *From Post-Industrial to Post-Modern Society: New Theories of the Contemporary World.* Wiley.

Lammers, J. 2003. "Know Your Ratios: Everyone Else Does." *Nonprofit Quarterly* 10(1): 1–4.

Lauren, P. G. 2011. *The Evolution of International Human Rights: Visions Seen.* Philadelphia: University of Pennsylvania Press.

Lipsky, M. 2010. *Street-Level Bureaucracy, 30th Anniversary Edition: Dilemmas of the Individual in Public Services.* New York: Russell Sage Foundation.

Maguire, E. R. 2003. *Organizational Structure in American Police Agencies: Context, Complexity, and Control.* New York: SUNY Press.

Marshall, J. H., and D. Suárez. 2014. "The Flow of Management Practices: An Analysis of NGO Monitoring and Evaluation Dynamics." *Nonprofit and Voluntary Sector Quarterly* 43(6): 1033–1051.

Marshall, T. H. 1964. *Class, Citizenship and Social Development.* Garden City, NY: Doubleday.

Matten, D., and A. Crane. 2005. "Corporate Citizenship: Toward an Extended Theoretical Conceptualization." *Academy of Management Review* 30(1): 166–179.

Mbaku, J. M. 1996. "Bureaucratic Corruption in Africa: The Futility of Cleanups." *Cato Journal* 16(1): 99–118.

McKeever, B. S. 2015. "The Nonprofit Sector in Brief 2015: Public Charities, Giving, and Volunteering." Urban Institute, October. https://www.urban.org/sites/default/files/publication/72536/2000497-The-Nonprofit-Sector-in-Brief-2015-Public-Charities-Giving-and-Volunteering.pdf.

McKeever, B., and S. Pettijohn. 2014. "The Nonprofit Sector in Brief: 2014." Urban Institute, October. https://www.urban.org/sites/default/files/publication/33711/413277-The-Nonprofit-Sector-in-Brief--.PDF.

Meyer, J. W. 2010. "World Society, Institutional Theories, and the Actor." *Annual Review of Sociology* 36: 1–20.

Meyer, J. W., and P. Bromley. 2013. "The Worldwide Expansion of Organization." *Sociological Theory* 31: 366–389.

Meyer, J. W., and R. L. Jepperson. 2000. "The 'Actors' of Modern Society: The Cultural Construction of Social Agency." *Sociological Theory* 18: 100–120.

Meyer, J. W., and B. Rowan. 1977. "Institutionalized Organizations: Formal Structure as Myth and Ceremony." *American Journal of Sociology* 83(2): 340–363.

Miller, P., and N. Rose. 1990. "Governing Economic Life." *Economy and Society* 19(1): 1–31.

———. 2008. *Governing the Present: Administering Economic, Social and Personal Life.* Cambridge, UK: Polity.

Mirabella, R. M. 2007. "University-Based Educational Programs in Nonprofit Management and Philanthropic Studies: A 10-Year Review and Projections of Future Trends." *Nonprofit and Voluntary Sector Quarterly* 36(4 Suppl.): 11S–27S.

Mirabella, R. M., G. Gemelli, M. J. Malcolm, and G. Berger. 2007. "Nonprofit and Philanthropic Studies: International Overview of the Field in Africa, Canada, Latin America, Asia, the Pacific, and Europe." *Nonprofit and Voluntary Sector Quarterly* 36(4 Suppl.): 110S–135S.

Mörth, U., ed. 2004. *Soft Law in Governance and Regulation: An Interdisciplinary Analysis.* Cheltenham, UK: Edward Elgar.

Musolf, L. D., and H. Seidman. 1980. "The Blurred Boundaries of Public Administration." *Public Administration Review* 40: 124–130.

Offenheiser, R. C., and S. H. Holcombe. 2003. "Challenges and Opportunities in Implementing a Rights-Based Approach to Development: An Oxfam America Perspective." *Nonprofit and Voluntary Sector Quarterly* 32: 268–301.

Orgtheory.net. 2012. https://orgtheory.wordpress.com/2012/09/22/non-profit-research-in-b-schools/.

Osborne, S. P. 2006. "The New Public Governance?" *Public Management Review* 8(3): 377–387.

———, ed. 2010. *The New Public Governance? Emerging Perspectives on the Theory and Practice of Public Governance.* London: Routledge.

Pache, A.-C., and F. Santos. 2012. "Inside the Hybrid Organization: An Organizational Level View of Responses to Conflicting Institutional Demands." *Academy of Management Journal* 56(4): 972–1001.

Parker, M. 1992. "Post-Modern Organizations or Postmodern Organization Theory?" *Organization Studies* 13(1): 1–17.

Pedersen, J. S., and F. Dobbin. 1997. "The Social Invention of Collective Actors: On the Rise of the Organization." *American Behavioral Scientist* 40(4): 431–443.

Perrow, C. 2009. *Organizing America: Wealth, Power, and the Origins of Corporate Capitalism.* Princeton, NJ: Princeton University Press.

Polletta, F., and J. M. Jasper. 2001. "Collective Identity and Social Movements." *Annual Review of Sociology* 27: 283–305.

Pope, S., P. Bromley, A. Lim, and J. W. Meyer. 2018. "The Pyramid of Nonprofit Responsibility: The Institutionalization of Organizational Responsibility Across Sectors." *Voluntas: International Journal of Voluntary and Nonprofit Organizations* 29(6): 1300–1314.

Power, M. 1999. *The Audit Society: Rituals of Verification.* Oxford, UK: Oxford University Press.

Presthus, R. 1962. *The Organizational Society: An Analysis and a Theory.* New York: Vintage Books.

Price, D. J. 1961. *Science Since Babylon.* New Haven, CT: Yale University Press.

Putnam, R. D., and D. E. Campbell. 2012. *American Grace: How Religion Divides and Unites Us.* New York: Simon and Schuster.

Ramirez, M. K., and S. A. Ramirez. 2017. *The Case for the Corporate Death Penalty: Restoring Law and Order on Wall Street.* New York: NYU Press.

Rhodes, R. A. W. 1996. "The New Governance: Governing Without Government." *Political Studies* 44: 652–667.

Robbins, K. C. 2006. "The Nonprofit Sector in Historical Perspective: Traditions of Philanthropy in the West." In *The Nonprofit Sector: A Research Handbook*, 2nd ed., ed. W. W. Powell and R. Steinberg, 13–31. New Haven, CT: Yale University Press.

Roy, K., and S. Ziemek. 2000. *On the Economics of Volunteering* (Discussion Papers on Development Policy #31). Bonn, Germany: Center for Development Research at the University of Bonn and the United Nations Volunteer Program. http://www.zef.de/fileadmin/webfiles/downloads/zef_dp/zef_dp31-00.pdf.

Ruggie, J. G. 1982. "International Regimes, Transactions, and Change: Embedded Liberalism in the Postwar Economic Order." *International Organization* 36(2): 379–415.

Salamon, L. M. 1987. "Of Market Failure, Voluntary Failure, and Third-Party Government: Toward a Theory of Government-Nonprofit Relations in the Modern Welfare State." *Nonprofit and Voluntary Sector Quarterly* 16(1): 29–49.

———. 1993. "The Global Associational Revolution: The Rise of Third Sector on the World Scene" (No. Occas. Pap. 15). Baltimore: Institution of Policy Studies, Johns Hopkins University.

Salamon, L. M., and H. K. Anheier. 1998. "Social Origins of Civil Society: Explaining the Nonprofit Sector Cross-Nationally." *Voluntas: International Journal of Voluntary and Nonprofit Organizations* 9(3): 213–248.

Schofer, E., and W. Longhofer. 2011. "The Structural Sources of Association." *American Journal of Sociology* 117(2): 539–585.

Schofer, E., and J. W. Meyer. 2005. "The Worldwide Expansion of Higher Education in the Twentieth Century." *American Sociological Review* 70(6): 898–920.

Scott, W. R. 2008. *Institutions and Organizations: Ideas and Interests.* Los Angeles: SAGE.

Sealander, J. 2003. "Curing Evils at Their Source: The Arrival of Scientific Giving." In *Charity, Philanthropy, and Civility in American History*, ed. L. J. Friedman and M. D. McGarvie, 217–240. New York: Cambridge University Press.

Stacy, H. 2009. *Human Rights for the 21st Century: Sovereignty, Civil Society, Culture.* Stanford, CA: Stanford University Press.

Stone, M. M. 1989. "Planning as Strategy in Nonprofit Organizations: An Exploratory Study." *Nonprofit and Voluntary Sector Quarterly* 18: 297–315.

Suárez, D. F. 2010. "Street Credentials and Management Backgrounds: Careers of Nonprofit Executives in an Evolving Sector." *Nonprofit and Voluntary Sector Quarterly* 39: 696–716.

———. 2011. "Collaboration and Professionalization: The Contours of Public Sector Funding for Nonprofit Organizations." *Journal of Public Administration Research and Theory* 21(2): 307–326.

Szper, R., and A. Prakash. 2011. "Charity Watchdogs and the Limits of Information-Based Regulation." *Voluntas: International Journal of Voluntary and Nonprofit Organizations* 22(1): 112–141.

Taylor, F. W. 1914. *The Principles of Scientific Management.* New York: Harper.

Tilly, C. 1990. *Coercion, Capital, and European States, AD 990–1990.* Cambridge, MA: Blackwell.

Tocqueville, A. de. (1836) 2003. *Democracy in America*, vol. 10. Washington, DC: Regnery.

Toulmin, S. 1992. *Cosmopolis: The Hidden Agenda of Modernity.* Chicago: University of Chicago Press.

Turco, C. J. 2016. *The Conversational Firm: Rethinking Bureaucracy in the Age of Social Media.* New York: Columbia University Press.

Union of International Associations. 2018. "Historical Overview of Number of International Organizations by Type." https://uia.org/sites/uia .org/files/misc_pdfs/stats/Historical_overview _of_number_of_international_organizations_by _type_1909-2013.pdf.

Wachhaus, A. 2013. "Governance Beyond Government." *Administration and Society* 46(5): 573–593.

Weber, E. 1976. *Peasants into Frenchmen: The Modernization of Rural France, 1870–1914.* Stanford, CA: Stanford University Press.

Weber, M. (1922) 1978. *Economy and Society: An Outline of Interpretive Sociology*, 2 vols., ed. G. Roth and C. Wittich. Berkeley: University of California Press.

Weisbrod, B. A. 1997. "The Future of the Nonprofit Sector: Its Entwining with Private Enterprise and Government." *Journal of Policy Analysis and Management* 16(4): 541–555.

———, ed. 1998. *To Profit or Not to Profit: The Commercial Transformation of the Nonprofit Sector.* New York: Cambridge University Press.

Wilensky, H. L. 1964. "The Professionalization of Everyone?" *American Journal of Sociology* 70: 137–158.

Williamson, O. E. 1979. "Transaction-Cost Economics: The Governance of Contractual Relations." *Journal of Law and Economics* 22(2): 233–261.

Wittberg, P. 2006. *From Piety to Professionalism— and Back? Transformations of Organized Religious Virtuosity.* Lanham, MD: Lexington Books.

World Development Indicators Online. 2018. "School Enrollment, Tertiary (Percent Gross)." Unesco Institute for Statistics. https://data .worldbank.org/indicator/SE.TER.ENRR.

World Management Survey. 2013. http://www .worldmanagementsurvey.org.

Young, D. R., and L. M. Salamon. 2002. "Commercialization, Social Ventures, and For-Profit Competition." In *The State of Nonprofit America*, ed. L. M. Salamon, 423–446. Washington, DC: Brookings Institution Press.

Zelizer, V. A. 1994. *Pricing the Priceless Child: The Changing Social Value of Children.* Princeton, NJ: Princeton University Press.

Chapter 5. Tangled Up in Tax: The Nonprofit Sector and the Federal Tax System

Americans for Tax Reform. 2018. "Contribute to ATR." https://www.atr.org/donate.

Andreoni, James. 1990. "Impure Altruism and Donations to Public Goods: A Theory of Warm-Glow Giving." *Economic Journal* 100(401): 464–477.

Aprill, Ellen P. 2011. "Regulating the Political Speech of Noncharitable Exempt Organizations After Citizens United." *Election Law Journal* 10(4): 363–405.

Aprill, Ellen P., and Daniel J. Hemel. 2018. "The Tax Legislative Process: A Byrd's Eye View." *Law and Contemporary Problems* 81(2): 99–136.

Bakija, Jon. 2013. "Tax Policy and Philanthropy: A Primer on the Empirical Evidence for the United States and Its Implications." *Social Research: An International Quarterly* 80(2): 557–584.

Banks, Adelle M. 2017. "Thousands of Faith Leaders Ask Congress to Protect Johnson Amendment." Religion News Service, August 16. https://religionnews.com/2017/08/16/thousands-of-faith-leaders-ask-congress-to-maintain-johnson-amendment.

Belson, Ken. 2015. "After Much Criticism, N.F.L.'s League Office Drops Tax-Exempt Status." *New York Times*, April 28. https://www.nytimes.com/2015/04/29/sports/football/nfls-league-office-to-drop-its-tax-exempt-status.html.

Bob Jones University v. United States, 461 U.S. 574 (1983).

C.F. Mueller Co. v. Commissioner, 190 F.2d 120 (2d Cir. 1951).

Clemens, Elisabeth S. 2006. "The Constitution of Citizens: Political Theories of Nonprofit Organizations." In *The Nonprofit Sector: A Research Handbook*, 2nd ed., ed. W. W. Powell and R. Steinberg, 207–270. New Haven, CT: Yale University Press.

Colinvaux, Roger. 2017. "The Importance of a Participatory Charitable Giving Incentive." *Tax Notes* 154(5): 605–614.

Colinvaux, Roger, Brian Galle, and Eugene Steuerle. 2012. *Evaluating the Charitable Contribution Deduction and Proposed Reforms*. Washington, DC: Urban Institute. https://www.urban.org/sites/default/files/publication/25491/412586-Evaluating-the-Charitable-Deduction-and-Proposed-Reforms.PDF.

Colvin, Gregory L. 2010. "Political Tax Law After *Citizens United*: A Time for Reform." *Exempt Organization Tax Review* 66(71).

Dees, J. Gregory. 1998. "Enterprising Nonprofits." *Harvard Business Review* (January–February): 55–67.

Foundation Center. 2014. "Fiscal Totals of the 50 Largest Foundations in the U.S. by Total Assets." http://data.foundationcenter.org/#/foundations/all/nationwide/top:assets/list/2013.

Freund, Paul A. 1969. "Public Aid to Parochial Schools." *Harvard Law Review* 82(8): 1680–1692.

Galle, Brian. 2010. "Keep Charity Charitable." *Texas Law Review* 88(6): 1213–1231.

———. 2016. "Pay It Forward? Law and the Problem of Restricted-Spending Philanthropy." *Washington University Law Review* 93(5): 1143–1207.

Galle, Brian, and David I. Walker. 2014. "Nonprofit Executive Pay as an Agency Problem: Evidence from U.S. Colleges and Universities." *Boston University Law Review* 94(6): 1881–1934.

Graham, Fred P. 1970. "High Court Backs Churches' Right to Tax Exemption." *New York Times*, May 5. https://www.nytimes.com/1970/05/05/archives/high-court-backs-churches-right-to-tax-exemption-holds-7-to-1-that.html.

Guillaume, Kristine E. 2018. "The Man for the Moment?" *Harvard Crimson*, May 23. https://www.thecrimson.com/article/2018/5/23/man-for-the-moment.

Hansmann, Henry B. 1980. "The Role of Nonprofit Enterprise." *Yale Law Journal* 89(5): 835–901.

———. 1989. "Unfair Competition and the Unrelated Business Income Tax." *Virginia Law Review* 75(3): 605–635.

Harding, Bertrand M. Jr. 2008. *The Tax Law of Colleges and Universities*, 3rd ed. Hoboken, NJ: Wiley.

Hayek, F. A. 1945. "The Use of Knowledge in Society." *American Economics Review* 35(4): 519–530.

———. 1982. *Law, Legislation, and Liberty: The Political Order of a Free People*. London: Routledge and Kegan Paul.

Hebrew Union College–Jewish Institute of Religion. n.d. "HUC-JIR Rabbinical, Cantorial and Educational Programs: Policies and Expectations." http://huc.edu/admissions/policies-and-expectations, accessed May 10, 2018.

Hendrie, Alexander. 2015. "Van Hollen's Liberal 'Action Plan' Is Nothing but Old Ideas and Failed Politics." Americans for Tax Reform, January 12. https://www.atr.org/van-hollens-liberal-action-plan-nothing-old-ideas-and-failed-policies.

Hines, James R. Jr., Jill R. Horwitz, and Austin Nichols. 2010. "The Attack on Nonprofit Status: A Charitable Assessment." *Michigan Law Review* 108(7): 1179–1220.

Jones, Daryll K. 2000. "The Scintilla of Individual Profit: In Search of Private Inurement and Excess Benefit." *Virginia Tax Review* 19(4): 575–681.

Kaplow, Louis. 1995. "A Note on Subsidizing Gifts." *Journal of Public Economics* 58(3): 469–477.

Kim, Anne. 2017. "The Push for College-Endowment Reform." *The Atlantic*, October 4. https://www .theatlantic.com/education/archive/2017/10/ the-bipartisan-push-for-college-endowment -reform/541140.

Klausner, Michael. 2003. "When Time Isn't Money: Foundation Payouts and the Time Value of Money." *Stanford Social Innovation Review* 1(1): 51–59.

Lemon v. Kurtzman, 403 U.S. 602 (1971).

Levmore, Saul. 1998. "Taxes as Ballots." *University of Chicago Law Review* 65(2): 387–431.

The Macaroni Monopoly: The Developing Concept of Unrelated Business Income of Exempt Organizations. 1968. *Harvard Law Review* 81(6): 1280–1294.

Malani, Anup, and Eric A. Posner. 2007. "The Case for For-Profit Charities." *Virginia Law Review* 93(8): 2017–2068.

Mankiw, N. Gregory. 2017. "The Peril of Taxing Higher Education." *New York Times*, December 22. https://www.nytimes.com/2017/12/ 22/business/the-peril-of-taxing-elite-higher -education.html.

Meek v. Pittenger, 421 U.S. 349, 372 (1975).

Merriam-Webster. n.d. "Entanglement." https:// www.merriam-webster.com/dictionary/ entanglement, accessed February 18, 2019.

Mysteryboy Inc. v. Commissioner, T.C. Memo 2010-13 (January 26, 2010).

NAACP v. Alabama ex rel. Patterson, 357 U.S. 449, 462 (1958).

National Council of Nonprofits. 2018. "Tax Cuts and Jobs Act, H.R. 1: Nonprofit Analysis of the Final Tax Law." February 22. https://www .councilofnonprofits.org/sites/default/files/ documents/tax-bill-summary-chart.pdf.

O'Daniel, Patrick L. 2001. "More Honored in the Breach: A Historical Perspective of the Permeable IRS Prohibition on Campaigning by Churches." *Boston College Law Review* 42(4): 733–769.

Pigou, A. C. 1907. "Some Aspects of the Problem of Charity." In *The Heart of the Empire: Discussions of Problems of Modern City Life in England*, ed. C.F.G. Masterman et al., 236–231. London: Unwin.

Pulliam Bailey, Sarah. 2015. "IRS Commissioner Promises Not to Revoke Tax-Exempt Status of Colleges That Oppose Gay Marriage." *Washington Post*, August 3. https://www.washingtonpost.com/news/ acts-of-faith/wp/2015/08/03/irs-commissioner -promises-not-to-revoke-tax-exempt-status-of -colleges-that-oppose-gay-marriage.

Rooney, Patrick. 2018. "How the New Estate Tax Rules Could Reduce Charitable Giving by Billions." *The Conversation*, April 13. http:// theconversation.com/how-the-new-estate -tax-rules-could-reduce-charitable-giving-by -billions-94879.

Rose-Ackerman, Susan. 1982. "Unfair Competition and Corporate Income Taxation." *Stanford Law Review* 34(5): 1017–1039.

Saez, Emmanuel. 2004. "The Optimal Treatment of Tax Expenditures." *Journal of Public Economics* 88(12): 2657–2684.

Simon, John G. 1987. "The Tax Treatment of Nonprofit Organizations: A Review of Federal and State Policies." In *The Nonprofit Sector: A Research Handbook*, ed. W. W. Powell, 67–98. New Haven, CT: Yale University Press.

Simon, John G., Harvey Dale, and Laura Chisholm. 2006. "The Federal Tax Treatment of Charitable Organizations." In *The Nonprofit Sector: A Research Handbook*, 2nd ed., ed. W. W. Powell and R. Steinberg, 267–306. New Haven, CT: Yale University Press.

Singer, Natasha, and Mike Isaac. 2015. "Mark Zuckerberg's Philanthropy Uses L.L.C. for More Control." *New York Times*, December 2. https:// www.nytimes.com/2015/12/03/technology/ zuckerbergs-philanthropy-uses-llc-for-more -control.html.

Smith, Steven R., and Kirsten A. Grønbjerg. 2006. "Scope and Theory of Government-Nonprofit Relations." In *The Nonprofit Sector: A Research Handbook*, 2nd ed., ed. W. W. Powell and R.

Steinberg, 221–242. New Haven, CT: Yale University Press.

Stiffman, Eden. 2016. "Dozens of 'Hate Groups' Have Charity Status, *Chronicle* Study Finds." *Chronicle of Philanthropy*, December 22. https://www.philanthropy.com/article/Dozens-of-Hate-Groups-/238748.

Sussman, Abigail B., and Christopher Y. Olivola. 2011. "Axe the Tax: Taxes Are Disliked More than Equivalent Costs." *Journal of Marketing Research* 48: S91–S101.

Taeb, Yasmine. 2017. "78 Organizations Call on Congress to Oppose the Repeal of the Johnson Amendment." Friends Committee of National Legislation, November 3. https://www.fcnl.org/updates/78-organizations-call-on-congress-to-oppose-the-repeal-of-the-johnson-amendment-1135.

Thurow, Lester C. 1971. "The Income Distribution as a Pure Public Good." *Quarterly Journal of Economics* 85(2): 327–336.

Tocqueville, Alexis de. (1840) 1899. *Democracy in America*, trans. Henry Reeve. New York: Adlard and Saunders.

Underwood, James L. 1976. "Permissible Entanglement Under the Establishment Clause." *Emory Law Journal* 25(1): 17–62.

USA Today Editorial. 2015. "Costs, Salaries, Out of Control in College Football." *News-Press*, January 5. https://www.news-press.com/story/opinion/2015/01/05/costs-salaries-control-college-football/21203721.

Vise, David A. 2005. "Google Starts Up Philanthropy Campaign." *Washington Post*, October 12. http://www.washingtonpost.com/wp-dyn/content/article/2005/10/11/AR2005101101788.html.

Walz v. Tax Commission of the City of New York, 397 U.S. 664 (1970).

Weaver, Warren Jr. 1970. "Blackmun Approved, 94–0; Nixon Hails Vote by Senate." *New York Times*, May 13. https://www.nytimes.com/1970/05/13/archives/blackmun-approved-940-nixon-hails-vote-by-senate-supreme-court.html.

Wolf, Alexander M. 2011. "The Problems with Payouts: Assessing the Proposal for a Mandatory Distribution Requirement for University Endowments." *Harvard Journal on Legislation* 48(2): 591–622.

Zelinsky, Edward A. 2012. "Do Religious Tax Exemptions Entangle in Violation of the Establishment Clause? The Constitutionality of the Parsonage Allowance Exclusion and the Religious Exemptions of the Individual Health Care Mandate and the FICA and Self-Employment Taxes." *Cardozo Law Review* 33(4): 1633–1677.

———. 2017. *Taxing the Church: Religion, Exemptions, Entanglement, and the Constitution*. New York: Oxford University Press.

Part II. Politics of the Public Sphere
Chapter 6. Political Theory and the Nonprofit Sector

Abizadeh, A. 2008. "Democratic Theory and Border Coercion: No Right to Unilaterally Control Your Own Borders." *Political Theory* 36(1): 37–65.

Achen, C. H., and L. M. Bartels. 2017. *Democracy for Realists: Why Elections Do Not Produce Responsive Government*. Princeton, NJ: Princeton University Press.

Anderson, E. 1993. *Value in Ethics and Economics*. Cambridge, MA: Harvard University Press.

———. 1999. "What Is the Point of Equality?" *Ethics* 109(2): 287–337.

———. 2017. *Private Government: How Employers Rule Our Lives (and Why We Don't Talk About It)*. Princeton, NJ: Princeton University Press.

Arneson, R. J. 2009. "The Supposed Right to a Democratic Say." In *Contemporary Debates in Political Philosophy*, ed. T. Christiano and J. P. Christman, 197–212. Hoboken, NJ: Wiley-Blackwell.

Arrow, K. J. 1951. *Social Choice and Individual Values*. New Haven, CT: Yale University Press.

Bartels, L. M. 2016. *Unequal Democracy: The Political Economy of the New Gilded Age*. Princeton, NJ: Princeton University Press.

Beerbohm, E. 2016. "The Free-Provider Problem: Private Provision of Public Responsibilities." In *Philanthropy and Democratic Societies: History, Institutions, Values*, ed. R. Reich, C. Cordelli, and L. Bernholz, 207–225. Chicago: University of Chicago Press.

Beitz, C. R. 1979. *Political Theory and International Relations*. Princeton, NJ: Princeton University Press.

———. 1989. *Political Equality: An Essay in Democratic Theory.* Princeton, NJ: Princeton University Press.

Berman, S. 1997. "Civil Society and the Collapse of the Weimar Republic." *World Politics* 49(3): 401–429.

Bishop, M., and M. Green. 2008. *Philanthrocapitalism: How the Rich Can Save the World.* New York: Bloomsbury Press.

Blake, M. 2001. "Distributive Justice, State Coercion, and Autonomy." *Philosophy and Public Affairs* 30(3): 257–296.

Bonica, A., N. McCarty, K. T. Poole, and H. Rosenthal. 2013. "Why Hasn't Democracy Slowed Rising Inequality?" *Journal of Economic Perspectives* 27(3): 103–124.

Brass, J. N. 2016. *Allies or Adversaries: NGOs and the State in Africa.* New York: Cambridge University Press.

Brighouse, H., and A. Swift. 2014. *Family Values.* Princeton, NJ: Princeton University Press.

Buchanan, A. 2002. "Political Legitimacy and Democracy." *Ethics* 112(4): 689–719.

Cammett, M., and L. M. MacLean, eds. 2014. *The Politics of Non-State Social Welfare.* Ithaca, NY: Cornell University Press.

Caney, S. 2006. *Justice Beyond Borders: A Global Political Theory.* Oxford, UK: Oxford University Press.

Chambers, S., and J. Kopstein. 2001. "Bad Civil Society." *Political Theory* 29(6): 837–865.

Ciepley, D. 2013. "Beyond Public and Private: Toward a Political Theory of the Corporation." *American Political Science Review* 107(1): 139–158.

Clough, E. 2017. "Exit, Voice, and Resources: How NGOs Shape State Performance in India." Doctoral diss., Harvard University.

Cohen, G. A. 1997. "Where the Action Is: On the Site of Distributive Justice." *Philosophy and Public Affairs* 26(1): 3–30.

Cohen, J. 2009. *Philosophy, Politics, Democracy: Selected Essays.* Cambridge, MA: Harvard University Press.

Cohen, J., and J. Rogers. 1995. *Associations and Democracy.* New York: Verso.

Cooter, R. D. 2003. "The Donation Registry." *Fordham Law Review* 72: 1981–1989.

Cordelli, C. 2011. "The Institutional Division of Labor and the Egalitarian Obligations of Nonprofits." *Journal of Political Philosophy* 20(2): 131–155.

———. 2016. "Reparative Justice and the Moral Limits of Discretionary Philanthropy." In *Philanthropy in Democratic Societies: History, Institutions, Values*, ed. R. Reich, C. Cordelli, and L. Bernholz, 245–266. Chicago: University of Chicago Press.

de Freytas-Tamura, K. 2017. "For Dignity and Development, East Africa Curbs Used Clothes Imports." *New York Times*, October 11, A4.

de Waal, A., ed. 2015. *Advocacy in Conflict.* London: Zed Books.

Douglas, J. A. 1983. *Why Charity? The Case for a Third Sector.* Beverly Hills, CA: SAGE.

Dryzek, J. S. 2012. "Global Civil Society: The Progress of Post-Westphalian Politics." *Annual Review of Political Science* 15(1): 101–119.

Dryzek, J. S., and S. Niemeyer. 2008. "Discursive Representation." *American Political Science Review* 102(4): 481–493.

Dunning, C. Forthcoming. *Nonprofit Neighborhoods: Poverty Policy and the Privatization of Boston, 1949–Present.* Chicago: University of Chicago Press.

Dworkin, R. 2000. *Sovereign Virtue: The Theory and Practice of Equality.* Cambridge, MA: Harvard University Press.

Elster, J. 1992. *Local Justice: How Institutions Allocate Scarce Goods and Necessary Burdens.* New York: Russell Sage Foundation.

Fleischer, M. P. 2009. "Theorizing the Charitable Tax Subsidies: The Role of Distributive Justice." *Washington University Law Review* 87: 505–566.

———. 2015. "Libertarianism and the Charitable Tax Subsidies." *Boston College Law Review* 56: 1345–1415.

Freeman, S. 2001. "Illiberal Libertarians: Why Libertarianism Is Not a Liberal View." *Philosophy and Public Affairs* 30(2): 105–151.

Friedman, M. 1962. *Capitalism and Freedom.* Chicago: University of Chicago Press.

Frumkin, P. 2009. *On Being Nonprofit: A Conceptual and Policy Primer.* Cambridge, MA: Harvard University Press.

Gaus, G. 2010. "Coercion, Ownership, and the Redistributive State: Justificatory Liberalism's Classical Tilt." *Social Philosophy and Policy* 27(1): 233–275.

Gilens, M. 2012. *Affluence and Influence: Economic Inequality and Political Power in America*. Princeton, NJ: Princeton University Press.

Gimmler, A. 2001. "Deliberative Democracy, the Public Sphere and the Internet." *Philosophy and Social Criticism* 27(4): 21–39.

Goodin, R. E. 1995. *Utilitarianism as a Public Philosophy*. Cambridge, UK: Cambridge University Press.

Grant, R. W., and R. O. Keohane. 2005. "Accountability and Abuses of Power in World Politics." *American Political Science Review* 99(1): 29–43.

Habermas, J. (1962) 1991. *The Structural Transformation of the Public Sphere: An Inquiry into a Category of Bourgeois Society*. Cambridge, MA: MIT Press.

Hall, P. D. 1992. *"Inventing the Nonprofit Sector" and Other Essays on Philanthropy, Voluntarism, and Nonprofit Organizations*. Baltimore: Johns Hopkins University Press.

Hansmann, H. 1987. "Economic Theories of Nonprofit Organizations." In *The Nonprofit Sector: A Research Handbook*, ed. W.W. Powell, 27–42. New Haven, CT: Yale University Press.

Hardin, R. 1982. *Collective Action*. Baltimore: Johns Hopkins University Press.

James, A. 2012. *Fairness in Practice*. New York: Oxford University Press.

Julius, A. J. 2003. "Basic Structure and the Value of Equality." *Philosophy and Public Affairs* 31(4): 321–355.

Kolodny, N. 2014a. "Rule over None I: What Justifies Democracy?" *Philosophy and Public Affairs* 42(3): 195–229.

———. 2014b. "Rule over None II: Social Equality and the Justification of Democracy." *Philosophy and Public Affairs* 42(4): 287–336.

Kymlicka, W. 2001. "Altruism in Philosophical and Ethical Traditions: Two Views." In *Between State and Market: Essays on Charities Law and Policy in Canada*, ed. J. Phillips, B. Chapman, and D. Stevens, 87–126. Montreal: McGill-Queens University Press.

———. 2002. "Civil Society and Government: A Liberal-Egalitarian Perspective." In *Civil Society and Government*, ed. N. L. Rosenblum and R. C.

Post, 79–110. Princeton, NJ: Princeton University Press.

Landemore, H. n.d. *Open Democracy: Reinventing Popular Rule for the 21st Century*. Unpublished manuscript.

Lechterman, T. M. 2018. "Of Sovereignty and Saints: When Is the Private Provision of Public Goods Illegitimate?" Paper presented at the American Political Science Association Annual Meeting and Exhibition, Boston, MA, August 31.

Lechterman, T.M. 2020. "The Effective Altruist's Political Problem." *Polity* 52, no. 1. doi: 10.1086/706867.

Lee, C., and L. Han. 2016. "Faith-Based Organization and Transnational Voluntarism in China: A Case Study of the Malaysia Airline MH370 Incident." *Voluntas: International Journal of Voluntary and Nonprofit Organizations* 27(5): 2353–2373.

Lin, J. 2015. "The Dynamics of Grassroots Environmental Protests in China: State-Protest Leader Interactions and Movement Trajectories." Doctoral diss., University of Chicago.

MacAskill, W. 2015. *Doing Good Better: How Effective Altruism Can Help You Make a Difference*. New York: Gotham Books.

Mayer, J. 2016. *Dark Money: The Hidden History of the Billionaires Behind the Rise of the Radical Right*. New York: Doubleday.

McGinnis Johnson, J. 2016. "Necessary but Not Sufficient: The Impact of Community Input on Grantee Selection." *Administration and Society* 48(1): 73–103.

Mill, J. S. 2015. *On Liberty, Utilitarianism, and Other Essays*. New York: Oxford University Press.

Miller, D. 2007. *National Responsibility and Global Justice*. Oxford, UK: Oxford University Press.

Murphy, L. B. 1998. "Institutions and the Demands of Justice." *Philosophy and Public Affairs* 27(4): 251–291.

Murphy, L. B., and T. Nagel. 2002. *The Myth of Ownership: Taxes and Justice*. New York: Oxford University Press.

Nagel, T. 2005. "The Problem of Global Justice." *Philosophy and Public Affairs* 33(2): 113–147.

Nozick, R. 1974. *Anarchy, State, and Utopia*. New York: Basic Books.

Oberman, K. 2011. "By Taxation or Donation: How Should Justice Be Funded?" Paper presented at the American Political Science Association Annual Meeting and Exhibition, Seattle, WA, September 1–4.

Okin, S. M. 1989. *Justice, Gender, and the Family.* New York: Basic Books.

Page, B. I., L. M. Bartels, and J. Seawright. 2013. "Democracy and the Policy Preferences of Wealthy Americans." *Perspectives on Politics* 11(1): 51–73.

Pettit, P. 1997. *Republicanism: A Theory of Freedom and Government.* Oxford, UK: Oxford University Press.

Pevnick, R. 2013. "Democratizing the Nonprofit Sector." *Journal of Political Philosophy* 21(3): 260–282.

Phillips, A. 1992. "Must Feminists Give Up on Liberal Democracy?" *Political Studies* 40(1 Suppl): 68–82.

Pitkin, H. F. 1967. *The Concept of Representation.* Berkeley: University of California Press.

Pogge, T. W. 2008. *World Poverty and Human Rights.* Cambridge, UK: Polity.

———. 2011. "How International Nongovernmental Organizations Should Act." In *Giving Well: The Ethics of Philanthropy*, ed. P. Illingworth, T. Pogge, and L. Wenar, 46–65. Oxford, UK: Oxford University Press.

Prewitt, K., M. Dogan, S. Heydemann, and S. Toepler, eds. 2006. *The Legitimacy of Philanthropic Foundations: United States and European Perspectives.* New York: Russell Sage Foundation.

Putnam, R. D. 2000. *Bowling Alone: The Collapse and Revival of American Community.* New York: Simon and Schuster.

Putnam, R. D., R. Leonardi, and R. Y. Nanetti. 1993. *Making Democracy Work: Civic Traditions in Modern Italy.* Princeton, NJ: Princeton University Press.

Rahman, K. S. 2018. "Infrastructural Regulation and the New Utilities." *Yale Journal on Regulation* 35: 911–939.

Rawls, J. 1971. *A Theory of Justice.* Cambridge, MA: Harvard University Press.

———. 1993. *Political Liberalism.* New York: Columbia University Press.

———. 2001. *The Law of Peoples.* Cambridge, MA: Harvard University Press.

Reckhow, S. 2013. *Follow the Money: How Foundation Dollars Change Public School Politics.* Oxford, UK: Oxford University Press.

Reich, R. 2011. "Toward a Political Theory of Philanthropy." In *Giving Well: The Ethics of Philanthropy*, ed. P. Illingworth, T. Pogge, and L. Wenar, 177–195. Oxford, UK: Oxford University Press.

———. 2018. *Just Giving: Why Philanthropy Is Failing Democracy and How It Can Do Better.* Princeton, NJ: Princeton University Press.

Ripstein, A. 2010. *Force and Freedom.* Cambridge, MA: Harvard University Press.

Roelofs, J. 2003. *Foundations and Public Policy: The Mask of Pluralism.* Albany: SUNY Press.

Rosenblum, N. 2000. *Membership and Morals: The Personal Uses of Pluralism in America.* Princeton, NJ: Princeton University Press.

———. 2002. "Feminist Perspectives on Civil Society and Government." In *Civil Society and Government*, ed. N. L. Rosenblum and R. C. Post, 151–178. Princeton, NJ: Princeton University Press.

Rosenblum, N. L., and R. C. Post, eds. 2002. *Civil Society and Government.* Princeton, NJ: Princeton University Press.

Rubenstein, J. 2015. *Between Samaritans and States: The Political Ethics of Humanitarian INGOs.* Oxford, UK: Oxford University Press.

Sangiovanni, A. 2007. "Global Justice, Reciprocity, and the State." *Philosophy and Public Affairs* 35(1): 3–39.

Satz, D. 2012. *Why Some Things Should Not Be for Sale.* Oxford, UK: Oxford University Press.

Saunders-Hastings, E. 2018. "Plutocratic Philanthropy." *Journal of Politics* 80(1): 149–161.

Saward, M. 2010. *The Representative Claim.* Oxford, UK: Oxford University Press.

Scalet, S., and D. Schmidtz. 2002. "State, Civil Society, and Classical Liberalism." In *Civil Society and Government*, ed. N. L. Rosenblum and R. C. Post, 26–47. Princeton, NJ: Princeton University Press.

Scheffler, S. 2015. "Distributive Justice, the Basic Structure and the Place of Private Law." *Oxford Journal of Legal Studies* 35(2): 213–235.

Schlesinger, M., S. Mitchell, and B. H. Gray. 2004. "Restoring Public Legitimacy to the Nonprofit

Sector: A Survey Experiment Using Descriptions of Nonprofit Ownership." *Nonprofit and Voluntary Sector Quarterly* 33(4): 673–710.

Schlozman, K. L., S. Verba, and H. E. Brady. 2012. *The Unheavenly Chorus: Unequal Political Voice and the Broken Promise of American Democracy.* Princeton, NJ: Princeton University Press.

Schnable, A. 2015. "Do-It-Yourself Aid: The Emergence of American Grassroots Development Organizations." Doctoral diss., Princeton University.

Sievers, B. 2010. *Civil Society, Philanthropy, and the Fate of the Commons.* Medford, MA: Tufts University Press.

Simmons, A. J. 1999. "Justification and Legitimacy." *Ethics* 109(4): 739–771.

Singer, P. 1972. "Famine, Affluence, and Morality." *Philosophy and Public Affairs* 1(3): 229–243.

———. 2015. *The Most Good You Can Do: How Effective Altruism Is Changing Ideas About Living Ethically.* New Haven, CT: Yale University Press.

Skocpol, T. 2003. *Diminished Democracy: From Membership to Management in American Civil Life.* Norman: University of Oklahoma Press.

Smith, W. K., M. Gonin, and M. L. Besharov. 2013. "Managing Social-Business Tensions: A Review and Research Agenda for Social Enterprise." *Business Ethics Quarterly* 23(3): 407–442.

Soskis, B. 2017. "The History of the Giving While Living Ethic." Atlantic Philanthropies, May 30. https://www.atlanticphilanthropies.org/research-reports/the-history-of-the-giving-while-living-ethic.

Steinberg, R. 2006. "Economic Theories of Nonprofit Organizations." In *The Nonprofit Sector: A Research Handbook*, 2nd ed., ed. W. W. Powell and R. Steinberg, 117–139. New Haven, CT: Yale University Press.

Su, F., M. Li, and R. Tao. 2018. "Bringing Politics Back in Charitable Giving: Evidence from Donations After China's Sichuan Earthquake." Paper presented at the American Political Science Association Annual Meeting and Exhibition, Boston, MA, August 31.

Taylor, C. 1990. "Modes of Civil Society." *Public Culture* 3(1): 95–118.

Taylor, R. S. 2018. "Donation Without Domination: Private Charity and Republican Liberty." *Journal of Political Philosophy* 26(4): 441–462.

Tocqueville, A. de. 2012. *Democracy in America.* Chicago: University of Chicago Press.

Tomasi, J. 2012. *Free Market Fairness.* Princeton, NJ: Princeton University Press.

Urbinati, N., and M. E. Warren. 2008. "The Concept of Representation in Contemporary Democratic Theory." *Annual Review of Political Science* 11(1): 387–412.

Waldron, J. 1987. "Theoretical Foundations of Liberalism." *Philosophical Quarterly* 37(147): 127–150.

———. 2016. *Political Political Theory: Essays on Institutions.* Cambridge, MA: Harvard University Press.

Weber, M. (1922) 1978. *Economy and Society: An Outline of Interpretive Sociology*, vol. 2, ed. G. Roth and C. Wittich. Berkeley: University of California Press.

Weisbrod, B. A. 1975. "Toward a Theory of the Voluntary Nonprofit Sector in a Three-Sector Economy." In *Altruism, Morality, and Economic Theory*, ed. E. S. Phelps, 171–195. New York: Russell Sage Foundation.

Wenar, L. 2016. *Blood Oil.* Oxford, UK: Oxford University Press.

Williams, B.A.O. 2005. *In the Beginning Was the Deed: Realism and Moralism in Political Argument.* Princeton, NJ: Princeton University Press.

Wu, T. 2018. *The Curse of Bigness: Antitrust in the New Gilded Age.* New York: Columbia Global Reports.

Young, I. M. 2000. *Inclusion and Democracy.* New York: Oxford University Press.

Chapter 7. Nonprofits as Boundary Markers: The Politics of Choice, Mobilization, and Arbitrage

Abbott, A. 2001. *Time Matters: On Theory and Method.* Chicago: University of Chicago Press.

Adams, C. 2007. "In the Public Interest: Charitable Association, the State, and the Status of *Utilité Publique* in Nineteenth-Century France." *Law and History Review* 25(2): 283–321.

Almond, G. A., and S. Verba. 1963. *The Civic Culture.* Princeton, NJ: Princeton University Press.

Andrews, K. T. 2001. "Social Movements and Policy Implementation: The Mississippi Civil Rights Movement and the War on Poverty, 1965–1971." *American Sociological Review* 66(1): 71–95.

Austin, M. J. 2003. "The Changing Relationship Between Nonprofit Organizations and Public Social Service Agencies in the Era of Welfare Reform." *Nonprofit and Voluntary Sector Quarterly* 32(1): 97–114.

Barman, E. 2013. "Classificatory Struggles in the Nonprofit Sector: The Formation of the National Taxonomy of Exempt Entities, 1969–1987." *Social Science History* 37(1): 103–141.

Beito, D. T. 2000. *From Mutual Aid to the Welfare State: Fraternal Societies and Social Services, 1890–1967*. Chapel Hill: University of North Carolina Press.

Bermeo, N., and P. Nord, eds. 2000. *Civil Society Before Democracy: Lessons from Nineteenth-Century Europe*. New York: Rowman and Littlefield.

Berry, J. M., with D. F. Arons. 2003. *A Voice for Nonprofits*. Washington, DC: Brookings Institution Press.

Blee, K. M. 2002. *Inside Organized Racism: Women in the Hate Movement*. Berkeley: University of California Press.

Bloom, J., and W. E. Martin. 2012. *Black Against Empire: The History and Politics of the Black Panther Party*. Berkeley: University of California Press.

Boris, E. T., and J. Krehely. 2003. "Civic Participation and Advocacy." In *The Resilient Sector: The State of Nonprofit America*, ed. L. Salamon, 299–330. Washington, DC: Brookings Institution Press.

Brown, Maoz. 2018. "Cooperation, Coordination, and Control: The Emergence and Decline of Centralized Finance in American Charity." *Social Science History* 42(3): 543–573.

Cammett, M. 2014. *Compassionate Communalism: Welfare and Sectarianism in Lebanon*. Ithaca, NY: Cornell University Press.

Cammett, M., and L. M. MacLean, eds. 2014. *The Politics of Non-State Social Welfare*. Ithaca, NY: Cornell University Press.

Castells, M. 1983. *The City and the Grassroots: A Cross-Cultural Theory of Urban Social Movements*. Berkeley: University of California Press.

Chambers, S., and J. Kopstein. 2001. "Bad Civil Society." *Political Theory* 29(6): 837–865.

Clemens, E. S. 1997. *The People's Lobby: Organizational Innovation and the Rise of Interest Group Politics in the United States, 1890–1925*. Chicago: University of Chicago Press.

———. 2006. "Lineages of the Rube Goldberg State: Public Finance and Private Governance, 1900–1940." In *Rethinking Political Institutions: The Art of the State*, ed. Ian Shapiro, Stephen Skowroneck, and Daniel Galvin, 187–215. New York: NYU Press.

———. 2017. "Reconciling Equal Treatment with Respect for Individuality: Associations in the Symbiotic State." In *The Many Hands of the State*, ed. K. Morgan and A. S. Orloff, 35–57. New York: Cambridge University Press.

———. 2020. *Civic Gifts: Voluntarism and the Making of the American Nation-State*. Chicago: University of Chicago Press.

Colley, L. 1992. *Britons: Forging the Nation 1707–1837*. New Haven, CT: Yale University Press.

Dai, J., and A. J. Spires. 2017. "Advocacy in an Authoritarian State: How Grassroots Environmental NGOs Influence Local Governments in China." *China Journal* 79 (January): 62–83.

Douglas, J. A. 1983. *Why Charity? The Case for a Third Sector*. Beverly Hills, CA: SAGE.

———. 1987. "Political Theories of Nonprofit Organization." In *The Nonprofit Sector: A Research Handbook*, ed. W.W. Powell, 43–54. New Haven, CT: Yale University Press.

Dresden, J. R., and M. M. Howard. 2016. "Authoritarian Backsliding and the Concentration of Political Power." *Democratization* 23(7): 1122–1143.

Eckstein, H. 1966. *Division and Cohesion in Democracy: A Study of Norway*. Princeton, NJ: Princeton University Press.

Edwards, B. 1994. "Semiformal Organizational Structure Among Social Movement Organizations: An Analysis of the U.S. Peace Movement." *Nonprofit and Voluntary Sector Quarterly* 23(4): 309–333.

Eliasoph, N. 1998. *Avoiding Politics: How Americans Produce Apathy in Everyday Life*. New York: Cambridge University Press.

———. 2011. *Making Volunteers: Civic Life After Welfare's End*. Princeton, NJ: Princeton University Press.

Elisha, O. 2010. "Evangelical Megachurches and the Christianization of Civil Society: An Ethnographic Case Study." In *Politics and Partnerships:*

The Role of Voluntary Associations in America's Political Past and Present, ed. E. S. Clemens and D. Guthrie, 269–296. Chicago: University of Chicago Press.

Ertman, T. 2000. "Liberalization, Democratization, and the Origins of a 'Pillarized' Civil Society in Nineteenth-Century Belgium and the Netherlands." In *Civil Society Before Democracy: Lessons from Nineteenth-Century Europe*, ed. N. Bermeo and P. Nord, 155–178. New York: Rowman and Littlefield.

Esping-Andersen, G. 1990. *The Three Worlds of Welfare Capitalism*. Princeton, NJ: Princeton University Press.

Finn, C. E. Jr., B. V. Manno, and G. Vanourek. 2000. *Charter Schools in Action: Renewing Public Education*. Princeton, NJ: Princeton University Press.

Fiorina, M. P. 1999. "Extreme Voices: A Dark Side of Civic Engagement." In *Civic Engagement in American Democracy*, ed. T. Skocpol and M. P. Fiorina, 395–425. Washington, DC: Brookings Institution Press.

Fleischacker, S. 1998. "Insignificant Communities." In *Freedom of Association*, ed. A. Gutmann, 273–313. Princeton, NJ: Princeton University Press.

Fox, J. 1997. "How Does Civil Society Thicken? The Political Construction of Social Capital in Rural Mexico." In *State-Society Synergy: Government and Social Capital in Development*, ed. P. Evans. Research Series 94. Berkeley: University of California Press.

Frumkin, P. 2002. *On Being Nonprofit: A Conceptual and Policy Primer*. Cambridge, MA: Harvard University Press.

Gamm, G., and R. D. Putnam. 1999. "The Growth of Voluntary Associations in America, 1840–1940." *Journal of Interdisciplinary History* 29(4): 511–557.

Ganz, M. 2000. "Resources and Resourcefulness: Strategic Capacity in the Unionization of California Agriculture, 1959–1966." *American Journal of Sociology* 105(4): 1003–1062.

Grønbjerg, K. A. 1993. *Understanding Nonprofit Funding: Managing Revenues in Social Services and Community Development Organizations*. San Francisco: Jossey-Bass.

Gutmann, A., ed. 1998. *Freedom of Association*. Princeton, NJ: Princeton University Press.

Habermas, J. (1962) 1991. *The Structural Transformation of the Public Sphere: An Inquiry into a Category of Bourgeois Society*. Cambridge, MA: MIT Press.

Hall, P. D. 1987. "A Historical Overview of the Private Nonprofit Sector." In *The Nonprofit Sector: A Research Handbook*, ed. W. W. Powell, 32–65. New Haven, CT: Yale University Press.

———. 1992. *"Inventing the Nonprofit Sector" and Other Essays on Philanthropy, Voluntarism, and Nonprofit Organizations*. Baltimore: Johns Hopkins University Press.

Hamlett, John C. 2017. "The Constitutionality of Russia's Undesirable NGO Law." *UCLA Journal of International Law and Foreign Affairs* 21(2): 246–310.

Han, H. 2016. "The Organizational Roots of Political Activism: Field Experiments on Creating a Relational Context." *American Political Science Review* 110(2): 296–307.

Hansmann, H. 1987. "Economic Theories of Nonprofit Organizations." In *The Nonprofit Sector: A Research Handbook*, ed. W. W. Powell, 27–42. New Haven, CT: Yale University Press.

Hoffman, S.-L. 2003. "Democracy and Associations in the Long Nineteenth Century: Toward a Transnational Perspective." *Journal of Modern History* 75 (June): 269–299.

Horvath, A., and W. W. Powell. 2016. "Contributory or Disruptive: Do New Forms of Philanthropy Erode Democracy?" In *Philanthropy in Democratic Societies: History, Institutions, Values*, ed. R. Reich, C. Cordelli, and L. Bernholz, 87–122. Chicago: University of Chicago Press.

Horvath, R. 2013. *Putin's "Preventive Counter-Revolution": Post-Soviet Authoritarianism and the Spectre of Velvet Revolution*. New York: Routledge.

Howard, M. M. 2003. *The Weakness of Civil Society in Post-Communist Europe*. New York: Cambridge University Press.

Hsu, J.Y.J., C. L. Hsu, and R. Hasmath. 2017. "NGO Strategies in an Authoritarian Context, and Their Implications for Citizenship: The Case of the People's Republic of China." *Voluntas: International Journal of Voluntary and Nonprofit Organizations* 28(3): 1157–1179.

Huard, R. 2000. "Political Association in Nineteenth-Century France: Legislation and Practice." In *Civil Society Before Democracy: Lessons from Nineteenth-Century Europe*, ed. N. Bermeo and P. Nord, 135–153. New York: Rowman and Littlefield.

Jenkins, J. C. 1987. "Nonprofit Organizations and Policy Advocacy." In *The Nonprofit Sector: A Research Handbook*, ed. W. W. Powell, 296–318. New Haven, CT: Yale University Press.

———. 1998. "Channeling Social Protest: Foundation Patronage of Contemporary Social Movements." In *Private Action and the Public Good*, ed. W. W. Powell and E. S. Clemens, 206–216. New Haven, CT: Yale University Press.

Kaufman, J. 2002. *For the Common Good? American Civic Life and the Golden Age of Fraternity*. New York: Oxford University Press.

Kendall, J. 2000. "The Mainstreaming of the Third Sector into Public Policy in England in the Late 1990s: Whys and Wherefores." *Policy and Politics* 28(4): 541–562.

Kuhnle, S., and P. Selle. 1992. "The Historical Precedent for Government-Nonprofit Cooperation in Norway." In *Government and the Third Sector: Emerging Relationships in Welfare States*, ed. B. Gidron, R. M. Kramer, and L. M. Salamon, 75–99. San Francisco: Jossey-Bass.

Lamoreaux, N. R., and J. J. Wallis, eds. 2017. *Organizations, Civil Society, and the Roots of Development*. Chicago: University of Chicago Press.

Lee, C. W., M. McQuarrie, and E. T. Walker. 2015. *Democratizing Inequalities: Dilemmas of the New Public Participation*. New York: NYU Press.

Levine, J. R. 2016. "The Privatization of Political Representation: Community-Based Organizations as Nonelected Neighborhood Representatives." *American Sociological Review* 81(6): 1251–1275.

Levy, J. 2017. "From Fiscal Triangle to Passing Through: Rise of the Nonprofit Corporation." In *Corporations and American Democracy*, ed. N. R. Lamoreaux and W. J. Novak, 213–244. Cambridge, MA: Harvard University Press.

Lichterman, P. 2005. *Elusive Togetherness: Church Groups Trying to Bridge America's Divisions*. Princeton, NJ: Princeton University Press.

Lindenmeyr, A. 1996. *Poverty Is Not a Vice: Charity, Society, and the State in Imperial Russia*. Princeton, NJ: Princeton University Press.

Ljubownikow, S., and J. Crotty. 2014. "Civil Society in a Transitional Context: The Response of Health and Educational NGOs to Legislative Changes in Russia's Industrialized Regions." *Nonprofit and Voluntary Sector Quarterly* 43(4): 759–776.

Ma, Q. 2002. "The Governance of NGOs in China Since 1978: How Much Autonomy?" *Nonprofit and Voluntary Sector Quarterly* 31(3): 305–328.

Malczewski, J. 2016. *Building a New Educational State: Foundations, Schools, and the American South*. Chicago: University of Chicago Press.

McCarthy, K. D. 2003. *American Creed: Philanthropy and the Rise of Civil Society, 1700–1865*. Chicago: University of Chicago Press.

McGarvie, M. D. 2003. "The *Dartmouth College* Case and the Legal Design of Civil Society." In *Charity, Philanthropy, and Civility in American History*, ed. L. J. Friedman and M. D. McGarvie, 91–105. New York: Cambridge University Press.

McVeigh, R. 2009. *The Rise of the Ku Klux Klan: Right-Wing Movements and National Politics*. Minneapolis: University of Minnesota Press.

Mettler, S. 2011. *The Submerged State: How Invisible Government Policies Undermine American Democracy*. Chicago: University of Chicago Press.

Mitchell, T. 1991. "The Limits of the State: Beyond Statist Approaches and Their Critics." *American Political Science Review* 85(1): pp. 77–96.

Moore, Barrington. 1966. *Social Origins of Dictatorship and Democracy: Lord and Peasant in the Making of the Modern World*. Boston: Beacon Press.

Morgan, K. J., and A. Campbell. 2011. *The Delegated Welfare State: Medicare, Markets, and the Governance of Social Policy*. New York: Oxford University Press.

Morone, J. A. 2003. *Hellfire Nation: The Politics of Sin in American History*. New Haven, CT: Yale University Press.

Nie, L., H. K. Liu, and W. Cheng. 2016. "Exploring Factors that Influence Voluntary Disclosure by Chinese Foundations." *Voluntas: International Journal of Voluntary and Nonprofit Organizations* 27(5): 2374–2400.

Nord, P. 2000. "Introduction." In *Civil Society Before Democracy: Lessons from Nineteenth-Century Europe*, ed. N. Bermeo and P. Nord, xiii–xxxiii. New York: Rowman and Littlefield.

North, D. C., J. J. Wallis, and B. R. Weingast. 2009. *Violence and Social Orders: A Conceptual Framework for Interpreting Recorded Human History.* New York: Cambridge University Press.

Novak, W. J. 2001. "The American Law of Association: The Legal-Political Construction of Civil Society." *Studies in American Political Development* 15(2): 163–188.

Oleinikova, O. 2017. "Foreign Funded NGOs in Russia, Belarus and Ukraine: Recent Restrictions and Implications." *Cosmopolitan Civil Societies: An Interdisciplinary Journal* 9(3): 85–94.

Osa, M. 2003. *Solidarity and Contention: Networks of Polish Opposition.* Minneapolis: University of Minnesota Press.

Pierson, P. 1994. *Dismantling the Welfare State? Reagan, Thatcher and the Politics of Retrenchment.* New York: Cambridge University Press.

Putnam, R. D. 2000. *Bowling Alone: The Collapse and Revival of American Community.* New York: Simon and Schuster.

Putnam, R. D., R. Leonardi, and R. Y. Nanetti. 1993. *Making Democracy Work: Civic Traditions in Modern Italy.* Princeton, NJ: Princeton University Press.

Reckhow, S. 2013. *Follow the Money: How Foundation Dollars Change Public School Politics.* Oxford, UK: Oxford University Press.

Reid, E. J. 1999. "Nonprofit Advocacy and Political Participation." In *Nonprofits and Government: Collaboration and Conflict*, ed. E. T. Boris and C. E. Steuerle, 291–325. Washington, DC: Urban Institute Press.

Riley, D. 2010. *The Civic Foundations of Fascism in Europe: Italy, Spain, and Romania, 1870–1945.* Baltimore: Johns Hopkins University Press.

Ronsavallon, P. 2007. *The Demands of Liberty: Civil Society in France Since the Revolution*, trans. Arthur Goldhammer. Cambridge, MA: Harvard University Press.

Rosenblum, N. L. 1998a. "Compelled Association: Public Standing, Self-Respect, and the Dynamic of Exclusion." In *Freedom of Association*, ed.

A. Gutmann, 75–108. Princeton, NJ: Princeton University Press.

———. 1998b. *Membership and Morals: The Personal Uses of Pluralism in America.* Princeton, NJ: Princeton University Press.

Salamon, L. M. 1987. "Partners in Public Service: The Scope and Theory of Government-Nonprofit Relations." In *The Nonprofit Sector: A Research Handbook*, ed. W. W. Powell, 99–117. New Haven, CT: Yale University Press.

Salamon, L. M., and H. K. Anheier. 1998. "Social Origins of Civil Society: Explaining the Nonprofit Sector Cross-Nationally." *Voluntas: International Journal of Voluntary and Nonprofit Organizations* 9(3): 213–248.

Skocpol, T. 1997. "The Tocqueville Problem: Civic Engagement in American Democracy." *Social Science History* 21(4): 455–480.

———. 2003. *Diminished Democracy: From Membership to Management in American Civic Life.* Norman: University of Oklahoma Press.

Skocpol, T., M. Ganz, and Z. Munson. 2000. "A Nation of Organizers: The Institutional Origins of Civic Voluntarism in the United States." *American Political Science Review* 94(3): 527–546.

Skocpol, T., M. Ganz, Z. Munson, B. Camp, M. Swers, and J. Oser. 1999. "How Americans Became Civic." In *Civic Engagement in American Democracy*, ed. T. Skocpol and M. P. Fiorina, 27–80. Washington, DC: Brookings Institution Press.

Small, M. L. 2009. *Unanticipated Gains: Origins of Network Inequality in Everyday Life.* Oxford, UK: Oxford University Press.

Smith, S. R., and M. Lipsky. 1993. *Nonprofits for Hire: The Welfare State in the Age of Contracting.* Cambridge, MA: Harvard University Press.

Spencer, S. B. 2011. "Culture as Structure in Emerging Civic Organizations in Russia." *Nonprofit and Voluntary Sector Quarterly* 40(6): 1073–1091.

Spires, A. J. 2011. "Contingent Symbiosis and Civil Society in an Authoritarian State: Understanding the Survival of China's Grassroots NGOs." *American Journal of Sociology* 117(1): 1–45.

Suleiman, E. 2003. *Dismantling Democratic States.* Princeton, NJ: Princeton University Press.

Thachil, T. 2011. "Embedded Mobilization: Nonstate Service Provision as Electoral Strategy in India." *World Politics* 63 (July): 434–469.

Tocqueville, A. de. 2004. *Democracy in America,* trans. A. Goldhammer. New York: Library of America.

Tuğal, C. 2017. "The Uneven Neoliberalization of Good Works: Islamic Charitable Fields and Their Impact on Diffusion." *American Journal of Sociology* 123(2): 426–464.

Ullman, C. F. 1998. *The Welfare State's Other Crisis: Explaining the New Partnership Between Non-profit Organizations and the State in France.* Bloomington: Indiana University Press.

Verba, S., K. L. Schlozman, and H. E. Brady. 1995. *Voice and Equality: Civic Voluntarism in American Politics.* Cambridge, MA: Harvard University Press.

Walker, E. T. 2014. *Grassroots for Hire: Public Affairs Consultants in American Democracy.* New York: Cambridge University Press.

Walzer, M. 1984. "Liberalism and the Art of Separation." *Political Theory* 12(3): 315–330.

Ware, A. 1989. *Between Profit and State: Intermediate Organizations in Britain and the United States.* Princeton, NJ: Princeton University Press.

Warren, M. E. 2001. *Democracy and Association.* Princeton, NJ: Princeton University Press.

Warren, M. R. 2001. *Dry Bones Rattling: Community Building to Revitalize American Democracy.* Princeton, NJ: Princeton University Press.

Weisbrod, B. A. 1988. *The Nonprofit Economy.* Cambridge, MA: Harvard University Press.

Wijkström, F., and A. Zimmer, eds. 2011. *Nordic Civil Society at a Cross-Roads: Transforming the Popular Movement Tradition.* Baden-Baden, Germany: Nomos Verlagsgesellschaft.

Wolch, J. R. 1992. *The Shadow State: Government and Voluntary Sector in Transition.* New York: Foundation Center.

Wuthnow, R., ed. 1991. *Between States and Markets: The Voluntary Sector in Comparative Perspective.* Princeton, NJ: Princeton University Press.

———. 1998. *Loose Connections: Joining Together in America's Fragmented Communities.* Cambridge, MA: Harvard University Press.

———. 1999. "Mobilizing Civic Engagement: The Changing Impact of Religious Involvement." In *Civic Engagement in American Democracy,* ed. T. Skocpol and M. P. Fiorina, 331–364. Washington, DC: Brookings Institution Press.

Xu, X. 2013. "Belonging Before Believing: Group Ethos and Bloc Recruitment in the Making of Chinese Communism." *American Sociological Review* 78(5): 773–796.

Young, M. P. 2002. "Confessional Protest: The Religious Birth of U.S. National Social Movements." *American Sociological Review* 67(5): 660–688.

Zollman, C. 1924. *American Law of Charities.* Milwaukee, WI: Bruce.

Zunz, O. 2012. *Philanthropy in America: A History.* Princeton, NJ: Princeton University Press.

Chapter 8. Politics, Philanthropy, and Inequality

Allied Media. 2017. "Changing the Conversation: Philanthropic Funding and Community Organizing in Detroit." https://www.alliedmedia.org/sites/default/files/funders_guidelines_2017_print.pdf, accessed December 11, 2018.

———. 2018. "The Transforming Power Fund Is Hiring Two Co-Directors." October 1. https://www.alliedmedia.org/news/2018/10/01/transforming-power-fund-hiring-two-co-directors.

Anderson, Michelle W. 2014. "The New Minimal Cities." *Yale Law Journal* 123(5): 1118–1625.

Atkinson, Anthony B., Thomas Piketty, and Emmanuel Saez. 2011. "Top Incomes in the Long Run of History." *Journal of Economic Literature* 49(1): 3–71.

Barkan, Joanne. 2013. "Plutocrats at Work: How Big Philanthropy Undermines Democracy." *Dissent.* https://www.dissentmagazine.org/article/plutocrats-at-work-how-big-philanthropy-undermines-democracy.

Barnum, Matt. 2018. "Internal Memo Offers Candid Postmortem of Charter Fight in Massachusetts." Chalkbeat, April 16. https://www.chalkbeat.org/posts/us/2018/04/16/internal-memo-offers-candid-postmortem-of-charter-fight-in-massachusetts/.

Bartels, Larry. 2008. *Unequal Democracy: The Political Economy of the New Gilded Age.* Princeton, NJ: Princeton University Press.

Bishop, Matthew, and Michael Green. 2010. *Philanthrocapitalism: How Giving Can Save the World.* New York: Bloomsbury Press.

Bonica, Adam, Nolan McCarty, Keith T. Poole, and Howard Rosenthal. 2013. "Why Hasn't

Democracy Slowed Rising Inequality?" *Journal of Economic Perspectives* 27(3): 103–124.

Callahan, David. 2017. *The Givers: Wealth, Power, and Philanthropy in a New Gilded Age.* New York: Knopf.

Chand, Daniel E. 2014. "Nonprofit Electioneering Post-Citizens United: How Organizations Have Become More Complex." *Election Law Journal* 13(2): 243–259.

de Graauw, Els. 2016. *Making Immigrant Rights Real: Nonprofits and the Politics of Integration in San Francisco.* Ithaca, NY: Cornell University Press.

DeVito, Lee. 2018. "More Corporations Come to Detroit's Rescue—and That's a Problem." *Detroit Metro Times*, December 11.

Donovan, Doug. 2016. "Billionaire Donors Laura and John Arnold Support Far More in Maryland than Police Surveillance." *Baltimore Sun*, August 26.

Downey, Davia C., and Sarah Reckhow. 2017. "Unnatural Disasters: Can Nonprofit Governance Promote Recovery in Detroit and Flint?" Michigan Applied Public Policy Brief. Institute for Public Policy and Social Research. Michigan State University.

Ember, Sydney, and Kenneth P. Vogel. 2017. "The Kochs Are Inching Closer to Becoming Media Moguls." *New York Times*, November 17. https://www.nytimes.com/2017/11/17/business/media/koch-brothers-time-meredith.html.

Fleishman, Joel. 2008. *The Foundation: A Great American Secret.* New York: Public Affairs.

Franz, Michael. 2013. "When Does Money Buy Votes? Campaign Contributions and Policymaking." In *New Directions in Interest Group Politics*, ed. Matt Grossmann, 165–184. London: Routledge.

Freedom to Marry. n.d. "The Roadmap to Victory." http://www.freedomtomarry.org/pages/Roadmap-to-Victory, accessed October 20, 2019.

Gilens, Martin. 2012. *Affluence and Influence: Economic Inequality and Political Power in America.* Princeton, NJ: Princeton University Press.

Gimpel, James G., Frances E. Lee, and Shanna Pearson-Merkowitz. 2008. "The Check Is in the Mail: Interdistrict Funding Flows in Congressional Elections." *American Journal of Political Science* 52(2): 373–394.

Goss, Kristin A. 2016. "Policy Plutocrats: How America's Wealthy Seek to Influence Governance." *PS: Political Science and Politics* 49(3): 442–448.

Grossmann, Matt. 2012. *The Not-So-Special Interests: Interest Groups, Public Representation, and American Governance.* Stanford, CA: Stanford University Press.

Hacker, Jacob, and Paul Pierson. 2011. *Winner-Take-All Politics: How Washington Made the Rich Richer—and Turned Its Back on the Middle Class.* New York: Simon and Schuster.

Holly, Christen, Tim Field, Juli Kim, Bryan C. Hassel, Maggie Runyan-Shefa, Michael Stone, and Davis Zaunbrecher. 2015. "Ten Years in New Orleans: Public School Resurgence and the Path Ahead–Executive Summary." New Orleans, LA: New Schools for New Orleans. http://www.newschoolsforneworleans.org/wp-content/uploads/2015/06/Public-School-Resurgence-Executive-Summary-FINAL.pdf.

Hood, Lauren, 2016. "Gentrification in Detroit." The Hub Detroit. https://www.thehubdetroit.com/gentrification-in-detroit/, accessed December 11, 2018.

Horvath, Aaron, and Walter W. Powell. 2016. "Contributory or Disruptive: Do New Forms of Philanthropy Erode Democracy?" In *Philanthropy in Democratic Societies: History, Institutions, Values*, ed. Rob Reich, Chiara Cordelli, and Lucy Bernholz, 87–122. Chicago: University of Chicago Press.

Jacobs, Lawrence, and Theda Skocpol. 2007. *Inequality and American Democracy: What We Know and What We Need to Learn.* New York: Russell Sage Foundation.

Kerlin, Janelle A., and Elizabeth J. Reid. 2010. "The Financing and Programming of Advocacy in Complex Nonprofit Structures." *Nonprofit and Voluntary Sector Quarterly* 39(5): 802–824.

Korn, Melissa. 2018. "Michael Bloomberg Commits $375 Million to Education Initiatives." *Wall Street Journal*, May 31. https://www.wsj.com/articles/michael-bloomberg-commits-375-million-to-education-initiatives-1527806842.

Krugman, Paul. 2014. "Why We're in a New Gilded Age." *New York Review of Books*, May 8.

Lemos, Margaret H., and Guy-Uriel Charles. 2018. "Public Programs, Private Financing." *Law and Contemporary Problems*, 81(3): 137–160.

Levine, Jeremy R. 2016. "The Privatization of Political Representation: Community-Based Organizations as Nonelected Neighborhood Representatives." *American Sociological Review* 81(6): 1251–1275.

Lowe, Kate, and Joe Grengs. Forthcoming. "Private Donations for Public Transit: The Equity Implications of Detroit's Public-Private Streetcar." *Journal of Planning Education and Research*.

Marwell, Nicole P. 2004. "Privatizing the Welfare State: Nonprofit Community-Based Organizations as Political Actors." *American Sociological Review* 69(2): 265–291.

McDonnell, Lorraine, and M. Stephen Weatherford. 2013. "Organized Interests and the Common Core." *Educational Researcher* 42(9): 488–497.

McDonald, Lauren. 2014. "Think Tanks and the Media: How the Conservative Movement Gained Entry into the Education Policy Arena." *Educational Policy* 28(6): 845–880.

McGooey, Linsey. 2016. *No Such Thing as a Free Gift: The Gates Foundation and the Price of Philanthropy*. New York: Verso.

Medvetz, Thomas. 2012. *Think Tanks in America*. Chicago: University of Chicago Press.

Miller, Claire Cain. 2013. "Laurene Powell Jobs and Anonymous Giving in Silicon Valley." *New York Times*, May 24. https://bits.blogs.nytimes.com/2013/05/24/laurene-powell-jobs-and-anonymous-giving-in-silicon-valley/.

Moran, Mary. 2015. "Howard Fuller Explains What's Happening in New Orleans." *Education Post*, August 7. https://educationpost.org/howard-fuller-explains-whats-happening-in-new-orleans/.

Morel, Domingo, and Sally Nuamah. Forthcoming. "Who Governs? How Shifts in Political Power Shape Perceptions of Local Government Services." *Urban Affairs Review*.

Omidyar Network. n.d. "A New Approach: Building a Philanthropic Investment Firm." https://www.omidyar.com/sites/default/files/file_archive/Omidyar%20Network%20Approach.pdf, accessed October 20, 2019.

Pacewicz, Josh. 2016. *Partisans and Partners: The Politics of the Post-Keynesian Society*. Chicago: University of Chicago Press.

Page, Benjamin I., Larry M. Bartels, and Jason Seawright. 2013. "Democracy and the Policy Preferences of Wealthy Americans." *Perspectives on Politics* 11(1): 51–73.

Pew Charitable Trusts. 2016. "Fiscal Health of Large U.S. Cities Varied Long After Great Recession's End." Issue Brief.

Pill, Madeleine. 2018. "The Austerity Governance of Baltimore's Neighborhoods: 'The Conversation May Have Changed but the Systems Aren't Changing.'" *Journal of Urban Affairs*. https://doi.org/10.1080/07352166.2018.1478226.

Piketty, Thomas. 2013. *Capital in the 21st Century*. Cambridge, MA: Harvard University Press.

Reckhow, Sarah. 2013. *Follow the Money: How Foundation Dollars Change Public School Politics*. Oxford, UK: Oxford University Press.

Reckhow, Sarah, Davia Downey, and Joshua Sapotichne. Forthcoming. "Governing Without Government: Nonprofit Governance in Detroit and Flint." *Urban Affairs Review*.

Reich, Rob. 2016. "On the Role of Foundations in Democracies." In *Philanthropy in Democratic Societies: History, Institutions, Values*, ed. Rob Reich, Chiara Cordelli, and Lucy Bernholz, 64–81. Chicago: University of Chicago Press.

———. 2018. *Just Giving: Why Philanthropy Is Failing Democracy and How It Can Do Better*. Princeton, NJ: Princeton University Press.

Rhodes, Jesse H., Brian F. Schaffner, and Raymond J. La Raja. 2018. "Detecting and Understanding Donor Strategies in Midterm Elections." *Political Research Quarterly* 71(3): 503–516.

Rich, Andrew. 2004. *Think Tanks, Public Policy, and the Politics of Expertise*. Cambridge, UK: Cambridge University Press.

Saez, Emmanuel, and Gabriel Zucman. 2014. "Wealth Inequality in the United States Since 1913: Evidennce from Capitalized Income Tax Data." National Bureau of Economic Research. Working Paper No. 20625.

Schlozman, Kay Lehman, Sidney Verba, and Henry E. Brady. 2012. *The Unheavenly Chorus: Unequal Political Voice and the Broken Promise of American Democracy*. Princeton, NJ: Princeton University Press.

Saunders-Hastings, Emma. 2018. "Plutocratic Philanthropy." *Journal of Politics* 80(1): 149–161.

Silverstein, Ken. 2015. "Where Journalism Goes to Die." Politico, February 27. https://www.politico.com/magazine/story/2015/02/ken-silverstein-the-intercept-115586.

Skocpol, Theda, and Alexander Hertel-Fernandez. 2016. "The Koch Network and Republican Party Extremism." *Perspectives on Politics* 14(3): 681–699.

Smith, Sandy, 2014. "Detroit's M-1 Rail Streetcar: A Next City Explainer." *Next City*, July 25. https://nextcity.org/daily/entry/detroit-m1-construction-starts-m1-streetcar-guide.

Stone, Clarence. 2015. "Reflections on Regime Politics: From Governing Coalition to Urban Political Order." *Urban Affairs Review* 51(1): 101–137.

Teles, Steven M. 2008. *The Rise of the Conservative Legal Movement: The Battle for Control of the Law.* Princeton, NJ: Princeton University Press.

Tompkins-Stange, Megan. 2016. *Policy Patrons: Philanthropy, Education Reform, and the Politics of Influence.* Harvard Education Press: Cambridge, MA.

Walker, Jack L. 1991. *Mobilizing Interest Groups in America: Patrons, Professions, and Social Movements.* Ann Arbor: University of Michigan Press.

Warren, Mark R., and Karen L. Mapp. 2011. *A Match on Dry Grass: Community Organizing as a Catalyst for School Reform.* New York: Oxford University Press.

Wemple, Erik. 2017. "Laurene Powell Jobs's Emerson Collective to purchase majority stake in the Atlantic." *Washington Post*, July 28. https://www.washingtonpost.com/blogs/erik-wemple/wp/2017/07/28/laurene-powell-jobss-emerson-collective-to-purchase-majority-stake-in-the-atlantic/?utm_term=.b509582387e3.

Whyte, Liz E. 2014. "Philanthropy Keeps the Lights on in Detroit." *Philanthropy* (January).

Wylie-Kellermann, Bill. 2015. "Gentrification and Race: Can We Have a Real Conversation?" *Detroit Metro Times*, April 25. https://www.metrotimes.com/news-hits/archives/2015/04/28/gentrification-and-race-can-we-have-a-real-conversation.

Zucman, Gabriel. 2019. "Global Wealth Inequality." National Bureau of Economic Research. Working Paper No. 25462.

Zunz, Olivier. 2012. *Philanthropy in America: A History.* Princeton, NJ: Princeton University Press.

Part III. Governance, Civic Capacity, and Communities

Chapter 9. Toward a Governance Framework for Government–Nonprofit Relations

Abzug, R. 1999. "Nonprofits in Organizational Sociology Research Traditions: An Empirical Study." *Nonprofit and Voluntary Sector Quarterly* 28(3): 330–338.

Anheier, H. K. 2009. "What Kind of Nonprofit Sector, What Kind of Society? Comparative Policy Reflections." *American Behavioral Scientist* 52(7): 1082–1094.

Anheier, H. K., and W. Seibel. 1997. "Germany." In *Defining the Nonprofit Sector: A Cross-National Analysis*, ed. L. M. Salamon and H. K. Anheier, 128–168. Manchester, UK: Manchester University Press.

Ansell, C., and A. Gash. 2008. "Collaborative Governance in Theory and Practice." *Journal of Public Administration Research and Theory* 18(4): 543–571.

Baas, M. 2013. *The Politics and Civics of National Service: Lessons from the Civilian Conservation Corps, VISTA, and AmeriCorps.* Washington, DC: Brookings Institution Press.

Barber, B. R. 1998. *A Place for Us: How to Make Society Civil and Democracy Strong.* New York: Hill and Wang.

Barman, E. 2016. *Caring Capitalism: The Meaning and Measure of Social Value.* Cambridge, UK: Cambridge University Press.

Battilana, J., B. Leca, and E. Boxenbaum. 2009. "How Actors Change Institutions: Towards a Theory of Institutional Entrepreneurship." *Academy of Management Annals* 3(1): 65–107.

Benjamin, L. M. 2012. "Nonprofit Organizations and Outcome Measurement: From Tracking Program Activities to Focusing on Frontline Work." *American Journal of Evaluation* 33(3): 431–447.

Ben-Ner, A., and B. Gui. 2003. "The Theory of Nonprofit Organizations Revisited." In *The Study of the Nonprofit Enterprise: Theories and Approaches*, ed. H. Anheier and A. Ben-Ner, 3–26. Boston: Springer.

Berger, P. L., and R. J. Neuhaus. 1996. *To Empower People: From State to Civil Society*, 2nd ed., ed. M. Novak. Washington, DC: American Enterprise Institute.

Bevir, M. 2011. "Governance as Theory, Practice, and Dilemma." In *The SAGE Handbook of Governance*, ed. M. Bevir, 1–16. Los Angeles: SAGE.

Bevir, M., and R.A.W. Rhodes. 2011. "The Stateless State." In *The SAGE Handbook of Governance*, ed. M. Bevir, 203–217. Los Angeles: SAGE.

Binder, A. 2007. "For Love and Money: Organizations' Creative Responses to Multiple Environmental Logics." *Theory and Society* 36(6): 547–571.

Boris, E. T., and C. E. Steuerle, eds. 2017. *Nonprofits and Government: Collaboration and Conflict*, 3rd ed. Lanham, MD: Rowman and Littlefield.

Brandsen, T., and U. Pape. 2015. "The Netherlands: The Paradox of Government–Nonprofit Partnerships." *Voluntas: International Journal of Voluntary and Nonprofit Organizations* 26(6): 2267–2282.

Brinkerhoff, J. M., and D. W. Brinkerhoff. 2002. "Government-Nonprofit Relations in Comparative Perspective: Evolution, Themes and New Directions." *Public Administration and Development* 22(1): 3–18.

Brodkin, E. Z. 2011. "Policy Work: Street-Level Organizations Under New Managerialism." *Journal of Public Administration Research and Theory* 21(suppl. 2): i253–i277.

Bromley, P., and J. W. Meyer. 2017. "'They Are All Organizations': The Cultural Roots of Blurring Between the Nonprofit, Business, and Government Sectors." *Administration and Society* 49(7): 939–966.

Brown, M. 2018. "Cooperation, Coordination, and Control: The Emergence and Decline of Centralized Finance in American Charity." *Social Science History* 42(3): 543–573.

Browning, P. C., and W. L. Sparks. 2015. *The Director's Manual: A Framework for Board Governance*. Hoboken, NJ: Wiley.

Bryson, J. M., B. C. Crosby, and L. Bloomberg. 2014. "Public Value Governance: Moving Beyond Traditional Public Administration and the New Public Management." *Public Administration Review* 74(4): 445–456.

Carman, J. G. 2007. "Evaluation Practice Among Community-Based Organizations: Research into the Reality." *American Journal of Evaluation* 28(1): 60–75.

———. 2009. "Nonprofits, Funders, and Evaluation: Accountability in Action." *American Review of Public Administration* 39(4): 374–390.

Carter, D. P. 2017. "Role Perceptions and Attitudes Toward Discretion at a Decentralized Regulatory Frontline: The Case of Organic Inspectors." *Regulation and Governance* 11(4): 353–367.

Chambers, S., and J. Kopstein. 2006. "Civil Society and the State." In *The Oxford Handbook of Political Theory*, ed. J. S. Dryzek, B. Honig, and A. Phillips, 363–381. Oxford, UK: Oxford University Press.

Chaskin, R. J. 2003. "Fostering Neighborhood Democracy: Legitimacy and Accountability Within Loosely Coupled Systems." *Nonprofit and Voluntary Sector Quarterly* 32(2): 161–189.

Chen, C. A. 2012. "Explaining the Difference of Work Attitudes Between Public and Nonprofit Managers: The Views of Rule Constraints and Motivation Styles." *American Review of Public Administration* 42(4): 437–460.

Child, C., E. Witesman, and R. Spencer. 2016. "The Blurring Hypothesis Reconsidered: How Sector Still Matters to Practitioners." *Voluntas: International Journal of Voluntary and Nonprofit Organizations* 27(4): 1831–1852.

Chin, J. J. 2009. "The Limits and Potential of Nonprofit Organizations in Participatory Planning: A Case Study of the New York HIV Planning Council." *Journal of Urban Affairs* 31: 431–460.

Clarke, L., and C. L. Estes. 1992. "Sociological and Economic Theories of Markets and Nonprofits: Evidence from Home Health Organizations." *American Journal of Sociology* 97: 945–969.

Clemens, E. S., and D. Guthrie, eds. 2010. *Politics and Partnerships: The Role of Voluntary Associations in America's Political Past and Present*. Chicago: University of Chicago Press.

Cumming, L. S. 2010. GONGOs. In *International Encyclopedia of Civil Society*, ed. H. K. Anheier, S. Toepler, and R. List, 779–783. New York: Springer.

da Cruz, N. F., P. Rode, and M. McQuarrie. 2019. "New Urban Governance: A Review of Current Themes and Future Priorities." *Journal of Urban Affairs* 41(1): 1–19.

Dai, H. 2014. "To Build an Extended Family: Feminist Organizational Design and Its Dilemmas in Women-Led Non-Governmental Elder Homes in China." *Social Forces* 92: 1115–1134.

de Wit, A., and R. Bekkers. 2016. "Government Support and Charitable Donations: A Meta-Analysis of the Crowding-Out Hypothesis." *Journal of Public Administration Research and Theory* 27(2): 301–319.

DiMaggio, P. J., and H. K. Anheier. 1990. "The Sociology of Nonprofit Organizations and Sectors." *Annual Review of Sociology* 16(1): 137–159.

DiMaggio, P. J., and W. W. Powell. 1991. "Introduction." In *The New Institutionalism in Organizational Analysis*, ed. W. W. Powell and P. J. DiMaggio, 1–38. Chicago: University of Chicago Press.

Dionne, E. J. Jr., ed. 1998. *Community Works: The Revival of Civil Society in America*. Washington, DC: Brookings Institution Press.

Dobbin, F. 2009. *Inventing Equal Opportunity*. Princeton, NJ: Princeton University Press.

Edwards, F. 2016. "Saving Children, Controlling Families: Punishment, Redistribution, and Child Protection." *American Sociological Review* 81(3): 575–595.

Eikenberry, A. M., and J. D. Kluver. 2004. "The Marketization of the Nonprofit Sector: Civil Society at Risk?" *Public Administration Review* 64(2): 132–140.

Emerson, K., T. Nabatchi, and S. Balogh. 2012. "An Integrative Framework for Collaborative Governance." *Journal of Public Administration Research and Theory* 22(1): 1–29.

Faulk, L. 2014. "Overcoming the Cause of Failure and the Role of Issue Salience: Toward a Comprehensive Theory for Nonprofit Activity and Competition in a Three-Sector Economy." *Nonprofit Policy Forum* 5(2): 335–365.

Frumkin, P. 2002. *On Being Nonprofit: A Conceptual and Policy Primer*. Cambridge, MA: Harvard University Press.

Frumkin, P., and J. Jastrzab. 2010. *Serving Country and Community: Who Benefits from National Service?* Cambridge, MA: Harvard University Press.

Fyall, R. 2016. "The Power of Nonprofits: Mechanisms for Nonprofit Policy Influence." *Public Administration Review* 76(6): 938–948.

Galaskiewicz, J. 1985. "Interorganizational Relations." *Annual Review of Sociology* 11: 281–304.

Garrow, E. E., and Y. Hasenfeld. 2014. "Social Enterprises as an Embodiment of a Neoliberal Welfare Logic." *American Behavioral Scientist* 58(11): 1475–1493.

Gray, B. H., ed. 1986. *For-Profit Enterprise in Health Care*. Washington, DC: National Academies Press.

Gray, B., and J. Purdy. 2014. "Conflict in Cross-Sector Partnerships." In *Social Partnerships and Responsible Business: A Research Handbook*, ed. M. M. Seitanidi and A. Crane, 205–225. New York: Routledge.

Hale, T., and D. Held, eds. 2011. *Handbook of Transnational Governance: Institutions and Innovations*. Cambridge, UK: Polity.

Hall, L. M., and S. S. Kennedy. 2008. "Public and Nonprofit Management and the 'New Governance.'" *American Review of Public Administration* 38(3): 307–321.

Hallett, T. 2010. "The Myth Incarnate: Recoupling Processes, Turmoil, and Inhabited Institutions in an Urban Elementary School." *American Sociological Review* 75(1): 52–74.

Hallett, T., and M. J. Ventresca. 2006. "Inhabited Institutions: Social Interactions and Organizational Forms in Gouldner's Patterns of Industrial Bureaucracy." *Theory and Society* 35(2): 213–236.

Handy, F., S. Seto, A. Wakaruk, B. Mersey, A. Mejia, and L. Copeland. 2010. "The Discerning Consumer: Is Nonprofit Status a Factor?" *Nonprofit and Voluntary Sector Quarterly* 39(5): 866–883.

Hansmann, H. B. 1980. "The Role of Nonprofit Enterprise." *Yale Law Journal* 89(5): 835–901.

Heinrich, C. J., L. E. Lynn Jr., and H. B. Milward. 2010. "A State of Agents? Sharpening the Debate over the Extent and Impact of the Transformation of Governance." *Journal of Public Administration Research and Theory* 20(Suppl. 1): i3–i19.

Hood, C. 1991. "A Public Management for All Seasons?" *Public Administration* 69: 3–19.

Hwang, H., and W. W. Powell. 2009. "The Rationalization of Charity: The Influences of Professionalism in the Nonprofit Sector." *Administrative Science Quarterly* 54(2): 268–298.

James, E. 1998. "Commercialism Among Nonprofits: Objectives, Opportunities, and Constraints." In *To Profit or Not to Profit: The Commercial Transformation of the Nonprofit Sector*, ed. B. A. Weisbrod, 271–286. New York: Cambridge University Press.

Kettl, D. F. 2006. "Managing Boundaries in American Administration: The Collaboration Imperative." *Public Administration Review* 66(s1): 10–19.

Kim, S. 2013. "Voluntary Organizations as New Street-Level Bureaucrats: Frontline Struggles of Community Organizations Against Bureaucratization in a South Korean Welfare-to-Work Partnership." *Social Policy and Administration* 47(5): 565–585.

Kingma, B. R. 1997. "Public Good Theories of the Non-Profit Sector: Weisbrod Revisited." *Voluntas: International Journal of Voluntary and Nonprofit Organizations* 8(2): 135–148.

Kissane, R. J., and J. Gingerich. 2004. "Do You See What I See? Nonprofit and Resident Perceptions of Urban Neighborhood Problems." *Nonprofit and Voluntary Sector Quarterly* 33(2): 311–333.

Knoke, D. 1990. *Political Networks: The Structural Perspective*. Cambridge, UK: Cambridge University Press.

Knutsen, W. 2016. "The Non-Profit Sector Is Dead, Long Live the Non-Profit Sector!" *Voluntas: International Journal of Voluntary and Nonprofit Organizations* 27(6): 1562–1584.

Knutsen, W. L., and R. S. Brower. 2010. "Managing Expressive and Instrumental Accountabilities in Nonprofit and Voluntary Organizations: A Qualitative Investigation." *Nonprofit and Voluntary Sector Quarterly* 39(4): 588–610.

Kramer, R. M. 1981. *Voluntary Agencies in the Welfare State*. Berkeley: University of California Press.

———. 2000. "A Third Sector in the Third Millennium?" *Voluntas: International Journal of Voluntary and Nonprofit Organizations* 11(1): 1–23.

Krashinsky, M. 1998. "Does Auspice Matter? The Case of Day Care for Children in Canada." In *Private Action and the Public Good*, ed. W. W. Powell and E. S. Clemens, 114–123. New Haven, CT: Yale University Press.

Laumann, E. O., J. Galaskiewicz, and P. V. Marsden. 1978. "Community Structure as Interorganizational Linkages." *Annual Review of Sociology* 4: 455–484.

Lee, Y. J. 2012. "Behavioral Implications of Public Service Motivation: Volunteering by Public and Nonprofit Employees." *American Review of Public Administration* 42(1): 104–121.

Lee, Y. J., and V. M. Wilkins. 2011. "More Similarities or More Differences? Comparing Public and Nonprofit Managers' Job Motivations." *Public Administration Review* 71(1): 45–56.

LeRoux, K. 2007. "Nonprofits as Civic Intermediaries: The Role of Community-Based Organizations in Promoting Political Participation." *Urban Affairs Review* 42(3): 410–422.

LeRoux, K., and M. K. Feeney. 2013. "Factors Attracting Individuals to Nonprofit Management over Public and Private Sector Management." *Nonprofit Management and Leadership* 24(1): 43–62.

Levine, J. R. 2016. "The Privatization of Political Representation: Community-Based Organizations as Nonelected Neighborhood Representatives." *American Sociological Review* 81(6): 1251–1275.

Lichterman, P., and N. Eliasoph. 2014. "Civic Action." *American Journal of Sociology* 120(3): 798–863.

Lipsky, M. 1980. *Street-Level Bureaucracy: Dilemmas of the Individual in Public Services*. New York: Russell Sage Foundation.

———. 2010. *Street-Level Bureaucracy, 30th Anniversary Edition: Dilemmas of the Individual in Public Services*. New York: Russell Sage Foundation.

Ljubownikow, S., and J. Crotty. 2016. "Nonprofit Influence on Public Policy: Exploring Nonprofit Advocacy in Russia." *Nonprofit and Voluntary Sector Quarterly* 45(2): 314–332.

Lu, J. 2018. "Fear the Government? A Meta-Analysis of the Impact of Government Funding on Nonprofit Advocacy Engagement." *American Review of Public Administration* 48(3): 203–218.

Lu, J., and C. Xu. 2018. "Complementary or Supplementary? The Relationship Between Government Size and Nonprofit Sector Size." *Voluntas: International Journal of Voluntary and Nonprofit Organizations* 29(3): 454–469.

Ma, J., and S. DeDeo. 2018. "State Power and Elite Autonomy in a Networked Civil Society: The Board Interlocking of Chinese Non-Profits." *Social Networks* 54: 291–302.

Maier, F., M. Meyer, and M. Steinbereithner. 2016. "Nonprofit Organizations Becoming Business-like: A Systematic Review." *Nonprofit and Voluntary Sector Quarterly* 45(1): 64–86.

Malani, A., and G. David. 2008. "Does Nonprofit Status Signal Quality?" *Journal of Legal Studies* 37(2): 551–576.

Marwell, N. P. 2004. "Privatizing the Welfare State: Nonprofit Community-Based Organizations as Political Actors." *American Sociological Review* 69(2): 265–291.

———. 2007. *Bargaining for Brooklyn: Community Organizations in the Entrepreneurial City.* Chicago: University of Chicago Press.

Marwell, N. P., and P. B. McInerney. 2005. "The Nonprofit/For-Profit Continuum: Theorizing the Dynamics of Mixed-Form Markets." *Nonprofit and Voluntary Sector Quarterly* 34(1): 7–28.

Maxwell, N. L., D. Rotz, and C. Garcia. 2016. "Data and Decision Making: Same Organization, Different Perceptions; Different Organizations, Different Perceptions." *American Journal of Evaluation* 37(4): 463–485.

Maynard-Moody, S., and S. Portillo. 2010. "Street-Level Bureaucracy Theory." In *The Oxford Handbook of American Bureaucracy*, ed. R. F. Durant, 252–277. New York: Oxford University Press.

Mayrl, D., and S. Quinn. 2016. "Defining the State from Within: Boundaries, Schemas, and Associational Policymaking." *Sociological Theory* 34(1): 1–26.

McQuarrie, M. 2012. "Community Organizations in the Foreclosure Crisis: The Failure of Neoliberal Civil Society." *Politics and Society* 41(1): 73–101.

Miller-Stevens, K., J. A. Taylor, and J. C. Morris. 2015. "Are We Really on the Same Page? An Empirical Examination of Value Congruence Between Public Sector and Nonprofit Sector Managers." *Voluntas: International Journal of Voluntary and Nonprofit Organizations* 26(6): 2424–2446.

Milward, H. B., and K. G. Provan. 2000. "Governing the Hollow State." *Journal of Public Administration Research and Theory* 10(2): 359–380.

Milward, H. B., K. G. Provan, A. Fish, K. R. Isett, and K. Huang. 2010. "Governance and Collaboration: An Evolutionary Study of Two Mental Health Networks." *Journal of Public Administration Research and Theory* 20(suppl. 1): i125–i141.

Morris, A. J. 2009. *The Limits of Voluntarism: Charity and Welfare from the New Deal Through the Great Society.* Cambridge, UK: Cambridge University Press.

Mosley, J. E. 2012. "Keeping the Lights On: How Government Funding Concerns Drive the Advocacy Agendas of Nonprofit Homeless Service Providers." *Journal of Public Administration Research and Theory* 22(4): 841–866.

Mosley, J. E., and C. M. Grogan. 2013. "Representation in Nonelected Participatory Processes: How Residents Understand the Role of Nonprofit Community-Based Organizations." *Journal of Public Administration Research and Theory* 23(4): 839–863.

Najam, A. 2000. "The Four-C's of Third Sector-Government Relations: Cooperation, Confrontation, Complementarity, and Co-optation." *Nonprofit Management and Leadership* 10(4): 375–396.

Nałęcz, S., E. Leś, and B. Pieliński. 2015. "Poland: A New Model of Government–Nonprofit Relations for the East?" *Voluntas: International Journal of Voluntary and Nonprofit Organizations* 26(6): 2351–2378.

Nowland-Foreman, G. 1998. "Purchase-of-Service Contracting, Voluntary Organizations, and Civil Society: Dissecting the Goose That Lays the Golden Eggs?" *American Behavioral Scientist* 42(1): 108–123.

Olasky, M. 1992. *The Tragedy of American Compassion.* Washington, DC: Regnery.

Orden, S. R. 1973. "The Impact of Community Action Programs on Private Social Service Agencies." *Social Problems* 20(3): 364–381.

Osborne, D., and T. Gaebler. 1993. *Reinventing Government: How the Entrepreneurial Spirit Is Transforming the Public Sector.* New York: Plume.

Pachucki, M. A., and R. L. Breiger. 2010. "Cultural Holes: Beyond Relationality in Social Networks and Culture." *Annual Review of Sociology* 36: 205–224.

Payne, A. A. 2009. "Does Government Funding Change Behavior? An Empirical Analysis of Crowd-Out." *Tax Policy and the Economy* 23: 159–184.

Peng, S., S. Pandey, and S. K. Pandey. 2015. "Is There a Nonprofit Advantage? Examining the Impact of Institutional Context on Individual–Organizational Value Congruence." *Public Administration Review* 75(4): 585–596.

Pfeffer, J., and G. R. Salancik. 1978. *The External Control of Organizations: A Resource Dependence Approach.* New York: Harper and Row.

Pierre, J. 2014. "Can Urban Regimes Travel in Time and Space? Urban Regime Theory, Urban Governance Theory, and Comparative Urban Politics." *Urban Affairs Review* 50(6): 864–889.

Pollitt, C., and P. Hupe. 2011. "Talking About Government: The Role of Magic Concepts." *Public Management Review* 13(5): 641–658.

Powell, W. W., and C. Rerup. 2017. "Opening the Black Box: The Microfoundations of Institutions." In *The SAGE Handbook of Organizational Institutionalism*, 2nd ed., ed. R. Greenwood, C. Oliver, T. B. Lawrence, and R. E. Meyer, 311–337. London: SAGE.

Provan, K. G., K. R. Isett, and H. B. Milward. 2004. "Cooperation and Compromise: A Network Response to Conflicting Institutional Pressures in Community Mental Health." *Nonprofit and Voluntary Sector Quarterly* 33(3): 489–514.

Provan, K. G., and P. Kenis. 2008. "Modes of Network Governance: Structure, Management, and Effectiveness." *Journal of Public Administration Research and Theory* 18(2): 229–252.

Provan, K. G., and H. B. Milward. 1994. "Integration of Community-Based Services for the Severely Mentally Ill and the Structure of Public Funding: A Comparison of Four Systems." *Journal of Health Politics, Policy and Law* 19(4): 865–894.

———. 1995. "A Preliminary Theory of Interorganizational Network Effectiveness: A Comparative Study of Four Community Mental Health Systems." *Administrative Science Quarterly* 40(1): 1–33.

Putnam, R. D. 2000. *Bowling Alone: The Collapse and Revival of American Community.* New York: Simon and Schuster.

Reckhow, S. 2013. *Follow the Money: How Foundation Dollars Change Public School Politics.* Oxford, UK: Oxford University Press.

Rhodes, R.A.W. 1996. "The New Governance: Governing Without Government." *Political Studies* 44: 652–667.

———. 2011. "One-Way, Two-Way, or Dead-End Street: British Influence on the Study of the Study of Public Administration in America Since 1945." *Public Administration Review* 71(4): 559–571.

Riggirozzi, P., and C. Wylde, eds. 2018. *Handbook of South American Governance.* New York: Routledge.

Rosenau, P. V., and S. H. Linder. 2003. "Two Decades of Research Comparing For-Profit and Nonprofit

Health Provider Performance in the United States." *Social Science Quarterly* 84(2): 219–241.

Rotolo, T., and J. Wilson. 2006. "Employment Sector and Volunteering: The Contribution of Nonprofit and Public Sector Workers to the Volunteer Labor Force." *Sociological Quarterly* 47(1): 21–40.

Salamon, L. M. 1987. "Of Market Failure, Voluntary Failure, and Third-Party Government: Toward a Theory of Government-Nonprofit Relations in the Modern Welfare State." *Nonprofit and Voluntary Sector Quarterly* 16(1): 29–49.

———. 1995. *Partners in Public Service: Government-Nonprofit Relations in the Modern Welfare State.* Baltimore: Johns Hopkins University Press.

———, ed. 2002. *The Tools of Government: A Guide to the New Governance.* Oxford, UK: Oxford University Press.

Salamon, L. M., and S. W. Sokolowski. 2016. "Beyond Nonprofits: Re-conceptualizing the Third Sector." *Voluntas: International Journal of Voluntary and Nonprofit Organizations* 27(4): 1515–1545.

Sanders, M. L., and J. G. McClellan. 2014. "Being Business-like While Pursuing a Social Mission: Acknowledging the Inherent Tensions in US Nonprofit Organizing." *Organization* 21(1): 68–89.

Schambra, W. A. 1997. "Building Community Top-Down or Bottom-Up? Local Groups Are the Key to America's Civic Renewal." *Brookings Review* 15: 20–22.

Scott, W. R. 2014. *Institutions and Organizations: Ideas, Interests, and Identities,* 4th ed. Los Angeles: SAGE.

Sellers, J. M. 2011. "State-Society Relations." In *The SAGE Handbook of Governance*, ed. M. Bevir, 124–141. Los Angeles: SAGE.

Selznick, P. 1949. *TVA and the Grass Roots.* Berkeley: University of California Press.

Smith, S. R. 2012. "Social Services." In *The State of Nonprofit America*, 2nd ed., ed. L. Salamon, 192–228. Washington, DC: Brookings Institution Press.

Smith, S. R., and K. A. Grønbjerg. 2006. "Scope and Theory of Government-Nonprofit Relations." In *The Nonprofit Sector: A Research Handbook,* 2nd ed., ed. W. W. Powell and R. Steinberg, 221–242. New Haven, CT: Yale University Press.

Smith, S. R., and M. Lipsky. 1993. *Nonprofits for Hire: The Welfare State in the Age of Contracting.* Cambridge, MA: Harvard University Press.

Soss, J., R. Fording, and S. F. Schram. 2011. "The Organization of Discipline: From Performance Management to Perversity and Punishment." *Journal of Public Administration Research and Theory* 21(suppl. 2): i203–i232.

Spires, A. J. 2011. "Contingent Symbiosis and Civil Society in an Authoritarian State: Understanding the Survival of China's Grassroots NGOs." *American Journal of Sociology* 117(1): 1–45.

Spitzmueller, M. C. 2016. "Negotiating Competing Institutional Logics at the Street Level: An Ethnography of a Community Mental Health Organization." *Social Service Review* 90(1): 35–82.

Steinberg, R. 1991. "Does Government Spending Crowd Out Donations? Interpreting the Evidence." *Annals of Public and Cooperative Economics* 62(4): 591–612.

———. 2006. "Economic Theories of Nonprofit Organizations." In *The Nonprofit Sector: A Research Handbook*, 2nd ed., ed. W. W. Powell and R. Steinberg, 117–139. New Haven, CT: Yale University Press.

Stoker, G. 1998. "Governance as Theory: Five Propositions." *International Social Science Journal* 50(155): 17–28.

Streeck, W., and P. C. Schmitter. 1985. "Community, Market, State—and Associations? The Prospective Contribution of Interest Governance to Social Order." *European Sociological Review* 1(2): 119–138.

Suárez, D. F., and N. Esparza. 2017. "Institutional Change and Management of Public–Nonprofit Partnerships." *American Review of Public Administration* 47(6): 648–660.

Taylor, J. 2010. "Public Service Motivation, Civic Attitudes and Actions of Public, Nonprofit and Private Sector Employees." *Public Administration* 88(4): 1083–1098.

Tocqueville, A. de. 2000. *Democracy in America*, ed. and trans. H. C. Mansfield and D. Winthrop. Chicago: University of Chicago Press.

van den Dool, L., A. Gianoli, F. Hendriks, and L. Schaap. 2015. "Good Urban Governance: Challenges and Values." In *The Quest for Good Urban Governance: Theoretical Reflections and International Practices*, ed. L. van den Dool, F. Hendriks, A. Gianoli, and L. Schaap, 11–28. Wiesbaden: Springer Fachmedian Wiesbaden.

Van Slyke, D. M. 2007. "Agents or Stewards: Using Theory to Understand the Government-Nonprofit Social Service Contracting Relationship." *Journal of Public Administration Research and Theory* 17(2): 157–187.

Vargas, R. 2016. *Wounded City: Violent Turf Wars in a Chicago Barrio.* New York: Oxford University Press.

Warren, R. L. 1967. "The Interorganizational Field as a Focus for Investigation." *Administrative Science Quarterly* 12(3): 396–419.

Weisbrod, B. A. 1975. "Toward a Theory of the Voluntary Nonprofit Sector in a Three-Sector Economy." In *Altruism, Morality, and Economic Theory*, ed. E. S. Phelps, 171–196. New York: Russell Sage Foundation.

Witesman, E. M., and S. Fernandez. 2013. "Government Contracts with Private Organizations: Are There Differences Between Nonprofits and For-Profits?" *Nonprofit and Voluntary Sector Quarterly* 42(4): 689–715.

Wuthnow, R. 1991. "Tocqueville's Question Reconsidered: Voluntarism and Public Discourse in Advanced Industrial Societies." In *Between States and Markets: The Voluntary Sector in Comparative Perspective*, ed. R. Wuthnow, 299–308. Princeton, NJ: Princeton University Press.

Young, D. R. 2000. "Alternative Models of Government-Nonprofit Sector Relations: Theoretical and International Perspectives." *Nonprofit and Voluntary Sector Quarterly* 29(1): 149–172.

Chapter 10. Social Service Nonprofits: Navigating Conflicting Demands

Alexander, J., R. Nank, and C. Stivers. 1999. "Implications of Welfare Reform: Do Nonprofit Survival Strategies Threaten Civil Society?" *Nonprofit and Voluntary Sector Quarterly* 28(4): 452–475.

Allard, S. W., and S. R. Smith. 2014. "Unforeseen Consequences: Medicaid and the Funding of Nonprofit Service Organizations." *Journal of Health Politics, Policy, and Law* 39(6): 1135–1172.

Andrews, R., and T. Entwistle. 2010. "Does Cross-Sectoral Partnership Deliver? An Empirical Exploration of Public Service Effectiveness, Efficiency, and Equity." *Journal of Public Administration Research and Theory* 20(3): 679–701.

Ansell, C., and A. Gash. 2008. "Collaborative Governance in Theory and Practice." *Journal of Public Administration Research and Theory* 18(4): 543–571.

Bekkers, R., and P. Wiepking. 2010. "A Literature Review of Empirical Studies of Philanthropy: Eight Mechanisms That Drive Charitable Giving." *Nonprofit and Voluntary Sector Quarterly* 40(5): 924–973.

Benjamin, L. M. 2012. "Nonprofit Organizations and Outcome Measurement: From Tracking Program Activities to Focusing on Frontline Work." *American Journal of Evaluation* 33(3): 431–447.

Benjamin, L. M., and D. C. Campbell. 2015. "Nonprofit Performance: Accounting for the Agency of Clients." *Nonprofit and Voluntary Sector Quarterly* 44(5): 988–1006.

Benton, A. D., and M. J. Austin. 2010. "Managing Nonprofit Mergers: The Challenges Facing Human Service Organizations." *Administration in Social Work* 34(5): 458–479.

Berger, P. L., and R. J. Neuhaus. 1977. *To Empower People: The Role of Mediating Structures in Public Policy.* Washington, DC: American Enterprise Institute for Public Policy Research.

Berry, J. M., with D. F. Arons. 2003. *A Voice for Nonprofits.* Washington, DC: Brookings Institution Press.

Birch, K., and M. Siemiatycki. 2016. "Neoliberalism and the Geographies of Marketization: The Entangling of State and Markets." *Progress in Human Geography* 40(2): 177–198.

Bode, I. 2017. "Governance and Performance in a "Marketized" Nonprofit Sector: The Case of German Care Homes." *Administration and Society* 49(2): 232–256.

Boris, E. T., de E. Leon, K. Roeger, and M. Nikolova. 2010. *Human Service Nonprofits and Government Collaboration: Findings from the 2010 National Survey of Nonprofit Government Contracting and Grants.* Washington, DC: Urban Institute. https://www.urban.org/research/publication/human-service-nonprofits-and-government-collaboration-findings-2010-national-survey-nonprofit-government-contracting-and-grants/view/full_report.

Brass, J. N. 2016. *Allies or Adversaries: NGOs and the State in Africa.* New York: Cambridge University Press.

Brest, P., and H. Harvey. 2018. *Money Well Spent: A Strategic Plan for Smart Philanthropy.* Stanford, CA: Stanford University Press.

Bromley, P., and J. W. Meyer. 2017. "'They Are All Organizations': The Cultural Roots of Blurring Between the Nonprofit, Business, and Government Sectors." *Administration and Society* 49(7): 939–966.

Brown, M. 2018. "The Moralization of Commercialization: Uncovering the History of Fee-Charging in the U.S. Nonprofit Human Services Sector." *Nonprofit and Voluntary Sector Quarterly* 47(5): 960–983.

Bushouse, B. K. 2009. *Universal Preschool: Policy Change, Stability, and the Pew Charitable Trusts.* Albany: SUNY Press.

Bushouse, B. K., and J. E. Mosley. 2018. "The Intermediary Roles of Foundations in the Policy Process: Building Coalitions of Interest." *Interest Groups and Advocacy* (September): 1–23.

Carroll, D. A., and K. J. Stater. 2009. "Revenue Diversification in Nonprofit Organizations: Does It Lead to Financial Stability?" *Journal of Public Administration Research and Theory* 19(4): 947–966.

Chaves, M., L. Stephens, and J. Galaskiewicz. 2004. "Does Government Funding Suppress Nonprofits' Political Activity?" *American Sociological Review* 69(2): 292–316.

Chaves, M., and W. Tsitsos. 2001. "Congregations and Social Services: What They Do, How They Do It, and With Whom." *Nonprofit and Voluntary Sector Quarterly* 30(4): 660–683.

Child, C., E. Witesman, and R. Spencer. 2016. "The Blurring Hypothesis Reconsidered: How Sector Still Matters to Practitioners." *Voluntas: International Journal of Voluntary and Nonprofit Organizations* 27(4): 1831–1852.

Clemens, E. S. 2006. "The Constitution of Citizens: Political Theories of Nonprofit Organizations." In *The Nonprofit Sector: A Research Handbook,* 2nd ed., ed. W. W. Powell and R. Steinberg, 207–220. New Haven, CT: Yale University Press.

Clemenson, B., and R. D. Sellers. 2013. "Hull House: An Autopsy of Not-for-Profit Financial Accountability." *Journal of Accounting Education* 31(3): 252–293.

Dean, R. J. 2018. "Counter-Governance: Citizen Participation Beyond Collaboration." *Politics and Governance* 6(1): 180–188.

de Graauw, E. 2016. *Making Immigrant Rights Real: Nonprofits and the Politics of Integration in San Francisco.* Ithaca, NY: Cornell University Press.

DiMaggio, P. J., and W. W. Powell. 1983. "The Iron Cage Revisited: Institutional Isomorphism and Collective Rationality in Organizational Fields." *American Sociological Review* 48(2): 147–160.

Dodge, J. 2010. "Tensions in Deliberative Practice: A View from Civil Society." *Critical Policy Studies* 4(4): 384–404.

Dolsak, N., and A. Prakash. 2015. "Government Contractors as Civil Society?" *Stanford Social Innovation Review,* November 9.

Duggan, M. 2004. "Does Contracting Out Increase the Efficiency of Government Programs? Evidence from Medicaid HMOs." *Journal of Public Economics* 88(12): 2549–2572.

Dunning, C. 2018. "New Careers for the Poor: Human Services and the Post-Industrial City." *Journal of Urban History* 44(4): 669–690.

Eikenberry, A. M., and J. D. Kluver. 2004. "The Marketization of the Nonprofit Sector: Civil Society at Risk?" *Public Administration Review* 64(2): 132–140.

Elstub, S., and L. Poole. 2014. "Democratising the Non-Profit Sector: Reconfiguring the State–Non -Profit Sector Relationship in the UK." *Policy and Politics* 42(3): 385–401.

Emerson, K., and T. Nabatchi. 2015. *Collaborative Govenance Regimes.* Washington, DC: Georgetown University Press.

Esping-Andersen, G. 2013. *The Three Worlds of Welfare Capitalism:* Hoboken, NJ: Wiley.

Field, J., and E. Peck. 2003. "Mergers and Acquisitions in the Private Sector: What Are the Lessons for Health and Social Services?" *Social Policy and Administration* 37(7): 742–755.

Fraser, N., and L. Gordon. 1994. "A Genealogy of Dependency: Tracing a Keyword of the U.S. Welfare State." *Signs* 19(2): 309–336.

Froelich, K. A. 1999. "Diversification of Revenue Strategies: Evolving Resource Dependence in Nonprofit Organizations." *Nonprofit and Voluntary Sector Quarterly* 28(3): 246–268.

Frumkin, P., and A. Andre-Clark. 2000. "When Missions, Markets, and Politics Collide: Values and Strategy in the Nonprofit Human Services." *Nonprofit and Voluntary Sector Quarterly* 29(1): 141–163.

Fyall, R., M. K. Moore, and M. K. Gugerty. 2018. "Beyond NTEE Codes: Opportunities to Understand Nonprofit Activity Through Mission Statement Content Coding." *Nonprofit and Voluntary Sector Quarterly* 47(4): 677–701.

Ganz, M., T. Kay, and J. Spicer. 2018. "Social Enterprise Is Not Social Change." *Stanford Social Innovation Review* (Spring): 59–60.

Giving USA. 2018. *Giving USA 2018: The Annual Report on Philanthropy for the Year 2017.* Chicago: Giving USA.

Grønbjerg, K. A. 1994. "Using NTEE to Classify Non -Profit Organisations: An Assessment of Human Service and Regional Applications." *Voluntas: International Journal of Voluntary and Nonprofit Organizations* 5(3): 301–328.

Hammack, D. C., and H. K. Anheier. 2010. "American Foundations: Their Roles and Contributions to Society." In *American Foundations: Roles and Contributions,* ed. H. K. Anheier and D. C. Hammack, 3–27. Washington, DC: Brookings Institution Press.

Hansmann, H. 1987. "Economic Theories of Nonprofit Organizations." In *The Nonprofit Sector: A Research Handbook,* ed. W. W. Powell, 27–42. New Haven, CT: Yale University Press.

Hasenfeld, Y., and E. E. Garrow. 2012. "Nonprofit Human-Service Organizations, Social Rights, and Advocacy in a Neoliberal Welfare State." *Social Service Review* 86(2): 295–322.

Heinrich, C. J., and Y. Choi. 2007. "Performance-Based Contracting in Social Welfare Programs." *American Review of Public Administration* 37(4): 409–435.

Hill, C. J., and L. E. Lynn. 2005. "Is Hierarchical Governance in Decline? Evidence from Empirical Research." *Journal of Public Administration Research and Theory* 15(2): 173–195.

Hodge, M. M., and R. F. Piccolo. 2005. "Funding Source, Board Involvement Techniques, and Financial Vulnerability in Nonprofit Organizations: A Test of Resource Dependence." *Nonprofit Management and Leadership* 16(2): 171–190.

Janus, K. K. 2018. "Creating a Data Culture." *Stanford Social Innovation Review*, March 2.

Johnston, E. W., D. Hicks, N. Nan, and J. C. Auer. 2011. "Managing the Inclusion Process in Collaborative Governance." *Journal of Public Administration Research and Theory* 21(4): 699–672.

Kania, J., and M. Kramer. 2011. "Collective Impact." *Stanford Social Innovation Review* (Winter): 36–41.

Kennedy, S. S. 2003. "Privatization and Prayer: The Challenge of Charitable Choice." *American Review of Public Administration* 33(1): 5–19.

Kettl, D. F. 2011. *Sharing Power: Public Governance and Private Markets*. Washington, DC: Brookings Institution Press.

Koning, P., and C. J. Heinrich. 2013. "Cream-Skimming, Parking and Other Intended and Unintended Effects of High-Powered, Performance-Based Contracts." *Journal of Policy Analysis and Management* 32(3): 461–483.

Lamothe, M., and S. Lamothe. 2009. "Beyond the Search for Competition in Social Service Contracting: Procurement, Consolidation, and Accountability." *American Review of Public Administration* 39(2): 164–188.

Levine, J. R. 2016. "The Privatization of Political Representation: Community-Based Organizations as Nonelected Neighborhood Representatives." *American Sociological Review* 81(6): 1251–1275.

Lu, J., and Q. Dong. 2018. "What Influences the Growth of the Chinese Nonprofit Sector: A Prefecture-Level Study." *Voluntas: International Journal of Voluntary and Nonprofit Organizations* 29(6): 1347–1359.

Lynch-Cerullo, K., and K. Cooney. 2011. "Moving from Outputs to Outcomes: A Review of the Evolution of Performance Measurement in the Human Service Nonprofit Sector." *Administration in Social Work* 35(4): 364–388.

Lyon, T. P., and J. W. Maxwell. 2004. "Astroturf: Interest Group Lobbying and Corporate Strategy." *Journal of Economics and Management Strategy* 13(4): 561–597.

Maier, F., M. Meyer, and M. Steinbereithner. 2016. "Nonprofit Organizations Becoming Business-like: A Systematic Review." *Nonprofit and Voluntary Sector Quarterly* 45(1): 64–86.

Marwell, N. P. 2004. "Privatizing the Welfare State: Nonprofit Community-Based Organizations as Political Actors." *American Sociological Review* 69(2): 265–291.

Marwell, N. P., and T. Calabrese. 2015. "A Deficit Model of Collaborative Governance: Government–Nonprofit Fiscal Relations in the Provision of Child Welfare Services." *Journal of Public Administration Research and Theory* 25(4): 1031–1058.

McBeath, B., and W. Meezan. 2010. "Governance in Motion: Service Provision and Child Welfare Outcomes in a Performance-Based, Managed Care Contracting Environment." *Journal of Public Administration Research and Theory* 20(Suppl. 1): i101–i123.

McLaughlin, K., E. Ferlie, and S. Osborne. 2002. *New Public Management*. London: Routledge.

Meagher, G., and K. Healy. 2003. "Caring, Controlling, Contracting and Counting: Governments and Non-Profits in Community Services." *Australian Journal of Public Administration* 62(3): 40–51.

Mettler, S. 2011. *The Submerged State: How Invisible Government Policies Undermine American Democracy*. Chicago: University of Chicago Press.

Meyer, J. W., and B. Rowan. 1977. "Institutionalized Organizations: Formal Structure as Myth and Ceremony." *American Journal of Sociology* 83(2): 340–363.

Michener, J. 2018. *Fragmented Democracy: Medicaid, Federalism, and Unequal Politics*. Cambridge, UK: Cambridge University Press.

Milward, H. B., and K. G. Provan. 2000. "Governing the Hollow State." *Journal of Public Administration Research and Theory* 10(2): 359–380.

Monsma, S. V. 2006. *Faith, Hope, and Jobs: Welfare-to-Work in Los Angeles*. Washington, DC: Georgetown University Press.

Morris, G., and D. Roberts. 2018. *A National Imperative: Joining Forces to Strengthen Human Services in America:* New York: Alliance for Strong Families and Communities. https://www

.alliance1.org/web/resources/pubs/national
-imperative-joining-forces-strengthen-human
-services-america.aspx.

Mosley, J. E. 2010. "Organizational Resources and
Environmental Incentives: Understanding the
Policy Advocacy Involvement of Human Service
Nonprofits." *Social Service Review* 84(1): 57–76.

———. 2012. "Keeping the Lights On: How Government Funding Concerns Drive the Advocacy
Agendas of Nonprofit Homeless Service Providers." *Journal of Public Administration Research
and Theory* 22(4): 841–866.

———. 2014. "Collaboration, Public-Private Intermediary Organizations, and the Transformation
of Advocacy in the Field of Homeless Services."
American Review of Public Administration 44(3):
291–308.

Mosley, J. E., and C. M. Grogan. 2013. "Representa-
tion in Nonelected Participatory Processes: How
Residents Understand the Role of Nonprofit
Community-Based Organizations." *Journal of
Public Administration Research and Theory* 23(4):
839–863.

Olasky, M. 1992. *The Tragedy of American Compassion*. Wheaton, IL: Crossway Books.

Olson, J., and A. Phillips. 2013. "Rikers Island: The
First Social Impact Bond in the United States."
Community Development Investment Review (1):
97–101.

Park, S. E., and J. E. Mosley. 2017. "Nonprofit Growth
and Decline During Economic Uncertainty."
*Human Service Organizations: Management,
Leadership and Governance* 41(5): 515–531.

Park, S. E., J. E. Mosley, and C. M. Grogan. 2018.
"Do Residents of Low-Income Communities
Trust Organizations to Speak on Their Behalf?
Differences by Organizational Type." *Urban
Affairs Review* 54(1): 137–164.

Payne, A. A. 1998. "Does the Government Crowd-
Out Private Donations? New Evidence from a
Sample of Non-Profit Firms." *Journal of Public
Economics* 69: 323–345.

Pfeffer, J., and G. R. Salancik. 1978. *The External
Control of Organizations: A Resource Dependence
Perspective*. New York: Harper and Row.

Piven, F. F., and R. A. Cloward. 1977. *Poor People's
Movements: Why They Succeed, How They Fail*.
New York: Pantheon Books.

Power, M. 2003. "Evaluating the Audit Explosion."
Law and Policy 25(3): 185–202.

Reckhow, S. 2013. *Follow the Money: How Foundation Dollars Change Public School Politics*.
Oxford, UK: Oxford University Press.

Reckhow, S., and M. Tompkins-Stange. 2018. "Financ-
ing the Education Policy Discourse: Philanthropic
Funders as Entrepreneurs in Policy Networks."
Interest Groups and Advocacy 7(3): 258–288.

Reich, R. 2016. "Repugnant to the Whole Idea of
Democracy? On the Role of Foundations in
Democratic Societies." *PS: Political Science and
Politics* 49(3): 466–472.

Salamon, L. M. 1987a. "Of Market Failure, Voluntary
Failure, and Third-Party Government: Toward
a Theory of Government-Nonprofit Relations
in the Modern Welfare State." *Nonprofit and
Voluntary Sector Quarterly* 16(1): 29–49.

Salamon, L. M. 1987b. "Partners in Public Service:
The Scope and Theory of Government-Nonprofit
Relations." In *The Nonprofit Sector: A Research
Handbook*, ed. W. W. Powell, 99–117. New Haven,
CT: Yale University Press.

Salamon, L. M. 1995. *Partners in Public Service:
Government-Nonprofit Relations in the Modern
Welfare State*. Baltimore: Johns Hopkins Univer-
sity Press.

Salamon, L. M., and H. K. Anheier. 1998. "Social Origins of Civil Society: Explaining the Nonprofit
Sector Cross-Nationally." *Voluntas: International
Journal of Voluntary and Nonprofit Organizations*
9(3): 213–248.

Sanders, M. L. 2015. "Being Nonprofit-like in a Market Economy: Understanding the Mission-Mar-
ket Tension in Nonprofit Organizing." *Nonprofit
and Voluntary Sector Quarterly* 44(2): 205–222.

Scott, W. R. 2014. *Institutions and Organizations:
Ideas, Interests, and Identities*, 4th ed. Los Angeles: SAGE.

Smith, A. 2007. *The Revolution Will Not Be Funded:
Beyond the Non-Profit Industrial Complex*. Cambridge, MA: South End Press.

Smith, S. R., and M. Lipsky. 1993. *Nonprofits for
Hire: The Welfare State in the Age of Contracting*.
Cambridge, MA: Harvard University Press.

Sosin, M. R., and S. R. Smith. 2006. "New Responsibilities of Faith-Related Agencies." *Policy Studies
Journal* 34(4): 533–562.

Spitzmueller, M. C. 2018. "Remaking 'Community' Mental Health: Contested Institutional Logics and Organizational Change." *Human Service Organizations: Management, Leadership and Governance* 42(2): 123–145.

Steinberg, R. 2006. "Economic Theories of Nonprofit Organizations." In *The Nonprofit Sector: A Research Handbook*, 2nd ed., ed. W. W. Powell and R. Steinberg, 117–139. New Haven, CT: Yale University Press.

Suárez, D. F. 2011. "Collaboration and Professionalization: The Contours of Public Sector Funding for Nonprofit Organizations." *Journal of Public Administration Research and Theory* 21(2): 307–326.

Thomson, A. M., and J. L. Perry. 2006. "Collaboration Processes: Inside the Black Box." *Public Administration Review* 66(1): 20–32.

Tompkins-Stange, M. E. 2016. *Policy Patrons: Philanthropy, Education Reform, and the Politics of Influence.* Cambridge, MA: Harvard Education Press.

Tufekci, Z. 2018. "Elon Musk Thinks He Can Fix Everything." *New York Times*, July 14.

Vanderwoerd, J. R. 2004. "How Faith-Based Social Service Organizations Manage Secular Pressures Associated with Government Funding." *Nonprofit Management and Leadership* 14(3): 239–262.

Van Slyke, D. M. 2003. "The Mythology of Privatization in Contracting for Social Services." *Public Administration Review* 63(3): 296–315.

———. 2007. "Agents or Stewards: Using Theory to Understand the Government-Nonprofit Social Service Contracting Relationship." *Journal of Public Administration Research and Theory* 17(2): 157–187.

Walker, E. T. 2016. "Between Grassroots and 'Astroturf': Understanding Mobilization from the Top-Down." In *The SAGE Handbook of Resistance*, ed. D. Courpasson and S. Vallas, 269–279. Thousand Oaks, CA: SAGE.

Weisbrod, B. A. 1988. *The Nonprofit Economy.* Cambridge, MA: Harvard University Press.

———. 1997. "The Future of the Nonprofit Sector: Its Entwining with Private Enterprise and Government." *Journal of Policy Analysis and Management* 16(4): 541–555.

Wolff, T., et al. 2017. "Collaborating for Equity and Justice: Moving Beyond Collective Impact." *Nonprofit Quarterly* 9 (January).

Wuthnow, R. 2004. *Saving America? Faith-Based Services and the Future of Civil Society.* Princeton, NJ: Princeton University Press.

Wuthnow, R., C. Hackett, and B. Y. Hsu. 2004. "The Effectiveness and Trustworthiness of Faith-Based and Other Service Organizations: A Study of Recipients' Perceptions." *Journal for the Scientific Study of Religion* 43(1): 1–17.

Chapter 11. Nonprofits as Urban Infrastructure

Addams, Carolyn T. 2014. *From the Outside In: Suburban Elites, Third-Sector Organizations, and the Reshaping of Philadelphia.* Ithaca, NY: Cornell University Press.

Addams, Jane. 1895. *Hull House Maps and Papers.* New York: Thomas Crowell.

Arena, John. 2012. *Driven from New Orleans: How Nonprofits Betray Public Housing and Promote Privatization.* Minneapolis: University of Minnesota Press.

Baggetta, Matthew. 2016. "Representative Bridging: Voluntary Associations' Potential for Creating Bridging Ties in Demographically Diverse Urban Areas." *Nonprofit and Voluntary Sector Quarterly* 45(1): 72S–94S.

Balogh, Brian. 2015. *The Associational State: American Governance in the Twentieth Century.* Philadelphia: University of Pennsylvania Press.

Beckert, Sven. 2001. *The Monied Metropolis: New York City and the Consolidation of the American Bourgeoisie, 1850–1896.* New York: Cambridge University Press.

Berry, Jeffrey M., with David F. Arons. 2003. *A Voice for Nonprofits.* Washington, DC: Brookings Institution Press.

Bielefeld, Wolfgang. 2000. "Metropolitan Nonprofit Sectors: Findings from NCCS Data." *Nonprofit and Voluntary Sector Quarterly* 29(2): 297–314.

Boli, John, and George M. Thomas. 1997. "World Culture in the World Polity: A Century of International Non-Governmental Organization." *American Sociological Review* 62(2): 171.

Braga, Anthony A., David Hureau, and Christopher Winship. 2008. "Losing Faith? Police, Black

Churches and the Resurgence of Youth Violence in Boston." *Ohio State Journal of Criminal Law* 6(1): 141–172.

Brandtner, Christof, and David Suárez. 2018. "The Structure of City Action: Collaborative Governance and Sustainability Practices in U.S. Cities." Working paper, Stanford University.

Carroll, Glenn R. 1985. "Concentration and Specialization: Dynamics of Niche Width in Populations of Organizations." *American Journal of Sociology* 90(6): 1262–1283.

Clemens, Elisabeth S. 2010. "In the Shadow of the New Deal: Reconfiguring the Roles of Government and Charity, 1928–1940." In *Politics and Partnerships: The Role of Voluntary Associations in America's Political Past and Present*, ed. Elisabeth S. Clemens and Doug Guthrie, 79–119. Chicago: University of Chicago Press.

Countryman, Matthew J. 2007. *Up South: Civil Rights and Black Power in Philadelphia*. Philadelphia: University of Pennsylvania Press.

Crockett, Karilyn. 2018. *People Before Highways: Boston Activists, Urban Planners, and a New Movement for City Making*. Amherst: University of Massachusetts Press.

Czarniawska, Barbara. 2002. *A Tale of Three Cities: Or the Glocalization of City Management*. Oxford, UK: Oxford University Press.

Deutsch, Sara. 2000. *Women and the City: Gender, Space, and Power in Boston, 1870–1940*. New York: Oxford University Press.

Domhoff, G. W. 2014. *Who Rules America: The Triumph of the Corporate Rich*, 7th ed. New York: McGraw-Hill.

Douglas, Gordon C. 2018. *The Help-Yourself City: Legitimacy and Inequality in DIY Urbanism*. Oxford, UK: Oxford University Press.

Dunning, Claire. 2018a. "New Careers for the Poor: Human Services and the Post-Industrial City." *Journal of Urban History* 44(4): 669–690.

———. 2018b. "Outsourcing Government: Boston and the Rise of Public-Private Partnerships." *Enterprise & Society* 19(4): 803–815.

Ferguson, Karen. 2013. *Top Down: The Ford Foundation, Black Power, and the Reinvention of Racial Liberalism*. Philadelphia: University of Pennsylvania Press.

Finger, Leslie K. 2018. "Giving to Government: The Policy Goals and Giving Strategies of New and Old Foundations." *Interest Groups and Advocacy* 7(3): 312–345.

Fleming, Lee, Charles King III, and Adam I. Juda. 2007. "Small Worlds and Regional Innovation." *Organization Science* 18(6): 938–954.

Fung, Archon. 2003. "Associations and Democracy: Between Theories, Hopes, and Realities." *Annual Review of Sociology* 29(1): 515–539.

Galaskiewicz, Joseph. 1985. "Interorganizational Relations." *Annual Review of Sociology* 11: 281–304.

———. 1997. "An Urban Grants Economy Revisited: Corporate Charitable Contributions in the Twin Cities, 1979–81, 1987–89." *Administrative Science Quarterly* 42: 445–471.

Galaskiewicz, Joseph, and Stanley Wasserman. 1989. "Mimetic Processes Within an Interorganizational Field: An Empirical Test." *Administrative Science Quarterly* 34(3): 454–479.

Gamm, Gerald H. 1999. *Urban Exodus: Why the Jews Left Boston and the Catholics Stayed*. Cambridge, MA: Harvard University Press.

Gans, Herbert J. 2002. "The Sociology of Space: A Use-Centered View." *City and Community* 1(4): 329–339.

Geismer, Lily. 2015. *Don't Blame Us: Suburban Liberals and the Transformation of the Democratic Party*. Princeton, NJ: Princeton University Press.

Gibbons, Joseph. 2014. "Does Racial Segregation Make Community-Based Organizations More Territorial? Evidence from Newark, NJ and Jersey City, NY." *Journal of Urban Affairs* 37(5): 600–619.

Goldstein, Brian D. 2017. *The Roots of Urban Renaissance: Gentrification and the Struggle over Harlem*. Cambridge, MA: Harvard University Press.

Granovetter, Mark. 1985. "Economic Action and Social Structure: The Problem of Embeddedness." *American Journal of Sociology* 91(3): 481–510.

Greenstone, David J., and Paul E. Peterson. 1973. *Race and Authority in Urban Politics: Community Participation and the War on Poverty*. New York: Russell Sage Foundation.

Greve, Henrich R., and Hayagreeva Rao. 2012. "Echoes of the Past: Organizational Foundings as Sources of an Institutional Legacy of Mutualism." *American Journal of Sociology* 118(3): 635–675.

Grønbjerg, Kirsten A., and Laurie Paarlberg. 2001. "Community Variations in the Size and Scope of the Nonprofit Sector: Theory and Preliminary Findings." *Nonprofit and Voluntary Sector Quarterly* 30(4): 684–706.

Guthrie, Doug, and Michael McQuarrie. 2008. "Providing for the Public Good: Corporate-Community Relations in the Era of the Receding Welfare State." *City and Community* 7(2): 113–139.

Hall, Peter D. 2006. "A Historical Overview of Philanthropy, Voluntary Associations, and Nonprofit Organizations in the United States, 1600–2000." In *The Nonprofit Sector: A Research Handbook*, 2nd ed., ed. Walter W. Powell and Richard Steinberg, 32–65. New Haven, CT: Yale University Press.

Hansmann, Henry. 1987. "Economic Theories of Nonprofit Organizations." In *The Nonprofit Sector: A Research Handbook*, ed. Walter W. Powell, 27–42. New Haven, CT: Yale University Press.

Higginbotham, Evelyn B. 1993. *Righteous Discontent: The Women's Movement in the Black Baptist Church, 1880–1920.* Cambridge, MA: Harvard University Press.

Hock, Jennifer. 2013. "Bulldozers, Busing, and Boycotts: Urban Renewal and the Integrationist Project." *Journal of Urban History* 39(3): 433–453.

Horvath, Aaron, Christof Brandtner, and Walter W. Powell. 2018. "Serve or Conserve: Mission, Strategy, and Multi-Level Nonprofit Change During the Great Recession." *Voluntas: International Journal of Voluntary and Nonprofit Organizations* 29(5): 976–993.

Hunter, Floyd. 1953. *Community Power Structure: A Study of Decision Makers.* Chapel Hill: University of North Carolina Press.

Hwang, Hokyu, and Walter W. Powell. 2009. "The Rationalization of Charity: The Influences of Professionalism in the Nonprofit Sector." *Administrative Science Quarterly* 54(2): 268–298.

Jacobs, Jane. 1992. *The Death and Life of Great American Cities.* New York: Random House.

Jones, Candace, Silviya Svejenova, Jesper S. Pedersen, and Barbara Townley. 2016. "Misfits, Mavericks and Mainstreams: Drivers of Innovation in the Creative Industries." *Organization Studies* 37(6): 751–768.

Katz, Michael B. 1996. *In the Shadow of the Poorhouse: A Social History of Welfare in America*, 2nd ed. New York: Basic Books.

Keyes, Langley Carleton Jr. 1969. *The Rehabilitation Planning Game: A Study in the Diversity of Neighborhood.* Cambridge, MA: MIT Press.

Klinenberg, Eric. 2002. *Heat Wave: A Social Autopsy of Disaster in Chicago.* Chicago: University of Chicago Press.

———. 2018. *Palaces for the People: How Social Infrastructure Can Help Fight Inequality, Polarization, and the Decline of Civic Life.* New York: Crown.

Kwon, Seok-Woo, Colleen Heflin, and Martin Ruef. 2013. "Community Social Capital and Entrepreneurship." *American Sociological Review* 78(6): 980–1008.

Laumann, Edward O., Joseph Galaskiewicz, and Peter V. Marsden. 1978. "Community Structure as Interorganizational Linkages." *Annual Review of Sociology* 4(1): 455–484.

Lecy, Jesse, and David Van Slyke. 2012. "Nonprofit Sector Growth and Density: Testing Theories of Government Support." *Journal of Public Administration Research and Theory* 23(1): 189–214.

Lee, Caroline W., Michael McQuarrie, and Edward T. Walker. 2015. *Democratizing Inequalities: Dilemmas of the New Public Participation.* New York: NYU Press.

Lee, Sonia Song-Ha. 2014. *Building a Latino Civil Rights Movement: Puerto Ricans, African Americans, and the Pursuit of Racial Justice in New York City.* Chapel Hill: University of North Carolina Press.

LeGates, Richard T., and Frederic Stout. 2015. *The City Reader.* London: Routledge.

Levine, Jeremy R. 2016. "The Privatization of Political Representation: Community-Based Organizations as Nonelected Neighborhood Representatives." *American Sociological Review* 81(6): 1251–1275.

———. 2017. "Urban Politics and the Study of Urban Poverty: Promising Developments and Future Directions." *Sociology Compass* 11(12): 1–9.

Levy, Jonathan. 2017. "From Fiscal Triangle to Passing Through: Rise of the Nonprofit Corporation." In *Corporations and American Democracy*, ed. Naomi R. Lamoreaux and William J. Novak, 213–244. Cambridge, MA: Harvard University Press.

Logan, John R., and Harvey L. Molotch. 1987. *Urban Fortunes: The Political Economy of Place*. Berkeley: University of California Press.

Longhofer, Wesley, Giacomo Negro, and Peter W. Roberts. 2018. "The Changing Effectiveness of Local Civic Action: The Critical Nexus of Community and Organization." *Administrative Science Quarterly* 63, https://doi.org/10.1177/0001839218762403.

Lounsbury, Michael. 2007. "A Tale of Two Cities: Competing Logics and Practice Variation in the Professionalizing of Mutual Funds." *Academy of Management Journal* 50(2): 289–307.

MacIndoe, Heather, and Emily Barman. 2013. "How Organizational Stakeholders Shape Performance Measurement in Nonprofits: Exploring a Multidimensional Measure." *Nonprofit and Voluntary Sector Quarterly* 42(4): 716–738.

Marquis, Christopher, and Julie Battilana. 2009. "Acting Globally but Thinking Locally? The Enduring Influence of Local Communities on Organizations." *Research in Organizational Behavior* 29: 283–302.

Marquis, Christopher, Gerald F. Davis, and Mary Ann Glynn. 2013. "Golfing Alone? Corporations, Elites, and Nonprofit Growth in 100 American Communities." *Organization Science* 24(1): 39–57.

Marquis, Christopher, Mary Ann Glynn, and Gerald F. Davis. 2007. "Community Isomorphism and Corporate Social Action." *Academy of Management Review* 32(3): 925–945.

Marquis, Christopher, Michael Lounsbury, and Royston Greenwood. 2011. "Introduction: Community as an Institutional Order and a Type of Organizing." In *Communities and Organizations: Research in the Sociology of Organizations*, vol. 33, ed. Christopher Marquis, Michael Lounsbury, and Royston Greenwood, ix–xxvii. Bingley, UK: Emerald.

Martin, John L. 2009. *Social Structures*. Princeton, NJ: Princeton University Press.

Marwell, Nicole P. 2004. "Privatizing the Welfare State: Nonprofit Community-Based Organizations as Political Actors." *American Sociological Review* 69(2): 265–291.

———. 2007. *Bargaining for Brooklyn: Community Organizations in the Entrepreneurial City*. Chicago: University of Chicago Press.

Matsunaga, Yoshiho, and Naoto Yamauchi. 2004. "Is the Government Failure Theory Still Relevant? A Panel Analysis Using US State Level Data." *Annals of Public and Cooperative Economics* 75(2): 227–263.

McAdam, Doug, Robert Sampson, Simon Weffer-Elizondo, and Heather MacIndoe. 2005. "'There Will Be Fighting in the Streets': The Distorting Lens of Social Movement Theory." *Mobilization: An International Quarterly* 10(1): 1–18.

McPherson, Miller. 1983. "An Ecology of Affiliation." *American Sociological Review* 48(4): 519–532.

McPherson, Miller, Lynn Smith-Lovin, and James M. Cook. 2001. "Birds of a Feather: Homophily in Social Networks." *Annual Review of Sociology* 27(1): 415–444.

McQuarrie, Michael. 2010. "Nonprofits and the Reconstruction of Urban Governance: Housing Production and Community Development in Cleveland, 1975–2005." In *Politics and Partnerships: The Role of Voluntary Associations in America's Political Past and Present*, ed. Elisabeth S. Clemens and Doug Guthrie, 237–268. Chicago: University of Chicago Press.

McQuarrie, Michael, and Nicole P. Marwell. 2009. "The Missing Organizational Dimension in Urban Sociology." *City and Community* 8(3): 247–268.

McRoberts, Omar. 2003. *Streets of Glory: Church and Community in a Black Urban Neighborhood*. Chicago: University of Chicago Press.

Mizruchi, Mark S. 1996. "What Do Interlocks Do? An Analysis, Critique, and Assessment of Research on Interlocking Directorates." *Annual Review of Sociology* 22: 271–298.

Mollenkopf, John. 1983. *The Contested City*. Princeton, NJ: Princeton University Press.

Molotch, Harvey. 1976. "The City as a Growth Machine: Toward a Political Economy of Place." *American Journal of Sociology* 82(2): 309–332.

Molotch, Harvey, William Freudenburg, and Krista E. Paulsen. 2000. "History Repeats Itself, but How? City Character, Urban Tradition, and the

Accomplishment of Place." *American Sociological Review* 65(6): 791–823.

Mumford, Lewis. 1937. "What Is a City." *Architectural Record* 82(5): 59–62.

O'Connor, Alice. 1996. "Community Action, Urban Reform, and the Fight Against Poverty: The Ford Foundation's Gray Areas Program." *Journal of Urban History* 22(5): 586–625.

———. 2001. *Poverty Knowledge: Social Science, Social Policy, and the Poor in Twentieth-Century U.S. History.* Princeton, NJ: Princeton University Press.

O'Mara, Margaret P. 2005. *Cities of Knowledge: Cold War Science and the Search for the Next Silicon Valley.* Princeton, NJ: Princeton University Press.

Orleck, Annelise, and Lisa Gayle Hazirjian, eds. 2011. *The War on Poverty: A New Grassroots History, 1964–1980.* Athens: University of Georgia Press.

Ortmann, Stephan. 2015. "The Umbrella Movement and Hong Kong's Protracted Democratization Process." *Asian Affairs* 46(1): 32–50.

Osman, Suleiman. 2011. *The Invention of Brownstone Brooklyn: Gentrification and the Search for Authenticity in Postwar New York.* New York: Oxford University Press.

Padgett, John F., and Walter W. Powell. 2012. *The Emergence of Organizations and Markets.* Princeton, NJ: Princeton University Press.

Pattillo, Mary. 2007. *Black on the Block: The Politics of Race and Class in the City.* Chicago: University of Chicago Press.

Paxton, Pamela. 2002. "Social Capital and Democracy: An Interdependent Relationship." *American Sociological Review* 67(2): 254–277.

———. 2007. "Association Memberships and Generalized Trust: A Multilevel Model Across 31 Countries." *Social Forces* 86(1): 47–76.

Pflieger, Géraldine, and Céline Rozenblat. 2010. "Introduction. Urban Networks and Network Theory: The City as the Connector of Multiple Networks." *Urban Studies* 47(13): 2723–2735.

Powell, Walter W., and Christof Brandtner. 2016. "Organizations as Sites and Drivers of Social Action." In *Handbooks of Sociology and Social Research*, ed. Seth Abrutyn, 269–291. Cham, Switzerland: Springer.

Powell, Walter W., Kenneth W. Koput, and Laurel Smith-Doerr. 1996. "Interorganizational Collab-

oration and the Locus of Innovation: Networks of Learning in Biotechnology." *Administrative Science Quarterly* 41(1): 116–145.

Putnam, Robert D. 2000. *Bowling Alone: The Collapse and Revival of American Community.* New York: Simon and Schuster.

Rabig, Julia. 2016. *The Fixers: Devolution, Development, and Civil Society in Newark, 1960–1990.* Chicago: University of Chicago Press.

Rackow, Ronald W. 2013. "Payments in Lieu of Taxes: The Boston Experience." *Land Lines* (January): 2–7.

Rao, Hayagreeva, and Henrich R. Greve. 2018. "Disasters and Community Resilience: Spanish Flu and the Formation of Retail Cooperatives in Norway." *Academy of Management Journal* 61(1): 5–25.

Reckhow, Sarah. 2013. *Follow the Money: How Foundation Dollars Change Public School Politics.* Oxford, UK: Oxford University Press.

Rockman, Seth. 2009. *Scraping By: Wage Labor, Slavery, and Survival in Early Baltimore.* Baltimore: Johns Hopkins University Press.

Safford, Sean. 2009. *Why the Garden Club Couldn't Save Youngstown: The Transformation of the Rust Belt.* Cambridge, MA: Harvard University Press.

Salamon, Lester M. 1995. *Partners in Public Service: Government-Nonprofit Relations in the Modern Welfare State.* Baltimore: Johns Hopkins University Press.

Sampson, Robert J. 2012. *Great American City: Chicago and the Enduring Neighborhood Effect.* Chicago: University of Chicago Press.

Sampson, Robert J., Doug McAdam, Heather MacIndoe, and Simon Weffer-Elizondo. 2005. "Civil Society Reconsidered: The Durable Nature and Community Structure of Collective Civic Action." *American Journal of Sociology* 111(3): 673–714.

Sassen, Saskia. 2012. *Cities in a World Economy*, 4th ed. Newbury Park, CA: Pine Forge Press.

Saxenian, AnnaLee. 1994. "Inside-Out: Regional Networks and Industrial Adaptation in Silicon Valley and Route 128." *Cityscape: A Journal of Policy Development and Research* 2(2): 41–60.

Schneiberg, Marc, Marissa King, and Thomas Smith. 2008. "Social Movements and Organizational Form: Cooperative Alternatives to Corporations in the American Insurance, Dairy, and Grain

Industries." *American Sociological Review* 73(4): 635–667.

Self, Robert O., and Thomas J. Sugrue. 2002. "The Power of Place: Race, Political Economy, and Identity in the Postwar Metropolis." In *A Companion to Post-1945 America, Blackwell Companions to American History*, ed. Jean-Christophe Agnew and Roy Rosenzweig, 23–43. Malden, MA: Blackwell.

Seligman, Amanda I. 2016. *Chicago's Block Clubs: How Neighbors Shape the City*. Chicago: University of Chicago Press.

Sewell, William H. Jr. 1992. "A Theory of Structure: Duality, Agency, and Transformation." *American Journal of Sociology* 98(1): 1–29.

Sharkey, Patrick, Gerard Torrats-Espinosa, and Delaram Takyar. 2017. "Community and the Crime Decline: The Causal Effect of Local Nonprofits on Violent Crime." *American Sociological Review* 82(6): 1214–1240.

Simon, William B. 2001. *The Community Economic Development Movement*. Durham, NC: Duke University Press.

Small, Mario L. 2004. *Villa Victoria: The Transformation of Social Capital in a Boston Barrio*. Chicago: University of Chicago Press.

———. 2009. *Unanticipated Gains: Origins of Network Inequality in Everyday Life*. Oxford, UK: Oxford University Press.

Small, Mario L., and Monica McDermott. 2006. "The Presence of Organizational Resources in Poor Urban Neighborhoods." *Social Forces* 84(3): 1697–1724.

Smith, Steven R., and Michael Lipsky. 1993. *Nonprofits for Hire: The Welfare State in the Age of Contracting*. Cambridge, MA: Harvard University Press.

Storper, Michael, Thomas Kemeny, Naji Makarem, and Taner Osman. 2015. *The Rise and Fall of Urban Economies: Lessons From San Francisco and Los Angeles*. Redwood City, CA: Stanford University Press.

Strang, David, and Sarah A. Soule. 1998. "Diffusion in Organizations and Social Movements: From Hybrid Corn to Poison Pills." *Annual Review of Sociology* 24: 265–290.

Sugrue, Thomas. 1996. *The Origins of the Urban Crisis: Race and Inequality in Postwar Detroit*. Princeton, NJ: Princeton University Press.

———. 2008. *Sweet Land of Liberty: The Forgotten Struggle for Civil Rights in the North*. New York: Random House.

Theoharis, Jeanne, and Komozi Woodward, eds. 2003. *Freedom North: Black Freedom Struggles Outside the South*. New York: Oxford University Press.

———. 2005. *Groundwork: Local Black Freedom Movements in America*. New York: NYU Press.

Tilcsik, András, and Christopher Marquis. 2013. "Punctuated Generosity: How Mega-Events and Natural Disasters Affect Corporate Philanthropy in U.S. Communities." *Administrative Science Quarterly* 58(1): 111–148.

Tompkins-Stange, Megan E. 2016. *Policy Patrons: Philanthropy, Education Reform, and the Politics of Influence*. Cambridge, MA: Harvard Education Press.

Vargas, Robert. 2016. *Wounded City: Violent Turf Wars in a Chicago Barrio*. New York: Oxford University Press.

Verba, Sidney, Kay L. Schlozman, and Henry E. Brady. 1995. *Voice and Equality: Civic Voluntarism in American Politics*. Cambridge, MA: Harvard University Press.

Vermeulen, Floris, Debra C. Minkoff, and Tom van der Meer. 2016. "The Local Embedding of Community-Based Organizations." *Nonprofit and Voluntary Sector Quarterly* 45(1): 23–44.

Whittington, Kjersten B., Jason Owen-Smith, and Walter W. Powell. 2009. "Networks, Propinquity, and Innovation in Knowledge-Intensive Industries." *Administrative Science Quarterly* 54(1): 90–122.

Woodsworth, Michael. 2016. *Battle for Bed-Stuy: The Long War on Poverty in New York City*. Cambridge, MA: Harvard University Press.

Zukin, Sharon. 2010. *Naked City: The Death and Life of Authentic Urban Places*. Oxford, UK: Oxford University Press.

Zunz, Olivier. 2012. *Philanthropy in America: A History*. Princeton, NJ: Princeton University Press.

Chapter 12. Immigrant Organizations: Civic (In)equality and Civic (In)visibility

Alba, Richard, and Victor Nee. 2003. *Remaking the American Mainstream: Assimilation and Contemporary Immigration*. Cambridge, MA: Harvard University Press.

Aleksynska, Mariya. 2011. "Civic Participation of Immigrants in Europe: Assimilation, Origin, and Destination Country Effects." *European Journal of Political Economy* 27(3): 566–585.

Andrews, Kenneth T., and Bob Edwards. 2004. "Advocacy Organizations in the U.S. Political Process." *Annual Review of Sociology* 30: 479–506.

Bauder, Harald, and Sita Jayaraman. 2014. "Immigrant Workers in the Immigrant Service Sector: Segmentation and Career Mobility in Canada and Germany." *Transnational Social Review* 4(2–3): 176–192.

Berry, Jeffrey M., with David F. Arons. 2003. *A Voice for Nonprofits.* Washington, DC: Brookings Institution Press.

Berry, John W. 2005. "Acculturation: Living Successfully in Two Cultures." *International Journal of Intercultural Relations* 29(6): 697–712.

Bloemraad, Irene. 2005. "The Limits of de Tocqueville: How Government Facilitates Organizational Capacity in Newcomer Communities." *Journal of Ethnic and Migration Studies* 31(5): 865–887.

———. 2006. *Becoming a Citizen: Incorporating Immigrants and Refugees in the United States and Canada.* Berkeley: University of California Press.

Bloemraad, Irene, Els de Graauw, and Rebecca Hamlin. 2015. "Immigrants in the Media: Civic Visibility in the United States and Canada." *Journal of Ethnic and Migration Studies* 41(6): 874–896.

Bloemraad, Irene, and Shannon Gleeson. 2012. "Making the Case for Organizational Presence: Civic Inclusion, Access to Resources, and Formal Community Organizations." In *Remaking Urban Citizenship: Organizations, Institutions, and the Right to the City: Comparative Urban and Community Research*, vol. 10, eds. Michael Peter Smith and Michael McQuarrie, 109–134. New Brunswick, NJ: Transaction.

Bloemraad, Irene, and Floris Vermeulen. 2014. "Immigrants' Political Incorporation." In *An Introduction to Immigrant Incorporation Studies: European Perspectives*, ed. Marco Martiniello and Jan Rath, 227–249. Amsterdam: Amsterdam University Press.

Bloemraad, Irene, Kim Voss, and Taeku Lee. 2011. "The Immigration Rallies of 2006: What Were They, How Do We Understand Them, Where Do We Go?" In *Rallying for Immigrant Rights: The Fight for Inclusion in 21st Century America*, ed. Kim Voss and Irene Bloemraad, 3–43. Berkeley: University of California Press.

Breton, Raymond. 1964. "Institutional Completeness of Ethnic Communities and the Personal Relations of Immigrants." *American Journal of Sociology* 70(2): 193–205.

Bruno, Andorra. 2015. *Refugee Admissions and Resettlement Policy.* Washington, DC: Congressional Research Service.

CCRT (Community Cohesion Review Team). 2001. *Community Cohesion: A Report of the Independent Review Team.* London: Home Office.

Chan, Elic. 2014. *Mahjonging Together: Distribution, Financial Capacity, and Activities of Asian Nonprofit Organizations in Canada.* PhD thesis, University of Toronto.

Chaudhary, Ali R., and Luis Eduardo Guarnizo. 2016. "Pakistani Immigrant Organisational Spaces in Toronto and New York City." *Journal of Ethnic and Migration Studies* 42(6): 1013–1035.

Cho, Esther Yoona. 2017. "Revisiting Ethnic Niches: A Comparative Analysis of the Labor Market Experiences of Asian and Latino Undocumented Young Adults." *Russell Sage Foundation Journal of the Social Sciences* 3(4): 97–115.

Chung, Angie Y. 2007. *Legacies of Struggle: Conflict and Cooperation in Korean American Politics.* Stanford, CA: Stanford University Press.

Coll, Kathleen M. 2010. *Remaking Citizenship: Latina Immigrants and New American Politics.* Stanford, CA: Stanford University Press.

Cordero-Guzmán, Héctor R. 2005. "Community-Based Organisations and Migration in New York City." *Journal of Ethnic and Migration Studies* 31(5): 889–909.

Cortés, Michael. 1998. "Counting Latino Nonprofits: A New Strategy for Finding Data." *Nonprofit and Voluntary Sector Quarterly* 27(4): 437–458.

Dahl, Robert A. 1961. *Who Governs? Democracy and Power in an American City.* New Haven, CT: Yale University Press.

de Graauw, Els. 2015. "Polyglot Bureaucracies: Nonprofit Advocacy to Create Inclusive City Governments." *Journal of Immigrant and Refugee Studies* 13(2): 156–178.

———. 2016. *Making Immigrant Rights Real: Nonprofits and the Politics of Integration in San Francisco.* Ithaca, NY: Cornell University Press.

de Graauw, Els, and Irene Bloemraad. 2017. "Working Together: Building Successful Policy and Program Partnerships for Immigrant Integration." *Journal on Migration and Human Security* 5(1): 105–123.

de Graauw, Els, and Shannon Gleeson. 2017. "Context, Coalitions, and Organizing: Immigrant Labor Rights Advocacy in San Francisco and Houston." In *The City Is the Factory: New Solidarities and Spatial Strategies in an Urban Age,* ed. Miriam Greenberg and Penny Lewis, 80–98. Ithaca, NY: Cornell University Press.

———. 2018. "Philanthropic Investments in Immigrant Rights During Turbulent Times." *Politics of Color,* February 14. http://politicsofcolor.com/philanthropic-investments-in-immigrant-rights-during-turbulent-times.

de Graauw, Els, Shannon Gleeson, and Irene Bloemraad. 2013. "Funding Immigrant Organizations: Suburban Free Riding and Local Civic Presence." *American Journal of Sociology* 119(1): 75–130.

de Graauw, Els, and Floris Vermeulen. 2016. "Cities and the Politics of Immigrant Integration: A Comparison of Berlin, Amsterdam, New York City, and San Francisco." *Journal of Ethnic and Migration Studies* 42(6): 989–1012.

de Leon, Erwin, Matthew Maronick, Carol J. De Vita, and Elizabeth T. Boris. 2009. *Community-Based Organizations and Immigrant Integration in the Washington, D.C., Metropolitan Area.* Washington, DC: Urban Institute Press.

Fennema, Meindert, and Jean Tillie. 1999. "Political Participation and Political Trust in Amsterdam: Civic Communities and Ethnic Networks." *Journal of Ethnic and Migration Studies* 25(4): 703–726.

Fine, Janice. 2006. *Worker Centers: Organizing Communities at the Edge of the Dream.* Ithaca, NY: Cornell University Press.

Foley, Michael W., and Dean R. Hoge. 2007. *Religion and the New Immigrants: How Faith Communities Form Our Newest Citizens.* New York: Oxford University Press.

Friesenhahn, Erik. 2016. "Nonprofits in America: New Research Data on Employment, Wages,

and Establishments." *Monthly Labor Review* 139: 1–12. https://www.bls.gov/opub/mlr/2016/article/nonprofits-in-america.htm.

Gans, Herbert. 1992. "Second-Generation Decline: Scenarios for the Economic and Ethnic Futures of the Post-1965 American Immigrants." *Ethnic and Racial Studies* 15(2): 173–190.

Gast, Melanie Jones, and Dina G. Okamoto. 2016. "Moral or Civic Ties? Deservingness and Engagement Among Undocumented Latinas in Nonprofit Organisations." *Journal of Ethnic and Migration Studies* 42(12): 2013–2030.

Gleeson, Shannon. 2012. *Conflicting Commitments: The Politics of Enforcing Immigrant Worker Rights in San Jose and Houston.* Ithaca, NY: Cornell University Press.

Gleeson, Shannon, and Irene Bloemraad. 2012. "Assessing the Scope of Immigrant Organizations: Official Undercounts and Actual Underrepresentation." *Nonprofit and Voluntary Sector Quarterly* 42(2): 344–368.

Gnes, Davide, and Floris Vermeulen. 2018. "Legitimacy as the Basis for Organizational Development of Voluntary Organizations." In *Handbook of Community Movements and Local Organizations in the 21st Century,* ed. Ram A. Cnaan and Carl Milofsky, 189–209. Cham, Switzerland: Springer.

Gordon, Milton M. 1964. *Assimilation in American Life: The Role of Race, Religion and National Origins.* New York: Oxford University Press.

Griffith, Kati L., and Shannon M. Gleeson. 2017. "The Precarity of Temporality: How Law Inhibits Immigrant Worker Claims." *Comparative Labor Law and Policy Journal* 39(1): 111–141.

Grønbjerg, Kirsten A. 1998. "Markets, Politics, and Charity: Nonprofits in the Political Economy." In *Private Action and the Public Good,* ed. Walter W. Powell and Elisabeth S. Clemens, 137–150. New Haven, CT: Yale University Press.

Grønbjerg, Kirsten A., and Laurie Paarlberg. 2001. "Community Variations in the Size and Scope of the Nonprofit Sector: Theory and Preliminary Findings." *Nonprofit and Voluntary Sector Quarterly* 30(4): 684–706.

———. 2002. "Extent and Nature of Overlap Between Listings of IRS Tax-Exempt Registration and Nonprofit Incorporation: The Case of Indiana." *Nonprofit and Voluntary Sector Quarterly* 31(4): 565–594.

Hagan, Jacqueline Maria. 1994. *Deciding to Be Legal: A Maya Community in Houston.* Philadelphia: Temple University Press.

Hansmann, Henry. 1987. "Economic Theories of Nonprofit Organizations." In *The Nonprofit Sector: A Research Handbook*, ed. Walter W. Powell, 27–42. New Haven, CT: Yale University Press.

Hein, Jeremy. 1997. "Ethnic Organizations and the Welfare State: The Impact of Social Welfare Programs on the Formation of Indochinese Refugee Associations." *Sociological Forum* 12(2): 279–295.

Hung, Chi-Kan R. 2007. "Immigrant Nonprofit Organizations in U.S. Metropolitan Areas." *Nonprofit and Voluntary Sector Quarterly* 36(4): 707–729.

Joassart-Marcelli, Pascale. 2013. "Ethnic Concentration and Nonprofit Organizations: The Political and Urban Geography of Immigrant Services in Boston, Massachusetts." *International Migration Review* 47(3): 730–772.

Jones-Correa, Michael. 1998. *Between Two Nations: The Political Predicament of Latinos in New York City.* Ithaca, NY: Cornell University Press.

Just, Aida, and Christopher J. Anderson. 2012. "Immigrants, Citizenship and Political Action in Europe." *British Journal of Political Science* 42(3): 481–509.

Kivisto, Peter. 2014. *Religion and Immigration: Migrant Faiths in North America and Western Europe.* Malden, MA: Polity.

Koopmans, Ruud, Paul Statham, Marco Giugni, and Florence Passy. 2005. *Contested Citizenship: Immigration and Cultural Diversity in Europe.* Minneapolis: University of Minnesota Press.

LaFrance Associates. 2005. "The 2005 Santa Clara County Nonprofit Benchmark Study." Santa Clara, CA: Community Foundation Silicon Valley and CompassPoint Nonprofit Services. http://www.siliconvalleycf.org/docs/1276CFSVreportF2.pdf, accessed December 10, 2018.

Lampkin, Linda M., and Elizabeth T. Boris. 2002. "Nonprofit Organization Data: What We Have and What We Need." *American Behavioral Scientist* 45(11): 1675–1715.

Levitt, Peggy, and Nina Glick Schiller. 2004. "Conceptualizing Simultaneity: A Transnational So-cial Field Perspective on Society." *International Migration Review* 38(3): 1002–1039.

Martinez, Lisa M. 2005. "Yes We Can: Latino Participation in Unconventional Politics." *Social Forces* 84(1): 135–155.

Marwell, Nicole P. 2007. *Bargaining for Brooklyn: Community Organizations in the Entrepreneurial City.* Chicago: University of Chicago Press.

McAdam, Doug. 1988. *Freedom Summer.* New York: Oxford University Press.

Milkman, Ruth. 2006. *L.A. Story: Immigrant Workers and the Future of the U.S. Labor Movement.* New York: Russell Sage Foundation.

Milkman, Ruth, and Veronica Terriquez. 2012. "'We Are the Ones Who Are Out in Front': Women's Leadership in the Immigrant Rights Movement." *Feminist Studies* 38(3): 723–752.

Minkoff, Debra. 1995. *Organizing for Equality: The Evolution of Women's and Racial-Ethnic Organizations in America, 1955–1985.* New Brunswick, NJ: Rutgers University Press.

Morales, Laura, and Marco Giugni. 2011. *Social Capital, Political Participation and Migration in Europe: Making Multicultural Democracy Work?* New York: Palgrave Macmillan.

Moya, José C. 2005. "Immigrants and Associations: A Global and Historical Perspective." *Journal of Ethnic and Migration Studies* 31(5): 833–864.

NASEM (National Academies of Sciences, Engineering, and Medicine). 2015. *The Integration of Immigrants into American Society.* Washington, DC: National Academies Press.

Nguyen, Angela-Minh T. D., and Verónica Benet-Martínez. 2013. "Biculturalism and Adjustment: A Meta-Analysis." *Journal of Cross-Cultural Psychology* 44(1): 122–159.

Nicholls, Walter J. 2013. *The DREAMers: How the Undocumented Youth Movement Transformed the Immigrant Rights Debate.* Stanford, CA: Stanford University Press.

Portes, Alejandro, and Min Zhou. 1993. "The New Second Generation: Segmented Assimilation and Its Variants." *Annals of the American Academy of Political and Social Science* 530: 74–96.

Ramakrishnan, S. Karthick, and Mark Baldassare. 2004. *The Ties That Bind: Demographics and Civic Engagement in California.* San Francisco: Public Policy Institute of California.

Ramakrishnan, S. Karthick, and Irene Bloemraad, eds. 2008. *Civic Hopes and Political Realities: Immigrants, Community Organizations, and Political Engagement*. New York: Russell Sage Foundation.

Ramakrishnan, S. Karthick, and Thomas J. Espenshade. 2001. "Immigrant Incorporation and Political Participation in the United States." *International Migration Review* 35(3): 870–907.

Roth, Benjamin J., Roberto G. Gonzales, and Jacob Lesniewski. 2015. "Building a Stronger Safety Net: Local Organizations and the Challenges of Serving Immigrants in the Suburbs." *Human Service Organizations: Management, Leadership, and Governance* 39(4): 348–361.

Santa Clara County Office of Human Relations. 2000. *Bridging Borders in Silicon Valley: Summit on Immigrant Needs and Contributions*. San Jose, CA: Santa Clara County Office of Human Relations, Citizenship and Immigrant Services Program.

Strolovitch, Dara Z. 2007. *Affirmative Advocacy: Race, Class, and Gender in Interest Group Politics*. Chicago: University of Chicago Press.

Sundeen, Richard A., Cristina Garcia, and Sally A. Raskoff. 2009. "Ethnicity, Acculturation, and Volunteering to Organizations: A Comparison of African Americans, Asians, Hispanics, and Whites." *Nonprofit and Voluntary Sector Quarterly* 38(6): 929–955.

Taylor, Marilyn, Gary Craig, and Mick Wilkinson. 2002. "Co-option or Empowerment? The Changing Relationship Between the State and the Voluntary and Community Sectors." *Local Governance* 28(1): 1–11.

Terriquez, Veronica. 2011. "Schools for Democracy: Labor Union Participation and Latino Immigrant Parents' School-Based Civic Engagement." *American Sociological Review* 76(4): 581–601.

———. 2012. "Civic Inequalities? Immigrant Incorporation and Latina Mothers' Participation in Their Children's Schools." *Sociological Perspectives* 55(4): 663–682.

———. 2015. "Intersectional Mobilization, Social Movement Spillover, and Queer Youth Leadership in the Immigrant Rights Movement." *Social Problems* 62(3): 343–362.

Truelove, Marie. 2000. "Services for Immigrant Women: An Evaluation of Locations." *Canadian Geographer* 44(2): 135–152.

UNDESA (United Nations Department of Economic and Social Affairs, Population Division). 2017. *International Migration Report 2017*. New York: United Nations. http://www.un.org/en/development/desa/population/migration/data/estimates2/estimatesmaps.shtml, accessed December 10, 2018.

van der Meer, Tom, and Jochem Tolsma. 2014. "Ethnic Diversity and Its Effects on Social Cohesion." *Annual Review of Sociology* 40: 459–478.

Verba, Sidney, Kay Lehman Schlozman, and Henry E. Brady. 1995. *Voice and Equality: Civic Voluntarism in American Politics*. Cambridge, MA: Harvard University Press.

Vermeulen, Floris. 2006. *The Immigrant Organising Process: Turkish Organisations in Amsterdam and Berlin and Surinamese Organisations in Amsterdam, 1960–2000*. Amsterdam: Amsterdam University Press.

Vermeulen, Floris, Debra C. Minkoff, and Tom van der Meer. 2016. "The Local Embedding of Community-Based Organizations." *Nonprofit and Voluntary Sector Quarterly* 45(1): 23–44.

Vertovec, Steven, and Susanne Wessendorf. 2010. "Introduction: Assessing the Backlash Against Multiculturalism in Europe." In *The Multicultural Backlash: European Discourses, Policies and Practices*, ed. Steven Vertovec and Susanne Wessendorf, 1–31. New York: Routledge.

Voicu, Bogdan. 2014. "Participative Immigrants or Participative Cultures? The Importance of Cultural Heritage in Determining Involvement in Associations." *Voluntas: International Journal of Voluntary and Nonprofit Organizations* 25(3): 612–635.

Voicu, Bogdan, and Monica Şerban. 2012. "Immigrant Involvement in Voluntary Associations in Europe." *Journal of Ethnic and Migration Studies* 38(10): 1569–1587.

Vongkiatkajorn, Kanyakrit. 2018. "Trump's Anti-Refugee Campaign Just Hit a New Low." *Mother Jones*, February 14. https://www.motherjones.com/politics/2018/02/trumps-anti-refugee-campaign-just-hit-a-new-low.

Voss, Kim, and Irene Bloemraad, eds. 2011. *Rallying for Immigrant Rights: The Fight for Inclusion in 21st Century America*. Berkeley: University of California Press.

Waters, Mary C., and Tomás R. Jiménez. 2005. "Assessing Immigrant Assimilation: New Empirical and Theoretical Challenges." *Annual Review of Sociology* 31(1): 105–125.

Wong, Janelle S. 2006. *Democracy's Promise: Immigrants and American Civic Institutions*. Ann Arbor: University of Michigan Press.

Yukich, Grace. 2013. "Constructing the Model Immigrant: Movement Strategy and Immigrant Deservingness in the New Sanctuary Movement." *Social Problems* 60(3): 302–320.

Part IV. Nonprofits, Mission, and the Market
Chapter 13. Economic Theories of the Social Sector: From Nonprofits to Social Enterprise

Akerlof, George, and Rachel Kranton. 2005. "Identity and the Economics of Organizations." *Journal of Economic Perspectives* 19(1): 9–32.

Benabou, Roland, and Jean Tirole. 2006. "Incentives and Prosocial Behavior." *American Economic Review* 96(5): 1652–1678.

Besley, Timothy, and Maitreesh Ghatak. 2005. "Competition and Incentives with Motivated Agents." *American Economic Review* 95: 616–636.

———. 2017a. "Profit with Purpose? A Theory of Social Enterprise." *American Economic Journal: Economic Policy* 9(3): 19–58.

———. 2017b. "Public-Private Partnership for the Provision of Public Goods: Theory and an Application to NGOs." *Research in Economics* 71(2): 356–371.

———. 2018. "Pro-social Motivation and Incentives." *Annual Review of Economics* 10: 411–438.

Bornstein, David. 2004. *How to Change the World: Social Entrepreneurs and the Power of New Ideas*. New York: Oxford University Press.

Brolis, Olivier. 2017. "Do Social Enterprises Attract Workers Who Are More Pro-socially Motivated than Their Counterparts in For-Profit Organizations to Perform Low-Skilled Jobs?" *International Journal of Human Resource Management* 29(20): 1–19.

Cassar, Lea, and Stephan Meier. 2018. "Nonmonetary Incentives and the Implications of Work as a Source of Meaning." *Journal of Economic Perspectives* 32(3): 215–238.

Coase, Ronald. 1960. "The Problem of Social Cost." *Journal of Law and Economics* 3(1): 1–44.

Culley, Rachel, and Jill R. Horwitz. 2015. "Profits v. Purpose: Hybrid Companies and the Charitable Dollar." In *A Subtle Balance: Expertise, Evidence, and Democracy in Public Policy and Governance, 1970–2010*, ed. Edward A. Parson, 158–182. Montreal: McGill-Queens University Press.

Dees, J. Gregory. 1998. "The Meaning of Social Entrepreneurship." Revised May 30, 2001. https://centers.fuqua.duke.edu/case/wp-content/uploads/sites/7/2015/03/Article_Dees_MeaningofSocialEntrepreneurship_2001.pdf.

Friedman, Milton. 1970. "The Social Responsibility of Business Is to Increase Its Profits." *New York Times Magazine*, September 13, 1970. http://umich.edu/~thecore/doc/Friedman.pdf.

Gibbons, Robert, and John Roberts. 2013. *Handbook of Organizational Economics*. Princeton, NJ: Princeton University Press.

Glaeser, Edward, and Andrei Shleifer. 2001. "Not-for-Profit Entrepreneurs." *Journal of Public Economics* 81: 99–115.

Handy, Femida. 1995. "Reputation as Collateral: An Economic Analysis of the Role of Trustees of Nonprofits." *Nonprofit and Voluntary Sector Quarterly* 24(4): 293–305.

Handy, Femida, Laurie Mook, Jorge Ginieniewicz, and Jack Quarter. 2007. "The Moral High Ground: Perceptions of Wage Differentials Among Executive Directors of Canadian Nonprofits." *The Philanthropist* 20(2): 109–127.

Hansmann, Henry B. 1980. "The Role of Nonprofit Enterprise." *Yale Law Journal* 89(5): 835–901.

———. 1987. "Economic Theories of Nonprofit Organizations." In *The Nonprofit Sector: A Research Handbook*, ed. Walter W. Powell, 27–42. New Haven, CT: Yale University Press.

Hirsch, Barry T., David A. Macpherson, and Anne E. Preston. 2017. "Nonprofit Wages: Theory and Evidence." In *Handbook of Research on Nonprofit Economics and Management*, 2nd ed., ed. Bruce Seaman and Dennis Young, 126–179. Northampton, MA: Edward Elgar.

Holmström, Bengt, and Paul Milgrom. 1991. "Multi-Task Principal-Agent Analyses: Incentive

Contracts, Asset Ownership, and Job Design." *Journal of Law, Economics and Organization* 7: 24–52.

Jones, Daniel B. 2015. "The Supply and Demand of Motivated Labor: When Should We Expect to See Nonprofit Wage Gaps?" *Labour Economics* 32: 1–14.

Katz, Robert A., and Antony Page. 2010. "The Role of Social Enterprise." *Vermont Law Review* 35: 59–103.

Kristof, Nicholas. 2007. "Do-Gooders With Spreadsheets." *New York Times*, January 30. https://www.nytimes.com/2007/01/30/opinion/30kristof.html.

Lee, Matthew, and Julie Battilana. 2013. "How the Zebra Got Its Stripes: Imprinting of Individuals and Hybrid Social Ventures." Working paper 14-005, Harvard Business School.

Levin, Jonathan, and Steven Tadelis. 2005. "Profit Sharing and the Role of Professional Partnerships." *Quarterly Journal of Economics* 120(1): 131–171.

Martin, Roger L., and Sally Osberg. 2007. "Social Entrepreneurship: The Case for Definition." *Stanford Social Innovation Review* (Spring): 29–39.

McKeever, Brice S. 2018. "The Nonprofit Sector in Brief 2018: Public Charites, Giving, and Volunteering." National Center for Charitable Statistics (NCCS), Urban Institute, November 2018. https://nccs.urban.org/publication/nonprofit-sector-brief-2018#the-nonprofit-sector-in-brief-2018-public-charites-giving-and-volunteering.

Ortmann, Andreas. 1996. "Modern Economic Theory and the Study of Nonprofit Organizations: Why the Twain Shall Meet." *Nonprofit and Voluntary Sector Quarterly* 25(4): 470–484.

Page, Antony, and Robert A. Katz. 2012. "The Truth About Ben and Jerry's." *Stanford Social Innovation Review* (Fall): 1–10.

Porter, Michael E., and Mark R. Kramer. 2011. "Shared Value." *Harvard Business Review* (January/February): 62–77.

Preston, Anne E. 1989. "The Nonprofit Worker in a For-Profit World." *Journal of Labor Economics* (7): 438–463.

Reiser, Dana Brakman. 2010. "Blended Enterprise and the Dual Mission Dilemma." *Vermont Law Review* 35: 105–116.

Salamon, Lester M., Megan A. Haddock, S. Wojciech Sokolowski, and Helen S. Tice. 2007. "Measuring Civil Society and Volunteering: Initial Findings from Implementation of the UN Handbook on Nonprofit Institutions." Working Paper No. 23, Johns Hopkins Center for Civil Society Studies.

Serra, Danila, Pieter Serneels, and Abigail Barr. 2011. "Intrinsic Motivations and the Non-Profit Health Sector: Evidence from Ethiopia." *Personality and Individual Differences* 51(3): 309–314.

Shiller, Robert. 2012. *Finance and the Good Society.* Princeton, NJ: Princeton University Press.

Strom, Stephanie. 2007. "Businesses Try to Make Money and Save the World." *New York Times*, May 6. https://www.nytimes.com/2007/05/06/business/yourmoney/06fourth.html.

Weisbrod, Burton A. 1988. *The Nonprofit Economy.* Cambridge, MA: Harvard University Press.

Werker, Eric, and Faisal Z. Ahmed. 2008. "What Do Nongovernmental Organizations Do?" *Journal of Economic Perspectives* 22(2): 73–92.

Yunus, Muhammad. 2007. *Creating a World Without Poverty: Social Business and the Future of Capitalism.* New York: Public Affairs.

———. 2011. "Sacrificing Microcredit for Megaprofits." *New York Times*, January 14. https://www.nytimes.com/2011/01/15/opinion/15yunus.html.

Chapter 14. Social Entrepreneurship: Research as Disciplined Exploration

Abbott, Andrew. 2004. *Methods of Discovery: Heuristics for the Social Sciences.* New York: Norton.

Anheier, Helmut K., and Gorgi Krlev. 2014. "Welfare Regimes, Policy Reforms, and Hybridity." *American Behavioral Scientist* 58(11): 1395–1411.

Anheier, Helmut K., and Lester M. Salamon. 2006. "The Nonprofit Sector in Comparative Perspective." In *The Nonprofit Sector: A Research Handbook*, 2nd ed., ed. Walter W. Powell and Richard Steinberg, 89–114. New Haven, CT: Yale University Press.

Austin, James, Howard Stevenson, and Jane Wei-Skillern. 2006. "Social and Commercial Entrepreneurship: Same, Different, or Both?" *Entrepreneurship: Theory and Practice* 30(1): 1–22.

Battilana, Julie, and Silvia Dorado. 2010. "Building Sustainable Hybrid Organizations: The Case of

Commercial Microfinance Organizations." *Academy of Management Journal* 53(6): 1419–1440.

Battilana, Julie, and Matthew Lee. 2014. "Advancing Research on Hybrid Organizing—Insights from the Study of Social Enterprises." *Academy of Management Annals* 8(1): 397–441.

Battilana, Julie, Metin Sengul, Anne-Claire Pache, and Jacob Model. 2015. "Harnessing Productive Tensions in Hybrid Organizations: The Case of Work Integration Social Enterprises." *Academy of Management Journal* 58(6): 1658–1685.

Becker, Howard S. 1966. *Outsiders: Studies in the Sociology of Deviance*. New York: Free Press.

Besharov, Marya, and Wendy Smith. 2014. "Multiple Logics in Organizations: Explaining Their Varied Nature and Implications." *Academy of Management Review* 39: 364–381.

Besley, Timothy, and Maitreesh Ghatak. 2017. "Profit with Purpose? A Theory of Social Enterprise." *American Economic Journal: Economic Policy* 9(3): 19–58.

Blau, Peter. M., and W. Richard Scott. 1962. *Formal Organizations: A Comparative Approach*. San Francisco: Chandler.

Blumer, Herbert. 1971. "Social Problems as Collective Behavior." *Social Problems* 18(3): 298–306.

Brakman Reiser, Dana. 2013. "Theorizing Forms for Social Enterprise." *Emory Law Journal* 62(4): 681–740.

Chliova, Myrto, Johanna Mair, and Alfred Vernis. Forthcoming. "Persistent Category Ambiguity: The Case of Social Entrepreneurship." *Organization Studies*.

Crucke, Saskia, and Mirjam Knockaert. 2016. "When Stakeholder Representation Leads to Faultlines: A Study of Board Service Performance in Social Enterprises." *Journal of Management Studies* 53(5): 768–793.

Dacin, M. Tina, Peter A. Dacin, and Paul Tracey. 2011. "Social Entrepreneurship: A Critique and Future Directions." *Organization Science* 22(5): 1203–1213.

Deeg, Richard, and Gregory Jackson. 2007. "Towards a More Dynamic Theory of Capitalist Variety." *Socio-Economic Review* 5(1): 149–179.

Dees, J. Gregory. 1994. "Social Enterprise: Private Initiatives for the Common Good." Harvard Business School, November 30.

———. 1998. "The Meaning of Social Entrepreneurship." Revised May 30, 2001. https://

centers.fuqua.duke.edu/case/wp-content/uploads/sites/7/2015/03/Article_Dees_MeaningofSocialEntrepreneurship_2001.pdf.

Dees, J. Gregory, and Beth Battle Anderson. 2002. "Blurring Sector Boundaries: Serving Social Purposes Through For-Profit Structures." CASE Working Paper Series, No. 2, Center for the Advancement of Social Entrepreneurship.

Defourny, Jacques, and Marthe Nyssens. 2017. "Fundamentals for an International Typology of Social Enterprise Models." *Voluntas: International Journal of Voluntary and Nonprofit Organizations* 28(6): 2469–2497.

Dey, Pascal, and Chris Steyaert. 2010. "The Politics of Narrating Social Entrepreneurship." *Journal of Enterprising Communities: People and Places in the Global Economy* 4(1): 85–108.

DiMaggio, Paul J., and Walter W. Powell. 1983. "The Iron Cage Revisited: Institutional Isomorphism and Collective Rationality in Organizational Fields." *American Sociological Review* 48(2): 147–160.

Dover, Graham, and Thomas B. Lawrence. 2012. "The Role of Power in Nonprofit Innovation." *Nonprofit and Voluntary Sector Quarterly* 41(6): 991–1013.

Drayton, William. 2006. "Everyone a Changemaker: Social Entrepreneurship's Ultimate Goal." *Innovations: Technology, Governance, Globalization* 1(1): 80–96.

Ebrahim, Alnoor, Julie Battilana, and Johanna Mair. 2014. "The Governance of Social Enterprises: Mission Drift and Accountability Challenges in Hybrid Organizations." *Research in Organizational Behavior* 34: 81–100.

Esping-Andersen, Gøsta. 1990. *The Three Worlds of Welfare Capitalism*. Princeton, NJ: Princeton University Press.

Galaskiewicz, Joseph, and Sondra N. Barringer. 2012. "Social Enterprises and Social Categories." In *Social Enterprises: An Organizational Perspective*, ed. Benjamin Gidron and Yeheskel Hasenfeld, 47–70. Basingstoke, UK: Palgrave Macmillan.

Ganz, Marshall, Tamara Kay, and Jason Spicer. 2018. "Social Enterprise Is Not Social Change." *Stanford Social Innovation Review* (Spring): 59–60.

Grohs, Stephan, Katrin Schneiders, and Rolf G. Heinze. 2017. "Outsiders and Intrapreneurs: The Institutional Embeddedness of Social Entrepreneurship in Germany." *Voluntas: International Journal of Voluntary and Nonprofit Organizations* 28(6): 2569–2591.

Gusfield, Joseph R. 1989. "Constructing the Ownership of Social Problems: Fun and Profit in the Welfare State." *Social Problems* 36(5): 431–441.

Hall, Peter A., and David W. Soskice. 2001. *Varieties of Capitalism: The Institutional Foundations of Comparative Advantage.* Oxford, UK: Oxford University Press.

Hall, Peter D. 2013. "Philanthropy and the Social Enterprise Spectrum." *Social Entrepreneurship* (2): 24–67.

Heckathorn, Douglas D. 1997. "Respondent-Driven Sampling: A New Approach to the Study of Hidden Populations." *Social Problems* 44(2): 174–199.

Hehenberger, Lisa, Johanna Mair, and Sara Seganti. 2018. "Impact Investing: Financing Social Entrepreneurs." In *Entrepreneurial Finance: The Art and Science of Growing Ventures*, ed. Luisa Alemany and Job J. Andreoli, 485–527. Cambridge, UK: Cambridge University Press.

Hilgartner, Stephen, and Charles L. Bosk. 1988. "The Rise and Fall of Social Problems: A Public Arenas Model." *American Journal of Sociology* 94(1): 53–78.

Humboldt, Alexander von, and Aimé Bonpland. 1807. *Ideen zu einer Geographie der Pflanzen.* Tübingen, Germany: Cotta.

Huysentruyt, Marieke, Johanna Mair, and Ute Stephan. 2016. "Market-Oriented and Mission-Focused: Social Enterprises Around the Globe." *Stanford Social Innovation Review*, October 19.

Huysentruyt, Marieke, Tomislav Rimac, Ute Stephan, and Suncica Vujic. 2017. "Sampling in Management Research: An Approach for Hard-to-Reach Populations." Paper presented at the annual meeting of the Academy of Management, Atlanta, GA, August 7.

Huysentruyt, Marieke, and Ute Stephan. 2017. "Social Enterprises, an Economic Force for Building More Inclusive Societies? Evidence from the SEFORÏS Study." *European Policy Brief*, June 15.

Kerlin, Janelle A. 2010. "A Comparative Analysis of the Global Emergence of Social Enterprise." *Voluntas: International Journal of Voluntary and Nonprofit Organizations* 21(2): 162–179.

———. 2013. "Defining Social Enterprise Across Different Contexts: A Conceptual Framework Based on Institutional Factors." *Nonprofit and Voluntary Sector Quarterly* 42(1): 84–108.

Kibler, Ewald, Virva Salmivaara, Pekka Stenholm, and Siri Terjesen. 2018. "The Evaluative Legitimacy of Social Entrepreneurship in Capitalist Welfare Systems." *Journal of World Business* 53(6): 944–957.

Lawrence, Thomas B., and Graham Dover. 2015. "Place and Institutional Work: Creating Housing for the Hard-to-House." *Administrative Science Quarterly* 60(3): 371–410.

Lawrence, Thomas B., Cynthia Hardy, and Nelson Phillips. 2002. "Institutional Effects of Interorganizational Collaboration: The Emergence of Proto-Institutions." *Academy of Management Journal* 45(1): 281–290.

Letts, Christine W., William Ryan, and Allen S. Grossman. 1997. "Virtuous Capital: What Foundations Can Learn from Venture Capitalists." *Harvard Business Review* (March–April): 36–44.

Light, Paul C. 2008. *The Search for Social Entrepreneurship.* Washington, DC: Brookings Institution Press.

Liu, Gordon, Teck-Yong Eng, and Sachiko Takeda. 2015. "An Investigation of Marketing Capabilities and Social Enterprise Performance in the UK and Japan." *Entrepreneurship: Theory and Practice* 39(2): 267–298.

Loseke, Donileen R. 2003. *Thinking About Social Problems.* New York: Routledge.

Mair, Johanna. 2010. "Social Entrepreneurship: Taking Stock and Looking Ahead." In *Handbook of Research on Social Entrepreneurship*, ed. Alain Fayolle and Harry Matlay, 16–33. Cheltenham, UK: Edward Elgar.

Mair, Johanna. 2018. "Scaling Innovative Ideas to Create Inclusive Labour Markets." *Nature Human Behaviour* 2(5): 884.

Mair, Johanna, Julie Battilana, and Julian Cardenas. 2012. "Organizing for Society: A Typology of Social Entrepreneuring Models." *Journal of Business Ethics* 111(3): 353–373.

Mair, Johanna, and Kate Ganly. 2008. "Social Entrepreneurship as Dynamic Innovation." *Innovations: Technology, Governance, Globalization* 3(4): 79–84.

Mair, Johanna, and Ignasi Martí. 2006. "Social Entrepreneurship Research: A Source of

Explanation, Prediction, and Delight." *Journal of World Business* 41(1): 36–44.

———. 2009. "Entrepreneurship in and Around Institutional Voids: A Case Study from Bangladesh." *Journal of Business Venturing* 24(5): 419–435.

Mair, Johanna, Ignasi Martí, and Marc J. Ventresca. 2012. "Building Inclusive Markets in Rural Bangladesh: How Intermediaries Work Institutional Voids." *Academy of Management Journal* 55(4): 819–850.

Mair, Johanna, Judith Mayer, and Eva Lutz. 2015. "Navigating Institutional Plurality: Organizational Governance in Hybrid Organizations." *Organization Studies* 36(6): 713–739.

Mair, Johanna, and Nikolas Rathert. Forthcoming. "Alternative Organizing with Social Purpose: Revisiting Institutional Analysis of Market-Based Activity." *Socio-Economic Review.*

Mair, Johanna, Nikolas Rathert, and Marieke Huysentruyt. 2018. "Novel and (Not So) Conventional? Exposing Heterogeneity of Social Enterprises Across Institutional Contexts." Paper presented at the Alberta Institutions Conference.

Mair, Johanna, Jeffrey Robinson, and Kai Hockerts. 2006. *Social Entrepreneurship.* Basingstoke, UK: Palgrave Macmillan.

Mair, Johanna, Miriam Wolf, and Alexandra Ioan. 2020. "Governance in Social Enterprises." In *Handbook on Advances in Corporate Governance: Comparative Perspectives,* ed. Helmut K. Anheier and Theodor Baums. Oxford, UK: Oxford University Press.

Mair, Johanna, Miriam Wolf, and Christian Seelos. 2016. "Scaffolding: A Process of Transforming Patterns of Inequality in Small-Scale Societies." *Academy of Management Journal* 59(6): 2021–2044.

Martin, Roger L., and Sally Osberg. 2007. "Social Entrepreneurship: The Case for Definition." *Stanford Social Innovation Review* (Spring): 29–39.

Minkoff, Debra C., and Walter W. Powell. 2006. "Nonprofit Mission: Constancy, Responsiveness, or Deflection." In *The Nonprofit Sector: A Research Handbook,* 2nd ed., ed. Walter W. Powell and Richard Steinberg, 591–609. New Haven, CT: Yale University Press.

Pache, Anne-Claire, and Filipe Santos. 2013. "Inside the Hybrid Organization: Selective Coupling as a Response to Conflicting Institutional Logics." *Academy of Management Journal* 56(4): 972–1001.

Sabeti, Heerad. 2011. "The For-Benefit Enterprise." *Harvard Business Review* (November): 98–104.

Salamon, Lester M., and Helmut K. Anheier, eds. 1997. *Defining the Nonprofit Sector: A Cross-National Analysis.* Manchester, UK: Manchester University Press.

———. 1998. "Social Origins of Civil Society: Explaining the Nonprofit Sector Cross-Nationally." *Voluntas: International Journal of Voluntary and Nonprofit Organizations* 9(3): 213–248.

Santos, Filipe M. 2012. "A Positive Theory of Social Entrepreneurship." *Journal of Business Ethics* 111(3): 335–351.

Schneiberg, Marc, and Elisabeth S. Clemens. 2006. "The Typical Tools for the Job: Research Strategies in Institutional Analysis." *Sociological Theory* 24(3): 195–227.

Scott, James C. 1990. *Domination and the Arts of Resistance: Hidden Transcripts.* New Haven, CT: Yale University Press.

Seelos, Christian, and Johanna Mair. 2005. "Social Entrepreneurship: Creating New Business Models to Serve the Poor." *Business Horizons* 48(3): 241–246.

———. 2007. "Profitable Business Models and Market Creation in the Context of Deep Poverty: A Strategic View." *Academy of Management Perspectives* 21(4): 49–63.

———. 2017. *Innovation and Scaling for Impact: How Effective Social Enterprises Do It.* Stanford, CA: Stanford University Press.

Seelos, Christian, Johanna Mair, Julie Battilana, and Tina Dacin. 2011. "The Embeddedness of Social Entrepreneurship: Understanding Variation Across Local Communities." In *Communities and Organizations: Research in the Sociology of Organizations,* vol. 33, ed. Christopher Marquis, Michael Lounsbury, and Royston Greenwood, 333–363. Bingley, UK: Emerald.

Seibel, Wolfgang. 2015. "Studying Hybrids: Sectors and Mechanisms." *Organization Studies* 36(6): 697–712.

Skloot, Edward. 1987. "Enterprise and Commerce in Nonprofit Organizations." In *The Nonprofit Sector: A Research Handbook*, ed. Walter W. Powell, 380–393. New Haven, CT: Yale University Press.

Smith, Wendy K., and Marya L. Besharov. 2019. "Bowing Before Dual Gods: How Structured Flexibility Sustains Organizational Hybridity." *Administrative Science Quarterly* 64(1): 1–44.

Stephan, Ute, Lorraine M. Uhlaner, and Christopher Stride. 2015. "Institutions and Social Entrepreneurship: The Role of Institutional Voids, Institutional Support, and Institutional Configurations." *Journal of International Business Studies* 46(3): 308–331.

Teasdale, Simon. 2012. "What's in a Name? Making Sense of Social Enterprise Discourses." *Public Policy and Administration* 27(2): 99–119.

Tracey, Paul, and Owen Jarvis. 2006. "An Enterprising Failure—Why a Promising Social Franchise Collapsed." *Stanford Social Innovation Review* 4(1): 66–70.

Vasi, Ion B. 2009. "New Heroes, Old Theories? Toward a Sociological Perspective on Social Entrepreneurship." In *An Introduction to Social Entrepreneurship: Voices, Preconditions, Contexts*, ed. Rafael Ziegler, 155–173. Cheltenham, UK: Edward Elgar.

Weber, Max. (1922) 1978. *Economy and Society: An Outline of Interpretive Sociology*, vol. 2, ed. G. Roth and C. Wittich. Berkeley: University of California Press.

Weick, Karl E. 1989. "Theory Construction as Disciplined Imagination." *Academy of Management Review* 14: 516–531.

Weisbrod, Burton A, ed. 1998. *To Profit or Not to Profit: The Commercial Transformation of the Nonprofit Sector*. New York: Cambridge University Press.

———. 2004. "The Pitfalls of Profits." *Stanford Social Innovation Review* 2(3): 40–47.

Wolf, Miriam, and Johanna Mair. 2019. "Purpose, Commitment and Coordination Around Small Wins: A Proactive Approach to Governance in Integrated Hybrid Organizations." *Voluntas: International Journal of Voluntary and Nonprofit Organizations* 30(3): 535–548.

Wry, Tyler, and Jeffrey G. York. 2017. "An Identity-Based Approach to Social Enterprise." *Academy of Management Review* 42(3): 437–460.

Zahra, Shaker A., Eric Gedajlovic, Donald O. Neubaum, and Joel M. Shulman. 2009. "A Typology of Social Entrepreneurs: Motives, Search Processes and Ethical Challenges." *Journal of Business Venturing* 24(5): 519–532.

Zhao, Eric Y., and Tyler Wry. 2016. "Not All Inequality Is Equal: Deconstructing the Societal Logic of Patriarchy to Understand Microfinance Lending to Women." *Academy of Management Journal* 59(6): 1994–2020.

Chapter 15. Nonprofits and the Environment: Using Market Forces for Social Good

Albersmeier, F., H. Schulze, and A. Spiller. 2009. "Evaluation and Reliability of the Organic Certification System: Perceptions by Farmers in Latin America." *Sustainable Development* 17(5): 311–324.

Anderson, R. C., and E. N. Hansen. 2004. "The Impact of Environmental Certification on Preferences for Wood Furniture: A Conjoint Analysis Approach." *Forest Products Journal* 54(3): 42–50.

Auld, G. 2010. "Assessing Certification as Governance: Effects and Broader Consequences for Coffee." *Journal of Environment and Development* 19(2): 215–241.

Auld, G., and L. H. Gulbrandsen. 2009. *To Inform or Empower? Transparency in Non-State Certification of Forestry and Fisheries*. Amsterdam: Conference on the Human Dimensions of Global Environmental Change.

Bacon, C. M., V. E. Méndez, S. R. Gliessman, D. Goodman, and J. A. Fox, eds. 2008. *Confronting the Coffee Crisis: Fair Trade, Sustainable Livelihoods and Ecosystems in Mexico and Central America*. Cambridge, MA: MIT Press.

Banerjee, A. V., S. Cole, E. Duflo, and L. Linden. 2007. "Remedying Education: Evidence from Two Randomized Experiments in India." *Quarterly Journal of Economics* 122(3): 1235–1264.

Banerjee, A., and B. D. Solomon. 2003. "Eco-Labeling for Energy Efficiency and Sustainability: A Meta-Evaluation of US Programs." *Energy Policy* 31(2): 109–123.

Barclay, P. 2004. "Trustworthiness and Competitive Altruism Can Also Solve the 'Tragedy of the Commons.'" *Evolution and Human Behavior* 25(4): 209–220.

Baron, David P., and D. Diermeier. 2007. "Strategic Activism and Nonmarket Strategy." *Journal of Economics and Management Strategy* 16(3): 599–634.

Bartley, T. 2007. "Institutional Emergence in an Era of Globalization: The Rise of Transnational Private Regulation of Labor and Environmental Conditions." *American Journal of Sociology* 113(2): 297–351.

Bass, S., and M. Simula. 1999. "Independent Certification/Verification of Forest Management." Paper prepared for the World Bank/WWF Alliance Workshop, Washington, DC.

Bass, T., R. Markopoulous, and G. Grah. 2001. *Certification's Impact on Forests, Stakeholders and Supply Chains: Instruments for Sustainable Private Sector Forestry Series.* London: Institute for Environment and Development.

Batte, M. T., N. H. Hooker, T. C. Haab, and J. Beaverson. 2007. "Putting Their Money Where Their Mouths Are: Consumer Willingness to Pay for Multi-Ingredient, Processed Organic Food Products." *Food Policy 2007* 32(2): 145–159.

Battilana, J., and S. Dorado. 2010. "Building Sustainable Hybrid Organizations: The Case of Commercial Microfinance Organizations." *Academy of Management Journal* 53(6): 1419–1440.

Battilana, J., M. Sengul, A.-C. Pache, and J. Model. 2015. "Harnessing Productive Tensions in Hybrid Organizations: The Case of Work Integration Social Enterprises." *Academy of Management* 58(6): 1658–1685.

Ben-Amar, W., M. Chang, and P. McIlkenny. 2017. "Board Gender Diversity and Corporate Response to Sustainability Initiatives: Evidence from the Carbon Disclosure Project." *Journal of Business Ethics* 142(2): 369–383.

Blackman, A., and J. Rivera. 2011. "Producer-Level Benefits of Sustainability Certification." *Conservation Biology* 25(6): 1176–1185.

Blamey, R. K., J. W. Bennett, J. J. Louviere, M. D. Morrison, and J. Rolfe. 2000. "A Test of Policy Labels in Environmental Choice Modeling Studies." *Ecological Economics* 32(2): 269–286.

Boström, M., and K. T. Hallström. 2010. "NGO Power in Global Social and Environmental Standard-Setting." *Global Environmental Politics* 10(4): 36–59.

Botanaki, A., K. Polymeros, E. Tsakiridou, and K. Mattas. 2005. "The Role of Food Quality Certification on Consumers' Food Choices." *British Food Journal* 108(2): 77–90.

Boyd, B., N. Henning, E. Reyna, D. Wang, M. Welch, and A. J. Hoffman. 2017. *Hybrid Organizations: New Business Models for Environmental Leadership.* London: Routledge.

Brès, L., E. Raufflet, and J. Boghossian. 2018. "Pluralism in Organizations: Learning from Unconventional Forms of Organizations." *International Journal of Management Reviews* 20(2): 364–386.

Brunsson, N., A. Rasche, and D. Seidl. 2012. "The Dynamics of Standardization: Three Perspectives on Standards in Organization Studies." *Organization Studies* 33(5–6): 613–632.

Büthe, T. 2010. "Global Private Politics: A Research Agenda." *Business and Politics* 12(3): 1–24.

Callery, P. J., and J. Perkins. 2017. "Unmasking Strategic Disclosure: Evidence from Voluntary Corporate Carbon Disclosures." *Academy of Management Proceedings* 2017(1): 11436.

Cao, K., J. Gehman, and M. Grimes. 2017. "Standing Out and Fitting In: Charting the Emergence of Certified B Corporations by Industry and Region." In *Hybrid Ventures: Advances in Entrepreneurship, Firm Emergence and Growth*, vol. 19, ed. A. C. Corbett and J. A. Katz, 1–38. Bingley, UK: Emerald.

Cashore, B. 2002. "Legitimacy and the Privatization of Environmental Governance: How Non-State Market-Driven (NSMD) Governance Systems Gain Rule-Making Authority." *Governance: An International Journal of Policy, Administration, and Institutions* 15(4): 503–529.

Cashore, B., G. Auld, and D. Newsom. 2004a. *Governing Through Markets: Forest Certification and the Emergence of Non-State Authority.* New Haven, CT: Yale University Press.

———. 2004b. "Legitimizing Political Consumerism: The Case of Forest Certification in North America and Europe." In *Politics, Products, and Markets: Exploring Political Consumerism Past and Present*, ed. M. Micheletti, A. Follesdal, and D. Stolle, 181–199. London: Transaction.

Chen, X., and T. Kelly. 2015. "B-Corps—A Growing Form of Social Enterprise: Tracing Their Progress and Assessing Their Performance." *Journal of Leadership and Organizational Studies* 22(1): 102–114.

Chiroleu-Assouline, M., and F. Wijen. Forthcoming. "Controversy over Voluntary Environmental Standards: A Socio-Economic Analysis of the Marine Stewardship Council." *Organization and Environment*.

Constance, D. H., and A. Bonanno. 2000. "Regulating the Global Fisheries: The World Wildlife Fund, Unilever, and the Marine Stewardship Council." *Agriculture and Human Values* 17(2): 125–139.

Coombs, W. T. 2014. "Nestlé and Greenpeace: The Battle in Social Media for Ethical Palm Oil Sourcing." In *Ethical Practice of Social Media in Public Relations*, ed. M. W. DiStaso and D. S. Bortree, 158–169. New York: Routledge.

Cooney, K., J. Koushyar, M. Lee, and H. Murray. 2014. "Benefit Corporation and L3C Adoption: A Survey." *Stanford Social Innovation Review*, December 5. https://ssir.org/articles/entry/benefit _corporation_and_l3c_adoption_a_survey.

Copeland, L., and Smith, E.R.A.N. 2014. "Consumer Political Action on Climate Change." In *Changing Climate Politics: U.S. Policies and Civic Action*, ed. Y. Wolinsky-Nahmias, 197–217. Washington, DC: CQ Press.

Corbett, C., and S. Muthulingam. 2007. "Adoption of Voluntary Environmental Standards: The Role of Signaling and Intrinsic Benefits in the Diffusion of the LEED Green Building Standards." Working paper, UCLA Anderson School of Management, Los Angeles, CA.

Cornes, R., and T. Sandler. 1996. *The Theory of Externalities, Public Goods and Club Goods*, 2nd ed. Cambridge, UK: Cambridge University Press.

Counsell, S., and K. T. Loraas. 2002. *Trading in Credibility: The Myth and Reality of the Forest Stewardship Council*. London: Rainforest Foundation.

Crespi, J. M., and S. Marette. 2005. "Eco-Labelling Economics: Is Public Involvement Necessary?" In *Environment, Information and Consumer Behavior*, ed. S. Krarup and C. S. Russell, 93–110. Northampton, MA: Edward Elgar.

Crutchfield, L. R., and H. M. Grant. 2012. *Forces for Good: The Six Practices of High-Impact Nonprofits*. San Francisco: Jossey-Bass.

Cummins, A. 2004. "The Marine Stewardship Council: A Multi-Stakeholder Approach to Sustainable Fishing." *Corporate Social Responsibility and Environmental Management* 11(2): 85–94.

Davies, A., A. Titterington, and C. Cochrane. 1995. "Who Buys Organic Food? A Profile of the Purchasers of Organic Food in Northern Ireland." *British Food Journal* 97(10): 17–23.

Dees, J. G. 1998. "Enterprising Nonprofits." *Harvard Business Review* (January–February): 54–69.

Delmas, M. A. 2002. "The Diffusion of Environmental Management Standards in Europe and in the United States: An Institutional Perspective." *Policy Sciences* 35(1): 91–119.

Delmas, M., and R. Clements. 2017. "Green Products Recognition, Understanding, and Preference: The Case of Coffee Eco-Labels." http://dx.doi .org/10.2139/ssrn.3091882.

Delmas, M. A., and D. Colgan. 2018. *The Green Bundle: Pairing the Market with the Planet*. Stanford, CA: Stanford University Press.

Delmas, M., and V. Cuerel Burbano. 2011. "The Drivers of Greenwashing." *California Management Review* 54(1): 64–87.

Delmas, M., V. Doctori, and K. Shuster. 2006. *Ceago Vinegarden: How Green Is Your Wine? Environmental Differentiation Strategy Through Ecolabels*. Working paper, University of California, Santa Barbara. https://escholarship.org/uc/ item/5k657745.

Delmas, M. A., D. Etzion, and N. Nairn-Birch. 2013. "Triangulating Environmental Performance: What Do Corporate Social Responsibility Ratings Really Capture?" *Academy of Management Perspectives* 27(3): 255–267.

Delmas, M. A., and L. E. Grant. 2014. "Eco-Labeling Strategies and Price-Premium: The Wine Industry Puzzle." *Business and Society* 53(1): 6–44.

Delmas, M. A., and N. Lessem. 2017. "Eco-Premium or Eco-Penalty? Eco-Labels and Quality in the Organic Wine Market." *Business and Society* 56(2): 318–356.

Delmas, M. A., and M. J. Montes-Sancho. 2010. "Voluntary agreements to improve environmental quality: Symbolic and substantive cooperation." Strategic Management Journal, 31(16): 576–601.

Delmas, M., M. J. Montes-Sancho, and J. P. Shimshack. 2010. "Information Disclosure Policies:
Evidence from the Electricity Industry." *Economic Inquiry* 48(2): 483–498.

Delmas, M. A., N. Nairn-Birch, and M. Balzarova.
2013. "Choosing the Right Eco-Label for Your
Product." *MIT Sloan Management Review* 54(4):
10.

Delmas, M. A., and A. K. Terlaak. 2001. "A Framework for Analyzing Environmental Voluntary
Agreements." *California Management Review*
43(3): 44–63.

Delmas, M. A., and O. R. Young, eds. 2009. *Governance for the Environment: New Perspectives.*
Cambridge, UK: Cambridge University Press.

Doherty, B., H. Haugh, and F. Lyon. 2014. "Social
Enterprises as Hybrid Organizations: A Review
and Research Agenda." *International Journal of
Management Reviews* 16(4): 417–436.

D'Souza, C., M. Taghian, and P. Lamb. 2006. "An
Empirical Study on the Influence of Environmental Labels on Consumers." *Corporate
Communications: An International Journal* 11(2):
162–173.

Duflo, E., and M. Kremer. 2005. "Use of Randomiza-
tion in the Evaluation of Development Effectiveness." In *Evaluating Development Effectiveness,*
ed. G. Pitman, O. Feinstein, and G. Ingram,
205–232. New Brunswick, NJ: Transaction.

Eikenberry, A. M., and J. D. Kluver. 2004. "The
Marketization of the Nonprofit Sector: Civil
Society at Risk?" *Public Administration Review*
64(2): 132–140.

EPA. 2010. *National Awareness of ENERGY STAR
for 2010: Analysis of 2010 CEE Household Survey.*
Environmental Protection Agency, Office of Air
and Radiation, Climate Protection Partnerships
Division.

EPA. 2012. *Celebrating 20 Years of ENERGY STAR.*
Environmental Protection Agency, Office of Air
and Radiation, Climate Protection Partnerships
Division. https://www.energystar.gov/ia/about/
20_years/ES_20th_Anniv_brochure_spreads.pdf
?1c89-fef6.

Fabrizio, K., and E.-H. Kim. 2016. "Voluntary
Disclosure and Information Intermediaries:
Evidence from the Carbon Disclosure Project."
Academy of Management Proceedings 2016(1).

Fairtrade International. 2016. *Monitoring the
Scope and Benefits of Fair Trade,* 9th ed. Bonn,
Germany: Fairtrade International. https://www
.fairtrade.org.uk/~/media/FairtradeUK/What
%20is%20Fairtrade/Documents/Policy%20and
%20Research%20documents/Monitoring
%20reports/Fairtrade%20Monitoring%20Report
_9thEdition%202016.pdf.

Feddersen, T. J., and T. W. Gilligan. "Saints and
Markets: Activists and the Supply of Credence
Goods." *Journal of Economics and Management
Strategy* 10(1): 149–171.

Feinberg, G., A. Leiserowitz, G. Auld, and B.
Cashore. 2008. "American and Canadian
Consumer Attitudes Toward Environmentally-
Friendly Products and Eco-Labeling." The GfK
Roper/Yale Survey on Environmental Issues.
New Haven, CT: Yale School of Forestry and
Environmental Studies.

Ferraro, P. J., T. Uchida, and J. M. Conrad. 2005.
"Price Premiums for Eco-Friendly Commodi-
ties: Are 'Green' Markets the Best Way to Protect
Endangered Ecosystems?" *Environmental and
Resource Economics* 32(3): 419–438.

Fischer, C., and T. P. Lyon. 2014. "Competing
Environmental Labels." *Journal of Economics and
Management Strategy* 23(3): 692–716.

Fisher-Vanden, K., and K. S. Thorburn. 2011. "Vol-
untary Corporate Environmental Initiatives and
Shareholder Wealth." *Journal of Environmental
Economics and Management* 62(3): 430–445.

Fleckinger, P., M. Glachant, and G. Moineville. 2017.
"Incentives for Quality in Friendly and Hostile
Informational Environments." *American Eco-
nomic Journal: Microeconomics* 9(1): 242–274.

Freris, N., and K. Laschefeski. 2001. "Seeing the
Wood from the Trees." *The Ecologist* 31(6):
40–43.

FSC (Forest Stewardship Council). 2007. *Stakeholder
Involvement in FSC-Certification: Guideline for
Stakeholders for Active Participation in FSC-Certification.* Forest Stewardship Council, Bonn,
Germany. http://www.fsc.dk/files/resource
_1/CoC%20dokumenter/FSC_stakeholder
_involvement_EN_1by1.pdf, accessed March
2012.

———. 2009. *FSC Impacts and Outcomes—Ex-
tracts from FSC Literature Review 2009.* Forest

Stewardship Council, Bonn, Germany. http://pre
.fsc.org/fileadmin/web-data/public/document
_center/publications/FSC_Policy_Series/Impacts
_lit_review_summary_EN.PDF, accessed
January 2012.

Gehman, J., and M. Grimes. 2017. "Hidden Badge
of Honor: How Contextual Distinctiveness
Affects Category Promotion Among Certified B
Corporations." *Academy of Management Journal*
60(6): 2294–2320.

Gerez Fernández, P., and E. Alatorre Guzman.
2003. *Challenges for Forest Certification and
Community Forestry in Mexico.* Unpublished
manuscript.

Global Reporting Initiative. 2016. Sustainability
Disclosure Database.

Golden, J. S. 2010. *An Overview of Eco-Labels
and Sustainability Certifications in the Global
Marketplace.* Corporate Sustainability Initiative,
Nicholas Institute for Environmental Policy
Solutions, Duke University.

Graves, S. B., S. Waddock, and K. Rehbein. 2001.
"Fad and Fashion in Shareholder Activism:
The Landscape of Shareholder Resolutions,
1988–1998." *Business and Society Review* 106(4):
293–314.

Grimes, M. G., J. Gehman, and K. Cao. 2018.
"Positively Deviant: Identity Work Through B
Corporation Certification." *Journal of Business
Venturing* 33(2): 130–148.

Griskevicius, V., J. M. Tybur, J. M. Sundie, R.
B. Cialdini, G. F. Miller, and D. T. Kenrick.
2007. "Blatant Benevolence and Conspicuous
Consumption: When Romantic Motives Elicit
Strategic Costly Signals." *Journal of Personality
and Social Psychology* 93: 85–102.

Grodsky, J. 1993. "Certified Green, the Law and
Future of Environmental Labeling." *Yale Journal
on Regulation* 10: 147–227.

Guay, T., J. Doh, and G. Sinclair. 2004. "Non-Governmental Organizaitons, Shareholder Activism,
and Socially Responsible Investments: Ethical,
Strategic, and Governance Implications." *Journal
of Business Ethics* 52(1): 125–139.

Gulbrandsen, L. 2006. "Creating Markets for
Eco-Labelling: Are Consumers Insignificant?"
International Journal of Consumer Studies 30(5):
477–489.

Hamilton, J. T. 1995. "Pollution as News: Media and
Stock Market Reactions to the Toxics Release
Inventory Data." *Journal of Environmental Eco-
nomics and Management* 28(1): 98–113.

Harbaugh, R., J. Maxwell, and B. Roussillon. 2011.
"Label Confusion: The Groucho Effect of Uncertain Standards." *Management Science* 57(9):
1512–1527.

Hardy, C., and M. Van Vugt. 2006. "Nice Guys Fin-
ish First: The Competitive Altruism Hypothesis."
Personality and Social Psychology Bulletin 32:
1402–1413.

Hickman, L., J. Byrd, and K. Hickman. 2014. "Explaining the Location of Mission-Driven Businesses: An Examination of B-Corps." *Journal of
Corporate Citizenship* 55: 13–25.

Honeyman, R. 2014. *The B Corp Handbook: How to
Use Business as a Force for Good.* San Francisco:
Berrett-Koehler.

Horne, R. E. 2009. "Limits to Labels: The Role of
Eco-Labels in the Assessment of Product Sustainability and Routes to Sustainable Consumption." *International Journal of Consumer Studies*
33(2): 175–182.

Huang, C. L. 1996. "Consumer Preferences and
Attitudes Toward Organically Grown Produce."
European Review of Agricultural Economics 23(3):
331–342.

Huang, C. L., and B. H. Lin. 2007. "A Hedonic Analysis of Fresh Tomato Prices Among Regional
Markets." *Review of Agricultural Economics*
29(4): 783–800.

Ibanez, L., and G. Grolleau. 2008. "Can Eco-Labeling
Schemes Preserve the Environment?" Environmental and Resource Economics 40(2): 233–249.

International Organization for Standardization. 2011.
"ISO/IEC Directives, Part 2: Rules for the Structure and Drafting of International Standards."
https://boss.cen.eu/ref/ISO_IEC_Directives
_Part2.pdf.

Jacobs, B. W., V. R. Singhal, and R. Subramanian.
2010. "An Empirical Investigation of Environmental Performance and the Market Value of the
Firm." *Journal of Operations Management* 28(5):
430–441.

Jacquet, J., D. Pauly, D. Ainley, S. Holt, P. Dayton,
and J. Jackson. 2010. "Seafood Stewardship in
Crisis." *Nature* 467(7311): 28.

Jaffee, D. 2007. *Brewing Justice: Fair Trade Coffee, Sustainability and Survival.* Berkeley: University of California Press.

Jahn, G., M. Schramm, and A. Spiller. 2005. "The Reliability of Certification: Quality Labels as a Consumer Policy Tool." *Journal of Consumer Policy* 28(1): 53–73.

Jira, C., and M. W. Toffel. 2013. "Engaging Supply Chains in Climate Change." *Manufacturing and Service Operations Management* 15(4): 559–577.

Jolly, D., and K. Norris. 1991. "Marketing Prospects for Organics and Pesticide-Free Produce." *American Journal of Alternative Agriculture* 6(4): 174–138.

Kahn, M. E. 2007. "Do Greens Drive Hummers or Hybrids? Environmental Ideology as a Determinant of Consumer Choice." *Environmental Economics and Management* 54(2): 129–145.

Kim, E.-H., and T. P. Lyon. 2011a. "Strategic Environmental Disclosure: Evidence from the DOE's Voluntary Greenhouse Gas Registry." *Journal of Environmental Economics and Management* 61(3): 311–326.

———. 2011b. "When Does Institutional Investor Activism Increase Shareholder Value? The Carbon Disclosure Project." *B.E. Journal of Economic Analysis and Policy* 11(1): Article 50.

Kirchhoff, S. 2000. "Green Business and Blue Angels." *Environmental and Resource Economics* 15(4): 403–420.

Kong, N., O. Salzmann, U. Steger, and A. Lonescu-Somers. 2002. "Moving Business/Industry Towards Sustainable Consumption: The Role of NGOs." *European Management Journal* 20: 109–127.

Kotchen, M. J. 2005. "Impure Public Goods and the Comparative Statics of Environmentally Friendly Consumption." *Journal of Environmental Economics and Management* 49(2): 281–300.

Kraft, M. E. 2001. "Influence of American NGOs on Environmental Decisions and Policies: Evolution over Three Decades." In *The Role of Environmental NGOs: Russian Challenges, American Lessons.* Washington, DC: National Academy Press.

———. 2011. *Environmental Policy and Politics*, vol. 589. New York: Longman.

Kremer, M. 2003. "Randomized Evaluations of Educational Programs in Developing Countries: Some Lessons." *American Economic Review* 93(2): 102–106.

Krier, J. M. 2007. *Fair Trade 2007: A Report on Fair Trade in 22 Consumer Countries. A Survey Prepared on Behalf of DAWS—Dutch Association of Worldshops.* http://www.european-fair-trade -association.org/efta/Doc/FT-E-2007.pdf.

Lee, S.Y., Y. S. Park, and R. D. Klassen. 2015. "Market Responses to Firms' Voluntary Climate Change Information Disclosure and Carbon Communication." *Corporate Social Responsibility and Environmental Management* 22(1): 1–12.

Leire, C., and A. Thidell. 2005. "Product-Related Environmental Information to Guide Consumer Purchases—A Review and Analysis of Research on Perceptions, Understanding and Use Among Nordic Consumers." *Journal of Cleaner Production* 13: 1061–1070.

Lewis, B. W., J. L. Walls, and G.W.S. Dowell. 2014. "Difference in Degrees: CEO Characteristics and Firm Environmental Disclosure." *Strategic Management Journal* 35(5): 712–722.

Li, D., M. Huang, S. Ren, X. Chen, and L. Ning. 2018. "Environmental Legitimacy, Green Innovation, and Corporate Carbon Disclosure: Evidence from CDP China 100." *Journal of Business Ethics* 150(4): 1089–1104.

Loureiro, M. L. 2003. "Rethinking New Wines: Implications of Local and Environmentally Friendly Labels." *Food Policy* 28(5–6): 547–560.

Loureiro, M. L., and J. Lotade. 2005. "Do Fair Trade and Eco-Labels in Coffee Wake Up the Consumer Conscience?" *Ecological Economics* 53(1): 129–138.

Lyon, T., ed. 2012. *Good Cop/Bad Cop: Environmental NGOs and Their Strategies Toward Business.* New York: Routledge.

Lyon, T., Y. Lu, X. Shi, and Q. Yin. 2013. "How Do Investors Respond to Green Company Awards in China?" *Ecological Economics* 94: 1–8.

Lyon, T. P., and J. W. Maxwell. 2011. "Greenwash: Corporate Environmental Disclosure Under Threat of Audit." *Journal of Economics and Management Strategy* 20(1): 3–41.

Magnusson, M. K., A. Arvola, U. Koivisto Hursti, L. Åberg, and P. Sjoden. 2001. "Attitudes Towards Organic Foods Among Swedish Consumers." *British Food Journal* 103(3): 209–227.

Martens, K. 2002. "Mission Impossible? Defining Nongovernmental Organizations." *Voluntas: Journal of Voluntary and Nonprofit Organizations* 13(3): 271–285.

Matisoff, D. C. 2013. "Different Rays of Sunlight: Understanding Information Disclosure and Carbon Transparency." *Energy Policy* 55: 579–592.

Matisoff, D. C., D. S. Noonan, and J. J. O'Brien. 2013. "Convergence in Environmental Reporting: Assessing the Carbon Disclosure Project." *Business Strategy and the Environment* 22(5): 285–305.

Matsumura, E. M., R. Prakash, and S. C. Vera-Muñoz. 2014. "Firm-Value Effects of Carbon Emissions and Carbon Disclosures." *Accounting Review* 89(2): 695–724.

Maxwell, J. W., T. P. Lyon, and S. C. Hackett. 2000. "Self-Regulation and Social Welfare: The Political Economy of Corporate Environmentalism." *Journal of Law and Economics* 43(2): 583–618.

Mayer, F., and G. Gereffi. 2010. "Regulation and Economic Globalization: Prospects and Limits of Private Governance." *Business and Politics* 12(3): 1–25.

Milgrom, P. 1981. "Good News and Bad News: Representation Theorems and Applications." *Bell Journal of Economics* 12: 380–391.

Milgrom, P., and J. Roberts. 1986. "Relying on the Information of Interested Parties." *RAND Journal of Economics* 17(1): 18–32.

Miller, G. F. 2009. *Spent: Sex, Evolution, and Consumer Behavior*. New York: Viking.

Moroz, P., O. Branzei, S. Parker, and E. Gamble. 2018. "Imprinting with Purpose: Prosocial Opportunities and B Corp Certification." *Journal of Business Venturing* 33: 117–129.

Munoz, P., G. Cacciotti, and B. Cohen. 2018. "The Double-Edged Sword of Purpose-Driven Behavior in Sustainable Venturing." *Journal of Business Venturing* 33: 149–178.

Murray, D., L. T. Raynolds, and P. L. Taylor. 2003. *One Cup at a Time: Poverty Alleviation and Fair Trade Coffee in Latin America*. Fort Collins: Colorado State University, Fair Trade Research Group.

Nilsson, H., B. Tunçer, and Å. Thidell. 2004. "The Use of Eco-Labeling Like Initiatives on Food Products to Promote Quality Assurance—Is

There Enough Credibility?" *Journal of Cleaner Production* 12(5): 517–526.

Olofsson, S., M. Hoveskog, and F. Halila. 2018. "Journey and Impact of Business Model Innovation: The Case of a Social Enterprise in the Scandinavian Electricity Retail Market." *Journal of Cleaner Production* 175: 70–81.

Organic Trade Association. 2006. "The OTA 2006 Manufacturer Survey Overview." http://www.ota.com/organic/mt.html, accessed January 2012.

Pache, A.-C., and F. Santos. 2010. "When Worlds Collide: The Internal Dynamics of Organizational Responses to Conflicting Institutional Demands." *Academy of Management Review* 35(3): 455–476.

Prag, A., T. Lyon, and A. Russillo. 2016. "Multiplication of Environmental Labelling and Information Schemes (ELIS)." OECD Environment working paper. https://doi.org/10.1787/19970900.

Peloza, J., and L. Falkenberg. 2009. "The Role of Collaboration in Achieving Corporate Social Responsibility Objectives." *California Management Review* 51(3): 95–113.

Potts, T., and M. Howard. 2007. "International Trade, Eco-Labelling, and Sustainable Fisheries—Recent Issues, Concepts and Practices." *Environment, Development and Sustainability* 9(1): 91–106.

Quinn, I. 2012. "'Frustrated' Tesco Ditches Eco-Labels." *The Grocer*, January 27. http://www.thegrocer.co.uk/companies/supermarkets/tesco/frustrated-tesco-ditches-eco-labels/225502.article.

Reid, E. M., and M. W. Toffel. 2009. "Responding to Public and Private Politics: Corporate Disclosure of Climate Change Strategies." *Strategic Management Journal* 30(11): 1157–1178.

Robson, R. 2015. "A New Look at Benefit Corporations: Game Theory and Game Changer." *American Business Law Journal* 52(3): 501–555.

Roe, B., M. F. Teisl, H. Rong, and A. S. Levy. 2001. "Characteristics of Consumer-Preferred Labeling Policies: Experimental Evidence from Price and Environmental Disclosure for Deregulated Electricity Services." *Journal of Consumer Affairs* 35(1): 1–26.

Rondinelli, D. A., and T. London. 2003. "How Corporations and Environmental Groups

Cooperate: Assessing Cross-Sector Alliances and Collaborations." *Academy of Management Perspectives* 17(1): 61–76.

Roper Organization and Johnson Wax. 1990. "The Environment: Public Attitudes and Individual Behavior." Ithaca, NY: Cornell University Press.

Segerson, K., and T. J. Miceli. 1998. "Voluntary Environmental Agreements: Good or Bad News for Environmental Protection?" *Journal of Environmental Economics and Management* 36(2): 109–130.

Sharma, G., A. Beveridge, and N. Haigh. 2018. "A Configural Framework of Practice Change for B Corporations." *Journal of Business Venturing* 33(2): 207–224.

Shin, H. S. 2003. "Disclosures and Asset Returns." *Econometrica* 71: 105–133.

Sustainable Foods News. 2011. "Farmed Fish Eco-Labels Fall Short of Protecting Environment, Says Report." *Sustainable Foods News*, December 7. https://sustainablefoodnews.com/?s=Farmed +Fish+Eco-Labels+Fall+Short+of+Protecting +Environment%2C+Says+Report.

Teisl, M. F., B. Roe, and R. L. Hicks. 2002. "Can Eco-Labels Tune a Market? Evidence from Dolphin-Safe Labeling." *Journal of Environmental Economics and Management* 43: 339–359.

TerraChoice Group. 2009. "The Seven Sins of Greenwashing." April. http://www .sinsofgreenwashing.org/findings/greenwashing -report-2009/, accessed July 10, 2019.

Tregear, A., J. B. Dent, and M. J. McGregor. 1994. "The Demand for Organically Grown Produce." *British Food Journal* 46(4): 21–25.

Utting, K. 2009. "Assessing the Impact of Fair Trade Coffee: Towards an Integrative Framework." *Journal of Business Ethics* 86(1): 127–149.

Utting-Chamorro, K. 2005. "Does Fair Trade Make a Difference? The Case of Small Coffee Producers in Nicaragua." *Development in Practice* 15(3–4): 584–599.

Vandenbergh, M. P., and B. Raker. 2017. "Private Governance and the New Private Advocacy." *Natural Resources and Environment* 32(2): 45–49.

Verrecchia, R. E. 1983. "Discretionary Disclosure." *Journal of Accounting and Economics* 5: 179–194.

Vogel, D. 2005. *The Market for Virtue: The Potential and Limits of Corporate Social Responsibility.* Washington, DC: Brookings Institution Press.

Wandel, M., and A. Bugge. 1997. "Environmental Concern in Consumer Evaluation of Food Quality." *Food Quality and Preferences* 8: 19–26.

Werker, E., and F. Z. Ahmed. 2008. "What Do Nongovernmental Organizations Do?" *Journal of Economic Perspectives* 22(2): 73–92.

Wilson, B. T. Takahashi, and I. Vertinsky. 2001. "The Canadian Commercial Forestry Perspective on Certification: National Survey Results." *Forestry Chronicle* 77(2): 309–313.

Chapter 16. The Outcomes Movement in Philanthropy and the Nonprofit Sector

Addy, C., M. Chorengel, M. Collins, and M. Etzel. 2019. "Calculating the Value of Impact Investing: An Evidence-Based Way to Estimate Social and Environmental Returns." *Harvard Business Review* (January–February): 102–109.

Andreoni, J. 1990. "Impure Altruism and Donations to Public Goods: A Theory of Warm-Glow Giving." *Economic Journal* 100(401): 464–477.

Arabella Advisors. 2012. "An Evaluation of the Nonprofit Marketplace Initiative." https://hewlett .org/wp-content/uploads/2016/08/Hewlett _Foundation_NMI_Evaluation_Exec_Sum.pdf _copy.pdf.

Arnold Ventures. 2019. https://www.arnoldventures .org/about/.

Arrillaga-Andreessen, L. 2011. *Giving 2.0: Transform Your Giving and Our World.* San Francisco: Jossey-Bass.

Ash Center for Democratic Governance and Innovation. n.d. "Compstat: A Crime Reduction Management Tool." https://www.innovations.harvard .edu/compstat-crime-reduction-management -tool, accessed July 11, 2019.

Ashoka. 2014. "Using Big Data for Social Good." *Forbes*, August 27. https://www.forbes.com/sites/ ashoka/2014/08/27/using-big-data-for-social -good/#64747a051425.

Bentham, J. 1830. *The Rationale of Reward.* London: Robert Heward.

Better Government Corporation. 1997. "Oklahoma Milestone Payment System." http://bgc

.pioneerinstitute.org/oklahoma-milestone
-payment-system/.

Brest, P. 2003. "What the Nonprofit Sector Can
Learn from Home Improvements." *Nonprofit Quarterly*, December 21. https://
nonprofitquarterly.org/2003/12/21/what-the
-nonprofit-sector-can-learn-from-home
-improvements/.

———. 2015. "Strategic Philanthropy and Its Discontents." *Stanford Social Innovation Review*,
April 27. https://ssir.org/up_for_debate/article/
strategic_philanthropy_and_its_discontents.

———. 2016. "Investing for Impact with Program-Related Investments." *Stanford Social
Innovation Review* (Summer). https://ssir.org/
articles/entry/investing_for_impact_with
_program_related_investments.

———. 2017. "Translating Science into Policy: The
Role of Decision Science." National Academies
of Sciences, Engineering, and Medicine, January
1. http://sites.nationalacademies.org/cs/groups/
pgasite/documents/webpage/pga_173231.pdf.

Brest, P., R. Gilson, and M. Wolfson. 2016. "How
Investors Can (and Can't) Create Social Value."
Stanford Social Innovation Review, December
8. https://ssir.org/up_for_debate/article/how
_investors_can_and_cant_create_social_value.

Brest, P., and H. Harvey. 2018. *Money Well Spent: A
Strategic Plan for Smart Philanthropy*. Stanford,
CA: Stanford University Press.

Brest, P., and L. H. Krieger. 2010. *Problem Solving,
Decision Making, and Professional Judgment*.
Oxford, UK: Oxford University Press.

Bridgespan. n.d. "About Bridgespan." https://www
.bridgespan.org/about-us/about-bridgespan,
accessed July 11, 2019.

Callahan, D. 2017. *The Givers: Wealth, Power, and
Philanthropy in a New Gilded Age*. New York:
Knopf.

Camber Collective. 2015. *Money for Good:
Revealing the Voice of the Donor in Philanthropic Giving*. http://static1.squarespace
.com/static/55723b6be4b05ed81f077108/t/
56957ee6df40f330ae018b81/1452637938035/$FG
+2015_Final+Report_01122016.pdf.

Campbell, D. T. 1979. "Assessing the Impact of
Planned Social Change." *Evaluation and Program
Planning* 2(1): 67–90. https://www-sciencedirect

-com.stanford.idm.oclc.org/science/article/pii/
014971897990048X?via%3Dihub.

Campbell, D. T., and J. C. Stanley. 1963. *Experimental
and Quasi-Experimental Designs for Research*.
Boston: Houghton Mifflin.

Cantor, A., and M. Gunther. 2018. "Charitable Giving: From the Heart or the Mind?" Philanthropy
Daily, June 15. https://www.philanthropydaily
.com/charitable-giving-from-the-heart-or-the
-mind/.

Chen, D. W. 2010. "Survey Raises Questions on
Data-Driven Policy." *New York Times*, February 8. https://www.nytimes.com/2010/02/09/
nyregion/09mayor.html.

Clayton, R. R., A. M. Cattarello, and B. M. Johnstone. 1996. "The Effectiveness of Drug Abuse
Resistance Education (Project DARE): 5-Year
Follow-Up Results." *Preventive Medicine* 25(3):
307–318.

Collins, D. 2004. "The Art of Philanthropy." In M. C.
Brown, *Just Money: A Critique of Contemporary
American Philanthropy*, ed. H. P. Karoff, 63–71.
Boston: TPI.

Drucker, P. F. 1999. *Management Challenges for the 21st Century*. Oxford, UK:
Butterworth-Heinemann.

Dunning, C. Forthcoming. *Nonprofit Neighborhoods:
Poverty Policy and the Privatization of Boston,
1949–Present*. Chicago: University of Chicago
Press.

Ebrahim, A., and C. Ross. 2012. *The Robin Hood
Foundation*. HBS No. 9-310-031. Boston: Harvard
Business School Press.

Executive Order No. 12866, 58 F.R. 51735 1993.

Farnham, P. G., and G. M. Guess. 2000. *Cases in
Public Policy Analysis*. Washington, DC: Georgetown University Press.

Fleishman, J. L. 2009. *The Foundation: A Great
American Secret; How Private Wealth Is Changing the World*. New York: Public Affairs.

Ford Foundation. 1949. *Report of the Study for the
Ford Foundation on Policy and Program*. https://
babel.hathitrust.org/cgi/pt?id=wu.89094310596&
view=1up&seq=7.

Foundation Center. n.d. "Philanthropy Classification
System." https://taxonomy.foundationcenter.org.

Freeman, H. E., P. H. Rossi, and S. R. Wright.
1979. *Evaluating Social Projects in Developing*

Countries. Paris, France: Development Centre of the Organisation for Economic Co-operation and Development.

Frumkin, P. 2008. *Strategic Giving: The Art and Science of Philanthropy.* Chicago: University of Chicago Press.

Fry Consultants. 1970. *Project Evaluation and the Project Appraisal Reporting System.* Agency for International Development. https://pdf.usaid .gov/pdf_docs/PNADW881.pdf.

Funnell, S. C., and P. J. Rogers. 2011. *Purposeful Program Theory: Effective Use of Theories of Change and Logic Models.* Hoboken, NJ: Wiley.

Gair, C. 2002. "A Report from the Good Ship SROI." Roberts Foundation. http://www.socialreturns .org/docs/good_ship_sroi_gair.pdf.

Gardner, H., M. Csikszentmihalyi, and W. Damon. 2001. *Good Work: When Excellence and Ethics Meet.* New York: Basic Books.

Gates, F. T. 1977. *Chapters in My Life.* New York: Free Press.

Giridharadas, A. 2018. *Winners Take All: The Elite Charade of Changing the World.* New York: Knopf.

GiveWell. 2017a. "Cost-Effectiveness." November. https://www.givewell.org/how-we-work/our -criteria/cost-effectiveness.

———. 2017b. "Our Criteria for Top Charities." August. https://www.givewell.org/how-we-work/ criteria.

Giving Compass. n.d. "Understanding Impact-Driven Philanthropy." https://cdn.givingcompass .org/wp-content/uploads/2017/10/21160854/ Impact-driven-Philanthropy.pdf, accessed July 11, 2019.

Giving USA. 2017. "Total Charitable Donations Rise to New High of $390.05 Billion." June 12. https:// givingusa.org/giving-usa-2017-total-charitable -donations-rise-to-new-high-of-390-05-billion/.

Gneezy, U., E. A. Keenan, and A. Gneezy. 2014. "Avoiding Overhead Aversion in Charity." *Science* 346(6209): 632–635.

Gregory, A. G., and D. Howard. 2009. "The Nonprofit Starvation Cycle." *Stanford Social Innovation Review* (Fall). https://ssir.org/articles/entry/ the_nonprofit_starvation_cycle.

Grossman, A., N. Greckol-Herlich, and C. Ross. 2009. *The Bridgespan Group: Chapter 2.* HBS No.

9-309-020. Boston: Harvard Business School Press.

Grossman, A., and J. Kalafatas. 2000. *The Bridgespan Group.* HBS No. 9-301-011. Boston: Harvard Business School Publishing.

Grossman, A., and A. Sesia. 2011. *Edna McConnell Clark Foundation—Enabling a Performance Driven Philanthropic Capital Market.* HBS No. 9-312-006. Boston: Harvard Business School Press.

GuideStar. n.d. "Welcome to Charting Impact." https://learn.guidestar.org/update-nonprofit -report/charting-impact, accessed July 11, 2019.

Gunther, M. 2018. "Giving in the Light of Reason." *Stanford Social Innovation Review* (Summer). https://ssir.org/articles/entry/giving_in_the _light_of_reason#.

Hart, K. 2010. "Is NCLB Intentionally Leaving Some Kids Behind?" http://www.nea.org/home/37772 .htm.

Hatry, H. P. 2013. "Sorting the Relationships Among Performance Measurement, Program Evaluation, and Performance Management." *New Directions for Evaluation* 137: 19–32.

Hazell, P. 2009. "Think Again: The Green Revolution." *Foreign Policy* (September 22). https:// foreignpolicy.com/2009/09/22/think-again-the -green-revolution/.

Hendricks, M., M. C. Plantz, and K. J. Pritchard. 2008. "Measuring Outcomes of United Way–Funded Programs: Expectations and Reality." *New Directions for Evaluation* 119: 13–135. http:// citeseerx.ist.psu.edu/viewdoc/download?doi=10 .1.1.498.8037&rep=rep1&type=pdf.

Hewlett Foundation. 2012a. *Outcome Focused Grantmaking: A Hard-Headed Approach to Soft-Hearted Goals.* https://hewlett.org/wp -content/uploads/2016/08/Outcome_Focused _Grantmaking_March_2012_0.pdf.

———. 2012b. "Performing Arts Program: Strategic Framework 2012–2017." https://hewlett.org/wp -content/uploads/2016/08/Performing_Arts _Strategic_Framework_October_2012.pdf.

Hope Consulting. 2010. "Money for Good: The US Market for Impact Investments and Charitable Gifts from Individual Donors and Investors." https://static1.squarespace .com/static/55723b6be4b05ed81f077108/t/

566efb6cc647ad2b441e2c55/1450113900596/
Money+for+Good+I.pdf.

Horvath, A. 2018. *Ideals of Order: Activists, Academics, Administrators, and the Ideal of Good Government in the United States.* Unpublished manuscript.

Impact Management Project. 2018. "Building Consensus for How We Measure and Manage Impact." https://impactmanagementproject.com.

Influence Watch. n.d. "Ford Foundation." https://www.influencewatch.org/non-profit/ford-foundation/, accessed July 11, 2019.

Meehan, W. F. III, and K. S. Jonker. 2017. *Engine of Impact: Essentials of Strategic Leadership in the Nonprofit Sector.* Stanford, CA: Stanford University Press.

Kania, J., M. Kramer, and P. Russell. 2014. "Strategic Philanthropy for a Complex World." *Stanford Social Innovation Review* 12(3): 26–37. https://ssir.org/up_for_debate/article/strategic_philanthropy.

Kaplan, R. S. 1992. "The Balanced Scorecard—Measures That Drive Performance." *Harvard Business Review* (January–February): 71–79.

Keystone Accountability. n.d. "Constituent Voice." http://keystoneaccountability.org/, accessed July 11, 2019.

Khare, R. 2017. "Addressing Recidivism in the Golden State through Pay for Success." November 21. https://medium.com/@info_88059/addressing-recidivism-in-the-golden-state-through-pay-for-success-a63a6325e464.

Kodali, S., J. Grossman, and G. Overholser. 2014. "The Massachusetts Juvenile Justice PFS Initiative." Third Sector Capital Partners. http://www.thirdsectorcap.org/wp-content/uploads/2015/02/TSCP_MAJJ-PFS-Project-Brief.pdf.

Korff, V. P. 2015. "Interstitial Organizations as Conversational Bridges." *Bulletin of the American Society for Information Science and Technology* 41(2): 34–38.

Kovick, D. 2005. "The Hewlett Foundation's Conflict Resolution Program: Twenty Years of Field-Building." Hewlett Foundation. https://hewlett.org/wp-content/uploads/2016/08/HewlettConflictResolutionProgram.pdf.

Lee, L. 2015 "Walter W. Powell: The Language of Nonprofits Is Changing." July 2. https://www.gsb.stanford.edu/insights/walter-w-powell-language-nonprofits-changing.

Lee, M. 2008. *Bureaus of Efficiency: Reforming Local Government in the Progressive Era.* Milwaukee, WI: Marquette University Press.

Letts, C. W., W. P. Ryan, and A. S. Grossman. 1997. "Virtuous Capital: What Foundations Can Learn from Venture Capitalists." *Harvard Business Review* (March–April): 36–44.

Levitt, L. 2003. "Crime Statistics Doubts Adding Up." NYPD Confidential, June 30. http://nypdconfidential.com/columns/2003/030630.html.

Lynch, R. L. 2007. "No Child Left Behind Act Wrongly Left the Arts Behind." The Hill, January 12. http://thehill.com/opinion/op-ed/7275-no-child-left-behind-act-wrongly-left-the-arts-behind.

MacAskill, W. 2016. *Doing Good Better: How Effective Altruism Can Help You Help Others, Do Work That Matters, and Make Smarter Choices About Giving Back.* New York: Avery.

Macdonald, D. 1989. *The Ford Foundation: The Men and the Millions.* New Brunswick, NJ: Transaction.

MacFarquhar, L. 2016. "What Money Can Buy." *New Yorker,* January 4. https://www.newyorker.com/magazine/2016/01/04/what-money-can-buy-profiles-larissa-macfarquhar.

Magat, R. 1979. *The Ford Foundation at Work: Philanthropic Choices, Methods and Styles.* New York: Ford Foundation.

Marshall, G., dir. 1939. *You Can't Cheat an Honest Man.* Motion picture. Universal Pictures.

Mathematica. n.d. "Case Study: Mathematica's Abstinence Evaluation: Responding to a Changing Policy Climate." https://www.mathematica-mpr.com/our-capabilities/case-studies/responding-to-a-changing-policy-climate, accessed July 11, 2019.

MDRC. n.d. History. https://www.mdrc.org/about/about-mdrc-history, accessed July 11, 2019.

Merry, S. E. 2016. *The Seductions of Quantification: Measuring Human Rights, Gender Violence, and Sex Trafficking.* Chicago: University of Chicago Press.

Morino, M. 2011. *Leap of Reason: Managing to Outcomes in an Era of Scarcity.* Washington, DC: Venture Philanthropy Partners.

Moses, P. 2005. "These Stats Are a Crime." *Village Voice*, November 1. https://web.archive.org/web/20070811035503/http://www.villagevoice.com/news/0544%2Cmoses%2C69552%2C5.html.

Muller, J. Z. 2018. *The Tyranny of Metrics*. Princeton, NJ: Princeton University Press.

Niehaus, P. 2014. "A Theory of Good Intentions." http://econweb.ucsd.edu/~pniehaus/papers/good_intentions.pdf.

O'Brien, D., and G. Revell. 2005. "The Milestone Payment System: Results Based Funding in Vocational Rehabilitation." *Journal of Vocational Rehabilitation* 23(2): 101–114.

Osborne, D., and T. Gaebler. 1992. *Reinventing Government: How the Entrepreneurial Spirit Is Transforming the Public Sector*. Reading, MA: Addison-Wesley.

Patrizi, P., and E. H. Thompson. 2010. "Beyond the Veneer of Strategic Philanthropy." *Foundation Review* 2(3) 55.

Patrizi, P., E. H. Thompson, J. Coffman, and T. Beer. 2013. "Eyes Wide Open: Learning as Strategy Under Conditions of Complexity and Uncertainty." *Foundation Review* 5(3): 50–65.

Patton, M. Q. 2008. *Utilization-Focused Evaluation*. Thousand Oaks, CA: SAGE.

Penna, R. M. 2011. *The Nonprofit Outcomes Toolbox: A Complete Guide to Program Effectiveness, Performance Measurement, and Results*. Hoboken, NJ: Wiley.

Petrosino, A., C. Turpin-Petrosino, M. E. Hollis-Peel, and J. G. Lavenberg. 2013. "'Scared Straight' and Other Juvenile Awareness Programs for Preventing Juvenile Delinquency." Wiley. https://www.ncbi.nlm.nih.gov/pubmed/23862186.

Police Executive Research Forum. 2013. "Compstat: Its Origins, Evolution, and Future in Law Enforcement Agencies." https://www.bja.gov/Publications/PERF-Compstat.pdf.

Porter, M. E., and M. R. Kramer. 1999. "Philanthropy's New Agenda: Creating Value." *Harvard Business Review* (November–December): 121–130.

Practical Concepts. n.d. "Guidelines for Teaching Logical Framework Concepts." https://pdf.usaid.gov/pdf_docs/pnaec576.pdf, accessed July 11, 2019.

President's Research Committee on Social Trends. 1933. *Recent Social Trends in the United States*. New York: McGraw-Hill.

Proscio, T. 2003. "The Foundations of Civil Society: A Review of Investments by the Atlantic Philanthropies in the Fundamentals of the U.S. Philanthropic Sector, 1984–2001." Atlantic Philanthropies. https://www.atlanticphilanthropies.org/wp-content/uploads/2016/02/The-Foundations-of-Civil-Society.pdf.

Quade, E. S. 1971. "A History of Cost-Effectiveness." RAND Corporation. http://www.dtic.mil/dtic/tr/fulltext/u2/730430.pdf.

Quote Investigator. 2011. "Not Everything That Counts Can Be Counted." September 5. https://quoteinvestigator.com/2010/05/26/everything-counts-einstein/.

REDF. n.d.a. "20 Years of Impact: An Investment That Works." http://redf.org/20th-anniversary/, accessed July 11, 2019.

———. n.d.b. "National Portfolio and Strategic Grants." http://redf.org/what-we-do/grant/, accessed July 11, 2019.

Reich, R. 2018. *Just Giving: Why Philanthropy Is Failing Democracy and How It Can Do Better*. Princeton, NJ: Princeton University Press.

Revesz, R. L., and M. A. Livermore. 2011. *Retaking Rationality: How Cost-Benefit Analysis Can Better Protect the Environment and Our Health*. Oxford, UK: Oxford University Press.

Ringwalt, C., S. T. Ennett, and K. D. Holt. 1991. "An Outcome Evaluation of Project DARE (Drug Abuse Resistance Education)." *Health Education Research* 6(3): 327–337.

Rockefeller Archive Center. n.d.a. "International Health Division." https://rockfound.rockarch.org/international-health-division#ftnref2.

———. n.d.b. "Malaria." https://rockfound.rockarch.org/malaria#_ftn1, accessed July 11, 2019.

———. n.d.c. "Precursors to a New Philanthropy." https://rockfound.rockarch.org/precursors-to-a-new-philanthropy#_edn2, accessed July 11, 2019.

———. n.d.d. "Rockefeller Sanitary Commission (RSC)." https://rockfound.rockarch.org/rockefeller-sanitary-commission, accessed July 11, 2019.

———. n.d.e. "Tuberculosis in France." https://rockfound.rockarch.org/tuberculosis-in-france, accessed July 11, 2019.

———. n.d.f. "Yellow Fever." https://rockfound.rockarch.org/yellow-fever, accessed July 11, 2019.

Rosegrant, S. 1998. "Oklahoma's Milestones Reimbursement System: Paying for What You Get." Harvard Kennedy School of Government. https://case.hks.harvard.edu/oklahomas-milestones-reimbursement-system-paying-for-what-you-get/.

Schambra, W. 2014. "The Coming Showdown Between Philanthrolocalism and Effective Altruism." Philanthropy Daily, May 22. https://www.philanthropydaily.com/the-coming-showdown-between-philanthrolocalism-and-effective-altruism/.

Sievers, B. 2004. "Philanthropy's Blindspots." In M. C. Brown, *Just Money: A Critique of Contemporary American Philanthropy*, ed. H. P. Karoff, 129–149. Boston: TPI.

Smith, C. 2018. "The Controversial Crime-Fighting Program That Changed Big-City Policing Forever." *New York Magazine* (March 2).http://nymag.com/daily/intelligencer/2018/03/the-crime-fighting-program-that-changed-new-york-forever.html.

Somerville, B., and F. Setterberg. 2008. *Grassroots Philanthropy: Field Notes of a Maverick Grantmaker*. Berkeley, CA: Heyday Books.

Soskis, B. 2013. "BJS Tobacco Report." Open Philanthropy Project. https://www.openphilanthropy.org/research/history-of-philanthropy.

———. 2015. "The Impact of Philanthropy on the Passage of the Affordable Care Act." Open Philanthropy Project. https://www.openphilanthropy.org/research/history-of-philanthropy.

Statista. n.d. "Number of Foundations in the United States from 1990 to 2015." https://www.statista.com/statistics/250878/number-of-foundations-in-the-united-states/.

Suchman, E. A. 1967. *Evaluative Research: Principles and Practice in Public Service and Social Action Programs*. New York: Russell Sage Foundation.

Teles, S., and M. Schmitt. 2011. "The Elusive Craft of Evaluating Advocacy." *Stanford Social Innovation Review* 9(3): 38–43.

Toenniessen, G., A. Adesina, and J. DeVries. 2008. "Building an Alliance for a Green Revolution in Africa." *Annals of the New York Academy of Sciences* 1136: 233–242.

Tompkins-Stange, M. E. 2016 *Policy Patrons: Philanthropy, Education Reform, and the Politics of Influence*. Cambridge, MA: Harvard Education Press.

Twersky, F., P. Buchanan, and V. Threlfall. 2013. "Listening to Those Who Matter Most, the Beneficiaries." *Stanford Social Innovation Review* (Spring). https://ssir.org/articles/entry/listening_to_those_who_matter_most_the_beneficiaries.

United Way of America. 1996. *Measuring Program Outcomes: A Practical Approach. Evaluation/Reflection* 47. https://digitalcommons.unomaha.edu/slceeval/47.

Waddington, M. E. 1995. "Total Quality Management: The Development, Application and Analysis of a Total Quality Management Paradigm in Healthcare." Doctoral diss., University of Huddersfield. http://eprints.hud.ac.uk/id/eprint/4875/1/DX194243.pdf.

Weinstein, M. M., and R. M. Bradburd. 2013. *The Robin Hood Rules for Smart Giving*. New York: Columbia Business School Publishing.

Weiss, C. H. 1972. *Evaluation Research: Methods for Assessing Program Effectiveness*. Englewood Cliffs, NJ: Prentice-Hall.

West, W. F. 2011. *Program Budgeting and the Performance Movement: The Elusive Quest for Efficiency in Government*. Washington, DC: Georgetown University Press.

W. K. Kellogg Foundation. 2004. *Logic Model Development Guide*. https://www.bttop.org/sites/default/files/public/W.K.%20Kellogg%20LogicModel.pdf.

Part V. Balancing Access and Inclusion
Chapter 17. Charitable Nonprofits and the Business of Health Care

Aldridge, Melissa D., Mark Schlesinger, Colleen L. Barry, R. Sean Morrison, Ruth McCorkle, Rosemary Hürzeler, and Elizabeth H. Bradley. 2014. "National Hospice Survey Results: For-Profit Status, Community Engagement, and Service." *JAMA Internal Medicine* 174(4): 500–506.

Alexander, Jeffrey A., Gary J. Young, Bryan J. Weiner, and Larry R. Hearld. 2008. "Governance and Community Benefit: Are Nonprofit Hospitals Good Candidates for Sarbanes-Oxley Type Reforms?" *Journal of Health Politics, Policy and Law* 33(2): 199–224.

Alliance for Advancing Nonprofit Health Care. 2012. "Basic Facts and Figures: Nonprofit Health Plans." http://www.nonprofithealthcare.org/resources/BasicFacts-NonprofitHealthPlans.pdf.

Amirkhanyan, Anna. 2008. "Privatizing Public Nursing Homes: Examining the Effects on Quality and Access." *Public Administration Review* 68(4): 665–680.

Amirkhanyan, Anna A., Hyun Joon Kim, and Kristina T. Lambright. 2008. "Does the Public Sector Outperform the Nonprofit and For-Profit Sectors? Evidence from a National Panel Study on Nursing Home Quality and Access." *Journal of Policy Analysis and Management* 27(2): 326–353.

Anderson, Michael, Carlos Dobkin, and Tal Gross. 2012. "The Effect of Health Insurance Coverage on the Use of Medical Services." *American Economic Journal: Economic Policy* 4(1): 1–27.

Axelrod, Jessica A. 1997. "The Future of the Corporate Practice of Medicine Doctrine Following *Berlin v. Sarah Bush Lincoln Health Center*." *DePaul Journal of Health Care Law* 2: 103–121.

Balhara, Kamna S., Lauren M. Kucirka, Bernard G. Jaar, and Dorry L. Segev. 2012. "Disparities in Provision of Transplant Education by Profit Status of the Dialysis Center." *American Journal of Transplantation* 12(11): 3104–3110.

Barry, Colleen L., Melissa D. A. Carlson, Jennifer W. Thompson, Mark Schlesinger, Ruth McCorkle, Stanislav Kasl, and Elizabeth H. Bradley. 2012. "Caring for Grieving Family Members: Results from a National Hospice Survey." *Medical Care* 50(7): 578–584.

Bazzoli, Gloria J., Jan P. Clement, and Hui-Min Hsieh. 2010. "Community Benefit Activities of Private, Nonprofit Hospitals." *Journal of Health Politics, Policy and Law* 35(6): 999–1026.

Bazzoli, Gloria J., Richard C. Lindrooth, Ray Kang, and Romana Hasnain-Wynia. 2006. "The Influence of Health Policy and Market Factors on the Hospital Safety Net." *Health Services Research* 41(4, pt. 1): 1159–1180.

Ben-Ner, Avner, and Ting Ren. 2015. "Comparing Workplace Organization Design Based on Form of Ownership: Nonprofit, For-Profit, and Local Government." *Nonprofit and Voluntary Sector Quarterly* 44(2): 340–359.

Blackwood, Amy, Katie L. Roeger, and Sarah L. Pettijohn. 2012. "The Nonprofit Sector in Brief: Public Charities, Giving, and Volunteering, 2012." Urban Institute Press. https://www.urban.org/sites/default/files/publication/25901/412674-The-Nonprofit-Sector-in-Brief-Public-Charities-Giving-and-Volunteering-.PDF.

Blackwood, Amy, Kennard T. Wing, and Thomas H. Pollak. 2008. "The Nonprofit Sector in Brief: Facts and Figures from the Nonprofit Almanac 2008: Public Charities, Giving, and Volunteering." Urban Institute Press. https://www.urban.org/sites/default/files/publication/31706/411664-Facts-and-Figures-from-the-Nonprofit-Almanac--.PDF.

Bloche, M. Gregg. 2006. "Tax Preferences for Nonprofits: From Per Se Exemption to Pay-for-Performance." *Health Affairs* 25(4): W304–W307.

———. 2009. "The Emergent Logic of Health Law." *Southern California Law Review* 82: 389–480.

Bourque, Monique. 2012. "Women and Work in the Philadelphia Almshouse, 1790–1840." *Journal of the Early Republic* 32(3): 383–413.

Brickley, James A., and R. Lawrence Van Horn. 2002. "Managerial Incentives in Nonprofit Organizations: Evidence from Hospitals." *Journal of Law and Economics* 45(1): 227–249.

Brieger, Gert H., ed. 1972. *Medical America in the Nineteenth Century: Readings from the Literature.* Baltimore: Johns Hopkins University Press.

Brody, Evelyn. 2007. "The States' Growing Use of a Quid-Pro-Quo Rationale for the Charity Property Tax Exemption." *Exempt Organization Tax Review* 56(3): 269–288.

———. 2016. "The 21st Century Fight over Who Sets the Terms of the Charity Property Tax Exemption." *Exempt Organization Tax Review* 77(4): 259–277.

Brooks, John M., Christopher P. Irwin, Lawrence G. Hunsicker, Michael J. Flanigan, Elizabeth A. Chrischilles, and Jane F. Pendergast. 2006. "Effect of Dialysis Center Profit-Status on Patient Survival: A Comparison of Risk-Adjustment and Instrumental Variable Approaches." *Health Services Research* 41(6): 2267–2289.

Brooks, Terri L. 2008. "Billions Saved in Taxes While Millions Underserved—What Has Happened to

Charitable Hospitals." *Houston Business and Tax Journal* 8: 391–424.

Bureau of the Census. 2018. "Table 174: Revenue for Selected Health Care Industries by Source of Revenue: 2016 [Physicians, Dentists, Hospitals, and Nursing and Residential Care Facilitates]." *ProQuest Statistical Abstract of the U.S.*, February. https://statabs.proquest.com/sa/docview.html ?table-no=174&acc-no=C7095-1.3&year=2018&z= 1D70047B58C4FB5BB0DE6931B82F3220F44BEF88.

Carlson, Melissa D. A., William T. Gallo, and Elizabeth H. Bradley. 2004. "Ownership Status and Patterns of Care in Hospice: Results from the National Home and Hospice Care Survey." *Medical Care* 42(5): 432–438.

Castaneda, Marco A., and Dino Falaschetti. 2008. "Does a Hospital's Profit Status Affect Its Operational Scope?" *Review of Industrial Organization* 33: 129–159.

Centers for Disease Control and Prevention. 2006. "Nursing Home Facilities: December 2006." https://www.cdc.gov/nchs/data/nnhsd/ nursinghomefacilities2006.pdf.

Centers for Disease Control and Prevention. 2017. "Table 179: Long-Term Care Facilities, Staff, And Clients By Provider Type and Selected Characteristics: 2014." *ProQuest Statistical Abstract of the U.S.*, December. https://statabs .proquest.com/sa/docview.html?table-no= 179&acc-n=C7095-1.3&year=2018&z=2907 FCCF2F58408E4D4A19D735834910DDD 01CA4.

Centers for Medicaid and Medicare Services. 2015. "Nursing Home Data Compendium 2015 Edition." https://www.cms.gov/Medicare/ Provider-Enrollment-and-Certification/ CertificationandComplianc/Downloads/ nursinghomedatacompendium_508-2015.pdf.

Chang, Tom, and Mireille Jacobson. 2012. "What Do Nonprofit Hospitals Maximize? Evidence from California's Seismic Retrofit Mandate." Unpublished manuscript. https://users.nber.org/ ~changt/ChangJacobson13apr9.pdf.

Cherlin, Emily J., Melissa D. A. Carlson, Jeph Herrin, Dena Schulman-Green, Colleen L. Barry, Ruth McCorkle, Rosemary Johnson-Hurzeler, and Elizabeth H. Bradley. 2010. "Interdisciplinary Staffing Patterns: Do For-Profit and Nonprofit Hospices Differ?" *Journal of Palliative Medicine* 13(4): 389–394.

Clemens, Jeffrey, and Joshua D. Gottlieb. 2017. "In the Shadow of a Giant: Medicare's Influence on Private Physician Payments." *Journal of Political Economy* 25(1): 1–39.

Cohen, Bernard I. 1954. *Benjamin Franklin: Some Account of Pennsylvania Hospital*. Baltimore: Johns Hopkins University Press.

Colombo, John D. 2002. "Commercial Activity and Charitable Tax Exemption." *William and Mary Law Review* 44(2): 487–567.

———. 2005. "The Failure of Community Benefit." *Health Matrix* 15: 29–65.

———. 2007a. "Federal and State Tax Exemption Policy, Medical Debt and Healthcare for the Poor." *Saint Louis University Law Journal* 51: 433–457.

———. 2007b. "Reforming Internal Revenue Code Provisions on Commercial Activity by Charities." *Fordham Law Review* 76: 667–691.

Commission on Hospital Care. 1947. *Hospital Care in the United States: A Study of the Function of the General Hospital: Its Role in the Care of All Types of Illness, and the Conduct of Activities Related to Patient Service, with Recommendations for Its Extension and Integration for More Adequate Care of the American Public*. New York: Commonwealth Fund.

Committee on the Costs of Medical Care. 1932. *Medical Care for the American People: The Final Report of the Committee on the Costs of Medical Care*, vol. 28. Chicago: University of Chicago Press.

Comondore, Vikram R., et al. 2009. "Quality of Care in For-Profit and Not-for-Profit Nursing Homes: Systematic Review and Meta-Analysis." *British Medical Journal* 339: 1–15.

Congressional Budget Office. 2006. "Nonprofit Hospitals and the Provision of Community Benefits." https://www.cbo.gov/sites/default/ files/109th-congress-2005-2006/reports/12-06 -nonprofit.pdf.

Conover, Christopher J., Mark A. Hall, and Jan Ostermann. 2005. "The Impact of Blue Cross Conversions on Health Spending and the Uninsured." *Health Affairs* 24(2): 473–482.

Corbett, Terry L. 2015. "Healthcare Corporate Structure and the ACA: A Need for Mission Primacy Through a New Organizational Paradigm." *Indiana Health Law Review* 12: 103–181.

Crossley, Mary. 2016. "Health and Taxes: Hospitals, Community Health and the IRS." *Yale Journal of Health Policy, Law and Ethics* 16: 51–110.

Dafny, Leemore S. 2005. "How Do Hospitals Respond to Price Changes?" *American Economic Review* 95(5): 1525–1547.

———. 2019. "Does It Matter If Your Health Insurer Is For-Profit? Effects of Ownership on Premiums, Insurance Coverage, and Medical Spending." *American Economic Journal: Economic Policy* 11(1): 222–265.

Dafny, Leemore, and David Dranove. 2009. "Regulatory Exploitation and Management Changes: Upcoding in the Hospital Industry." *Journal of Law and Economics* 52(2): 223–250.

Dalrymple, Lorien S., Kirsten L. Johansen, Patrick S. Romano, Glenn M. Chertow, Yi Mu, Julie H. Ishida, Barbara Grimes, George A. Kaysen, and Danh V. Nguyen. 2014. "Comparison of Hospitalization Rates Among For-Profit and Nonprofit Dialysis Facilities." *Clinical Journal of the American Society of Nephrology* 9: 73–81.

Decker, Frederic H. 2011. "Profit Status of Home Health Care Agencies and the Risk of Hospitalization." *Population Health Management* 14(4): 199–204.

DiMaggio, Paul. 2006. "Nonprofit Organizations and the Intersectoral Division of Labor in the Arts." In *The Nonprofit Sector: A Research Handbook*, 2nd ed., ed. Walter W. Powell and Richard Steinberg, 432–461. New Haven, CT: Yale University Press.

Dorner, Zachary. 2016. "Manufacturing Pharmaceuticals, Credit, and Empire in the Eighteenth-Century British Atlantic." PhD diss., Brown University.

Dowling, Harry F. 1982. *City Hospitals: The Undercare of the Underprivileged*. Cambridge, MA: Harvard University Press.

Dranove, David, Craig Garthwaite, and Christopher Ody. 2017. "How Do Nonprofits Respond to Negative Wealth Shocks? The Impact of the 2008 Stock Market Collapse on Hospitals." *RAND Journal of Economics* 48(2): 485–525.

Eggleston, Karen, Yu-Chu Shen, Joseph Lau, Christopher H. Schmid, and Jia Chan. 2008. "Hospital Ownership and Quality of Care: What Explains the Different Results in the Literature?" *Health Economics* 17(12): 1345–1362.

Eldenburg, Leslie G., Katherine A. Gunny, Kevin W. Hee, and Naomi Soderstrom. 2011. "Earnings Management Using Real Activities: Evidence from Nonprofit Hospitals." *Accounting Review* 86(5): 1605–1630.

Fei, Fan, James R. Hines Jr., and Jill R. Horwitz. 2016. "Are PILOTs Property Taxes for Nonprofits?" *Journal of Urban Economics* 94: 109–123.

Ferdinand, Alva O., Josué P. Epané, and Nir Menachemi. 2014. "Community Benefits Provided by Religious, Other Nonprofit, and For-Profit Hospitals: A Longitudinal Analysis 2000–2009." *Health Care Management Review* 39(2): 145–153.

Fichter, Andrew. 2006. "Owning a Piece of the Doc: State Law Restraints on Lay Ownership of Healthcare Enterprises." *Journal of Health Law* 39(1): 1–76.

Folkerts, Laura L. 2009. "Do Nonprofit Hospitals Provide Community Benefit? Critique of the Standards for Proving Deservedness of Federal Tax Exemptions." *Journal of Corporation Law* 34: 611–640.

Fox, Daniel M. 2013. "A Once Charitable Enterprise: Hospitals and Health Care in Brooklyn and New York, 1885–1915, David Rosner. Cambridge, UK: Cambridge University Press, 1982, 1992, 2004; Princeton, NJ: Princeton University Press, 1986." *Nonprofit Policy Forum* 4(1): 99–103.

———. 2015. "Policy Commercializing Nonprofits in Health: The History of a Paradox from the 19th Century to the ACA." *Milbank Quarterly* 93(1): 179–210.

Frakt, Austin B. 2011. "How Much Do Hospitals Cost Shift? A Review of the Evidence." *Milbank Quarterly* 89(1): 90–130.

Friesenhahn, Erik. 2016. "Nonprofits in America: New Research Data on Employment, Wages, and Establishments." *Monthly Labor Review* 139: 1–12. https://www.bls.gov/opub/mlr/2016/article/nonprofits-in-america.htm.

Gaynor, Martin, Kate Ho, and Robert J. Town. 2015. "The Industrial Organization of Health-Care

Markets." *Journal of Economic Literature* 53(2): 235–284.

Gertler, Paul, and Jennifer Kuan. 2009. "Does It Matter Who Your Buyer Is? The Role of Nonprofit Mission in the Market for Corporate Control of Hospitals." *Journal of Law and Economics* 52(2): 295–306.

Goodman, Michele. 2009. "Putting the Community Back in Community Benefit: Proposed State Tax Exemption Standard for Nonprofit Hospitals." *Indiana Law Journal* 84: 713–742.

Gore, Thomas B. 2013. "A Forgotten Landmark Medical Study from 1932 by the Committee on the Cost of Medical Care." *Proceedings (Baylor University Medical Center)* 26(2): 142–143.

Grabowski, David C., Zhanlian Feng, Richard Hirth, Momotazur Rahman, and Vincent Mor. 2013. "Effect of Nursing Home Ownership on the Quality of Post-Acute Care: An Instrumental Variables Approach." *Journal of Health Economics* 32(1): 12–21.

Grabowski, David C., and Richard A. Hirth. 2003. "Competitive Spillovers Across Non-Profit and For-Profit Nursing Homes." *Journal of Health Economics* 22(1): 1–22.

Grabowski, David C., Haiden A. Huskamp, David G. Stevenson, and Nancy L. Keating. 2009. "Ownership Status and Home Health Care Performance." *Journal of Aging and Social Policy* 21(2): 130–143.

Grabowski, David C., and David G. Stevenson. 2008. "Ownership Conversions and Nursing Home Performance." *Health Services Research* 43(4): 1184–1203.

Gray, Bradford H., and Mark Schlesinger. 2009a. "The Accountability of Nonprofit Hospitals: Lessons from Maryland's Community Benefit Reporting Requirements." *Inquiry* 46(2): 122–139.

———. 2009b. "Charitable Expectations of Nonprofit Hospitals: Lessons from Maryland." *Health Affairs* 28(5): w809–w821.

Hall, Mark A. 1988. "Institutional Control of Physician Behavior: Legal Barriers to Health Care Cost Containment." *University of Pennsylvania Law Review* 137: 431–536.

———. 2013. "There Oughta Be a Law." *Hastings Center Report* 43(4): 7–8.

Hall, Mark A., and Christopher J. Conover. 2006. "For-Profit Conversion of Blue Cross Plans: Public Benefit or Public Harm?" *Annual Review of Public Health* 27: 433–463.

Hall, Mark A., and Carl E. Schneider. 2008. "Patients as Consumers: Courts, Contracts, and the New Medical Marketplace." *Michigan Law Review* 106: 643–689.

Hall, Mark A., Carl E. Schneider, and Lois L. Shepherd. 2006. "Rethinking Health Law." *Wake Forest Law Review* 41: 341–345.

Hamadi, Hanadi, Emma Apatu, and Aaron Spaulding. 2018. "Does Hospital Ownership Influence Hospital Referral Region Health Rankings in the United States." *International Journal of Health Planning and Management* 33(1): e168–e180.

Hansmann, Henry B. 1981. "Reforming Nonprofit Corporation Law." *University of Pennsylvania Law Review* 129(3): 497–623.

Hellinger, Fred Joseph. 2009. "Tax-Exempt Hospitals and Community Benefits: A Review of State Reporting Requirements." *Journal of Health Politics, Policy, and Law* 34(1): 37–61.

Herndon, Ruth Wallis. 2012. "Poor Women and the Boston Almshouse in the Early Republic." *Journal of the Early Republic* 32(3): 349–381.

Herrera, Cristian A., Gabriel Rada, Lucy Kuhn-Barrientos, and Ximena Barrios. 2014. "Does Ownership Matter? An Overview of Systematic Reviews of the Performance of Private For-Profit, Private Not-for-Profit and Public Healthcare Providers." *PLOS One* 9(12): 1–18.

Hill, Frances R., and Douglas M. Mancino. 2002. *Taxation of Exempt Organizations*. Eagan, MN: Warren Gorham and Lamont of RIA.

Hillmer, Michael P., Walter P. Wodchis, Sudeep S. Gill, Geoffrey M. Anderson, and Paula A. Rochon. 2005. "Nursing Home Profit Status and Quality of Care: Is There Any Evidence of an Association?" *Medical Care Research and Review* 62(2): 139–166.

Hirth, Richard A., Michael E. Chernew, and Sean M. Orzol. 2000. "Ownership, Competition, and the Adoption of New Technologies and Cost-Saving Practices in a Fixed-Price Environment." *Inquiry* 37(3): 282–294.

Hirth, Richard A., David C. Grabowski, Zhanlian Feng, Momotazur Rahman, and Vincent Mor.

2014. "Effect of Nursing Home Ownership on Hospitalization of Long-Stay Residents: An Instrumental Variables Approach." *International Journal of Health Care Finance and Economics* 14(1): 1–18.

Horwitz, Jill R. 2003. "Why We Need the Independent Sector: The Behavior, Law, and Ethics of Not-for-Profit Hospitals." *UCLA Law Review* 50: 1345–1411.

———. 2005. "Making Profits and Providing Care: Comparing Nonprofit, For-Profit, and Government Hospitals." *Health Affairs* 24(3): 790–801.

———. 2006. "Nonprofit Ownership, Private Property, and Public Accountability." *Health Affairs* 25(4): W308–W311.

———. 2007. "Does Corporate Ownership Matter? Service Provision in the Hospital Industry." *Yale Journal on Regulation* 24(1): 139–204.

———. 2009. "Nonprofits and Narrative: Piers Plowman, Anthony Trollope, and Charities Law." *Michigan State Law Review* 4: 989–1016.

———. 2016. "Nonprofit Healthcare Organizations and the Law." In *The Oxford Handbook of U.S. Health Law*, ed. Glenn Cohen, Allison K. Hoffman, and William M. Sage, 535–555. New York: Oxford University Press.

Horwitz, Jill, and David Cutler. 2015. "The ACA's Hospital Tax-Exemption Rules and the Practice of Medicine." *Health Affairs*, March 3.

Horwitz, Jill R., and Austin Nichols. 2009. "Hospital Ownership and Medical Services: Market Mix, Spillover Effects, and Nonprofit Objectives." *Journal of Health Economics* 28(5): 924–937.

———. 2011. "Rural Hospital Ownership: Medical Service Provision, Market Mix, and Spillover Effects." *Health Services Research* 46(5): 1452–1472.

House Committee on Ways and Means. 2005. *The Tax-Exempt Hospital Sector: Hearing Before the Committee on Ways and Means. U.S. House of Representatives.* Serial No. 109-17, 109th Cong. (2005).

Hyman, David A., and William M. Sage. 2006. "Subsidizing Health Care Providers Through the Tax Code: Status or Conduct?" *Health Affairs* 25(4): W312–W315.

Institute of Education Sciences, National Center for Education Statistics. 2018. *The Condition of Education 2018*. https://nces.ed.gov/pubs2018/2018144.pdf.

IRS (Internal Revenue Service). 2014. "IRS Exempt Organizations (TE/GE) Hospital Compliance Project Final Report." https://www.irs.gov/pub/irs-tege/frepthospproj.pdf.

Jha, Ashish, and Arnold Epstein. 2010. "Hospital Governance and the Quality of Care." *Health Affairs* 29(1): 182–187.

Jones, Daniel B., Carol Propper, and Sarah Smith. 2017. "Wolves in Sheep's Clothing: Is Non-Profit Status Used to Signal Quality?" *Journal of Health Economics* 55: 108–120.

Kaiser Family Foundation. 2016. "Health Insurance Coverage of the Total Population." https://www.kff.org/other/state-indicator/total-population.

Kane, Nancy M. 2006. "Tax-Exempt Hospitals: What Is Their Charitable Responsibility and How Should It Be Defined and Reported." *Saint Louis University Law Journal* 51: 459–473.

Kerson, Toba Schwaber. 1981. "Almshouse to Municipal Hospital: The Baltimore Experience." *Bulletin of the History of Medicine* 55(2): 203–220.

Kett, Joseph F. 1968. *The Formation of the American Medical Profession: The Role of Institutions, 1780–1860.* New Haven, CT: Yale University Press.

Kinney, Eleanor D. 2010. "For Profit Enterprise in Health Care: Can It Contribute to Health Reform?" *American Journal of Law and Medicine* 36: 405–435.

Klebes, Katharine. 2015. "For-Profit Healthcare in Connecticut: New Requirements Under the Patient Protection and Affordable Care Act and the Emerging For-Profit Hospital Model in Connecticut." *Quinnipiac Health Law Journal* 18: 239–286.

Konetzka, R. Tamara, William Spector, and Thomas Shaffer. 2004. "Effects of Nursing Home Ownership Type and Resident Payer Source on Hospitalization for Suspected Pneumonia." *Medical Care* 42(10): 1001–1008.

Kutney-Lee, Ann, G. J. Melendez-Torres, Matthew D. McHugh, and Barbra Mann Wall. 2014. "Distinct Enough? A National Examination of Catholic Hospital Affiliation and Patient Perceptions of Care." *Health Care Management Review* 39(2): 134–144.

Lamboy-Ruiz, Melvin A., James N. Cannon, and Olena V. Watanabe. 2017. "Does State Community Benefits Regulation Influence Charity Care and Operational Efficiency in US Non-Profit Hospitals?" *Journal of Business Ethics* (December): 1–25.

Lancet Editorial. 2017. "40 Years of Percutaneous Coronary Intervention: Where Next?" *The Lancet* 390(August 19): 715.

Lee, Donald K. K., Glenn M. Chertow, and Stefanos A. Zenios. 2010. "Reexploring Differences Among For-Profit and Nonprofit Dialysis Providers." *Health Services Research* 45(3): 633–646.

Leone, Andrew J., and R. Lawrence Van Horn. 2005. "How Do Nonprofit Hospitals Manage Earnings?" *Journal of Health Economics* 24(4): 815–837.

Levitt, Jane. 1986. "The Corporatization of Health Care." In *Health Care Delivery in the United States*, ed. Steven Jonas. New York: Springer.

Lieber, Ethan M. J. 2018. "Does Health Insurance Coverage Fall When Nonprofit Insurers Become For-Profits?" *Journal of Health Economics* 57: 75–88.

Lindrooth, Richard C., and Burton A. Weisbrod. 2007. "Do Religious Nonprofit and For-Profit Organizations Respond Differently to Financial Incentives? The Hospice Industry." *Journal of Health Economics* 26(2): 342–357.

Mars, Sara. 1997. "The Corporate Practice of Medicine: A Call for Action." *Health Matrix* 7: 241–300.

McGregor, Cecilia M. J. 2007. "The Community Benefit Standard for Non-Profit Hospitals: Which Community, and for Whose Benefit." *Journal of Contemporary Health Law and Policy* 23: 302–340.

McKeever, Brice S. 2015. "The Nonprofit Sector in Brief 2015: Public Charities, Giving, and Volunteering." Urban Institute Press, October. https://www.urban.org/sites/default/files/publication/72536/2000497-The-Nonprofit-Sector-in-Brief-2015-Public-Charities-Giving-and-Volunteering.pdf.

Miller, Keaton S., and Wesley W. Wilson. 2018. "Governance Structure and Exit: Evidence from California Hospitals." *Review of Industrial Organization* 53: 31–55.

Molk, Peter. 2012. "Reforming Nonprofit Exemption Requirements." *Fordham Journal of Corporate and Financial Law* 17: 475–543.

Morris, Theresa, Kelly McNamara, and Christine H. Morton. 2017. "Hospital-Ownership Status and Cesareans in the United States: The Effect of For-Profit Hospitals." *Birth* 44(4): 325–330.

National Center for Education Statistics. 2018. "Private School Enrollment." https://nces.ed.gov/programs/coe/indicator_cgc.asp.

National Hospice and Palliative Care Organization. 2017. "Facts and Figures: Hospice Care in America." Revised April 2018. https://www.nhpco.org/sites/default/files/public/Statistics_Research/2017_Facts_Figures.pdf.

O'Halloran, Kerry. 2012. *The Profits of Charity: International Perspectives on the Law Governing the Involvement of Charites in Commerce.* Oxford, UK: Oxford University Press.

Packard, Francis R. 1963. *History of Medicine in the United States.* New York: Hafner.

Paul, Jomon A., Benedikt Quosigk, and Leo MacDonald. 2017. "Factors Impacting Market Concentration of Not-for-Profit Hospitals." *Journal of Business Ethics* (March 1): 1–19.

Pettijohn, Sarah L. 2013. "The Nonprofit Sector in Brief: Public Charities, Giving, and Volunteering, 2013." Urban Institute Press. https://www.urban.org/sites/default/files/publication/24041/412923-The-Nonprofit-Sector-in-Brief-Public-Charities-Giving-and-Volunteering-.PDF.

Pihlblad, T. C. 1938. "A Study of Missouri Almshouses." *Southwestern Social Science Quarterly* 19(2): 201–210.

Price, R. M. 1985. "A Case Book of the Philadelphia Almshouse Infirmary Dr. James Rush Attending Physician." *Bulletin of the History of Medicine* 59(3): 383–389.

Quigley, William P. 1997. "Reluctant Charity: Poor Laws in the Original Thirteen States." *University of Richmond Law Review* 31: 111–178.

Reich, Adam D. 2014a. "Contradictions in the Commodification of Hospital Care." *American Journal of Sociology* 119(6): 1576–1628.

———. 2014b. *Selling Our Souls: The Commodification of Hospital Care in the United States.* Princeton, NJ: Princeton University Press.

Richmond, Kelly A., and Pamela C. Smith. 2005. "Machiavellian Tendencies of Nonprofit Health Care Employees." *Journal of Health Care Finance* 32(2): 19–31.

Roeger, Katie L., Amy Blackwood, and Sarah L. Pettijohn. 2011. "The Nonprofit Sector in Brief: Public Charities, Giving, and Volunteering, 2011." Urban Institute Press. https://www.urban .org/sites/default/files/publication/26636/412434 -The-Nonprofit-Sector-in-Brief-Public-Charities -Giving-and-Volunteering-.PDF.

Ronald, Lisa A., Margaret J. McGregor, Charlene Harrington, Allyson Pollock, and Joel Lexchin. 2016. "Observational Evidence of For-Profit De- livery and Inferior Nursing Home Care: When Is There Enough Evidence for Policy Change?" *PLOS Medicine* 13(4): 1–12.

Rosenau, Pauline V., and Stephen H. Linder. 2003. "Two Decades of Research Comparing For-Profit and Nonprofit Health Provider Performance in the United States." *Social Science Quarterly* 84(2): 219–241.

Rosenbaum, Sara. 2016. "Hospital Community Benefit Spending: Leaning In on the Social Determinants of Health." *Milbank Quarterly* 94(2): 251–254.

Rosenbaum, Sara, David A. Kindig, Jie Bao, Maureen K. Byrnes, and Colin O'Laughlin. 2015. "The Value of the Nonprofit Hospital Tax Exemption Was $24.6 Billion in 2011." *Health Affairs* 34(7): 1225–1233.

Rosenberg, Charles E. 1977. "And Heal the Sick: The Hospital and the Patient in the 19th Century America." *Journal of Social History* 10(4): 428–447.

Rosner, David. 1982. *A Once Charitable Enterprise: Hospitals and Health Care in Brooklyn and New York 1885–1915.* New York: Cambridge University Press.

Rothstein, William G. 1972. *American Physicians in the Nineteenth Century: From Sects to Science.* Baltimore: Johns Hopkins University Press.

Rubin, Daniel B., Simone R. Singh, and Peter D. Jacobson. 2013. "Evaluating Hospitals' Provision of Community Benefit: An Argument for an Outcome-Based Approach to Nonprofit Hospital Tax Exemption." *American Journal of Public Health* 103(4): 612–616.

Rubin, Daniel B., Simone R. Singh, and Gary J. Young. 2015. "Tax-Exempt Hospitals and Community Benefit: New Directions in Policy and Practice." *Annual Review of Public Health* 36: 545–557.

Sage, William M. 2016. "Assembled Products: The Key to More Effective Competition and Antitrust Oversight in Health Care." *Cornell Law Review* 101: 609–700.

Schirra, Jeremy J. 2011. "A Veil of Tax Exemption: A Proposal for the Continuation of Federal Tax -Exempt Status for Nonprofit Hospitals." *Health Matrix* 21: 231–277.

Schlesinger, Mark, and Bradford H. Gray. 2006a. "How Nonprofits Matter in American Medicine, and What to Do About It." *Health Affairs* 25(4): W287–W303.

———. 2006b. "Nonprofit Organizations and Health Care: Some Paradoxes of Persistent Scrutiny." In *The Nonprofit Sector: A Research Handbook,* 2nd ed., ed. Walter W. Powell and Richard Steinberg, 378–414. New Haven, CT: Yale University Press.

Schneider, Helen. 2007. "Paying Their Way? Do Nonprofit Hospitals Justify Their Favorable Tax Treatment?" *Inquiry* 44(2): 187–199.

Senate Finance Committee. 2006. *Taking the Pulse of Charitable Care and Community Benefits at Nonprofit Hospitals: Hearing Before the S. Fin. Comm.,* 109th Cong. (2006).

Shen, Yu-Chu, Karen Eggleston, Joseph Lau, and Christopher H. Schmid. 2007. "Hospital Ownership and Financial Performance: What Explains the Different Findings in the Empirical Literature?" *Inquiry* 44(1): 41–68.

Shen, Yu-Chu, and Glenn Melnick. 2004. "The Effects of HMO Ownership on Hospital Costs and Revenues: Is There a Difference Between For-Profit and Nonprofit Plans?" *Inquiry* 41(3): 255–267.

Shugarman, Lisa R., Nancy Nicosia, and Cynthia R. Schuster. 2007. "Comparing For-Profit and Not-for-Profit Health Care Providers: A Review of the Literature." Working paper, RAND Cor- poration. https://www.rand.org/pubs/working _papers/WR476.html.

Silverman, Elaine, and Jonathan Skinner. 2004. "Medicare Upcoding and Hospital Ownership." *Journal of Health Economics* 23(2): 369–389.

Singer, Lawrence E. 2008. "Leveraging Tax-Exempt Status of Hospitals." *Journal of Legal Medicine* 29(1): 41–64.

Singh, Simone R., Gary J. Young, Lacey Loomer, and Kristin Madison. 2018. "State-Level Community Benefit Regulation and Nonprofit Hospitals' Provision of Community Benefits." *Journal of Health Politics, Policy, and Law* 43(2): 229–269.

Sloan, Frank A. 2000. "Not-for-Profit Ownership and Hospital Behavior." *Handbook of Health Economics* 1: 1141–1174.

Smith, Janice M., and John V. Woodhull. 2017. "Lay of the Land—Where Does Property Tax Exemption for Health Care Entities Stand Now?" *Tax of Exempts* 28(3): 38–46.

Sosinsky, Laura S., Heather Lord, and Edward Zigler. 2007. "For-Profit/Nonprofit Differences in Center-Based Child Care Quality: Results from the National Institute of Child Health and Human Development Study of Early Child Care and Youth Development." *Journal of Applied Developmental Psychology* 28(5): 390–410.

Stenbacka, Rune, and Mihkel Tombak. 2018. "Optimal Reimbursement Policy in Health Care: Competition, Ownership Structure and Quality Provision." *B.E. Journal of Economic Analysis and Policy* 18(1): 1–19.

Stevens, Rosemary. 1989. *In Sickness and in Wealth: American Hospitals in the Twentieth Century.* New York: Basic Books.

Stevenson, David G., David C. Grabowski, Nancy L. Keating, and Haiden A. Huskamp. 2016. "Effect of Ownership on Hospice Service Use: 2005–2011." *Journal of the American Geriatrics Society* 64(5): 1024–1031.

Stewart, Katie. 2009. "Property Tax Exemptions for Nonprofit Hospitals: The Implications of *Provena Covenant Medical Center v. Department of Revenue.*" *Tax Lawyer* 62(4): 1157–1196.

Stone, Deborah A. 1993. "The Struggle for the Soul of Health Insurance." *Journal of Health Politics, Policy and Law* 18(2): 287–317.

Straube, Barry M. 2014. "Do Health Outcomes Vary by Profit Status of Hemodialysis Units?" *Clinical Journal of the American Society of Nephrology* 9(1): 1–2.

Swogier, Jillian A. 2017. "Finding a Fit for Nonprofit Hospitals: A National Perspective of State Property Tax Exemption Laws." *Seton Hall Legislative Journal* 41(2): 469–498.

Szczech, L. A., P. S. Klassen, B. Chua, S. S. Hedayati, M. Flanigan, W. M. McClellan, D. N. Reddan, R. A. Rettig, D. L. Frankenfield, and W. F. Owen. 2006. "Associations Between CMS's Clinical Performance Measures Project Benchmarks, Profit Structure, and Mortality in Dialysis Units." *Kidney International* 69(11): 2094–2100.

Tahk, Susannah C. 2014. "Tax-Exempt Hospitals and Their Communities." *Columbia Journal of Tax Law* 6: 33–85.

Thamer, Mae, Yi Zhang, James Kaufman, Dennis Cotter, Fan Dong, and Miguel A. Hernán. 2007. "Dialysis Facility Ownership and Epoetin Dosing in Patients Receiving Hemodialysis." *Journal of the American Medical Association* 297(15): 1667–1674.

Thomasson, Melissa A. 2002. "From Sickness to Health: The Twentieth-Century Development of US Health Insurance." *Explorations in Economic History* 39(3): 233–253.

Thompson, Jennifer W., Melissa D. A. Carlson, and Elizabeth H. Bradley. 2012. "US Hospice Industry Experienced Considerable Turbulence from Changes in Ownership, Growth, and Shift to For-Profit Status." *Health Affairs* 31(6): 1286–1293.

Titmuss, Richard M. 1970. *The Gift Relationship: From Human Blood to Social Policy.* London: Allen and Unwin.

Town, Robert, Roger Feldman, and Douglas Wholey. 2004. "The Impact of Ownership Conversions on HMO Performance." *International Journal of Health Care Finance and Economics* 4(4): 327–342.

Tyrrell, James E. III. 2010. "Non-Profits Under Fire: The Effects of Minimal Charity Care Requirements Legislation on Not-for-Profit Hospitals." *Journal of Contemporary Health Law and Policy* 26: 373–402.

Urban Institute. 2007. "The Nonprofit Sector in Brief: Facts and Figures from the Nonprofit Almanac 2007." https://www.hplct.org/assets/uploads/files/Nonprofit%20Almanac.pdf.

U.S. Government Accountability Office. 2008. "Nonprofit Hospitals: Variation in Standards and Guidance Limits Comparison of How Hospitals

Meet Community Benefit Requirements."
https://www.gao.gov/new.items/d08880.pdf.

Vansant, Brian. 2016. "Institutional Pressures to Provide Social Benefits and the Earnings Management Behavior of Nonprofits: Evidence from the
US Hospital Industry." *Contemporary Accounting
Research* 33(4): 1576–1600.

Vladeck, Bruce C. 1983. "Nursing Homes." In
*Handbook of Health, Health Care, and the Health
Professions*, ed. David Mechanic. New York: Free
Press.

Vlassopoulos, Michael. 2009. "Quality, Reputation
and the Choice of Organizational Form." *Journal
of Economic Behavior and Organization* 71(2):
515–527.

Vogel, Morris J. 1978. "Patrons, Practitioners, and
Patients: The Voluntary Hospital in Mid-Victo-
rian Boston." In *Sickness and Health in America:
Readings in the History of Medicine and Public
Health*, ed. Judith W. Leavitt and Ronald L.
Numbers. Madison: University of Wisconsin
Press.

Wachterman, Melissa W., Edward R. Marcantonio,
Roger B. Davis, and Ellen P. McCarthy. 2011.
"Association of Hospice Agency Profit Status
with Patient Diagnosis, Location of Care, and
Length of Stay." *Journal of the American Medical
Association* 305(5): 472–479.

Watson, Sidney D. 2010. "From Almshouses to
Nursing Homes and Community Care: Lessons
from Medicaid's History." *Georgia State University Law Review* 26: 937–969.

Weisbrod, Burton A., ed. 1998. *To Profit or Not to
Profit: The Commercial Transformation of the
Nonprofit Sector*. New York: Cambridge Univer-
sity Press.

White, Kenneth R., and Roberto Dandi. "2009.
"Intrasectoral Variation in Mission and Values:
The Case of the Catholic Health Systems." *Health
Care Management Review* 34(1): 68–79.

Wilson, Nathan E. 2016. "For-Profit Status and
Industry Evolution in Health Care Markets: Evidence from the Dialysis Industry." *International
Journal of Health Economics and Management*
16(4): 297–319.

Wing, Kennard T., Katie L. Roeger, and Thomas H.
Pollak. 2009. "The Nonprofit Sector in Brief:
Public Charities, Giving, and Volunteering,

2009." Urban Institute Press. https://www.urban
.org/sites/default/files/publication/28606/412085
-The-Nonprofit-Sector-in-Brief.PDF.

Yetman, Michelle H., and Robert J. Yetman.
2008. "Why Do Nonprofits Have Taxable
Subsidiaries?" *National Tax Journal* 61(4, pt. 1):
675–698.

You, Kai, Yue Li, Orna Intrator, David Stevenson,
Richard Hirth, David Grabowski, and Jane
Banaszak-Holl. 2016. "Do Nursing Home Chain
Size and Proprietary Status Affect Experiences
with Care?" *Medical Care* 54(3): 229–234.

Young, Gary J., Chia-Hung Chou, Jeffrey Alexander,
Shoou-Yih Daniel Lee, and Eli Raver. 2013. "Provision of Community Benefits by Tax-Exempt
US Hospitals." *New England Journal of Medicine*
368(16): 1519–1527.

Cases Cited

AHS Hospital Corp. v. Town of Morristown, 28
N.J.Tax 456 (2015).

Berlin v. Sarah Bush Lincoln Health Ctr., 179 Ill.2d 1
(1997).

*California Med. Ass'n, Inc. v. Regents of Univ. of
California*, 79 Cal.App.4th 542, 200 (Cal. Ct.
App. 2000).

*California Physicians' Serv. v. Aoki Diabetes Research
Inst.*, 163 Cal.App.4th 1506 (2008).

Carter-Shields, M.D. v. Alton Health Inst., 201 Ill.2d
441 (2002).

Grp. Health Ass'n v. Moor, 24 F.Supp. 445 (D.D.C.
1938).

Michigan Attorney General, Nonprofit Corporation
Act, Op. Mich. Att'y Gen. 6770 (Sept. 17, 1993),
http://www.ag.state.mi.us/opinion/datafiles/
1990s/op06770.htm.

*People ex rel. State Bd. of Med. Examiners v. Pac.
Health Corp.*, 82 P.2d 429 (Cal. 1938).

Provena Covenant Med. Ctr. v. Dep't of Revenue, 236
Ill.2d 368 (2010).

Chapter 18. Education and the Nonprofit Sector: Schools and Organizational Intermediaries

Arum, R., and J. Roksa. 2011. *Academically Adrift*.
Chicago: University of Chicago Press.

Balogh, B. 2015. *The Associational State: American
Governance in the Twentieth Century*. Philadelphia: University of Pennsylvania Press.

Berends, M., and G. Zottola. 2009. "Social Perspectives on School Choice." In *Handbook of Research on School Choice*, ed. Mark Berends, 35–54. New York: Routledge.

Bulkley, K. 2004. "Balancing Act: Educational Management Organizations and Charter School Autonomy." In *Taking Account of Charter Schools: What's Happened and What's Next*, ed. K. E. Buckley and P. Wohlstetter, 121–141. New York: Teachers College Press.

Calvin, A. 2000. "Use of Standardized Tests in Admissions in Postsecondary Institutions of Higher Education." *Psychology, Public Policy and Law* 6(1): 20–32.

Carey, K. 2016. *The End of College: Creating the Future of Learning and the University of Everywhere*. New York: Riverhead Books.

Clemens, E. S. 2006. "Lineages of the Rube Goldberg State: Building and Blurring Public Programs, 1900–1940." In *Rethinking Political Institutions: The Art of the State*, ed. I. Shapiro, S. Skowronek, and D. Galvin, 187–189. New York: NYU Press.

Cole, J. R. 2016. *Toward a More Perfect University*. New York: Public Affairs.

Crouse, J., and D. Trusheim. 1988. *The Case Against the SAT*. Chicago: University of Chicago Press.

Davies, S., and J. Mehta. 2018. "The Deepening Interpenetration of Education in Modern Life." In *Education in a New Society: Renewing the Sociology of Education*, ed. J. Mehta and S. Davies, 83–114. Chicago: University of Chicago Press.

DiMaggio, P. J., and W. W. Powell. 1983. "The Iron Cage Revisited: Institutional Isomorphism and Collective Rationality in Organizational Fields." *American Sociological Review* 48(2): 147–160.

Eaton, C. 2018. *The Ivory Tower Tax Haven: The State, Financialization, and the Growth of Wealth College Endowments*. Haas Institute for a Fair and Inclusive Society, University of California. http://haasinstitute.berkeley.edu/justpublicfinance.

Eaton, C., J. Habinek, A. Goldstein, C. Dioun, D. G. Santibáñez Godoy, and R. Osley-Thomas. 2016. "The Financialization of US Higher Education." *Socio-Economic Review* 14(3): 507–535.

Eaton, J. S. 2012. "The Future of Accreditation." *Society for College and University Planning* 40(3): 8–15.

Federal Student Aid. 2017. "Official Cohort Default Rates for Schools." https://www2.ed.gov/offices/OSFAP/defaultmanagement/schooltyperates.pdf.

Fiala, R., and A. Gordon-Lanford. 1987. "Educational Ideology and the World Educational Revolution, 1950–1970." *Comparative Education Review* 31(3): 315–332.

Foundation Center. 2015. *Key Facts on U.S. Foundations, 2014*. http://foundationcenter.org/gainknowledge/research/keyfacts2014/pdfs/Key_Facts_on_US_Foundations_2014.pdf.

Frankenberg, E., G. Siegel-Hawley, and J. Wang. 2011. "Choice Without Equity: Charter School Segregation." *Education Policy Analysis Archives* 19(1). http://epaa.asu.edu/ojs/article/view/779.

Furgeson, J., et al. 2012. "Charter-School Management Organizations: Diverse Strategies and Diverse Student Impacts." Mathematica Policy Research and Center on Reinventing Public Education. https://www.crpe.org/sites/default/files/pub_cmofinal_Jan12_0.pdf.

Gulosino, C., and C. d'Entremont. 2011. "Circles of Influence: An Analysis of Charter School Location and Racial Patterns at Varying Geographic Scales." *Education Policy Analysis Archives* 19(8). http://epaa.asu.edu/ojs/article/view/842.

Gumport, P. J., and S. K. Snydman. 2006. "Higher Education: Evolving Forms and Emerging Markets." In *The Nonprofit Sector: A Research Handbook*, 2nd ed., ed. W. W. Powell and R. Steinberg, 462–484. New Haven, CT: Yale University Press.

Guthrie, D., R. Arum, J. Roksa, and S. Damaske. 2008. "Giving to Local Schools: Corporate Philanthropy, Tax Incentives, and the Ecology of Need." *Social Science Research* 37(3): 856–873.

Henig, J. R. 2008. *Spin Cycle: How Research Gets Used in Policy Debates—The Case of Charter Schools*. New York: Russell Sage Foundation.

Honig, B. 2004. "Entrepreneurship Education: Toward a Model of Contingency-Based Business." *Academy of Management Learning and Education* 3(3): 258–273.

Howard, C. 1999. *The Hidden Welfare State: Tax Expenditure and Social Policy in the United States*. Princeton, NJ: Princeton University Press.

Jacob, B., B. McCall, and K. M. Stange. 2013. "College as a Country Club: Do Colleges Cater to Students' Preferences for Consumption?" NBER

Working Paper No. w18745. National Bureau of Economic Research.

Kamenetz, A. 2010. *DIY U: Edupunks, Edupreneurs, and the Coming Transformation of Higher Education.* White River Junction, VT: Chelsea Green.

Kirp, D. L. 2003. *Shakespeare, Einstein, and the Bottom Line: The Marketing of Higher Education*, vol. 139. Cambridge, MA: Harvard University Press.

Lagemann, E. C. 1992. *The Politics of Knowledge: The Carnegie Corporation, Philanthropy, and Public Policy.* Chicago: University of Chicago Press.

Lemann, N. 2000. *The Big Test: The Secret History of the American Meritocracy.* London: Macmillan.

Malczewski, J. 2016. *Building a New Educational State: Foundations, Schools, and the American South.* Chicago: University of Chicago Press.

Malczewski, J. 2017. "Interstitial Collaboration: Education Reform in the Jim Crow South." *Studies in American Political Development* 31(2): 238–258.

Martin, J. C. 1994. "Accrediting Agencies in Postsecondary Education." *Law and Contemporary Problems* 57: 121–149.

McDonald, J. P., et al. 2014. *American School Reform: What Works, What Fails, and Why.* Chicago: University of Chicago Press.

Mettler, S. 2011. *The Submerged State: How Invisible Government Policies Undermine American Democracy.* Chicago: University of Chicago Press.

———. 2014. *Degrees of Inequality: How the Politics of Higher Education Sabotaged the American Dream.* New York: Basic Books.

Meyer, J. W. 1977. "The Effects of Education as an Institution." *American Journal of Sociology* 83(1): 55–77.

Meyer, J. W., and B. Rowan. 1977. "Institutionalized Organizations: Formal Structure as Myth and Ceremony." *American Journal of Sociology* 83(2): 340–363.

Meyer, J. W., R. Scott, and T. E. Deal. 1981. "Institutional and Technical Sources of Organizational Structure: Explaining the Structure of Educational Organizations." In *Organization and the Human Services*, ed. H. D. Stein, 151–178. Philadelphia: Temple University Press.

Miller, B. 2018. "The Student Debt Problem Is Worse Than We Imagined." *New York Times*, August 25. https://www.nytimes.com/interactive/2018/08/

25/opinion/sunday/student-debt-loan-default -college.html.

Miron, G., and C. Gulosino. 2013. *Profiles of For-Profit and Nonprofit Education Management Organizations: Fourteenth Edition 2011–2012.* Boulder, CO: National Education Policy Center.

National Science Board. 2010. *Science and Engineering Indicators 2010.* Alexandria, VA: National Science Foundation.

———. 2018. *Science and Engineering Indicators 2018.* Alexandria, VA: National Science Foundation.

Owen-Smith, J., and W. W. Powell. 2003. "The Expanding Role of University Patenting in the Life Sciences: Assessing the Importance of Experience and Connectivity." *Research Policy* 32(9): 1695–1711.

Perry, A. M. 2017. "How Charter Schools Are Prolonging Segregation." Brookings Institution, December 11. https://www.brookings.edu/blog/ the-avenue/2017/12/11/how-charter-schools-are -prolonging-segregation/.

Pfeffer, J., and G. R. Salancik. 2003. *The External Control of Organizations: A Resource Dependence Perspective.* Stanford, CA: Stanford Business Classics.

Reckhow, S., and J. W. Snyder. 2014. "The Expanding Role of Philanthropy in Education Politics." *Educational Researcher* 43(4): 186–195.

Salamon, L. M. 2012. "The Nonprofit Sector at a Crossroads: The Case of America." In *Third Sector Policy at the Crossroads*, 29–47. Abingdon: Routledge.

Salamon, L. M., and H. K. Anheier. 1992. "In Search of the Non-Profit Sector. I: The Question of Definitions." *Voluntas: International Journal of Voluntary and Nonprofit Organizations* 3(2): 125–151.

Schofer, E., and J. W. Meyer. 2005. "The Worldwide Expansion of Higher Education in the Twentieth Century." *American Sociological Review* 70(6): 898–920.

Scott, W. R. 2015. "Higher Education in America: Multiple Fields Perspective." In *Remaking College: The Changing Ecology of Higher Education*, ed. M. W. Kirst and M. L. Stevens, 19–38. Stanford, CA: Stanford University Press.

Sedlacek, W. E. 2003. "Alternative Admissions and Scholarship Selection Measures in Higher Education." *Measurement and Evaluation in Counseling and Development* 35(January): 263–272.

Slaughter, S., and G. Rhoades. 2004. *Academic Capitalism and the New Economy: Markets, State, and Higher Education.* Baltimore: Johns Hopkins University Press.

Snyder, T. D., C. de Brey, and S. A. Dillow. 2019. *Digest of Education Statistics (53rd Edition): 2017.* National Center for Education Statistics. https:// nces.ed.gov/pubsearch/pubsinfo.asp?pubid= 2018070.

State Higher Education Officers. 2018. "State Higher Education Finance FY 2017." https://sheeo.org/ wp-content/uploads/2019/02/SHEEO_SHEF _FY2017_FINAL-1.pdf.

Stevens, M. L. 2007. *Creating a Class: College Admissions and the Education of Elites.* Cambridge, MA: Harvard University Press.

Stevens, M. L., E. A. Armstrong, and R. Arum. 2008. "Sieve, Incubator, Temple, Hub: Empirical and Theoretical Advances in the Sociology of Higher Education." *Annual Review of Sociology* 34: 127–151.

Stevens, M. L., and B. Gebre-Medhin. 2016. "Association, Service, Market: Higher Education in American Political Development." *Annual Review of Sociology* 42: 121–142.

Stevens, M., and M. W. Kirst. 2015. *Remaking College: The Changing Ecology of Higher Education.* Stanford, CA: Stanford University Press.

Stewart, D. M., P. R. Kane, and L. Scruggs. 2012. "Education and Training." In *The State of Nonprofit America,* ed. L. M. Salamon, 137–191. Washington, DC: Brookings Institution Press.

Tocqueville, A. de. (1836) 2003. *Democracy in America,* vol. 10. Washington, DC: Regnery.

Tompkins-Stange, M. E. 2016. *Policy Patrons: Philanthropy, Education Reform, and the Politics of Influence.* Cambridge, MA: Harvard Education Press.

Tyack, D., and T. James. 1986. "State Government and American Public Education: Exploring the 'Primeval Forest.'" *History of Education Quarterly* 26(1): 39–69.

Tyack, D., and W. Tobin. 1994. "The 'Grammar' of Schooling: Why Has It Been So Hard to Change?" *American Educational Research Journal* 31(3): 453–479.

Weick, K. E. 1976. "Educational Organizations as Loosely Coupled Systems." *Administrative Science Quarterly* 21(1): 1–19.

Worcester, K., and E. Sibley. 2001. *Social Science Research Council, 1923–1998.* New York: Social Science Research Council.

Chapter 19. Nonprofit Arts Organizations: Sustainability and Rationales for Support

Abzug, Rikki, and Joseph Galaskiewicz. 2001. "Nonprofit Boards: Crucibles of Expertise or Symbols of Local Identities?" *Nonprofit and Voluntary Sector Quarterly* 30(1): 51–73.

Accominotti, Fabien, Shamus Khan, and Adam Storer. 2018. "How Cultural Capital Emerged in Gilded Age America: Musical Purification and Cross-Class Inclusion at the New York Philharmonic." *American Journal of Sociology* 123(6): 1743–1783.

Alexander, Victoria. 1996. "From Philanthropy to Funding: The Effects of Corporate and Public Support on American Art Museums." *Poetics* 24(2–4): 87–129.

Americans for the Arts. 2017a. "Americans for the Arts Releases Statement on Tax Reform and the Charitable Deduction." https://blog .americansforthearts.org/news-room/americans -for-the-arts-news/americans-for-the-arts -releases-statement-on-tax-reform-and-the -charitable-deduction.

———. 2017b. "Statement on Tax Reform and the Charitable Deduction." https://www .americansforthearts.org/news-room/arts -mobilization-center/statement-on-tax-reform -and-the-charitable-deduction.

Anderson, Sheila M. 2007. "The Foundation of Theater Arts Philanthropy in America: W. McNeil Lowry and the Ford Foundation, 1957–65." In *Angels in the American Theater,* ed. Robert A. Schanke, 173–189. Carbondale: Southern Illinois University Press.

Andersson, Fredrik O., and Daniel G. Neely. 2017. "Examining the Role and Diversity of Fiscal Sponsors in the Nonprofit Sector." *Nonprofit and Voluntary Sector Quarterly* 46(3): 488–504. First published online August 25, 2016. https://journals.sagepub.com/doi/10.1177/ 0899764016664030.

Baumol, William J., and William G. Bowen. 1965. "On the Performing Arts: The Anatomy of Their Economic Problems." *American Economic Review* 55 (1/2): 495–502.

———. 1966. *Performing Arts—The Economic Dilemma: A Study of Problems Common to Theater, Opera, Music, and Dance.* New York: Twentieth Century Fund.

Berrey, Ellen. 2018. "Social Enterprise Law in Action: The Organizational Characteristics of U.S. Benefit Corporations." *Transactions: The Tennessee Journal of Business Law* 20(1): 21–114.

Borwick, Doug. 2012. *Building Communities, Not Audiences: The Future of the Arts in the United States.* Winston-Salem, NC: ArtsEngaged.

Brown, Alan S., and Jennifer L. Novak-Leonard. 2011. "Getting In On the Act: How Arts Groups Are Creating Opportunities for Active Participation." October. San Francisco: James Irvine Foundation. https://irvine-dot-org.s3 .amazonaws.com/documents/12/attachments/ GettingInOntheAct2014_DEC3.pdf.

Brown, Alan, and Rebecca Ratzkin. 2013. "New World Symphony: Summary Report: 2010–2013 Concert Format Assessment." San Francisco: Wolf Brown. http://cuttime.com/wp-content/ uploads/2013/11/nws-final-assessment-report-on -new-concert-formats.pdf.

Burgess, Chris N., and David B. Pankratz. 2008. "Interrelations in the Arts and Creative Sector." In *Understanding the Arts and Creative Sector in the U.S.*, ed. Joni M. Cherbo, Ruth A. Stewart, and Margaret J. Wyszomirski, 28–38. New Brunswick, NJ: Rutgers University Press.

Cherbo, Joni M., Harold L. Vogel, and Margaret J. Wyszomirski. 2008. "Toward an Arts and Creative Sector." In *Understanding the Arts and Creative Sector in the U.S.*, ed. Joni M. Cherbo, Ruth A. Stewart, and Margaret J. Wyszomirski, 9–27. New Brunswick, NJ: Rutgers University Press.

Conner, Lynne. 2013. *Audience Engagement and the Role of Arts Talk in the Digital Era.* New York: Palgrave Macmillan.

Cowen, Tyler. 2010. *Good and Plenty: The Creative Successes of American Arts Funding.* Princeton, NJ: Princeton University Press.

Cox, Gordon. 2014. "The Complicated Relationship Between Commercial and Not-for-Profit The-

atres." *American Theatre* (March). https://www .americantheatre.org/2014/03/13/relationship -between-commercial-not-for-profit-theatres/.

Dietz, Nathan, Melissa S. Brown, Lawrence McGill, Kiley K. Arroyo, Jim Bildner, and Sarah Reibstein. 2013. "Birth and Mortality Rates of Arts and Cultural Organizations, 1990–2010." Working paper, National Endowment for the Arts. https://www.arts.gov/artistic-fields/research -analysis/research-art-works-study-findings/ research-art-works-full-listing.

DiMaggio, Paul J. 1986a. "Cultural Entrepreneurship in Nineteenth-Century Boston." In *Nonprofit Enterprise in the Arts: Studies in Mission and Constraint*, ed. Paul J. DiMaggio, 41–61. New York: Oxford University Press.

———. 1986b. "Introduction." In *Nonprofit Enterprise in the Arts: Studies in Mission and Constraint*, ed. Paul J. DiMaggio, 3–13. New York: Oxford University Press.

———. 1986c. "Support for the Arts from Independent Foundations." In *Nonprofit Enterprise in the Arts: Studies in Mission and Constraint*, ed. Paul J. DiMaggio, 113–139. New York: Oxford University Press.

———. 2006. "Nonprofit Organizations and the Intersectoral Division of Labor in the Arts." In *The Nonprofit Sector: A Research Handbook*, 2nd ed., ed. Walter W. Powell and Richard Steinberg, 432–461. New Haven, CT: Yale University Press.

DiMaggio, Paul, and Francie Ostrower. 1992. *Race, Ethnicity and Participation in the Arts.* Washington, DC: Seven Locks Press.

Donahue, Tim, and Jim Patterson. 2010. *Stage Money: The Business of the Professional Theater.* Columbia: University of South Carolina Press.

Farrell, Betty. 2008. "Changing Culture and Practices Inside Organizations." In *Entering Cultural Communities: Diversity and Change in the Nonprofit Arts*, ed. Diane Grams and Betty Farrell, 38–63. New Brunswick, NJ: Rutgers University Press.

Giving USA. 2018. *Giving USA: The Annual Report on Philanthropy for the Year 2017.* Chicago: Giving USA.

Grams, Diane. 2008. "Building Arts Participation Through Transactions, Relationships, or Both." In *Entering Cultural Communities: Diversity and Change in the Nonprofit Arts*, ed. Diane Grams and Betty Farrell, 13–37. New Brunswick, NJ: Rutgers University Press.

Hager, Mark, and Mary Kopczynski. 2003. *The Value of the Performing Arts in Five Communities: A Comparison of Household Survey Data in Alaska, Cincinnati, Denver, Pittsburgh, and Seattle.* Washington, DC: Urban Institute Press.

Hansmann, Henry B. 1980. "The Role of Nonprofit Enterprise." *Yale Law Journal* 89(5): 835–901.

———. 1986. "Nonprofit Enterprise in the Performing Arts." In *Nonprofit Enterprise in the Arts: Studies in Mission and Constraint*, ed. Paul J. DiMaggio, 17–40. New York: Oxford University Press.

Harlow, Bob. 2014. "The Road to Results: Effective Practices for Building Arts Audiences." New York: The Wallace Foundation. http://www .wallacefoundation.org/knowledge-center/ Documents/The-Road-to-Results-Effective -Practices-for-Building-Arts-Audiences.pdf.

Ivey, Bill. 2005. "America Needs a New System for Supporting the Arts." *Chronicle of Higher Education*, February 4.

———. 2008. *Arts, Inc.: How Greed and Neglect Have Destroyed Our Cultural Rights.* Berkeley: University of California Press.

Joynes, D. Carroll, and Diane Grams. 2008. "Leaders Bridging the Culture Gap." In *Entering Cultural Communities: Diversity and Change in the Nonprofit Arts*, ed. Diane Grams and Betty Farrell, 64–90. New Brunswick, NJ: Rutgers University Press.

Keating, Elizabeth K., and Geeta Pradhan. 2012. "Passion and Purpose Revisited: Massachusetts Nonprofits and the Last Decade's Financial Roller Coaster." Boston Foundation. http:// www.tbf.org/~/media/TBFOrg/Files/Reports/ PP2012Final.pdf.

Kim, Mirae, Sheela Pandey, and Sanjay Pandey. 2018. "Why Do Nonprofit Performing Arts Organizations Offer Free Public Access?" *Public Administration Review* 78(1): 139–150.

Kreidler, John. 1996. "Leverage Lost: The Nonprofit Arts in the Post-Ford Era." *Motion*, February 16. http://www.inmotionmagazine.com/lost.html.

Kushner, Roland J., and Randy Cohen. 2016. "National Arts Index 2016: An Annual Measure of the Vitality of Arts and Culture in the United States: 2002–2013." Americans for the

Arts. http://www.americansforthearts.org/ sites/default/files/2016%20NAI%20%20Final %20Report%20%202-23-16.pdf.

LeRoux, Kelly, and Anna Bernadska. 2014. "Impact of the Arts on Individual Contributions to U.S. Civil Society." *Journal of Civil Society* 10(2): 144–164. https://www.arts.gov/sites/default/files/ Research-Art-Works-Chicago.pdf.

Lewis, Justin. 2000. "Designing a Cultural Policy." In *The Politics of Culture: Policy Perspectives for Individuals, Institutions and Communities*, ed. Gigi Bradford, Michael Gary, and Glenn Wallach, 79–93. New York: New Press.

Marks, Peter. 2011. "New Chairman Provokes Heated Debate: How Much Art Is Too Much?" *Washington Post*, February 13. http://www .washingtonpost.com/wp-dyn/content/article/ 2011/02/10/AR2011021007122.html.

McCarthy, Kevin, Arthur C. Brooks, Julia Lowell, and Laura Zakaras. 2001. "The Performing Arts: Trends and Their Implications." Santa Monica, CA: RAND Corporation. http://www.rand.org/ pubs/research_briefs/RB2504/index1.html.

McCarthy, Kevin F., and Kimberly Jinnett. 2001. *A New Framework for Building Participation in the Arts.* Santa Monica, CA: RAND Corporation. http://www.rand.org/content/dam/rand/pubs/ monograph_reports/2005/MR1323.pdf.

McCarthy, Kevin, Elizabeth Ondaatje, and Jennifer Novak. 2007. *Arts and Culture in the Metropolis: Strategies for Sustainability.* Santa Monica, CA: RAND Corporation.

McCarthy, Kevin, Elizabeth Ondaatje, Laura Zakaras, and Arthur Brooks. 2005. *Gifts of the Muse: Reframing the Debate About the Benefits of the Arts.* Santa Monica, CA: RAND Corporation.

McDonnell, Terence E., and Steven J. Tepper. 2014. "Culture in Crisis: Deploying Metaphor in Defense of Art." *Poetics* 43(1): 20–42.

McKeever, Brice S., Nathan Dietz, and Saunji D. Fyffe. 2016. *The Nonprofit Almanac: The Essential Facts and Figures for Managers, Researchers, and Volunteers*, 9th ed. Lanham, MD: Rowman and Littlefield.

Mulcahy, Kevin V. 2000. "The Government and Cultural Patronage: A Comparative Analysis of Cultural Patronage in the United States, France, Norway, and Canada." In *The Public Life of the Arts in America*, ed. Joni M. Cherbo and Margaret J. Wyszomirski, 138–170. New Brunswick, NJ: Rutgers University Press.

NEA (National Endowment for the Arts). 2012. *How the U.S. Funds the Arts*. Washington, DC: National Endowment for the Arts.

———. 2015. *A Decade of Arts Engagement: Findings from the Survey of Public Participation in the Arts, 2002–2012*. Washington, DC: National Endowment for the Arts. https://www.arts.gov/sites/default/files/2012-sppa-jan2015-rev.pdf.

———. 2018. *U.S. Trends in Arts Attendance and Literary Reading: 2002–2017: A First Look at Results from the 2017 Survey of Public Participation in the Arts*. Washington, DC: National Endowment for the Arts. https://www.arts.gov/sites/default/files/2017-sppapreviewREV-sept2018.pdf.

Nelson, Susan, Juliana Koo, Alison M. Crump, and Nathalie Woolworth. 2014. "Capitalization, Scale and Investment: Does Growth Equal Gain? A Study of Philadelphia's Arts and Culture Sector 2007 to 2011." William Penn Foundation. http://www.williampennfoundation.org/Doc/DoesGrowthEqualGain_2.pdf.

Novak-Leonard, Jennifer, Patience Baach, Alexandria Schultz, Betty Farrell, Will Anderson, and Nick Rabkin. 2014. *The Changing Landscape of Arts Participation: A Synthesis of Literature and Expert Interviews*. Chicago: NORC.

Novak-Leonard, Jennifer L., and Alan S. Brown. 2011. "Beyond Attendance: A Multi-Modal Understanding of Arts Participation." National Endowment for the Arts Research Report #54. https://www.arts.gov/sites/default/files/2008-SPPA-BeyondAttendance.pdf.

Nytch, Jeffrey. 2013. "Beyond Marketing: Entrepreneurship, Consumption, and the Quest to Rebuild Audiences for the Performing Arts." *Journal of Marketing Development and Competitiveness* 7(4): 87–93.

Ostrower, Francie. 2002. *Trustees of Culture*. Chicago: University of Chicago Press.

———. 2013. "Diversity on Cultural Boards: Implications for Organizational Value and Impact." Working paper, National Endowment for the Arts. https://www.arts.gov/sites/default/files/Research-Art-Works-UTX-Austin.pdf.

Ostrower, Francie, and Thad Calabrese. 2019. "Audience Building and Financial Health in the Nonprofit Performing Arts: Current Literature and Unanswered Questions." A Building Audiences for Sustainability: Research and Evaluation study report, University of Texas at Austin. https://www.wallacefoundation.org/knowledge-center/Documents/Audience-Building-Financial-Health-Nonprofit-Performing-Arts.pdf.

Ottoni-Wilhelm, Mark. 2009. "Arts and Culture Giving." Lilly Family School of Philanthropy. https://scholarworks.iupui.edu/bitstream/handle/1805/6068/2009PPSArtsandCulture.pdf.

Pompe, Jeffrey, and Lawrence Tamburri. 2016. "Fiddling in a Vortex: Have American Orchestras Squandered Their Supremacy on the American Cultural Scene?" *Journal of Arts Management, Law, and Society* 46(2): 63–72.

Powell, Walter, and Rebecca Friedkin. 1986. "Politics and Programs: Organizational Factors in Public Television Decision Making." In *Nonprofit Enterprise in the Arts: Studies in Mission and Constraint*, ed. Paul J. DiMaggio, 245–269. New York: Oxford University Press.

Pulh, Mathilde, Séverine Marteaux, and Rémi Mencarelli. 2008. "Positioning Strategies of Cultural Institutions: A Renewal of the Offer in the Face of Shifting Consumer Trends." *International Journal of Arts Management* 10(3): 4–20.

Reich, Robert. 2011. "Toward a Political Theory of Philanthropy." In *Giving Well: The Ethics of Philanthropy*, ed. Patricia Illingworth, Thomas Pogge, and Leif Wenar, 177–195. Oxford, UK: Oxford University Press.

Reidy, Brent. 2014. "Why 'Where'? Because 'Who': Arts Venues, Spaces, and Tradition." James Irvine Foundation. https://irvine-dot-org.s3.amazonaws.com/documents/161/attachments/WhyWhereBecauseWho_2014DEC3.pdf.

Reiser, Dana Brakman. 2012. "The Next Big Thing: Flexible Purpose Corporations." *American University Business Law Review* 2(1): 55–83.

Rosenstein, Carole. 2010. *Live from Your Neighborhood: A National Study of Outdoor Arts Festivals*. National Endowment for the Arts Research Report #51. https://www.arts.gov/sites/default/files/Festivals-Report.pdf.

———. 2018. *Understanding Cultural Policy*. New York: Routledge.

Rosenstein, Carole, and Amy Brimer. 2005. "Nonprofit Ethnic, Cultural, and Folk Organizations: Baseline Data from the National Center for

Charitable Statistics." *Journal of Arts Management, Law, and Society* 35(3): 189–203.

Rushton, Michael. 2014. "Hybrid Organizations in the Arts: A Cautionary View." *Journal of Arts Management, Law, and Society* 44(3): 145–152.

———. 2015. "Are Nonprofit Arts Organizations Special?" AJBlogs, April 16. https://www.artsjournal.com/worth/2015/04/are-nonprofit-arts-organizations-special/.

Sidford, Holly, and Alexis Frasz. 2017. *Not Just Money: Equity Issues in Cultural Philanthropy.* Helicon Collaborative. http://heliconcollab.net/wp-content/uploads/2017/08/NotJustMoney_Full_Report_July2017.pdf.

Smith, James A. 2010. "Foundations as Cultural Actors." In *American Foundations,* ed. Helmut Anheier and David Hammack, 262–282. Washington, DC: Brookings Institution Press.

Stallings, Stephanie, and Bronwyn Mauldin. 2016. "Public Engagement in the Arts: A Review of Recent Literature." Los Angeles County Arts Commission. https://www.lacountyarts.org/sites/default/files/pdfs/lacac_pubenglitrev.pdf.

Stern, Mark J. 2011. "Age and Arts Participation: A Case Against Demographic Destiny." National Endowment for the Arts Research Report #53. https://www.arts.gov/sites/default/files/2008-SPPA-Age.pdf.

Stern, Mark, and Susan Seifert. 2017. "The Social Wellbeing of New York City's Neighborhoods: The Contribution of Culture and the Arts." Social Impact of the Arts Project. https://repository.upenn.edu/cgi/viewcontent.cgi?article=1001&context=siap_culture_nyc.

Tepper, Steven. 2008. "The Next Great Transformation: Leveraging Policy and Research to Advance Cultural Vitality." In *Engaging Art: The Next Great Transformation of America's Cultural Life,* ed. Steven J. Tepper and Bill Ivey, 363–366. New York: Routledge.

Throsby, David. 2010. *The Economics of Cultural Policy.* Cambridge, UK: Cambridge University Press.

Toepler, Stefan, and Margaret J. Wyszomirski. 2012. "Arts and Culture." In *The State of Nonprofit America*, 2nd ed., ed. Lester M. Salamon, 229–265. Washington, DC: Brookings Institution Press.

Undercofler, James. 2012. "Organizational Models in the Arts and Culture Sector." In *Building Com-* munities, Not Audiences: The Future of the Arts in the United States*, ed. Doug Borwick, 132–145. Winston-Salem, NC: ArtsEngaged.

U.S. Trust and Lilly Family School of Philanthropy. 2018. *The 2018 U.S. Trust Study of High Net Worth Philanthropy: Portraits of Generosity.* Bank of America Corporation. https://scholarworks.iupui.edu/bitstream/handle/1805/17667/high-net-worth2018.pdf.

Voss, Zannie Giraud, and Glenn Voss. 2017. "Arts and Culture Are Closer Than You Realize: U.S. Nonprofit Arts and Cultural Organizations Are a Big Part of Community Life, Economy, and Employment—and Federal Funding Enhances the Impact." SMU National Center for Arts Research, March. https://sites.smu.edu/Meadows/NCARPaperonNationalArtsandCultural%20Field_FINAL.PDF.

Voss, Zannie Giraud and Glenn Voss, with Brooke Awtry and Jennifer Armstrong. 2018. "NCAR Arts Vibrancy Index IV: Hotbeds of America's Arts and Culture." SMU National Center for Arts Research, July. https://sites.smu.edu/Meadows/NCAR%20VibrancyIndex%20July2018_7.9.pdf.

Wali, Alaka, Rebecca Severson, and Mario Longoni. 2002. *Informal Arts: Finding Cohesion, Capacity and Other Cultural Benefits in Unexpected Places.* Chicago Center for Arts Policy. https://www.artplaceamerica.org/view/pdf?f=public://pictures/informal_arts_full_report.pdf.

Walker, Chris, and Stephanie Scott-Melnyk, with Kay Sherwood. 2002. "Reggae to Rachmaninoff: How and Why People Participate in Arts and Culture." Washington, DC: Urban Institute.

Zakaras, Laura, and Julia F. Lowell. 2008. *Cultivating Demand for the Arts: Arts Learning, Arts Engagement, and State Arts Policy.* Santa Monica, CA: RAND Corporation. http://www.rand.org/content/dam/rand/pubs/monographs/2008/RAND_MG640.pdf.

Part VI. Advocacy, Engagement, and the Public

Chapter 20. Advocacy, Civic Engagement, and Social Change

Alliance for Justice. 2015. *Philanthropy Advocacy Handbook.* Washington, DC: Alliance for Justice.

Almog-Bar, Michal, and Hillel Schmid. 2014. "Advocacy Activities of Nonprofit Human Service

Organizations." *Nonprofit and Voluntary Sector Quarterly* 43(1): 11–35.

Andrews, Kenneth T., and Bob Edwards. 2004. "Advocacy Organizations in the U.S. Political Process." *Annual Review of Sociology* 30: 479–506.

Ansell, Chris, and Alison Gash. 2008. "Collaborative Governance in Theory and Practice." *Journal of Public Administration Research and Theory* 18(4): 543–571.

Avner, Marcia. 2010. "Advocacy, Lobbying, and Social Change." In *The Jossey-Bass Handbook of Nonprofit Leadership and Management*, ed. David Renz, 347–374. San Francisco: Jossey-Bass.

Baggetta, Matt. 2009. "Civic Opportunities in Associations: Interpersonal Interaction, Governance Experience and Institutional Relationships." *Social Forces* 88(1): 175–199.

Barman, Emily. 2006. *Contesting Communities: The Transformation of Workplace Charity*. Stanford, CA: Stanford University Press.

Barman, Emily, and Heather MacIndoe. 2012. "Institutional Pressures and Organizational Capacity: The Case of Outcome Measurement." *Sociological Forum* 27(1): 70–93.

Bartley, Tim. 2007. "How Foundations Shape Social Movements: The Construction of an Organizational Field and the Rise of Forest Certification." *Social Problems* 54(3): 229–255.

Bass, Gary, David Arons, Kay Guinane, and Matthew F. Carter. 2007. *Seen But Not Heard: Strengthening Nonprofit Advocacy*. Washington, DC: Aspen Institute.

Baumgartner, Frank R., Jeffrey M. Berry, Marie Hojnacki, David C. Kimball, and Beth L. Leech. 2009. *Lobbying and Policy Change: Who Wins, Who Loses, and Why*. Chicago: University of Chicago Press.

Baumgartner, Frank R., and Beth L. Leech. 1998. *Basic Interests: The Importance of Groups in Politics and in Political Science*. Princeton, NJ: Princeton University Press.

Berry, Jeffrey M. 1977. *Lobbying for the People: The Political Behavior of Public Interest Groups*. Princeton, NJ: Princeton University Press.

———. 1999. *The New Liberalism: The Rising Power of Citizen Groups*. Washington, DC: Brookings Institution Press.

———. 2005. "Nonprofits and Civic Engagement." *Public Administration Review* 65(5): 568–578.

Berry, Jeffrey M., with David F. Arons. 2003. *A Voice for Nonprofits*. Washington, DC: Brookings Institution Press.

Boris, Elizabeth, and John Krehely. 2002. "Civic Participation and Advocacy." In *The Resilient Sector: The State of Nonprofit America*, ed. Lester Salamon, 299–330. Washington, DC: Brookings Institution Press.

Bromley, Patricia, and John W. Meyer. 2017. "'They Are All Organizations': The Cultural Roots of Blurring Beween the Nonprofit, Business, and Government Sectors." *Administration and Society* 49(7): 939–966.

Bromley, Patricia, and Walter W. Powell. 2012. "From Smoke and Mirrors to Walking the Talk: Decoupling in the Contemporary World." *Academy of Management Annals* 6(1): 483–530.

Bryson, John, Barbara Crosby, and Melissa Middleton Stone. 2015. "Designing and Implementing Cross-Sector Collaborations: Needed and Challenging." *Public Administration Review* 75(5): 647–663.

Buffardi, Anne, Robert Pekkanen, and Steven R. Smith. 2015. "Shopping or Specialization: Venue Targeting Among Nonprofits Engaged in Advocacy." *Policy Studies Journal* 43(3): 188–206.

Burstein, Paul. 1998. "Social Movement Organizations, Interest Groups, and Political Parties: A Theoretical Synthesis." In *Social Movements and American Political Institutions*, ed. Anne Costain and Andrew McFarland, 39–56. Lanham, MD: Rowman and Littlefield.

Bushouse, Brenda. 2016. "Leveraging Nonprofit and Voluntary Action Research to Inform Public Policy." *Policy Studies Journal*, 45(1): 50–73.

Campbell, David E. 2008. *Why We Vote: How Schools and Communities Shape Our Civic Life*. Princeton, NJ: Princeton University Press.

Chaves, Mark, Laura Stephens, and Joseph Galaskiewicz. 2004. "Does Government Funding Suppress Nonprofits' Political Activity?" *American Sociological Review* 69(2): 292–316.

Child, Curtis D., and Kirsten A. Grønbjerg. 2007. "Nonprofit Advocacy Organizations: Their Characteristics and Activities." *Social Science Quarterly* 88(1): 259–281.

Clemens, Elisabeth S. 1993. "Organizational Repertoires and Institutional Change: Women's Groups and the Transformation of U.S. Politics, 1890–1920." *American Journal of Sociology* 98(4): 755–798.

———. 1997. *The People's Lobby: Organizational Innovation and the Rise of Interest Group Politics in the United States, 1890–1925.* Chicago: University of Chicago Press.

———. 2006. "The Constitution of Citizens: Political Theories of Nonprofit Organizations." In *The Nonprofit Sector: A Research Handbook*, 2nd ed., ed. Walter W. Powell and Richard Steinberg, 207–220. New Haven, CT: Yale University Press.

Clemens, Elisabeth S., and Doug Guthrie, eds. 2010. *Politics and Partnerships: The Role of Voluntary Associations in America's Political Past and Present.* Chicago: University of Chicago Press.

Cohen, Joshua, and Joel Rogers. 1992. "Secondary Associations and Democratic Governance." *Politics and Society* 20(4): 393–472.

Cress, Daniel. 1997. "Nonprofit Incorporation Among Movements of the Poor." *Sociological Quarterly* 38(2): 343–360.

Crowley, Jocelyn E., and Theda Skocpol. 2001. "The Rush to Organize: Explaining Associational Formation in the United States, 1860s–1920s." *American Journal of Political Science* 45(4): 813–829.

Crutchfield, Leslie, and Heather McLeod Grant. 2012. *Forces for Good: The Six Practices of High-Impact Nonprofits.* San Francisco: Jossey-Bass.

de Figueiredo, John M., and Brian K. Richter. 2014. "Advancing the Empirical Research on Lobbying." *Annual Review of Political Science* 17(1): 163–185.

DiMaggio, Paul J., and Walter W. Powell. 1983. "The Iron Cage Revisited: Institutional Isomorphism and Collective Rationality in Organizational Fields." *American Sociological Review* 48(2): 147–160.

Edwards, Bob. 1994. "Semiformal Organizational Structure Among Social Movement Organizations." *Nonprofit and Voluntary Sector Quarterly* 23(4): 309–333.

Eikenberry, Angela M., and Jodie D. Kluver. 2004. "The Marketization of the Nonprofit Sector: Civil Society at Risk?" *Public Administration Review* 64(2): 132–140.

Frumkin, Peter. 2005. *On Being Nonprofit: A Conceptual and Policy Primer.* Cambridge, MA: Harvard University Press.

Fyall, Rachel. 2016a. "Nonprofits as Advocates and Providers: A Conceptual Framework." *Policy Studies Journal* 45(1): 121–143.

———. 2016b. "The Power of Nonprofits: Mechanisms for Nonprofit Policy Influence." *Public Administration Review* 76(6): 938–948.

Fyall, Rachel, and Michael McGuire. 2015. "Advocating for Policy Change in Nonprofit Coalitions." *Nonprofit and Voluntary Sector Quarterly* 44(6): 1274–1291.

Galaskiewicz, Joseph, Wolfgang Bielefeld, and Myron Dowell. 2006. "Networks and Organizational Growth: A Study of Community Based Nonprofits." *Administrative Science Quarterly* 51(3): 337–380.

Gamm, Gerald, and Robert D. Putnam. 1999. "The Growth of Voluntary Associations in America, 1840–1940." *Journal of Interdisciplinary History* 29(4): 511–557.

Goss, Kristin A. 2016. "Policy Plutocrats: How America's Wealthy Seek to Influence Governance." *PS: Political Science and Politics* 49(3): 442–448.

Grønbjerg, Kirsten A., and Aseem Prakash. 2017. "Advances in Research on Nonprofit Advocacy and Civic Engagement." *Voluntas: International Journal of Voluntary and Nonprofit Organizations* 28(3): 877–887.

Grønbjerg, Kirsten A., and Lester M. Salamon. 2002. "Devolution, Marketization, and the Changing Shape of Government-Nonprofit Relations." In *The State of Nonprofit America*, ed. Lester M. Salamon, 447–470. Washington, DC: Brookings Institution Press.

Guo, Chao, and Juliet Musso. 2007. "Representation in Nonprofit and Voluntary Organizations: A Conceptual Framework." *Nonprofit and Voluntary Sector Quarterly* 36(2): 308–326.

Guo, Chao, and Greg Saxton. 2010. "Voice In, Voice Out: Constituent Participation in Nonprofit Advocacy." *Nonprofit Policy Forum* 1(1): 1–25.

———. 2014. "Tweeting Social Change: How Social Media Are Changing Nonprofit Advocacy."

Nonprofit and Voluntary Sector Quarterly 43(1): 57–79.

Hall, Peter D. 1992. *"Inventing the Nonprofit Sector" and Other Essays on Philanthropy, Voluntarism, and Nonprofit Organizations.* Baltimore: Johns Hopkins University Press.

———. 2006. "A Historical Overview of Philanthropy, Voluntary Associations, and Nonprofit Organizations in the United States, 1600–2000." In *The Nonprofit Sector: A Research Handbook*, 2nd ed., ed. Walter W. Powell and Richard Steinberg, 32–65. New Haven, CT: Yale University Press.

Han, Hahrie. 2014. *How Organizations Develop Activists: Civic Associations and Leadership in the 21st Century.* New York: Oxford University Press.

———. 2016. "The Organizational Roots of Political Activism: Field Experiments on Creating a Relational Context." *American Political Science Review* 110(2): 296–307.

Han, Hahrie, and Lisa Argyle. 2016. *A Program Review of the Promoting Electoral Reform and Democratic Participation (PERDP Initiative of the Ford Foundation).* New York: Ford Foundation.

Hojnacki, Marie. 1997. "Interest Groups' Decisions to Join Alliances or Work Alone." *American Journal of Political Science* 41(1): 61–87.

Hojnacki, Marie, David C. Kimball, Frank R. Baumgartner, Jeffrey M. Berry, and Beth L. Leech. 2012. "Studying Organizational Advocacy and Influence: Reexamining Interest Group Research." *Annual Review of Political Science* 15: 379–399.

Hwang, Hokyu, and Walter W. Powell. 2009. "The Rationalization of Charity: The Influences of Professionalism in the Nonprofit Sector." *Administrative Science Quarterly* 54(2): 268–298.

Hwang, Hokyu, and David Suárez. 2019. "Beyond Charity: Institutional Influences and Advocacy in the San Francisco Nonprofit Sector." In *Actors, Agents and Actorhood: Research in the Sociology of Organizations*, vol. 61, ed. Hokyu Hwang, Jeannette Colyvas, and Gili Drori (forthcoming). Bingley, UK: Emerald.

Jenkins, J. Craig. 1987. "Nonprofit Organizations and Political Advocacy." In *The Nonprofit Sector: A Research Handbook*, ed. W. W. Powell, 296–320. New Haven, CT: Yale University Press.

———. 1998. "Channeling Social Protest: Foundation Patronage of Contemporary Social Movements." In *Private Action and the Public Good*, ed. Walter W. Powell and Elisabeth S. Clemens, 206–216. New Haven, CT: Yale University Press.

———. 2006. "Nonprofit Organizations and Political Advocacy." In *The Nonprofit Sector: A Research Handbook*, 2nd ed., ed. Walter W. Powell and Richard Steinberg, 307–332. New Haven, CT: Yale University Press.

Jenkins, J. Craig, and Chris M. Eckert. 1986. "Channeling Black Insurgency: Elite Patronage and Professional Social Movement Organizations in the Development of the Black Movement." *American Sociological Review* 51: 812–829.

Karl, Barry. 1998. "Volunteers and Professionals: Many Histories, Many Meanings." In *Private Action and the Public Good*, ed. Walter W. Powell and Elisabeth S. Clemens, 245–257. New Haven, CT: Yale University Press.

Kelleher, Christine, and Susan Webb Yackee. 2009. "A Political Consequence of Contracting: Organized Interests and State Agency Decision Making." *Journal of Public Administration Research and Theory* 19(3): 579–602.

Kettl, Donald. 1997. "The Global Revolution in Public Management: Driving Themes, Missing Links." *Journal of Policy Analysis and Management* 16(3): 446–462.

Kim, Mirae. 2017. "Characteristics of Civically Engaged Nonprofit Arts Organizations." *Nonprofit and Voluntary Sector Quarterly* 46(1): 175–198.

Kim, Mirae, and Dyana Mason. 2018. "Representation and Diversity, Advocacy, and Nonprofit Arts Organizations." *Nonprofit and Voluntary Sector Quarterly* 47(1): 49–71.

Knoke, David. 1986. "Associations and Interest Groups." *Annual Review of Sociology* 12: 1–21.

Leech, Beth. 2006. "Funding Faction or Buying Silence? Grants, Contracts, and Interest Group Lobbying Behavior." *Policy Studies Journal* 34(1): 17–35.

Leroux, Kelly. 2007. "Nonprofits as Civic Intermediaries: The Role of Community-Based Organizations in Promoting Political Participation." *Urban Affairs Review* 42(3): 410–422.

———. 2009. "The Effects of Descriptive Representation on Nonprofits' Civic Intermediary Roles: A

Test of the 'Racial Mismatch' Hypothesis in the Social Services Sector." *Nonprofit and Voluntary Sector Quarterly* 38(5): 741–760.

———. 2011. "Examining Implementation of the National Voter Registration Act by Nonprofit Organizations: An Institutional Explanation." *Policy Studies Journal* 39(4): 565–589.

Leroux, Kelly, and Holly T. Goerdel. 2009. "Political Advocacy by Nonprofit Organizations: A Strategic Management Explanation." *Public Performance and Management Review* 32(4): 514–536.

Levine, Jeremy R. 2016. "The Privatization of Political Representation: Community-Based Organizations as Nonelected Neighborhood Representatives." *American Sociological Review* 81(6): 1251–1275.

Lichterman, Paul, and Nina Eliasoph. 2014. "Civic Action." *American Journal of Sociology* 120(3): 798–863.

Longhofer, Wesley, Giacomo Negro, and Peter W. Roberts. 2018. "The Changing Effectiveness of Local Civic Action: The Critical Nexus of Community and Organization." *Administrative Science Quarterly* 64(1): 203–229.

Lu, Jiahuan. 2018a. "Fear the Government? A Meta-Analysis of the Impact of Government Funding on Nonprofit Advocacy Engagement." *American Review of Public Administration* 48(3): 203–218.

———. 2018b. "Organizational Antecedents of Nonprofit Engagement in Policy Advocacy: A Meta-Analytical Review." *Nonprofit and Voluntary Sector Quarterly* 47(4S): 177S–203S.

Lyon, Christina. 2014. "Nonprofit Groups and Partisan Politics." *CQ Researcher* 24(41): 961–984.

MacIndoe, Heather. 2010. "Advocacy Organizations." In *Leadership in Nonprofit Organizations: A Reference Handbook*, ed. Kathryn Agard, 155–162. Thousand Oaks, CA: SAGE.

———. 2014. "How Competition and Specialization Shape Nonprofit Engagement in Policy Advocacy." *Nonprofit Policy Forum* 5(2): 307–333.

MacIndoe, Heather, and Ryan Whalen. 2013. "Specialists, Generalists, and Policy Advocacy by Charitable Nonprofit Organizations." *Journal of Sociology and Social Welfare* 40(2): 119–149.

Maier, Florentine, and Michael Meyer. 2011. "Managerialism and Beyond: Discourses of Civil Society

Organizations and their Governance Implications." *Voluntas: International Journal of Voluntary and Nonprofit Organizations* 22(4): 731–756.

Maier, Florentine, Michael Meyer, and Martin Steinbereithner. 2016. "Nonprofit Organizations Becoming Business-like: A Systematic Review." *Nonprofit and Voluntary Sector Quarterly* 45(1): 64–86.

Marshall, Jeffery, and David Suárez. 2014. "The Flow of Management Practices: Monitoring and Evaluation in NGOs." *Nonprofit and Voluntary Sector Quarterly* 43(6): 1033–1051.

Marwell, Nicole P. 2004. "Privatizing the Welfare State: Nonprofit Community Organizations as Political Actors." *American Sociological Review* 69(2): 265–291.

———. 2007. *Bargaining for Brooklyn: Community Organizations in the Entrepreneurial City*. Chicago: University of Chicago Press.

———. 2010. "Privatizing the Welfare State: Nonprofit Community-Based Organizations as Political Actors." In *Politics and Partnerships: The Role of Voluntary Associations in America's Political Past and Present*, ed. Elisabeth S. Clemens and Doug Guthrie, 209–236. Chicago: University of Chicago Press.

McAdam, Doug, John McCarthy, and Mayer N. Zald, eds. 1996. *Comparative Perspectives on Social Movements: Political Opportunities, Mobilizing Structures, and Cultural Framings*. Cambridge, UK: Cambridge University Press.

McAdam, Doug, Robert Sampson, Simon Weffer-Elizondo, and Heather MacIndoe. 2005. "'There Will Be Fighting in the Streets': The Distorting Lens of Social Movement Theory." *Mobilization: An International Quarterly* 10(1): 1–18.

McFarland, Andrew. 1984. *Common Cause: Lobbying in the Public Interest*. Chatham, NJ: Chatham House.

———. 2010. "Interest Group Theory." In *The Oxford Handbook of American Political Parties and Interest Groups*, ed. L. Sandy Maisel and Jeffrey M. Berry, 37–56. Oxford, UK: Oxford University Press.

Meyer, David S., and Sidney Tarrow, eds. 1998. *The Social Movement Society*. Lanham, MD: Rowman and Littlefield.

Meyer, Michael, Renate Buber, and Anahid Aghamanoukjan. 2013. "In Search of Legitimacy: Managerialism and Legitimation in Civil Society Organizations." *Voluntas: International Journal of Voluntary and Nonprofit Organizations* 24(1): 167–193.

Milward, H. Brinton, and Keith G. Provan. 2000. "Governing the Hollow State." *Journal of Public Administration Research and Theory* 10(2): 359–380.

Minkoff, Debra. 1994. "From Service Provision to Institutional Advocacy: The Shifting Legitimacy of Organizational Forms." *Social Forces* 72(4): 943–969.

———. 1999. "Bending with the Wind: Organizational Change in American Women's and Minority Organizations." *American Journal of Sociology* 104(6): 1666–1673.

———. 2002. "The Emergence of Hybrid Organizational Forms: Combining Identity-Based Service Provision and Political Action." *Nonprofit and Voluntary Sector Quarterly* 31(3): 377–401.

———. 2016. "The Payoffs of Organizational Membership for Political Activism in Established Democracies." *American Journal of Sociology* 122(2): 425–468.

Minkoff, Debra, Silke Aisenbrey, and Jon Agnone. 2008. "Organizational Diversity in the U.S. Advocacy Sector." *Social Problems* 55(4): 525–548.

Minkoff, Debra, and Walter Powell. 2006. "Nonprofit Mission: Constancy, Responsiveness, or Deflection?" In *The Nonprofit Sector: A Research Handbook*, 2nd ed., ed. Walter W. Powell, 591–609. New Haven, CT: Yale University Press.

Mintrom, Michael, and Sandra Vergari. 1996. "Advocacy Coalitions, Policy Entrepreneurs, and Policy Change." *Policy Studies Journal* 24(3): 420–434.

Mosley, Jennifer E. 2010. "Organizational Resources and Environmental Incentives: Understanding the Policy Advocacy Involvement of Human Service Nonprofits." *Social Service Review* 84(1): 57–76.

———. 2011. "Institutionalization, Privatization, and Political Opportunity: What Tactical Choices Reveal About the Policy Advocacy of Human Services Nonprofits." *Nonprofit and Voluntary Sector Quarterly* 40(3): 435–457.

———. 2012. "Keeping the Lights On: How Government Funding Concerns Drive the Advocacy Agendas of Nonprofit Homeless Service Providers." *Journal of Public Administration Research and Theory* 22(4): 841–866.

———. 2013. "The Beliefs of Homeless Service Managers About Policy Advocacy: Definitions, Legal Understanding, and Motivations to Participate." *Administration in Social Work* 37(1): 73–89.

Mosley, Jennifer E., and Joseph J. Galaskiewicz. 2015. "The Relationship Between Philanthropic Foundation Funding and State-Level Policy in the Era of Welfare Reform." *Nonprofit and Voluntary Sector Quarterly* 44(6): 1225–1254.

Nicholson-Crotty, Jill. 2007. "Politics, Policy, and the Motivations for Advocacy in Nonprofit Reproductive Health and Family Planning Providers." *Nonprofit and Voluntary Sector Quarterly* 36(1): 5–21.

———. 2011. "Nonprofit Organizations, Bureaucratic Agencies, and Policy: Exploring the Determinants of Administrative Advocacy." *American Review of Public Administration* 41(1): 61–74.

Osborne, Stephen P., ed. 2010. *The New Public Governance? Emerging Perspectives on the Theory and Practice of Public Governance*. London: Routledge.

Paxton, Pamela. 1999. "Is Social Capital Declining in the United States? A Multiple Indicator Assessment." *American Journal of Sociology* 105(1): 88–127.

Pekkanen, Robert, Steven Smith, and Yutaka Tsujinaka, eds. 2014. *Engaging Community and Government in an Era of Retrenchment*. Baltimore: Johns Hopkins University Press.

Powell, Walter W. 1990. "Neither Market nor Hierarchy: Network Forms of Organization." *Research in Organizational Behavior* 12: 295–336.

Powell, Walter W., Aaron Horvath, and Christof Brandtner. 2016. "Click and Mortar: Organizations on the Web." *Research in Organizational Behavior* 36: 101–120.

Putnam, Robert D. 1995. "Bowling Alone: America's Declining Social Capital." *Journal of Democracy* 6(1): 65–78.

———. 2000. *Bowling Alone: The Collapse and Revival of American Community*. New York: Simon and Schuster.

Quinn, Rand, Megan Tompkins-Stange, and Debra Meyerson. 2014. "Beyond Grantmaking: Philanthropic Foundations as Agents of Change and Institutional Entrepreneurs." *Nonprofit and Voluntary Sector Quarterly* 43(6): 950–968.

Reckhow, Sarah. 2013. *Follow the Money: How Foundation Dollars Change Public School Politics.* Oxford, UK: Oxford University Press.

Reid, Elizabeth. 1999. "Nonprofit Advocacy and Political Participation." In *Nonprofits and Government: Collaboration and Conflict*, ed. Elizabeth T. Boris and C. Eugene Steuerle, 291–327. Washington, DC: Urban Institute Press.

———. 2000. "Understanding the Word 'Advocacy': Context and Use." In *Structuring the Inquiry into Advocacy*, vol. 1, ed. Elizabeth Reid, 1–7. Washington, DC: Urban Institute Press.

Rich, Andrew. 2004. *Think Tanks, Public Policy, and the Politics of Expertise.* Cambridge, UK: Cambridge University Press.

Salamon, Lester M. 1995. *Partners in Public Service: Government-Nonprofit Relations in the Modern Welfare State.* Baltimore: Johns Hopkins University Press.

Sampson, Robert J., Doug McAdam, Heather MacIndoe, and Simon Weffer-Elizondo. 2005. "Civil Society Reconsidered: The Durable Nature and Community Structure of Collective Civic Action." *American Journal of Sociology* 111(3): 673–714.

Schadler, Holly. 2018. *The Connection: Strategies for Creating and Operating 501(c)(3)s, 501(c)(4)s, and Political Organizations*, 4th ed. Washington, DC: Alliance for Justice.

Schlesinger, Arthur M. 1944. "Biography of a Nation of Joiners." *American Historical Review* 50(1): 1–25.

Schlozman, Kay L., Sidney Verba, and Henry E. Brady. 2012. *The Unheavenly Chorus: Unequal Political Voice and the Broken Promise of American Democracy.* Princeton, NJ: Princeton University Press.

Scott, W. Richard. 2001. *Institutions and Organizations*, 2nd ed. Thousand Oaks, CA: SAGE.

Skocpol, Theda. 2003. *Diminished Democracy: From Membership to Management in American Civic Life.* Norman: University of Oklahoma Press.

———. 2004. "Voice and Inequality: The Transformation of American Civic Democracy." *Perspectives on Politics* 2(1): 3–20.

Skocpol, Theda, and Morris P. Fiorina, eds. 1999. *Civic Engagement in American Democracy.* Washington, DC: Brookings Institution Press.

Skocpol, Theda, Marshall Ganz, and Ziad Munson. 2000. "A Nation of Organizers: The Institutional Origins of Civic Voluntarism in the United States." *American Political Science Review* 94(3): 527–546.

Small, Mario L. 2006. "Neighborhood Institutions as Resource Brokers: Childcare Centers, Interorganizational Ties and Resource Access Among the Poor." *Social Problems* 53(2): 274–292.

Smith, Steven R., and Michael Lipsky. 1993. *Nonprofits for Hire: The Welfare State in the Age of Contracting.* Cambridge, MA: Harvard University Press.

Staggenborg, Suzanne. 1988. "The Consequences of Professionalization in the Pro-Choice Movement." *American Sociological Review* 53: 585–605.

Strolovitch, Dara Z. 2007. *Affirmative Advocacy: Race, Class, and Gender in Interest Group Politics.* Chicago: University of Chicago Press.

Suárez, David F. 2009. "Nonprofit Advocacy and Civic Engagement on the Internet." *Administration and Society* 41(3): 267–289.

———. 2011. "Collaboration and Professionalization: The Contours of Public Sector Funding for Nonprofit Organizations." *Journal of Public Administration Research and Theory* 21(2): 307–326.

———. 2012. "Grantmaking as Advocacy: The Emergence of Social Justice Philanthropy." *Nonprofit Management and Leadership* 22(3): 259–280.

Suárez, David F., and Nicole Esparza. 2017. "Institutional Change and Management of Public-Nonprofit Partnerships." *American Review of Public Administration* 47(6): 648–660.

Suárez, David F., Kelly Husted, and Andreu Casas. 2018. "Community Foundations as Advocates: Social Change Discourse in the Philanthropic Sector." *Interest Groups and Advocacy* 7(3): 206–232.

Suárez, David, and Hokyu Hwang. 2008. "Civic Engagement and Nonprofit Lobbying in California." *Nonprofit and Voluntary Sector Quarterly* 37(1): 92–112.

Theiss-Morse, Elizabeth, and John R. Hibbing. 2005. "Citizenship and Civic Engagement." *Annual Review of Political Science* 8: 227–249.

Tocqueville, Alexis de. (1835) 1969. *Democracy in America*, ed. J. P. Mayer, trans. George Lawrence. Garden City, NY: Doubleday.

Tompkins-Stange, Megan. 2016. *Policy Patrons: Philanthropy, Education Reform, and the Politics of Influence*. Cambridge, MA: Harvard Education Press.

Verba, Sidney, and Norman Nie. 1972. *Participation in America: Political Democracy and Social Equality*. New York: Harper and Row.

Walker, Edward T. 2014. *Grassroots for Hire: Public Affairs Consultants in American Democracy*. New York: Cambridge University Press.

Walker, Edward T., John D. McCarthy, and Frank Baumgartner. 2011. "Replacing Members with Managers? Mutualism Among Membership and Nonmembership Advocacy Organizations in the United States." *American Journal of Sociology* 116(4): 1284–1337.

Walker, Jack L. 1991. *Mobilizing Interest Groups in America: Patrons, Professions, and Social Movements*. Ann Arbor: University of Michigan Press.

Weir, Margaret, and Marshall Ganz. 1997. "Reconnecting People and Politics." In *The New Majority: Toward a Popular Progressive Politics*, ed. Stanley Greenberg and Theda Skocpol, 149–171. New Haven, CT: Yale University Press.

Chapter 21. The Changing Face of Nonprofit Advocacy: Democratizing Potentials and Risks in an Unequal Context

Aldrich, H. E., and C. M. Fiol. 1994. "Fools Rush In? The Institutional Context of Industry Creation." *Academy of Management Review* 19(4): 645–670.

Ananny, M., and D. Kreiss. 2011. "A New Contract for the Press: Copyright, Public Domain Journalism, and Self-Governance in a Digital Age." *Critical Studies in Media Communication* 28(4): 314–333.

Andrews, K. T., and B. Edwards. 2004. "Advocacy Organizations in the U.S. Political Process." *Annual Review of Sociology* 30: 479–506.

Andrews, K. T., B. Edwards, A. Al-Turk, and A. K. Hunter. 2016. "Sampling Social Movement Organizations." *Mobilization: An International Quarterly* 21(2): 231–246.

Andrews, K. T., M. Ganz, M. Baggetta, H. Han, and C. Lim. 2010. "Leadership, Membership, and Voice: Civic Associations That Work." *American Journal of Sociology* 115(4): 1191–1242.

Asencio, H., and R. Sun, eds. 2015. *Cases on Strategic Social Media Utilization in the Nonprofit Sector*. Hershey, PA: IGI Global.

Bail, C. A., T. W. Brown, and M. Mann. 2017. "Channeling Hearts and Minds: Advocacy Organizations, Cognitive-Emotional Currents, and Public Conversation." *American Sociological Review* 82(6): 1188–1213.

Barber, B. 1984. *Strong Democracy: Participatory Politics for a New Age*. Berkeley: University of California Press.

Bass, F. 2016. "After Citizens United, a Surge in 'Dark Money' Groups." Maplight, May 12. https://maplight.org/story/after-citizens-united-a-surge-in-dark-money-groups/.

Bennett, W. L., and A. Segerberg. 2013. *The Logic of Connective Action: Digital Media and the Personalization of Contentious Politics*. New York: Cambridge University Press.

Berghmans, M., M. Simons, and J. Vandenabeele. 2017. "What Is Negotiated in Negotiated Accountability? The Case of INGOs." *Voluntas: International Journal of Voluntary and Nonprofit Organizations* 28(4): 1529–1561.

Berman, E. P. 2011. *Creating the Market University: How Academic Science Became an Economic Engine*. Princeton, NJ: Princeton University Press.

Bertrand, M., M. Bombardini, R. Fisman, and F. Trebbi. 2018. *Tax-Exempt Lobbying: Corporate Philanthropy as a Tool for Political Influence*. NBER Working Paper No. 24451.

Best, R. K. 2012. "Disease Politics and Medical Research Funding: Three Ways Advocacy Shapes Policy." *American Sociological Review* 77(5): 780–803.

Bishop, M., and M. Green, 2010. *Philanthrocapitalism: How Giving Can Save the World*. New York: Bloomsbury Press.

Blee, K. M. 2012. *Democracy in the Making: How Activist Groups Form*. New York: Oxford University Press.

Bonikowski, B., and P. DiMaggio, 2016. "Varieties of American Popular Nationalism." *American Sociological Review* 81(5): 949–980.

Bosso, C. J. 2005. *Environment, Inc.: From Grassroots to Beltway.* Lawrence: University Press of Kansas.

Boutyline, A., and R. Willer. 2016. "The Social Structure of Political Echo Chambers: Variation in Ideological Homophily in Online Networks." *Political Psychology* 38(3): 551–569.

Brady, H. E., K. L. Schlozman, and S. Verba. 1999. "Prospecting for Participants: Rational Expectations and the Recruitment of Political Activists." *American Political Science Review* 93(1): 153–168.

Braunstein, R., B. R. Fulton, and R. L. Wood. 2014. "The Role of Bridging Cultural Practices in Racially and Socioeconomically Diverse Civic Organizations." *American Sociological Review* 79(4): 705–725.

Brown, H. 2015. "The Institutional Digital Divide: Immigrant-Serving Nonprofit Organization Adoption of Social Media." *Social Science Computer Review* 33(6): 680–695.

———. 2016. *Immigrants and Electoral Politics: Nonprofit Organizing in a Time of Demographic Change.* Ithaca, NY: Cornell University Press.

Bump, P. 2015. "How Citizens United Is—and Isn't—to Blame for the Dark Money President Obama Hates So Much." *Washington Post*, January 21. https://www.washingtonpost.com/news/the-fix/wp/2015/01/21/how-citizens-united-is-and-isnt-to-blame-for-the-dark-money-president-obama-hates-so-much/.

Cnaan, R. A., K. Jones, A. Dickin, and M. Salomon. 2011. "Nonprofit Watchdogs: Do They Serve the Average Donor?" *Nonprofit Management and Leadership* 21(4): 381–397.

Cordery, C., and R. Sinclair. 2013. "Measuring Performance in the Third Sector." *Qualitative Research in Accounting and Management* 10(3/4): 196–212.

Costa, D. L., and M. E. Kahn. 2003. "Civic Engagement and Community Heterogeneity: An Economist's Perspective." *Perspective on Politics* 1(1): 103–111.

Cunningham, K., and M. Ricks. 2004. "Why Measure? Nonprofits Use Metrics to Show That They Are Efficient. But What If Donors Don't Care?" *Stanford Social Innovation Review* 2(1): 44–51.

Dart, R. 2004. "Being 'Business-like' in a Nonprofit Organization: A Grounded and Inductive Typology." *Nonprofit and Voluntary Sector Quarterly* 33(2): 290–310.

Earl, J. 2006. "Pursuing Social Change Online: The Use of Four Protest Tactics on the Internet." *Social Science Computer Review* 24(3): 362–377.

———. 2015. "The Future of Social Movement Organizations: The Waning Dominance of SMOs Online." *American Behavioral Scientist* 59(1): 35–52.

Earl, J., and K. Kimport. 2011. *Digitally Enabled Social Change: Activism in the Internet Age.* Cambridge, MA: MIT Press.

Earl, J., K. Kimport, G. Prieto, C. Rush, and K. Reynoso. 2010. "Changing the World One Webpage at a Time: Conceptualizing and Explaining Internet Activism." *Mobilization: An International Quarterly* 15(4): 425–446.

Earl, J., A. Martin, J. D. McCarthy, and S. A. Soule. 2004. "The Use of Newspaper Data in the Study of Collective Action." *Annual Review of Sociology* 30: 65–80.

Earl, J., H. McKee Hurwitz, A. Mejia Mesinas, M. Tolan, and A. Arlotti. 2013. "This Protest Will Be Tweeted: Twitter and Protest Policing During the Pittsburgh G20." *Information, Communication and Society* 16(4): 459–478.

Earl, J., and A. Schussman. 2008. "Contesting Cultural Control: Youth Culture and Online Petitioning." In *Civic Life Online: Learning How Digital Media Can Engage Youth*, ed. W. L. Bennett, 71–95. Cambridge, MA: MIT Press.

Edwards, M. 2008. *Just Another Emperor? The Myths and Realities of Philanthrocapitalism.* New York: Demos.

Espeland, W. N., and M. Sauder. 2007. "Rankings and Reactivity: How Public Measures Recreate Social Worlds." *American Journal of Sociology* 113(1): 1–40.

Fiorina, M. P. 1999. "Extreme Voices: A Dark Side of Civic Engagement." In *Civic Engagement in American Democracy*, ed. T. Skocpol and M. P. Fiorina, 395–425. Washington, DC: Brookings Institution Press.

Fung, A. 2003. "Associations and Democracy: Between Theories, Hopes, and Realities." *Annual Review of Sociology* 29(1): 515–539.

Gainous, J., and K. M. Wagner. 2013. *Tweeting to Power: The Social Media Revolution in American Politics.* New York: Oxford University Press.

Galaskiewicz, J., and M. S. Colman. 2006. "Collaboration Between Corporations and Nonprofit

Organizations." In *The Nonprofit Sector: A Research Handbook*, 2nd ed., ed. W. W. Powell and R. Steinberg, 180–204. New Haven, CT: Yale University Press.

Ganuza, E., and G. Baiocchi. 2012. "The Power of Ambiguity: How Participatory Budgeting Travels the Globe." *Journal of Public Deliberation* 8(2): Article 8.

Gibelman, M., and S. R. Gelman. 2004. "A Loss of Credibility: Patterns of Wrongdoing Among Nongovernmental Organizations." *Voluntas: International Journal of Voluntary and Nonprofit Organizations* 15(4): 355–381.

Gill, S., and T. Freedman. 2014. "Climbing the Mountain: An Approach to Planning and Evaluating Public-Policy Advocacy." *Foundation Review* 6(3): 7.

Givel, M. 2007. "Consent and Counter-Mobilization: The Case of the National Smokers Alliance." *Journal of Health Communication: International Perspectives* 12(4): 339–357.

Gladwell, M. 2010. "Small Change." *New Yorker*. https://www.newyorker.com/magazine/2010/10/04/small-change-malcolm-gladwell.

Goldkind, L. 2014. "E-Advocacy in Human Services: The Impact of Organizational Conditions and Characteristics on Electronic Advocacy Activities Among Nonprofits." *Journal of Policy Practice* 13(4): 300–315.

Gross, N., T. Medvetz, and R. Russell. 2011. "The Contemporary American Conservative Movement." *Annual Review of Sociology* 37(1): 325–354.

Guo, C., and G. D. Saxton. 2014. "Tweeting Social Change: How Social Media Are Changing Nonprofit Advocacy." *Nonprofit and Voluntary Sector Quarterly* 43(1): 57–79.

Hall, P. D. 2006 "A Historical Overview of Philanthropy, Voluntary Associations, and Nonprofit Organizations in the United States, 1600–2000." In *The Nonprofit Sector: A Research Handbook*, 2nd ed., ed. W. W. Powell and R. Steinberg, 32–65. New Haven, CT: Yale University Press.

Han, H. 2014. *How Organizations Develop Activists: Civic Associations and Leadership in the 21st Century.* New York: Oxford University Press.

———. 2016. "The Organizational Roots of Political Activism: Field Experiments on Creating a Relational Context." *American Political Science Review* 110(2): 296–307.

Hansen, W. L., M. S. Rocca, and B. L. Ortiz. 2015. "The Effects of Citizens United on Corporate Spending in the 2012 Presidential Election." *Journal of Politics* 77(2): 535–545.

Himmelstein, J. L. 1992. *To the Right: The Transformation of American Conservatism.* Berkeley: University of California Press.

Howard, P. N., and M. M. Hussain. 2013. *Democracy's Fourth Wave? Digital Media and the Arab Spring.* New York: Oxford University Press.

Hwang, H., and W. W. Powell. 2009. "The Rationalization of Charity: The Influences of Professionalism in the Nonprofit Sector." *Administrative Science Quarterly* 54(2): 268–298.

Jenkins, G. W. 2010. "Who's Afraid of Philanthrocapitalism." *Case Western Reserve Law Review* 61(3): 753–821.

Jenkins, J. C. 1998. "Channeling Social Protest: Foundation Patronage of Contemporary Social Movements." In *Foundations for Social Change*, ed. D. R. Faber and D. McCarthy, 206–233. Lanham, MD: Rowman and Littlefield.

———. 2006. "Nonprofit Organizations and Political Advocacy." In *The Nonprofit Sector: A Research Handbook*, 2nd ed., eds. W. W. Powell and R. Steinberg, 307–332. New Haven, CT: Yale University Press.

Jepson, P. 2005. "Governance and Accountability of Environmental NGOs." *Environmental Science and Policy* 8(5): 515–524.

Jordan, G., and W. A. Maloney. 1997. *The Protest Business? Mobilising Campaign Groups.* Manchester, UK: Manchester University Press.

Kanter, B., and A. Fine. 2010. *The Networked Nonprofit: Connecting with Social Media to Drive Change.* New York: Wiley.

Karpf, D. 2010. "Online Political Mobilization from the Advocacy Group's Perspective: Looking Beyond Clicktivism." *Policy and Internet* 2(4): 7–41.

———. 2012. *The MoveOn Effect: The Unexpected Transformation of American Political Advocacy.* New York: Oxford University Press.

———. 2016. *Analytic Activism: Digital Listening and the New Political Strategy.* New York: Oxford University Press.

King, D. 2017. "Becoming Business-like: Governing the Nonprofit Professional." *Nonprofit and Voluntary Sector Quarterly* 46(2): 241–260.

Kraatz, M. S., and E. J. Zajac. 1996. "Exploring the Limits of the New Institutionalism: The Causes and Consequences of Illegitimate Organizational Change." *American Sociological Review* 61(5): 812–836.

Lee, C. W., K. McNulty, and S. Shaffer. 2013. "'Hard Times, Hard Choices': Marketing Retrenchment as Civic Empowerment in an Era of Neoliberal Crisis." *Socio-Economic Review* 11(1): 81–106.

Lee, C. W., M. McQuarrie, and E. T. Walker. 2015. *Democratizing Inequalities: Dilemmas of the New Public Participation*. New York: NYU Press.

Levitsky, S., and D. Ziblatt. 2018. *How Democracies Die*. New York: Crown.

Lichterman, P. 2006. "Social Capital or Group Style? Rescuing Tocqueville's Insights on Civic Engagement." *Theory and Society* 35(5–6): 529–563.

Lipton, E., and R. Abrams. 2016. "EpiPen Maker Lobbies to Shift High Costs to Others." *New York Times*, September 16. https://www.nytimes.com/2016/09/16/business/epipen-maker-mylan-preventative-drug-campaign.html.

Little, A. T. 2015. "Communication Technology and Protest." *Journal of Politics* 78(1): 152–166.

Lowell, S., B. Trelstad, and B. Meehan. 2005. "The Ratings Game." *Stanford Social Innovation Review* 3(2): 38–45.

Martin, I. W. 2013. *Rich People's Movements: Grassroots Campaigns to Untax the One Percent*. New York: Oxford University Press.

———. 2015. "The Fiscal Sociology of Public Consultation." In *Democratizing Inequalities: Dilemmas of the New Public Participation*, ed. C. W. Lee, M. McQuarrie, and E. T. Walker, 102–124. New York: NYU Press.

Marwell, N. P. 2004. "Privatizing the Welfare State: Nonprofit Community-Based Organizations as Political Actors." *American Sociological Review* 69(2): 265–291.

Mayer, J. 2016. *Dark Money: The Hidden History of the Billionaires Behind the Rise of the Radical Right*. New York: Doubleday.

McCarthy, J. D., and E. T. Walker. 2004. "Alternative Organizational Repertoires of Poor People's Social Movement Organizations." *Nonprofit and Voluntary Sector Quarterly* 33(3 suppl.): 97S–119S.

McCarthy, J. D., and M. N. Zald. 1973. *The Trend of Social Movements in America: Professionalization and Resource Mobilization*. Morristown, NJ: General Learning Press.

———. 1977. "Resource Mobilization and Social Movements: A Partial Theory." *American Journal of Sociology* 82(6): 1212–1241.

McGann, J. G., and R. K. Weaver, eds. 2002. *Think Tanks and Civil Societies: Catalysts for Ideas and Action*, rev. ed. New Brunswick, NJ: Transaction.

McInerney, P.-B. 2014. *From Social Movement to Moral Market: How the Circuit Riders Sparked an IT Revolution and Created a Technology Market*. Palo Alto, CA: Stanford University Press.

McNutt, J. 2008. "Advocacy Organizations and the Organizational Digital Divide." *Currents: Scholarship in the Human Services* 7(2): 1–16.

Medvetz, T. 2012. *Think Tanks in America*. Chicago: University of Chicago Press.

Minkoff, D., S. Aisenbrey, and J. Agnone. 2008. "Organizational Diversity in the U.S. Advocacy Sector." *Social Problems* 55(4): 525–548.

Mizruchi, M. S. 2013. *The Fracturing of the American Corporate Elite*. Cambridge, MA: Harvard University Press.

Munson, Z. W. 2008. *The Making of Pro-Life Activists: How Social Movement Mobilization Works*. Chicago: University of Chicago Press.

Norris, P. 2011. *Democratic Deficit: Critical Citizens Revisited*. New York: Cambridge University Press.

Peschek, J. G. 1987. *Policy-Planning Organizations: Elite Agendas and America's Rightward Turn*. Philadelphia: Temple University Press.

Phillips-Fein, K. 2009. *Invisible Hands: The Making of the Conservative Movement from the New Deal to Reagan*. New York: Norton.

Polonsky, M., and S. L. Grau. 2010. "Assessing the Social Impact of Charitable Organizations— Four Alternative Approaches." *International Journal of Nonprofit and Voluntary Sector Marketing* 16(2): 195–211.

Portes, A. 1998. "Social Capital: Its Origins and Applications in Modern Sociology." *Annual Review of Sociology* 24(1): 1–24.

Portes, A., and P. Landolt. 2000. "Social Capital: Promise and Pitfalls of Its Role in Development." *Journal of Latin American Studies* 32(2): 529–547.

Portes, A., and E. Vickstrom. 2011. "Diversity, Social Capital, and Cohesion." *Annual Review of Sociology* 37(1): 461–479.

Prewitt, K. 2006. "Foundations." In *The Nonprofit Sector: A Research Handbook*, 2nd ed., ed. W. W. Powell and R. Steinberg, 355–377. New Haven, CT: Yale University Press.

Putnam, L., and T. Skocpol. 2018. "Middle America Reboots Democracy." *Democracy Journal*, February 20. https://democracyjournal .org/arguments/middle-america-reboots -democracy/.

Putnam, R. D. 2000. *Bowling Alone: The Collapse and Revival of American Community.* New York: Simon and Schuster.

———. 2007. "E Pluribus Unum: Diversity and Community in the Twenty-First Century—The 2006 Johan Skytte Prize Lecture." *Scandinavian Political Studies* 30(2): 137–174.

Rich, A. 2005. *Think Tanks, Public Policy, and the Politics of Expertise.* Cambridge, UK: Cambridge University Press.

Rothman, S. M., V. H. Raveis, A. Friedman, and D. J. Rothman. 2011. "Health Advocacy Organizations and the Pharmaceutical Industry: An Analysis of Disclosure Practices." *American Journal of Public Health* 101(4): 602–609.

Sampson, R. J., D. McAdam, H. MacIndoe, and S. Weffer-Elizondo. 2005. "Civil Society Reconsidered: The Durable Nature and Community Structure of Collective Civic Action." *American Journal of Sociology* 111(3): 673–714.

Sarat, A., and S. A. Scheingold. 1998. *Cause Lawyering: Political Commitments and Professional Responsibilities.* New York: Oxford University Press.

Scheingold, S., and A. Sarat. 2004. *Something to Believe In: Politics, Professionalism and Cause Lawyering.* Palo Alto, CA: Stanford University Press.

Sheingate, A. D. 2016. *Building a Business of Politics: The Rise of Political Consulting and the Transformation of American Democracy.* New York: Oxford University Press.

Shulman, S. W. 2009. "The Case Against Mass E-Mails: Perverse Incentives and Low Quality Public Participation in U.S. Federal Rulemaking." *Policy and Internet* 1(1): 23–53.

Skocpol, T. 1999. "Associations Without Members." *American Prospect* 10 (45): 66–73.

———. 2003. "Diminished Democracy: From Membership to Management in American Civic Life." Norman: University of Oklahoma Press.

———. 2004. "Voice and Inequality: The Transformation of American Civic Democracy." *Perspectives on Politics* 2(1): 3–20.

Skocpol, T., and A. Hertel-Fernandez. 2016. "The Koch Network and Republican Party Extremism." *Perspectives on Politics* 14(3): 681–699.

Skocpol, T., and V. Williamson. 2016. *The Tea Party and the Remaking of Republican Conservatism.* New York: Oxford University Press.

Sloan, M. F. 2009. "The Effects of Nonprofit Accountability Ratings on Donor Behavior." *Nonprofit and Voluntary Sector Quarterly* 38(2): 220–236.

Smith, D. H. 1997. "The Rest of the Nonprofit Sector: Grassroots Associations as the Dark Matter Ignored in Prevailing 'Flat Earth' Maps of the Sector." *Nonprofit and Voluntary Sector Quarterly* 26(2): 114–131.

Soss, J., and L. R. Jacobs. 2009. "The Place of Inequality: Non-Participation in the American Polity." *Political Science Quarterly* 124(1): 95–125.

Southworth, A. 2004. "Conservative Lawyers and the Contest over the Meaning of Public Interest Law." *UCLA Law Review* 52: 1223–1278.

Stein, L. 2009. "Social Movement Web Use in Theory and Practice: A Content Analysis of US Movement Websites." *New Media and Society* 11(5): 749–771.

Steinert-Threlkeld, Z. C. 2017. "Spontaneous Collective Action: Peripheral Mobilization During the Arab Spring." *American Political Science Review* 111(2): 379–403.

Steinmetz, K. 2016. "Inside Airbnb's Plan to Build a Political Movement." *Time*, July 21. http://time .com/4416136/airbnb-politics-sharing-economy -regulations-housing/.

Steuerle, C. E. 1999. *Will Donor-Advised Funds Revolutionize Philanthropy?* Washington, DC: Urban Institute Press.

Sunstein, C. R. 2018. *#Republic: Divided Democracy in the Age of Social Media.* Princeton, NJ: Princeton University Press.

Swarts, H. 2011. "Drawing New Symbolic Boundaries over Old Social Boundaries: Forging Social Movement Unity in Congregation-Based Community Organizing." *Sociological Perspectives* 54(3): 453–477.

Szper, R., and A. Prakash. 2011. "Charity Watchdogs and the Limits of Information-Based Regulation." *Voluntas: International Journal of Voluntary and Nonprofit Organizations* 22(1): 112–141.

Teles, S. M. 2008. *The Rise of the Conservative Legal Movement: The Battle for Control of the Law.* Princeton, NJ: Princeton University Press.

Teles, S., and M. Schmitt. 2011. "The Elusive Craft of Evaluating Advocacy." *Stanford Social Innovation Review* 9(3): 38–43.

Tilly C., and L. J. Wood. 2013. *Social Movements 1768–2012.* Boulder, CO: Paradigm.

Tocqueville, A. de. (1835) 2003. *Democracy in America.* Washington, DC: Regnery.

Tufekci, Z. 2014. "Big Questions for Social Media Big Data: Representativeness, Validity and Other Methodological Pitfalls." *ICWSM* 14: 505–514.

———. 2017. *Twitter and Tear Gas: The Power and Fragility of Networked Protest.* New Haven, CT: Yale University Press.

Tufekci, Z., and C. Wilson. 2012. "Social Media and the Decision to Participate in Political Protest: Observations from Tahrir Square." *Journal of Communication* 62(2): 363–379.

Van Iwaarden, J., T. Van Der Wiele, R. Williams, and C. Moxham. 2009. "Charities: How Important Is Performance to Donors?" *International Journal of Quality and Reliability Management* 26(1): 5–22.

Van Laer, J., and P. Van Aelst. 2010. "Internet and Social Movement Action Repertoires." *Information, Communication and Society* 13(8): 1146–1171.

Verba, S., K. L. Schlozman, and H. E. Brady. 1995. *Voice and Equality: Civic Voluntarism in American Politics.* Cambridge, MA: Harvard University Press.

Vogel, D. 1996. *Kindred Strangers: The Uneasy Relationship Between Politics and Business in America.* Princeton, NJ: Princeton University Press.

Walker, E. T. 2008. "Contingent Pathways from Joiner to Activist: The Indirect Effect of Participation in Voluntary Associations on Civic Engagement." *Sociological Forum* 23(1): 116–143.

———. 2009. "Privatizing Participation: Civic Change and the Organizational Dynamics of Grassroots Lobbying Firms." *American Sociological Review* 74(1): 83–105.

———. 2013a. "Signaling Responsibility, Deflecting Controversy: Strategic and Institutional Influences on the Charitable Giving of Corporate

Foundations in the Health Sector." In *Research in Political Sociology*, vol. 21, 181–214. Bingley, UK: Emerald.

———. 2013b. "Voluntary Associations and Social Movements." In *The Blackwell Encyclopedia of Social and Political Movements*, ed. D. A. Snow, D. della Porta, B. Klandermans, and D. McAdam, 1385–1388. New York: Blackwell.

———. 2014. *Grassroots for Hire: Public Affairs Consultants in American Democracy.* New York: Cambridge University Press.

Walker, E. T., and J. D. McCarthy. 2004. "Alternative Organizational Repertoires of Poor People's Social Movement Organizations." *Nonprofit and Voluntary Sector Quarterly* 33(3): 97S–119S.

———. 2010. "Legitimacy, Strategy, and Resources in the Survival of Community-Based Organizations." *Social Problems* 57(3): 315–340.

Walker, E. T., J. D. McCarthy, and F. Baumgartner. 2011. "Replacing Members with Managers? Mutualism Among Membership and Nonmembership Advocacy Organizations in the United States." *American Journal of Sociology* 116(4): 1284–1337.

Walker, E. T., and C. M. Rea. 2014. "The Political Mobilization of Firms and Industries." *Annual Review of Sociology* 40(1): 281–304.

Walker, E. T., and L. M. Stepick. 2014. "Strength in Diversity? Group Heterogeneity in the Mobilization of Grassroots Organizations." *Sociology Compass* 8(7): 959–975.

———. Forthcoming. "A Theory of Authenticity in Social Movements." *Mobilization: An International Quarterly.*

Warren, M. R. 2001. *Dry Bones Rattling: Community Building to Revitalize American Democracy.* Princeton, NJ: Princeton University Press.

Weir, M., and M. Ganz. 1997. "Reconnecting People and Politics." In *The New Majority: Toward a Popular Progressive Politics*, ed. S. Greenberg and T. Skocpol, 149–171. New Haven, CT: Yale University Press.

Weisbrod, B. A. 1977. *The Voluntary Nonprofit Sector: An Economic Analysis.* Lexington, MA: Lexington Books.

Winkler, A. 2018. *We the Corporations: How American Businesses Won Their Civil Rights.* New York: Norton.

Wolin, S. S. 2017. *Democracy Incorporated: Managed Democracy and the Specter of Inverted Totalitar-*

ianism—New Edition. Princeton, NJ: Princeton University Press.

Wood, R. L. 2002. *Faith in Action: Religion, Race, and Democratic Organizing in America.* Chicago: University of Chicago Press.

Young, J. A. 2017. "Facebook, Twitter, and Blogs: The Adoption and Utilization of Social Media in Nonprofit Human Service Organizations." *Human Service Organizations: Management, Leadership, and Governance* 41(1): 44–57.

Chapter 22. Advocating for What?
The Nonprofit Press and Models
of the Public

Aitamurto, Tanja. 2016. "Crowdsourcing in Open Journalism: Benefits, Challenges, and Value Creation." In *The Routledge Companion to Digital Journalism Studies,* ed. Bob Franklin and Scott Eldridge, 185–193. London, UK: Routledge.

American Society of Newspaper Editors. 2017. American Society of Newspaper Editors Diversity Survey. October. https://www.asne.org/diversity-survey-2017.

Ananny, Mike. 2014. "Networked Press Freedom and Social Media: Tracing Historical and Contemporary Forces in Press-Public Relations." *Journal of Computer-Mediated Communication* 19(4): 938–956.

———. 2018. *Networked Press Freedom: Creating Infrastructures for a Public Right to Hear.* Cambridge, MA: MIT Press.

Ananny, Mike, and Leila Bighash. 2016. "Why Drop a Paywall? Mapping Industry Accounts of Online News Decommodification." *International Journal of Communication* 10: 3359–3380.

Anderson, B. 1983. *Imagined Communities,* rev. ed. London, UK: Verso.

Baker, C. Edwin. 1998. "The Media That Citizens Need." *University of Pennsylvania Law Review* 147(2): 317–408.

———. 2007. *Media Concentration and Democracy: Why Ownership Matters.* Cambridge, UK: Cambridge University Press.

Barnhurst, Kevin G., and John Nerone. 2001. *The Form of News: A History.* New York: Guilford Press.

Beam, Randal A. 1993. "The Impact of Group Ownership Variables on Organizational Professional-

ism at Daily Newspapers." *Journalism Quarterly* 70(4): 907–918.

Bell, Emily, and Taylor Owen. 2017. *The Platform Press: How Silicon Valley Reengineered Journalism.* http://towcenter.org/wp-content/uploads/2017/03/The_Platform_Press_Tow_Report_2017.pdf.

Benson, Rodney. 2006. "News Media as a 'Journalistic Field': What Bourdieu Adds to New Institutionalism, and Vice Versa." *Political Communication* 23(2): 187–202.

———. 2017. "Can Foundations Solve the Journalism Crisis?" *Journalism* 19(8): 1059–1077.

Benson, Rodney, and Erik Neveu, eds. 2005. *Bourdieu and the Journalistic Field.* Cambridge, UK: Polity.

Berkowitz, Dan. 1992. "Non-Routine News and Newswork: Exploring a What-a-Story." *Journal of Communication* 42(1): 82–94.

Bezanson, Randall P. 2003. "The Structural Attributes of Press Freedom: Private Ownership, Public Orientation, and Editorial Independence." In *Journalism and the Debate over Privacy,* ed. Craig LaMay, 17–60. London, UK: Routledge.

Boczkowski, Pablo J. 2004. *Digitizing the News: Innovation in Online Newspapers.* Cambridge, MA: MIT Press.

———. 2009. "Rethinking Hard and Soft News Production: From Common Ground to Divergent Paths." *Journal of Communication* 59(1): 98–116.

Bradlee, Benjamin C. 1975. *Conversations with Kennedy.* New York: Norton.

Braun, Joshua A., and Tarleton Gillespie. 2011. "Hosting the Public Discourse, Hosting the Public: When Online News and Social Media Converge." *Journalism Practice* 5(4): 383–398.

Breese, Elizabeth B. 2011. "Mapping the Variety of Public Spheres." *Communication Theory* 21(2): 130–149.

Butsch, Richard. 2008. *The Citizen Audience: Crowds, Publics, and Individuals.* New York: Routledge.

Calhoun, C. 1998. "The Public Good as a Social and Cultural Project." In *Private Action and the Public Good,* ed. Walter W. Powell and Elizabeth S. Clemens, 20–35. New Haven, CT: Yale University Press.

Carlson, Matt. (2015a). "The Many Boundaries of Journalism." In *Boundaries of Journalism: Professionalism, Practices and Participation*, ed. Matt Carlson and Seth C. Lewis, 1–18. New York: Routledge.

———. 2015b. "Metajournalistic Discourse and the Meanings of Journalism: Definitional Control, Boundary Work, and Legitimation." *Communication Theory* 26(4): 349–488.

Center for Collaborative Media. 2018. "Collaborative Journalism—About Us." https://collaborativejournalism.org/about/.

Chadwick, Andrew. 2013. *The Hybrid Media System: Politics and Power*. Oxford, UK: Oxford University Press.

Chittum, Ryan. 2011. "Nonprofit News and the Tax Man." *Columbia Journalism Review*, November 17. http://archives.cjr.org/the_audit/nonprofit _news_and_the_tax_man.php.

Chomsky, Daniel. 2006. "'An Interested Reader': Measuring Ownership Control at the *New York Times*." *Critical Studies in Mass Communication* 23(1): 1–18.

Christians, Clifford G., Theodore L. Glasser, Denis McQuail, Kaarle Nordenstreng, and Robert A. White. 2009. *Normative Theories of the Media*. Urbana: University of Illinois Press.

Christin, Angele. Forthcoming. *Metrics at Work: How Web Journalists Make Sense of Their Algorithmic Publics in the United States and France*. Princeton, NJ: Princeton University Press.

Curran, James, and Jean Seaton. 2009. *Power Without Responsibility: The Press and Broadcasting in Britain*, 7th ed. London, UK: Routledge.

Darnton, Robert. 1975. "Writing News and Telling Stories." *Daedalus* 104(2): 175–194.

Deuze, Mark, and Tamara Witschge. 2017. "Beyond Journalism: Theorizing the Transformation of Journalism." *Journalism* 19(2): 165–181.

Dewey, John. 1954. *The Public and Its Problems*. New York: Swallow Press.

DiMaggio, Paul J., and Walter W. Powell. 1991. Introduction. In *The New Institutionalism in Organizational Analysis*, ed. Walter W. Powell and Paul J. DiMaggio, 1–38. Chicago: University of Chicago Press.

Downey, John, Sabina Mihelj, and Thomas König. 2012. "Comparing Public Spheres: Normative Models and Empirical Measurements." *European Journal of Communication* 27(4): 337–353.

Ettema, James S., and Theodore L. Glasser. 1998. *Custodians of Conscience*. New York: Columbia University Press.

Fung, Archon. 2003. "Recipes for Public Spheres: Eight Institutional Design Choices and Their Consequences." *Journal of Political Philosophy* 11(3): 338–367.

Gans, Herbert. 1979. *Deciding What's News*. New York: Vintage Books.

Gardner, Howard, Mihaly Csikszentmihalyi, and William Damon. 2002. "Good Work in Journalism Today." In *Good Work: When Excellence and Ethics Meet*, 179–206. New York: Basic Books.

Glasser, Theodore L., and James S. Ettema. 1993. "When the Facts Don't Speak for Themselves: A Study of the Use of Irony in Daily Journalism." *Critical Studies in Mass Communication* 10(4): 322–338.

Graham, Katherine. 1998. *A Personal History*. New York: Vintage Books.

Habermas, Jürgen. 1989. *The Structural Transformation of the Public Sphere: An Inquiry into a Category of Bourgeois Society*. Cambridge, MA: MIT Press.

Hallin, Daniel C. 1985. "The American News Media: A Critical Theory Perspective." In *Critical Theory and Public Life*, ed. John F. Forester, 121–146. Cambridge, MA: MIT Press.

———. 1986. *The "Uncensored War": The Media and Vietnam*. New York: Oxford University Press.

Halperin, Terri D. 2016. *The Alien and Sedition Acts of 1798*. Baltimore: Johns Hopkins University Press.

Hamilton, James T. 2006. *All the News That's Fit to Sell*. Princeton, NJ: Princeton University Press.

Held, D. 2006. *Models of Democracy*, 3rd ed. Stanford, CA: Stanford University Press.

Herbst, Susan. 1995. *Numbered Voices: How Opinion Polling Has Shaped American Politics*. Chicago: University of Chicago Press.

Jian, Lian, and Jieun Shin. 2015. "Motivations Behind Donors' Contributions to Crowdfunded Journalism." *Mass Communication and Society* 18(2): 165–185.

Jian, Lian, and Nikki Usher. 2014. "Crowd-Funded Journalism." *Journal of Computer-Mediated Communication* 19(2): 155–170.

John, Richard R. 1998. *Spreading the News: The American Postal System from Franklin to Morse.* Cambridge, MA: Harvard University Press.

———. 2012. *The American Postal Network, 1792–1914.* New York: Routledge.

Kelty, Chris M. 2008. *Two Bits: The Cultural Significance of Free Software.* Durham, NC: Duke University Press.

Konieczna, Magda. 2018. *Journalism Without Profit: Making News When the Market Fails.* Oxford, UK: Oxford University Press.

Konieczna, Magda, and Elia Powers. 2017. "What Can Nonprofit Journalists Actually Do for Democracy?" *Journalism Studies* 18(12): 1542–1558.

Lee, Deron. 2017. "The Pleasure and Pain of Going Nonprofit." *Columbia Journalism Review* (Spring). https://www.cjr.org/local_news/nonprofit-news-local-tulsa-frontier.php.

Levy, David A. L., and Robert G. Picard, eds. 2012. "Is There a Better Structure for News Providers? The Potential in Charitable and Trust Ownership." *Journalism Practice* 6(4): 586–587.

Lewis, Seth C. 2011. "Journalism Innovation and Participation: An Analysis of the Knight News Challenge." *International Journal of Communication* 5: 1623–1648.

Lipari, Lisbeth. 1996. "Journalistic Authority: Textual Strategies of Legitimation." *Journalism and Mass Communication Quarterly* 73(4): 821–834.

Lippmann, Walter. 1922. *Public Opinion.* New York: Free Press.

McLellan, Michele, and Jesse Holcomb. 2018. "The State of Nonprofit News." Institute for Nonprofit News, October. https://inn.org/wp-content/uploads/2018/10/INN.Index2018FinalFullReport.pdf.

Mouffe, Chantal. 2005. *On the Political.* London, UK: Routledge.

Murdock, Graham. 1977. *Patterns of Ownership: Questions of Control.* Milton Keynes, UK: Open University Press.

———. 1982. "Large Corporations and the Control of the Communications Industries." In *Culture, Society and the Media*, ed. Michael Gurevitch, Tony

Bennett, James Curran, and Janet Woollacott, 118–150. New York: Methuen.

Napoli, Philip M. 2011. *Audience Evolution: New Technologies and the Transformation of Media Audiences.* New York: Columbia University Press.

Napoli, Philip M., and Robyn Caplan. 2017. "Why Media Companies Insist They're Not Media Companies, Why They're Wrong, and Why It Matters." *First Monday* 22(5).

Neff, Gina. 2015. "Learning from Documents: Applying New Theories of Materiality to Journalism." *Journalism* 16(1): 74–78.

Nerone, John. 2015. *The Media and Public Life: A History.* London, UK: Polity.

New York Times. 2017. "A New Role for Janet Elder." September 1. https://www.nytco.com/a-new-role-for-janet-elder/.

Nielsen, Rasmus K., and Sarah Anne Ganter. 2017. "Dealing with Digital Intermediaries: A Case Study of the Relations Between Publishers and Platforms." *New Media and Society* 20(4): 1600–1617.

Nonprofit Media Working Group. 2013. "The IRS and Nonprofit Media: Toward Creating a More Informed Public." Council on Foundations, March 4. https://www.cof.org/nonprofitmedia.

Owen, Laura H. 2017. "'Won't Work for Exposure': The Financial Nitty-Gritty of Commercial–Nonprofit News Partnerships." Nieman Lab, May 18. http://www.niemanlab.org/2017/05/wont-work-for-exposure-the-financial-nitty-gritty-of-commercial-nonprofit-news-partnerships/.

Picard, Robert G., and Aldo van Weezel. 2008. "Capital and Control: Consequences of Different Forms of Newspaper Ownership." *International Journal on Media Management* 10(1): 22–31.

Pickard, Victor, and Alex T. Williams. 2014. "Salvation or Folly? The Promises and Perils of Digital Paywalls." *Digital Journalism* 2(2): 195–213.

Prior, M. 2007. *Post-Broadcast Democracy: How Media Choice Increases Inequality in Political Involvement and Polarizes Elections.* Cambridge, UK: Cambridge University Press.

ProPublica. n.d. "News Apps: ProPublica's News Applications, Graphics, Databases and Tools." http://www.propublica.org/tools/, accessed July 24, 2019.

Protess, David L., Fay L. Cook, Jack C. Doppelt, James S. Ettema, Margaret T. Gordon, Donna R. Leff, and Peter Miller. 1991. *Journalism of Outrage: Investigative Reporting and Agenda Building in America.* New York: Guilford Press.

Rogers, Everett M., James W. Dearing, and Soonbum Chang. 1991. "AIDS in the 1980s: The Agenda-Setting Process for a Public Issue." *Journalism Monographs* 126: 1–86.

Salmon, Charles T., and Theodore L. Glasser. 1995. "The Politics of Polling and the Limits of Consent." In *Public Opinion and the Communication of Consent*, ed. Theodore L. Glasser and Charles T. Salmon, 437–458. New York: Guilford Press.

Schiller, Dan. 1979. "An Historical Approach to Objectivity and Professionalism in American News Reporting." *Journal of Communication* 29(4): 46–57.

Schmidt, Christine. 2018. "No Print, No Private Owners, Fewer Problems? Quebec's 134-Year-Old La Presse Is Going Nonprofit." Nieman Lab, May 9. http://www.niemanlab.org/2018/05/no-print-no-private-owners-fewer-problems-quebecs-134-year-old-la-presse-is-going-nonprofit/.

Schudson, Michael. 1978. *Discovering the News: A Social History of American Newspapers.* New York: Basic Books.

———. 1995. "Question Authority: A History of the News Interview." In *The Power of News*, 72–93. Cambridge, MA: Harvard University Press.

———. 1998. *The Good Citizen: A History of American Public Life.* New York: Free Press.

———. 2000. "The Sociology of News Production Revisited (Again)." In *Mass Media and Society*, ed. James Curran and Michael Gurevitch, 175–200. London: Arnold.

Squires, Catherine R. 2002. "Rethinking the Black Public Sphere: An Alternative Vocabulary for Multiple Public Spheres." *Communication Theory* 12(4): 446–468.

Stonbely, Sarah. 2017. "Comparing Models of Collaborative Journalism." Monclair State University, September. https://collaborativejournalism.org/wp-content/uploads/2017/09/Models-for-Collaborative-Journalism-research-paper.pdf.

Stroud, Natalie J. 2011. *Niche News: The Politics of News Choice.* Oxford, UK: Oxford University Press.

Thornton, Paul. 2013. "On Letters from Climate-Change Deniers." *Los Angeles Times*, October 8. http://www.latimes.com/opinion/opinion-la/la-ol-climate-change-letters-20131008-story.html.

Tuchman, Gaye. 1978. *Making News: A Study in the Social Construction of Reality.* New York: Free Press.

Villalonga, Belen, and Raphael Amit. 2006. "How Do Family Ownership, Control and Management Affect Firm Value?" *Journal of Financial Economics* 80(2): 385–417.

Wagner, Michael W., and Timothy P. Collins. 2014. "Does Ownership Matter? The Case of Rupert Murdoch's Purchase of the *Wall Street Journal*." *Journalism Practice* 8(6): 758–771.

Wahl-Jorgensen, Karin. 2007. *Journalists and the Public: Newsroom Culture, Letters to the Editor, and Democracy.* Cresskill, NJ: Hampton Press.

Wang, Shan. 2016. "'No Single, One-Size-Fits-All Approach': Challenges and Possibility in the Philly Newspapers' Nonprofit Reorganization." Nieman Lab, June 15. http://www.niemanlab.org/2016/06/no-single-one-size-fits-all-approach-challenges-and-possibility-in-the-philly-newspapers-nonprofit-reorganization/.

Wojdynski, Bartosz W. 2016. "The Deceptiveness of Sponsored News Articles: How Readers Recognize and Perceive Native Advertising." *American Behavioral Scientist* 60(12): 1475–1491.

Young, Iris M. 2000. *Inclusion and Democracy.* New York: Oxford University Press.

Zelizer, Barbie. 2017. *What Journalism Could Be.* New York: Polity.

Part VII. Motivation, Meaning, and Prosocial Behavior

Chapter 23. What Influences Charitable Giving?

Adelman, C., B. Schwartz, and E. Riskin. 2016. *Index of Global Philanthropy and Remittances 2016.* Washington, DC: Hudson Institute.

Andreoni, J. 1990. "Impure Altruism and Donations to Public Goods: A Theory of Warm Glow Giving." *Economic Journal* 100(401): 464–477.

Andreoni, J., E. Brown, and I. Rischall. 2003. "Charitable Giving by Married Couples: Who Decides and Why Does It Matter?" *Journal of Human Resources* 38(1): 111–133.

Andreoni, J., and A. A. Payne. 2003. "Do Government Grants to Private Charities Crowd Out Giving or Fund-Raising?" *American Economic Review* 93(3): 792–812.

———. 2011. "Is Crowding Out Due Entirely to Fundraising? Evidence from a Panel of Charities." *Journal of Public Economics* 95(5–6): 334–343.

Arnold, C., with T. Conway and M. Greenslade. 2011. *Cash Transfers: Evidence Paper.* London: Department for International Development.

Arrow, K. 1972. "Gifts and Exchanges." *Philosophy and Public Affairs* 1(4): 343–362.

Balsam, S., and E. E. Harris. 2013. "The Impact of CEO Compensation on Nonprofit Donations." *Accounting Review* 89(2): 425–450.

Barman, E. 2016. "Caring Capitalism: The Meaning and Measure of Social Value." Cambridge, UK: Cambridge University Press.

Bail, C. A. 2016a. "Combining Natural Language Processing and Network Analysis to Examine How Advocacy Organizations Stimulate Conversation on Social Media." *Proceedings of the National Academy of Sciences* 113(42): 11823–11828.

———. 2016b. "Cultural Carrying Capacity: Organ Donation Advocacy, Discursive Framing, and Social Media Engagement." *Social Science and Medicine* 165, 280–288.

Bail, C. A., T. W. Brown, and M. Mann. 2017. "Channeling Hearts and Minds: Advocacy Organizations, Cognitive-Emotional Currents, and Public Conversation." *American Sociological Review* 82(6): 1188–1213.

Becker, G. S. 1974. "A Theory of Social Interactions." *Journal of Political Economy* 82(6): 1063–1093.

Bekkers, R., and P. Wiepking. 2011a. "A Literature Review of Empirical Studies of Philanthropy: Eight Mechanisms That Drive Charitable Giving." *Nonprofit and Voluntary Sector Quarterly* 40(5): 924–973.

———. 2011b. "Who Gives? A Literature Review of Predictors of Charitable Giving. Part One: Religion, Education, Age and Socialisation." *Voluntary Sector Review* 2(3): 337–365.

Bergstrom, T. C., L. Blume, and H. Varian. 1986. "On the Private Provision of Public Goods." *Journal of Public Economics* 29(1): 25–50.

Berman, J. Z., A. Barasch, E. E. Levine, and D. Small. 2018. "Impediments to Effective Altruism: The Role of Subjective Preferences in Charitable Giving." *Psychological Science* 29(5): 834–844.

Bick, J. 2007. "Write a Check? The New Philanthropist Goes Further." *New York Times*, March 19. http://www.nytimes.com/2007/03/18/business/yourmoney/18legacy.html.

Brest, P., and H. Harvey. 2018. *Money Well Spent: A Strategic Plan for Smart Philanthropy.* Stanford, CA: Stanford University Press.

Bronfman, C., and J. R. Solomon. 2010. *The Art of Giving: Where the Soul Meets a Business Plan.* San Francisco: Jossey-Bass.

Brown, E., and J. M. Ferris. 2007. "Social Capital and Philanthropy: An Analysis of the Impact of Social Capital on Individual Giving and Volunteering." *Nonprofit and Voluntary Sector Quarterly* 36(1): 85–99.

Calabrese, T. D. 2011. "Do Donors Penalize Nonprofit Organizations with Accumulated Wealth?" *Public Administration Review* 71(6): 859–869.

Castillo, M., R. Petrie, and C. Wardell. 2014. "Fundraising Through Online Social Networks: A Field Experiment on Peer-to-Peer Solicitation." *Journal of Public Economics* 114: 29–35.

Caviola, L., N. Faulmüller, J. A. Everett, J. Savulescu, and G. Kahane. 2014. "The Evaluability Bias in Charitable Giving: Saving Administration Costs or Saving Lives?" *Judgment and Decision Making* 9(4): 303.

Charity Navigator. 2010. "CEO Compensation Study." https://www.charitynavigator.org/__asset__/studies/2010_CEO_Compensation_Study_Revised_Final.pdf.

Clotfelter, C. 1985. *Federal Tax Policy and Charitable Giving.* Chicago: University of Chicago Press.

Cobb, N. K. 2002. "The New Philanthropy: Its Impact on Funding Arts and Culture." *Journal of Arts Management, Law, and Society* 32(2): 125–143.

Croson, R., and J. Shang. 2013. "Limits of the Effect of Social Information on the Voluntary Provision of Public Goods: Evidence from Field Experiments." *Economic Inquiry* 51(1): 473–477.

de Wit, A., and R. Bekkers. 2016. "Government Support and Charitable Donations: A Meta-Analysis of the Crowding-Out Hypothesis." *Journal of Public Administration Research and Theory* 27(2): 301–319.

Eckel, C. C., and P. J. Grossman. 2008. "Subsidizing Charitable Contributions: A Natural Field Experiment Comparing Matching and Rebate Subsidies." *Experimental Economics* 11(3): 234–252.

Espeland, W. N., and M. L. Stevens. 2008. "A Sociology of Quantification." *European Journal of Sociology* 49(3): 401–436.

Friedman, E. 2013. *Reinventing Philanthropy: A Framework for More Effective Giving*. Washington, DC: Potomac Books.

Frey, B. S., and S. Meier. 2004. "Social Comparisons and Pro-social Behavior: Testing 'Conditional Cooperation' in a Field Experiment." *American Economic Review* 94(5): 1717–1722.

Frumkin, P. 2002. *On Being Nonprofit: A Conceptual and Policy Primer*. Cambridge, MA: Harvard University Press.

———. 2008. *Strategic Giving: The Art and Science of Philanthropy*. Chicago: University of Chicago Press.

Gee, L. K., and M. J. Schreck. "Do Beliefs About Peers Matter for Donation Matching? Experiments in the Field and Laboratory." *Games and Economic Behavior* 107: 282–297.

Giving USA. 2018a. *Giving USA 2018: The Annual Report on Philanthropy for the Year 2017*. Chicago: Giving USA.

Giving USA. 2018b. *Special Report on the Data on Donor-Advised Funds: New Insights You Need to Know*. Chicago: Giving USA.

Glazer, A., and K. A. Konrad. 1996. "A Signaling Explanation for Charity." *American Economic Review* 86(4): 1019–1028.

Gneezy, U., E. A. Keenan, and A. Gneezy. 2014. "Avoiding Overhead Aversion in Charity." *Science* 346(6209): 632–635.

Gregory, A. G., and D. Howard. 2009. "The Nonprofit Starvation Cycle." *Stanford Social Innovation Review* 7(4): 49–53.

Hall, M. H. 2001. "Measurement Issues in Surveys of Giving and Volunteering and Strategies Applied in the Design of Canada's National Survey of Giving, Volunteering and Participating."

Nonprofit and Voluntary Sector Quarterly 30(3): 515–526.

Hanlon, J., A. Barrientos, and D. Hulme. 2010. *Just Give Money to the Poor: The Development Revolution from the Global South*. Sterling, VA: Kumarian Press.

Harbaugh, W. T. 1998. "The Prestige Motive for Making Charitable Transfers." *American Economic Review* 88(2): 277–282.

Harbaugh, W. T., U. Mayr, and D. R. Burghart. 2007. "Neural Responses to Taxation and Voluntary Giving Reveal Motives for Charitable Donations." *Science* 316: 1622–1625.

Harris, E. E., and J. A. Ruth. 2015. "Analysis of the Value of Celebrity Affiliation to Nonprofit Contributions." *Nonprofit and Voluntary Sector Quarterly* 44(5): 945–967.

Haushofer, J., and J. Shapiro. 2016. "The Short-Term Impact of Unconditional Cash Transfers to the Poor: Experimental Evidence from Kenya." *Quarterly Journal of Economics* 131(4): 1973–2042.

Havens, J. J., M. O'Herlihy, and P. G. Schervish. 2006. "Charitable Giving: How Much, by Whom, to What, and How?" In *The Nonprofit Sector: A Research Handbook*, 2nd ed., ed. W. W. Powell and R. Steinberg, 542–567. New Haven, CT: Yale University Press.

Hodgkinson, V. A. 1990. "The Future of Individual Giving and Volunteering: The Inseparable Link Between Religious Community and Individual Generosity." In *Faith and Philanthropy in America: Exploring the Role of Religion in America's Voluntary Sector*, ed. R. Wuthnow, V. A. Hodgkinson, and Associates, 284–312. San Francisco: Jossey-Bass.

Hopkins, B. R., 2011. *The Law of Tax-Exempt Organizations*, 10th ed. Hoboken, NJ: Wiley.

Independent Sector. 2002. *Faith and Philanthropy: The Connection Between Charitable Behavior and Giving to Religion*. Washington, DC: Independent Sector.

Institute for Local Government. 2010. "Pondering Public/Nonprofit Collaborations: What a Form 990 Says About a Nonprofit." http://www.ca-ilg .org/sites/main/files/file-attachments/what_a _form_990_says_about_a_nonprofit.pdf.

Jackson, E. F., M. D. Bachmeier, J. R. Wood, and E. A. Craft. 1995. "Volunteering and Charitable

Giving: Do Religious and Associational Ties Promote Helping Behavior?" *Nonprofit and Voluntary Sector Quarterly* 24(1): 59–78.

Jacobs, F. A., and N. P. Marudas. 2009. "The Combined Effect of Donation Price and Administrative Inefficiency on Donations to US Nonprofit Organizations." *Financial Accountability and Management* 25(1): 33–53.

James, R. N. III, and D. L. Sharpe. 2007. "The Nature and Causes of the U-Shaped Charitable Giving Profile." *Nonprofit and Voluntary Sector Quarterly* 36(2): 218–238.

Karlan, D., and J. A. List. 2007. "Does Price Matter in Charitable Giving? Evidence from a Large-Scale Natural Field Experiment." *American Economic Review* 97(5): 1774–1793.

Karlan, D., J. A. List, and E. Shafir. 2011. "Small Matches and Charitable Giving: Evidence from a Natural Field Experiment." *Journal of Public Economics* 95(5–6): 344–350.

Karlan, D., and D. H. Wood. 2017. "The Effect of Effectiveness: Donor Response to Aid Effectiveness in a Direct Mail Fundraising Experiment." *Journal of Behavioral and Experimental Economics* 66: 1–8.

Kingma, B., and R. McClelland. 1995. "Public Radio Stations Are Really, Really Not Public Goods." *Annals of Public and Cooperative Economics* 66(1): 65–76.

Kolm, S. C. 1969. "The Optimal Production of Social Justice." In *Public Economics: An Analysis of Public Production and Consumption and Their Relations to the Private Sectors*, ed. J. Margolis and H. Guitton, 145–200. London: Macmillan.

Krishnan, R., M. H. Yetman, and R. J. Yetman. 2006. "Expense Misreporting in Nonprofit Organizations." *Accounting Review* 81(2): 399–420.

List, J. A. 2011. "The Market for Charitable Giving." *Journal of Economic Perspectives* 25(2): 157–180.

List, J. A., and D. Lucking-Reiley. 2002. "The Effects of Seed Money and Refunds on Charitable Giving: Experimental Evidence from a University Capital Campaign." *Journal of Political Economy* 110(1): 215–233.

MacAskill, W. 2015. *Doing Good Better: How Effective Altruism Can Help You Make a Difference.* New York: Gotham Books.

Martin, R., and J. Randal. 2009. "How Sunday, Price, and Social Norms Influence Donation Behaviour." *Journal of Socio-Economics* 38(5): 722–727.

Meer, J. 2011. "Brother, Can You Spare a Dime? Peer Pressure in Charitable Solicitation." *Journal of Public Economics* 95(7–8): 926–941.

———. 2017. "Does Fundraising Create New Giving?" *Journal of Public Economics* 145: 82–93.

Meer, J., D. Miller, and E. Wulfsberg. 2017. "The Great Recession and Charitable Giving." *Applied Economics Letters* 24(21): 1542–1549.

Mesch, D. J., P. M. Rooney, K. S. Steinberg, and B. Denton. 2006. "The Effects of Race, Gender, and Marital Status on Giving and Volunteering in Indiana." *Nonprofit and Voluntary Sector Quarterly* 35(4): 565–587.

Molino, M. 2011. *Leap of Reason: Managing to Outcomes in an Era of Scarcity.* Washington, DC: Venture Philanthropy Partners.

Moody, M., 2008. "'Building a Culture': The Construction and Evolution of Venture Philanthropy as a New Organizational Field." *Nonprofit and Voluntary Sector Quarterly* 37(2): 324–352.

Newland, K., A. Terrazas, and R. Munster. 2010. *Diaspora Philanthropy: Private Giving and Public Policy.* Washington, DC: Migration Policy Institute.

O'Neill, M. 2001. "Research on Giving and Volunteering: Methodological Considerations." *Nonprofit and Voluntary Sector Quarterly* 30(3): 505–514.

Ott, J. S., and L. A. Dicke, eds. 2012. *Understanding Nonprofit Organizations: Governance, Leadership, and Management.* Boulder, CO: Westview Press.

Ottoni-Wilhelm, M. 2017. "Overview of Overall Giving: Based on Data Collected in 2015 About Giving in 2014." Indiana University Lilly Family School of Philanthropy. http://generosityforlife.org/wp-content/uploads/2017/10/Overall-Giving-10.5.17-jb-CJC.pdf.

Pallotta, D. 2009. *Uncharitable: How Restraints on Nonprofits Undermine Their Potential.* Medford, MA: University Press of New England.

Paxton, P., K. Velasco, and R. Ressler. 2019. "Does Use of Emotion Increase Donations and Volunteers for Nonprofits?" Working paper.

Reich, R. 2010. "Toward a Political Theory of Philanthropy." In *Giving Well: The Ethics of Philanthropy*, ed. Patricia Illingworth, Thomas Pogge, and Leif Wenar, 177–195. Oxford, UK: Oxford University Press.

———. 2016. "Keynote Address." Speech given at the 45th Association for Research on Nonprofits and Voluntary Associations Conference, "Nonprofits, Philanthropy, and Government: Policy and Partnerships in an Era of Change," Washington, DC, November 17–19.

Ressler, R., P. Paxton, and K. Velasco. 2018. "The Social Context of Donations." Working paper.

Rondeau, D., and J. A. List. 2008. "Matching and Challenge Gifts to Charity: Evidence from Laboratory and Natural Field Experiments." *Experimental Economics* 11(3): 253–267.

Rooney, P. M., M. S. Brown, B. H. Milner, X. Wei, T. Yoshioka, and D. A. Fleischhacker. 2007. *Patterns of Household Charitable Giving by Income Group, 2005*. Indianapolis, IN: Center on Philanthropy.

Rooney, P., K. Steinberg, and P. G. Schervish. 2004. "Methodology Is Destiny: The Effect of Survey Prompts on Reported Levels of Giving and Volunteering." *Nonprofit and Voluntary Sector Quarterly* 33(4): 628–654.

Rose-Ackerman, S. 1996. "Altruism, Nonprofits, and Economic Theory." *Journal of Economic Literature* 34: 701–786.

Salamon, L. M. 1987. "Of Market Failure, Voluntary Failure, and Third-Party Government: Toward a Theory of Government-Nonprofit Relations in the Modern Welfare State." *Nonprofit and Voluntary Sector Quarterly* 16(1): 29–49.

———. 2003. "The Resilient Sector: The Future of Nonprofit America." In *The State of Nonprofit America*, 2nd ed., ed. L. M. Salamon, 3–86. Washington, DC: Brookings Institution Press.

Salamon, L. M., S. Sokolowski, and R. List. 2004. *Global Civil Society*, vol. 2. Bloomfield, CT: Kumarian Press.

Sargeant, A. 1999. "Charitable Giving: Towards a Model of Donor Behaviour." *Journal of Marketing Management* 15(4): 215–238.

Sargeant, A., and J. Shang. 2010. *Fundraising Principles and Practice*, vol. 17. Hoboken, NJ: Wiley.

Schervish, P. G., and J. J. Havens. 1997. "Social Participation and Charitable Giving: A Multivariate Analysis." *Voluntas: International Journal of Voluntary and Nonprofit Organizations* 8(3): 235–260.

Sen, A. K. 1977. "Rational Fools: A Critique of the Behavioral Foundations of Economic Theory." *Philosophy and Public Affairs* 6(4): 317–344.

Shang, J., and R. Croson. 2009. "A Field Experiment in Charitable Contribution: The Impact of Social Information on the Voluntary Provision of Public Goods." *Economic Journal* 119(540): 1422–1439.

Shang, J., A. Reed, and R. Croson. 2008. "Identity Congruency Effects on Donations." *Journal of Marketing Research* 45(3): 351–361.

Singer, P. 1972. "Famine, Affluence, and Morality." *Philosophy and Public Affairs* 1(3): 229–243.

———. 2010. *The Life You Can Save: How to Do Your Part to End World Poverty*. New York: Random House.

Smith, B., S. Shue, J. L. Vest, and J. Villareal. 1999. *Philanthropy in Communities of Color*. Bloomington: Indiana University Press.

Smith, S., F. Windmeijer, and E. Wright. 2015. "Peer Effects in Charitable Giving: Evidence from (Running) Field." *Economic Journal* 125(585): 1053–1071.

Snibbe, A. C. 2006. "Drowning in Data." *Stanford Social Innovation Review* 4(3): 39–45.

Soskis, B. 2017. "Giving Numbers: Reflections on Why, What, and How We Are Counting." *Nonprofit Quarterly*, November 1.

Stack, C. B. 1997. *All Our Kin: Strategies for Survival in a Black Community*. New York: Basic Books.

Szper, R., and A. Prakash. 2011. "Charity Watchdogs and the Limits of Information-Based Regulation." *Voluntas: International Journal of Voluntary and Nonprofit Organizations* 22(1): 112–141.

Tinkelman, D., and K. Mankaney. 2007. "When Is Administrative Efficiency Associated with Charitable Donations?" *Nonprofit and Voluntary Sector Quarterly* 36(1): 41–64.

Tucker, C. 2014. "Why the Ice Bucket Challenge Proved Such a Runaway Success." Yahoo Tech, October 18. https://finance.yahoo.com/news/why-the-ice-bucket-challenge-proved-such-a-runaway-100262238434.html.

Tuckman, H. P., and C. F. Chang. 1991. "A Methodology for Measuring the Financial Vulnerability of

Charitable Nonprofit Organizations." *Nonprofit and Voluntary Sector Quarterly* 20(4): 445–460.

U.S. Trust. 2014. *The 2014 U.S. Trust Study of High Net Worth Philanthropy: Issues Driving Charitable Activities Among Wealthy Households*. Indianapolis: Lilly Family School of Philanthropy at Indiana University.

Verhaert, G. A., and D. Van den Poel. 2012. "The Role of Seed Money and Threshold Size in Optimizing Fundraising Campaigns: Past Behavior Matters!" *Expert Systems with Applications* 39(18): 13075–13084.

Vesterlund, L. 2006. "Why Do People Give?" In *The Nonprofit Sector: A Research Handbook*, 2nd ed., ed. W. W. Powell and R. Steinberg, 568–587. New Haven, CT: Yale University Press.

Weinstein, M. M., and R. M. Bradburd. 2013. *The Robin Hood Rules for Smart Giving*. New York: Columbia Business School Publishing.

Wiepking, P., and R. Bekkers. 2012. "Who Gives? A Literature Review of Predictors of Charitable Giving. Part Two: Gender, Family Composition and Income." *Voluntary Sector Review* 3(2): 217–245.

Weisbrod, B. A. 1977. *The Voluntary Nonprofit Sector: An Economic Analysis*. Lexington, MA: Lexington Books.

Weisbrod, B. A., and N. D. Dominguez. 1986. "Demand for Collective Goods in Private Nonprofit Markets: Can Fundraising Expenditures Help Overcome Free-Rider Behavior?" *Journal of Public Economics* 30(1): 83–96.

Wicks, P. 2014. "The ALS Ice Bucket Challenge— Can a Splash of Water Reinvigorate a Field?" *Amyotrophic Lateral Sclerosis and Frontotemporal Degeneration* 15(7–8): 479–480.

Woodruff, P., ed. 2018. *The Ethics of Giving: Philosophers' Perspectives on Philanthropy*. New York: Oxford University Press.

Wuthnow, R. 1990. "Religion and the Voluntary Spirit in the United States: Mapping the Terrain." In *Faith and Philanthropy in America: Exploring the Role of Religion in America's Voluntary Sector*, ed. R. Wuthnow, V. A. Hodgkinson, and Associates, 3–21. San Francisco: Jossey-Bass.

———. 1991. *Acts of Compassion: Caring for Others and Helping Ourselves*. Princeton, NJ: Princeton University Press.

Yaffe-Bellany, D. 2018. "A Viral Facebook Fundraiser Has Generated More Than $20 Million for Immigration Nonprofit RAICES." *Texas Tribune* (Austin, TX), June 27.

Yan, W., and M. F. Sloan. 2016. "The Impact of Employee Compensation and Financial Performance on Nonprofit Organization Donations." *American Review of Public Administration* 46(2): 243–258.

Chapter 24. The Altruism Budget: Measuring and Encouraging Charitable Giving

Adena, M., and S. Huck. "Giving Once, Giving Twice: A Two-Period Field Experiment on Intertemporal Crowding in Charitable Giving." *Journal of Public Economics* 172 (2019): 127–134.

Alpizar, F., F. Carlsson, and O. Johansson-Stenman. 2008. "Anonymity, Reciprocity, and Conformity: Evidence from Voluntary Contributions to a National Park in Costa Rica." *Journal of Public Economics* 92: 1047–1060.

Alston, M., C. Eckel, J. Meer, and W. Zhan. 2018. "High Income Donors' Preferences for Charitable Giving." Working paper, Texas A&M University.

Andreoni, J. 2006a. "Leadership Giving in Charitable Fund-Raising." *Journal of Public Economic Theory* 8(1): 1–22.

———. 2006b. "Philanthropy." In *Handbook of the Economics of Giving, Altruism and Reciprocity*, vol. 2, ed. S.-C. Kolm and J. M. Ythier, 1201–1269. Amsterdam: Elsevier.

Andreoni, J., and B. D. Bernheim. 2009. "Social Image and the 50-50 Norm: A Theoretical and Experimental Analysis of Audience Effects." *Econometrica* 77(5): 1607–1636.

Andreoni, J., W. G. Gale, and J. K. Scholz. 1996. *Charitable Contributions of Time and Money*. Working paper, University of Wisconsin–Madison.

Andreoni, J., and L. K. Gee. 2012. "Gun for Hire: Delegated Enforcement and Peer Punishment in Public Goods Provision." *Journal of Public Economics* 96(11–12): 1036–1046.

Andreoni, J., and J. M. Rao. 2011. "The Power of Asking: How Communication Affects Selfishness, Empathy, and Altruism." *Journal of Public Economics* 95(7–8): 513–520.

Andreoni, J., J. M. Rao, and H. Trachtman. 2017. "Avoiding the Ask: A Field Experiment on Altruism, Empathy, and Charitable Giving." *Journal of Political Economy* 125(3): 625–653.

Ariely, D., A. Bracha, and S. Meier. 2009. "Doing Good or Doing Well? Image Motivation and Monetary Incentives in Behaving Prosocially." *American Economic Review* 99(1): 544–555.

Bakija, J., and B. T. Heim. 2011. "Incentive and Distributional Consequences of Tax Expenditures: How Does Charitable Giving Respond to Incentives and Income? New Estimates from Panel Data." *Economic Analysis of Tax Expenditures* 64(2): part 2.

Bekkers, R. 2015. "When and Why Matches Are More Effective Subsidies Than Rebates." In *Replication in Experimental Economics: Research in Experimental Economics*, vol. 18, ed. C. A. Deck, E. Fatas, and T. Rosenblat, 186–211. Bingley, UK: Emerald.

Bekkers, R., and P. Wiepking. 2011. "A Literature Review of Empirical Studies of Philanthropy: Eight Mechanisms That Drive Charitable Giving." *Nonprofit and Voluntary Sector Quarterly* 40(5): 924–973.

Bénabou, R., and J. Tirole. 2006. "Incentives and Prosocial Behavior." *American Economic Review* 96(5): 1652–1678.

Blanken, I., N. van de Ven, and M. Zeelenberg. 2015. "A Meta-analytic Review of Moral Licensing." *Personality and Social Psychology Bulletin* 41(4): 540–558.

Blumkin, T., and E. Sadka. 2007. "A Case for Taxing Charitable Donations." *Journal of Public Economics* 91(7–8): 1555–1564.

Bracha, A., and L. Vesterlund. 2017. "Mixed Signals: Charity Reporting When Donations Signal Generosity and Income." *Games and Economic Behavior* 104: 24–42.

Brown, A. L., J. Meer, and J. F. Williams. 2018. "Why Do People Volunteer? An Experimental Analysis of Preferences for Time Donations." *Management Science* 65(4): 1455–1468.

Brown, E., and H. Lankford. 1992. "Gifts of Money and Gifts of Time Estimating the Effects of Tax Prices and Available Time." *Journal of Public Economics* 47(3): 321–341.

Brown, S., M. N. Harris, and K. Taylor. 2012. "Modelling Charitable Donations to an Unexpected Natural Disaster: Evidence from the U.S. Panel Study of Income Dynamics." *Journal of Economic Behavior and Organization* 84(1): 97–110.

Cairns, J., and R. Slonim. 2011. "Substitution Effects Across Charitable Donations." *Economics Letters* 111(2): 173–175.

Castillo, M., R. Petrie, and A. Samek. 2017. "Time to Give: A Field Experiment on Intertemporal Charitable Giving." Working paper.

Castillo, M., R. Petrie, and C. Wardell. 2014. "Fundraising Through Online Social Networks: A Field Experiment on Peer-to-Peer Solicitation." *Journal of Public Economics* 114: 29–35.

Chaudhuri, A. 2011. "Sustaining Cooperation in Laboratory Public Goods Experiments: A Selective Survey of the Literature." *Experimental Economics* 14(1): 47–83.

Clotfelter, C. T. 1985. *Federal Tax Policy and Charitable Giving.* Chicago: University of Chicago Press.

Corazzini, L., C. Cotton, and P. Valbonesi. 2015. "Donor Coordination in Project Funding: Evidence from a Threshold Public Goods Experiment." *Journal of Public Economics* 128: 16–29.

Council of Economic Advisers. 2017. *Evaluating the Anticipated Effects of Changes to the Mortgage Interest Deduction.* November. https://www .whitehouse.gov/sites/whitehouse.gov/files/ images/Effects%20of%20Changes%20to%20the %20Mortgage%20Interest%20Deduction %20FINAL.pdf.

Dahl, G. B., and M. R. Ransom. 1999. "Does Where You Stand Depend on Where You Sit? Tithing Donations and Self-Serving Beliefs." *American Economic Review* 89(4): 703–727.

Damgaard, M. T., and C. Gravert. 2018. "The Hidden Costs of Nudging: Experimental Evidence from Reminders in Fundraising." *Journal of Public Economics* 157: 15–26.

DeAngelo, G., and L. K. Gee. 2018. *Peers or Police? Detection and Sanctions in the Provision of Public Goods* (No. 11540). Institute for the Study of Labor (IZA).

Deck, C., and J. Murphy. 2018. "Donors Change Both Their Level and Pattern of Giving in Response to Contests Among Charities." *European Economic Review* 112 (2019): 91–106.

DellaVigna, S., J. A. List, and U. Malmendier. 2012. "Testing for Altruism and Social Pressure in Charitable Giving." *Quarterly Journal of Economics* 127(1): 1–56.

Deryugina, T., and B. Marx. 2015. *Do Causes Crowd Each Other Out? Evidence from Tornado Strikes.* Working paper.

Eckel, C., D. Herberich, and J. Meer. 2017. "A Field Experiment on Directed Giving at a Public University." *Journal of Behavioral and Experimental Economics* 66: 66–71.

———. "It's Not the Thought That Counts: A Field Experiment on Gift Exchange at a Public University." In *The Economics of Philanthropy*, ed. K. Scharf and M. Tonin, 145–160. Cambridge, MA: MIT Press, August 2018.

Elfenbein, D. W., R. Fisman, and B. McManus. 2012. "Charity as a Substitute for Reputation: Evidence from an Online Marketplace." *Review of Economic Studies* 79(4): 1441–1468.

Elfenbein, D. W., and B. McManus. 2010. "A Greater Price for a Greater Good? Evidence That Consumers Pay More for Charity-Linked Products." *American Economic Journal: Economic Policy* 2: 28–60.

Exley, C. L. 2015. "Excusing Selfishness in Charitable Giving: The Role of Risk." *Review of Economics Studies* 83(2): 587–628.

———. 2017. "Incentives for Prosocial Behavior: The Role of Reputations." *Management Science* 64(5): 2460–2471.

———. 2018. *Using Charity Metrics as an Excuse Not to Give.* Working paper.

Exley, C. L., and R. Petrie. 2018. "The Impact of a Surprise Donation Ask." *Journal of Public Economics* 158: 152–167.

Falk, A. 2007. "Gift Exchange in the Field." *Econometrica* 75: 1501–1511.

Feldman, N. E. 2010. "Time Is Money: Choosing Between Charitable Activities." *American Economic Journal: Economic Policy* 2(1): 103–130.

Filiz-Ozbay, E., and N. Uler. 2018. "Demand for Giving to Multiple Charities: An Experimental Study." *Journal of the European Economic Association.* https://doi.org/10.1093/jeea/jvy011.

Gee, L. K. 2011. "The Nature of Giving Time to Your Child's School." *Nonprofit and Voluntary Sector Quarterly* 40(3): 552–565.

Gee, L. K., and M. J. Schreck. 2018. "Do Beliefs About Peers Matter for Donation Matching? Experiments in the Field and Laboratory." *Games and Economic Behavior* 107: 282–297.

Giving USA. 2018. *Giving USA 2018: The Annual Report on Philanthropy for the Year 2017.* Chicago: Giving USA.

Glazer, A., and K. A. Konrad. 1996. "A Signaling Explanation for Charity." *American Economic Review* 86(4): 1019–1028.

Gneezy, U., A. Imas, and K. Madarász. 2014. "Conscience Accounting: Emotion Dynamics and Social Behavior." *Management Science* 60(11): 2645–2658.

Gneezy, U., E. A. Keenan, and A. Gneezy. 2014. "Avoiding Overhead Aversion in Charity." *Science* 346(6209): 632–635.

Harbaugh, W. T. 1998a. "The Prestige Motive for Making Charitable Transfers." *American Economic Review* 88(2): 277–282.

———. 1998b. "What Do Donations Buy? A Model of Philanthropy Based on Prestige and Warm Glow." *Journal of Public Economics* 67: 269–284.

Harwell, H., D. Meneses, C. Moceri, M. Rauckhorst, A. Zindler, and C. Eckel. 2015. "Did the Ice Bucket Challenge Drain the Philanthropic Reservoir?" Working paper, Economic Research Laboratory, Texas A&M University.

Jason, L. A., T. Rose, J. R. Ferrari, and R. Barone. 1984. "Personal Versus Impersonal Methods for Recruiting Blood Donations." *Journal of Social Psychology* 123(1): 139–140.

Jones, D. B. 2015. "The Supply and Demand of Motivated Labor: When Should We Expect to See Nonprofit Wage Gaps?" *Labour Economics* 32: 1–14.

Joulfaian, D. 2001. "Charitable Giving in Life and at Death." In *Rethinking Estate and Gift Taxation*, ed. W. G. Gale, J. R. Hines, and J. B. Slemrod, 350–374. Washington, DC: Brookings Institution Press.

———. 2005. "Choosing Between Gifts and Bequests: How Taxes Affect the Timing of Wealth Transfers." *Journal of Public Economics* 89(11–12): 2069–2091.

Kamdar, A., S. D. Levitt, J. A. List, B. Mullaney, and C. Syverson. 2015. *Once and Done: Leveraging Behavioral Economics to Increase Charitable Con-*

tributions. SPI Working Paper No. 25, Science of Philanthropy Initiative (SPI) Working Paper Series.

Karlan, D., and J. A. List. 2012. "How Can Bill and Melinda Gates Increase Other People's Donations to Fund Public Goods?" NBER Working Paper No. 17954.

Kessler, J. 2017. "Announcements of Support and Public Good Provision." *American Economic Review* 107(12): 3760–3787.

Kessler, J. B., K. L. Milkman, and C. Y. Zhang. "Getting the Rich and Powerful to Give." *Management Science*, April 26. https://pubsonline.informs.org/doi/10.1287/mnsc.2018.3142.

Krieg, J., and Samek, A. 2017. "When Charities Compete: A Laboratory Experiment with Simultaneous Public Goods." *Journal of Behavioral and Experimental Economics* 66: 40–57.

Kumru, C. S., and L. Vesterlund. 2010. "The Effect of Status on Charitable Giving." *Journal of Public Economic Theory* 12(4): 709–735.

Lacetera, N., M. Macis, and R. Slonim. 2012. "Will There Be Blood? Incentives and Displacement Effects in Pro-social Behavior." *American Economic Journal: Economic Policy* 4(1): 186–223.

Landry, C. E., A. Lange, J. A. List, M. K. Price, and N. G. Rupp. 2010. "Is a Donor in Hand Better than Two in the Bush? Evidence from a Natural Field Experiment." *American Economic Review* 100(3): 958–983.

Ledyard, J. O. 1995. "Public Goods: A Survey of Experimental Research." In *Handbook of Experimental Economics*, ed. J. Kagel and A. Roth, 111–194. Princeton, NJ: Princeton University Press.

Lilley, A., and R. Slonim. 2014. "The Price of Warm Glow." *Journal of Public Economics* 114: 58–74.

List, J. A., and M. K. Price. 2009. "The Role of Social Connections in Charitable Fundraising: Evidence from a Natural Field Experiment." *Journal of Economic Behavior and Organization* 69(2): 160–169.

List, J. A., and D. Rondeau. 2003. "The Impact of Challenge Gifts on Charitable Giving: An Experimental Investigation." *Economics Letters* 79(2): 153–159.

Look to the Stars. 2018. "Marcus Samuelsson and Ethan Hawke Join the Y for New Video Series."

February 19. https://www.looktothestars.org/news/17615-marcus-samuelsson-and-ethan-hawke-join-the-y-for-new-video-series.

Meer, J. 2011. "Brother, Can You Spare a Dime? Peer Pressure in Charitable Solicitation." *Journal of Public Economics* 95(7–8): 926–941.

———. 2013. "The Habit of Giving." *Economic Inquiry* 51(4): 2002–2017.

———. 2014. "Effects of the Price of Charitable Giving: Evidence from an Online Crowdfunding Platform." *Journal of Economic Behavior and Organization* 103: 113–124.

———. 2017. "Does Fundraising Create New Giving?" *Journal of Public Economics* 145: 82–93.

Meer, J., and H. S. Rosen. 2009. "Altruism and the Child-Cycle of Alumni Donations." *American Economic Journal: Economic Policy* 1(1): 258–286.

———. 2011. "The ABCs of Charitable Solicitation." *Journal of Public Economics* 95(5–6): 363–371.

———. 2012. "Does Generosity Beget Generosity? Alumni Giving and Undergraduate Financial Aid." *Economics of Education Review* 31(6): 890–907.

———. 2013. "Donative Behavior at the End of Life." *Journal of Economic Behavior and Organization* 92: 192–201.

Meier, S. 2007. "Do Subsidies Increase Charitable Giving in the Long Run? Matching Donations in a Field Experiment." *Journal of the European Economic Association* 5(6): 1203–1222.

Merriam-Webster. n.d. "Altruism," def. 2. https://www.merriam-webster.com/dictionary/altruism, accessed August 28, 2018.

Ottoni-Wilhelm, M., L. Vesterlund, and H. Xie. 2017. "Why Do People Give? Testing Pure and Impure Altruism." *American Economic Review* 107(11): 3617–3633.

Potters, J., M. Sefton, and L. Vesterlund. 2005. "After You—Endogenous Sequencing in Voluntary Contribution Games." *Journal of Public Economics* 89(8): 1399–1419.

———. 2007. "Leading-by-Example and Signaling in Voluntary Contribution Games: An Experimental Study." *Economic Theory* 33(1): 169–182.

Price, M. K. 2008. "Fund-Raising Success and a Solicitor's Beauty Capital: Do Blondes Raise More Funds?" *Economics Letters* 100(3): 351–354.

Raihani, N. J., and S. Smith. 2015. "Competitive Helping in Online Giving." *Current Biology* 25(9): 1183–1186.

Rand, D. G., and M. A. Nowak. 2013. "Human Cooperation." *Trends in Cognitive Sciences* 17(8): 413–425.

Reinstein, D. A. 2011. "Does One Charitable Contribution Come at the Expense of Another?" *BE Journal of Economic Analysis and Policy* 11(1): 1–54.

Rosen, H. S., and S. T. Sims. 2011. "Altruistic Behavior and Habit Formation." *Nonprofit Management and Leadership* 21(3): 235–253.

Ruhm, C., and C. Borkoski. 2003. "Compensation in the Nonprofit Sector." *Journal of Human Resources* 38(4): 992–1021.

Samuelson, P. A. 1993. "Altruism as a Problem Involving Group Versus Individual Selection in Economics and Biology." *American Economic Review* 83(2): 143–148.

Sanders, M., and S. Smith. 2016. "Can Simple Prompts Increase Bequest Giving? Field Evidence from a Legal Call Centre." *Journal of Economic Behavior and Organization* 125: 179–191.

Scharf, K. A., S. Smith, and M. Wilhelm. 2017. *Lift and Shift: The Effect of Fundraising Interventions in Charity Space and Time.* CEPR Discussion Paper No. DP12338, September. https://ssrn.com/abstract=3047325.

Schmitz, J. 2018. "Is Charitable Giving a Zero-Sum Game? The Effect of Competition Between Charities on Giving Behavior." Working paper, ETH Zurich.

Shang, J., and R. Croson. 2009. "A Field Experiment in Charitable Contribution: The Impact of Social Information on the Voluntary Provision of Public Goods." *Economic Journal* 119(540): 1422–1439.

Small, D. A., and G. Loewenstein. 2003. "Helping a Victim or Helping the Victim: Altruism and Identifiability." *Journal of Risk and Uncertainty* 26(1): 5–16.

Smith, S., F. Windmeijer, and E. Wright. 2015. "Peer Effects in Charitable Giving: Evidence from the (Running) Field." *Economic Journal* 125(585): 1053–1071.

Soskis, B. 2017. "Giving Numbers: Why, What, and How Are We Counting?" Urban Institute, March. https://urban.org/sites/default/files/publication/89406/giving_numbers_1.pdf.

Steel, E. 2014. "'Ice Bucket Challenge' Has Raised Millions for ALS Association." *New York Times*, August 17. http://nytimes.com/2014/08/18/business/ice-bucket-challenge-has-raised-millions-for-als-association.html.

Steinberg, R. 1990. "Taxes and Giving: New Findings." *Voluntas: International Journal of Voluntary and Nonprofit Organizations* 1(2): 61–79.

Van Diepen, M., B. Donkers, and P. H. Franses. 2009. "Dynamic and Competitive Effects of Direct Mailings: A Charitable Giving Application." *Journal of Marketing Research* 46(1): 120–133.

Vesterlund, L. 2003. "The Informational Value of Sequential Fundraising." *Journal of Public Economics* 87(3–4): 627–657.

———. 2006. "Why Do People Give?" In *The Nonprofit Sector: A Research Handbook*, 2nd ed., ed. W. W. Powell and R. Steinberg, 168–190. New Haven, CT: Yale University Press.

Yeomans, M., and O. Al-Ubaydli. 2018. "How Does Fundraising Affect Volunteering? Evidence from a Natural Field Experiment." *Journal of Economic Psychology* 64: 57–72.

Yörük, B. K. 2009. "How Responsive Are Charitable Donors to Requests to Give?" *Journal of Public Economics* 93(9–10): 1111–1117.

Chapter 25. What Do Volunteers Do?

Alexander, J. 2006. *The Civil Sphere*. New York: Oxford University Press.

Bayat, A. 2010. *Life as Politics*. Amsterdam: Amsterdam University Press.

Bonetti, M., and G. Riccardo. 2015. "Blurring the Borders of Voluntary Action in Times of Crisis: The Program of Short-Term Volunteering of Expo Milan 2015." Tenth Annual Conference in Interpretive Policy Analysis, University of Lille, Lille, France.

Carlsen, H. A. B. 2019. "Habits and Flows in Refugee Solidarity Activism: An Interactional Approach by Digital Means." Doctoral diss., University of Copenhagen.

Clément, K. 2015. "Unlikely Mobilisations: How Ordinary Russian People Become Involved in Collective Action." *European Journal of Cultural and Political Sociology* 2(3–4): 211–240.

———. 2017. "Social Imagination and Solidarity in Precarious Times: The Case of Lower Class People in Post-Soviet Russia." *Russian Sociological Review* 16(4): 28–45.

Daniels, A. K. 1988. *Invisible Careers: Women Civic Leaders from the Volunteer World.* Chicago: University of Chicago Press.

Dewey, J. 1920. *Reconstruction in Philosophy.* New York: Holt.

Elias, N. (1939) 1982. *The History of Manners* (The Civilizing Process #1), trans. Edmund F. N. Jephcott. New York: Pantheon.

Eliasoph, N. 1998. *Avoiding Politics: How Americans Produce Apathy in Everyday Life.* New York: Cambridge University Press.

———. 2011. *Making Volunteers: Civic Life After Welfare's End.* Princeton, NJ: Princeton University Press.

———. 2016. "The Mantra of Empowerment Talk: An Essay." *Journal of Civil Society* 12(3): 247–265.

Eliasoph, N., and P. Lichterman. 2003. "Culture in Interaction." *American Journal of Sociology* 108(4): 735–794.

Elsayed, Y. 2018. "At the Intersection of Social Entrepreneurship and Social Movements: The Case of Egypt and Arab Spring." *Voluntas: International Journal of Voluntary and Nonprofit Organizations* 29: 819–831. https://link.springer.com/epdf/10.1007/s11266-017-9943-0.

Garrow, E., and Y. Hasenfeld. 2014. "Institutional Logics, Moral Frames, and Advocacy: Explaining the Purpose of Advocacy Among Nonprofit Human-Service Organizations." *Nonprofit and Voluntary Sector Quarterly* 48: 80–98.

Gaventa, J. 1980. *Power and Powerlessness: Acquiescence and Rebellion in an Appalachian Valley.* Urbana: University of Illinois Press.

Grootegoed, E. 2013. *Dignity of Dependence: Welfare State Reform and the Struggle for Respect.* PhD diss., University of Amsterdam.

Grootegoed, E., B. Bröer, and J. W. Duyvendak. 2013. "Too Ashamed to Complain: Cuts to Publicly Financed Care and Clients' Waiving of Their Right to Appeal." *Journal of Social Policy* 12(3): 475–486.

Hamidi, C. 2010. *La société civile dans les cites: Engagement associatif et politisation dans des associations de quartier.* Paris: Economica.

Handy, F., et al. 2010. "A Cross-Cultural Examination of Student Volunteering: Is It All About Resume Building?" *Nonprofit and Voluntary Sector Quarterly* 39(3): 498–523.

Helander, V., and S. Sundback. 1998. "Defining the Nonprofit Sector: Finland." *Working Papers of the Johns Hopkins Comparative Nonprofit Sector Project*, no. 34, ed. L. M. Salamon and H. K. Anheier. Baltimore: Johns Hopkins Institute for Policy Studies.

Henriksen, L. S., S. R. Smith, and A. Zimmer. 2015. "Welfare Mix and Hybridity: Flexible Adjustments to Changed Environments." *Voluntas: International Journal of Voluntary and Nonprofit Organizations* 26: 1591–1600.

Hillman, A. 1960. *Neighborhood Centers Today.* New York: National Federation of Settlements and Neighborhood Centers.

Hustinx, L., and E. De Waele. 2015. "Managing Hybridity in a Changing Welfare Mix: Everyday Practices in an Entrepreneurial Nonprofit in Belgium." *Voluntas: International Journal of Voluntary and Nonprofit Organizations* 26: 1666–1689.

Hustinx, L., and F. Lammertyn. 2003. "Collective and Reflexive Styles of Volunteering: A Sociological Modernization Perspective." *Voluntas: International Journal of Voluntary and Nonprofit Organizations* 14: 167–187.

Krinsky, J., and M. Simonet. 2016. *Who Cleans the Park? Public Work and Urban Governance in New York City.* Chicago: University of Chicago Press.

Kropotkin, P. (1892) 2006. *The Conquest of Bread.* Chico, CA: AK Press.

Lichterman, P. 2005. *Elusive Togetherness: Church Groups Trying to Bridge America's Divisions.* Princeton, NJ: Princeton University Press.

Lichterman, P., and N. Eliasoph. 2014. "Civic Action." *American Journal of Sociology* 120(3): 798–863.

Luhtakallio, E. 2012. *Practicing Democracy: Local Activism and Politics in France and Finland.* London: Palgrave.

McQuarrie, M. 2011. "Nonprofits and the Reconstruction of Urban Governance: Housing Production and Community Development in Cleveland, 1975–2005." In *Politics and Part-*

nerships: The Role of Voluntary Associations in America's Political Past and Present, ed. E. S. Clemens and D. Guthrie, 237–268. Chicago: University of Chicago Press.

Meilvang, M. L., H. B. Carlsen, and A. Blok. 2018. "Methods of Engagement: On Civic Participation Formats as Composition Devices in Urban Planning." *European Journal of Cultural and Political Sociology* 5(1–2): 12–41.

Meriluoto, T. 2018. "Neutral Experts or Passionate Participants? Renegotiating Expertise and the Right to Act in Finnish Participatory Social Policy." *European Journal of Cultural and Political Sociology* 5(1–2): 116–139.

Mische, A. 2009. "Projects and Possibilities: Researching Futures in Action." *Sociological Forum* 24(3): 694–704.

Mosley, J. 2012. "Keeping the Lights On: How Government Funding Concerns Drive the Advocacy Agenda of Nonprofit Homeless Service Providers." *Journal of Public Administration Research and Theory* 4: 2–26.

Muelebach, A. 2012. *The Moral Neoliberal: Welfare and Citizenship in Italy.* Chicago: University of Chicago Press.

Norgaard, K. 2011. *Living in Denial: Climate Change, Emotions, and Everyday Life.* Cambridge, MA: MIT Press.

Ramirez, B. 2016. "Three 'Styles' of Immigrant Aid in California: Publicizing Stories, Helping One at a Time, and Protesting Unjust Policies." Unpublished seminar paper, Contemporary Theory Seminar, USC Sociology Department, Los Angeles.

Rosaldo, M. Z. 1982. "The Things We Do with Words: Ilongot Speech Acts and Speech Act Theory in Philosophy." *Language in Society* 11(2): 203–237.

Salamon, L. M., H. K. Anheier, R. List, S. Toepler, and S. W. Sokolowski. 2003. *Global Civil Society: An Overview.* Baltimore: Johns Hopkins Center for Civil Society Studies.

Sanyal, P. 2014. *Credit to Capabilities.* New York: Cambridge University Press.

Scott, J. 1990. *Domination and the Arts of Resistance.* New Haven, CT: Yale University Press.

Shachar, I. Y., L. Hustinx, L. Roza, and L.C.P.M. Meijs. 2016. "A New Spirit Across Sectors: Con-

structing a Common Justification for Corporate Volunteering." *European Journal of Cultural and Political Sociology* 5(1–2): 90–115.

Shachar, I. Y., and L. Hustinx. 2019. "Settling the Neoliberal Contradiction Through Corporate Volunteering: Governing Employees in the Era of Cognitive Capitalism." *Journal of Contemporary Ethnography.* https://doi.org/10.1177/0891241619828442.

Smith, S. R., and M. Lipsky. 1993. *Nonprofits for Hire: The Welfare State in the Age of Contracting.* Cambridge, MA: Harvard University Press.

Spires, A. 2011. "Organizational Homophily in International Grantmaking: US-Based Foundations and Their Grantees in China." *Journal of Civil Society* 7(3): 305–331.

Stauber, J., and S. Rampton. 1996. *Toxic Sludge Is Good for You: Lies, Damn Lies and the Public Relations Industry.* Monroe, ME: Common Courage Press.

Swidler, A., and S. C. Watkins. 2009. "'Teach a Man to Fish': The Sustainability Doctrine and Its Social Consequences." *World Development* 37(7): 1182–1196.

Talpin, J. 2011. *How Ordinary Citizens (Sometimes) Become Competent in Participatory Budgeting Institutions.* Colchester, UK: ECPR Press.

Thompson, E. P. 1969. "The Moral Economy of the English Crowd in the Eighteenth Century." *Past and Present* 50(1): 76–136.

Tocqueville, A. de. (1835) 1969. *Democracy in America,* ed. J. P. Mayer, trans. G. Lawrence. Garden City, NY: Doubleday.

Toubøl, J. 2017. "Differential Recruitment to and Outcomes of Solidarity Activism: Ethics, Values and Group Style in the Danish Refugee Solidarity Movement." Doctoral diss., University of Copenhagen.

Tugal, C. 2017. *Caring for the Poor: Islamic and Christian Benevolence in a Liberal World.* New York: Routledge.

Varieties of Democracy Project. 2018. https://www.v-dem.net/en/.

Verhoeven, I., and E. Tonkens. 2013. "Talking Active Citizenship: Framing Welfare State Reform in England and the Netherlands." *Social Policy and Society* 12: 415–426.

Walker, E. T. 2014. *Grassroots for Hire: Public Affairs Consultants in American Democracy.* New York: Cambridge University Press.

Wilson, J. 2012. "Volunteerism Research: A Review Essay." *Nonprofit and Voluntary Sector Quarterly* 41(2): 176–212.

Wolfe, A. 1989. *Whose Keeper?* Berkeley: University of California Press.

World Bank. 2012. "When Do Participatory Development Projects Work?" http://www. worldbank .org/en/news/press-release/2012/11/14/when-do -participatory-development-projects-work.

Xu, B. 2017. *The Politics of Compassion: The Sichuan Earthquake and Civic Engagement in China.* Stanford, CA: Stanford University Press.

Zhuravlev, O., S. Yerpyleva, and N. Saveleva. 2017. "Nationwide Protest and Local Action: How Anti-Putin Rallies Politicized Russian Urban Activism." *Russian Analytical Digest* 210: 15–19.

Chapter 26. Religious Organizations: Crosscutting the Nonprofit Sector

Albert, S., and D. A. Whetten. 1985. "Organizational Identity." *Research in Organizational Behavior* 7: 263–295.

Alvesson, M. 2012. *Understanding Organizational Culture.* Thousand Oaks, CA: SAGE.

Amirkhanyan, A. A., H. J. Kim, and K. T. Lambright. 2008. "Does the Public Sector Outperform the Nonprofit and For-Profit Sectors? Evidence from a National Panel Study on Nursing Home Quality and Access." *Journal of Policy Analysis and Management* 27(2): 326–353.

Ammerman, N. T. 2005. *Pillars of Faith: American Congregations and Their Partners.* Berkeley: University of California Press.

Austin, T. S., D. P. King, A. Hemphill, and B. R. Fulton. 2018. *Identity and Activity of Nonprofit Humanitarian Organizations: Defining and Estimating the Reach of Religious Affiliation in the U.S. and Beyond.* Paper presented at the Association for Research on Nonprofit Organizations and Voluntary Action Annual Meeting, Austin, TX, November 15.

Baggett, J. P. 2000. *Habitat for Humanity: Building Private Homes, Building Public Religion.* Philadelphia: Temple University Press.

Barbee, D. 2004. "Finding Sanctuary." *Fort Worth (TX) Star-Telegram*, December 5.

Barnes, T. 2014. "Tennessee Says NSPIRE Outreach Isn't 'Who They Say They Are.'" *Tennessean*, December 29.

Battilana, J., and T. D'Aunno. 2009. "Institutional Work and the Paradox of Embedded Agency." In *Institutional Work: Actors and Agency in Institutional Studies of Organizations*, ed. T. Lawrence, R. Suddaby, and B. Leca, 31–58. New York: Cambridge University Press.

Beckford, J. A. 1985. "Religious Organizations." In *The Sacred in a Secular Age*, ed. P. E. Hammond, 124–138. The Hague: Mouton.

Berger, J. 2003. "Religious Nongovernmental Organizations: An Exploratory Analysis." *Voluntas: International Journal of Voluntary and Nonprofit Organizations* 14(1): 15–39.

Berger, P. L. 1967. *The Sacred Canopy: Elements of a Sociological Theory of Religion.* New York: Doubleday.

Bielefeld, W., and W. S. Cleveland. 2013a. "Defining Faith-Based Organizations and Understanding Them Through Research." *Nonprofit and Voluntary Sector Quarterly* 42(3): 442–467.

———. 2013b. "Faith-Based Organizations as Service Providers and Their Relationship to Government." *Nonprofit and Voluntary Sector Quarterly* 42(3): 468–494.

Biscotti, D., and N. W. Biggart. 2014. "Organizing Belief: Interfaith Social Change Organizations in the Religious-Environmental Movement." *Research in the Sociology of Organizations* 41: 413–439.

Boddie, S. C., and R. A. Cnaan. 2012. *Faith-Based Social Services: Measures, Assessments, and Effectiveness.* New York: Routledge.

Boone, C., and S. Özcan. 2016. "Ideological Purity Vs. Hybridization Trade-Off: When Do Islamic Banks Hire Managers from Conventional Banking?" *Organization Science* 27(6): 1380–1396.

Bostwick, H. 2007. "What Constitutes a Church Under Federal Laws?" https://www.legalzoom .com/articles/what-constitutes-a-church-under -federal-laws.

Brandsen, T., W. Van de Donk, and K. Putters. 2005. "Griffins or Chameleons? Hybridity as a Permanent and Inevitable Characteristic of the

Third Sector." *International Journal of Public Administration* 28(9–10): 749–765.

Brauer, S. G. 2017. "How Many Congregations Are There? Updating a Survey-Based Estimate." *Journal for the Scientific Study of Religion* 56(2): 438–448.

Braunstein, R., B. R. Fulton, and R. L. Wood. 2014. "The Role of Bridging Cultural Practices in Racially and Socioeconomically Diverse Civic Organizations." *American Sociological Review* 79(4): 705–725.

Brown, T. J., P. A. Dacin, M. G. Pratt, and D. A. Whetten. 2006. "Identity, Intended Image, Construed Image, and Reputation: An Interdisciplinary Framework and Suggested Terminology." *Journal of the Academy of Marketing Science* 34(2): 99–106.

Burchardt, M. 2013. "Faith-Based Humanitarianism: Organizational Change and Everyday Meanings in South Africa." *Sociology of Religion* 74(1): 30–55.

Cadge W., and M. E. Konieczny. 2014. "'Hidden in Plain Sight': The Significance of Religion and Spirituality in Secular Organizations." *Sociology of Religion* 75(4): 551–563.

Cadge, W., and R. Wuthnow, eds. 2006. *Religion and the Nonprofit Sector*. New Haven, CT: Yale University Press.

Cameron, H. 2004. "Typology of Religious Characteristics of Social Service and Educational Organizations and Programs—A European Response." *Nonprofit and Voluntary Sector Quarterly* 33(1): 146–150.

Candid. 2019. *501c3 Organizational Data*. GuideStar Pro database.

Chan-Serafin, S., A. P. Brief, and J. M. George. 2013. "How Does Religion Matter and Why? Religion and the Organizational Sciences." *Organization Science* 24(5): 1585–1600.

Charity Navigator. 2018. *Charity Navigator Advisories*. https://www.charitynavigator.org/index.cfm?bay=search.cnadvisories.

Chaves, M. 1993. "Intraorganizational Power and Internal Secularization in Protestant Denominations." *American Journal of Sociology* 99(1): 1–48.

———. 1996. "Ordaining Women: The Diffusion of an Organizational Innovation." *American Journal of Sociology* 101(4): 840–873.

———. 2002. "Religious Organizations: Data Resources and Research Opportunities." *American Behavioral Scientist* 45(10): 1523–1549.

———. 2004. *Congregations in America*. Cambridge, MA: Harvard University Press.

Cimino, R. P., and C. Smith. 2014. *Atheist Awakening: Secular Activism and Community in America*. New York: Oxford University Press.

Clarke, M., and V.-A. Ware. 2015. "Understanding Faith-Based Organizations: How FBOs Are Contrasted with NGOs in International Development Literature." *Progress in Development Studies* 15(1): 37–48.

Clerkin, R. M., and K. A. Grønbjerg. 2007. "The Capacities and Challenges of Faith-Based Human Service Organizations." *Public Administration Review* 67(1): 115–126.

Cnaan, R., and D. Curtis. 2013. "Religious Congregations as Voluntary Associations: An Overview." *Nonprofit and Voluntary Sector Quarterly* 42(1): 7–33.

Cornwell, T. W. Jr. 2017. *Nonprofit Management Education in Seminaries*. PhD diss., Wilmington University.

DiMaggio, P. J., and H. K. Anheier. 1990. "The Sociology of Nonprofit Organizations and Sectors." *Annual Review of Sociology* 16(1): 137–159.

Doherty, B., H. Haugh, and F. Lyon. 2014. "Social Enterprises as Hybrid Organizations: A Review and Research Agenda." *International Journal of Management Reviews* 16(4): 417–436.

Dyck, B., F. A. Starke, H. Harder, and T. Hecht. 2005. "Do the Organizational Structures of Religious Places of Worship Reflect Their Statements of Faith? An Exploratory Study." *Review of Religious Research* 47(1): 51–69.

Ebaugh, H. R., J. S. Chafetz, and P. F. Pipes. 2006. "Where's the Faith in Faith-Based Organizations? Measures and Correlates of Religiosity in Faith-Based Social Service Coalitions." *Social Forces* 84(4): 2259–2272.

———. 2007. "Collaborations with Faith-Based Social Service Coalitions." *Nonprofit Management and Leadership* 18(2): 175–191.

Ebrahim, A. 2012. "Enacting Our Field." *Nonprofit Management and Leadership* 23(1): 13–28.

Eby, J., E. Iverson, J. Smyers, and E. Kekic. 2011. "The Faith Community's Role in Refugee Resettlement in the United States." *Journal of Refugee Studies* 24(3): 586–605.

Edwards, K. L. 2008. "Bring Race to the Center: The Importance of Race in Racially Diverse Religious Organizations." *Journal for the Scientific Study of Religion* 47(1): 5–9.

Edwards, K. L., B. Christerson, and M. O. Emerson. 2013. "Race, Religious Organizations, and Integration." *Annual Review of Sociology* 39: 211–228.

Eliasoph, N., and P. Lichterman. 2003. "Culture in Interaction." *American Journal of Sociology* 108(4): 735–794.

Emerson, M. O., and D. Hartman. 2006. "The Rise of Religious Fundamentalism." *Annual Review of Sociology* 32: 127–144.

Fine, G. A. 2012. "Group Culture and the Interaction Order: Local Sociology on the Meso-Level." *Annual Review of Sociology* 38: 159–179.

Fine, G. A., and T. Hallett. 2014. "Group Cultures and the Everyday Life of Organizations: Interaction Orders and Meso-Analysis." *Organization Studies* 35(12): 1773–1792.

Fitzgerald, S. 2009. "Cooperative Collective Action: Framing Faith-Based Community Development." *Mobilization: An International Quarterly* 14(2): 181–198.

Friedland, R., and R. R. Alford. 1991. "Bringing Society Back In: Symbols, Practices and Institutional Contradictions." In *The New Institutionalism in Organizational Analysis*, ed. W. W. Powell and P. J. DiMaggio, 232–263. Chicago: University of Chicago Press.

Fu, J. S., K. R. Cooper, and M. Shumate. 2017. *Beyond Funding: The Role of Religiosity in Faith-Based Partnerships*. Paper presented at the Association for Research on Nonprofit Organizations and Voluntary Associations Annual Meeting, Grand Rapids, MI, November 16.

Fulton, B. R. 2011. "Black Churches and HIV/AIDS: Factors Influencing Congregations' Responsiveness to Social Issues." *Journal for the Scientific Study of Religion* 50(3): 617–630.

———. 2016a. "Network Ties and Organizational Action: Explaining Variation in Social Service Provision Patterns." *Management and Organizational Studies* 3(3): 1–20.

———. 2016b. "Trends in Addressing Social Needs: A Longitudinal Study of Congregation-Based

Service Provision and Political Participation." *Religions* 7(5): 51–67.

———. 2017. "Fostering Muslim Civic Engagement Through Faith-Based Community Organizing." *Journal of Muslim Philanthropy and Civil Society* 1(1): 23–39.

Fulton, B. R., M. Oyakawa, and R. L. Wood. Forthcoming. "Critical Standpoint: Leaders of Color Advancing Racial Equality in Predominantly White Organizations." *Nonprofit Management and Leadership*.

Fulton, B. R., and R. L. Wood. 2017. "Achieving and Leveraging Diversity Through Faith-Based Organizing." In *Religion and Progressive Activism*, ed. R. Braunstein, T. N. Fuist, and R. H. Williams, 29–55. New York: NYU Press.

———. 2018. "Civil Society Organizations and the Enduring Role of Religion in Promoting Democratic Engagement." *Voluntas: International Journal of Voluntary and Nonprofit Organizations* 29(5): 1068–1079.

Gidron, B., and Y. Hasenfeld. 2012. *Social Enterprises: An Organizational Perspective*. Basingstoke, UK: Palgrave Macmillan.

Gioia, D. A., S. D. Patvardhan, A. L. Hamilton, and K. G. Corley. 2013. "Organizational Identity Formation and Change." *Academy of Management Annals* 7(1): 123–193.

Gioia, D. A., K. N. Price, A. L. Hamilton, and J. B. Thomas. 2010. "Forging an Identity: An Insider-Outsider Study of Processes Involved in the Formation of Organizational Identity." *Administrative Science Quarterly* 55(1): 1–46.

Giving USA. 2019. *Giving USA 2019: The Annual Report on Philanthropy for the Year 2018*. Chicago: Giving USA.

Graddy, E. A., and K. Ye. 2006. "Faith-Based Versus Secular Providers of Social Services—Differences in What, How, and Where." *Journal of Health and Human Services Administration* 29(3): 309–335.

Grammich, C., K. Hadaway, R. Houseal, D. E. Jones, A. Krindatch, R. Stanley, and R. H. Taylor. 2012. *2010 U.S. Religion Census: Religious Congregations and Membership Study*. Lenexa, KS: Association of Statisticians of American Religious Bodies.

Greenwood, R., M. Raynard, F. Kodeih, E. R. Micelotta, and M. Lounsbury. 2011. "Institutional

Complexity and Organizational Responses." *Academy of Management Annals* 5(1): 317–371.

Grønbjerg, K. A., and B. Never. 2004. "The Role of Religious Networks and Other Factors in Types of Volunteer Work." *Nonprofit Management and Leadership* 14(3): 263–289.

GuideStar. 2018a. *Profile for Campus Crusade for Christ.* GuideStar Premium database. https://www.guidestar.org/profile/95-6006173.

———. 2018b. *Profile for World Vision International* GuideStar Premium database. https://www.guidestar.org/profile/95-3202116.

Gümüsay, A. A. 2015. "Entrepreneurship from an Islamic Perspective." *Journal of Business Ethics* 130(1): 199–208.

———. 2017. "The Potential for Plurality and Prevalence of the Religious Institutional Logic." *Business and Society*, December 7. https://doi.org/10.1177%2F0007650317745634.

He, H., and A. D. Brown. 2013. "Organizational Identity and Organizational Identification: A Review of the Literature and Suggestions for Future Research." *Group and Organization Management* 38(1): 3–35.

Herzog, K. L. 2016. *Perceptions of Executive Leadership in the YMCA.* Fond du Lac, WI: Marian University.

Hinings, C. R., and M. Raynard. 2014. "Organizational Form, Structure, and Religious Organizations." *Research in the Sociology of Organizations* 41: 159–186.

Hodge, D. R. 2011. "Using Spiritual Interventions in Practice: Developing Some Guidelines from Evidence-Based Practice." *Social Work* 56(2): 149–158.

Hopkins, B. R. 2016. *The Law of Tax-Exempt Organizations*, 11th ed. Hoboken, NJ: Wiley.

Hopkins, B. R., and D. Middlebrook. 2008. *Nonprofit Law for Religious Organizations: Essential Questions and Answers.* Hoboken, NJ: Wiley.

Hugen, B., and R. Venema. 2009. "The Difference of Faith: The Influence of Faith in Human Service Programs." *Journal of Religion and Spirituality in Social Work* 28(4): 405–429.

Hwang, H., and W. W. Powell. 2009. "The Rationalization of Charity: The Influences of Professionalism in the Nonprofit Sector." *Administrative Science Quarterly* 54(2): 268–298.

Jäger, U., and T. Beyes. 2010. "Strategizing in NPOs: A Case Study on the Practice of Organizational Change Between Social Mission and Economic Rationale." *Voluntas: International Journal of Voluntary and Nonprofit Organizations* 21(1): 82–100.

Jay, J. 2013. "Navigating Paradox as a Mechanism of Change and Innovation in Hybrid Organizations." *Academy of Management Journal* 56(1): 137–159.

Jeavons, T. H. 1998. "Identifying Characteristics of Relgious Organizations: An Exploratory Proposal." In *Sacred Companies: Organizational Aspects of Religion and Religious Aspects of Organizations*, ed. N. J. Demerath, P. D. Hall, T. Schmitt, and R. H. Williams, 79–95. New York: Oxford University Press.

———. 2004. "Religious and Faith-Based Organizations: Do We Know One When We See One?" *Nonprofit and Voluntary Sector Quarterly* 33(1): 140–145.

Johnson, T. M., and B. J. Grim. 2013. *The World's Religions in Figures: An Introduction to International Religious Demography.* Hoboken, NJ: Wiley.

Kissane, R. J. 2008. "How Do Faith-Based Organizations Compare to Secular Providers? Nonprofit Directors' and Poor Women's Assessments of FBOs." *Journal of Poverty* 11(4): 91–115.

Kraatz, M. S., and E. S. Block, eds. 2008. *Organizational Implications of Institutional Pluralism.* London: SAGE.

Kreiner, G. E., E. Hollensbe, M. L. Sheep, B. R. Smith, and N. Kataria. 2015. "Elasticity and the Dialectic Tensions of Organizational Identity: How Can We Hold Together While We Are Pulling Apart?" *Academy of Management Journal* 58(4): 981–1011.

Kreutzer, K., and U. Jäger. 2011. "Volunteering Versus Managerialism: Conflict over Organizational Identity in Voluntary Associations." *Nonprofit and Voluntary Sector Quarterly* 40(4): 634–661.

Lainer-Vos, D. 2012. "Manufacturing National Attachments: Gift-Giving, Market Exchange and the Construction of Irish and Zionist Diaspora Bonds." *Theory and Society* 41(1): 73–106.

LaVigne, N. G., D. Brazzell, and K. Small. 2007. *Evaluation of Florida's Faith- and Character-Based*

Institutions. Washington, DC: Urban Institute Press.

Lawrence, T., B. Leca, and T. Zilber. 2013. "Institutional Work: Current Research, New Directions and Overlooked Issues." *Organization Studies* 34(8): 1023–1033.

Lawrence, T., and R. Suddaby. 2006. "Institutions and Institutional Work." In *The Sage Handbook of Organization Studies*, 2nd ed., ed. S. R. Clegg, C. Hardy, T. Lawrence, and W. R. Nord, 215–254. London: SAGE.

Lawrence, T., R. Suddaby, and B. Leca. 2009. *Institutional Work: Actors and Agency in Institutional Studies of Organizations*. New York: Cambridge University Press.

Leondar-Wright, B. 2014. *Missing Class: How Seeing Class Cultures Can Strengthen Social Movement Groups*. Ithaca, NY: Cornell University Press.

Levin, J. 2014. "Faith-Based Initiatives in Health Promotion: History, Challenges, and Current Partnerships." *American Journal of Health Promotion* 28(3): 139–141.

Leviton, L. C., C. Herrera, S. K. Pepper, N. Fishman, and D. P. Racine. 2006. "Faith in Action: Capacity and Sustainability of Volunteer Organizations." *Evaluation and Program Planning* 29(2): 201–207.

Lichterman, P. 1995. "Piecing Together Multicultural Community: Cultural Differences in Community Building Among Grassroots Environmentalists." *Social Problems* 42(4): 513–534.

———. 2012. "Religion in Public Action: From Actors to Settings." *Sociological Theory* 30(1): 15–36.

Lim, C., and C. A. MacGregor. 2012. "Religion and Volunteering in Context: Disentangling the Contextual Effects of Religion on Voluntary Behavior." *American Sociological Review* 77(5): 747–779.

Lindsay, D. M. 2010. "Organizational Liminality and Interstitial Creativity: The Fellowship of Power." *Social Forces* 89(1): 163–184.

Marti, G., and G. Ganiel. 2014. *The Deconstructed Church: Understanding Emerging Christianity*. New York: Oxford University Press.

Martin, J., and P. Frost. 2011. "The Organizational Culture War Games." In *Sociology of Organizations: Structures and Relationships*, ed. M.

Godwyn and J. H. Gittell, 315–326. Thousand Oaks, CA: Pine Forge Press.

McKeever, B. S. 2018. *The Nonprofit Sector in Brief 2018: Public Charities, Giving, and Volunteering*. Washington, DC: Urban Institute Press.

Meyer, J. W., and B. Rowan. 1977. "Institutionalized Organizations: Formal Structure as Myth and Ceremony." *American Journal of Sociology* 83(2): 340–363.

Minkoff, D. C. 2002. "The Emergence of Hybrid Organizational Forms: Combining Identity -Based Service Provision and Political Action." *Nonprofit and Voluntary Sector Quarterly* 31(3): 377–401.

Monsma, S. V. 2009. *Putting Faith in Partnerships: Welfare-to-Work in Four Cities*. Ann Arbor: University of Michigan Press.

Mundey, P., D. P. King, and B. R. Fulton. 2019. "The Economic Practices of U.S. Congregations: A Review of Current Research and Future Opportunities." *Social Compass*, June 4. https://doi.org/ 10.1177/0037768619852230.

Netting, F. E., M. K. O'Connor, and G. Yancey. 2006. "Belief Systems in Faith-Based Human Service Programs." *Journal of Religion and Spirituality in Social Work* 25(3–4): 261–286.

Nite, C., J. N. Singer, and G. B. Cunningham. 2013. "Addressing Competing Logics Between the Mission of a Religious University and the Demands of Intercollegiate Athletics." *Sport Management Review* 16(4): 465–476.

Pache, A.-C., and F. Santos. 2013. "Inside the Hybrid Organization: Selective Coupling as a Response to Competing Institutional Logics." *Academy of Management Journal* 56(4): 972–1001.

Packard, J. 2011. "Resisting Institutionalization: Religious Professionals in the Emerging Church." *Sociological Inquiry* 81(1): 3–33.

Perry, S. L. 2013. "She Works Hard(er) for the Money: Gender, Fundraising, and Employment in Evangelical Parachurch Organizations." *Sociology of Religion* 74(3): 392–415.

Pew Research Center. 2015. *America's Changing Religious Landscape*. Washington, DC: Pew Research Center.

Picardo, R. 2015. *Ministry Makeover: Recovering a Theology for Bi-Vocational Service in the Church*. Eugene, OR: Wipf and Stock.

Powell, D. 2009. "Skilled and Satisfied: Research Findings Regarding Executive Pastors." *Christian Education Journal* 6(2): 229–249.

Powell, W. W., ed. 1987. *The Nonprofit Sector: A Research Handbook*. New Haven, CT: Yale University Press.

Pratt, M. G., and P. O. Foreman. 2000. "Classifying Managerial Responses to Multiple Organizational Identities." *Academy of Management Review* 25(1): 18–42.

Ravasi, D. 2016. "Organizational Identity, Culture, and Image." In *Oxford Handbook of Organizational Identity*, ed. M. G. Pratt, M. Schultz, B. E. Ashforth, and D. Ravasi, 65–78. New York: Oxford University Press.

Ressler, R. W., B. R. Fulton, and P. Paxton. 2019. "Finding Faith: Uncovering Religiously-Identified Organizations in the Nonprofit Sector." Unpublished manuscript.

Ressler, R. W., P. Paxton, K. Velasco, and N. Reith. 2018. *Nonprofits as Social Entities: Using the New IRS Data to Predict Donations*. Paper presented at the Association for Research on Nonprofit Organizations and Voluntary Action Annual Meeting, Austin, TX, November 15.

Schein, E. H. 2010. *Organizational Culture and Leadership*. Hoboken, NJ: Wiley.

Scheitle, C. P. 2010. *Beyond the Congregation: The World of Christian Nonprofits*. New York: Oxford University Press.

Scheitle, C. P., and J. D. McCarthy. 2018. "The Mobilization of Evangelical Protestants in the Nonprofit Sector: Parachurch Foundings Across U.S. Counties, 1998–2016." *Journal for the Scientific Study of Religion* 57(2): 238–257.

Scheitle, C. P., E. J. Dollhopf, and J. D. McCarthy. 2016. "Exploring Religious Congregations' Registration with the IRS." *Nonprofit and Voluntary Sector Quarterly* 45(2): 397–408.

Schneider, J. A., and P. Wittberg. 2011. "Comparing Practical Theology Across Religions and Denominations." *Review of Religious Research* 52: 405–426.

Sider, R. J., and H. R. Unruh. 2004. "Typology of Religious Characteristics of Social Service and Educational Organizations and Programs." *Nonprofit and Voluntary Sector Quarterly* 33(1): 109–134.

Sinha, J. W. 2013. "Unintended Consequence of the Faith-Based Initiative: Organizational Practices and Religious Identity Within Faith-Based Human Service Organizations." *Nonprofit and Voluntary Sector Quarterly* 42(3): 563–583.

Skelcher, C., and S. R. Smith. 2015. "Theorizing Hybridity: Institutional Logics, Complex Organizations, and Actor Identities: The Case of Nonprofits." *Public Administration* 93(2): 433–448.

Smith, H., and R. Marranca. 2009. *The World's Religions*. New York: Harper.

Smith, S. R., and M. R. Sosin. 2001. "The Varieties of Faith-Related Agencies." *Public Administration Review* 61(6): 651–670.

Spear, R. 2010. "Religion and Social Entrepreneurship." In *Values and Opportunities in Social Entrepreneurship*, ed. K. Hockerts, J. Mair, and J. Robinson, 31–51. New York: Palgrave Macmillan.

Starling, V. T. 2010. *Faith-Based Social Venture Enterprise: A Model for Financial Sustainability*. PhD diss., Walden University.

Sveningsson, S., and M. Alvesson. 2003. "Managing Managerial Identities: Organizational Fragmentation, Discourse and Identity Struggle." *Human Relations* 56(10): 1163–1193.

Syakhroza, M. A., L. Paolella, and K. Munir. 2018. "Holier Than Thou? Identity Buffers and Adoption of Controversial Practices in the Islamic Banking Category." *Academy of Management Journal*, October 29. https://doi.org/10.5465/amj.2016.1017.

Taylor, B. J. 2015. "Responses to Conflicting Field Imperatives: Institutions and Agency Among Evangelical Christian Colleges." *Sociological Spectrum* 35(2): 207–227.

Thomas, M. L. 2009. "Faith and Collaboration: A Qualitative Analysis of Faith-Based Social Service Programs in Organizational Relationships." *Administration in Social Work* 33(1): 40–60.

Thornton, P. H., and W. Ocasio. 1999. "Institutional Logics and the Historical Contingency of Power in Organizations: Executive Succession in the Higher Education Publishing Industry, 1958–1990." *American Journal of Sociology* 105(3): 801–843.

Torry, M. 2014. *Managing Religion: The Management of Christian Religious and Faith-Based Organizations*. New York: Springer.

———. 2017. *Managing God's Business: Religious and Faith-Based Organizations and Their Management.* New York: Routledge.

Tracey, P. 2012. "Religion and Organization: A Critical Review of Current Trends and Future Directions." *Academy of Management Annals* 6(1): 87–134.

Tracey, P., N. Phillips, and M. Lounsbury. 2014. "Taking Religion Seriously in the Study of Organizations." *Research in the Sociology of Organizations* 41: 3–21.

U.S. Department of the Treasury. Internal Revenue Service. 2015. *Tax Guide for Churches and Religious Organizations (Publication 1828).* Washington, DC: U.S. Government Printing Office.

———. 2017. *Social Security and Other Information for Members of the Clergy and Religious Workers (Publication 517).* Washington, DC: U.S. Government Printing Office.

Urban Institute. 2004. *Volunteer Management Capacity in America's Charities and Congregations: A Briefing Report.* Washington, DC: Urban Institute Press.

Walker, E. T., and L. M. Stepick. 2014. "Strength in Diversity? Group Heterogeneity in the Mobilization of Grassroots Organizations." *Sociology Compass* 8(7): 959–975.

Warner, R. S. 1993. "Work in Progress Toward a New Paradigm for the Sociological Study of Religion in the United States." *American Journal of Sociology* 98(5): 1044–1093.

———. 1994. "The Place of the Congregation in the Contemporary American Religious Configuration." In *American Congregations: New Perspectives in the Study of Congregations*, vol. 2, ed. J. P. Wind and J. W. Lewis, 54–99. Chicago: University of Chicago Press.

Weaver, G. R., and J. M. Stansbury. 2014. "Religion in Organizations: Cognition and Behavior." *Research in the Sociology of Organizations* 41: 65–110.

Whetten, D. A. 2006. "Albert and Whetten Revisited: Strengthening the Concept of Organizational Identity." *Journal of Management Inquiry* 15(3): 219–234.

Wilde, M. J., K. Geraty, S. L. Nelson, and E. A. Bowman. 2010. "Religious Economy or Organizational Field? Predicting Bishops' Votes at the Second Vatican Council." *American Sociological Review* 75(4): 586–606.

Wong, E. C., B. R. Fulton, and K. P. Derose. 2018. "Prevalence and Predictors of Mental Health Programming Among US Religious Congregations." *Psychiatric Services* 69(2): 154–160.

Wood, J. R. 1989. "Review of *The Nonprofit Sector: A Research Handbook* by Walter W. Powell." *American Journal of Sociology* 94(6): 1442–1443.

Wood, R. L., and B. R. Fulton. 2015. *A Shared Future: Faith-Based Organizing for Racial Equity and Ethical Democracy.* Chicago: University of Chicago Press.

Yamada, A.-M., K. K. Lee, and M. A. Kim. 2012. "Community Mental Health Allies: Referral Behavior Among Asian American Immigrant Christian Clergy." *Community Mental Health Journal* 48(1): 107–113.

Yukich, G., B. R. Fulton, and R. L. Wood. 2019. "Representative Group Styles: How Ally Immigrant Rights Organizations Promote Immigrant Involvement." *Social Problems*, August 21. https://doi.org/10.1093/socpro/spz025.

Part VIII. Global and Comparative Perspectives

Chapter 27. The Global Rise of Nongovernmental Organizations

Afsharipour, Afra. 1999. "Empowering Ourselves: The Role of Women's NGOs in the Enforcement of the Women's Convention." *Columbia Law Review* 99(1): 129–172.

Almond, Gabriel, and Sidney Verba. 1963. *The Civic Culture: Political Attitudes and Democracy in Five Nations.* Newbury Park, CA: SAGE.

Banks, Nicola, David Hulme, and Michael Edwards. 2015. "NGOs, States, and Donors Revisited: Still Too Close for Comfort?" *World Development* 66: 707–718.

Boli, John, and George Thomas, eds. 1999. *Constructing World Culture: International Non-Governmental Organizations Since 1875.* Stanford, CA: Stanford University Press.

Boulding, Kenneth. 1989. *Three Faces of Power.* Newbury Park, CA: SAGE.

Brady, Henry E., Sidney Verba, and Kay Lehman Schlozman. 1995. "Beyond SES: A Resource

Model of Political Participation." *American Political Science Review* 89(2): 271–294.

Brass, Jennifer N. 2016. *Allies or Adversaries: NGOs and the State in Africa.* New York: Cambridge University Press.

Brass, Jennifer, Wesley Longhofer, Rachel Sullivan Robinson, and Allison Schnable. 2018. "NGOs and International Development: A Review of Thirty-Five Years of Scholarship." *World Development* 112: 136–149.

Bratton, Michael. 1989. "The Politics of Government-NGO Relations in Africa." *World Development* 17(4):569–87.

Bromley, Patricia, and John W. Meyer. 2016. *Hyper-Organization: Global Organizational Expansion.* Oxford, UK: Oxford University Press.

Bromley, Patricia, and Walter W. Powell. 2012. "From Smoke and Mirrors to Walking the Talk: Decoupling in the Contemporary World." *Academy of Management Annals* 6(1): 483–530.

Bromley, Patricia, Evan Schofer, and Wesley Longhofer. 2018. "Organizing for Education: A Cross-National, Longitudinal Study of Civil Society Organizations and Education Outcomes." *Voluntas: International Journal of Voluntary and Nonprofit Organizations,* 29(3): 526–540.

———. Forthcoming. "Resisting World Culture: The Rise of Legal Restrictions on Foreign Funding to NGOs, 1994–2015." *Social Forces.*

Campbell, Catherine. 2003. *Letting Them Die: Why HIV/AIDS Prevention Programmes Fail.* Bloomington: Indiana University Press.

Cole, Wade M. 2017. "World Polity or World Society? Delineating the Statist and Societal Dimensions of the Global Institutional System." *International Sociology* 32(1): 86–104.

Dill, Brian. 2009. "The Paradoxes of Community-Based Participation in Dar es Salaam." *Development and Change* 40(4): 717–743.

DiMaggio, Paul J., and Walter W. Powell. 1983. "The Iron Cage Revisited: Institutional Isomorphism and Collective Rationality in Organizational Fields." *American Sociological Review* 48(2): 147–160.

Dupuy, Kendra, James Ron, and Aseem Prakash. 2016. "Hands Off My Regime! Governments' Restrictions on Foreign Aid to Non-Governmental Organizations in Poor and Middle-Income Countries." *World Development* 84: 299–311.

Edwards, Michael, and David Hulme. 1996. "Too Close for Comfort? The Impact of Official Aid on Nongovernmental Organizations." *World Development* 24(6): 961–973.

Ferguson, James. 1990. *The Anti-Politics Machine: Development, Depoliticization, and Bureaucratic Power in Lesotho.* Cambridge, UK: Cambridge University Press.

Fligstein, Neil, and Doug McAdam. 2015. *A Theory of Fields.* New York: Oxford University Press.

Fourcade, Marion, and Evan Schofer. 2015. "Political Structures and Political Mores." *Sociological Science* 3: 414–443.

Fourcade-Gourinchas, Marion, and Sarah Babb. 2002. "The Rebirth of the Liberal Creed: Paths to Neoliberalism in Four Countries." *American Journal of Sociology* 108(3): 533–579.

Fowler, Alan. 1991. "The Role of NGOs in Changing State-Society Relations: Perspectives from Eastern and Southern Africa." *Development Policy Review* 9(1): 53–84.

Freedom House. 2018. *Freedom in the World 2018.* Washington, DC: Freedom House.

Gauri, Varun, and Julia Galef. 2005. "NGOs in Bangladesh: Activities, Resources, and Governance." *World Development* 33(12): 2045–2065.

Guillén, Mauro. 2018. "Symbolic Unity, Dynastic Continuity, and Countervailing Power: Monarchies, Republics, and the Economy." *Social Forces* 97(2): 607–648.

Hansmann, Henry. 1987. "Economic Theories of Nonprofit Organizations." In *The Nonprofit Sector: A Research Handbook,* ed. W. W. Powell, 2–42. New Haven, CT: Yale University Press.

Hironaka, Ann. 2014. *Greening the Globe: World Society and Environmental Change.* New York: Cambridge University Press.

———. 2017. *Tokens of Power: Rethinking War.* New York: Cambridge University Press.

Hwang, Hokyu. 2006. "Planning Development: Globalization and the Shifting Locus of Planning." In *Globalization and Organizational Change,* ed. Gili S. Drori, John W. Meyer, and Hokyu Hwang, 69–90. New York: Oxford University Press.

Hwang, Hokyu, and Walter W. Powell. 2009. "The Rationalization of Charity: The Influences of Professionalism in the Nonprofit Sector." *Administrative Science Quarterly* 54(2): 268–298.

Iriye, Akira. 1999. "A Century of NGOs." *Diplomatic History* 23(2): 421–435.

Jepperson, Ronald. 2002. "Political Modernities: Disentangling Two Underlying Dimensions of Institutional Differentiation." *Sociological Theory* 20(1): 61–85.

Jepperson, Ronald L., and John W. Meyer. 1991. "The Public Order and the Construction of Formal Organizations." In *The New Institutionalism in Organizational Analysis*, ed. W. W. Powell and P. J. DiMaggio, 204–231. Chicago: University of Chicago Press.

Joyce, Michael S., and William A. Schambra. 1996. "A New Civic Life." In *To Empower People: From State to Civil Society*, 2nd ed., ed. Michael Novak, 15–25. Washington, DC: AEI Press.

Kaldor, Mary, Henrietta L. Moore, and Sabine Selchow, eds. 2012. *Global Civil Society 2012: Ten Years of Critical Reflection*. Basingstoke, UK: Palgrave Macmillan.

Kallman, Meghan Elizabeth, and Terry Nichols Clark. 2016. *The Third Sector: Community Organizations, NGOs, and Nonprofits*. Urbana: University of Illinois Press.

Kamat, Sangeeta. 2004. "The Privatization of Public Interest: Theorizing NGO Discourse in the Neoliberal Era." *Review of International Political Economy* 11(1): 155–176.

Katz, Jonathan M. 2013. *The Big Truck That Went By: How the World Came to Save Haiti and Left Behind a Disaster*. New York: St. Martin's Griffin.

Keck, Margaret E., and Kathryn Sikkink. 1998. *Activists Beyond Borders: Advocacy Networks in International Politics*. Ithaca, NY: Cornell University Press.

Kerrissey, Jasmine, and Evan Schofer. 2013. "Unions and Political Participation in the U.S." *Social Forces* 91(3): 895–928.

Longhofer, Wesley, and Evan Schofer. 2010. "National and Global Origins of Environmental Association." *American Sociological Review* 75(4): 505–533.

Meyer, John W. 2010. "World Society, Institutional Theories, and the Actor." *Annual Review of Sociology* 36: 1–20.

Meyer, John W., John Boli, George Thomas, and Francisco O. Ramirez. 1997. "World Society and the Nation-State." *American Journal of Sociology* 103(1): 144–181.

Meyer, John W., and Brian Rowan. 1977. "Institutionalized Organizations: Formal Structure as Myth and Ceremony." *American Journal of Sociology* 83(2): 340–363.

Meyer, John W., and W. Richard Scott. 1983. *Organizational Environments: Ritual and Rationality*. Beverly Hills, CA: Sage.

Mosse, David, and David Lewis. 2005. *The Aid Effect: Ethnographies of Development Practice and Neo-Liberal Reform*. London: Pluto.

Murdie, Amanda. 2014. *Help or Harm: The Human Security Effects of International NGOs*. Stanford, CA: Stanford University Press.

OECD Development Assistance Committee, ed. 2015. *Aid for CSOs*. Paris: OECD.

Otto, Diane. 1996. "Nongovernmental Organizations in the United Nations System: The Emerging Role of International Civil Society." *Human Rights Quarterly* 18(1): 107–141.

Putnam, Robert D. 2000. *Bowling Alone: The Collapse and Revival of American Community*. New York: Simon and Schuster.

Rahman, Sabeel. 2006. "Development, Democracy and the NGO Sector." *Journal of Developing Societies* 22(4): 451–473.

Reimann, Kim D. 2006. "A View from the Top: International Norms and the Worldwide Growth of NGOs." *International Studies Quarterly* 50(1): 45–68.

Risse, Thomas. 1999. "The Power of Norms Versus the Norms of Power: Transnational Civil Society and Human Rights." In *The Third Force: The Rise of Transnational Civil Society*, ed. Ann M. Florini, 177–209. Washington, DC: Carnegie Endowment for the Peace.

Robertson, Roland. 1992. *Globalization: Social Theory and Global Culture*. London: Sage.

Ruggie, John G. 1998. "Globalization and the Embedded Liberalism Compromise: The End of an Era?" In *Internationale Wirtschaft, Nationale Demokratie*, ed. Wolfgang Streeck, 79–98. Frankfurt: Campus.

Salamon, Lester. 1994. "The Rise of the Nonprofit Sector." *Foreign Affairs* 73(4): 109–122.

Schnable, Allison. 2015. "New American Relief and Development Organizations: Voluntarizing Global Aid." *Social Problems* 62(2): 309–329.

Schofer, Evan, and Marion Fourcade-Gourinchas. 2001. "The Structural Contexts of Civic

Engagement. Voluntary Associations Membership in Comparative Perspective." *American
Sociological Review* 66(6): 806–828.

Schofer, Evan, David J. Frank, Ann Hironaka,
and Wesley Longhofer. 2014. "Sociological
Institutionalism and World Society." In *The
New Blackwell Companion to Political Sociology*,
ed. Edwin Amenta, Kate Nash, and Alan Scott,
57–68. Oxford, UK: Blackwell.

Schofer, Evan, and Ann Hironaka. 2005. "The Effects
of World Society on Environmental Protection
Outcomes." *Social Forces* 84(1): 25–47.

Schofer, Evan, and Wesley Longhofer. 2011. "The
Structural Sources of Association." *American
Journal of Sociology* 117(2): 539–585.

Schofer, Evan, John W. Meyer, and Julia C. Lerch.
2018. "Illiberal Reactions to the University in
the 21st Century." Paper presented at the annual
meeting of the American Sociological Association, Philadelphia, PA, August 14.

Schuller, Mark. 2009. "Gluing Globalization: NGOs
as Intermediaries in Haiti." *PoLAR: Political and
Legal Anthropology Review* 32(1): 84–104.

———. 2012. *Killing with Kindness: Haiti, International Aid, and NGOs*. New Brunswick, NJ:
Rutgers University Press.

Skocpol, Theda. 2003. *Diminished Democracy:
From Membership to Management in American
Civic Life*. Norman: University of Oklahoma
Press.

Skocpol, Theda, and Morris P. Fiorina, eds. 1999.
Civic Engagement in American Democracy.
Washington, DC: Brookings Institution Press.

Shihata, Ibrahim F. I. 1992. "World Bank and
Non-Governmental Organizations." *Cornell Law
Journal* 25: 623–641.

Stroup, Sarah. 2012. *Borders Among Activists:
International NGOs in the United States, Britain,
and France*. Ithaca, NY: Cornell University
Press.

Swidler, Ann, and Susan C. Watkins. 2017. *A Fraught
Embrace: The Romance and Reality of AIDS
Altruism in Africa*. Princeton, NJ: Princeton
University Press.

Tarrow, Sidney. 1998. *Power in Movement: Social
Movements and Contentious Politics*, 2nd ed.
Cambridge, UK: Cambridge University Press.

UNCTAD 2007. *World Investment Report*. New York:
United Nations.

Union of International Associations, ed. 2019. *Yearbook of International Organizations, 2019–2010*.
Brussels: Union of International Associations.

USAID. 2016. *CSO Sustainability Index*. Washington,
DC: USAID.

Watkins, Susan C., Ann Swidler, and Thomas Han-
nan. 2012. "Outsourcing Social Transformation:
Development NGOs as Organizations." *Annual
Review of Sociology* 38(1): 285–315.

Weisbrod, Burton. 1977. *The Voluntary Nonprofit
Sector: An Economic Analysis*. Lexington, MA:
Lexington Books.

———. 1978. "Problems of Enhancing in the Public
Interest: Towards a Model of Government
Failures." In *Public Interest Law*, ed. Burton A.
Weisbrod, John F. Handler, and Neil K. Berkeley,
30–41. Berkeley: University of California Press.

Werker, Eric, and Faisal Z. Ahmed. 2008. "What Do
Nongovernmental Organizations Do?" *Journal
of Economic Perspectives* 22(2): 73–92.

World Bank. 2018. *Civil Society*. Washington, DC:
World Bank.

Chapter 28. Global Backlash Against Foreign Funding to Domestic Nongovernmental Organizations

Andreas, P. 2000. *Border Games: Policing the
US-Mexico Divide*. Ithaca, NY: Cornell University Press.

Banks, N., D. Hulme, and M. Edwards. 2015. "NGOs,
States, and Donors Revisited: Still Too Close for
Comfort?" *World Development* 66: 707–718.

Bauhr, M., N. Charron, and N. Nasiritousi. 2013.
"Does Corruption Cause Aid Fatigue? Public
Opinion and the Anti-Corruption Paradox."
International Studies Quarterly 57: 568–579.

Bob, C. 2002. "Merchants of Morality." *Foreign Policy*
129 (March–April): 36–45.

Bratton, M. 1989. "The Politics of Government-NGO
Relations in Africa." *World Development* 17(4):
569–587.

Bräutigam, D. A., and S. Knack. 2004. "Foreign Aid,
Institutions, and Governance in Sub-Saharan
Africa." *Economic Development and Cultural
Change* 52: 255–285.

Burger, R., T. Owen, and A. Prakash. 2018. "Global
Nonprofit Chains and the Challenges of De-
velopment Aid Contracting." *Nonprofit Policy
Forum* 9(4): 1–12.

Chahim, D., and A. Prakash. 2014. "NGOization, Foreign Funding, and the Nicaraguan Civil Society." *Voluntas: International Journal of Voluntary and Nonprofit Organizations* 25(2): 487–513.

Chandhoke, N. 2002. "The Limits of Global Civil Society." In *Global Civil Society Yearbook 2002*, ed. M. Glasius, M. Kaldor, and H. Anheier, 35–54. Oxford, UK: Oxford University Press.

Cooley, A., and J. Ron. 2002. "The NGO Scramble: Organizational Insecurity and the Political Economy of Transnational Action." *International Security* 27(1): 5–39.

Cornwall, A., and C. Nyamu-Musembi. 2004. "Putting the 'Rights-Based Approach' to Development into Perspective." *Third World Quarterly* 25(8): 1415–1437.

Diamond, L. 2015. "Facing Up to the Democratic Recession." *Journal of Democracy* 26(1): 141–155.

Dietrich, S. 2013. "Bypass or Engage? Explaining Donor Delivery Tactics in Foreign Aid Allocation." *International Studies Quarterly* 57(4): 698–712.

Dugger, C. W. 2008. "In a Crackdown, Zimbabwe Curbs Aid Groups." *New York Times*, June 4. http://www.nytimes.com/2008/06/04/world/africa/04zimbabwe.html.

Dupuy, K., and A. Prakash. 2018. "Do Donors Reduce Bilateral Aid to Countries with Restrictive NGO Laws? A Panel Study, 1993–2012." *Nonprofit and Voluntary Sector Quarterly* 47(1): 89–106.

Dupuy, K., J. Ron, and A. Prakash. 2015. "Who Survived? Ethiopia's Regulatory Crackdown on Foreign-Funded NGOs." *Review of International Political Economy* 22(2): 419–456.

———. 2016. "Hands Off My Regime! Governments' Restrictions on Foreign Aid to Non-Governmental Organizations in Poor and Middle-Income Countries." *World Development* 84, 299–311.

Easterly, W. 2006. *The White Man's Burden: Why the West's Efforts to Aid the Rest Have Done So Much Ill and So Little Good.* New York: Penguin.

Edwards, M., and D. Hulme. 1996. "Too Close for Comfort? The Impact of Official Aid on Nongovernmental Organizations." *World Development* 24(6): 961–973.

Englebert, P., and D. M. Tull. 2008. "Postconflict Reconstruction in Africa: Flawed Ideas About Failed States." *International Security* 32(4): 106–139.

Fowler, A. 1991. "The Role of NGOs in Changing State-Society Relations: Perspectives from Eastern and Southern Africa." *Development Policy Review* 9(1): 53–84.

Freedom House. 2012. *Freedom in the World 2012.* Washington, DC: Freedom House.

Hamm, B. 2001. "A Human Rights Approach to Development." *Human Rights Quarterly* 23(4): 1005–1031.

Hansmann, H. B. 1980. "The Role of Nonprofit Enterprise." *Yale Law Journal* 89(5): 835–901.

Hathaway, O. A. 2007. "Why Do Countries Commit to Human Rights Treaties?" *Journal of Conflict Resolution* 51(4): 588–621.

Hearn, J. 2007. "African NGOs: The New Compradors?" *Development and Change* 38(6): 1095–1110.

Henderson, S. 2003. *Building Democracy in Contemporary Russia: Western Support for Grassroots Organizations.* Ithaca, NY: Cornell University Press.

———. 2011. "Civil Society in Russia." *Problems of Post-Communism* 58(3): 11–27.

Human Rights Watch. 2008. "Zimbabwe: Surge in State-Sponsored Violence." April 25. http://www.hrw.org/news/2008/04/25/zimbabwe-surge-state-sponsored-violence.

———. 2010. "'One Hundred Ways of Putting Pressure': Violations of Freedom of Expression and Association in Ethiopia." New York: Human Rights Watch.

———. 2013. "Ecuador: Clampdown on Civil Society: Decree's 'Big Brother' Powers Undermine Groups' Independence." August 12. http://www.hrw.org/news/2013/08/12/ecuadorclampdown-civil-society.

International Crisis Group. 2009. "Zimbabwe: Engaging the Inclusive Government." Africa Briefing No. 59. April 20. https://www.crisisgroup.org/africa/southern-africa/zimbabwe/zimbabwe-engaging-inclusive-government.

Jalali, R. 2008. "International Funding of NGOs in India: Bringing the State Back In." *Voluntas: International Journal of Voluntary and Nonprofit Organizations* 19: 161–188.

Jalali, R. 2013. "Financing Empowerment? How Foreign Aid to Southern NGOs and Social Move-

ments Undermines Grass-Roots Mobilization."
Sociology Compass 7(1): 55–73.

Johnson, E., and A. Prakash. 2007. "NGO Research
Program: A Collective Action Perspective."
Policy Sciences 40(3): 221–240.

Kaufman, B. I. 1992. "Trade and Aid: Eisenhower's
Foreign Economic Policy, 1953–1961." Baltimore:
Johns Hopkins University Press.

Keck, M., and K. Sikkink. 1998. *Activists Beyond Borders: Advocacy Networks in International Politics.*
Ithaca, NY: Cornell University Press.

Kipkorir, B. 1997. "Testimony Before the Trade
Sub-Committee of the House Ways and Means
Committee." *Hearing on the African Growth
and Opportunity End of Dependency Act of 1996.*
April 29.

Lacey, M. 2005. "Ethiopia's Capital, Once Promising, Finds Itself in Crisis." *New York Times.*,
November 14. http://www.nytimes.com/2005/11/
14/international/africa/14ethiopia.html.

Lancaster, C. 2008. *Foreign Aid: Diplomacy, Development, Domestic Politics.* Chicago: University of
Chicago Press.

Lewis, D., and T. Wallace. 2000. *New Roles and
Relevance: Development NGOs and the Challenge
of Change.* West Hartford, CT: Kumarian Press.

Lewis, T. 2003. "Environmental Aid: Driven by Recipient Need or Donor Interests?" *Social Science
Quarterly* 84(1): 144–161.

Levine, A. 2002. "Convergence or Convenience?
International Conservation NGOs and Development Assistance in Tanzania." *World Development* 30(6): 1043–1055.

Levitsky, S., and L. Way. 2015. "The Myth of Democratic Recession." *Journal of Democracy* 26(1):
45–58.

Lipschutz, R. 1992. "Reconstructing World Politics:
The Emergence of Global Civil Society." *Millennium* 21: 389–420.

Lundsgaarde, E., C. Breunig, and A. Prakash. 2010.
"Instrumental Philanthropy: Trade and the
Allocation of Foreign Aid." *Canadian Journal of
Political Science* 43(3): 733–761.

Maizels, A., and M. K. Nissanke. 1984. "Motivations
for Aid to Developing Countries." *World Development* 12(9): 879–900.

McKinley, R. D., and R. Little. 1979. "The US Aid
Relationship: A Test of the Recipient Need and

the Donor Interest Models." *Political Studies*
27(2): 236–250.

Meyer, J. W., J. Boli, G. Thomas, and F. O.
Ramirez. 1997. "World Society and the Nation-State." *American Journal of Sociology* 103(1):
144–181.

Mishler, W., and R. Rose. 1997. "Trust, Distrust and
Skepticism: Popular Evaluations of Civil and Po-
litical Institutions in Post-Communist Societies."
Journal of Politics 59(2): 418–451.

Mitlink, D., S. Hickey, and A. Bebbington. 2007.
"Reclaiming Development? NGOs and the
Challenge of Alternatives." *World Development*
35: 1699–1720.

Murdie, A., and T. Bhasin. 2011. "Aiding and
Abetting: Human Rights INGOs and Domestic
Protest." *Journal of Conflict Resolution* 55(2):
163–191.

Nelson, P. 1995. *The World Bank and Non-
Governmental Organizations: The Limits of
Apolitical Development.* New York: St. Martin's
Press.

Neumeyer, E. 2003. "Do Human Rights Matter in Bilateral Aid Allocation? A Quantitative Analysis
of 21 Donor Countries." *Social Science Quarterly*
84(3): 650–666.

OECD Development Assistance Committee, ed.
2015. *Aid for CSOs.* Paris: OECD.

Olivier, J., et al. 2015. "Understanding the Roles of
Faith-Based Health-Care Providers in Africa:
Review of the Evidence with a Focus on Magni-
tude, Reach, Cost, and Satisfaction." *The Lancet*,
October 31.

Osborne, D. 1993. "Reinventing Government." *Public
Productivity and Management Review* 16(4):
349–356.

Ostrom, E. 1990. *Governing the Commons.* New
York: Cambridge University Press.

Parmar, I. 2012. "Foundation Networks and American Hegemony." *European Journal of American
Studies* 7(1): 1–29.

Plattner, M. F. 2015. "Is Democracy in Decline?"
Journal of Democracy 26(1): 5–10.

Polanyi, K. 1944. *The Great Transformation.* Boston:
Beacon Press.

Prakash, A., and M. K. Gugerty, eds. 2010. *Advocacy
Organizations and Collective Action.* New York:
Cambridge University Press.

Putnam, R. D. 1995. "Bowling Alone: America's Declining Social Capital." *Journal of Democracy* 6(1): 65–78.

Reimann, K. D. 2006. "A View from the Top: International Politics, Norms and the Worldwide Growth of NGOs." *International Studies Quarterly* 50(1): 45–68.

Reyes, Che de los. 2011. "In Ecuador, Closure of 16 Foreign NGOs an Omen for Other International Groups?" August 8. https://www.devex.com/news/in-ecuador-closure-of-16-foreign-ngosan-omen-for-other-international-groups-75569.

Roberts, L., and M. Enserink. 2007. "Did They Really Say . . . Eradication?" *Science* 318(5856): 1544–1545.

Rugumayo, E. 2004. "Trade Not Aid, Says Minister." New Vision, May 26. https://www.newvision.co.ug/new_vision/news/1099925/trade-aid-minister.

Sachs, J. 2006. *The End of Poverty.* New York: Penguin.

Salamon, L. 1994. "The Rise of the Nonprofit Sector." *Foreign Affairs* 73(4): 109–122.

Salamon, L. M., and H. K. Anheier. 1998. "Social Origins of Civil Society: Explaining the Nonprofit Sector Cross-Nationally." *Voluntas: International Journal of Voluntary and Nonprofit Organizations* 9(3): 213–248.

Schofer, E., and W. Longhofer. 2011. "The Structural Sources of Association." *American Journal of Sociology* 117(2): 539–585.

Schraeder, P. J., S. W. Hook, and B. Taylor. 1998. "Clarifying the Foreign Aid Puzzle: A Comparison of American, Japanese, French, and Swedish Aid Flows." *World Politics* 50: 294–323.

Scurlow, R., N. Dolsak, and A. Prakash. 2019. "Recovering from Scandals: Twitter Coverage of Oxfam and Save the Children Scandals." *Voluntas: International Journal of Voluntary and Nonprofit Organizations.* August. doi:10.1007/s11266-019-00148-x.

Sell, S., and A. Prakash. 2004. "Using Ideas Strategically: Examining the Contest Between Business and NGO Networks in Intellectual Property Rights." *International Studies Quarterly* 48(1): 143–175.

Smith, D. 2012. "AIDS NGOs and Corruption in Nigeria." *Health and Place* 18(3): 475–480.

Smith, S. R., and M. Lipsky. 1993. *Nonprofits for Hire: The Welfare State in the Age of Contracting.* Cambridge, MA: Harvard University Press.

Sundstrom, L. M. 2006. *Funding Civil Society: Foreign Assistance and NGO Development in Russia.* Palo Alto, CA: Stanford University Press.

Taleb, N., and C. Sandis. 2014. "The Skin in the Game Heuristic for Protection Against Tail Events." *Review of Behavioral Economics* 1(1–2): 115–135.

U.S. Agency for International Development (USAID). 2015. *2015 CSO Sustainability Index for Sub-Saharan Africa.* Washington, DC: USAID.

UNICEF. 2016. *Situation Analysis of Children in Somalia 2016.* https://www.unicef.org/somalia/resources_18507.html.

Vakil, A. C. 1997. "Confronting the Classification Problem: Toward a Taxonomy of NGOs." *World Development* 25(12): 2057–2070.

Van Rooy, A., ed. 1998. *Civil Society and the Aid Industry: The Politics and Promise.* London: Earthscan.

Vernon, R. 1957. "Foreign Aid: 'A Proposal' Re-examined." *World Politics* 9: 579–592.

Wapner, P. 1995. "Politics Beyond the State: Environmental Activism and World Civic Politics." *World Politics* 47: 311–340.

Weisbrod, B. 1977. *The Voluntary Nonprofit Sector: An Economic Analysis.* Lexington, MA: Lexington Books.

Williamson, J. 1993. "Democracy and the 'Washington Consensus.'" *World Development* 21(8): 1329–1336.

Yagub, A., and K. Mtshali. 2015. "The Role of Non-Governmental Organizations in Providing Curative Health Services in North Darfur State, Sudan." *African Health Sciences* 15(2): 1049–1055.

Young, D. R. 2000. "Alternative Models of Government-Nonprofit Sector Relations: Theoretical and International Perspectives." *Nonprofit and Voluntary Sector Quarterly* 29(1): 149–172.

Zakaria, F. 1997. "The Rise of Illiberal Democracy." *Foreign Affairs* 76: 22–43.

Chapter 29. Social Movements in a Global Context: History, Content, and Form

Adams, Nick. 2015. "Contention and Control: How U.S. Cities and Police Responded to the Occupy

Campaigns of 2011." PhD diss., University of California, Berkeley.

Andrews, Kenneth T. 2004. *Freedom Is a Constant Struggle: The Mississippi Civil Rights Movement and Its Legacy.* Chicago: University of Chicago Press.

Aptheker, Herbert. 1937. "American Negro Slave Revolts." *Science and Society* 1(4): 512–538.

Armstrong, Elizabeth A., and Mary Bernstein. 2008. "Culture, Power, and Institutions: A Multi-Institutional Approach to Social Movements." *Sociological Theory* 26(1): 74–99.

Arrighi, Giovanni. 2009. *The Long 20th Century: Money, Power, and the Origins of Our Times.* New York: Verso.

Ashworth, John. (1995) 2007. *Slavery, Capitalism, and Politics in the Antebellum Republic: Volume 1, Commerce and Compromise, 1820–1850.* Cambridge, UK: Cambridge University Press.

Baldassarri, Delia, and Peter Bearman. 2007. "Dynamics of Political Polarization." *American Sociological Review* 72(5): 784–811.

Baran, Paul, and Paul Sweezy. 1966. *Monopoly Capital: An Essay on the American Economic and Social Order.* New York: Monthly Review Press.

Barker, Colin, Laurence Cox, John Krinsky, and Alf Gunvald Nilsen, eds. 2013. *Marxism and Social Movements.* Chicago: Haymarket Books.

Bearman, Peter, and Kevin Everett. 1993. "The Structure of Social Protest, 1961–1983." *Social Networks* 15(2): 171–200.

Bender, Thomas, John Ashworth, David Brion Davis, and Thomas Haskell. 1992. *The Antislavery Debate: Capitalism and Abolitionism as a Problem in Historical Interpretation.* Berkeley: University of California Press.

Bennett, Lance W. 2005. "Social Movements Beyond Borders: Understanding Two Eras of Transnational Activism." In *Transnational Protest and Global Activism,* ed. Donatella della Porta and Sidney Tarrow, 203–226. Oxford, UK: Rowman and Littlefield.

Berman, Sheri. 1997. "Civil Society and the Collapse of the Weimar Republic." *World Politics* 49(3): 401–429.

Blackett, Richard J. M. 1983. *Building an Antislavery Wall: Black Americans in the Atlantic Abolitionist Movement, 1830–1860.* Baton Rouge: Louisiana State University Press.

———. 2000. *Divided Hearts: Britain and the American Civil War.* Baton Rouge: Louisiana State University Press.

———. 2013. *Making Freedom: The Underground Railroad and the Politics of Slavery.* Chapel Hill: University of North Carolina Press.

Blee, Kathleen, and Kimberly Creasap. 2010. "Conservative and Right-Wing Movements." *Annual Review of Sociology* 36: 269–286.

Bob, Clifford. 2002. "Merchants of Morality." *Foreign Policy* 129(March–April): 36–45.

———, ed. 2009. *The International Struggle for New Human Rights.* Philadelphia: University of Pennsylvania Press.

———. 2010. "The Market for Human Rights." In *Advocacy Organizations and Collective Action,* ed. Aseem Prakash and Mary Kay Gugerty, 133–154. Cambridge, UK: Cambridge University Press.

Bobel, Chris. 2007. "'I'm Not an Activist, Though I've Done a Lot of It': Doing Activism, Being Activist and the 'Perfect Standard' in a Contemporary Movement." *Social Movement Studies* 6(2): 147–159.

Boli, John, and George Thomas, eds. 1999. *Constructing World Culture: International Non-Governmental Organizations Since 1875.* Stanford, CA: Stanford University Press.

Borinski, Ernst. 1961. "Review. European Socialism: A History of Ideas and Movements." *Social Forces* 39(3): 269–271.

Borras, Saturnino, Marc Edelman, and Cristóbal Kay. 2009. *Transnational Agrarian Movements Confronting Globalization.* New York: Wiley-Blackwell.

Boschee, Elizabeth, Jennifer Lautenschlager, Sean O'Brien, Steve Shellman, James Starz, and Michael Ward. 2018. "ICEWS Coded Event Data." Harvard Dataverse. https://dataverse.harvard.edu/dataset.xhtml?persistentId=doi:10.7910/DVN/28075, accessed August 27, 2019.

Bourdieu, Pierre. (1979) 1984. *Distinction: A Social Critique of the Judgment of Taste,* trans. Richard Nice. Cambridge, MA: Harvard University Press.

Braudel, Fernand. 1977. *Afterthoughts on Material Civilization and Capitalism,* trans. Patricia M.

Ranum. Baltimore: Johns Hopkins University Press.

Bringel, Breno. 2011. "A Busca de Uma Nova Agenda de Pesquisa Sobre os Movimentos Sociais e o Confronto Político." *Política and Sociedade* 10(18): 1–24.

———. 2013. "MST's Agenda of Emancipation: Interfaces of National Politics and Global Contestation." In *Brazil Emerging: Inequality and Emancipation*, ed. Jan N. Pieterse and Adalberto Cardoso, 97–120. New York: Routledge.

———. 2015. "Social Movements and Contemporary Modernity: Internationalism and Patterns of Global Contestation." In *Global Modernity and Social Contestation*, ed. Breno M. Bringel and Jose M. Domingues, 122–138. Los Angeles: SAGE.

———. 2016. "The Long June: The 2013 Demonstrations and the Future of Social Movements in Brazil." In *Understanding Southern Social Movements*, ed. Simin Fadaee, 153–167. London: Routledge.

———. 2019. "Latin American Perspectives in Social Movement Research." In *Latin American Sociologies: Key Texts from Latin American Sociologists*, ed. Fernanda Beigel, 339–359. Los Angeles, CA: SAGE.

Bringel, Breno, and Heriberto Cairo, eds. 2019. *Critical Geopolitics and Regional (Re)Configurations: Interregionalism and Transnationalism between Latin America and Europe*. London: Routledge.

Bringel, Breno, and Geoffrey Pleyers. 2017. "Protesta e Indignación Global." Consejo Latinoamericano de Ciencias Sociales, Buenos Aires, Argentina. http://biblioteca.clacso.edu.ar/clacso/se/20171204044413/Protesta_e_indignacion_global.pdf.

———. 2019. "June 2013, Five Years Later: Polarization, Reconfiguration of Activism, and Challenges for Brazilian Left." In *The Brazilian Left in the 21st Century: Conflict and Conciliation in Peripheral Capitalism*, ed. Luis F. Miguel and Vladimir Puzone, 237–258. New York: Palgrave.

Brown, Christopher Leslie. 2006. *Moral Capital: Foundations of British Abolitionism*. Chapel Hill: University of North Carolina Press.

Buechler, Steven. 2000. *Social Movements in Advanced Capitalism: The Political Economy and Cultural Construction of Social Activism*. New York: Oxford University Press.

Cabral, Amilcar. (1964) 2010. "Is Neocolonialism Rationalized Imperialism?" In *Africa and the West: From Colonialism to Independence, 1875 to the Present*, ed. William H. Worger, Nancy L. Clark, and Edward A. Alpers, 179–183. New York: Oxford University Press.

Caren, Neal, Sarah Gaby, and Catherine Herrold. 2017. "Economic Breakdown and Collective Action." *Social Problems* 64(1): 133–135.

Carey, Brycchan. 2005. *British Abolitionism and the Rhetoric of Sensibility*. New York: Palgrave Macmillan.

Castells, Manuel. 2013. *Networks of Outrage and Hope: Social Movements and the Internet Age*. Cambridge, UK: Polity.

Chen, Xi, and Dana Moss. 2018. "Authoritarian Regimes and Social Movements." In *The Wiley Blackwell Companion to Social Movements*, ed. David A. Snow, Sarah A. Soule, Hanspeter Kriesi, and Holly J. McCammon, 666–681. Hoboken, NJ: Wiley-Blackwell.

Clemens, Elisabeth S. 2006. "The Constitution of Citizens: Political Theories of Nonprofit Organizations." In *The Nonprofit Sector: A Research Handbook*, 2nd ed., ed. Walter W. Powell and Richard Steinberg, 207–220. New Haven, CT: Yale University Press.

Collins, Henry. 1962. "Karl Marx, the International and the British Trade Union Movement." *Science and Society* 26(4): 400–421.

Crenshaw, Kimberlé. 1991. "Mapping the Margins: Intersectionality, Identity Politics, and Violence Against Women of Color." *Stanford Law Review* 43(6): 1241–1299.

della Porta, Donatella. 2015. *Social Movements in Times of Austerity: Bringing Capitalism Back in to Protest Analysis*. Malden, MA: Polity.

DiMaggio, Paul. 2001. "Introduction: Making Sense of the Contemporary Firm and Prefiguring Its Future." In *The Twenty-First Century Firm: Changing Economic Organization in International Perspective*, ed. P. DiMaggio, 3–30. Princeton, NJ: Princeton University Press.

DiMaggio, Paul, Manish Nag, and David Blei. 2013. "Exploring Affinities Between Topic Modeling and the Sociological Perspective on Culture:

Application to Newspaper Coverage of U.S. Government Arts Funding." *Poetics* 41: 570–606.

Domingues, José Maurício. 2012. *Global Modernity, Development, and Contemporary Civilization: Towards a Renewal of Critical Theory*. New York: Routledge.

Drescher, Seymour. (1977) 2010. *Econocide: British Slavery in the Era of Abolition*. Chapel Hill: University of North Carolina Press.

Du Bois, W.E.B. 2007. *The Suppression of the African Slave-Trade to the United States of America*, ed. Henry L. Gates. New York: Oxford University Press.

Dufour, Pascale, Dominique Masson, and Dominique Caouette, eds. 2011. *Solidarities Beyond Borders: Transnationalizing Women's Movements*. Vancouver: University of British Columbia Press.

Edwards, Richard. 1979. *Contested Terrain: The Transformation of the Workplace in the Twentieth Century*. New York: Basic Books.

Estanque, Elísio, Hermes Augusto Costa, and José Soeiro. 2013. "The New Global Cycle of Protest and the Portuguese Case." *Journal of Social Science Education* 1: 1–23.

Fanon, Frantz. (1963) 2004. *The Wretched of the Earth*, trans. Richard Philcox. New York: Grove Press.

Ferguson, John-Paul, Thomas Dudley, and Sarah A. Soule. 2017. "Osmotic Mobilization and Union Support During the Long Protest Wave, 1960–1995." *Administrative Science Quarterly* 63(2): 441–477.

Finnemore, Martha, and Kathryn Sikkink. 1998. "International Norm Dynamics and Political Change." *International Organization* 52(4): 887–917.

Fisher, Dana R., Kevin Stanley, David Berman, and Gina Neff. 2005. "How Do Organizations Matter? Mobilization and Support for Participants at Five Globalization Protests." *Social Problems* 52(1): 102–121.

Fligstein, Neil, Jonah Stuart Brundage, and Michael Schultz. 2017. "Seeing Like the Fed: Culture, Cognition, and Framing in the Failure to Anticipate the Financial Crisis of 2008." *American Sociological Review* 82(5): 879–909.

Fraser, Nancy. 2009. *Scales of Justice: Reimagining Political Space in a Globalizing World*. New York: Columbia University Press.

French, John. 2000. "The Latin American Labor Studies Boom." *International Review of Social History* 45: 279–308.

Friedman, Thomas. 2005. *The World Is Flat: A Brief History of the Twenty-First Century*. New York: Farrar, Strauss and Giroux.

Galbraith, John Kenneth. (1967) 2007. *The New Industrial State*. Princeton, NJ: Princeton University Press.

Ganz, Marshall. 2018. "How to Organize to Win." *The Nation*, March 16. https://www.thenation.com/article/how-to-organize-to-win/.

Glasius, Marlies. 2013. "Dissident Writings as Political Theory on Civil Society and Democracy." In *Civil Society Activism Under Authoritarian Rule: A Comparative Perspective*, ed. Francesco Cavatorta, 34–56. London: Routledge.

Gohn, Maria da Glória. 2011. "Movimentos Sociais Na Contemporaneidade." *Revista Brasileira de Educação* 16(47): 333–361.

Goodwin, Jeff, and James Jasper. 2004. "Caught in a Winding, Snarling Vine: The Structural Bias of Political Process Theory." In *Rethinking Social Movements: Structure, Meaning, and Emotion*, ed. Jeff Goodwin and James M. Jasper, 3–30. Lanham, MD: Rowman and Littlefield.

Goodwin, Jeff, and Theda Skocpol. 1989. "Explaining Revolutions in the Contemporary Third World." *Politics and Society* 17(4): 489–509.

Gould, Roger. 2005. "Historical Sociology and Collective Action." In *Remaking Modernity: Politics, History, and Sociology*, ed. Julia Adams, Elizabeth S. Clemens, and Ann S. Orloff, 286–299. Durham, NC: Duke University Press.

Hancock, Ange-Marie. 2016. *Intersectionality: An Intellectual History*. New York: Oxford University Press.

Herod, Andrew. 2003. "Geographies of Labor Internationalism." *Social Science History* 27(4): 501–523.

Hetland, Gabe, and Jeff Goodwin. 2013. "The Strange Disappearance of Capitalism from Social Movement Studies." In *Marxism and Social Movements*, ed. Colin Barker, Laurence Cox, John Krinsky, and Alf G. Nilsen, 83–102. Chicago: Haymarket Books.

Howard, Philip N., and Muzammil M. Hussain. 2011. "The Role of Digital Media." *Journal of Democracy* 22(3): 35–48.

Huntington, Samuel. 1991. *The Third Wave: Democratization in the Late Twentieth Century*. Norman: University of Oklahoma Press.

Inclán, María de la Luz. 2008. "From the ¡Ya Basta! to the Caracoles: Zapatista Mobilization Under Transitional Conditions." *American Journal of Sociology* 113(5): 1316–1350.

Ingram, Paul, and Brian Silverman. 2016. "The Cultural Contingency of Structure: Evidence from Entry to the Slave Trade in and Around the Abolition Movement." *American Journal of Sociology* 122(3): 755–797.

Jeffrey, Julie Roy. 1998. *The Great Silent Army of Abolitionism: Ordinary Women in the Antislavery Movement*. Chapel Hill: University of North Carolina Press.

Kaplan, Sarah, and Keyvan Vakili. 2015. "The Double-Edged Sword of Recombination in Breakthrough Innovation." *Strategic Journal of Management* 36(10): 1435–1457.

Keck, Margaret E., and Kathryn Sikkink. 1998. *Activists Beyond Borders: Advocacy Networks in International Politics*. Ithaca, NY: Cornell University Press.

Ketelaars, Pauline. 2016. "What Strikes the Responsive Chord? The Effects of Framing Qualities on Frame Resonance Among Protest Participants." *Mobilization: An International Quarterly* 21(3): 341–360.

Khagram, Sanjeev, James Riker, and Kathryn Sikkink. 2002. *Restructuring World Politics: Transnational Social Movements, Networks, and Norms*. Minneapolis: University of Minnesota Press.

Kimball, Roger. 2000. *The Long March: How the Cultural Revolution of the 1960s Changed America*. San Francisco: Encounter Books.

Klandermans, Bert. 1994. "Transient Identities?" In *New Social Movements: From Ideology to Identity*, ed. Enrique Laraña, Hank Johnston, and Joseph R. Gusfield, 168–184. Philadelphia: Temple University Press.

Landauer, Carl. 1959. *European Socialism: A History of Ideas and Movements*. Berkeley: University of California Press.

Levi, Margaret, and Gillian Murphy. 2006. "Coalitions of Contention: The Case of the WTO Protests in Seattle." *Political Studies* 54(4): 651–670.

Levine, Daniel. 1988. "Assessing the Impacts of Liberation Theology in Latin America." *Review of Politics* 50(2): 241–263.

Lin, Jean. 2020. *A Spark in the Smokestacks: Environmental Organizing in Beijing Middle-Class Communities*. New York: Columbia University Press.

Long, Yan. "Domesticating a Dragon: The Contradictory Impact of Transnational Aids Institutions on State Repression in China, 1989–2013." *American Journal of Sociology*, 2018.

Longhofer, Wesley, and Evan Schofer. 2010. "National and Global Origins of Environmental Association." *American Sociological Review* 75(4): 505–533.

Löwy, Michael. 1998. "Por um Novo Internacionalismo." Recherches Internationales. http://www4.pucsp.br/neils/downloads/v5_artigo_michael.pdf, accessed April 20, 2018.

Luders, Joseph. 2010. *The Civil Rights Movement and the Logic of Social Change*. Cambridge, UK: Cambridge University Press.

Lukes, Steven. (1974) 2005. *Power: A Radical View*. New York: Palgrave Macmillan.

Mamdani, Mahmood. 1995. *African Studies in Social Movements and Democracy*. Oxford, UK: African Books Collective.

Mann, Michael. 1984. "The Autonomous Power of the State: Its Origins, Mechanisms, and Results." *European Journal of Sociology* 25(2): 185–213.

———. 1997. "Has Globalization Ended the Rise and Rise of the Nation-State?" *Review of International Political Economy* 4(3): 472–496.

Manza, Jeff, and Michael McCarthy. 2011. "The Neo-Marxist Legacy in American Sociology." *Annual Review of Sociology* 37: 155–183.

Marcuse, Herbert. 1972. *Counterrevolution and Revolt*. Boston: Beacon Press.

Mariátegui, José Carlos. 2005. *Por um Socialismo Indo-Americano*. Rio de Janeiro: Editora UFRJ.

Martínez-Torres, María Elena, and Peter M. Rosset. 2010. "La Vía Campesina: The Birth and Evolution of a Transnational Social Movement." *Journal of Peasant Studies* 37(1): 149–175.

Marx, Karl. (1864) 2000. "Inaugural Address of the International Working Men's Association." https://www.marxists.org/archive/marx/works/1864/10/27.htm, accessed August 28, 2019.

Marx, Karl, and Friedrich Engels. (1848) 1978. "Manifesto of the Communist Party." In *The Marx-Engels Reader*, ed. Robert C. Tucker, 469–500. New York: Norton.

McAdam, Doug. (1982) 1999. *Political Process and the Development of Black Insurgency, 1930–1970.* Chicago: University of Chicago Press.

McAdam, Doug, and William H. Sewell. 2001. "It's About Time: Temporality in the Study of Social Movements and Revolutions." In *Silence and Voice in the Study of Contentious Politics*, ed. Ronald R. Aminzade et al., 89–125. Cambridge, UK: Cambridge University Press.

McAdam, Doug, and Sidney Tarrow. 2010. "Ballots and Barricades: On the Reciprocal Relationship between Elections and Social Movements." *Perspectives on Politics* 8(2): 529–542.

McCarthy, John D., and Mayer N. Zald. 1977. "Resource Mobilization and Social Movements: A Partial Theory." *American Journal of Sociology* 82(6): 1212–1241.

McKenna, Elizabeth. 2019. "The Life and Death of Brazil's New Republic." *Berkeley Review of Latin American Studies* (Fall): 14–19, 56–59.

Meyer, David S., and Suzanne Staggenborg. 1996. "Movements, Countermovements, and the Structure of Political Opportunity." *American Journal of Sociology* 101(6): 1628–1660.

Midgley, Clare. 1996. "Slave Sugar Boycotts, Female Activism, and the Domestic Base of British Anti-Slavery Culture." *Slavery and Abolition* 17(3): 137–162.

Morris, Aldon D. 1984. *The Origins of the Civil Rights Movement.* New York: Free Press.

Munson, Ziad W. 2008. *The Making of Pro-Life Activists: How Social Movement Mobilization Works.* Chicago: University of Chicago Press.

Murray, David. 1980. *Odious Commerce: Britain, Spain and the Abolition of the Cuban Slave Trade.* Cambridge, UK: Cambridge University Press.

Nash, Jennifer C. 2017. "Intersectionality and Its Discontents." *American Quarterly* 69(1): 117–129.

Newman, David, and Sharon Block. 2006. "Probabilistic Topic Decomposition of an Eighteenth-Century American Newspaper." *Journal of the Association for Information Science and Technology* 57(6): 753–767.

Oliver, Pamela, and Gerald Marwell. 1992. "Mobilizing Technologies for Collective Action." In *Frontiers in Social Movement Theory*, ed. A. D. Morris and C. M. Mueller, 251–272. New Haven, CT: Yale University Press.

Oommen, T. K. 2012. "Methods and Methodological Issues in the Analysis of Social Movements: An Overview." *CNAS Journal* 39: 1–20.

Ortiz, David, Daniel Myers, Eugene Walls, and Maria-Elena Diaz. 2005. "Where Do We Stand with Newspaper Data?" *Mobilization: An International Quarterly* 10(3): 397–419.

Padawangi, Rita. 2013. "The Cosmopolitan Grassroots City as Megaphone: Reconstructing Public Spaces Through Urban Activism in Jakarta." *International Journal of Urban and Regional Research* 37(3): 849–863.

Paige, Jeffrey. 1975. *Agrarian Revolution: Social Movements and Export Agriculture in the Underdeveloped World.* New York: Free Press.

Paschel, Tianna. 2016. *Becoming Black Political Subjects: Movements and Ethno-Racial Rights in Colombia and Brazil.* Princeton, NJ: Princeton University Press.

Pierson, Paul. 2015. "Goodbye to Pluralism? Studying Power in Contemporary American Politics." Paper presented at the Wildavsky Forum for Public Policy, April 2015, Goldman School of Public Policy.

Piven, Frances Fox, and Jon Shefner. 2014. "A New Popular Movement for Social Justice in the United States and Beyond." In *Social Justice and the University*, ed. Jon Shefner, 295–308. New York: Palgrave Macmillan.

Polletta, Francesca, and James M. Jasper. 2001. "Collective Identity and Social Movements." *Annual Review of Sociology* 27: 283–305.

Ray, Raka, and Mary Fainsod Katzenstein. 2005. *Social Movements in India: Poverty, Power, and Politics.* Oxford, UK: Rowman and Littlefield.

Robinson, Cedric. (1983) 2000. *Black Marxism: The Making of the Black Radical Tradition.* Chapel Hill: Universtiy of North Carolina Press.

Rodríguez, Dylan. 2007. "The Political Logic of the Non-Profit Industrial Complex." In *The Revolution Will Not Be Funded: Beyond the Non-Profit Industrial Complex.*, ed. Incite! Women of Color Against Violence, 21–40. Cambridge, MA: South End Press.

Santos, Boaventura de Sousa, and Hermes Augusto Costa. 2005. "Introdução: Para Ampliar o Cânone do Internacionalismo Operário." *Revista de Cultura e Política* 64: 17–26.

Sassen, Saskia. 1983. "Labor Migrations and the New International Division of Labor." In *Women, Men, and the International Division of Labor*, ed. June Nash and María P. Fernández-Kelly, 175–204. Albany: SUNY Press.

———. 2002. "Global Cities and Diasporic Networks: Microsites in Global Civil Society." In *Global Civil Society*, ed. Marlies Glasius, Mary Kaldor, and Helmut Anheier, 217–238. Oxford, UK: Oxford University Press.

Schlossberg, Joseph. 1935. *The Workers and Their World: Aspects of the Workers' Struggle at Home and Abroad: Selected Essays*. New York: A.L.P. Committee.

Schoenberger, Erica. 1988. "Multinational Corporations and the New International Division of Labor: A Critical Appraisal." *International Regional Science Review* 11(2): 105–119.

Schrodt, Philip A., and David Van Brackle. 2013. "Automated Coding of Political Event Data." In *Handbook of Computational Approaches to Counterterrorism*, ed. V. S. Subrahmanian, 23–50. New York: Springer.

Seguin, Charles. 2016. "Cascades of Coverage: Dynamics of Media Attention to Social Movement Organizations." *Social Forces* 94(3): 997–1020.

Sewell, William H. 1996a. "Historical Events as Transformations of Structures: Inventing Revolution at the Bastille." *Theory and Society* 25(6): 841–881.

———. 1996b. "Three Temporalities: Toward an Eventful Sociology." In *The Historic Turn in the Human Sciences*, ed. Terrence J. McDonald, 245–280. Ann Arbor: University of Michigan Press.

Shorter, Edward, and Charles Tilly. 1974. *Strikes in France: 1830–1968*. London: Cambridge University Press.

Sikkink, Kathryn. 1993. "Human Rights, Principled Issue-Networks, and Sovereignty in Latin America." *International Organization* 47(3): 411–441.

Sikkink, Kathryn, and Jackie Smith. 2002. "Infrastructures for Change: Transnational Organizations, 1953–1993." In *Restructuring World Politics: The Power of Transnational Agency and Norms*, ed. Sanjeev Khagram, James V. Riker, and Kathryn Sikkink, 24–44. Minneapolis: University of Minnesota Press.

Simpson, Adam. 2013. "An 'Activist Diaspora' as a Response to Authoritarianism in Myanmar: The Role of Transnational Activism in Promoting Political Reform." In *Civil Society Activism Under Authoritarian Rule: A Comparative Perspective*, ed. Francesco Cavatorta, 181–218. London: Routledge.

Singer, Thea. 2016. "Using Big Data to Monitor Societal Events Shows Promise, but the Tech Needs Work." Phys.Org, September 30. https://phys.org/news/2016-09-big-societal-events-coding-tech.html.

Skocpol, Theda, and Alexander Hertel-Fernandez. 2016. "The Koch Network and Republican Party Extremism." *Perspectives on Politics* 14(3): 681–699.

Small, Albion W. 1897. "The Meaning of the Social Movement." *American Journal of Sociology* 3: 340–354.

Smith, Jackie. 2001. "Globalizing Resistance: The Battle of Seattle and the Future of Social Movements." *Mobilization: An International Quarterly* 6(1): 1–19.

———. 2008. *Social Movements for Global Democracy*. Baltimore: Johns Hopkins University Press.

Smith, Jackie, Charles Chatfield, and Ron Pagnucco. 1997. *Transnational Social Movements and Global Politics: Solidarity Beyond the State*. Syracuse, NY: Syracuse University Press.

Smith, Jackie, et al. 2014. *Global Democracy and the World Social Forums*. New York: Paradigm.

Smucker, Jonathan. 2017. *Hegemony How-To: A Road Map for Radicals*. Chico, CA: AK Press.

Snow, David, and Dana Moss. 2014. "Protest on the Fly: Toward a Theory of Spontaneity in the Dynamics of Protest and Social Movements." *American Sociological Review* 79(6): 1122–1143.

Stavenhagen, Rodolfo. 2003. "Mexico's Unfinished Symphony: The Zapatista Movement." In *Mexico's Politics and Society in Transition*, ed. Joseph S. Tulchin and Andrew D. Selee, 109–126. Boulder, CO: Lynne Rienner.

Stepan, Nancy. 1982. "Race and the Return of the Great Chain of Being, 1800–50." New York: Macmillan.

Tarrow, Sidney. 1993. "Cycles of Collective Action: Between Moments of Madness and the Repertoire of Contention." *Social Science History* 17(2): 281–307.

———. 2001. "Transnational Politics: Contention and Institutions in International Politics." *Annual Review of Political Science* 4(1): 1–20.

———. 2005. *The New Transnational Activism.* Cambridge, UK: Cambridge University Press.

———. 2007. "Inside Insurgencies: Politics and Violence in an Age of Civil War." *Perspectives on Politics* 5(3): 587–600.

Taylor, Verta. 1989. "Social Movement Continuity: The Women's Movement in Abeyance." *American Sociological Review* 54(5): 761–775.

Thomas, David, and Sharoni Mitra. 2017. "Global Civil Society and Resistance to Canadian Mining Abroad: Building and Enhancing the Boomerang Model." *Studies in Political Economy* 98(1): 48–70.

Tilly, Charles. 1978. *From Mobilization to Revolution.* Reading, MA: Addison-Wesley.

———. 1995. "Contentious Repertoires in Great Britain, 1758–1834." In *Repertoires and Cycles of Collective Action*, ed. Mark Traugott, 15–42. Durham, NC: Duke University Press.

Toscano, Emanuele, ed. 2019. *Researching Far-Right Movements: Ethics, Methodologies, and Qualitative Inquiries.* Boca Raton, : CRC Press.

Tufekci, Zeynep. 2014. "Social Movements and Governments in the Digital Age: Evaluating a Complex Landscape." *Journal of International Affairs* 68(1): 1–19.

———. 2017. *Twitter and Tear Gas: The Power and Fragility of Networked Protest.* New Haven, CT: Yale University Press.

Tuğal, Cihan. 2014. "End of the Leaderless Revolution." *Berkeley Journal of Sociology*, October 7. http://berkeleyjournal.org/2014/10/end-of-the-leaderless-revolution/.

Walder, Andrew. 2009. "Political Sociology and Social Movements." *Annual Review of Sociology* 35: 393–412.

Wallerstein, Immanuel. 1974. "The Rise and Demise of the Capitalist World System." *Comparative Studies in Society and History* 16(4): 387–415.

Wang, Dan, and Sarah A. Soule. 2012. "Social Movement Organizational Collaboration: Networks of Learning and the Diffusion of Protest Tactics,

1960–1995." *American Journal of Sociology* 17(6): 1674–1722.

Wang, Wei, Ryan Kennedy, David Lazer, and Naren Ramakrishnan. 2016. "Growing Pains for Global Monitoring of Society Events." *Science* 353(6307): 1502–1503.

Waterman, Peter. 1998. *Globalization, Social Movements and the New Internationalisms.* London: Mansell.

Weber, Max. (1922) 1946. "Class, Status, Party." In *From Max Weber: Essays in Sociology*, ed. Hans E. Gerth and C. Wright Mills, 180–195. New York: Oxford University Press.

Wendt, Alexander. 1999. *Social Theory of International Politics.* New York: Cambridge University Press.

Wolf, Eric. 1969. *Peasant Wars of the Twentieth Century.* Norman: University of Oklahoma Press.

Chapter 30. Comparative Nonprofit Sector Research: A Critical Assessment

Abbott, A. 2016. *Processual Sociology.* Chicago: University of Chicago Press.

Abramson, A., and K. Billings. Forthcoming. "New Legal Forms for Hybrid Organizations." In *The Routledge Companion to Nonprofit Management*, ed. H. K. Anheier and S. Toepler. London: Routledge.

Acheson, N., B. Harvey, and A. Williamson. 2005. "State Welfare and the Development of Voluntary Action: The Case of Ireland, North and South." *Voluntas: International Journal of Voluntary and Nonprofit Organizations* 16(2): 181–202.

Ahlquist, J. S., and C. Breunig. 2012. "Model-Based Clustering and Typologies in the Social Sciences." *Political Analysis* 20(1): 92–112.

Aksartova, S. 2009. "Promoting Civil Society or Diffusing NGOs?" In *Globalization, Philanthropy, and Civil Society: Projecting Institutional Logics Abroad*, ed. D. C. Hammack and S. Heydemann, 160–191. Bloomington: Indiana University Press.

Almog-Bar, M., and D. R. Young. 2016. "Policy Towards Nonprofits in International Perspective: Current Trends and Their Implications for Theory and Practice." *Nonprofit Policy Forum* 7(2): 85–93.

Alscher, M., E. Priller, S. Ratka, and R. G. Strachwitz. 2017. *The Space for Civil Society: Shrinking?*

Growing? Changing? (Opuscula #104). Berlin: Maecenata Institut für Philanthropie und Zivilgesellschaft.

Amenomori, T. 1998. *The Nonprofit Sector in Japan.* Manchester, UK: Manchester University Press.

Anheier, H. K. 2014. *Nonprofit Organizations: Theory, Management, Policy,* 2nd ed. Abingdon, UK: Routledge.

———, ed. 2018. "Philanthropic Foundations in Comparative Perspectives: Assessments from Twelve Countries." Special issue in 2 vols. *American Behavioral Scientist,* forthcoming.

Anheier, H., and S. Daly, eds. 2007. *The Politics of Foundations: A Comparative Analysis.* London: Routledge.

Anheier, H. K., and D. C. Hammack, eds. 2010. *American Foundations: Roles and Contributions.* Washington, DC: Brookings Institution Press.

Anheier, H. K., and G. Krlev. 2015. "Guest Editors' Introduction: Governance and Management of Hybrid Organizations." *International Studies of Management and Organization* 45(3): 193–206.

Anheier, H. K., M. Lang, and S. Toepler. 2019. "Civil Society in Times of Change: Shrinking, Changing and Expanding Spaces and the Need for New Regulatory Approaches." *Economics: The Open-Access, Open-Assessment E-Journal* 13(2019-8): 1–27.

Anheier, H. K., and D. Leat. 2018. *Performance Measurement in Philanthropic Foundations: The Ambiguity of Success and Failure.* Oxford, UK: Routledge.

Anheier, H., D. Leat, and S. Toepler. 2018. *Philanthropic Foundations: From Promise to Sustainable Contributions.* Policy brief prepared for Task Force 8: Social Cohesion, T20 Policy Brief. https://t20argentina.org/publicacion/philanthropic-foundations-from-promise-to-sustainable-contributions/.

Anheier, H. K., and R. List. 2005. *A Dictionary of Civil Society, Philanthropy and the Non-Profit Sector.* London: Routledge.

Anheier, H. K., G. Rudney, and L. M. Salamon. 1994. "Non-Profit Institutions in the United Nations System of National Accounts: Country Applications of SNA Guidelines." *Voluntas: International Journal of Voluntary and Nonprofit Organizations* 4(4): 486–501.

Anheier, H. K., and W. Seibel. eds. 1990. *The Third Sector: Comparative Studies of Nonprofit Organizations.* Berlin: De Gruyter.

———. 2001. *The Nonprofit Sector in Germany: Between State, Economy, and Society.* Manchester, UK: Manchester University Press.

Anheier, H. K., and S. Toepler, eds. 1999. *Private Funds, Public Purpose: Philanthropic Foundations in International Perspective.* New York: Springer.

Anheier, H. K., S. Toepler, and R. List, eds. 2010. *International Encyclopedia of Civil Society.* New York: Springer.

Archambault, E. 1997. *The Nonprofit Sector in France.* Manchester, UK: Manchester University Press.

———. 2017. "The Evolution of Public Service Provision by the Third Sector in France." *Political Quarterly* 88(3): 465–472.

Archambault, E., E. Priller, and A. Zimmer. 2014. "European Civil Societies Compared: Typically German—Typically French?" *Voluntas: International Journal of Voluntary and Nonprofit Organizations* 25(2): 514–537.

Banfield, J. D., and A. E. Raftery. 1993. "Model-Based Gaussian and Non-Gaussian Clustering." *Biometrics* 49(3): 803–821.

Barthélemy, M. 2000. *Associations: un nouvel âge de la participation?* Paris: Presses de Sciences Po.

Benevolenski, V. B., and S. Toepler. 2017. "Modernising Social Service Delivery in Russia: Evolving Government Support for Non-Profit Organisations." *Development in Practice* 27(1): 64–76.

Ben-Ner, A., and T. Van Hoomissen. 1991. "Nonprofit Organizations in the Mixed Economy." *Annals of Public and Cooperative Economics* 62(1): 519–550.

Borzaga, C., and A. Santuari. n.d. *Social Enterprises and New Employment in Europe.* Bolzano, Italy: Regione Autonomica Trentino-Alto Adige.

Brandsen, T., T. Steen, and B. Verschuere. Forthcoming. "Co-production." In *The Routledge Companion to Nonprofit Management,* ed. H. K. Anheier and S. Toepler. London: Routledge.

Breunig, C., and J. S. Ahlquist. 2014. "Quantitative Methodologies in Public Policy." In *Comparative and Methodological Challenges,* ed. I. Engeli, 109–130. Basingstoke, UK: Palgrave Macmillan.

Brudney, J. L., and R. E. England. 1983. "Toward a Definition of the Coproduction Concept." *Public Administration Review* 43(1): 59–65.

Burger, A., P. Dekker, S. Toepler, and H. K. Anheier. 1999. "Netherlands." In *Global Civil Society: Dimensions of the Nonprofit Sector*, ed. L. M. Salamon, H. K. Anheier, R. List, S. Toepler, and S. W. Sokolowski, 145–162. Baltimore: Johns Hopkins Center for Civil Society Studies.

Cardoso, F. 2004. *We the Peoples: Civil Society, the United Nations and Global Governance Report of the Panel of Eminent Persons on United Nations–Civil Society Relations*. United Nations A/58/817.

Carothers, T. 2015. *The Closing Space Challenge: How Are Funders Responding?* Washington, DC: Carnegie Endowment for International Peace.

Carothers, T. 1999. "Think Again: Civil Society." *Foreign Policy* 117 (Winter): 18–24, 26–29.

Carothers, T., and S. Brechenmacher. 2014. *Closing Space: Democracy and Human Rights Support Under Fire*. Washington, DC.: Carnegie Endowment for International Peace.

Choudry, A., and D. Kapoor. 2013. *NGOization: Complicity, Contradictions and Prospects*. London: Zed Books.

Christensen, D., and J. M. Weinstein. 2013. "Defunding Dissent: Restrictions on Aid to NGOs." *Journal of Democracy* 24(2): 77–91.

Coppedge, M., et al. 2018. *V-Dem Codebook v8*. Varieties of Democracy (V-Dem) Project.

Dahrendorf, R. 1997. *After 1989: Morals, Revolution, and Civil Society*. New York: St. Martin's Press.

Daucé, F. 2014. "The Government and Human Rights Groups in Russia: Civilized Oppression?" *Journal of Civil Society* 10(3): 239–254.

Defourny, J., K. Grønbjerg, and L. Meijs. 2016. "Voluntas Symposium: Comments on Salamon and Sokolowski's Re-conceptualization of the Third Sector." *Voluntas: International Journal of Voluntary and Nonprofit Organizations* 27(4): 1546–1561.

Dewey, J. 1927. *The Public and Its Problems*. University Park: Pennsylvania State University Press.

DiMaggio, P. J., and H. K. Anheier. 1990. "The Sociology of Nonprofit Organizations and Sectors." *Annual Review of Sociology* 16(1): 137–159.

Doyle, L. 1996. *Funding Europe's Solidarity: Resourcing Foundations, Associations, Voluntary Organisations and NGOs in the Member States of the European Union*. Brussels: Association for Innovative Cooperation in Europe.

Dupuy, K., J. Ron, and A. Prakash. 2016. "Hands Off My Regime! Governments' Restrictions on Foreign Aid to Non-Governmental Organizations in Poor and Middle-Income Countries." *World Development* 84, 299–311.

Edwards, M., and D. Hulme. 1996. *Beyond the Magic Bullet: NGO Performance and Accountability in the Post–Cold War World*. West Hartford, CT: Kumarian Press.

Eikenberry, A. M., and J. D. Kluver. 2004. "The Marketization of the Nonprofit Sector: Civil Society at Risk?" *Public Administration Review* 64(2): 132–140.

Esping-Andersen, G. 1990. *The Three Worlds of Welfare Capitalism*. Princeton, NJ: Princeton University Press.

Fisher, J. 1998. *Non Governments, NGOs and the Political Development of the Third World*. West Hartford, CT: Kumarian Press.

Fraley, C., and A. Raftery. 1998. "How Many Clusters? Which Clustering Method? Answers via Model-Based Cluster Analysis." *Computer Journal* 41(8): 578–588.

Gaskin, K., and J. D. Smith. 1995. *A New Civic Europe? A Study of the Extent and Role of Volunteering*. London: Volunteer Centre UK.

Gellner, E. 1994. *Conditions of Liberty: Civil Society and Its Rivals*. London: Hamish Hamilton.

Goddeeris, J. H., and B. A. Weisbrod. 1998. "Conversion from Nonprofit to For-Profit Legal Status: Why Does It Happen and Should Anyone Care?" *Journal of Policy Analysis and Management* 17(2): 215–233.

Gray, B., and M. Schlesinger. 2012. "Health Care." In *The State of Nonprofit America*, 2nd ed., ed. L. M. Salamon, 89–135. Washington, DC: Brookings Institution Press.

Grønbjerg, K. A., and S. R. Smith. 2015. *The Changing Dynamics of the Nonprofit-Government Relationship*. Revised version of paper presented at the 2014 International Society for Third-Sector Research Conference, Münster, Germany. https://www.researchgate.net/publication/ 301291814_The_Changing_Dynamics_of _Government-Nonprofit_Relations_Advancing _the_Field_-_A_Review_Essay.

Guo, C., and G. D. Saxton. 2014. "Tweeting Social Change: How Social Media Are Changing Non-profit Advocacy." *Nonprofit and Voluntary Sector Quarterly* 43(1): 57–79.

Habermas, J. 1989. *The Structural Transformation of the Public Sphere: An Inquiry into a Category of Bourgeois Society.* Cambridge, MA: MIT Press.

Haddad, T. 2017. "Analysing State–Civil Society Associations Relationship: The Case of Lebanon." *Voluntas: International Journal of Voluntary and Nonprofit Organizations* 28(4): 1742–1761. https://doi.org/10.1007/s11266-016-9788-y.

Hall, P. A., and D. W. Soskice, eds. 2001. *Varieties of Capitalism: The Institutional Foundations of Comparative Advantage.* Oxford, UK: Oxford University Press.

Hall, P. D. 1992. *"Inventing the Nonprofit Sector" and Other Essays on Philanthropy, Voluntarism, and Nonprofit Organizations.* Baltimore: Johns Hopkins University Press.

Hammack, D. C., and H. K. Anheier. 2013. *A Versatile American Institution: The Changing Ideals and Realities of Philanthropic Foundations.* Washington, DC: Brookings Institution Press.

Hansmann, H. 1987. "Economic Theories of Non-profit Organizations." In The *Nonprofit Sector: A Research Handbook*, ed. W. W. Powell, 27–42. New Haven, CT: Yale University Press.

———. 1990. "The Economic Role of Commercial Nonprofits: The Evolution of the US Savings Bank." In *The Third Sector: Comparative Studies of Nonprofit Organizations*, ed. H. K. Anheier and W. Seibel, 65–75. Berlin: De Gruyter.

Heydemann, S., and S. Toepler. 2006. "Foundations and the Challenge of Legitimacy in Comparative Perspective." In *The Legitimacy of Philanthropic Foundations: United States and European Perspectives*, ed. K. Prewitt, M. Dogan, S. Heydemann, and S. Toepler, 3–26. New York: Russell Sage Foundation.

Hulme, D., and M. Edwards. 1997. *Too Close for Comfort? NGOs, States and Donors.* London: St. Martin's.

Hustinx, L., F. Handy, and R. A. Cnaan. 2012. "Student Volunteering in China and Canada: Comparative Perspectives." *Canadian Journal of Sociology* 37(1): 55–83.

Hustinx, L., F. Handy, R. A. Cnaan, J. L. Brudney, A. B. Pessi, and N. Yamauchi. 2010. "Social and Cultural Origins of Motivations to Volunteer: A Comparison of University Students in Six Countries." *International Sociology* 25(3): 349–382.

Jackson, S. K., S. Guerrero, and S. Appe. 2014. "The State of Nonprofit and Philanthropic Studies Doctoral Education." *Nonprofit and Voluntary Sector Quarterly* 43(5): 795–811.

James, E. 1983. "How Nonprofits Grow: A Model." *Journal of Policy Analysis and Management* 2(3): 350–365.

———. 1987. "The Nonprofit Sector in Comparative Perspective." In *The Nonprofit Sector: A Research Handbook*, ed. W. W. Powell, 397–415. New Haven, CT: Yale University Press.

———, ed. 1989. *The Nonprofit Sector in International Perspective: Studies in Comparative Culture and Policy.* Oxford, UK: Oxford University Press.

Ju, C. B., and S.-Y. Tang. 2010. "Path Dependence, Critical Junctures, and Political Contestation: The Developmental Trajectories of Environmental NGOs in South Korea." *Nonprofit and Voluntary Sector Quarterly* 40(6): 1048–1072.

Kabalo, P. 2009. "A Fifth Nonprofit Regime? Revisiting Social Origins Theory Using Jewish Associational Life as a New State Model." *Nonprofit and Voluntary Sector Quarterly* 38(4): 627–642.

Kala, K. 2008. "The Social Origins of the Estonian Nonprofit Sector." *Journal of the Humanities and Social Sciences* 12(4): 441–449.

Kaldor, M. 2013. *Global Civil Society: An Answer to War.* Hoboken, NJ: Wiley.

Kamerāde, D., J. Crotty, and S. Ljubownikow. 2016. "Civil Liberties and Volunteering in Six Former Soviet Union Countries." *Nonprofit and Voluntary Sector Quarterly* 45(6): 1150–1168.

Keane, J. 1998. *Civil Society: Old Images, New Visions.* Stanford, CA: Stanford University Press.

———. 2005. "Eleven Theses on Markets and Civil Society." *Journal of Civil Society* 1(1): 25–34.

Kendall, J., and M. Knapp. 1997. *The Nonprofit Sector in the United Kingdom.* Manchester, UK: Manchester University Press.

Kerlin, J. A. 2010. "A Comparative Analysis of the Global Emergence of Social Enterprise." *Voluntas: International Journal of Voluntary and Nonprofit Organizations* 21(2): 162–179.

Kim, S. E., and Y. H. Kim. 2015. "Measuring the Growth of the Nonprofit Sector: A Longitudinal Analysis." *Public Administration Review* 75(2): 242–251.

Kim, Y. H., and S. E. Kim. 2016. "What Accounts for the Variations in Nonprofit Growth? A Cross-National Panel Study." *Voluntas: International Journal of Voluntary and Nonprofit Organizations* 29(3): 481–495.

Kingma, B. R. 2003. "Public Good Theories of the Nonprofit Sector." In *The Study of the Nonprofit Enterprise,* ed. H. Anheier, 53–65. New York: Springer.

Kramer, R. M. 1981. "Voluntary Agencies in the Welfare State." Berkeley: University of California Press.

———. 1987. "Voluntary Agencies and the Personal Social Services." In *The Nonprofit Sector: A Research Handbook,* ed. W. W. Powell, 240–257. New Haven, CT: Yale University Press.

Krashinsky, M. 2003. "Stakeholder Theories of the Nonprofit Sector." In *The Study of Nonprofit Enterprise: Theories and Approaches,* ed. H. K. Anheier and A. Ben-Ner, 125–136. Heidelberg, Germany: Springer.

Kumar, K. 1993. "Civil Society: An Inquiry into the Usefulness of an Historical Term." *British Journal of Sociology* 44(3): 375–395.

Lajevardi, N., M. R. Bussell, J. Stauch, and N. Rigillo. 2017. "Room to Flourish: Lessons for Canadian Grantmaking Foundations from Sweden, Germany and the Netherlands." *Canadian Journal of Nonprofit and Social Economy Research* 8(2): 80–96.

Lecy, J. D., and D. M. Van Slyke. 2013. "Nonprofit Sector Growth and Density: Testing Theories of Government Support." *Journal of Public Administration Research and Theory* 23(1): 189–214.

Lee, E. W. Y. 2005. "Nonprofit Development in Hong Kong: The Case of a Statist–Corporatist Regime." *Voluntas: International Journal of Voluntary and Nonprofit Organizations* 16(1): 51–68.

Lehner, O. M. 2011. "The Phenomenon of Social Enterprise in Austria: A Triangulated Descriptive Study." *Journal of Social Entrepreneurship* 2(1): 53–78.

Lewis, D. 2014. *The Management of Non-Governmental Development Organizations: An Introduction.* London: Routledge.

Lundström, T., and F. Wijkström. 1997. *The Nonprofit Sector in Sweden.* Manchester, UK: Manchester University Press.

Mahoney, J., and K. Thelen. 2010. *Explaining Institutional Change: Ambiguity, Agency, and Power.* Cambridge, UK: Cambridge University Press.

Mirabella, R., J. Hvenmark, and O. S. Larsson. 2015. "Civil Society Education: International Perspectives." *Journal of Nonprofit Education and Leadership* 5(4): 213–218.

Mirabella, R., and M. McDonald. 2012. "University-Based Education Programs in Nonprofit Management and Philanthropic Studies: Current State of the Field and Future Directions." In *Human Resource Management in the Nonprofit Sector,* ed. R. J. Burke and C. L. Cooper, 243–255. Northampton, MA: Edward Elgar.

Morris, S. 2000. "Defining the Nonprofit Sector: Some Lessons from History." *Voluntas: International Journal of Voluntary and Nonprofit Organizations* 11(1): 25–43.

Mosley, J., T. Weiner-Davis, and T. Anasti. Forthcoming. "Advocacy and Lobbying." In *The Routledge Companion to Nonprofit Management,* ed. H. K. Anheier and S. Toepler. London: Routledge.

Nielsen, W. A. 1972. *The Big Foundations.* New York: Columbia University Press.

Nissan, E., M.-S. Castaño, and I. Carrasco. 2012. "Drivers of Non-Profit Activity: A Cross-Country Analysis." *Small Business Economics* 38(3): 303–320.

Olson, M. 1965. *Logic of Collective Action: Public Goods and the Theory of Groups. Harvard Economic Studies,* vol. 124. Cambridge, MA: Harvard University Press.

Ortmann, A., and M. Schlesinger. 2003. "Trust, Repute, and the Role of Nonprofit Enterprise." In *The Study of Nonprofit Enterprise: Theories and Approaches,* ed. H. K. Anheier and A. Ben-Ner, 77–114. Heidelberg, Germany: Springer.

Ostrom, E. 1975. *The Delivery of Urban Services: Outcomes of Change.* Beverly Hills, CA: SAGE.

———. 1996. "Crossing the Great Divide: Coproduction, Synergy, and Development." *World Development* 24(6): 1073–1087.

Poppe, A. E., and J. Wolff. 2017. "The Contested Spaces of Civil Society in a Plural World: Norm Contestation in the Debate About Restrictions on International Civil Society Support." *Contemporary Politics* 23(4): 469–488.

Powell, W. W., ed. 1987. *The Nonprofit Sector: A Research Handbook*. New Haven, CT: Yale University Press.

Prewitt, K. 2006. "American Foundations: What Justifies Their Unique Privileges and Powers." In *The Legitimacy of Philanthropic Foundations: United States and European Perspectives*, ed. K. Prewitt, M. Dogan, S. Heydemann, and S. Toepler, 27–48. New York: Russell Sage Foundation.

Putnam, R. D. 1994. *Making Democracy Work: Civic Traditions in Modern Italy*. Princeton, NJ: Princeton University Press.

———. 2000. *Bowling Alone: The Collapse and Revival of American Community*. New York: Simon and Schuster.

Quigley, K. F. 1997. *For Democracy's Sake: Foundations and Democracy Assistance in Central Europe*. Washington, DC: Woodrow Wilson Center Press.

Rutzen, D. 2015. "Civil Society Under Assault." *Journal of Democracy* 26(4): 28–39.

Sachße, C. 1994. "Subsidiarität: Zur Karriere eines sozialpolitischen Ordnungsbegriffes." *Zeitschrift für Sozialreform* 40(11): 717–738.

Salamon, L. M. 1995. *Partners in Public Service: Government-Nonprofit Relations in the Modern Welfare State*. Baltimore: Johns Hopkins University Press.

Salamon, L. M., and H. K. Anheier. 1992a. "In Search of the Nonprofit Sector I: The Question of Definitions." *Voluntas: International Journal of Voluntary and Nonprofit Organizations* 3(2): 125–161.

———. 1992b. "In Search of the Nonprofit Sector II: The Problem of Classification." *Voluntas: International Journal of Voluntary and Nonprofit Organizations* 3(3): 267–309.

———. 1996. *The Emerging Nonprofit Sector: An Overview*. Manchester, UK: Manchester University Press.

———. 1997. *Defining the Nonprofit Sector: A Cross-National Analysis*. Manchester, UK: Manchester University Press.

———. 1998. "Social Origins of Civil Society: Explaining the Nonprofit Sector Cross-Nationally." *Voluntas: International Journal of Voluntary and Nonprofit Organizations* 9(3): 213–248.

Salamon, L. M., H. K. Anheier, R. List, S. Toepler, and S. W. Sokolowski, eds. 1999. *Global Civil Society: Dimensions of the Nonprofit Sector*. Baltimore: Johns Hopkins Center for Civil Society Studies.

Salamon, L. M., and S. W. Sokolowski. 2016. "Beyond Nonprofits: Re-Conceptualizing the Third Sector." *Voluntas: International Journal of Voluntary and Nonprofit Organizations* 27(4): 1515–1545.

Salamon, L. M., S. W. Sokolowski, and M. A. Haddock. 2017. *Explaining Civil Society Development*. Baltimore: Johns Hopkins University Press.

Salamon, L. M., and S. Toepler. 2015. "Government-Nonprofit Cooperation: Anomaly or Necessity?" *Voluntas: International Journal of Voluntary and Nonprofit Organizations* 26(6): 2155–2177.

Schiff, J., and B. Weisbrod. 1991. "Competition Between For-Profit and Nonprofit Organizations in Commercial Markets." *Annals of Public and Cooperative Economics* 62(4): 619–640.

Schlüter, A., V. Then, and P. Walkenhorst, eds. 2001. *Foundations in Europe*. London: Directory of Social Change.

Schneider, M., and M. Paunescu. 2012. "Changing Varieties of Capitalism and Revealed Comparative Advantages from 1990 to 2005: A Test of the Hall and Soskice Claims." *Socio-Economic Review* 10(4): 731–753.

Selle, P., and D. Wollebæk. 2010. "Why Social Democracy Is Not a Civil Society Regime in Norway." *Journal of Political Ideologies* 15(3): 289–301.

Shier, M. L., and F. Handy. 2014. "Research Trends in Nonprofit Graduate Studies: A Growing Interdisciplinary Field." *Nonprofit and Voluntary Sector Quarterly* 43(5): 812–831.

Skokova, Y., U. Pape, and I. Krasnopolskaya. 2018. "The Non-Profit Sector in Today's Russia: Between Confrontation and Co-Optation." *Europe-Asia Studies* 70(4): 531–563.

Slivinski, A. 2003. "The Public Goods Theory Revisited." In *The Study of the Nonprofit Enterprise*, ed. H. Anheier, 67–74. New York: Springer.

Smith, D. H. 2013. "Growth of Research Associations and Journals in the Emerging Discipline of Altruistics." *Nonprofit and Voluntary Sector Quarterly* 42(4): 638–656.

Smith, D. H., R. A. Stebbins, and J. Grotz, eds. 2017. *The Palgrave Handbook of Volunteering, Civic Participation, and Nonprofit Associations*. London: Springer.

Smith, S. R., and K. Grønbjerg, eds. 2018. "Special Issue: Nonprofits and Policy." *Nonprofit and Voluntary Sector Quarterly* 47(4 suppl.).

Smith, S. R., and M. Lipsky. 1993. "Nonprofits for Hire: The Welfare State in the Age of Contracting." Cambridge, MA: Harvard University Press.

Steinberg, R. 2006. "Economic Theories of Nonprofit Organizations." In *The Nonprofit Sector: A Research Handbook*, 2nd ed., ed. W. W. Powell and R. Steinberg, 117–139. New Haven, CT: Yale University Press.

Suleiman, L. 2013. "The NGOs and the Grand Illusions of Development and Democracy." *Voluntas: International Journal of Voluntary and Nonprofit Organizations* 24(1): 241–261.

Svidroňová, M., G. Vaceková, and V. Valentinov. 2016. "The Theories of Non-Profits: A Reality Check from Slovakia." *Lex Localis* 14(3): 399–418.

System of National Accounts (SNA). 2009. *System of National Accounts 2008*. https://unstats.un.org/unsd/nationalaccount/docs/SNA2008.pdf.

Tarasenko, A. 2018. "Russian Non-Profit Organisations in Service Delivery: Neoliberal and Statist Social Policy Principles Intertwined." *Europe-Asia Studies* 70(4): 1–17.

Teets, J. C. 2014. *Civil Society Under Authoritarianism: The China Model*. Cambridge, MA: Cambridge University Press.

Tocqueville, A. de. (1836) 2003. *Democracy in America*, vol. 10. Washington, DC: Regnery.

Toepler, S. 2016. "Foundations in Germany and the US: Comparative Observations." In *German Philanthropy in Transatlantic Perspective*, 23–39. Heidelberg, Germany: Springer.

———. 2018a. "Public Philanthropic Partnerships: The Changing Nature of Government/Foundation Relationships in the US." *International Journal of Public Administration* 41(8): 657–669.

———. 2018b. "Toward a Comparative Understanding of Foundations." *American Behavioral Scientist* 62(13): 1956–1971.

Toepler, S., U. Pape, and V. Benevolenski. Forthcoming. "Subnational Variations in Government-Nonprofit Relations: A Comparative Analysis of Regional Differences within Russia." *Journal of Comparative Policy Analysis*. https://doi.org/10.1080/13876988.2019.1584446.

Tranvik, T., and P. Selle. 2007. "The Rise and Fall of Popular Mass Movements: Organizational Change and Globalization: The Norwegian Case." *Acta Sociologica* 50(1): 57–70.

United Nations. 2003. *Handbook on Non-Profit Institutions in the System of National Accounts*. ST/ESA/STAT/SER.F/91. New York: United Nations.

Wagner, A. 2000. "Reframing 'Social Origins' Theory: The Structural Transformation of the Public Sphere." *Nonprofit and Voluntary Sector Quarterly* 29(4): 541–553.

Weisbrod, B. A. 1975. "Toward a Theory of the Voluntary Nonprofit Sector in a Three-Sector Economy." In *Altruism, Morality, and Economic Theory*, ed. E. S. Phelps, 171–195. New York: Russell Sage Foundation.

———. 1988. *The Nonprofit Economy*. Cambridge, MA: Harvard University Press.

Wiepking, P., and F. Handy. 2016. *The Palgrave Handbook of Global Philanthropy*. London: Springer.

Wollebæk, D., and P. Selle. 2008. "A Social Democratic Model of Civil Society?" In *Changing Images of Civil Society. From Protest to Governance*, ed. B. Jobert and B. Kohler-Koch, 47–69. London: Routledge.

Worms, J. P. 2002. "France: Old and New Civic and Social Ties in France." In *Democracies in Flux: The Evolution of Social Capital in Contemporary Society*, ed. R. D. Putnam, 137–188. Oxford, UK: Oxford University Press.

Wuthnow, R., V. A. Hodgkinson, and Associates 1990. *Faith and Philanthropy in America: Exploring the Role of Religion in America's Voluntary Sector*. San Francisco: Jossey-Bass.

Yu, J., and K. Chen. 2018. "Does Nonprofit Marketization Facilitate or Inhibit the Development of Civil Society? A Comparative Study of China and the USA." *Voluntas: International Journal of Voluntary and Nonprofit Organizations* 29(5): 925–937.

Zhao, R., Z. Wu, and C. Tao. 2016. "Understanding Service Contracting and Its Impact on NGO Development in China." *Voluntas: International Journal of Voluntary and Nonprofit Organizations* 27(5): 2229–2251.

Walter W. Powell is Jacks Family Professor of Education and (by courtesy) Sociology, Organizational Behavior, Management Science and Engineering, and Communication at Stanford University and a faculty fellow at the Center for Advanced Study in the Behavioral Sciences. He has been a Co-Director of the Center on Philanthropy and Civil Society since its founding in 2006. His interests focus on the processes through which practices move across organizations and the role of networks in facilitating or hindering the transfer of ideas. He is the author or editor of *Books: The Culture and Commerce of Publishing*, with Lewis Coser and Charles Kadushin (Basic Books, 1982); *Getting into Print: The Decision-Making Process in Scholarly Publishing* (University of Chicago Press, 1985); *The New Institutionalism in Organizational Analysis*, with Paul DiMaggio (University of Chicago Press, 1991); *Private Action and the Public Good*, with Elisabeth Clemens (Yale University Press, 1997); *The Nonprofit Sector*, 2nd ed., with Richard Steinberg (Yale University Press, 2006), and *The Emergence of Organizations and Markets*, with John Padgett (Princeton University Press, 2012).

Patricia Bromley is an Assistant Professor of Education and (by courtesy) Sociology at Stanford University. Her research spans a range of fields including comparative education, organization theory, the sociology of education, and public administration and policy. Her work focuses on the rise and globalization of a culture emphasizing rational, scientific thinking and expansive forms of rights. Empirically, much of her research focuses on two settings—education systems and organizations. Recent publications examine the rise of emphases on human and minority rights, environmentalism, and diversity in textbooks from countries around the world and investigate the global expansion of formal organization worldwide, which has increased in numbers and internal complexity. She is co-author of *Hyper-Organization: Global Organizational Expansion*, with John W. Meyer (Oxford University Press, 2015).

Helmut K. Anheier is past President and Professor of Sociology at the Hertie School, and on the faculty at the Luskin School of Public Affairs at UCLA. His research centers on social innovation, culture, philanthropy, organizational studies, and indicator systems.

Anheier, author of over 450 publications, many in leading journals, has received various international awards for his scholarship. He is founding editor-in-chief of Global Perspectives, University of California Press.

Mike Ananny is an Associate Professor of Communication and Journalism at the University of Southern California's Annenberg School for Communication and Journalism, and an Affiliated Faculty member with USC's Science, Technology and Society research cluster. He studies the intersection of journalism practice and technology design, the public significance of networked news infrastructures, and the ethics of algorithmic systems. He has published in various academic and popular venues, is the author of *Networked Press Freedom* (MIT Press, 2018), is currently writing a book on absence and silence in online journalism (Yale University Press), and is co-editor of *Bauhaus Futures*, with Laura Forlano and Molly Wright Steenson (MIT Press, 2019).

Richard Arum is Dean of the School of Education and Professor of Education and (by courtesy) Sociology, Criminology, Law and Society at the University of California, Irvine. He is the author of *Judging School Discipline: A Crisis of Moral Authority* (Harvard University Press, 2003) and coauthor of *Academically Adrift: Limited Learning on College Campuses*, with Josipa Roska (University of Chicago Press, 2011).

Irene Bloemraad is the Class of 1951 Professor of Sociology and the Thomas Garden Barnes Chair of Canadian Studies at the University of California, Berkeley. Her research examines how immigrants become incorporated into the political and civic life of the places where they live, as well as the consequences of immigration for politics, policy, and understandings of citizenship. In addition to articles published in journals spanning sociology, political science, history, and ethnic/migration studies, she is the author or co-editor of *Handbook of Citizenship* (Oxford University Press, 2017), *Migrants, Minorities, and the Media* (Routledge, 2017), *Rallying for Immigrant Rights* (University of California Press, 2011), *Civic Hopes and Political Realities* (Russell Sage Foundation, 2008), and *Becoming a Citizen* (University of California Press, 2006). She is the Founding Director of the Berkeley Interdisciplinary Migration Initiative.

Christof Brandtner is a postdoctoral fellow at the Mansueto Institute for Urban Innovation and the Department of Sociology at the University of Chicago. His research investigates how new ideas and routines related to rational organizing—such as strategic planning, performance evaluation, and voluntary certification—change organizations and places in which democratic and community values loom large. His work has appeared in *Sociological Theory*, the *Socio-Economic Review*, *Voluntas*, *Urban Studies*, and *Organization Studies*.

Paul Brest is Former Dean and Professor Emeritus (active) at Stanford Law School, a Lecturer at the Stanford Graduate School of Business, and Co-Director of the Stanford Law and Policy Lab. He is co-author of *Money Well Spent: A Strategic Guide to Smart Philanthropy*, 2nd ed. (Stanford University Press, 2018), *Problem Solving, Decision Making, and Professional Judgment* (Oxford University Press, 2010), and articles on constitutional law, philanthropy, and impact investing.

Breno Bringel is Professor of Sociology at the Institute of Social and Political Studies at the State University of Rio de Janeiro (IESP-UERJ). His current research addresses the reconfiguration of activism, social movements, and contemporary internationalism as well as the geopolitical and theoretical construction of Latin American sociology.

Maoz Brown is a PhD candidate in Sociology at the University of Chicago with research interests in the social organization and political economy of altruism, philanthropy, and social welfare services. His latest research explores the social construction of organizational effectiveness and program evaluation standards in the U.S. nonprofit human services sector. He recently joined the Wharton Social Impact Initiative, where he leads research projects on impact investing, social enterprise, and other topics at the intersection of business and philanthropy.

Elisabeth S. Clemens is William Rainey Harper Professor of Sociology at the University of Chicago and editor of the *American Journal of Sociology*. Her research explores the role of social movements and organizational innovation in political change. She is the author of *The People's Lobby: Organizational Innovation and the Rise of Interest Group Politics in the United States, 1890–1925* (University of Chicago Press, 1997) as well as *What Is Political Sociology?* (Polity, 2016). She has co-edited multiple volumes, including *Remaking Modernity: Politics, History and Sociology* (Duke University Press, 2005) and *Politics and Partnerships: Voluntary Associations in America's Past and Present* (University of Chicago Press, 2010). She is currently completing *Civic Gifts*, which traces the tense but powerful entanglements of benevolence and liberalism in the development of the American nation-state.

Els de Graauw is Associate Professor of Political Science at Baruch College, the City University of New York. Her research centers on the nexus of immigration and citizenship, civil society organizations, urban and metropolitan politics, and public policy, with a focus on building institutional capacity for immigrant integration and representation. Her book *Making Immigrant Rights Real: Nonprofits and the Politics of Integration in San Francisco* (Cornell University Press, 2016) analyzes the role of nonprofit organizations in advocating for immigrant integration policies in San Francisco, with a focus on immigrant language access, labor rights, and municipal ID cards.

Magali (Maggie) Delmas is Professor of Management at the University of California, Los Angeles Anderson School of Management and the Institute of the Environment & Sustainability and the director of the Center for Corporate Environmental Performance. She conducts research in strategy and corporate sustainability and has published more than eighty articles, book chapters, and case studies on the subject. She currently works on developing effective information strategies to promote conservation behavior and the development of green markets. Her latest book is *The Green Bundle: Pairing the Market with the Planet* (Stanford University Press, 2018).

Kendra Dupuy is a Senior Researcher at the Peace Research Institute Oslo (PRIO) and an affiliated researcher at the Chr. Michelsen Institute (CMI). She studies the political repression of civil society, education in crisis and conflict-affected contexts, natural resource and environmental management, and foreign aid.

Claire Dunning is an Assistant Professor at the School of Public Policy at the University of Maryland–College Park. An urban and political historian, she received her PhD in History from Harvard University and was a Postdoctoral Fellow at Stanford University's Center on Philanthropy and Civil Society. Her work has appeared in the *Journal of Urban History* and *Enterprise & Society*. She is currently finishing a book on nonprofit organizations, poverty policy, and urban governance from 1950 to the present.

Nina Eliasoph is Professor of Sociology at the University of Southern California. She studies everyday interaction in voluntary associations, nonprofits, and activist organizations. Her publications include *Avoiding Politics: How Americans Produce Apathy in Everyday Life* (Cambridge University Press, 1998) and *Making Volunteers: Civic Life at Welfare's End* (Princeton University Press, 2011) as well as articles in the *American Journal of Sociology*. Currently, she is working on two projects: a computational linguistics study documenting the global presence of organizations that share "the mantra of empowerment" and an ethnography of local activism within political parties in the United States, especially focusing on how activists imagine the future, when our current futures are all unimaginable.

Yotala Oszkay is a PhD candidate in the Department of Sociology at the University of California, Los Angeles. She is currently examining the local dynamics that undergird market participation in what is popularly termed the "sharing economy," with a specific focus on the sector of home-sharing. This work is part of a larger dissertation project that examines how these new forms of participation then constitute particular local politics over the regulation of such "sharing economy" markets.

Brad R. Fulton is Assistant Professor at Indiana University in the O'Neill School of Public and Environmental Affairs. His research draws on organizational theory and network analysis to examine the social, political, and economic impact of community-based organizations. Fulton is the lead researcher for the National Study of Community Organizing Organizations—a multi-level study that examines grassroots efforts to address socioeconomic inequality. He is Co-Principal Investigator for the Observing Civic Engagement project, the National Study of Congregations' Economic Practices, and the Indiana Data Partnership project. Fulton's work has been published in the *American Sociological Review* and *Sociological Methods and Research*. His courses *Managing Diversity* and *Statistics for the Social Sciences* have been published on Apple Podcasts.

Laura K. Gee is an Associate Professor of Economics at Tufts University. Her work has appeared in the *Journal of Labor Economics*, the *Journal of Public Economics*, *Management Science*, and *Experimental Economics*. Her research is in behavioral economics, with a particular focus on how individual decision making is influenced by group dynamics. She currently has two main lines of research; one concerns the provision of public goods including charitable contributions, and the second addresses the relationship between behavioral factors/social networks and labor markets.

Maitreesh Ghatak is Professor of Economics at the London School of Economics (LSE). He works on the economics of organizations and development economics. His main areas of interest are nonpecuniary motivation and incentives, nonprofits, social enterprise, inequality and occupational choice, poverty traps, microfinance, property rights, tenancy, and land reform. He has been the Director of the Development Economics Programme at the Suntory and Toyota International Centres for Economics and Related Disciplines at the LSE since 2005. He is a co-editor of *Economica*, an elected Fellow of the British Academy, and a founding member of research networks on Economics of Social Sector Organisations and Non-profits, Governments, and Organizations.

Shannon Gleeson is an Associate Professor of Labor Relations, Law, and History at Cornell University's School of Industrial and Labor Relations. Her books include *Building Citizenship from Below: Precarity, Migration, and Agency*, edited with Marcel Paret (Routledge, 2017), *Precarious Claims: The Promise and Failure of Workplace Protections in the United States* (University of California Press, 2016), *The Nation and Its Peoples: Citizens, Denizens, Migrants*, edited with John Park (Routledge, 2014), and *Conflicting Commitments: The Politics of Enforcing Immigrant Worker Rights in San Jose and Houston* (Cornell University Press, 2012). Her work examines consular protection and transnational migrant advocacy strategies (with Xóchitl Bada), the role of civil society and local governments in implementing the 2012 Deferred Action for Childhood Arrivals (DACA) program (with Els de Graauw), and the impacts of temporary legal status on immigrant workers (with Kate Griffith). She is currently documenting the responses of the labor movement to immigration policy under the Trump administration.

Daniel J. Hemel is an Assistant Professor at the University of Chicago Law School. His research focuses on taxation, nonprofit organizations, administrative law, and federal courts. His academic work has appeared in numerous publications including the *California Law Review*, *Cornell Law Review*, *Columbia Law Review*, *NYU Law Review*, *Supreme Court Review*, *Tax Law Review*, *Texas Law Review*, *University of Chicago Law Review*, and *Yale Law Journal*.

Aaron Horvath is a PhD candidate in Sociology at Stanford University and a member of the Civic Life of Cities Lab. His research centers on the interplay of ideational, organizational, and political developments with a particular interest in the processes by which novel or transgressive ideas become imprinted into organizational forms and the political consequences thereof. Horvath's dissertation traces the evolving ideals of administrative expertise and rational governance in the United States from the late nineteenth to the mid-twentieth century.

Jill R. Horwitz is Vice Dean for Faculty and Intellectual Life and Professor of Law at the University of California, Los Angeles. Her research explores the legal regulation of health care and nonprofit organizations, law and economics, and tort law. Most recently she has been studying the relationship between state and provincial regulation on opioid prescribing and various outcomes such as dispensing to patients and hospitalizations in the United States and Canada. She is the Reporter for the American Law Institute Restatement, First, of Charitable Nonprofit Organizations as well as a Research Associate at the National Bureau of Economic Research, an Adjunct Professor of Economics at the University of Victoria Department of Economics in British Columbia, and a member of the Bar of the Commonwealth of Massachusetts.

Sean Jackson is an undergraduate math/economics student and research assistant at the University of California, Los Angeles. He worked on this volume with Professor Magali Delmas and Professor Tom Lyon as part of the Sustainable Los Angeles Undergraduate Research Scholar Program.

Jacob L. Kepins is a PhD student of Education Policy and Social Context in the School of Education at the University of California, Irvine. His research focuses on school structures, organizations, and processes, and the role they play in the transition from secondary to postsecondary education. He is specifically interested in differences in curriculum, grading, and discipline across school sectors and contexts.

Markus Lang is a researcher at the Max Weber Institute of Sociology at Heidelberg University. His current interests lie in the impact of patent, trademark, and copyright policy on global inequality. His most recent publication is "Open to Feedback? Formal and Informal Recursivity in Create Commons' Transnational Standard-Setting" (*Global Policy*, 2017), with Leonhard Dobusch and Sigrid Quack.

Ted Lechterman is a Visiting Scholar at the Hertie School of Governance in Berlin. His research principally concerns how democratic ideals apply to economic practices. His work has appeared in *Polity*, the *Journal of Practical Ethics*, and *Raisons Politiques*.

Wesley Longhofer is an Associate Professor of Organization and Management in the Goizueta Business School at Emory University, where he also holds courtesy appointments in Sociology, Ethics, and the Emory Global Health Institute. Some of his published work on charitable organizations, environmental protection, and international law has appeared in the *American Sociological Review*, *American Journal of Sociology*, *Administrative Science Quarterly*, *Social Forces*, *Sociological Science*, and *Scientific Reports*.

Thomas P. Lyon holds the Dow Chair of Sustainable Science, Technology and Commerce at the University of Michigan, with appointments in both the Ross School of Business and the School of Environment and Sustainability. He is President of the Alliance for Research on Corporate Sustainability. He uses economic analysis to understand corporate environmental strategy, especially in the energy industry, and how it is shaped by emerging government regulations, nongovernmental organizations, and consumer demands. He is the author of *Corporate Environmentalism and Public Policy* (Cambridge University Press, 2004). His current research focuses on environmental information disclosure, private politics, regulatory compliance, and eco-certification.

Johanna Mair is Professor of Organization, Strategy and Leadership at the Hertie School of Governance in Berlin. Her research focuses on the nexus of organizations, institutions, and societal challenges. Her focus in recent work is on mechanisms that enable organizations to transform social systems and make progress on social problems. She is the Academic Editor of *Stanford Social Innovation Review* and Co-Director of the Global Innovation for Impact Lab at the Stanford Center on Philanthropy and Civil Society. In addition to her book *Innovation and Scaling—How effective Social Entrepreneurs create Impact*, co-authored with Christian Seelos (Stanford University Press, 2017), she has published in the *Academy of Management Journal, Organization Studies, Academy of*

Management Discoveries, Academy of Management Perspectives, and *Journal of Business Venturing*.

Nicole P. Marwell is an Associate Professor in the University of Chicago School of Social Service Administration. Her research examines urban governance, with a focus on the diverse intersections between nonprofit organizations, government bureaucracies, and politics. She is author of *Bargaining for Brooklyn: Community Organizations in the Entrepreneurial City* (University of Chicago Press, 2007). Her work draws on an interdisciplinary set of insights and tools from sociology, organization studies, ethnic studies, political science, and public administration, and uses qualitative, quantitative, and historical methods to explore how changes in this meso level of social structure affect urban cohesion, inequality, and exclusion; current research examines the role of data in urban governance.

Elizabeth McKenna is a postdoctoral fellow at the Agora Institute at Johns Hopkins University. She studies social movements and political organizing in the United States and Brazil. She is the co-author of *Groundbreakers: How Obama's 2.2 Million Volunteers Transformed Campaigning in America*, with Hahrie Han (Oxford University Press, 2014).

Jonathan Meer is Professor of Economics at Texas A&M University, a Private Enterprise Research Enterprise Center Professor, and a Research Associate at the National Bureau of Economic Research. He is the author of more than thirty peer-reviewed articles on charitable giving, the economics of education, and the impact of the minimum wage.

Jennifer E. Mosley is an Associate Professor in the University of Chicago's School of Social Service Administration. Her research focuses on the political engagement of nonprofit organizations, particularly social service agencies, community-based organizations, and philanthropic foundations. Recent projects explore the relationship between advocacy and improved democratic representation, how social service organizations balance self-interest with larger community goals, and how public administration and nonprofit management trends, particularly collaborative governance and contracting, affect nonprofits' advocacy role. Her research has appeared in the *Journal of Public Administration Research and Theory, Nonprofit and Voluntary Sector Quarterly, Social Service Review*, and *Urban Affairs Review*.

Francie Ostrower is Professor at the University of Texas at Austin in the LBJ School of Public Affairs and College of Fine Arts, Director of the Portfolio Program in Arts and Cultural Management and Entrepreneurship, and a Senior Fellow in the RGK Center for Philanthropy and Community Service. She has been a visiting professor at IAE de Paris/Sorbonne graduate Business School and is an Urban Institute affiliated scholar. She has authored numerous publications on philanthropy, nonprofit governance, and arts participation that have received awards from the Association for Research on Nonprofit and Voluntary Action (ARNOVA) and Independent Sector. Her many past and current professional activities include serving as a board member and president of ARNOVA, and an editorial board member of the *Nonprofit and Voluntary Sector Quarterly*.

Pamela Paxton is the Linda K. George and John Wilson Professor of Sociology at the University of Texas at Austin. She has intersecting research interests in prosocial behavior, politics, gender, and methodology. Her research has appeared in the *American Sociological Review*, *American Journal of Sociology*, *Social Forces*, *Comparative Politics*, *International Studies Quarterly*, and *Legislative Studies Quarterly*. With Melanie Hughes, she co-authored *Women, Politics, and Power: A Global Perspective* (SAGE, 2016). She is also an author of *Nonrecursive Models: Endogeneity, Reciprocal Relationships, and Feedback Loops* (SAGE, 2011). Her current research explores how nonprofits improve the well-being of communities and how the use of emotion in nonprofit mission statements can increase both donations and volunteers.

Aseem Prakash is Professor of Political Science, the Walker Family Professor for the College of Arts and Sciences, and the Founding Director of the Center for Environmental Politics at University of Washington, Seattle. He is the General Editor of the Cambridge University Press Series in Business and Public Policy and the Associate Editor of *Business and Society*. He serves as a member of the National Academies of Sciences, Engineering, and Medicine's Board on Environmental Change and is a Society and International Research Fellow at the Center for Corporate Reputation at the University of Oxford.

Sarah Reckhow is an Associate Professor of Political Science at Michigan State University. Her research focuses on urban politics and policy and the role of nonprofits and philanthropy in the political process. Her book, *Follow the Money: How Foundation Dollars Change Public School Politics* (Oxford University Press, 2012), examines the role of major foundations in urban school reform. Her newest research lies at the intersection of two trends: the weakening of local governments in some parts of the country due to public-sector austerity and the rising importance of resources for urban public policy initiatives from private-sector philanthropy. Her research has appeared in *Educational Researcher*, *Urban Affairs Review*, *Journal of Urban Affairs*, and *Policy Studies Journal*.

Rob Reich is Professor of Political Science and (by courtesy) Philosophy and Education at Stanford University. He is Co-Director of the Stanford Center on Philanthropy and Civil Society and Director of the Center for Ethics in Society. His recent scholarship includes *Just Giving: Why Philanthropy Is Failing Democracy and How It Can Do Better* (Princeton University Press, 2018) and the edited volume, with Chiara Cordelli and Lucy Bernholz, *Philanthropy in Democratic Societies* (University of Chicago Press, 2016).

Evan Schofer is Professor of Sociology at the University of California, Irvine. His research in comparative political sociology explores cross-national differences in political participation and the historical growth of voluntary associations. In other work, he examines the global expansions of environmentalism, science, and educational systems. Much of his work seeks to develop and extend world society theory, to better understand global patterns of social change. His work has appeared in the *American Sociological Review*, *American Journal of Sociology*, *International Organization*, and *Social Forces*.

Benjamin Soskis is a Research Associate in the Center on Nonprofits and Philanthropy at the Urban Institute and the Co-Founder and Co-Editor of *HistPhil*, a web publication dedicated to the history of the nonprofit and philanthropic sectors. He is a frequent contributor to the *Chronicle of Philanthropy* and the co-author of *The Battle Hymn of the*

Republic: A Biography of the Song that Marches On (Oxford University Press, 2013) and *Looking Back at 50 Years of US Philanthropy* (Hewlett Foundation, 2016).

David Suárez is an Associate Professor at the Evans School of Public Policy and Governance, University of Washington. His current projects include research on public–nonprofit partnerships in national parks and schools, monitoring and evaluation practices in development NGOs, the emergence and growth of nonprofit management programs in universities, and the role of foundations in generating social change. His work has appeared in the *Journal of Public Administration Research and Theory, American Review of Public Administration, Administration and Society, Nonprofit and Voluntary Sector Quarterly, Voluntas,* and *Sociology of Education.*

Stefan Toepler is Professor of Nonprofit Studies and Director of the MPA in the Schar School of Policy and Government, George Mason University in Virginia. His research covers nonprofit policy and management broadly, and he has written extensively on philanthropic foundations comparatively as well as on global civil society. His publications include *The Legitimacy of Philanthropic Foundations: US and European Perspectives,* edited with Kenneth Prewitt and Steve Heydemann (Russell Sage Foundation, 2006), and *Private Funds, Public Purpose: Philanthropic Foundations in International Perspective,* co-edited with Helmut Anheier (Springer, 1999). He is co-editor (with Helmut Anheier) of two forthcoming volumes, the *Routledge Companion to Nonprofit Management* and a second edition of the *International Encyclopedia of Civil Society.*

Edward T. Walker is Professor, Vice Chair, and Director of Graduate Studies in the Department of Sociology at the University of California, Los Angeles. His research investigates the mobilization and outcomes of advocacy both by social movement organizations and by business firms and trade associations; his focus in recent work is on contention surrounding hydraulic fracturing for natural gas as well as efforts by activists to pressure companies to improve their political disclosure practices. He is author of *Grassroots for Hire: Public Affairs Consultants in American Democracy* (Cambridge University Press, 2014) and co-editor of *Democratizing Inequalities: Dilemmas of the New Public Participation* (NYU Press, 2015). His research has appeared in the *American Sociological Review, American Journal of Sociology,* and *Social Problems.*

INDEX

abeyance, 697n2 (ch. 29)

abolitionist movement, 33–35, 637–638, 698n11

accountability, 194, 228–230, 234, 240–241, 261–263, 351–352, 511–512. *See also* governance; transparency

accrediting agencies, higher education, 464–465, 466

activism, 34–37, 57–60, 293, 518–519, 600–601, 632, 634–636, 643–644, 646–647, 697n2 (ch. 29). *See also* grassroots; social movements

activists, as term, 640–641, 697n1

Addams, Jane, 283

additionality, 405–406

admissions testing in higher education, 465, 466

advisors, philanthropic, 407

advocacy: about, 491–493, 507–508, 520; account-ability pressures, 511–512; civic voice and, 312–313; collaboration in, 501–502; contemporary landscape, 493–497; democracy and, 491–492; drivers and determinants, 499–504; external operational environment, 500; funding model, 502–503; future research, 504–505; inequalities, negotiating, 512–514; managerialism in, 500–501; mission and, 503; mobilizing *versus* organizing, 516–518; nonprofit organizational structures and, 508–511; as nonprofit role, 497–499, 659; organi-zational, 492; organizational fields, 503; policy, 57–58, 394–396; political intermediaries in, 514–516; relational embeddedness, 502; techno-logical environment and, 518–520; transnational, 188–189. *See also* nonprofit press

advocacy organizations, defined, 508

Affordable Care Act, 396, 440

affordable housing coalitions, 244–245

agentic (principled-actor) perspective, 620, 697n3 (ch. 28), 697n4

aggregated opinions (public type), 532, 534–535

agonism and contestation (public type), 532, 534–535

aid, transnational. *See* foreign aid

"aid fatigue," 623, 627, 628

Allentown, Pennsylvania, 282

almshouses, 6, 281, 415, 425–429

ALS ice bucket challenge, 553–554

altruism, 205, 368, 426, 540, 558–564; altruism *versus* warm glow, 547, 552, 554, 556, 559–560. *See also* charitable giving; philanthropy; grants

altruism budget: about, 558–559; asks, 560, 565, 695n5; components, 561; explicit benefits from donations, 559, 560; flexibility *versus* fixedness, 562–565; future research, 565; image concerns, 559–560

American Anti-Slavery Society, 34

American Bible Society, 30, 33

American Colonization Society, 34

American Commission for Relief in Belgium, 47–48

American Council of Voluntary Agencies for For-eign Service, 50

American Enterprise Institute, 65

American exceptionalism, 53, 198

American Fund for Public Service, 100

American Red Cross, 46, 47, 48

American Revolution, 25–27

American Social Science Association, 90

Printed and bound by CPI Group (UK) Ltd, Croydon, CR0 4YY

16/04/2025

14658409-0001